Handbook of Internal Accounting Controls
Second Edition

Handbook of Internal Accounting Controls

Second Edition

Wanda A. Wallace, Ph.D., CPA, CMA, CIA

PRENTICE HALL
Englewood Cliffs, New Jersey 07632

Prentice-Hall International, Inc., *London*
Prentice-Hall of Australia, Pty. Ltd., *Sydney*
Prentice-Hall Canada Inc., *Toronto*
Prentice-Hall of India Private Ltd., *New Delhi*
Prentice-Hall of Japan, Inc., *Tokyo*
Prentice-Hall of Southeast Asia Pte. Ltd., *Singapore*
Whitehall Books, Ltd., *Wellington, New Zealand*
Editora Prentice-Hall do Brasil, Ltda, *Rio de Janeiro*

© 1991, 1984
Prentice-Hall, Inc.
Englewood Cliffs, N.J.

Library of Congress Cataloging-in-Publication Data

Wallace, Wanda A.
  Handbook of internal accounting controls/Wanda A. Wallace.—2nd ed.
    p.   cm.
  Includes bibliographical references and index.
  ISBN 0-13-388059-1
  1. Auditing, Internal.   2. Managerial accounting.   I. Title.
HF5668.25.W35   1991
658.15′4—dc20
                                                            91–25621
                                                            CIP

PRENTICE HALL
Career & Personal Development
Englewood Cliffs, NJ 07632

A Simon & Schuster Company

Printed in the United States of America

Dedication

To my husband, James J. Wallace,
a good friend and inspiration.

About the Author

Wanda A. Wallace is a Certified Public Accountant, Certified Management Accountant, and Certified Internal Auditor. Her education includes a Master of Professional Accountancy and a Ph.D. in Accounting and Finance, with a Statistics Research Skill. Dr. Wallace has worked in public accounting, with the firms of Arthur Andersen & Co. and Ernst & Ernst (now Ernst & Young). For over a decade, she was the Regression Consultant to the World Firm of Price Waterhouse, extensively involved in the design of specifications for microcomputer software that performs regression analysis, tailored to the auditor's needs, as well as in the development of related training materials. Dr. Wallace has also consulted with the National Office of Peat, Marwick, Mitchell & Co. (now KPMG Peat Marwick), and she has also developed course materials for that firm's training program for senior auditors concerning the assessment of control risk. She has consulted with Arthur Andersen & Co. concerning audit methodology, and with Peterson Consulting Limited Partnership on sampling applications and numerous business issues. Although her teaching experience spans the full extent of accounting course offerings at both the undergraduate and graduate level, Dr. Wallace has primary teaching interests in auditing and has taught at several universities as well as having instructed courses for managers and partners of Price Waterhouse concerning regression analysis. Two grants have been awarded to Professor Wallace by the Excellence in Audit Education program of Coopers & Lybrand. She currently holds the Deborah D. Shelton Systems Professorship of

Accounting at Texas A&M University. Dr. Wallace has conducted extensive research in the area of internal control evaluation and reporting responsibilities which has been supported by the Research Opportunities in Auditing Program of Peat Marwick. Her research has also been supported by Deloitte, Haskins & Sells (now Deloitte & Touche), Price Waterhouse, the Prochnow Foundation of the Banking School of the University of Wisconsin, the National Science Foundation, the Canadian General Accountants' Research Foundation, and The Institute of Internal Auditors. Additional grants received through the Research Opportunities in Auditing Program of KPMG Peat Marwick have supported research on the influence of the Foreign Corrupt Practices Act on Management Letters, on the Peer Review Process, and on the association of auditing practices and cost of capital. Her publication, *The Economic Role of the Audit in Free and Regulated Markets*, with an accompanying *Instructor's Manual*, was financed by the Aid to Education Program of Touche Ross & Co. and has been adopted for use at universities across the country, as well as internationally. She was awarded the 1981 Wildman Medal for this publication, which is the American Accounting Association-Deloitte Haskins & Sells Award for the article, monograph, book, or other work published during the three calendar years preceding the year of the award which is judged to have made or to be likely to make the most significant contribution to the advancement of the public practice of accountancy, including audit, tax, and management services. This same publication won the first American Woman's Society of Certified Public Accountants' Literary Award (1981) and has been translated into Japanese for use in that country's universities. She is a co-author of a chapter on "The Environment of Auditing," published in *Research Opportunities in Auditing: The Second Decade*, and the winner of the 1990 Wildman Gold Medal. Her research on stock options and stock appreciation rights received the fourth annual American Woman's Society of Certified Public Accountants' Literary Award. In 1990, she was identified as the "Most Prolific Author in the Past Decade (1979–1988) in 24 academic accounting journals" in a research study appearing in *The International Journal of Accounting*. Dr. Wallace has authored over 12 books and monographs and over 90 articles in such journals as: *Contemporary Accounting Research*; *Journal of Accounting, Auditing and Finance*; *Research in Accounting Regulation*; *Accounting Horizons*; *Managerial Auditing Journal*; *Issues in Accounting Education*; *Directors & Boards*; *Management International Review*; *The Wall Street Journal*; *The CPA Journal*; *Accounting Review*; *Journal of Accounting Research*; *Auditing: A Journal of Practice and Theory*; *Bankers Monthly*; *The Woman CPA*; *Financial Executive*; and the *Harvard Business Review*. She currently serves on the editorial board of seven national journals.

A member of the AICPA, IIA, AAA, NAA, Texas Society of CPAs, AWSCPA, and AAA Auditing and Government and Non-Profit Sections, she has been involved on numerous committees, including AAA Subcommittees that formally respond to exposure drafts of the Auditing Standards Board and FASB, and the AAA Auditing Standards Committee which interfaces with both the Auditing Standards Board and The Institute of Internal Auditors. She was the chairman of the Auditing Standards Committee of the American Accounting Association in 1982–1983, and has served three times on the national Council of the AAA, as an officer of the Auditing Section, and as Chair of the Government and Nonprofit Section. She is currently serving a two-year term as Vice President of the American Accounting Association. Dr. Wallace is active in the Auditing Section of the American Accounting Association (AAA), currently serving as Editor of *The Auditor's Report*. On February 12, 1991, Dr. Wallace was invited by Charles A. Bowsher, Comptroller General of the United States, to serve on the Government Auditing Standards Advisory Council. Her professional activities include serving on a joint task force of the AICPA and Canadian Institute of Chartered Accountants and on the 1982–84 Board of Regents of The Institute of Internal Auditors. In 1990–91, Dr. Wallace served as a member of the Consulting Panel for the Financial Executive Institutes' Project on "Integrated Guidance on Internal Control." Her past honors include receipt of the Certificate of Distinguished Performance for the total score received on the 1980 CMA Examination, an Ernst & Whinney Doctoral Dissertation Award, and an American Accounting Association Fellowship. She was also awarded the 1981 Highest Achievement Award (Gold Medal) for having received the highest score on the International Certified Internal Auditor Examination.

Dr. Wallace is extremely active in the academic profession, having screened applicants for Fulbright Scholar awards from 1985 to 1988, served on the resident faculty of the AAA Doctoral Consortium on two occasions, and been on the faculty of the New Faculty Consortium in 1990. She served on the faculty of the 1991 Senior Faculty Consortium. In fall of 1991, she will be an associate editor for *Accounting Horizons*. She has been a Visiting Scholar at both the University of Manchester in England and the Norwegian School of Economics and Business Administration in Bergen, Norway.

On September 1, 1991, Dr. Wallace joins the College of William & Mary as the John N. Dalton Professor of Business Administration and Associate Dean of Academic Affairs.

Acknowledgments

I would like to thank those who were involved in seeing this book through its preparation and production phases. For the first edition Zeke Kilbride was the editor at Prentice-Hall during the initial formation of this project. Susan Clarey has provided useful editorial comments and has been responsible for launching the book. I appreciate the assistance of both of these professionals. The second edition has proceeded, working with Ronald Cohen, Senior Editor at Prentice-Hall and Tom Curtin in Production.

The manuscript for the first edition was typed, in large part, by the word processing department at the Edwin L. Cox School of Business at Southern Methodist University, and I'd like to thank the individuals who did so with such painstaking care:

Edith Benham
Madelon Gafford
Wanda Hanson
Mary Kesner
Patricia Sheild
Beth Vick

The second edition has been prepared with the administrative assistance of Sindy L. Rabold, who has done her usual impeccable job. I am most appreciative of her contributions.

Also, I appreciate the suggestions regarding the manuscript from an anonymous technical reviewer at Prentice-Hall.

Professional experiences have added important insights into relevant questions described herein. The contributions of practitioner colleagues to my formulation of ideas expressed herein are far too numerous to mention but are gratefully acknowledged. Numerous discussions of practical problems, as well as my research endeavors, have had an important influence on this book. To those who have shared their experiences, posed challenging questions, and shared their resolution of issues, I express thanks.

Introduction

External and internal auditors, system designers, and operating managers are constantly faced with the task of designing internal accounting controls and evaluating existing systems of control, including the advisability of recommending and implementing changes to existing control systems. The *Handbook of Internal Accounting Controls, Second Edition* presents a workable, intuitive approach to designing and/or evaluating both existing and proposed controls. It explains the reasons why particular controls are important, the practical factors that often diminish the effectiveness of well-designed controls, and the effect that can be expected if a particular control is omitted. In other words, the *Handbook of Internal Accounting Controls, Second Edition* has been carefully designed to address the "why" of control evaluation procedures as well as the "how."

The focus on control structure, fraud detection issues, industry-specific control problems, the effects of technology on control, and evolving reporting and regulatory issues should be of interest to all who are involved in economic activities. Increased attention is directed to control concepts relevant to litigation support, as well as practical considerations in sampling.

WHAT THIS HANDBOOK WILL DO FOR YOU

This *Handbook* describes a practical approach to an essential element of the audit process: the assessment of control risk to determine the nature, extent, and timing of the audit process. It has been designed to provide valuable guidance for making decisions about the critical questions that arise during an audit engagement. Many of these decisions are also faced by system designers and those responsible for implementing controls.

This *Handbook* shows you, for example:

—How to design controls
—How to evaluate existing controls
—The assessment of control risk for an owner-manager operation
—What are reportable conditions

—Whether an observed weakness in controls is material

—Which tools to use in evaluating controls

—How to test a particular control

—How to address common practice problems when applying statistical sampling

—What mix of substantive tests and tests of control is optimal

—What the control implications are of microcomputers, minicomputers, or other computer environments

—How to prepare a management letter or a report on internal accounting control

—Cost savings possibilities such as coordinating internal control documentation internally with that prepared for the audit engagement

—The acceptability of the content of Management's Reports concerning internal controls

—Implications of The Treadway Commission's findings

—How to integrate research on fraudulent reporting when developing systems and assessing control risk

—How controls interrelate to error incidence

—What requirements exist in the *Yellow Book* related to internal controls and reports thereon

—What has been learned about quality controls in professional firms

—What control problems arise that are peculiar to personal computers

—How the outcomes of controls can be checked through applying analytical procedures

—Possible applications for expert systems

—The relevance of control concepts to litigation support services

—What control problems are common in banks, thrifts, defense contracting, and other industries

Until now, the procedures for evaluating internal accounting controls and assessing control risk have been outlined in the literature either in vague generalities or in excruciating detail, neither of which can be practically applied in the audit setting.

In contrast, the *Handbook of Internal Accounting Controls, Second Edition* describes in practical terms, with examples, the critical elements of internal accounting control. Then, it provides a step-by-step applications guide to show how these critical elements can be evaluated and improved upon for each of the major operating cycles of a business. It offers you the following useful features:

Charts for each operating cycle. Operating cycle charts which effectively capture

—the critical segregation of duties per cycle

—the effect of not having such a segregation

—the basis for effectively evaluating the completeness of accounting records

—the consequences of an incomplete data base

—the essential elements in an effective control environment

—the basis for assessing the risk exposure of the client

—available means of enhancing operating efficiency.

These charts should prove invaluable in the field, both as a guide and as a basis for documenting the auditor's understanding and evaluation of client controls. By integrating marginal notes, the charts or checklists can be tailored to each client and incorporated in the working papers.

Ways to achieve efficiencies in evaluating controls. For auditors striving for efficiency, the *Handbook* offers creative "walk through" procedures, flowcharting techniques, risk exposure worksheets, and internal accounting control checklists.

Guidelines for selecting a mix of substantive tests and tests of control. A critical decision for the auditor, once control risk has been assessed, is whether to perform tests of controls or substantive tests and how to integrate such tests in the audit plan. This *Handbook* provides suggestions concerning the selection of a mix of substantive tests and tests of control and examples of effective means of performing tests of controls. The advantages of statistical sampling techniques and computer auditing techniques in performing tests of control are demonstrated.

A special separate section on control concerns unique to EDP systems. Special attention is given to minicomputers, as their proliferation can pose unique control problems for the auditor, system designer, and operating management. The advantages and disadvantages of integrating the review of EDP and Manual Controls are discussed and suggestions are made as to how to proceed in an EDP environment. New technologies are considered, including control implications of interactive systems, paperless systems, expert systems and various decision support systems, database management systems, and electronic data interchange (EDI) systems. Personal computers raise such control problems as portability and accessibility which are given particular attention.

Fraud detection issues. Recent developments in the profession, such as concerns for Fraudulent Financial Reporting and findings of the Treadway Commission are described. Ideas on approaching fraud detection are provided, including the application of analytical procedures. Distinctions between control structure and fraud prevention are described, including limitations and relative costs.

Tests of controls via statistical methods. Statistics are addressed in a very friendly "How To" manner, describing challenges when testing controls using statistical techniques. The relevance of system changes, software changes, macro spreadsheet development, and similar common practices to those performing statistical tests is described. Implications of human nature are also explored.

Guidelines for distinguishing material weaknesses. The auditor is responsible for communicating reportable conditions and may wish to report material weaknesses in internal accounting control. This *Handbook* explains how to distinguish those weaknesses which are material and provides examples of such weaknesses.

Valuable assistance for preparing management letters and increasing a firm's revenues from management advisory services. The understanding of a client's operations and controls provides the basis for recommending means of improving the control system as well as the operating efficiency of a client. Although there is no requirement that auditors provide management letters to their clients, the profession has traditionally offered this service as a by-product of the audit. This guide considers operating efficiency suggestions that should be of interest to auditors who are striving to improve the quality of management letters, as well as to increase their firms' revenue from management advisory services.

Such suggestions can be invaluable to internal auditors who are responsible for generating control recommendations; in addition, operating suggestions that can generate cost savings are described. Internal auditors and operating managers frequently have responsibility for responding to external auditors' management letters, and the *Handbook* provides these individuals with useful insights as to how the management letter points are prepared, as well as a basis for evaluating the quality of the letters currently being prepared.

By integrating control and operating suggestions within each cycle of a business, this *Handbook* shows you how to recognize problems and potential savings, and presents some possible solutions to those problems or shortcomings. The distinction between *desirable* and *necessary* control is described, as is the ability to achieve adequate accounting control without foregoing operating efficiencies, if proper planning is performed when designing the control system. The use of risk exposure worksheets to evaluate the adequacy of proposed or existing controls can aid the CPA in explaining the expected effects of a management advisory engagement, or help the system designer and internal auditor in describing the ramifications of control recommendations.

Suggestions for handling comprehensive reviews of internal accounting control systems. Documentation and reporting issues related to such engagements are covered, as well as the distinction between the objectives and approach to comprehensive review engagements and the evaluation of controls as an integral part of the audit. Another reporting issue involves management reports, which are becoming commonplace and which typically discuss internal controls. This *Handbook* describes the usual content of management reports that relates to internal accounting controls, as well as those topics which the CPA might suggest to management for coverage in such reports. The discussion of management reports has particular relevance to directors, managers, and internal auditors who are likely to share responsibility for drafting such disclosures. Recent regulatory proposals are described, as are the proposed attestation standards associated with control reports and management's reports on control.

Control problems by industry type. Patterns identified within particular industries are described. Both inherent risk and control risk are explored, as is their interaction.

Assistance in adapting control design and evaluation procedures to governmental and other not-for-profit entities. Fund accounting is reconciled with the cycle approach, and critical operating distinctions that influence controls are identified. In addition, the areas of operation and types of information—including social performance measures—over which controls are likely to be designed and reviewed as a means of facilitating monitoring by management, regulators, and other interested parties are described. Control issues for governmental units, hospitals, and churches are given special attention. The *Yellow Book* revision includes considerable coverage of internal control reports, as described. Moreover, the General Accounting Office has cited control considerations at various governmental entities and examples are discussed.

Litigation support considerations. Helpful advice is provided concerning the assimilation of evidence, evaluation of the effectiveness of control practices in others' assimilation of evidence, and communication of how control has been established and monitored in the evidence collection and presentation process.

WHO CAN BENEFIT BY USING THIS HANDBOOK

Although this *Handbook* was written with the CPA in mind, its content should prove useful to internal auditors, system designers, controllers, operating managers, and directors. Any individual who desires to gain an understanding of the critical concepts underlying the evaluation of control, an awareness of useful tools and techniques for both designing and evaluating control including how they are applied in the field, and an appreciation for the CPA's professional and reporting responsibilities, will find this *Handbook* appealing. Its joint consideration of rationale and procedure makes it a valuable learning tool as well as a handy reference. Specifically:

Internal auditors will find that the *Handbook's* coverage of operating efficiency will be of particular use in evaluating controls beyond the internal accounting control system as they perform operational audits.

Governmental auditors will find the *Handbook's* adaptation to not-for-profit entities to be particularly useful in their evaluation of controls.

System designers are likely to find the *Handbook's* discussion of how the approach to evaluating controls can be adapted to a systems design engagement to be tailor-made for their reference.

Controllers accept primary responsibility for the integrity of the accounting reporting system and can find numerous suggestions for ways of increasing their assurance that their information system is complete, accurate, and operating efficiently.

Operating managers are the key decision-makers who determine whether to implement, change, or retain a particular set of controls, and who are often required to respond formally to internal and external auditors' findings. To do so effectively, an understanding of controls and report forms is critical and is obtainable from this *Handbook*.

Directors who frequently cannot be thoroughly familiar with an entity's control system are expected to exercise oversight of internal and external audit activities and overall operations. In order to interpret the information made available to them in such documents and management letters, directors need this *Handbook* as a reference manual.

Those involved with small business will find detailed consideration of control in the small business environment, with particular emphasis on the owner-manager's role within the control system. Those involved in litigation support will find the discussion of control concepts applicable to gathering, evaluating, and presenting evidential matter, to be of substantial use.

HOW TO USE THIS HANDBOOK

The *Handbook of Internal Accounting Controls, Second Edition* has been chronologically constructed to answer questions that are likely to arise during the course of accepting and planning an engagement and performing the necessary procedures to meet professional and reporting responsibilities:

Chapter 1 describes the importance of quality to economic success and a number of alternative taxonomies of control. The audit risk model is explained, as are its limitations. The chapter also pinpoints your objectives in evaluating internal accounting controls in both audit engagements and comprehensive review engagements. Key reasons for understanding control structure, assessing control risk, and evaluating controls are provided. Quality, a necessary ingredient for economic success, depends on an effective control structure. Continuous controls are increasingly required due to real-time information access. To create and maintain an effective control environment, understanding is essential. The advantages of expertise in control systems to those performing management advisory services are described.

Chapter 2 introduces terminology, concepts, and the broad approach to controls that permeates managers', directors', auditors', and regulators' current thinking. The control structure is defined, as is the interaction of the components of control structure. Concepts of control risk assessment are developed, as are implications for managers, directors, auditors, regulators, and other third parties.

Chapter 3 addresses how controls have been influenced by technology. Electronic data interchange (EDI) systems expand control considerations beyond an individual entity. Paperless systems, decision support systems, management systems' implications for controls, and personal computers' general effect on control structure are discussed.

Chapter 4 reports on recent developments in the profession, such as concerns for Fraudulent Financial Reporting and findings of the Treadway Commission, as well as ideas on approaching fraud detection. Research implications are detailed, including how to use analytical procedures to uncover problems. An efficient markets application is also described, whereby risk exposure from the client's reaction to market performance can be assessed.

Chapter 5 explains why particular elements of control are important and presents the *Handbook's* recommended approach to designing and evaluating controls. It provides insights as to how to evaluate and respond to such typical comments as the following:

—"My operation is too small to have a control system. . . ."

—"The owner-manager doesn't know accounting. . . ."

—"Well, that's the way we say we do things, but the way we really do things is. . . ."

—"I just initial the form and forward it through the system. . . . I don't know why I have to, but that's what the auditors check for."

—"Computers only automate the accounting process. . . ."

—"When I'm running out of time, I do my operating duties. My control duties can wait."

Chapter 6 of the *Handbook* explains how controls can be efficiently evaluated by using "Six Useful Tools of the Trade":

(1) Internal Accounting Control Checklists
(2) Flowcharting Techniques
(3) The "Walk-Through"
(4) Computer Auditing Techniques
(5) Statistical Sampling Techniques
(6) Risk Exposure Worksheets

Chapter 7 addresses statistics in a very friendly "How To" manner and describes challenges in testing controls using statistical techniques. The relevance of system changes, software changes, and similar common practices to those performing statistical tests is described. Implications of "human nature" and current practice are explored.

Chapter 8 expands upon how an audit plan is formulated. Special emphasis is placed on how the mix of substantive tests and tests of control is selected, and what constitutes a test of control.

Chapters 9 through 11 apply the concepts of Chapter 5 to the key operations of an entity:

—The Revenue or Income-Producing Cycle,
—The Cost of Sales or Production Cycle, and
—Financing and Nonroutine Transactions.

A number of common exhibits are contained in Chapters 9, 10, and 11, summarizing five key considerations. The first consideration relates to the precise duties that should be segregated; examples are provided from a broad cross-section of profit and not-for-profit entities of factors that influence the effectiveness of the formal segregation of duties in day-to-day operations.

The second consideration is an outline of the critical documents that comprise the accounting and audit trail of an entity for each cycle. While these documents are likely to vary in format and may be in manual or computer-readable form, the basic content of the documents is essential in assuring that the accounting records are complete. In an EDP system, a log and password sign-on may replace the initials of the preparer of a document, and a programmed edit check may replace the initials of a second person verifying the mathematical accuracy of that document. Yet a one-to-one correspondence of existing checks and logs to those implied by the documents outlined in exhibits of Chapters 9 through 11 should be identifiable.

The third consideration addresses the evaluation of the control environment. This checklist is almost identical per cycle, with the exception of its tailored emphasis on the content of the procedures manuals for each cycle. This redundancy in checklists is to encourage reconsideration of the overall control environment as each distinct cycle of operations is approached. Since general controls can preclude the effectiveness of detailed controls, completion of such an exhibit is a prerequisite to evaluating the detailed control risks that are present in any system.

The fourth consideration reminds the evaluator of three basic problems that can arise in any control system: (1) loss of documents or input of bogus documents; (2) inaccurate recording of transactions; and (3) removal of assets. The common controls that are intended to address such problems are identified. The related exhibit then focuses on the critical risks of each cycle.

The fifth consideration relates to showing some examples of how operating efficiency considerations can be effectively integrated with control concerns. The examples, once again, are drawn from a wide variety of entities and should prove useful to you in formulating control and operating suggestions.

Chapter 9 has an increased focus on services and attendant control difficulties related to revenue recognition. *Chapter 10* describes the advent of Just in Time Inventory Systems and related control effects. *Chapter 11* has expanded treatment of financial instruments, problems entailed in three-party transactions, and control implications of leveraged buy-outs and financial restructuring.

Chapter 12 discusses how computers affect the evaluation of internal accounting control. Special emphasis is given to minicomputers, service centers, and the control implications of a data base management system. General and specific controls are discussed, as well as means of integrating the review of EDP and manual controls. The primary role of personal computers and the exposures related to linking systems are described. Electronic Data Interchange (EDI) and computer viruses are described. Working paper documentation is illustrated. The five key considerations described for the application in Chapters 9 through 11 also relate to Chapter 12; exhibits are included emphasizing the segregation of duties, suggested documentation procedures, key elements of the control environment, critical risks, and operating efficiency considerations in the computer environment.

Chapter 13 of the *Handbook* describes how to combine the analysis per cycle into an audit plan. Risk exposure worksheets, described in Chapter 6, are used to evaluate the entity's risk exposure from observed weaknesses in control. A flowchart is provided to assist in the identification of material weaknesses, and some examples of material weaknesses are provided. The interpretation of the results of tests of control is discussed, as are the CPA's responsibilities for investigating and reporting illegal acts.

Chapter 13 also discusses how the approach to evaluating controls that is described in this *Handbook* can be adapted to a systems design engagement, i.e., a management advisory service. Since the principles and examples described in Chapters 1 through 12 apply to the design of a new system just as they apply to the improvement of an existing system, the adaptation process is reasonably straightforward.

Examples are provided on how to link risk assessment to testing, cost-benefit considerations, and overall evaluation of controls. Related working paper documentation of such linkages is illustrated.

Chapter 14 discusses the advantages and potential disadvantages of issuing a management letter. A suggested form for such letters is presented, as well as examples of how specific suggestions should be drafted. The capability of management letters to enhance revenue from auditing, management advisory, and tax services is explained.

Chapter 15 describes the objectives of a comprehensive review engagement and the implications of such objectives in terms of the differing procedures to be performed for review and audit engagements. The savings that can accrue from combining comprehensive review engagements and audits are also described. The ability of clients to effectively reduce the cost of a CPA's services by documenting their control systems themselves is likewise acknowledged.

Chapter 16 describes control problems by industry type. Based on a review of over 500 management letters, classified by industry type, suggestions are made as to useful control practices by specific line of business and size of entity. In addition, attention is directed to financial institutions, defense contractors, and service organizations (focusing on CPA firms).

Chapter 17 discusses reporting issues. A synopsis of the reporting options permitted under Statement on Auditing Standards No. 30 is provided. In addition, managers' past practices in making disclosures related to internal controls are described. The means by which the quality of these disclosures might be improved are discussed.

Proposals of the Securities and Exchange Commission are described, as are the requirements of the General Accounting Office. Implications of demand for interim information is likewise explored.

Chapter 18 describes how the *Handbook's* approach to designing and evaluating controls can be adapted to government and not-for-profit entities. Examples of material weaknesses in government and not-for-profit settings are provided, as is a rather in-depth description of control design for a church. The importance of expanding the scope of controls for not-for-profit entities beyond the typical accounting system orientation of controls is explained. The prevalence of performance measures directed at service and output results in a demand for increased attention to control over the general information system. The importance of third-party donors and payors, as well as regulators' oversight, frequently requires the accumulation of data on a broader scope than would be required for financial reporting purposes.

Chapter 19 describes how control considerations are relevant to litigation support activities. Helpful advice is provided on assimilating evidence, evaluating the effectiveness of control practices in others' assimilation of evidence, and communicating how control has been established and monitored in the evidence collection and presentation process.

Chapter 20 brings closure to the topics addressed and gives attention to pending proposals in the regulatory setting, debates in practice, and promises regarding future streams of research.

The objective of this *Handbook* is to ingrain the critical concepts underlying the evaluation of control in the minds of its readers. Its combination of theory and practice is intended to enhance its usefulness for instructional purposes and for field applications. Readers are encouraged to contact the author as to their experiences with the guide and their suggestions as to how it may be improved to better meet its objectives in future editions.

The *Handbook* is intended to be a self-contained reference manual on a reasonably broad scope of topics—from computer auditing to reporting issues, the reader is provided with explanations, instructions, and examples that incorporate flowcharting, statistical sampling, and checklist techniques. The numerous business and not-for-profit examples of control issues provided in the *Handbook* should serve as benchmarks to which parallels can be drawn from other businesses in identifying problems and in formulating suggestions.

Professionals' judgment is their primary asset, and if this *Handbook* serves to improve their thinking process and subsequent control-related judgments, it will have served its primary objective.

Wanda A. Wallace

Table of Contents

Chapter 3: THE EFFECTS OF TECHNOLOGY ON CONTROL   69

Chapter 6: SIX USEFUL TOOLS OF THE TRADE—THEIR APPLICATION IN THE DESIGN AND EVALUATION OF CONTROLS 219

Chapter 12: HOW TO HANDLE CONTROL CONCERNS UNIQUE TO COMPUTER SYSTEMS

Chapter 13: PUTTING IT ALL TOGETHER: HOW TO PRODUCE A GLOBAL PICTURE OF AN ENTITY'S CONTROLS   627

Table of Exhibits

1

Key Reasons for Understanding Control Structure, Assessing Control Risk, and Evaluating Controls

"The success of each is dependent upon the success of the other."

John D. Rockefeller, Jr.[1]

As this quote suggests, interdependencies are pervasive. This is perhaps best evidenced by the ripple effects of the thrift industry on the economy, including recessionary consequences, tax levies, stewardship expectations, fraud revelations, mismanagement controversies, and proposed regulations. As epitaphs are written on various debacles among financial institutions, the resounding question

---

[1] *The Executive's Quotation Book*, Edited by James Charlton (New York: St. Martin's Press, 1983), p. 22.

is "What went wrong?" While theories vary on the relative importance of numerous causal and environmental factors, some consensus seems to have evolved that a key element of success was missing: CONTROL!

The concept of "control" is central to managing economic entities, be they profit-oriented, governmental, or not-for-profit organizations. In the absence of adequate control, risks will fail to be identified and will not be effectively addressed when identified. Success will be by happenstance rather than by design. More frequently, failure will result. A need exists to understand control as a complete system that accomplishes a number of integrated objectives, including continuing improvement. By recognizing interrelationships and focusing on control as an integrative process, you can be more effective in both designing and evaluating controls in an organization.

THE FOCUS ON QUALITY AS THE NECESSARY INGREDIENT FOR ECONOMIC SUCCESS DEPENDS ON AN EFFECTIVE CONTROL STRUCTURE

Hand-in-hand with continued improvement is the notion of quality. For the past 25 years, W. Edwards Deming has been revered in Japan as the "Father of Quality Control"; indeed, he is given a large share of the credit for Japan's postwar economic recovery.[2] Deming espouses the philosophy that higher quality means lower cost. Moreover, managers must know that they and their workers are responsible for improving the system and this can best be accomplished by forging a partnership between worker and supplier, including continuous knowledge of the customer feedback loop and the process feedback loop. Management's responsibility encompasses practices and policies that govern people, methods, equipment, materials, and the environment. Deming further sets forth essential actions by top management to facilitate continuous improvement, including

- top management must work on itself
- a positive focus for change must exist
- the whole organization must be involved
- all must understand there are substantial unknown costs of a dissatisfied customer or employee
- a climate must be created for gathering data and solving problems to take priority over technological change.[3]

Widely applied is the Deming improvement cycle: Plan-Do-Check-Action (PDCA cycle). This recognizes the importance of a team effort that identifies what are its important planned accomplishments, desirable changes, and required information to guide the change, process or test to achieve and monitor the change, and statistics necessary to communicate with one another. Such a PLANNING

---

[2] For related discussions, see Myron Tribus, "Deming's Way," *New Management* (vol. 1, Spring 1983), pp. 22–25.

[3] Alan Hodgson, "Deming's Never-Ending Road to Quality," *Personnel Management* (vol. 19, no. 7, July 1987), pp. 40–44.

phase is followed by DOING, which entails looking for answers to questions posed in phase one and executing the change or test, often on a small scale initially. The third phase of CHECKING observes the effects of the change or test. The fourth phase of ACTION studies the results to answer the question "What did we learn?"[4] This PDCA approach can be viewed as a sort of control structure guiding improvement.

Such a cycle reflects commitment of management to quality enhancement, a clear planning process intrinsically linked with ongoing communications, an assessment process that can be characterized as monitoring and feedback, and an explicit action plan that has been well controlled by the very process through which it has been developed, executed, and reassessed. While the language changes when one shifts from the Deming philosophy to the management, accounting, auditing, and regulatory prescriptions concerning control, a clear one-to-one mapping of critical aspects of a coherent control framework exists between the PDCA cycle and a control structure for an economic entity.

ALTERNATIVE TAXONOMIES OF CONTROL

Controls in the business literature have been characterized and classified in a number of ways. Some appeal to the typical functions in a business and differentiate controls peculiar to:

Executive Management	Marketing and Sales
Treasury and Finance	Distribution
Research and Development	Human Resources Management and Labor Relations
Purchasing	Information Systems
Production	Accounting and Control
Quality Control	Risk Management, including
Inventory Management	Legal Matters
Facilities Management and Security	Public Relations

Others have described broad areas of the control environment such as:

- managerial control
- operational control
- internal control
- risk and fraud prevention

The levels of risk and exposure have likewise provided a taxonomy:

Fraud, embezzlement, and/or fraudulent financial reporting	Excessive costs/deficit revenues
	Competitive disadvantage

---

[4] Edward M. Baker and Harry L. Artinian, "The Deming Philosophy of Continuing Improvement in a Service Organization: The Case of Windsor Export Supply," *Quality Progress* (June 1985), pp. 61–69. Also see W. Edwards Deming, *Quality, Productivity, and Competitive Position* (Cambridge, Mass: Massachusetts Institute of Technology, Center for Advanced Engineering Study, 1982) and "Deming's Way Out of the Crisis," *Industry Week* (June 20, 1988), p. 91.

Business interruption

Erroneous record keeping

Loss or destruction of assets

Unacceptable accounting

Erroneous management decisions

Statutory sanctions

These[5] and other classifications by business cycle, by area for control, and by method for control all differ in the element of the control structure upon which they construct a framework for viewing controls.

Yet, regardless of the perspective from which controls are viewed, the "big picture" must be retained. Exhibit 1–1 is an example of one internal audit director's view of how controls permeate the organization and the interplay between business precepts and control dimensions. Importantly, the diagram bears out the need for control, the process being controlled, and the tone of the organization which determines to a substantial degree the effectiveness of the controlling process.

OBJECTIVES IN ASSESSING CONTROL RISK FOR EXTERNAL AUDITING PURPOSES

The reasons for a CPA assessing an entity's control risk and gaining an understanding of the control structure depend on the type of engagement. A CPA cannot plan or carry out an audit without understanding the entity's internal accounting structure and the second standard of field work requires that the auditor obtain "A sufficient understanding of the internal control structure to . . . plan the audit and to determine the nature, timing, and extent of tests to be performed." [Statement on Auditing Standard (SAS) No. 55, p. 3]

Questions to be addressed include:

- Which mix of tests of control and substantive tests is likely to be an optimum approach to performing the audit examination?

- Should the client's controls, including the accounting control environment and internal audit department, be considered to lower control risk and to what extent?

- What should be the nature, timing, and extent of the audit procedures performed?

- Do the results of the tests of controls require a reevaluation of the quality of control and an adjustment of the audit plan?

The auditor's assessment of control risk is performed at both the financial statement level and at the level of particular classes of transactions and balances. This is essential when striving to answer these questions. Both assessing control risk and understanding the control structure are critical facets of an external audit engagement.

---

[5] Wanda A. Wallace, Howard L. Siers, James K. Loebbecke, William D. Hall, and Keagle W. Davis, "Integrated Guidance on Internal Control" (July 1989) describe such taxonomies.

Exhibit 1–1

Components of an Organization's Control Culture

Control Environment	*Business Planning*
1. Tone at the Top—the board's and management's *integrity and ethical* values 2. Communications and Openness 3. Behavior—supporting concepts of control and addressing control issues proactively (words and deeds) 4. Proactive Self-Evaluation of Controlling Process 5. Ownership and Accountability Defined (This component establishes the tone and behavioral support for the other three components of the control culture).	1. Setting objectives or primary mission 2. Identifying and analyzing exposures that impede achieving objectives or mission 3. Identifying infrastructure of business fundamentals within the organization and its resources to address exposures 4. Managing change (This component establishes *need* for controlling.)
The Controlling Process It is comprised of tasks that people do daily at all levels of the organization, such as: 1. Monitoring 7. Communicating 2. Analyzing 8. Observing 3. Reconciling 9. Comparing 4. Auditing 10. Approving 5. Checking 11. Authorizing 6. Reporting • It is dependent on business fundamentals to function • Its focus is on achieving control objectives (This component relates to an *effective* process and encompasses the controlling actions of people.)	*Infrastructure of Business Fundamentals* 1. Organizing responsibilities, authority, and accountability 2. Establishing policies, procedures, plans, budgets, etc. 3. Establishing network of management information, operating, and financial systems. (This component relates to an *adequate* process and serves as the basis for the *actions of people*.)

Source: Roger N. Carolus, NCNB Corporation, Charolotte, NC 28255.

AN OVERVIEW

The auditor's consideration of a client's internal control structure in a financial statement audit is described in considerable depth in SAS 55.[6] Exhibit 1–2 provides

Exhibit 1–2

The Auditor's Consideration of the Internal Control Structure

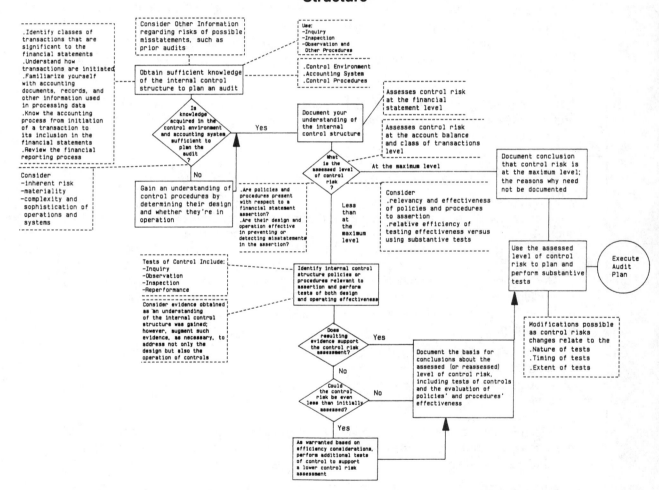

Source: Adapted from Robert H. Temkin and Alan J. Winters, "SAS No. 55: The Auditor's New Responsibility for Internal Control," *Journal of Accountancy* (May 1988), pp. 86–98 and SAS No. 55 (AICPA, 1988).

---

[6] "Consideration of the Internal Control Structure in a Financial Statement Audit" (New York: AICPA, April 1988).

an overview of its general provisions, clarifying both audit procedures applied, relevant considerations, expected judgments, and documentation requirements. This overview is intended to provide an organizational context for subsequent chapters' detailed treatment of relevant aspects of control structure to the audit process.

An entity's internal control structure can be thought of as the nerve center of its operations and is comprised of the control environment, the accounting system, and control procedures. Historically, the accounting literature distinguished between administrative and accounting controls. However, the definitions of administrative and internal accounting controls are by no means mutually exclusive. Hence, in 1988, the profession discarded the distinction between accounting and administrative controls (though the demarcation persists in certain legislation such as the Foreign Corrupt Practices Act).

Generally accepted auditing standards (GAAS) now recognize the total spectrum of internal control structure policies and procedures relevant to an audit as requiring attention by the auditor. [SAS 55] "Relevant" recognizes that the auditor focuses on an "entity's ability to record, process, summarize, and report financial data consistent with management's assertions embodied in the financial statements" or on data used to apply auditing procedures to test such assertions. [SAS 55, p. 29]

The key role of assertions in approaching an audit is graphically depicted in Exhibit 1–3. As one proceeds to consider assertions across the financial statements, assurance can be gained through inherent risk assessments, control risk assessments, and detection risk assessment (which relates to tests of controls as well as substantive test work). Before proceeding with our discussion of the role of control risk assessment, it is helpful to review the audit risk model and the concept of business risk.

THE AUDIT RISK MODEL[7]

According to professional standards [SAS 47, Section 312], the auditor must quantify the audit risk (AR) in light of (1) the risk of material misstatement in the financial statements, (2) the cost of reducing the risk, and (3) the effect of the potential misstatement on the use and understanding of the financial statements.

The risk of material misstatement is generally acknowledged as depending on management's integrity, the entity's internal accounting control system, and the entity's overall economic position. The cost-benefit considerations related to audit risk rest with the CPA, except that professional standards are expected to set some ceiling on the amount of risk that a CPA can accept. Some CPAs avoid high-risk clients, though others are willing to accept such risks, as they believe that the higher audit fees will offset the costs associated with a greater risk of

---

[7] This discussion is based on the author's writing in *Auditing* Second Edition (Boston, MA: PWS-Kent, 1991).

Exhibit 1–3

The Fundamental Role of Assertion in the Audit Process

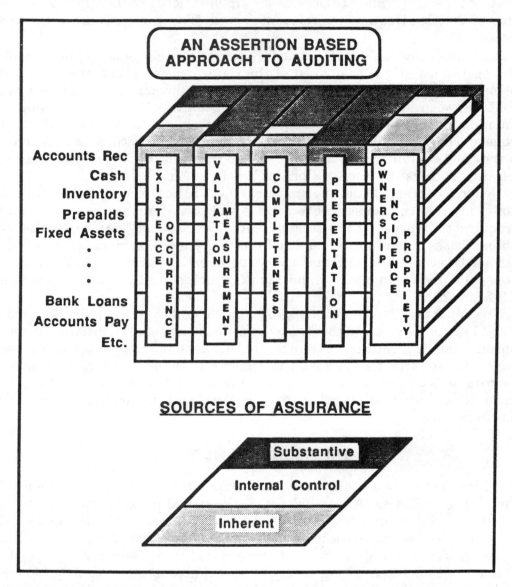

Source: Donald A. Leslie, Stephen J. Aldersley, Donald J. Cockburn, Carolyn J. Reiter, "An Assertion Based Approach to Auditing," *Auditing Symposium VIII* (The University of Kansas, 1987)

unfavorable publicity or legal sanctions. Of course, factors other than economic considerations influence the acceptance of clients, including a desire to serve the public. The "effect of material misstatement on the users" depends on which user group is involved—for example, public or private companies. A closely held private company may give its financial statements only to its banker and 10 stockholders, all of whom will be familiar with its operations, anyway. But a public company sends its financial statements to many users and so is subject to numerous regulatory agencies' reviews. In addition, class action suits can mean big-dollar liability to investors.

Its Use In Planning

With all these considerations in mind, the CPA will determine the acceptable risk of issuing an opinion on financial statements that may be incorrect because of undetected material errors and irregularities. To plan an audit that can control AR, the auditor will rely on internal controls (IC), analytical procedures (AP), and substantive tests of details (TD). Professional standards permit any combination of these procedures but do not permit a complete reliance on controls. This audit planning approach is described in the following risk model:

$$AR = IC \times AP \times TD$$

where AR = audit risk
IC = risk assessment that the internal control structure will fail to detect errors equal to the tolerable error
AP = risk assessment that analytical procedures will fail to detect errors equal to the tolerable error
TD = risk assessment that substantive tests of details will fail to detect errors equal to the tolerable error

The model merely points out that if, for example, internal controls are strong and warrant an assessment of control risk at less than a maximum level, then fewer tests of details will be needed. Similarly, extensive use of analytical procedures should reduce the extent of detailed test work needed. Exhibit 1–4 illustrates the audit risk model using an analogy to a hailstorm that represents the potential errors and misstatements. If the series of checkpoints or screens designed to prevent errors and misstatements from reaching the financial statements or to detect them during the audit (i.e., the control structure, analytical procedures, and tests of details, are effective) the risk of hailstones reaching the financial statements is reduced. "Depending on the intensity of the downpour or the size of an individual error, it is conceivable that any one of the screens could prevent cumulatively material errors and misstatements from reaching the financial statements."[8] In Exhibit 1–4 note that both client controls and audit procedures screen

---

[8] Lynford E. Graham, "Audit Risk—Part I," *The CPA Journal* (August 1985), p. 20. Reprinted with permission from *The CPA Journal,* August 1985, copyright 1985.

Exhibit 1–4

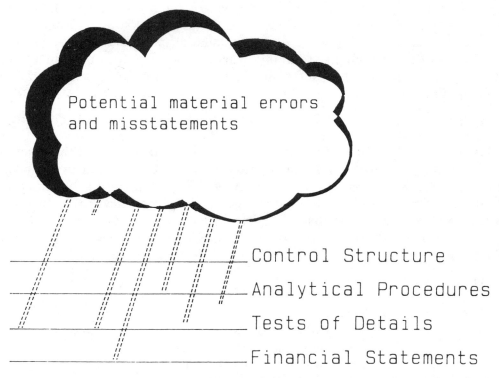

Hailstorm Audit Risk Analogy

Potential material errors and misstatements

Control Structure

Analytical Procedures

Tests of Details

Financial Statements

Source: Adapted from Lynford E. Graham "Audit Risk—Part I," *The CPA Journal* (August 1985), p. 20. Reprinted with permission from *The CPA Journal,* August 1985, copyright 1985.

errors and if collectively effective, a material error will rarely reach the audited financial statements.

In planning an engagement, if the auditor determines, based on experience and judgment that he or she wants an audit risk level of .05 and believes that controls might fail to detect aggregate errors equal to the tolerable error 50% of the time, and analytical procedures might fail to detect such error 30% of the time, the allowable risk of incorrect acceptance for a specific substantive test of details would be 33%, calculated as follows:

$$TD = \frac{AR}{IC \times AP} = \frac{.05}{.50 \times .30} = .33$$

If it were possible to reduce *AP* to 10%, the formula would imply that no substantive tests of detail would be necessary (beyond those tied directly to the analytical procedures). Just as the above computation solves for *TD*, the relationship can also be adjusted algebraically to solve for *IC*, *AP*, or the implied *AR*, depending on how much is known about the effectiveness of various procedures and the planned audit approach.

Assumptions

The professional standards also offer the following assumptions about the audit risk model:

1. The risk factors are assumed to be independent of one another. In other words, it is assumed that there is no significant causal relationship between errors of one type and errors of another. Yet, both *AP* and *TD* are widely acknowledged to depend, in part, on *IC*.
2. The auditor is assumed to be able to assess *IC* and *AP* subjectively and with reasonable accuracy.
3. Nonsampling risk, such as the auditor's failure to recognize errors or to select the appropriate audit test, is assumed to be negligible, being effectively controlled through planning, supervision, review, and careful selection of audit procedures whenever weaknesses are a concern [SAS 22, Section 311].

Problems with the Model

Other problems with the model are that other factors may influence the determination of individual risk components. One of these factors is inherent risk, or the risk that monetary errors equal to tolerable error would have occurred without internal accounting controls over the account balance or class of transactions. The concept of inherent risk will be developed in the next subsection of this chapter; however, the point raised by those who critique the audit risk model is that if the auditor were given credit for the fact that some clients have less inherent risk, then actual risk would be reduced below the risk calculated in the model's current form.

There is also an aggregation problem, in that the model is likely to be applied to sets of transactions and account balances on a disaggregated level, whereas the AR is related conceptually to an aggregate judgment on the set of financial statements. Just as there are no directions as to how to aggregate the audit risk models' various applications, there also are no directions as to how to evaluate audit risk model's various applications, there also are no directions as to how to evaluate audit cost factors when establishing *AR*. The final warning is the necessity of using the audit risk model solely for planning purposes, as distinct from using it as an iterative evaluation tool. In other words, the *AR* result would not be accurate if the auditor were to set *AP*, *IC*, and *TD*; perform *AP*, look at the results; and then readjust the *AP* value. Every time such a readjustment is made, the audit risk inferred from the model understates the actual risk. At the extreme, if an auditor iteratively evaluated *AP*, *IC*, and *TD* at all possible levels, the audit risk would actually be .1998 (assuming that the probability of intolerable error is 1), despite the model's computation of a .05 risk.[9]

Inherent Risk

As already noted, inherent risk is the probability that without controls, there will be a material error in the accounting process. This probability is likely to be affected by the state of the economy; the client's ownership; geographical location; and management's reputation. For example, closely held entities may present more inherent risk with respect to understatements of income, due to tax minimization incentives, and publicly held entities may pose more inherent risk with respect to overstatements of income, due to the structure of incentive plans for top management.

Statement No. 47, Section 312 suggests that an audit risk (AR) model recognize three key components: inherent risk (IR), control risk (CR), and detection risk (DR): $AR = IR \times CR \times DR$. Control risk is the probability that material errors cannot be prevented or detected on a timely basis by the internal control structure. Detection risk is the probability that material errors not detected or corrected by the internal control structure will also not be detected by the audit procedures. This AR model is an extension of SAS No. 39.

Note that IR and CR assessment are typically subjective judgments, whereby detection risk may be set to attain the desired AR. Also note that the higher levels of materiality will enable lower audit risk (if all else is held constant).

Exhibit 1–5 illustrates how inherent risk can influence an audit objective and the procedures which become a part of the audit plan.

Research has demonstrated that assessments of internal control are dependent on the level of the susceptibility of the process to errors (inherent risk).[10]

Overview

Exhibit 1–6 depicts each of the basic audit risk components. Exhibit 1–7 sketches, in general terms, the approach to developing an overall audit plan in light of such risks. It emphasizes the iterative nature of an audit plan.

Business Risk

The concept of business risk is the probability that auditors will suffer some loss or injury to their professional reputation as a result of a particular client relationship. In addition, auditors can also lose money because of litigation and/

---

[9] William R. Kinney, Jr., "A Note on Compounding Probabilities in Auditing," *Auditing*: A *Journal of Practice & Theory*, Spring 1983, pp. 13–22.

[10] R. Libby, J. T. Artman, and J. J. Willingham, "Process Susceptibility, Control Risk, and Audit Planning," *Accounting Review* (April 1985), pp. 212–230.

Exhibit 1–5

Examples of Responding to Inherent Risk Assessments

The following examples illustrate possible responses to identified inherent risks or changes in inherent risks:

(1) Description: A regulatory agency has issued a ruling that all communications equipment henceforth manufactured in the U.S. must have an expanded capacity to receive additional frequencies.

Classification: A condition

Balance(s): Inventory
Allowance for Returned Merchandise

Audit Objective(s): Inventory—Valuation (pricing), in light of possible obsolescence of products not having the expanded capacity.

Allowance—Adequacy, in light of products recently sold, still subject to return and more likely to be returned because of obsolescence.

Procedures: Inventory—Discuss with management their response to this condition. If they demonstrate that they will try to sell current inventory at a reduced price, consider the impact of a forecasted price of the current product when performing the standard lower-of-cost-or-market test. Perform the test at or near year end using the latest available relevant data, and review again for reasonableness at the time of engagement sign-off. If management intends to modify units to add the additional capacity, review estimates of additional costs to complete and proposed selling prices at year end, and review again for reasonableness at time of sign off. Allowance—Consider this when performing standard review of the adequacy of the allowance. Additionally, obtain information from next year-end and early into the next period (prior to sign-off) to track the actual experience on returns.

(2) Description: Client invests in marketable securities. Fluctuating value and ready marketability make these items inherently risky. Client's trading activity near year end is usually insignificant.

Exhibit 1–5 (continued)

Classification:	**Conclusion**
Balance(s):	Inherent risk, which includes factors within and outside of the scope of the client's existing internal control system, is often a crucial component of audit risk. To make an adequate assessment of inherent risk, we should:
Audit Objective(s):	
Procedures:	

Characteristic

Marketable securities

Accuracy of securities pricing

Completeness and validity

Volatility of price suggests a year-end pricing test. Low activity expectation and excellent client security and record-keeping procedures justifies observing the count of securities at a time prior to year end (e.g., 12/1). Review activity to year end and reconsider need for additional counts at year end. A "standard" review of the physical security over these items is sufficient.

Inherent risk, which includes factors within and outside of the scope of the client's existing internal control system, is often a crucial component of audit risk. To make an adequate assessment of inherent risk, we should:

- Be sensitive to the dynamics of the client's business, including the client's key competitors, customers, suppliers, and other related parties.
- Keep abreast of developments in the general business environment and the environment within which the client operates.
- Maintain ongoing communications, both formal and informal, with a broad spectrum of client personnel.
- Constantly relate the audit findings to the accumulated knowledge of the client's business and to audit risk.
- Maintain a posture of professional skepticism at all times.

Source: Lynford E. Graham, "Audit Risk—Part II," *CPA Journal* (September 1985), p. 40. Reprinted with permission from *The CPA Journal*, September 1985, copyright 1985.

Exhibit 1–6

Basic Audit Risk Components

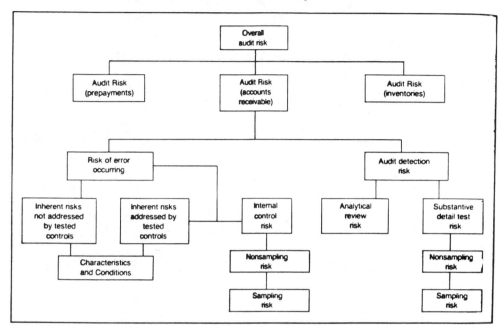

Source: Lynford E. Graham, "Audit Risk—Part II," *CPA Journal* (September 1985), p. 40. Reprinted with permission from *The CPA Journal,* September 1985, copyright 1985.

or sanctions imposed by regulators. Business risk thus may also affect insurance coverage and billing rates.[11]

WHY THE ATTENTION TO CONTROL?

Internal control encompasses the management information system for planning, control, decision-making, and reporting purposes. That portion of the system that affects reported accounting numbers is commonly referred to as the internal accounting control system of an entity. This subsystem is the focal point of the CPA for external auditing purposes.

The reason for the auditor's attention to the internal accounting control system of a client is its intrinsic role in generating the financial statements upon which he or she intends to express an opinion. Without an understanding of the internal accounting system and its controls, the auditor cannot describe information flows in a manner that facilitates the planning of an audit or the subsequent collection and testing of a data set. At times, in the process of initially reviewing controls, the CPA may determine that the design and control over the organization's information flow is so poor that the client is unauditable.

---

[11] See Craig A. Brumfield, Robert K. Elliott, and Peter D. Jacobson, "Business Risk and the Audit Process," *Journal of Accountancy*, April 1983, pp. 60–68.

Exhibit 1–7

Development of Overall Audit Plan

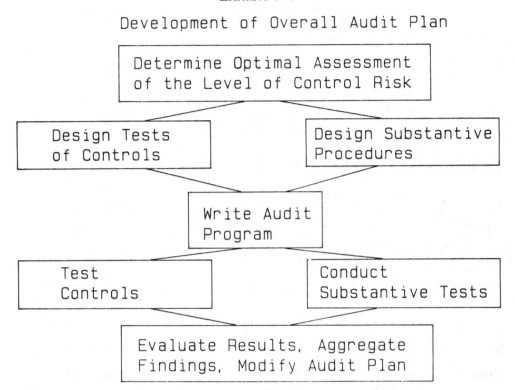

Source: Lynford E. Graham, "Audit Risk—Part V," *CPA Journal* (December 1985), p. 28. Reprinted with permission from *The CPA Journal,* December 1985, copyright 1985.

Objective #1: To Assess Whether the Entity Is Auditable

The initial decision the CPA must make concerning a prospective or new client is whether or not the entity is auditable. The decision is similar to the surgeon's decision as to whether or not a patient is operable, or to the attorney's decision as to whether a person has some legitimate defensible claim that can be taken to court. Just as the physician requires the presence of some minimum conditions before proceeding to prepare a patient for an operation, basic requirements must be met before an audit can be performed. However, just as the physician's judgment may assume the use of support devices external to the patient, such as breathing machines, the CPA's judgment may well assume the use of information sources external to an entity as a means of making an otherwise unauditable entity into an auditable operation.

The CPA's basic requirement is either that the entity to be audited has maintained some record of every transaction in which it has been involved or that some other party(ies) can create the equivalent of such a record. Once the CPA is sure that the information base is reasonably complete or can be made so without excessive cost, the entity can be audited. The audit process will test the completeness and overall reasonableness of the financial statements that are summarized from the information base to ascertain that the client's operations are fairly presented. However, the "garbage-in, garbage-out" adage would apply if the information set of the client were incomplete or incorrect as the result of double-recording of transactions, bogus documentation, or errors in documentation. No matter how well the client accumulates and transmits the data from the information set into the financial accounting records, in such a circumstance the initial or source documents for such records would contain errors that inevitably would become part of the financial representations. The means of compensating for shortcomings in the client's initial information set in order to make what appears to be an unauditable entity into an auditable one will be discussed in Chapter 5.

At times the CPA will determine that merely expanding audit procedures cannot compensate for the missing or erroneous data in the information set and will judge the entity, in its present condition, to be unauditable. Such was the case with the City of Cleveland.

> In Cleveland, Price Waterhouse studied the books, looked up, and announced that they were unauditable.[12]

Yet, as the phrase "in its present condition" suggests, an unauditable entity can be transformed into an auditable one through management's actions. By establishing procedures to ensure the initial documentation of all transactions with reasonable accuracy and researching historical transactions to acquire the detail necessary for proper contemporary records, management can frequently create an auditable entity in a relatively short time. One obvious means of expediting such a transformation is to have the CPA who judged the entity to be unauditable make some suggestions as to how to establish those critical attributes of its information system that could facilitate an audit. In fact, a typical process for privately held businesses that plan to register their securities with the Securities and Exchange Commission (SEC) is to establish a client relationship with a CPA at least three to five years in advance of going public. This practice provides the companies with an opportunity to improve their information system and accounting records to whatever extent is necessary to facilitate an audit.

Objective #2: To Assess Control Risk

Once a client is judged to be auditable, the next question is how to perform the audit in the most efficient and effective manner. A basic issue that the auditor must address is whether tests of control could be performed in lieu of some substantive tests and, if so, which mix of tests would be optimal in cost/benefit terms. The thought process for the CPA, in general terms, proceeds as follows:

---

[12] Peter F. Rousmaniere, "Auditing the Cities," The *Wall Street Journal* (May 7, 1979), p. 22.

(1) Which controls appear to be adequate, in terms of their design?
(2) What substantive tests could be reduced or omitted if these controls were relied upon?
(3) What are the relative costs of the proposed tests of control?
(4) If the cost savings from (2) exceed the costs of (3) and the probability of compliance with the controls described in (1) is expected to be high, proceed with the tests of control.
(5) If the tests of control support the adequacy of controls, assess control risk at less than the maximum level and reduce or omit substantive tests, as deemed appropriate.

The thought process clarifies how much auditors' judgments as to the level of control risk depend upon control system design capabilities, system performance, and the relative efficiency of audit procedures. A poorly designed system cannot be relied upon despite total compliance with the system, and a well-designed system cannot be relied upon if compliance is not observed. Furthermore, since compliance with some controls can be difficult if not impossible to observe, the cost of control test procedures or their ineffectiveness can result in a well-designed system, with which employees and managers comply, not being relied upon. *Note that the concept of reliance on internal control has been rephrased in GAAS into a concept of assessing control risk at less than a maximum level.*

Objective #3: To Plan the Nature, Timing, and Extent of Audit Procedures

Once the extent of potential reliance on controls is determined, the detailed plans as to the nature, timing, and extent of audit procedures can be laid.

Determining the nature of tests. The nature of tests depends on the planned assessment of control risk, as well as the audit objectives for the engagement. Audit procedures, while commonly delineated as either tests of control or substantive tests, are frequently dual-purpose tests. In other words, while the testing of controls is performed, evidence is frequently obtained regarding whether the dollar balances in the accounts are properly stated. Obviously, once a sample is drawn and the document is being examined by the auditor, the marginal cost of checking dollar amounts in addition to collecting evidence of control compliance is minor. In fact, in many cases the amount must be checked in order to collect sufficient evidence of compliance; in such a case, the substantive evidence is obtained at essentially zero cost.

In planning an audit, an awareness of control reliance possibilities allows a CPA to develop the most efficient mix of tests, generating dual-purpose evidence whenever possible. Beyond a control and/or substantive test objective, the auditor applies a judgment process as to the type of evidence necessary to form a sufficient basis for an audit report. The plans concerning the nature of this evidence encompass considerations ranging from trivial (how are particular types of documents filed by a client?) to critical (how reliable are the various sources of evidence and what is the more effective audit procedure for collecting such evidence?).

The reliability and effectiveness of various audit procedures will depend on the particular circumstances of the engagement. For example, despite the fact that auditing standards imply that detailed testing provides stronger evidence than inquiry procedures, such a generalization is not of any practical use in the multitude of situations where detailed testing alternatives are unavailable or where such evidence, due to its "snapshot" and possible "superficial" nature, is of limited value. To illustrate this latter point, a sample of 60 purchase orders for the past six months or operations will provide evidence for 60 specific points in time (i.e., 60 "snapshots") that authorization initials were placed on the purchase orders. However, whether the authorization was given subsequent to the performance of thorough prescribed procedures or, instead, was given on blank forms prior to the actual purchases, in an obviously superficial manner, cannot be detected by merely examining the completed purchase orders. Frequently, inquiry procedures can provide the desired continuity of evidence over the audit period, as well as some perspective as to whether there has been compliance in substance or only in form. Hence, if the objective of the auditor is to assess the competency with which control procedures are being performed, such as the example provided whereby initials are required to authorize a purchase, the more reliable evidence may well be collected through inquiry and direct observation procedures, rather than through detailed testing procedures.

Similarly, the general presumption that confirmation procedures are more reliable than auditing procedures such as vouching is erroneous when the parties to whom confirmations are being distributed happen to be related parties. In other words, the nature of tests is dependent on the audit circumstances but in all cases requires an understanding of the client's operations, information system, and controls. How else could the CPA discern who are the related parties with whom business is transacted, or how effective a particular test procedure is likely to be relative to some alternative testing approach?

Factors involved in the timing of audit procedures. In addition to establishing the nature of the test, the auditor must select the timing of the audit procedures. Timing encompasses PERT (Program Evaluation Review Technique)[13] considerations as well as audit risk assessments. With respect to the former, certain audit procedures must be performed at particular points in time, such as inventory observations and year-end cash counts; others require substantial lead time, such as first and second requests for confirmations; and certain procedures are most efficiently performed chronologically, such as the review of internal accounting control preceding substantive test work or the use of analytical procedures as a directing device for substantive test work. These considerations suggest a role for a PERT or network approach to planning an audit, as a means of assuring that critical paths are recognized and that the audit process proceeds in a systematic manner.

---

[13] PERT is a tool to assist managers in controlling large scale projects, such as a construction job or, in this case, an audit engagement. PERT diagrams typically show critical sequential and concurrent events (as circles) connected by arrows that represent various activities drawn in the necessary chronological order of performance. Activity times and costs can be estimated probabilistically and used to assess critical paths for use in planning and in evaluating the cost of delays in carrying out a particular activity.

The other issue to be considered in the course of planning an audit involves audit risk. The term "busy season" is well recognized as referring to CPAs' work overload from calendar year end to the end of tax season. Since work overloads result in higher costs of doing business due to overtime pay rates and the adverse results of fatigue and staff shortages, CPAs prefer to spread audit work to interim periods, i.e., to times other than at year-end. However, the ability to perform interim work as a basis for drawing inferences for the entire year of operations under review depends heavily upon the quality of the control system of the client. If controls are poor, the audit risk from performing extensive interim work in lieu of year-end work would very likely preclude such a trade off, whereas good controls could support this approach to an audit. Of course, whenever interim work is performed, some audit evidence pertaining to the period of time from the interim date to year end must be collected, regardless of the extent of reliance on controls. In part, this is because reliance on controls (assessment of control risk at less than the maximum level) requires testing for compliance with controls for the full period of time under review. Audit judgment will be the basis for (1) evaluating the relative risks of performing various audit procedures mid-year, at the end of the third quarter, at year end, or at some other point in time, (2) the alternative means of gaining assurance that financial statements are fairly presented for the period subsequent to interim work, and (3) the cost savings and efficiencies gained from differential timing of audit procedures (including advantages to a more continuous type of auditing strategy, i.e., a greater frequency of client contacts during the period under review).

Determining the extent of testing. The final aspect of planning that relates to the CPA's objectives in evaluating internal accounting controls concerns the extent of testing. The extent of substantive tests obviously depends on the level of control risk which is affected, in turn, by the extent and results of tests of control. A generally accepted approach to auditing is to first determine the level of control risk and then to reduce the extent of substantive testing, as appropriate, in light of the quality of the control system. For example, if the auditor rates a control system excellent, the extent of substantive testing will be less than if the system were judged to be good. Again, audit judgment is the focal point in determining the approximate extent of testing; however, such judgment requires a thorough understanding of controls as a foundation for decision making.

THE ROLE OF THE CONTROL EVALUATION IN THE COMPREHENSIVE REVIEW

The CPA offers services beyond an audit, one of which is commonly termed a comprehensive review of internal accounting controls. This distinct service is not a required part of an audit but represents a more extensive study and evaluation of internal accounting controls for the purpose of expressing an opinion on the system. In fact, this service can be provided to either an audit or a nonaudit client. Frequently, if this review engagement is combined with that of an audit, efficiencies can accrue in documentation, in the process of gaining a good understanding as to the client's operations and control systems, and in testing. Although the objectives of the two engagements are distinct, requiring that the CPA must be ever cognizant of both sets of objectives as the joint engagement is performed, many opportunities for cost savings exist. However, these opportunities may be overlooked if the CPA is not careful in considering both engagements during the planning stage. As an example, the comprehensive review engagement will require testing of all significant control procedures, whereas the audit engagement only requires tests of controls on which the auditor intends to rely because it is cost-beneficial to do so, relative to a substantive testing approach. If the CPA is requested to perform both a comprehensive review and an audit, the cost/benefit picture changes. Given that tests of control are to be performed anyway, to what extent can such tests (directed primarily at the objectives of a comprehensive review) be utilized to justify a reduction of the substantive tests that are planned for the audit engagement? Obviously any reduction translates to a cost savings relative to two separate engagements being performed, i.e., a comprehensive review and an audit.

Rather than focusing on audit risk and financial reporting problems, the CPA who performs a comprehensive review focuses on the significant control areas within the internal accounting control system. The objective of the CPA is to assess whether the system as a whole provides reasonable, but not absolute, assurance that (1) assets are being safeguarded, (2) transactions are being executed as authorized, and (3) records are being maintained in a manner that will facilitate the preparation of financial statements that follow generally accepted accounting principles. The CPA defines reasonable assurance by applying a materiality threshold. That threshold relates to the definition of a material weakness that is provided in the professional literature and is a topic that will be explored in depth in a later chapter.

Key Differences Between Control Evaluations Performed for a Comprehensive Review and for an Audit

A key difference in the role of the control evaluation for a comprehensive review and that performed for an audit is that the former is intended to disclose all material weaknesses, whereas the latter is not. In addition, the former will result in disclosure of all material weaknesses, while the audit report is not typically affected by material weaknesses and required disclosures of reportable conditions are limited to either oral or written communication to senior management and the board of directors or audit committee. The breadth of both testing and reporting with respect to internal accounting controls can be considerably wider for a comprehensive review engagement relative to an audit, particularly if little reliance on accounting controls is planned for the audit engagement (i.e., if control risk is assessed at the maximum level).

The Growing Interest in Disclosures Regarding Internal Accounting Control

The comprehensive review engagement with a related public report is a service that has been made a part of generally accepted auditing standards and is presently being revisited to consider an attestation standard for reporting on management's report on the effectiveness of an entity's internal control structure over financial reporting. While it is unclear what the market demand from other user groups will be for such a service, history has suggested that regulators have an interest in disclosures concerning internal accounting control. Exhibit 1–8 summarizes the recent history of proposals, pronouncements, and regulations related to internal accounting control. The clear implication to be drawn from this table is that regulators applied pressure to the profession and other participants in the market to provide disclosures regarding internal accounting control. Statement on Auditing Standards (SAS) No. 30, "Reporting on Internal Accounting Control," was the final formal response of the profession, after the regulators postponed the proposed rules that (1) reports on internal accounting control be mandatory disclosures, and (2) an auditor's opinion be required on such reports. This SAS will be discussed in greater depth in a later chapter, but an historical perspective on how this service evolved may help the CPA in gaining an understanding of the service and in describing it to clients. Further attention will be accorded to the proposed attestation standard in later chapters.

HOW A CAREFUL STUDY OF CONTROLS CAN BE INVALUABLE FOR ADVISING MANAGEMENT

Management Advisory Services encompass any means by which the CPA can assist the client in improving operations, as related to both accounting and non-accounting matters. Opportunities to assist a client are frequently suggested to the CPA in the course of providing other services, such as an audit or comprehensive review engagement. An important technique that permits the CPA to assist a client in identifying trouble spots as well as those aspects of operations that are conducive to productivity gains through the application of new controls, systems, reporting practices, or new technology, is the CPA's practice of evaluating a client's control system, an integral part of the audit and, of course, the comprehensive review engagement. Similarly, the particular means of eliminating trouble spots and/or enhancing operating efficiency is often suggested to the auditor through a careful study of controls.

Just as economies can be realized by integrating the CPA's review and audit engagements, an advisory service that is performed by a CPA who is performing a comprehensive review and/or audit can be expected to generate cost savings. The primary additional consideration that arises is that of independence. However, the profession seems capable of selecting and performing advisory services that are consistent with maintaining independence as evidenced, in part, by the Public

Exhibit 1–8

Recent Proposals, Pronouncements, and Regulations Related to Internal Accounting Controls

Securities and Exchange Commission (SEC) (Securities Exchange Act Release No. 13185)	—Proposed requirement that management maintain an adequate system of internal control	January 19, 1977
	—Expressed interest in requiring internal control reports to shareholders	
The Commission on Auditor's Responsibilities (Report of Tentative Conclusions) (see also the Report, Conclusions, and Recommendations, 1978)	—Recommended auditor's report on material weaknesses to management, "including, if appropriate, the audit committee or the full board" (p. 39)	1977
	—Recommended a report by management on internal controls and management's response to the auditor's suggestions for correction of weaknesses	
	—Recommended a report by the auditor "on whether he agrees with management's description of the company's controls" that would also "describe material uncorrected weaknesses not disclosed in that report" (p. 61)	
American Institute of Certified Public Accountants (AICPA) Auditing Standards Board (Statement on Auditing Standards No. 20)	—Required communication of material weaknesses in internal accounting controls	August, 1977
Congress [Foreign Corrupt Practices Act of 1977 (FCPA)]	—Required public companies to maintain adequate systems of internal accounting controls	December 19, 1977

Exhibit 1–8 (continued)

Securities and Exchange Commission (Accounting Series Release No. 242)	—Advised companies to "review their accounting procedures, systems of internal accounting controls and business practices in order that they may take any actions necessary to comply with the requirements contained in the Act" (FCPA) (43FR7752)	February 16, 1978
Financial Executives Institute (FEI) (Guidelines for Preparation of A Statement of Management Responsibility for Financial Statements)	—Endorsed the furnishing of management reports, including "Management's assessment of the effectiveness of the internal accounting control system" (p. 1)	June, 1978
AICPA, Reports by Management Special Advisory Committee (Tentative Conclusions and Recommendations)	—Tentatively concluded that annual reports to shareholders should include a management report which should discuss internal accounting control	December 8, 1978
Securities and Exchange Commission (Statement of Management on Internal Accounting Control; delayed for 1979 per AICPA [December 10, 1979, p. 1])	—Proposed rules that would require a management statement and an auditor's opinion on internal accounting control by all SEC registrants	April, 1979
AICPA, Auditing Standards Board (Exposure draft: Reporting on Internal Accounting Control)	—Provides guidance on reports made as part of an engagement to study and evaluate internal accounting control, as well as reports based solely on the review of controls made as part of an audit	December 31, 1979
Securities and Exchange Commission (Statement on Withdrawal of Proposal to Require Reports on Internal Accounting Controls)	—Withdrew rules proposed in April, 1979, and announced the SEC's intention to monitor voluntary private-sector initiatives in this area through the spring of 1982 and then to reconsider regulatory action	June 6, 1980

Exhibit 1–8 (continued)

AICPA, "Reporting on Internal Accounting Control" Statement on Auditing Standards No. 30	—Final form of above described exposure draft	July 1980
The Treadway Commission [National Commission on Fraudulent Reporting]	—Recommends that its sponsoring organizations "cooperate in developing integrated guidance on internal controls" and calls for broader controls that can address management override risks	October 1987
AICPA, "Consideration of the Internal Control Structure in a Financial Statement Audit," Statement on Auditing Standards No. 55	—Altered second standard of field work to focus on control structure	April 1988
Securities and Exchange Commission Proposed Report of Management's Responsibilities (Release No. 33-6789)	—Proposed requirement of registrants to report on management's responsibilities for the preparation of the registrant's financial statements and other financial information, and for establishing and maintaining a system of internal control directly related to financial reporting, including management's assessment of the effectiveness of the system of internal control, including a statement as to management's response to significant recommendations on controls made by internal and independent accountants (a materiality threshold is included as is a point-in-time focus)	July 1988
Securities and Exchange Commission Item 303 of Regulation S-K (SAR No.	—Management Discussion and Analysis disclosures address liquidity and other condi-	May 18, 1989

Exhibit 1–8 (continued)

6231, 1980) and interpretive Release Nos. 33-6835; 34-2683; IC-16961; FR-36	tions related to financing and operations; may influence need for internal control standards	
Congressman Dingell and Wyden Proposed Amendment to the S&L Crime Bill	—Would have required a management report on the adequacy of the internal control system and an auditor's report on management's assessment (also would have codified related party, illegal acts, and going concern auditing standards, and called for direct reporting to the SEC by auditors of illegal acts)	1990
AICPA, Proposed Statement on Standards for Attestation Engagements: "Reporting on Management's Report on the Effectiveness of an Entity's Internal Control Structure Over Financial Reporting" (File Reference No. 4287)	—Provides guidance to a CPA engaged to examine and report on management's report (assertion) on the effectiveness of an entity's internal control structure over financial reporting, including annual and interim financial statements	September 12, 1990

Source: Wanda A. Wallace, "Internal Control Reporting Practices in the Municipal Sector," *The Accounting Review* (July, 1981, p. 667); *Reporting of the National Commission on Fraudulent Financial Reporting* (October 1987), p. 11; AICPA Pronouncements; SEC Proposals; Congressional activities

Oversight Board's inability to identify any adverse effect on independence of CPAs' regular involvement in advisory service engagements.[14]

An understanding of a client's operations is essential to the CPA, whether the planned engagement is an audit, a comprehensive review, or an advisory service. If a client selects three CPAs to perform the three services rather than one CPA, the cost of the CPAs' gaining of a basic understanding of the business will essentially be paid three times. The additional cost of the three CPAs becoming acquainted with the control systems can be substantial, compared to the cost of utilizing one CPA who is already familiar with both operations and controls through having provided other services for the client in past periods. Of course, while audits require CPAs, advisory services are offered by numerous consulting companies as well as by CPAs. The CPAs' ability to evaluate internal controls is one of the attributes that clearly distinguish their experience from that of other consultants.

While not a separable management advisory service, the common issuance of the so-called "management letters" or "control-point suggestions" is part of the service package typically provided by the auditor. Such reports are facilitated and enhanced by the CPA's understanding and evaluation of controls. Even when a management suggestion is related to such operating characteristics as cash management, the idea that a problem existed probably arose during the CPA's review of controls over cash-related activities of the client, during either the evaluation or the testing phase of the CPA's analysis of controls. Management letters, although not required by professional standards, are regularly provided to audit clients. The implication is that such letters are probably a joint product with the audit and are regularly demanded by the clients. Hence, from a competitive perspective, the CPA wishes to prepare a consistently useful list of suggestions for management, and one means of assimilating such a report is to be well informed as to the control system of the client's entity. Note that generally accepted auditing standards require communication of reportable conditions, as will be discussed in a later chapter. These are likely to considerably overlap the management letter content.

OBJECTIVES IN EVALUATING INTERNAL CONTROLS FOR INTERNAL AUDITING PURPOSES

Internal auditing departments are responsible for exercising control over an entity's system of internal control as a service to management. The purview of their interest expands beyond internal accounting controls, as many of their assignments relate to operational audits. The purpose of their review is to ascertain whether the control system provides reasonable assurance that the organization's objectives will be met efficiently. The review activity will encompass the entire

---

[14] *Scope of Services by CPA Firms—Public Oversight Board Report* (New York: American Institute of Certified Public Accountants), 1979.

management process and hence, in addition to internal accounting controls, the entity's administrative controls, management controls, operational controls, and output controls are all of concern to the internal auditor.

The review is intended to provide reasonable assurance that

—appropriate objectives have been established;
—plans have been made to authorize, monitor and periodically compare assets to the accounting records, as well as to document such activities to the extent required to attain the entity's objectives; and
—objectives and goals are achieved.

In addition, internal auditors are required to be alert to the possibility of intentional wrongdoing, errors and omissions, inefficiency, waste, ineffectiveness and conflicts of interest. (The Institute of Internal Auditors, *Standards for the Professional Practice of Internal Auditing.* Altamonte Springs: IIA, 1978. Guideline 280.1.)

The Statement on Internal Auditing Standard No. 1 entitled "Control: Concepts and Responsibilities" emphasizes that control is any action taken by management to enhance the likelihood that established objectives and goals will be achieved and results from management's planning, organizing, and directing. Internal auditing is expected to examine and evaluate the planning, organizing, and directing processes to determine whether reasonable assurance exists and that objectives and goals will be achieved, with all systems, processes, operations, functions, and activities within the organization being subject to internal auditing's evaluations.

OBJECTIVES OF SYSTEM DESIGNERS IN EVALUATING INTERNAL CONTROLS

Obviously, system designers have a joint objective: first, to design a system that will meet the information and operating needs of the various user groups, and second, to ensure the reliability and efficiency of that system. It is the latter concern that provides an incentive for the system designer to explicitly evaluate existing and proposed internal control dimensions of any system. The fact that controls can be more efficiently built into a system at the planning phase than added to a system at some later date is another important motivation for entities to hire system designers who are also specialists in evaluating internal controls.

OBJECTIVES IN EVALUATING INTERNAL CONTROLS IF YOU'RE NEITHER AN AUDITOR NOR A SYSTEM DESIGNER

Just as the internal auditor has an interest in whether management's objectives are being achieved, operating managers and directors who have primary responsibility for meeting their objectives have an incentive to analyze the overall control system, which is intended to assist them in carrying out and monitoring their activities. Any opportunity for cost-justified control enhancements or operating improvements can increase the probability of achieving stated objectives. In addition, the recognition of control problems and related risks can be critical to effective decision-making. A legal obligation also exists; the Foreign Corrupt Practices Act requires that public companies have adequate controls. Internal control evaluations are of concern to controllers as well as to line managers. The integrity of the financial accounting reporting system is heavily dependent upon the internal accounting control system. Threats to such systems include the addition of unauthorized or bogus transactions, the loss of information, and the inaccuracy of reported numbers. Controls must be established to address each of these threats.

As depicted in Exhibit 1–8, regulators are increasingly interested in controls and related reports thereon. Most believe that some mandatory report on controls by management is likely to be a part of regulation either from the Securities and Exchange Commission or from Congress in the next few years. Should that be the case, it is increasingly important for directors and top management to thoroughly understand the concept of control and how it can most effectively be achieved.

Real-Time Considerations

In this age of real-time information access, an increased need exists for continuous controls. Management requires information to effectively manage, yet if this information is faulty, the consequences can be devastating. It is insufficient to wait until month-end, quarter-end, or year-end, to gain assurance that the information system is credible. Effective controls are essential to ensuring useful information for decision making.

Employees' Understanding

Literature on quality control has emphasized a key role for quality education system classes for employees, brainstorming toward problem solutions, and suggestions from line personnel.[15] To institute modern methods of on-the-job training and to break down barriers between departments are two critical recommendations put forth by W. Edwards Deming.[16] All of these processes involve achieving real understanding by workers and managers alike of what control is. Recognition of problems, the ability to propose solutions, and assumed understanding by decision makers of key tradeoffs and related consequences are capabilities being attributed to employees that require knowledge.

---

[15] Craig R. Waters, "Quality Beings at Home," *Inc.* (Vol. 7, No. 8, August 1985), pp. 68–71.

[16] Jackie Roth, "The Stuff That Quality Is Made Of," *Industrial Management* (Canada) (Vol. 9, No. 7, August 1985), pp. 18–19 and Bradford W. Parkinson, "Factory Automation Without Frustration," *Chief Executive* (no. 28, Summer 1984), pp. 30–32.

It has been pointed out that Japanese industry devotes on average one of five days to employees' education; American industry is woefully behind in this regard. The content of this book is one example of a place to start in achieving employees' understanding of control concepts and their role in iteratively improving both control and, consequently, the success of an enterprise.

Directors' Responsibilities

Since 1978, the New York Stock Exchange has required audit committees to be formed, comprised of nonemployee directors. In 1989, NASDAQ created a similar rule except that only a majority of the members must be nonemployees. The concept underlying these requirements is that corporate governance would be enhanced through these committees' oversight of reporting, auditing, and control practices of the entity.

In a sense, the SEC's pressure for audit committees has given more power to the CPAs when interacting with management, because of their direct reporting link with outside directors. The general definition of an audit committee, its responsibilities, and its typical means of discharging committees' responsibilities are outlined in Exhibit 1–9.

Unfortunately, cases have arisen in which audit committees' effectiveness has been questioned. MiniScribe is facing a number of lawsuits totaling hundreds of millions of dollars and among the major defendants are "Officers and directors individually and . . . the firms employing two audit committee members . . . described as 'deep-pocket defendants.' "[17] The MiniScribe audit committee met only once in 1987 and once in 1986 according to the proxy statements, whereas an average of four audit committee meetings per year for the industry in general is a norm. Indeed, for the entire board questions have been raised since "Board meetings were not regularly scheduled in advance, and several took place by telephone. . . . Sufficiently detailed materials were often not made available to directors in advance of meetings."[18] One clear implication of such problem cases is that directors need to understand control structure and how they can effectively fulfill their corporate governance responsibilities.

Litigation Support Settings

As suggested by the liability exposure of directors, litigation is an ever increasing element in business. Beyond providing, additional incentives for designing and monitoring effective controls, litigation itself involves the accumulation of information and relevant evidence to demonstrate the facts involved in a dispute and the economic consequences of various events. The litigation process

---

[17] Curtis C. Verschoor, "The Aftermath of Audit Committee Ineffectiveness at MiniScribe," *Internal Auditing* (Vol. 6, No. 1, Summer 1990), pp. 25–28, quote on p. 26.

[18] MiniScribe Form 8-K Current Report dated September 12, 1989, p. 11.

Exhibit 1-9

Audit Committees

- Audit committees are typically composed of three to five directors who are outside directors; preferably at least one member will have financial experience.

- Responsibilities should include
  —the nomination of the independent accountants and discussion of their work with them.
  —the review and evaluation of reports on control weaknesses.
  —follow-up to ascertain whether management has taken appropriate action on these recommendations.
  —a review of financial statements and interim reports with the independent accountants.
  —establishing a direct line of communications between the directors and independent accountants.
  —appraisal of the effectiveness of the audit effort, including discussion of scope, opinion, and desirable areas for special emphasis.
  —determination that management placed no restrictions on the auditors.
  —inquiry into the effectiveness of the company's management in financial and accounting functions and the absence of illegal or improper payments.
  —evaluation of the internal audit department's effectiveness.
  —review of limited review engagements, including asking about large or unusual transactions, the adequacy of disclosure, accounting developments affecting reporting practices, and changes in accounting and operating controls.

- To discharge such responsibilities, three to four meetings a year are commonly held, and those present may include legal counsel and others with information relevant to auditing, accounting, and disclosure issues. Auditors should be permitted to request a special meeting with the audit committee to discuss topics requiring special attention. Assuming four meetings a year, the likely agenda for each meeting would be
  1. the objectives and scope of the audit process, including attention to reporting requirements, recent developments in financial reporting, and the overall audit plan.
  2. the audit's status after interim work and problems needing attention before year-end.
  3. review of the financial statements to be submitted to the board, including a review of the auditor's report and consideration of the independent accountants' need to meet with the board.
  4. a final review of the audit and preparation of a committee report to the full board.

Adapted from Price Waterhouse, *The Audit Committee: The Board of Directors and the Independent Accountant* (New York: Price Waterhouse, 1976), pp. 1–12.

requires the implementation of control concepts to ensure the integrity of the data bases accessed, formulated, analyzed, and otherwise applied in the course of deliberations, trials, or other resolutions. An understanding of control permits better assessment of various types of risk exposure, strengths and weaknesses of alternative evidential sources, and means by which improved assurance can be obtained as to the credibility of information being gathered and evaluated. These considerations are the subject matter of Chapter 19.

Control Consciousness

The attitude of organizations constitutes their "control consciousness"—how that attitude is developed and how it is maintained as part of the corporate culture will determine whether control methods are developed and applied or set aside. Too often controls are circumvented not due to sinister motives but merely due to a lack of understanding of the purpose of control, its positive effects, and the manner in which one control element interrelates with a variety of other elements in the control system. A virtual snowball effect can result from individuals lacking a control consciousness. If you're neither an auditor nor a system designer, this book is nonetheless directed toward your needs, since control consciousness must permeate an effective economic entity and by definition you are a part of that control consciousness.

SYNOPSIS

A CPA's objectives in evaluating internal accounting controls may relate to an external audit engagement, a comprehensive review service, or a management advisory client setting. If the client is to be audited, the internal accounting control evaluation process encompasses three primary decisions:

—whether the entity is auditable,

—the appropriate degree of reliance to place on internal accounting controls (i.e., the level of control risk), and

—how to plan the nature, timing, and extent of auditing procedures.

An Appendix to this chapter provides an historical perspective of the GAAS framework for evaluating control in an audit setting Pre SAS No. 55. Recall that Exhibit 1–2 reflects SAS No. 55. If instead of an audit a comprehensive review is being performed, the CPA must gain an understanding of the internal accounting control system and must also test the system to see whether or not reasonable control is present. The management advisory services provided by a CPA can range from special projects, such as an inventory control problem, to accounting and control systems design. While the latter obviously requires an understanding of existing controls and expertise regarding control systems, the former also requires an understanding of the client's operations and present controls. Control issues permeate all types of CPA engagements and are formalized not only in auditors' working papers, but also in informal reports to the client, commonly termed management letters, a service that might be described as a management advisory by-product of the audit engagement.

Internal auditors review the entire control system of an organization in order to ascertain that it provides reasonable assurance that objectives and goals will be met efficiently. System designers' concern for controls stems from their objective of ensuring the reliability and efficiency of systems. Operating managers can increase the probability of achieving stated objectives by evaluating the strengths and weaknesses of controls and by implementing cost-justified control enhancements. Directors and managers have a legal obligation under the Foreign Corrupt Practices Act to maintain an adequate internal accounting control system. Controllers have particular concern for the integrity of the reporting system, which is determined largely by the adequacy of controls. Employees' contributions to controls and enhancement of the effectiveness of overall operations are largely a function of them first understanding control structure. Similarly, those involved in litigation support activities can more effectively discharge their responsibilities—in both helping to assemble and to analyze information relevant to the facts of the case and the economic consequences of various events in dispute—by applying control concepts to the process of gathering, maintaining, and evaluating evidence.

GAAS: The Historical Framework for Control Assessment Pre SAS No. 55

I. TO APPROPRIATELY EVALUATE SPECIFIC CONTROLS, THE AUDITOR SHOULD HAVE AN UNDERSTANDING OF THE ENVIRONMENT OR GENERAL CONTROLS OF THE CLIENT

Related Statements on Auditing Standards

A. *Objective*

To fulfill the auditor's *second standard of field-work*

B. *Attitude*

The auditor should plan and perform an examination with an attitude of professional *skepticism*, recognizing that the application of auditing procedures may produce evidential matter indicating the possibility of errors on irregularities. (AU § 327.06)

C. *Awareness*

There are *inherent limitations* that should be recognized in considering the potential effectiveness of any system of accounting control, including possibilities for errors arising from

- misunderstanding of instructions,
- mistakes of judgment,
- personal carelessness,
- distraction,
- fatigue,
- collusion,
- management override,

- changes in conditions making controls inadequate, and
- deterioration of the degree of compliance.

(AU § 320.33)

D. *Environment*

Reasonable assurance that the objectives of accounting control are achieved depends on

- the *competence* and integrity of personnel,
- the independence of their assigned functions, and
- their understanding of the prescribed procedures.

These factors provide an *environment conducive to ac-counting control.* (AU § 320.35–320.36)

Incompatible functions for accounting control purposes are those which place any person in a position both to per-petrate and to conceal errors or irregularities in the normal course of his duties. (AU § 320.36)

The independent auditor should acquire an understand-ing of the *internal audit function* as it relates to his study and evaluation of internal accounting control. (AU § 322.03)

The organization and procedures required to accomplish those (control) objectives may be influenced by the method of *data processing* used. (AU § 320.33 and 321)

E. Other Concerns

The study and evaluation of internal control frequently provides a basis for *constructive suggestions to clients* concerning improvements in internal control. (AU § 320.07)

The auditor should inquire about the client's policies relevant to the prevention of *illegal acts* and internal communications, such as directives issued by the client and periodic representations obtained by the client from management at appropriate levels of authority concerning compliance with laws and regulations. (AU § 328.08)

II. AS A MEANS OF SELECTING THOSE SPECIFIC CONTROLS FOR FURTHER STUDY, IDENTIFY THOSE FINANCIAL STATEMENT CAPTIONS, GENERAL LEDGER ACCOUNTS, OR ASSETS THAT ARE POTENTIAL SOURCES OF MATERIAL FINANCIAL STATEMENT ERROR

Related Statements on Auditing Standards

Identify those controls that have an important bearing on the *reliability* of financial records for external reporting purposes—while such controls are expected to be primarily accounting controls, some administrative controls are likely to be critical in an auditor's evaluation of internal control. (AU § 320.12, AU § 320.19)

Identify those controls that are concerned mainly with the *safeguarding* of assets against loss from unintentional or intentional errors or irregularities. (AU § 320.19)

Identify all significant accounts and valuable moveable assets underlying significant financial statement amounts

Study and evaluate only those controls which will assist in determining whether the organization is auditable or upon which the auditor may choose to rely in determining the nature, timing, and extent of audit procedures

CONSIDER:

SALES
- of inventory
- of services
- of other assets
- of stock including original issue

RECEIPTS (Other than on Loans)

PURCHASES
- of inventory
- of services
- of other assets
- of stock

PAYMENTS (Other than on Loans)

SHIPMENTS

EXCHANGES

III. DOCUMENT THE DIRECT FLOW OF ACCOUNTING INFORMATION FROM THE POINT AT WHICH IT ENTERS THE PROCESSING SYSTEM UNTIL ITS ULTIMATE COMPILATION IN THE GENERAL LEDGER FOR SETS OF RELATED ACCOUNTS AS A MEANS OF DEMONSTRATING AN UNDERSTANDING OF THE INFORMATION SYSTEM AND TO PROVIDE A FRAMEWORK FOR CONTROL EVALUATION

Related Statements on Auditing Standards

DEBT-RELATED

Other Capital Transactions

Foreign Currency Exchange

A. *Objective*

To fulfill the first phase of a study to evaluate internal control: the auditor is required to gain

Knowledge and understanding of the procedures and methods prescribed—referred to as the review of *the system.* Typically this understanding is gained by inquiry, review of clients' documentation, and a tracing of the transactions which are documented in a form which suits the auditor's needs or preferences, and facilitate a preliminary evaluation (assuming satisfactory compliance with the prescribed system). (AU § 320.50–320.54)

B. *Transaction Cycle Emphasis*

Controls and weaknesses affecting different classes of transactions are not offsetting in their effect. The auditor's

review of the system of accounting control and his tests of compliance should be related to the purposes of his evaluation of the system. For this reason, *generalized or overall evaluations are not useful* for auditors because they do not help the auditor decide the extent to which auditing procedures may be restricted. (AU § 320.66)

Transactions are the basic components of business operations and, therefore, are the primary subject matter of internal control, including exchanges of assets or services with parties outside the business entity and transfers or use of assets or services within it. (AU § 320.20)

For purposes of analyzing internal controls first focus on information flows related to exchanges and nonreciprocal transaction types, allocations, and valuations to insure the review of controls is comprehensive

C. *Critical Information Flow*

The primary functions involved in the flow of transactions and related assets include:

- the *authorization* of transactions
  —either general authorization, concerned with the definition or identification of the general conditions under which transactions are authorized without regard to the specific parties or transactions, or
  —specific authorization, referring to a single transaction and comprehending both the conditions under which transactions are authorized and the parties involved in the transaction;
- the *execution* of transactions which includes the entire cycle of steps necessary to complete the exchange of assets between the parties or the transfer or use of assets within the business;
- the *recording* of transactions which comprehends all records maintained with respect to the transactions and the resulting assets or services and all functions performed with respect to such records—thus, the preparation and summarization of records and the posting thereof to the general ledger and subsidiary ledger are included; and
- the *accountability* for resulting assets which results from following assets from the time of their acquisition in one transaction until their disposition or use in another by maintaining records and making periodic comparisons of these records with the related assets.

(AU § 320.20–320.25)

Document information flows to all significant accounts identified

IV. DOCUMENT AND TEST BOUNDARY CONTROLS, DOCUMENT SAFEGUARD CONTROLS, DOCUMENT PROCESSING CONTROLS, AND IF BOUNDARY CONTROLS ARE TO BE RELIED UPON, DOCUMENT PROCESSING CONTROLS. FOCUS UPON CONTROL POINTS WHERE POPULATION AND ACCURACY ERRORS COULD OCCUR.

Related Statements on Auditing Standards

A. *A Logical Approach to Control Evaluation*

A conceptually logical approach to the auditor's evaluation of accounting control, which focuses directly on the purpose of preventing or detecting material errors and irregularities in financial statements is to apply the following steps in considering each significant class of transactions and related assets involved in the audit:

a. Consider the *types of errors and irregularities* that could occur.

b. Determine the accounting control *procedures that* should *prevent or detect* such errors and irregularities.

c. Determine whether the necessary *procedures* are *prescribed* and *are being followed* satisfactorily.

d. *Evaluate any weaknesses*—i.e., types of potential errors and irregularities not covered by existing control procedures—to determine their effect on (1) the nature, timing, or extent of auditing procedures to be applied and (2) suggestions to be made to the clients.

(AU § 320.65)
B. *Objective*
The objective of accounting control with respect to the *recording of transactions* requires that

• they be recorded at the amounts,
• they be recorded in the accounting periods in which they were executed, and
• they be classified in appropriate accounts.

(AU § 320.37)

V. COMPLIANCE TEST PROCESSING AND SAFEGUARD CONTROLS

A. *Objective*
To fulfill the second phase of a study to evaluate internal control the auditor is required to obtain *a reasonable degree of assurance* that controls are in use and are operating as planned—referred to as tests of compliance. Such tests are required for reliance on controls in determining the nature, timing, or extent of substantive tests of particular classes of transactions or balances, but are not necessary if the procedures are not to be relied upon for that purpose. Nonreliance can result from the auditor's conclusion.

Identify controls over capturing the data which take place at the boundary of the entity: BOUNDARY CONTROLS

Boundary controls are directed at
• POPULATION ERRORS—errors in the number of items of data and/or
• ACCURACY ERRORS—discrepancies between items of information captured or processed and the true items of information.

Identify controls over the custody of property: SAFEGUARD CONTROLS—focus on control points where population and accuracy errors might occur.
Identify controls over processing exchange data, allocations, and valuations: PROCESSING CONTROLS—focus on control points where population and accuracy errors might occur.

Related Statements on Auditing Standards

• that the procedures are not satisfactory for that purpose or
• that the audit effort required to test compliance with the procedures to justify reliance on them in making substantive tests would exceed the reduction in effort that could be achieved by such reliance.

(AU § 320.50–320.55)

The purpose of comparing recorded accountability with assets is *to determine whether the actual assets agree with* the *recorded accountability*, providing evidence of unrecorded or improperly recorded transactions. Such a comparison should

- be made independently,
- be made as frequently as the nature and amount of the assets involved and the cost of making the comparison suggest is reasonable for safeguarding purposes,
- be made as frequently as the materiality of assets and their susceptibility of loss through errors or irregularities suggest for record reliability purposes, and
- result in appropriate action with respect to any discrepancies revealed by the comparison of recorded accountability with assets. Such action will depend primarily on the nature of the asset, the system in use, and the amount and cause of the discrepancy.

(AU § 320.43–320.48)

B. *Compliance Tests*

Obtaining reasonable assurance that *transactions* are *executed as authorized* requires independent evidence

- that authorizations are issued by persons acting within the scope of their authority, and
- that transactions conform with the terms of the authorizations.

(AU § 320.37)

The objective of safeguarding assets requires that *access to assets* be *limited* to authorized personnel. (AU § 320.42)

Tests of compliance are concerned primarily with these questions:

- *Were necessary procedures performed?*
- *How were they performed?*
- *By whom were they performed?*

(AU § 320.57)

C. *Dual Purpose Evidence*

Auditing procedures often *concurrently provide* evidence of compliance with accounting control procedures as well as *evidence required for substantive purposes.* (AU § 320.56)

D. *EDP*

Situations involving the more complex EDP applications ordinarily will require that the auditor apply *specialized expertise in EDP* in the performance of necessary audit procedures. (AU § 321.04)

VI. DETERMINE EXTENT OF RELIANCE ON INTERNAL CONTROL AND THE EFFECTS OF CONTROL EVALUATION, INCLUDING COMPLIANCE TEST RESULTS, ON THE NATURE, TIMING, AND EXTENT OF SUBSTANTIVE TESTING

Related Statements on Auditing Standards

A. The Adequacy of Controls for Auditing Purposes

Prescribed *procedures and compliance* therewith are *satisfactory* for the auditor's purpose if the auditor's review and tests disclose no condition he believes to be a material weakness—a condition in which the auditor believes the prescribed procedure or the degree of compliance with them does not provide reasonable assurance that errors or irregularities in amounts that would be material in the financial statements being audited would be prevented or detected within a timely period by employees in the normal course of performing their assigned functions. (AU § 320.69)

B. Disclosure Responsibilities

If in the course of complying with generally accepted auditing standards, the auditor becomes aware of a *material weakness* in internal accounting control, communication to senior management and to the board of directors or its audit committee (or the equivalent level of authority, such as a board of trustees) at the earliest practicable date following the completion of the examination or at an interim date is required. Although generally accepted auditing standards permit oral communication, given appropriate notations are made to the working papers to document the discussion (AU § 323.05), it is firm policy to require a written report of material weaknesses, to avoid any possible misunderstanding.

C. Limitations on Control Reliance

The second standard [of field work] does *not* contemplate that the auditor will place *complete reliance* on internal control to the exclusion of other auditing procedures with respect to material *amounts* in the financial statements. (AU § 320.71)

If compliance tests indicate that controls are functioning effectively, then reliance may reasonably be placed on the controls tested and the nature, timing, and extent of the related substantive procedures may be modified

When compliance deviations are unacceptable

- compensating audit procedures may be available,
- the cause of such deviations should be considered for reporting in the management letter and for follow-up if illegal acts are suggested, and
- the relationship of deviations and weaknesses to other phases of the audit should be considered.

2

The Control Structure

"Every great man of business has got somewhere a touch of the idealist in him."

Woodrow Wilson, 1913[1]

To initiate a useful discussion of control structure, it is helpful to first develop some perspective as to a number of control principles that affect organizations. Foremost in this perspective is a personal view that the foundation of good control is ethical behavior. Not only is ethical behavior of value, in and of itself, but it is also true that good ethics is good business. Or, to put this idea differently, ethical organizations are likely to be more successful than unethical organizations. This implies that it is in an organization's best interest, economic and otherwise, to be ethical. For this to occur, in part, means that its individual employees must believe that ethical behavior is in their best interest. A reputation for integrity and "fairness" has to be valued, rewarded, and nurtured within the operations of the organization. Internal control is both an indication of ethical behavior and a device through which ethical behavior can be developed and maintained.

These and expanded ideas were developed and influenced by some discussions and joint efforts of myself and a team of professionals with diverse backgrounds. Specifically, that team was comprised of (1) Howard L. Siers, retired General Auditor of E.I. DuPont de Nemours & Co., (2) James K. Loebbecke, past Auditing

---

[1] Michael Jackman, *The Macmillan Book of Business & Economic Quotations* (New York, New York: Macmillan Publishing Company, 1984), p. 76.

Standards Board member, former partner of Touche Ross, and presently an academician at the University of Utah, (3) William D. Hall, retired partner of Arthur Andersen & Co. and former Managing Director of Accounting Principles and Auditing Procedures and Chairman of the firm's Committee on Professional Standards, as well as present Chairman of the Quality Control Inquiry Committee of the SEC Practice Section of the American Institute of Certified Public Accountants, (4) Keagle W. Davis, former audit partner of Touche Ross and National Director of Computer Auditing from 1968 to 1973 and currently consulting, and (5) myself. The results of our joint efforts in describing our combined perspective on internal control are presented in Exhibit 2–1. These ideas provide an excellent starting point for exploring control structure.

Exhibit 2–1
Perspectives on Internal Control

An Attitude Problem . . .

Control is largely a function of attitude. In order to have good control, there must be a positive attitude toward control throughout the organization. As research studies have found, such attitudes must start from the top. Top management must consider control to be important and communicate that belief down the organization. Such communication must be consistent and effective. Actions must support words. For example, violators of important control policies should not be excused. Similarly, there should be no reprisals for "whistle-blowing."

Faced with pressure for reflecting forecasts or higher levels of earnings per share (EPS), financial managers may succumb to such pressure by "managing" numbers, thereby sending a message through the entire accounting organization of the entity. The tone at the top must actively deter such behavior and resultant attitudes.

An important economic basis for control is that the cost of controls is exceeded by the benefits they derive. It is important for reinforcement of a positive attitude toward control that management be aware of the benefits that controls obtain, and that they make employees aware of those benefits in turn. The objective should be that all in the organization come to believe that good control is part of the corporate culture, for the reasons that it contributes to the essential well-being of the organization and all its members in very real terms.

Grassroots: *Completing the Circle* . . .

At the same time as top management emphasizes the importance of control, there must be grassroots activities that continually reinforce such statements by management. In other words, there must be discipline in the organization that calls the importance of good control habits and practices to the attention of all employees on a continuing basis. For example, we would propose that a common grassroots element across all economic units is some incidence of expense reimbursement procedures that apply to most employees and "set the stage" as to whether controls

Exhibit 2–1 (continued)

are taken seriously. If a form exists that fits the purpose, has clear instructions, is reasonable in its expectations, and is sequentially processed in a manner consistent with controls to ensure that only legitimate expenditures are reimbursed, a sense of the control attitudes of the organization is established. Indeed, we believe that you can determine the quality of the control environment of an organization by reviewing expense reporting practices. If top management has sloppy expense reporting practices, this permeates the organization and this sloppiness is not limited to expense reporting practices. People who are allowed to submit sloppy expense reports tend to be careless in other areas of their work. Internal controls break down and ultimately, a disaster results. On the other hand, strong support at every layer of the organization for good expense reporting practices will deliver a message. Install an accounting review for documentation support prior to approval to avoid embarrassing the employee or the manager, and you deliver a message to advocate adherence to internal controls. Since expense reports are very personal and directly affect so many individuals, this is a good area for an entity to deliver its message on strict adherence to internal control procedures.

Consistent with our grassroots notion, the system of internal controls, to the maximum extent possible should be self-checking, i.e., not subject to dependency on audits for disclosure. They should also be constructed in such a manner as to have self-checking quality control type inspection features built in so as to give the earliest possible warning of system problems or errors, i.e., before rather than after the problem develops. (Despite this self-checking attribute, however, the internal control system should be monitored by an extensive program of oversight by management and internal auditing,[1]* appropriately coordinated with external audit.)

Yet, too often occasions arise such as the following:

- a manager, desirous of a computer-based accounting system, appropriately controlled, is deterred from its implementation by either (1) too stringent a set of controls that preclude long-term benefit programs, favoring shorter term gains or (2) an unwillingness by other managers to go up the chain of command to secure the necessary approval;
- an employee who incurs a borderline acceptable type of exposure is instructed by a manager to report the expense under a different "acceptable" expense category.

Of course, the resourceful "entrepreneur" will often elect to pursue his or her ends via piecemeal authorization of the new computer system or inappropriate classification of expenditures. Such employee abuse invites trouble and total disregard for other controls is the next step.

People: the Critical Ingredients of Competency and Integrity . . .

This raises the point that the most important element of control is people. As controls permit flexibility and work not to pose barriers to getting the job done effectively

---

* See notes at end of Exhibit 2–1.

Exhibit 2–1 (continued)

and efficiently, they presume some degree of competency and integrity on the part of the individuals operating within the economic unit. In other words, can we trust the individuals to make reasonable acquisition decisions, if we impose minimal constraints on certain types of acquisitions? How can we ensure timely detection of abuses to such trust? What evolves is a very clear sense that control entails operational, managerial, and accounting considerations. Specifically, hiring and training practices, supervision, monitoring, and reporting all combine to deter problems and to detect those which nonetheless arise. Internal controls should be subject to constant review, revision, and update by competent people who are keeping pace with new technology and changes in the entity's operations. Otherwise, controls will be in place to support previously discarded procedures or technology and will often create substantial problems due to the failure to recognize such changes or to be able to be sufficiently flexible to take the changes into account within the control framework. A cost-benefit framework applies in designing, implementing, and monitoring the "package of controls" to induce a well-controlled economic unit.

The internal control system should be cost-effective, i.e., the cost of the control system should not exceed the value of the benefits being obtained. Our experience is that often too much time is devoted to "counting cash" versus establishing controls over areas of substance. Internal controls should be administered flexibly, i.e., subject to reasoned and properly supported override, but not subject to "management" override to avoid a problem. Competent, honest people allow that to be done.

Controls should be viewed as a valuable asset of each entity rather than as a hindrance to progress. In fact, properly constructed and maintained controls are reflective of the quality of the organization. A well-managed company will organize to use the most cost-effective technology applicable to its business, the talents of a well-trained and properly motivated staff, and appropriate levels of internal control that are the glue that holds systems together and ensures quality operations.

Processes: The Critical Ingredient in Facilitating Compliance with the System of Internal Control

The existence of and effectiveness of systems of internal control cannot be determined, analyzed, monitored, or measured, unless the system has been captured in a set of well defined processes—and not just computer processes and systems. Personnel can not be expected to comply with a set of directives which are nonexistent, or rely for direction exclusively on the varying, and ever changing, interpretations of their supervision and management.

People are the key ingredient in a successful system of internal control, but they need tools to help them do the job in a manner which can be effectively measured and evaluated. The "tools" are processes, systems, and procedures, and these tools should be under constant scrutiny as to their adequacy in the current environment. When problems arise, you fix the causes, that is the processes, first, and the people second.

Exhibit 2–1 (continued)

Computers, a Control Challenge . . .

Over the past two decades, computerized systems have proliferated as the main mode of capturing, transmitting, analyzing, and reporting information. The information that is used by companies for higher-level decision making as well as day-to-day operations can be viewed as the corporate data base. That data base will be maintained in computerized form to some extent in all companies. In many, particularly large, public companies, it will be computerized virtually 100%. Thus, computerization is pervasive and reliance on a corporate data base for many essential functions mandates effective control over the data and the processes that capture, maintain, and report it.

Furthermore, the advantages of increased familiarity with computers and a proliferation of information are also disadvantages. The accessibility of data internally within an organization between families of systems in shared data environments, through individual terminals, physically movable data (diskettes, and so on), networks, and communication systems—as well as externally through all kinds of access devices—has a material and growing effect on the system of internal control.

Previous conceptions of the role of internal versus external factors on management and the system of internal control are no longer accurate in an environment which includes the exposure of instantaneous access to information assets from within the organization, between functions in the organization, and from outside the organization. Widespread access to proprietary information and the repository of asset and liability records, in tandem with the problem of so many reports that none are used, can create temptation and invite error.

Exposure from system failures or their destruction has often not been recognized or effectively addressed as a critical facet of the control setting. At times, the controls are undercut by the necessity of responding to customers when computers are "down"—a foreseeable problem for which direction is often incomplete, if even available. A system which fails to address contingencies is one that is difficult to take seriously. The saying that a chain is only as strong as its weakest link would seem to apply: the development of bad habits in times of emergencies, have a way of pointing the way to circumvention of an entire control system and erosion of control.

Internal controls should recognize and deal with the pervasive, integration of computerized operation of most management information systems. Security and reliability are key considerations here. Most companies are absolutely dependent on computer adequacy and accuracy, but fail to give adequate recognition to this element of their operations from the standpoint of the value of information and other assets, liabilities, budgetary controls, and security.

A critical realization is that good people could make even a poor manual system work, whereas strong personnel alone will not succeed in establishing an effective computer interface in the absence of well-defined and good processes, methods, procedures, and systems. The basic nature of computer processing requires that a control structure exist and that it be analyzed, documented, and maintainable.

Exhibit 2–1 (continued)

The Entire Information System Must Be Controlled . . .

The chain of controls must encircle not merely financial information, but the information system which affects financial information, even indirectly. Again, the concern is one of a consistent atmosphere of controls, as well as the creation of a setting which facilitates monitoring. Entities in which managers regularly perform analytical procedures are observed to have more effective controls and fewer errors.[2] These entail financial and nonfinancial information, as well as externally-generated benchmarks, likely to be captured as a facet of the information system. It is difficult to make a misrepresentation in financial data without it being detected through operations and vice versa, if both are controlled and periodically monitored.

The internal control system should ensure that financial and operating data are both reliable and timely. The nature of the information being processed will influence the type of control structure required, as security concerns, dollar implications, and industry exposures will vary. The means of measuring, classifying, and reporting data must be monitored to ensure their propriety and accuracy.

Intrusion of controls into purely operational areas, such as resource allocation and investment policies should be limited. A fine line exists between financial or management operating data that become the basis for entries to the books of account versus operational judgments and decisions. In the laboratory area, as an example, controls should exist over safeguarding the product of experimentation (timely signing and witnessing of lab notebooks), but not over the type of experimentation. The methods used to measure, classify, and report data are clearly covered by the control system, as is the use of overtime hours rather than the expansion of the labor force. Reporting of travel expense should be subject to internal accounting controls, but not whether travel should be incurred—beyond some control process as to the relative advisability of travel in various settings.

Following are two examples of incidents that occurred at a major Fortune 500 company and are in the public domain. They illustrate the importance of internal controls over operating data that affect financial statements. They furthermore reflect our project team's experience with recognizing where the fine line to which we refer lies in practice.

Exhibit 2–1 (continued)

Illustration of the Importance of Control Over Operating Data Affecting Financial Statements

- Stringent internal controls over repair orders charged to cost on a current basis caused many people to exaggerate the effect of a repair order—to read the work order, you would conclude that the equipment to be worked on would be better than new. As a result, the Internal Revenue Service wanted to capitalize several years of repair orders involving millions of dollars for the entire period under audit—a potential disaster to the bottom line. This was a case of using internal accounting controls to accomplish operational objectives. We had to restate our internal controls to ensure that the operating information was properly stated as repair expense. Production management had to use other methods to achieve their management objectives. Although operational in nature, the consequences of failing to use proper internal controls could have had a significant effect on the financial statements if the Internal Revenue Service had prevailed.

- Parts shortages and skyrocketing costs in the mid-70s led a number of plants to stockpile spare parts. To get around internal controls on stores investments, the plants purchased parts and charged them to current cost. (A production man would never allow a plant to shut down because of lack of a spare part.) Although this was clearly evident, in retrospect, on cost sheets and other reports, it was overlooked because of a satisfactory level of profit margins. When the company became aware of the problem, they had to capitalize a very significant multi-million dollar inventory of spare parts, write off many millions of dollars in obsolete parts, and pay the Internal Revenue Service 50% of the amount capitalized, plus interest. This led to a strong campaign to adhere to established internal controls. This was endorsed by top management and extended through every level of the company. Compliance with internal controls was introduced as part of each plant's quality control program, and included in each management performance review.

Operating Controls Can Not Be Separated from Their Effects on Financial Numbers . . .

An interesting aspect of financial accounting is that it reflects actual operations which can be altered to affect reported numbers. Cutoff adjustments through holding shipments or working overtime to speed them up, approving credit without performing prescribed procedures, or assembling of related parties to time a material transaction permitting revenue recognition are the types of operating activities that have ripple

Exhibit 2–1 (continued)

effects on reporting practices. An atmosphere that strives toward controlling operations to avoid "form over substance" adjustments, in and of itself, will deter entities from entering the slippery slope of fraudulent financial reporting—the initial phase of discretionary accounting to the fruition of material misstatement.

In considering how financial managers and internal auditors can deal with a number of aspects of operational efficiency and effectiveness, it is helpful to consider several questions. How can such staffs with a cost-beneficial mix of specialists have the expertise or qualifications to review a research and development budget? Or, at a more mundane level, how would such staff be able to appraise store location decisions for a retail chain? What is reasonable to expect is that the staff could see that the right people in the organization were involved and that decisions were properly supported and documented. However, the efficiency and effectiveness of the decisions depend on the quality of the personnel making the decisions and the quality of information available to them to make those decisions. For example, in assessing the adequacy of systems development methodology and system testing in both development and maintenance functions, entity-wide participation in setting the requirements for new systems and systems changes is a key determinant of the success or failure of the system of internal control.

Post facto performance auditing is clearly feasible, but *a priori* evaluation of effectiveness is problematic. Yet, operations managers making the decisions can not have primary responsibility for operational control over their own decisions. The point is that the definition of controls should be circumscribed as they relate to operational objectives, to acknowledge the limitations in assessing efficiency and effectiveness before the fact. If certain procedures for decision making were generally accepted as essential to lead to efficient and effective decisions, then management, or auditors, could assess whether such procedures were followed. But this is more of a compliance orientation than an effectiveness assessment.

AN OPERATIONAL DEFINITION OF CONTROL

Internal controls encompass: (1) the plan of organization; (2) methods and procedures adopted within a business to ensure that goals and objectives are met; (3) encouragement of adherence to prescribed managerial policies; (4) means of ensuring that there is compliance with laws and regulations; (5) methods and measures to safeguard assets against waste, loss, and misuse; (6) methods of promoting operational efficiency; (7) means of gaining assurance that data obtained, maintained, and utilized by management are complete, accurate, and reliable; and (8) means of gaining assurance that the adequacy of such data is also adequate in facilitating both the preparation of financial statements and the maintenance of accountability for assets and responsibility for liabilities. This definition is our blending of several that appear in existing literature.

The above definition of internal control is central to two related dimensions: first, the broad objectives of internal control that give rise to the eight components of the

Exhibit 2–1 (continued)

definition, and second, the various types of control methods that can be integrated and employed within any control system to accomplish these objectives. The following matrix relates those objectives and methods. The contents subsume the classifications of management, administration, and accounting.

The critical perspective used in defining control is the importance of the attitude of the organization, its "control consciousness," how that attitude is developed, and how it is maintained as part of the corporate culture. In that regard, we believe that many control methods not only provide control, but foster control consciousness and the benefits of control consciousness, in much the same manner as quality control can foster a higher quality product or service. At the same time, a high level of control consciousness provides a basis for the development and effective use of control methods. Indeed, large compendiums of internal controls already exist, but often are not used because "control consciousness" is not a part of the corporate environment.

The structure of internal control analysis must change from one of identifying and reporting on the existence of errors to one of control system process, defect identification, measurement and analysis, and eradication. The existence of the problem or defect or error is not the key point. The deficiencies in the methods and processes which allow it to happen is the key point.

Artificial intelligence and expert systems for internal control analysis are being developed and are likely to be useful as tools in future system development. Fourth (and "fifth") generation systems development tools, including systems analysis and design packages, macro level languages, prototyping, and flowcharting systems, are of likely use to system designers and to those striving to analyze controls over data and program operations.

In considering diverse approaches to analysis and documentation, we would offer a premise that there is nothing about a system that an auditor needs to know that management, users, and MIS should not have been concerned with (and have documented) first.

Exhibit 2–1 (continued)

An Operational Definition of Objectives for Control and Related Control Methods

CONTROL METHODS	BROAD OBJECTIVES FOR CONTROL							
	CREATE AND MAINTAIN APPROPRIATE ORGANIZATION AND CULTURE	SET AND MEET CORPORATE OBJECTIVES	ADHERENCE TO MANAGEMENT'S POLICIES	OBEY LAWS AND REGULATIONS	SAFEGUARDING OF ASSETS	OPERATIONAL EFFICIENCY	COMPLETE AND ACCURATE MANAGEMENT REPORTS	COMPLETE AND ACCURATE FINANCIAL STATEMENTS
PLANNING SYSTEMS		X						
MONITORING SYSTEMS	X	X	X	X	X	X		
ORGANIZATION STRUCTURE	X	X	X		X	X		
MANAGEMENT POLICIES	X	X	X	X	X	X	X	
MANAGEMENT STYLE	X		X					
AUDIT COMMITTEE			X	X	X			X
OUTSIDE ADVISORS				X				X
COMMUNICATION SYSTEMS	X	X	X	X		X	X	
CODE OF CONDUCT	X		X	X	X	X		X
MANAGEMENT INFORMATION/ ACCOUNTING SYSTEMS		X	X	X	X	X	X	X
BUDGETING SYSTEMS			X			X	X	X
INTERNAL AUDIT	X		X	X	X	X	X	X
SYSTEM-LEVEL PREVENTION AND DETECTION CONTROLS			X	X	X	X	X	X
ADEQUATE & COMPETENT PERSONNEL	X	X	X	X	X	X	X	X

Exhibit 2–1 (concluded)

Endnotes

[1] This conclusion is similarly drawn in the *Treadway Report—Report of the National Commission on Fraudulent Financial Reporting* (October 1987), p. 37.

[2] This evidence is provided by Richard W. Kreutzfeldt and Wanda A. Wallace, in their articles entitled "Error Characteristics in Audit Populations: Their Profile and Relationship to Environmental Factors," *Auditing: A Journal of Practice & Theory* (Fall 1986), pp. 20–43 and "Control Risk Assessments: Do They Relate to Errors?", in a supplement to the same journal (1991), as well as in related working papers.

Source: Wanda A. Wallace, Howard L. Siers, William D. Hall, James K. Loebbecke, and Keagle W. Davis, "Our Perspectives on Internal Control" (1989)

THE AUDITING LITERATURE'S DESCRIPTION OF CONTROL STRUCTURE

Professional literature evolves over time, both in form and in substance. Statement on Auditing Standards No. 55 which was cited in Chapter 1 has introduced an entirely new set of terminology to the area of control.[2] The old and new terms follow:

Old Terminology	New Terminology
Internal control system	Internal control structure
Study and evaluation of internal control	Assessing control risk
Review of system and compliance tests	Test of controls
Reliance on internal control	Assessed level of control risk
Accounting controls and administrative controls	Internal control structure policies and procedures relevant to an audit

SAS no. 55 explains that control structure encompasses the control environment, the accounting system, and control procedures.

The Three Components of Control Structure

The control environment entails the collective effect of a number of factors on establishing, enhancing, or mitigating the effectiveness of specific policies and procedures. The factors include management philosophy and operating style

---

[2] The following discussion of internal control and related documentation requirements was concurrently developed for this book and a textbook on *Auditing*, Second Edition, 1991 from PWS-Kent.

- organizational structure
- the function of the board of directors and its committees
- methods of assigning authority and responsibility
- management control methods
- the internal audit function
- personnel policies and practices
- external influences concerning the entity.

The accounting system refers to "methods and records established to identify, assemble, analyze, classify, record, and report an entity's transactions and to maintain accountability for the related assets and liabilities." [SAS 55, p. 28]

Control procedures are other policies and procedures beyond the environment and accounting system that "management has established to provide reasonable assurance that specific entity objectives will be achieved." In tandem, all "policies and procedures established to provide reasonable assurance that specific entity objectives will be achieved" constitute the *internal control structure*.

Minimum Documentation Requirements

As depicted in Exhibit 2–2, auditors are required to document their understanding of the internal control structure obtained to plan the audit. The form and extent of documentation is influenced by an entity's size and complexity and nature of the internal control structure. Exhibit 2–2 provides an illustration of the type of information likely to be included in such documentation. The modes of documentation are the subject matter of later chapters.

The review of control structure will entail judging whether an entity is auditable and assessing the client's risk profile. The review should provide the auditor with an understanding of the accounting control environment and the flow of transactions through the accounting system. In gaining an understanding, the auditor is required to know how internal control policies and procedures are designed and whether an entity is actually using such policies and procedures.

CONTROL RISK ASSESSMENT

Once the auditor understands management's and the board of directors' attitude, awareness, and actions concerning the control environment, the implications of this understanding for overall control risk must be considered. One element of such risk relates to management integrity. Can the auditor expect full disclosure of problems or will a setting exist where the "right questions" must be asked in order to discover the material risks confronted by the client? Are records merely available but not acted upon? For example, budgetary reports contribute to control only if effectively analyzed at intermittent periods. For significant account balances and classes of transactions, the auditor must know the nature

Exhibit 2–2

**Exemplary Information of Use in Documenting An Understanding
of Control Structure**

NATURE OF BUSINESS	Manufacturer	Retailer
NUMBER OF LOCATIONS	3 Plants	100 Stores
CORPORATE STRUCTURE	Single Entity	Consolidated Entity
OWNERSHIP	Sole owner	Public Company
TRADING OF COMMON STOCK	No Common Stock	New York Stock Exchange
CONTROL STRUCTURE	50 Personnel with 1 Top Manager and 3 in Accounting	5,000 Personnel with 7 Top Managers and 50 in Accounting
CONTROL DESIGN	Limited Segregation of Duties	Good Segregation of Duties
PRIOR AUDITS	Historically, Adjustments Have Related to Inventory and Closing	No Significant Adjustments Historically
CLIENT DOCUMENTATION	Nominal Documentation of Controls	Good Internal Documentation
AUDIT COMMITTEE	No Audit Committee	Audit Committee Meets 4 Times a Year
INTERNAL AUDIT	No Internal Audit Function	Internal Audit Function Performs both Financial and Operational Audits
	Micro Computers Used for the Accounting System	Mainframe Computer Used for the Accounting System
	Decentralized Data Processing with No Data Processing Personnel	Centralized Data Processing with 40 Data Processing Personnel
	Batch Processing	On-line Entry Batch Update

Exhibit 2–2 (continued)

Per Class of Transactions, Document
- How the transaction is initiated
- The accounting records, supporting documents, machine readable information, and specific accounts involved in the processing of transactions
- Financial reporting process

In the Permanent File, Document An Understanding of the Control Structure Potentially Using

- Checklists
- Flowcharts
- Memoranda.

Often, a control environment checklist or questionnaire is used. A flowchart of the accounting system and memoranda of control procedures are prepared and a memorandum summarizing potential risks of material misstatements is used (e.g., risks attendant to a situation where access to computer files is unrestricted.)

Source: Adapted, in part, from "Guide for the Consideration of Internal Control Structure in a Financial Statement Audit" (AICPA, January 7, 1989)

---

and complexity of the transactions and significant processing activities. In gaining an understanding of how transactions are initiated and recorded, some knowledge of control procedures will likely be obtained. As an example, the auditor will likely find out who reconciles the bank statement. If an auditor can identify potential misstatements and design substantive tests, then sufficient information is at hand.

However, the auditor may determine that in order for some assertions to be audited cost-effectively, an understanding of specific control procedures is required. Examples most frequently relate to the completeness assertion: to plan how to ascertain that all cash contributions are recorded by nonprofit entities such as churches, an understanding of control procedures over cash receipts may be essential. Similarly, efficient physical inventory observation procedures may depend on understanding of a client's control procedures, while taking such physical counts.

Minimum Documentation

If control risk is determined to be at a maximum level, this conclusion must be documented, though it need not be explained in the working papers. If such risk is expected to be less than the maximum level, then support for such a reduction can be based on evidence (a) collected as an understanding of the control structure was obtained, (b) based on prior years' audits, or (c) identified through additional tests of controls for policies and procedures.

Procedures Toward an Understanding

An understanding of controls will entail consideration of previous experiences with the client and evidence obtained via inquiry, inspection, and/or observation procedures. The assessment of control risk may combine inherent (susceptibility of the process to errors in the absence of controls) and control risk considerations and should be assessed for assertions related to material account balances or transactions.

Note that while an understanding of controls requires assurance that policies and procedures are placed in operation, the assessment of control risk relates to operating effectiveness, i.e., the consistency with which the policy or procedure is used and who is applying it. Such effectiveness can be stated qualitatively or quantitatively and it is quite likely that assessments will vary across assertions, e.g., some will be of maximum control risk, while others may well be moderate or low in control risk. The actual timing of tests of controls will relate to audit efficiency considerations and audit risk. The more effective an internal control structure, the lower the risk of misstatement, and the less evidence required from substantive tests. Importantly, auditors may evaluate the degree of control risk anywhere along the range from a maximum level to a minimum level. Tests of controls may include tests of large numbers of individual transactions, but need not involve such sampling.

In determining the extent of procedures to obtain a sufficient understanding of control risk, prior permanent file documentation of such understanding will reduce the extent of procedures, often leading only to additional inquiry procedures. Similarly, if a client extensively documents control, the auditor can quickly evaluate design via far less extensive inquiry and observation procedures. Should a client operate in a new or specialized industry, conduct complex and material transactions, face high inherent risk, and have extensive computer processing, such considerations will lead to different and possibly more extensive audit procedures.

An understanding of control influences audit staffing, overall audit strategy, and the degree of professional skepticism applied in the course of the audit.

An Historical Perspective

Of particular interest in considering the manner in which an audit strategy is formulated, is the thought process of one of the original drafters of literature related to control risk: Kenneth W. Stringer. He reviewed two studies of irregularities which had been conducted by insurance companies providing fidelity insurance. The studies found that approximately 10% of the claims had been the result of collusion, forgery, and so on. This experience led him to the idea that total reliance on internal control was inappropriate. Deloitte, Haskins & Sells, the firm with which Mr. Stringer was associated, adopted a practice of not allowing reliance on control to exceed 87½% (i.e., not below a 12½% control risk level).[3]

Summarizing Control Risk Assessment

A useful approach to documentation is to prepare a summary of relevant internal control structure policies and procedures and related tests of controls for all assertions where control risk is assessed at less than a maximum level. In such a summary, inherent and control risk assessments should be related to the nature, timing, and extent of substantive audit procedures.

Exhibit 2–3, illustrates a portion of such a document as it might relate to sales and accounts receivable transactions and, in particular, the valuation and allocation assertion for two different companies. The second example depicts a summary of the audit approach, including the nature of substantive tests to be performed.

Exhibit 2–3

Excerpts from a Summary of Control Risk Assessment

Example 1

Valuation and Allocation:

Gross Valuation of Receivables and Sales.

Internal control structure policies and procedures include good user department controls in sales over changes to the master price files. Inquiries of the sales manager and employees in the sales manager's office on 5/1/x5, and examination of selected "was-is" computer reports of master price file changes (See W/P XX-4-3; Not illustrated here) indicate that this aspect of valuing gross receivables is carefully reviewed. Supporting documentation for selected price changes was also examined and no exceptions were noted.

Invoice quantities, however, are not subject to the same control procedures. Past history indicates that immaterial quantity errors do occur during heavy seasonal periods. This history appears not to have changed based upon review of correspondence with customers and responses to inquiries of accounts receivable personnel. However, no such errors were noted in the current period that approached amounts equivalent to tolerable misstatement. Also, a greater concern exists relative to receivables involving the Texas operation because of high turnover of personnel.

---

[3] Recounted by James J. Tucker II, Rutgers University, in his working paper "An Early Contribution of Kenneth W. Stringer: Development and Dissemination of the Audit Risk Model," p. 13.

Based on these tests of controls, control risk is assessed as moderate for all operations except the Texas operation, where control risk is assessed at slightly below the maximum.

Net Valuation of Receivables

Control risk is assessed at the maximum.

Example 2

SUMMARY OF AUDIT APPROACH

CLIENT: ___VINCO, INC.___   BALANCE SHEET DATE: __12/31/X4__
Prepared by: ___Roger Smith___   Date: ___9/15/X4___
Reviewed by: ___Paul Harmon___   Date: ___10/2/X4___
    Account(s): ___Receivables/Revenues___
    Assertion(s): ___Valuation (Realizable Value Objective)___

Summary of Inherent Risks:

• Average of 2–3 months sales in receivables
• Annual write-offs average 3% of sales

Summary of Relevant Internal Control Structure Policies and Procedures:

• Good control procedures to determine reserve (see R-60)

    However, some audit adjustments have historically been made in this area due to its volatile and subjective nature.

Summary of Tests of Controls:

• Control procedures to determine reserve are tested using a "dual purpose" testing approach in connection with substantive tests.

Risk Assessment:

• Moderate risk of errors in the reserve due to its volatile and subjective nature.

Summary of Substantive Tests:

• Analytical procedures (comparison of aging statistics and write-offs between years, comparison of reserve to agings).
• Discuss with management the reserve requirements needed for past due accounts by customer, product line and region of the country (this is a "dual purpose" test because it provides evidence of the effectiveness of management's reserve estimates).

Guide for the Consideration of Internal Control Structure in a Financial Statement Audit (AICPA: exposure draft from January 7, 1989), pp. 149–219.

Further consider a setting in which you combine your inherent and control risk assessment. The concept is first to focus on what errors would be likely in the absence of controls. A broad interpretation of this concept would be to broadly assess the client's exposure to such threats of loss as:

—theft,

—regulatory changes, or

—expropriation of assets and effects of similar political actions.

Hence, the inherent risk would increase as assets became more liquid or mobile, regulators are able to more directly influence operations, and foreign business interests are expanded into more unstable countries.

Other inherent risk indicators may include the

—personality of management and

—type of user groups receiving the financial statements.

Then, second control risk is considered. Assume you decide that it is appropriate to assess the control risk at less than the maximum level with respect to cut-off practices. Specifically, you form the following assessments (analogous to examples provided in Exhibit 1–5) and would gather related information on client procedures.

Inherent Risk:	Client's fiscal year end coincides with his busiest season, possibly leading to relatively high cut-off risks for sales and shipments at year end.
Classification:	The foregoing is a characteristic (for this client)
Balance(s):	Inventory/Cost of Sales Accounts Receivable/Sales
Audit Assertion(s):	Inventory/Cost of Sales—existence or validity and completeness Accounts Receivable/Sales—existence or validity and completeness
Procedures:	Inventory/Cost of Sales—Client has established extensive procedures to ensure accurate shipment cut-off and has an effective perpetual inventory system that is supplemented by a test of selected department and location inventories at or near year end.

This could then form the basis for proposing an audit strategy.

As strategies are developed, keep in mind that the means of gaining assurances as to controls such as effective segregation of duties tend to be via observation and evaluation of control design. Samples cannot be drawn to test controls such as the segregation of duties, but inquiry procedures can be quite effective, as can observation of how procedures are performed and by whom. Auditability and the completeness of documents can be assessed by evaluating control design, testing compliance with that design, and/or performing substantive test work. For example, the auditor can confirm that document logs are in use, that monthly statements are mailed, and that time cards or similar records are used and can test for numerical sequence. Typically, such tests of control are not based on samples, but rather emphasize inquiry, observation, or a check on the total sequence of documents of interest. The control environment is implied by the design of controls as well as the results of both tests of control and substantive test work.

AN EMERGING DEFINITION

Internal control has been defined in a variety of ways; one proposal that is currently being discussed by the same sponsoring organizations who supported the Treadway Report and now are pursuing the objective set forth by the Treadway Commission of integrating guidance on controls, follows:

Internal control comprises the environment, plans, policies, systems, and procedures

—established, executed, and monitored by an entity's board of directors, management, and other personnel

—to foster achievement of the entity's objectives

—in compliance with applicable laws and ethical standards

—and in a prudent, cost-effective manner.

The advantages of this definition include its focus on broad management control, its acknowledgment of the critical role of objectives that have an acceptable legal and ethical basis, and its explicit recognition of cost-benefit considerations (i.e., suggesting reasonable assurance rather than absolute assurance is sought, in view of economic implications).

With this sort of definition as a framework, various components of control can be explored and tied directly to such a definition.[4] As an example, the management level of activities suggests that management integrity as well as management style, corporate culture, and ethical values would be relevant ingredients for a well controlled environment. Corporate governance in the form of directors' and audit committees' oversight is likewise relevant, in tandem with an appropriate organization structure.

---

[4] The definition and some of the framework described is elaborated upon in an "Internal Control Discussion Paper" authored by James K. Loebbecke (September 15, 1990). Note also, that a similar internal control model elaborating upon planning controls, implementation controls, and analytical controls is described by William R. Kinney, Jr., Michael W. Maher, and David W. Wright, "Assertions-Based Standards for Integrated Internal Control" (October 19, 1989 and revised May 31, 1990), subsequently published in *Accounting Horizons*.

Integrity

In trying to apply the notion of management integrity, I have found the following interpretation to be helpful. If you picture all clients with whom you have dealt along a continuum, then place at the furthest end those clients who are extremely open with you and, in fact, seek out your counsel whenever key decisions are to be made that might have important financial consequences to the entity. When problems arise, these clients can be counted on to share details and discuss implications, just as they do when good news is at hand. Now, at the opposite end of the continuum, place the client who is uncooperative. Not only is information not shared, misleading information is commonly provided.

As you no doubt guess, the open discussion-oriented client would represent the highest integrity, while the closed-mouth or misleading disclosure client would be viewed as lacking integrity. The more interesting set of clients to consider is the list that will give you the right answer when asked, but you must first find the right question. In other words, the client is not always forthcoming at highlighting risks and problems, but if you pose your inquiry correctly and thoroughly, you can count on the client representations being an accurate response to the precise question posed. Such a client would be described as possessing moderate integrity. The point is that the client knows that risk exposures are relevant to the CPA and should be forthcoming as to related problems.

Ethical Values

Recent debates have made it patently evident that grey areas arise in ethics and, in fact, ethical dilemmas are not always recognized by decision makers. The question likewise arises of how ethical issues can be recognized by those designing and evaluating controls. One framework that has been proposed is depicted in Exhibit 2–4. After providing some examples of ethical dilemmas, the approach to analysis is outlined and our focus is likely to be upon the testing of options. Not only are the notions of legality, virtue, and benefit cited, but two key questions that should particularly help those grey matters: would you be comfortable with your family's reactions, were they told of your decision and would you be comfortable if all read about your decision on the front page of the newspaper tomorrow?

Exhibit 2–4

Ethical Dilemmas

- A fellow employee makes a copy of a supplier's competitive proposal and expresses an intent to show it to a competitor whose proposal has not yet been submitted.
- To avoid a budget constraint, entertainment expenses are intentionally misclassified as advertising.

Exhibit 2–4 (continued)

- A prospective borrower requests financing for expansion of his business in legal pornography.
- An employee is judged ready for promotion, yet the supervisor knows that a freeze on hiring will prevent that employee's replacement and is aware that a vice president is lobbying heavily to get his son hired into the position for which the employee is eligible.
- A copy of a major competitor's cost data is received anonymously, marked "confidential and personal."
- When on expense account, do you order prime ribs or "the usual?"
- When requesting engineering data, can you say it is more urgent than it really is to ensure that you get it on time?
- Should preference be given to local suppliers?
- Should design procedures be followed to a T even if you think you have identified a better way?
- Can you use a coupon for a free drink provided when you check into a motel?
- If you are offered $50 to stay in a motel, is it reasonable to select that motel when traveling?
- What do you owe the long time employee who seems incapable of learning how to utilize new machinery?
- What do you owe a community no longer producing business?

ANALYZE THESE BY

- RECOGNIZING AND DEFINING THE DILEMMA
- GETTING THE FACTS
- LISTING THE OPTIONS
- TESTING THE OPTIONS
  —ARE THEY LEGAL
  —ARE THEY RIGHT?
  —ARE THEY BENEFICIAL?
  —HOW WOULD YOU FEEL IF YOUR FAMILY FOUND OUT ABOUT YOUR DECISION?
  —HOW WOULD YOU FEEL IF YOU SAW IT PRINTED IN THE NEWS-PAPER?

Adapted from: Alan L. Otten, "Ethics on the Job: Companies Alert Employees to Potential Dilemmas," *Wall Street Journal* (July 14, 1986), Section 2, p. 17.

From a control design perspective, some have posed the interesting question of whether compensation through bonuses based on reported accounting numbers is ethical in the sense that it would seem to implicitly be encouraging employees to behave in a potentially biased manner. The same query has been posed with respect to the practice of implicitly encouraging if not rewarding the padding of budgets. Would these questions elicit different responses if you knew the bonus could be over 100% of normal compensation of an employee? What if other competitors use similar compensation programs?

Undoubtedly, the question is one of balance. To have incentives that have potentially ill consequences if abused is not problematic if monitoring or incentive devices exist to deter the abusive action. Hence, the element of ethical values in the corporate culture may be a critical offset to other aspects of an incentive system that could otherwise throw off "mixed signals" from a motivational perspective.

Organizational Structure

A related example is whether problems arise due to the structuring of operations. Is decentralization creating too much discretion at the operating location level, such that local optimal activities are pursued at the cost of the optimal choices at an overall organizational level? Is this not a potential incentive for abuse, thereby suggesting some fault on the part of management? Indeed, MiniScribe's debacle, in part, has been attributed to problems arising from:

—location of the business in Colorado, while the Chief Executive Officer managed from California

—an intimidating style of management by Q. T. Wiles

—formation of 20 minicompanies in which turmoil was the norm since many reorganizations occurred (literally every quarter) and firings were common

—sole success criterion was a financial goal that could range up to 100% of an individual's salary

—managers lacked financial training

—significant accounting judgments were permitted to be made by divisional controllers.[5]

Oversight and Self-Assessment

Many aspects of management style, corporate culture, and structure can be prevented from becoming overly idiosyncratic or oppressive by merely ensuring effective corporate governance oversight by a board and audit committee. Moreover, if managers continually self-assess their performance and the system, balance should be maintained.

In a very interesting discussion of directors' responsibilities, Roderick M. Hills, former Chairman of the U.S. Securities and Exchange Commission and

---

[5] MiniScribe Form 8-K Current Report dated September 12, 1989, p. 4 and related discussion by Curtis C. Verschoor, "MiniScribe: A New Example of Audit Committee Ineffectiveness," *Internal Auditing* (Vol. 5, No. 4, Spring 1990), pp. 13–19.

director of several entities shared his personal views on corporate governance. In particular, he observed that too many board members shared the four D's:

- Dismay
- Disillusionment
- Disinterest
- Disgust

Unfortunately, those feeling disgust are the ones that leave, while the former stay even, at times, in the worst of settings. He proceeded to explain the importance of creating a sort of 8-K disclosure process whereby directors' departures had to be reported to regulators in a similar manner as changes in auditors are now reported. Commentary would be provided by the director as to why he or she had left the board if departure precedes normal tenure. A reporting approach by management, with either support or disagreement expressed by the director would be an alternative approach to the same issue.

Mr. Hills further elaborated on the importance of having external and internal auditors meet with the board members and audit committee and legal counsel. Substantive one-hour meetings should be held. Moreover, he expressed the belief that involved directors would make a point to have a lunch to get to know the individuals on whom they were relying in their governance function. If an audit committee is not available, then external auditors should be requested to report on control weaknesses to the board.

A related issue addressed was the composition of the board of directors. A critical control element in Mr. Hills's opinion was the existence of an independent nomination committee for directors.[6] Legitimate concerns have been raised as to the composition of some boards, as reflected in a reprinted editorial from *The Wall Street Journal* in Exhibit 2–5.

In research concerning "Methodological Implications of the Corporate Governance Mechanism—The Board of Directors," I and Karen S. Cravens find that nominating committees and management ownership appear to act as substitute corporate governance mechanisms, as do the proportion of external directors and both management ownership and institutional ownership. A complementary relationship appears to exist between the size of the board and both institutional ownership and nominating committees. Similarly, audit committees and a lower proportion of insiders seem to be complementary board traits. The implications of such research is that the control structure of a company entails not merely the presence of a nominating or audit committee, but also the context in which these particular governance mechanisms are observed. Indeed, board composition, characteristics, structure, and process are observed to be highly relevant to corporate performance. Well controlled environments will likely mix and match a variety

---

[6] Roderick M. Hills, Luncheon Address on "Management's Responsibilities—New Initiatives by the SEC and Congress," Executive Enterprises, Inc. program in New York on December 4, 1990.

Exhibit 2–5

Are Outside Directors Put on Boards Just for Show?

Last month's firing of 10 Continental Illinois directors is reminiscent of the attention directed to the Penn Square debacle. A congressional hearing concerning the collapse of the "shopping center" bank in Oklahoma noted that the directors for the bank had insufficient expertise to question its practices. One House Banking Committee member is reported to have said that the testimony represented "an indictment of the regulatory system that placed too much reliance on outside directors who are lay persons."

As numerous groups, particularly regulators, have promoted the advantages of

---

Manager's Journal

by Wanda A. Wallace

---

outside, "independent" directors, they have failed to stress the importance of getting qualified individuals for the job. Yet, in contrast to Penn Square, the list of the fired directors at Continental Illinois includes an impressive number of corporate chief executive officers. Despite the presence of these corporate chieftains, the FDIC pointed out that the Continental directors who served before 1980 permitted the disastrous management policies that eventually dragged the business down.

The attention directed at boards warrants reexamination of their responsibilities and suggestions for changing the approach to selecting board members.

Taking Committee Responsibilities Seriously. In recent years, board members' legal responsibilities have been increased. In fact, the New York Stock Exchange and

actions by the Financial Executives Institute now require boards to maintain active audit committees. Directors on these committees are supposed to actively oversee control practices of both internal and external auditors' examinations. However, regular monthly exchanges of information between audit committees and external auditors is unusual, and regular review of even executive summaries of internal audit reports by audit committee members is virtually nonexistent. Regulators have been known to challenge directors—at Penn Square, for example—as to why they were not aware of the extent of troubled loans and the poor documentation practices of management with respect to new loans. Indeed, few professionals working with board members would expect any understanding of such detail by directors.

Even more interesting than an investigation of the depth of directors' oversight activities would be the polling of external auditors as to whether they believe that audit committees have been beneficial with respect to improving corporate governance. An informal survey I conducted has uncovered a split vote. The overriding concern is with the expertise of directors and the time that they reasonably can be expected to devote to oversight activities.

Board Members Should Complement Management. Inside directors are likely to be top-level generalists with substantial company experience. It is therefore desirable that outside directors should complement the insiders' experience. If the CEO's background is production, the outside directors should add finance and accounting expertise. Similarly, if the CEO's background is marketing or finance, getting an outside director with an engineering back-

ground makes sense. (All businesses seek counsel with attorneys and creditors, and these individuals have incentives to monitor operations without formally serving as directors.) The board should enlarge the pool of resources available to top management rather than merely replicating it.

Resist Hiring Local Celebrities. A review of annual reports quickly discloses a tendency for companies to bring "celebrity types" onto the board. These individuals can be telltale signs of managers wanting a rubber stamp rather than the advice of professionals with technical expertise.

Instead of focusing on highly visible presidents or deans of universities, companies ought to explore the potential candidates who have particular expertise in areas where detailed counsel is needed. A chemist, engineer, accountant, computer scientist, or marketing analyst who is active in state-of-the-art lines of inquiry can provide the technical expertise that may prove crucial when the economy slumps, industry-growth slows or controls fail. Similarly, other companies' line managers and technically oriented project managers may serve as far better complements to a board than other companies' CEOs. CPAs and internal auditors could offer obvious advantages to audit committees, just as compensation consultants could prove invaluable to compensation committees.

The Incentive System. The incentive for younger board members to more actively participate in boards' oversight functions is tied to their interest in signaling the labor market as to their capabilities. At the age of 65, a director faces very limited risk; it's not as though future livelihood and long-term professional reputation depend on his performance as a director. In

contrast, a 40-year-old who imperils his or her reputation by performing poorly on a board can imperil a substantial amount of potential future income.

Increased incentives in the form of compensation may be needed, given that audit-committee membership (as one example) typically results in only $5,000 to $10,000 of incremental fees. On the other hand, the relative attractiveness of such income to professionals below the CEO income may increase the incentive for active monitoring by non-CEO-level directors.

Directors Must Adapt to Informatics. As microcomputers proliferate, tremendous data bases are available within seconds, and analytical tools are at the fingertips of all who are literate in computers and statistical techniques. Innovation yields benefits to professionals who undergo continuing education and imposes penalties on those who do not adapt. How many directors are comfortable with micros, large data bases, descriptive data, probability theory, simulation, statistical tests and modeling? Yet, use of these resources can provide powerful oversight capabilities for directors.

Avoid Rigid Prerequisites. I would no more encourage the total replacement of experience with technical expertise than I would endorse the current imbalance that seems to stress experience over innovative technical knowledge. A blend is needed. Directors must receive monthly financial statements, operating statistics, press releases, capital-expenditure plans, product developments, technical-innovation reports, and auditors' reports and have access to data bases on the industry and economy. Each board member should be prepared to provide timely advice, particularly with regard to his or her respective areas of expertise, and this advice ought to be tapped by managers.

Ms. Wallace is Marilyn R. and Leo F. Corrigan Jr. Trustee professor at the Edwin L. Cox School of Business, Southern Methodist University.

THE WALL STREET JOURNAL.
Published since 1889 by
DOW JONES & COMPANY, INC.

Source: Wanda A. Wallace, *The Wall Street Journal*, Monday, January 21, 1985, editorial page.

---

of governance techniques, suggesting that one dimension should not be viewed in isolation. As one example of the results of research to date, if managers hold more than 20 percent of outstanding shares of large public New York Stock Exchange companies, those boards are likewise observed to have a greater proportion of private investors on their boards and to be less likely to have a large proportion of CEOs and similar duality on their board. These companies are also less likely to have a nominating committee. The idea may be that the alignment of ownership and manager incentives makes it less necessary to implement a nominating committee mechanism. Of course, the possibility also arises of entrenched management who controls the board composition. If this were the case, an expectation arises that stockholders would initiate a board governance mechanism that includes establishment of a nominating committee.

Planning

The process of planning not only identifies goals and objectives, but evaluates related risks and ensures consideration of the need for change, as well as the management of change. Planning provides a benchmark of use in checking and preparing for action. Identified risks can sometimes be diversified away, insured against, or merely accepted but continually monitored in a manner where action could be taken if suddenly deemed advisable. Whenever change arises, risk tends to be increased due to the very process of control required. However, the absence of change can likewise pose risks—consider the business failure inevitable for those not changing from the buggy whip industry to transportation.

Planning controls are those that are based on management's short-run and long-run expectations. The realism of such plans is important. Assumptions about the environment, physical constraints, economic setting, and competition should likewise be realistic. Threats to achieving plans should be delineated and, to the extent feasible, addressed in the strategic planning process.

Communication

Both formal and informal communication are important to establishing controls. Informal signals emerge from watching whether those not complying with controls are punished or rewarded, relative to those who choose to comply. The direction of communication should be in all directions and include coordination among peers.

Monitoring and Feedback

Numerous "gauges" are set to check on control processes and the achievement of objectives. Information systems are intended to provide the raw data as well as necessary graphics, statistical tests, or the like that assist in the checking function. Internal auditing and external auditing provide important monitoring services and feedback. Outside sources providing feedback loops include customers, suppliers, creditors, the investment community, regulators, and various users of information on operations, such as academic researchers. Early warning signals should be attainable through applying statistical check and analytical procedures as controls.

Action

Some sort of timely response mechanism or action is essential for effective control. This could range from a triggering process geared to a statistical test of the results of some change, to a routine variance analysis or the like that explains why projections or standards are not being achieved. Clearly, the response must be in substance, not mere form, and the nature of the response must be appropriate for the issue at hand.

Other Personnel and Prudent Care

The role of other than top management and the board is cited and the message must include a need for qualified, competent personnel who are thereby able to exercise due care. Unless an understanding of control is possessed, an appreciation of the why of particular procedures is lacking, and controls can be inadvertently abused.

Control Procedures

The procedures for control, if not understood can be undercut. For example, if an employee knows that extra permission is required when an invoice exceeds $100 and chooses to avoid the extra paperwork by splitting invoices apart whenever they exceed $100, likely does not understand the why of the $100+ control procedure. If the employee were to understand the why, including protection against his or her unintentional mistake, then compliance is far more likely to occur. Furthermore, implementation controls could include the broad span of administrative and internal accounting controls, encouraging compliance through incentives and feedback, as well as the overall control environment.

SYNOPSIS

The control structure entails a broader approach to controls than in the traditional internal accounting controls literature. Indeed, the move toward integrating definitions of internal controls involves a management control focus, substantially beyond a financial reporting orientation. The "Tone at the Top" is widely acknowledged to be an essential element of a control environment and literally sets the stage for the remaining dimensions of control. The generally accepted auditing standards distinguish the control environment from accounting system and control procedures but acknowledge their interrelationship in comprising an internal control structure. Control risk assessment entails consideration of each facet of the control structure, is permitted to use information from prior engagements, and often depends on observation and inquiry procedures rather than necessarily tests of sample items. The implications of control risk for managers, directors, and regulators relate to operational, liability, and regulatory exposure. As stated in Chapter 1, increasing pressures are evolving for managers to take formal responsibility for the adequacy of controls through a management report. Indeed, Congress has proposed an auditor's report thereon. Since corporate governance is closely linked to reporting and disclosure practices, such reporting has direct responsibility linkages to the directors and, in particular, audit committees.

Third party implications of control risks and control structure are numerous. The likelihood of creditors, stockholders, or customers being harmed in some manner can be substantially reduced through specification and control of risks. For example, adaptability to changing market conditions makes failure far less likely, leading to lowered exposure of creditors and investors to losses. Similarly, careful evaluation and approval processes of suppliers is less likely to lead to contamination of some sort that might harm a consumer either physically or economically.

As suggested in the introduction of Chapter 1, the thrift industry has had numerous ripple effects, including an enormous tax bill. This third-party implication to taxpayers suggests that business environments may not have established, in some cases, the sort of comprehensive control structure described herein. Through increased understanding of the control process, such third parties, alongside regulators, can be expected to bring to bear pressures to require attention to these broader based control considerations. An appendix to this chapter reports an Executive Summary of related control guidance from The Institute of Internal Auditors.

Appendix

Executive Summary of Guidance on Controls by the Institute of Internal Auditors

This statement provides guidance to internal auditors on the nature of control and the roles of the participants in its establishment, maintenance, and evaluation. It does not provide guidance on tools and techniques utilized in the performance of audit work.

It includes interpretations of sections 300.02 through 300.04 of the *Standards for the Professional Practice of Internal Auditing* and new guidelines relating to concepts of control and management and internal auditing responsibilities.

Major conclusions include:
1. Control has two aspects:

   - *Control* results from management's planning, organizing, and directing.
   - A *control* is any action taken by management to enhance the likelihood that established objectives and goals will be achieved.

2. The many variants of the term control (for example, administrative control, management control, internal control) can be incorporated within the generic term.

3. The overall system of control is conceptual in nature. It is the integrated collection of systems used by an organization to achieve its objectives and goals.

4. Management's basic responsibility relating to control is to plan, organize, and direct in such a fashion as to provide reasonable assurance that established objectives and goals will be achieved.

5. Internal auditing's basic responsibility relating to control is to examine and evaluate management's planning, organizing, and directing to determine whether reasonable assurance exists that objectives and goals will be achieved. Internal auditing's review encompasses the entire management process and provides information to appraise the overall system of control.

Source: Draft of a Statement on Internal Auditing Standards (SIAS) on the subject of Control: Concepts and Responsibility (The Institute of Internal Auditors, Inc., May 1, 1983).

3

The Effects of
Technology on Control

"A computer does not substitute for judgment any more than
a pencil substitutes for literacy. But writing without a pencil is
no particular advantage."

Robert McNamara[1]

As the quote suggests, computers and technology are unavoidable tools,
though fraught with limitations.

This chapter will provide an overview of key issues related to computers'
effect on control, as well as implications of other aspects of technology. A later
chapter will develop concepts mentioned herein with far greater depth.

DEVELOPMENTS SINCE THE FIRST PERSONAL COMPUTER

The first personal computer was assembled by John Blankenbaker in 1971
and dubbed the Kenbak[2], and the consequences of the PC expansion since that

---

[1] *The Executive's Quotation Book: A Corporate Companion,* Edited by James Charlton (New
York: St. Martin's Press, 1983), p. 63.

[2] William M. Bulkeley, "Who Built the First PC? Hint: His Name Isn't Wozniak or Jobs," *The
Wall Street Journal* (May 14, 1986), p. 29. This discussion is largely adapted from "Personal Computers and Their Impact on EDP Auditing," *Spectrum* (Fall 1986), pp. 44–49, by Wanda A. Wallace.

date are substantial. Exhibit 3–1 defines key types of computer systems. A paperless environment prevails. Where books and ledgers once accumulated, computer disks and tapes are now accrued. Obviously, computer literacy becomes essential in such an environment; otherwise, the records of an organization are unintelligible. This necessity for basic skills has led to a large group of generalists rather than specialists. Research in natural language processing and voice recognition, in tandem with "fifth generation" system architecture and the evolution of artificial intelligence applications (expert systems) will likely push user friendliness to its limits.[3] In other words, user groups are by no means computer specialists. In fact, many restrict their knowledge intentionally to the bare necessities.

Exhibit 3–1

Definition of Computer Systems

Micros	Minis	Mainframes

| Small computer that can easily fit onto a desk | Medium computer | Large fast multiple-user computer |

| Designed for single user, though can be multi-user systems | | Becoming a peripheral device for microcomputer work stations |

| Likely to be in networking of a large number of microcomputers, as well as a large mainframe system | | • Millions of instructions per seconds (MIPS) can be processed
• Mid-1980s: 5–10 MIPS
• Super Computers: 100s of MIPS
• By 1999: > 1000 MIPS |

---

[3] Andrew D. Bailey, Jr., Lynford E. Graham, and James V. Hansen, "Technological Development & EDP," *Research Opportunities in Auditing: The Second Decade* (American Accounting Association Auditing Section, 1988).

FRUSTRATIONS FACED BY NOVICE USERS

Unfortunately, it is difficult for a novice to define such necessities, so we witness the exasperation of PC users when information is lost from a disk, files seem to disappear, the hardware does not work appropriately, the software will not do what it is intended to do, and the memory constraint becomes binding. Given these common problems with relatively novice users—who are committed to retain their novice status—it quickly becomes apparent that an inability to limit access and effectively exercise data base protection is a critical problem. The development of new applications without implementing control standards for those applications can lead to costly errors and irregularities. Exhibit 3–2 describes common microcomputer characteristics.

Exhibit 3–2

Microcomputer Characteristics

- No separate data processing staff
- The personnel process and training is oriented toward the computer applications
- Computer and peripherals sit on a desk or stand instead of being in a computer area or computer center
- Virtually no physical security exists for the computer
- A rigid (hard) disk is used for system software and programs in use, with auxiliary storage on flexible floppy disks

---

All of us have heard the story of someone inadvertently writing a message with a diskette underneath, thereby ruining the files on that disk. Indeed, diskettes take care, as described in Exhibit 3–3. Similarly, turnover of personnel with insufficient on-the-job-training can lead to destruction of data files by the new employee or disgruntled employees. Then there is the type of story that Donn Parker (a well-known computer fraud specialist) likes to tell: by just calling up a business's employees and claiming to be a member of top management, he was able to obtain information on how to log onto the business's computer system, including details as to passwords and the retrieval of files.[4] Parker points out the necessity of educating employees as to the sensitivity of the information handled in an EDP setting. In a sense, the terminal is a key to the vaults of an organization. Layers of passwords are essential, alongside frequent changes of such passwords. Development of "read only" files, as well as encryption/decryption of data, can

---

[4] Tom Alexander, "Waiting for the Great Computer Rip-Off," *Fortune* (July 1974), p. 148.

Exhibit 3–3

Treat Disks Carefully

- Oil in a fingerprint will disrupt the disk surface it touches
- Use only felt tip pens with a light touch, as ballpoints and pencils will destroy information by destroying the surface of the disk
- Heat from hot lamps, radiators, direct sunlight, or glove compartments can melt disks and even if not melted, the disk surface can be distorted
- Do not bend the disk; if it becomes bent, try to copy it and then discard the original
- Avoid magnetic fields including

    —telephone bells
    —transformers in florescent desk lamps
    —motors in electric typewriters
    —color television sets
    —magnetic memo & paper clip holders,

  as they will destroy disks
- Back up everything
- Use a "patch" program to recover information on a damaged disk (programs costs $25 to $75)

help protect against unauthorized alteration or access. Audit trails of user IDs, files used, duration of use, types of transactions performed, and denied access can be effective means of control. The personal computers' familiarity has bred a number of "bad habits": disks lay on table tops with no protection by lock and key or by password; if passwords exist, they can be "guessed" by friends or are provided to all who are curious on a piece of paper taped to the wall or on the side of the terminal! Even hard disks are frequently left unlocked and if a key is issued, the key is often accessible to a large number of individuals; in addition, one key frequently locks or unlocks a number of hard disk drives!

ENHANCING PHYSICAL SECURITY

Since it takes seconds to copy a diskette, security is a really big problem. Some entities enhance physical security by disabling a micro each night by removing critical software, then restoring it each morning. Alteration of programs can similarly be deterred to some extent by placing compiled versions of programs on-line and then removing source code from the system. Not only does this deter modification, but compiled versions can be executed more quickly. The relative ease of copying and adjustment of files leads to a related consequence of personal computers: multiple sets of books. Too often three copies of key records are in three different hands, one copy gets updated on an individual's disk and not on others—or, the party responsible for updating the main source file fails to do so and three individuals "post" separate adjustments and fail to tie in to a timely total. Many a CPA has stories to share concerning a meeting with the client where the CPA's trial balance, the controller's worksheet, and the vice president's numbers fail to correspond.

Advanced computer systems have as a foundation data communications and data base technologies. Micro-to-mainframe linkages in distributed processing add risks related to the concentration of previously scattered information-gathering, record-keeping, and accounting functions.[5]

NETWORKING CHALLENGES

As already suggested, the key problem with generating up-to-date information is an absence of effective networking. Exhibit 3–4 describes common data communication networks. The basic task of networking can be difficult. I recently had a need to print a diskette while editing another and after trying five different computer configurations of colleagues, losing letters off the side and obtaining representations of the strangest language symbols, I gave up. The problem is that everyone has a different micro, different software with unique commands, and printers of an even wider range of makes and capabilities. The concept of networking such a hodge-podge of personal computers is challenging to say the least. Those companies with foresight, cared about compatibility. Others, due to forecast errors concerning their needs, technological changes, and possible applications, have faced the nightmare of networking. Again, the generalist problem rears its head. In the traditional setting, a mainframe computer system had echo checks, read back confirmations, and a variety of similar hardware equipment controls to ensure full transmission of data. As "make-do" networking evolves, some similar assurance of effective communication between terminals is needed.

Moreover, networks increasingly pool software access, with little available in the form of documentation or training help to the large number of potential users. Attendant risks include misuse of software and inadequate appreciation of software limitations for certain applications.

ANALYTICAL PROCEDURES

Personal computers have a set of predictable effects. The information explosion and information systems orientation have led to more widespread application of analytical procedures. An increasing number of managers are familiar with the ease of use of Lotus, relatives to VISICALC (e.g., 1-2-3, SuperCalc, and FlashCalc), Windows, EXCEL, and numerous statistical packages which can gen-

---

[5] S. D. Halper, G. C. Davis, P. Jarlath O'Neil-Dunne, and Pamela R. Pfau, *Handbook of EDP Auditing* (New York: Warren, Gorham & Lamont, 1986), Supplement.

Exhibit 3–4

Data Communication Networks

Characteristic Network Configurations	"Local Area Networks" (LAN)

—Microcomputers and their peripherals
—nodes linking mainframe computers
—concurrent communications of data, video, and voice

Point-to-Point
Multipoint
Star

- "Upload": transfer data from micro to larger computer
- "Down load": data transferred from larger computer to micro
- MODEMS/Communications interface hardware
- Communications Software—can "emulate" more than one standard terminal

---

Local Area Networks

- Increase security risk
- Should support concurrent processing and the locking of various levels of files and records
- Password protection is essential
- Audit trails are important to maintain

Micro-Mainframe Link

- Can download data, then do whatever one wishes with that information
- Requires extra security

—Call back device (calls back modem at predetermined number)
—Note that preprogramming abilities of communications software expose a system to substantial risk

---

erate descriptive profiles, ratios, histograms, trend lines, and even more sophisticated models for analysis of operations. The good news about such activities by managers is that timely detection of problems is more likely. Moreover, these activities serve as a sort of "user control" over the EDP setting. if the various problems already described have taken a toll on the accuracy of the information system, they are likely to come to light as managers compare their performance to that of competitors and budgeted data.

USER CONTROLS

Yet, reliance should not be placed on management's analytical procedures to monitor operations, since time and operating demands on these individuals could easily lead to suspension of such checks. User controls, routinely applied by key user groups should be established. Any questions as to the reasonableness of reported numbers should lead to follow up. Given the ease of tailoring reports to user needs, micros have increased the need for feedback on report forms. Of course, the "other side" of this case of tailoring of report forms is that no two reports need have the same format. Users may request diskettes of data or spreadsheets and tailor their format to their decision-making style. For a third party striving to reconcile reports or merely to review control environment steps taken by management, these diverse report forms can be problematic.

CONTROL PROBLEMS

When reviewing an entity with microcomputers, the systems evaluator quickly identifies a multitude of control problems—most often linked to the lack of segregation of duties, inadequate competency of personnel, and insufficient safeguards of equipment, data, and other assets. The microcomputer environment is often analogous to a one-bookkeeper accounting department. This is due to the commonality with which computer accessibility facilitates authorization, custody, and accounting of a single transaction. When users perform EDP in a personal computer environment, one user should be asked to perform as a sort of independent control, maintaining logs of (1) transaction balance by type of transaction, (2) master file control totals, and (3) control total comparisons, made based on estimated totals. Increased use of dual controls can also be helpful.

REINVENTING THE WHEEL

A prevalent problem, tied in part to documentation problems in many microcomputer environments, is on-line use of untested or inadequately tested software. For both hardware and software, there is a lack of standardization across vendors which affects both backup and portability of programs. Controls are often an afterthought and easily removable. Quality control varies widely. Companies by the thousands "reinvent the wheel," programming software from scratch and then implementing it prematurely. Can auditors cite a single client that has not used, on-line, software with a critical error at some point in the past? One survey reports that only 13% to 32% of entities require user-developed micro applications to be tested and/or reviewed, in spite of the micro's use for decision support in 69% of these entities.[6] Exhibit 3–5 offers some suggestions on spreadsheet design. This is just one example of the areas in which training is needed by both developers and users of macros. It is hardly surprising that companies can go out of business

---

[6] Norman O. Schultz and Debra D. Hoglund, "Microcomputer Spreadsheets: A Case for Controls," *The Internal Auditor* (February 1986), pp. 46–50.

Exhibit 3–5

Ten Steps to Better Spreadsheet Design

- Do not start without a plan.
- Use your cell protect feature. (To avoid overwriting)
- Do not mingle data entry areas with calculations. (Allows display to focus on users' needs)
- Make your data input resemble existing forms.
- Use the input area as a data capture form. (Hard copy to match input form)
- Enter data in either rows or columns, not both. (Avoids moving cursor)
- Use manual recalculation when entering data into *large* spreadsheets (For speed)
- Place instructions an identification in the spreadsheet.

  —who built the spreadsheet,
  —when it was created,
  —what input is expected,
  —under what file name it is saved,
  —what date it was last used, and
  —when it was last audited.

- Back up your files.
- Always test your spreadsheet

Source: *InfoWorld* (Feb. 11, 1985), p. 27.

---

before anyone even detects an error in software that can critically damage operations: errors in billings, improper application of credit limits, or similar critical flaws. Testing should include contrived systems whereby deliberate faults and errors are input, as well as real systems whereby representative real data are processed, such as the prior month's transactions. Tests of all software should be run periodically to detect deterioration effects, as well as possible coding errors. All assumptions underlying user-written micro programs should be documented, as well as all program testing and sample transactions. A clear narrative description of each program should also be available. Restrictions on development and circularization of software are essential to deter ill-effects. Beyond tests of programs, the tests of data entry are of paramount importance in creating and maintaining a credible data base on which decision makers can rely. Exemplary of the types of correctness edit checks which should be applied upon entry of data onto the micro are: field content checks of alpha versus numeric input, coding checks of number of digits, legitimacy of code checks, agreement to batch totals, check digits to detect transposition errors, and recalculations of all additions and extensions.

COMMON PROBLEMS

The problems with the integrity of software and data entry are closely linked to common problems in a personal computer environment: inadequate

—audit trails,

—backup, and

—assignment of responsibility.

Logs ought to be maintained to reflect who has accessed and altered what programs, data sets, or report forms. In other words, micro system software should strive for some of the "automatic" control assurances provided by the traditional mainframe system. Run instructions should be complete and an operations log should reflect the date, job runs, reasons for a re-run, problems, and machine failures. Backup may be the most difficult problem, because many get impatient with copying files and wait . . . unfortunately, until it is too late to do so. Many forget that RAM represents temporary storage, and if not backed up before turning off the computer, will be lost. (Exhibit 3–6 describes these similar terms applicable to the configuration of micros). I would venture a guess that every client has at times lost data and related analyses. A disk was too full and wouldn't execute the save command, or the power went off and retrieval was effectively precluded. An acquaintance of mine worked as a small business trouble-shooter for a major computer company and recounted an unbelievable number of stories where an entity had succeeded in virtually destroying its own records.

Exhibit 3–6

Terms Applicable to Micro-Configuration

Information storage

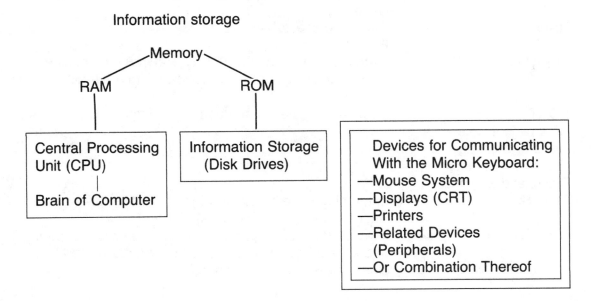

Exhibit 3–6 (continued)

An Operating System Has Four Primary Functions

1) Governs allocation of resources of the machine

   - controlling use of memory
   - sending output to CRT or printer

2) Coordinates activities of CPU and disk drives
3) Maintains disk files for the system
4) Provides utility programs to maintain

   - disk directories
   - edit and copy files
   - execute command sequences automatically

Jargonese

BIT:	An on or off state recognized by the CPU as being meaningful—a series of bits can represent a set of numbers in binary notation
BYTE:	A collection of bits that contains an instruction or piece of data—typically 8 bits long, although 16-bit and 32-bit instructions are in use (e.g., IBM PCAT is 16)
ASCII:	American Standard Code for Information Interchange defines 128 codes (using 7 bits)
PARITY INDICATOR:	The last bit used to verify the information contained in the other seven bits—last digit makes it even or odd—which is compared between receiving and sending machine
RAM:	Random Access Memory
ROM:	Read Only Memory
Kilobyte (K):	Memory Measurement—64K typical in 8 bit machine; 768K machines exist (K = 1024 or 2 to the tenth power)
PORT:	Doorway or gateway through which information is sent
"Floppy" Flexible Disks or Diskettes, "Hard" Winchester Disks, and Magnetic Tape Storage:	External storage media, storing 5, 10, 15, 20, and 40 "megabytes" (1 million bytes)
CHIP:	Integrated circuit chip, the basic electronic component of a PC—a tiny piece of etched silicon embedded in a plastic carrier with wire leads

Exhibit 3–6 (continued)

MOTHERBOARD:
Central part of computer containing microprocessor, memory, chips for coordinating memory and input/output, a power supply, and connection slots for peripheral interfaces

"BOOT" DISK:
Disk containing operating system—so called because the machine "pulls itself up by the bootstraps"

"booting":
Process of reading in the operating systems

Automatic backup:
A feature in which the program automatically creates a copy of the document while you are working on it, so if, for example, electrical service is interrupted, the back up copy is preserved.

Data Base Manager

dBASE II: relational data base manager

Standard Commands will
    —retrieve
    —sort
    —list
single items or groups of items by all or part of any field value, e.g., search title entry for text strings "and liab" to identify things to do with auditors' liability

---

Comparisons of Storage Devices

Hard Disk:
greater speed
greater precision

Removable Cartridge Hard Disk Drives:
removability allows for essentially unlimited capacity but introduces the potential for greater numbers of mechanical failures

RAM "disk" operating storage:
part of RAM is configured to look like a disk drive to the operating system in order to speed access and processing but unless backed up by batteries, if power goes off, RAM disk goes away—user must remember not to turn the machine off until storing RAM disk onto magnetic disk

Exhibit 3–6 (continued)

Video Laser Disk Technology: High capacity external storage of 1 to 10 gigobytes (one billion bytes or 1500 300-page books)

Dominant Languages in Programming

BASIC   easy to learn but slow and nonstandard, encouraging messy code

PASCAL   fast and standard but requires major software support and memory; also, quite inflexible

ASSEMBLY   very fast to utilize all machine capabilities, but machine dependent and tedious to scope

Other Languages

COBOL—business applications

FORTRAN—science and engineering

C—useful in systems design

FORTH—a systems development language

LOGO—uses a lot of graphics

LISP—standard language of artificial intelligence

Prologue—also used for artificial intelligence

With backup practices so poor, it should not be a surprise to hear that disaster plans are virtually nonexistent. Responsibilities are so poorly assigned and supported, that some micro environments will find themselves grinding to a halt merely because one individual is out-of-town. For example, "no one *else* knows how to "capture a file" other than in hard-copy form. . . ." Whenever one person is "indispensable" with regard to hardware (or the "I'm the Only Genius" syndrome is permitted) at an entity, a high risk situation arises. This is because the other individuals involved have "chosen ignorance" about the topic. Such a strategy creates "opportunities" for the EDP person which have to be carefully monitored.

One means of deterring breakdowns is to recognize such culprits to disaster as the environment; Exhibit 3–7 discusses some of these exposures. The procedure of father-son-grandson from mainframe environments creates and retains three generations of master files that ensure lost and destroyed data can be regenerated from other master files in concert with transaction data. Envision the updating of an accounts receivable subsidiary ledger, where last month's balances are retained, as are documents supporting billings and collections. In a disk file setting, as distinct from a magnetic tape system, this updating backup concept is difficult to implement because when records are updated on disk, new data is written over old data. In other words, the updating process is destructive. While a similar problem might arise in a tape environment, the economics are such that retaining several generations of tape files is feasible and common practice. Exhibit 3–7 offers suggestions for a micro environment.

Exhibit 3–7

Environmental Problems

Heat:	Do not block fans and cooling vents by equipment, disks, or other items: a fan is useless if the air around the machine is warm (above 90 degrees F)

- Too warm a machine will function erratically
  —Screen display will go
  —Disk drives will go
  —If severe, will cause permanent damage

- If running machine for a very long time, remove cover to maximize air circulation (if in a secure location)

Smoke and Dust:	Electronic devices are very sensitive to cigarette smoke, dust, and other small particles. They will attract tar from cigarettes
Static Electricity:	Since these charges in an individual can be thousands of volts, they can destroy isolated integrated circuit chips
Liquid:	Even tears have been known to short-circuit a keyboard; chemical deposits like sugar or coffee can damage the machine
Unreliable Power Supplies:	Erratic circuits such as those with sudden loads like blowers for air conditioning systems can be a problem and programs can be lost if power is lost

- voltage spike protection circuits can be installed ($50 to $500)
- batteries can be acquired to save programs if power reliability is a major problem ($400 to $800)

Wear and Tear:	Moving parts can break
Theft:	Be certain they are secured and insured
Data Backup:	Should maintain three generations

(1) Grandparent
(2) Parent
(3) Child
In three *different* locations
Program backup is important
Also, date accurately to avoid use of outdated data (e.g., old tax tables or old prices)

COMPUTER AUDITING

Now that the typical effects on a client have been reviewed, consider the typical EDP auditing techniques. A key segmentation of such auditing is between system testing and transaction testing. A systems-based approach to auditing requires an evaluation and testing of the control environment *and* its essential systems features, such as administrative and/or application controls surrounding the computer system being used.

Such a process is likely to involve external auditors, internal auditors, and clients' management information systems staff. With an understanding of organizational, equipment, and processing controls, including computer programs, the tests of detailed procedures can proceed.

An EDP environment often produces computer-generated error listings, for which tests of control can be used, as for a manual accounting system. When there is no visible evidence, tests of control will require computer auditing tools. System testing can be viewed as a sort of general or environmental control concern. The testing of software before it is released for on-line applications is an example of system testing. In contrast, transaction testing would focus, as an example, on whether a particular transaction is processed effectively. For example, did the name included in test data which was not on the approved vendor listing generate an exception report? System testing as a test of general EDP control is a prerequisite to effective transactions testing. Exhibit 3–8 reminds us of attitudes for skeptical systems evaluators.

Ample generalized audit software (GAS) is available. Firms originally developed GAS to extract and manipulate data from sequential files and have only recently sought to develop tools to audit direct access files. For some data base management systems (DBMSs), no GAS is yet available.

In order to apply GAS to complex data structures, it may be necessary to create an intermediate flat file, creating questions as to the completeness and correctness of original data representation. Complexity also tends to make audit queries more cumbersome. One problem with GAS is its limited ability to verify processing logic and its non-trivial propensity for error.[7]

More common GAS is virtually identical for micro and mainframe environments except that less sophisticated software is available on the micro, creating a need for auditors' development of programs or use of a micro as a dummy terminal, tying into mainframe software. On the micro, the auditor can consider writing extract programs using client query software or report-writer programs to parallel the GAS capabilities.

---

[7] Andrew D. Bailey, Jr., Lynford E. Graham, and James V. Hansen, "Technological Development & EDP," *Research Opportunities in Auditing: The Second Decade* (American Accounting Association: Auditing Section, 1988). Also see R. Weber, "Some Characteristics of the Free Recall of Computer Controls by EDP Auditors," *Journal of Accounting Research* (Vol. 18, No. 1), pp. 214–241.

Exhibit 3–8

Micro Risks

Keep in Mind . . .

A computer's software is not difficult to change.

Idiosyncratic, complex coding methods are common.

DOCUMENT AND TEST USER-WRITTEN MICRO PROGRAMS AND
AUDIT PERIODICALLY FOR VERIFICATION OF CORRECTNESS

- All assumptions of program
- All program testing
- Sample transactions
- A narrative description

USE COMPILED VERSION OF PROGRAM AND REMOVE SOURCE
CODE FROM SYSTEM

- Less likely to be modified if not in an interpreted version of BASIC
- Can be executed more quickly

A COMPUTER WILL NOT ALWAYS BE RIGHT.

- Hardware circuitry can be faulty
- Programs may not be sufficiently debugged

Micro Risks Include:

— Physical Security of Hardware

THEFT

Secure at a workstation or keep locked in a cabinet designed to house
a micro.

Rollable, lockable cabinets are available.

DAMAGE

Many computers have a routine that must be followed before relocation.
- Moving read/write head on fixed disk drive to an unused portion of
  disk
- Locking read/write head to prevent damage

— Physical Security of Software

- PASSWORD PROTECTION (multiple password levels, especially for
  use of disk)
- AUDIT TRAILS (Record User ID, files used, duration of use, types of
  transactions performed, and denied access)
- DATA ENCRYPTION/DECRYPTION (prevents reading of data)
- COPY PROTECTION

SHOULD TEST PERIODICALLY

- Billing errors
- Improper application of credit limits

COMPANIES CAN GO OUT OF BUSINESS BEFORE ANYONE EVEN
DETECTS AN ERROR!

USE OF "DUMMY TERMINALS"

By using micros as "dummy terminals" and accessing more memory, computing capabilities are improved. Since many clients will still have primary account records on a mainframe, the interface of micro to mainframe will be essential for pulling machine-readable data from the mainframe for audit purposes. Of course, one problem is that others can download data and then do whatever they wish with that information. Hence, control over micro-mainframe linkage is critical. Extra security like call back devices and layers of password protection are critical. An advantage of mainframe linkage is that the auditor may wish to retrieve information from such national data banks as NAARS, Citibank, Compustat, and *The New York Times* or similar media services for the purpose of performing analytical procedures or to obtain prototypes for checking the phrasing of disclosures.

An advantage of performing audit applications on a micro level is the friendliness and diversity of software. SPSS, a popular statistical package for mainframes, has been converted to micros. It facilitates statistical analyses, data manipulation, profile analysis, and similar studies. Both SAS and TSP are among numerous available statistical packages for micros. However, as with other programs, users need to be trained on both the use of the software and its limitations. A set of controls over software acquisitions is advisable, and selection should consider

—ease of learning

—ease of use

—error handling

—performance

—versatility

—overall evaluation.

QUESTIONS AS YET UNANSWERED

In considering the auditing of hardware controls, research is still being directed toward

—whether an examination of vendor specifications is sufficient for all hardware,

—which hardware can be substituted for other hardware,

—what set of controls is advisable and where to minimize the risk of exposure, and

—can software be used to automatically verify the correct operation of hardware controls.[8]

---

[8] Andrew D. Bailey, Jr., "Technological Development & EDP," *Research Opportunities in Auditing: The Second Decade* (American Accounting Association: Auditing Section, 1988, p.77.

EXPERT SYSTEMS

Expert systems are steadily evolving to address

—internal control evaluations,
—EDP audit controls,
—bad debt write-offs,
—loan loss reserve estimates, and
—tax planning issues.

Analytical procedure applications are probable in the near future. Care must be taken in understanding the underlying knowledge base, the rule-oriented approach, and the scope of such systems. Otherwise, garbage in–garbage out problems can dominate. A key advantage of expert systems is its "why" capabilities: systems will tell the reasoning used to derive the result given.

Technological developments may quickly enhance the largest problem with effective artificial intelligence (AI) applications in auditing. That problem relates to interfacing an expert system with a data base. This retrieval linkage is critical. The problem is that while data base retrieval systems (relational data base managers) are available, as are rule-based and other types of expert systems, dual use—the obvious ideal—is not yet developed. One reason stems from the past applications of AI when contrasted with potential accounting and auditing questions. Past expert systems have had to construct knowledge bases to which rules were applied, whereas accounting and auditing have data bases in terms of the underlying records to which expert systems are intended to be applied. While it is obviously possible to access data with a retrieval data base software, and to then apply various software for analyses of such data, this process primarily represents mechanization. In order to integrate logic into the scenario, based on the expertise of key decision makers, in an efficient manner, far more development in technology is required. A key obstacle in AI is widely acknowledged to be the development of an associative memory, flexible enough to retrieve stored experiences that approximately match an arbitrary new situation.

LEGAL ISSUES RELATED TO AI

Hand-in-hand with technological developments are legal issues. Recently, I have been told, the IRS has expressed its intent to hold software developers of tax return packages liable for underpayment penalties due to errors in their packages. The unanswered question is how the quality of audit evidence generated by expert systems will be assessed in the courtroom setting. Since a wide variety of approaches are used in knowledge base development and the specification of related rules, questions could arise as to the legitimacy of certain systems. As one example, many systems are based on a research method known as protocol analysis. This means that individuals describe their decision processes and this description is used to develop that expert's decision process into an expert system.

Yet, as Robert Elliott, a partner at Peat, Marwick, Main has reported: an experiment in which a group of partners were asked to describe swimming led to protocols which never mentioned "water!" The point, of course, is that people may either not understand their decision processes or may be woefully lacking in their ability to communicate those processes. How knowledge is represented includes the use of networks, frames, and or rule-based IF/THEN commands.

Accounting and control issues in the EDP audit area relate to the completeness, accuracy, and integrity of the accounting data as it enters and is processed through the accounting system. As important is the timeliness with which accounting changes are reflected in the accounting records being subjected to EDP analyses. Of course, this goal of timeliness can inversely relate to the need for adequate testing of software and system changes before revised or new applications are put on line.

NEURAL NETWORKS

An alternative to AI which is reportedly cheapest to access is neural net technology: it mimics the brain's complex network of neurons, the cells that transmit and store the nervous system's messages and learns to make its judgments similar to human beings.[9] While early in development, and limited in the lack of clarity as to how problems are solved or how large a problem can be tackled, neural networks are predicted to teach themselves a broad cross-section of skills: wherever pattern recognition is important. Successes have been observed in detection of defective motors and faulty paint finishes; such inspections out perform bored or fatigued human inspectors. While too early to hypothesize control issues, the black-box nature of neural networks could lead to similar problems as hypothesized for AI.

FRAUD

Finally, the fraud issue is a significant concern. The tales of EDP fraud are plentiful. While many merely replace the pencil with the keyboard and are not truly "computer frauds," the nature of a computer environment facilitates repetitive processing of immaterial errors, in a manner that eventually aggregates to a material amount. It has been pointed out that computers can easily be programmed to lie or conceal the truth, and security specialists point out the absence of external evidence of frauds:

> Sherlock Holmes . . . can't come in and find any heel marks. There's no safe with its door blown off. [Moreover, the] first thing the interloper would do is to corrupt the audit-trail software itself.[10]

---

[9] Brian O'Reilly, "Computers That Think Like People," *Fortune* (February 27, 1989), pp. 90–93.

[10] Tom Alexander, "Waiting for the Great Computer Rip-Off," *Fortune* (July 1974), p. 146.

The cleverness of defrauders is reflected in a case reported by the *Wall Street Journal*.[11] It seems that a Mr. Slyngstad, a programmer for the State of Washington, wrote checks to Stanley Lyngstad and reported that no bank ever questioned the missing "S" in his last name. Of interest is the fact that an auditor who applied the matching capability of GAS to compare recipients of vocational rehabilitation checks with employees' names would not have generated an exception report. The point is that an EDP systems evaluator must be creative, in designing control-oriented program checks, perhaps focusing on subsets of names when running matching procedures. Otherwise, a defrauder's move to transpose two letters in their names can virtually undermine a host of machine-based checks. In addition, attention to the number of transactions through an account rather than merely its balance can prove helpful in detecting accounts used to "pass through" questionable transactions. For example, dormant accounts should be reviewed as to the frequency of the activity in such accounts as a specified control procedure. Donn Parker, Senior Management Systems Consultant at SRI International states that at least three conditions are necessary to perpetrate a computer fraud: knowledge, access, and resources. These conditions are far more prevalent in the 1990s than in past years, implying greater threats to control.[12]

Estimates of losses incurred due to computer fraud range from $3 billion to $5 billion annually in the United States alone. Estimates of reported cases as a percentage of committed computer fraud cases range from 5% to 20%.[13] Domestic problems are similarly experienced internationally. A survey in England, Wales, and Scotland reported that 8% of 943 respondents had suffered computer fraud in the prior five years.

LIMITATIONS OF TECHNOLOGY[14]

Technology has strengths and limitations. The skeptical nature of the systems evaluator should reflect an understanding of technology and innovation, with an appreciation of potential pitfalls. I have concerns that so much technology has been placed at the fingertips of today's professionals that those with an inclination toward innovation may be too quick to perceive that "nothing can go wrong" as sophistication of method is enhanced. I cringe when I hear tale of a Lotus regression application that uses six data points. As I review approaches to expert systems which lop off branches of the decision tree largely due to size constraints of the

---

[11] Erik Larson, "Crook's Tool: Computers Turn Out to Be Valuable Aid in Employee Crime," *Wall Street Journal* (January 14, 1985), p. 1.

[12] Ernst & Whinney, *Computer Fraud* (1987), p. 6.

[13] Ernst & Whinney, *Computer Fraud* (1987). [This also is the source of information on the survey in England, Wales, and Scotland.]

[14] This discussion is an adaptation from "Educating the Partner of the Year 2000," *Auditor Productivity in the Year 2000, 1987 Proceedings of the Arthur Young Professors' Roundtable*, Andrew Bailey, Editor, Ohio State University (The Council of Arthur Young Professors Reston International Center, 1988), pp. 245–251.

system on which the prototype is intended to operate, my concern grows. We must have sophisticated consumers of technology and nurture skepticism.

As technology is applied to enhance effectiveness and efficiency, the human element behind the technology must be appreciated. I recently heard an anecdote of an accomplished system designer who was replaced. He left a farewell present for his past employer. Every year, on his birthday, the entire company's system freezes and terminals flash with a message like "Happy Birthday Harry." Despite repeated attempts by his replacement to find the source of this prank, I understand that now, six years following Harry's departure, his message persists.

I share this story as an example of how technology can operate effectively for 364 out of 365 days of the year, yet be undermined by a virtual needle in the haystack on that 365th day. Awareness of the vulnerability of technology to knowledgeable professionals should be a key lesson.

To address such potential problems, competency is an essential trait of personnel responsible for controls. In addition, creativity has to be nurtured, along with understanding of such issues as why post facto sampling will not cover the risk exposure to data base management systems. Creative generating of rules for on-line exception reports is essential to provide useful and adequate continuous audit coverage. Most importantly, can we change a mindset from resistance to change to embracing technology, yet retain healthy skepticism as to the risks, inherited through innovation?

Forewarned Is Forearmed

The prevalence of computer technology in supporting clients' operations and audit technology leads to a set of unique considerations about which the systems evaluator must be kept painstakingly aware. I will provide some examples in the spirit of demonstrating how forewarned may mean forearmed.

Each day, over $400 billion is transferred, unencoded over the financial networks such as SWIFT, CHIPS, and FEDWIRE. Many predict a financial community catastrophe on the order of Chernobyl. One must be leery of the business attitude: "It can't happen here."[15] Auditors must assess the risk encompassed by such transactions, as well as changes in such risk due to technological developments or shifts in business practices.

Research suggests that of the computer abuses discovered,

32%	are discovered by accident
45%	are discovered via normal systems controls
8%	are discovered by computer security officers
4.5%	are discovered by all auditors.

This evidence supports attention to system controls but it also implies room for improvement of auditors' effectiveness in detecting computer fraud. Given the

---

[15] Adapted from Paul L. Tom, *Managing Data as a Corporate Resource.*

number of undiscovered abuses is thought to far exceed the number discovered, care must be directed to assisting future auditors in recognizing the motivations and effects of abuse, alongside recognizing opportunity for abuse.

Reportedly, motivations include:

30% for personal gain
25% due to ignorance of proper conduct
20% through misguided playfulness
10% as maliciousness

These motivations both intentional and unintentional, lead to abuse of a variety of assets, including:

	Estimates
Computer Services	46%
Data	26%
Programs	16%
Hardware	12%

Auditors who regularly access client data for their testing needs must be alert to the potential for data contamination.

Exposure to abuse includes a broad number of occupations:

	Estimates
Application Programmers	18%
Clerical Personnel	14%
System Users	14%
Students	12%
Managers	11%
Systems Analysts	6%
Machine Operators	6%
Top Executives	4%
Other EDP Staff	3%
Data Entry Staff	3%
Systems Programmers	3%
Consultants	3%
Accountants	2%
Security Officers	1%

Reportedly, controllers and auditors are not yet represented.[16] Such research dissipates notions that the auditor's key exposure is among EDP personnel. The users and clerical personnel pose an equivalent threat. Given their number, the threat may well be greatest from other than EDP professionals.

---

[16] All statistics are based on DPMA, ABA, AICPA and similar research accumulated for course instruction in the systems area at the University of Minnesota.

One means of enhancing control is to ensure that the computer security officer reports to the chief information officer and is hierarchically independent of the data base administrator and the managers of both systems development and systems operations. Such independent status is as critical to the future auditor as the more traditional attention to the internal auditor's independence.

System Decentralization

The decentralization of computing power has led to a number of organizational control issues as to how much autonomy to permit, relative to central control over distributed databases. One observable trend in companies is to appoint a senior executive as *chief information officer* (CIO) to coordinate strategic management information system (MIS) activities for the entire organization. Preferably, this person reports to the chief executive officer and supervises a computer security officer, a systems development manager, a database administrator, and a systems operations manager. This desired organizational chart is depicted in Exhibit 3–9.

Exhibit 3–9

Desired Organization Chart

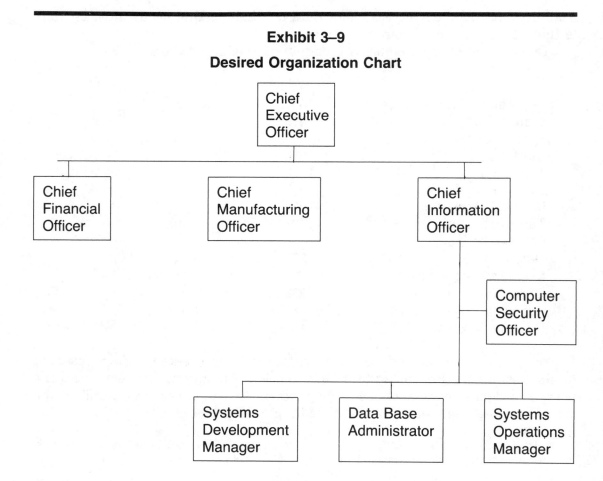

The smaller computer systems that evolve in decentralized settings often involve "turnkey software packages" which require a determination of what controls have been built in by the vendors, since user-developed documentation is unlikely to be complete. Similarly, attention to separation of duties and backup and recovery are more likely to be casual.

Local area networks (LANs)—one form of decentralized operation already described—are expected to entail workstation controls of multi-level passwords, separation of duties as they relate to the initiation of transactions, distribution of source documents for confirmation (e.g., customers' confirmation of sales), and workstation restrictions as to the type of processing permitted.[17]

Questions should be posed as to the degree of oversight by a CIO. Decentralization could lend itself to a superior degree of separation of duties, relative to a centralized operation, with proper control design.[18] Recent research has suggested means of measuring EDP management effectiveness, which could prove useful in assessing control risk.[19]

Risk Assessment

As technology becomes increasingly advanced, including eventual software technology which is capable of maintenance and modification of programs, businesses' exposure to disaster recovery will continually increase. In fact, a formal concept referred to as Maximum Time to Belly Up (MTBU) demands substantial attention by those relying on computers in real time in sensitive aspects of their business.[20] Given extended auditors' responsibilities in assessing going concern, EDP considerations of this nature will likely grow in their particular relevance to CPAs.

The point of each of these examples is that as technology becomes increasingly positive in both the client's and auditor's operations, focus must be directed to a total integrated picture of risk. Volume of transactions, existence of abuse, potential controls, the implications of reliance upon computers, and ill-effects of "bad habits" tied to ease of access combine to affect both audit risk and the CPA's business risk.

Those evaluating systems must design on-line sampling considering creative strata based on time, scope, thresholds, nature of transactions, and frequency of occurrence. Sampling from redefined populations such as exception reports may

---

[17] Robert M. Harper, "AHP Judgment Models of EDP Auditors' Evaluations of Internal Control for Local Area Networks," Workpaper at Louisiana State University (1988).

[18] Some of these concepts are developed by Andrew D. Bailey, Jr., Lynford E. Graham, and James V. Hansen, "Technological Development & EDP," *Research Opportunities in Auditing: A Second Decade* (American Accounting Association: Auditing Section, 1989).

[19] James H. Gerlach, "A Model for Testing the Reliability of Computer Programs and EDP Management: Internal Control Implications," *Auditing: A Journal of Practice & Theory* (Spring 1988), pp. 61–76.

[20] Adapted from Donn B. Parker, *Crime by Computer*.

well be beneficial. Just as one auditor reportedly discovered a fraud in dormant accounts of a bank by testing the number of transactions through an account, *rather than* its ending balance, intelligent auditing must be engendered among those charged with assessing control risk. As always, it is the smart application of the innovative technology, rather than its mere existence, which makes all the difference.

Among the open questions tied to the auditing of complex technology include:

- How can the auditor assess the quality of evidence produced by embedded software?
- What are the appropriate times to gather evidence and does it vary per type of control?
- How do data structures affect evidence requirements?
- Can effective test data be developed for advanced computing systems programmed controls, given control failures are difficult to detect for some software yet reliance on programmed controls raise the costs of a control that is not functioning appropriately.[21]

Software engineering is moving toward more computer assisted design (CAD), computer assisted engineering (CAE), and maintenance-free characteristics. Research is currently underway to consider the integration of security and reliability features in design software. Initial work has similarly been performed on experts' decision rules when evaluating EDP-related control risk dimensions.[22]

Technology is so pervasive that it has been cited as likely to affect

- evidence collection
  —type
  —source
  —mode of collection
  —quality
- scope expansion
- audit administration
- professional education
- professional standards

---

[21] Andrew D. Bailey, Jr., Lynford E. Graham, and James V. Hansen, "Technological Development & EDP," *Research Opportunities in Auditing*: *The Second Decade* (American Accounting Association: Auditing Section, 1988).

[22] Stanley F. Biggs, William F. Messier, Jr., and James V. Hansen, "A Descriptive Analysis of Computer Audit Specialists' Decision-Making Behavior in Advanced Computer Environments," *Auditing*: *A Journal of Practice & Theory* (Spring 1987), pp. 1–21.

- staffing
- legal liability.[23]

Obviously, technology affects control and, in turn, those responsible for designing evaluations and testing control structure.

SYNOPSIS

Technology permeates every corner of an organization's operations and hence is intrinsically related to controls. While later chapters provide far more elaboration, rudimentary terms in personal computer settings and more sophisticated systems are introduced, with examples of attendant control risks. The appendix to this chapter includes a case related to microcomputers. While developed well before SAS 55, its lessons are a useful demonstration of control concepts. Computer auditing, fraud exposure, and expert systems are among the topics addressed. The need for professional skepticism in evaluating and using technology is discussed.

---

[23] Adapted from Andrew D. Bailey, Jr., Lynford E. Graham, James V. Hansen, "Technological Development & EDP," *Research Opportunities in Auditing: The Second Decade* (American Accounting Association: Auditing Section, 1988).

APPENDIX

A Case from Practice:
Internal Control Considerations in a Microcomputer Environment

Contributed by Price Waterhouse

Introduction

The second standard of field work requires that an audit include "a proper study and evaluation of the existing internal control as a basis for reliance thereon and for the determination of the resultant extent of the tests to which auditing procedures are to be restricted." SAS 3, **The Effects of EDP on the Auditor's Study and Evaluation of Internal Control,** states that this review is required whether the client maintains a manual accounting system or an accounting system that includes EDP operations. In the latter case, the review considerations are equally pertinent whether a mainframe, minicomputer or microcomputer is utilized to generate financial statement information.

Given the increasing use of microcomputers by many businesses today, the auditor must be cognizant of the potential internal control weaknesses that may be inherent in a microcomputer environment. Such knowledge is crucial if the auditor is to make a proper assessment of the related controls and to plan an effective and efficient audit approach.

In the following case study, assume you are participating in the audit of XYZ Company and the following background information has been obtained during the planning phase. Consider the potential effects on internal control that have been introduced by the microcomputer applications and assess how those effects may alter the audit plan for the current year.

Background Information

XYZ Company is a wholesale distributor of electric appliances. The Company's sales in each of the last two years have been approximately $40,000,000. All accounting applications are handled at the Company's corporate office.

The data processing operations have historically centered around an onsite minicomputer. The computer applications include accounts payable and cash disbursements, payroll, inventory and general ledger. Accounts receivable and fixed asset records have been prepared manually in the past. Internal controls in all areas have been considered strong in the last few years.

During the past year financial management decided to automate processing of sales, accounts receivable and fixed asset transactions and accounting. Management also concluded that purchasing a microcomputer and related available software was more cost-effective than increasing the minicomputer capacity and hiring a second computer operator. The controller and accounting clerks have been encouraged to find additional uses for the microcomputer and to "experiment" with it when they are not too busy.

The accounts receivable clerk is enthusiastic about the microcomputer, but the fixed asset clerk seems somewhat apprehensive about it because he has no prior experience with computers. The accounts receivable clerk explained that the controller had purchased a "very easy to use" accounts receivable software application program for the microcomputer which enables her to quickly input the daily information regarding billings and payments received. The controller has added some programming of his own to the software to give it better report-writing features.

During a recent demonstration, the accounts receivable clerk explained that the program required her only to input the customer's name and invoice amount in the case of billings, or the customer's name and check amount in the case of payments. The microcomputer then automatically updates the respective customer's account balance. At the end of every month, the accounts receivable trial balance is printed and reconciled by the clerk to the general ledger balance. The reconciliation is reviewed by the controller.

The fixed asset program was also purchased from an outside

vendor. The controller indicated that the software package had just recently been put on the market and that it was programmed to compute tax depreciation based on recent changes in the federal tax laws. He also stated that because of the fixed asset clerk's reluctance to use the microcomputer, he had input all the information from the fixed asset manual records. He indicated, however, that the fixed asset clerk would be responsible for the future processing related to the fixed asset files and for generating the month-end and year-end reports used to prepare the related accounting entries.

The various accounts receivable and fixed asset diskettes are all adequately labeled as to the type of program or data file and are arranged in an organized manner in a diskette holder located near the microcomputer.

Suggested Solution

Internal Control Implications

Although the addition of the microcomputer may well prove beneficial to the Company, a number of apparent internal control weaknesses exist that could have serious ramifications.

—The diskettes are stored openly near the microcomputer, and employees are "encouraged" to experiment with the microcomputer. Thus, many employees appear to have access to the accounts receivable and fixed asset diskettes. Such access could result in improper alterations to the related data or programs.

—The accounts receivable program was partially reprogrammed by the controller and thus appears readily susceptible to change. Tampering with a "live" program could result in the improper processing of data.

—The accounts receivable program does not leave an audit trail. Account balances are updated, but no transaction record of the individual billings and payments is made (i.e., only invoice or check amounts are entered into the system, and not invoice numbers, dates, etc.). As a result, it would be very time consuming to investigate any differences that might arise between the accounts receivable detail and general ledger balance or between the Company's and customers' records.

—No mention was made of whether the fixed asset program was adequately tested. Although it is supposedly "state-of-the-art," it may not compute depreciation and net book value on a basis consistent with the Company's policy.

—The fixed asset clerk's reluctance to use the microcomputer implies that proper training may not

have taken place. In addition, adequate systems or application documentation may not exist for him to teach himself. Accordingly, improper use of the fixed asset program is not an unreasonable possibility.

—The fixed asset processing appears to lack adequate segregation of duties. The fixed asset clerk will be responsible for processing future fixed asset transactions and generating general ledger entries. Based on the descriptions provided by the Company, no cross-checking controls exist.

—It is relatively simple to use a microcomputer to access data files in a minicomputer. No mention was made as to whether any controls were established to prevent this from occurring, and thus it may be possible for the minicomputer data files or programs to be improperly altered by using the microcomputer as a terminal.

Implications for the Audit Plan

The auditor would need to make inquiries to confirm whether some of the potential internal control weaknesses mentioned above could impact the audit or are mitigated by other controls and procedures. However, based on the available information, the apparent weaknesses are significant enough to cause serious concern as to whether controls surrounding the microcomputer applications are sufficiently reliable to produce proper financial statement information.

If the auditor determines that the internal control weaknesses are not mitigated by other controls and procedures, the audit approach in the fixed asset and accounts receivable areas would probably be based largely on substantive testing. For example, the auditor might perform the circularization of accounts receivable at year-end rather than interim in order to make certain that the detailed trial balance can be used to support the general ledger balance and to assess the reserve for bad debts.

The auditor must be aware that many of the control features that apply in larger minicomputer or "mainframe" installations typically will not be present in the microcomputer environment. When microcomputers are used in applications or situations similar to the XYZ Company example, control over accounting applications may be jeopardized by less segregation of duties, reduced processing controls and a casual operating environment. When these circumstances are encountered, the auditor should inquire regarding other controls, such as (1) management involvement in the form of review and approval of transactions and reports and (2) clear and distinct audit trails over transaction processing, to determine if reliance on controls in microcomputer-based systems is warranted.

Source: *The Auditor's Report* (Vol. 7, No. 2, Summer 1983), pp. 5, 6.

4

Special Attention to Fraud Detection Issues

"Where large sums of money are concerned, it is advisable to trust nobody."

Agatha Christie[1]

A commonly cited saying is that a person can be defrauded only by someone he or she trusts. Hence, Agatha Christie's words may be particularly important to keep in mind when considering exposure to fraud. The moral of the saying is never to place undue reliance on a single individual.[2] This concept is often difficult to accept, particularly by many small businesses which tend to view their long-time employees as being "above reproach." The problem with such a belief is that the personal circumstances of an employee may change in a manner which supersedes any employer/employee relationship. For example, severe illness in a family, financial difficulties, or personal problems leading to blackmail or gambling debts can arise which lead to even a loyal employee's temptation. Obviously, this

---

[1] *The Executive's Quotation Book: A Corporate Companion*, Edited by James Charlton (New York: St. Martin's Press, 1983), p. 6.

[2] The following discussions were jointly developed for this *Handbook* and related work authored by W. Wallace, as published in *Financial Accounting* (South-Western Publishers) and *Auditing*, 2nd edition (PWS-KENT).

temptation is greatest when complete "trust" has been placed in the employee's hands, with few if any checks and balances; similarly, an employer's exposure is greatest in such a circumstance. The bare necessity, in terms of control procedures, is to purchase *fidelity bonding insurance coverage.* This basically involves a check by the insurer into the background of the employee and then the creation of an insurance policy which will reimburse the employer for losses due to defalcations (fraudulent activities) of an employee. A small business with a single employee who had a good employment history could likely obtain a $40,000 employee dishonesty bond for $100 a year. Both individual and blanket (i.e., covering all employees) bond coverage is available to businesses, often as an integral part of their commercial insurance coverage.

In addition to the inherent risk of trusting in an employee, an employer should be alert to casual substitutions of employees for one another. It is well documented that defrauders often are given "opportunity" by offering assistance to a colleague who is performing a task which is incompatible with their responsibilities. One means by which a company can evaluate whether this is happening is to periodically ask employees to describe their jobs day-to-day and, in particular, to list the names of those with whom they interact regularly (this is referred to as positional analysis). If interaction is noted among individuals whose duties should not typically cause them to meet on the job, a problem could be on the horizon. Since research suggests that most fraud is perpetuated unilaterally (80% is the estimate), segregation of duties both formally and informally can operate as an important deterrent to fraud.

A system is most vulnerable to errors and irregularities during a system change or personnel change. Careful hiring practices are essential. In addition, training and promotion must be handled with care to ensure the quality and competence of employees. Plenty of on-the-job-training (OJT) is essential to deter inadvertent errors as well as intentional irregularities. Whenever possible, the old system or departing personnel should overlap with the new operations to ensure things are operating effectively and are well controlled before transitions are finalized.

OPPORTUNITIES TO COMMIT FRAUD

An important aspect of control strategy is to reduce opportunities for fraud. Researchers have examined actual fraud settings and suggest key considerations in identifying possible opportunities for fraud. These are presented in Exhibit 4–1.

Employee Control Problems/Risks (Theft and Fraud)

A key problem faced by business is employee theft. Exhibit 4–2 reprints an article on this topic which discusses both the typical control problems and means

Exhibit 4–1

Opportunities Allowing Individuals to Commit Fraud Against the Company

1. Do any of the key executives have close associations with suppliers or key individuals who might have motives inconsistent with the company's welfare?
2. Does the company fail to inform employees about rules of personal conduct and the discipline of fraud perpetrators?
3. Is the company experiencing a rapid turnover of key employees, either through their quitting or being fired?
4. Have any of the key executives recently failed to take annual vacations of more than one or two days, or has the company failed periodically to rotate or to transfer key personnel?
5. Does the company fail to use adequate personnel screening policies when hiring new employees to fill positions of trust (i.e., check on secondary references)?
6. Does the company lack explicit and uniform personnel policies?
7. Does the company fail to maintain accurate personnel records of dishonest acts or disciplinary actions?
8. Does the company fail to require executive disclosures and examinations (i.e., personal investments, incomes)?
9. Does the company appear to have a dishonest or unethical management?
10. Is the company dominated by only one or two individuals?
11. Does the company appear to operate continually on a crisis basis?
12. Does the company fail to pay attention to details (i.e., are accurate accounting records unimportant)?
13. Does the company place too much trust in key employees and overlook traditional controls?
14. Is there a lack of good interpersonal relationships among the key executives in the company?
15. Does the company have unrealistic productivity measurements or expectations?
16. Does the company have poor compensation practices? Is pay commensurate with level of responsibility?
17. Does the company lack a good system of internal security (i.e., locks, safes, fences, gates, guards)?
18. Does the company lack adequate training programs?
19. Does the company have an inadequate internal control system or does it fail to enforce the existing controls?

Source: W. Steve Albrecht, "Understanding Fraud," *The Accounting Forum*, vol. 55 (December 1985/January 1986), pp. 11, 12.

Exhibit 4–2

The High Cost of Employee Theft

The news was dramatic, and it put the spotlight on something that most companies would rather not talk about. Last month, newspaper headlines proclaimed that the International Business Machines Corp. has just fired and sued three employees, accusing them of stealing and trying to sell company secrets. Such information is seldom made public, and that may explain why so few people, from corporate executives on down, realize how really big employee theft is.

The fact is, it's a crime that amounts to 1% of the Gross National Product, or some $40 billion a year, and just about every employee this side of sainthood will commit it some time during his working life. Moreover, it accounts for 80% of all crime against corporations, and, with economic hard times joining ever-present greed as a motivating force, it is growing. Even the spread of barter is helping the trend. An appliance worker who swipes a food processor from his company no longer has to find some criminal to fence it; he may be able to trade it to his local service station for a tankful of gasoline.

Employee theft can threaten the very life of an enterprise, as a Pennsylvania construction-materials firm learned. One of its financial officers, who was selling commercial paper to help fund two subsidiaries, set up dummy subsidiaries to which he channeled some of the proceeds. After the deception was discovered three years later, the legitimate subsidiaries were forced into bankruptcy court. All told, one out of every 10 companies that fails each year does so as a direct result of employee theft, the Commerce Department estimates; the U.S. Chamber of Commerce has an even higher estimate: a frightening 30%.

Yet while employee theft thrives, most corporations make only perfunctory efforts to solve the problem. . . .

Security experts divide internal crime into three categories: the theft of things such as raw materials, finished products, cash and tools; the theft of information; and fraud.

The theft of raw materials occurs primarily in the manufacturing and construction businesses. For a manufacturing firm, it most often occurs in the shipping and receiving or warehouse end of the operation, where controls are notoriously lax. With hundreds of shipments going in and out of a docking area each day, keeping an eye on materials is taxing, and the opportunity for theft astounding.

The crimes are often simple, but costly. For instance, a manufacturer of vacuum tubes may receive a shipment of copper wire. A dishonest employee might sign for 100 reels, unload them from the truck and then hide two reels on his way from the receiving area to the warehouse. He then simply recovers the two reels later. The employee could also unload only

Exhibit 4–2 (continued)

98 reels but sign for 100 and split the proceeds from the sale of the two extras with the driver of the truck.

At construction sites, there are often hundreds of workers performing a wide variety of tasks and trucks coming and going with materials. So it's relatively easy for an employee to slip off the job to nab some lumber, plasterboard or insulating material and stash it in his pick-up truck, or to arrange for a friend with a commercial truck to pick up material and haul it away. Fred Bornhoffen, head of security for Sun Co. Inc., maintains that many construction companies do not even monitor who goes in and out of a site and whether they are authorized to take materials out.

The theft of semifinished and finished products occurs in all industries. One security consultant tells the sad tale of a leading bottler of antifreeze in the Midwest. When the price of antifreeze, like oil, rose in the mid-70s, the bottler began to notice a good deal of unfamiliar antifreeze being stocked by gas stations that previously had bought only from him. When he investigated, he discovered that as antifreeze rose in price from $1.50 to $8 a gallon, some of his employees were tempted to come into the warehouse area at night, load antifreeze onto company trucks, repackage it and distribute it at a discount.

The illegal siphoning off of crude and refined oil plagues the oil industry. The measurement of how much oil goes into a tank is relatively imprecise, so employees are able, undetected, either to siphon oil from a storage tank or to pump only part of the oil in a tanker truck into a tank. And as Bornhoffen of Sun points out: "If you are able to tamper with the meter of the tank— and some people are—that is just a license to steal."

In the retail area, Arthur Young & Co., recently surveyed 127 companies with a total of 25,000 individual store locations and total sales of $53 billion and found that inventory shrinkage amounted to slightly more than $1 billion. About half, or about 1% of total sales, was due to employee theft. Twenty percent was attributed to accounting errors and 30% to shoplifting.

Internal theft occurs in a variety of places at a retail organization—at the shipping and receiving dock, at the warehouse and while moving goods from one store to another—but most often it occurs right in the store. An employee may work alone, merely taking merchandise from the shelves or ringing up less than the purchase price and pocketing the difference; or he may work with an outside accomplice who buys something to which the employee adds additional goods at no charge. Stealing cash directly from the register is somewhat infrequent in large department stores because most purchases are made with credit cards.

The Arthur Young survey found that employee theft is most likely to occur just before the store opens, when employees can wander about the premises and security staffers usually aren't around.

Exhibit 4–2 (continued)

Small convenience stores and gas stations are extremely vulnerable to the theft of cash by employees. Security director M. W. McBee of Ashland Oil Inc., explains that because service station jobs tend to be low paying, managers often do not thoroughly check out new employees. As a result, thefts occur. "It is not at all uncommon for an employee at a service station to take in $4,000 in cash in one shift and then skip town and the state with the money," he says, "We've certainly had it happen to us, and we are no exception."

When it comes to the outright theft of money, banks are where the big action is. Wells Fargo bank was the victim of one of the biggest recent ripoffs. An employee in the operations department fiddled with customer accounts entered in the bank computers and embezzled about $21 million in a two-year period before he was caught.

A blank purchase order is simply another form of cash, but companies often leave the drawer with these orders unlocked when they would not dream of doing so with cash. Michael Moritz, director of security for United Telephone Systems, tells of a worker at the warehouse of a New England firm who took four purchase orders from an unlocked cabinet and wrote out at least two requiring his company to ship pumps to another company he had set up to receive just these items. After two of these orders came through the purchasing department, another employee noted that the numbers were out of sequence. The company investigated and found the pumps had been loaded onto an unmarked truck and whisked away.

The theft of tools and equipment is rampant in the construction and energy business. Energy companies had a particularly tough problem keeping expensive drill bits and valves during . . . the domestic drilling boom, when these items were in short supply. Often, no one was keeping track of who received how many drill bits or valves. A similar absence of records also hurts the construction industry.

"The theft from outside of a $200,000 bulldozer gets lots of publicity. But if 2,000 workers each walk off with $100 worth of drills and hammers and saws, which would not be uncommon, the loss adds up the same," says Brian Deery, who heads up the division on theft of construction equipment at the Association of General Contractors. And it's the public that ultimately pays. Some contractors routinely add 5% to their estimates to cover the cost of internal and external theft, Deery reports.

Holding on to office supplies can be equally difficult. Pens, paper, scissors, staplers, calculators and cassette recorders are all small items that can be easily hidden in a large purse or an executive briefcase. Because these items are relatively low in value, few managers keep track of them or even bother to lock them up at night. One security consultant reports that office supplies tend to disappear faster in August than in any other

Exhibit 4–2 (continued)

month as parents outfit their children for the September return to school. And so it goes, similarly, with the use of the office telephone for personal long-distance calls, the use of office postage and the office copier.

Theft of information, though less prevalent than the theft of objects or services, can be disastrous. The energy industry is a frequent target of such thefts. Seismic surveys and exploration data, which cost millions of dollars to collect, have been pilfered from major oil companies and sold to small, independent drillers or to foreign concerns.

Bornhoffen of Sun says his company has been offered such information, but has always turned the seller away. "We know the information has been stolen from one of our competitors," he notes.

Fraudulent schemes are the most costly form of employee theft. "The creation of dummy or shell companies is on the upswing, and it is not especially difficult to arrange," says Errol M. Cook, a security expert at Arthur Young. He tells of one executive who formed an "offshore" insurance company. This executive had the authority to place insurance, so he bought a policy from the dummy company and pocketed the premiums. Cook notes that "where phony insurance companies are used, the type of insurance placed is usually where claims would not be occurring—officers' and directors' liability and bonding insurance, for example."

The general counsel at a major corporation devised another nifty scheme. He set up a dummy legal firm and submitted bills from it to his corporation for legal work he claimed had been performed. Dummy companies are found in the advertising end of a company also.

Schemes between purchasers and suppliers are also common. A purchasing agent for a company may merely turn a company's business over to a favored supplier. The sales manager of the supplier, in return for the business, gives the purchasing agent a kickback—either cash or valuable goods or services. This, of course, raises the cost of business.

Employees in a payroll department can easily rip off a company. At a Baltimore hospital, a woman worker added the names of two friends to the payroll, and managed to funnel $40,000 their way before she was caught.

Today's glamour theft, of course, is so-called computer crime. No computer is tamper proof, and dishonest employees are constantly making fictitious entries, switching accounts and the like. While the losses from any of these scams can be huge, as the Wells Fargo caper testifies, the extent to which computers are used to steal from companies isn't really known, "It is easier for a person to take information out of a computer than it is to know that the information has been taken out," observes the computer security expert of a major East Coast conglomerate.

Often, a theft is discovered only by accident, as happened with an employee of a major utility who was using the computer to switch payments

Exhibit 4–2 (continued)

from the company to his dummy bank account. He was caught only after his car was stolen, then recovered and found to contain incriminating evidence.

The most distressing thing about employee theft, security experts say, is that companies make it so easy. They leave vulnerable items unlocked or do not check to see that supplies actually exist. "It is just astounding the number of the top 500 corporations in America that have woefully inadequate security systems. . . ."

Setting up a [security] system involves both physical and procedural controls. In the physical control area, a company can make sure that its assets are under lock and key. It can separate the shipping area from the receiving area, so that incoming goods come in only one door and outgoing shipments only out another. Retailers can use closed circuit television to monitor their sales clerks. Oil companies can put serial numbers on some of their equipment and record the numbers with an industry data bank so that another firm does not mistakenly purchase stolen items.

Clarkson Construction Co., a major Midwest construction firm, cut its insurance premiums in half over a nine year period when it set up physical controls. The foreman at every construction site keeps a record of who has been issued what tools. The tools must be returned at the end of the day, when they are locked up. "Good controls and constant supervision are the keys to our program," says security director Ed DeMoss, "along with excellent support from the head of the company."

Procedural controls are perhaps the most important step. The access and the control of any item, service or piece of information should be separated among employees. For instance, the person who authorizes the use of [the] company computer should not have access to it, and vice versa. Employees should be rotated from one operation to another. While critics of this practice contend that a purchasing manager skilled in the business of buying steel should not be moved to purchasing aluminum because the company would suffer the loss of his accumulated knowledge, most security experts believe that the benefits of keeping the agent free from entangling alliances with suppliers far outweighs the loss of expertise.

Companies should also insist that employees take vacations and should be suspicious if a worker refuses promotion. Security consultants say that white-collar employees involved in fraud are often reluctant to take vacations or accept promotions for fear their schemes will come to light while they are away. Determining whether ghost suppliers are being used can be done relatively simply. "A check of Dun & Bradstreet reports will quickly reveal a company's nonexistence," says Cook of Arthur Young.

Some security directors urge companies to encourage whistle blowing, but others frown on it. Whistle-blowing is popular among retailers. Some

Exhibit 4-2 (continued)

reward all employees when inventory shrinkage is reduced; others pay individual employees a monetary reward for turning in a dishonest employee.

Once controls are set up, there are numerous danger signals that something is rotten in the corporate Denmark. Customer complaints should be examined carefully. "For some blasted reason, when a company gets a complaint from a customer, the company official usually argues with the customer and assumes the problem to be at the customer's end. That is wrong, because customers are often the best tip-off that internal crime has taken place," says Moritz.

Paperwork that is either redone or frequently lost is another danger signal. Repeated shortages of materials can also indicate employee fraud, and so can large discrepancies in the cost of businesses between two facilities of equal size.

The question of whether to prosecute or not to prosecute a thieving employee and under what circumstances is a decision that must be made by top management. Some firms merely dismiss the offending employee, others keep him as long as he makes up for the goods or services stolen, while still others have a strict policy of prosecuting the thief. Any of these approaches can work. The important thing is to be consistent.

Of course, too much security can present a danger, too. If employees perceive that management does not trust them with a single paper clip or that they are being continually watched, morale can suffer. "The controls a corporation sets up should be tasteful, tactful and logical," says [Louis] Tyska [director of Security at Revlon Inc.]. Indeed, says Moritz, "Fostering a concentration camp atmosphere where employees don't trust their fellow workers can be more costly than too lax a security program." An angered employee who might otherwise be honest could turn to sabotage.

by which they can be addressed. Note, in particular, the article's acknowledgment of the need for

—safeguarding of assets,
—accountability for assets,
—authorization procedures,
—segregation of duties,
—prenumbering of documents,
—rotation of duties,

—use of information external to the organization (such as Dun & Bradstreet),

—attention to customers' complaints,

—monitoring the overall reasonableness of operating results,

—consistent management policies, and

—cost-benefit evaluation of controls.

Many of these ideas are likewise highlighted in Exhibit 4–1. A subtle point emerges from the insurance example provided in Exhibit 4–2 and discussion of fictitious advertising companies. Any acquisition of services has a less rigorous audit trail than the acquisition of goods. For example, no receiving report exists for many service acquisitions. As a result, irregularities are more likely to occur due to the very nature of the underlying transaction.

One type of fraud that can be extremely difficult to detect is *lapping*. This means that an employee steals from one customer's account and then attempts to cover up the theft by applying to that account later collections from another customer. "Robbing Peter to pay Paul" characterizes this approach. It is most likely to occur when a company does not provide the segregation of the following duties: opening the mail and scheduling of receipts, preparation of deposit slips, trips to the bank to make deposits, and entering receipts into the journal.

The other common defalcation involving cash is referred to as *kiting*. This fraud is perpetuated through the use of multiple bank accounts. Money is transferred from Bank A to Bank B, reflected as a deposit at Bank B, but not concurrently reflected as a withdrawal from Bank A. Because kiting is frequently done at year-end, it is often referred to as a "cut-off problem." This is because the cut-off of deposits and withdrawals is not parallel if kiting exists.

Related parties have been identified as a potential source of additional risk exposure. These might include employees' involvement in transactions. One step in evaluating the scope and potential need for enhanced controls over such transactions is to perform a computer match on various purchasing and customer records. Yet, this can be a challenging procedure to execute. As an example, consider a scenario where an employee named John Doe Smith may go by J. D. Smith, John Smith, D. Smith, or even Jonathan Smith. Further assume that this related party is a key executive in the controller's department and has been claiming large travel advances. If an auditor or systems designer wanted to peruse the records to obtain an overall assessment of any large-dollar payments to Mr. Smith, then scanning—assuming alertness to the various forms of his name in use—could be an effective review procedure. The effectiveness of the computer in performing such a task relies on *a priori* knowledge of all the potential names that might be in use by Mr. Smith. Computers' adaptiveness has not yet reached that of humans—although such adaptiveness is the very aspect of humans which often makes scanning a useful audit procedure.

AN APPROACH TO ASSESSING THE LIKELIHOOD OF FRAUD

One assessment approach suggested in the literature on fraud detection is to consider the presence or absence of three key criteria:

(1) "the degree to which conditions are such that a material irregularity could be committed"
(2) "the degree to which the person or persons in positions of authority and responsibility in the entity have a reason or motivation to commit an irregularity," and
(3) "the degree to which the person or persons in positions of authority and responsibility in the entity have an attitude or set of ethical values such that they would allow themselves (or even seek) to commit an irregularity."[3]

The contention is that in the presence of all three of these criteria, material irregularity is deemed highly likely, while the absence of any one of the criteria transforms the setting to one of being highly unlikely that a material irregularity has occurred or is likely to occur.

A Test of the Model. To test this model, its developer reviewed the AAERs of the SEC issued from 1982 to mid-1987 and inferred that SAS No. 53 is useful but that it fails to highlight the possibility of

- dominance by management being a small group rather than one person,
- magnitude of a single difficult-to-audit transaction being of paramount importance, rather than the frequency of such transactions,
- the relevance of related party conditions in creating an opportunity for management fraud, and
- some factors being primary, while others are secondary in their weight.

For example, the model's developer contends that management dominance, a difficult-to-audit material transaction or transactions, related parties, weak control environment, and material judgmental accounts are primary factors allowing material irregularities to be committed. Primary factors providing motivation to commit an irregularity include poor performance and compensation arrangements which are performance based. Primary factors indicating attitudes allowing irregularities include a poor management reputation in the business community,

---

[3] James K. Loebbecke, "Assessing the Risk of Material Irregularities," Working Paper, University of Utah (February 10, 1988).

past experience which indicates dishonesty, and overly aggressive attitudes toward financial reporting. The latter are shown by evasive responses, opinion shopping, false statements to the prior auditors, and disputes.

The Results

The research reports that in 49 of 93 cases covered by AAERs, management fraud existed and in another 22 cases, it appeared to be present. The three components of the model were observed in 71% of the cases examined, two were present in 23%, one was present in 4%, and none in 2% of the comprehensive management fraud cases.

Of added interest is the observation that management fraud most often involved over valuation of assets, improper revenue recognition, specious audit judgment, omitted or misleading disclosures, and unrecorded transactions or events.[4]

Multiple Causes

The notion of multiple causes of deceptive financial-reporting schemes is similarly a characteristic of research based on panel discussions of cases designed to analyze fraudulent and questionable financial reporting. Specifically, multiple causes include incentives for deceptive reporting via performance targets and incentive compensation plans, failure to establish effective controls and to administer severe penalties on those discovered to be engaged in deceptive reporting practices, and failure to provide adequate moral guidance and leadership via the delineation and communication of procedures, their importance, and codes of conduct.

Recognizing Fraudulent Financial Reporting

In analyzing questionable financial-reporting practices, six questions were considered by expert panels which may be of use to an auditor or party evaluating control exposures to fraud:

1] Could the practice be viewed as inconsistent with GAAP?
2] Is the treatment attempting to disguise the entity's long-tem trends rather than merely smoothing short-term perturbations?
3] Would a perceptive analyst be deceived, given the disclosure provided?
4] How material is the effect, i.e., does it make a substantial difference?
5] What period of time does the practice affect, i.e., monthly, quarterly, or annual results?
6] What is the direction of the effect, e.g., does it overstate or understate assets and liabilities?

---

[4] James K. Loebbecke, "Assessing the Risk of Material Irregularities," Working Paper, University of Utah (February 10, 1988).

If a practice is inconsistent with GAAP, disguises long-term trends, is inadequately disclosed, is material in its effect, influences annual results, and either overstates assets or understates liabilities (rather than being conservative), the less favorable the reporting practice.[5] Exhibit 4–3 describes determinants of accounting method selection. Problems arise when these varied and often conflicting determinants lead to distortion of reported financial performance. For example, if bonus plans based on accounting numbers entail the usual floor and ceiling specification, as reflected in Exhibit 4–4, then either "Big Bath" behavior or biases linked to attempts to maximize continuous bonus payments are potential exposures. Consider how to operationalize Exhibit 4–3. Indeed, at least one country has tried to direct auditors to disclose the aggressiveness of accounting practices in use by their client.

Exhibit 4–3

Determinants of Accounting Method Selection

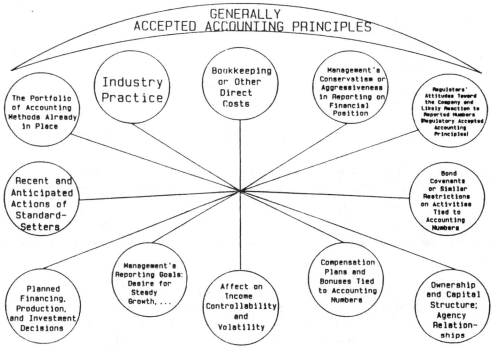

---

[5] Kenneth A. Merchant, *Fraudulent and Questionable Financial Reporting: A Corporate Perspective* (New Jersey: Financial Executives Research Foundation, 1987). For a discussion of determinants of accounting practices, see Ross L. Watts and Jerold L. Zimmerman, *Positive Accounting Theory* (Englewood Cliffs, New Jersey: Prentice-Hall, 1986).

Exhibit 4–4

Incentives Created By
Management Bonus Plans

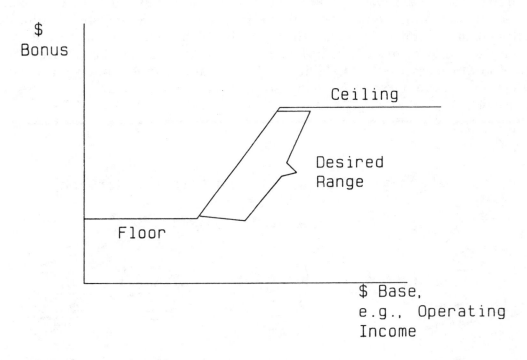

Adapted from Paul Healy, "The Impact of Bonus Schemes on the Selection of
Accounting Principles," *Journal of Accounting and Economics*, 7 (April
1985).

The problem of the auditor in confronting such regulators' expectations is
reflected in the following discussion appearing in a Canadian journal, referring
to an opinion sought by Section 295 of the Act Respecting Trust Companies and
Savings Companies in Quebec. (See boxed material on next page.)

While somewhat discouraging as a hypothetical, the point is made that the
profession needs to direct attention to building consensus as to what constitute
"unduly aggressive" accounting practices.

The issue of fraudulent financial reporting has been examined by the National
Commission on Fraudulent Financial Reporting (the Treadway Commission). The
final report of the Commission emphasized the importance of an ethical "tone at

"The regulator," according to the interpretation guideline, is "primarily interested in knowing, in cases where GAAP allows alternative accounting treatments, whether the methods selected by management are not unduly aggressive, and whether the accounting principles and methods applied by the company have not been systematically selected to show the financial situation in the most favourable light."

Ignoring the unstated matters in which the regulator may have a secondary interest, there are no criteria against which "unduly aggressive" (as opposed to merely aggressive) can be measured. Let's imagine a conversation between the auditor of a financial institution and its chief financial officer.

Auditor: "I intend to qualify my report because your method of accounting for losses is unduly aggressive."

Client: "I presume you can back up your claim in court by reference to criteria for measuring whether or not a policy is unduly aggressive, as opposed to merely aggressive?"

Auditor: "Well, uh, no. There are no such criteria."

Client: "I see, no criteria. So you can't prove that our policy is unduly aggressive."

Auditor: "Um, no."

Client: "Guess you'd be on pretty shaky ground if you qualify your report. We will certainly sue for damages. Still going to tell the regulator?"

Auditor: "Um, er (gulp), I guess not.'"

Client: "Wonderful, what other matters did you want to discuss?"

Auditor: "Um, er (gulp), nothing, I guess."

Source: "Trying to live up to regulators' expectations," *Auditing* (Edited by Donald J. Cockburn, FCA and Clarkson Gordon, Toronto), p. 48.

the top," effective controls, written codes of conduct,[6] internal[7] auditors, and audit committees[8] as deterrents of fraudulent reporting. These topics have been discussed in earlier chapters and will be revisited later in this chapter.

---

[6] Examples of excerpts from such codes are provided in the monograph by Kenneth A. Merchant, *Fraudulent and Questionable Financial Reporting: A Corporate Perspective* (New Jersey: Financial Executives Research Foundation, 1987).

[7] Indeed, internal auditors' responsibilities for "Deterrence, Detection, Investigation, and Reporting of Fraud," Detailed in Statement on Internal Auditing Standards No. 3—May 1985 (IIA), would be expected to enhance overall control.

[8] *Report of the National Commission on Fraudulent Financial Reporting* (October 1987).

Some Infamous Frauds and Corresponding Lessons Regarding Controls

Unfortunately, weaknesses in controls often are not evidenced until it is literally too late. Many infamous frauds demonstrate the importance of the various controls described to this point, as well as the inherent limitations of internal controls. Lack of care in complying with control duties, override of designed controls by top management, fraud, and similar potential problems can undermine the designed control structure.

As one example, consider the infamous "salad oil king." An individual with a questionable record approached a public warehouse to arrange for storage of inventory. The public warehouse was affiliated with American Express and had a great deal of credibility in the marketplace. The "salad oil king" used this "good name" to borrow substantial funds in the marketplace. Receipts from the public warehouse were used as collateral to obtain investment and creditor funds. Yet, the receipts were bogus inventory! The problem was that the warehouse took the "word" of the "salad oil king" that a specified quantity of salad oil had been stored on a given day. In fact, huge vats claimed to be filled with oil were actually filled with water. Only a small layer of salad oil floated on top, to give the impression that the inventory was valid. The fraud grew to such a level that the recorded inventory represented close to the world's supply of salad oil! This particular scheme bears out the importance of established controls that require the reputation of those with whom one transacts business to be checked, much as one screens prospective employees. In this case, a background check on the individual would have forewarned a problem. In addition, a "receiving dock" type control where the warehouse observed and tested the inventory being stored may have detected the water content.[9]

Another fraud was of such major scope that it resulted in a "television movie" which described how the large "bubble" burst at Equity Funding, a high-growth company. The interesting part of this fraud is the role computers played. Essentially, they were used to perpetrate and cover up the fraud, which involved what is known as "re-insurance." This means that company A sells an insurance policy to individual B and then sells the rights to all future premiums to company C. The amount of the selling price is less than the total amount of premiums because company C assumes the risk of collectibility and payment of claims. Equity Funding, acting as company A in this scenario, took advantage of a missing control within the industry. At the time the fraud was perpetrated, it was standard procedure for company C to buy policies from company A without confirming anything with customer B. Knowing this fact, Equity Funding, which had some liquidity problems, deduced that it could "sell" fictitious insurance policies. This idea, originally intended to get the company past hard times, mushroomed quickly.

In a sense, the company found the process so easy that it was hard to resist

---

[9] See the *Wall Street Journal,* "The Case of the Phantom Salad Oil," December 1963, for a detailed discussion.

the temptation of increased growth. Reportedly, a number of employees knew about the fraud and, in fact, it was well known that "midnight parties" were held to fabricate insurance policies, birth and death certificates, and medical records in support of fictitious insurance policies for inspection by the external auditors. Apparently, the employees used cigarettes to age the paper and got fairly sophisticated in their forgeries. The use of computers stemmed from the defrauders' realization that if the reinsurance policies failed to perform in line with the industry's experiences, questions might be raised. This created a need to study legitimate policies' experiences with respect to cancellations and claims. By using actual experiences as a prototype, Equity Funding was able to simulate actual experience for the pool of fictitious policies. This led, for example, to claiming that some fictitious policyholders had died, generating even more cash for the defrauders.

The "bubble" burst when a disgruntled employee was fired and called the Securities and Exchange Commission with a tip. As the fraud unraveled, it became clear that while the segregation of duties might reduce the likelihood of fraud, such segregation of duties most certainly did not preclude fraud. In fact, extensive collusion had occurred at Equity Funding with no apparent leakage for a considerable length of time. The fraud made it apparent that while monitoring operations could be effective, mere comparison to industry or historical norms as a control procedure might well fail to detect anything. This is due to the defrauders' own practice of emulating such experiences in fabricating numbers for fictitious transactions. Importantly, this fraud demonstrates how some lack of control within the structure of operations, such as no confirmation procedure with new customers acquired in reinsurance transactions, creates an opportunity for abuse.[10]

Unfortunately, the list of frauds could go on and on, but generally, a few elements are present. First, a tendency exists to take advantage of a weakness in the system or somebody else's "good name." Second, greed is typically present and results in excessive returns to the defrauders which, by their very size, increase the risk of discovery. Third, the fraudulent transactions are typically spread across a large number of individuals, so that nobody really sees the "whole picture" or entire scope of the fraud. With the salad oil fraud, American Express was "used," salad oil inventories approached world market proportions, and numerous creditors and investors held the "bogus inventory" receipts. In Equity Funding, defrauders took advantage of the failure of insurance companies to confirm policies with individual customers, leading to growth in reinsurance that literally would have represented the entire market within a five-year period, had the growth rates been sustained. Several companies were involved on the other side of the transaction, just as a number of creditors were involved in the Salad Oil fraud.

Many more recent examples of frauds, that are mirror images of these three key problems, are available from merely picking up the newspaper. Often, they

---

[10] U.S. v. Weiner F. 2nd. 757 (9th Cir. 1978); also see AICPA, "Report of the Specific Committee on Equity Funding," 1975.

resemble a sort of "shell game," where "assets" are moved to avoid detection of overvaluation. To some extent that was the underlying problem of United American Bank of Knoxville in which brothers "covered" for one another as the bank auditors performed their examinations.[11] Similarly, in Penn Square Bank's failure, pooled loans misdirected attention from the adequacy of underlying collateral to overall rates of return, with implied buyback guarantees from the bank which eventually failed.[12] In many cases, problems involved related party transactions and such rapid growth that controls are virtually nonexistent over the scope of transactions into which the entity had expanded.

While Equity Funding demonstrates the use of the computer as a tool to assist in defrauding, the defalcation was by no means a computer fraud. Yet, because computers process a large number of transactions in a routine manner over a fairly short time frame, it is possible for individuals to use so-called "camouflaged" code to remove assets from an entity. As one example, a programmer initiated a payroll computation routine which rounded off calculations and put the "rounded" amount into his personal account. Needless to say, for a large operation, pennies from payroll can add up! With the growth of the personal computer and generally high levels of knowledge of computers by the average person, external exposure to organizations from computer fraud has become a significant risk.

Exhibit 4–5 on "The Anatomy of a Fraud" points out key considerations for auditors, which also hold relevance for system designers and managers.

The Fraud Scale

Research on the prevention of fraud has suggested that the likelihood of fraud relates to the degree of situational pressures (such as personal problems due to illness or spending habits), opportunities to commit fraud (such as poor control or lax management), and personal integrity. The fraud scale considers these three criteria and argues that close to a 50% likelihood of fraud exists in the presence of low integrity, and very moderate levels of situational pressure and opportunity to commit fraud. The likelihood increases to a high level if low integrity and high situational pressure as well as high opportunity to commit fraud exists.[13]

Effect of the Foreign Corrupt Practices Act (FCPA)

The widely publicized questionable or dubious payments made by more than 300 major U.S. corporations to foreign governments led to Congressional action.[14]

---

[11] See the *Wall Street Journal,* "Knoxville Bank's Fall: Fair Had a Hand in It, As Did Lending Policy, March 15, 1983, p. 22.

[12] Further details are provided in "Annual of Finance: Funny Money—I, II, and III," *The New Yorker* (April 29, 1985), pp. 42–91; (also see May 6, 1985, pp. 49–109).

[13] The Institute for Financial Crime Prevention, 716 West Avenue, Austin, Texas 78701, brochure entitled "Red Flags: What Every Manager Should Know About Internal Crime" (1986).

[14] John S. Estey and David W. Marston, "Pitfalls (and Loopholes) in the Foreign Bribery Law," *Fortune* 98, No. 7 (October 1978), p. 182.

Exhibit 4–5

The Anatomy of a Fraud Presented to the American Accounting Association
The Auditing Section

remarks by Robert J. Sack[1]

. . . It seems to me that there is a close analogy between the education of a medical doctor and the education of a professional accountant. It is true that a medical autopsy is often performed to determine whether a crime has been committed and to make an assessment of possible guilt. But it is also true that another objective of a medical autopsy is simply to learn what went wrong, and to make a judgment as to what might have been done differently. Unfortunately some patients do not respond to treatment—medicine after all does not have all the answers. The medical profession tries to learn from those failures, to expand its list of answers. Unfortunately the financial reporting process sometimes fails too, because the practice of accounting and auditing—like medicine—is still imperfect. We must find a way for accountants to use those financial reporting failures in the expansion of our knowledge base.

In the same way that an aspiring doctor learns the hard facts of this practice from an autopsy, so must aspiring accountants learn the hard facts of "what went wrong," as detailed, for example, in an enforcement release. Clearly, young accountants have a great deal to learn today, in that they are faced with new technology and an expanding range of accounting services. But in addition to the need to learn about procedures and techniques, and concepts and principles, accounting students must learn about professional conduct. Aspiring accountants must be confronted with the difficulties of applying their new knowledge in a high-pressure, competitive environment. I believe live case studies, drawn from our enforcement experiences can help them anticipate that world.

The facts in the SEC's various enforcement and disciplinary actions are documented in Accounting and Auditing Enforcement Releases, published by the Commission. Not every AAER has instructional value, but out of the forty or fifty cases which are published each year I believe that at least half can illustrate one or more important issues. That's not to say that you won't have to use your imagination. Please remember as you study an SEC Enforcement Release that it is a legal document. As a result, the release details only those facts which the Commission believes it can prove in court. After an investigation we are usually confident that we can prove what happened in a particular case, but it is often much more difficult to develop convincing evidence as to why some-

[1] Mr. Sack was then Chief Accountant of the Enforcement Division of the Securities and Exchange Commission. The Securities and Exchange Commission, as a matter of policy, disclaims responsibility for any private publication or statement by any of its employees. The views expressed herein are those of the author and do not necessarily reflect the views of the Commission or of the author's colleagues on the staff of the Commission.

Exhibit 4–5 (continued)

thing may have happened. When using the Enforcement Releases as a teaching tool, you may have to help . . . surmise the motivations of the principals.

Similarly, because Enforcement Releases are legal documents, the rights of individuals must be protected. You may, as you read Enforcement Releases wonder what roles other people in the Company or the accounting firm may have played, and ask yourself why the Commission chose not to comment on the role (for instance) of the audit committee or the board of directors or the concurring partner. The legal process guards against tarring passive bystanders with our enforcement brush, even where the staff believes that the bystander had an obligation to be more than passive. Because the Enforcement Releases are legal documents, they will only deal with people directly involved in the transactions. Finally, most SEC enforcement and disciplinary cases are settled on a consent basis, where the respondent consents to the Commission's action without admitting or denying the Commission's allegations. As a result, the Commission's allegations will not have been tested in a court of law, and the respondent will not have been found by adjudication of a court to have been legally culpable for the action.

With those cautions, I believe that the Commission's Accounting and Auditing Enforcement Releases provide wonderful opportunities for teaching. They deal with timely topics, they almost always provide an exhaustive analysis of the facts, they cite the GAAP and GAAS authorities for the Commission's position—and most important they are real.

From my own perspective, I believe that the last several year's Enforcement Releases teach a number of critical lessons to aspiring public accountants and internal auditors and candidates for other accounting positions. You might consider . . . benefits from those practical lessons. For example:

An auditor must be a business person first. In recent years the profession has moved aggressively toward a quantification of audit risks. That quantified, risk analysis approach is logical and appropriate. Economic pressures demand that auditors be efficient with the use of their time, and litigation exposures demand that auditors be in a position to justify their judgments. To the extent that a quantitative approach replaces an audit mystique, everyone benefits. But quantified analysis can never take the place of business acumen. The profession is rightly recognizing that need for business judgment with its renewed emphasis on Analytical Review. Enforcement cases teach us that an auditor who is confronted with a difficult or unique transaction must ask whether the deal makes business sense. Enforcement cases teach us that auditors sometimes get into trouble when they comply with all of the required procedures but fail to view the transaction or the client with a sufficiently skeptical business eye. For example, see AAER 78 where the Commission alleged that

Exhibit 4–5 (continued)

the auditors received a carefully worded accounts receivable confirmation from a middleman, but did not see that the substance of the transaction required the commitment of the end user.

As a professional, an auditor must not participate in GAAP abuse. The essence of professionalism in accounting is the ability to exercise an independent judgment, even when that judgment runs contrary to the client's wishes, and especially where the judgment cannot be supported by a clear statement in the literature.

Written accounting principles cannot begin to comprehend all transactions—and in fact it appears that some transactions are specifically designed to skirt the requirements of written GAAP. Auditors must first define the business substance of the transaction, and then find the accepted accounting principle which does the best job of reporting that substance. That analysis, and the resulting judgments are often difficult, but that's why the profession has been trusted with the attestation responsibility. Many of our Enforcement Releases provide case studies illustrating this substance/form problem. See for example AAER 45 where the Commission alleged that an auditor did not take exception when his client channeled loss operations through an affiliate in apparent compliance with a literal reading of the consolidation principles, but where the substance of that relationship called for consolidation of the client financial statements and those of its affiliate.

An auditor must remember who the real client is. A profession is by definition a service business, and the public accounting profession is rightly proud of the service it has rendered to society and to specific clients. CPAs who are business people as well as technical experts find that they are able to use their business acumen to advise client management and help the client company be better off. But when CPAs wear their auditor hats it is vitally important that they remember that client management—the CEO they work with on a daily basis, the managers they try to help manage better and the CFO who pays their fee—are not their ultimate clients. Public accounting is different from any of the other professions in that the real client is amorphous and does not have a voice with which to communicate its needs. An auditor must be able to visualize that very real, but very distant, client and keep its interest foremost in mind as he/she deals with very tangible client people, sitting directly across the desk. Because a confusion of loyalties is subjective and difficult to document and prove, no enforcement case makes this point explicitly. However, a number of the Commission's Enforcement actions against accountants suggest that idea: It seems to be especially true in those cases involving the smaller CPA firms. See for example AAERs 66 and 67 where the Commission alleged that a CPA failed to recognize that when his client became publicly-held it was necessary to put the compensation owed to the president of the company (and the principal sales person) on an accrual

Exhibit 4–5 (continued)

basis rather than on the more tax-advantaged cash basis.

The most important internal controls are the ones which cannot be drawn on a flow chart. Most of the egregious fraud cases occur not because of a breakdown in a classic internal control procedure, but because management at the top overrides the control system. To a degree all top managements are in a position to override basic controls and are beyond the reach of many fundamental controls. But all managements could be subject to the control exercised by the oversight of the Board of Directors or the Audit committee. In many enforcement cases where the Commission charges a CEO with fraud involving his company's financial statements, I have often asked myself how the Audit Committee or the Board of Directors could have allowed that to happen.

The Board will obviously not see transaction details, but they will see the CEO in action and, being people of the world, must be in a position to make a judgment as to that officer's integrity. Said more directly, the Board and the Audit committee are in a position to observe whether the CEO has a propensity to cut a corner to achieve an objective. A board member who has serious concerns about the integrity of corporate management, must push for circumscribing controls or a change in management, or the board member must consider resigning and sending a signal with that department.

In the same way, auditors work with company management day to day and they also have an opportunity (and an obligation) to make a judgment on that management's integrity: An auditor must not take too much comfort from his/her detail work in the face of management of questionable integrity. The audit process is too tenuous, and life is too short to be associated with questionable clients. We have seen several 8-Ks this year where CPA firms have resigned, citing the loss of a professional relationship.

As in many things, in auditing two heads are better than one. It seems to be a given that public accounting is more complex than ever and as a corollary it is more difficult for one individual to provide all services to the client. That axiom is true for most every client—consider the need for expertise in computer auditing, for specialized industry knowlede, for the ability to unwind financing transactions and for the ability to evaluate tax effects. But that need for differing perspectives is equally true in the substance of the audit. The public accounting business is more competitive than it ever was, clients show a greater propensity to shop for auditing services and complex transactions require the exercise of greater judgment. That environment puts incredible pressure on the engagement partner at the top of the pyramid and it is vital that he/she recognizes his/her vulnerability.

Individual practitioners, confronted with a complex client, need a second perspective. The profession has gradually stepped up to the need for an independent, objective, concurring partner perspective, at least for SEC

Exhibit 4–5 (continued)

clients. The procedure is in place, through the AICPA SEC Practice Section requirement, but the substance of that idea—a collegial, testing challenge of the critical issues in the audit—must be embraced by the engagement people responsible for the job. See AAER 62 where the Commission alleged that the engagement people responsible for the audit put off the required second partner review, diminishing its effectiveness.

Because an audit is done on a test basis the tests must be complete. Exceptions to an audit test are by definition, problems. They require extra time and effort to search for missing documents, they require extra partner/manager time to analyze and detail challenged transactions, and often they require unpleasant confrontations with otherwise pleasant client people. However, most every exception has significant information potential and

must be followed up. That follow-up must include an analysis of the exception—what do those facts tell the auditor about the account under review, about the system of control, and about client integrity. See for example AAER 109A, where the Commission alleged a failure to follow-up on confirmation replies (and non-returns) which pointed to a client fraud.

* * * * * * *

These then are some of the auditing lessons I've observed from my work with the SEC's enforcement cases. But you will agree with me, I'm sure, that a good case study is rich in possibilities, beyond the observations of any one individual. Most every person who works with a case, whether practitioner, student or teacher, brings a unique perspective to the analysis of the case and sees some new and different learning experience.

Source: *The Auditor's Report* (Vol. 10, No. 2, Winter 1987), pp. 1–3.

As discussed in an earlier chapter, the *Foreign Corrupt Practices Act* in 1977 made bribes to politicians, both domestically and in foreign countries an illegal act, punishable by both fines of up to $1 million on companies and up to $10,000 for each individual and imprisonment for up to five years. Penalties have been harshened in subsequent regulations. As part of an omnibus trade bill passed in August 1988, the FCPA was amended to limit criminal penalties to those who knowingly fail to comply with them and increase bribery penalties to $2,000 for companies and $100,000 for individuals. This amendment also defined "reasonable detail" and "reasonable assurances" to mean a level of detail and degree of assurance that would satisfy prudent officials in the conduct of their own affairs. Entities owned 50 percent or less are to be influenced to maintain a system of controls, with public companies being expected to be able to demonstrate they proceeded in good faith to use such influence.

The Foreign Corrupt Practices Act (FCPA) had far-reaching effects beyond prohibiting bribes and similar illegal payments. Specifically, the FCPA mandates that controls be established which are adequate to either prevent or detect illegal payments, with a reasonably high probability. The Act uses the professional auditing literature to describe the objectives of controls and the requirement that "adequate" controls be established. A cost-benefit dimension is incorporated in the Act, whereby managers are not required to establish controls that are not cost-justified.

Many credit the FCPA for focusing managers' attention onto controls and leading to enhancements in documentation and overall improvement in control structure. In particular, internal auditing departments in large organizations were reported to have directors earning six-figure salaries, with reporting privileges directly to the Board and CEO. The internal auditor provides a service to management by overseeing operations for effectiveness, efficiency, economy, and control. The Treadway Commission, a national independent group which considered how to deter fraudulent financial reporting concluded in 1987 that internal auditors were an important facet of control which had fraud deterrent capabilities.

CODES OF BUSINESS CONDUCT

Codes of business conduct are intended to enhance the control environment of an organization. The topics likely to be included in such codes, according to the Treadway Report, include those listed in Exhibit 4–6.

A key concern, given this primary role of management in establishing and monitoring the control system, is whether a high likelihood exists of *management override* (i.e., circumvention) of the control system. Decentralized operations, incentive compensation tied to reported accounting numbers, and the lack of independence of parties with whom business is transacted are among the conditions associated with a higher probability of management override. Many organizations have established *exception reporting systems*, whereby any employee requested to ignore some aspect of the control system is expected to document the unusual handling of the transaction. If the circumvention is essential for effective operations in an unusual circumstance, then the manager or person requesting the circumvention should have no problem with a documentation of the override being generated. This is a signal to the employee if the individual is told not to make an exception report, that "collusion" is being requested. Such a request should lead to "whistle-blowing," although, admittedly, this is an unpopular action.

ETHICAL CONSIDERATIONS

In addition to developing Codes of Conduct, businesses are increasingly recognizing the multiple dimensions of their decision making and the importance of ethics. As reflected in Exhibit 4–7, beyond profitability, a number of other goals merit consideration, including public responsibility. To sensitize decision makers to evaluate ethical dimensions of decision settings, increased resources are being

Exhibit 4–6
Content of Codes of Conduct

- **public service expectations**

- **respect for assets of the company**

- **moonlighting and related conflict-of-interest issues**

- **political contributions and questionable payments**

- **financial interests and insider information**

- **tips, gifts, and entertainment**

- **accurate reporting**

- **use of personal information about employees**

- **information about customers, prospects and suppliers**

directed to training personnel in ethics. One important responsibility is to learn to recognize when an ethical dilemma has presented itself.

Recall the pragmatic framework already provided for analyzing ethical problems. It can be of considerable use in sensitizing people to think about their public and ethical responsibilities as they perform day-to-day activities in diverse settings. To provide insight as to the diverse types of social matters and ethical considerations facing businesses, Exhibit 4–8 describes the subject matter of Hearings before the Securities and Exchange Commission.

ERRORS AND IRREGULARITIES . . . MODES OF DETECTION

Errors and irregularities differ in accordance with the element of intent. Intentional irregularities are the focal point for fraud detection. Yet, beyond the research already discussed related to fraud detection, research results on error detection lend insights as to those tools available for detecting problems, which, in turn, can be evaluated as to whether an intentional alteration is involved.

Exhibit 4–7

Multiattribute Problems: Industrial Multicriteria

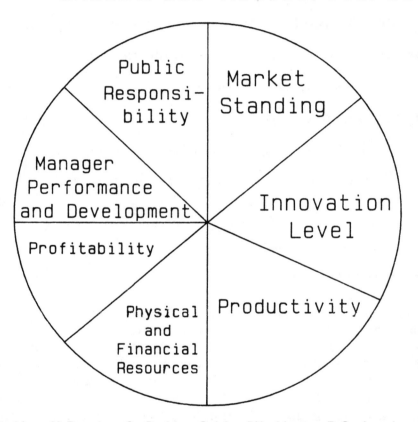

Adapted from K. Duncker, *On Problem Solving* (Washington, D.C.: American Psychological Association, Psychological Monographs, 58, No. 5,000) cited by Kenneth J. Arrow and Hervé Raynaud, *Social Choice and Multicriterion Decision-Making* (Cambridge, Massachusetts: The MIT Press, 1986).

Exhibit 4–8

Social Matters Submitted by "Ethical Investors" in Hearings Before the Securities and Exchange Commission

Advertising practices; all advertising costs; "false" advertising; contract disputes; patent disputes; compliance with antitrust laws; limitations on competition; concentration in an industry; consumer protection activities and consumer affairs posture; any activities likely to lead to litigation; all litigation (issues, disposition); all litigation but for that settled or dismissed without "conformance of corporate activities" to the substance of the complaint; degree of compliance with applicable regulations; all government hearings; all agency actions; a textual summary of agency actions; charitable contributions; company activities undertaken without a goal of profit maximization; community activities; commitment to the "human community"; corporate external relations; "good things a company had done"; financial practices; energy conservation; distribution of resources; investment practices; marketing practices; pricing practices; expenditures in the land grant college system; receipt of federal subsidies; corporate practices that are damaging to "interests of other investors," the "overall economy," or to "property"; biographical information, including race and sex, regarding directors; interlocking directorates; the existence of a corporate environmental department; control within a corporation; the role of the board of directors; all subsidiaries; all benefits received by directors; "commerciogenic" malnutrition; food production; in-house nutritional research; registrant's impact on the world food crisis; contractual commitments to purchase crops; a division-by-division breakdown of the number of employees in agri-business companies; foreign investments; nature of operations in South Africa; U.S.-Soviet trade; marketing efforts of drug companies outside the U.S.; employment practices in foreign facilities; registrant's participation in the "flight of companies making hazardous goods to foreign countries"; registrant's participation in the Arab boycott; exports; products made in foreign countries; foreign military goods contracts; foreign beneficial ownership; purchases from, and sales to, communist countries; activities which would be illegal in the U.S. but which are conducted abroad; registrant's impact on unemployment; compliance with the Fair Labor Standards, the Occupational Safety and Health, and the National Labor Relations Acts; health hazards in plants; health standards; effects on the unionized work force of company politics and technology; employee relations other than wages, hours, and working conditions; the psychological work environment; pension and health protection; management opportunities for women and minorities; the costs of giving "preferential treatment" to blacks and females; safety records; employee training and education; employee benefits, relations and satisfactions; discrimination against persons less than six feet tall; lobbying

Exhibit 4–8 (continued)

efforts; political influence; political contributions; all products by brand name; all product lines; product-by-product financial statements; product purity (recalls, reasons for corrective action); toxic substances produced; product reliability; customer complaints; tobacco products manufactured; alcoholic beverages produced; gambling equipment manufactured; strip mining; defense contracts and military goods produced; nuclear energy production; banking operations; with respect to agricultural machinery companies, manpower displacement research; tax loophole savings; tax law compliance; all state and federal tax returns; all tax disputes; beneficial ownership; racial justice; prospective legislation; and the willingness to disclose corporate information to shareholders.

Source: Robert E. Jensen, "Phantasmagoric Accounting: Research and Analysis of Economic, Social and Environmental Impact Of Corporate Business," *Studies in Accounting Research #14*, American Accounting Association, 1976 p. 209. Securities and Exchange Commission Release No. 5627, October 14, 1975, pp. 45–46.

Researchers have analyzed 1,506 errors detected in 260 audit engagements. The following modes of detection were identified by the audit teams:

Audit Procedure	Errors
Expectation from Experience in Prior Years	287
Discussion with Client Management or Employees	504
Tests of Control	7
Predictive/Analytical Testing	293
Analysis of Accounts and Inspection of Detail	767
Evaluation of Accounting Estimates	202
Recomputations & Clerical Accuracy Tests	162
Cutoff Tests	155
Circularization, Observation, and Other Tests of Detail	205
	2,582

The total exceeds the number of errors as reported by the audit team, since more than one mode of detection often applied to an error, suggesting synergy in the audit process.[15]

---

[15] Richard W. Kreutzfeldt, and Wanda A. Wallace, "Error Characteristics in Audit Populations: Their Profile and Relationship to Environmental Factors," *Auditing: A Journal of Practice & Theory* (Fall 1986), p. 31.

Of particular interest is the effectiveness of analytical procedures at identifying errors or unreasonable, unexpected balances.

THE USE OF ANALYTICS TO DETERMINE PROBLEMS, INCLUDING FRAUD

Analytical procedures are powerful audit tools in both an internal and external audit setting, as well as from a manager's perspective. Indeed, empirical evidence exists that the incidence of errors is significantly lower for companies in which management regularly applies analytical procedures as a monitoring tool. Moreover, analyses of companies at which fraud has been detected suggest that certain analytical procedures might have been effective at discovering the operating and reporting problems at an earlier date.

Generally accepted auditing standards require the use of analytical procedures in the planning and overall review stages of an audit. The basic premise of such procedures is that plausible relationships among data may reasonably be expected to exist and continue in the absence of known conditions to the contrary (e.g., business changes, accounting changes, or misstatements). Hence, the application of analytical procedures can assist auditors in planning the nature, timing, and extent of other procedures and in performing an overall review of the financial information in the final review stage of the audit. The extent to which analytical procedures are used as a substantive test of particular assertions will depend on the relative effectiveness and efficiency of such procedures, relative to alternative audit steps. From a systems reviewer's perspective, the application of analytical procedures can serve as evidence on the effectiveness of various controls in avoiding material misstatements. Moreover, research has demonstrated that the incidence of error is lower when managers apply analytical procedures to regularly monitor their operations.[16]

Judgment

There are a number of analytical procedures in use. Research in 1984 found that 90% of auditors surveyed used judgmental-based analytical procedures.[17] Yet, given the possibility of biases affecting human judgments, subsequent research has explored how auditors make judgments related to analytical procedures. One study described analytical procedures as five interrelated steps:

(1) preliminary information search and goal setting,
(2) information acquisition,

---

[16] Richard W. Kreutzfeldt and Wanda A. Wallace, "Error Characteristics in Audit Populations: Their Profile and Relationship to Environmental Factors," *Auditing: A Journal of Practice & Theory* (Vol. 6, No. 1, Fall, 1986), pp. 20–43.

[17] S. F. Biggs and J. J. Wild, "A Note on the Practice of Analytical Review," *Auditing: A Journal of Practice and Theory* (Spring 1984), pp. 68–79.

(3) information evaluation,

(4) combining of evaluated information to take action or make a choice, and

(5) feedback.[18]

The evaluation of information entails comparing unaudited values with expectations.

Past research has identified a finding that auditors tend to be biased in the direction of unaudited book values when formulating their expectations.[19] This has the troublesome implication that greater risk of not detecting material errors can ensue from the ready availability of unaudited book values during an audit. However, subsequent research has noted that less bias arises when more audited information became available to auditors in an experimental setting, suggesting that in a more complex and realistic task situation, auditors' judgments may not be affected by unaudited data. Another interesting research finding is that auditors are able to extrapolate simple and commonly occurring patterns in financial data.[20] However, other research has found that auditors had difficulty in recognizing and explaining a pattern of unexpected changes in several accounts caused by a particular error.[21] Thus, there is mixed evidence about the presence of this important skill when applying analytical procedures.

Non-statistical procedures have been demonstrated to provide increased audit effectiveness and efficiency, particularly when applied to monthly data rather than annual balances.[22]

Given the audit process tends to be sequential, involving the formation of beliefs and then revision of such beliefs as more evidence is gathered, questions can be posed of how auditors react to evidence received throughout such an iterative process. Research indicates that auditors are prone to revise their beliefs when new evidence is received and that such revision is greater when the evidence received disconfirms their current beliefs.[23] Other studies have demonstrated auditors' ability to identify crucial audit problems embedded in a case via analytical procedures.[24]

---

[18] S. Biggs, T. Mock and P. Watkins *Analytical Review Procedures and Processes in Auditing*, The Canadian General Accountants Research Foundation Monograph Number 14 (1989), p. 18.

[19] W. R. Kinney and W. C. Uecker, "Mitigating the Consequences of Anchoring in Auditor Judgments," *The Accounting Review* (January 1982), pp. 55–69.

[20] Stanley F. Biggs and John J. Wild, "An Investigation of Auditor Judgment in Analytical Review," *The Accounting Review* (October 1985), pp. 607–633.

[21] J. Beddard and S. Biggs "Processes of Pattern Recognition and Hypothesis Generation in Analytical Review," unpublished manuscript, University of Connecticut (1989).

[22] W. Robert Knechel, "The Effectiveness of Nonstatistical Analytical Review Procedures Used as Substantive Audit Tests," *Auditing: A Journal of Practice and Theory* (Fall 1988), pp. 87–107.

[23] Alison Hubbard Ashton and Robert H. Ashton, "Sequential Belief Revision in Auditing," *The Accounting Review* (October 1988), pp. 623–641.

[24] Stanley F. Biggs, Theodore J. Mock, and Paul R. Watkins, "Auditor's Use of Analytical Review in Audit Program Design," *Accounting Review* (January 1988), pp. 148–161.

Traditional Tests

A number of types of analytical procedures are in use, beyond a purely judgmental approach. Prior year to current year comparisons, often referred to as flux analysis is one tool. But rather than emphasizing the previous year, longer-term trends are particularly useful.

Budgeted data can also be applied as a benchmark. Beyond applying financial budget information, nonfinancial data is also of use in evaluating reasonableness. On the following pages a chart outlines exemplary analytical procedures; the "overall tests" can provide a useful picture of the reasonableness of reported numbers.

Ratios

When applying ratios, a combination of financial and nonfinancial information may be used. The common ratios computed for financial statement evaluation are cited in Exhibit 4–9. Also provided is a practice case, preceding SAS 59 on going concern issues, but of similar relevance.

One research study has demonstrated how joint consideration of deviations in several ratios can be useful in actually identifying the type of error likely to arise. For example, an increased accounts receivable turnover accompanied by a decreased inventory turnover might suggest fictitious credit sales; a decrease in accounts receivable turnover accompanied by an increased inventory turnover might, on the other hand, suggest the possibility of omitted credit purchases.[25] Such findings have led to recommendations that computer-assisted pattern search techniques which help the auditor evaluate patterns of related ratios be developed. Industry and economic data can be useful in enhancing the objectivity of the auditor's evaluation of context when assessing the reasonableness of reported numbers.

Structural Modeling

Along with descriptive data and ratios, sophisticated modeling is a powerful analytical procedure. Simulation research has demonstrated that regression analysis increased audit effectiveness relative to an audit strategy that did not use such analytical procedures and also increased audit efficiency. The use of monthly data in modeling greatly increased overall effectiveness in detecting potentially material misstatements.[26] One type of modeling used to assess risk relates to bankruptcy models. These are described later in this chapter.

---

[25] William R. Kinney, Jr., "Attention Directing Analytical Review Using Accounting Ratios: A Case Study," *Auditing: A Journal of Practice and Theory* (Spring 1987), pp. 59–73.

[26] W. Robert Knechel, "The Effectiveness of Statistical Analytical Review as a Substantive Auditing Procedure: A Simulation Analysis," *Accounting Review* (January 1988), pp. 74–95.

Recommended Detail for Analysis	Tie-In To	Past (P) Budget (B) Industry (I) Comparisons	Particular Ratios or Analyses [overall tests]
SALES BY: —Product Line —Location —Largest Customer RECEIVABLES BY: —Sales Routes —Distribution Channels —Other Marketing Units —Age —Customer	Sales to Inventory Purchases Sales to Production Statistics Returns, Discounts and Allowances to Sales Credits to Receivables Cost of Sales to Sales Selling expense, sales tax, commissions or other relevant sales-related costs to sales Collections subsequent to year-end with Receivable Balances Bad Debt Allowance to Receivables Provision for Bad Debts to Sales Provision for Bad Debts to Write-Offs Scrap Sales to Production Levels	P, B —Revenues —Returns, Discounts & Allowances —Receivables —Intercompany Revenue —Intercompany Receivables	[Total Units Sold × Average Selling Price] [Maximum Sales Possible Based on Capacity and Selling Price Compared to Reported Sales, Adjusting for Vacancy and Utilization Rates] [Total Units Returned × Average Selling Price] [Reported Revenues × Fixed Percentage Commissions, Royalties, or Sales Tax] Number of Days Sales in Accounts Receivable Aged Receivable Balances to Allowance for and Historical Experience with Uncollectibles Relate Recorded Revenues and Receivables from Various Miscellaneous Sources to Knowledge of Operations

		P, B, I	
PRODUCTION VOLUME IN DOLLARS AND UNITS BY: —Major Product Line —Location	Production Costs to Sales	—Comparative Unit Costs of Raw Materials and Finished Goods by Cost Element and Review on Monthly or Quarterly Basis	[Annualize Monthly Sublease Rental Income, Compare to Recorded Amount]
PERCENTAGE OF MATERIAL, LABOR, AND OVERHEAD IN TOTAL PRODUCTION COSTS BY: —Major Product Line —Location	Production Costs to Production Statistics	—Expenditures for Expensed Supply and Maintenance Materials	[Total Units Produced × Estimated Average Cost]
COST OF SALES AS A PERCENT OF SALES BY: —Major Product Line —Location	Inventory Shrinkage to Sales Scrap Losses to Sales Internal Use Data to Sales	—Monthly Operating Statements	Cost Variances and the Reasonableness of Allocations to Ending Inventory
OVERHEAD ABSORPTION BY: —Major Product Line —Location	Inventory Shrinkage to Sales Scrap Losses to Sales Internal Use Data to Sales	—Inventory Turnover Statistics	[Maximum Capacity of Potential Storage Areas in Total, by Location, etc. Compared to Reported Inventory Quantities]
UNIT QUANTITIES OF INVENTORY BY: —Major Product Line —Location	Intracompany and Intercompany Profits in Inventories to Volume of Intracompany and Intercompany Purchases	—Available Information on Commodity Prices, Selling Price Indices, or Other Market Value Indicators in Relation to Reported Amounts	[Adjust Quantity at Beginning of Period for Purchases, Production, and Sales of the Period to Formulate Estimate of Inventory Quantity on Hand (and Compare to Reported Quantities)]
UNIT QUANTITIES OF INVENTORY TO USAGE PROJECTIONS BY: —Product Line —Location		—Provisions for Obsolete Inventories	Compare Material Purchased and Other Production Costs for the Last Fiscal Period Prior to the Cutoff Date with Those for the First Fiscal Period Subsequent to the Cutoff Date

Recommended Detail for Analysis	Tie-In —To—	Past (P) Budget (B) Industry (I) Comparisons	Particular Ratios or Analyses [overall tests]
GROSS MARGIN PERCENTAGES BY: —Major Product Line —Location	Cost of Sales Changes to Gross Margin Changes Shifts in Product Mix to Profitability Changes	P, B, I —Gross Margin Percentages on a Monthly, Quarterly and Annual Basis —Differences from Expectations —Profitability Statistics for the Industry	Compare Gross Margin Percentage to First Fiscal Period Subsequent to the Cutoff Date, by Product Line and Location
PROVISIONS FOR OBSOLETE INVENTORIES BY: —Product Line —Location			Review Management Reports Concerning Studies and Adjustments Necessary to Record Inventories at the Lower of Cost or Market and Compare to Accounting Records
INTRACOMPANY AND INTERCOMPANY PROFITS BY: —Product Line —Location			Review Appropriate Management Reports Dealing with Amounts of Intracompany and Intercompany Inventories and Related Profits or Losses Eliminated and Compare to Accounting Records
			[Estimate Aggregate Intracompany and Intercompany Inventory Quantities on Hand at End of Period, Adjusting for Purchases, Produc-

CURRENT YEAR ADDITIONS BY: —Class of Assets			tion, and Sales of the Period and Apply Appropriate Gross Margin Percentages]
BALANCES BY: —Class of Assets		P, B, I —Current Year Additions	Review Board of Directors Minutes, Capital Budgets, and Tie to Accounting Records
CURRENT YEAR DEPRECIATION, DEPLETION, AND AMORTIZATION TO BOOK VALUES BY: —Class —Location	Current Year Depreciation, Depletion, and Amortization Charges to Book Values	—Current Year Depreciation, Depletion and Amortization Charges	[Apply Estimated Average Depreciation, Depletion, and Amortization Rates to Recorded Book Values by Class of Assets]
DETAILS OF RECORDED PRODUCTIVE ASSETS BY: —Type —Location —Age	Repair and Maintenance to Productive Assets Repair and Maintenance to Total Expenses	—Repair and Maintenance Amounts —Repair and Maintenance to Productive Assets on Industry Basis	Compare Details of Recorded Productive Assets to Cumulative Audit Knowledge of the Business
COMPARE COMPENSATION COST BY: —Department —Production Line COMPARE CURRENT NUMBER OF EMPLOYEES BY: —Department —Production Line COMPARE TOTAL DEDUCTIONS BY: —Type of Gross Payroll	Total Deductions to Gross Payroll	P, B —Compensation Costs —Period-end Liabilities	[Multiply Total Number of Employees (By Department, Production Line, etc.) by Average Annual Rate]

Recommended Detail for Analysis	Tie-In —To—	Past (P) Budget (B) Industry (I) Comparisons	Particular Ratios or Analyses [overall tests]
ACTUAL COSTS BY: —Plan —Benefit Program	Benefit Costs to Compensation Costs Benefit Costs to the Number of Eligible Employees Post-Employment Benefits to the Number of Eligible Employees	P, B —Actual Cost —Employee Data Supplied to the Actuary —Employee Benefit Costs by Account —Aggregate Payments Made by Plan —Current Balance of Accrued Liability Account —Pensions, Deferred Compensation, Vacation, etc.	(Actuarial Estimates Less Realized Costs) (Post-Employment Benefits Divided by Payroll Costs)
COMPARE RECEIPTS OR TOTAL CASH AND CREDIT SALES BY: —Account —Location —Entity —Daily, Weekly, and Monthly COMPARE CASH DISBURSEMENTS BY: —Account —Location —Entity —Expense Category COMPARE CASH BALANCES BY:	Total Cash Disbursements to Total Costs and Expenses, Adjusted for Accruals and Other Significant Uses of Cash	P, B —Customer Remittances —Total Cash and Credit Sales —Volume of Cash Receipt and Disbursement Transactions	Review Inventory Shrinkage, Gross Profit, and Related Operating Data, and Appropriate Management Reports for Evidence of Unrecorded Cash Sales, Primarily for Retail Stores, Restaurants, Supermarkets, and Similar Businesses

		P, B, I	
—Account —Location			
Investments —by type of investment —by related party nature	Accrued Income to Total Investments Accrued Income to Bond Investments Accrued Income to Equity Investments Accrued Income to Cash Equivalents Accrued Income to Other Investments Income on Related Party Investments	P, B, I —Sales Transactions —Dividends —Interest —Other Income —Accrued Investment Income —Investment Balances —Detailed Investment Records —PBGC and Similar Groups' Expected Rate of Return —Mix of Related Party Investments and Extent of Influence	Review Aggregate Purchase Transactions in Relation to Such Factors as Prior Activity, the Client's Investment Plans and Business Conditions Review Aggregate Sales Transactions in Relation to Such Factors as Prior Activity, the Client's Investment Plans, and Business Conditions [Aggregate Face Amount of Interest-Bearing Investments × Estimated Average Interest Rate] Estimate Total Accrued Income Based on Current Investment Amounts
Debt—Current —by maturity date —by call provision —by hybrid features	Costs of Issuance to Principal Extraordinary Gain on Early Retirement of Debt to Principal and to Income	P, B, I —Amortization Amounts for Premiums and Discounts —Current Interest Costs, Including Allocation Between	Relate Reported Details Concerning New Borrowings to Appropriate Management Reports Relate Reported Details of Debt Issue Costs and Debt Premium or Dis-

Recommended Detail for Analysis	Tie-In To	Past (P) Budget (B) Industry (I) Comparisons	Particular Ratios or Analyses [overall tests]
		Amounts Capitalized and Expensed —Debt Ratio	count to Appropriate Management Reports, Prospectuses, and Other Pertinent Documents
Leases	Footnote Disclosures on Present Value of Lease Payments to Cash Flow	Convert Operating Leases with Longer than One-Year Term to Capitalized Basis for Debt Analysis	Review Lease Classification Treatment Given to New or Changed Leases Relative to Past Leasing Practices and the Use of Standard Lease Terms
COMPARE PAYABLE BALANCES BY: —Significant Vendor —Location —Subsidiary for Multi-Location Companies	Purchased Inventory to Cost of Goods Sold, Adjusted by Inventory Increments or Decrements Other Production Costs to Cost of Goods Sold, Adjusted by Inventory Increments or Decrements Credits, Adjustments, and Allowances to Purchases Cash Disbursements to Reported Purchases	P, B —Reported Expenses —Credits, Adjustments, and Allowances on Purchases Separately or in Total —Daily, Weekly, or Monthly Cash Disbursements	[For Recurring Expenditures, multiply the Typical Amount Per Period by the Appropriate Number of Periods to Determine Reasonableness of Reported Purchases] [Compare Recorded Volume or Quantity of Pertinent Purchases with Known Capacity, Level of Current Operations and/or Similar Benchmarks to Assess Reasonableness of Reported Purchased

Quantity and Multiply Quantity by Approximate Price to Assess Reasonableness of Reported Purchases]	Incidence of Low Bid Selection and Other Criteria Applied	Time from Order to Delivery	Debt—Noncurrent —by maturity date —by call provision —by hybrid features
Compare Credits, Adjustments, and Allowances from Major Suppliers			
[Multiply Total Number of Units Returned by Average Purchase Price to Determine Reasonableness of Credit Recorded]			
Estimate Liability for Recurring Charges (e.g., one month's activity) and Compare to Recorded Amount			
Relate Reported Details on Payments and Redemption to Appropriate Management Reports	P, B —Current Debt —Noncurrent Debt (Reclassification of Noncurrent Debt to Current) —Amortization Amounts for Premiums and Discounts	Costs of Issuance to Principal Extraordinary Gain on Early Retirement of Debt to Principal	
Relate Details Concerning Aggregate Interest Costs, Including Amounts Capitalized, to Appropriate Management Reports			
[Average Interest Rate, As Appropriate × Approximate Average Debt Outstanding]			

Recommended Detail for Analysis	Tie-In —To—	Past (P) Budget (B) Industry (I) Comparisons	Particular Ratios or Analyses [overall tests]
	Debt to Equity	—Current Interest Costs, Including Allocation Between Amounts Capitalized and Expensed	[Approximate Average Applicable Interest Rate × Approximate Average Applicable Amount of Qualifying Assets]
	Interest to Debt		Relate Reported Details of Outstanding Debt to Appropriate Management Reports
	Debt Capacity to Outstanding Debt		
Equity —By shares of investor —Held by management and/or directors —Institutional ownership —Outstanding equity claims	Primary Earnings for Share to Fully Diluted EPS to Assess Degree of Dilution	P —Current Year Dividend Amounts —Current Year Balances of Common and Preferred Stock —Current Year Balance of Treasury Stock —Warrants, Options, and Convertibles	Relate Reported Details Concerning Issuances, Redemptions and Repurchase to Appropriate Management Reports [Total Shares × Stated Prices or Appropriate Average Market Prices] [For Redeemed Preference Shares, Relate Details to the Call or Redemption Provisions of the Class of Security Involved and to the Company's By-Laws and Charter] [Reconcile Total Dividends Paid to Totals Obtained by Multiplying

Income Taxes	Deferred Income Tax Provision to Pretax Accounting Income	P, I —Deferred Income Tax Provisions —Current Tax Liability Accounts —Individual Items Comprising Differences Between Book and Tax Income	Accounting Income × Statutory Income Tax Rate Tax Notes Comparison for Industry Experience
Other Assets & Liabilities	Prepaid Expenses to Related Income Statement Accounts Accrued Expenses to Related Income Statement Accounts	P —Prepaid Expense Balance —Deposits —Cash Surrender Value of Life Insurance —Deferred Costs and Intangibles —Amortization of Intangibles —Accrued Expenses —Warranty Obligations	the Number of Shares Outstanding as of the Record Dates by the Rates Approved by the Board of Directors] Compare Existing Insurance Coverage to Evaluate Whether Significant Insurable Risks and Assets Are Adequately Covered Review Percentage Changes in Accounts

Exhibit 4–9

An Overview of Ratio Analysis

- RATIO ANALYSIS is a key tool applied to financial statements to examine interrelationships among accounts and evaluate liquidity, solvency, profitability, and activity, among other traits.
- Ratios have the advantage of extracting size and thereby permit comparisons among highly diverse companies.

The major types of ratios and the dimension of performance that each formula was designed to measure include.

- LIQUIDITY RATIOS

$$\text{—current ratio} = \frac{\text{current assets}}{\text{current liabilities}}$$

$$\text{—quick ratio (acid-test ratio)} = \frac{\text{quick assets}}{\text{current liabilities}}$$

$$\text{—no credit interval} = \text{defensive assets} - \frac{\text{actual liabilities}}{\text{projected daily expenditures}}$$

$$\text{—accruals ratio} = \frac{\text{receivables}}{\text{payables}}$$

- DEBT RATIO or Financial Leverage Metric

$$\text{—debt ratio} = \frac{\text{total liabilities}}{\text{total liabilities plus owners' equity}}$$

- COVERAGE RATIOS

$$\text{—times interest earned} = \frac{\text{net income} + \text{interest expense adjusted by the tax rate}}{\text{interest expense adjusted by the tax rate}}$$

$$\text{—book value per share} = \frac{\text{common stockholders' equity}}{\text{outstanding shares}}$$

- ACTIVITY RATIOS

$$\text{—accounts receivable turnover} = \frac{\text{credit sales}}{\text{average net trade receivables}}$$

$$\text{—number of days' sales in receivables} = \frac{\text{receivables}}{\text{average daily sales}}$$

Exhibit 4–9 (continued)

—inventory turnover ratio $= \dfrac{\text{cost of goods sold}}{\text{average inventory}}$

—number of days' sales in inventory $= \dfrac{\text{inventory}}{\text{average cost of goods sold per day}}$

- CAPITAL TURNOVER RATIO

—asset turnover $= \dfrac{\text{net sales}}{\text{average total assets}}$

- PROFITABILITY RATIOS

—earnings per share (EPS) $= \dfrac{\text{net income} - \text{preferred stock dividends}}{\text{weighted average number of common stock shares outstanding}}$

—return on sales $= \dfrac{\text{net income}}{\text{net sales}}$

—rate of return on assets $= \dfrac{\text{net income}}{\text{total assets}}$

—return on stockholders' equity $= \dfrac{\text{net income} - \text{preferred dividends}}{\text{average common stockholders' equity}}$

—price-earnings ratio (P/E) $= \dfrac{\text{market price of a share of common stock}}{\text{earnings per share}}$

- CASH FLOW AND DIVIDEND POLICY RATIOS

—payout ratio $= \dfrac{\text{cash dividends}}{\text{net income} - \text{preferred dividends}}$

Also useful are common-size statements and various trend analyses.

- COMMON-SIZE income statements translate to percentage terms, facilitating comparisons across time and across companies. Effectively, net sales are set at 100% then everything else on the income statement is translated to percentage-of-sales terms.
- These statements are also referred to as VERTICAL PERCENTAGE ANALYSIS.

Exhibit 4–9 (continued)

- TREND ANALYSIS is a year-to-year comparison, often for five to 10 years. Longitudinal comparisons must be applied within context, i.e., giving attention to changes in business, the economy, and accounting treatments.
- PATTERNS IN RATIOS may provide insight as to the likely nature of any errors and misstatements.

A Case from Practice

Contributed by Peat, Marwick, Mitchell & Co.

Case Study on Potential Problems

Introduction

SAS 34 states that, in performing an audit of financial statements according to generally accepted auditing standards, the auditor is not required to ". . . search for evidential matter relating to the entity's continued existence because, in the absence of information to the contrary, an entity's continuation is usually assumed in financial accounting." (Since, updated.)

Although the auditor need not look for evidence that the entity may have going concern problems, contrary information cannot be ignored. The indications of contrary information for which the auditor should be alert are also known as "red flags."

"Red flags" are indicators of potential problems the auditor observes during the course of planning and conducting the audit engagement. Being sensitive to "red flags" is important to the auditor, especially during difficult economic times.

If during these difficult economic times the auditor fails to increase his sensitivity for such "red flags," he might miss the severity of a client's cash flow problems or the complexity of transactions or other events that may indicate a going concern problem or a need for special consideration on the auditor's part.

Case Study

Read the Zark Company's situation below and:

- Identify any "red flags" and any factors that tend to mitigate these "red flags."
- Discuss the implications of these "red flags" and mitigating factors.
- List what additional facts you would want to know before proceeding any further, i.e., what questions would you like answered?

Exhibit 4–9 (continued)

While you are reading, assume the economic situation is poor, i.e., a serious recession has strongly impacted the client's industry. Assume further that these poor conditions are expected to last for at least another year.

The Zark Company

The Zark Company manufactures mobile homes sold throughout the United States by dealers authorized by the Company. Because the prices of conventional homes have increased over the past several years (until the last year or so), the management of Zark believed that the future of American housing was in manufactured mobile homes. As a result, the Company began a long-range plan to produce more units and to stockpile more raw materials. The following are some key financial data for the Zark Company for the past several years:

(Dollars in Thousands)

| | 1983 1st Quarter | December 31 | | |
		1982	1981	1980
Sales	25,000	185,000	206,000	205,000
Net Income	1,500	14,000	20,000	15,000
Gross profit %	15%	20%	25%	20%
Total assets	265,000	250,000	200,000	180,000
Inventory	190,000	175,000	125,000	95,000
Equity	110,500	109,000	95,000	75,000

The Company's policy has been to sell the mobile homes through dealers who found their own third-party financing; therefore, Zark's receivables are not a significant part of its asset base.

So far, the Company's financing of its own activities has been relatively easy. Zark has a revolving line of credit with a group of banks. This loan provides that under certain circumstances (i.e., when certain net worth conditions exist) the Company must put up its inventory as collateral. A portion of this inventory was already pledged under other debt agreements. During the first quarter of 1983 these conditions existed, and now all of the inventory has been pledged. However, the banks have indicated to the Company that they can loan an additional $10,000,000 if the Company also pledges its fixed assets as collateral for the loans. In addition, the banks postponed the dates when principal payments would be required. A representative of the lead lending institution indicated to one of Zark's V.P.'s that these modifications were made because Zark has never been late with any of its interest payments.

Exhibit 4–9 (continued)

Suggested Solution

A number of "red flags" should come to the auditor's attention:

- Management's plans include increasing production in a period when sales trends have been decreasing.
- Inventory balances are at record levels and appear to be increasing significantly, even though sales have been decreasing.
- Several negative trends are evident:
    - Decreasing sales
    - Increasing debt-to-equity ratio
    - Decreasing net income
    - Decreasing gross profit %.
- Almost all of Zark's assets have been pledged as collateral to the lending institutions to secure the line of credit. (Conditions are such that this debt modification was required.)

Although from the information provided it is difficult to determine the economic condition of Zark with any real accuracy, it is apparent that the Company has some difficult problems. If the Company cannot sell the inventory that it already has, it may have to take a large writedown this year. Without the new sales in the near future, it is going to get harder for Zark to carry the excess inventory, especially with the large amount of debt that the Company has on its books. Cash flow problems may be evident in the very near future, and more serious liquidity and going concern problems may develop if the current problems relating to inventory are not solved.

The only mitigating factor mentioned in the exercise is the willingness of the banks to modify the debt agreement and the availability of the additional $10,000,000 financing.

The ability to borrow an additional $10,000,000 may help the Company with any short-term cash flow problems. However, to be effective, the Company probably needs to deal directly with its overstocked inventory problem. If the Company continues in the same direction toward producing more inventory, the $10,000,000 will not go very far. A definitive management plan is probably required before the Company's problems get worse.

With the small amount of knowledge that we have at this point, we really cannot make any judgments. The "red flags" indicate that definite problems related to overstocked inventory, lower sales and increasingly larger amounts of debt exist. Because we do not know how serious the problem is, we need to ask management about its overall course of action and any specific plans for the near future (from a few months to the next few years). Some things that we may want to find out are:

Exhibit 4–9 (continued)

- Does management intend to sell some of the older inventory at reduced prices?
- Does it intend to provide other incentives to sell the inventory?
- Is there a plan specifically to reduce the debt-to-equity ratio?
- How does the Company intend to meet its short-term cash needs if sales keep falling? Will the $10,000,000 be sufficient?

In addition, we probably should request a cash flow analysis from management that covers at least the next six quarters.

We will have to use judgment to determine whether the answers to these questions and the assumptions used to come up with these answers are reasonable.

Source: *The Auditor's Report* (Winter, 1983), pp. 3, 4.

Relative Effectiveness

Assurance from analytical procedures is provided by the consistency of the recorded amounts with expectations developed from data derived from other sources. The degree of assurance is related to the reliability of the data gathered. GAAS specifies that factors influencing such reliability include

- "Whether the data was obtained from independent sources outside the entity or from sources within the entity
- Whether sources within the entity were independent of those who are responsible for the amount being audited
- Whether the data was developed under a reliable system with adequate controls
- Whether the data was subjected to audit testing in the current or prior year
- Whether the expectations were developed using data from a variety of sources" (SAS 56, p. 5).

As mentioned earlier, the study of 260 audit engagements reported that about 40% of the errors were detected using 'high-level' audit procedures such as analytical testing or discussions with the client.[27]

---

[27] Richard W. Kreutzfeldt and Wanda A. Wallace, "Error Characteristics in Audit Populations: Their Profile and Relationship to Environmental Factors," *Auditing: A Journal of Practice and Theory* (Fall, 1986), pp. 20–43.

Exhibit 4–10

Key Analytics: An Overview

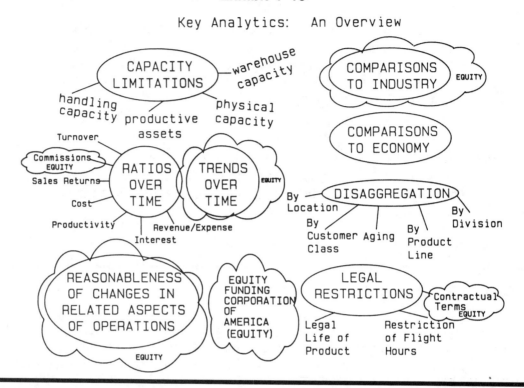

An Example

To demonstrate the usefulness of analytical procedures in highlighting problems, reconsider the Equity Funding case described earlier in this chapter. The overstatement of income which resulted was $115 million. Had a time-series model been analyzed, whereby historical relationships of commission expenses to commission income, commission contract ratios, industry commission rates, and the quantity of new business, were examined, the problem may well have come to light at an earlier date. This expectation is based on the fact that Equity Funding did not record commission expense (typically 50% of commission income) on fictitious income. Given the fictitious income from 1964 to 1968 ranged from 15% to 49% of annual commission income, the model would have borne out results inconsistent with expectations.[28]

Exhibit 4–10 depicts the various comparisons expected to be of use as analytical procedures based on researchers' analysis of past SEC enforcement actions and related law suits.[29] The cloud-shaped markings highlight those comparisons

---

[28] Report of the Trustee of Equity Funding Corporation of America, United States District Court: Central District of California (October 31, 1974).

[29] Frank Coglitore and R. Glen Berryman, "Analytical Procedures: A Defensive Necessity," *Auditing: A Journal of Practice and Theory* (Spring 1988), pp. 150–163.

which relate to Equity Funding! For details on how the comparisons illustrated in Exhibit 4–10 might be helpful in other cases, a suggested reading is "Analytical Procedures: A Defensive Necessity.[30] The Appendix to this chapter applies the same type of framework described in Exhibit 4–10 to other past fraud cases.

Obviously, the size of misstatement is an important determinant of the success of analytical procedures.[31] In addition, the degree of sophistication of the tool applied is associated with the relative effectiveness in detecting problems.[32]

Assessing the Risk of Misrepresentation

SAS 53 requires the auditor to assess the risk of management misrepresentation, detailed in Exhibit 4–11, and to consider the effect of such risks in setting overall audit strategy and the expected conduct and scope of the audit. The planning and performance of an audit are to be carried out by an auditor with an attitude of professional skepticism. "The auditor neither assumes that management is dishonest nor assumes unquestioned honesty" (p. 8). Objective evaluation is essential, alongside continual professional skepticism. For difficult-to-substantiate assertions, the auditor is expected to give special recognition to the importance of management integrity. Yet, dishonesty is by no means presumed, as persuasive rather than conclusive evidence is gathered regarding management representations. Moreover, an audit which challenged the genuineness of all records and documents obtained from a client would be unreasonably costly as well as impractical. Once some comfort is obtained as to the quality of representations made, analytical tools using such data can be applied.

Predictive Models[33]

One type of model available relates to bankruptcy prediction which can be used to assess risk. E. I. Altman developed a model directed at the prediction of business failure, referred to as the z-score model which is based on a set of ratios. The z-score is computed as $z = 1.2x_1 + 1.4x_2 + 3.3x_3 + .6x_4 + 1.0x_5$ where $x_1 =$ working capital/total assets; $x_2 =$ retained earnings/total assets; $x_3 =$ earnings before interest and taxes/total assets; $x_4 =$ market value of equity/book value of total debt and $x_5 =$ sales/total assets. A z value greater than or equal to 2.99 is considered a safe position, a z value between 1.82 and 2.98 is in a gray area, and a z value below 1.81 is considered a troubled company. This z-score model has

---

[30] *ibid.*

[31] W. R. Kinney, Jr., "Attention-Directing Analytical Review Using Accounting Ratios: A Case Study," *Auditing: A Journal of Practice and Theory* (Spring 1987), pp. 59–73.

[32] J. K. Loebbecke and P. J. Steinbart, "An Investigation of the Use of Preliminary Analytical Review to Provide Substantive Audit Evidence," *Auditing: A Journal of Practice and Theory* (Spring 1987), pp. 74–89.

[33] This discussion is largely adapted from Paul Barnes, "The Analysis and Use of Financial Ratios: A Review Article," *Journal of Business, Finance & Accounting* (Winter 1987), pp. 449–461.

Exhibit 4–11

Considerations When Assessing the Risk of Management Misrepresentation

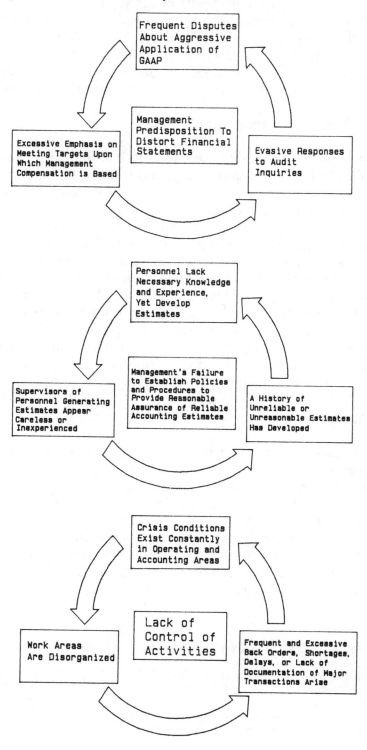

Exhibit 4–11 (continued)

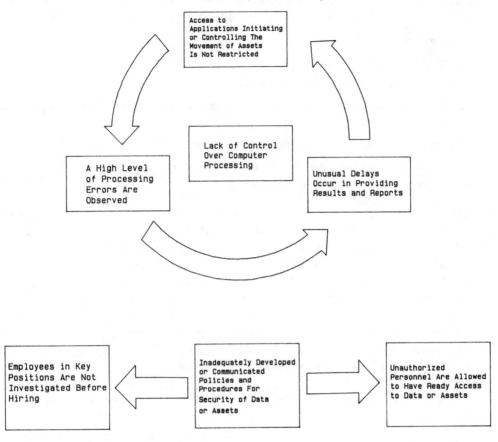

Adapted from SAS 53 [Section 316], "The Auditor's Responsibility to Detect and Report Errors and Irregularities," (New York: AICPA, April 1988), p. 6.

been successfully marketed for credit analysis and investment analysis. Similar analyses have been made of different countries and industries (particularly problem banks and related lending decisions and capital adequacy evaluation). Ratios have been effective in projecting betas (risk measures tied to stock prices), as well as in projecting rates of return on common stock. Past research demonstrates that risk-adjusted security returns are associated most with return on investment ratios, followed by effects of capital turnover, inventory turnover, receivable turnover, and financial leverage. Each of these ratio sets is significantly associated with the security return.[34]

---

[34] William S. Hopwood and Thomas F. Schaefer, "Incremental Information Content of Earnings- and Nonearnings-based Financial Ratios," *Contemporary Accounting Research* (Fall 1988), pp. 318–342.

Ratios have been suggested as useful in estimating the likelihood of auditors expressing a going concern uncertainty. The ratios suggested include:

—current ratio

—change in current ratio

—retained earnings/total assets

—long-term debt (including current portion and excluding deferred taxes)/ total assets

—income from continuing operations/total assets

—recurring operating losses for three consecutive years

—cash flow from operations/total liabilities

The cash flow from operations can be computed by dividing working capital from operations adjusted by changes in noncash working capital accounts (except for short-term debt and the current portion of long-term debt).[35]

Zeta analysis extended z-score to include accounting changes, such as the capitalization of leases. Others have observed that bankrupt firms' ratios have more instability and that such instability grows over the period preceding bankruptcy. The point has been made that predictability requires stability, yet ratios change over time and interrelationships among variables fluctuate over time. Moreover, since tests of models have often been performed on matched samples, with 50% failed and 50% nonfailed, their performance appears better than it would in the "real world" where bankruptcy is still a rare event. In 1932, the failure rate of companies varied from 1.54% in 1932 to .04% in 1945. The 1983 failure rate was 1.1%.[36]

One study reports that the five financial ratios described as the best predictors of bankruptcy in past research are:

1. Cash Flow/Total Debt
2. Net Income/Total Assets
3. Total Debt/Total Assets
4. Working Capital/Total Assets
5. Current Assets/Current Liabilities[37]

Of interest is statistical work which has tried to identify patterns of ratios that appear to have distinctive descriptive information. One study identified seven factors which appear relatively stable over time: (1) return on investment, (2) capital turnover, (3) inventory turnover, (4) financial leverage, (5) receivables

---

[35] Krishnagopal Menon and Kenneth B. Schwartz, "An Empirical Investigation of Audit Qualification Decisions in the Presence of Going Concern Uncertainties," *Contemporary Accounting Research* (Spring, 1987), pp. 302–315.

[36] Dun & Bradstreet, *The 1982–1983 Business Failure Record* (New York: Dun & Bradstreet, 1985).

[37] W. H. Beaver, "Financial Ratios as Predictors of Failure," *Empirical Research in Accounting: Selected Studies*, Supplement to *Journal of Accounting Research* (vol. 4, 1966), pp. 71–111.

turnover, (6) short-term liquidity, and (7) cash position. A number of ratios could be selected from each major attribute of interest, but only a set of seven[38] would seem to be necessary to form a fairly comprehensive picture of operations.

Bond Covenants

In addition to bankers' and other lenders' use of ratios in predictive models, ratios are used to constrain borrowers' activities. Specifically, by including ratios in indenture agreements, lenders can ensure that the firm is not liquidated from under them (e.g., through excess dividend declarations), that borrowing is not increased to such an extent that risk is out of line with what was anticipated by lenders in setting the rate of interest, or that other activities harmful to those extending credit are deterred. Three ratios which commonly appear in bond covenants are

$$(1) \quad \frac{\text{dividends}}{\text{unrestricted retained earnings}}$$

$$(2) \quad \frac{\text{income}}{\text{interest expense}}$$

$$(3) \quad \frac{\text{net tangible assets}}{\text{long-term debt}} [39]$$

In assessing risk, the presence of covenants and compliance with such covenants are important aspects to consider.

Early Warning Focus

In Philip B. Chenok's [President of the American Institute of Certified Public Accountants (AICPA)] testimony before the Subcommittee on Oversight and Investigations on the "Financial Fraud Detection and Disclosure Act of 1986," he cited "Early Warning Responsibility" of the profession as a function "closely related to the effectiveness of the auditor's report as a communication device" (p. 8). A special task force of the AICPA has been exploring ways to improve present disclosure of the risks and uncertainties facing a business. Of special interest are Philip Chenok's words:

> It is the AICPA's view that many of the current concerns raised about the effectiveness of independent audits are linked to the volatility of today's business environment. (p. 4)

---

[38] G. E. Pinches, K. A. Mingo, and J. K. Caruthers, "The Stability of Financial Patterns in Industrial Organizations," *Journal of Finance* (June 1973), pp. 389–396.

[39] R. Bowen, J. Lacey, and E. Noreen, "Determinants of the Corporate Decision to Capitalize Interest," *Journal of Accounting and Economics* (August 1981), pp. 151–179.

Obviously, to enhance communication of such volatility and related risks, auditors must first recognize the presence of change and the magnitude of its effects.[40] Such effects can have important control risk implications.

Efficient Markets

For the past two decades, both finance and accounting literature has applied the capital asset pricing model (CAPM) and efficient markets paradigm to evaluate the effects of a wide variety of events on the market. Despite theoretical criticisms,[41] anomalies,[42] and the postulation of alternative pricing models (such as the arbitrage pricing model), the CAPM is "alive and well" as a useful theoretical model based on expectations. CAPM can be empirically applied to market realizations by means of the market model. Such an analysis allows inferences to be drawn concerning market expectations and reactions. However, little attention has been given in the literature to the plausibility of auditors applying CAPM as a potentially useful tool for assessing auditees' special risks and uncertainties.

Smoothing literature and agency theory, as well as both theoretical and empirical evidence concerning market behavior, demonstrate the plausibility of CAPM's effective use as an audit tool. In particular, such a tool can address the "emerging issue in auditing" of how to identify and communicate "early warning" signals to users of the financial statements.

Scenarios of interest would include:

(1) How does our client's return compare to the market?

(2) What changes have occurred over time and what is the cumulative result?

(3) Have specific events been perceived as good news or bad news?

(4) What are the incentives to litigate?

(5) Is this a troubled company with bleak prospects? Should the company be viewed as a going concern?

THE SMOOTHING HYPOTHESIS

There are numerous reasons why deviations can arise between expected book values and recorded client balances. While most of these are likely to be perfectly legitimate, there can exist special audit risks if a client's "smoothing activities" cause material distortion of the financial statements.

---

[40] This discussion is taken from Wanda A. Wallace, "An "Early Warning" Signal From the Market: Its Potential As An Audit Tool," *Advances in Accounting: Supplemental Volume* (Supplement 1, 1989), pp. 205–231.

[41] R. Roll, "A Critique of the Asset Pricing Theory's Tests. Part I: On Past and Potential Testability of the Theory," *Journal of Financial Economics* (March 1977), pp. 129–179.

[42] Thomas R. Dyckman and Dale Morse, *Efficient Capital Markets and Accounting: A Critical Analysis*, Second Edition (Englewood Cliffs, New Jersey: Prentice-Hall, 1986).

In 1964, Myron Gordon[43] formulated a theory of managerial choice of accounting techniques, commonly referred to as the smoothing hypothesis. He makes three basic assumptions:

(1) that managers maximize their utility,
(2) that corporate stock prices are a positive function of the level of and rate of growth of accounting earnings and a negative function of the variance of accounting earnings changes, and
(3) that corporate managers' compensation depends on the corporation's stock price.

In light of these assumptions, Professor Gordon suggests that managers select accounting techniques to increase reported earnings and the growth rate of reported earnings and to decrease the variance of earnings changes. The smoothing literature[44] designed to test Gordon's theory has failed to provide conclusive empirical evidence of smoothing. Besides methodological problems and the testing of a joint hypothesis in empirical applications, there are at least two credible explanations for the absence of such evidence, given smoothing occurs. First, it is extremely plausible that monthly financial figures are adjusted to yield smooth annual earnings, and hence the comparison of annual earnings alone will fail to uncover smoothing activities.[45] Second, rather than evident smoothing activities via major changes in accounting techniques as investigated by Gordon, Horwitz and Meyers,[46] management may adjust financial statements through operating policies[47] that affect revenue realization and expense recording. In fact, when

---

[43] Myron J. Gordon, "Postulates, Principles, and Research in Accounting," *Accounting Review* (April, 1964), pp. 251–263.

[44] For example see:
Michael Schiff, "Accounting Tactics and the Theory of the Firm," *Journal of Accounting Research IV*, No. 1 (Spring, 1966), pp. 62–67;
Nicholas Dopuch and David Drake, "The Effect of Alternative Accounting Rules for Nonsubsidiary Investments," Empirical Research in Accounting: Selected Studies (1966) Supplement to Vol. IV, *Journal of Accounting Research*, pp. 192–219;
R. M. Barefield and E. E. Comiskey, "The Smoothing Hypothesis: An Alternative Test," *Accounting Review* 47 (April 1972), pp. 291–298; and
J. Ronen and S. Sadan, *Smoothing Income Numbers: Objectives, Means, and Implications* (Reading, Mass.: Addison-Wesley, 1981).

[45] Beaver et al (1980) discuss how temporal aggregation can disguise the character of the underlying series and in the limit all securities' earnings behave identically at the annual level. This is an important observation when considering the smoothing literature involving time-series models (e.g., Ball and Watts, 1972).

[46] Myron J. Gordon, Bertrand N. Horwitz, and Philip T. Meyers, "Accounting Measurements and Normal Growth of the Firm," in *Research in Accounting Measurements*, Robert K. Jaedicke, Yuji Ijiri and Oswald Nielsen (eds.) (Evanston, Illinois: American Accounting Association, 1966).

[47] R. M. Copeland, "Income Smoothing," *Emperical Research in Accounting: Selected Studies 1968*, Supplement to Volume 6 of *Journal of Accounting Research* (1968), pp. 101–116, discusses this point:
a smoothing device should not force management to disclose the fact of its manipulation and obviously must not cause the auditor to qualify his opinion. Disclosure may obviate the benefits of manipulation. (p. 104)
This is particularly clear in circumstances where manipulation is motivated by covenant restrictions or political and regulatory costs.

Stirling Homex, Great Southwestern, and the practices of land development companies prior to the AICPA's activities to develop firmer accounting standards are considered, the plausibility of manipulations within the framework of existing accounting techniques by a company's management increases. Of course, a complication in this literature is the set of diverse incentives faced by management. For example, Professor Paul Healy[48] explains that managers have incentives for both over- and understatements of operating income and various financial measures due to the wealth effects of bonus plans.

It is recognized by the author that a great deal of earnings management may be deemed perfectly legitimate by the auditor and even recommended to clients for tax purposes. For example, the timing of fixed asset purchases in the right period to qualify for the investment tax credit would be a recommended maneuver and would affect both depreciation and tax expense. In addition, the smoothing activities across months or even quarters will be of less concern than across years due to auditors' primary responsibility for annual financial statements. However, smoothing activities are of concern to the auditor if material, especially if they distort the going concern status of an entity. In light of the number of frauds which apparently began as a minor "smoothing" adjustment in the recording practices of monthly transactions (e.g., the first week of the next month's sales are "prerecorded"), it would appear that concern for smoothing activities by the auditor is warranted. Once discovered, auditors' judgment concerning the legitimacy of the smoothing activity would be required.

There is a basic problem with Professor Gordon's development of the smoothing hypothesis: his model assumes a mechanical relation between stock prices and accounting earnings. This concept of "fooling" the market is inconsistent with the considerable evidence on the efficient markets hypothesis (EMH). An interesting paper which builds on the EMH is Beaver et al[49]; the paper examines forecasting models which incorporate price data in much greater depth than earlier work. An inference that can be drawn is that auditors may find market prices to be informative beyond their traditional use in raw form. More specifically, Beaver et al[50] cite the contemporaneous association between earnings and prices and

---

[48] Healy, Paul, "The Impact of Bonus Schemes on the Selection of Accounting Principles," *Journal of Accounting and Economics* 7 (April 1985).

[49] William Beaver, Richard Lambert, and Dale Morse, "The Information Content of Security Prices," *Journal of Accounting and Economics* 2 (March 1980), pp. 3–28.
Also see
E. F. Fama, "Efficient Capital Markets: A Review of Theory and Empirical Work," *Journal of Finance* (May, 1970), pp. 383–417;
Thomas R. Dyckman, and Dale Morse, *Efficient Capital Markets and Accounting: A Critical Analysis*, Second Edition (Englewood Cliffs, New Jersey: Prentice-Hall, 1986);
Ross L. Watts, and Jerold L. Zimmerman, *Positive Accounting Theory* (Englewood Cliffs, New Jersey: Prentice-Hall, 1986).
Note, however, that anomalies have been documented, inconsistent with EMH. Noise trading and limitations on arbitrage activities are two explanations of observed inefficiencies.

[50] William Beaver, Richard Lambert, and Dale Morse, "The Information Content of Security Prices," *Journal of Accounting and Economics* 2 (March 1980), pp. 3–28.

Exhibit 4–12

Prices As Surrogates For Information Beyond The Financial Statements

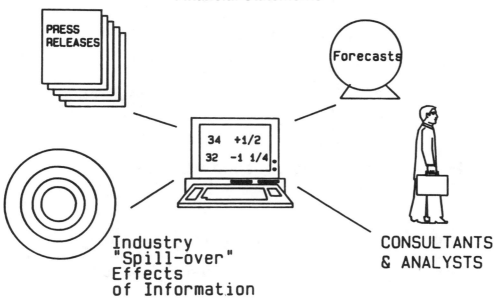

RATIONAL EXPECTATIONS

note that price can be viewed as a surrogate for additional information available to market participants. As Exhibit 4–12 illustrates, the clearing price should reflect press releases, the information content available from forecasts and other companies' disclosures (i.e., "spillover effects" from competitors' reports), as well as specialists' information and expectations. Rational expectations theory implies that the clearing price is the "best available" measure of expected future earnings as perceived by market participants.

The rationale provided for prices conveying more information than financial statements has at least three dimensions, as summarized in Exhibit 4–13. First, annual earnings are necessarily aggregate numbers, whereas stock prices track daily information, in preaggregated form. Second, by definition, financial statements are historical in nature. In contrast, many other sources of information are directed to the future, particularly forecasts. Third, earnings are thought to be a compound process which can blur information relative to stock prices. Of course, since auditors have access to transaction-level information, management forecasts, and details as to the influence of underlying assumptions and accounting

Exhibit 4–13

**Rationale For Prices Conveying Information About Future
Earnings**

I.

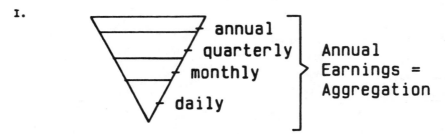

Prices = f (preaggregated information)

II. F/S ────────────── Events Affecting Future Earnings ────▶
   Historical   │   Impounded in Price

III. Earnings = Compound process with
              > 1 Stochastic variable

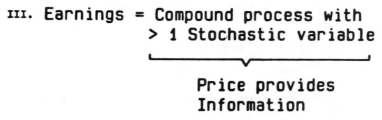

Price provides
Information

Due, in part to the
"Garble Factor" in
Earnings

Source: Adapted from William Beaver, Richard Lambert, and Dale Morse, "The
Information Content of Security Prices," *Journal of Accounting and Economics* 2 (March 1980), pp. 3–28.

___

practices, some may contend that the market price would not necessarily enhance
their information set. This is essentially an empirical question that, in part, will
depend on relative cost-benefit considerations.

Expanding on Exhibit 4–13, Beaver et al[51] propose a model that decomposes

___

[51] William Beaver, Richard Lambert, and Dale Morse, "The Information Content of Security
Prices," *Journal of Accounting and Economics* 2 (March 1980), pp. 3–28.

events affecting earnings into two elements: those events related to stock prices and those events independent of prices. This decomposition suggests that earnings reflect events related to stock prices with a lag. The second process is called the garbling process and it is independent of price changes. The key concept underlying this work is that security prices may be analyzed to extract information regarding expectations of market participants.

If earnings do reflect stock prices with a lag, it is possible to form earnings expectations for comparison with clients' recorded earnings. The divergence of expected and recorded earnings may reflect "garbling," some of which may be intentional "smoothing." This could effectively be an "early warning" signal of risk.

ASSESSMENT OF RISK EXPOSURE FROM CLIENT'S REACTION TO MARKET PERFORMANCE

The implementation of the market model, well developed in past literature and summarized in the next subsection, as an audit tool can alert the auditor as to probable client reactions to its stock market performance and to specific economic events. Audit risk associated with internal control system overrides, financial statement manipulation, and frauds is particularly difficult to control through traditional auditing techniques. The market model can assist the auditor in assessing the incentives of management to distort financial statements.

The Market Model

A well-developed and widely used technique for measuring a company's market performance due to firm-specific events is illustrated in Fama, Fisher, Jensen and Roll.[52] This technique provides a way to purge the time series of returns (or percentage price changes) for a stock of the effects due to industry- and market-wide influences. This well-known "market model" adjusted for industry factors can be written:

$$\text{Log}\,(1 + R_t) = a + b_{-1} \cdot \text{Log}\,(1 + R_{m,t-1} + b \cdot \text{Log}\,(1 + R_{m,t})$$
$$+ b_{+1} \cdot \text{Log}\,(1 + R_{m,t+1}) + c_{-1} \cdot \text{Log}\,(1 + I_{t-1}) + c \cdot \text{Log}\,(1 + I_t)$$
$$+ c_{+1} \cdot \text{Log}\,(1 + I_{t+1}) + u_t$$

$$\text{where } R_t = \frac{(P_t - P_{t-1}) + D_t}{P_t}$$

P_t = the closing price of the client's stock at time t

P_{t-1} = the price one day earlier at time $t - 1$

---

[52] Eugene F. Fama, Lawrence Fisher, Michael C. Jensen, and Richard Roll, "The Adjustment of Stock Prices to New Information," *International Economic Review X* (February, 1969), pp. 1–21. Also see Brown and Warner, "Measuring Security Price Performance," *Journal of Financial Economics* 8 (September 1980), pp. 205–258.

$(P_t - P_{t-1})$ = the capital gain or loss for day t

D_t = the dividend (if any) paid on the client's stock at time t

Log: reflection of continously compounded daily rates of return (natural logarithm)

a: the average return on the specific client's stock on all days which is not due to the market and industry components

bR_{mt}: that part of the return for day t which is due to market-wide factors and is therefore associated with the market returns, R_{mt} (an equally-weighted R_{mt} is utilized due to empirical advantages over the theoretically preferred value-weighted R_{mt}

cI_t: that part of the return for day t due to industry-wide factors and is therefore associated with the industry return, I_t

u_t: that part of the return on the client of interest for day t which is due to factors unique to that client for day t

$t - 1$ and $t + 1$ subscripts: represents returns on the related indices for the previous day and next day to avoid problems emanating from the non-trading phenomenon[53]

The factors "a" and "u_t" are both unique to the client, with "a" reflecting normal and u_t reflecting abnormal returns.

Given such a purged return series, an index of abnormal returns (i.e., abnormal price changes) due primarily to factors specific to the given client can be created. By examining the sum of such compounded abnormal (u_t) returns around the time of considering a prospective client or reviewing the auditor's risk exposure related to a current client, some measure of special audit risk due to management's incentive to distort financial performance can be derived. *Note that a simple regression model without the industry factor or log transformation, i.e., the so-called market model, may well suffice for the more complicated approach to estimating the CAPM that is described herein.*

News Announcements

Currently available data bases make the news announcements for a client accessible at fairly low cost; the effect of a particular piece of information can be measured by examining abnormal returns (u_t) around the time of public announcement (i.e., estimating the percentage change in price which is associated with that information). By examining u_t, the news announcements can be classified as good or bad news and assist the auditor in assessing the economic impact of particular events, as well as possible management activities in light of this effect. While many information items could be intuitively classified as good or bad news, the market model provides an aggregate assessment of not only the direction of the effect, but its relative importance in determining future cash flows. For ex-

---

[53] Myron Scholes and Joseph Williams, "Estimating Betas From Nonsynchronous Data," *Journal of Financial Economics* (December, 1977).

ample an announcement of increased regulatory activities may increase the probability of intervention sufficiently to encourage reductions in reported rates of return by one client, while having had no effect on another client in the same industry. Negative cumulative abnormal returns (CARs) worse than a .4 level are observed for several companies involved in litigation and bankruptcy, well in advance of these events. This suggests the advisability of monitoring CARs as an analytical approach.

Summary

Exhibit 4–14 summarizes the broad continuum of available analytical procedures, from judgmental approaches to more sophisticated modeling. The application of bankruptcy, efficient market, and client tailored regression models can be powerful tools in assessing risk.

OVERVIEW

Recent developments in the profession have included a number of initiatives directed at deterring and detecting fraud. While failsafe systems are prohibitively expensive, a number of steps can be taken to both discourage fraud and to recognize its relative risk for purposes of evaluating cost-benefit tradeoffs in considering alternative control structures. Exhibit 4-15 outlines sources of increased risk exposure to a company and are factors that have been identified by those performing epitaphs on past frauds. The manner by which frauds are perpetrated can be quite diverse. However, those involved in evaluating diverse fraud cases (such as those operating fraud hotlines) have suggested the following deterrents to fraud:

> effective audit trails; safeguarding of equipment, including logs of equipment use and guards around the premises; effective segregation of duties; effective custody controls; internal audit monitoring of control compliance; clear designation of authorization power to individuals who do not have incompatible duties assigned to them; and effective administrative controls.

This chapter not only provides a discussion of the nature of fraud-related problems and research implications regarding such problems, it suggests how analytical procedures might be applied to uncover problems. Ethics-related matters are discussed, as are various findings and recommendations of such groups as the Treadway Commission.

It is important to keep in mind that a distinction exists between control structure and fraud prevention. Limitations exist in any control structure, yet the elimination of limitations is not feasible from a relative cost perspective, given fraud continues to be a comparatively rare event. As a result, in tandem with preventive measures, detection has to be a key concern. Analytical procedures, including the monitoring of such information as market performance, can be very helpful early warning signals to potential fraud problems.

Exhibit 4–14

The Continuum of Available Analytical Procedures

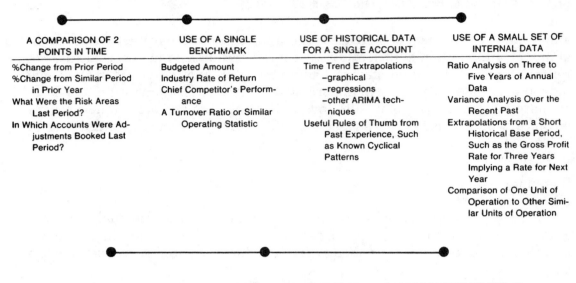

A COMPARISON OF 2 POINTS IN TIME	USE OF A SINGLE BENCHMARK	USE OF HISTORICAL DATA FOR A SINGLE ACCOUNT	USE OF A SMALL SET OF INTERNAL DATA
%Change from Prior Period %Change from Similar Period in Prior Year What Were the Risk Areas Last Period? In Which Accounts Were Adjustments Booked Last Period?	Budgeted Amount Industry Rate of Return Chief Competitor's Performance A Turnover Ratio or Similar Operating Statistic	Time Trend Extrapolations –graphical –regressions –other ARIMA techniques Useful Rules of Thumb from Past Experience, Such as Known Cyclical Patterns	Ratio Analysis on Three to Five Years of Annual Data Variance Analysis Over the Recent Past Extrapolations from a Short Historical Base Period, Such as the Gross Profit Rate for Three Years Implying a Rate for Next Year Comparison of One Unit of Operation to Other Similar Units of Operation

USE OF A SMALL SET OF INTERNAL/EXTERNAL DATA	USE OF A LARGE NUMBER OF DATA POINTS GENERATED INTERNALLY	USE OF A LARGE NUMBER OF DATA POINTS GENERATED INTERNALLY AND EXTERNALLY
Comparison of Recent Experience to the Industry, Including Ratio Analysis Market Share Performance Economic Benchmarks –for the industry –for the company –for particular regions Operating Statistics' Comparison to the Environment, e.g., A Utility's Comparison to Weather Statistics Extrapolations from a Short Historical Base Period, Such as the Relationship of Degree Days to Gas Production Statistics for Three Years Implying a Relationship for Next Year	Structural Regression Models –time series comparisons of accounts and internal operating statistics –cross-sectional comparisons of units of operation Judgmental Comparisons	Structural Regression Models –time series comparisons of accounts, internal operating statistics, industry statistics, environmental attributes, and economic barometers Judgmental Comparisons

ATTRIBUTES THAT DIFFER ACROSS AVAILABLE PROCEDURES
 –EASE OF USE
 –NUMBER OF DATA POINTS UTILIZED
 –SOURCE OF DATA INTEGRATED
 –BUSINESS APPROACH FACILITATED
 –HISTORICAL PERSPECTIVE PROVIDED
 –OBJECTIVITY OF INFERENCES DRAWN
 –RELIABILITY OF PROJECTIONS FORMULATED

SOURCES OF DATA FOR USE IN ANALYTICAL PROCEDURES
 –ACCOUNTING DEPARTMENT
 –CLIENT'S LONG-RANGE FORECASTING DEPARTMENT
 –MARKETING, PRODUCTION, AND OTHER OPERATING DEPARTMENTS
 –GOVERNMENT
 –TRADE JOURNALS, MOODY'S, STANDARD & POOR'S, VALUE LINE, AND SIMILAR SERVICES
 –ON-LINE DATA BASES, INCLUDING
  • NAARS
  • DISCLO
  • NEXIS
  • DIALOG & ORBIT
  • THE NEW YORK TIME INFORMATION BANK
  • THE DOW JONES NEWS/RETRIEVAL SYSTEM
  • CITIBANK

Source: Wanda A. Wallace, "Analytical Review: Misconceptions, Applications and Experience—Part 1," *CPA Journal*, January 1983, p. 30. Reprinted with permission from *The CPA Journal*, January 1983, copyright 1983.

Exhibit 4–15
Sources of Increased Risk Exposure

Management Objectives

- trading off customer satisfaction for profitability, to an unethical degree
- encouragement of high-risk taking
- bonuses tied to pretax income, encouraging earnings management
- risk-taking behavior, in excess of similar industry participants
- unrealistic goals

Management Style

- excessive laissez-faire management style, with a decentralized organizational structure
- a philosophy pervades that the ends justify the means
- over-emphasis on revenue-generating activities without adequate attention to controls, especially supervisory and monitoring responsibilities
- use of aggressive accounting practices
- unwillingness to admit mistakes or failures

Corporate Governance

- related parties asked to serve on boards (e.g., family and employees)
- consensus camouflaging of financial condition
- collusion to mislead auditors
- tendency to override control procedures
- inexperienced directors
- directors with substantial business connections to the company being named to the audit committee
- preoccupation of directors with other than financial and control matters
- no audit committee

Communication

- board failure to establish communication channels outside of top management
- poor communication channels linking suspecting employees to legal counsel or board

Resources

- unskilled managers
- excessive power over financial officers, due to lack of alternative, comparable employment opportunities

Exhibit 4–15 (continued)

Inaction

- inertia with respect to the information system
- inertia in responding to any demands for change
- failure to adapt controls to international settings, particularly addressing compensating controls needed due to regulatory differences
- inadequate documentation
- unresponsiveness to communications by auditors as to control procedure deficiencies
- not requiring dual signatures
- no documentation of circumvention of controls
- inadequate information system for decision making
- no internal audit department
- no internal review function over the control system

Overt Activities

- selling off a majority of stockholdings
- working after hours or off the premises

Results

- abnormal performance

Appendix

Examples of How Modern Analytical Techniques Might Have Been Applied to Engagements Involved in Past Court Decisions and U.S. Securities and Exchange Commission Actions to Identify Critical Problems

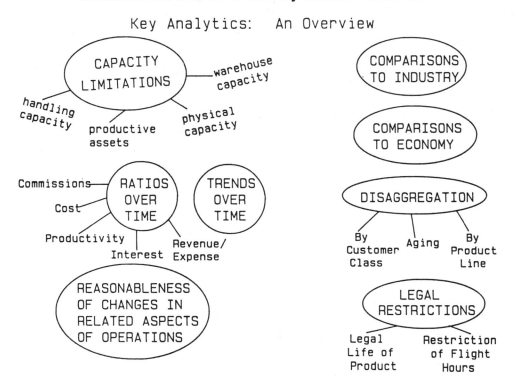

This template will be applied to a variety of legal cases to highlight its possible effectiveness as a monitoring tool of entities' operations.

Cases for Consideration

- Cenco Medical Health/Supply Corporation
  [ASR 196 (1976)]
- Dunkin, Inc.
  [Lorber vs. Beebe (1975)]
- Flight Transportation Corporation
  [SEC Accounting and Auditing Enforcement Release No. 81 (1986)]
- Florafax International, Inc.
  [SEC Accounting and Auditing Enforcement Release No. 44 (1984)]
- Generics Corporation
  [ASR 210 (1977)]
- Marsh and McLennan Companies, Inc.
  [SEC Accounting and Auditing Enforcement Release No. 124 (1987)]
- Mattel
  [ASR (1981)]
- Photon, Inc.
  [ASR 212 (1977)]
- Saxon Industries, Inc.
  [SEC Accounting and Auditing Enforcement Release No. 127 (1987)]
- Seaboard
  [ASR 78 (1957)]
- Whittaker Corporation
  [ASR 157 (1974)]

Note: Each of these examples is adapted from a working paper entitled "Analytical Procedures: A Defensive Necessity" by Frank Coglitore and R. Glen Berryman (1987).

Cenco Medical Health/Supply Corporation (CENCO)

Problem: Overstated Inventory

Year	*Overstatement*
1973	$16 million
1974	$20 million (50% of reported inventory)

Approach: Time-Series Model Comparing Key Factors Longitudinally (Prior Years to Present)

Modern Analytic Technique:

Inventory $\cong$ * SALES
                              * PRODUCT MIX
                              * INVENTORY TURNOVER RATE FOR INDUSTRY
                              * QUALITY AND QUANTITY OF EQUIPMENT AND LABOR PRODUCTIVITY MEASURES
                                  • revenue dollars per salesperson
                                  • revenue dollars per service technicians

Conclusion: Inventory increases were significantly greater than sales increases. Inventory turnover rates were significantly below prior years and the industry average. (Increases were claimed for certain products, implying a shift in product mix of sales which had not occurred.)

Production per unit of labor would raise questions on whether it was physically possible to reach reported production levels.

Source: SEC Accounting Series Release No. 196 (1976).

Key Analytics: An Overview

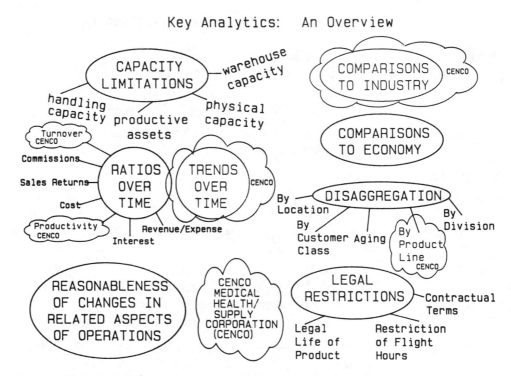

Note: Clouds highlight aspects of the template of particular use in warning that risks of misstatements existed.

Dunkin, Inc. (DUNKIN)

Problem: Understated Interest Expense

Approach: Time-Series Model Comparing Key Factors Longitudinally (Prior Years to Present)

Modern Analytic Techniques:

Interest Expense $\cong$ * PRINCIPAL OUTSTANDING
                                   * MARKET RATE OF INTEREST

Conclusion: Early years of loan understated interest expense by recording an equal amount of interest each year, rather than reflecting an effective interest method.

Source: Lorder versus Beebe, 407 F. Supp. 279 (1975).

Key Analytics: An Overview

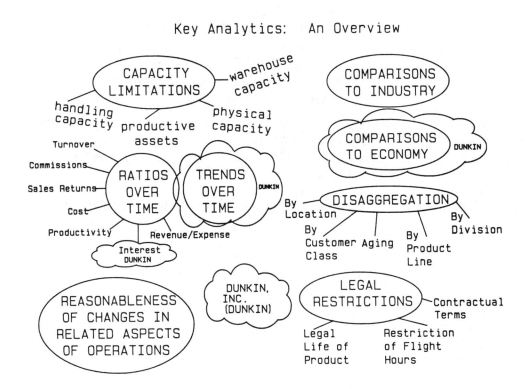

Flight Transportation Corporation (FTC)

Problem: Overstated Revenue

Year	Overstatement	% of Revenue
1980	$ 5 million	62%
1981	$13 million	54%
1982	$23 million	32%

Approach: Time-Series Model Comparing Key Factors Longitudinally (Prior Years to Present)

Modern Analytic Technique:

Revenue   ≅   * CAPACITY OF AIRCRAFT
                           • Available Seats
                           • Seat miles
                         * ROUTES FLOWN
                         * REGULATORY LIMIT ON FLIGHT HOURS
                           (1000 PER YEAR)
                         * NUMBER OF PILOTS EMPLOYED
                         * DOWNTIME
                         * ESTABLISHED OR PUBLISHED PRICES
                         * INDUSTRY CONDITION MEASURE
                         * ECONOMIC INDICATOR

Conclusion: Revenue exceeds physical capacity and regulatory restriction of flight hours. Revenue growth over time was
inverse to both the economy and industry which were in
a recession.

Source: SEC Accounting and Auditing Enforcement Release No. 81 (1986).

Key Analytics: An Overview

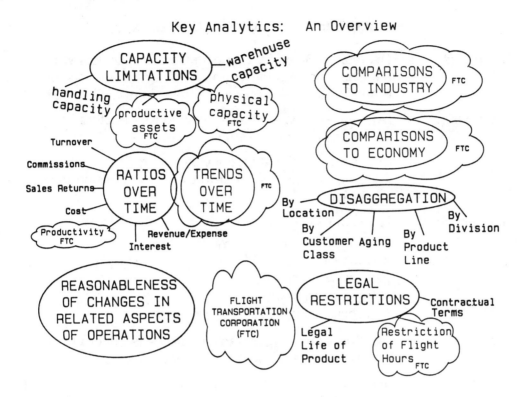

Florafax International, Inc. (FLORAFAX)

Problem: Overstated Sales By Shipping Certain Products With-
                    out Customer Authorization And With An Unconditional
                    Right To Return—Returns Ranged From 28% to 69%

Approach: (A) Time-Series Model Comparing Key Factors Longi-
                         tudinally (Prior Years to Present)

                    (B) Cross-Sectional Model Comparing One Product
                         Line To Another, Year-to-Date, and Division to Di-
                         vision

Modern Analytic Techniques:

(A)   (B)
Sales $\cong$ * SALES RETURNS   SALES = SALES RETURNS
                    * INDUSTRY NORM FOR
                    SALES RETURNS
                    * PRODUCT MIX

Conclusions: (A) Sales returns substantially exceeded prior years'
                         experience, as well as the industry's norm.

                    (B) The holiday container program was that product
                         line for which shipments of unordered products
                         were made.

Source: SEC Accounting and Auditing Enforcement Release No. 44 (1984).

Key Analytics: An Overview

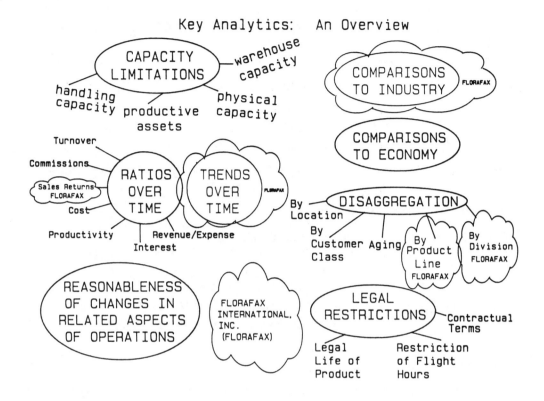

Generics Corporation (GENERICS)

Problem: Overstated Inventory

Year   *Overstatement*

1972 $2   million
1973 $3   million
1974 $4.4 million

Approach: Time-Series Model Comparing Key Factors Longitudinally (Prior Years to Present)

Modern Analytic Techniques:

(A) Inventory   ≅   * ECONOMIC INDICATOR
                       * INDUSTRY AVERAGE TURNOVER RATIO
                       * AGE OF INVENTORY LESS LEGAL
                         LIFE OF INVENTORY
                       * MONTHS' SALES IN INVENTORY
                         LESS LEGAL LIFE OF INVENTORY
                       * SALES

(B) Gross Profit = Units Sold

Conclusion: (A) Inventory turnover declined from 1.3 to .8 from 1972
                       to 1974 and this meant 15 months of inventory were
                       on hand, some in excess of acceptable sales dates.
                  (B) Gross profit margins increased from 36% in 1972 to
                       43% in 1974.

Source: SEC Accounting Series Release No. 210 (1977)

Key Analytics: An Overview

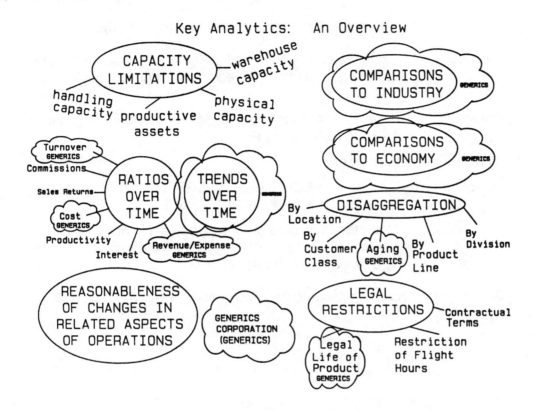

Marsh and McLennan Companies, Inc. (M&M)

Problem: Understated liabilities and assets by $1.2 billion by not reporting repurchase agreements for government securities

Approach: Time-Series Model Comparing Key Factors Longitudinally (Prior Years to Present)

Modern Analytic Techniques:

Interest Income $\cong$ * SECURITIES INVESTED
                               * MONEY MARKET RATE

Conclusion: Net interest income on unreported securities was recorded, resulting in a 16% to 17% yield versus an average money market rate of 9.5%

Source: SEC Accounting and Auditing Enforcement Release No. 124 (1987).

Key Analytics: An Overview

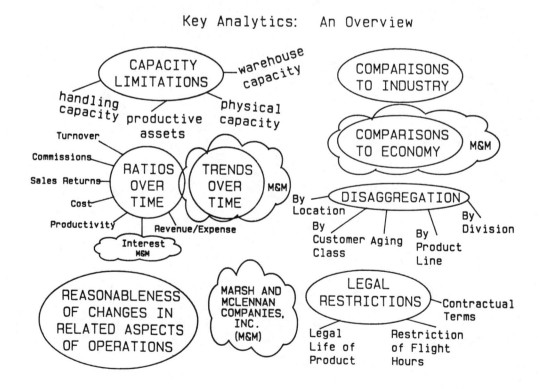

Mattel, Inc. (MATTEL)

Problem: Overstated Sales By $15 Million In The Last Month Of
                     The Fiscal Year And Understated The Provision For In-
                     ventory Obsolescence

Approach: Time-Series Model Comparing Key Factors Longitudi-
                     nally (Prior Years to Present)

Modern Analytic Techniques:

Sales   ≅   * ECONOMIC INDICATOR
                       * INDUSTRY INDICATOR
                       * SEASONAL ADJUSTMENT VARIABLES
                       * NUMBER OF CUSTOMERS

Inventory   ≅   * INDUSTRY TURNOVER RATIO
                       * ECONOMIC INDICATOR
                       * INDUSTRY INDICATOR
                       * SEASONAL ADJUSTMENTS
                       * CREDITS EXTENDED TO RETAILERS
                          OR SIMILAR PROMOTIONAL PROGRAMS
                       * PRODUCT MIX
                       * AGE OF INVENTORY
                       * PRACTICAL LIFE OF PRODUCT
                       * PROVISION FOR INVENTORY
                          OBSOLESENCE OR CHARGE
                          THERETO
                       * SALES (Corrected Basis)

Conclusions: Sales increased 7% when the economy and toy indus-
                     try were declining. Fictitious sales were recorded to ex-
                     isting customers, raising the issue of the reasonable-
                     ness of more sales per customer being realized.
                     Corresponding months over time were inconsistent:
                     35% change from January 1971 to 1972, 65% drop in
                     two months relative to prior years. Sales for one month
                     were negative. In 1972, $2.3 million of inventory parts
                     were scrapped and portions of inventory were sold at
                     prices below costs. The practical life of products in the
                     toy industry is very short.

Source: SEC Accounting Series Release No. 292 (1981).

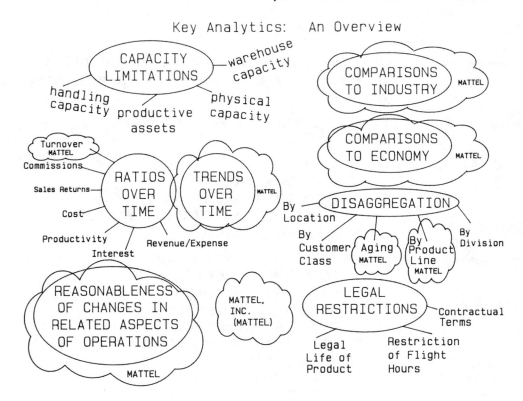

Photon, Inc. (PHOTON)

Problem: Overstated Sales and Accounts Receivable—15% of
                    1970 and 1971 Sales and Related Receivables Were
                    15% of Total Assets

Approach: Time-Series Models Comparing Key Factors Longitudi-
                    nally (Prior Years to Present)

Modern Analytic Technique:

(A) Accounts Receivable   ≅   * SALES
                                * INDUSTRY TURNOVER

(B) Gross Profit = Units Sold

Conclusion: (A) The turnover rate declined as the accounts receiv-
                        able increased significantly over time.
                    (B) Cost of goods sold were not recorded for the ficti-
                        tious sales, resulting in an inflated gross profit per-
                        centage relative to prior years.

Source: SEC Accounting Series Release No. 212 (1977).

Key Analytics: An Overview

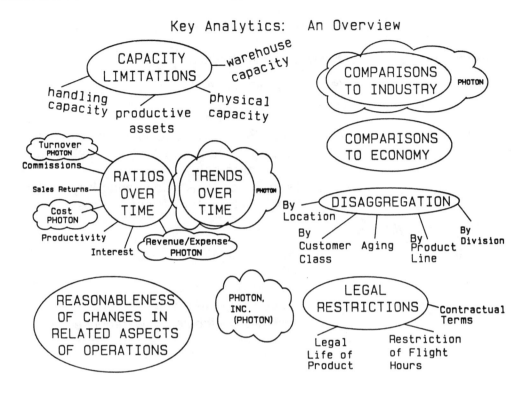

Saxon Industries, Inc. (SAXON)

Problem: Overstated Inventories

                Year   *Overstatement*

                1981 $86 million

Approach: (A) Cross-Sectional Model Comparing Warehousing Location to Location (Peak Values and Year-to-date)

                (B&C) Time-Series Model Comparing Key Factors Longitudinally (Prior Years to Present)

Modern Analytic Techniques:

(A) Inventory   ≅   * APPROXIMATE CAPACITY PER WAREHOUSE
- handling capacity
- cubic feet (square feet)
- physical attributes of warehouse and product

                                  * TURNOVER MEASURE

(B) Inventory (Consider Disaggregation By Product Line)   ≅
- * SALES
- * INDUSTRY TURNOVER RATIO
- * PRODUCT MIX OF INVENTORY
- * PRODUCT MIX OF SALES
- * MARKET SHARE
- * AGE OF INVENTORY ON HAND (e.g., Average Months Since Acquisition)

(C) Production   ≅   UNITS OF CAPACITY
LABOR
INDUSTRY NORM FOR PRODUCTION PER UNIT OF PHYSICAL CAPACITY AND PER UNIT OF LABOR

CONCLUSIONS:

(A) One location reported $532,000 of copier paper when $200,000 was the capacity of that warehouse.

(B) In the context of a competitive industry, slow-moving inventory would raise questions of marketability. This is particularly the case given much of the inventory related to outmoded product lines.

(C) Product per unit declined over time due to 30% overstatement of plant and equipment.

Source: SEC Accounting and Auditing Enforcement Release No. 127 (1987).

Key Analytics: An Overview

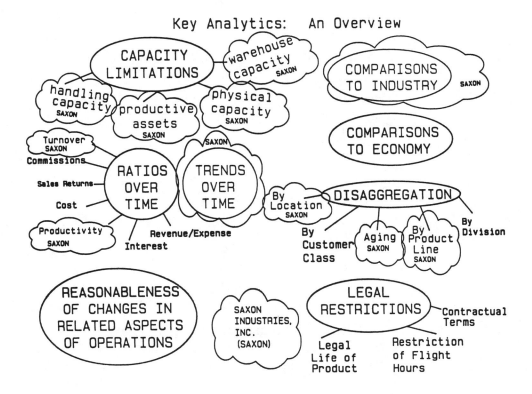

Seaboard

Problem: Extended bank credit from $807,000 to $4.1 million to five deteriorating customers.

Approach: Time-Series Model Comparing Key Factors Longitudinally (Prior Years to Present)

Modern Analytic Technique:

| Accounts Receivable (Consider Disaggregation by Customer, Industry, Size, Maturity, or Similar Attributes) | $\cong$ | * SALES
* CUSTOMER MIX
* AVERAGE AGE
* ALLOWANCE ACCOUNT OR RESERVE ADJUSTMENT
* PERCENTAGE OF RECEIVABLES IN LARGEST TEN CUSTOMER ACCOUNTS (OR SIMILAR CONCENTRATION MEASURE) |

Conclusion: Five customers accounted for 50% of total assets and merit in-depth investigation. Reserve adjustment was inadequate. Non-payment of old balances rather than an increase in the volume of business led to the increased account balances.

Source: SEC Accounting Series Release No. 78 (1957).

Key Analytics: An Overview

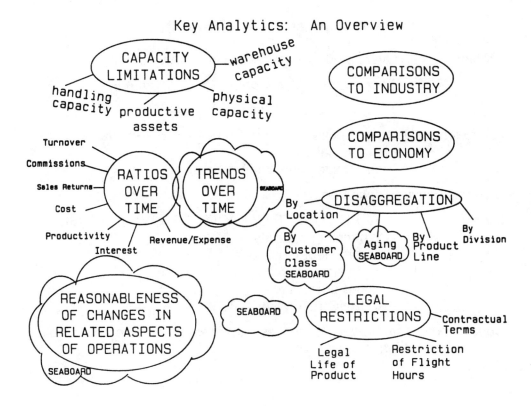

Whittaker Corporation (WHITTAKER)

Problem: Overstated Inventories at Crown Aluminum

Year	Overstatement	% of Inventory
1971	$4.4 million	48%

Approach: Cross-Sectional Model Comparing Warehousing Loca-
                  tion to Location
                  (Peak Values and Year-to-date)

Modern Analytic Technique:

Inventory $\cong$ * APPROXIMATE CAPACITY PER WAREHOUSE
                    • handling capacity
                    • cubic feet (square feet)
                    • physical attributes of warehouse
                      and product
                 * TURNOVER MEASURE

Conclusion: Inventory list quantities exceeded warehouse and handling
                  capacity.

Source: SEC Accounting Series Release No. 157 (1974).

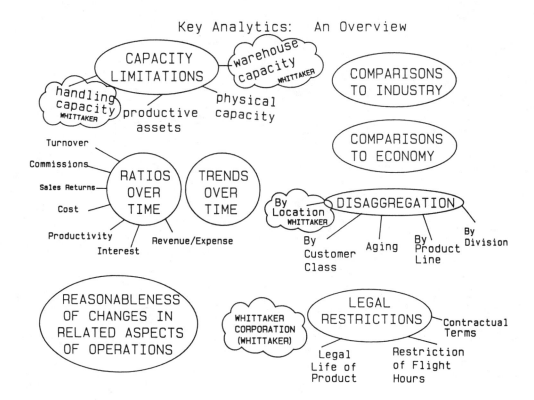

Key Analytics: An Overview

5

A Recommended Approach to Designing and Evaluating Controls: Identify the Critical Elements of Internal Accounting Control

"You can observe a lot just by watching."

Yogi Berra[1]

Such wisdom has much to recommend itself to those responsible for designing and evaluating controls. Observational skills can be used to identify exposures, assess controls that are in place, and to monitor changes in such control.

This *Handbook's* recommended approach to the design and evaluation of internal control will now be described. To set the stage for the detailed discussion

---

[1] Cited by George W. Downs and Patrick D. Larkey, *The Search For Government Efficiency* (Philadelphia: Temple University Press, 1986), p. 74.

Exhibit 5–1

**The Recommended Approach to Designing and Evaluating
Controls: An Overview**

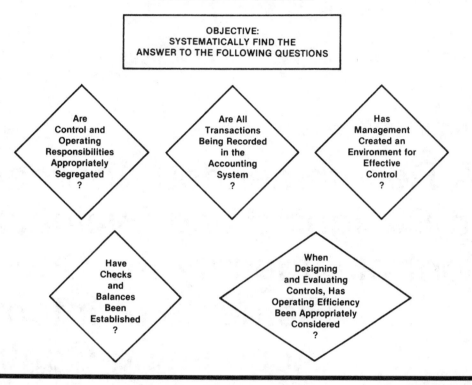

OBJECTIVE:
SYSTEMATICALLY FIND THE
ANSWER TO THE FOLLOWING QUESTIONS

Are
Control and
Operating
Responsibilities
Appropriately
Segregated
?

Are All
Transactions
Being Recorded
in the
Accounting
System
?

Has
Management
Created an
Environment for
Effective
Control
?

Have
Checks
and
Balances
Been
Established
?

When
Designing
and Evaluating
Controls, Has
Operating Efficiency
Been Appropriately
Considered
?

of the critical elements of internal accounting control, an overview of the *Handbook's* approach is presented in Exhibit 5–1.

HOW TO DETERMINE WHETHER CONTROL AND OPERATING RESPONSIBILITIES ARE APPROPRIATELY SEGREGATED

The segregation of duties is one of the critical elements of control which you must be capable of designing and evaluating. The presumption is that if collusion is required to perpetrate a fraud, the probability of defalcation is substantially reduced. The implication is that no single individual should have control over an entire transaction.

Three-Way Division of Job Responsibilities

The typical approach to segregating responsibilities is to separate the authorization, custody of assets, and record-keeping functions. The underlying concept in this approach is that a person with the ability to authorize a transaction must be capable of obtaining custody of some assets and of controlling the related record of the transaction if a defalcation is to be perpetrated without others' cooperation or subsequent detection via routine checks and balances or the audit process. Similarly, a person having custody of assets must be able to authorize their removal and to adjust the books that inventory them if a misuse of assets is to occur without detection. Of course, the record keeper can accrue no direct benefit from altering records unless assets can be obtained with appropriate approval—two distinct functions, controlled, in part, by the segregation of responsibilities across at least two individuals. Unless an individual can authorize transactions, take custody of assets, and account for the transaction, the single-handed perpetration of a fraud that is not detected in the normal course of operations is improbable.

Adequate Controls Can Be Established for the Small Business

The realization that a three-way division of job responsibilities can achieve an adequate segregation of duties facilitates the establishment of adequate controls for a small business. As long as the entity has at least three employees, the critical segregation of duties can be maintained. In fact, even if the entity has only two employees involved in day-to-day operations, a careful allocation of duties could ensure that neither individual would control a transaction from its initiation to its completion and record in the books of the entity.

While a larger number of employees permits the development of numerous checks and balances, the critical control obtainable through segregating duties is feasibly obtained in a small operation. Often, the difficulty is the lack of formality in the operations of a small entity.

Another problem with controls that can plague you in evaluating the compliance of a client or a company with a reasonably well-designed system is what is done when employee(s) go to lunch or are on vacation. With two or three employees, the segregated duties often become fiction rather than fact due to practical operating "adaptations" made in the interest of maintaining smooth and efficient operations. One of the tasks involved in designing controls is to anticipate such operating necessities as covering the duties of absent employees and to provide instructions as to which "adaptations" can be made with the least loss in control. One resource of particular importance to the small entity is the owner-manager.

The Control Capabilities of the Owner-Manager Can Be Substantial

The owner-manager of a small entity typically understands all phases of the operations and has day-to-day contact with employees as well as tremendous oversight capabilities. This individual has incentives that are similar to those of other owners and can operate as a control that has no counterpart in larger organizations. This is true, in part, because of the owner-manager's accessibility to all operating departments and, in larger part, to the owner-manager's ability to assess the reasonableness of authorizations, assets-on-hand, and records, in relationship to the total entity's operations.

The problem of what to do when employees are absent due to lunch time or vacation time can be easily solved by requiring secondary approval of transactions by the owner-manager whenever the person to whom such duties are regularly assigned is unavailable. A second, though not as practical, solution is to have the owner-manager actually perform those tasks that would be incompatible for others to perform whenever the regular employees are absent. With respect to custody and record-keeping responsibilities, if the owner-manager chooses not to assume such tasks during others' absence, an additional oversight policy should be established whereby the owner-manager regularly reviews those tasks that are being performed by persons to whom the tasks are not routinely assigned.

Regardless of the absenteeism situation, the owner-manager should exercise oversight through procedures similar to those regularly assigned to treasurers, controllers, and internal auditors in large entities. For example, the bank reconciliation, the second signature for acquisitions and disbursements over some set dollar amount, a test of detailed documentation, and a periodic balancing of the subsidiary ledger to the general ledger can all be assigned responsibilities of the owner-manager as a means of enhancing control. In addition, the owner-manager should be made aware of easy analytical procedures to test the reasonableness of recorded operations and should be encouraged to use observation and inquiry procedures to retain vigilance over operations.

In small operations the owner-manager frequently knows all the employees well and is able to establish a trust and loyalty in the employer-employee relationship superior to the relationship common in larger organizations. Of course, the potential hazard of misplaced loyalty in an environment that is more easily abused because of the fewer controls typically established in smaller, more informal operations can be substantial. You should encourage the owner-manager to exercise prudence in establishing formal controls, and you will often be able to demonstrate planning and financial advantages to the more formalized approach, even if the owner-manager perceives no necessity for the formal control in terms of the assets' risk exposure from maintaining an informal system. *Note*: In all cases, the client should have fidelity bonding for all employees who handle a significant amount of assets for the entity (not merely a significant amount of cash).

Reliance on the Owner-Manager Can Be Risky

While the owner-manager represents an effective control over operations, excessive reliance on the owner-manager poses substantial risk. The primary risk exposure stems from management-override capabilities of an owner-manager. If the key person in an organization instructs others or chooses, himself, to process a transaction in a nonroutine manner, such a request is likely to be followed and in all probability that request will not be reported to some third party. Furthermore, the owner-manager's excellent knowledge of the business and its controls facilitates the abuse of the system. Who better can recognize the weaknesses in a system than the owner who, most likely, either established or had a critical role in designing the control system?

Your Assessment of Controls Should Reflect the Incentives of the Owner-Manager

The question arises as to what incentives would motivate an owner-manager to override or abuse controls. If the owner-manager is the sole owner and has no credit extended by third parties, no incentive other than the avoidance of taxes appears to exist. If, on the other hand, multiple owners and creditors for the business are assumed to exist, the reward to an owner-manager from extracting assets of the business is the other owners' and creditors' share of those assets. Although the interests of an owner-manager are similar to those of silent co-owners, the ability of management to benefit from perquisites such as "plush offices" can encourage the owner-manager to take actions that are not in the best long-term interests of the business.

Your assessment of controls, particularly when the owner-manager assumes a critical role in the control system, should reflect the incentives of the individuals responsible for that system. If the risk of management override is judged to be minor, reliance on the owner-manager represents little risk exposure for the auditor or other individual who is evaluating a control system. However, generally speaking, increased reliance on owner-managers within any control system increases the risk from management override.

Exhibit 5–2 summarizes those duties that should be segregated from one another and the oversight role of owner-managers. As emphasized in the exhibit, both formal and informal segregation of duties is essential in order to maintain control.

Caution: Be on the Lookout for the Informal System Behind the Formal System Design

Whether relying on the control activities of the owner-manager or of other personnel, you must determine whether or not the formally designed separation of responsibilities corresponds to the informal day-to-day operations of the client. One example of a common troublespot was provided earlier: what happens over lunch time and during vacations? Are controls maintained or does the segregation of duties become blurred? Similarly, how accessible are accounting records, computer terminals, and assets to the regular employees? If everyone has access to accounting records, the formal separation of duties is inoperative. If employees can literally walk off with inventory because the loading platform is not controlled

Exhibit 5–2

Appropriate Segregation of Duties

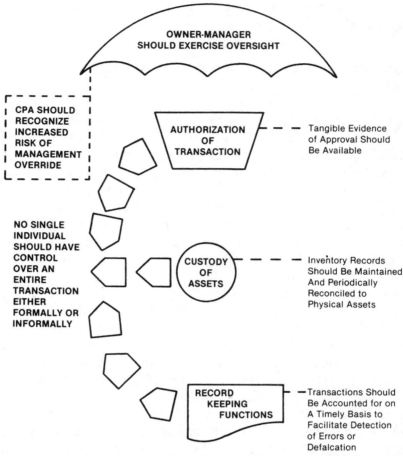

via observation or check-out procedures, the formally assigned "custody of assets" job description has little meaning as a control technique.

More specific examples can be provided of informality in performing control duties which makes the formal segregation of responsibilities for specific tasks inoperative:

—If a bank statement, not yet reconciled, is left open on a desk, easily accessible to all, checks could be removed or substituted to cover up a defalcation by an individual who, according to the formal design of the system, is being "checked" by the "separate" reconciliation function.

—Similarly, if custody of marketable securities is controlled by issuing one set of keys to an individual who then leaves those keys in the top drawer of a desk that is accessible to everyone, custody of assets is not being well segregated from the authorization and record-keeping functions.

—If dual signatures are required on checks, but one individual signs blank checks to expedite the making of disbursements, the informal system is not complying with the design of the formal system of controls.

—If a storekeeper, despite instructions to complete and verify a requisition slip before releasing materials, in fact encourages employees to "take what they need and just leave a requisition slip on the counter," the deterioration of intended control over the custody of assets is considerable.

The point is that you must evaluate not only the formal system design with respect to the segregation of duties, but also the design changes that have been made informally in the course of actual operations.

Employees' Understanding of Control-Related Duties Has Both Benefits and Risks

One reason for the informal deterioration of system design is the lack of understanding of control-related duties. An employee in accounting may see no harm in asking the cashier to substitute for an account clerk who is on vacation, if that employee does not understand that the employer, for good reasons, wishes to segregate the custody of assets from record-keeping. Of course, providing an explanation for such segregation poses two risks:

(1) The employee may become indignant at the idea that the business intentionally has designed a means of deterring fraud, thereby impugning some employees' integrity.
(2) Once knowledgeable as to controls, the employees are better able to beat the system, either by recognizing the flaws in system design or by colluding with one another.

Managing the risks. You can handle the first risk by stressing to the employees the fact that you are striving for a system of checks and balances over "honest mistakes," as opposed to looking for intentional defalcations. The second risk is not as manageable, except through the improvement of system controls to correct weaknesses and the careful selection and evaluation of employees. The extent of the second risk can be controlled, in part, by providing minimal instructions as to the objectives of control, with an emphasis on their importance. By integrating control system compliance measures into the performance evaluation system, you better motivate employees to give adequate attention to control procedures.

To secure the proper handling of keys, bank statements, and similar items, one employee must clearly assume responsibility for their use and control. If the employee in the example given above comprehends that any missing marketable securities could result in loss of employment, and thus sees the possible real cost of neglectfully leaving keys in the top drawer of a desk accessible to other employees and to customers, that employee would most likely exercise due care in handling such keys.

Overall, the employees should be taught that controls are an integral part of operations and that control duties are as important to the entity's success and to the evaluation of employees' performance as are operating duties. Furthermore, the importance of complying with formal job descriptions and not informally sharing or trading off various job responsibilities should be stressed in employee training programs.

The costly consequences that can result when employees do not understand control-related duties. While the weaknesses of existing controls need not be explained, the philosophy underlying existing controls does need an explanation. The epitome of the potential consequence of an employee's not understanding some prescribed control-related duty is demonstrated by the following example:

> An employee was asked to take a sample of 50 invoices for inventory purchases and retrace them into the inventory records as a follow-up check on recorded balances, to assure that the 50 recorded balances were correct. Not understanding the purpose of the procedure, the employee expanded the original sample of 50 every time a discrepancy was found between the invoice and recorded balances until 50 correctly recorded invoices were identified. Then the employee reported that 50 correctly recorded invoices had been found.

Obviously, the employee had no understanding of the control procedure to be performed and, in fact, provided information from which others were likely to draw erroneous conclusions. If the employee pulled 100 invoices before finding 50 correctly recorded inventory items, a recording system that was only 50% accurate was being reported as 100% accurate.

The costs of such poor information could include misstated financial reports, poor customer relations when inventory records did not correspond to inventory items actually available for sale, and inaccurate planning of purchases, profit margin, and other key operating characteristics. Had the objective of the control procedure been described in advance, the problems might have been avoided. The example clearly demonstrates the risks that stem from employees' *not understanding* their control-related duties, which are likely to be greater than those stemming from their *understanding* of such duties. When one considers that employees who wish to steal will not easily be prevented from learning about existing controls, the added risk due to training—that a knowledgeable employee will abuse the control system—appears to be low. However, the problem is considered to have some merit, as regulatory bodies like the Federal Home Loan Bank Board have a basic policy of not making public those reports which discuss control weaknesses, for fear that the information could be used to "beat" the respective entities' control system. You should make a client or company aware of the benefits and risks associated with the alternative approaches to improving employees' understanding of controls. The informal deterioration of controls caused when employees frequently substitute for other employees during lunch times, breaks, vacations, and other absences is much less likely to occur if they understand the importance of segregated duties.

How to Overcome the High Risk to Control Presented by Electronic Data Processing

One important area of wide misunderstanding concerns the role of computers, particularly with respect to controls. Common practice has been to computerize as large a segment of operations as possible, assuming, somehow, that the computer is always well controlled. This is in spite of the fact that when a client has a computerized information system, documentation that was typically segregated in a manual system through the assignment of responsibilities to different individuals is all processed through a centralized electronic data processing (EDP) system. This combination of duties poses a potentially high risk to control and must be explicitly evaluated and, where possible, compensated for through alternative control procedures.

Treat the EDP as though it were one individual. A conservative approach to evaluating the effect of such centralized computer processing upon the desired segregation of duties framework is to treat the EDP processing as though it represented one individual. Then, every time EDP performs incompatible functions, the risk exposure can be assessed. The underlying logic of the approach is that EDP personnel tend to have access to all documentation flowing through the computer, and key people, particularly the system designer, programmer, and operator, could have extensive access to all areas of operations that are either processed or retained on the computer. The conservative aspect of the approach concerns the prevalence with which compensating controls are established.

Establish compensating controls. As the name suggests, compensating controls are intended to compensate for a weakness in one control by adding another control that corrects the particular weakness. For example, when the purchasing department has purchase orders processed by EDP at the same time that the cashier is having disbursements processed by EDP, the question arises as to the effects of combining the authorization and custody functions. By establishing strong input and user review controls, you can gain assurance that documents were not added to or removed from the data base. If you require passwords and similar access controls and maintain a computer log of who performs the processing, you can establish responsibility for particular EDP activities. These types of control can partially compensate for dual access to authorization forms and rights to assets, in the form of disbursement checks. If you monitor disbursements through dual control over any facsimile signature plate, as well as through careful count controls, you can assure minimal risk exposure from EDP's assumption of two typically incompatible operations.

The key to maintaining adequate segregation in spite of EDP. The key to maintaining adequate segregation of responsibilities, in spite of central processing by EDP, is to assign input and output control responsibilities to non-EDP personnel, to keep tight control over highly exposed processing activities

Exhibit 5–3

Controlling Centralized Data Processing

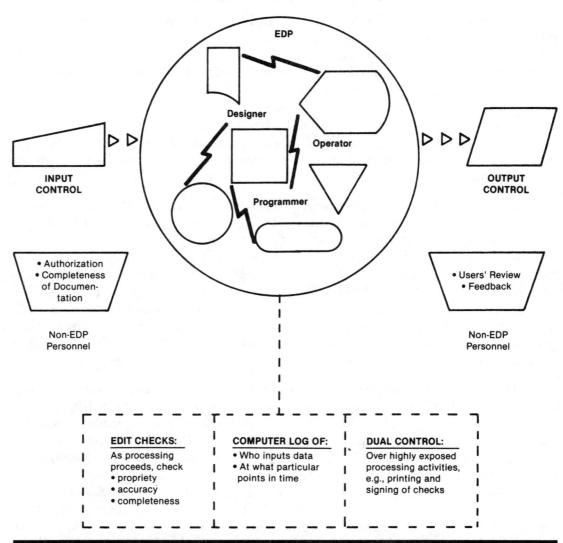

such as the computerized printing and signing of checks, and to clearly delineate job responsibilities within the EDP department, maintaining file access controls and efficiently incorporating edit checks for propriety, accuracy, and completeness of processing activities. These compensating controls, illustrated in Exhibit 5–3, can lead to an adequate system of control with respect to the segregation of duties.

HOW TO ASCERTAIN WHETHER ALL TRANSACTIONS ARE BEING RECORDED IN THE ACCOUNTING SYSTEM

Once you have considered the adequacy with which controls have been segregated, the next critical question to be addressed is whether all transactions are being recorded in the accounting system. Since most of your tests focus on recorded transactions, reasonable assurance must be obtained that all transactions are, in fact, recorded.

How to Establish the Audit Trail

The key question is whether an audit trail can be established. When business transactions occur with third parties, is it reasonable to expect that evidence of these transactions will be created internally? While errors may occur from the point in time when the original documentation is created until the numbers are recorded in the accounting ledgers, such misstatements can be uncovered in the course of the audit if there is some evidence of the transaction within the accounting system. However, if no documentation is available, the error is likely to be undetectable.

You must be able to identify the means by which all types of transactions that involve a given client are reflected in the accounting system and then must understand the movement of the source record of transactions into the accounting ledgers. The path from original source document to its final record in the ledgers is typically termed the audit trail.

Identify transactions that affect financial operations. To establish the audit trail, you should first identify those transactions that affect the financial operations of the entity. Generally speaking, these will include

—acquisition of capital,

—acquisition of assets,

—purchases of services,

—selling of goods or services,

—collection of receivables,

—payment for assets and services,

—investments,

—management of pensions and profit-sharing arrangements,

—disposal of assets, and

—paying off of capital-related commitments.

Determine whether documentation exists for routine and nonroutine transactions. You must gain assurance that both routine and nonroutine transactions are documented and that such documentation is maintained for a sufficient period of time and in reasonable order to facilitate an audit.

Consider the auditability of the flow through the system. As the source document flows through the system, the designer of internal accounting controls should specifically consider the auditability of the flow through the system. For example, assume that a client or company plans to use a service bureau to generate payroll checks and customer billings. If no control was established over the number of time cards and the billing source documents that are transferred to the service bureau, then despite the completeness of original records, the amounts recorded in the ledgers could be incomplete if documents were lost and not appropriately processed by the service bureau. On the other hand, if controls were established whereby the number of documents transferred was known and the number of documents returned from the service bureau was recorded, then the records could be checked for completeness and an audit trail would exist for the accounting functions performed by the service bureau.

Establish document control. In designing an audit trail, control over documents can often be established through merely prenumbering printed forms, retaining voided forms, and periodically accounting for the numerical sequence of such documents as they flow through the accounting system. Beyond merely providing a means of gaining assurance that all transactions have been processed, the audit trail should provide answers to the questions of who has processed the documents and how have they been processed. Often, job descriptions will designate who is supposed to do the processing, but who actually does the processing may differ from prescriptions. An audit trail is easily established by requiring that the employee who approves a document, checks its mathematical accuracy, or performs other control responsibilities, also initials it to establish who processed the form and what has been done to it.

Maintaining an Audit Trail

The audit trail must result in tangible sources of evidence that an auditor can test to gain assurance that all transactions are being recorded in the accounting system and that prescribed control procedures are being performed. When operating efficiency and technological developments lead to such operating procedures as real time input of data onto computer files, rather than a manual input process, the entity should maintain an audit trail. This can easily be done through the maintenance of a computer log that identifies who inputs data, at what particular points in time, and through edit checks which confirm that all data entering the initial processing point are transmitted through each phase of the processing.

Similarly, a wire transfer, intended to expedite the typical paper transmittal of funds, should nevertheless be accompanied by an audit trail so that loss of funds could be identified, as could responsibility for errors. Without an audit trail, neither you nor your client can have assurance that all transactions are being recorded in the accounting system. The process of establishing an audit trail is summarized in Exhibit 5–4.

Is the Entity Auditable?

If an audit trail can be established for all transactions in which the entity is involved, the entity is auditable. This does not, of course, mean that the entity

Exhibit 5–4

Establishing the Audit Trail

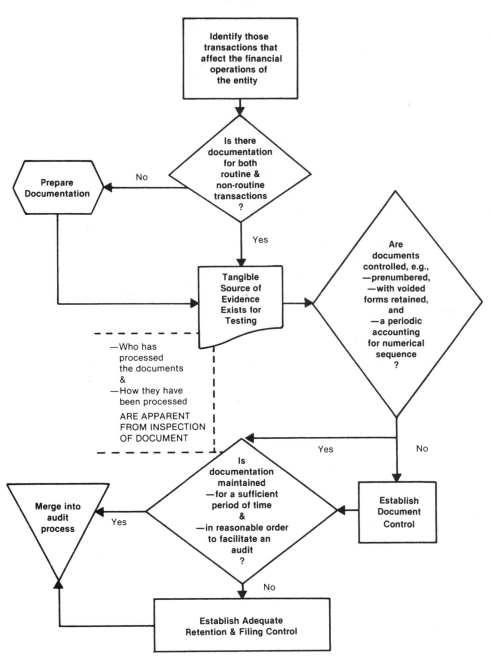

will receive a clean audit report, or that it has all the information necessary to issue financial statements that comply with generally accepted accounting principles (GAAP). It merely confirms that an audit can be performed which, in turn, will result in the evidence necessary for the formulation of an audit report that, in addition to other attributes, assesses whether or not GAAP compliance has been achieved by the client.

Substantive Testing When Audit Trails Are Nonexistent

More often than not, a client or company will not have an established audit trail for all transactions, particularly in the case of nonroutine transactions. For example, if a client had a good opportunity to acquire additional credit at a reasonable interest rate, and persuaded an existing creditor to verbally waive a bond covenant provision to facilitate the transaction, an audit trail documenting the waiver was probably not established. However, inquiry procedures could provide the information necessary to acquire tangible evidence of the waiver through a formal written confirmation procedure.

A critical element of control for which tangible audit trails are frequently nonexistent is the proper segregation of duties within an entity. Although job descriptions and procedures manuals may be available, the compliance with such manuals, for many day-to-day operations, can be confirmed only through inquiry and observation procedures. The absence of an audit trail that can be compliance tested using sampling procedures does not result in the entity being unauditable; it merely requires that substantive testing augment tests of control as a basis for the audit report. In fact, inquiry and observation procedures can provide important assurance that aid in evaluating the control system, as well as the reasonableness of the financial statements.

In other words, the inability to test controls has a compensating audit procedure—the substantive test. However, the inability to perform either tests of controls or substantive tests makes the entity unauditable. Consider the following examples, where the ability to substantively test the available data and to draw audit conclusions regarding particular balances is questionable.

Example 1. Cash disbursements are made from several checking accounts. The checks are not prenumbered. The cashier numbers the checks as they are issued, discards voided checks, and simply reuses the check number for any checks that are voided.

—In such a case, the designed controls over disbursements are inadequate for reliance and the substantive test question concerns whether all disbursements have been recorded and whether they are all appropriate expenditures for the entity. The balances of concern include cash and accounts payable, as a minimum.

—Bank reconciliations are available; however, if the cashier performs such reconciliations and if outstanding checks are listed in the reconciliation, the obvious means of reviewing the propriety of disbursements and the completeness of records are ineffective.

Example 2. A client has an estimated $400,000 of fixed assets, most of which were acquired over 10 years ago. Records of original cost have not been maintained, and since depreciation has not been recorded in prior years, separate asset records for bulk purchases have not been established.

—The substantive test objective is to obtain assurance that recorded asset and related depreciation accounts are fairly stated. Obviously, tests of control cannot be applied to data 10 years old as a basis for relying on asset acquisition, maintenance, and disposal control procedures, as an alternative approach, since on these dates the individual historical costs were not recorded, suggesting that neither the tests of control nor substantive audit trails are available. In addition, there is no suitable substitute for concurrent observation and inquiry procedures, in terms of assuring that employees were competent and duties over such assets were sufficiently segregated to permit reliance on the 10-year-old control procedures.

—Physical observation of assets would permit an inventory to be taken, and statistics may well be available as to the assets' resale and/or replacement value. Appraisers could provide independent estimates of reasonable valuations. However, the historical documentation required for compliance with the historical costing principle of valuation under GAAP is nonexistent.

Example 3. A client receives most cash receipts by mail. The bookkeeper opens the mail and records the receipts, then forwards them to the cashier for deposit in the bank.

—The handling of assets by the person in charge of generating accounting records is a major control problem. It is possible for the bookkeeper to extract cash receipts, and never to have recorded that receivable in the books, to have adjusted the books to remove the receivable, or to suppress the future billings to a customer, thereby removing assets without detection. The substantive test question relates primarily to the cash and receivables balance. Have all receipts been appropriately reflected on the books?

—Confirmation procedures could be used to substantively test recorded receivables, but what of receivables that have not been recorded or those to which adjustments were made to secure the "proper balance" without recording cash receipts (i.e., accounts in which sales allowances were recorded)? Although receipts can be tested from the point when they are recorded by the bookkeeper to the time they reach the bank, how can you gain assurance that all receipts were initially recorded?

Alternative Approaches

Alternative approaches are available when you face particular accounts or an entity that would be unauditable if only typical audit procedures were applied. One approach is to try to create an audit trail, as suggested in the example involving the client who had a debt covenant verbally waived by a creditor. Another approach is to collect information from sources that were not necessarily involved in the transaction to validate the reasonableness of recorded transactions, such as the use of the appraiser in the fixed asset example. Should the available audit trails suggest that the entity is not auditable, you should consider whether the entity can, in fact, be made auditable.

How to Make an Entity Auditable

Any entity can be made auditable, given a sufficient period of time. This is because a control and information system can be designed from scratch, implemented, and, at some subsequent date, subjected to an audit. However, the pressing issue to be addressed is whether a practical means exists by which the entity can be made auditable for the current period.

Reduce the scope of the audit or audit report. In many cases the means of making an entity auditable will be a reduction in the scope of the audit and/ or the scope of the audit report. For example, a first-time audit client will typically receive an audit report that covers only the balance sheet, because beginning inventory, which is the primary determinant of cost of goods sold, cannot be adequately verified. A company that has an unauditable subsidiary may decide to have an audit performed for the company's operations, excluding that particular subsidiary. A common occurrence for municipalities undergoing an audit is to accept a qualification in the audit report concerning the valuation of fixed assets. Since cities and towns frequently have no records as to historical costs for city halls and similar municipal buildings, appraisal values are commonly used for reporting purposes. This creates an audit trail for the current and subsequent periods but is contrary to the historical cost principle.

Perform an extended scope audit. Other than accepting a restriction on the scope of an audit or a qualified audit report, the only alternative to no audit is an extended scope audit that makes the entity auditable.

Example. In the example where the bookkeeper handled cash receipts, the means by which assurance could be obtained that all receipts were being recorded would encompass the following steps:

—reconcile the customer list to whom sales were made to the receivables on the books;

—send confirmations to all customers with whom the entity has carried on business in the past year, for whom receivables are not recorded, asking that they indicate their balance due; and

—take a sample of customers for whom sales allowances and similar adjusting entries affected the receivables balances, and send confirmation or detail test available supporting evidence that such an adjustment was made and was reasonable.

The last step could be performed under the guise of a customer service objective of the client. These three steps would, of course, augment the normal confirmation procedure and would suffice only if the sales function and underlying documentation were properly segregated from the bookkeeping and if invoices were subjected to numerical control, from which a customer list was available. In other words, the particular means by which the auditor gains assurance that all receipts are recorded will depend on the client's control and information systems.

Example. The disbursements example, in which controls did not include numerical control over checks, physical retention of voided checks, or the separate reconciliation of the bank statements, can be addressed similarly:

—An extended sampling of recorded disbursements and their correspondence to the approved supplier listing would be performed, as would an examination of supporting purchase documentation to ensure the propriety of individual purchases.

—A confirmation would be mailed to suppliers regarding their current accounts payable balances, particularly to suppliers for whom zero balances are recorded.

—The cut-off bank statements would, as usual, be received by the person performing the audit, but extended work would include the application of inquiry, confirmation, or some other follow-up procedure to outstanding checks.

—An extended testing of the bank reconciliation procedure would be performed, particularly the mathematical accuracy, the tie-in of canceled checks to recorded disbursements, the reasonableness of endorsements, and any adjusting entries related to outstanding checks. If any canceled checks listed on the bank statement are missing, follow-up procedures with the bank may be necessary unless the disbursements can be located in the books and follow-up procedures applied to the payable.

—Of particular interest in this setting is whether the banks have been instructed not to cash checks made out to Cash and whether the authorized check signers and endorsers for checks made payable to the company are correctly recorded at the bank. Direct inquiry procedures at the banks, particularly to confirm with the tellers that the person in charge of disbursements has not cashed checks payable to cash or to the company, may be deemed necessary.

Again, the extent of additional audit procedures and external data collected before you judge that the company's records are complete and auditable will depend on the company's system and the evidence collected through the extended procedures. Often, added assurance that the accounting records are complete can be obtained by merely looking one step beyond the accounting system.

Using Operating Data to Check the Completeness of Accounting Records

Assume that cost accounting statistics that underlie recorded cost of sales are not well controlled, and you are uncertain as to whether or not they're complete. Certain operating statistics may assist you in gaining assurance that the recorded numbers are reasonable.

Benchmarks for assessing recorded cost of sales. The production capacity statistics and normal production levels, as indicated by the number of labor shifts and total amount of raw material purchases, can provide one benchmark for assessing whether recorded cost of sales is feasible. The management information system will frequently maintain operating statistics that typically are not used in the cost accounting department but can help you to formulate an expected value for cost of sales. In purchasing, competitive bidding practices and special project studies may generate an average cost benchmark for raw materials put into production. The production quality review department may periodically analyze products as to their composition and as to how the labor/material mix and quality compares to competitors. The sales department probably maintains statistics for salesmen as to number of customers visited, number of units sold, and the product classifications for units sold, which, of course, suggests a certain amount as reasonable for recorded cost of sales. The marketing department would probably have prepared some profile analysis of the percentage of market share held by the company and the growth expected for that market share in the current period. This information, combined with externally generated data concerning the market and competitors' operating performance, could provide an extremely useful barometer for assessing the reasonableness of recorded cost of goods sold.

Formulating expectations that can be compared to recorded book values. Statement on Auditing Standards [SAS] No. 56, which describes analytical procedures, stresses the concept of formulating an expectation to which recorded book values can be compared. The expectations cited in the SAS include prior year activities and historical patterns, budgeted data, and industry statistics. The objective is to identify predictable patterns and to utilize such patterns to formulate expectations which can, in turn, be applied as benchmarks in reaching an audit conclusion as to the reasonableness of the financial statements. This audit procedure can be of particular use in making an entity auditable, in the sense that when no clear assurance is available through established procedures that the accounting records of the company are complete, analytical procedures applied to assess the reasonableness of the recorded numbers may provide such necessary assurance. You should make a practice of reviewing the management information system and externally generated industry data in order to gain a well-rounded business perspective as to the client's or the company's operations, the adequacy of controls, and the reasonableness of the financial statements; in particular, the external validation process of using industry data can assist in checking the completeness of accounting records.

Exhibit 5–5 summarizes the various means of making an entity auditable, including the use of operating statistics to gain confidence as to the completeness of the information base. Your selection of a particular approach from this set of alternatives will largely depend on the client's control and information system, the time frame available to make the entity auditable, and the relative efficiency and effectiveness of the available extended audit procedures.

Exhibit 5–5

Making an Entity Auditable

Reduction in the Scope of the Audit Report

Reduction in the Scope of the Audit

Acceptance of a Qualified Audit Report

Available Alternatives

Extended Scope Audit

Using Operating Data to Check the Completeness of Accounting Records

LONG-RANGE ALTERNATIVE: Establish an Adequate Audit Trail

Typically a substantive testing approach is applied

The selection of particular procedures will be tailored to clients' control and information system

SAS No. 56
Analytical Procedures

Use of
• prior year data
• historical patterns
• budgets
• industry statistics
To Assess Completeness and Reasonableness of Information Set

HOW TO DETERMINE WHETHER MANAGEMENT HAS CREATED AN ENVIRONMENT FOR EFFECTIVE CONTROL

Traditionally the professional literature distinguished between accounting and administrative controls. The former referred to controls that directly affected the numbers that were recorded in the accounting system and eventually were reported on the financial statements. Administrative controls were more operating than accounting in nature, only indirectly affecting the financial statement figures. The example of administrative control commonly used in the literature is the requirement that salesmen submit a detailed listing of which customers were visited during the month. Such a reporting practice is clearly distinct from the accounting process of recording sales, yet exercises operating control over salesmen and facilitates their performance evaluation. The accounting literature focused on accounting controls with the stipulation that any administrative controls that might affect accounting numbers should be subjected to review.

As the business approach to the audit process became more pronounced in the accounting literature, it became generally recognized that before giving attention to detailed accounting controls, the CPA should begin the review and evaluation process by analyzing general controls, typically referred to as the control environment of an entity. More recently, SAS No. 55 has adopted the term control structure, one component of which is the control environment.

Control environments are often discussed as informal controls, including: competence, trust, shared values, strong leadership, high expectations, clear accountability, openness, and high ethical standards. These can be contrasted with more formal control mechanisms such as policies, procedures, regulations, laws, organizational structure, and bureaucracy. Some suggest that low level formal controls can be effectively complemented with a high level of informal controls.[2]

SAS No. 55 and Management Control

The content of SAS No. 55 recognizes that

> An entity's control structure consists of the policies and procedures established to provide reasonable assurance that specific entity objectives will be achieved. (paragraph 6)

This broader perspective relates to economic decision making and how management runs a business. Actions by the board of directors, management, and other competent personnel that ensure achievement of established goals are a critical aspect of controls. These actions include setting objectives, implementing plans, and monitoring operations. While keeping track of internal and external events and attendant risks, management sets strategies and establishes organizational

---

[2] B. J. White, *Internal Control in U.S. Corporations* (Financial Executives Research Foundation, 1980).

structures, information systems, and control procedures. One objective is to ensure the reliability and integrity of information. Of particular importance is the employment of competent people to carry out such activities.

This view of management control over resources and activities entails compliance with applicable laws and ethical standards, along with achievement of the entity's objectives. Prudent cost-effectiveness is an expected evaluation criterion.

In assessing business processes, evaluators of controls should consider how:

—ownership and accountability are established and maintained,

—processes are evaluated as effective via the measurement of key indicators and trends,

—processes are modified to compensate for changing conditions,

—key people gain an understanding of processes,

—economic, management, and external factors are evaluated as to their effect on key business processes—including concerns for the entity's survival, competitiveness, and financial strength,

—key dependencies on systems are evaluated, as well as applications of such systems, and

—affects of changes in technology, staff, and business practices are evaluated.

Risk exposures can be mitigated through information security, separation of duties, education and training, quality programs, and formation of alliances—such as feedback from customers.

A Workshop Approach

Among alliances fostered in some entities is internal auditors' effort to maintain open lines of communication with employees. For example, some departments regularly meet with operating personnel and ask them to identify their key goals, primary control responsibilities, and ideas for improvement. The General Auditor of Gulf Canada Resources Limited in Calgary, Alberta uses half-day workshops in which operating divisions perform self assessments of controls, past improvements, concerns as to what could be improved, and action plans (including recommendations and target dates). He notes that such workshops create incentives to specify objectives and encourage information sharing. A broader look at the whole company is facilitated. In drawing comparisons to past practices, he has found that more information on accountability and key risks are obtained from the workshops than were identified via more traditional internal audit procedures. A team worker attitude is nurtured and knowledge engineering is a skill fostered among internal auditors.

An interesting observation shared by Mr. Paul G. Makosz, the General Auditor of Gulf Canada Resources Limited was that access to the entire company each and every year through such workshops provided greater assurance of alignment of ethical values among employees and stakeholders. He pointed out that while stakeholders include the general public, government representatives, and investors, a small group of directors and officers might lose sight of the broader expectations of such diverse groups. Indeed, when problems have arisen in companies, often evidence emerges that managers were "caught up" in saving their company and started to rationalize their activities. By accessing employees' views on company policies, a far better "mirror" of stakeholders is provided, which implicitly acts as a deterrent to unethical behavior.

Corporate Personalities

Willard E. Hick, Second Vice President of Corporate Audit for Massachusetts Mutual Life Insurance Company similarly observes that since a legal entity has the rights and privileges of a person, it has a personality viewed from both the inside and out. This personality is intrinsically linked to management's personalities. He observes how quickly perceptions of personalities can change, citing Union Carbide in India, Gerber's experience with baby food (juice) press coverage, and the Chicago Board of Trade's Investigation. The influence of Drexel Burnham on the personality of Wall Street, the linkage of Morton Thiokal with the Challenger disaster, and Exxon's Valdez experience similarly demonstrate the point. To develop an ethics orientation, all associates must share basic ethical values and preferably apply the age old golden rule. Leadership is crucial and sentiments such as "You are all auditors" develops a joint sense of responsibility for control.

Management Override Possibilities Must Be Assessed

One key question that should be posed regarding the control environment of an entity is what possibility exists for management override. Once these possibilities are identified, you must assess the probability of override and what effect the probability has on your evaluation of the overall control system. No matter how well designed a control system, if it can easily be circumvented without subsequent detection of such circumvention and if such circumvention is deemed probable, you cannot rely on specific controls in the course of the audit.

Exception reporting. The possibilities of management override will depend, in part, on how employees are instructed to react to managers' requests that some aspects of controls or normal processing procedures be circumvented. As described in an earlier chapter, some companies have instructed employees to formally document any "unusual handling" of a transaction; preprinted forms are provided that request detailed answers to these questions:

—Who made the request that the system be circumvented?

—What type of transaction was involved?

—How was the transaction handled?

—How does the handling of this transaction differ from normal practice?

This manner of exception reporting ensures that you, as well as top management, can review those cases where override occurred, monitor the use of override, and have reasonable assurance that undetected override of the system is unlikely.

Of course, the "reporting of overrides" control could itself be overridden. However, the probability of this occurring can be minimized by setting clear policies whereby responsibility for reporting the circumvention of the system is accepted by employees and by disciplining any parties who do not appropriately comply with such a requirement. An employee's cooperation with a manager is less likely if that employee believes that such cooperation will imperil future employment. Of course, practically speaking, "blowing the whistle" on one's boss is not a popular activity, so some risk of noncompliance with exception reporting will persist, regardless of the clarity with which the entity's policies are set.

Be on the Lookout for Operating Conditions Conducive to Management Override

Certain operating conditions increase the possibility of management override.

Branch operations. In a branch operation where controls are decentralized, the power that can be exercised by the branch manager, including the power of circumventing established controls, can be substantial. In part this is due to more esprit de corps at the branch level than at the entity level, and if competition exists across branches and the manager can persuade employees that "other branches are similarly circumventing controls," the cooperation of employees in the overriding of controls is more likely.

Manner in which duties are segregated. The segregation of duties similarly affects the possibility of management override. In a small operation where the owner-manager assumes a key role in controlling several phases of operations, the possibility of overriding the system without detection is much greater than in an operation where each manager controls only one function in each phase of operations. If one manager authorizes transactions, while other managers have custody and record-keeping responsibilities, the likelihood of one manager's overriding of the system without subsequent detection by one of the others is slim.

Incentive systems for employees. Another facet of operations influencing the possibility of override is the incentive system for the entity. Using the branch manager example, if bonuses are awarded based on reported branch performance, there are greater incentives for favorably biasing reported statistics, and these incentives may encourage collusion, thereby circumventing the designed segregation of duties.

Incentives for third parties. The possibility of overriding controls similarly depends on the incentives of parties with whom business is transacted. For example, if suppliers are dependent on a company for substantial amounts of business, or if business is frequently transacted with related parties, there is the possibility of circumventing such controls as those over purchasing that are designed to prevent kickbacks, through gaining the cooperation of third parties. Third parties with vested interests have been known to create bogus documentation of transactions to facilitate biased reporting and the circumvention of established controls.

These factors that suggest the possibility of management override must be evaluated in order to assess the probability of the control system being circumvented. Several aspects of the entity's control environment will affect how probable management override is; the most important of these is likely to be the overall competence of the employees.

How to Evaluate the Competence of Employees

The propensity of managers to override a control system will depend in part on their understanding of the importance of controls, the risk of establishing a precedent of circumvention, and the ramifications of abusing established controls should subsequent discovery occur; and in part on their basic integrity and professionalism. The control environment of an entity depends heavily on competent management.

Steps a company can take to ensure competence. A company can take overt actions to ensure competence and professionalism by carefully selecting new employees. A formal job description establishing minimum experience, educational, and professional requirements, a thorough substantiation and confirmation of reported credentials, and the requirement of letters of reference from particular types of associates (such as past employers or colleagues in business, rather than only social acquaintances) can be useful employee selection tools.

In some cases an entrance exam is appropriate, and if the employee will have access to assets of high value, a bonding company's check and approval provides additional assurance as to the quality of the individual being considered for employment. Some companies have employed lie-detection tests, and some have even utilized investigation agencies to report on prospective employees. Of course, how well the selection process operates will depend on the quality of the individuals evaluating the applicants:

—Can they discern the difference between relevant and irrelevant experience?

—Do they recognize the different quality standards maintained by various educational institutions?

—Are they reasonable judges of character?

—Do they use good judgment in selecting how to confirm particular qualifications (for example, do they require that transcripts be mailed directly to them from the universities or is a telephone confirmation at a phone number provided by the applicant considered sufficient)?

Once the entry point is passed, questions regarding employee competence are more dependent upon existing training programs, continuing education policies, job manuals, employee turnover, performance evaluation and promotion practices, compensation levels, and prescribed procedures during absenteeism.

How to Evaluate Employment Practices

You can evaluate these practices by reviewing documentation, making inquiries, and assessing how an entity compares to similar entities, i.e., are the employees' skills commensurate with their responsibilities? Interviews with employees can be very effective in providing insight into how well operating and control duties are understood, as well as into employees' attitudes concerning the importance of control duties and the priorities of top management with respect to day-to-day operations.

You should evaluate the competence of employees, identify where risk areas are likely to be, and utilize such information in designing the audit tests for the client. In addition to making a general review of the company's procedures relating to the hiring of qualified employees and to their continued education, you will subsequently test those areas of the control system where reliance is planned; such tests will provide some confirmation as to employees' competence in actually performing their assigned control duties.

Why Clarifying the Company's Policy with Regard to Controls Is Essential to Prevent Loss, Operating Problems, and Defalcations

No matter how competent the employees, if the entity does not establish a clear policy with regard to controls, which stresses the importance of control duties and their relevance to performance evaluations, those employees cannot be expected to conscientiously meet their control-related responsibilities. Priorities are a fact of life, as is the limitation of such resources as time. When operations are busy, overtime is common, and time is tight, the tendency of employees is to give priority to operating duties, to slough off the performance of control duties, and to rationalize that such is the preferred strategy. Of course, whenever controls are ignored or are untimely, the risk of loss to the entity increases and operating problems can go undetected, as can misstatements and defalcations in recorded accounts which, in turn, typically influence future operations.

Unless a company can persuade employees that controls are an integral part of operations, that compliance with designed controls is a key objective of top management, and that through assisting in the maintenance of controls the employees can expect overall operations to be more efficient, including their own job performance, the control system will not work, simply because control duties will receive a low priority relative to operating duties. The effectiveness of controls depends on the care that is exercised in performing control-related duties. If the employees perceive control duties as unimportant, they are less likely to invest the time necessary to gain a clear understanding of such duties or to perform them with due care and diligence.

Nonroutine Processing of Transactions Should Be Documented

If control duties are not understood or are thought to be unimportant, their absence with respect to some transactions is less likely to be noted, resulting in the potential absence of an audit trail for nonroutine transactions or nonroutine processing of routine transactions.

Example. As an example, assume that a company leases a new word processor on a trial basis and that it has never before leased equipment. With no prescribed procedures, the administrative director over secretaries verbally arranged for the machine to be delivered, gave a phone call to the disbursement clerk, and informed the clerk that lease payments would be made out of petty cash over this trial period, so to increase the petty cash balance. If the control environment is weak in the sense that the importance of control duties, compliance with the designed system, and the existence of a complete audit trail are all unrecognized, such handling of a nonroutine transaction might be permitted. The result could well be

—no record of the lease,

—no physical control over the word processor,

—a precedence for other "circumventions" of the check disbursement system through petty cash,

—increased risk exposure and subsequent losses from the maintenance of a large petty cash fund, and

—an overall weakness in the segregation of duties, particularly with respect to present and future leasing transactions.

If, instead, employees were cognizant of the importance of controls and audit trails, they would have raised questions as to how to adequately document this nonroutine transaction. Preferably, despite the temporary nature of the lease, a routinized means of processing such transactions would be developed.

What should have been done. In this instance, the lease payment should have been processed through normal disbursements and the person responsible for physical custody of assets should have been notified of the lease transaction. The lease agreement should have been filed with the department that would typically be involved in arranging loans and financing for the acquisition of equipment. If, for efficiency reasons, such a routine handling of the new transaction was deemed unnecessary, a procedure should exist whereby nonroutine or new transactions are documented in some manner. The exception reporting described earlier whereby management overrides of a system were formally documented should similarly apply to the nonroutine processing of transactions.

Exhibit 5–6

Factors Affecting the CPA's Assessment of the Probability of Management Override

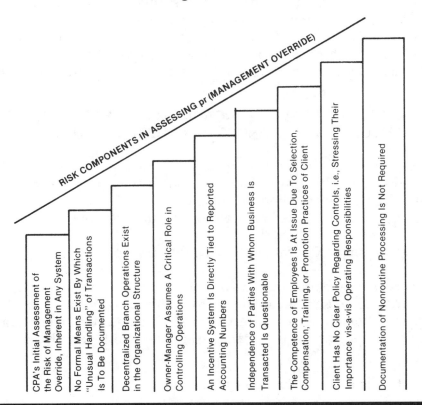

Exhibit 5–6 illustrates the various considerations that contribute to an increased risk of management override. As it suggests, if employees are competent, the importance of control duties stressed, and the documentation of nonroutine processing required, the probability of management override should be low, and the control environment thereby established can be expected to be effective.

The Problem of Overpaid Employees

Ironically, one of the key risk indicators in an entity may well be overpaid, satisfied employees. If an employee is unable to secure a comparable employment position elsewhere, then a much higher likelihood exists that he or she will "go along to get along," thereby facilitating management override.

In numerous settings of control breakdowns, when questioned as to whether they realized the problems at hand, employees by and large admit their knowledge. However, they express concern over being fired, had they reported the situation. Moreover, often times they admit their inability to easily secure a comparable position elsewhere. In other words, a certain "hush money" type of environment can be fostered through excessive compensation practices. Remember the Keating Hearings' revelations as to salary levels of numerous employees of questionable qualifications. One regulator told of how Keating had offered him a lucrative position, apparently hoping to quiet regulatory attention to Lincoln Savings. Hence, when evaluating employees' competence, not only should an evaluator question whether skills are sufficient to handle a particular job, but that evaluator should also ask whether compensation levels are commensurate with such skills.

APPLYING THE CYCLE APPROACH TO DETERMINE WHETHER CHECKS AND BALANCES HAVE BEEN ESTABLISHED

Once assurance is gained that general controls are in place and that the control environment is likely to be effective, you must begin to evaluate the specific controls established by the client or company. One of the more effective means of evaluating specific controls has been termed the cycle approach.

Identify Key Cycles of Operations or Account Groups

Every organization may have its own unique accounting and control system, but it will tend to be similar to all other organizations in terms of the general types of transactions in which it participates which, in turn, can be categorized as general operating cycles. For example, entities will tend to have

—a revenue or income-producing cycle,

—a cost of sales or production cycle, and

—a financing and nonroutine transaction cycle, which operates as a catchall.

Obviously these cycles can be subclassified to provide such detail as whether a particular obligation is to vendors or to employees, or can be augmented to include financial reporting concerns explicitly, rather than considering the event an integral part of each of the cycles, most likely relating to financing transactions. In applying the three-cycle approach, you must identify the account groups affected by each cycle by becoming familiar with the types of transactions in which an entity is involved.

For example, the revenue or income-producing cycle would involve

—the selection of customers,

—the extension of credit,

—the acceptance of orders,

—the filling of orders,

—the billing of credit customers,

—the collection of receivables,

—the handling of receipts from cash sales,

—the handling of returns and allowances, and

—the earning of interest, rental, royalty, and similar income.

These transactions imply effects on the following accounts:

Revenue,
Returns and Allowances,
Accounts Receivable,
Allowance for Doubtful Accounts,
Cash, and
Interest, Rental, Royalty, and Miscellaneous Income.

By grouping transaction types and their related accounts, it is easier to identify similarities across entities and across cycles within an entity, which simplifies the evaluation of controls. Since, in the normal course of business, the business process flows through operating cycles as opposed to through the accounting system, the cycle approach tends to be an effective framework to apply when determining whether control checks and balances have been established for an entity.

Document the Operating Objectives

Once the cycles are identified, you must gain an understanding of the operating objectives of each cycle. For example, the revenue cycle is likely to have the objective of optimizing revenue through adequate customer service, reasonable credit-granting practices, timely billings, sufficient follow-up of old receivables, and good investment and cash management practices. These operating objectives imply control objectives such as ensuring that customers are appropriately approved, as are credit returns and allowances, that the custody of cash and receivables is effectively handled, and that records are complete and accurate as to income-producing transactions. Once the objectives are comprehended, one can proceed to evaluate whether such objectives are likely to be met.

What Could Go Wrong?

An effective way of evaluating an internal accounting control system is to pose the question: what could go wrong? For example, in the revenue cycle

—credit could be granted inappropriately,

—sales could be made to unapproved customers,

—orders could be accepted which could not be filled,

—sales could go unrecorded,

—sales could be recorded inaccurately,

—sales could be recorded twice,

—billings to customers could reflect the errors in sales or create an additional set of errors,

—collections could be mishandled,

—collections could be recorded in error,

—cash sales receipts could be mishandled,

—returns and allowances could be granted inappropriately and/or recorded in error, and

—other income could go unreported or be inaccurately reflected on the books.

As soon as the types of errors and problems that could arise within a given cycle have been identified, this critical question of the means by which such errors and problems are avoided, detected, and/or corrected, can be addressed.

How to Detect or Avoid Errors and Defalcations

There must be a shift from general questions of what could go wrong to specific replies as to how the pitfalls and inaccuracies can be avoided or detected. Obviously, avoiding problems is preferred to merely detecting problems, but at times the former will not be cost/beneficial, and as long as the latter is done on a timely basis, in the normal course of operations, it can result in adequate control over an entity.

Consider the revenue cycle's potential problems or errors:

1. *Inappropriate credit granting could be avoided* by prescribing reasonably effective procedures for evaluating potential customers and by requiring written approval of such credit extensions, so that responsibility is assigned to a particular individual. This tends to motivate those granting credit to comply with prescribed procedures. Inappropriate credit granting could be detected not only through eventual collection experiences and comparisons to competitors, but also through periodically testing for written approvals and documentation of the decision process.

2. *Incomplete or inaccurate recording of sales or returns and allowances* could be avoided by periodically checking for the numerical sequence of prenumbered purchase orders, billings, and credit memos, and by requiring tests of prices and the mathematical accuracy of extensions and totals on the billings.

3. *Handling of collections and other cash receipts* is more likely to comply with prescribed procedures if duties are appropriately segregated.

4. *Mishandling of funds* can frequently be detected through independent bank reconciliation procedures and through customers' feedback.

The specific control can come in a variety of forms, but whatever the form, it should be capable of avoiding possible errors and intentional misstatements or of detecting problems that do occur. Often a control system, by design, will have more than one means of avoiding an error or detecting a past error.

How Much Redundancy Is Desirable: The Issue of Compensating Controls

Due to fatigue, oversight, or intentional noncompliance with a particular control, or due to other inherent limitations in the effectiveness of individual control procedures, errors may not be avoided or may not be detected if only one control capable of addressing what could go wrong were included in a control system. Therefore, system designers will commonly build in redundant controls, in order that a second or third control mechanism might compensate for the ineffectiveness of the primary control procedure. The question of how much redundancy is desirable in a control system is a cost/benefit question. The risk exposure from a potential error will frequently determine whether redundant controls are desirable, although the effectiveness of the primary control will also influence the decision as to whether secondary or even tertiary controls are advisable.

The ability of one control to compensate for another is of particular value to the auditor. In testing controls, those control procedures for which audit trails are available can be selected for testing, and should one control prove ineffective, the testing of a redundant one may nevertheless support reliance on controls (i.e., a reduction of control risk below the maximum level). Furthermore, the potential problems arising from a flaw in controls may be insignificant in their effects, largely due to compensating controls that would be sensitive to material errors. Designed redundancy in a control system has the objective of achieving greater reliability for the system and relates to the engineering and statistical principles of how likely malfunctioning of controls happens to be, what the price would be should the malfunctioning occur, and the cost of compensating for malfunctioning controls. An important consideration in assessing the last issue is whether overlapping controls have an adverse effect on operating efficiency.

BUILDING OPERATING EFFICIENCY INTO CONTROL SYSTEMS

Obviously, operating efficiency is a primary goal of every organization. When control systems are designed, they should dovetail, as far as possible, with operations, in order to facilitate operating efficiency.

"Selling" Controls to Employees

The benefits of control may be understood by employees, but if such benefits are obtained only at substantial cost, particularly in the form of decreased operating efficiency, the control system is unlikely to be effective. Both you and the entity's management should consider how the controls can and have been "sold."

The selling of controls to employees requires an emphasis on the benefits, a clarification of the costs, and, whenever possible, assurance that the employees will not be penalized for decreased operating efficiency that stems from complying with prescribed controls. If employees cannot be motivated to willingly perform their control duties, the problem may well be that operating efficiency was not appropriately considered when the control system was designed.

For example, if all purchases are to be authorized by a single individual who is regularly out of town reviewing new raw material products and enhancing supplier relations, the inefficiency of postponing the processing of a purchase order, the time wasted in confirming that the person who is to authorize the order is or is not available, and the frustration of having no clear policy as to who else may authorize orders, all combine to encourage those employees with related operating responsibilities to ignore the authorization control procedure.

Similarly, if a storekeeper is to account for all materials issued to the production line, but inevitably is a bottleneck in the sense that lines build up and the paperwork for requisitions is excessive, employees will requisition more materials than required simply to avoid subsequent lines. Control over raw materials is thereby lost, and waste is likely to occur.

When such problems occur, the employees should be encouraged to describe why they do not "buy" the controls, in the sense of recognizing them as reasonable checks and balances that could, in fact, lead to operating efficiency. At times, the mere clarification of policy may suffice, such as a listing of who can authorize purchases, who the back-up people are, and who should know where to find these individuals and be able to direct one of them to the spot where authorization is required. With the requisitioning example, an attempt to cut down the paperwork or to utilize two storekeepers to cut the waiting time of employees may effectively eliminate the deterrent to control compliance. By demonstrating an interest in establishing efficient controls, management will more easily be able to sell those controls.

Ensuring Against Circumvention of Controls

Despite a general acceptance of control responsibilities, whenever operating gains are attainable by circumventing controls there is a risk that such circumvention will occur. The design of a control system should explicitly consider such a risk. For example, if employees are expected not to bother to obtain proper authorization, the system should include a checkpoint beyond which processing of the purchase order will not occur without such an authorization. If the purchase orders are returned for such approval, that control probably will not be circumvented in the future.

Similarly, if limits to the amount of raw materials that can be requisitioned at a particular point in time are established, the opportunity for circumventing raw material control by requisitioning excessive amounts of materials is greatly diminished. These explicit checkpoints and restrictive limits can provide some assurance that controls will not be circumvented. Of course, the most effective means of avoiding circumvention is by making the compliance with controls a key objective and responsibility of employees.

Using Performance Evaluations to Ensure That Employees Respect Both Operating and Control Responsibilities

In order to set control compliance as an objective for employees, performance evaluation must encompass both operating and control responsibilities. Management has to demonstrate that to enhance operating performance at the expense of control is unacceptable, by penalizing those individuals who make such trade-offs. An evaluation approach that balances the credit given to operating as well as to control-related duties will motivate employees to comply with established controls.

For example, individuals who are responsible for purchasing activities should be evaluated not only as to their ability to purchase quality raw materials at minimum cost but also as to their performance with respect to control-related duties, including the securing of proper documentation of approval, of the use of competitive bidding procedures, and of the selection of only approved vendors. The party responsible for requisitioning raw materials for the production line should be evaluated on the smoothness with which the production line is able to operate due to the steady and timely availability of material inputs, as well as the gap between goods requisitioned and goods put into production (to penalize for waste and stockpiling of materials) and the extent to which all control-related paperwork was properly completed. Of course, if the control-related duties have obvious operating effects, particularly in the sense of helping the employee to be more efficient, the motivation for control compliance will increase substantially.

Creative Thinking Can Accomplish a Dual Purpose: Better Controls and Greater Operating Efficiencies

Assume that the person who is to authorize purchase transactions has 20 years of experience, knows all the suppliers well, and is aware of their reliability, terms of sale, differential quality, and financial situation. While obtaining approval for purchases to fulfill control requirements, the employee arranging for the purchase receives information as to the likelihood of the order being filled to meet the desired specifications, within the necessary time frame. Problems with meeting commitments, based on past record or based on current financial troubles, can be identified at this point of approval, and the possibility of improving quality and/or price through an alternative supplier or through extended negotiations can be brought to the employee's attention.

In this situation, approval serves a dual purpose—that of control and that of gaining valuable information to make an operating decision. It is essential to secure authorization in such a setting, since both operating and control responsibilities are met through complying with the requirement. The likelihood of not having supplies when needed, of having an unfavorable price variance, or of foregoing a better purchasing opportunity is decreased by complying with what is typically viewed as a control requirement.

If management thinks creatively in designing control duties, dual-purpose controls that offer operating efficiencies when utilized can become commonplace, greatly improving the probability of compliance.

Note: Often, the dual-purpose dimension requires no more than the careful selection of the one who is to perform the control check (e.g., the party who will authorize the purchase) and an expanded job description that encourages that individual to be concerned with operating efficiency (e.g., to consider whether the proposed purchase is optimal, in light of the available information).

In the storekeeper example, if the person issuing raw materials helps to identify substitute materials that are of higher quality and/or are cheaper and of similar quality, making it possible to improve the reported operating performance of the production department, employees are likely to seek such valuable advice by complying with normal requisitioning procedures. Similarly, if the employee obtaining materials understands that without his or her accurate and timely completion of requisition forms the storekeeper may not have an accurate inventory and may therefore be unable to fill future requisitions, resulting in a slow-down if not a halt in production, that employee is likely to recognize the importance of the formal requisition control requirements and will properly comply with them.

The other dimension of a control system, beyond its control and operating objectives, is the timeliness with which controls operate to prevent or detect problems in the normal course of operations. This dimension can be represented as the frequency with which controls are administered.

Determine an Optimum Frequency of Control Activities

While certain controls should be operative at all times, operating efficiency and practicality suggest that the cost of applying all controls in such a manner frequently exceeds any related benefits. In addition, if the controls are perceived by employees to be excessive, compliance with such controls is likely to deteriorate.

Ways to Vary the Frequency of Controls

One means of varying the frequency of controls is by stratifying the types of transactions that are subjected to daily control from those subject to interim checks. For example, purchase authorizations may be required only for orders exceeding a particular dollar amount. However, smaller purchase transactions may be periodically tested by the party authorizing the larger expenditures or by internal auditors. The requirement of a second check signer on disbursements over a certain dollar amount is an analogous variation of the frequency of control that is a common practice.

Earlier it was suggested that one means of avoiding the circumvention of controls was to assign limits to the number of goods that could be requisitioned at one point in time. Such a limitation is effective, if not too extreme. If the limit is too low, requiring completion of formal paperwork on too frequent a basis, employees are likely to become resentful of the control and seek means by which it can be circumvented.

Weigh the Benefits of Frequent Controls Against the Cost

To determine the optimum frequency of control activities, the management of a company should evaluate the cost of the increased frequency of controls relative to its benefit. The cost will be the direct cost of actually performing the control check, as well as the indirect cost of lowering employees' morale and harming operating efficiency, if the frequency of control becomes excessive and cumbersome. the benefits of the increased frequency will be greater control over the dollars of transactions processed and assets under management.

Sampling Procedures and the "Threat Value" of Possible Control Checks

The relative benefit is a critical question, which is often a function of how effective sampling procedures can be and whether the "threat value" of possible control checks motivates employees to competently perform their operating duties in the absence of such checks. A random sample of all small purchase transactions, subject to the same information and general control system, can provide a reasonable basis for determining the accuracy and propriety with which similar transactions are being processed. If the party who records asset disposals and maintains fixed asset records knows that periodically a comparison of such records to physical assets will be made by some third party, this knowledge alone could motivate effective performance of operating duties, even if the comparison is made only once in three years. An annual review may be excessively costly, with no relative advantage when compared to a review at varying points in time but, on average, no more than once in three years.

Factors That Affect Frequency of Controls

Certain routine checks can be performed daily on all transactions, such as a check of the mathematical accuracy of all invoices prior to payment, while other checks, such as a confirmation that customers' interest charges are being correctly calculated by the computer, would be required only when program changes were made or at long intervals of time, to provide assurance that unauthorized program changes had not been made. No need exists, however, to test all computations made by the computer! Sometimes the desirable frequency of control activities is apparent due to observed employee turnover, system changes, variations in business operations, and the general competence of current employees. At other times, operating efficiency will dictate control design. For example, control checks related to production can typically be integrated most effectively at the start, regular breaking points, or end of the production line; to interrupt the production process is neither practical nor cost-beneficial.

Key Factors to Consider When Establishing the Optimum Frequency of Control Activities

The optimum frequency of control activities can be assessed by using a decision framework that integrates

- —operating efficiency concerns,
- —control procedures' effectiveness considerations,
- —sampling alternatives,
- —an accurate understanding of the effectiveness of "threats of possible control checks" as distinct from the actual checks,
- —the plausible effects of changes in the control environment, including personnel and system changes, and
- —an evaluation of the specific costs or benefits to increasing or decreasing the frequency of control, in light of the above considerations.

SYNOPSIS

The recommended approach to designing and evaluating controls, as described in this chapter, entails systematically answering the following questions:

- —Are control and operating responsibilities appropriately segregated?
- —Are all transactions being recorded in the accounting system?
- —Has management created an environment for effective control?
- —Have checks and balances been established?
- —When designing and evaluating controls, has operating efficiency been appropriately considered?

The means of making this approach operational will become apparent as you work through the core cycle chapters which demonstrate the approach in detail, providing you with useful decision aids and suggestions. Before this in-depth cycle analysis, it will be beneficial to consider some available tools of the trade that have been found in seeking the answers to the queries described in this chapter.

6

Six Useful Tools of the Trade—Their Application in the Design and Evaluation of Controls

Dear Sir:

In the affair of so much importance to you, wherein you ask my advice, I cannot, for want of sufficient premises, advise you what to determine, but if you please I will tell you how. When those difficult cases occur, they are difficult, chiefly because while we have them under consideration, all the reasons pro and con are not present to the mind at the same time; but sometimes one set present themselves, and at other times another, the first being out of sight. Hence the various purposes or inclinations that alternatively prevail, and the uncertainty that perplexes us. To get over this, my way is to divide half a sheet of paper by a line into two columns; writing over the one Pro, and over the other Con. Then, during three or four days consideration, I put down under the different heads short hints of the different motives, that at different times occur to me, for or against the measure. When I have thus got them all together in one view, I endeavor to estimate their respective weights; and where I find two, one on each side, that seem equal, I strike them both out. If I find a reason pro equal to some two reasons con, I strike out the three. If I judge some two reasons con, equal to some three reasons pro, I strike out the five; and thus proceeding I find at length where the balance lies; and if, after a day or two of further consideration, nothing new that is of importance occurs on either side, I come to a determination accordingly. And, though the weight of reasons cannot be taken with the precision of algebraic quantities, yet when each is thus considered, separately and comparatively, and the whole lies before me, I think I can judge better, and am less liable to make a rash step, and in fact I have found greater advantage from this kind of equation, in what may be called moral and prudential algebra.

Wishing sincerely that you may determine for the best, I am ever, my dear friend, your most affectionately.

B. Franklin,[1] London, September 19, 1772

The introductory quote describes an approach to evaluating alternatives and reaching a conclusion, which is the essence of evaluating controls.

You should be familiar with those tools that are typically considered useful in the process of designing and evaluating controls. Six tools will be described here:

—internal accounting control checklists,

—flowcharting techniques,

—the "walk-through,"

—computer auditing techniques,

—statistical sampling techniques, and

—risk exposure worksheets.

Each of these topics could by itself provide the subject matter for a book, and in fact several books have been written on the topics of internal accounting control checklists and statistical sampling. The purpose of this chapter is to describe the basic concepts underlying each tool and the situations in which each tool's application can prove to be particularly useful with respect to internal control-related activities. A short case example in which each of the tools is applied will be provided. This background should facilitate both your recognition of settings in which the tools could be usefully applied and your actual field application of the tools in various client settings.

---

[1] Cited by George W. Downs and Patrick D. Larkey, *The Search for Government Efficiency* (Philadelphia: Temple University Press, 1986), pp. 107–108. These authors express indebtedness to Kenneth R. MacCrimmon for this letter.

INTERNAL ACCOUNTING CONTROL CHECKLISTS

To help in evaluating an internal accounting control system, many firms prepare a standardized internal accounting control checklist. Such a form (1) provides a means of ensuring that a comprehensive review of the core set of expected controls for all operating entities is performed, (2) documents findings, (3) serves as a linkage of the tests of control and substantive testing approach for the engagement, and (4) facilitates review of the working papers. While touted for their memory-jogging advantages, the checklists are criticized for their lack of a custom-tailored inquiry approach and their encouragement of rote completion of questions, as distinct from insightful evaluations. To curb the latter problem, firms have changed from traditional itemizing of account-specific control procedures to an objectives-oriented checklist format. If the preparer of the questionnaire understands the objective of various dimensions of a control system, recognizes that such objectives can be reached in a variety of ways, and is encouraged to identify those procedures meeting a particular objective as well as the consequences of no such procedure, that preparer is much less likely to perform the task in a mechanical fashion.

The custom-tailoring problem is similarly addressed by encouraging the adaptation of the standard form to the particular client setting. This may mean the deletion of certain parts of the checklist and the addition of control objectives that reflect control concerns peculiar to a particular client. Often such peculiarities will be due to the industry specialization of the client or to the organizational structure of the client. Some CPA firms prepare industry-tailored internal control checklists to reduce the task of adapting the general form to the client setting. When different controls are established at the branch, divisional, and/or entity level, several control checklists will be prepared for a client, to reflect the various subsystems of control. This approach results in a slightly more tailored approach to the multi-unit client or decentralized organization.

The Basic Structure of Control Checklists

Internal accounting control checklists address the same issues as are considered in the recommended approach to designing and evaluating controls, described in the previous chapter. The segregation of duties, the completeness of data, the attributes of the control environment, the particular checks and balances in the system, and the effects of controls on operating efficiency are all encompassed in the checklists. Typically, the checklist directed at the general environment will be distinct from the checklists per cycle to facilitate the separation of the various sections of the document within the working papers, if desired. In this manner the questionnaire for the revenue cycle, for example, can be filed with the flowchart of the revenue cycle and related control and substantive test results. Even if the questionnaire is not separated into parts, cross-references are encouraged to ease the tie-in to related working papers for the person preparing the checklist, as well as for the reviewers of the engagement.

Within each section of the checklist, a similar structure will be used that

1st—summarizes the objectives of the control subsystem;

2nd—distinguishes between the objectives that are internal accounting control-related and those that are operations-related;

3rd—considers the potential errors if the objectives are not achieved;

4th—summarizes the general types of controls that might meet each objective;

5th—cross-references the flowcharts or other supporting documentation that has a bearing on evaluating which controls are or are not present;

6th—requires an assessment of whether or not an objective is apparently met by the design of the system as well as an evaluation of the effect of such an assessment;

7th—ties into the subsequent test work on controls and the consequential substantive testing effects; and

8th—provides space for an explanation of specific controls in use, resolution of queries formulated during the review process, and extensions of or deletions from the checklist.

Sample Format for an Internal Accounting Control Checklist

Exhibit 6–1 summarizes a useful working paper format for an internal accounting control checklist. Generally speaking, questions on the checklist are worded to solicit a "yes" or "no" response, and a "no" response is expected to initiate follow-up procedures. These follow-up procedures may be merely inquiry and observation procedures, or they may entail the identification of a compensating control. In any case, some explanation of what was done with respect to the "no" response, including the source of any information used in evaluating the effects of the missing control, will be essential in order to document the control evaluation process. If no compensating control is present, the effects of the "no" response must be evaluated, as must its effects on the planned substantive test work for the engagement. The "yes/no" standardization of responses facilitates the review process. Since the "no" response is intended to represent a potential weakness in control, a third response is preferable when particular control attributes are absent due merely to their inapplicability to the client's line of business; that response is N/A and should appear under the "yes" response column if an N/A column is not provided.

One Drawback to the "Yes/No" Approach—and How to Avoid It

One drawback to the standardized "yes/no" approach is the possibility that rather than carefully considering each questionnaire item, the person checking

Exhibit 6–1

A Useful Approach to Structuring Internal Accounting Control Checklists

OBJECTIVE TO BE ACHIEVED

EXAMPLE: Internal Accounting Control-Related: All receipts are to be accurately recorded and deposited.
Operations Related: The collection, recording, and depositing activities are to be performed in an efficient manner.

POTENTIAL ERRORS IF OBJECTIVE IS NOT ACHIEVED

Receipts may either not be recorded or not deposited, or if recorded, the amount, account, or period affected could be in error.

CONTROLS WHICH ARE USEFUL IN ACHIEVING THE OBJECTIVE

WORKING PAPER FORMAT										
Key Controls	Are Such Controls Present?					Are Such Controls to Be Tested for Possible Reliance?		Evaluation of Control after Testing		
								Reliance		
	Yes	No	N/A	Explanation	W/P Ref.	Yes	No	Yes	No	W/P Ref.
Is the handling of cash receipts segregated from the accounting for such receipts?	√				Flowchart CR 1					
Is a lock box utilized for collecting customers' payments?	√				Flowchart CR 1					
Are cash registers used with controlled-access cash register tapes?			√	Cash sales are rare						
Does one person have responsibility for listing cash receipts by mail for subsequent reconciliation to deposits?	√				Flowchart CR 1	√		√		CR 21

the list may be tempted to automatically respond "yes," knowing that, in some sense, it is the preferred and expected response. To avoid this tendency, you should purposefully paraphrase some questions in order to solicit an assortment of "yes" and "no" verbal responses, even though the checklist may document all responses as "yes." For example, if one questionnaire item is phrased like this:

Is the handling and listing of cash receipts segregated from the posting to the sales and general ledgers?

it could easily be revised as follows:

> Does one individual handle and list cash receipts, as well as do posting to the
> sales and general ledgers?

A "no" response to the latter question, with a follow-up inquiry as to how these tasks are segregated, could provide the basis for a "yes" response on the checklist. In this manner, game-playing is avoided, and you are likely to obtain a higher quality set of responses. In the course of the interview you should use the opportunity to enhance the available information base on the client or company's operations, mode of management, attitudes toward and understanding of controls, and overall objectives. This approach can break the monotony of a question-answer session and may well prove useful in evaluating the risk exposure of the client.

Testing Is Required in Order to Rely on Controls

A critical difference exists between a "yes" response on the internal accounting control checklist and the effective operation of such a control in a manner that facilitates reliance on that control for audit purposes. The initial "yes/no" information relates to the design of controls rather than to the operation of controls. The former must be evaluated in all audit engagements, while the latter is relevant only when reliance on controls is planned (i.e., control risk is assessed at less than the maximum level). In order to rely on controls, tests are required to assure that controls are operating as designed and are effective in preventing or detecting errors or misstatements. The reasons for not testing controls may be (1) the poor design of controls, (2) the cost of such tests, (3) the relative low cost and/or effectiveness of substantive tests, or (4) the immateriality of the accounts affected by the controls being reviewed. This discussion assumes that tests of control are a possible alternative to substantive tests whenever controls are well designed. This assumption is valid, provided that the yes/no responses to the checklist are well thought-out by the list's preparer.

For example, suppose you inquire, "Is someone responsible for authorizing purchase transactions over $1,000?" If the response is "yes," the follow-up question required to appropriately complete the checklist is: "What visible evidence of this authorization procedure is available?" If no initials, signature, or similiar verifiable evidence that particular documents have been authorized is available, the appropriate checklist response is "no." In other words, "yes" responses regarding control procedures require that such procedures have an audit trail. The only exception to the requirement that tangible evidence be available to support "yes" responses on internal accounting control checklists relates to the concept of segregation of duties. You never have much more than inquiry and observation procedures available to evaluate whether duties are appropriately segregated, hence a "yes" response in an interview will be reflected as a "yes" on the checklist, unless disconfirming evidence that this was the case happens to come to your attention.

Expanding the Checklist to Cover Operating Control

The internal accounting control checklist will frequently be expanded to consider operating control. You are thereby provided with a better knowledge of client operations, as well as a basis for making comments in a letter to management concerning control.

Note: In preparing such a letter you should be careful to discern the difference between the basis upon which you evaluate controls and the basis used by the client or company. You may stress material effects on the financial statements, while the entity focuses on the cost/benefit justification for controls. In all cases the CPA is obliged to report material weaknesses to management. Internal auditors or system evaluators similarly would want to report material weaknesses. If an immaterial weakness is known not to be cost/beneficial, this fact should either be acknowledged in the letter of comments or that particular control recommendation should be deleted. Of course, the letter of comments with respect to immaterial control weaknesses is purely a voluntary service typically provided by the CPA, so its content is discretionary, other than its possible use as the means for disclosing material control weaknesses and reportable conditions.

Practical Applications for Internal Accounting Control Checklists

For new clients. Internal accounting control checklists are indispensable as a means of becoming familiar with a new client's system of controls. In subsequent years, the checklist need only be updated for changes in the control system. Frequently, CPA firms will nevertheless require that a new questionnaire be completed every three years, as a means of ensuring that changes in the control system are not inadvertently overlooked due to the "marginal update" approach to documenting the controls of prior years' clients.

For smaller clients. The extent to which control checklists are useful for smaller clients will, in large part, depend upon the ease with which the checklist can be adapted to smaller operations. Many firms have developed a separate checklist for smaller clients, focusing on the critical role of the owner-manager. Similar to industry-tailored checklists, these client-size-tailored checklists offer efficiencies to both the CPA completing the form and the CPA reviewing the working papers on an engagement.

Sample special purpose checklist. Exhibit 6–2 provides an example of a checklist directed at the evaluation of owner-manager controls.

Evaluating risk exposure. The checklists are useful not only in gaining an understanding of companies' control systems but also in evaluating companies' risk exposure. As already suggested, the checklists bridge the planning process

Exhibit 6-2

A Special Purpose Checklist: Evaluating Owner/Manager Controls*

Yes	No	Explanation	Working Paper Reference	Owner/Manager Controls
				1. Are the owner/manager's objectives compatible with the auditor's objectives with respect to: a) the revenue or income-producing cycle? b) the cost of sales or production cycle financing? c) nonroutine transactions?
				2. Is the owner/manager competent to perform the management and control duties for which (s)he has responsibility? a) Is accounting information effectively utilized in the management process? b) Can (s)he identify unusual items and differences from expectations? c) Are explanations sought for unusual fluctuations? d) Are such explanations understood? e) Are basic control concepts understood?
				3. Does the owner/manager have a high level of integrity? a) Are past and present business and personal activities consistent with a high level of personal integrity? b) Are business and personal finances and life style such that personal integrity is not being threatened by unusual economic or social conditions?
				4. Is the owner/manager control conscious? a) Does the organizational structure maximize the segregation of duties? (For example, are nonaccounting employees, such as receptionists, used to perform control functions to maximize the segregation of incompatible duties?) b) Are incompatible functions performed by the owner/manager structured to involve other employees, as a check on the owner/manager? c) Does the owner/manager communicate an attitude that controls are important to the entity's employees? d) Are procedures set for handling absenteeism of either employees or the owner/manager? e) Does the owner/manager review activities subsequent to being absent from operations? f) Are employees qualified for their duties? g) Is the owner/manager's authorization required for large or unusual transactions and essential prior to **the release of assets (e.g., prior to payment)**? h) Are controls commensurate with risk? i) Are the owner/manager's duties performed at a point in time when errors can frequently be prevented, rather than merely detected?
				5. Does it appear that the owner/manager has complied with the designed system of internal control?

* Adapted from material presented by D. D. Raiborn, "Auditing Research Monograph #5: Audit Problems Encountered in Small Business Engagements" (New York: American Institute of Certified Public Accountants, 1982).

to the flowcharting and system documentation work, summarizing the changes in plans due to the evaluation of control design or control test results, and describing the substantive test mix that results from the assessment of control risk. To assist in evaluating risk, the internal accounting control checklists will frequently be divided into an overall control environment analysis and a specific control-oriented analysis. The former allows you to evaluate override possibilities, employees' competency, the clarity of control policies, and the extent to which nonroutine processing of transactions is documented. The effects of this evaluation upon specific controls are then intended to be assessed by you as the specific control-oriented checklists are completed. The control environment checklist is particularly valuable as a reminder of what general controls can affect the operation of specific accounting controls.

Evaluating the internal audit function. For clients that have an internal auditing department, the CPA can reduce testing by relying on the work of the internal audit staff, just as the auditor relies on other facets of the internal accounting control system. Statement on Auditing Standards No. 9, "The Effects of an Internal Audit Function on the Scope of the Independent Auditor's Examination," requires that the CPA evaluate the competence, objectivity, and performance of internal auditors as a means of determining the appropriate degree of reliance thereon. (At the time of this writing an exposure draft is pending to revise SAS No. 9. Its content is generally consistent with the checklist.) Exhibit 6–3 provides one checklist that could be used in evaluating the internal audit function.

Exhibit 6–3

A Checklist for Evaluating an Internal Audit Function

Yes	No	Explanation	Attributes of the Internal Audit Department
			1. Is the internal audit department relatively autonomous and independent? a. Does it report to top management, the board of directors, or the audit committee? (Top management means vice-president or higher.) b. Does it give such reports regularly? c. Does it have full access to the company's operations and records to perform an unlimited scope audit (i.e., is it permitted to investigate any aspect of the entity's activities)? d. Is there a separate systems and procedures function that is independent of the internal audit department? e. Are temporary assignments of internal audit staff to a line or accounting function prohibited (including substitution for operational responsibilities of vacationing employees)? f. Are professional staff periodically rotated? g. Are individual internal auditors in a position to be independent with respect to the matters they review?

Exhibit 6–3 (Cont.)

Yes	No	Explanation	Attributes of the Internal Audit Department
			2. Does the internal audit department have a Statement of Responsibility with approved objectives for the department?
			3. Has the organization had an internal audit department for a number of years, providing some assurance of stability and clarity of purpose (the median age of departments is about ten years)?
			4. Is an internal audit schedule covering the scope of internal audit activities established annually? a. Is this schedule approved by top management, the board of directors, or the audit committee? b. Does the schedule reflect an overall audit strategy that is tailored to the critical risk areas of accounting, auditing, and management concern? c. Is the schedule developed in consultation with the organization's external auditors? d. Are a charter, policies, and budgets formalized for the internal audit department?
			5. Does the internal audit department have adequate staffing? a. Are education and business and audit experience of the professional staff commensurate with responsibilities? b. Are professional staff knowledgeable of company operations, processes, and procedures? c. Do minimum requirements exist with respect to education and experience? d. Do the sources of personnel suggest that hiring practices will provide the necessary expertise for the professional staff's needs? e. Do some of the professional staff have public accounting experience? f. Do some of the professional staff hold professional certifications? g. Are professional staff active in professional organizations? h. Is staff turnover at a reasonable level? i. Does the organization try to avoid fixed or limited terms of duty in the internal audit department, i.e., are career opportunities available within the department? j. Are salaries of professional staff competitive? k. Do the professionals engage in continuing education?
			6. Is the internal audit department adequately supervised? a. Are job descriptions formalized? b. Do job assignments reflect normal job descriptions? c. Are up-to-date audit manuals available? d. Are staff properly instructed prior to commencing an examination? e. Is the work of staff members monitored? f. Is appropriate on-the-job training received? g. Are audits periodically reviewed by superiors and by someone not participating in the particular examination? h. Does the review cited in (g) include a review of 1. goals 2. personnel 3. documentation 4. whether innovative techniques like computer and statistical auditing procedures are properly controlled and applied, and 5. reports? i. Are periodic performance reviews required? j. Is the internal audit function centralized with the manager of internal auditing coordinating all internal auditing activities?

Exhibit 6–3 (Cont.)

Yes	No	Explanation	Attributes of the Internal Audit Department
			7. Do the following requirements exist? a. Internal auditors must follow generally accepted auditing standards. b. Written audit programs must be prepared. c. Audit programs are to be modified to respond to current circumstances. d. Audit program steps are to be initialed at the completion of each test procedure. e. All tests are to be comprehensively documented in the working papers, including the detailed procedure applied and the results of such tests. f. Work is to be adequately supported, particularly with respect to the follow-up work and disposition of exceptions. g. A written report, adequately supported by the working papers and following a prescribed form, is to be prepared for each examination. h. Written reports should summarize all significant matters; no management influence will be permitted to suppress the reporting of audit findings. i. The findings and recommendations of the audit are to be reviewed with management on a higher level than the head of the audited organization. j. Audit reports must be regularly distributed to top executives. k. Mandatory reply procedures exist within the company, whereby auditors formally respond to the internal audit department regarding its reports. l. All reports are subjected to follow-up, with an emphasis on the correction of reported deficiencies and the formal responses by affected areas. m. Management relies on the audit reports, encourages corrective action, and regularly provides feedback to the internal audit department. n. All physical facilities are periodically scheduled for review by internal auditing. o. Operational and administrative controls are reviewed on a clerical basis. p. Periodic reports are to be submitted by the internal auditing department to report its progress with respect to the planning schedule and budget.
			8. Are file retention systems adequate? a. Is there a written description of the filing system? b. Are files organized efficiently? c. Is the retention period for working papers sufficient for external auditors' purposes?

In an Auditing Procedure Study of the AICPA entitled *The Independent Auditor's Consideration of the Work of Internal Auditors*,[2] a summary is provided as to independent auditors' consideration of the work of internal auditors:

(1) the internal audit function can affect the assessment of the control environment;

(2) work performed independently by internal auditors can be used to assess control risk and design substantive tests; and

(3) the independent auditors can plan and supervise internal auditors' work as an intrinsic part of the audit process.

Phase (1) links to a departmental review, while both phases (2) and (3) could link to particular individuals or projects in the internal audit department. For the overall internal audit function, an important source of information to a systems evaluator is an external review of quality assurance policies and procedures by other internal auditors, independent auditors, or management consulting firms. These often provide insights concerning the objectivity, competence, and performance of such departments. If organizational status and the quality assurance program provide reasonable assurance of the department's objectivity and competence, detailed evaluation of these traits of individual staff members is unnecessary. If such assurance is not available, then project-specific review of working papers and individual internal auditors may nonetheless provide a sufficient basis to permit the use of specific work by internal auditors.

Quality attributes tied to internal auditing that have been found to track error rates are summarized in Exhibit 6–4.

The checklist as a source of ideas for improving controls and operating efficiency. Beyond the audit setting, the internal accounting control checklist provides an important source of ideas as to how you might advise the client to improve existing controls and operating efficiency. Through the use of careful, in-depth inquiry procedures, you may uncover problems with the structuring of controls, employees' understanding of controls, or the mode of compliance with controls, which over the long term could pose operating as well as control problems. The insights gained can be communicated in a letter to management and can, of course, lead to management advisory service revenue to the CPA firm that provides useful suggestions.

FLOWCHARTING TECHNIQUES

The old adage that "a picture can tell a thousand words" underlies the popularity of flowcharting techniques as a means of documenting various clients' systems of internal accounting control. Often a ten-page memo delineating internal control procedures and information flow can be captured in a one-page flowchart

---

[2] A Joint Study by: American Institute of Certified Public Accountants and Canadian Institute of Chartered Accountants (New York: AICPA and CICA, 1989).

Exhibit 6-4

Descriptive Statistics for Strata Defined by Quality Attributes Tied to Internal Auditing

Rating of Internal Audit Function on a 1 to 9 Scale Where 1 = Very Poor 9 = Excellent	Mean (Standard Deviation) Sample Size	Median (Minimum) Maximum	Average Number of Errors [Overall Assessment of the Client's Internal Control Environment*] Per Engagement for Strata Formed Based on Internal Audit Criterion			Spearman Correlation Coefficient (Significance) [Sample Size] Sum of Total Dollar Error
			Poor (1–3)	Medium (4–6)	High (7–9)	
Comprehensively addressing key financial statement audit risk areas	4.55 (1.71) 97	4 (1) 8	4.71 [6.55] 31	4.29 [7.22] 49	3.24 [7.47] 17	−.04 (.74) [75]
Training, experience and ability to enable management to rely upon the validity of their work?	5.52 (1.42) 98	5 (2) 8	3.33 [6.67] 9	4.72 [6.90] 58	3.55 [7.48] 31	.27 (.02) [76]
Independence (in terms of reporting to an appropriate level of management)?	6.10 (1.80) 98	7 (1) 9	7.78 [6.56] 9	4.63 [6.61] 38	3.29 [7.49] 51	.02 (.89) [76]
Following-up on the disposition of their recommendations?	5.79 (1.69) 98	6 (1) 9	4.36 [6.45] 11	4.79 [6.77] 48	3.49 [7.59] 39	.29 (.01) [76]
Effectiveness in detecting material errors in the financial statements?	4.52 (1.77) 95	4 (1) 8	3.68 [6.81] 31	4.94 [6.94] 48	3.75 [7.63] 16	.06 (.61) [75]

231

Exhibit 6-4 (continued)

Rating of Internal Audit Function on a 1 to 9 Scale Where 1 = Very Poor 9 = Excellent	Mean (Standard Deviation) Sample Size	Median (Minimum) Maximum	Average Number of Errors [Overall Assessment of the Client's Internal Control Environment*] Per Engagement for Strata Formed Based on Internal Audit Criterion			Spearman Correlation Coefficient (Significance) [Sample Size] Sum of Total Dollar Error
			Poor (1–3)	Medium (4–6)	High (7–9)	
Testing the effectiveness of the transaction processing systems?	5.81 (1.71) 98	6 (1) 9	3.91 [6.18] 11	5.23 [6.91] 43	3.32 [7.43] 44	.25 (.03) [76]
Establishing or approving the scope of the work of the internal audit function	5.46 (1.68) 98	5 (1) 8	5.69 [6.54] 13	3.69 [6.98] 52	4.48 [7.39] 33	.06 (.62) [76]
Promptly evaluating and, if appropriate, implementing the recommendations of the internal audit function	5.76 (1.39) 98	6 (2) 8	6.20 [5.80] 5	4.30 [6.79] 61	3.78 [7.78] 32	.15 (.19) [76]
Company Descriptives for Total Sample						
Total revenue	182,577,255 (551,708,868) 260	25,898,000 (1) 4,634,021,000	**	**	**	.47 (.0001) [225]
Total assets	425,794,019 (1,514,025,165) 260	43,686,500 (767,000) 13,591,137,000	**	**	**	.39 (.0001) [225]

Company has Audit Committee 1 = Yes 2 = No	1.53 (.50) 257	2 (1) 2	**	**	**	−.07 (.30) [222]
Overall assessment of the client's internal accounting control *environment*: 1 = Very Poor 9 = Excellent	6.48 (1.28) 260*	7 (1) 9	**	**	**	−.07 (.31) [225]
Total number of errors	5.75 (5.65) 260	1 (3–4) 21+	**	**	**	**
Total dollar errors	3,337,203 (13,774,276) 225	512,000 (3,000) 178,116,000	**	**	**	**

* The overall control environment entails the collective effect of a number of factors on establishing, enhancing, or mitigating the effectiveness of specific policies and procedures. These factors include management philosophy and operating style, organizational structure, audit committees, methods of assigning authority and responsibility, management control methods, and external influences such as monitoring by regulators [AICPA, 1988, SAS No. 55].

** Not applicable

Note: Companies without internal audit departments (165 companies) average 6.56 errors and a 6.17 rating on their overall control environment.

Source: Wanda A. Wallace and Richard W. Kreutzfeldt, "Distinctive Characteristics of Entities with An Internal Audit Department the Association of the Quality of Such Departments with Errors," *Contemporary Accounting Research*, forthcoming 1991.

233

that is easier to evaluate and substantially easier to review or use in becoming acquainted with entities' operations.

Common Flowcharting Symbols

Although standard flowcharting symbols exist and advantages can accrue from some consistency across the profession, many CPA firms have developed their own set of symbols, including their own templates for ease of use, while other firms have encouraged creative flowcharting, as long as it's clear. The result is that flowcharts appear in an endless variety of forms, with diagrams frequently interspersed with flowchart shapes. Exhibit 6–5 illustrates common flowcharting symbols and how such symbols can be tailored for use in flowcharting control systems.

The Basic Structure of Flowcharts

Despite the variety of practices, certain structural rules generally apply to the flowcharting process. For example, information flow tends to move in sequence, from top to bottom and left to right on a flowchart, and distinctions are made as to the form of the information being described (e.g., punched card, magnetic tape, or documents) and the mode of processing (i.e., manual, distributed system, terminal input, or some similar mode). Whenever the linkages are not left to right or top to bottom, arrowheads are required. Information flows across departmental lines are typically identified, as well as the processing and control activities of each department with respect to that information.

Two approaches to flowcharts: their advantages and drawbacks. Individuals differ in their attitude as to whether flowcharts should diagram all primary information flow or should focus on the information trail that leads from the source document to the accounting ledgers. In the former case, the disposition of all four copies of a customer order form, purchase order, shipping form or some similar document is clearly shown in the flowchart, while in the latter case, only the copy that flows into the accounting records is traced. One advantage of the former approach is that a more comprehensive understanding of information flow and company operations is obtained, and often the entity likes to have this type of detailed documentation made available for internal use, subsequent to the initial audit. One disadvantage is the greater difficulty in distinguishing between information flows that have an effect on reported accounting numbers and those that have no such effect.

Key points to keep in mind when using flowcharts. Regardless of the approach that you prefer, a few basic principles are important to keep in mind if the flowcharting tool is to be used to its full potential:

—The simpler the flowchart, the better;
—complexities can be better explained in attached memoranda or on control checklists;

Exhibit 6–5

Flowcharting Symbols

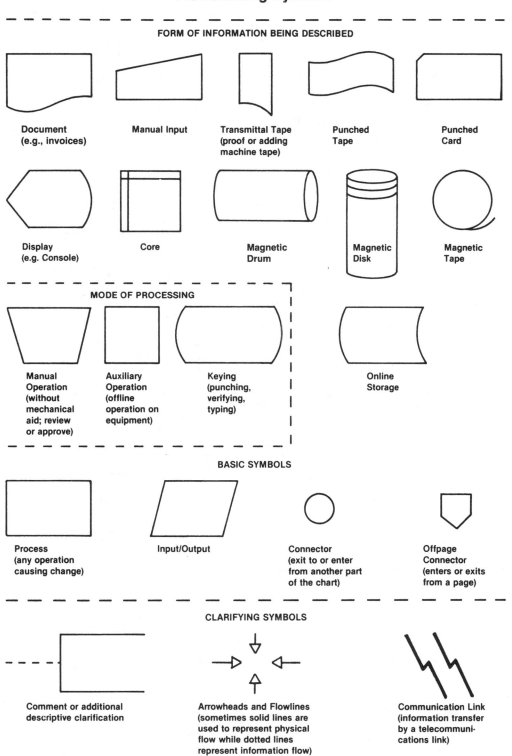

FORM OF INFORMATION BEING DESCRIBED

Document
(e.g., invoices)

Manual Input

Transmittal Tape
(proof or adding
machine tape)

Punched
Tape

Punched
Card

Display
(e.g. Console)

Core

Magnetic
Drum

Magnetic
Disk

Magnetic
Tape

MODE OF PROCESSING

Manual
Operation
(without
mechanical
aid; review
or approve)

Auxiliary
Operation
(offline
operation on
equipment)

Keying
(punching,
verifying,
typing)

Online
Storage

BASIC SYMBOLS

Process
(any operation
causing change)

Input/Output

Connector
(exit to or enter
from another part
of the chart)

Offpage
Connector
(enters or exits
from a page)

CLARIFYING SYMBOLS

Comment or additional
descriptive clarification

Arrowheads and Flowlines
(sometimes solid lines are
used to represent physical
flow while dotted lines
represent information flow)

Communication Link
(information transfer
by a telecommuni-
cations link)

Exhibit 6–5 (continued)

- -

PROGRAMMING SYMBOLS

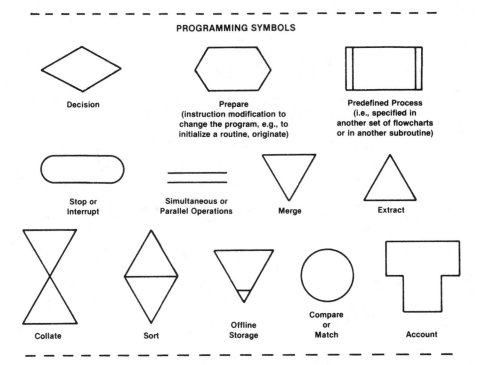

Decision	Prepare (instruction modification to change the program, e.g., to initialize a routine, originate)	Predefined Process (i.e., specified in another set of flowcharts or in another subroutine)

Stop or Interrupt	Simultaneous or Parallel Operations	Merge	Extract

Collate	Sort	Offline Storage	Compare or Match	Account

- -

TAILORED CONTROL SYMBOLS

To distinguish between processes involving assets, accounting entries, or control events, use a consistent marking within the symbol:

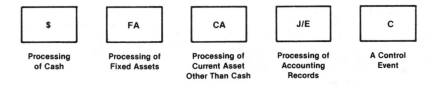

$	FA	CA	J/E	C
Processing of Cash	Processing of Fixed Assets	Processing of Current Asset Other Than Cash	Processing of Accounting Records	A Control Event

To distinguish between original source documents and those that have been authorized and to indicate those documents that are attached to other documents:

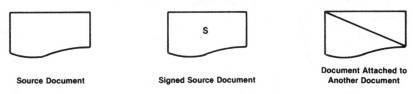

Source Document	Signed Source Document (S)	Document Attached to Another Document

To distinguish between types of files and to signify the manner of filing:

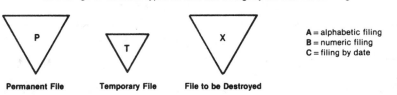

Permanent File (P)	Temporary File (T)	File to be Destroyed (X)	A = alphabetic filing B = numeric filing C = filing by date

Typically:

- *Each vertical column in a flowchart corresponds to an organizational unit.*
- *The name of each document is included within the document symbol.*
- *When possible, the names of persons performing the particular processes are shown.*
- *As the auditor evaluates how the flowchart relates to the internal control checklist, details are recorded as to completeness of documentation, the use of control totals, and the performance of control checks on the flowchart.*

- -

—unless the flowchart is clear to the reader, its comparative advantage as an illustration of the system, as distinct from a mere description in the form of a memorandum, is lost.

—Do not clutter the flowchart:

—a symbol (not to be used sparingly) commonly termed the connector can tie several pages of flowcharts together, providing continuity without clutter;

—otherwise, the usefulness of the flowchart for risk analysis will be significantly reduced.

—While creativity can be useful, remember that the key objective is communication:

—do not use obscure flowcharting symbols or difficult-to-interpret diagrams, and include a key to the flowcharting symbols;

—try to standardize the flowcharting approach applied to various parts of the internal accounting control system being reviewed.

—Focus on cycles rather than on accounts:

—for example, the billing cycle or payroll cycle is likely to be a more useful subject for a flowchart than the cash account;

—only in this manner can the role with respect to control of the various departments in the organization be appropriately appreciated, as well as the interrelated nature of the accounts.

—Prepare the flowchart with the preferences and requirements of the intended reader in mind:

—frequently an overview flowchart without detailed document flows will be sufficient for evaluating certain aspects of the control system;

—even if a detailed flowchart is required, an accompanying overview flowchart will help the reader to understand the overall process before analyzing the detailed processing.

Innovative Ways to Use Flowcharts to Diagram Control Duties and Decision Processes

In addition to being used to illustrate general control systems' operations, flowcharts can be effectively used to diagram specific control duties and decision processes. For example, if one person performs several control-related duties, the nature of which is determined by the particular attributes of the transaction being controlled, a flowchart of that person's duties might prove useful in gaining an understanding of the business.

Such a person might be the employee who authorizes purchases. Typically, when competitive bids have to be obtained, such questions as to whether quantity discounts should apply, whether negotiated terms should be sought, and the lead time allotted for the delivery process are all questions that will vary according to size, type, and timing of purchases. In certain cases, the supporting documentation required for a particular purchase will vary as a function of the mode of ordering—e.g., buy-and-hold purchase arrangements versus telephone orders versus lease-purchase transaction terms. A flowchart that summarizes the task of the employee who authorizes purchases can be a useful addition to the job description manual for that position in the organization.

Decision analysis and its use in planning an audit. While commonly termed a decision tree, a diagram of the possible alternatives faced by a decision maker, the assessed probability of each alternative, and the results of the various choices can be viewed as a type of flowchart. Such a decision tree can be useful in the planning phase of an audit. Essentially, the person in charge of the audit should consider the potential for overreliance and underreliance on the client's control system (i.e., error in assessing the level of control risk), and probability of such errors occurring, and the results of utilizing other than an optimal audit approach. Exhibit 6–6 presents a simple decision tree overview of the auditor's risk exposure and efficiency. A decision tree is read from the furthest branch on the right side. Each of these branches is conditioned by the prior probabilities relating to the various states of nature that can exist, reported to the left of each final branch.

Updating flowcharts and decision trees to reflect system changes. Whenever flowcharts, decision trees, or similar tools are utilized from year to year, occasions will arise when the diagrams will require updating to reflect system changes. Rather than starting from scratch, you should photocopy the original diagrams and make the necessary adjustments on these copies. *Note:* It is important that the original illustrations remain unaltered, in order to provide permanent records of the systems that were reviewed in prior years' engagements.

THE "WALK-THROUGH"

Once you believe you have a basic understanding of the entity's information flows and both general and specific control procedures, as documented via internal accounting control checklists and related flowcharts, an easy means is available by which you can perform a preliminary check as to whether such beliefs are accurate. This check is commonly termed a "walk-through."

What the Walk-Through Accomplishes

As suggested by its name, the walk-through enables you to see whether transactions are processed as expected when you accompany the transactions through the system, or walk through the audit trail generated by some small set of two or three transactions. While far from being a definitive test of operations and the effectiveness of controls, this tool does help you to understand the structure of the internal accounting control system. The technique serves a primary function of "disproving" a checklist or flowchart, since, by design, the small sample is

Exhibit 6-6

An Overview of the Auditor's Risk and Efficiency Probabilities in Decision Tree Format

State of Nature
of Interest to the Auditor

Effectiveness of the Internal
Accounting Control System

- Effective System pr(A)
  - Auditor Correctly Assesses System pr(1)
  - Auditor Incorrectly Assesses System pr(2)
- Ineffective System pr(B)
  - Auditor Correctly Assesses System pr(3)
  - Auditor Incorrectly Assesses System pr(4)

Fairness of the Financial
Statements

- Fairly Stated pr(C)
  - Auditor Correctly Opines on the Statements pr(5)
  - Auditor Incorrectly Opines on the Statements pr(6)
- Not Fairly Stated pr(D)
  - Auditor Correctly Opines on the Statements pr(7)
  - Auditor Incorrectly Opines on the Statements pr(8)

Optimal Mix of Tests of Control
and Substantive Tests for
Correctly Evaluating the
Fairness of the Financial
Statements

- Optimal Mix Includes Reliance
  on Tests of Control pr(E)
  - Auditor Relies on Controls pr(9)
  - Auditor Does Not Rely on Controls pr(10)
- Optimal Mix Includes No Reliance
  on Tests of Control pr(F)
  - Auditor Relies on Controls pr(11)
  - Auditor Does Not Rely On Controls pr(12)

Assessment of auditor's risk of not detecting problems or errors when they exist (States of Nature—B&D): Σ pr(4), pr(8).
Assessment of auditor's risk of detecting errors when none exist (States of Nature—A&C): Σ pr(2), pr(6).
Assessment of auditor's inefficiency (States of Nature—E&F): Σ pr(10), pr(11).

incapable of proving anything at all. In fact, the effectiveness of a walk-through may in large part depend on your ability to be inconspicuous during the walk-through process. Otherwise, the employees may comply with what they know to be prescribed procedures, merely for your benefit, despite the fact that these procedures are not routinely performed. Of course, if the employees were totally unaware of prescribed controls, even a conspicuous observer could gain valuable information from a walk-through.

When to Perform the Walk-Through

The walk-through is a "soft" but important test of your comprehension of both information flows and internal accounting controls. It should be performed as part of the review and evaluation of internal accounting controls, prior to performing any tests of controls. By timing the walk-through in the early part of the audit, you can plan a more efficient audit approach due to your improved knowledge base concerning client or company operations. The comprehension of information flows, types of documentation, methods of filing and retrieval of information, and control procedures facilitates efficient and effective testing procedures.

For example, if you wish to draw a sample of invoices for testing control-related procedures, you will know how such documents are filed (for example, by number, chronologically, by customer, or by geographical region) and the implications of such filing procedures for sample selection and testing. This point is explored in further depth later in this chapter.

COMPUTER AUDITING TECHNIQUES

The advent of computers has not only reduced the clerical burden of clients while increasing their ability to generate useful management information, but has also reduced the clerical burden of auditors while increasing their ability to effectively and efficiently audit clients' records. The auditor's use of the computer as an audit tool can generally be classified as being either

—a generalized audit software application, or

—an auditing technique tailored to a computerized accounting system for the purpose of testing that system.

The use of generalized audit software is primarily directed at testing data, whereas system-testing techniques fall into the second classification. However, the two approaches overlap in that the performance of a system can be inferred by analyzing data, just as the data can be judged as being of reasonable quality if the system is operating effectively.

Generalized Audit Software

The computer's speed and accuracy provide the capacity to perform audit procedures that would be impractical to apply manually. Extensions of invoices, inventories, and payroll, as well as computations of interest, depreciation, and leases can be performed on a 100% basis in a matter of minutes. Furthermore, the aging of receivables, the matching of receivables with subsequent cash receipts, the reclassifying of debit balances, the stratification of receivables for sampling purposes, and the generation of confirmations, ready for mailing, are just a small subset of the kinds of procedures a generalized audit software package is capable of performing. Exhibit 6–7 summarizes the major functions of generalized audit software packages, with an example of a practical application, given each of these capabilities.

In general, software packages are easy to use with a minimum amount of computer knowledge and frequently require no programming expertise whatsoever. The exception is the case where the auditor wishes to perform some function not generally available and chooses to add special-purpose programmed routines. In such circumstances, it is clear that an understanding of programming and the necessary test procedures for new programs is imperative.

Planning Procedures for Computer-Assisted Audit Techniques

For both routine and nonroutine applications of computer-assisted audit techniques, certain conditions and planning procedures are essential to ensure that the techniques are effective and efficiently used. Specifically, lead time must be available for planning, developing, and testing the particular technique of interest. Such planning will include a review by a CPA who is experienced in computer-assisted techniques, as well as an allocation of computer time, files, programs, and EDP personnel by the company or client, as required to perform the selected techniques. The planning must also provide sufficient time for reviewing the output from the technique and performing the necessary follow-up work. Basic problems with available computer time, policies on retaining data files, and the general controls over the computer system can make a planned computer auditing application implausible in the absence of adequate planning. Exhibit 6–8 summarizes those procedures that are recommended for both the planning and the performance of computer-assisted audit techniques.

System-Testing Techniques

One of your objectives is to form a conclusion on the performance of those aspects of the client's or company's control system upon which you intend to rely. One means of testing both accounting processes and internal control procedures that are embedded in an EDP system is through the use of system-testing techniques.

Using test decks. A popular approach involves the use of test decks. This term refers to data supplied by the auditor, to be processed by the entity's system, for the purpose of checking whether the system operates as designed. For example, if an editing check is programmed for the system to detect any exception report debit charges to payables, customers' accounts exceeding stated credit limits,

Exhibit 6-7

Generalized Audit Software Packages: Capabilities and Applications

Major Functions of Generalized Audit Software Packages	Specific Capabilities	Example of Audit Application
The Reorganization of Data Files	Merger of Two Files	Merge two receivables files to provide one population from which to draw a random sample.
• Determining the Attributes of the Data File	Update Function	Add names and addresses to an invoice file to facilitate confirmation procedures.
• Comparing Information to Assess the Consistency with Which Data Is Processed	Sort Function	Put purchase orders in the order of largest dollar amount to lowest dollar amount to facilitate stratified tests that can reflect differing controls over large-dollar orders.
• Discovering Variations Between Two Files	Matching Two Files	Compare the auditor's test counts to the client's inventory file to detect differences.
• Resequencing Data	Generate Files and Save Files	Prepare a copy of client's file for processing to be retained by CPA, to facilitate the mailing of second requests for confirmation. Otherwise, there is a risk that the file will be updated prior to the mailing, and effective control over the data will not have been maintained.
	Summarize Function	Read through the voucher file, combining records with same vendor coding, and prepare a summary record with the totals of these cards for use in confirming payables.
Totalling or Subtotalling Within the File	Levels of Totals	Subtotal accounts receivable by division and report total receivables, to provide a means of evaluating how reasonable the balances are per division as well as a means of confirming that all receivables comprising the ledger balance were processed.
• Summarizing Data		
• Testing Completeness of Data and the Processing of Data		

Major Functions of Generalized Audit Software Packages	Specific Capabilities	Example of Audit Application
Mathematical Computations Involving Information in the Data Files • Testing Mathematical Accuracy • Determining the Attributes of the Data File • Performing Ratio Analysis	Add, Subtract, Multiply, Divide Compute Means, Variances, Square Roots, and Exponents	Verify the net pay calculations for employees' payroll. Compute the average inventory value per inventory classification and review for reasonableness.
Extraction of Records from Data Files • Facilitates Tests of Data Subsets	Apply Procedures to a Subset of Records	Extract only those cost records that are coded Department 010 and subtotal those costs.
Logic Functions • Determining the Attributes of the Data File • Searching Files and Selecting Significant or Unusual Items • Simulating Production Program Logic • Reviewing the Quality and Correctness of Data	Move and Conditional Operations (greater than, less than, equal)	Select and print all receivable values less than zero to allow reclassification of debit balances.
Selecting Records from the File, Using Some Statistical Technique • Selection of Items for Testing	Interval, Random, and Sampling Proportionate to Size Selection Approaches	Select the sample of invoices to be subjected to control testing.
Printing Reports in Formats Specified by the User(s) • Printing of Audit Samples and Confirmations • Automatic Report Formatting	User-Specified Columns, Headings, Subheadings, Totals; Histograms, Bar Graphs, and Graphic Analyses	Prepare an aging schedule, summarizing balances less than 30 days, those 30 days and over but less than 60 days, 60 days and over but less than 90 days, and 90 days and over.

243

Exhibit 6–7 (Cont.)

Major Functions of Generalized Audit Software Packages	Specific Capabilities	Example of Audit Application
Miscellaneous Functions—Utility Programs • Editing of User's Specifications • Multiple-Pass Capability • Editing of Input Files for Data Format Errors • Test Options • Exits to the User's Programmed Routines	Flexible Data Management and Data Analysis	Prior to rechecking payroll calculations, confirm that all of the data fields that are to be complete are, in fact, filled with information.
Statistical Sampling Capabilities • Attribute Sampling • Variable Sampling • Discovery Sampling • Sampling Proportionate to Size • Stop-or-Go Sampling • Cluster or Multistage Sampling	Random Number Tables Random Number Generator Stratification Sampling Evaluation of Sample Results	The sample size required to indicate that controls are in effect, can be determined.
Modeling Capabilities—Timesharing Programs and Microcomputers • Analyze Data in Terms of Meaningful Trends, Relationships, and Product Mix Effects • Present Value and Cash Flow Analyses	Linear Programming Trend-Line Analysis Correlation Analysis Simple and Multiple Regression Analysis	Analytical procedures can be performed on financial statement accounts via regression analysis.

Exhibit 6–8

Planning and Performing Computer-Assisted Audit Techniques

Step 1: Define the audit objective of the technique.

Step 2: Investigate the feasibility of applying the technique:
- what data are available in machine-readable form?
- can such data be easily processed with available audit software?
- is computer time available on the client's equipment and is it compatible with available software, or are alternative arrangements necessary?

Step 3: Plan the application:
- document the data files' format, the technique's approach, and the planned approach;
- obtain feedback from other members of the audit team on means of improving the application.

Step 4: Test the application:
- prepare specification forms for the generalized audit software package;
- run a small sample of data to confirm that the processing is being performed as planned and that the output meets the auditor's needs.

Step 5: Confirm that the necessary files will be available for the time period required for the actual application of the computer-assisted audit technique and that computer time and required assistance by client employees will likewise be available.

Step 6: Maintain control of the actual processing.

Step 7: Analyze the results.

Step 8: Document the application, investigation, follow-up, and findings.

mathematical extensions, account codings, and similar transaction attributes, you can create data that are expected to trigger these editing checks and to generate exception reports. In this manner, controls that would otherwise lack an audit trail can be effectively documented. Of course, the documentation is only for the point in time at which the test deck is processed. Inferences beyond that point in time will depend on the existing controls over programs and program changes.

The test decks will include both normal and atypical data and are intended to check all the important processing and control points of a system. In fact, the test deck approach should begin with the data conversion stage and flow through the system to the final output stage, in order to form a basis for evaluating the system under study. To be effective, test decks should be merged with actual data and be indistinguishable by employees; otherwise you face the risk that the test deck will be processed differently from the routine data received by the system. The test deck is thereby limited in its inferential value when (1) identifiable by employees, (2) submitted for processing by only a subset of the system routine, and (3) capable of evaluating only a subset of the program logic steps. These limitations are aggravated by the practical problems of merging artificial data with actual data and trying to anticipate all possible combinations of data entry or processing errors that are to be detected by the system, in order to test such detection routines. It should be noted, however, that automated methods of creating test decks do exist and are called test data generators.

ITF. Probably the most important uncertainty with test decks is whether the system being tested was, in fact, the system in operation over the period under audit. For this reason, an extended test deck approach has evolved, known as an integrated test facility or ITF.

An ITF essentially is an ongoing test deck approach. Throughout the period, test data are processed and documented as a means of creating a continuous compliance check on the system. The practical problems of an ITF relative to the use of test decks can be substantial. Unless the test data are automatically reversed out of the accounting system in a well-controlled manner, the integrity of the accounting records is threatened. As steps are taken to ensure that actual data are not contaminated, the risk of employees' detection of the test data increases and the effectiveness of the audit technique wanes.

Tagging and tracing. A similar audit technique that avoids the data contamination problem but effectively generates an audit trail for testing is an approach called tagging and tracing. This technique may be used as either a data or a system test routine. Essentially, certain actual transactions are "tagged" and as they proceed through the system, a data file is created that traces the processing through the system and permits you to subsequently review that processing.

Concurrent processing. In addition to tagged transactions, a data file might automatically be created for certain classes of transactions to facilitate your review. This technique is termed concurrent processing. An example might be the generation of an exception report every time a disbursement check is cut for more than $50,000, or every time a pay rate change is initiated. These data files, which can then be tested for propriety, simplify the application of audit-testing procedures. This approach relies on your ability to interact with the client during the design phase of the system; without such interaction it is unlikely that the integration of automatic audit-related data files and documentation will be possible—or economical to implement.

Parallel simulation. An alternative approach to auditing a system, called parallel simulation, uses the auditor's computer system for testing. The primary logic of the auditee's computerized edit and control checks and processing routines is replicated in a program created by the auditor. Data that were processed by the auditee's system are reprocessed through the auditor's program to determine if the output obtained matches the output generated by the auditee. Certain deviations will be expected due to the replication of only a subset of the auditee's program; however, such variations should be easily explained, permitting you to focus on real control or processing problems.

Program code checking and flowchart verification. This audit technique is similar to an audit procedure whereby you review the program logic in detail (a technique known as program code checking or, when automated, as a flowchart vertification routine) as both techniques, if tailored, would require indepth knowledge of programming. However, generalized audit software exists for capturing the primary processing logic of a system. Hence, if this less tailored approach to simulating a program is sufficient, you could apply parallel simulation and yet not be acquainted with programming, beyond identifying the key processing logic that is to be included in the program for testing purposes.

Mapping and controlled processing or reprocessing. When programming expertise is available, mapping can be applied, in conjunction with controlled processing or reprocessing. These terms, as well as the other system-testing techniques described herein, are defined in Exhibit 6–9. In addition, the shortcomings of the various techniques are delineated.

SPECIALIZED AUDIT SOFTWARE

Due to limitations in GAS, specialized audit software has been developed, including such applications as:

- programs to map the logic of an application program and
- programs to capture significant events while application programs are running, such as a concurrent monitor that records all interrupts of an application.

Exhibit 6–9

System-Testing Techniques—a Synopsis

Technique	Description	Shortcomings
Test Deck (Test Data)	Input data containing normal and atypical data are processed by the clients' system to trigger logic routines to provide evidence that processing and control checks are operating as expected.	• Program tested may not be the one used by the client over the period under audit. • Different programs could nevertheless generate the same output for a test deck. • All of the important logic of the program may not be effectively tested due to practical problems in generating test data.
Integrated Test Facility	Concurrent processing of test data with live data by the client's system, on a continuous basis, to test the system's performance.	• The above shortcomings hold, except that the continuous basis of ITFs reduces the risk that a program other than the one being tested was in operation during the period. • Client data may be destroyed or contaminated in the course of processing and adjusting out the test files.
Tagging and Tracing and Concurrent Processing	Client data are marked or classes of transactions are identified that will trigger the creation of an audit data file that documents the processing of and control checks on that data at various points in the processing, for use in auditing the system.	• All of the important logic of the program may not be effectively tested by the tagged transactions. • If the client can identify tagged data or the points at which data files are created, the test could be effectively circumvented.
Parallel Simulation	An auditor-created set of application programs is used to simulate the client's processing functions on a set of data and results are compared to the client's output.	• Inferences cannot be drawn beyond the particular data set that is analyzed. • Mere comparability of input and output does not necessarily imply the comparability of the processing logic.
Program Code Checking and Flowchart Verification	Detailed analysis of the client's process code, possibly with the assistance of a software routine that can generate a logic flowchart.	• Requires programming and flowcharting expertise, is time consuming, and tends to be inefficient. • Human, software, and practical limitations exist with respect to the thoroughness and accuracy of a line-by-line review of a program code.

Exhibit 6–9 (continued)

Technique	Description	Shortcomings
Mapping and Controlled Processing or Reprocessing	Logical paths in a process are identified, with an emphasis on paths that have and have not been crossed in a particular application; then under the control of the auditor the client's system is used to process or reprocess data to authenticate the consistency of the client's current or past output with expected and actual output from that program.	• Requires programming expertise. • Malicious code could be effectively camouflaged in prior processing by the client. • The exceptions noted will tend to be limited to those that are expected.

Problems include expense of development and adaptation to systems change. Models are being developed to identify structural changes so that the auditor need only modify audit procedures where changes occur.[3]

Concurrent auditing techiques, including the previously described Integrated Test Facility (ITF), Snapshot and Extended Record (SER), and System Control Audit Review File (SCARF) techniques, have been applied to advanced systems. The approaches help in creating systems, training, and may well aid in developing a new generation of GAS.

Expert Systems

Expert systems can be viewed as a type of audit software increasingly applied in the field. As examples of such systems, consider EDPXPERT[4] developed to assist in auditing general EDP systems and AUDITPLANNER,[5] used to assess materiality. Exhibit 6–10 reprints an article that introduces the topic of expert systems and provides examples of applications. To extend that discussion, consider QUESTOR,[6] which evaluates the internal audit department's role in the organization, measures of resource availability, and measures of performance, focusing on the company, department, and internal audit director.

---

[3] Yair Wand and Ron Weber, "A Model of Control and Audit Procedure Change in Evolving Data Processing Systems," *Accounting Review* (January 1989), pp. 87–107.

[4] J. V. Hansen and W. F. Messier, "A Knowledge-Based Expert System for Auditing Advanced Computer Systems," *European Journal of Operations Research* (September 1986), pp. 371–379.

[5] P. Steinbart, "The Construction of a Rule-Based Expert System as a Method for Studying Materiality Judgments," *Accounting Review* (January 1987). Note that C. E. Brown provides "Accounting Expert Systems: A Comprehensive Annotated Bibliography," *USC Expert Systems Review* (Spring–Summer 1989).

[6] Arun Sen and Wanda A. Wallace, "An Expert Systems Assistance to Internal Audit Department Evaluation," *Expert Systems With Applications* (An International Journal, Pergamon Press) forthcoming in 1991.

Exhibit 6–10

Expert Systems in Auditing: The State-of-the-Art

by John Chandler
University of Illinois

I. Overview

One of the most controversial questions in business today is the long-term impact of artificial intelligence (AI). The most common realization of AI research has been the expert system. Many expert system applications are in the hard sciences: medicine, geology, and petro-chemistry. But what is happening in auditing with respect to AI and expert systems? What does the future hold? This article addresses these two questions. First, however, the general characteristics of an expert system are described and the proper role of expert systems in the AI field is explained. A review of the research and development activities in the auditing field is then presented, followed by a discussion of the potential of expert systems for auditing.

II. What is an Expert System?

The term artificial intelligence (AI) brings many bizarre impressions to mind from HAL in "2001: A Space Odyssey" to chess-playing computers. The real issue lies in the difficulty of defining intelligence, real or artificial. But, be that as it may, artificial intelligence is the study of all forms of intelligence, human or otherwise. Furthermore, it examines how computers can be made more useful to human decision making. These goals do not imply replacing human decision makers, but rather studying how to improve judgments by analyzing models of how decision makers think and by building systems to augment decision making.

Early AI research efforts attempted to build models of the basic information processing functions of humans such as vision, speech, memory, and decision making (for example, Ernst & Newell, 1969). The idea was that by building models of these basic processes, one could then combine them to form a complete model of human information processing (HIP). Although these models provide valuable insights into HIP, when they were applied to specific decision making situations, however, they had serious problems. It became apparent to the AI community that decision making was made up of not only efficient information processing mechanisms, but also of knowledge about the decision environment. Hence, a movement began to develop mechanisms to represent and capture this knowledge resulting in what is now called expert systems.

One of the first key findings that researchers discovered in developing expert systems was that the amount of knowledge that a human possesses, about even the smallest decision, is immense. Furthermore, the more general the decision, the broader the base of knowledge and the less structured the relationships among the items of knowledge. This made representing decisions very difficult and acquiring the corresponding knowledge almost impossible, leading researchers to attack very narrow decision environments where the relevant

Exhibit 6–10 (continued)

knowledge was of a concentrated nature. The "expert" can be characterized as an individual producing high quality results in minimal time, usually employing heuristics and insights gained from experience (Hayes-Roth, 1983). Using experts as models, however, has problems because human expertise is not usually evaluated objectively and there is controversy over the definition and importance of subjective criteria. Also, there are differing opinions as to the existence of consensus among experts (Joyce, 1979 and Einhorn, 1976).

The central element in an expert system is the knowledge base. It is a collection of facts and relationships about the decision environment under scrutiny (called the knowledge domain). This knowledge can be represented in many alternative methods, but the most common form is the production (or IF-THEN) rule. Knowledge is represented in a conditional format: IF a given condition exists THEN take a certain action. It should be noted that any method only represents the system builder's ("knowledge engineer's") external perception of the expert's knowledge and does not imply that the expert actually represents knowledge, internally, in that format.

Expert systems operate in an interactive mode with decision makers. The system asks for information about the specific decision situation from the individual and then either makes a suggestion or asks for more data. The system's response may include not only a final recommendation, but also intermediate conclusions, chains of reasoning, and explanations.

The heart of an expert system's processing is called the inference engine. This software applies the human's input to the existing knowledge base and may involve updating probabilities, realigning relationships, evaluating hypotheses, restructuring data or logic, and so on. How it performs these tasks is a function of the knowledge representation format and the knowledge engineer's assumptions about information processing. But the decision maker (the use of the expert system) does not have to worry about these details.

The process of developing an expert system follows an evolutionary pattern; that is, one is continually revising previous versions of the system as a result of new knowledge, further examples, or changing decision making strategies. The first step in building an expert system, however, is probably the most critical; choosing an appropriate decision to support. Too broad a decision can lead to an intractable system. Too narrow a decision can lead to a simplistic system, not worth the effort to build.

After choosing a decision, the most difficult step must be performed; representing the knowledge of decision makers. There is no prescribed method for accomplishing this task, but all depend on decision makers eliciting accurate descriptions of their current or past thought processes. Because people cannot explain exactly how they make a decision, only what they perceive, one is never sure that the knowledge and decision processes that the knowledge engineer has captured within the expert system are accurate or complete.

The third step is essentially never ending, it is the refinement step. The initial expert system is now tested by the decision maker. Ideally, real world examples are used to validate the results and reasoning of the system. Any discrepancies between the system and the expert are noted and used to redesign

Exhibit 6–10 (continued)

the system for another round of tests. The process never ends because decision needs will change, decision makers may use different decision processes, and new data may become available. At some point in time, the expert will be satisfied with the quality of response from the system and put it into use.

III. Expert Systems in Auditing: Goals

Given that the development of an expert system may take several person-years (or more) and that the decision that it supports may be very narrow, then why are such systems built? There are both research and practice goals for constructing expert systems. How auditors make decisions has been an important research topic in auditing (see Libby [1981] and Ashton [1982] for critical surveys). Most of the techniques employed, however, have examined the actual decision making process as a "black box," i.e., focusing on how final decisions (outputs) are affected by various forms of information provided (inputs). Expert systems offer an approach for opening up the black box. Insights into the interactions and processes of human decision making may be found by examining and testing the expert system.

Expert systems can also provide a powerful research tool. Because of the computer program nature of expert systems, decision situations can be replayed, modified, and analyzed many times. Sensitivity analysis can be performed on the various assumptions of the model (e.g., relationships and probabilities) to determine the limits and usefulness of the model. Other techniques become static after the decision situation has been captured, whereas expert systems can be used dynamically.

There are also several practical uses of expert systems. The ultimate use of an expert system is on-the-job decision support. This can range from automatically collecting data and recommending courses of action (such as in geology or oil exploration) to interactively leading the human through an efficient path of analysis (such as in medicine). In all cases the human is still left with the task of making the final decision. One benefit is that the human may not have to waste time collecting and evaluating unnecessary data, the expert system can request only relevant data. Another benefit is that the expert system will attempt to link related data items to maximize their impact on the decision. And finally, the expert system can act as a reminder to the human of data to collect, questions to ask, or decisions to make in the audit. The formulation of a hypothesis has been shown to have significant effect on what data decision makers look for, how they evaluate new data, and the correctness of their final decision [Elstein et al., 1978; Biggs and Mock, 1980].

A more long-term practical benefit of expert systems involves the training of non-experts. By capturing the decision rules of experts, expert systems can lead to a more consistent approach to making audit decisions and to teaching how to make audit decisions. In the medical profession, some rule-bases are being used as textbooks for advanced diagnosis classes in medical schools. A similar use could be made in universities and in-house training in accounting firms. The computer program nature of expert systems also allows novices to

Exhibit 6–10 (continued)

see the effect of their own decision choices and compare them to those of the experts.

IV. Expert Systems in Auditing: The State of the Art

The first expert system in an auditing environment was developed by Dungan and Chandler [1981]. They studied the auditor's evaluation of a client's Allowance for Bad Debts for commercial clients, using the AL/X system developed by Michie [Paterson, 1981], a rule-based system. Rigorous validation tests were applied to the prototype system. Insights into the decision making process also resulted from the study [Dungan, 1983].

At about the same time, Hansen and Messier began a study of EDP control evaluation using an expert system approach [Hansen & Messier, 1983]. They also employed the AL/X system. Because the scope of the decision environment is greater than other studies, the resultant rule base will be much larger and more complex. They are currently engaged in validation and have a significant portion of the rule base built.

A different form of expert system analysis was used by Bailey et al. [1985]. Their system, TICOM (The Internal Control Monitor), performs an analysis of the flow of documents and effectiveness of controls. It suggests additional controls and identifies potential weaknesses. They are currently adding an intelligent analyzer (i.e., expert system) that will evaluate the output of TICOM.

Braun and Chandler [1983] are investigating the auditor's determination of the Allowance for Bad Debts in the health care industry, in particular with respect to hospital audits. This project is using the AL/X system to develop a prototype expert system. They are also testing the viability of using "rule inductance" software as an initial step in constructing the knowledge base of an expert system. Such software analyzes examples and attempts to discover structural relationships among attributes of the examples. This study is using ACLS (Analog Concept Learning System) [Paterson and Niblett, 1982].

Biggs joined the Hansen and Messier team in a continuation of the study of EDP auditing [1985]. The current study is focused on the analysis of the decision making processes followed by computer audit specialists. A characterization of the steps and strategies employed in EDP audit analysis is one of their goals.

In a more practical vein, Willingham and Wright [1985] have recently been developing an expert system to aid in the audit of the collectibility of bank loans. Wright used the MI development system, spending a year at Peat, Marwick, Mitchell and Co. The system is currently being field tested. The goal is to have it operational in 1985 for use by PMM auditors in the field. This is the first truly practical project to date.

Two recent Ph.D. dissertations at Michigan State University are broadening the scope of expert system research in accounting and auditing. Steinbart developed an expert system to study the nature of materiality [1984]. Gal is examining internal control in the revenue cycle [1985].

It should be noted that, of the above eight research projects, all but two

Exhibit 6–10 (continued)

(Gal and Steinbart) were funded by the Peat, Marwick, Mitchell & Co. Research Opportunities in Auditing Program. PMM is also attempting the first commercial application as a result of the Willingham and Wright study.

V. Assessment of the Future of Expert Systems in Auditing

This area is still in its infancy, but growing rapidly. The viability of expert systems in the auditing and accounting field has been demonstrated, but the practicality has yet to be proven. The Willingham and Wright study should provide some important results and insights.

Recent technological advances in both hardware and software should make practical applications more feasible and more easily developed. Many of the above research projects were accomplished with developmental software that had to run on mainframes. This makes development awkward when using experts because the interface is slow, tedious, and unnatural. Many of the projects also used prototype or educational versions of the knowledge based systems. The current expert system development environment, however, includes personal computers, user-friendly software interfaces, and knowledge based systems that are commercial quality. These factors will have a tremendous impact on the ease of knowledge acquisition, system refinement, and operational feasibility.

From a research perspective, more rigorous testing needs to be done on the existing expert systems. Studies comparing the results of expert system research to the more traditional HIP methodologies must be conducted. A key question is whether the effort expended in the construction of expert systems produces more cost-effective models of HIP or the resulting decisions than earlier approaches. Also, more "live" data needs to be made available. Expert systems are created from real decision situations and, thus, researchers and developers need to have access to such data or the people (experts) who generate it. Peat Marwick is to be commended for their leadership in this area.

With respect to practical applications, we are only now starting to get close. But a first area of use could well be in training. Here the goal is to demonstrate different chains of reasoning, the impact of judgments, and the importance of evidence to novice decision makers. A much less precise system is needed here than for those developed for field use. Development time is also much faster. Through the use of such systems in a simulation mode, the novice decision maker may become an experienced decision maker more quickly. Research has found the experts can also improve their decision making by using and examining expert systems.

Expert systems can potentially aid in many areas of auditing. In general, expert system applications can be categorized as planning, analysis, and design [Hayes-Roth, 1983]. A planning concern of auditors is the design of the audit program. Scheduling scarce resources into many concurrent tasks under the pressure of competitive fees makes this a prime area.

Analysis and diagnosis applications probably have the potential for widest use. Many research projects are examining analytic review to assist in identify-

Exhibit 6–10 (continued)

ing problems in an organization. A second area is internal control evaluation. This judgment is complicated by the number of controls, complexity of interactions, and the subjectivity of control. A third area of the audit process is the final review in which all of the evidence must be evaluated together.

A relatively new area involves continuous auditing where the operations of the organization are closely monitored, especially in a computer-based environment. The continuous auditing system collects data on the organization's activities and reports exceptions to management. The determination of when exceptions have occurred, what caused them, and what to do about them are all appropriate for expert systems.

A final area of application for expert systems is in design, i.e., suggesting changes to the organization. The internal control evaluation mentioned above can be extended to identification of possible new controls or elimination (or rearrangement) of existing controls. Another design application involves the analysis of analytic evidence. Such analysis can indicate deficiencies in the system, whether other auditing tests should be performed, and what types of tests to perform.

References

Ashton, R. H., *Human Information Processing in Accounting*, Sarasota, Florida: American Accounting Association, 1982.

Bailey, A. D., Jr.; Duke, G. L.; Gerlach, J.; Ko, C.; Meservy, R. D.; and Whinston, A. B., "TICOM and the Analysis of Internal Controls," *Accounting Review*, LX, 2, 1985, pp. 186–201.

Biggs, S. F.; Messier, W. F., Jr.; and Hansen, J. V., "A Study of the Predecisional Behavior of Computer Audit Specialists in Advanced EDP Environments," ARC Working Paper No. 84–1, University of Florida, 1985.

Biggs, S. F. and Mock, T. J., "Auditor Information Search Processes in the Evaluation of Internal Controls," Working Paper 2-80-6, University of Wisconsin, Madison, February 1980.

Braun, H. M. and Chandler, J. S., "Development of an Expert System to Assist Auditors in the Investigation of Analytic Review Fluctuations," research project for Peat, Marwick, Mitchell & Co., 1983.

Braun, H. M. and Chandler, J. S., "Development of Knowledge-Based Expert Systems to Model Auditors' Decision Processes," research project for Peat, Marwick, Mitchell & Co., 1981.

Dungan, C. W., "A Model of an Audit Judgment in the Form of an Expert System," Ph.D. Dissertation, Department of Accountancy, University of Illinois at Urbana, 1983.

Dungan, C. W. and Chandler, J. S., "Development of Knowledge-Based Expert Systems to Model Auditors' Decision Processes," research project for Peat, Marwick, Mitchell & Co., 1981.

Einhorn, H. J., "Expert Judgment: Some Necessary Conditions and an Example," *Journal of Applied Psychology*, Vol. 59 (October 1974), pp. 562–571.

Elstein, A. S.; Shulman, L. E.; and Sprafka, S. A., *Medical Problem Solving: An Analysis of Clinical Reasoning*, Cambridge, MA: Harvard University Press, 1978.

Ernst, G. W. and Newell, A., *GPS: A Case Study in Generality and Problem Solving*, Academic Press, 1969.

Gal, G., "Using Auditor Knowledge to Formulate Data Model Constraints: Expert Sys-

Exhibit 6–10 (continued)

tems for Internal Control Evaluation," Ph.D. Dissertation (in progress), Department of Accounting, Michigan State University, 1985.

Hansen, J. V. and Messier, W. F., Jr., "Continued Development of a Knowledge-Based Expert System for Auditing Advanced Computer Systems," Preliminary Report submitted to Peat, Marwick, Mitchell Foundation, 1984.

Hayes-Roth, F.; Waterman, D. A.; and Lenat, D. B. (eds), *Building Expert Systems*, Addison-Wesley, Reading MA, 1983.

Joyce, E. J., "Expert Judgment in Audit Program Planning," *Studies in Human Information Processing in Accounting*, Supplement to the *Journal of Accounting Research*, Vol. 14, 1976, pp. 29–60.

Libby, R., *Accounting and Human Information Processing*, P-H, 1981.

Paterson, A., *AL/X User Manual*, Intelligent Terminals Ltd., Oxfordshire, 1981.

Paterson, A. and Niblett, T., *ACLS User Manual*, Department of Computer Science, Class Note, 8 CS347/397d, University of Illinois at Urbana, Fall 1982.

Steinbart, P., "The Construction of an Expert System to Make Materiality Judgments," Ph.D. Dissertation, Accounting Department, Michigan State University, 1984.

Willingham, J. and Wright, W., "Development of a Knowledge-Based System for Auditing the Collectibility of a Commercial Loan," research proposal, 1985.

Source: John Chandler, "Expert Systems in Auditing: The State-of-the-Art," *The Auditor's Report* (Volume 8, Number 3, Summer, 1985), pp. 1–4.

Rules used in expert systems tend to be of the if/then variety, such as

if < director of internal audit is evaluated by controller > then < indep company > prob = 10

This implies that other than the controller should be the evaluator if independence is to be maintained (i.e., 10 = high risk). In substance, such questions would pattern the type detailed in the earlier exhibit on evaluating internal audit.

The general architecture for QUESTOR is depicted in Exhibit 6–11. The overall inferencing should have four major components: the evidence combination mechanism; the procedure for selecting the top ranked hypothesis; the query selection mechanism that directs the user-system dialogue based on the top ranked hypothesis; and a top level controller for selecting the partitions within the rule base. Using the evidence obtained, the system should rank conclusions or hypotheses; and select a query, the response to which is likely to support the top ranked hypothesis. An example of the knowledge base would be the following measure of resource availability:

a rule-of-thumb in past literature is an average standard of one internal auditor per 1,000 employees.

The use of a decision tool such as QUESTOR is one facet of an evaluation of internal audit, as described in Exhibit 6–12 (where iad represents internal audit department).

Exhibit 6–11

The Architecture of the QUESTOR System

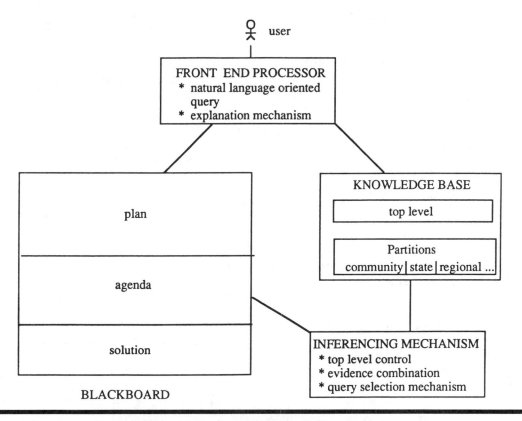

STATISTICAL SAMPLING TECHNIQUES

The number and complexity of daily transactions of businesses and not-for-profit entities preclude the auditor from performing a 100% examination of operations. Instead, you are interested in a means of examining some subset of a period's transactions, for the purpose of drawing inferences for all of the period's transactions. The means by which this can be accomplished is through sampling, and two possible approaches are commonly applied: statistical and nonstatistical sampling.

How Statistical Sampling Works

Statistical sampling means that the sample of transactions to be tested is selected and evaluated using mathematical theorems of probability to arrive at quantitative measures of (1) the likelihood that the sample results will reflect the larger group's characteristics, and (2) the accuracy with which the sample results are measured. In contrast, these mathematical measures cannot be calculated

Exhibit 6–12

Event Diagram of Internal Audit Department Evaluation

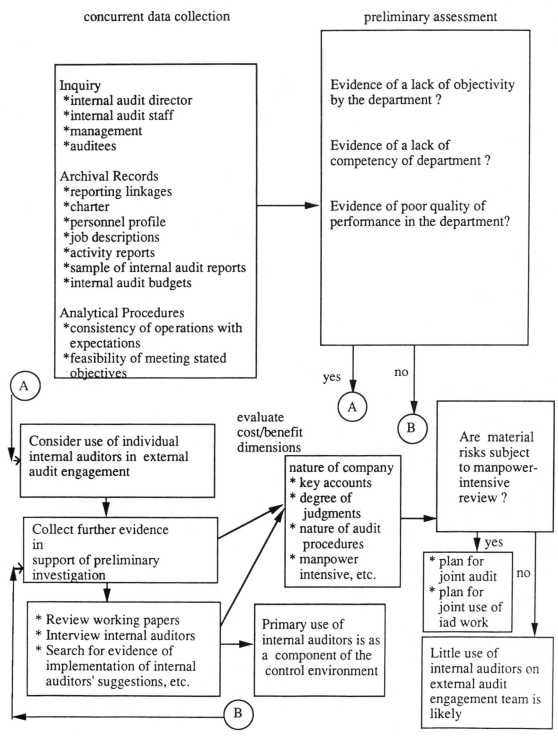

for nonstatistical samples because there is no available assurance that the underlying assumptions for the mathematical theorems to hold have been met. It is nevertheless advisable to select and analyze nonstatistical samples in a manner that parallels that process used for statistical applications, as a means of gaining some insight as to the quality of the inferences that can reasonably be drawn from the nonstatistical process. A study of the big 8 firms and four other large accounting firms found that the following policies were in place in the mid 1980s:

Policy	Number of Firms
Statistical Sampling strongly encouraged or required	5
Statistical Sampling preferred	3
Statistical or non-statistical at the auditor's discretion	3
Non-statistical Sampling preferred	1
	12[7]

The basic concepts underlying statistical sampling are intuitively appealing and have, most likely, guided CPAs since long before the technical concepts of statistical sampling entered the auditor's professional literature. The objective of the selection process is to ensure that every unit or transaction that corresponds to a larger set of transactions on which the auditor wishes to draw inferences has an equal chance of being selected. Underlying this objective is the presumption that the auditor

(1) has identified the set of data about which (s)he wishes to generalize—commonly termed the population;
(2) has defined the sampling unit or individual item to be tested from the population; and
(3) has confirmed that the sampling unit is both feasible and practical and corresponds to the population to which inferences are to be drawn.

Identifying the population. The presumption is important in order to appreciate the context of random selection methods. If you wish to test compliance with internal accounting control you must first identify the population of interest, in light of a specific audit objective. For example, if the objective is to test that no cash disbursements were made without adequate documentation, the population of interest is the total set of disbursements, whereas, if the objective was to test that receiving reports were obtained prior to making disbursements to suppliers, the population would focus only on disbursements to suppliers of goods that are received, as distinct from disbursements for services.

Defining the sampling unit. The objective of the audit test should make the relevant population obvious. A classic example of objectives directing audit

---

[7] Barry E. Cushing and James K. Loebbecke, *Studies in Accounting Research #26: Comparison of Audit Methodologies of Large Accounting Firms* (American Accounting Association, 1986), p. 25.

procedures is provided by the distinction between vouching and retracing. To test that all recorded sales are valid, vouching is appropriate; in contrast, to test that all sales were recorded, retracing is required. The sampling unit would be recorded sales in the first case, whereas the sampling unit in the latter case would be the initial document representing a sale such as the customer's order.

Feasibility considerations. The thought process includes feasibility considerations. For example, if the cash disbursement procedures are documented by check copies that are filed with their corresponding vouchers and, presumably, the documents supporting those vouchers, then the voucher is a more practical sampling unit than the check copy. To accept such a substitution of sampling units would require the auditor to test that all checks had at least one corresponding voucher number. Whether selecting a statistical or a nonstatistical sample, (s)he would need to be concerned about the objective of sampling, the population of interest, the unit to be sampled, and the practicality of the planned approach. The difference in planning involves the exact means by which items are selected and sample sizes are computed.

The selection method. In order to ensure that every possible combination of sampling units has an equal probability of being a part of the sample, you should use random numbers (whereby the sampling units are defined to correspond to a random number table or generator) or a systematic sampling technique (whereby every nth item is selected, with several random starts). If, in contrast, nonstatistical approaches are taken, such as walking up to a file cabinet and selecting 20 vouchers from the drawers, there is no assurance that the selection will be random. Human factors, such as the auditor's height, the tendency not to want to stoop, and a right-hand inclination, can all unintentionally bias the selection method.

For this reason, you should consider a statistically random selection method even if nonstatistical sampling is being applied. It is imperative to recognize that these sampling approaches do not preclude getting large dollar coverage, testing particular points in time that are of interest, or focusing on items thought to have a greater probability of error. These factors merely define the population(s) of interest, e.g., those expenditures over $10,000 and those under, those expenditures made in the month of July (when the disbursements supervisor was on vacation), or employee receivables in addition to tests of accounts receivable.

The selection methods can also be altered to reflect specific auditor concerns. For example, stratified sampling approaches whereby higher-dollar items have a greater probability of selection can be applied, or if systematic selection is planned and the order of filing of documents is found to be related to the item of audit interest (for example, vouchers are filed by customers, in geographical subsets, and each of these factors might affect the ability of a systematic selection-based sample to equitably represent the entire population), a change to a random number table approach would be appropriate.

The audit objective and sampling unit will tend to direct you in your (1) selection from a number of available sampling approaches, (2) definition of an error, (3) determination of sample size, and (4) interpretation of findings. This discussion intentionally focuses on attribute sampling, since it is the type of sampling plan that is most applicable to the testing of internal accounting controls.

Attributes sampling. An attributes plan gets its name from the focal point of the sampling procedure: an attribute or characteristic of a sampling unit, rather than a dollar amount orientation. While the attribute of interest might be whether the dollar amount was accurately footed, it can just as easily be a qualitative attribute, such as whether or not a particular item has been approved. The objective of an attribute approach is to estimate the rate of occurrence or nonoccurrence of the attribute in the population. Often the rate of occurrence is an error rate, defined as the number of times a deviation from prescribed control procedures is observed. The deviation is an error in the sense of compliance, yet may result in no dollar error on the financial records of the client. The idea, of course, is to infer how likely dollar errors are, in light of the internal accounting controls and the extent of compliance with these controls. All statistical terms can be thought of in layman terms, as to what one is trying to quantify. For example, in regard to test of control, precision refers to the accuracy or range within which an error rate can be measured. The error rate is the frequency of deviations from the prescribed internal control procedures. One cannot expect the sample's error rate to be exactly the same as the error rate of the population.

Reliability is the assurance that identically constructed sample plans, performed repeatedly, should obtain consistent results.

Precision for substantive tests is commonly stated in dollars and is related to materiality. One common guide used in two-tailed tests is to set precision at one-half of materiality, as then the difference in the limits of confidence intervals will represent materiality, reinforcing the concept that book values within those intervals will be acceptable. Accuracy in attributes tests relate to error rate ranges.

Reliability tends to be related to the reasonableness assurance concept and is referred to as confidence level. Reliability and precision are interdependent and inseparable. In fact, to cite precision without citing reliability is meaningless. Auditors use tests of detail and analytical procedures. The tests of detail can range from testing 100% of the detail in a particular account, to scanning. The evidence required to form an opinion is a matter of audit judgment, but the ideal sample size must balance the cost to auditing with fairness of presentation.

When considering attributes sampling, it is important to recognize that the upper precision or error limit is not the same as a complement of the percentage of effectiveness of controls, as a single sample is only one piece of the pool of evidence for the control structure. The gaining of an understanding of controls, walk-through, and related control risk assessment procedures all lead to the eventual evaluation of controls.

The audit judgments affecting testing of controls will be discussed in a later chapter; for the purposes of this discussion, assume that the statistical planning requirements of defining objectives, deviation conditions, population, corresponding sampling unit, and selection method have been met. Your next task is to select the sample size.

Sample size determination. The required number of sampling units is affected by the rate of error that can be tolerated in the sample, the expected rate of error in the population, the size of the population, and the acceptable risk level of the auditor (i.e., what probability can exist that you have, in fact, overrelied on internal accounting control or under-estimated the level of control risk?). To demonstrate how these considerations affect sample size, Exhibit 6–13 was prepared. The selection of values for these parameters that affect sample size requires audit judgment. Rules of thumb, however, have been discussed in the auditing literature. Specifically, if you plan to assess control risk at less than a maximum level, the tolerable error rate should not exceed 20%. If limited reliance is anticipated, a tolerable rate from 11% to 20% would be typical; for moderate reliance, a 6% to 12% rate; and for substantial reliance, a 2% to 7% rate.[8] The key element in the decision is the auditor's assessment of control risk. If planned to be at less than the maximum level the tolerable rate will likely range from 2% to 7% (based on AICPA guidelines), whereas slightly less than the maximum level suggests a tolerable rate from 11% to 20%. The tolerable error, other things being equal, moves inversely with sample size. If certain conditions remain constant, a 2% tolerable rate will require a sample size of 149. If the error frequency is expected to be high and the tolerable error rate is low, then an auditor may need to shift from a sampling approach to a 100% examination or re-evaluate the efficiency of the planned audit approach. In other words, substantive testing may be more cost beneficial than testing of controls. The dominant risk level accepted by CPAs is 5%, providing a 95% probability (confidence level) that estimates from the sample correspond to the population's characteristics; however, practice does vary, typically ranging from 1% to 20%. The expected population deviation rate must be less than the tolerable error rate for the sample. It should be estimated, based on (1) the auditor's knowledge of client operations, (2) the client's internal accounting control system, (3) past experience with testing controls, and (4) recent changes in the client's system or personnel. In a new client setting, a pilot sample of 30 to 50 items could be drawn as a basis for making estimates necessary for sample size determination. The rule-of-thumb of 30 to 50 stems from the Central Limit Theorem which predicts that many observations will tend to have a distribution approaching normality. The advantage of such a distribution is that its mean or average value is likely to be a meaningful estimate. Typically, the population is sufficiently large that no adjustment to the sample size is required.

Both computer programs and statistical tables are readily available for your use, so it is unnecessary in this overview to discuss the underlying computations

---

[8] AICPA, "Exposure Draft: Proposed Audit Guide, Audit Sampling" (March 1, 1982), pp. 26–27.

Exhibit 6–13

What Affects Attribute Sample Sizes and How Much?

Factors Affecting Sample Size	Quantification* of Effect on Sample Size
Tolerable Rate of Error As the Tolerable Rate ↑, Sample Size ↓	As the tolerable rate moves from 2% to 8% the sample size drops from 149 to 36, if a large population size with an expected deviation rate of zero and a 5% chance of overreliance is assumed. From 2% to 4% and from 4% to 6%, the sample size halves itself and then the decline slows down.
Expected Rate of Error in Population As the Expected Rate ↑, Sample Size ↑	As the expected rate of error in the population moves from 0% to 2%, sample size climbs from 59 to 181, almost doubling per percentage point, if a large population with a tolerable rate of error of 5% and a 5% chance of estimating control risk at too low a level.
Population Size As the Population Size ↑, Sample Size ↑, Only Slightly Beyond a Population Size of 4,000	As the population size grows from 50 to 500, the sample size grows from 45 to 87 and then merely climbs to 93 for a 100,000 population, assuming an expected error rate of 1% and a tolerable error rate of 5%.
Acceptable Risk Level As the Acceptable Risk ↑, Sample size ↓	As the acceptable risk of estimating control risk at too low a level moves from 1% to 10%, the sample size declines from 165 to 77, if a large population size with an expected deviation rate of 1% and a tolerable error rate of 5% is assumed.

* These descriptions were adapted from the "Exposure Draft: Proposed Audit Sampling," American Institute of Public Accountants (March 1, 1982), since published.

and statistical theories for the determination of sample size. While tables appear in various formats, the following excerpt demonstrates how easy they are to apply in computing sample sizes.[9]

5% Risk of Setting Control *Risk at Too Low a Level*	*Tolerable Rate*	
Expected Population *Deviation Rate*	*5%*	*10%*
1%	93	46
2%	181	46

If you designate 5% risk, an expected population deviation rate of 2%, but a tolerable error rate of 10%, you would select a sample of 46. This sample size reflects an expectation of only one error in the sample. If more than one error is found, the tolerable error rate will be exceeded.

An example. Assume you are testing whether or not cash disbursements are properly authorized. Specifically, you are examining whether checks are signed by both authorized check signers. A total of 10,000 checks have been written. You decide that control risk will be sufficiently low if this control procedure does not fail more than 6% of the time (i.e., this is the maximum error rate the auditor can tolerate). A 90% confidence level is sufficient. The estimated true error rate in the population is 1%. An examination of a table produces a sample size of 64 with one deviation permitted to achieve the tolerable rate of 6%.

To use the formula approach, we must revisit the notion of one-tailed and two-tailed tests since 8% confidence is unacceptable. We must focus on how to reconcile the right half of the two-tailed curve to a one-tailed perspective. Since only an upper-limit is desired, to use a two-tailed formula, we will convert 90% to 95%, convert the 6% upper precision level to a 3% maximum per tail, and presume that only 1.5% or half of this is expected to lie in the upper-tail. This permits a calculation as follows:

$$\frac{(1.96)^2 \, (.015) \, (.985)}{.03^2} = 63.07$$

Sample evaluation. This leads to the concept of sample evaluation. Assume that a sample of 46 was drawn, using random numbers, whereby voucher numbers were tied to the last five digits in a column on the random number table, and two

---

[9] Ibid, p. 93.

errors were found when the tests were performed. Again, tables are readily available to determine the implications of the sample result.[10]

5% Risk of Setting Control Risk Too Low	Actual Number of Deviations			
Sample Size	0	1	2	3
45	6.4	10.1	13.3	16.3

A sample of 46 with two errors implies a maximum population error rate of 13.3%, rather than the desired 10%, at a 95% level of confidence (i.e., the reliability of this statistic is such that only 5% of the time, given this sample result, would the population error rate exceed 13.3%). In such a situation, you can (1) expand the sample size if you continue to expect the 10% maximum rate, believing that the sample of 46 items was unrepresentative, or (2) perform additional substantive tests in lieu of relying on the controls that were tested.

Now, assume that 64 sampling units, mentioned in describing sample size, have been examined and none of the items lack evidence of proper authorization. This means a zero error for an occurrence rate of zero in a population of 10,000 and a one-tailed reliability level of 90%. Keep in mind that we wish to draw a one-tailed conclusion as to the upper precision limit. Given zero errors and a sample size of 60, the upper limit is 3.8%. Since the sample size was actually 64, it is slightly better than this if you wanted to interpolate. However, given 3.8% is well under the 6% tolerable rate, the sample evaluation provides evidential support of the auditor's control risk assessment. The auditor may actually reduce the assessed level of control risk further, now that an upper limit has been quantified at 3.8% (rather than the tolerable rate within the original audit plan of 6%).

The sample result must be evaluated both quantitatively and qualitatively. The quantitative evaluation for a test of control determines the error rate, and the qualitative evaluation determines the type and severity of any errors.

In all cases, consideration should be given to the effectiveness of other control procedures in serving as secondary or compensating controls. If the error rates are higher than acceptable, the substantive testing will need to be increased, or its timing will have to be shifted to the balance sheet date. In performing tests of control, the auditor should also watch the deviation rate.

Evaluating samples may also pose practical problems. For example, assume

---

[10] Ibid, p. 95.

that in testing customers' orders on an ith, or interval, basis, the auditor discovers a customer order to which no shipping documents are attached. Upon investigation, he or she finds that the customer was never billed. Does this constitute an "error?" Should the next customer order that is "matched" with a shipping report be selected in lieu of the former?

Advantages of Statistical Sampling over Nonstatistical Approaches

While the approach to describing an attribute sampling application has been rather cursory, the coverage is intended merely to demonstrate the ease of use and the intuitive appeal of statistical sampling tools. In fact, a large variety of sampling approaches are available, including some that provide two-sided estimates of the population error rate—e.g., at a 5% risk of setting control risk too low, the error rate lies between 7% and 9%. The appropriate technique will depend on the auditor's objectives. However, each statistical sampling approach shares numerous advantages over nonstatistical approaches.

(1) There is an objective basis for estimating sample size and for evaluating sample results.
(2) Probability estimates quantify the population error rate at a set level of reliability.
(3) Risk is explicitly controlled in the sampling approach and a measure of sampling risk is thereby provided.
(4) Requiring, at the planning stage, a formal assessment of factors known to affect sample size selection avoids the problems that could arise if such issues were not considered in a nonstatistical approach.
(5) The formal objective approach ensures an efficient sample size and a measure of the sufficiency of the evidence collected.

While nonstatistical sampling is widely used, the statistical sampling alternative will frequently be cost-beneficial in light of these advantages and the ease of use of such techniques (particularly with the advent of computers, as well as readily available tables for the auditor's reference). You should utilize this efficient, objective tool to test internal accounting controls whenever it is practical to do so.

HOW TO USE RISK EXPOSURE WORKSHEETS FOR DESIGNING AND EVALUATING CONTROLS

In designing controls, in evaluating the cost-benefit picture for the adoption of new controls or the elimination of existing controls, and in assessing the overall risk exposure from existing weaknesses in control, risk exposure worksheets can prove to be a valuable tool. Whether it is termed a formalized risk exposure assessment or a step in an overall cost/benefit evaluation, the worksheet addresses the critical objective of estimating both the worst case and the likely case of exposure. The general concepts of cost/benefit analysis are well known to auditors, as they are an implicit part of capital budgeting and similar investment analyses.

The direct and indirect costs that will be incurred as a result of the event, be it an acquisition of a piece of equipment or the failure of a control, are compared to the incremental benefits of the event relative to other possible events. The net benefit can either support the selection of equipment or control procedures or, if negative, can support a decision not to select that particular alternative. Costs and benefits that do not change as an event occurs are irrelevant to the analyzing of the net benefit of the investment. Both quantitative and qualitative considerations are to be assessed, including the effects of uncertainty on underlying estimates. In assessing risk, numerous information services are available. For example, if political risks posed by a client's international operations are of interest, you might reference Frost & Sullivan's *Political Risk Yearbook*[11] which annually addresses countries' economic, social, and political setting, such as the likely influence of international debt or protectionism policies. A sensitivity analysis as to when the decision to adopt some alternative would be reversed is useful in evaluating the importance of underlying estimates to the decision process. Given the diversity of qualitative and quantitative characteristics that are likely to influence the cost/benefit analysis of various controls, as well as the wide range of possible compliance conditions with related probability profiles, a useful analysis approach is to convert such characteristics to some common denominator. The most effective measure is typically dollars. The idea is to identify dollar categories that are sufficiently distinctive to make differences of opinion by those evaluating controls unlikely.

Quantifying Risk

Two dimensions of the risk exposure form related to control weaknesses are

(1) the expected error or loss from one occurrence, and
(2) the frequency with which this one occurrence is likely to be observed.

A common approach to quantifying these dimensions, initially applied in the evaluation of computer systems, is to set up a table with a wide range of values by using some power (i.e., exponent) such as 2, 5, or 10. The use of powers ensures substantial gaps between categories but permits the categories to reasonably correspond to the size of the entity being analyzed. Exhibit 6–14 provides examples of plausible tables that reflect powers of 2, 5, and 10 for both the magnitude of error or loss and the frequency of occurrence. These tables are easily applied to a calculation of the risk exposure from a particular occurrence. For example, if the magnitude of the expected error or loss from an unauthorized purchase order is assessed to be in the $5 category and is expected to occur five times per day, the calculation would be

$$\$5 \times 5 \text{ times per day} \times 260 \text{ business days} = \$6,500.$$

---

[11] Home office for Providers of Political Risk Services: Frost & Sullivan, Inc., 106 Fulton Street, New York, N.Y. 10038.

Exhibit 6–14

Quantifying Risk

Magnitude of Expected Error or Loss from One Occurrence

For Use by Small Operation			For Use by Large Operation
$1	$1	...	$1
2	5		10
4	25		100
8	125		1,000
16	625		10,000
32	3,125		100,000
64	15,625		1,000,000
128	78,125		10,000,000

Frequency of Occurrence

16 per day	625 per day	...	10,000 per day
8 per day	125 per day		1,000 per day
4 per day	25 per day		100 per day
2 per day	5 per day		10 per day
1 per day	1 per day		1 per day
once in 2 days	once in 5 days		once in 10 days
once in 4 days	once in 1 month		once in 3⅓ months
once in 1 week(+)	once in 4 months		once in 3 years(−)
once in 2 weeks(+)	once in 2 years		once in 28 years(−)
once in 1 month(+)	once in 10 years		once in 278 years(−)
once in 2 months(+)	once in 50 years		virtually impossible
	virtually impossible		

The real problem is uncertainty in selecting across categories. What if you believe that there is some risk that a $3,125 error will occur once in four months? In other words, the error would occur three times per year. That assessment implies

$$\$3,125 \times 3 = \$9,375$$

risk exposure on an annual basis. Hence, two exposures are estimated to arise from unauthorized purchase orders.

Sample Risk Exposure Worksheet

To facilitate an analysis of the range of the risk exposure for a particular accounting control, a worksheet is recommended on which all of the possible risks can be summarized. Exhibit 6–15 provides such a worksheet. After completing the relevant boxes, you should try to narrow the uncertainty in the two factors to a subset of columns or lines on the worksheet. The perusal of the worksheet

Exhibit 6–15

Risk Exposure Worksheet

Internal Accounting Control Weakness under Evaluation:

_____

Nature of Cost/Benefit Characteristics:

_____
_____
_____

Possible Risk Exposures:

Magnitude of Expected Error or Loss	Frequency of Occurrence								
	Once in					Times per day			
	10 years	2 years	4 months	1 month	5 days	1	5	25	125
$15,625									
3,125			$9,375						
625									
125									
25									
5					$6,500				
1									

Worst Case of Exposure $_____
Expected Exposure $_____
Further Actions Recommended _____

_____
_____

would then permit an assessment of the range of the risk, as well as your expectations. In Exhibit 6–15, if it was determined that no loss over $1,000 would occur without detection due to some secondary control over disbursements, then the maximum exposure if the two completed blocks included all possibilities would be $6,500. Obviously, worksheets with the upper righthand corner blocks filled and deemed to be probable would represent high risk exposure where adjustments to the control system are likely to be cost/beneficial.

Other Risk-Related Considerations

In using a risk worksheet and evaluating subsequent actions with respect to internal control recommendations, you should document the explicit considerations in deriving the cost and frequency parameters, as well as those factors that were purposefully excluded from the analysis. For example, the low turnover of personnel, prior years' tests of control results, and qualitative concerns like the effect on the control environment of an undetected error may all have been relevant considerations. This description of an auditor's thought process (or of management's thought process) will facilitate the updating, improvement, and comprehension of past and present risk assessments.

In considering the frequency of problems as well as the benefits, you must be careful in indentifying what could go wrong and in identifying the nature of the controls that are intended to prevent and/or detect such problems. For example, is a primary or a secondary control operative? Are controls sequential or parallel in operation? Do controls overlap, are they redundant, or is the operation of a control independent of the operation of other controls? The answer to such inquiries will suggest the frequency of the problem, the likelihood of large errors or occurrences going undetected, and, most importantly, the optimality of the current system relative to possible changes to the system. Some redundant or overlapping controls may be dispensable, i.e., eliminated in the interest of operating efficiency, with only a negligible effect on the client's risk exposure. Often, there are compensating controls that can be expected to reduce the risk exposure from control weaknesses.

Tips for Making Risk Analysis Operational

Useful tips in making risk analysis operational include the five listed here:

(1) a group of decision makers, with reasonable consensus on the selection of values from Exhibit 6–14, should be identified;

(2) intangible assets and qualitative considerations in cost/benefit applications must be incorporated when assessing risk;

(3) the role of limited resources should be explicitly considered in making suggestions for control;

(4) decision makers should be encouraged to consider the fact that a "no risk" state is not likely to be optimal; and

(5) risk analyses can be applied incrementally, for analyzing one control at a time, and for evaluating combinations of controls.

A CASE EXAMPLE ILLUSTRATING HOW ALL SIX TOOLS OF THE TRADE ARE USED IN PRACTICE

To illustrate the application of the six useful tools of the trade described herein, the payroll system of a client will be analyzed.

The Facts of the Case

Assume that you have the following general understanding of operations:

Every other Friday, Jack, a payroll clerk, reviews the payroll department files to determine that all the names listed are current employees, and he prepares time cards for a two-week period. A timekeeper distributes these cards every other Monday and regularly observes the punching of the time cards. The foreman reviews and approves the time cards at the end of each day, initialing the normal hours and, when applicable, initialing the overtime hours. A plant supervisor is responsible for approving the foreman's time card. The foreman prepares a summary of normal and overtime hours worked, in duplicate. The copy of this summary is forwarded to Joan, a second payroll clerk, along with the time cards.

After computing the normal and overtime hours and comparing them to the summary prepared by the foreman, Joan obtains the information from the payroll files concerning employment status, wage rates, and payroll deductions, all of which are updated as needed, based on information from personnel. Joan computes gross and net payroll and prepares the payroll register.

Jack verifies that gross and net pay are calculated correctly and that the payroll register foots and cross-foots. The payroll supervisor is then responsible for approving the payroll.

The EDP department prints the payroll checks and produces a report of the numerical sequence of checks written and the total dollars of gross pay, net pay, and each type of deduction. This summary report is tied into the payroll register by the payroll supervisor.

A manager from the treasurer's department supervises the stamping of the check signatures and then delivers the checks to the cashier's department. Employees pick up their payroll checks at the cashier's department, where they are required to present their company identification card and are asked to sign a sheet indicating their receipt of the check. Any checks that are not claimed within two weeks from the payroll date are forwarded to the treasurer's department for follow-up.

Preparing the Internal Control Checklist

To formalize this understanding of the client's payroll system, you may prepare an internal control descriptive memorandum. In addition or in lieu of such an approach, an internal control checklist is often used. Exhibit 6–16 exemplifies a typical payroll-related control checklist. The descriptive memo did not explicitly address questions 1(f), 2, 6, 7, 8, 9, 10, 11, 12, 13, or 15. Hence, the control checklist ensures that certain pertinent aspects of control are not overlooked. Assume that inquiries resulted in "yes" responses to each of the items in Exhibit 6–13 except for #6 and #12. Although payroll is periodically compared with employees' payroll records, it has not been company practice to also compare payroll to personnel records. Item #12 is not applicable since the client has no internal auditing department.

Preparing the Flowchart

Now you are in a position to illustrate the payroll system of the client. Based on the initial memorandum and the additional information obtained from using a control checklist, a flowchart can be prepared. The flowchart presented in Exhibit 6–17 would be cross-referenced to Exhibit 6–16 to support and clarify the "yes" responses. Note that Exhibit 3–17 distinguishes between signed (S) and unsigned

---

Exhibit 6–16

An Internal Accounting Control Checklist for Payroll

> OBJECTIVE TO BE ACHIEVED

Authorized payroll is accurately processed and appropriately recorded. This process is done in an efficient and timely manner..

> POTENTIAL ERRORS
> IF OBJECTIVE
> IS NOT ACHIEVED

Fictitious employees could be paid, improper amounts could be distributed, or accounting records could be incomplete or in error.

Are Such Controls Present?			Working Paper Reference	Key Payroll Controls
Yes	No	Explanation		

				1. Are written authorizations required for
				    (a) new employees?
				    (b) employee terminations?
				    (c) changes in pay rates?
				    (d) payroll deductions?
				    (e) overtime?
				    (f) adjustment forms for erroneous deductions, severance pay, vacation advances and other variations from normal pay procedures?

				2. Is there a separation among those maintaining employment records, those authorizing payroll changes, those preparing payroll, and those disbursing payroll checks?
				3. Does an approved time card, job ticket, or attendance sheet support each payroll check?
				4. Are clerical operations in the preparation of payrolls checked in the following manner: (a) Extensions and totals of time records recalculated?

Exhibit 6–16 (continued)

					(b) Rates of pay verified? (c) Gross earnings calculated? (d) Deductions calculated? (e) Net pay calculated?
					5. Is the total net pay of the checks prepared calculated and tied to payroll records?
					6. Does some independent employee periodically compare payrolls with employment records?
					7. Does some independent employee periodically compare payroll with hours worked and quantities produced?
					8. Is an imprest payroll bank account used?
					9. Are dollar limits established for payroll checks and printed on the face of the checks?
					10. Are time limits established for cashing payroll checks and printed on the face of the checks?
					11. At payroll distribution is employee identification verified?
					12. Does internal auditing periodically perform surprise pay distributions?
					13. Is accounting control maintained over unclaimed pay?
					14. Are unclaimed paychecks in the custody of an employee with no other cash responsibility?
					15. Are tests made periodically for duplicate payroll checks?
					OPERATING CONSIDERATIONS: Are available opportunities for the use of mechanized or computerized processing being used to their potential?
					Potential Management Letter Suggestions: _____ _____ _____ _____

Exhibit 6-17

Payroll System Flowchart

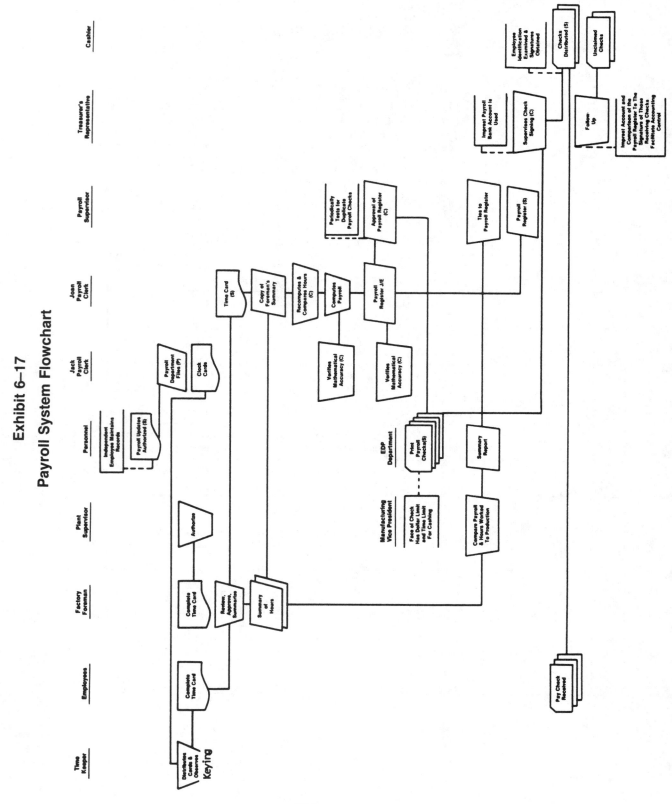

documents, identifies permanent (P) files, and indicates the nature of the various processing activities (i.e., $, C, or J/E).

Performing a Walk-Through

To confirm that the flowchart, checklist, and accompanying memoranda correspond to actual information flows and control points in the client's system, you will perform a walk-through. Based on the flowchart and accompanying documentation, you would, most likely, begin with the personnel files and sample about four employees—one just hired, one for whom a pay change has recently been authorized, one recently terminated, and one who is a foreman. The audit trail would then be followed.

(1) The payroll department file would be examined to see that it reflects these changes and that supporting documentation was properly authorized.

(2) Inquiry procedures would confirm that Jack reviewed the payroll department files as a basis for preparing time cards.

(3) Casual observation would confirm that the timekeeper distributes time cards and observes the punching of time cards, both in and out. Inquiry procedures could also be used.

(4) The time card for each of the four employees sampled would be reviewed to confirm their accuracy and approval by the appropriate party of both regular and overtime hours.

(5) The summary report prepared by the factory foreman would be reviewed, with attention directed at obtaining evidence that it had been recomputed by Joan and compared to the time cards. Similarly, the payroll computations by Joan should bear some physical evidence that they were verified by Jack, as should the payroll register. The register should also bear a signature from the payroll supervisor.

(6) Inquiry procedures can confirm the division of duties and the participation by EDP, the manufacturing vice president, the treasurer's representative, and the cashier in the processing of payroll.

(7) An inspection of the four employees' checks would confirm that a dollar limit and time limit were printed on the face of checks and that the checks were appropriately signed. The presence of numerical control over checks would be documented in the summary report, bearing some indication of the payroll supervisor's confirmation that the report tied to the payroll register.

(8) The imprest basis of the payroll account could be checked by inquiry procedures and by examining a bank reconciliation.

(9) The cashier should have physical evidence that the four employees picked up their checks, and inquiry or observation procedures could confirm that employees' identification cards were appropriately checked.

(10) A comparison of the list of signatures to the payroll register facilitates the identification of unclaimed checks, one of which could be walked through to the treasurer's department to verify that follow-up actions were taken and appropriately reflected in the records.

The walk-through is simply the physical tracing of the client's information flow to ensure that the auditor understands that flow and can identify evidence of the performance of control procedures.

Computer Auditing

This walk-through sets the basis for planning audit tests. For example, EDP prints payroll checks and generates a summary report. Generalized audit software could be used to recheck the accuracy with which the summary report was prepared or to check for duplicate payroll checks. It could likewise be used to match a personnel file with the payroll run to confirm that only current employees processed through personnel are being paid. Or, generalized audit software might be used to draw a sample of employees' checks for tests of control purposes. Assume that you choose to verify that the employees on the payroll check file correspond to personnel records, as no periodic check is made by the client to ensure that this is the case [recall Exhibit 6–16, item #6]. Exhibit 6–18 describes what might be done in an application, the relevant file layout required to perform the application, and the desired report format. The printed list of new hirees and terminations during the period can be reviewed for reasonableness or can be used to perform a test of payroll changes.

One computer-assisted auditing technique that could be applied to check the editing routines in the client's program would be test decks. Data that went beyond the limit test and a duplicate payment to a single employee could be processed to confirm that the appropriate checks are triggered with their corresponding exception reports. The alternative uses of the computer are plentiful, even in a limited EDP environment.

Statistical Sampling

Assume that you consider the design of controls over payroll to be sufficiently good to warrant assessment of control risk at less than the maximum level, if the controls are being effectively applied. One possible test of control over payroll would be an examination of time cards for an indication of proper approval of those cards. You can easily confirm the population size because time cards are prenumbered. It is sufficiently large that no effect on sample size is expected. The sampling unit is the individual time card. Since a correspondence between time card numbers and random numbers can easily be defined, you select a random number table selection method. A 6% risk of assessing control risk too low is considered to be acceptable, and since you plan a substantial level of reliance on

Exhibit 6–18

A Summary of One Generalized Audit Software Application: Payroll Application Chart

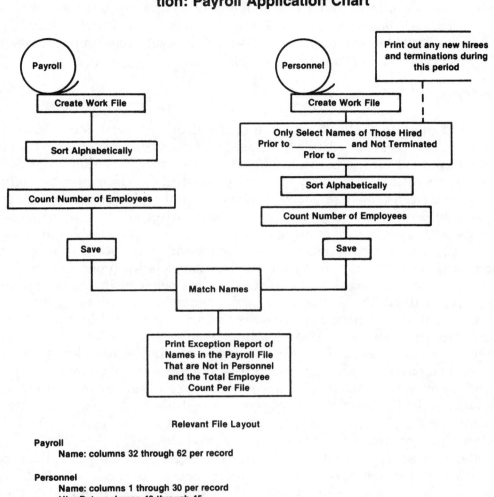

Relevant File Layout

Payroll
    Name: columns 32 through 62 per record

Personnel
    Name: columns 1 through 30 per record
    Hire Date: columns 40 through 45
    Termination Date: columns 47 through 52

Desired Report Format
Names in Payroll Not in Personnel File

Name	Total No. of Employees: Payroll File _____	Total No. of Employees: Personnel File _____

New Hirees and Terminations
For the Period Beginning _____ and Ending _____
Per Personnel File

Name	Hire Date	Termination Date

the authorization control, you specify a 5% tolerable rate. The population deviation rate that is expected, based on past experience, is no more than 1%. The sample size, based on generally available tables, would be 78 time cards. If this sample were taken, examined, and all cards found to be approved, the available tables for evaluation would indicate a 3.9% upper limit on the error rate for the pop-, ulation, at a 95% level of confidence. Clearly, this result would support assessment of control risk at less than the maximum level.

Evaluating Risk Exposure

In evaluating the risk exposure of the firm, one focal point would be the apparent weakness in controls, indicated by Exhibit 6–16, item #6. No periodic check of payroll files to personnel files is performed. To evaluate the risk from the absence of this check, you must first consider the chances of personnel not notifying payroll of changes, such notifications getting lost, such notifications not being accurately reflected in the files, or unauthorized changes being made to the file. Even if these errors or irregularities occurred, the question arises of how likely they are to remain undetected. With payroll, employees can be expected to monitor their paychecks. In the event that someone has informed an employee of a raise, special vacation payment, or similar change in compensation, that employee is likely to ask questions if the change is not properly processed. In addition, the termination of employees should be signalled by the absence of a time card, the absence of a party claiming the check, or the absence of an appropriate identification card by that party who is trying to claim the paycheck.

As a means of quantifying possibilities and probabilities, expected value computations often prove useful. Assume that based on the above, as well as the check amount limits, the possible risk exposure is estimated at $2,000 for 50% of the circumstances, $10,000 for 40%, and $40,000 for 10%. The expected value of the dollar exposure would be ($2,000 $\times$ .5) + ($10,000 $\times$ .4) + ($40,000 $\times$ .1) or $9,000. Now, using the Exhibit 6–13 tables for a company for which the exponent of 10 is deemed appropriate, a magnitude of expected loss of $10,000 can be selected. The frequency of occurrence information should reflect the total number of payroll changes, adjusted for that number which is expected to be processed correctly. In this setting, again referring to Exhibit 6–13, once in every third month is the expected frequency of occurrence. Therefore, in the course of one year, $9,000 $\times$ 4 = $36,000 would be a slightly overstated estimate of the risk exposure to the firm from not having the periodic check of the personnel file. Of course the important question is how probable it is that this risk exposure will be realized. In many cases a risk exposure work sheet is primarily used as a "worst-case" reminder of what could go wrong if the existing control weaknesses were recognized and intentionally abused. Such analyses can prove particularly useful when assessing the current or potential materiality of a particular recommendation.

SYNOPSIS

Six of the most useful tools of the trade in assessing control risk (i.e., evaluating and testing accounting controls) are

(1) internal accounting control checklists,
(2) flowcharting techniques,
(3) the walk-through,
(4) computer auditing techniques,
(5) statistical sampling techniques, and
(6) risk exposure worksheets.

This chapter describes these tools, with an emphasis on their application in the audit setting. A case example is provided in which each of the tools is used to address control-related questions about a payroll system and how it might be effectively tested. A wide variety of opportunities for applying these tools exists in the field; you need only remain alert for means of improving the effectiveness and efficiency of your work by applying one or more of these techniques.

7

Expanded Treatment of Tests of Controls Via Statistical Methods . . . Practical Considerations

"When you can measure what you are speaking about, and express it in numbers, you know something about it; when you cannot express it in numbers, your knowledge is of a meager and unsatisfactory kind."

Lord Kelvin[1]

While somewhat extreme, the introductory quote suggests that the ability to quantify when describing something of interest adds untold information to a decision process. Indeed, when evaluating control structures and, in particular,

---

[1] Lord Kelvin, British physicist. Cited in Donald A. Leslie, Albert D. Teitlebaum, and Rodney J. Anderson, *Dollar-Unit Sampling* (Toronto: Copp Clark Pitman, 1979), p. 46.

assessing control risk levels, it is helpful to be able to quantify risk exposure in terms of error rates. While the prior chapter introduced the concept of sampling as one of a potpourri of tools available to a systems evaluator, this chapter expands on the notion of statistics from a practical applications perspective. A "how to" approach is taken, with an emphasis on the practice problems common when approaching a sampling application.

THE SPECTRUM OF TOOLS AVAILABLE

Sampling primarily involves two types of statistical approaches: variables sampling and attributes sampling. The former has the objective of estimating a number such as average dollar sales or the value of inventory. The latter deals with some qualitative attribute which is evaluated as a "yes" or "no" and will be quantified as a percentage of occurrence rate. In the majority of systems evaluation settings, attributes sampling is the focus of attention. Commonly, specific controls are identified which are to be tested to determine the rates of compliance, or alternatively, the rates of exceptions. This is the source of the idea of "error rate." The systems evaluator might, as one example, be interested in whether the invoicing system uses the proper price listing. A control procedure might be that the preparer of the invoice is to refer to a standard price listing and confirm the accuracy of the initial order. By testing a sample of invoices back to the standard price listing, the number of discrepancies can be tracked and an error rate can be formulated.

At times the systems evaluator will be interested in the amount of a transaction being tested, this may be due to different controls applying to transactions of differing magnitudes. Alternatively, this could be due merely to a desire to have a number of dollars covered in the testing process. Tools available to the systems evaluator include: distinct definitions of multiple populations, each of which is subjected to unique controls; stratified sampling to ensure certain testing coverage of transactions of various amounts; or dollar unit sampling that combines certain aspects of attributes and variables testing in the sense that it ensures a higher likelihood of selection of larger dollar items. The selection from among such tools is an important decision process of the person performing statistical sampling.

These tools will be described in this chapter in tandem with basic concepts underlying sampling, diverse terminology is use, and practical considerations in selecting a sampling approach and executing a sampling plan in the face of various problems that can arise in a field application.

BASIC SAMPLING CONCEPTS

The idea of statistical sampling is that it is possible to draw a subset of a population and then to draw inferences from that sample to characterize the larger population. The jargon already emerges. A population is the total body of items about which a systems evaluator wants to draw conclusions. However the population is described, it will guide the rest of the sampling procedure. It is very important that the population is defined in a manner relevant to the systems evaluator's goal and that it is homogeneous with respect to those characteristics about which the evaluator wants to draw conclusions.

In a control structure setting, it is often the case that a population of transactions, such as all invoices, can differ with respect to what is being billed, to whom it is being billed, the type of documentation expected to accompany the billing, the control procedures applied to such a billing, and the magnitude that is being billed. The systems evaluator must first ask the question of whether any such differences affect the relevance or approach to drawing inferences regarding control risk. Typically, the design of the control system guides population definitions and, in particular, the specific things to be tested about that population.

Let us assume that a unique control system applies to invoices in excess of 100,000 and only 40 of these transactions arise in a system over a calendar year. Such a fact suggests the possible wisdom of doing a 100% examination of that population and then sampling invoices below 100,000. This ensures dollar coverage and, importantly, recognizes that the nature of the control system is nonhomogeneous.

The next question to be considered is whether a complete listing of the population is available from which a sample can be drawn. For example, is there a computer listing that can be tied into the audited accounting records that could be sorted to set aside all invoices in excess of 100,000 and then list all invoices below 100,000 to facilitate the identification of a sample? If not, is there some way in which a complete listing might be formulated? Remember that in order for a statistically valid sample to be drawn from the population and inferences to be drawn to the whole population from a sample drawn, all items in the population must have an equal likelihood of selection. If some items are not listed in the population when a sampling plan is designed, they would have no chance of selection, and as a result any inferences drawn from the sample can only represent those items in the population's listing. The acceptability of such a limitation is just one of a number of critical judgments to be made by a systems evaluator.

Beyond differences in the dollar amount of transactions of the control procedures unique to various classes of transactions, a systems evaluator should also consider the nature of the problems anticipated and their interaction with human nature. For example, one might hypothesize that people naturally take a more careful approach to a large-dollar transaction when processing it, suggesting that a differential error rate might emerge for such transactions. If intentional misstatement is expected, then one must consider two conflicting effects: (1) the larger sized transaction creates a better opportunity to remove larger amounts of resources from the entity; however (2) since the larger sized transactions may be scrutinized more closely, the risk of detection may be viewed as higher. The results of these conflicting considerations can go either way, depending on their relative net effect on a potential defrauder. In some cases, spreading misstatements across a large number of very small amounts can result in a large defalcation within the commensurate risk of detection. Moreover, it is sometimes possible to re-structure what would have been a very large transaction into numerous documents that spread the effect and avoid certain procedures that only kick into amounts over a given threshold. For example, if a special credit approval is needed for customers in excess of $50,000, sales to that customer of $60,000 might be written up as two sales of $30,000 each, thereby intentionally avoiding the added oversight. If the transaction is being designed to remove unauthorized funds from the system, then detection of such a maneuver will depend on the design of tests in a manner to ensure examination of transactions below $50,000.

Let us now assume that the relevant population or populations have been defined and that a complete listing of the items in such a population have been obtained from which a sample is to be drawn.

VARIABILITY OF THE POPULATION

A critical ingredient of sample size requirements relates to the anticipated variability of the population. With respect to attributes testing, the question is directed at the likelihood of any given draw being in compliance with the prescribed control or not in compliance. The greatest uncertainty would arise if the probability were 50–50, such as a flip of the coin. The least uncertainty would be if one were certain that the system would be in total compliance, i.e., 100–0. Exhibit 7–1 portrays a contrast of two populations from which samples could be drawn. The urn pictured on the left is homogeneous, representing marbles all of which are one color. If a systems evaluator had assurance that all were one color and were asked to determine the color of such marbles, then a sample size of one would suffice: any single marble would convey information on the color of every other marble in the population. This is the certainty case. In stark contrast, the urn on the right of the illustration in Exhibit 7–1 indicates that a number of different colors are in the urn. If the charge were handed to the systems evaluator to determine what colors were represented and what proportion of all marbles each color represented, it is obvious that a sample of one should be woefully insufficient. Hence, a basic premise of sampling emerges: THE GREATER THE DISPERSION IN THE POPULATION, THE LARGER THE REQUIRED SAMPLE SIZE.

In addressing variability of the population, the systems evaluator must keep in mind what is to be tested and the broadest spectrum of differences among such traits. As an example, if testing invoices, in addition to the standard price list comparison, we may choose to establish that the customer is authorized, credit has been approved, goods were received prior to invoicing, the goods shipped matched the goods ordered which, in turn, matched the goods billed, and similar characteristics. It is perfectly acceptable to test numerous controls on a single sample. Yet, in defining sample size, it is likely that the variability of error rates is diverse across such characteristics. For example, it may be that virtually zero

Exhibit 7–1

Sample Size Determinants

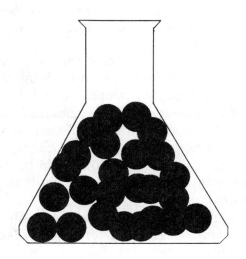 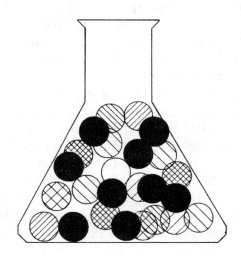

DISPERSION OF POPULATION

---

errors are anticipated on customer list and credit approval, while nonagreement with the order and shipped merchandise could be 25% for the system at hand. Since the attributes test is a yes/no dichotomy, this suggests a variability of 0/100 and 25/75. As dispersion approaches 50/50, it increases and sample size demands increase.

This explains why different sampling plans may be designed for disparate control procedures: their variability may be so diverse as to suggest a testing approach that is not sampling based or that uses a different sampling unit to identify the core concern. Specifically, if the concern is short-shipments, whereby not all the order is filled in the initial shipment to customers, then a shipping log may be a preferable population list on which to focus, rather than invoices. This is particularly so if the company often bills for services, apart from goods. This might be the case, for example, if the company happens to be in the design business.

EXPECTATIONS

The variability of the population is an inherent characteristic of the data set and can only be altered by redefining the relevant population. However, the other two key ingredients in a sampling plan are at the discretion of the systems evaluator: accuracy and reliability. The sample can be drawn to fulfill any desired expectations, although if too demanding, in light of the variability of the population, the entire population might have to be examined.

Accuracy is the notion of precision, described in the last chapter. The question is if an error rate of 25% is expected, is a point estimate that is accurate to 5% sufficient, at a stated level of reliability? In other words would it be acceptable that the actual population might well have a 20% accuracy or even a 30% accuracy? Would such a range meet the decision maker's needs?

Exhibit 7–2 highlights a commonplace problem: not realizing that sample size can only be assessed as to adequacy if one knows both accuracy and reliability. The point of reliability is to answer the question: if repeated samples were taken of a similar size, how likely would the point estimates formed approximate that of the initial sample? In evaluating reliability expected from a sample, one key query is whether a reliability interval (two-sided range) or a one-sided range is desired. For example, does the systems evaluator care that the 25% could be as low as 20% and as high as 30%, or is [s]he solely interested in the rate not being over 30% (a so-called, one-tailed testing concern).

Exhibit 7–3 depicts the ability to convert between one-tailed and two-tailed reliability intervals. As depicted, the level of confidence of 90% for a one-tailed confidence level can be easily translated to an 80% two-tailed confidence interval. The question is what level of confidence is being expected from the sampling plan. Is it sufficient that 80% of similar samples would be expected to form a point estimate within the precision range of the point estimate for the initial sample?

A conventional benchmark in common use is 95% confidence, leaving 5% in

---

Exhibit 7–2

Demand The Full Story

You have likely noticed the frequency with which announcers of polls will state that some finding has a margin for error of 2 percent. While that information is useful, as it implies the width of the precision interval, it is only part of the information you need to evaluate how much reliance you might be willing to place on a sample result. You also need to be given a confidence level. Without some idea of the reliability level provided by the sample result, the precision alone is virtually meaningless.

the "tail of the distribution" (i.e., normal curve as depicted in Exhibit 7–3). However, if the evaluator wants to be very demanding from the sample, a 99% confidence level might be invoked. By the same token if the objectives can be met with a less stringent reliability level being imposed, tables are available for virtually any confidence level desired. The auditing literature displays a number of confidence levels over 50%. The idea seems to be that any testing procedures should be capable of providing information better than a flip of a coin, but occasions could well arise where 60% or 70% reliability was deemed sufficient for the particular objective of interest (in the context of the decision maker).

The reliability level selected for the sampling plan is translated into a normal curve area factor, to depict the corresponding area in the tail or tails of the distribution (recall Exhibit 7–3, e.g., area C or D). Two-tailed and one-tailed factors based on a normal distribution curve that converts confidence level percentages to standard deviation units for a sample size of reasonable magnitude (e.g., in excess of 100) follow:

Exhibit 7–3

Conversion of One-Sided Upper Precision Limit to Two-Sided Confidence Interval

To compute analogous two-sided confidence intervals, consider the following graphic illustration based on the normal curve:

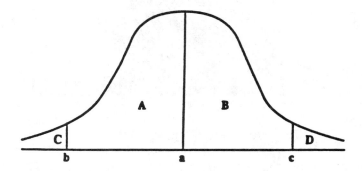

Where:

a—unknown population mean
b—lower precision limit
c—upper precision limit

A 90% one-sided upper precision limit says that one can be 90% confident that the population mean lies to the left of point c. The range ABC incorporates 90% of the area under the normal curve, and range D accounts for the remaining 10%.

Exhibit 7–3 (*Cont.*)

In converting to a two-sided confidence interval, in which the lower precision limit is employed, the population mean is expected to lie between points *b* and *c*. The degree of confidence with which it can be expected to lie between *b* and *c* is 80%, the area *AB*. The confidence level is reduced from the 90% one-sided interval by the additional 10% risk in area *C*.

Another graphic illustration enforces the point:

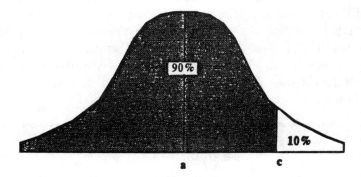

90% One-Sided Confidence Interval

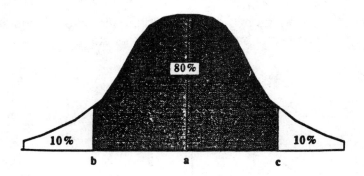

80% Two-Sided Confidence Interval

Source: The author appreciates the provision of this pedagogical tool by Bob Dougherty of Peterson & Co. Consulting.

Confidence Level	Two-Tailed Factor	One-Tailed Factor
99.9%	3.29	3.10
99%	2.58	2.33
95%	1.96	1.64
90%	1.64	1.29
85%	1.44	1.14
80%	1.26	.85

Confidence Level	Two-Tailed Factor	One-Tailed Factor
75%	1.15	.68
70%	1.04	.53
60%	.84	.26

SAMPLE SIZE COMPUTATION

The sample size formula for an attributes test follows:

$$n = \frac{P(1-P)\,U_R^2}{A^2}$$

where n = sample size

P = proportion of qualitative trait of interest (e.g., error rate)

$(1-P)$ = complement of P, i.e., $100\% - P$

U_R = reliability factor associated with the confidence level selected

A = accuracy or precision expected (i.e., width of confidence interval that is acceptable around the point estimate, in a two-tailed test)

By plugging into the formula, you can see that at a 95% level of confidence for a two-tailed test in which the proportions were 50–50 and a desired 5% precision level were set, the sample size would be 385. Holding precision and confidence constant, this is the "worst case" resulting from variability in the sample, since a 50–50 is the greatest dispersion possible. If this set of proportions shifted to 10% and 90%, then the sample size under the same conditions of confidence and precision drops to 138.24, or 139, since rounding is always done in a conservative fashion. The sample size matrix in Exhibit 7–4, reflecting a two-tailed confidence level, further demonstrates the point.

Exhibit 7–5 summarizes the fact that due to the formula's nature (of sample size determination) and the generally accepted nature of statistical sampling procedures, once the three ingredients are determined, everyone would be expected to compute identical sample sizes.

SAMPLE SELECTION

Once the sample size is determined, the question arises of how to select the sampling units. Statistical sampling presumes a random selection which means,

Exhibit 7–4

Sample Size Matrix

Assumed Error Rate

Precision	30%	25%	20%	15%	10%	5%
2%	2,017	1,801	1,537	1,225	864	456
3%	896	800	683	544	384	203
4%	504	450	384	306	216	114
5%	323	288	246	196	138	73
6%	224	200	171	136	96	51
7%	165	147	125	100	71	37
8%	126	113	96	77	54	29
9%	100	89	76	60	43	23
10%	81	72	61	49	35	18
11%	67	60	51	40	29	15
12%	61	55	47	37	26	14

Note: Confidence Level = 95% (two-tailed)

Exhibit 7–5

Required Input for Attributes Sample

In an attributes sample, three pieces of information are needed: the acceptable average incidence, the precision desired around that average, and the level of confidence desired. If interested in the rate of error in a data base that has been assembled for analysis, you might state that you wish an error rate to average 2 percent, are willing to permit a precision around that rate of 3 percent, and have set the required reliability at a 95 percent confidence. With these three pieces of information, all individuals would determine the same sample size, given some idea of the size of the population being tested.

as already noted, that every item in the population has an equal chance of selection. In this day of microcomputer access, a random number generator on such readily available software packages as SYMPHONY OR SPSSPC, among others, is one of the more promising approaches. A one to one mapping needs to be made between sampling units and the random numbers generated. Also, since some random numbers may turn out to be inapplicable to the population, it is a good idea to generate more random numbers than one expects will be needed. However, in taking such an approach, it is critical to keep in mind that sample units must be examined up to a given cut-off point. In other words, care should be taken not to examine the excess random numbers unless needed, since they cannot merely be substituted for earlier applicable random numbers.

An alternative to a random number generator is a random number table, available in a variety of statistical books. When using such tables, a random starting point should be selected and then a systematic use of columns and rows must be made. Often times, those designing sample points will close their eyes and choose a starting point or will look at a dollar bill and use its serial number to select a page, column, and row number from a book of random numbers.

Even if population items are not prenumbered in a manner that simply tracks one-for-one to a random number scheme, use your imagination, as tractability can be arranged. As an example, if no listing exists or prenumbering, but an estimation can be made of the number of inches' depth of the files from which sampling units are to be drawn, then numbers can be mapped to number of inches in a given drawer or stack or box. Such an approach is far less likely to suffer from a lack of randomness due to such physical traits of the person drawing the sample as their height or inclination to bend and stretch!

SYSTEMATIC, INTERVAL OR EVERY Nth ITEM SAMPLING

Often, in lieu of random numbers, sample plan designers opt to use interval sampling, often referred to as every Nth item. This frequently entails dividing the number of the population items by the computed sample size and then drawing every item at that interval starting at the front of the population items and proceeding to the end. The problem with this approach is that it may create distortions due to patterns in the manner in which a population is arranged. For example, if the customers were arranged by their nature, industry, location, magnitude of purchases, sales agent, or the like, then drawing a sample of every Nth item would potentially produce an unrepresentative sample with respect to the population at large. In other words, the individual planning a sample draw should consider the order of the population and whether that order has any possibility of influencing the interpretation of the results.

Even if no pattern is anticipated, the designer of a sampling plan should strive to vary the Nth interval approach to make it more random. As an example, multiple random starts are encouraged, as well as random variation of the Nth unit drawn. For example, if every 100th unit was to be originally drawn, to make three random starts, simply pull every 300th item the first pass and then make a random draw the second round, pulling every 300th item, and on the third round, with a third random start, choose every 300th item again. Keep in mind that random interval sampling, once it fixes a starting point and repeatedly draws every Nth item changes the likelihood of an individual item being drawn. Hence, in a technical sense, pure equivalence to a random number generator is not obtained. However, the practical significance of the variation depends on the likelihood of a pattern in the population having a relationship to the nature of the inference to be drawn from the sample.

OVERVIEW

Exhibit 7–6 summarizes the key concepts introduced to this point. It bears out that before drawing sample units, the population must be defined and checked as to completeness. If the random selection approach intended is systematic sampling, then particular attention has to be directed to whether a pattern exists in the population that might adversely affect the ability to draw conclusions to the general population based on the resulting sample. The potential need for strat-

Exhibit 7–6

Key Considerations In Sampling

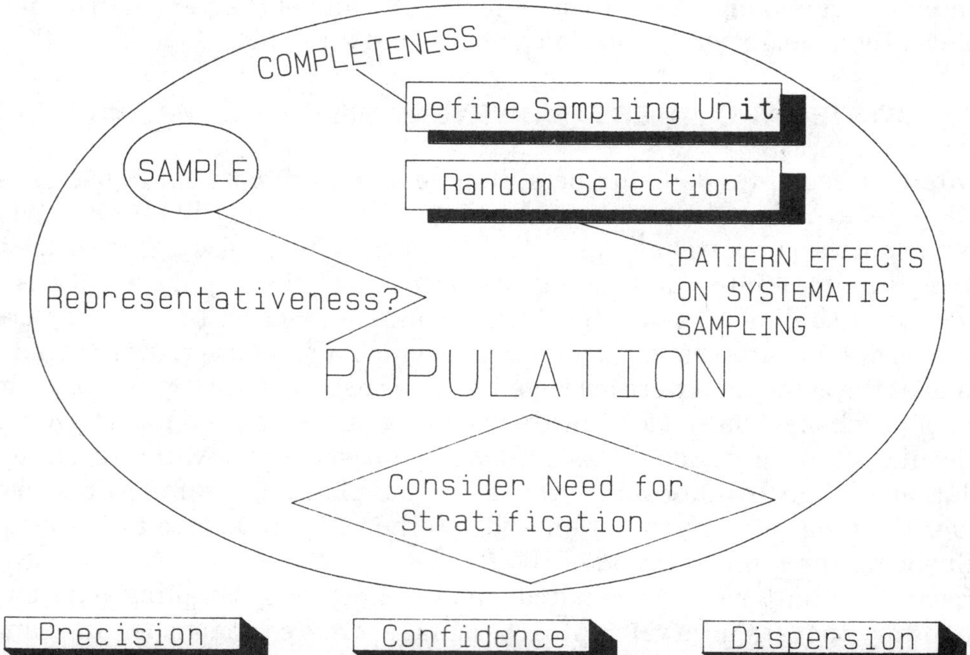

ification is noted, as are the three ingredients for sample size determination: precision, confidence, and dispersion.

A particularly relevant concern is whether the sample that results is representative of the population. If statistical sampling plans are well planned and executed, then the sample should be representative. However, it is useful to watch for telltale signs of a sample lacking representativeness. Remember that 95% reliability means that a 5% risk still exists that a sample will fail to be representative. To ascertain that a sample is likely to represent the population from which it was drawn, one useful approach is to consider how the sample compares to what is known about the population. For example, what is the average size of transaction in the sample, relative to the population? Are certain types of customers totally omitted or too dominant in the sample units? These sorts of intuitive checks on representativeness can alert the systems evaluator to a possible need to expand a sample.

BACKGROUND NECESSARY FOR DESIGNING SAMPLING PLANS

Before approaching any test of controls, it is imperative that the systems evaluator understand how the control procedure to be tested operates and assists in achieving the control objective of interest. The various exceptions that can arise need to be understood as well as possible, with a clear approach to identifying exceptions in the course of executing the test of controls. In tandem with such exceptions, the risks associated with each exception need to be understood in terms of their implications.

Often this type of background is obtainable by interviewing those responsible for the procedure and by observing the performance of the procedures. Both the formal and informal nature of documenting the performance of control procedures needs to be understood. Questions can be effective means of ensuring one understands how documents are prepared, how retrievable the documents are, and the complete listing of population items available for sampling definition purposes. In the questioning process, use open-ended questions to encourage elaboration or general descriptions.

PILOT SAMPLES

In designing a sample plan, if the designer is uncertain as to the diversity of the population items or the nature of the procedures and the exceptions that might arise, a pilot sample is advisable. Pilot samples are commonly drawn as 30 to 50 items (recall this is based, in part, on the Central Limit Theorem). If care is taken to use a sample selection process that is consistent with that planned, then the pilot results can be integrated with the fuller sample. This approach may help to ensure adequate sample size determination and the identification of needed stratification or alternative testing procedures.

FINITE CORRECTION FACTOR

When the systems evaluator is testing a finite population for which the sample size is expected to exceed 5% of the population size (as a general rule of thumb commonly applied), a finite correction factor can be invoked to lower the required sample size. The factor is defined as the sample size commonly computed, divided by $1 + (n/N)$ where N is the population size and n is the sample size prior to applying the finite correction factor.

STRATIFICATION

Keep in mind that stratification will improve efficiency only if it is possible to predict segments of the population that have a higher error rate than other segments. In such a case, strata are defined in a manner that keeps expected errors of similar size in the same stratum. In attributes sampling, it is unlikely that a stratification based on dollar amounts will not be accompanied by differences in systems, which means that the strata will actually become different populations for testing purposes.

OTHER PERIPHERAL FACTORS AFFECTING SAMPLE SIZES

As population increases, sample size increases, but this influence is negligible if the population is large, i.e., in excess of 5,000 units. As expected error gets closer to tolerable error in a sampling approach, the required sample size increases. The point, of course, is that too much fineness of sampling results is so demanding that it may not be achievable in a cost-effective manner. The term tolerable error is meant to represent the maximum rate of deviation from the prescribed control procedure which would be acceptable without having to alter the intended assessment of control risk. The expected population deviation rate or expected error rate is the expected rate of occurrence, which refers to the proportions discussed earlier.

Alpha risk is viewed as the complement of reliability, e.g., a 95% level of confidence translates to a 5% level of risk. As already described, sample size increases as the level of reliability desired increases or, alternatively worded, as risk declines. Exhibit 7–7 provides a means of considering the concepts of alpha and beta risk or Type I and Type II error as they are discussed in sampling and other statistical literature. Assume that the reality depicted is either that the control structure is effective (i.e., the IS RELATED box) or that the control structure is not effective (the IS NOT RELATED box). Furthermore, assume that the statistical test in this case is the test of controls and that it could indicate the control structure is effective (IS RELATED) or is inoperative at the desired level (IS NOT RELATED). The best of all worlds are the two boxes with Xs, since they suggest that the test corresponds to reality and gives appropriate information to the systems evaluator. The worst of all worlds can be represented as having test

Exhibit 7–7

Type I and Type II Errors

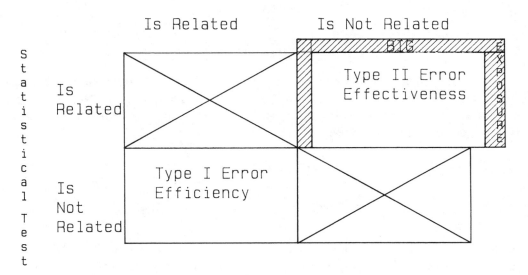

REALITY

Null Hypothesis: Is Related
Type II -- a false null hypothesis
is incorrectly accepted

results that suggest control is effective when, in reality, it is not effective. This is what the literature refers to as a Type II error, representing BETA risk. This is represented as an effectiveness exposure since the results of the testing are ineffective in capturing reality and could lead to an ineffective decision as to the control risk level. To reduce beta risk and Type II error, sample sizes need to be increased.

The other alternative result is that the test of control depicts a problem of some sort that, in reality is not a problem. This would be a Type I error, with efficiency implications; such errors are also known as sources of ALPHA risk. While potentially troublesome in the sense that inefficiency results during the process of system evaluation, the presumption is that with extended testing, reality would be revealed. Exhibit 7–7 uses an explanation that refers to the null hypothesis "is related" which, in the example at hand is the concept of controls being operative. The Exhibit clarifies that Type I and Type II error categories are statistical concepts rather than being peculiar to accounting or auditing, and their definition depends on how the null hypothesis is defined. Throughout the auditing literature, the null hypothesis tends to be viewed as financial statements being fairly stated, leading to a false null hypothesis yielding a type II error always relating to an audit effectiveness threat. In other words, things look better than they are and can lead to faulty risk assessment. Yet, from a purely statistical point of view, it would be possible to phrase the null hypothesis differently which, in turn would change the Type Error demarcations. Interpretation of Exhibit 7–7 maps "IS RELATED" to "CONTROL TESTS THAT SUGGEST CONTROLS ARE OPERATIVE RELATE TO REALITY."

TERMINOLOGY

Over the years, a number of terms have evolved in their use for statistical sampling applications. The following compares terms in SAS No. 39, related statistical terms from typical statistics courses, and more recent adjustment of terms to focus on risk measures:

SAS No. 39	Statistics Courses	Risk-Oriented Terminology
Risk	Reliability Confidence Level	Risk
Risk of Overreliance on Internal Accounting Control for Compliance Testing	Beta Risk Risk of Type II Errors	Assessing Control Risk Too Low
Risk of Incorrect Acceptance for Substantive Testing	Beta Risk Risk of Type II Errors	Assessing Control Risk Too Low
Risk of Underreliance on Internal Accounting Control for Compliance Testing	Alpha Risk Risk of Type I Errors	Assessing Control Risk Too High
Risk of Incorrect Rejection of an Account Balance for Substantive Testing	Alpha Risk Risk of Type I Errors	Assessing Control Risk Too High
Tolerable Error	Precision	Misstatement
Allowance for Sampling Risk	Precision	Misstatement

Important changes invoked by the American Institute of Certified Public Accountants in recent times include: replacement of the term compliance tests with the term tests of controls; alteration of the notion of study and evaluation of internal controls with terminology as to the need to obtain an understanding of the internal control structure and formation of a control risk assessment; and replacement of the term internal control system with internal control structure.

While these distinctions are promoted by the AICPA, depending on when particular pronouncements and guides were written, all of the terms will appear in various publications by not only the AICPA but by other professional groups dealing with system design and testing issues. Hence, in this *Handbook*, a variety of these terms appear interchangeably.

PRACTICAL PROBLEMS

A number of practical problems pervade settings in which tests of controls are being planned. For example, a system change may have occurred in the time frame of interest, storage of supporting documents may be in multiple locations, population listings may be incomplete, the systems evaluator may wish to draw inferences beyond those originally intended, the proportions found may not be what was expected, and a decision might be made to expand a sample beyond its originally intended size. Moreover, documents may be missing for sampling units selected and units drawn may be discovered to lack relevance to the control objective of interest. The obvious question is how should these types of common questions be answered in the field.

SYSTEM CHANGES

The advent of system changes increases the likelihood of problems with implementing and complying with controls. A useful approach to testing is to treat the pre-change, during change, and post-change periods as separate populations. In such a case, reason may exist for having the greatest attention to the "during change" time frame.

An important idea to keep in mind is that only the population subjected to testing can be represented by the selected sample. In other words, if interim testing is performed, the transactions post-interim testing are not part of the population to which the sample inferences can be drawn. Either an expanded sample or a separate sample is necessary to cover such transactions.

MULTIPLE LOCATIONS

Despite separate location of the sampling units, no reason exists to have separate sampling plans. If the locations are homogeneous in the nature of populations represented and a single sample is desired, the sampling plan should merely map the random numbers to the population units at each of the locations. Then the sampling units can be retrieved as appropriate. Either the population can be stratified and sampled proportionate to the number of items per location, or a general random sample can be drawn. If the latter approach is taken, it is a good idea to compare the proportionate split among locations for the population relative to the sample. This could act as one test of the representativeness of the selected sample.

POPULATION COMPLETENESS

If the population to be tested is not listed in some central location, but is partially inventoried, then steps have to be taken to achieve a complete listing or to limit the inferences to that population for which an inventory is available. One plausible approach is to find a larger population listing that incorporates the population of interest in a comprehensive manner, although also including less relevant sampling units. As an example, if invoices for materials are desired, yet a receivables listing is deemed complete though including services, the receivables listing can be the population from which sampling units are drawn. Whenever services are involved in an outstanding balance, that would be deemed an inapplicable selection and the next random number would be drawn until the sample size of units only related to purchases of goods had been identified.

In considering the completeness question, remember the distinction in vouching and tracing. If the accounts receivable subsidiary ledger were used for sampling, the procedure is analogous to vouching, in that the question would be addressed of whether documents existed in support of each of the items on the books. This idea is captured in Exhibit 7–8. If doubt exists as to the completeness of the accounts receivable subsidiary ledger, then a tracing procedure is necessary to test for possible omissions. As depicted in Exhibit 7–9, this will require sampling of documents such as invoices and tracing of such documents into the receivables subsidiary ledger.

UNEXPECTED OBJECTIVES

After drawing a sample and examining the units to draw inferences, at times a systems evaluator may decide he or she wishes to draw additional inferences beyond those originally planned. For example, if several individuals are involved

---

Exhibit 7–8

Vouching

Question: Were the transactions recorded valid? Or, are bogus transactions included in the books?

To find out, a vouching procedure is necessary.

VOUCH FROM ⬚ Journal   TO ⬚ Documents

e.g.: Sales Journal to Shipping Documents and/or Sales Orders
       Purchases Journal to Receiving Reports and/or Purchase Orders
       Payroll Journal to Timecards and/or Personnel Records

Exhibit 7–9

Tracing

Question: Were all transactions recorded?

To find out, a tracing procedure is necessary.

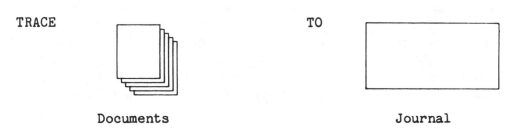

TRACE   TO

            Documents   Journal

e.g.:   Receiving Reports to Purchases Journal
         Shipping Documents to Sales Journal
         Timecards to Payroll Journal

in control procedures, one objective might be to evaluate how effectively each individual performs. To do so, sample size would need to be stratified by person or expanded to acquire sufficient sampling units to draw conclusions with the desired precision and reliability on a per employee basis. There is no reason why the original sampling units cannot be used as part of the extended sample, but it is highly unlikely that the original sample will be sufficient in size to draw the per-person inferences. Of course, if the system evaluator is willing to give up a great deal of precision and lower reliability expectations, then it may be that the original sample will support the extended inferences of interest.

EXPECTATIONS NOT MET

What happens if the proportions expected within the population are other than found in the sample? For example, what if expected proportions were 10% and 90% but upon testing, found to be 20% and 80%? This would mean that the sample drawn is incapable of delivering the desired reliability and accuracy. It is possible to review the original formula for sample size and pose the question. What sample size would have been required had the proportions in the population been known when the sample size was originally defined? The actual sample drawn can be placed into the formula, reliability held constant, and the actual precision achieved computed. Alternatively, the precision and sample size could be held constant, and the reliability achieved could be inferred.

It is important to re-evaluate the sample plan in light of the actual findings of the sample. Otherwise, presumptions as to the types of inferences that can be drawn may overstate what is actually demonstrable from the testing procedure.

EXPANDING THE SAMPLE

Assume the results are worse than expected but reason exists to question the representativeness of the sample. In such a setting, one approach is to expand the sample size to see if the results from a larger sample corroborate expectations after all (i.e., add to the representativeness of the sample). With careful planning, the added sample can be combined with the original sample as though a single sample had been drawn in the first place. The key is that the manner of selection is followed consistently and that the sample size is sufficient to cover the "stop and go" nature of the sampling process. In a sense, a price is to be paid for "peeking" at the data midway. If the population's control deviation rate is high, a sequential approach would result in a larger sample size than a typical fixed sampling plan.

MISSING DOCUMENTS

If a sampling unit is missing, the typical approach is to consider it an exception, i.e., presume it is in error or has the qualitative trait that is problematic. This is conservative and is capable of retaining the statistical sampling inferential power desired in the initial planning process. However, there may sometimes be an alternative to considering missing documents to be errors. For example, if the auditor wants to examine evidence that goods were in fact shipped to a customer and a shipping report is not attached to the invoice as expected, inquiry procedures may be used to locate elsewhere in the system where shipping reports are on file and then those alternative documents in support could be examined. Of course, the plausibility of such an approach heavily depends on the nature of the sampling objective. If attachment of the shipping documentation to the invoice as part of the control procedures is considered important, then its absence is an exception whether or not it is retrievable elsewhere.

VOIDED OR UNISSUED UNITS

When drawing a sample, the possibility likewise exists that a selected sampling unit has been voided or was not issued. In such a circumstance the auditor should test the propriety of the voided or unissued status. If proper, then the voiding or lack of issuance becomes an irrelevant sampling unit and another random number is drawn to replace that originally defined sampling unit.

QUALITATIVE INTERPRETATION OF FINDINGS

In evaluating sampling results, it is important to augment quantitative interpretation with a qualitative review of the results. For example, were all exceptions similar in some manner? Could it be that one party among several who are expected to perform a control duty continually does some facet of that procedure in error? Do problems arise when overtime is prevalent? Do problems arise when system changes arise? Do errors cluster in some manner?

It has been suggested that patterns of noncompliance arise due to the likely causes of some of the problems being tested. If fatigue or distraction is a source of error, then it seems intuitively appealing that once distracted, several clustered items may suffer from similar problems before that distraction wanes. This speaks to some desirability of further investigating an exception in accordance with other transactions or population units adjacent to the selected sampling unit. This may be particularly crucial when employee turnover or system changes have occurred.

COMBINING TESTS AT DIFFERENT POINTS IN TIME

It has already been suggested that points in time may suggest redefinition of populations or a stratified approach. Yet, it may be that samples drawn at different points in time were always intended to be combined. The best of all approaches in such a case is to have an *a prior* sample plan that designates the sampling units to be drawn as they become available or time is allocated to such testing. On the other hand, if a single front-end sample plan was not formulated, the possibility exists of treating the time frames as strata and combining the results based on a reasonable combinatorial rule, such as proportionate to the number of transactions processed. However, any combination needs to, in retrospect, clearly depict the likelihood of selection per stratum and the similarity of reliability and accuracy demands placed on each of the strata.

SYSTEM TESTING VERSUS STATISTICAL TESTING OF CONTROLS

Some have suggested that with the advent of computers and the similarity of processing of repetitive transactions, systems testing should and will take precedence over the traditional statistical sampling performed in manual systems. While systems testing is an important aspect of auditing through the computer and understanding the control structure, it cannot totally displace statistical testing. For one thing, camouflaged code, system changes, and system breakdowns are among numerous risks associated with computerized systems that call for some sort of detective control, in tandem with various preventive controls. While walk-through sorts of understanding associated with systems and the testing of systems may well be the focal point in many systems evaluations, an important means of acquiring comfort that controls are operating as designed and as apparent from documentation is to look at the results. Results tend to be tested through sampling.

The likelihood exists that sampling, systems testing, analytical procedures, and various other tools already described in earlier chapters will be integrated by systems evaluators in reaching judgments related to control. As Exhibit 7–10 suggests, sampling will focus on the nature of what is being asked, the objectives set forth in the plan, the ability of the sample to represent the population, the effectiveness at addressing practical problems, the careful drawing of inferences, and the possibility of blending findings with such related tools as modeling.

DISCOVERY SAMPLING

A type of attributes sampling that is sometimes applied is known as discovery sampling. This approach is expected to provide assurance that some critical attribute would have appeared in the sample under certain conditions. For example, if a random sample of 300 accounts receivable balances were to be tested with regard to some control, from a population of 2,000 items, at a 95% reliability, the sample would have encountered at least one bogus customer had 1% of the population units been inappropriately handled with respect to the control procedures necessary to avoid such fraudulent occurrences. Tables are available in various statistical sampling books to facilitate the application of discovery sampling. An excerpt follows: PROBABILITY IN PERCENT OF FINDING ONE ERROR IF TOTAL NUMBER OF ERRORS IN UNIVERSE IS AS INDICATED[2]

	Population Size of 1,000 (2,000) With Expected Number of Errors of:			
	5	*10*	*20*	*30*
Sample Sizes				
75				90.7
100				96
150			96	99 (90.5)
250		94.5	99.7 (93.2)	(98.2)
400	92.3	99.4	(98.9)	(99.9)
500	96.9	99.9 (94.4)	(99.7)	

DOLLAR UNIT SAMPLING

As already mentioned, dollar unit sampling applies attributes sampling to individual dollars to form quantitative estimates, similar to variables sampling. The sample size is determined by dividing the upper error limit in dollars by the appropriate upper error limit factor, available from tables and based on sampling theory. As one example, if the tolerable basic precision were $150,000, an error size limit assumption was 100% (i.e., total misstatement is possible but no more

---

[2] Adapted from Richard L. Ratliff, Wanda A. Wallace, James K. Loebbecke, and William G. McFarland, *Internal Auditing: Principles and Techniques* (Altamonte Springs, Florida: The Institute of Internal Auditors, 1988).

Exhibit 7–10

Key Steps in Planning and Evaluating Samples

SAMPLING
. **Question Being Addressed**
. **Sampling Plan**
. **Representativeness**
. **Practical Problems**
. **Drawing Inferences**
. **Combining With Modeling**

than 100% misstatement), and reliability is set at 95%, then an average sampling interval can be calculated using a factor of 3:

$$\frac{\$150,000}{3 \times 100\%} = \$50,000$$

Given a population size of $5,600,000, divided by such a sampling interval would yield a sample size of 112. Note that each dollar bill within the total balance of some item being tested (such as outstanding receivables) represents a sampling unit. Hence, the likelihood of any balance being drawn is proportionate to the number of dollars in that particular balance. In that sense, a stratified sample, in relationship to dollar magnitude of balance results.

RELATED CAVEATS

When considering dollar unit sampling for attributes testing, a number of caveats apply. First, some reason should exist for giving larger amounts a higher proportionate chance of selection. Unless control systems vary, there would seem to be little reason to test controls relative to the dollar amount of a transaction that happens to be processed. An added concern with Dollar Unit Sampling (DUS and sometimes referred to as sampling proportionate to size) is that it does not give any chance of selection to credit balances or zero balances, by definition. Moreover, the DUS approach is most tailored to one-sided overstatement assessment and is most efficient in low error rate populations. As a result, testing would have to proceed with attention through alternative means to zero balances, credit balances, and high error rate items of interest.

SYNOPSIS

In developing a sampling plan, the systems evaluator should specify:

- The population definition
- Sampling unit specification
- The nature of the errors or misstatements to be identified
- The method of selection
- Sampling risk

Exhibit 7–11

Statistical Sample Sizes for Testing of Controls 5% Risk of Assessing Control Risk at Too Low a Level (with number of expected errors in parentheses) [one-sided upper precision limits at 95% confidence]

Expected Population Deviation Rate	Tolerable Rate										
	2%	3%	4%	5%	6%	7%	8%	9%	10%	15%	20%
0.00%	149(0)	99(0)	74(0)	56(0)	49(0)	42(0)	36(0)	32(0)	29(0)	19(0)	14(0)
.25	236(1)	157(1)	117(1)	93(1)	78(1)	66(1)	58(1)	51(1)	46(1)	30(1)	22(1)
.50	*	157(1)	117(1)	93(1)	78(1)	66(1)	58(1)	51(1)	46(1)	30(1)	22(1)
.75	*	208(2)	117(1)	93(1)	78(1)	66(1)	58(1)	51(1)	46(1)	30(1)	22(1)
1.00	*	*	156(2)	93(1)	78(1)	66(1)	58(1)	51(1)	46(1)	30(1)	22(1)
1.25	*	*	156(2)	124(2)	78(1)	66(1)	58(1)	51(1)	46(1)	30(1)	22(1)
1.50	*	*	192(3)	124(2)	103(2)	66(1)	58(1)	51(1)	46(1)	30(1)	22(1)
1.75	*	*	227(4)	153(3)	103(2)	88(2)	77(2)	51(1)	46(1)	30(1)	22(1)
2.00	*	*	*	181(4)	127(3)	88(2)	77(2)	68(2)	46(1)	30(1)	22(1)
2.25	*	*	*	208(5)	127(3)	88(2)	77(2)	68(2)	61(2)	30(1)	22(1)
2.50	*	*	*	*	150(4)	109(3)	77(2)	68(2)	61(2)	30(1)	22(1)
2.75	*	*	*	*	173(5)	109(3)	95(3)	68(2)	61(2)	30(1)	22(1)
3.00	*	*	*	*	195(6)	129(4)	95(3)	84(3)	61(2)	30(1)	22(1)
3.25	*	*	*	*	*	148(5)	112(4)	84(3)	61(2)	30(1)	22(1)
3.50	*	*	*	*	*	167(6)	112(4)	84(3)	76(3)	40(2)	22(1)
3.75	*	*	*	*	*	185(7)	129(5)	100(4)	76(3)	40(2)	22(1)
4.00	*	*	*	*	*	*	146(6)	100(4)	89(4)	40(2)	22(1)
5.00	*	*	*	*	*	*	*	158(8)	116(6)	40(2)	30(2)
6.00	*	*	*	*	*	*	*	*	179(11)	50(3)	30(2)
7.00	*	*	*	*	*	*	*	*	*	68(5)	37(3)

*Sample size is too large to be cost effective for most audit applications.
Note: This table assumes a large population.
From AICPA Statistical Sampling Subcommittee, Audit and Accounting Guide: *Audit Sampling* (New York: AICPA, 1983), p. 106.

- The sample size
- Both the evaluation and interpretation of sample results (quantitative and qualitative factors, as already discussed).

If stratification is chosen, it need not be based on dollar values, but could reflect a change in controls or other meaningful subcategories. If the information needed for sample size determination is uncertain, a pilot sample can be helpful.

While formulas have been discussed herein, Exhibits 7–11 through 7–16 provide sample size and evaluation standard tables for one-sided upper precision limits at 95% and 90% confidence levels.

Exhibit 7–12

Statistical Sample Sizes for Testing of Controls 10% Risk of Assessing Control Risk at Too Low a Level (with number of expected errors in parentheses) [one-sided upper precision limits at 90% confidence]

Expected Population Deviation Rate	__	__	__	__	__	Tolerable Rate	__	__	__	__	__
	2%	3%	4%	5%	6%	7%	8%	9%	10%	15%	20%
0.00%	114(0)	76(0)	57(0)	45(0)	38(0)	32(0)	28(0)	25(0)	22(0)	15(0)	11(0)
.25	194(1)	129(1)	96(1)	77(1)	64(1)	55(1)	48(1)	42(1)	38(1)	25(1)	18(1)
.50	194(1)	129(1)	96(1)	77(1)	64(1)	55(1)	48(1)	42(1)	38(1)	25(1)	18(1)
.75	265(2)	129(1)	96(1)	77(1)	64(1)	55(1)	48(1)	42(1)	38(1)	25(1)	18(1)
1.00	*	176(2)	96(1)	77(1)	64(1)	55(1)	48(1)	42(1)	38(1)	25(1)	18(1)
1.25	*	221(3)	132(2)	77(1)	64(1)	55(1)	48(1)	42(1)	38(1)	25(1)	18(1)
1.50	*	*	132(2)	105(2)	64(1)	55(1)	48(1)	42(1)	38(1)	25(1)	18(1)
1.75	*	*	166(3)	105(2)	88(2)	55(1)	48(1)	42(1)	38(1)	25(1)	18(1)
2.00	*	*	198(4)	132(3)	88(2)	75(2)	48(1)	42(1)	38(1)	25(1)	18(1)
2.25	*	*	*	132(3)	88(2)	75(2)	65(2)	42(1)	38(1)	25(1)	18(1)
2.50	*	*	*	158(4)	110(3)	75(2)	65(2)	58(2)	38(1)	25(1)	18(1)
2.75	*	*	*	209(6)	132(4)	94(3)	65(2)	58(2)	52(2)	25(1)	18(1)
3.00	*	*	*	*	132(4)	94(3)	65(2)	58(2)	52(2)	25(1)	18(1)
3.25	*	*	*	*	153(5)	113(4)	82(3)	58(2)	52(2)	25(1)	18(1)
3.50	*	*	*	*	194(7)	113(4)	82(3)	73(3)	52(2)	25(1)	18(1)
3.75	*	*	*	*	*	131(5)	98(4)	73(3)	52(2)	25(1)	18(1)
4.00	*	*	*	*	*	149(6)	98(4)	73(3)	65(3)	25(1)	18(1)
5.00	*	*	*	*	*	*	160(8)	115(6)	78(4)	34(2)	18(1)
6.00	*	*	*	*	*	*	*	182(11)	116(7)	43(3)	25(2)
7.00	*	*	*	*	*	*	*	*	199(14)	52(4)	25(2)
					*	*					

*Sample size is too large to be cost effective for most audit applications.

Note: This table assumes a large population.

From AICPA Statistical Sampling Subcommittee, Audit and Accounting Guide: *Audit Sampling* (New York: AICPA, 1983), p. 107.

Exhibit 7–13

Statistical Sample Results: Evaluation Table for Tests of Control—Upper Limits at 5% Risk of Assessing Control Risk at Too Low a Level
[one-sided upper precision limits at 95% confidence]

Sample Size	Actual Number of Deviations Found										
	0	1	2	3	4	5	6	7	8	9	10
25	11.3	17.6	*	*	*	*	*	*	*	*	*
30	9.5	14.9	19.6	*	*	*	*	*	*	*	*
35	8.3	12.9	17.0	*	*	*	*	*	*	*	*
40	7.3	11.4	15.0	18.3	*	*	*	*	*	*	*
45	6.5	10.2	13.4	16.4	19.2	*	*	*	*	*	*
50	5.9	9.2	12.1	14.8	17.4	19.9	*	*	*	*	*
55	5.4	8.4	11.1	13.5	15.9	18.2	*	*	*	*	*
60	4.9	7.7	10.2	12.5	14.7	16.8	18.8	*	*	*	*
65	4.6	7.1	9.4	11.5	13.6	15.5	17.4	19.3	*	*	*
70	4.2	6.6	8.8	10.8	12.6	14.5	16.3	18.0	19.7	*	*
75	4.0	6.2	8.2	10.1	11.8	13.6	15.2	16.9	18.5	20.0	*
80	3.7	5.8	7.7	9.5	11.1	12.7	14.3	15.9	17.4	18.9	*
90	3.3	5.2	6.9	8.4	9.9	11.4	12.8	14.2	15.5	16.8	18.2
100	3.0	4.7	6.2	7.6	9.0	10.3	11.5	12.8	14.0	15.2	16.4
125	2.4	3.8	5.0	6.1	7.2	8.3	9.3	10.3	11.3	12.3	13.2
150	2.0	3.2	4.2	5.1	6.0	6.9	7.8	8.6	9.5	10.3	11.1
200	1.5	2.4	3.2	3.9	4.6	5.2	5.9	6.5	7.2	7.8	8.4

*Over 20 percent.

Note: This table presents upper limits as percentages and assumes a large population.

From: AICPA Statistical Sampling Subcommittee, Audit and Accounting Guide: *Audit Sampling* (New York: AICPA, 1983), p. 108.

Exhibit 7–14

Statistical Sampling Results: Evaluation Table for Tests of Control—Upper Limits at 10% Risk of Assessing Control Risk at Too Low a Level
[one-sided upper precision limits at 90% confidence]

Sample Size	Actual Number of Deviations Found										
	0	1	2	3	4	5	6	7	8	9	10
20	10.9	18.1	*	*	*	*	*	*	*	*	*
25	8.8	14.7	19.9	*	*	*	*	*	*	*	*
30	7.4	12.4	16.8	*	*	*	*	*	*	*	*
35	6.4	10.7	14.5	18.1	*	*	*	*	*	*	*
40	5.6	9.4	12.8	16.0	19.0	*	*	*	*	*	*
45	5.0	8.4	11.4	14.3	17.0	19.7	*	*	*	*	*
50	4.6	7.6	10.3	12.9	15.4	17.8	*	*	*	*	*
55	4.1	6.9	9.4	11.8	14.1	16.3	18.4	*	*	*	*
60	3.8	6.4	8.7	10.8	12.9	15.0	16.9	18.9	*	*	*
70	3.3	5.5	7.5	9.3	11.1	12.9	14.6	16.3	17.9	19.6	*
80	2.9	4.8	6.6	8.2	9.8	11.3	12.8	14.3	15.8	17.2	18.6
90	2.6	4.3	5.9	7.3	8.7	10.1	11.5	12.8	14.1	15.4	16.6
100	2.3	3.9	5.3	6.6	7.9	9.1	10.3	11.5	12.7	13.9	15.0
120	2.0	3.3	4.4	5.5	6.6	7.6	8.7	9.7	10.7	11.6	12.6
160	1.5	2.5	3.3	4.2	5.0	5.8	6.5	7.3	8.0	8.8	9.5
200	1.2	2.0	2.7	3.4	4.0	4.6	5.3	5.9	6.5	7.1	7.6

*Over 20 percent.

Note: This table presents upper limits as percentages and assumes a large population.

From: AICPA Statistical Sampling Subcommittee, Audit and Accounting Guide: *Audit Sampling* (New York: AICPA, 1983), p. 109.

Exhibit 7–15

**One-Sided Upper Precision Limits
for 95% Confidence Level**

Sample Size	Occurrence Rate								
	12	14	16	18	20	25	30	40	50
100	18.7	21.2	23.3	25.6	27.7	33.1	38.4	48.7	56.6
200	16.4	18.7	20.9	23.1	25.2	30.5	35.7	47.0	56.8
300	15.5	17.7	19.8	22.0	24.1	29.1	34.1	44.1	54.1
400	15.0	17.2	19.2	21.2	23.2	28.2	33.2	43.2	53.2
500	14.6	16.7	18.6	20.7	22.6	27.6	32.6	42.6	52.6
600	14.2	16.2	18.2	20.2	22.2	27.2	32.2	42.2	52.2
700	13.9	15.9	17.9	19.9	21.9	26.9	31.9	41.9	51.9
800	13.7	15.7	17.7	19.7	21.7	26.7	31.7	41.7	51.7
900	13.5	15.5	17.5	19.5	21.5	26.5	31.5	41.5	51.5
1000	13.4	15.4	17.4	19.4	21.4	26.4	31.4	41.4	51.4

Exhibit 7–16

**One-Sided Upper Precision Limits
for 90% Confidence Level**

Sample Size	Occurrence Rate								
	12	14	16	18	20	25	30	40	50
100	17.3	19.6	21.7	24.0	26.1	31.4	36.6	46.9	56.8
200	15.5	17.7	19.8	22.0	24.0	29.3	34.5	44.4	54.4
300	14.7	16.9	19.0	21.1	23.2	28.2	33.2	43.2	53.2
400	14.3	16.5	18.5	20.5	22.5	27.5	32.5	42.5	52.5
500	14.1	16.1	18.1	20.1	22.1	27.1	32.1	42.1	52.0
600	13.7	15.7	17.7	19.7	21.7	26.7	31.7	41.7	51.7
700	13.5	15.5	17.5	19.5	21.5	26.5	31.5	41.5	51.5
800	13.3	15.3	17.3	19.3	21.3	26.3	31.3	41.3	51.3
900	13.2	15.2	17.2	19.2	21.2	26.2	31.2	41.2	51.2
1000	13.1	15.1	17.1	19.1	21.1	26.1	31.1	41.1	51.1

8

How to Formulate an Audit Plan: Selecting the Right Mix of Tests of Control, Substantive, and Dual Purpose Tests

"Just as no society operates entirely on the command principle,
so none operates entirely through voluntary cooperation."

Milton Friedman, 1979[1]

As implied by the introductory quote, a balance between prescribed procedures and voluntary compliance has to be struck in any society and, in turn, within such societal entities as economic units. This is achieved through design of an

---

[1] Michael Jackman, *The Macmillan Book of Business & Economic Quotations* (New York: Macmillan Publishing Company, 1984), p. 170.

effective control structure and periodic oversight of such structure through a variety of monitoring practices. One aspect of such monitoring is the role assumed by external auditors. In formulating their audit plan, the primary objective under present generally accepted auditing standards is to form an opinion regarding the fairness of presentation of financial statements. Tremendous latitude exists as to whether this objective is accomplished via tests of control or substantive testing. However, this chapter is devoted to discussing some of the considerations likely to influence the manner in which an audit plan is designed.

Three general types of tests are available as means of gathering evidence: tests of control, substantive, and dual purpose. *Tests of control* are intended to provide reasonable assurance that the accounting control procedures are being applied as designed. *Substantive tests* provide evidence as to the validity and propriety of financial statement balances and their underlying transactions. Any tests that provide both tests of control and substantive evidence are termed *dual-purpose tests*. Confirmation letters to customers with accounts receivable balance are one example of a dual-purpose test, despite its common classification as a substantive test. In other words, the demarcation between tests of control and substantive tests is hazy at best.

Most audit engagements are likely to have all three testing approaches incorporated in an audit plan. Tests of control not only assist the auditor in establishing that an entity is auditable, but also provide the basis for modifying the nature, timing, and/or extent of related substantive audit procedures. The purpose of this chapter is to show how you can evaluate these alternative types of tests and combinations thereof when formulating an audit plan. Primary attention will be directed toward those considerations of particular importance when designing a testing approach directed to controls.

GUIDELINES FOR THE EXTERNAL AUDITOR WHEN CHOOSING A TESTING STRATEGY

Generally accepted auditing standards permit the external auditor to select an audit plan. That plan could represent primarily a substantive testing approach, a testing strategy for controls, a fairly balanced hybrid of the two approaches, or any combination of the two strategies. Relevant directions provided to the auditor by existing standards are listed here.

(1) Internal accounting controls must be tested if the auditor plans to assess control risk at less than the maximum level on such controls.

(2) If setting control risk at less than the maximum level is warranted, substantive testing can be reduced based on the test of control work; specifically, the nature, timing, and/or extent of substantive testing can be altered.

(3) The critical consideration, beyond gaining a sufficient evidential base, is efficiency; tests of control should be applied only when cost/beneficial—

in other words, the planned reduction in substantive tests is expected to at least offset the time and costs directed to tests of control.

(4) When these are plausible, dual-purpose tests can frequently provide both tests of control and substantive test results more efficiently than either approach separately applied; therefore, you should routinely consider the possibility of performing such tests.

What should be obvious from the sparse directions is that it is the auditor's judgment that forms the basis of the audit plan, rather than one prescribed testing approach delineated in the standards. This auditor's choice facilitates the efficient tailoring of an audit approach to each client's particular control and information system.

Which Audit Procedures Will Be Most Effective for a Particular Client?

The relative effectiveness of various audit procedures in light of the particular client's setting is an important determinant of the audit plan. For example, in spite of a design for internal accounting controls that is excellent in a particular area of operations, the capability of performing an efficient and effective substantive test for less expense than performing a test of controls of that well-designed system would preclude a testing of control strategy for that facet of the transaction cycle. At times, the performance of tests of control may similarly be precluded by the absence of an audit trail that could document control compliance. In such cases you must evaluate the effectiveness of observation and inquiry techniques as an evidential basis for reducing substantive work.

The Auditor's Choice of a Testing Strategy

Your choice of a testing strategy is broadly outlined in Exhibit 8–1. Since the design and evaluation of internal accounting controls will be given in-depth attention in Chapters 9 through 12, this chapter will assume that you have evaluated the design of controls as befitting assessment of control risk at less than the maximum level, if the tests of control confirm that the system is operating as designed. Your decision then focuses on whether tests of control or substantive tests are more efficient. However, before proceeding with the efficiency comparisons, your responsibilities as auditor will be described, should control risk be assessed at the maximum level.

STATEMENT ON AUDITING STANDARDS NO. 55

The April 1988 pronouncement of the AICPA altered the second standard of field work to read:

> A sufficient understanding of the internal control structure is to be obtained to plan the audit and to determine the nature, timing, and extent of tests to be performed.

Exhibit 8–1

The External Auditor's Choice of a Testing Strategy

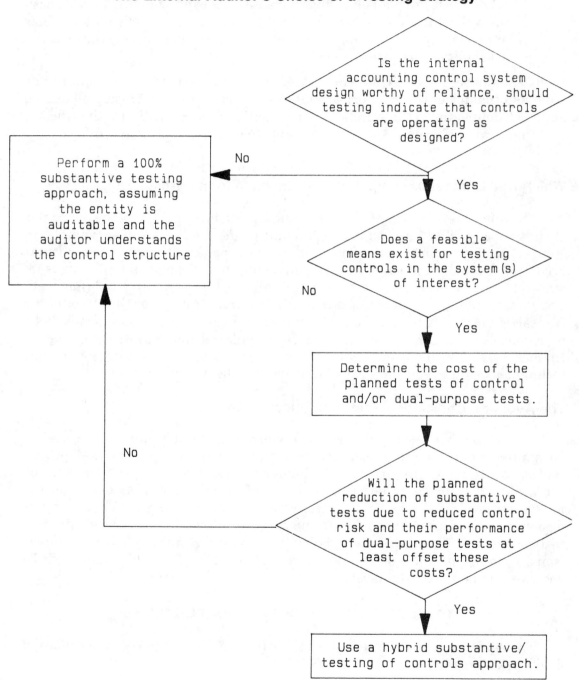

Once an understanding is reached, the auditor is expected to assess control risk and if that control risk is set at the maximum level, the understanding obtained serves as a basis for determining the nature, timing, and extent of substantive tests. The understanding obtained is expected to include knowledge about the system design and operation. In particular, the auditor is expected to determine that the entity is using designed controls. If no reduction in control risk is intended as a basis for reducing substantive test work, then the auditor is not responsible for determining operating effectiveness.

An understanding of the internal control structure first and foremost provides a basis for assessing whether an entity is auditable. Secondly, it provides a framework for planning the audit approach. The manner in which an understanding is obtained will likely include prior audit experience, an understanding of the industry in which the client operates), assessments of inherent risk, materiality, and the influence of computer operations. Greater complexity and sophistication in a control and information system will likely demand increased attention to obtaining the understanding required under GAAS.

Care is needed to focus on the substance, rather than merely the form of control procedures, including the role of top management and the board of directors. An understanding of the accounting system entails recognition of significant classes of transactions, how they are initiated, processed, and carried forward to the financial reporting process, with particular attention to accounting estimates and disclosure practices. Ordinarily, the GAAS prescribed understanding of controls does not require an understanding of control procedures at the account or transaction level. Nonetheless, some information on procedures is likely to be gained as the understanding of both the control environment and the accounting system is obtained.

Inquiries, inspection of documents and records, observation of operations, and prior experience will be the primary means of obtaining the understanding required under GAAS. The degree or work required in this process, in part, will reflect the auditor's assessments of materiality and inherent risk.

DOCUMENTATION

SAS No. 55 specifically requires that the auditor document the understanding of the internal control structure elements. This is often achievable through use of flowcharts, questionnaires, decision tables, and/or memoranda. The extent of documentation is expected to reflect the complexity of the underlying control structure being described.

The auditor may list the reasons for deciding not to extend the testing of the control structure past the understanding phase required in the professional standards but is not required to do so. Such a judgment may reflect the auditor's

—belief that further study and evaluation of controls are unlikely to justify any restriction of substantive testing, and/or

—conclusion that the audit effort required to study and evaluate the system's design and to test compliance exceeds that audit effort for substantive testing procedures that could be reduced as a result of the reliance on controls due to
- the nature of transactions or balances involved,
- the amount of transactions or balances involved,
- the data processing methods in use, and/or
- the substantive testing procedures that are available.

The former circumstances might arise if unusually high turnover has occurred and the auditor doubts the experience and competence levels of the new employees that have been hired or if the risk of management override is judged to be excessive. The latter circumstance may indicate that the size of the engagement is more conducive to a substantive testing approach, particularly due to poor control over documentation that might otherwise have facilitated testing of controls.

The objective of gaining an understanding of controls is to ensure the auditor has general knowledge of, among other aspects of control:

—organizational structure,

—the means by which the entity communicates responsibility and authority,

—the methods utilized by management to supervise the system,

—the presence and role of an internal audit function,

—the various types of transactions, and

—the means of authorizing, executing, initially recording, and subsequently processing transactions of the entity.

This is expected to require inquiry and observation procedures, as well as the review of prior-year working papers, client-prepared descriptions of the system, and other related materials. Of course, previous experience with an entity will also be relevant to completing this phase of the review process.

Consider the Client's Risk Profile

In performing a review of the control environment of an entity, you ought to consider the entity's risk profile. Past survey studies involving internal auditors have asked that they rank various risk attributes suggested in existing literature in the order of their importance to the internal auditor in evaluating audit risk. In order of importance, the risk factors deemed to be of some significance are listed here:

(1) poor design and/or past performance of internal controls;
(2) managers with a lower level of competence than desired;
(3) managers with less integrity than desired;
(4) units of substantial size that face larger potential losses;
(5) a recent change in systems, particularly the accounting system;

(6) operations of high complexity;

(7) highly liquid assets present in greater proportion to total assets than is typical for audit settings;

(8) lack of continuity in key personnel;

(9) units with poor economic conditions;

(10) rapid growth in operations;

(11) extensive computerization of data processing;

(12) greater than usual lapse of time since the last audit (e.g., due to a randomized rotational plan being in use);

(13) increased performance pressures on management to meet target objectives;

(14) extensive government regulation, adding an element of unpredictability (e.g., rate case decisions);

(15) low employee morale;

(16) lack of coverage of a unit by the external auditors;

(17) political exposure of the company (e.g., its manufacture of defense products or involvement in nuclear plant construction could lead to adverse publicity). (See Patton et al, 1981.)

Such risk factors are likely to be of similar relevance to the external auditor, except that #16 would be appropriately adjusted to reflect both the lack of past coverage by the external auditor and the lack of past or recent coverage by the internal auditors. General information regarding these risk factors can be obtained through observation and inquiry procedures in the early phase of control risk assessment.

Now that the minimal requirements have been delineated, return to the more common assumption that some control reliance is anticipated. In such a case, the decision as to whether the tests of control to facilitate reduction of control risk to less than a maximum level are cost/beneficial necessitates a comparison of the efficiency of tests of control relative to substantive tests.

KEY FACTORS TO CONSIDER WHEN MAKING EFFICIENCY COMPARISONS

The efficiency of testing controls will primarily depend on the

—strength of designed controls,

—stability of the control system,

—nature of the audit trail,

—timing of the audit procedures, and

—actual compliance with designed controls.

These efficiency considerations, once evaluated, form the basis for comparing a strategy of testing controls to that of a substantive testing approach. As a general guideline, a control test should be considered only in those circumstances that offer an opportunity to realize "savings" from reduced substantive tests.

In other words, the value of a test of control in the audit context is purely as a means of reducing substantive work. Of course, qualitative considerations like "client service" commitments may lead to testing of controls, as would an expanded engagement intended to report on internal accounting controls. However, these rationales for testing controls are adjustments to, rather than being an intrinsic part of, an audit plan.

Factors to Consider When Evaluating the Control Design

Compliance with poorly designed controls is meaningless. Hence, the first question you must answer is whether an entity's control design warrants reliance.

Identify these key controls. You must identify each of the important controls relating to the financial statement accounts on which you plan to form an opinion and assess their ability to provide assurance that

—only authorized transactions are being recorded,

—no such transactions are omitted, and

—all recorded transactions are accurate.

Can weaknesses be overcome by compensating controls? The controls may at times be redundant controls, in which case you should select only one of the controls for testing. At other times, a control will appear to be missing, but a broader review of the information and control system will reveal that a compensating control is operating as designed. The assurance this provides must then be evaluated in order to estimate the potential value of control test results in forming an audit opinion. Sometimes parallel controls are in operation, both of which may require testing as a basis for control reliance. When key controls are sequential, testing should proceed sequentially, as a severe weakness at early points in processing the transaction may preclude reliance on the related controls. If the client's designed controls overlap, you should be attentive to efficiency gains from testing such overlap only once.

Look for opportunities to test an overall control. You should be particularly alert for opportunities to test an overall control that effectively meets the objectives of various individual controls. For example, good control over the bank reconciliation procedure may effectively test various individual controls over multiple phases of the cash disbursement function. In selecting which control to test, evaluate the objectives to which the control relates. Frequently, several objectives can be met by one test of control, permitting the efficient reduction of several substantive test procedures based on a single control test procedure.

Evaluate the quality of the control. While a control may exist over the generation, processing, and accumulation of accounting information, you must evaluate the quality of that control with respect to its design. For example, is mathematical accuracy checked by someone other than the individual who performed the initial calculations? If supporting documentation for cash disbursements are filed with check copies, are such documents canceled? If a file of authorized purchase orders is maintained and these orders are matched to receiving reports before making disbursements, does the control system require the file of unmatched purchase orders to be periodically reviewed for follow-up? Are controls designed so that employees are not reviewing the work of their supervisors who have responsibility for the employees' performance evaluation?

Controls are frequently evaluated as good, fair, or poor. If poor, tests of control would generally be undesirable as an audit approach. If the controls are good, tests of control offer one viable audit strategy. The control areas with only a fair design are likely to require the most thorough analysis in determining whether it would be potentially cost effective to perform tests of control. Design considerations primarily provide information on the advisability of considering tests of control as an audit strategy, whereas other considerations will lead to a decision on whether the audit plan will actually include tests of control.

Focus on the entire control cycle. In evaluating design, you should focus on an entire cycle that leads to the various financial balances of interest. The old adage that "a chain is only as strong as its weakest link" has some applicability to control design. For example, a preliminary review of purchasing and receiving activities may suggest that purchases are properly authorized, receiving reports are completed on a timely basis, and these reports are required as a basis for cash disbursements to suppliers. However, the discovery that people who authorized purchase orders had access to blank receiving reports and uncanceled historical documentation that could be reused would cast a shadow over the operation of the entire control system over purchasing, receiving, and disbursements. Before allocating time to testing any single control, you should make sure that the design of that control is not tainted by some critical flaw in related controls. This phase of test work is frequently referred to as a test of general controls, as distinct from a test of specific controls. The point suggests the saying, "Don't lose sight of the forest for the trees." Unless the general controls are reasonably designed, the testing of specific controls is inappropriate.

Classifying Controls to Determine Which Will Be Tested

One aspect of controls that may be useful in evaluating their adequacy and in selecting which ones are to be tested is their classification as preventive, detective, or corrective. The terms are relatively self-explanatory. *Preventive controls* are intended to prevent the occurrence of an error or irregularity. Authorizations are an example of a preventive control intended to prevent unauthorized transactions, such as purchases. *Detective controls* are intended to detect problems that have occurred. A bank reconciliation is a detective control, intended to detect errors in cash receipts and cash disbursements. *Corrective controls* would relate to corrections of errors once they are detected. The requirements that one individual take responsibility for investigating and resolving customers' disputes, and that adjusting journal entries to correct detected errors be approved, are examples of controls directed at activities that correct records for detected errors. Many times, a detective control can compensate for a weak preventive control if it is operative on a timely basis. *Note*: Generally, if a preventive control exists, it will be the control selected for testing.

Exhibit 8–2 depicts the relationship of the various components of the control structure with the classification scheme of preventive and detective controls,

---

Exhibit 8–2

The Relationship of Control Structure Policies As They Relate to Objectives, Financial Statement Assertions, and Classification of Preventive and Detective Controls

Control Environment: *Preventive Control Policy or Procedure*	*Entity's Objective*	*Assertion*
A background check is performed on all prospective employees	To ensure qualified personnel and avoid those personnel known to lack integrity	All assertions, to the extent they are affected by competent personnel possessing integrity
Control Environment: *Detective Policy or Procedure*		
The Vice President of finance compares the budget with actual results each quarter and investigates significant variances	Control expenses	The presentation and disclosure of expenses
Accounting System: *Preventive Control*		
Receiving reports are matched with purchase orders before processing cash disbursements	To prevent payment for goods not received	Allocation of purchases to the appropriate time frame and propriety of purchase
Accounting System: *Detective Control*		
Reconciles bank statement on a monthly basis	To detect mishandling of cash and assure proper recording of cash transactions	Existence, completeness, allocation, and presentation of cash

Control Procedures:
Preventive Control
Policy or Procedure

| Owner/Manager approves credit terms | Reduce losses from uncollectibles | Valuation of accounts receivable |

Control Procedures:
Detective Control
Policy or Procedure

| Sales manager reviews summary of accrued commissions in light of sales activity per salesperson | Monitor sales performance | Completeness of sales revenue |

---

entities' objectives, and financial statement assertions. While not reflected, a corrective control is frequently a subsequent concern to assessing preventive or detective controls. For example, the reconciliation of a bank statement commonly prompts such corrective action as recording an entry to reflect non-sufficient funds checks and an eventual adjusting journal entry to write-off very old outstanding checks.

How to Determine the Stability of the Control System

After the design of the control system has been evaluated, the question of stability must be addressed. These factors should be considered:

—*New versus established system*. Is the control system newly designed or has it been in operation for some time?

—*Rigidity versus adaptability*. Does the system appear to be rigid over time or has it effectively adapted to changes in operations?

—*Manual versus computerized system*. Is the information system a manual or a computerized operation and how do frequent changes in hardware and software affect the stability of controls?

—*Effects of employee turnover*. How has employee turnover affected the stability of the control system, particularly compliance with that system, in past years?

—*Effects of the type or level of operations*. Do operating characteristics suggest any problems with system stability? For example, has the client been operating above normal capacity, with excessive overtime, making the likelihood of noncompliance with control procedures greater than usual due to the competing time demands of normal operating responsibilities?

How Many Control Systems Have Been in Operation?

The control system's stability is particularly important in evaluating the feasibility of control reliance. If three control systems have been operating within the past year over accounts payable, due to a gradual transition from a manual, to a mechanized, to a computerized system, how feasible would it be for you to test all three systems? If the controls are to provide a basis for evaluating all transactions recorded for that account area for the past year, it is not enough merely to test the "current" control system. You must also find out whether or not the two former control systems operated effectively.

In a similar manner, the turnover of a key person in a control cycle, such as the director of the electronic data processing department (EDP), may well merit your decision that two control systems were in operation for the past year—the control system directed by the predecessor and the one managed by the current director of EDP. Again, you must determine the feasibility of testing the two systems.

Consider the Likelihood of a System Change

You should also consider the likelihood of a system change subsequent to interim testing of controls. If controls are not expected to remain the same for the rest of the fiscal year, you must evaluate the economic feasibility of testing the two systems that will have been in operation by year-end. Such factors as the length of the time period in which the new system will be in operation and the magnitude of the transactions to be processed by that system will influence the extent of testing of controls that would be required at year-end.

A system may be thought of as unstable, yet have no clear demarcations as to new employees or new procedures that would facilitate the testing of separate systems in operation over a period of time. In such a case, you should consider the worst case of stability. For example, if the greatest instability stems from cyclical operations that overly pressure employees into trading off control duties, how bad is this "instability," and is otherwise "fair" to "good" control design likely to break down due to the control system's inability to adapt to full capacity operations? If the instability is due to continual changes in the lines of business of a conglomerate, does some "floor" exist below which controls are not permitted to fall? In particular, would such a "floor" warrant assessment of control risk at less than a maximum level if operating as designed?

Certain aspects of a system might be unstable, yet have no effect on the plausibility of assessing control risk at less than the maximum level. For example, a computerized system may be implemented, leaving a parallel manual system in operation throughout the first period of the transition to an EDP environment. The instability typical of a control system design for a newly computerized cycle of operations would have been avoided for the transition period, enabling you to give your full attention to the manual system in the year of transition (and on the computerized system in subsequent periods).

In an organization undergoing growth, an internal audit department may be established to exercise a check on controls. While this particular aspect of a control environment is likely to be unstable until the department's charter is established, its responsibilities are outlined, and experience is gained by the professional staff, you could nevertheless rely on the designed controls of the system that are to be subjected to the additional check of the internal audit department. The internal audit activities will be of greater use to you as the development stage stabilizes; however, in any case, improved controls that are unstable or checks on controls that are unstable should not serve as deterrents to your reliance on existing controls. If anything, the mere ongoing development and improvement of controls encourages reliance thereon. Instability in controls that is caused by timely on-going adaptation to achieve optimal controls is desirable, in contrast to the maintenance of a rigid, static (though admittedly "stable") control system.

Determining Whether the Audit Trail Can Be Tested

An important consideration in assessing the efficiency of control testing is whether or not there is an audit trail that can be tested in an expedient and effective manner. Several dimensions of the audit trail are relevant:

—existence of a trail,

—control over the quantity of documents comprising the trail,

—documentation control to ensure that an adequate trail, once generated, remains intact,

—accessibility of the audit trail, and

—ability of the auditor to draw samples for testing of controls.

Does the audit trail exist? The existence of an audit trail was addressed to some extent when the auditability issue was resolved. However, existence at this point encompasses more than the mere assurance that all transactions involving the operating entity get recorded in some traceable form. Your concern as you consider the control testing mode is whether the audit trail from the point at which it is generated to the point at which it enters the accounting journals and ledgers is sufficiently testable to serve as a basis for reducing control risk below the maximum level.

Look for adequate controls over the quantity of documentation. Often an audit trail will exist in the form of shipping and receiving documentation but will not indicate the potential for control reliance because of the relative absence of quantity controls. Are shipping documents and receiving reports prenumbered? If not, what assurance is there of the availability of a complete population of transactions from which a sample can be drawn for the purpose of drawing inferences to the relevant population of all shipments and purchases, respectively?

Be alert to the problem of physical documentation control. A related problem can arise even if documents are prenumbered; that problem relates to the physical control over documentation. Often documents are filed at various locations throughout the entity. As questions or disputes arise, employees often feel free to "pull" the original documentation from the files for follow-up. The problem arises when that documentation is not appropriately returned to the files. If you as auditor design a sampling plan and fail to obtain the original documentation corresponding to that plan's random selection, you are likely to obtain unacceptable results. This is largely due to the fact that any document that cannot be located must be deemed to be in error. In fact, controls may have been appropriately applied to that transaction, and the sole problem may well be the physical security over the documentation that's potentially capable of establishing that fact.

The log system: an easy solution. Of course, an easy solution is to establish logs over documentation so that any employee removing materials from the files has to check them out. Such a system establishes responsibility for the materials and facilitates location of missing documents that are part of the sample that has been drawn.

If numerical filing of documentation is not available, a log system becomes even more important due to the difficulty of defining a population. If one defines "all documents stored in these file cabinets" as the population from which a sample is to be drawn, the presumption is that the population sampled is equivalent to the population of interest. Obviously, if documents are missing, such a presumption is erroneous. An additional cost of applying a test of control when a log system is not in operation and numerical controls are not easily established over documentation is the cost of gaining assurance that the population to be tested corresponds to the population of primary interest.

Is Documentation Accessible?

Difficulties with locating documentation of interest are not confined to situations in which controls over documentation are lacking.

Storage conditions. Despite the presence of controls, the storage conditions of documents may make the audit trail, practically speaking, inaccessible. For example, if all raw data for a particular cycle are boxed and stored at a separate location after three months, you may well find an alternative document or testing procedure to be a preferable, more efficient auditing approach.

Branch offices. Similarly, if an entity has numerous branches, geographically disbursed, maintaining documentation that is not available on a centralized basis, you face a situation where economics preclude accessibility to 100% of the population. In most cases a multi-location sampling plan is applied. However, the relevant populations from which samples are drawn must be redefined, and the resulting audit coverage should be compared in a cost/benefit framework to alternative substantive testing approaches.

Determining which controls can be tested by sampling. Assuming an audit trail exists, is complete, is well controlled, and is accessible, the final dimension of particular interest to an auditor is its ability to be tested through some sampling approach. The typical dichotomy between controls that can and cannot be sampled is described in Exhibit 8–3. Examples of those specific tests of control that can be applied to meet each of the common test of control objectives are also provided in Exhibit 8–3. What should be evident is that the inability to sample often, by default, leaves you with no more than observation and inquiry procedures. However, most of these techniques, as seen in Exhibit 8–3, serve as prerequisites for the application of normal control test procedures. They tend to check out the reasonableness of the other attributes of the audit trail: existence, completeness, and control.

How secure is the audit trail? While accessibility of the documents is a practical concern in an auditor's sampling, it also has relevance to the segregation of duties issue presented in Exhibit 8–3. One of the valuable assets of an entity is its information base. It's imperative to the integrity of the company's financial records that the documents not be altered in any unauthorized fashion. Defalcations have involved such obvious alterations of documents as the "white-out" of endorsements on canceled checks and the removal of canceled checks from a bank statement, replacing such checks with substitute documents. Alteration involves not only substitution, but also the addition of documentation to the information system. For example, entities have been known to secure blank bills of lading and similar documents that facilitated bogus inflation of recorded inventory and other assets on the books of an entity. Obviously, in order to enter the financial records, such documentation would have to enter the audit trail after the receiving department's point of control but before the initial recording of inventory or other assets in the accounting records. Of course, any established control to compare receiving activity to accounting records would have to be satisfied for the bogus transactions. This may not be difficult, however, if many people have easy access to blank and/or completed receiving reports. The security of an audit trail is essential to a testing of controls audit approach.

Timing of the Audit Procedures: Avoiding the Busy Season "Crunch"

Interim versus year-end. In selecting an audit approach, an important consideration is when those audit procedures are to be applied. A widely acknowledged advantage of control test work is the CPA's ability to perform the procedures at an interim date. However, when tests are performed at interim, assurance of control is gained for only that period tested, i.e., from the beginning of the fiscal year to the date of interim testing. At year-end the CPA must apply other procedures or extend the sample drawn at the interim date in order to gain assurance that controls were in place for the remainder of the year. The length of time that elapses from the interim date to year-end, the magnitude of transactions to be processed during this period, the stability of controls, the results of

Exhibit 8–3

Control Test Objectives Intended to Detect Invalid, Unauthorized, Incorrect, Misclassified, and Unrecorded Transactions That Are Due to Noncompliance with Designed Controls as Well as Both Inadequate Controls and Unsegregated Duties

Internal Accounting Controls for Which Samples Cannot Be Drawn to Test Controls

Segregation of Duties	Existence of Records or Procedures That Are Deemed to Be Essential
Observe that segregation exists by watching how procedures are being performed and who performs them.	Confirm that documents are prenumbered.
	Confirm that document logs are in use.
Observe whether access to valuable and/or highly pilferable assets is restricted.	Inquire as to the existence of clients' credit and related policies and their reasonableness.
	Observe whether monthly statements are mailed.
Inquire as to the job duties of each employee.	Inquire whether time cards and/or similar control records are used.
	Observe whether a restricted endorsement is used on cash receipts.
	Inquire whether internal auditors perform confirmation procedures; if so, observe them.
	Inquire about and review internal audit work.

Internal Accounting Controls for Which Samples Can Be Drawn to Test Controls

Approval	Dual Control via Signatures	Cancellation of Documents	Checking Procedures
Examine documents for evidence of approval.	Examine documents for evidence of dual approval.	Confirm that supporting documents for disbursements (including petty cash) were properly canceled.	Compare dates and amounts across corresponding documents against authorized files, and into the accounting records.
Trace investments, capital expenditures, and similar transactions to the minutes of the board of directors' meetings.	When dual access to signature plates, lock boxes, and valuable assets is required, confirm that both required signatures are documented for each time that access was granted.	Account for the sequence of checks and proper voiding of unissued past disbursements.	Confirm that the mathematical accuracy of books was checked.
Compare authorized signatures file to signatures used to gain access to marketable securities, signature plates, and so on.			Distribute payroll on a surprise basis.
			Check for the reconciliation of accounts to subsidiary and control accounts.

the interim test procedures, and the planned substantive test work will all influence the nature of the "other procedures" to be performed as of year-end.

Design a sampling plan that covers the year's transactions. If you can estimate the size of the population of transactions for the entire year, as of the interim date, you can design a sampling plan that addresses the total year's transactions. Obviously, only the sampled items as of the interim date can be examined at the time the sampling plan is formulated, but at year-end the transactions corresponding to the remaining sampling units can be examined. In this manner, your conclusion as to the client's compliance with designed controls relates to the entire period under audit.

Be aware of this drawback. Of course, this sampling approach has a drawback: no conclusion regarding controls can be drawn at the interim date. Hence, an assessment of control risk at less than the maximum level may turn out to be inappropriate if, at year-end, a number of deviations from controls are identified in the sampling units that were unavailable for examination at the interim date.

Continuous monitoring. Another aspect of timing that relates to the nature of the audit trail is the plausibility of a continuous monitoring approach. The concept of an integrated test facility discussed earlier is an example of a mechanism that can provide continuous feedback to an auditor.

A less formal but nevertheless important source of continuous monitoring is the periodic observation and inquiry techniques applied during the period to be audited. For some large clients, a CPA may have a permanent office at the client's business, as (s)he may be involved in audit, acquisition, tax, and advisory services for the entire year. When a CPA has this type of continual access to a client and has the potential of "blending into the normal day-to-day operating setting," (s)he can acquire a very good sense of the control environment of that entity.

In a similar manner, the CPA for a small business or nonprofit entity who provides various advisory and tax services in the course of a year may be able to infer, in fairly accurate terms, the nature of the client's control environment. Frequent visits to a client offer an opportunity for surprise observations of operations and the manner in which employees carry out their day-to-day responsibilities.

One of the most difficult aspects of checking those controls that cannot be tested through sampling (as exemplified in Exhibit 8–3) is the fact that observation and inquiry procedures tend to be "snapshots." While providing some assurance of controls that are currently in operation, such one-time examinations tell you nothing about past or future controls. Yet, just as a number of photographs flipped quickly can give the impression of a continuous motion picture, a number of "snapshots" in the course of a fiscal year (particularly if made on an unannounced basis) can provide a reasonably complete picture of controls for the auditor.

Weigh the costs and benefits of applying particular procedures at interim rather than year-end. The importance of timing to the efficiency of alternative approaches to an audit is largely due to the seasonal nature of audit work. The infamous busy season is in large part created by the dominance of calendar year audit clients who also have tax work demands at year-end. Filings with many regulatory agencies are required within two months of year-end, and many substantive audit procedures can be performed only as of year-end (such as end-of-year inventory observation procedures). These factors lead to excessive workloads for CPAs at year-end, which translate to overtime costs, fatigue and morale problems with professional staff members, and other unfavorable consequences. Hence, any audit procedure that can be applied at other than year-end offers economic and efficiency advantages over applying that same procedure at year-end. The relevant question is, "What are the costs and benefits of applying a particular procedure at interim, relative to some alternative procedure that is thought to provide similar or improved audit assurance at year-end?"

Rating Actual Compliance with Designed Controls

Beyond the design and stability of a control system, a critical factor you should consider is the anticipated level of compliance with such controls, as well as the capability of efficiently determining the extent of actual compliance. The latter has been addressed in discussions of the nature of the audit trail and the alternatives that exist with respect to the timing of audit procedures. The former is a separate judgment that has substantial bearing on the selection of an efficient auditing approach.

The typical convention is to rate various controls as good, fair, or poor, and to rely only on good and fair controls with which employees regularly comply. You can estimate the likelihood of compliance with controls based on

—the client's control environment, with particular attention to the quality of staffing and the frequency of employee turnover.

—past audit experience, i.e., the extent of compliance that was observed in prior years' audits, and

—recent observation and inquiry-based evidence.

Control environment, staffing, and past experience. For example, if the client has understaffed the accounting department, tends to have little or no formal training, has few if any procedures manuals, has had a control system that has not warranted control reliance in prior years, and has recently been observed to be operating in what appears to be an unorganized, unsupervised manner, you would not anticipate that good test of control results would be obtained. On the other hand, if staffing by a well-trained, rather stable work force is observed and controls have been tested in prior years and have warranted reliance thereon, you have every reason to believe that tests of control would support the auditor's assessment of control risk at less than the maximum level.

Evaluate effect of expected compliance with designed controls to help determine sample size. As described earlier, the auditor's estimated population error rate (or compliance deviation rate) is an input to the formula that serves as a basis for determining sample size. In order to draw a reasonably small sample size, the expected rate of deviation needs to be fairly low. Should the expected rate of deviation from controls be expected to be high, a control testing approach is likely to be inefficient, if not inappropriate. You should take care to design control tests that are applied to a sufficiently large sample that some deviations can be tolerated, since human error is likely to cause a few exceptions for an extremely strong system of controls.

Dual-Purpose Testing Opportunities

A final efficiency consideration for the auditor is whether the use of a dual-purpose testing approach is preferred to a control or substantive testing approach. Practically speaking, a test of controls is one that is applied to a control with a specified control objective, while a substantive test is directed at the propriety of an account balance. Whenever a test provides evidence of both compliance with a control objective and propriety of an account balance, that procedure can be termed a dual-purpose test. From examining one sample, you can frequently draw conclusions as to dollar amounts and control in almost half the time required to separately perform control testing and substantive testing procedures. Many times the complete performance of a test of control automatically provides information as to dollar balances. This will become clear as the nature of a test of control is discussed in further depth.

SYNOPSIS

The attributes that affect the relative efficiency of testing control and substantive testing approaches are illustrated in Exhibit 8–4. A composite picture of these factors for each audit engagement and for each control cycle within a particular engagement provides the basis for selecting an audit plan that will efficiently accomplish the varied audit objectives.

WHAT'S INVOLVED IN PERFORMING A TEST OF CONTROL?

Should the efficiency comparisons guided by Exhibit 8–4 indicate that testing of controls is desirable, you must then plan and execute the necessary procedures that will disclose the appropriate level of control risk. The judgments regarding efficiency and the selection of particular procedures rely on your understanding of what constitutes a test of control.

Exhibit 8–3 provided some examples of tests of control that may appear to be rather straightforward. However, consider one of the descriptions provided in this exhibit: "Examine documents for evidence of approval." To make sense of such a description, the control test must be placed in the context of a control cycle with a particular control objective of interest.

Exhibit 8–4

Relevant Attributes Affecting the Efficiency of Alternative Audit Approaches

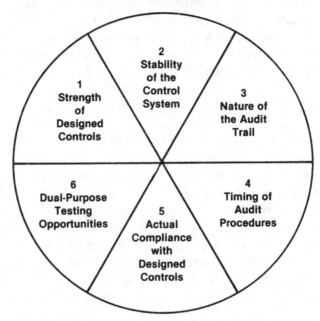

• Only authorized transactions are being recorded

• All authorized transactions are recorded

• Transactions are recorded accurately

• Apparent weaknesses may be overcome by compensating controls

• Quality of controls (appropriate timing, follow-up, and segregation of duties) is relevant

• Focus should be upon the entire control cycle

Consider:

• New vs. established system

• Rigidity vs. adaptability of system

• Manual vs. computerized system—effects of changing technology

• Effects of employee turnover

• Effects of the level of operations

• How many different systems are in operation in the course of a year?

Relevant dimensions include:

• Existence

• Control over the quantity of documents

• Documentation control

• Accessibility

• Flexibility to be sampled

Consider:

• Interim vs. year-end

• Ability to draw conclusions regarding the entire period under audit

• Continuous monitoring possibilities

• "Busy season" effects

• Consider the control environment, past audit experience, and recent observation- and inquiry-based evidence

• Evaluate the effect of the expected compliance with designed controls as an input for determining sample size

• Select a test capable of providing evidence re:

  —compliance with controls and

  —propriety of account balances

• The efficiency of using one sample for two testing objectives should be apparent

Assume that the cycle of interest is the purchasing cycle. You are interested in determining whether all purchase orders have been properly authorized. Assume that the employee who is responsible for written authorization of purchase orders has been instructed to confirm that

(1) all vendors are on the approved vendor listing,
(2) no purchase of over $20,000 is made without the vice president's approval,
(3) competitive bids are on file for suppliers of units that cost more than $1,000 each, and
(4) for raw material acquisitions, the reorder point has been flagged in the perpetual inventory records.

Under these circumstances, what will constitute an effective control test of authorization?

Why Reperformance of Control Procedures Is Essential

A simplistic response would be that you need only check for the initials or signature of the employee who has responsibility for the formal authorization of purchases. If written evidence is available, you could point to such evidence as support for a client's compliance with prescribed authorization procedures.

Why mere inspection is not sufficient. However, is mere inspection of initials or signatures an adequate check for compliance? Would it not be possible for an employee, caught short of time, to merely affix his or her authorization on the documents of interest without performing the prescribed procedures? If this were the case, would reliance upon the affixed signature be appropriate? Would prescribed controls be operative? Obviously, the controls would not be operating as designed, yet the mere examination of signatures would not detect such noncompliance. The relevant question is, "What would constitute a test of prescribed authorization procedures for the purchasing cycle?"

Steps You Should Take to Perform a Test of Control

If you wish to test compliance with prescribed authorization procedures, you must actually reperform such procedures for each sampling unit selected for testing. In other words, for a sample of purchase orders you would

(1) check for written authorization,
(2) check that the vendor's name also appeared on the approved vendor listing,
(3) check if the purchase is over $20,000 and, if so, that the vice-president's approval is documented,
(4) check the files for competitive bids on purchases involving units that cost more than $1,000 each, and
(5) trace raw material acquisitions to the corresponding inventory item on

the perpetual inventory records to confirm that the reorder point has been reached.

Only by reperforming the procedures is it possible for you to test compliance. If this complete test of control were performed and the partial test of control results became part of the evidential base in a litigation suit, the plaintiff's attorney might be able to demonstrate that "not only were few purchase orders examined, but for the few documents that were examined, errors were present, yet were not detected by the CPA." What would be the Court's reasonable reaction to the demonstration that *bogus suppliers* and *unsupported prices in excess of the $1,000* appeared on purchase orders that were sampled by the CPA? Obviously, the prudent care of the CPA in examining the various items could very well be the subject of some dispute.

The question of what constitutes a test of control is best answered as the reperformance of all control-related duties being tested for each sampling unit selected. Hence, when an employee is to check the mathematical accuracy of a purchase order and is then supposed to initial the order to document that such a check has been performed, in order to test compliance, you must both

—examine the document for physical evidence of an accuracy check, i.e., the employee's initials, and

—recompute the math on the purchase order to confirm that the math is accurate.

One Key Advantage of a Complete Test of Control

One advantage of a complete test of control is that it will frequently provide quantitative results that could be used in fulfilling dual-purpose test objectives. For example, if you are interested in testing the recorded cost of production and/ or accounts payable, the examination of the purchase orders that enter the books as raw material purchases and other payable obligations can provide some assurance as to the accuracy of the recorded balances.

Determining What Constitutes a Compliance Deviation

In addition to recognizing the fact that tests of control encompass the reperformance of prescribed control duties and often provide dual-purpose information, it is essential that you know what constitutes a compliance deviation. In the planning phase of control testing, you must determine what will constitute a compliance deviation as you reperform the prescribed control duties of primary interest. In the purchase order example, the obvious potential compliance deviations would include

—no written evidence of approval,

—the use of a vendor not on the approved vendor listing,

—no approval by the vice-president of purchases that exceed $20,000,

—no competitive bid file on purchases involving units that cost more than $1,000 each, and

—no indication that a reorder point had been reached according to the perpetual inventory records when the raw materials were purchased.

However, what if the party authorizing purchase orders notes on the order that the vendor is not on the approved listing, yet was verbally approved by the vice president? What if no competitive bid file is located and inquiry procedures suggest that such bids are irrelevant to the selected purchase because only one supplier is available for those particular items being purchased? What if a reorder point was not flagged on the perpetual inventory records, yet inquiry procedures indicated that this was due to notification by that particular supplier that an extra two-week lead time would be necessary on orders due to a strike situation at that supplier's plant? What if you observe that a $30,000 purchase was split across two purchase orders to effectively circumvent the $20,000 authorization procedure?

In each of these settings, you would most likely not declare such occurrences to be compliance deviations. Based on a review and understanding of operations and the control system, you would be aware of "authorized" and "acceptable" exceptions to the rule. On the other hand, the effective circumvention of the $20,000-procedure, while not a deviation, suggests the lack of a control environment.

What to look for. The focal point of compliance deviations is the potential for error in the financial statements as a result of the deviations, rather than the actual error or lack thereof in the transactions under review. The profession has referred to compliance deviations as the "smoke" that can dissipate without error ("fire") in the accounting records or that can, in fact, cause error in those same statements. When exceptions to prescribed controls are permitted or when control checks are easily circumvented, you must evaluate the control over such exceptions and the ramifications of effective circumvention. If variations from prescribed duties must be documented and if there is a compensating control for those controls that were or apparently could be circumvented, no control deviations may be present.

On the other hand, if a post-facto justification of noncompliance is proposed, with no physical evidence that the noncompliance was traceable to a particular finding, such as the availability of only one supplier for a particular good, that noncompliance is likely to be deemed a compliance deviation. Yet, it should be acknowledged that the use of a vendor who was not on the vendor listing may not cause any error in the accounting records. The purchase may be business related, at a preferable price. The potential errors of (1) using bogus suppliers, (2) making nonbusiness purchases, or (3) having unsupported expenditures may not have occurred for the sampling unit. A conservative rule of thumb is that only one out of three compliance deviations leads to error in the financial statements (sometimes referred to as the three-to-one ratio of "smoke" to "fire"). By defining what constitutes a test of control, reperforming control duties, and carefully describing control deviations before performing control test procedures, you can be sure that the actual tests will be complete and interpretable, even in the absence of a one-to-one correspondence to financial statement errors.

Key point to keep in mind. The critical point to keep in mind is that tests of control are intended to provide evidence about the operation of controls, not about the individual transactions being controlled. Hence, a deviation is significant even if the particular transaction being tested is not in error. The question of interest is what the implications of having a control in operation that is not appropriately applied 1%, 2%, or 6% of the time. A deviation need not correspond to an error to affect the auditor's strategy in formulating an audit opinion. In fact, all deviations have a bearing on the reasonableness of your assessment of control risk.

How should dollar amounts be considered in relation to control testing? It is the relative absence of a dollar amount conclusion from control testing procedures that accounts for the auditor's lack of concern for the dollar amount of the various transactions that are tested. While stratified sampling, whereby a greater number of large dollar transactions are tested than small dollar transactions, is a popular audit approach in substantive testing, it is typically unrelated to a control testing approach.

When dollar amounts should be considered. The reason for using the term "typically" is that the design of controls can make the dollar magnitude of transactions a relevant consideration in planning tests of control.

For example, in the purchasing example described earlier, the vice president's approval was required for purchases over $20,000. This implies two different subsystems of control: those applicable to purchases less than or equal to $20,000, and those that apply to purchases in excess of $20,000. Such a designed control could be the basis for a stratification of transactions into two subgroups for the purpose of separately testing those transactions that are and those that are not subjected to the vice-president's approval.

Dual-purpose testing. Another reason that the term "typically" is appropriate is that if a sample is to be used for dual-purpose testing, an efficiency argument can be made for selecting higher dollar values for the sample. In such a case, a possibility that should be considered is that the control test results do not accurately reflect the level of compliance with controls when applied to lower dollar items. When the sampling bias is combined with the unintentional human bias of taking greater care with large-dollar transactions, the findings could be substantially distorted.

Client service. One other reason for using the term "typically" relates to client service. Some practicing CPAs believe that, in addition to testing the compliance with controls for reliance purposes, the CPA is expected to test a certain percentage of dollar transactions that are subject to control and to report this percentage to the audit client.

Note: If the client wishes such a report, it should be considered as a separate, though joint, service with no necessary relationship to the required evidential base for formulating an audit report. To bias a test of control sample toward larger dollar amounts is inappropriate if controls are to be applied to all transactions regardless of their magnitude. The question to be answered is how well did controls operate in processing transactions, not how well did controls operate in processing large dollar transactions!

As compliance deviations are detected you should keep in mind the expected number of deviations utilized in designing sample size. Obviously if four deviations are expected for a sample of 60 items and the first three items tested have deviations, the level of compliance is not as expected and further testing of the sample would be fruitless. The test of control in such a situation is appropriately terminated and an alternate audit approach is selected.

Look for These Potential Causes of Compliance Deviations

Compliance deviations can result for a variety of reasons.

New or untrained employees. For a new employee, the misunderstanding of instructions or the absence of on-the-job training can easily account for observed problems. A learning curve is likely to be observed for new employees. Mistakes will occur more frequently as the employees are first learning their duties. The substitution of one employee who is unfamiliar with the specific duties to be assumed, for another employee who is on vacation, can cause problems similar to those observed for new employees, and yet such a circumstance is more difficult to detect due to the absence of the signal provided by employees' turnover.

Inadequate staffing. If the staffing in the accounting department or in other operating departments is inadequate, the likelihood of error due to employees' fatigue and carelessness increases. This is particularly true if the employees are regularly required to work overtime.

Seasonality of operations. A related cause of compliance deviations is the seasonality of operations. Retail clients have the Christmas rush, ski lodge operations are besieged by customers through the holiday season, and numerous lines of business experience monthly and quarterly peaks and troughs. Those peaks may, by definition, represent periods of "understaffing" that will tend to increase the frequency of errors by tired employees who become more careless as their weariness grows.

Related Party Considerations. In evaluating risks, the auditor must try to identify any related parties [SAS 45, Section 1020]; however, an "examination made in accordance with generally accepted auditing standards cannot be expected to provide assurance that all related party transactions will be discovered."[2] Hence, noncompliance could be the result of an undetected related party relationship. Exhibit 8–5 summarizes the types of procedures that are useful in identifying and examining related-party transactions, including those that are unreported. If a client is having economic trouble, a related party may provide free services, such as computer time or consultations, thus distorting the entity's financial operating picture.

---

[2] Statement on Auditing Standards No. 6, "Related Party Transactions" (New York: AICPA, July 1975), par. 09.

Exhibit 8–5

Identifying and Examining Related Party Transactions

Key Sources of Information

Filings, including proxy material, with the Securities and Exchange Commission and other regulatory bodies.

Information on pension and other trusts established for employees, emphasizing the names of officers and trustees.

Stockholder listings of closely held companies.

Predecessor, principal, or other auditors.

Minutes of board of director meetings, emphasizing material transactions authorized or discussed.

Conflict-of-interest statements completed by management.

Major customer, supplier, borrower, and lender listings.

Large, unusual, or nonrecurring transactions or balances in accounting records.

Confirmations of compensating balance arrangements.

Invoices from law firms.

Confirmations of loans receivable and payable for indications of guarantees.

Contracts involving material transactions.

Management.

Audit Procedures

Review written sources and ask management about related parties and their transactions.

Keep a central listing of related parties in the continuing or permanent audit file, and make certain that all audit staff members are familiar with these names in conducting their audit work, in order to facilitate the identification of related party transactions.

Evaluate the entity's procedures for identifying and properly accounting for related party transactions.

Exhibit 8–5 (continued)

Per related party transaction:

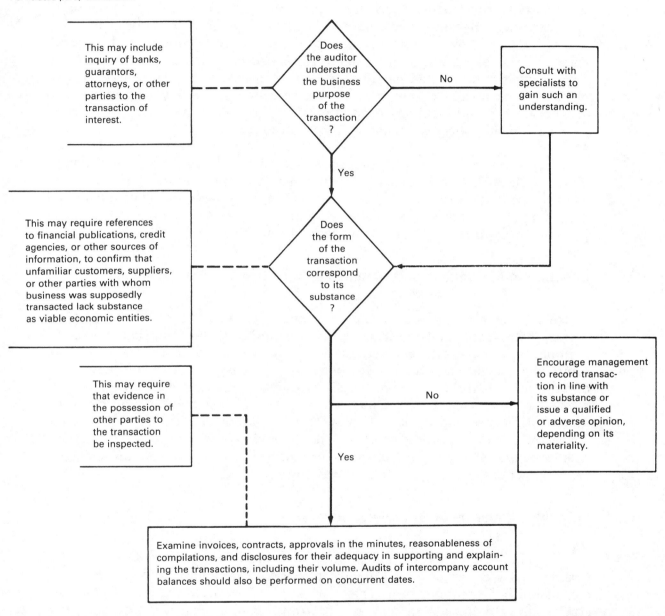

This may include inquiry of banks, guarantors, attorneys, or other parties to the transaction of interest.

Does the auditor understand the business purpose of the transaction?

No → Consult with specialists to gain such an understanding.

Yes

This may require references to financial publications, credit agencies, or other sources of information, to confirm that unfamiliar customers, suppliers, or other parties with whom business was supposedly transacted lack substance as viable economic entities.

Does the form of the transaction correspond to its substance?

No → Encourage management to record transaction in line with its substance or issue a qualified or adverse opinion, depending on its materiality.

This may require that evidence in the possession of other parties to the transaction be inspected.

Yes

Examine invoices, contracts, approvals in the minutes, reasonableness of compilations, and disclosures for their adequacy in supporting and explaining the transactions, including their volume. Audits of intercompany account balances should also be performed on concurrent dates.

Related parties increase the likelihood of collusion in order to promote joint interests. For example, property and services may be exchanged or sold at other than their fair market value, or borrowing may be arranged at below market rates with rather vague payment terms. These types of transactions can materially distort financial statements. The form of the related-party transactions must be compared with their substance. If a loan is not supposed to be repaid, then contributed capital may well be the substance of the financing arrangement. Below-market interest rates will distort an entity's true cost of debt, and consequently, the reported return on funds borrowed will not indicate the future expected returns to stockholders. Because of related-party transactions' greater risk, the planning process should allow time to investigate them, in accordance with the overall perceived risk exposure. In designing controls, special care needs to be directed toward identifying related parties and then monitoring such transactions commensurate with their higher risk. In testing controls, if a deviation or circumvention is observed involving related parties, corrective action may be merited to sever economic ties or otherwise improve the control setting.

Fraud. Of course, the possibility exists that the compliance deviation is intentional. Such a situation can have far-reaching implications. You must consider the possibility that fraud has occurred or that some event requiring special disclosure and potentially affecting the financial statement balances has taken place—such as a related party transaction or an illegal act.

Interpreting the Causes and Ramifications of Compliance Deviations

Whenever a compliance deviation is identified, you should investigate and interpret its causes and ramifications. For example, if the cause is a change in staffing, how many transactions are likely to be subject to the same type of compliance deviation? Should the client be requested to review and adjust, as appropriate, the transactions processed by the new employee during the first two weeks on the job, based on the fact that formal orientation and training did not occur until the second week of employment? If the cause of the deviation stems from staff overload during peak periods, should you stratify the transactions processed and select more from the peak period, in order to get an adequate reflection of employees' compliance with controls?

Be Alert to Patterns or Systematic Errors

The clue to interpreting compliance deviations is to be alert to systematic errors or patterns in observed deviations. As an example, if three clerks have responsibility for testing the extension accuracy of invoices, and if every time an error occurs the initials on that invoice are those of clerk #1, the cause of the error and the potential scope of the compliance deviations become easier to identify. If you are testing the extension of payroll and observe a systematic overstatement of withholding taxes of two cents, the source of the problem may be a programming error or, as uncovered in some past examinations, an intentional defalcation that over time and across a large number of employees can represent a material loss to an entity. Unintentional errors with immaterial financial statement effects are expected to be randomly distributed, suggesting no systematic pattern or repetition in the population of interest.

Your Role in Reporting Compliance Deviations

You should be alert to the client service potential for reporting to the client on compliance deviations and on means of improving controls. As discussed in a later chapter, the management letter is a useful form for reporting on control test results and making recommendations to the client that have operating efficiency and control advantages.

EXAMPLES OF TESTS OF CONTROL AND THEIR RELATIONSHIP TO SUBSTANTIVE AUDIT PROCEDURES

Control test procedures depend on the particular control procedure being tested. As demonstrated in Exhibit 8–3, some controls can be tested only through inquiry and observation procedures, while other controls can be tested through sampling procedures involving the inspection of supporting documentation.

When Inquiry Procedures Can Be Especially Helpful

Inquiry procedures can be particularly helpful in evaluating

—employees' understanding of controls,

—employees' perceptions as to their and others' compliance with prescribed controls, and

—the day-to-day effective segregation of duties.

Look for Both Informal and Formal Procedures

In all organizations, informal groups and practices tend to develop parallel to formal organizations, and the result can be deviations from formally prescribed procedures. The auditor can attempt to uncover the nature of informal operations by making open-ended inquiries of various key employees. For example, by asking employees to describe their primary working relationships, including the individuals involved, the nature of the tasks performed, and the time spent carrying out the various activities, the auditor can gain an understanding of how operations are actually conducted. The auditor should explicitly design inquiry procedures to gain such insight as to both formal and informal procedures, particularly as to the effect that informality has upon controls.

Examples of Tests of Control to Conduct Per Major Cycle of Operations

The walk-through procedure described earlier, if appropriately designed—i.e., to interface with a sampling plan—can be considered as part of the test of transactions. Exhibit 8–6 provides numerous examples of tests of control per major cycle of operations. Many of these tests are dual-purpose.

Exhibit 8-6

Examples of Tests of Control Per Cycle

REVENUE OR INCOME-PRODUCING CYCLE	COST OF SALES OR PRODUCTION CYCLE	FINANCING AND NONROUTINE TRANSACTIONS
Check whether billing documents are prenumbered and account for their numerical sequence.	Observe • payroll distribution.	Obtain and review • organization chart • accounting policy and procedures manual
Select invoices and sales return and allowance memos and test for • credit department approval • pricing against price lists • extensions and footings.	Inspect • employee compensation plans for compliance with ERISA • requisitions of raw materials • transfer slips to and from work-in-process • time records and related reports and trace to payroll and production accounts	• fidelity bond coverage • documentation underlying balance sheet estimates • closing journal entries • standard reporting forms for all operating units • consolidation schedules • financial report
Select invoices and sales return and allowance memos and trace • to shipping and receiving records, respectively, with special attention to cutoff • to entries in detail records.	• invoices for purchases and tie to recorded payables • shipping documents.	• employees' stock purchase plans • propriety of unissued and canceled certificates
Test client's procedure of soliciting confirmations from customers periodically by observing the sending of statements and by investigating the differences and discrepancies reported by customers.	Test accuracy of payroll calculations and related reports as well as pension-related computations and stock option grants.	• opinion from lawyer that the issue of shares has complied with state and SEC requirements • summary of changes in equity balances, recompute, test for board of directors' approval, and reconcile to records.
Compare customers' orders to copies of billings sent to customers; check for evidence that any unusual discounts taken were appropriately approved.	Evaluate • reasonableness of overhead allocation and accuracy of related contributions • reasonableness of standard costs and related variance analyses	Trace documentation of stock issues and dividends to records.
Test extensions and footings of • journal entries • journals and ledgers.	• reasonableness of inventory valuation by comparing to invoices, purchase commitments, pricing policies, and uncompleted contracts.	Trace proceeds and disbursements to records and check their accuracy.
Examine the records for evidence of periodic reconciliation of subsidiary ledgers and journals to the general ledger and check for accuracy.	Reconcile related accounts: e.g., work-in-process credits to finished goods debits.	Review the client's calendar of principal payments and interest payments.
Review cash receipt records and tie to bank statements, testing for accuracy.	Trace entries to supporting documentation, e.g., payable vouchers, invoices, payroll records, and requisitions.	Examine company policies regarding the use of an imprest bank account for dividend payments and ascertain that such a policy is in effect, if applicable.

338

Observe opening of mail and prelisting of cash receipts; observe the restriction of employees' and other parties' access to cash.

Test deposit activities and processing on a "live" basis; observe the controller receiving deposit slips and bank statements directly from the bank, then review and test the bank reconciliation that the controller prepares.

Test entries in receivable records to underlying source documents.

Discuss with the client the established criteria for extending credit and ascertain the reasonableness of such criteria.

Review collectibility procedures, including those directed at accounts that were previously written off.

Review the client's aging schedules for accounts receivable, noting the timeliness of their preparation and their accuracy.

As invoices are processed, verify account distribution, its accuracy and approval thereof.

Check compliance with inventory observation procedures and tie in test counts; especially note cutoff and handling of consignments.

Coordinate compliance counting with inventory records and test accuracy of compilation of inventory.

Ascertain whether invoices, shipping reports, bills of lading, receiving reports, and intercompany transfers are recorded in proper period.

Examine the records for evidence of periodic reconciliation of subsidiary ledgers and journals to the general ledger and check for accuracy.

Test evidence of ownership, i.e., deeds and property tax receipts, of property.

Observe use of property and its existence.

Test accuracy of depreciation calculations.

Trace depreciation entries to ledger accounts.

Check compliance with property purchase procedures and abandonment procedures.

Review lease-related procedures.

Inquire whether standard journal entries are used to amortize the balances of intangibles and review such entries.

Inquire whether in-house legal counsel review and evaluate pending litigation on a routine basis and review their analyses.

Inquire whether effective control exists over redeemed notes and bonds, canceled equity securities and unissued securities, and examine evidence of such control; ascertain whether stock certificates are prenumbered and account for their numerical sequence.

Inquire whether an internal auditing department exists; review evidence of the internal auditors' competency and independence and examine their working papers and audit reports to evaluate the quality and scope of their work.

Five-Step Approach to Selecting Tests of Control

However, the relevant question is how the auditor selects among the available tests of control, or, for that matter, among the numerous controls to which such tests can be applied.

Your approach should be a five-step process:

(1) Consider the primary audit objective.
(2) Select the substantive tests that when applied would achieve the audit objective.
(3) Evaluate what controls, if operative, would cost/beneficially reduce substantive tests by altering their
   —nature,
   —timing, or
   —extent.
(4) Select the control(s) which meet the control objective identified in Step 3.
(5) If more than one control relates to the objective, select the key control for testing that is expected to be most efficient and effective in meeting the audit objective.

Examples of How Tests of Control Relate to Substantive Audit Procedures

Examples of how tests of control relate to substantive audit procedures are provided in Exhibit 8–7. You must carefully evaluate, prior to performing any tests of control, how the planned substantive tests will be affected by evidence of control compliance. Unless the control test is cost-justified in this manner, it ought not to be performed for audit purposes. The possibility always exists, of course, that client requests or a complementary engagement to report on controls will lead to control related test work which would not have been performed if the audit report had been your sole concern.

SYNOPSIS

The external auditor must make a choice as to what combination of control, substantive, and dual-purpose tests will be most efficient in providing a sufficient evidential base to form an audit opinion. If tests of control are to be omitted, the auditor is nonetheless required to gain an understanding of the control structure and to document such understanding. If tests of control are to be performed, i.e., if control risk is assessed at less than a maximum level, the control structure is to be documented in sufficient depth to facilitate an evaluation of the controls' design and the selection of those controls for testing that, if operating as prescribed, will reduce substantive test work. The expected reduction of substantive work should generate cost savings that exceed the costs of performing the planned tests of control; if not, the tests will not be performed for audit purposes. Several

Exhibit 8-7

The Relationship of Control Testing to Substantive Audit Procedures

OBJECTIVE	CONTROL TEST WORK	EXPECTED REDUCTION OF SUBSTANTIVE TEST WORK
	REVENUE OR INCOME-PRODUCING CYCLE	
Accuracy of recorded sales and receivables.	Test for effectiveness of segregated duties through inquiry and observation procedures.	• Smaller sample sizes for sales cutoff tests.
	Match orders from customers to billings, checking reasonableness of dates and agreement of amounts.	• Less documentation of allowance for doubtful accounts must be examined.
	Examine shipping and billing documents to determine if they are prenumbered and that the sequence of numbers used is complete.	• Reduce the number of confirmations mailed to customers.
	Match recorded sales to shipping documents and ascertain that the client follows up on "open items," i.e., unmatched shipping documents or sales without shipping document support.	• Utilize negative confirmation requests instead of positive requests. • Perform confirmation procedures prior to year-end.
	Review cash receipts records and tie to bank statements.	
	Discuss with the client the criteria for extending credit and assess the reasonableness of such criteria.	
Investments Related		
Existence of marketable securities	If access is restricted at client's office —observe whether restrictions are followed —compare signature files of authorized personnel to signatures in records of those gaining access.	• Certificates could be examined prior to year-end.
	If held by a trust company —examine agreement for safekeeping and report by trust company's auditors as to the control over securities held for third parties —inquire as to the reputation of the trust company and its financial position.	• Confirmation procedures with the trust company could be applied in lieu of physical inspection of securities.

Exhibit 8–7 (continued)

OBJECTIVE	CONTROL TEST WORK	EXPECTED REDUCTION OF SUBSTANTIVE TEST WORK
	COST OF SALES OR PRODUCTION CYCLE	
Accurate inventory records	If no standard cost system —dates on receiving reports, invoices, and inventory records correspond, as do the quantities entered in the records —dates on shipping documents, billings, and inventory records reasonably correspond, as do the quantities entered in the records. If standard cost system —review system and analyses of variances for completeness and the reasonableness of explanations —test a sample of actual material, labor, and overhead costs, and gain assurance that they are being compared to the appropriate standards.	• Inventory observation can be performed prior to year-end. • Test counts and the scope of observation can be reduced. • Smaller samples can be drawn for vouching inventory costs to ascertain the reasonable valuation of inventory. • The vouching of inventory costs for the purpose of checking the valuation of inventory can be performed prior to year-end.
Accurate payroll expense	Assuming the use of time cards —examine cards for numerical control and proper approval —inquire as to the adequate segregation of duties and use observation techniques as well —on a surprise basis, distribute payroll checks to gain additional evidence that controls have been effective.	• Apply analytical procedures to payroll expenses rather than detailed testing. • Reduce the sample size for detailed testing.
Accurate depreciation expense	Assuming the presence of internal auditors —review internal audit working papers that reflect the department's review of depreciation schedules.	• Reduce the quantity of depreciation calculations that are independently checked.

OBJECTIVE	CONTROL TEST WORK	EXPECTED REDUCTION OF SUBSTANTIVE TEST WORK
FINANCING AND NONROUTINE TRANSACTIONS		
Accuracy of long-term debt balances	Through inquiry procedures ascertain that the board of directors' approval is required for all borrowings. Tie the authorizations in the minutes to the general ledger.	• Reduce the search for unrecorded borrowings by confirmation and related procedures.
Accuracy of stock balances and recorded dividend payments	Inquire whether independent transfer agents and registrars are used and whether an imprest bank account has been established for dividend payments.	• Eliminates the need to examine the stockbook; instead, a confirmation procedure is sufficient. • Decrease the sample size for examining dividend payments.

examples of control tests and their relationship to substantive test work were provided. However, to effectively design such tests, the auditor must have in-depth knowledge of the related operating cycle's controls. Chapters 9 through 11 will provide detailed guidance as to how internal accounting controls should be designed and evaluated for the

—revenue or income-producing cycle,

—cost of sales or production cycle, and

—financing and nonroutine transactions of an entity.

REFERENCES

American Institute of Certified Public Accountants, Statement on Auditing Standards No. 55, "Consideration of the Internal Control Structure in a Financial Statement Audit" (New York: AICPA, April 1988).

Patton, James M., John H. Evans III, and Barry L. Lewis, *A Framework for Evaluating Internal Audit Risk*, Research Report No. 25 (Florida: The Institute of Internal Auditors, Inc., 1982).

9

How to Design and Evaluate Internal Accounting Controls for the Revenue- or Income-Producing Cycle

"The value of a thing means the quantity of some other thing,
or things in general, which it exchanges for."

John Stuart Mill, 1848[1]

The simplicity of representing revenue as the value given up for goods or services is conceptually elegant but operationally fraught with problems. A number of judgments are involved in evaluating the earning process and determining when that process is complete, or is at some point deemed reasonable for beginning the recognition of related revenue. The controls over the revenue cycle relate to

---

[1] Michael Jackman, *The Macmillan Book of Business & Economic Quotations* (New York, Macmillan Publishing Company, 1984), p. 151.

both the judgmental process and the underlying transactions that enter, are processed, and eventually are summarized for various decision makers' reference in evaluating the income stream of an enterprise.

The revenue or income-producing cycle encompasses both

—revenue—order entry, credit granting, shipping, billing, sales returns and allowances, and investment income, and

—receipts—credit and collections, maintenance of receivable records, and cash receipts.

Controls can be designed and existing controls evaluated for the revenue or income-producing cycle through the implementation of the approach outlined in prior chapters. In this chapter are examples of control problems that have been observed at companies representing a wide cross-section of industries, with details as to how these problems can be identified and corrected by using the recommended approach to analyzing controls.

SEGREGATING INCOMPATIBLE FUNCTIONS

Generating revenue requires the authorization of sales and other income-producing activities, the execution of the sale or investment, the recording of the related transactions, and the accountability for the assets that accrue from the revenue-producing transactions. Duties are incompatible if a single person can perpetrate and conceal errors and irregularities in the course of performing day-to-day activities. Only three functions have to be segregated to ensure that duties are effectively separated: authorization, custody, and accounting. However, such general titles are of limited use; the question of concern to the systems designer or evaluator is this:

Which specific responsibilities within the revenue or income-producing cycle should be assigned to different individuals to achieve effective control? Exhibit 9–1 details the critical segregation of duties that is desirable.

Interpreting Exhibit 9–1

Exhibit 9–1 is organized with the owner-manager as an overall means of control. Should a desirable separation of duties not be present in an entity, the owner-manager can intervene and review the work of those individuals who are responsible for incompatible functions. Such intervention can result in a fairly effective control system. Earlier discussions in this guide have stressed the ability of a three-man operation to accrue many of the benefits of segregated duties, simply by recognizing the basic control concept of separating the duties of authorization, custody of assets, and accounting for transactions. Exhibit 9–1 uses a three-column structure to emphasize this critical concept. However, the maximum benefits from such segregation will be realized if each of the duties delineated in Exhibit 9–1 is performed by a different person within each of the departments

Exhibit 9–1

Critical Segregation of Duties for the Revenue- or Income-Producing Cycle

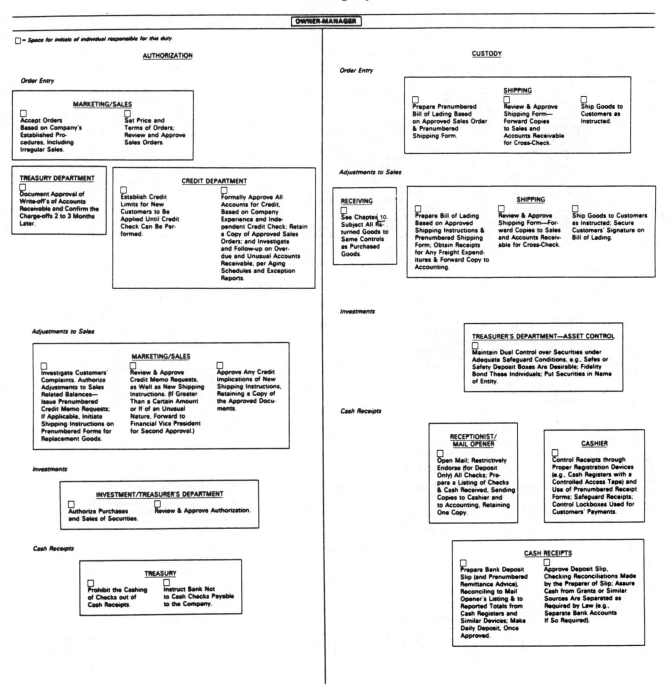

Exhibit 9–1 (continued)

OWNER-MANAGER

ACCOUNTING

Order Entry

ACCOUNTS RECEIVABLE

☐ Account for the Sequence of Pre-numbered Customer Order Forms, Following Up on Open Orders to Detect Unbilled Shipments; Generate Prenumbered Invoices, Matching Them to Approved Customer Orders, Shipping Documentation, or Other Evidence of Services Provided; Attach Proofs of Delivery to the Associated Billings.

☐ Review & Approve Billing Package for Distribution
—Independently Check Prices, Terms, Extensions and Footings
—Account for the Sequence of Sales Invoices
—Compare Data on Invoices with Order Entry Forms and Shipping or Service Documentation.

☐ Maintain the Subsidiary Accounts Receivable Ledger; Prepare an Aging Schedule of Accounts Receivable, Forwarding a Copy to the Credit Department; Periodically Prepare a Report on Write-offs and Recoveries for Approval by the Treasurer; Maintain a Separate Listing of Accounts Written-off for Subsequent Follow-Up and Billing, If Appropriate; Control and Mail Monthly Statements to Customers.

GENERAL LEDGER ACCOUNTING

☐ Maintain the Control Accounts; Review Exception Reports Based on Reasonableness or Limit Checks of Sales and Credit Granted, as Well as Reports of Credit Balances.

☐ Review & Approve Journal Entries, Reconcile Subsidiary with General Ledger, Reconcile Daily Billings Totals with Total Receivables Postings, Compare Production and Inventory Records with Shipping and Billing Documentation, Match Shipping Advices from Independent Shippers to Internal Documentation, and Review Open and Unmatched Files and Unaccounted For Documents, e.g., Any Unfilled Customer Orders or Unmatched Shipping Documents.

Adjustments to Sales

ACCOUNTS RECEIVABLE

☐ Account for the Sequence of Prenumbered Credit Memo Requests, Match Them to Receiving Reports, When Applicable. Generate Prenumbered Credit Memos to Customers, Attaching Supporting Documentation That Is Canceled.

☐ Review & Approve Credit Package for Distribution; Independently Check Support, Extensions, Sequence, and Agreement of Credit Memos to Requests, to Receiving Information.

☐ Maintain the Subsidiary Accounts Receivable Ledger.

GENERAL LEDGER ACCOUNTING

☐ Maintain the Control Accounts.

☐ Review & Approve Journal Entries, Reconcile Subsidiary with General Ledger, Reconcile Daily Credit Requests to Credit Memos, to Total Receivables Postings.

Investments

GENERAL LEDGER ACCOUNTING

☐ Prepare Necessary Journal Entries to Reclassify and/or Revalue Recorded Securities; Reconcile Brokers' Statements to General Ledger.

☐ Review & Approve Journal Entries; Reconcile Investment Ledger to General Ledger; Review Reconciliation of Brokers' Statements to General Ledger.

INVESTMENT LEDGER

☐ Maintain Record of Certificate Numbers, Descriptive Details, Cost, Market Value, and Physical Location of Securities; Receive Investment Advices and Brokers' Monthly Statements and Record Activity; Propose Reclassification of Investments Representing Equity Holdings of Affiliates, Subsidiaries, et cetera.

Cash Receipts

ACCOUNTS RECEIVABLE

☐ Update Cash Receipts Journal Daily to Reflect Receipts; Account for Sequence of Receipt Forms and Remittance Advices and for Agreement of Registration Devices' Records and Cash Receipts Per Mail Opener and Cashiers.

☐ Maintain the Subsidiary Accounts Receivable Ledger.

GENERAL LEDGER ACCOUNTING

☐ Maintain the Control Accounts.

☐ Review & Approve Journal Entries; Reconcile Subsidiary with General Ledger; Reconcile Total Receipts with Total Accounts Receivable Postings and Accounts Receivable Balances to the Accounts Receivable Aging Schedule.

☐ Compare Authenticated Deposit Ticket to Record of Incoming Remittances, Cash Book, and Postings to Other Accounting Records; Investigate Deposits or Collection Items Charged Back By Bank (e.g., Due to Insufficient Funds); Prepare Bank Reconciliation.

indicated. Since the exhibit is subdivided into four components of the revenue or income-producing cycle, focus on the first subdivision: those transactions related to order entry. The three-man operation would be expected to separate the sales, credit, and treasury department activities from the shipping and accounts receivable functions. Within the authorization function, it is desirable to have one party accept and prepare orders, another party approve orders, a credit department set credit limits and approve credit per customer, and the treasury department approve write-offs of accounts receivable. However, the ability to separate these four to five functions will depend upon the number of available employees. An important premise of internal control is reflected throughout Exhibit 9–1, including that part of it directed at the authorization function: one can never check oneself as thoroughly as can an independent third party. Two people are unlikely to make the same mistake, and collusion would be required to perpetrate a defalcation. Partly to reflect this fact, Exhibit 9–1 describes 42 different tasks for segregation, yet the exhibit does not imply a minimum staff of 42. For example, the person in general ledger accounting who reviews and approves journal entries related to order entry, adjustments to sales, investments, and cash receipts could be one individual. In smaller entities, the owner-manager may be assigned several of the responsibilities described in the exhibit as a means of achieving reasonable control.

How to Use Exhibit 9–1

Become familiar with operations and put the initials of the person performing each of the 42 tasks on Exhibit 9–1 in the spaces indicated. Initials appearing more than once within one of the three columns on the exhibit cause little concern, although the absence of cross-checks increases the risk exposure to careless errors. If the same initials appear as both the originator and the reviewer of a document or a transaction, no real protection against error exists; this is particularly true if a single individual is accounting for a transaction from its beginning to the end of the accounting trail. The real control concerns arise whenever duties are not appropriately segregated across the three columns. Exhibit 9–1 should permit the identification of control flaws and assist in the interpretation of the added risk exposure that can arise from combining the incompatible functions. The combination of functions may be either direct or indirect; often, mere access to records and assets processed by others is enough to create a situation in which the segregation of duties is ineffective.

> EXAMPLE: An electric equipment company has the policy of having checks that are received by mail logged by the receptionist, then forwarded first to the credit department and then back to order entry for distribution to the accounts receivable department. Giving the accounts receivable clerk such access to cash receipts creates the potential for errors and irregularities. Furthermore, the unnecessary handling of cash receipts by the credit department before deposit can result in lost checks or slower deposits. The result of the control problems is that bank reconciliations are being performed on the basis

of checks recorded which do not necessarily reflect checks received. In addition, the opportunity exists for the sales department to change the price, total amount, or other terms offered, after the credit department's review.

Be alert for ineffective controls. Sometimes a segregation of duties appears to exist, but further inquiry or the applying of test procedures shows the separation to be a facade. For example, dual control may be implied by a formal preventive control, but if such a control is not applied consistently or is applied post-facto, and there is no back-up detection control to compensate for the problem, designed controls become ineffective in their application. This is sometimes more likely to occur when a third party is relied upon for the back-up detection control.

EXAMPLE: An insurance carrier employs an investment accounting technician who initiates wire transfers to purchase short-term securities by telephoning the bank, identifying himself, and indicating the account number and bank to which the funds are to be transferred. Subsequently, the carrier sends the bank a wire transfer approval form, signed by two officers of the bank. The bank is supposed to call the carrier if no approval terms are received within a reasonable time, yet for two transfers no forms were submitted and no calls were received.

SOLUTION: To establish an effective control over wire transfers, the carrier should require that the bank confirm all requests for wire transfers by calling a person independent of the individual requesting the transfer. This confirmation should be made before the bank executes the wire transfer.

Obviously, Exhibit 9–1 is easiest to use in designing controls; yet the general terms used should facilitate the matching of any existing entity's personnel to the individual tasks listed, as well as the interpretation of the risk exposure that results from the fact that certain duties are not optimally segregated. However, it is more than a mere matching process; the access to assets and records and the timing of such access must also be considered, as illustrated in the two previous examples. In addition to the problems resulting from unrestricted access, many other factors can adversely affect the adequacy of control and, in particular, the effectiveness with which duties are segregated.

Watch for These Factors That Can Adversely Affect Control and Segregation of Duties

Controls are not effectively used. At times, the task descriptions on Exhibit 9–1 will appear to match an existing design system, yet the apparent prescriptions may not be in operation.

EXAMPLE: The hospital administrator's secretary prepares an initial list of all cash receipts as she opens the mail. However, this apparent strength is negated in that once the list is prepared, it is never compared to either the daily deposit of receipts or the postings to the accounting records.

SOLUTION: A hospital official without any cash receipts responsibilities should compare the initial listing of daily receipts to those recorded on the books and received by the bank. Otherwise, time is effectively wasted, save for its illusory threat value, by preparing any initial listing of receipts!

EXAMPLE: Similarly, a bank's tellers have access to supervisors' audit keys, allowing them to process override transactions. In addition, tellers' terminal tapes are not reviewed by a responsible official when removed. The result is that tellers can process unauthorized transactions and such unusual items are unlikely to be detected.

SOLUTION: Supervisory personnel should maintain sole access to audit keys and review terminal tapes for unusual items. Otherwise, such potential controls serve no function.

Employees have the power to negate controls. Rather than these obvious settings in which existing controls are not being used effectively, consider the more deceptive case in which adverse control effects stem from the fact that employees have additional power to carry out transactions that can effectively negate established controls.

EXAMPLE: A company with a fundamentally sound sales and accounts receivable system faces one weakness that could have significant consequences. That weakness concerns the assignment to the credit manager of the power to void sales invoices once they have entered the system. Although a daily voided invoice listing is generated by the system, it is reviewed only by the credit manager, that person empowered to authorize the voiding of invoices.

The potential abuse inherent in such a system is great. Through collusion with customers, valid sales can be voided in the system by one individual, with no outside controls.

SOLUTION: In order to ensure that this situation does not develop, the daily voided invoice listing should be distributed to the corporation's controller or other party authorized to be responsible for investigating the propriety of any large or unusual voided invoices. This control would be inexpensive, yet important in significantly reducing the entity's risk exposure that exists from assigning the credit manager the power to authorize the voiding of invoices.

In this latter situation, a detective control is selected to compensate for a basic lack of segregated duties with respect to the voiding of sales. While collusion has been emphasized in the example, the credit manager could unilaterally create a customer and perpetrate a one-party fraud on the entity. However, a review of voided sales by some third party substantially increases the risk of detection of such a defalcation by the credit manager.

Assets from related parties. In segregating duties and evaluating the effectiveness of designed controls, the nature of the particular assets and accounts that are being placed under control is an important consideration. One such issue could be termed "assets from related parties."

EXAMPLE: A retail store does not review and collect employees' receivables on a timely basis. Yet such receivables are more exposed to misstatement and even collectibility problems, since the normal credit check is not performed on employees.

SOLUTION: Miscellaneous receivables, particularly employees' receivables, should be reconciled to general ledger controls at least quarterly during the year. The subsidiary trial balances of all such receivables should be reviewed with operating personnel to ascertain the status and ultimate collectibility of individual amounts. Since there are greater incentives for misstating such assets and greater opportunity to create a misstatement, special care in setting and administering controls is essential.

Employees' vacations. A factor that can influence the effectiveness of segregated duties and overall control is the manner in which employees' vacation periods are handled. Duties of vacationing personnel should be assigned to other trained individuals who perform no incompatible duties. In other words, the temporary assumption of another's duties by that particular party is not expected to impair the control system. Of course, one way of avoiding the coupling of incompatible duties is to avoid reassigning vacationers' tasks.

> EXAMPLE: An advertising agency's clerk, typically responsible for depositing cash receipts, went on vacation for two weeks and no one assumed the clerk's responsibilities. Both checks and currency that were received were simply placed in an envelope awaiting the clerk's return.

> SOLUTION: It is imperative that employees' responsibilities be assumed while they are on vacation, particularly those duties relating to cash receipts!

Vacations and Employee Rotation Can Serve as a Control Check

The timely assumption of duties not only serves to safeguard assets, but it also ensures an independent check of an employees' duties and complicates his or her ability to perpetrate a long-term fraud. For this reason, vacations should be required of all employees as a control measure. Of course, the effectiveness of the measure rests entirely on the assumption of the vacationing employee's duties by another competent employee, who carries on no duties that could be deemed incompatible with those being assumed.

A routine way to get the same type of control check as provided by an annual vacation is via rotation. Consider the following setting.

> EXAMPLE: A dairy products company has several drivers, assigned various customer routes, who are responsible for cash receipts. Yet drivers are not rotated, nor do supervisors accompany drivers on their routes.

> SOLUTION: Since such procedures could prove to be an effective deterrent to misappropriation of company funds, they should be enforced at all locations.

Rotational procedures, as well as the involvement of supervisors and owner-managers, can be important considerations in reducing the adverse effects of unsegregated duties.

Code Exhibit 9–1 for These Adverse Factors

The systems evaluator must remain aware of potential adverse factors and the means of offsetting such factors when evaluating controls. Code initials onto Exhibit 9–1 that reflect

(a) family and related party relationships,
(b) those that assume permanent and temporary duties in other operating areas,
(c) the apparent access by others to assets or to documentation under particular individuals' controls, and
(d) the handling of specific transactions known to involve a conflict of interest.

The use of this type of a coding scheme will enable the evaluator to better assess the effectiveness with which duties have been segregated.

MAINTAINING COMPLETE ACCOUNTING RECORDS

Once the systems designer has established the critical segregation of duties or the systems evaluator has identified the apparent separation of duties and related strengths and weaknesses, what information is available to document that each of the tasks outlined in Exhibit 9–1 has in fact been performed? As discussed earlier in this guide, tests of control frequency involve observation and inquiry techniques. However, a strong control system is expected to create an accounting trail that documents employees' performance of both operating and control duties. Such a trail stresses the employees' accountability for their activities and provides physical evidence that control procedures are currently in operation.

Forms for Assuring Complete Accounting Records

Exhibit 9–2 provides the systems designer and evaluator with a standard or benchmark against which the completeness of an accounting trail can be evaluated. The documents presented underlie the revenue or income-producing cycle. If these documents are properly completed and controlled, they will be the basis for an entity's recording of all valid and authorized transactions in the appropriate amount, account, and time period. Obviously, the format of each document, as well as the particular terms applied to each of the forms, must be tailored to each client's operations. However, as noted in Exhibit 9–2, each document has a purpose which should be common across entities and is intended to assist the system designer in understanding the "why" of each form. In addition to the documents, a formal set of journals, subsidiary ledgers, and a general ledger, routinely reconciled, are required, as is a management reporting system that is designed to meet management's needs. Nevertheless, the source documents are an important means by which control over summary accounting records and management reports is obtained, and are the critical basis for any entity's information system. The manual, automated, or computerized mode of processing such an information system is but a secondary consideration. Although Exhibit 9–2 gives an overall impression of a manual accounting system, identical information should be collected for any system, only in a machine-readable format that is accessible by terminal or print-out and is easy to use.

Exhibit 9–2

**Assuring Complete Accounting Records—Use and Control
of the Following Forms Will Assist in Recording All Valid
and Authorized Revenue- or Income-Producing
Transactions in the Appropriate Amount, Account,
and Time Period**

CUSTOMER ORDER FORM

\# _____   Date _____

Name _____

Address _____ Apt ____

City _____

State _____ Zip _____

Description	Code	Quantity	Price Each	Total Price

Total Order

Desired Delivery Date
(Maximum Acceptable Delivery Date): _____ (_____)

Shipping Instructions: _____

Expected Discount Terms: _____

Signature _____

Salesman _____

Approval of Order _____

Credit Dept. Approval _____

—Retain First Copy in Marketing.
—Forward Copies Two Through Five to Credit Department for Approval.
—Forward Approved Second and Third Copies to Shipping.
—Forward Approved Fourth Copy to Accounts Receivable.
—Have Shipping Forward Third Copy to Customer as a Packing Slip.

Purpose: To initially record customers' orders and document credit approval and shipping
    instructions.

Exhibit 9–2 (continued)

CUSTOMER'S RECORD

\# _____   Date _____

Customer's Name _____

Customer's Address _____

_____

Customer's Code _____

Credit Check: _____

_____

Other Relevant Data: _____

_____

Purchasing Agent: _____

General Shipping Instructions: _____

_____

General Terms Offered: _____

Sales Tax Terms: _____

Credit Limit: _____

Expressed or Implied Warranty: _____

If Long-Term Commitment, Review by Legal Counsel

: _____

Signature _____

Supervisor's Signature _____

Purpose: To record results of credit check and information that can ensure adequate customer service and documentation of business commitments.

Exhibit 9–2 (continued)

```
SHIPPING ORDERS

# _____                                                    Date _____

Supporting Customer Order Number: _____

Description _____

Quantities _____ Unit of Measure _____

Method of Counting, Weighing, or Measuring _____

                        Counter's Signature _____

Comparison With Customer Order

     Agreement          _____

     Partial Shipment   _____

     Shortage           _____

     Overage            _____

     Substitution       _____

     Action Taken       _____

                        Signature _____

                        Supervisor's Signature _____
```

Purpose: To document shipments and variations of shipments from customers' orders.

```
BILL OF LADING

# _____                                                    Date _____

Customer's Name/Account _____

Customer's Address _____

| Description | Coding | Quantity |
|-------------|--------|----------|
|             |        |          |
|             |        |          |
|             |        |          |

                        Preparer _____

Customer's Signature,
   Acknowledging Receipt
   of Goods              _____
```

—First Copy to Accounting.
—Second Copy to Customer.
—Third Copy on File in Shipping Department.

Purpose: To document items delivered and to provide proof of delivery.

Exhibit 9–2 (continued)

COMPANY'S NAME

INVOICE

\# _____ Date _____

Customer's Name/Account _____

Customer's Address _____

_____

Payment Due Date _____

Sale Date	Reference Number	Description	Code	Quantity	Price Each	Total Amount
					TOTAL DUE	

Discount Terms: _____

Amount Due if Remitted Prior to _____: $ _____

—First Copy to Customer,
—Second Copy Stamped with Following:

REVIEW PROCEDURES

Initials (Date)

Reconciled to Order _____
Reconciled to Shipping _____
Recalculation _____
Checked Price, Terms,
   & Approvals _____
Final Approval _____

—Review procedures completed before first copy was mailed.

Purpose: To bill customers and to document review procedures performed prior to mailing the invoice.

Exhibit 9–2 (continued)

COMPANY'S NAME

CUSTOMER'S STATEMENT

\# _____   Date _____

Customer's Name/Account _____

Customer's Address _____

_____

Payment Due Date _____

Beginning Balance

Sale Date	Reference Number	Description	Code	Quantity	Price Each	Total Amount

Current Month's Activity

Sale Date	Reference Number	Description	Code	Quantity	Price Each	Total Amount

Payment Activity

Date Remitted	Total Amount
BALANCE	

Purpose: To provide a monthly report to customers on both sales and collection activities on a cumulative basis (operating as a check on the accuracy and completeness of customers' records and encouraging payment).

Exhibit 9–2 (continued)

Date _____

AGED TRIAL BALANCE FOR

ACCOUNTS RECEIVABLE

Customer Name	Coding	Credit Limit	Total Balance	0–30 days	31–60 days	61–90 days	Over 90 days

Total Accounts Receivable _____ ___ % of Total ____ % of Total ___ % of Total ____ % of Total

Preparer _____

Supervisor's Signature _____

Credit Department's Review _____

Suggested Action: _____

Purpose: To assist management in monitoring receivables and estimating uncollectibles.

Exhibit 9–2 (continued)

SALES ADJUSTMENTS

REQUEST FOR CREDIT MEMO

\# _____   Date _____

Customer's Account _____

Customer's Name _____

Customer's Address _____

_____

Nature of Problem _____

_____

Description of Goods Returned _____

_____

Description of Goods on Which Credit Is to Be Granted _____

_____

_____

Total Credit _____

Signature _____

Supervisor's Signature _____

If Greater Than $ _____, Vice President's Signature _____

If Credit Implications, Credit Department Approval _____

Purpose: To authorize sales returns and allowances, documenting nature of problem to
facilitate management's oversight.

Exhibit 9–2 (continued)

SALES RETURNS

(RECEIVING REPORT)

\# _____   Date _____

Cross-Reference to Credit Request \# _____

Postage, if applicable \$ _____

Description _____

Quantities _____ Units of Measure _____

(If scales are used, record gross and tare scale weights.)

Method of Counting, Weighing, or Measuring _____

Counter's Signature _____

Condition of Goods _____

Handling of Unidentified Receipts _____

Handling of Damaged Goods _____

Signature _____

Supervisor's Signature _____

Purpose: To establish control over goods returned by customers, documenting the condition of goods and subsequent handling.

Exhibit 9–2 (continued)

COMPANY'S NAME

CREDIT MEMO

_____   Date _____

Cross-Reference to Credit Request # _____

Cross-Reference to Sales Returns Receiving Report# _____

Customer's Name/Account _____

Customer's Address _____

_____

Date Credit Was Issued	Related Sale: Reference No.	Description	Code	Quantity Returned	Amount of Credit Granted

TOTAL CREDIT [_____]

Signature _____

Signature _____

Purpose: To credit customers for their returns and allowances.

Exhibit 9–2 (continued)

Preparer _____

Approval _____

RECORD OF INVESTMENTS

Issuer of Security	Nature of Security	Par or Face Value	# of Units	Serial Numbers	Premium or Discount

Date of Issue	Date of Maturity	Term	Interest or Dividend Rate	Interest or Dividend Dates	Cumulative Dividends

Stock Dividends	Tax Status	Callable @ $ ___	When Callable	Rights	Conversion Privileges

Registered in Name Of	Physical Location	Other Data (e.g., If Mortgage, Property Appraisal & Insurance Coverage)

Date	Bought From or Sold To (or Name of Broker)	Purchases Quantity/ Cost	Sales Quantity/ Proceeds	Balances Average Value	Amount

Dividend or Interest Income

Date	Amount	Other Data

Purpose: To establish control over investment securities and related investment income.

Exhibit 9–2 (continued)

CASH RECEIPTS

CASH SALES SLIP

\# _____   Date _____

Cashier \# _____

Description	Code	Quantity	Price of Each	Total
			TOTAL DUE	

Purpose: To initially record cash sales and establish control over cash receipts.

COMPANY'S NAME

REMITTANCE ADVICE

\# _____   Date _____

Customer's Name/Account _____

Customer's Address _____

_____

Payment Due Date _____

Statement Date _____

Balance _____

Enter Amount Enclosed \$ _____

Check Here for Change of Address ☐

New Address _____

_____

PLEASE REMIT WITH PAYMENT. MAKE CHECK PAYABLE IN U.S. DOLLARS TO
_____ . INCLUDE ACCOUNT NUMBER ON CHECK OR
MONEY ORDER. NO CASH PLEASE.

Purpose: To facilitate proper crediting of customers' payments and the maintenance of up-to-date addresses for customers.

Exhibit 9–2 (continued)

DAILY REMITTANCE LIST			
# _____		Date _____	
Customer Name (or other source)	Currency?	Check?	Amount
TOTALS			
Preparer _____			

—First Copy Retained by Preparer.
—Second Copy Forwarded with Receipts.
—Third Copy Forwarded to Accounts Receivable for Reconciliation to Reported Bank Deposits.
—Fourth Copy Forwarded to Treasurer for Reconciliation to Bank Statement.

Purpose: To establish control over cash receipts from customers' remittances.

Exhibit 9–2 (continued)

Front Side

DEPOSIT SLIP

\# _____   Date _____

ACCOUNT NAME

C A S H	Currency		
	Coin		
Checks			
TOTAL from reverse side			
TOTAL			
LESS CASH RECEIVED			
NET DEPOSIT			

Reverse Side

Checks Listed Singly	Dollars	Cents
1		
2		
3		
4		
5		
6		
7		
. . .		
TOTAL THIS SIDE		

IMPORTANT: Enter the total in the space provided on front. (Send authenticated copy to Treasurer.)

Purpose: To document the cash receipts deposited in the bank, thereby maintaining control over them.

Exhibit 9–2 (continued)

OPEN CUSTOMER ORDERS

_____   Date _____

Those Beyond Delivery Period

Customer Order #   Action Taken (Reason)

_____   _____

_____   _____

_____   _____

Terms Less Than Current Prices

Customer Order #   Action Taken (Reason)

_____   _____

_____   _____

_____   _____

Signature _____

Supervisor's Signature _____

Purpose: To ensure follow-through on a timely basis of all unfilled customers' orders.

UNMATCHED SHIPPING FORMS

_____   Date _____

Shipping Form # (Description)	Date of Shipment	Reason	Action Taken
_____	_____	_____	_____
_____	_____	_____	_____
_____	_____	_____	_____
_____	_____	_____	_____

Signature _____

Supervisor's Signature _____

Purpose: To control the risk exposure from unbilled shipments.

Exhibit 9–2 (continued)

UNMATCHED CREDIT REQUESTS & SALES RETURNS

(RECEIVING REPORTS)

\# _____   Date _____

CREDIT REQUEST NUMBER	SALES RETURN NUMBER	ACTION TAKEN (REASON)
_____	_____	_____
_____	_____	_____
_____	_____	_____
_____	_____	_____
_____	_____	_____

Signature _____

Supervisor's Signature _____

Purpose: To ensure follow-through on a timely, basis of all unfilled requests for sales returns and allowances (this is particularly important to maintaining good customer relations).

Exhibit 9–2 (continued)

Write-off & Recovery Report

\# _____   Date _____

Proposed Write-offs:

Customer Name	Code	Balance	Reason/Collection Action to Be Taken

Proposed by _____

Approved by _____

Treasurer's Approval _____

Recovery of Accounts Previously Written Off:

Customer Name	Code	Balance	Means of Collection

Preparer _____

Supervisor's Signature _____

Purpose: To document rationale for and authorization of write-offs and to ensure proper recording of reinstated accounts.

How to Use the Forms

Match the system's forms to these source documents. Compare the source documents that have been proposed for a new system or that are used in an existing system, for the revenue or income-producing cycle, to those outlined in Exhibit 9–2. A one-to-one comparison should be possible, although it is likely that some forms may be combined or subdivided. Any missing form will flag a break in the accounting trail and a possible weakness in controls.

For example, assume that no shipping form is prepared by the entity. The customer order is the source document that initiates a shipment and also serves as the basis for billings. The obvious effects of such a lack of documentation is that billings could be made for orders that have not yet been shipped, resulting in overstated sales, poor customer relations, and potentially lost revenue. Similarly, shipments might be made but unbilled, due to loss of customer orders and the fact that there is no shipping documentation available to flag a problem. If no bills of lading were prepared and no signed bills were received back from customers, requests for proof of delivery might become difficult to fulfill and might also lead to a loss of revenue. The risk of exposure from such possibilities can be evaluated to formulate an opinion of particular areas of control.

Compare the contents of each document. After a one-to-one match to Exhibit 9–2, examine the content of each document, comparing its format to the format proposed in the exhibit. Any missing information may flag a break in the accounting trail and related weakness in controls. For example, if an entity has investments, some record of these investments should be created immediately upon receipt.

EXAMPLE: It is not uncommon to make such discoveries as a bank's investment division maintaining no listing of original bonds and securities held *prior* to sending them to their servicing department for photographing.

SOLUTION: A list or photocopy should be prepared before sending the documents for filming to avoid the risk of loss in transit.

Similarly, if assets are held for some third party, particularly customers, documentation is essential for control.

EXAMPLE: Banks, as a customer service, will often safekeep assets. Yet many banks retain no formal record of items held in safekeeping.

SOLUTION: A prenumbered multi-copy safekeeping form should be used as follows:

Original—retained by bank in numerical sequence or as a permanent record.
Copy 1—distributed to the customer as a receipt
Copy 2—filed by customer name to serve as a register of outstanding items
Copy 3—filed by maturity date for follow-up on maturities and interest payments

When items are released from safekeeping, the original should be signed by the customer. The other copies should be pulled from the files and may be destroyed after the receipt for the release of the item(s) is obtained. As a minimum, a safekeeping control book should be maintained with receipts issued upon receipt of items and signatures obtained upon their release. Since safekeeping of customers' items increases the bank's risk and produces no income, customers should be requested to open safe deposit boxes. This would reduce, if not eliminate, the recordkeeping demands.

Be alert to lack of control over available documentation. Rather than the omission of documentation, the problem may be the lack of effective control over the available information.

EXAMPLE: A separate general ledger control account is being maintained for delinquent accounts. Yet despite the need for tighter control over such accounts and for timely follow-up, the client does not maintain a trial balance of such accounts.

SOLUTION: A separate trial balance should be set up for delinquent accounts and reconciled to the general ledger on a monthly basis.

Destruction of data. At times, information is originally available in an information system but is destroyed during processing.

EXAMPLE: A textile mill programmed its computer to delete the accounts receivable records for any customer who made a payment prior to the tenth day of the month, as the accounts receivable aged trial balance is prepared. This practice, which was intended to suppress the printing of collected items that need not concern those employees who review the aging of accounts, has substantial recordkeeping ramifications. The audit trail is lost since the payment is not listed on the aged trial balance and the receivable is deleted.

The destruction of data can particularly distort the information that is made available to management for its decision-making.

EXAMPLE: An airline company transfers old receivables into a receivable suspense account. When such transfers are made, they are recorded as current receivables for the purposes of preparing an aging of accounts receivable. As a result, the original aging of receivables is not accurately reflected in the records. The visibility of an account's actual age is camouflaged by this practice.

SOLUTION: The recording process should be adjusted so that the original aging of receivables is appropriately reflected in the suspense account and integrated in the aging report.

Watch for needless redundancy. Even when data have not been destroyed, they may be of highly limited use if not filed in an easily accessible manner. To facilitate the efficient and reasonably accurate preparation of financial statements, data may have to be collected in what appears to be a rather redundant manner.

EXAMPLE: A company dealing in leather products files shipping documents in the shipping department by the date of shipment. However, bills of lading are not filed in numerical sequence by date shipped. The result is that a shipping cutoff is difficult to obtain. The company should maintain a daily shipping log that includes the

—date of shipment,
—customer name,
—invoice number, and
—name of carrier.

Such a log would facilitate an accurate cutoff.

Of course, there is such a thing as too much redundancy. Sometimes the duplication of efforts can be detected by performing a one-to-one match of the documents in Exhibit 9–2 to the entity's information system.

EXAMPLE: Although redundant procedures can enhance control, they can be extremely inefficient with nominal advantages as control measures. A chemical company has a duplication of effort that illustrates this. A clerk from the accounts receivable department and a clerk from the credit department both update, on a daily basis, separate copies of the accounts receivable trial balance, based on remittances received. Such a duplication of effort can and ought to be eliminated without any adverse control consequences.

Two Critical Points to Consider: Consistent Use of Documents and Proper Sequencing

Perhaps two of the most critical points to be recognized in gaining familiarity with the documentation of an entity's system are (1) existing documents may not be used consistently, and (2) the order in which the documents are completed and actions are taken is critical.

Inconsistent use of documents. With respect to #1, consider the following companies' practices.

EXAMPLE: A wholesaler of durable goods records invoices for sales that are made to non-repeat customers on a cash basis, as remittances are received. To recognize revenue at the point of sales and to facilitate follow-up, accounts receivable ledger cards should be maintained.

In this setting, despite the availability of a complete receivables' documentation system, it was not consistently applied to all sales. Those invoices to non-repeat customers were processed in a manner that had both control and financial reporting ramifications.

EXAMPLE: An interior designer decided, as a cost of savings measure, not to send monthly statements unless the customer's account was past due or the customer specifically requested a statement.

The merits of such a procedure must be carefully evaluated against the increase in the collection period, as well as uncollectibles that will probably result from the designer's "cost savings" measure. Perhaps more importantly, the control feature of customers' feedback on a timely basis is lost by such an inconsistent issuance of customers' statements.

EXAMPLE: Similarly, a bank adopted a policy of not mailing checking statements to customers until the ledger sheet is filled, unless specifically requested to do otherwise by the customer. Over-the-counter statements are held until they are picked up, regardless of the time that elapses.

While some operating cost savings might accrue from this policy, the potential losses from the poor controls that result could be substantial. The regular rendering of customers' statements is an important element of internal controls, as it serves as a form of direct verification of balances with the customer. All customers' statements should be mailed at least quarterly. All over-the-counter statements should be carefully controlled and mailed, if not picked up within a three-month period. The inconsistent timing of customers' statements thwarts the apparent effectiveness of designed controls.

EXAMPLE: For a slightly different reason, a general merchandise store has a policy of not mailing monthly statements to those customers who have credit memos outstanding. The management attributes its ability to ultimately write off several credit balances to miscellaneous income each year to this policy.

The problem with adopting such an apparent income-producing policy is that its control implications, which could well result in losses that more than offset the apparent gains, have not been recognized by management. The policy has negated the entire set of established controls that separate the control and mailing of monthly statements from bookkeepers and billing clerks in order to create effective deterrents to the lapping of accounts and the misappropriation of cash receipts. When statements are not sent to certain customers, variances from customers' records cannot be discovered on a timely basis.

Order in which documents are processed. Shifting to the second point, not only is the consistency of timing important, but the actual order in which documents are processed, within a time period, has to be considered. The improper sequence of control procedures can eliminate the potential effectiveness of reasonable documentation of these activities.

> EXAMPLE: The credit limits for the customers of an electronic equipment company are not regularly reviewed prior to entering an order. The result is that shipments are frequently made before any automatic credit check is made.

Obviously, a credit check after the goods are "out the door" is of limited value, if indeed of any value at all. While it may help to prevent future sales to a poor credit risk, it has failed in its primary objective: to avoid current sales to bad credit risks.

Caution: a physical trail of forms can be deceptive. Exhibit 9–2 helps to assure that controls are not overlooked and in that sense can direct the accountant through the control procedures of the revenue or income-producing cycle. The alert evaluator will consider the

—gaps in information,

—needless redundancy in data or in documented procedures,

—inconsistent applications of documents,

—untimely use of documentation, and

—other than optimal sequencing of control duties

in assessing the adequacy of documentation and control. It is imperative that the evaluator recognize that a physical trail of forms can be deceptive.

> EXAMPLE: A chemical and allied products company uses prenumbered bills of lading but does not account for their numerical sequence.

> SOLUTION: Each shipping location should be given a unique series of prenumbered bills of lading and should account for their sequence, at least monthly. Corporate accounting departments should reconcile the bills of lading numbers with invoices billed, as a means of lessening the possibility of making shipments to customers and not billing such shipments.

> EXAMPLE: Similarly, a trucking company uses unissued freight revenue invoices in the manual preparation and billing of miscellaneous revenues. As a result, no control is maintained over unused invoices and the sequence of invoices is not accounted for. Additionally, these invoices are issued from multiple locations within the company's home office.

SOLUTION: Prenumbered invoices with a different sequence than regular freight revenue invoices should be used for miscellaneous revenue. Only one central location at the home office should issue invoices.

Each of these settings illustrates how the existence of prenumbered forms can be deceptive; the evaluator of a system cannot assume that simply because forms are prenumbered, they will be accounted for. Of course, to assure that the accounting records are complete, the sequence of prenumbered forms must be periodically checked and missing items must be investigated. The probability that an entity will maintain a reasonably complete set of accounting records will largely rest on the presence of an overall control environment.

WHAT TO LOOK FOR WHEN EVALUATING THE CONTROL ENVIRONMENT

The effective performance of control duties requires that employees understand their control responsibilities and that management recognizes the need for control and its involvement in the development and maintenance of controls.

Checklist for Determining Whether There Is an Effective Environment for Control

While concerns for the overall control environment are essentially the same for all cycles, as described earlier in this guide, Exhibit 9–3 provides a checklist to remind the systems evaluator of the primary factors to consider when evaluating whether an entity has an environment conducive to effective control, with particular emphasis on the revenue or income-producing cycle. In reviewing Exhibit 9–3 consider the revenue cycle's transactions.

For example, does the organizational structure clearly define the responsibilities of marketing, the credit department, the treasury department, shipping, cash receipts, and the accounts receivable department? Exhibit 9–3 is intended to be a basis for predicting the plausibility of specific or detailed controls operating effectively. The overall control consciousness of an entity should be evaluated at the initial stages of an engagement, so that its effect on detailed controls can be anticipated as detailed control review and tests of control are planned. As the engagement proceeds, the results of analyzing the control environment should be continually considered and should be updated to reflect information gained during the course of the systems review, as well as during subsequent audit procedures.

Do Employees Understand Control Policies?

No matter how well designed a control system, if employees do not understand control procedures, the effectiveness with which detailed controls will be applied becomes suspect.

Exhibit 9–3

Checklist to Determine Whether There Is an Environment
for Effective Control
(Emphasis Is Placed upon the Revenue-
or Income-Producing Cycle)

— 1. Is the organizational structure conducive to control, providing a clear definition of responsibilities and segregating the duties of authorization, custodianship, and recordkeeping?

— 2. Are accounting policies and procedures and job descriptions communicated via manuals? If so, do the following manuals provide instructions as to each of the procedures delineated below?

ORDERING MANUAL
— Customer Acceptance Criteria
— Credit Approval Requirements
— Coordination of Sales with Customers, Production, and Market Research
— Authorized Levels of Approval
— Follow-up Responsibilities
— Long-term Sales Commitments: Contract Negotiating
— Interface with Transportation, Shipping, Accounting, Top Management, and Legal Counsel
— Deviations from Established Procedures
— Company Policy Regarding:
  • Intercompany Sales
  • Sales to Employees

INVESTMENTS MANUAL
— Purchasing Criteria
— Interface Between Investment Department, Accounting Department, Board of Directors, and Broker
— Authorized Levels of Approval
— Deviations from Established Procedures
— Periodic Inventory Procedures
— Safeguarding Procedures

SHIPPING MANUAL
— Quantity Verification Criteria
— Coordination with Receiving
— Interface with Sales and Accounting
— Authorized Levels of Approval
— Company Policy Regarding:
  • Partial Shipments
  • Over or Under Shipments
  • Handling of Returned Goods
  • Goods on Consignment at Others' Locations
— Safeguarding Procedures

CASH RECEIPTS MANUAL
— Restriction of Disbursements out of Receipts
— Coordination with Accounts Receivable, General Ledger Accounting, Payors, and the Bank
— Authorized Levels of Approval
— Safeguarding Procedures

— 3. Are personnel selection methods, company training programs, supervisory practices, and performance evaluation techniques conducive to control, providing assurance that an adequate number of employees are available to perform both operating and control duties within the revenue or income-producing cycle?

Exhibit 9–3 (continued)

___ 4. Are vacations mandatory, and are provisions made for competent replacements to perform all of the assigned duties of the vacationing employees?

___ 5. For positions of trust, are employees' duties rotated, including bookkeepers' rotation among the various ledgers and cashiers' rotation from the responsibility of receiving incoming mail? (Note that cash on hand should be counted and reconciled before rotating custodians, and similar accountability checks should be invoked prior to rotation of other jobs.)

___ 6. Is Board designation of authorized credit approvers and handlers of investments required and are signature files of authorized personnel maintained?

___ 7. Is fidelity bonding insurance coverage adequate? (Employees handling cash receipts, investments, and similar valuables should be bonded.)

___ 8. Are there provisions for reasonable protection against fire, explosion, other natural disaster, and/or malicious destruction of records or processing facilities, and of other assets of the entity? Such provisions should include adequate loss-of-records insurance coverage as well as adequate insurance coverage of assets.

___ 9. Is access to investments, cash receipts, accounting records, and critical forms—both issued and unissued—permitted only in accordance with management criteria which reflect control objectives (i.e., is access limited to those persons whose duties require such access)?

___ 10. Is record retention adequate?

___ 11. Are accounting data periodically reviewed, tested, and compared to budgets, variance and exception reports, and nonfinancial reports generated outside of the accounting department by internal auditors or by individuals who are independent of generating the accounting data? Do operating personnel rely on such data for decision making?

___ 12. Are recorded balances of investments, cash receipts, and similar related transaction activity periodically substantiated and evaluated through physical inventory, confirmation, and a review of legal documents? Are the adjusting journal entries that result consistent with an adequate control environment?

EXAMPLE: For security purposes, copies of income notes were made; however, all the duplicate notes were filed with the original notes.

SOLUTION: The duplicates should be stored in a separate labeled file. Apparently, the employees who prepared the duplicates did not understand the purpose of making copies of such notes.

EXAMPLE: Despite the presence of several edit and audit checks and the identification of pricing errors, the detected errors are being processed in the billing cycle because the employees are using manual override procedures to enter the data, without correcting the errors that have been flagged.

SOLUTION: Exception reports should be prepared and corrective, well-controlled actions should be taken on a timely basis.

Again the employees apparently do not understand the purpose of edit checks or the necessity of correcting errors as they are detected, rather than perpetuating the errors.

Sometimes a lack of understanding of control duties is not as obvious as in the above settings. For example, an indirect signal that employees did not know how to handle certain types of transactions may be received only when the content of miscellaneous accounts is analyzed.

EXAMPLE: The miscellaneous receivables account of a manufacturing company was used as a catchall account for items that accounting personnel could not post elsewhere. This practice is all too common when account titles are rather nondescript.

SOLUTION: The general accounting manager should periodically analyze and review this account to insure that items are properly classified and are collectible.

At other times, employees will veer from prescribed duties because of general misconceptions.

EXAMPLE: A trucking and warehousing company had many old receivables that had not been considered in estimating bad debts. Inquiry procedures indicated that most of the old accounts were from large, well-known companies, so the employees were reluctant to write off the accounts. Yet no documentation was available as to why the items were not paid, nor had steps been taken to prompt collections.

SOLUTION: Efforts for final settlement should be increased. Penn Central and W. T. Grant were, after all, large, well-known companies! Employees' perceptions as to what constitutes uncollectibles influenced the manner in which prescribed duties were performed.

EXAMPLE: A communications company does not write off any accounts receivable until the credit department has judged that there is no possibility of collection. As a result, bad debts get charged late.

SOLUTION: To provide management with a more current appraisal of operations, collectibility should be analyzed on a quarterly basis. Again, employees' perceptions that write-offs were a last resort led to an untimely application of prescribed duties.

The misconceptions of employees may be such blatant "laymen's" errors in perception or may stem from accounting training that has misled the employee as to the objectives of control and the financial reporting system.

EXAMPLE: At times, conservatism is invoked as support for a rather lopsided recording system which increases control problems and can result in lost revenue. An electronics equipment company, as a normal operating procedure, contracts with customers for future sales of transformers. The company properly recognizes a liability for any transformers that have not been shipped, based on the current market price. In some instances, the company is permitted to charge its customers for changes in market price from the purchase date, i.e., an escalation clause is included in some contracts. However, the estimated potential receivable from the escalation is not recognized until the transformer is actually shipped.

SOLUTION: Such receivables due from escalation should be recognized to reflect actual activity and ensure that the additional revenue is appropriately billed.

The improper interpretation and application of a control and/or the demonstrated ignorance of controls by employees when performing either operating control or accounting control activities implies an ineffective control environment in the sense of checklist items #2, 3, 4, and 11 of Exhibit 9–3. When this situation exists, employees must be trained as to the objectives of controls and their importance.

Be Alert for Sloppy Application of Controls

Even with trained employees, problems can arise in a well-designed control system due to the sloppy application of controls. Often the sloppy application is detectable only if control or dual-purpose test procedures are applied.

The following two examples of controls applied in a sloppy manner were detected through control test work on credit policies and through the application of confirmation procedures.

EXAMPLE: A bakery has established credit policies, including the requirement that

—a credit file be established for balances in excess of $1,000,
—lines of credit be set per customer, and
—no sales be made before a credit ruling is received.

Yet no credit files were available for three account balances over $10,000. Sales were made in excess of the established credit limit for four different customers. A sale in excess of $1,000 was made before a credit rule was completed. Two customers for whom credit was not established and for whom directions were given to salesmen that only COD terms were to be used were nevertheless permitted to buy on credit. When questioned, salesmen stated that

—credit limits were out of date,
—the time required to establish a credit ruling was excessive, and
—records were not showing a balance in excess of the set credit limit

when sales were made to three of the four customers with established credit rulings.

SOLUTION: Management should reevaluate credit limits and update them periodically. Furthermore, any deviations from established credit terms should be approved by the credit office.

EXAMPLE: An auditor prepared and mailed positive confirmations of recorded accounts receivable. In their replies to these confirmation notices, many customers reported that the balances had been paid prior to the confirmation date. Subsequent follow-up indicated that payments had indeed been received by the client before the date of confirmation, yet had not been applied against the individual customers' accounts. Not only does slow accounting thwart the effectiveness and efficiency of audit procedures, it also makes it impossible for a client to follow up on disputed items.

SOLUTION: Payment details should be applied on a timely basis.

EXAMPLE: Similarly, many of the accounts receivable confirmation differences that were reported related to credits granted but not reported to the accounting department.

SOLUTION: All credit memos, upon approval, should be sent to accounting for a timely clearance of erroneous or disputable items that might delay collection and/or affect relations with customers. The absence of current reporting increases the possibility of improper handling of accounts.

At times, despite the availability of safeguards, they are not applied on a consistent basis.

EXAMPLE: A company in communications has a number of certificates of deposit that are kept in a locked safe at the company's place of business, yet some stock certificates are kept in an unlocked file cabinet during business hours.

SOLUTION: To reduce the possibility of loss or misuse, all these certificates should be placed in a safe deposit box in a financial institution, to which access is limited. At a minimum, all certificates should be stored in the locked safe at all times.

Some businesses have established procedures, the purpose of which they understand, yet they sporadically apply such procedures.

EXAMPLE: An operator of an electronic game room is supposed to take meter readings and customer signatures to document cash collections and for use in recording cash receipts, yet such procedures are used only sporadically. The result, of course, is ineffective control.

To effectively apply controls, employees must understand their purpose and consistently apply whatever specific procedures are necessary to fulfill the control objective. For example, financial transactions are to be recorded accurately, in the appropriate period, and in a manner that fairly reflects their effect on an entity's financial position. It is not enough merely to ensure that all transactions are recorded.

EXAMPLE: A mining company makes loans on which interest income is front-end loaded. By recognizing such interest at payment dates, no interest income will be booked in the latter years of the loans.

SOLUTION: For a more reasonable picture of the investment activities of the entity, the interest income should be spread over the total repayment period. Any other recording practice would be sloppy.

The sloppy application of controls can effectively destroy a potentially adequate control system; as a minimum, the control environment is adversely affected. The sloppy application of controls would be reflected in Exhibit 9–3 as mixed responses to items #1, 2, 3, 6, 8, and 9.

Check for Circumvention of Existing Controls by Employees

Rather than being sloppy in applying controls, either intentionally or due to ignorance, some employees and managers will actually circumvent established controls, effectively eliminating any potential positive effects of a well-designed control system.

EXAMPLE: Despite the company's well-controlled receivables and revenue cycle, a large receivable and related revenue were not recorded until the cash was actually received. Upon investigation, it was discovered that the marketing research department had billed the customer directly for work performed by the department. In this manner, established procedures were circumvented.

SOLUTION: The company must take special action to emphasize to all departments that they are to adhere strictly to established billing procedures. In this manner the company can gain assurance that all revenue is recorded promptly and accurately.

EXAMPLE: A trucking and warehousing company records all unapplied cash receipts as revenue. Typically, these receipts represent payments on accounts receivable that the system was unable to match.

SOLUTION: The receipts should be recorded as a liability and later matched with related invoices, when investigative procedures have identified the related receivable. Any unmatched receipts should be adequately investigated to ensure that they constitute revenue. To enhance customer relations, the customers should be notified of the possibility that they have made a duplicate payment.

The direct crediting to revenue upon receipt (the current practice), tends to remove these receipts from the normal processing cycle and has, in fact, resulted in unrecorded cash receipts, discovered only upon reconciliation of bank deposits. In addition to the above procedures, the unapplied cash receipts should be processed through the normal cash receipts system. A separate file should be established for unmatched cash receipts and this file compared to the open accounts receivable whenever the master file is updated, to ensure that matched items are appropriately eliminated from both files. A detail listing of the individual unapplied cash file should be printed periodically for investigation and follow-up by the accounts receivable clerk.

The current practice constitutes an effective circumvention of the designed controls over cash receipts, eliminating their potential positive effect on the propriety of recorded balances and the safeguarding of assets.

Often the circumvention of controls is effectively initiated from outside the entity, due simply to a customer's or other party's unusual or unprescribed action.

EXAMPLE: A small manufacturer's large customers take discounts that are not offered when remitting payment. The client fears the loss of customers if demands are made for full payment. As a result of large customers' "claimed discounts," prescribed control procedures intended to verify the propriety of billings and receipts cannot be effectively performed, since numerous exceptions would have to be reported, although the cause of the exceptions was understood.

SOLUTION: Any such unusual discounts should require explicit approval prior to processing, in order to integrate such unusual or unprescribed customer actions into the control system, rather than permitting the system to be circumvented.

Of course, the most common cause of circumvention of controls is likely to be a lack of clarity as to exactly what the prescribed controls are in a variety of circumstances.

EXAMPLE: A retailer has no set policy statement regarding write-offs and control over collections of amounts that were previously written off. Without criteria for determining which receivables should have an inactive status, when accounts should be turned over to a collection agency or attorney, and what steps personnel should take to collect accounts that have been written off, it is possible to have unauthorized write-offs and improper handling of collections from delinquent accounts.

SOLUTION: A formal policy statement on both write-offs and collection activities should be formulated and distributed to all personnel involved. A control trial balance ought to be established at each location and periodically reviewed by internal auditing.

By clarifying what controls apply in particular circumstances, how the unusual transactions are to be processed, and the importance of processing transactions through the normal operating and control cycles even if their nature or source is atypical, the entity can reduce the frequency with which controls are circumvented. Many companies have initiated a reporting system whereby any variations from routine processing procedures are to be documented. The person instructed to take some unusual action, particularly to process a transaction in other than the routine manner, is to complete an information form as to who authorized such actions, what actions were taken, and which transactions were involved.

To effectively block the circumvention of a control system by employees, a control environment must be established with trained personnel who understand their job responsibilities; affirmative replies to items #1, 2, and 3 of Exhibit 9–3 are essential.

Telltale Signs of Control Problems

In the course of a systems view, evidence is often gathered that flags control problems. While the exact source of the problem may be operating management, staff personnel or other employees, and be difficult to identify, the observed conditions will be telltale signs of weakness in the entity's control environment.

Questionable organization of certain operations. One such sign may be in the organization of a particular facet of operations.

EXAMPLE: A common revenue source for banks is the rental of safe deposit boxes, yet things are not always as they seem. For example, one bank had safe deposit boxes in its basement, space that was rented to an insurance agency. The safe deposit boxes were operated by the agency's employees on behalf of the bank. Such an arrangement may pose liability problems. Furthermore, controls over safe deposit box operations leave something to be desired. For example:

—Signature cards are not on file for all safe deposit box renters.
—The locks on surrendered safe deposit boxes are not changed before the boxes are rented to another customer.
—The vault custodian does not always accompany the customer when the safe deposit box is removed or replaced in the vault.
—When a key is lost, the lock is not changed.

Operations "after hours." An even stronger sign of an entity's control problems is often provided by a casual look at operations "after hours."

EXAMPLE: After normal working hours, undeposited receipts were frequently left lying on desk tops, lacking a "for deposit only" endorsement or any safeguard provision for currency.

SOLUTION: All checks should be restrictively endorsed immediately upon receipt and, if not deposited on the day of receipt, should be kept in a locked safe at night.

This disregard of basic safeguard procedures may suggest that other procedures are being similarly disregarded.

No apparent controls. At times, the telltale sign comes in the form of an action taken or a service performed over which no controls appear to exist in either design or application.

EXAMPLE: Often stock and similar investments are transferred to businesses as a payment by customers. At times these stock certificates and similar items may be deemed worthless, and destroyed.

SOLUTION: In order to control the company's assets, certificates of document destruction should be executed and approved prior to any such action. Without any formal approval or documentation procedures, certificates are subject to inadvertent destruction or irregular handling with subsequent claims that the certificates in question were destroyed.

EXAMPLE: Banks frequently hold collateral on loans that is subject to substitution, yet frequently no formal procedures are established for collateral substitution or collateral removal by customers, when the debt reaches maturity.

SOLUTION: The loan officer should be required to formally request in writing that the collateral clerk release the physical collateral. When the collateral is returned to the customer, the collateral clerk should prepare a cover letter for transmittal to the customer and maintain one copy of the transmittal letter with the officer's request in the department's file. The daily transaction journal should list all collateral movement. A copy of this journal should be supplied to the collateral clerk for agreement with the retained copy of the transmittal letter, and the clerk should initial the journal to document this procedure. If any letters are missing from the transaction journal, prompt follow-up action is appropriate.

The absence of current control exposes the bank to claims that collateral is still being held which has, in fact, been substituted. In addition, a borrower can substitute worthless collateral for valuable collateral if no formal approval procedures exist over substitution practices.

EXAMPLE: A company in the air transportation business has an equipment trust certificate trustee, yet no reports are received showing the investment activity of the trust fund.

SOLUTION: It is important that companies monitor their investments and related income.

EXAMPLE: A company that wholesales farm machinery receives most of its cash receipts via a bank lockbox. Therefore, the company has set no controls over checks that come directly into the company's offices.

SOLUTION: Even unusual or infrequent activities in immaterial amounts should be subjected to control procedures. This is particularly true when the assets involved are highly liquid.

Weigh Telltale Signs of Control Problems Against Risk Exposure

The importance of telltale signs of control problems depends entirely upon the risk exposure from the apparent weaknesses in the control environment. Telltale signs, indicated by mixed responses to items #1, 2, 3, 8, 9, 10, 11, and 12 of Exhibit 9–3, cannot be translated into errors and loss of control. For example, accounts receivable that range from seven to thirty months old, unsupported credits in an accounts receivable ledger, and a continuing accrual of interest on delinquent notes receivable are all telltale signs of control problems, yet there may be compensatory controls to reduce the effect of such problems. In order for a systems evaluator to gain perspective as to the relative importance of observed flaws in the control environment and in specific control procedures, (s)he must consider (as discussed earlier in this guide)

—the types of errors and irregularities that can occur, and

—the accounting control procedures that should prevent or detect such errors and irregularities.

Completion of Exhibit 9–3 makes the evaluator cognizant of potential problems but does not provide an assessment of the risk exposure of the company.

GUIDELINES FOR ASSESSING RISK EXPOSURE

Generally speaking, three major risks exist for an entity's system of control:

(1) It can lose valid documents, failing to record the underlying transactions, or it can permit bogus documents to enter the data base.
(2) It can inaccurately record transactions.
(3) It can permit the removal of assets.

What Can Go Wrong—and How to Prevent or Detect Errors and Defalcations

These three risks are presented in Exhibit 9–4, with those controls that are typically present in a control system over the revenue or income-producing cycle in order to reduce such risks. This general list is intended to provide a reference for the designer of a control system as (s)he selects controls and for the systems evaluator as (s)he recommends how to improve controls.

Caution: However, such a general listing should not be interpreted as "all these controls are preferred to fewer controls." The systems designer and evaluators should consider the benefits of control redundancy and the efficiency implications of the various available controls. A cost/benefit evaluation of available controls will serve as the basis for selecting the particular controls to be implemented in a given entity. This evaluation will, of course, reflect certain basic controls, the absence of which would result in a critical weakness in controls.

Critical Sources of Risk

Within the sales or income-producing cycle there are four primary sources of risk, as delineated in Exhibit 9–5. Also presented in this exhibit are those key controls that could be expected to prevent or detect both the misappropriation of resources and the accounting cover-up of such misappropriations. The systems evaluator must recognize that each critical source of risk exists and that there is no accounting control procedure to prevent or detect such an error or irregularity, if those key controls outlined in Exhibit 9–4 are missing (and not effectively compensated for by alternative controls).

Estimates Involved in the Revenue Cycle

A special source of risk can also stem from the nature of estimates. Generally accepted auditing standards make the auditor responsible for evaluating the reasonableness of clients' accounting estimates, in the context of the financial statements taken as a whole. Both subjective and objective factors should be considered by the auditor with an attitude of professional skepticism. This is particularly important in considering subjective factors due to the potential for

Exhibit 9–4

**What Could Go Wrong and What Controls Can Preclude
or Detect Such Errors and Defalcations?
The Risk Profile of the Revenue- or Income-Producing
Cycle**

GENERAL TYPES OF RISKS AND RELATED CONTROLS TO REDUCE THESE RISKS

Loss of Documents or Input of Bogus Documents	Inaccurate Recording of Transactions	Removal of Assets
—Authorization Procedures	—Authorization Procedures	—Authorization Procedures
—Competent Employees	—Competent Employees	—Formal, Well-Controlled Hiring Practices
—Segregation of Duties	—Segregation of Duties	—Segregation of Duties
—Initial Listing of Receipts	—Utilization of Performance Measures Conducive to Accurate Reporting	—Access Restriction and Physical Safeguards
—Batch Controls	—Batch Controls	—Automatic Accounting Checks
—Systematic Stamping of Time and Date on Documents, upon Receipt	—Clerical Checks of Original Documents and Intermediate Summaries	—Periodic Reconciliation of Books-to-Physical—Cycle Counts
—Systematic Filing of Documents	—Validity Checks	
—Filing of Support Documents with Related Vouchers	—Limit Checks	
—Sign-out Log When Documents Are Removed from an Area	—Review of "Was-Is" Reports (to Summarize, for Example, Changes to a Master File)	
—Set Policy of Only Permitting Copies of Documents to Leave the Filing Area	—Exception Reports	
—Stamping of Duplicate Documents	—Tickler Files for Accruals (Chronological Reminders of When to Record What Entries)	
—Clear Voiding and Retention of Documents	—Independent Review of Journal Entries and Postings	
—Cancellation of Used Documents	—Independent Reconciliation of Subsidiaries to Controlling Accounts	
—Accounting for Numerical Sequence	—Comparison of Independently Generated Reports Such as Customer Orders with Shipping Documents with Billings	
—Periodic Inventory of Unissued Forms	—Reconciliation of Customers' Confirmation with Accounts Receivable	
—Matching of Key Documents	—Quick Follow-up on Customers' and Others' Complaints	
—Follow-up on Unmatched, Unpaid, and Open Items	—Recount of Physical Inventory of Investments (by an Independent Count Team)	
—Periodic Independent Tests, Both Vouching and Retracing	—Confirmation of Asset Balances Held Elsewhere	
	—Utilization of Imprest Basis Funds	

385

Exhibit 9–4 (continued)

Critical Sources of Risk in the Revenue- or Income-Producing Cycle and Controls Intended to Reduce Such Risk

What Could Go Wrong?	Key Controls to Prevent or Detect Extraction of Resources	Key Controls to Detect Accounting Cover-Up
UNRECORDED CASH RECEIPTS COULD BE MISAPPROPRIATED	— Require Two Individuals to Open Mail and Make Collections. — Use Lock Boxes, Automatic Registration Mechanical Devices, and Independent Preparation of Prenumbered Sales Tickets to Control Receipts. — Compare Receipts to Independently Generated Information Such as Published Dividend Information. — Prenumber Remittance Advices, Control the Advices, Account for the Sequence of Advices. — Restrictively Endorse All Checks Immediately and Make Daily Deposits.	• Require an Independent Party to Compare Accounts Receivable Postings to Cash Receipts Deposited. • Require an Independent Party to Handle Customers' Confirmations and Customers' Inquiries. • Require an Independent Party to Test the Detailed Transactions Underlying the General Ledger Accounts (Emphasize Sales Returns and Allowances as Well as Write-Offs; Review Adjusting Journal Entries; Check Footings).
RECORDED CASH RECEIPTS COULD BE MISAPPROPRIATED	— Require an Independent Party to Compare Deposits, Per Initial Listing, to Books and to Bank Deposits (or Cash on Hand). — Require a Synchronizing of Cash Verification with Securities Verification to Eliminate the Possibility of Cross-Substitution. — Restrictively Endorse All Checks Immediately and Make Daily Deposits. — Do Not Permit Disbursements to Be Made from Cash Receipts.	

SHIPMENTS COULD BE MISAPPRO-PRIATED	— Require Approved Customer Orders as Documentation for Shipments. — Require an Independent Party to Reconcile Customer Orders to Shipping Documentation to Billings. — Institute Safeguarding Procedures for Storage and Movement of Goods.	• Require an Independent Party to Periodically Compare Tangible Assets to Detailed Inventory Records. • Require an Independent Party to Periodically Compare Tangible Assets to Detailed Inventory Records. • Require an Independent Party to Periodically Review Adjusting Entries to Inventory Related Accounts. • Require an Independent Party to Handle Customers' Complaints and Inquiries—Particularly Regarding Short Shipments or Goods Not Delivered.
INVESTMENTS COULD BE MISAPPRO-PRIATED	— Use Dual Authorization Procedures. — Apply Safeguarding Procedures, Including Dual Access to Safe Deposit Boxes. — Process Investment Purchases and Income Through Normal Cash Receipts and Disbursements Operations. — Require an Independent Party to Compare Activity to Broker's Statements and Market Information, i.e., to Reconcile Records With Brokers' Reports.	• Require an Independent Party to Periodically Compare Investments to Detailed Investment Records Through Physical Inspection. • Require an Independent Party to Periodically Review the Adjusting Entries to Investment Related Accounts, to Test Detailed Investment Transactions, and to Compare the Reasonableness of Account Balances to Externally Generated Market Information.

bias. SAS 57 identifies the following examples of accounting estimates[2] which relate to the revenue cycle

Receivables:	Revenues:
Uncollectible receivables	Airline passenger revenue
Allowance for loan losses	Subscription income
Uncollectible pledges	Freight and cargo revenue
	Dues income
Contracts:	Losses on sales contracts
Revenue to be earned	

The auditor will review and test management's process of formulating estimates, or choose to either develop an independent expectation for corroboration of the estimate's reasonableness or review subsequent events occurring prior to the completion of fieldwork to assess such reasonableness [SAS 57].

The internal control structure may reduce the likelihood of material misstatements of accounting estimates. To assess such a possible reduction, the auditor directs attention to how management

- communicates the need for proper estimates
- accumulates relevant, sufficient, and reliable data on which to base an accounting estimate,
- ensures that accounting estimates are prepared by qualified personnel,
- adequately reviews and approves accounting estimates by appropriate levels of authority, including review of
    —relevant factors,
    —development of assumptions,
    —the reasonableness of assumptions and resulting estimates,
    —specialists' role, and
    —changes in previously established methods to arrive at accounting estimates,
- compares prior accounting estimates with subsequent results to assess the reliability of the process used to develop estimates, and
- considers whether the resulting accounting estimate is consistent with the operational plans of the entity.

As the auditor evaluates assumptions, he or she should consider sensitivity to variations, deviations from historical patterns, and whether the assumptions are subjective and susceptible to misstatement and bias. [SAS 57] A systems evaluator should consider whether the control design effectively addresses risks associated with accounting estimates.

---

[2] "Auditing Accounting Estimates" (New York, AICPA, April 1988), p. 8.

A STARK LOOK AT PENN SQUARE

The Facts

From 1974 to 1981 assets grew 15-fold, from $35 million to $525 million. Eighty percent of the loan portfolio were energy-related loans. These loans were based on 75 percent of the gross value of claimed proven reserves of oil and gas, as collateral. A total of $2.5 billion energy-related loans were made, and $2 billion of these were sold to major "upstream" banks with the tacit guarantee that they would be repurchased on demand. This guarantee, coupled with the loan participants' knowledge that Penn Square Bank had the greatest relative exposure to loan losses, served as an effective means of marketing loan participation.

An example of how analytical procedures can be helpful in identifying problems with revenue-related estimates is provided by examining the Penn Square case facts.

Some problem loans that Penn Square Bank sold were taken back and then were sold to Hal Clifford, who was concurrently extended new loans by Penn Square. Clifford Resources owed $60 to $65 million to banks. As problem loans arose within Penn Square, the bank made a practice of making principal and interest payments to larger correspondent banks who shared in the problem loans, on behalf of the delinquent borrowers. This practice resulted in more than $2 million of interest payments in 1981 and by Spring of 1982, $10 million.

An estimated 20% of problem loans involved insiders. One director alone received $200 million; the Chairman of the Board received $18 million in loans. An executive vice president and director received loans totaling $167,720 for a mortgage and two family members. Virtually all directors and their related interests were found to have received loans from the bank. At least 21 loans were classifiable as being preferential to insiders.

Some customers of Penn Square Bank received a very large amount of credit; for example, one borrower was extended a loan for $125 million.

Early in 1980, Penn Square Bank was placed on a list of problem banks by Federal bank regulators and ordered to correct several problems. From the beginning of 1980 through July of 1982, five exams were performed by the comptroller's office.

Industry Knowledge

Federal Banking Law in 1978 restricted direct loans to executives, setting limits of:

- $60,000 for mortgages
- up to $20,000 for educational purposes, and
- $10,000 for consumer loans.

Under this banking regulation, each bank designates which officers come under this lending limit restriction.

Beyond the above restriction, banks may not lend more than 10 percent of their capital to any one party. Penn Square had $35 million of capital.

The common banking practice when lending to oil and gas entities is to accept about half of a company's claimed proven reserves of oil and gas and then base loans on just 30 percent of that figure because of inflationary expectations.

With respect to the oil and gas industry, the number of rigs drilling in Oklahoma had increased from fewer than 200 in 1974 to 689 in 1981. Oil and gas prices had increased 10-fold from 1973 to 1980.

Inflation and interest rates have increased the cost of drilling, and the lowering of the maximum tax rate on earned income from 70% to 50% has substantially affected the attractiveness of oil and gas tax shelters.

With respect to regulation, the number of bank examiner positions has declined by 12 percent, and those banks with less than $1 billion in assets are receiving less coverage by examiners.

Local Knowledge

Hal Clifford is known as the "debt junkie" in Oklahoma City. In the last four to five years $4 billion to $4.5 billion net new energy loans were generated in Oklahoma, with only $1 to $1.5 billion handled inside the area. The Senior Executive Vice President at Penn Square has a reputation for bizarre personal and banking behavior. The omission of vice presidents' and directors' names from the list of officers to whom lending limit restrictions apply is a widespread practice of banks in Oklahoma.

Auditors' Activities

Penn Square prevented its own internal auditors from reviewing many of the energy-related loans.

Peat, Marwick, Mitchell & Co. inspected 15% of the bank's loans.

At the end of a letter from the former Vice President of Continental Illinois to Penn Square's Executive Vice President, saying "he had assured a group purchasing the Penn Square Loans that 'we would take the credits out at maturity or whenever they felt unconfident,'" the external auditors noted: "no disclosure of this informal takeout agreement was proposed."

The Third Party Picture

Chase Manhattan Bank purchased $212 million of loans generated from Penn Square. Since Chase had PMM&Co. as auditors, it requested that the auditor provide information regarding its loan participations with Penn Square.

Continental Illinois National Bank of Chicago, in the middle of the depressed Great Lakes economy, readily purchased more than $1 billion of energy-related loans from Penn Square. We already know the rest of that story . . .

Another heavy purchaser was Seattle–First National Bank.

Other Points to Ponder

Each of the parties from bank officials to auditors and Federal Regulators blamed someone else for the collapse. The Board of Directors said that they relied on PMM&Co. and the Comptroller and did not look at any specific loans. In addition, the Board had insufficient expertise to question the practices. One Banking Committee member said the testimony represented "an indictment of the regulatory system that places too much reliance on outside directors who are lay persons." The testimony at the Congressional hearing indicated that "each watch dog, in many respects relied on another in concluding that the bank's condition was not so bad."

The Comptroller said that PMM&Co. should have looked at 80 percent of the outstanding loans.

Following Penn Square, Continental Illinois National Bank of Chicago reported that 3.7% of its loans are currently in the nonperforming category, twice the rate of other banks its size.

Loan-Loss Provisions at the Largest Banks

	2nd qtr. 1982 Loan-Loss Provision ($ Million)	2nd qtr. 1982 Loan-Loss Provision as a Percent of Total Loans and Leases (Annual Rate)
Continental Illinois	$262.0	3.03
First Interstate	35.6	.62
Bank America	100.5	.54
Marine Midland	15.0	.53
Bankers Trust	24.0	.50
Wells Fargo	22.6	.48
First Chicago	25.0	.47
Chase Manhattan	55.0	.42
Citicorp	80.0	.40
Security Pacific	20.6	.35
Chemical	24.7	.33
Manufacturers Hanover	34.3	.32
Irving Trust	7.9	.30
Crocker National	9.8	.25
Morgan Guaranty	17.0	.23

Source: Keefe, Bruyette, & Woods, Inc. (cited in *N.Y. Times* August 2, 1982)

Borrowers from Penn Square have told such tales as: "They loaned me $2.5 million hardly asking any questions and then sold the loan to Continental."

Thirty cases for possible criminal prosecution related to $70 million of transactions are under consideration, involving

- kickbacks,
- misapplication of bank funds,
- conspiracy,
- bank fraud
- concealment,
- wire fraud,
- falsified books and records, and
- interstate transportation of stolen property.

Note: All of these details have been extracted from media coverage appearing in *The New York Times* and *The Wall Street Journal*.

For consideration:

What analytical procedures could have been applied, and what would they have brought to light?

SUGGESTED POINTS FOR CONSIDERATION

As the Penn Square auditor, a comparison of the bank's practices to the industry practices would have raised questions as to

- the undiversified portfolio of loans,
- the collateral basis of oil and gas loans,
- the tacit guarantee issued to those participating in loans, and
- whether the entity is complying with bank regulations.

REASONABLENESS TESTS/TRADITIONAL TESTS

Internal	External
% Growth, in light of regulatory requirement that no more than 10% of the bank's capital could be loaned to any one party	% Growth, relative to industry growth
% of loan portfolio relating to energy loans—80%	Diversification is generally deemed to be a desirable practice, particularly in light of the economic reasons for oil and gas growth
% of problem loans sold to Hal Clifford	Financial status of Clifford Resources
$ Cash outflow to correspondent banks	Inquiry as to who is paying on which loans

Internal (Cont'd.)	*External (Cont'd.)*
% of loans to insiders (particularly, problem loans); review list of who is subject to rules	Regulator's findings—past reports; extent of scrutiny
Total loans to officers	Compliance with bank regulation
Collateral value 75% gross value of claimed reserves	Industry Practice: ½ claimed reserves x 30%
Tacit guarantee to those participating in loans—growth of contingency	Industry Practice
Reasonableness of board's oversight—expertise available	Knowledge of those participating in loans—% loans in & out of Oklahoma (remember the ammonia fertilizer "shell game"?—Who has the total picture?—some analogies could be drawn)
Nonperforming loans (As they were "covered up" through sales to Hal Clifford, this percentage may well be unbelievably low)	Nonperforming loans at other institutions

Note Re: Regulator's Findings—
@ Penn Square

A 5-point rating scale is utilized for banks: 1 & 2 = soundness, 4 = unsafe, and 5 = serious risk of failing. As of October, 1982, a rating of 5 was assigned to 15 banks, 4 to 49 banks, and 3 to 299 banks. A rating of 1 & 2 was held by 4,130 banks or 92% of banks. As of January 1, 1981, Penn Square has a 3 rating. [Source: *Wall Street Journal* (12/31/82), p. 12, col. 3]

The global picture of analytical procedures entails far more than ratios and structural models; it involves thinking about the client's business and identifying the right questions that will provide a fair picture of operations and related risk. Some would refer to this process as "soft evidence," yet these are the critical questions for understanding the client and clearly create or lead to hard evidence, as the investigation of unusual fluctuations progresses. It was the recognition of a troubled entity making poor decisions that led to regulators' actions and subsequent discovery of the scope of activities for which criminal prosecution is possible. Post-facto, the flags are obvious. However, our task is to try to identify the flags before they become obvious . . .

Consider United American Bank of Knoxville, Tennessee, where

Ernst & Whinney issued an unqualified audit opinion three weeks before the bank's failure. Similar flags abound: a disproportionate number of loans to insiders and to the World's Fair-related projects; inadequate collateral; informal lending procedures; and extensive regulatory interest in current operations. The shifting of loans across related financial institutions and the resulting restriction on the auditors' ability to identify and review problem loans are similar to Penn Square's Hal Clifford transactions and the client's assumption of cash disbursement of interest and principal responsibilities for troubled loans. Three analytical procedures could have led to directed detail tests which were capable of defining the scope of the problem:

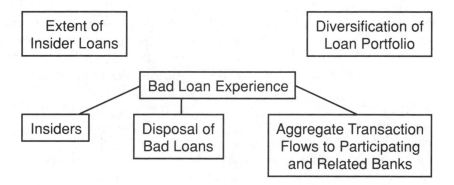

Controls for Prevention and Detection

As the systems designer or evaluator considers what could go wrong, one concern is the timeliness with which a problem will be detected. Of course, if at all possible, preventive controls are preferred to detective controls. For example, dual control over cash receipts should prevent the extraction of cash, unless the two employees collude. This is preferable to merely detecting a shortage at some later date, based upon a customer's complaint. Effective detective controls applied at frequent time intervals can help to limit losses as well as deter irregularities, since they increase the probability of catching the party involved in such a misappropriation of resources. The important use of Exhibit 9–4 is in identifying those specific controls that are critical to the revenue or income-producing cycle, as well as measuring the implied risk exposure from either not having such controls in the design of the system or having them in the design but operating ineffectively. The latter circumstance can be identified through testing of controls.

CONSIDERING OPERATING EFFICIENCY:
COMMON PROBLEMS AND PROVEN SOLUTIONS

The evaluation of a control system requires an in-depth knowledge of operations that permits an assessment of the entity's risk exposure and the formulation of means by which an entity can become more effective and efficient in exercising both accounting and operating control over transactions. Within the revenue or income-producing cycle, numerous problems are common per facet of operations, and various solutions have been put to use and proven to be effective in a variety of entities—both businesses and not-for-profit organizations. Several of these problems and solutions are presented in Exhibit 9–5.

Exhibit 9–5

Operating Efficiency Considerations—Means of Enhancing Operating and Internal Controls and Responding to Common Problems Encountered in the Revenue- or Income-Producing Cycle

ORDER ENTRY

PROBLEM: Discount terms are verbally agreed upon with no formal documentation. Customers' recollection of the terms does not always match with the sales representatives' recollection. As a result, excessive sales discounts have been given to customers and revenues have been lost.

SOLUTION: Discount terms should be in writing and should be approved by a responsible company official. Accounting personnel should periodically test the approved discounts to the invoices issued.

PROBLEM: Revenue has been lost due to misclassification of receivables involving various third-party payors.

SOLUTION: Set up a review procedure to confirm proper classification prior to any billings to increase the efficiency of billings and to improve the likelihood of collection.

PROBLEM: Employees' receivables have grown to rather large balances due to an absence of any limit on the receivables or a limitation on the time that accounts can remain unpaid.

SOLUTION: Adopt a policy whereby employees' receivable balances are deducted from their paychecks after a certain period of time.

PROBLEM: Sundry and miscellaneous accounts receivable contain several old and disputed items.

SOLUTION: Place sundry and miscellaneous receivables under the control of the credit department to facilitate their timely collection and disposition.

CREDIT CHECKS:

PROBLEM: Credit checks take one week to perform and a rather large amount of receivables have been uncollectible for those sales that have been

Exhibit 9–5 (continued)

made to new customers for whom a credit rating, as yet, was unavailable.

SOLUTION: Preliminary credit limits should be established for new customers while the credit report is being obtained.

PROBLEM: Sales that result in customers' credit balances exceeding established credit limits occur frequently.

SOLUTION: Program the computer to automatically flag orders that will cause the customer's account balance to exceed the established credit limit.

CUSTOMER RELATIONS AND RECORDKEEPING:

PROBLEM: No correspondence has been mailed to either new or old customers, missing an excellent marketing and control opportunity.

SOLUTION: Send "goodwill" letters to new customers and to those customers who are closing their accounts. Such letters, distributed by employees who do not handle customers' accounts or receipts, will promote good customer relations, confirm name, address, and the balance of each new account, and confirm the closing of all accounts.

PROBLEM: An efficient means of documenting the completeness of customers' files is desired.

SOLUTION: Document the review of files' completeness on the file cover of each customer by using a checklist of the appropriate documents to be included in each file.

PROBLEM: Customer service records are maintained on a "wheel" that is rather cumbersome to handle, access, and update.

SOLUTION: Automate the customer service records using in-house data processing, including the use of controls to assure that information posted agrees with other financial source records, especially sales and commissions. Computerization of related receivable balances will facilitate collections.

PROBLEM: Each year when a company's internal and external auditors distribute confirmations, a substantial number are returned by the postal service due to incorrect mailing addresses.

SOLUTION: Each year when the confirmation is mailed, it should contain a request that customers indicate changes in their billing address or status. Then, any information received could be updated periodically.

PROBLEM: Accounts receivable detail records are individual customer statements that are awkward to handle and to maintain. Such statements

Exhibit 9–5 (continued)

provide an opening balance with no detail, requiring the client to go to the original statement to which the balance applies if any investigation of particular prior months' items is needed.

SOLUTION: An open invoice statement should be used in lieu of the current customer statement. Such a statement would show the detail invoices that make up the opening balance.

PROBLEM: Accounts receivable invoices are maintained in an open invoice file and are difficult to use and to control.

SOLUTION: Establish an accounts receivable subsidiary ledger for more effective internal control. Consider using an EDP service bureau to prepare and maintain the subsidiary. In addition, have the bureau prepare an aging analysis for all accounts as a useful management tool for controlling receivables.

SHIPPING:

PROBLEM: Efficient ways of establishing the shipping and receiving cutoffs at year-end do not exist. Each year a substantial amount of time is spent reviewing detailed records in an effort to establish a cutoff, *post facto*.

SOLUTION: Indicate "before inventory" and "after inventory" on each shipping and receiving document for the period surrounding the physical inventory.

PROBLEM: A high percentage of charge-backs involve shortages in shipment.

SOLUTION: A credit memo request system should be established to facilitate prompt and timely identification of disputed items. Explanations for short shipments, provided on a timely basis, are likely to improve collection chances.

BILLING:

PROBLEM: Two months' billings are generally in accounts receivable at any point in time, due primarily to billings not being sent to the customers until approximately two weeks after month-end.

SOLUTION: Accelerate the billing process by estimating the activity for the last several days of the month, sending billings on, or close to, the last day of the month, adjusting the balances as needed in the following month. In addition, the setting of target levels of days sales in receivables can assist management in monitoring receivable balances.

Exhibit 9–5 (continued)

PROBLEM: At times it is difficult to establish a distinct sales cutoff between time periods.

SOLUTION: Use different serial number codes for different time periods when prenumbering invoices.

PROBLEM: Verifying the unit values used in billings is a time-consuming process.

SOLUTION: Use exception reports that are based on reasonableness checks or limit checks, applied to total billings and to unit values.

PROBLEM: Significant past-due balances are in the receivables account. Inquiry procedures discovered that several customers had long-standing balances which they were unaware existed.

SOLUTION: Mail monthly statements to all customers, so that items that are at variance with customer records can be determined and followed up promptly.

PROBLEM: The passage of time reduces the collectibility of any amounts in dispute. It is imperative that differences can be identified promptly, yet for companies that use brokers, differences in billings and payments commonly arise, unnoticed until the receipt of cash.

SOLUTION: Try to identify those agents who have habitually served the customers who pay less than the company's billings. Frequently, agents are unwilling to rebill their customers when discrepancies arise in the agents' original billing and the billing by the company. Yet, if agents' prices were reviewed and information as to price changes was provided to the agents on a timely basis, the number of disputes should be diminished. When payment differences do arise, they should be investigated and resolved promptly to increase the likelihood of eventual collection.

COLLECTIONS:

PROBLEM: Collections are being slowed down by chronic abusers of our credit policies—customers who regularly request that proof of delivery be furnished prior to their payment.

SOLUTION: To resolve these frequent requests on a timely basis, the company should request a signed copy of the bill of lading from the customer upon receipt of the merchandise.

PROBLEM: Customers are extremely slow in paying off their accounts.

SOLUTION: Institute a monthly service charge on receivables to encourage prompt payment.

Exhibit 9–5 (continued)

PROBLEM: Several accounts receivable are over 180 days past due, yet the company has every confidence that the account will eventually be paid off. However, time has value, particularly the extension of credit over time.

SOLUTION: In those states where contract requirements and usury laws permit such a practice, the original sales on account should be arranged so that they are automatically replaced by notes at the end of 180 days, at a rate that is either a set rate that reasonably reflects the market or a rate that is keyed to a market measure, like the prime rate.

PROBLEM: Interest is not typically charged on receivables unless the credit manager deems it to be helpful in motivating payment. When interest is billed, it is booked as an account receivable. Yet, rarely is it collected, resulting in the write-off of the accounts in later months.

SOLUTION: To avoid unnecessary postings to the journal entries, only record this interest income on a cash basis. The controls over the billing and cash receipts process should be strong if such a solution is used, and the amounts of interest income involved should only be minor amounts.

PAST DUE ACCOUNTS:

PROBLEM: Managers and salesmen are so lax in following up on past due accounts that the average age of receivables exceeds 90 days.

SOLUTION: Motivate employees to take action in checking credit and following up on uncollected billings, by charging units of operation for the costs associated with past-due accounts.

PROBLEM: Bad debts are climbing.

SOLUTION: Develop standardized collection letters to improve follow-up on past-due accounts. Assign individuals the function of following up receivable collections, requiring that such follow-up include telephone calls and personal visits to customers. Require that credit limits be set for each customer based on both collection experience and independent credit reports. Include the limits in the receivables ledger and require that any excess of receivables over the limit be reported to management for action. Such action should include an investigation of whether the credit limit should be raised and whether subsequent orders ought to be processed prior to the payment of existing receivables.

Exhibit 9–5 (continued)

AGING SCHEDULES:

PROBLEM: To facilitate the manual updating of the accounts receivable aging schedule, customers' cash receipts are given to the credit department each day. This additional handling of checks increases the possibility of loss and misappropriation and delays bank deposits.

SOLUTION: Use photostatic copies of checks or remittance advices to notify the credit department of payments.

PROBLEM: Since most aged accounts receivable are over 90 days, the aging schedule is not of much use in following up on potential uncollectibles.

SOLUTION: Recognize the nature of customers' payment practices; if the customers normally remit in a period that is over 60 days, adjust the aging schedule accordingly. The headings on the aging report should be current, over 90, over 120, and over 180 days in order to provide management with a better tool for identifying past-due accounts.

PROBLEM: Delinquency reports are prepared based on an aging of accounts receivable, yet problems persist with excessive uncollectibles.

SOLUTION: The delinquency reports should also consider credit limits. Any accounts that are in excess of established credit limits should be highlighted, and salesmen should be required to justify the extension of excessive credit. In addition, four practices that are distorting the accounts receivable aging process should be avoided:

    —cash remittances on customers' accounts are being applied on a FIFO basis rather than against specific invoices,

    —large customers' balances are being aged on a billed basis rather than on a payment basis,

    —rebills are being recorded according to the date the rebill is printed, and

    —charge-backs are classified in the current category of the aging schedule, based on the date of charge-back rather than the date of the original invoice to which it relates; to facilitate a more accurate aging process, as well as daily balancing, all charge-backs should have both the date of the original invoice and the issuance date for the charge-back.

ADJUSTMENTS TO SALES:

PROBLEM: A fairly large number of charge-backs have been recorded.

SOLUTION: Analyze the nature of charge-backs to facilitate follow-up and corrective action on a timely basis:

Exhibit 9–5 (continued)

—stratify charge-backs and open credit memos by the reason they were issued, e.g., returned goods or disallowed discounts,

—calculate the percentage of open credit memos that are applicable to charge-backs, as well as the percentage of sales for which charge-backs are issued,

—age both charge-backs and credit memos as a basis for determining the adequacy of the allowance for doubtful accounts, and

—report the disposition of charge-backs on a monthly basis, e.g., the amount collected, the amount removed from receivables, etc.

PROBLEM: Both sales and return and allowance accounts are inflated by the practice of "double charges" accruing from sales adjustments that are actually corrections of errors made in the initial invoicing of customers.

SOLUTION: In order to generate useful internal statistics as to sales and sales returns and allowances, those entries that are actually corrections of errors in initial invoicing should be matched to the original invoice. The difference in the original and corrected invoice should be charged to the sales account.

INVESTMENTS:

PROBLEM: Recalculation of interest income can be very time-consuming.

SOLUTION: Graph the approximate annual interest rate, to date, for certificates of deposit and similar investments and compare it to total interest income as a reasonableness check. Performing such a check monthly can be the basis for performing recalculations for only a sample of investments on a periodic basis, e.g., quarterly.

CASH RECEIPTS:

PROBLEM: Many cash receipts are received at various district offices where the segregation of duties is not possible.

SOLUTION: Use outside lockboxes to strengthen internal accounting controls by using outside parties to handle the receipt of checks and cash.

PROBLEM: Preparation of an initial listing of receipts by the receptionist is an extremely time-consuming process.

SOLUTION: Have the receptionist prepare an adding machine tape and reconcile the total against the receipts recorded on the books and those deposited at the bank.

PROBLEM: Maintaining adequate control over cash sales.

Exhibit 9–5 (continued)

SOLUTION: Use a cash register or similar machine that has a controlled access cash register tape.

PROBLEM: Some customers who have more than one account number do not include remittance advices with their checks, and the payments are frequently applied to the wrong account number.

SOLUTION: A copy of such checks should be made and attached to the remittance advice to provide a reference for correcting any posting errors on a timely basis.

PROBLEM: The posting of cash receipts from customers is inefficient and frequently errors occur. The remittances have to be matched to the appropriate bill and microencoded for posting to the trial balance. In addition, they originally have to be sorted to distinguish between customers who are remitting payments versus those who have arranged for direct payment through some other means, such as a transfer from another related account.

SOLUTION: The volume of processing justifies the use of pre-encoded payment remittance advices to accompany customers' payments; such an approach will cut the time necessary to sort remittances and to match payments with billings and will eliminate the time commitment to encoding payments.

Tradeoffs Between Control and Operating Objectives

Many of the problems and solutions reflect tradeoffs in control objectives and operating objectives.

EXAMPLE: What appear to be good ideas for marketing and the enhancement of sales often fail due to poor design and disregard for control. As an example, a distributor of grocery products to grocery stores established a "free goods" program, whereby customers were rewarded for exceeding sales volume quotas. Performance was calculated on a quarterly basis. The problems with the program were numerous:

(1) by placing larger orders within a single quarter a customer can qualify for free goods, even if the annual orders are lower than in prior periods;
(2) since customers sell the goods awarded to retail customers, an environment is created for even lower sales overall, due to the program;
(3) the program is expensive and may well yield no net benefits; and
(4) control over cost is not maintained, due to the possibility of quarterly manipulations of sales.

Often, by considering the operating efficiency effects of various control and operating procedures, opportunities for improvement can be identified.

EXAMPLE: A special trade contractor has experienced rather long delays in the invoicing for goods that have been shipped. The delays have ranged from one to two weeks for regular products and up to a month for special products. The delays in the invoicing of products occur when inventory is not maintained by the company, but is shipped directly from the vendor to the customer. In these instances, the initial order for the inventory is entered by the corporate office. Once the vendor's invoice is received, processed, and paid by corporate office, it is forwarded to the applicable sales district, at which time the district invoices the customer for the inventory shipped. By the time the sales district invoices the customer, approximately two to four weeks have passed since the time the inventory was originally shipped from the vendor to the customer.

The significant delays in invoicing products have numerous financial short-comings.

—A timely and accurate cutoff of revenues cannot be achieved on a month-end basis. Only by performing a detailed review of all unbilled shipments at year-end can the company be assured that all products shipped have been invoiced in the appropriate period.

—By delaying the invoicing of products from one week to a month, the company is, in effect, carrying its customers' receivables for that extra time since the company will not receive payment for these shipments for that additional time.

—Additional employees' time and expense are incurred in processing, recording, tracking, and filing invoices.

A means of speeding up the invoicing process that maintains control over billings and shipments needs to be designed.

The consideration of operating efficiency will frequently suggest changes in the timing of control procedures.

EXAMPLE: Many companies prepare all the forms necessary to generate a sale before the credit department reviews the package. Should the credit department refuse the sale, both time and forms have been wasted and might even be used to process an unauthorized sale. By delaying the completion of documentation until after the credit department has approved the sale, cost savings can accrue.

A popular means of generating cost savings in control and information systems has been automation and computerization. However, any time the processing medium is altered, controls over the transition are essential.

EXAMPLE: Any new automated system should be carefully tested, yet an insurance carrier that used such a system to prepare all parts of schedule D of its statutory annual statements failed to identify unreconciled discrepancies in the par values, accrued interest, and interest received on certain loans.

For new systems, reconciliation procedures should be implemented and further controls established that test the overall reasonableness of the items involved.

While management's needs are a primary consideration in designing information systems, these needs must be augmented by the demands of financial reporting practices.

EXAMPLE: A trucking and warehousing company maintains cargo and accident claim registers that facilitate management control but are inadequate in meeting financial reporting needs. To facilitate the establishment of claim reserves for financial statement purposes, the claims register should be expanded to provide details as to

> —the date freight was picked up,
> —the amount, date, and check number for each payment,
> —the date each claim was closed, i.e., that date when no further liability is believed to exist, and
> —the amount that has been charged back to owner-operators.

Operating efficiency and effectiveness must be balanced. At the other extreme from the trucking and warehousing company is the entity that stresses the financial reporting presentation of cash to such an extent that substantial losses of revenue result.

EXAMPLE: A company has established a procedure of liquidating all short-term commercial paper at the end of each quarter and then reinvesting the proceeds on the first business day of the next quarter. Due to the amount of cash held at year-end, this procedure results in a loss of approximately $10,000 in interest income.

Typically, if the systems designer and evaluator consider both control needs and efficiency implications, they will discover that many procedures effectively fulfill both objectives.

EXAMPLE: A training school improved its ability to identify problem accounts early and prevent the build-up of large, uncollectible balances, by establishing a maximum amount that a student can be in arrears.

EXAMPLE: A hospital gained assurance, at low cost, that all patient charges were being recorded by accounting for prenumbered charge slips for services, drugs, and ambulance use on a daily basis.

EXAMPLE: A chain of schools found that it could more effectively monitor its receivables by performing comprehensive analytical procedures on trends by school. The type of information that was collected and reviewed included

> —properly aged receivable balances with comparative amounts for prior periods,
> —average receivable balance per active subject,
> —percentage change in receivable balances over various time periods,
> —cash collections by month in total and per active student, and
> —cash collections by month as a percentage of tuition revenue.

The use of this data fulfilled control objectives efficiently and provided a useful information base for managers' decision-making.

By considering the numerous suggestions in Exhibit 9–5, as well as those that have just been described, the systems evaluator can gain a good understanding of how control and operating efficiency interrelate. Occasions will arise when tradeoffs have to be made; however, frequently both control and operating efficiency objectives can be reasonably met by a carefully designed internal accounting control system. In fact, a good systems evaluator can enhance the operating efficiency of the revenue or income-producing cycle as the internal controls of an entity are strengthened.

UNIQUE CONSIDERATIONS INVOLVING SERVICES AS THE PRIMARY REVENUE SOURCE

Today's economy is increasingly directed away from goods, toward services. As a result, many of the facets of the revenue-generating process that simplify control design when goods are involved are unavailable. As an example, shipping documents provide a control center in tracking sources of revenue and completion of certain revenue-generating activities. In stark contrast, the primary evidence available on completion of a revenue process is a verbal or written representation by the provider of services. Poor recollection, rationalization that cooperation with a client is acceptable, fatigue, human error, desire to come in under budget, realization concerns, and insufficient timeliness in preparing time reports are among the problems that can arise in the reporting and billing process.

Understanding Is Critical

As with many areas of control design, professionals providing services need to gain an understanding of the importance of the accuracy of their input as a basis for initiating the accounting and control process. The need to have time reports that capture the substance of the revenue-generating process in a manner that reflects the financial performance of the provider of services has to be appreciated by those initiating the accounting trail. Cooperation with clients in a manner that distorts the revenue realization process has to be understood to be an aspect of fraudulent financial reporting, just as the case would be if goods were shipped to customers who had not placed orders as a means to increase reported revenue.

Addressing Critical Risks: Initiating Client Relationships

In establishing controls, beyond the employees' understanding of the importance of accounting records, control practices should be designed to permit operating effectiveness and efficiency but at the same time ensure adequate checks and balances at points of critical risk exposure. For example, one might characterize the initiation of client contacts as particularly critical to professional service entities, due to the importance of reputation effects. Who a professional is associated with can reflect on his or her reputation and suggests a need to evaluate a prospective client on a number of dimensions, beyond mere credit worthiness. A number of data bases are available to check media coverage on prospective clients, as well as litigation cases in which they have been involved. Beyond checking such public data bases, some firms use detective agencies to do a background check on prospective clients. The degree to which formal practices are standardized, as well as the scope of such procedures will no doubt vary, depending on the nature of the services to be provided. Moreover, personal references often provide a key source of information to decision makers concerning judgments on initiating a professional relationship.

Just as dual check signers are a common procedure, dual authorization and approval of a prospective client is a desirable control practice. The second party can add an objective perspective to evaluating the new relationship and often can be asked to evaluate the proposed client from a firmwide perspective. For example, some professional services try to diversify their client base and may find it troublesome if they have too large a proportion of clients in a particular industry. Similarly, certain clients may pose costs for a firm in the form of technology acquisition and development and employee training. Whether such investment is justifiable, in light of other client prospects, is a business dimension of a professional service firm that merits attention in the design of controls.

Retention of Clients

The types of controls suggested for new clients should likewise be applied to ongoing relationships. Periodically, existing client portfolios should be reviewed to determine whether continued associations are desirable. In speaking with a CPA who had operated a firm of 20 to 30 professionals for a number of years, he indicated that one of the wisest moves he had made was to ask his professional staff whether they would recommend retention of a client and why. He stated that professionals have a very good understanding of aspects of a client that are not always obvious from accounting records. For example, some clients may be less cooperative, slow in paying, complaining regarding fees, risk takers or overly aggressive in their decisions on financial and tax matters, or otherwise aggravating in a manner that is inconsistent with the objectives of the professional firm. Hence, a facet of controls that should be considered is a formal review process where such input is sought.

Competency-Related Considerations

In the provision of services, competency takes on added importance from the perspective of hiring qualified personnel, keeping these personnel up-to-date through continuing education, and having resources available in the form of reference materials, libraries, and similar necessary materials. An evaluation system needs to be in place to monitor the process of hiring professionals and ensuring their professional development. Feedback needs to be timely and should problems arise, a system for fair and expedient action should be in place.

Such concerns suggest control procedures to verify applications and vita-related details, including confirmation with universities or other educational institutions from which the candidate has graduated. An interview process is also an important means of evaluating candidates. Research suggests that three individuals' points of view, developed into a consensus, will outperform a single individual's judgment process. Hence, a control procedure involving three people making judgments on hiring would be a research-based recommendation.

The provision of resources for day-to-day reference includes granting access to specialists and encouraging consultations. Professionals should have reasonable latitude to acquire resources they deem appropriate, although controls are needed to avoid duplication or waste in authorizing such expenditures. Continuing education may be pursued internally and through various third parties. Care needs to be taken to ensure effective education, tailored to the needs of the professional staff. Records should be maintained for use in staff assignment and also for purposes of complying with a number of continuing education requirements increasingly established for professionals by regulatory agencies and professional associations.

An evaluation system that periodically reviews all staff and makes a point to provide feedback to professionals on a timely basis throughout and after completion of key projects is an important aspect of a professional service firm's quality control. Written and oral feedback is useful, and steps toward addressing weaknesses should be initiated. These steps may include supporting further education of the staff, increasing supervision, or otherwise working with the staff member on skills such as interpersonal and communication dimensions that might have created problems. A common practice is to invite the individuals being evaluated to formally respond to the feedback and propose an action plan for self-improvement. Exhibit 9–6 gives an example of a performance evaluation form used by public accounting firms.

Supervision

An aspect of quality control in a professional services setting that is intrinsically linked with competency considerations is the adequacy of the supervisory process. The revenue-generating process needs a quality control monitoring system and that is most likely to be in the form of a supervisory system. Policies should ensure the accessibility of well trained supervisors to professional staff. Some formal documentation of the supervisory process is advisable.

Critical Incident Program

When a critical incident arises, a program should be in place that provides guidance as to the appropriate handling of the matter. To provide an example, assume it is discovered that a professional staff member did not perform the steps which he or she represented as being completed. Swift definitive action is an important part of maintaining a control environment conducive to avoiding such occurrences in the future. That action may well be termination of the employee, to send a strong signal to all other professional staff as to the gravity of the

Exhibit 9–6

Performance Evaluations—An Illustration

Audit Staff Rating Form
(To Be Completed on a Timely Basis for Each Engagement)

Staff Member Being Rated: _____

Engagement on Which Rating Is Based: _____

Job Title and Related Responsibilities: _____

	Poor	Fair	Average	Above Average	Excellent
Technical Competence					
1. Knowledge of Accounting					
2. Knowledge of Auditing					
3. Industry Expertise					
4. Ability to Gain an Understanding of Client's System and Operations					
5. Soundly Approached Problems					
6. Analytical Abilities					
7. Displayed Initiative in Attacking Problems					
Execution					
1. Willing to Follow Instructions					
2. Able to Reach Objective with Minimal Instructions					
3. Capable and Willing to Assume Responsibility					
4. Effective at Supervising Others' Work and Delegating Work When Appropriate					
5. Capable of Adequately Documenting Work					
6. Able to Discriminate Between Important and Unimportant Items					
7. Adequately Planned Work Performed					
8. Carefully Analyzed Findings; Effective Decision Maker					
9. Able to Recognize Significant Findings					
10. Met Reasonable Time Limits on Assignments					
Communication					
1. Oral Presentation Skills					
2. Adequacy of Discussions Regarding Findings					
3. Clarity of Working Paper Documentation					
4. Ability to Write Reports					
Interpersonal Skills					
1. Tactful in Gaining Client's Cooperation in Obtaining Data As Well As the Cooperation of Others					
2. Able to Deal with Management Personnel					
3. Attitude Toward Associates					
4. Attitude Toward Supervisors					
5. Approachable So That Others Can Seek Help As Needed					
6. Can Sustain a Position Without Creating Resentment When Disagreement Occurs					
7. Ability to Stimulate Others to Participate in Decision Making					
8. Can Criticize Others Constructively					
9. Able to Concede Graciously When Shown to Be in Error					
10. Versatile in Handling Unusual Situations					
11. Personal Appearance					
12. Behavior on and Away from Job					
Advancement Potential					
1. Capacity for Growth and Development					
2. Interest in Work					
3. Ability to Accept Increased Responsibility					
4. Understanding and Adherence to Required Standards of Conduct and Ethics					
5. Awareness of Cost/Benefit Dimensions of Audit Work					
6. Leadership Skills					
7. Training Skills					
8. Motivation					

Exhibit 9–6 (continued)

Performance Evaluations—An Illustration

Do you feel that this employee is ready for a promotion or increased job responsibility? Justify your recommendations. (For example, does employee possess a CPA certificate for advancement?)

_____

_____

_____

_____

Recommendations regarding employee's training and development: _____

_____

Other Comments: _____

_____

_____

_____

Evaluated by _____

Date _____

Reviewed by _____

Employee's Comments: _____

_____

_____

Assignment Preferences: _____

_____

Signature of Employee _____

Date _____

Comments on Conference Held With Employee on _____
                                              Date

_____

_____

_____

_____

Adapted from William E. Fergusson and Dianne S. Fergusson, *The Internal Audit Training Program*, Research Report 23 (Altamonte Springs, Fla.: Institute of Internal Auditors, 1980), pp. 78–83; and "Compliance Review Program Guidelines," Division for CPA Firms Peer Review Program (New York: AICPA, 1981), pp. 63–72.

situation. If the individual is retained, some means must be pursued not to leave the impression that this is acceptable behavior. As an example of an explanation that might justify retention of the professional is that some other procedure had been performed which he or she viewed as the equivalent of that which had been reported. The result of such an explanation would be to clarify the importance of having the reporting process align with the actual procedures performed. The fact that the critical incident arose suggests a need for training throughout the professional staff to avoid similar problems in the future.

Clear control procedures should be available for identifying critical incidents, reporting such incidents, and taking necessary action. Termination-related procedures are particularly critical in light of the legal implications that can arise if such termination is not appropriately handled.

A number of very sensitive critical incidents can be hypothesized to be relevant to professional service firms, including: discovery of fraud; reporting responsibilities related to such fraud; disagreements with clients that include threatened litigation and public disclosure practices; and risk exposures to professionals linked to international travel needs and the like. The more forward-looking a professional firm is at identifying such risk exposures and having a system, familiar to professional staff, in place, the more likely that risks will be appropriately controlled.

Overview

While some of the issues described herein overlap the cost of sales and finance cycles of a professional firm, the decision was made to focus on quality control procedures for professional firms within the revenue cycle discussion. Additional attention is directed to such issues in Chapter 16 of this *Handbook*, which shares lessons learned from the peer review process presently applied to a number of public accounting firms. Exhibit 9–7 summarizes some key control suggestions when designing and evaluating professional service firms.

DATABASE MANAGEMENT SYSTEMS (DBMS) IMPLICATIONS

In considering various means of assisting employees in understanding their own critical role in the accounting process, one opportunity that comes to mind is the plausibility of using database management systems (DBMS) to communicate. DBMS use relational accounting systems that conceptualize a model of a business in a manner that tells a story and is easy to understand, with little if any grounding in accounting. The conceptual models cross organizational boundaries, integrating accounting information with that generated through various operating arms of the organization, including manufacturing, marketing, and distribution. By using semantic specifications that tell a story, not only is a DBMS easier to understand, but it is also possible that the system could draw inferences and learn through processing. This could make the system capable of responding to incomplete or ambiguous questions and take advantage of decision support system technology that is increasingly available.

To envision the process of story telling, consider the script of an economic entity, with various scenes related to buying product for resell, advertising and selling that product, and spending resources on various support activities. The

Exhibit 9–7

Key Control Suggestions For Professional Firms

- Ensure all professionals understand the need for accurate reporting of services rendered
  —the control culture should clearly state that realization issues, budget variations, and similar considerations are separate from the reporting process for the accounting system; in other words, it is imperative that actual time spent, budget required, and billings desired are a part of the information system whether such quantities are eventually billed or not
  —the control culture should make it clear that "cooperation" with clients regarding billing and payment practices is to be kept distinct from the revenue recognition process, intended to track with the delivery of services, i.e., with the earning process
- Dual approval of all new clients, following a background check on those attributes of the clients deemed relevant
  —procedures should consider diversification implications for the firm
  —necessary investments related to client acceptance should be evaluated prior to accepting a new client
- A periodic review of existing clients should be required to determine if retention is desirable
- Hiring, professional development, and supervisory practices should be commensurate with the competency levels required for the services to be rendered
  —access to consultants should be available
  —formal evaluation procedures should be in place
  —adequate training and supervisory practices must be established
  —reporting practices should be in place to assist in assignment of professional staff and to comply with various regulatory and professional bodies
- Procedures should be in place for handling critical incidents including discovery of fraudulent activities and termination of professional staff
- Analytical procedures should be used to monitor the reasonableness of reported numbers; for example, are the professionals humanly able to have worked for the number of hours reported?

roles are assumed by a number of interested parties including employees, suppliers, and customers. Then the props would be the inventory purchased for resell, the cash changing hands upon selling, and a number of items used in carrying out business, such as facilities.[3] This type of nontechnical manner of communi-

[3] For additional information on such systems, see W. E. McCarthy, "An Entity-Relationship View of Accounting Models, *The Accounting Review*, 54 (October 1979), pp. 667–686 and "The REA

cating the critical ingredients in the revenue process and related activities of an entity can go a long way in enhancing understanding and ensuring effective communication among individuals with diverse backgrounds.

ADDITIONAL EXAMPLES

The Appendix to this chapter provides further examples of the tie-in of errors, control risk, tests of control, and substantive tests (Exhibits 9–8 and 9–9), as well as related documentation for the revenue cycle (Exhibit 9–10). In particular, the concept of a bridging working paper is illustrated, whereby the CPA describes his or her objective, the related system controls, tests of control, substantive procedures, and overall conclusion. Such a documentation process clarifies the interrelationship of various aspects of an engagement. Its general form likewise could be used in an internal control reporting engagement, linking testing objective to design, procedure, test, and conclusion.

Accounting Model: A Generalized Framework for Accounting Systems in a Shared Data Environment," *The Accounting Review* 57 (July, 1982), pp. 554–578. A related example tied to tax matters is provided by W. E. McCarthy and E. Outslay in an article entitled "An Analysis of the Applicability of Artificial Intelligence Techniques to Problem Solving in Taxation Domains," *Accounting Horizons* (June, 1989), pp. 14–27.

APPENDIX

Exhibit 9–8

The Tie-in of Possible Errors, Controls, Related Tests, and Substantive Test Work in the Revenue Cycle

	Controls		Tests of Control		Substantive Tests	
Error	Preventive	Detective	Preventive	Detective	Interim	Final
Goods shipped but not billed.	—Controlled access to shipping area. —Segregated duties. —Prenumbered shipping documents, sales orders, and invoices. —Matching of sales orders, shipping documents, and invoices.	—Independent review of sequence of prenumbered documents. —Independent review of unmatched shipping documents. —Independent review of reasonableness of sales and inventory shortages.	—Observe shipping area. —Observe separate sales orders, billings, and inventory control areas. —Examine used and unused documents for prenumbering. —Examine system of numbering incoming sales orders. —Examine logs or system in place for matching documents.	—Examine initials supporting review. —Examine evidence of separate reasonableness tests, e.g., in the internal audit work papers. —Examine evidence of separate review of inventory shortages.	—Trace shipping documents to invoices, accounting for description and quantity. —Trace sales orders to invoices to ensure all sales received were billed.	—Review all sales orders and shipping documents, determining most likely error.
Goods returned but no credit given to customer	—Separate receiving department to handle returned goods. —Prenumbered receiving slips for returned goods. —Prenumbered credit memoranda. —Matching of receiving slips with credit memoranda.	—Independent review of sequence of prenumbered documents. —Independent review of unmatched credit memoranda and receiving slips. —Investigation of overdue accounts receivable records. —Investigation of customers' complaints.	—Examine documentation supporting write offs. —Examine initials on write-offs indicating independent review before recording of write-offs.	—Examine initials supporting review. —Examine evidence of review of overdue accounts receivable. —Examine evidence of how customer complaints have been handled.	—Trace returned goods on receiving slips to credit memoranda. —Confirm invoices with customer, especially if overdue. —Examine correspondence from customers in credit department files	—Confirm accounts receivable or unpaid older invoices at year end. —For last month of fiscal year, trace returned goods on receiving reports to credit memoranda.

Exhibit 9–8 (continued)

Cash not recorded or deposited.	—Require two people to be present when mail is opened. —For over the counter receipts, use locked box or a cash register with standard controls.	—Separate cash receipts from accounts receivable. —Send monthly statements to customers, using a person other than the one posting detailed receivable records. —Investigate customers' complaints. —Regularly review aged trial balance and independently inquire into problems with collections.	—Observe opening of mail. —Observe system for handling over-the-counter cash receipts.	—Observe segregation of duties. —Observe practice of sending monthly statements, noting separation of duties. —Examine work papers or reports that document how customers' complaints have been handled. —Examine aged trial balance and related analyses performed.	—Confirm open accounts receivable, particularly if overdue. —Examine correspondence from customers in credit department files. —Prepare daily totals of receipts and trace to deposits, accounting for unusual variations in amounts deposited.	—Confirm year-end accounts receivable.
Unauthorized write-offs of accounts either collectible or already collected and not deposited.	—Require write-offs to be supported by documentation of collection attempts and response, if any, from customer. —Approval of write-off by someone independent from the credit granting and cash receipts functions.	—Compare amount written off against new sales to "reasonableness" benchmark (based on past experience and industry experience). —Review approvals by independent party, as well as substantiation for write-offs.	—Examine documentation supporting a reasonableness review of write-offs. —Examine initials indicating independent review was made of support for write-offs.	—Examine working papers supporting reasonableness review of write-offs. —Examine initials indicating an independent review of the support for write-offs.	—Confirm write-offs with customers. —Examine correspondence or other documentation supporting write-offs.	—Extend interim work to additional write-offs between interim date and year-end.

Adapted from Jay M. Smith, "An Analysis of the Effectiveness and Efficiency of Substantive Auditing Procedures," working paper, Brigham Young University, 1980.

Exhibit 9–9

An Example of the Linkage Between Internal Control Risk Assessment and Substantive Testing

Problem:

You are the in-charge accountant examining the financial statements of the Gutzler Company for the year ended December 31, 19X6. During late October 19X6, you, with the help of Gutzler's controller, completed an internal control questionnaire and prepared the appropriate memoranda describing Gutzler's accounting procedures. Your comments regarding cash receipts are as follows.

All cash receipts are sent directly to the accounts receivable clerk with no processing by the mail department. The accounts receivable clerk keeps the cash receipts journal, prepares the bank deposit slip in duplicate, posts from the deposit slip to the subsidiary accounts receivable ledger, and mails the deposit to the bank.

The controller receives the validated deposit slips directly (unopened) from the bank. He also receives the monthly bank statement directly (unopened) from the bank and promptly reconciles it.

At the end of each month, the accounts receivable clerk notifies the general ledger clerk by journal voucher of the monthly totals of the cash receipts journal for posting to the general ledger.

Each month, the general ledger clerk makes an entry in the general ledger cash account, to record the total debits to cash from the cash receipts journal. In addition, the general ledger clerk sometimes makes debit entries in the general ledger cash account from sources other than the cash receipts journal, e.g., funds borrowed from the bank.

You have already performed certain standard auditing procedures as listed below in the audit of cash receipts. The extent to which you have performed these procedures is not relevant to the question.

- Total and cross-total all columns in the cash receipts journal.
- Trace postings from the cash receipts journal to the general ledger.
- Examine remittance advices and related correspondence to support entries in the cash receipts journal.

Required:

Considering Gutzler's internal control over cash receipts and standard auditing procedures already performed, list all other auditing procedures and the reasons they should be performed to obtain sufficient audit evidence regarding cash receipts. Do not discuss the procedures for cash disbursements and cash balances and the extent to which any of the procedures are to be performed. Assume there are adequate controls to ensure that all sales transactions are recorded.

Solution:

Other audit procedures	Reason for other audit procedures	Other audit procedures	Reason for other audit procedures
1. Sources of debit entries in the general ledger cash account, other than from the cash re-	1. Because the auditor, using standard procedures, examines only the cash receipts journal, he	2. There should be a surprise examination of cash receipts. Before the accounts receiv-	2. Because there are no initial controls over cash receipts before the accounts receivable

Exhibit 9–9 (continued)

Other audit procedures	Reason for other audit procedures	Other audit procedures	Reason for other audit procedures
ceipts journal, should be investigated, and supporting documents should be examined.	or she must investigate the validity of all other sources of cash receipts that are not recorded in these journals.	able clerk obtains the cash receipts, the auditor should make a list of them without the clerk's knowledge. The undeposited mail receipts should then be controlled after completion of their preparation for deposit and after postings have been made to the subsidiary accounts receivable ledger. The deposit slip should be totaled and compared with the remittances and the list prepared by the auditor for accuracy. Individual items on the deposit slip should be compared with postings to the subsidiary accounts receivable ledger. The auditor should then supervise the mailing of the deposit to the bank. The auditor should ask Gutzler to ask the bank to send the statement containing this deposit directly to the auditor.	clerk obtains the cash, a surprise examination is the only method of determining whether cash receipts are being recorded and deposited properly.
3. Postings from other deposit slips should	3. Because there is no separation of	4. A proof-of-cash working paper	4. Because internal control over cash

Exhibit 9–9 (continued)

Other audit procedures	Reason for other audit procedures	Other audit procedures	Reason for other audit procedures
be traced to the cash receipts journal and the subsidiary accounts receivable ledger. Also, entries in the subsidiary accounts receivable ledger should be traced to the cash receipts journal and to the deposit slips.	duties between cash receipts and accounts receivable, the accounts receivable clerk may have been careless in performing his or her posting duties. This procedure may also disclose whether the accounts receivable clerk may have been lapping the accounts.	should be prepared that reconciles total cash receipts with credits per bank statements. The opening and closing reconciliation of the proof of cash should be compared with the comparable reconciliation prepared by the controller.	receipts is weak, the auditor should perform this overall check to ensure that he or she has investigated all material items during his or her detail tests.
5. Review the subsidiary accounts receivable ledger, and confirm accounts that have abnormal transaction activity, such as consistently late payments.	5. See 3 above.	6. Prepare a ratio analysis of monthly collections to total sales of the preceding month or monthly collections to total accounts receivable at the beginning of the month and compare this analysis with a similar analysis for the preceding year.	6. Because internal control over cash receipts is weak, this overall test may highlight any irregularities
7. If Gutzler allows customers to take discounts, the amount of such discounts and the discount period should be checked.	7. Because there is no separation of duties between cash receipts and accounts receivable, the accounts receivable clerk may have appropriated discounts that could have been, but were not, taken or may have been careless in checking the appropriateness of discounts taken.	8. Visit the client on the balance sheet date or the next business day to determine whether there has been an appropriate cutoff of cash receipts.	8. Because internal control over cash receipts is weak, the auditor needs to satisfy himself or herself that cash receipts are recorded in the appropriate period.
9. Dates and amounts of daily deposits per bank statements should be compared with en-	9. Because there are no initial controls over cash receipts before the accounts receivable clerk ob-	10. For those periods for which the above audit procedures were not performed and for	10. Because internal control over cash receipts is weak, the auditor should perform this re-

Exhibit 9–9 (continued)

Other audit procedures	Reason for other audit procedures	Other audit procedures	Reason for other audit procedures
tries in the cash receipts journal.	tains the cash, he or she may have become careless about promptly depositing the daily receipts.	a period after the balance sheet date, scan the cash receipts journal and bank statements for unusual items.	view to ensure that he or she has investigated all material items not covered during his or her other tests.

CPA exam adapted, May 9, 1974, question 3.

Exhibit 9–10

Dividend Revenue: Example of a Bridging Working Paper

W/P Ref. No.
Preparer
Date

Bridging Working Paper

Audit Objective: Reported dividend revenue represents the actual amount earned from investments, is recorded in the proper period, and has been appropriately recorded to reflect dividends receivable and collections of such receivables.

System Controls: The design of controls over cash receipts is good and encompasses not only receipts from inventory sales but also nonroutine receipts such as investment revenue. A separate investment ledger is maintained that is routinely reviewed and matched with actual receipts. See W/P No. __.

Tests of Control: The investment ledger was tied to the general ledger; controls over cash receipts were tested and found to be effective. See W/P No. __.

Substantive Procedures: Investment securities were inspected. Cash balances were confirmed with the bank, and a cutoff bank statement was audited. Dividend revenue was tied to publicly available dividend records printed by Standard & Poor's. See W/P No. __.

Exhibit 9–10 (continued)

Overall Conclusion: Dividend revenue is accurately stated in the proper period, and receivables tie to dates of declaration on securities for which the payment date has not yet arrived, whereas all other dividend revenue has been collected, as appropriate.

10

How to Design and Evaluate Internal Accounting Controls for the Cost of Sales or Production Cycle

> "I should never have made my success in life if I had not bestowed upon the least thing I have ever undertaken the same attention and care that I have bestowed upon the greatest."
>
> **Charles Dickens[1]**

The attention to detail implied in the introductory quote is particularly appropriate in considering controls associated with the cost of sales or production cycle. The nuances of operations necessary to produce the revenue cycle described in Chapter 9 are numerous, all of which need to be controlled. This chapter will describe both the design and evaluation of internal accounting controls for the cost of sales or production cycle.

---

[1] James Charlton, Editor, *The Executive's Quotation Book: A Corporate Companion* (New York: St. Martin's Press, 1983), p. 40.

The cost of sales or production cycle encompasses both

—expenditures—purchasing, transportation, receiving, trade payables, payroll, and cash disbursements, and

—production or conversion—inventory, manufacturing, cost accounting, scrap, and property accounts.

How to design controls and evaluate existing controls for this operating cycle by implementing the approach outlined in prior chapters will now be explained. The explanations provided will include examples of control problems that have been observed for a wide cross-section of industries and details as to how these problems would be identified and could be corrected by using the recommended approach to control analysis.

SEGREGATING INCOMPATIBLE FUNCTIONS

Any flow of transactions and related assets, as described earlier in this guide, involves the authorization of transactions, the execution of transactions, the recording of transactions, and the accountability for the assets that result from such transactions. Functions are said to be incompatible when one person is in a position both to perpetuate and to conceal either errors or irregularities while performing his or her normal duties. Generally speaking, such an undesirable combination of normal duties is avoided by separating three functional areas: authorization, custody, and accounting. However, when reviewing an entity's organization chart and job descriptions and discussing day-to-day operations, which are the specific responsibilities that should be assigned to different individuals to achieve effective control? Exhibit 10–1 details the critical segregation of duties desirable for the cost of sales or production cycle.

Interpreting Exhibit 10–1

As was Exhibit 9–1, Exhibit 10–1 is organized with the owner-manager as an overall means of control. Whenever an entity lacks a desired separation of duties, the intervention of the owner-manager into the cycle and his or her review of the work of individuals who are performing incompatible functions can result in a reasonably effective system of control. The three-man operation, as suggested earlier in this guide, can accrue many of the benefits available from segregating duties by applying the three-column structure of Exhibit 10–1; however, the benefits of segregating duties can be maximized if each of the duties delineated in the exhibit is performed by a different person within each of the departments indicated. Exhibit 10–1 is subdivided into five components of the cost of sales or production cycle. Focusing on the first subdivision, we find expenditures for inventory; services other than payroll; property, plant, and equipment; and other assets. The three-man operation would be expected to separate the purchasing

Exhibit 10–1

Critical Segregation of Duties for the Cost of Sales or Production Cycle

OWNER-MANAGER

□ = Space for initials of individual responsible for this duty.

AUTHORIZATION	CUSTODY

Expenditures—Purchasing of: inventory; services other than property, plant and equipment; other assets | *Expenditures—Purchasing of: inventory; services other than property, plant and equipment; other assets*

PURCHASING

□ Approved Purchase (or Check) Requisition from Operating Departments (Including the Transportation Department) or from the Board of Directors Initiates Purchase Activity.

□ Prepare Purchase Order (Including Work Orders) Based on Requisition.

□ Review & Approve Purchase Order (Send Copy to Party Making Request and to Accounting for Cross-check and Retain a Copy for Control); Mail to Vendor.

□ Investigate Complaints and Correspond with Vendors.

RECEIVING

□ Prepare Receiving Report (May Include Interface with Inspection Department; Goods Will Include Returns).

□ Review & Approve Receiving Report—Forward Copies to Purchasing and Accounts Payable for Cross-Check.

□ Forward Goods to Warehousing & Storeroom.

Expenditures—Payment of purchase obligations | *Expenditures—Payment of purchase obligations*

TREASURY

□ Check Signer (Reviews Voucher Package Before Signing.)

□ Countersignature (Reviews Voucher Package Before Signing.)

CASH DISBURSEMENTS

□ Distribute Checks to Payee (This task is controlled by the last check signer.)

□ Maintain Check Register (Have Custody of Unissued Checks and Debit Memoranda.)

□ Cancel Voucher and Supporting Documents and Return Them to Accounting, Noting Check Number Issued.

Expenditures—Payroll | *Expenditures—Payroll*

PERSONNEL

□ Maintain Employee Master File: Approve Additions, Deletions, and Changes to Payroll Master File with Hiring Consensus from Operating Department.

TIMEKEEPING

□ Maintain Time Cards with Approval of Hours Worked.

TREASURY

□ Control Signature Plate.

CASH DISBURSEMENTS

□ Deposit Net Payroll Amount in Payroll Imprest Bank Account Based on Voucher.

PAYROLL DISTRIBUTION

□ Distribute Checks (or Pay Envelopes), Returning Unclaimed Checks to a Cash Disbursements Employee with No Other Cash Responsibilities.

Production or Conversion | *Production or Conversion*

PRODUCTION CONTROL

□ Initiate Movement or Transfer Forms.

WAREHOUSING & STOREROOM

□ Account for Goods from the Receiving Department and for Requisitions.

□ Custody of Inventory and Property.

□ Safeguarding of Property.

PRODUCTION CONTROL

□ Control Inventory Movement.

PHYSICAL INVENTORY TAKING

□ Cycle Counts and Annual Physical Inventory; at Least a Triannual Inventory of Property, Plant and Equipment.

Petty Cash | *Petty Cash*

TREASURY

□ Verify Imprest Basis of Petty Cash Fund, Approving Voucher for Reimbursement.

□ Check Signer (Reviews Voucher Package Before Signing, Cancels Petty Cash Vouchers and Supporting Documents, and Notes the Check Number Issued.)

□ Countersignature (Reviews Voucher Package Before Signing, Checks for Cancellation, and Returns Voucher Package to Accounting).

PETTY CASH CUSTODIAN

□ Responsible for Petty Cash Fund (Including the Cashing of Reimbursement Checks).

□ Countersignature on Petty Cash Voucher.

Exhibit 10–1 (continued)

OWNER-MANAGER

ACCOUNTING

Expenditures—Purchasing of: inventory; services other than property, plant and equipment; other assets

ACCOUNTS PAYABLE

☐ Prepare Voucher: Comparing Purchase Order, Receiving Report, and Invoice—Checking Extensions and Propriety (Alternative Forms of Support for Claims and Professional Services May Be Appropriate).

☐ Review & Approve Voucher Package for Payment (Including Approval of Account Distribution).

☐ Prepare Check—and Forward Voucher Package for Payment.

☐ Maintain the Voucher Register, and Files of Open Purchase Orders, Unmatched Receiving Reports, Unmatched Invoices, and Unmatched Records of Returns and Claims.

☐ Maintain the Subsidiary Account Payable Ledger.

GENERAL LEDGER ACCOUNTING

☐ Maintain the Control Accounts.

☐ Review & Approve Journal Entries, Reconcile Subsidiary with General Ledger, Reconcile Vendor Statements, Review Open and Unmatched Files and Unaccounted-for Documents.

Expenditures—Payment of purchase obligations

ACCOUNTS PAYABLE

☐ Update Voucher Register to Reflect Vouchers Paid.

☐ Maintain the Subsidiary Accounts Payable Ledger.

PURCHASE & EXPENSE LEDGER

☐ Maintain Detailed Expense Ledger (Including Prepaid Expense Items for Which Check Requisitions Were Properly Authorized).

GENERAL LEDGER ACCOUNTING

☐ Maintain the Control Accounts.

☐ Review & Approve Journal Entries, Reconcile Subsidiary with General Ledger and Vendor Statements, and Account for Usage of Checks and Debit Memoranda.

☐ Prepare Bank Reconciliation (Separate General and Dividend Accounts Should Be Maintained).

Expenditures—Payroll

PAYROLL PREPARATION

☐ Prepare Payroll, Reconciling Job Time Tickets to Time Clock Cards, and Record Labor Distribution.

☐ Prepare Payroll Checks.

☐ Signing Payroll Checks (Signature Plate Separately Controlled from Accounting).

☐ Maintain Employee Records.

ACCOUNTS PAYABLE

☐ Review Payroll—Checking Extensions and Propriety—and Prepare Voucher.

☐ Review & Approve Voucher for Payroll.

GENERAL LEDGER ACCOUNTING

☐ Maintain the Control Accounts; Review Exception Reports Based on Reasonableness or Limit Checks of Sales and Credit Granted, as Well as Reports of Credit Balances.

☐ Review & Approve Journal Entries, Reconcile Subsidiary with General Ledger, Reconcile Daily Billings Totals with Total Receivables Postings, Compare Production and Inventory Records with Shipping and Billing Documentation, Match Shipping Advices from Independent Shippers to Internal Documentation, and Review Open and Unmatched Files and Unaccounted For Documents, e.g., Any Unfilled Customer Orders or Unmatched Shipping Documents.

Production or Conversion

COST ACCOUNTING

☐ Maintain Inventory and Manufacturing Records (Stock Ledger Entries); Maintain Detailed Plant Records (Maintain Separate Records on Goods on Consignment and Goods Belonging to Third Parties.)

☐ Prepare Production and Inventory Reports, Reviewing Detailed Records.

GENERAL LEDGER ACCOUNTING

☐ Maintain the Control Accounts.

☐ Approve Journal Entries and Adjustments.

☐ Reconcile Inventory Cost System with General Ledger; Reconcile Transfers from Finished Goods with Quantities Charged to Customers; Review Periodic Management Reports.

☐ Reconcile Physical Inventory to Books, Confirm Inventory Held by Outsiders.

Petty Cash

ACCOUNTS PAYABLE

☐ Review Petty Cash Vouchers for Propriety and Prepare Voucher for Reimbursement.

☐ Prepare Check Payable to Custodian and Forward Voucher Package for Payment.

PURCHASE & EXPENSE LEDGER

☐ Update Purchase & Expense Ledger for Petty Cash Disbursements.

GENERAL LEDGER ACCOUNTING

☐ Maintain the Control Accounts.

☐ Approve Journal Entries and Adjustments.

☐ Prepare Bank Reconciliation.

function from the receiving and accounts payable functions. Within the purchasing function it is desirable to have one party approve purchase and check requisitions, another party prepare the related purchase order, a third party review and approve the order, and a fourth party investigate vendors' complaints. What is the rationale for having four separate tasks within purchasing?

The first two parties can be thought of as a separation of authorization and custody responsibilities within the authorization function. The authorizer of a purchase order cannot extract resources by submitting bogus purchase orders for which support does not exist unless (s)he has access to or custody of the purchase orders. Furthermore, the third party proves to be an accounting type of function, as (s)he accounts for the proper authorization of the purchase order and the appropriate completion of the purchase order form. A final check on the three key subfunctions of purchasing is the availability of a fourth party to whom vendors can complain. Note that the self-interest of creditors provides a protective feature for accounts payable, as vendors can be expected to speak up if payments for their goods and services are not received. However, their complaints to parties who have made the error or who are perpetrating a fraud are likely to fall on deaf ears. In contrast, an independent party can effectively capitalize on an available source of control—the vendor. One might also question the necessity of having one party review and approve a purchase order prepared by someone else. The intention is to increase the likelihood of detecting errors; one can never check oneself as thoroughly as can an independent third party. It is unlikely that the same error will be repeated by two people; moreover, a defalcation could not be expected to be exposed by the perpetrator's review of his own work. A final common-sense consideration is warranted in reviewing whether this four-man segregation of duties within the authorization function is achieved for a given entity. To whom does each individual report, and are the incentives of each person to effectively perform his job? For example, if the reviewer and approver of the purchase order is subject to performance reviews by the preparer of the purchase order, one can hardly expect the reviewer to be anxious to uncover and to report the errors of his or her "boss."

Each of the boxes in Exhibit 10–1 can be scrutinized in the same detail as the purchasing function and the same major ideas will persist:

—Within each of the department functions a subclassification of authorization, custody, and accounting-type duties is identifiable.

—Someone independent of the preparer of a document should review and approve the document.

—Some party not involved in originating and approving initial transactions should have overview, testing, and follow-up responsibilities.

Exhibit 10–1 lists 62 different tasks for segregation but does not imply a minimum staff of 62. For example, the party preparing the bank reconciliations for purchases, payroll, and petty cash could be one individual and no loss of control would result. Similarly, the party in general ledger accounting who reviews and approves journal entries in each of the five subdivisions of the cycle could be one person. In smaller organizations, both these functions would typically be the review responsibility of the owner-manager. The central question arises—how is Exhibit 10–1 utilized in control design and evaluation?

How to Use Exhibit 10–1

Become familiar with operations and put the initials of the party performing each of the 62 tasks on the exhibit in the spaces provided. Initials appearing more than once within one of the three columns on the exhibit cause little concern, although the absence of cross-checks increases the risk exposure to careless errors. If the same initials appear as originator and reviewer, no real protection against error exists; this is particularly the case if one individual accounts for a transaction from the beginning to the end of the accounting trail. The real control concerns arise when duties are not appropriately segregated across the three columns. Exhibit 10–1 should permit one to both identify the control flaw and interpret the added risk exposure that arises from combining incompatible functions.

EXAMPLE: In a shoe store retail operation, the accounts payable manager assigns vendor numbers to new vendors as they are needed and prepares the data to be put onto the master file of approved vendors by the EDP department.

A review of Exhibit 10–1 reminds the system reviewer that the approved vendor file is part of the authorization function, while the accounts payable manager is principally expected to control accounting functions.

The detailed tasks permit the reviewer to outline what could go wrong: the accounts payable manager could input a bogus vendor on the master file, and the authorization procedure whereby the purchasing department determines to whom a purchase order is to be mailed (including comparison to the approved vendor listing) becomes an ineffective control. Despite no direct access to cash, the accounts payable manager has structured a means of obtaining cash via a bogus supplier.

SOLUTION: Obviously, risk exposure or possibility is distinct from probability. This combination of incompatible functions could be offset by adding a task within the purchasing department of reviewing "was-is reports" on changes to the master vendor file. In addition, vendors added to the master file could be subject to approval first by the appropriate buyer and his merchandising manager. Such a strategy essentially transfers authorization responsibilities away from the accounting function.

EXAMPLE: In a Federal Reserve Bank, tellers and bookkeepers regularly accept instructions to turn over customer statements to an officer or other employee for special attention. In addition, due to the size of the operation, both tellers and bookkeepers are used in preparing and mailing customer statements. It is common practice that change-of-address requests from customers are received by tellers and updated on the books.

Tellers are typically expected to have custody responsibilities, while bookkeepers have accounting duties and officers have authorization responsibilities.

In this setting, a careful scrutiny of Exhibit 10–1, particularly the payment subdivision, clarifies the overlapping of the three columns, with respect to both receipts and payments to customers (or suppliers of capital, if this perspective clarifies the cost of sales and production cycle of banks).

SOLUTION: The recommendations for improved control in this setting would be

> —to prohibit tellers and bookkeepers from accepting such instructions from officers or employees, as it is imperative that executives authorizing transactions do not have access to accounting records (this is actually an example of overriding the established control system— a risk discussed earlier in this guide);
> —to maintain an assignment sheet with the names of employees preparing customer statements and rotate these employees in the preparation and mailing process; and
> —to verify all changes in address by mailing a written confirmation to the old address.

Obviously, Exhibit 10–1 is easiest to use as a basis for designing controls; however, it is presented in sufficiently general terms that any critical segregation of duties that is missing in an organization can be identified by matching specific people to the individual duties and interpreting the consequence with respect to risk exposure. The probability of such risks will be clarified in the next stage of system analysis, but first consider potential adverse effects of other factors upon what otherwise appears to be an effective separation of duties.

Watch for These Factors That Can Adversely Affect Control and Segregation of Duties

At times, the use of initials on Exhibit 10–1 will not identify weaknesses in controls because other factors are relevant in evaluating the effectiveness of the apparent segregation of duties.

Family ties.

EXAMPLE: The bookkeeper for a utility company is related to one of the warehouse salesmen.

Family ties result in a higher-than-normal risk of collusion and should be considered by the business when hiring and by anyone who is reviewing a control system in which employees are related.

Assumption of permanent or temporary duties in other operating areas.

EXAMPLE: A small interior decorating store has a bookkeeper and a cashier who substitute for each other during lunch hours.

Stated responsibilities will often differ from actual operating procedures. In this setting, no real separation of accounting and custody is achieved.

Access to assets which should be strictly controlled.

EXAMPLE: A credit agency maintains Series E Bonds and travelers' checks in locked boxes, the keys to which are stored in the assistant manager's desk drawer, accessible to all personnel.

In this setting, no segregation of authorization, custody, or accounting exists with respect to these assets. The keys should be strictly controlled if the segregation of duties is to be effective.

Potential conflicts of interest.

EXAMPLE: A drug company permits authorized check signers to sign checks releasing funds for their own business expenditures.

Although such expenditures may be entirely legitimate and business related, the appearance of impropriety to other nonactive owners of the company, as well as the risk exposure to improper authorization, would be minimized if another check signer was required for this type of disbursement.

Code Exhibit 10–1 for these adverse factors. The systems evaluator must remain aware of such potential adverse factors when evaluating controls. A useful approach is to code initials onto Exhibit 10–1 that reflect (a) family relationships, (b) those assuming permanent and temporary duties in other operating areas, (c) the apparent access by others to assets under particular individuals' control, and (d) the handling of specific transactions known to involve a conflict of interest. The use of such a coding scheme will enable the evaluator to better assess the effectiveness of segregated duties as an accounting and operating control.

MAINTAINING COMPLETE ACCOUNTING RECORDS

Once the systems designer has established the critical segregation of duties or the systems evaluator has identified the apparent separation of duties and related strengths and weaknesses, what information is available to document that each of the tasks outlined in Exhibit 10–1 has in fact been performed? As discussed earlier in this guide, tests of control frequently involve observation and inquiry techniques. However, a strong control system will create an accounting trail which requires employees to document the performance of both operating and control duties, thereby stressing the employees' accountability and providing physical evidence that control procedures are in operation.

Forms for Assuring Complete Accounting Records

Exhibit 10–2 provides the systems designer and evaluator with a standard by which to assess the completeness of the accounting trail. The documents presented underlie the cost of sales or production cycle and, if properly completed and controlled, can be expected to assist an entity in recording all valid and authorized transactions in the appropriate amount, account, and time period. Obviously, the format of each document, as well as the terms applied to each of the forms, should be tailored to the client's operations. However, as noted in Exhibit 10–2, each document has a purpose which should be common across

Exhibit 10–2

**Assuring Complete Accounting Records—Use and Control
of the Following Forms Will Assist in Recording Ail Valid
and Authorized Cost of Sales or Production Cycle
Transactions in the Appropriate Amount, Account, and
Time Period**

EXPENDITURES

\# _____   PURCHASE REQUISITION   Date _____

Description _____

Quantities _____   Units of Measure _____

Expected Cost _____

Quality Standard _____

Desired Delivery Date _____

Transportation Arrangements _____

Expected Discount Terms _____

Maximum Cost Authorized _____

Maximum Acceptable Delivery Period _____

Signature _____

Supervisor's Signature _____

Special Approval of Long-Term Commitments _____

Requested Approval by Purchasing Department of Variation from Above Terms:

Description of Variation _____

If Approve, Authorizing Signature _____

Supervisor's Signature _____

Purpose: To authorize purchase, documenting specifications regarding quality, price, and
delivery.

Exhibit 10–2 (continued)

_____   CHECK REQUISITION   Date _____

Description of Services _____

Time Limit for Services _____ Days _____ Hours

Price Limit for Services _____

Required Inspection Procedures _____

Appropriate Accounting Treatment (e.g., Prepaid Charge-Off Period)_____

MAINTENANCE & REPAIR OF FIXED ASSETS

Reason for Requisition _____

Estimated Cost _____

Detail Plant or Expense Account to Be Charged _____

Description and Original Cost of Displaced Plant _____

Instructions _____

PROPERTY, PLANT & EQUIPMENT

Description _____

Expected Cost _____

Asset Account to Be Charged _____

Expected Service Life _____ Years _____ Months

Estimated Salvage Value _____

Suggested Depreciation Method _____

Instructions (Delivery, Routing, Discount Terms, Inspection)_____

Approval of Depreciation Method by Tax Department _____

                    Signature _____

                    Supervisor's Signature _____

If Greater Than $ _____ , Board of Directors' Authorizing Signature _____

ROUTINE EXPENDITURES

Telephone _____

Utilities _____

Municipal Taxes _____

Lease Obligations _____

Postage _____

Other _____

                    Signature _____

Purpose: To authorize payment for services, maintenance and repair of fixed assets, acqui-
        sition of property, plant, and equipment, and routine expenditures (with docu-
        mentation of types, amount, and timing of expenditures).

Exhibit 10–2 (continued)

_____   PURCHASE ORDER   Date _____

Supporting Requisition Number _____

Accounting Distribution _____

Description _____

Quantities _____ Unit of Measure _____

Total Cost _____

Transportation Arrangements _____

Special Delivery Instructions _____

If Telephone Order Was Placed, Date _____

Required Testing and Inspection Procedures by Receiving Department _____

Signature _____

Supervisor's Signature _____

—Forward First Two Copies to Vendor, Requesting That the Copy Be Returned to Acknowledge Receipt of Order
—Retain Third Copy for Control
—Forward Fourth Copy to Receiving Department
—Forward Fifth Copy to Accounting Department
—Forward Sixth Copy to Source of Requisition

Purpose: To initiate actual purchase, documenting telephone orders, the supporting requisition(s), and special instructions for the receiving department.

Exhibit 10–2 (continued)

_____   BUYER'S RECORD   Date _____

Supporting Purchase Order Number _____

Competitive Bids _____

Market Price Data _____

Rationale for Vendor Selection:

    Price Competitiveness _____

    Discounts Offered _____

    Transportation Costs _____

    Credit Terms _____

    Legal Restrictions (Import Quotas) _____

    Conflict of Interest Concerns _____

    Reciprocity _____

    Timely Delivery _____

    Quality of Merchandise _____

    Service _____

    Expressed or Implied Warranty _____

    Other (e.g., Alternative Use) _____

Compliance with Company Policy: Authorized Vendor Listing _____

    [If Not, Authorized Signature _____]

    Recent Check on Financial Status of Vendor _____

    Maintenance of Multiple Suppliers _____

    Use of Local Suppliers _____

    Sales Tax Terms _____

    If Long-term Commitment, Review by Legal Counsel _____

                Signature _____

        Supervisor's Signature _____

Purpose: To document basis for vendor selection and compliance with company policy
(if applicable, will document long-term purchase commitments).

Exhibit 10–2 (continued)

```
#_____                    RECEIVING REPORT            Date_____

Postage, if Applicable $_____

Description_____

Quantities_____  Units of Measure_____
(If scales are used, record gross and tare scale weights.)

Method of Counting, Weighing, or Measuring_____

                    Counter's Signature_____

Comparison with Purchase Order #_____

    Agreement_____

    Partial Shipment_____

    Shortage_____

    Overage_____

    Action Taken_____

Handling of Unidentified Receipts_____

Handling of Goods on Consignment_____

Handling of Goods Held for Third Parties_____

Compliance with Required Testing and Inspection Procedures:

Damaged Goods Returned_____

Claims Filed_____

                    Signature_____

            Supervisor's Signature_____
```

Purpose: To document goods received and variations from purchase orders, including performance of inspection procedures and return of damaged goods.

Exhibit 10–2 (continued)

_____   VOUCHER   Date _____

Invoice # _____

Purchase Order # _____

Receiving Report # _____

Other Supporting Document # _____ Type _____

    Agreement _____

    Action Taken on Differences _____

Approval of Incorrect or Incomplete Invoice Adjustments _____
                                            Signature

Note Completion of Following Procedures with Initials:

    All Forms Stamped as to Date and Hour Received _____

    Duplicate Invoices Stamped as Copies _____

    Recalculated Footings and Extensions _____

    Checked Vendor File for Propriety of Name, Address, and Prices _____

    Recomputed Discount _____

Approval for Payment _____
                                        Signature

Account Distribution _____ Approval of Account _____

Date upon Which Payment Is to Be Made _____
(Utilize this date to file in the Tickler File.)

               Review Procedures   Initials (Date)

Reconciled Vendor's Statement to Accounts Payable   _____

Effective Cancellation of Voucher and All Supporting
Documents   _____

Check Number Issued # _____   _____

Entered in Inventory   _____

Entered in Property Ledger   _____

Purpose: To authorize payment through reference to necessary supporting documents and to document performance of prescribed review duties.

Exhibit 10–2 (continued)

```
#_____              COMPLETION REPORT              Date_____

Description of Services_____

Comparison with Check Requisition #_____

    Agreement_____

    Action Taken if Not in Agreement_____

Compliance with Required Inspection Procedures_____

    Claims Filed_____

                         Signature_____

              Supervisor's Signature_____
```

Purpose: To authorize payment for services by documenting the completion of specified
work and compliance with required inspection procedures (if applicable, claims
filed are also documented).

```
#_____              DEBIT MEMORANDA                Date_____

                                Unit of      Basis
          Description  Quantity  Measure     of Claim    Amount

          _____   _____   _____     _____    _____

          _____   _____   _____     _____    _____

Payee_____

              Authorized Signature_____

              Supervisor's Signature_____
```

Required Procedures:

—Comparison to Original Record of Goods Returned or Claims Made_____
                                                                     initials

—Comparison of Prices to Original Invoice_____
                                                              initials

—Check of Extensions and Footings_____
                                                        initials

—Controlled by Voucher #_____

Purpose: To debit suppliers' accounts for claims, returns and allowances, and document
related review procedures.

Exhibit 10–2 (continued)

FOLLOW-UP

```
#_____          OPEN PURCHASE ORDERS          Date_____

              Those Beyond Delivery Period

        P.O.#          Action Taken (Reason)
        ____           _____
        ____           _____
        ____           _____


              Terms in Excess of Current Prices

        P.O.#          Action Taken (Reason)
        ____           _____
        ____           _____
        ____           _____


              Signature _____
        Supervisor's Signature _____
```

Purpose: To ensure follow-through on a timely basis of all unfilled purchase orders.

```
#_____          UNMATCHED RECEIVING REPORTS          Date_____

  Receiving Report #      Date of                    Action
    (Description)         Receipt       Reason        Taken
  _____       _____      _____        ____
  _____       _____      _____        ____
  _____       _____      _____        ____

              Signature _____
        Supervisor's Signature _____
```

Purpose: To facilitate follow-up on goods received but not yet billed by suppliers.

Exhibit 10–2 (continued)

PAYMENT

# _____	CHECK	Date _____
Payee _____		$ _____
Amount _____dollars		
Voucher # _____	Signature _____	
	Signature _____	

—Issue Original to Payee.
—Retain Copy as Check Register.
—If Branch, Forward Copy to Home Office.
—Reference Check Number on Voucher and Cancel All Supporting Documents.
—Use Check Protector or Computer to Print Amount and Use Imprinted Prenumbered
 Checks.
—If This Was a Petty Cash Fund Check It Would Be Signed by the Custodian.
—Establish a Printed Dollar Limit on Payroll Checks as Well as a Time Limit.

Purpose: To make authorized payment of funds, documenting the voucher to which payment relates.

# _____	PETTY CASH VOUCHER	Date _____
Payee _____		$ _____
Amount _____		
Purpose _____dollars		
(Cashing of Personal Checks Is Prohibited.)		
Account Distribution _____		
Payee's Signature _____		
Custodian's Signature _____		
Supervisor's Signature _____		

—Prepare in ink.

Purpose: To document expenditures from petty cash, including their purpose, account, and amount (payee's signature constitutes authorization).

Exhibit 10–2 (continued)

# _____	WRITTEN BANK AUTHORIZATION			Date _____
Account	**Authorized Check Signer**	**Signature Sample**	**Unacceptable Payees**	**Instructions**
General	_____	_____	Bearer Cash Company	Dual Signatures Required
Payroll	_____	_____	Bearer Cash Company	Dual Signatures Required No Payment in Excess of $5,000 Is to Be Honored, as Stated on Face of Payroll Checks
Petty Cash	_____	_____	All, Other Than the Custodian: _____	Dual Signatures Required No Payment in Excess of $500 Is to Be Honored

Check Signers No Longer Authorized:

Account _____ Name _____

Account _____ Name _____

Official's Signature _____

Official's Countersignature _____

Purpose: To inform bank as to authorized check signers for each bank account and to provide instructions regarding unacceptable payees, dual signature requirements, and payment limits.

Exhibit 10–2 (continued)

PRODUCTION OR CONVERSION

_____ STORES' RECEIPT OF INVENTORY Date _____

Description	Quantity	Unit of Measure	Condition
_____	_____	_____	_____
_____	_____	_____	_____
_____	_____	_____	_____

Signature _____

Please Forward to Accounting Department

For Accounting Use Only: Initials

Reconciled to Receiving Report _____

Posted to Detailed Inventory Records _____

Purpose: To establish control over goods moved from receiving to stores.

Exhibit 10–2 (continued)

_____   PRODUCTION ORDER   Date _____
(Including Self-Constructed Assets)

Description _____

Specifications

Inputs:

    Labor _____

    Material _____

    Overhead _____

Predetermined Rates:

    Indirect Costs _____

    Spoilage _____

    Idle Labor _____

    Idle Machine Time _____

Standard Costs:

    Material _____

    Labor _____

    Overhead _____

Cost Accounting Standards Board and/or IRS Considerations _____

Comparison with Customer Order # _____

    Agreement _____

    If Not in Agreement, Action Taken _____

Compliance with Inspection Procedures:

    Results _____

    Handling of Rejects or Rework Items _____

Desired Starting Date _____ Desired Completion Date _____

                Signature _____

       Supervisor's Signature _____

Purpose: To establish control over production, documenting specifications and inspection procedures.

Exhibit 10–2 (continued)

_____   STOCKROOM REQUISITION   Date _____

Description	Quantity	Unit of Measure	Unit Cost	Amount
_____	_____	_____	_____	_____
_____	_____	_____	_____	_____
_____	_____	_____	_____	_____

Comparison With: Bill of Materials # _____

                 Production Order # _____

_____   Engineering Order # _____

Initials of   Sales Order # _____
Issuer

                 Shipping Order # _____

       Requisitioner's Signature _____

Purpose: To establish control over goods moved from stores to the production line.

_____   WORK ORDERS FOR INTERDEPARTMENTAL   Date _____
                 MOVEMENT OF MATERIALS & FIXED ASSETS

Description	Quantity	Unit of Measure	From	To
_____	_____	_____	_____	_____
_____	_____	_____	_____	_____
_____	_____	_____	_____	_____

            Signature _____

Purpose: To establish control over goods and fixed assets moved between departments.

Exhibit 10–2 (continued)

# _____	SCRAP & WASTE			Date _____

Production Order # _____

Units Worked On	Good Units Worked On	Normal Spoilage	Abnormal Spoilage	Scrap
_____	_____	_____	_____	____
_____	_____	_____	_____	____
_____	_____	_____	_____	____

Materials Scrapped _____

Work-in-Process Scrapped _____

Describe Disposition _____

Compare Scrap to Predetermined Norm or Standard _____

Signature _____

Supervisor's Signature _____

—Matched spoilage reports with subsequent dispositions of scrap.
—Compare prices received for scrap with published prices.

Purpose: To establish control over and monitor the magnitude of scrap, documenting
its source and disposition.

Exhibit 10–2 (continued)

```
# _____                    JOB TICKET              Date _____

Employee # _____

Job or Production Order # _____

Operation _____

Account _____

Department _____

Start Time _____ Stop Time _____

Rate _____ Amount _____

Pieces Worked _____

Pieces Rejected _____

Pieces Completed _____

Idle Time _____

    Explanation of Idle Time _____

                    Signature _____

            Supervisor's Signature _____
```

Purpose: To document labor on particular jobs and monitor idle time, as well as pieces rejected.

Exhibit 10–2 (continued)

| # _____ | | | TIMECARD | | | Week Ending _____ |

Name _____

Employee # _____

Department _____

Date	AM		PM		Excess Hours		Total Hours
	In	Out	In	Out	In	Out	

Regular Time _____ Hours @ _____ = _____

Overtime Premium _____ Hours @ _____ = _____

Authorization for Overtime _____
                                            Signature

Gross Earnings _____

Supervisor's Approval _____
                                            Signature

—Can be adapted to a piecework basis.
—Check hours with job tickets.

Purpose: To document hours worked per employee and to authorize overtime.

Exhibit 10–2 (continued)

PAYROLL

| # _____ | PERSONNEL AUTHORIZATION FOR PAYROLL | Date _____ |

New Employees

- -

Name	Rate	Deductions
_____	_____	_____
_____	_____	_____

Changes In Pay

- -

Name	Old Rate	New Rate	Old Deductions	New Deductions
_____	_____	_____	_____	_____
_____	_____	_____	_____	_____

Terminated Employees

- -

Name	Rate	Deductions
_____	_____	_____
_____	_____	_____

General Policy Changes

- -

	Union Contract	Sick Pay	Vacation Pay	Bonuses	Overtime	Pensions	Other
Old	_____	___	_____	_____	_____	_____	___
New	_____	___	_____	_____	_____	_____	___

Signature _____

Supervisor's Signature _____

Purpose: To authorize all changes to payroll master file or related calculations.

Exhibit 10–2 (continued)

# _____							PAYROLL				Date _____		
Employee	Hours	Rate	Gross	Federal	State	FICA	Insurance	United Way	Pension	Profit-Sharing	Other	Net
——	——	——	——	——	——	——	——	——	——	——	——	——
——	——	——	——	——	——	——	——	——	——	——	——	——
——	——	——	——	——	——	——	——	——	——	——	——	——

Reconciled Job Time Tickets to Time Cards _____ Canceled Tickets & Time Cards _____
                                    Initials   Initials

Reviewed for Overtime Approval _____
                                        Initials

Labor Distribution _____

Total Net Pay _____

               Signature _____

      Supervisor's Signature _____

General Ledger Accounting: Reconciled Payroll to Master File,
                     Production Records, and Deductions _____
                                               Signature

Purpose: To record payroll and document review procedures, including tie-in to supporting documents.

Exhibit 10–2 (continued)

# _____	CASH PAYROLL RECEIPT	Date _____

$ _____ Amount Received _____

Signature of Employee _____

Signature of Observer _____

Verified Employee Identification _____

                                        Signature

Purpose: To establish control over all cash payroll payments to employees (signature of employee documents payment was made).

# _____	UNCLAIMED WAGES	Date _____

Employee Name   **Wages Not Distributed**

_____   _____

_____   _____

_____   _____

        Total   _____

Paymaster's Signature _____

Acceptance of Unclaimed Wages and Related Report _____

Purpose: To establish control over all unclaimed cash payroll payments.

Exhibit 10–2 (continued)

INVENTORY

# _____	PHYSICAL INVENTORY COUNT SHEETS	Date _____

Location _____ Reminder: Review Physical Inventory Instructions Before Proceeding

Purpose (Surprise Count; Cycle Count; Year-End Count) _____

Tag#	Part#	Unit	First Count Quantity	Stage of Completion, Description, Condition, etc.	Second Count Quantity	Comments; Disposition of Differences
____	____	____	_____	_____	_____	_____
____	____	____	_____	_____	_____	_____
____	____	____	_____	_____	_____	_____

First Counter _____

Second Counter _____

For Property Not Inventoried, Explain Procedures Taken (e.g., comparison to engineering records, blueprints, and similar independent data) _____
_____

Description	Quantity Assessed Through Comparison to Independent Data	Comments
_____	_____	_____
_____	_____	_____

Signature _____

Supervisory Signature _____

Purpose: To document periodic checks as to quantity and condition of inventory.

Exhibit 10–2 (continued)

```
# _____                                              Date _____
                  INVENTORY AND PROPERTY CONFIRMATION
                  FOR ASSETS HELD BY OUTSIDERS FOR _____

     Description   Quantity   Unit of Measure   Condition   Location

     _____    _____    _____    _____    _____

     _____    _____    _____    _____    _____

     _____    _____    _____    _____    _____

Please Confirm Your Possession of the Above Goods by Providing Your:

                  Signature _____

                  Title _____

                  Company _____

Reconciliation to Accounting Records _____ _____
                                            Initials           Date
```

Purpose: To document periodic confirmation of quantity and condition of goods held on consignment or by other third parties.

```
# _____                    INVENTORY WORKSHEETS        Date _____

     Part #   Description   Unit   Cost per Unit   Quantity   Total

     _____   _____    ____   _____    _____   _____

     _____   _____    ____   _____    _____   _____

     _____   _____    ____   _____    _____   _____

                  Signature _____

                  Supervisor's Signature _____

-----------------------------------------------------------------------

To Document Accounting Checks:                    Initials

     Verified Cost per Unit                        _____

     Recalculated Extensions and Footings          _____

     Reconciled Total to Books                     _____
```

Purpose: To document tie-in of physical inventory to valuation records, including the performance of prescribed review procedures.

Exhibit 10–2 (continued)

| # _____ | CONTROL OVER INVENTORY TAGS, COUNT SHEETS, AND WORK SHEETS | | | Date _____ |

Inventory Location	# of Tags Issued	# of Tags Returned	# of Tags Voided	# of Tags Unissued
_____	_____	_____	_____	_____
_____	_____	_____	_____	_____

Inventory Location	# of Count Sheets Issued	# of Count Sheets Returned	# of Count Sheets Voided	# of Count Sheets Unissued
_____	_____	_____	_____	_____
_____	_____	_____	_____	_____

Inventory Location	# of Work Sheets Issued	# of Work Sheets Returned	# of Work Sheets Voided	# of Work Sheets Unissued
_____	_____	_____	_____	_____
_____	_____	_____	_____	_____

Signature _____

Supervisor's Signature _____

Purpose: To establish numerical control over documents related to physical inventory and its extension to valuation records.

Exhibit 10–2 (continued)

PROPERTY

```
#_____        APPROVAL FOR REMOVAL OR          Date_____
                DISASSEMBLY OF PROPERTY

     Property                      Description of
    Description    Original Cost   Work Authorized    Disposition

    _____      _____       _____      _____

    _____      _____       _____      _____

    _____      _____       _____      _____


Other Instructions _____

              Signature _____

    Supervisor's Signature _____
```

Purpose: To authorize the removal or disassembly of property and to document its disposition.

```
#_____             INSURANCE COVERAGE           Date_____

     Inventory      Inventory     Other Property    Insurance
     Location        Value           Value          Coverage

     _____       _____       _____         _____

     _____       _____       _____         _____

     _____       _____       _____         _____


Fidelity Bonding Insurance _____

Reviewed and Deemed Adequate by _____
                                              Signature
```

Purpose: To document insurance coverage to facilitate its periodic review.

Exhibit 10–2 (continued)

DECENTRALIZED OPERATIONS

```
#_____            BRANCH OPERATIONS WEEKLY REPORT      Date_____

Key Operating Figures:

    Sales _____
    Collections _____
    Cost of Sales _____
    Requested Disbursements _____
    Inventory Turnover _____
    Advertising Expense _____
    Travel & Entertainment _____

            Amount                    Description (Business Purpose)

    _____      _____

    _____      _____

                    Signature _____
```

Purpose: To establish control over branch operations via a weekly report covering performance and expenditures.

---

entities and is intended to assist the system designer in understanding the "why" of each form. The documents should be augmented by a formal set of journals, subsidiary ledgers, and a general ledger, routinely reconciled, as well as a management reporting system tailored to users' needs. The source documents, however, are the means by which control over summary accounting records and management reports is obtained and form the critical foundation of any entity's information system. Although this exhibit appears to be documentation for a manual accounting system, identical information should be collected for a computerized accounting system. A user number coding may replace initials and the mode of data entry is likely to be a terminal rather than a pencil, but other than such superficial differences, the basic information content summarized in Exhibit 10–2 should be available in machine-readable form on master files and accessible, in the form of users' reports, as needed.

How to Use the Forms

Match the system's forms to these source documents. Compare the source documents proposed or being maintained by the entity of its cost of sales or production cycle to those outlined in Exhibit 10–2. A one-to-one comparison should be possible, although some forms may be combined or subdivided. A missing form will flag a break in the accounting trail and a possible weakness in controls.

For example, the lack of a purchase or check requisition indicates the absence of formal, separate authorization of purchases by operating departments and a lack of operating control over purchases (i.e., there is no avenue for formally specifying purchase terms and standards or the desired accounting treatment of purchases, such as those delineated in the requisition presented in Exhibit 10–2. The effects that are predictable including the making of unauthorized purchases, the acceptance of below-quality (or excessively high-quality) merchandise on dates beyond the desired delivery period, the use of other than optimal transportation arrangements, and more frequent emergency purchases and stock-outs.

Compare the contents of each document and look for missing information. After a one-to-one match, scrutinize the contents of each document, comparing the format with Exhibit 10–2. Any missing information may flag a break in the accounting trail and related weaknesses in controls. For example, if only one signature is required, as opposed to a required countersignature by the supervisor, the controls are not as thorough as those implied in Exhibit 10–2. However, this would not constitute a break in the accounting trail and the effect of this difference would be only a marginal increase in possible errors; no weakness in controls would be implied.

In contrast, the absence of initials on the voucher that support the completion of review procedures and the cancellation of documents would make it difficult to distinguish which procedures were and were not performed, would increase the risk of paying twice and in the wrong amount for merchandise that had not been received, and would represent a break in the accounting trail and a weakness in control. Exhibit 10–2 helps to assure that controls are not overlooked and in that sense can direct the accountant through the control procedures of the cost of sales or production cycle.

Caution: a physical trail of forms can be deceptive. However, such a physical trail of forms can also be deceptive. For example, if a form is signed and the appropriate review procedures are not performed or if the sequence of prenumbered forms is not periodically checked, the apparent completeness of accounting records and existence of controls will be a facade. The probability of an entity maintaining a complete set of accounting records will rest largely on the presence of an overall control environment.

WHAT TO LOOK FOR WHEN EVALUATING THE CONTROL ENVIRONMENT

The proper performance of control duties requires employees' understanding of control responsibilities and management's recognition of control requirements and its involvement in the development and maintenance of controls.

Checklist for Determining Whether There Is an Effective Environment for Control

While concerns for the overall control environment are essentially the same for all cycles, as described earlier in this guide, Exhibit 10–3 provides a checklist

Exhibit 10–3

Checklist to Determine Whether There Is an Environment for Effective Control (Emphasis Is Placed Upon the Cost of Sales or Production Cycle)

___ 1. Is the organization structure conducive to control, providing a clear definition of responsibilities and segregating the duties of authorization, custodianship, and recordkeeping?

___ 2. Are accounting policies and procedures and job descriptions communicated via manuals?

    If so, do the following manuals provide instructions as to each of the procedures delineated below?

PURCHASING MANUAL

___ Vendor Selection Criteria
___ Competitive Bidding Requirements
___ Coordination of Purchasing with User Groups
___ Authorized Levels of Approval (Prohibition re: signing blank purchase orders)
___ Follow-up Responsibilities
___ Long-term Commitments: Contract Negotiation
___ Interface with Transportation, Receiving, Inspection, Accounting, Top Management and Legal Counsel
___ Deviations from Established Procedures
___ Company Policy Regarding:
    • Conflict of Interest Concerns
    • Employee Purchases

RECEIVING MANUAL

___ Quantity Verification Criteria
___ Coordination with Inspection Department (Defined Tolerances)
___ Interface with Purchasing, Stores, and Accounting
___ Authorized Levels of Approval
___ Company Policy Regarding:
    • Partial Shipments
    • Over or Under Shipments
    • Drop Shipments
    • Handling of Damaged Merchandise
    • Goods on Consignment from Others and Third Parties' Merchandise
    • Unidentified Receipts
___ Safeguarding Procedures

PRODUCTION MANUAL

___ Planning, Transmitting Input Needs, and Receiving Inputs
___ Control over Processing
___ Interface with Inspection and Quality Control Personnel, Accounting, Warehousing, and Shipping
___ Company Policy Regarding:
    • Unions
    • Physical Inventory
    • Standard Costing and Management Reports
___ Receipt, Installation, and Testing of Equipment and Production Processes

PAYROLL MANUAL

___ Hiring Criteria; Verification of Applications
___ Coordination Between Payroll, Personnel, Timekeeping, Cost Distribution, Accounts Payable, General Ledger Accounting, Shops, Cash Disbursements, and the Bank
___ Authorized Levels of Approval
___ Reporting of Payroll Tax Information
___ Company Policy Regarding:
    • Conflict of Interest Concerns
    • Unions
    • Overtime, Sick Pay, Vacation Pay
    • Profit Sharing, Pensions, Stock Purchase Plans, and Management Compensation Plans
    • Insurance
    • Employee Advances
    • Unclaimed Wages
    • Surprise Payoffs

INVENTORY MANUAL

_____ Ordering Criteria
_____ Interface Between Receiving, Stores,· Production, User Groups, Purchasing, and Accounting
_____ Authorized Levels of Approval
_____ Handling of Merchandise Which Is Not the Company's Property
_____ Deviations from Established Procedures
_____ Handling of Obsolete and Damaged Goods
_____ Handling of Goods on Consignment, Merchandise in Public Warehouses, and Drop Shipments
_____ Physical Inventory Procedures
_____ Safeguarding Procedures

INSPECTION AND QUALITY CONTROL MANUAL

_____ Specification Criteria
_____ Coordination with Purchasing, Receiving, Production, User Groups, Accounting, Vendors, and Top Management
_____ Authorized Levels of Approval
_____ Statistical Sampling Requirements
_____ Handling of Rejects and Rework Items
_____ Handling of Disputes

_____ 3. Are personnel selection methods, company training programs, supervisory practices, and performance evaluation techniques conducive to control, providing assurance that an adequate number of employees are available to perform both operating and control duties?

_____ 4. Are vacations mandatory, and are provisions made for competent replacements to perform all of the assigned duties of the vacationing employees?

_____ 5. For positions of trust, are employees' duties rotated, including bookkeepers' rotation among the various ledgers and paymasters' rotation from the distribution of payroll? (Note that physical inventory of high-valued items should be taken whenever storekeepers are rotated, petty cash should be counted and reconciled before rotating custodians, and similar accountability checks should be invoked prior to rotation of other jobs.)

_____ 6. Is Board designation of authorized check signers required and are signature files of authorized personnel maintained?

_____ 7. Is fidelity bonding insurance coverage adequate? (Employees handling cash, securities, and other valuables should be bonded.)

_____ 8. Are there provisions for reasonable protection against fire, explosion, other natural disaster, and/or malicious destruction of records, of processing facilities, and of other assets of the entity? Such provisions should include adequate loss-of-records insurance coverage as well as adequate insurance coverage of assets.

_____ 9. Is access to property, inventory, production processing areas, accounting records, and critical forms—both issued and unissued—permitted only in accordance with management criteria which reflect control objectives (i.e., is access limited to those persons whose duties require such access)?

_____ 10. Is record retention adequate?

_____ 11. Are accounting data periodically reviewed, tested, and compared to budgets, variances and exception reports, and nonfinancial reports generated outside of the accounting department by internal auditors or by individuals who are independent of generating the accounting data? Do operating personnel rely on such data for decision-making?

_____ 12. Are recorded balances of inventory, property, and related transaction activity periodically substantiated and evaluated through physical inventory, confirmation, and a review of legal documents? Are the adjusting journal entries that result consistent with an adequate control environment?

CASH DISBURSEMENTS MANUAL

_____ Payment Criteria: All Disbursements by Check (Except for Petty Cash)
_____ Coordination with Accounts Payable, General Ledger Accounting, Payees, and the Bank
_____ Authorized Levels of Approval (Prohibition re: signing blank checks or checks payable to cash or to bearer)
_____ Safeguarding Procedures (particularly over signature plates)
_____ Petty Cash Fund Procedures
_____ Separate Payroll, Dividend, and Branch Bank Accounts—Imprest Basis

to remind the systems evaluator of the primary factors to consider when evaluating whether an entity has an environment that is conducive to effective control. Exhibit 10–3 is slightly tailored to the cost of goods sold or production cycle and should be reviewed with particular regard to that cycle's transactions.

For example, does the organizational structure clearly define the responsibilities of purchasing, receiving, inventory management, production, inspection, payroll, and cash disbursements, and are personnel selection techniques and vacation policies in these departments conducive to control? Exhibit 10–3 is intended to be a basis for predicting the plausibility of specific controls operating effectively and should be reviewed by the systems evaluators as one of the first steps in their review of controls. The results of the analysis should be considered throughout the review of specific controls and updated to reflect information gained during the course of the systems review.

Do Employees Understand Control Policies?

Comprehension of control policies by middle management is a prerequisite to effective control, yet the following management letter comment to an equipment supplier by an auditor is atypical:

> EXAMPLE: An internal control questionnaire was developed and circulated to Group and Divisional Controllers. A review of their responses noted a consistent lack of understanding regarding the need for a formal documentation of controls and procedures at the local level. Most respondents believe that this is a corporate responsibility.

Control can be viewed as a pyramid with two essential components. Its foundation is the execution of control procedures at the operating level, and its apex is a clear direction from top management that establishes a control environment.

Direct inquiry is not the sole means of detecting a lack of understanding of controls.

> EXAMPLE: A drug company had an understaffed accounting department. Whenever an employee was on vacation, his functions generally were not performed until his return.
> The company's management had said that vacations were mandatory for accounting personnel, yet the objective of this policy from a control perspective obviously was not understood. Furthermore, no continuity of accurate up-to-date information for decision-making existed during vacation periods.

> EXAMPLE: A business in the communications industry used prenumbered checks but did not write them in sequential order; furthermore, voided checks were discarded.
> The objective of prenumbering and the desire for a complete accounting trail of issued, unissued, and voided documents had not been understood by the personnel in the cash disbursements area.

> EXAMPLE: An equipment manufacturer prepared an exception report for payroll that listed excessive hours and pay and was 60 pages long.

For control purposes, such a lengthy report cannot be an exception report and suggests some misunderstanding as to the purpose of such reports.

SOLUTION: Parameters to determine exceptions should be adjusted to produce an effective report.

EXAMPLE: Tags were issued by area for the physical inventory of a motor vehicle parts and accessories operation. When count teams had completed their areas, rather than returning unused tags to the tag control clerk, they used these tags to assist in counting other areas not specifically assigned to them.

The control ramifications of such actions had not been explained to the counters; they may not have even been understood by management. Since tags were not confined to the area to which they had been issued, they could not be accounted for until the end of the inventory. Missing tags could not be isolated to a specific area, and the result was increased time, effort, and cost, and decreased tag control for the physical inventory.

In other words, the improper application of a control and/or the demonstrated ignorance of controls by employees when performing either operating control or accounting control activities imply an ineffective control environment in the sense of checklist items #2, 3, 4, and 11 of Exhibit 10–3. A lack of understanding of control is primarily an education problem, but what of sloppy disregard for controls?

Be Alert for Sloppy Application of Controls

Despite knowledge of the rationale underlying specific control procedures, employees can effectively destroy a potentially adequate control system through the sloppy application of controls.

EXAMPLE: A producer of durable goods makes records of unclaimed payroll checks and then mails all unclaimed payroll checks to employees.

Apparently, the company has ignored the risk possibilities of such a practice.

SOLUTION: Unclaimed checks should be picked up from the cashier in person except for very unusual situations which should require special approval. The sloppy, uncontrolled handling of signed payroll checks (i.e., the direct mailing of such checks) thwarts effective control possibilities.

EXAMPLE: A dairy business had a side door for the warehouse connected to an alarm system. However, the door was used by both warehouse and office employees as a route in and out of the building, regularly sounding the alarm; hence, no one paid attention to the alarm.

The affirmative response that inventory is safeguarded by an alarm system misrepresents the control environment.

SOLUTION: Management should require employees to stop using the side door as an entrance and exit, and, if necessary, should either lock the door or limit access to the door. Employees apparently were willing to disregard controls for day-to-day convenience.

EXAMPLE: The authorized signatories confirmed by savings and loans and credit unions with which a business service client had banking relationships included past officers, retirees, and other managers who had left the business service involuntarily.

The risk exposure of such a lapse in control was apparently overlooked or disregarded.

SOLUTION: Whenever authorized signatories change due to retirement, rotation, or termination, financial institutions should be formally notified of such changes on a timely basis.

EXAMPLE: A salaried employee of a manufacturing company was paid for two months after termination. Furthermore, several stock options were not properly canceled upon employees' termination.

Obviously, controls over the information flow from personnel to payroll are inadequate, with regard both to termination and to those employees eligible for supplemental compensation benefits that may require follow-up.

SOLUTION: Personnel should inform payroll of all terminations on a timely basis. The existence of supplemental compensation benefits affected by such terminations should be brought to the attention of those responsible for benefit programs.

While information links apparently exist, the employees are sloppy in using such communication links on a timely basis.

In addition to being sloppy in applying controls (as flagged by mixed responses to items #1, 2, 3, 6, 8, and 9 on Exhibit 10–3), employees may intentionally circumvent controls.

Check for Circumvention of Existing Controls By Employees

The effectiveness of controls depends on the employees' compliance with the substance of the control techniques, regardless of the ease with which the controls could be circumvented.

EXAMPLE: The cash disbursements department of a wholesaler of photographic equipment and supplies commonly avoided the requirement of two check signers for checks over $1,000 because often only one signatory was in the office at the time the check was to be issued.

This practice obviously made nonsense of the signing limits and implied either a lack of appreciation for the control or a lack of management's involvement in setting appropriate and practical control procedures.

EXAMPLE: A shoe store established a special check system intended to be used for special payments to vendors that required immediate attention. Yet the system was regularly abused by being utilized to process magazine subscriptions, donations, and numerous other expenditures.

SOLUTION: Since the special check system effectively circumvents the normal control system over accounts payable, an effective control environment would set up strict guidelines as to what disbursements are to be allowed through the special check system. Check authorizers and issuers ought to be told to refuse payments that should go through the normal disbursements system. The absence of such guidelines reflects some problems with management's means of evaluating the control implications of operating decisions (such as the establishment of two check systems), particularly the effect of facilitating the circumvention of controls.

EXAMPLE: A credit agency maintained kitties of tellers' overages and shortages of less than a set dollar amount. Such a practice eliminated the ability to evaluate specific tellers' performance or to appropriately record a particular day's cash settlement.

SOLUTION: Stop the practice.

EXAMPLE: A finance company's tellers notified accounting whenever customers requested that no mail be sent to them.

SOLUTION: Since such customer accounts effectively prohibit communication between the company (or its auditors) and the customer, written authorizations should be obtained as a minimum general control over all transactions not handled in a routine manner. Regular rendering of customers' statements is an important element of internal control, serving as a form of direct verification of balances with the customer. The management's tolerance of verbal communications suggests a lack of appreciation for the related control implications and the employees' ability to circumvent controls.

A control environment requires sufficient training of personnel and delineation of job responsibilities to deter the circumvention of the control system by employees; in other words, affirmative replies to items #1, 2, and 3 of Exhibit 10–3 are required. An integration of control duties with employees' performance evaluations is one means of motivating employees to comply with control guidelines, i.e., in the above examples: encouraging the use of two check signers, restricting the use of a special check system to its intended purpose, recording actual shortages and overages rather than averaging such items across time, and securing written authorization for customers' requests not to mail regular reports on transactions that affect their accounts.

Telltale Signs of Control Problems

In addition to problems with employees' comprehension of controls, sloppy application of controls, and deliberate circumvention of controls, all of which suggest some shortcomings in the control environment, evidence gathered in the course of a systems review will often flag control problems. While the source of the problem may be operating management, staff personnel or other employees, and may be difficult to identify, the observed conditions will be telltale signs of weakness in the entity's control environment.

Insufficient controls

EXAMPLE: A grocery store utilizing an inventory comptometer service failed to detect the excursion of "live" inventory sheets from compilation due to the mixing of such sheets with voided sheets.

The implication is that controls are not strong enough at the comptometer company and that management has not sufficiently investigated the controls of the service agency, has not established compensatory controls for problems known to exist, or has not achieved compliance with such controls.

SOLUTION: Effective control would require testing of the books when returned from the comptometer service, and recompilation of the inventory if excessive error is detected. Whenever service bureaus are utilized, their financial stability and reliability should be checked and where possible, an on-site review of control procedures should be performed.

Lack of standards

EXAMPLE: For an equipment manufacturer, work orders are established prior to the development of a standard cost, and transfers must sometimes be made at zero cost because no standard is yet available. On the date the standard is input, the transfer is recorded. As a result, the recorded date is not the actual date of transfer and no record of actual movement appears in the work-in-process inventory listings.

SOLUTION: For control purposes the transfer from work-in-process should be recorded on the date of transfer and identified as an exception on the report of such transfers (flagging the zero cost assignments). The standards should be established on a timely basis to permit the avoidance of such recording problems. Otherwise, no control over asset movements exists and faulty operating decisions could be made due to an inappropriate interpretation of reports regarding goods available for sale and work-in-process.

Unreliable budgets

EXAMPLE: A hospital equipment manufacturer reported significant differences between the original budget and actual results. Investigation indicated that while the existing mechanical budget procedures were functioning effectively, in some cases realistic goals were not being established.

SOLUTION: Evidently, additional training of personnel, recognition of the entity's sensitivity to current and forecasted business conditions, and consideration of historical trends may be required to yield an effective budget.

Lack of controls

EXAMPLE: An electronic equipment manufacturer kept blank drafts in a vault that was open to all office personnel during working hours, and a facsimile signature plate in an unlocked box on a shelf in the computer department. The numerical sequence of checks printed on the computer was accounted for by the same control clerk who processed the checks through the signature machine, and signed checks were returned to persons who prepared input for draft preparation. Bank statements, although delivered unopened to the preparer of reconciliations, were left open on a desk for a day prior to completion of the reconciliation.

Such a combination of procedures that disregard control effects communicates to the system evaluator either a complete lack of knowledge of control procedures or a complete lack of concern for control by both management and employees.

Caution: Telltale signs of control problems must be weighed against risk exposure. Inappropriate reliance on service bureaus, incomplete data bases, absurd budgets, and the good faith of employees and passers-by are all telltale signs of control problems. However, the importance of such signs entirely depends upon the risk exposure from apparent weaknesses in the control environment. Consider the following company policy and its effects on the risk exposure of the business:

> EXAMPLE: A retailer pays employees discounts on their purchases by having a cashier disburse cash based on cash receipts for purchases presented by the employee.
>
> Such a procedure indicates no concern over control, as the employee could easily submit fallacious cash receipts, including those picked up from customers or from the floor, for a discount.
>
> SOLUTION: As a minimum, some other party's signature should be required to approve the discount payments, and when goods are returned by the employee, repayment of discounts should be required.

The example raises questions concerning potential risk exposure; however, the probable extent of abuse will depend on the overall control environment. For example, is a cashier likely to identify and report those employees who appear to be receiving excessive cash discounts? Is a mechanism for reviewing sales returns, particularly those from employees, in regular use, and can it be depended upon to flag actual risk exposure? Is it possible to tie recorded sales to employees to the discounts paid by the cashier?

In other words, telltale signs of control problems (flagged by mixed responses to items #1, 2, 3, 8, 9, 10, 11, and 12 of Exhibit 10–3), cannot be translated into errors and loss of control. A physical inventory of blank checks, an accounting for the numerical sequence of checks, and a thorough testing of monthly bank statements may well indicate that the electronic equipment manufacturer has not actually lost control over cash, as was deemed possible in the example provided. Compensatory controls may exist, as suggested earlier in this guide, for flaws that are observed in the control system. For the systems evaluator to gain perspective on the relative importance of flaws in the control environment and in specific control procedures, (s)he must consider (as discussed earlier in this guide)

—the type of errors and irregularities that can occur, and

—the accounting control procedures that should prevent or detect such errors and irregularities

Completion of Exhibit 10–3 makes the evaluator aware of potential problems, but does not permit an assessment of the risk exposure of the company.

GUIDELINES FOR ASSESSING RISK EXPOSURE

Generally speaking, three major risks exist for an entity's control system:

(1) It loses valid documents, failing to record the underlying transactions, or it permits bogus documents to enter the data base.
(2) It inaccurately records transactions.
(3) It permits the removal of assets.

What Can Go Wrong—and How to Prevent or Detect Errors and Defalcations

These three risks are presented in Exhibit 10–4 with those controls that are typically present in a control system to reduce such risks. This general list is intended to provide a reference for the systems designer in selecting controls and for the systems evaluator in recommending the improvement of controls. *Caution:* However, such a general listing cannot be interpreted as "all of these controls are preferred to fewer controls." Recall the earlier discussions in this guide of redundancy in control systems and efficiency considerations; it is unlikely that every conceivable control could or should be implemented in a given entity. What is likely, however, is that if certain basic controls are not present, a critical weakness in controls will exist.

Critical Sources of Risk

Within the cost of sales or production cycle there are six primary sources of risk, as delineated in Exhibit 10–4. Also presented in the exhibit are those key controls that would be expected to prevent or detect both the extraction of resources and the accounting cover-up of such an extraction. The systems evaluator must recognize the existence of these critical sources of risk and the lack of accounting control procedures to prevent or detect such an error or irregularity, if the key controls outlined in the exhibit are missing (and not effectively compensated for by alternative controls).

Controls for Prevention and Detection

In evaluating what could go wrong, the systems evaluator must be concerned with the timeliness of detection, and the relative strength of prevention controls when compared to detection controls. For example, the use of two check signers who review supporting documents for cash disbursements is a preventive control, while the comparison of paid checks with initial payroll disbursement records is a control intended to detect errors and defalcations after the fact. Controls for detection must be applied frequently in order to be effective and are expected primarily to limit rather than prevent losses. The prevention capabilities of "a priori" reviews, rather than "post facto" investigations, make preventive controls stronger than detective controls in reducing an entity's risk exposure. However, the direct cost of applying preventive controls is frequently higher than the direct cost of detective controls, resulting in a possible economic advantage to the latter. In addition, the mere threat value of detection controls can often deter defalcations and errors as effectively as prevention controls themselves, due to employees' fear of discovery. It is this capability of detection controls that leads to the definition of what constitutes a material weakness in a control system:

> . . . a condition in which the systems evaluator believes the prescribed pro-
> cedure or the degree of compliance with the procedure does not provide rea-

Exhibit 10–4

What Could Go Wrong and What Controls Can Preclude or Detect Such Errors and Defalcations? The Risk Profile of the Cost of Sales or Production Cycle

GENERAL TYPES OF RISKS AND RELATED CONTROLS TO REDUCE THESE RISKS

Loss of Documents or Input of Bogus Documents

—Authorization Procedures
—Competent Employees
—Segregation of Duties
—Batch Controls
—Systematic Stamping of Time and Date on Documents upon Receipt
—Systematic Filing of Documents
—Filing of Support Documents with Related Vouchers
—Sign-out Log When Documents Are Removed from an Area
—Set Policy of Only Permitting Copies of Documents to Leave the Filing Area
—Stamping of Duplicate Invoices
—Clear Voiding and Retention of Documents
—Cancellation of Used Documents
—Accounting for Numerical Sequence
—Periodic Inventory of Unissued Forms
—Matching of Key Documents
—Follow-up on Unmatched, Unpaid, and Open Items
—Periodic Independent Tests, Both Vouching and Re-tracing

Inaccurate Recording of Transactions

—Authorization Procedures
—Competent Employees
—Segregation of Duties
—Utilization of Performance Measures Conducive to Accurate Reporting
—Batch Controls
—Clerical Checks of Original Documents and Intermediate Summaries
—Validity Checks
—Limit Checks
—Review of "Was-Is" Reports (to Summarize, for Example, Changes to a Master File)
—Exception Reports
—Tickler Files for Accruals (Chronological Reminders of When to Record What Entries)
—Independent Review of Journal Entries and Postings
—Independent Reconciliation of Subsidiaries to Controlling Accounts
—Comparison of Independently Generated Reports Such as Purchase Orders with Receiving Reports and Invoices
—Reconciliation of Vendors' Statements with Accounts Payable
—Quick Follow-up On Vendors,' Employees,' and Others' Complaints
—Recount of Physical Inventory Before Book to Physical Adjustment (by an Independent Count Team)
—Confirmation of Asset Balances Held Elsewhere
—Utilization of Imprest Basis Funds

Removal of Assets

—Authorization Procedures
—Formal, Well-Controlled Hiring Practices
—Segregation of Duties
—Access Restrictions and Physical Safeguards
—Automatic Accounting Checks
—Periodic Reconciliation of Books-to-Physical-Cycle-Counts

Exhibit 10-4 (continued)

What Could Go Wrong?	Key Controls to Prevent or Detect Extraction of Resources	Key Controls to Detect Accounting Cover-Up
IMPROPER VOUCHERS COULD BE PREPARED	—Require Check Signers to Examine Supporting Documents. —For Cash Disbursements or Reimbursement of Funds, Require an Independent Party to Review Supporting Documents.	• Require an Independent Party to Compare Recorded Disbursements with Subsidiary Accounts Payable Ledger. • Require an Independent Party to Reconcile to Vendor. • Require an Independent Party to Test the Detailed Transactions Underlying the General Ledger Accounts (Including Adjusting Journal Entries).
UNSUPPORTED CHECKS COULD BE ISSUED	—Require Two Check Signers. —Require an Independent Party to Compare Paid Checks with the Initial Cash Disbursement Records. —Require an Independent Party to Test Supporting Documents.	
SIGNED CHECKS COULD BE MISAPPROPRIATED	—Require That the Second Check Signer Mail Checks Directly to Payees. —Require an Independent Examination of Paid Checks for Unusual Features.	
PAYROLL COULD BE IMPROPERLY DISBURSED	—Require an Independent Party to Test Initial Payroll Disbursement Records. —Require an Independent Party to Compare Paid Checks with Initial Payroll Disbursement Records. —Require an Independent Party to Test Payroll Disbursements to Persons Who Participate in Payroll Disbursements and to Persons Who Reconcile Payroll Bank Accounts.	• Require an Independent Party to Prepare and to Handle Employee Earnings Notifications and Related Employee Inquiries.
CASH ON HAND OR ON DEPOSIT, INCLUDING PAYROLL CASH, COULD BE MISAPPROPRIATED	—Require a Surprise Count of Undeposited Cash Receipts and of Imprest or Other Funds to Be Made by an Independent Party Periodically. —Require an Independent Test of Supporting Documents for Miscellaneous Disbursements or Vouchers. —Synchronize the Verification of Cash and Securities to Eliminate Possibility of Cross-Substitution.	• Require an Independent Party to Compare Recorded Disbursements with Detailed Payroll Records. • Require an Independent Party to Test the Detailed Cash Transactions.
TANGIBLE ASSETS COULD BE MISAPPROPRIATED	—Institute Safeguarding Procedures for Storage and Movement of Assets.	• Require an Independent Party to Periodically Compare Tangible Assets to Detailed Property Ledgers. • Require an Independent Party to Periodically Review Adjusting Entries to Property Related Accounts.

464

sonable assurance that errors or irregularities in amounts that would be material in the financial statements being audited would be prevented *or* detected within a timely period by employees in the normal course of performing their assigned functions. (AU§320.69 of Statements on Auditing Standards)

The testing of controls, discussed in depth earlier in this guide, can be applied to the controls in each operating cycle. The important use of Exhibit 10–4 is in identifying those specific controls that are critical to the cost of goods sold or production cycle and the implied risk exposure from either not having these controls or discovering through tests of control that they are ineffective.

AUDITING COST OF SALES—RELATED ACCOUNTING ESTIMATES

The auditor is required by GAAS to evaluate the reasonableness of the client's accounting estimates in the context of the financial statements taken as a whole. Both subjective and objective factors should be considered by the auditor with an attitude of professional skepticism, especially in relation to subjective factors. SAS 57 identifies the following examples of accounting estimates related to the cost of sales or production cycle:

Inventories:

Obsolete Inventory
Net Realizable Value
Losses in Purchase Commitments
Production Facilities, Natural,
   Resources, and Intangibles

Contracts:

Costs to be Incurred
Leases
• Initial Direct Costs
• Executory Costs
• Residual Values

Accruals:

Property and Casualty Insurance
   Co.
Loss Reserves
Warranty Claims
Taxes on Real and Personal
   Property
Actuarial Assumptions in Pension
   Costs[2]

Chapter 9 described the various procedures likely to contribute to an auditor's assessment of control structure associated with estimates.

---

[2] AICPA, Statement of Auditing Standards, "Auditing Accounting Estimates" (New York: AICPA, April, 1988).

CONSIDERING OPERATING EFFICIENCY: COMMON PROBLEMS AND PROVEN SOLUTIONS

The evaluation of controls involves gathering an in-depth knowledge of operations, assessing the risk exposure of the entity, and suggesting the means by which an entity can become more effective and efficient in exercising both accounting and operating control over transactions. Within the cost of goods sold and production cycle, numerous problems are common per facet of operations, and various solutions have been put to use and proven to be effective in a variety of businesses; several of these problems and solutions are presented in Exhibit 10–5.

Tradeoffs Between Control and Operating Objectives

Many of the problems and solutions reflect tradeoffs in control objectives and operating objectives. Such a tradeoff can be exemplified by the following experience of a retailer:

EXAMPLE: Items on the sales floor had price tags indicating a price higher than the price at which the item was charged to stock. The buyer explained that the item would actually be sold at the lower price and give the customer a feeling that he or she was "getting a good deal."

While such a marketing policy may be effective, the control over this type of transaction when using a retail inventory method is minimal, as the item could be sold at the higher price or inventoried at the higher price in error.

SOLUTION: For effective control, a set pricing policy should be followed.

In addition to conflicts in operating and control objectives, often the means of performance evaluation will adversely affect operating and control effectiveness.

EXAMPLE: A retailer's employees regularly reported markup cancellations instead of markdowns, even when no markups were previously recorded, and often did not aggressively use markdowns to liquidate old-season inventories. The reason was that they wanted to stay within the budgeted dollar amount of markdowns.

This substitution practice improperly depressed the mark-on complement and thereby increased the cost of ending inventory, reduced the cost of goods sold, and impaired analytic comparisons by department between years. Moreover, by emphasizing budgeted markdowns, excessive quantities of inventory from past seasons had to be maintained and potential revenue from aggressive marketing was lost.

SOLUTION: A company must provide incentives for employees to act in the interests of the company. When slow inventory is a problem, plant managers should be provided with an incentive to identify and dispose of obsolete inventory on a timely basis, rather than encouraged to comply with some budgeted obsolescence quota that results in holding obsolete inventory for an excessive period.

By considering the specific suggestions in Exhibit 10–5 and being cognizant of necessary tradeoffs between control and operating efficiency and potential con-

Exhibit 10-5

Operating Efficiency Considerations—Means of Enhancing Operating and Internal Controls and Responding to Common Problems Encountered in the Cost of Sales or Production Cycle

PURCHASES

PROBLEM: Authorization procedures can be time consuming.

SOLUTION: Permit general authorization for the purchase of regular operating needs, including inventory, requiring specific authorization by a limited number of people for less routine expenditures, including the acquisition of capital assets.

PROBLEM: Inventory is a sizable investment, demanding substantial working capital. Informal or uncontrolled purchasing practices can be disastrous for an entity's operations.

SOLUTION: Utilize available management science techniques in planning purchases and monitor suppliers' performance. Consider implementing the following suggestions:

Maximize Synergy

- If purchasing is decentralized, coordinate purchases so that departments and branches do not compete with each other and purchasing power can be maximized via nationwide buying contracts and blanket purchase commitments;
- maintain good communication between purchasing, production planning, sales forecasting, and developers of formal material requirement schedules;
- have qualified traffic personnel furnish routing for purchase commitments;
- have purchasing agents participate in programs for standardization, value analysis, lease versus buy analysis, and negotiations for options to purchase in lease agreements;
- try to work with vendors to study cost reduction possibilities.

Establish an Information System

- Maintain supplier evaluation files concerning the adequacy of suppliers' delivery, quality, and cost performances as well as their supplier capabilities;
- have a listing of possible combinations between location, major account code, and type of inventory used or stored, for reference in checking purchase orders for reasonableness;
- have exception reports prepared and reviewed that list all nonstandard orders received (these can be identified by reference to a master file of standard products and to approvals of production orders for non-standard production by the engineering department);
- document procurement plans including material requirements schedule, capital expenditures budget, and economic order quantities;
- have purchase authorizations indicate when requested materials are required and the technical and performance specifications for the requested materials;
- have requisitioners authorize methods and periods for amortizing deferred costs, including property to assist in purchasing and in accounting for purchases;
- facilitate supplier negotiations by providing summaries of commodity buying volumes and supplier buying volumes;
- maintain records of competitive bids obtained periodically for recurring purchases.

Standardize Procedures

- Require at least three competitive bids to be solicited per purchase and supplement such formal bids by phone contacts;
- require purchase requisitions to be submitted with sufficient lead time for purchasing to shop the market for the best supplier;
- set dollar limitations on the extent to which a given employee may commit the company;
- restrict purchases for employees (as they are costly and can be an annoyance to both vendors and the purchasing department);
- avoid unwarranted favoritism to particular vendors;
- preprint terms on purchase order forms based on industry practice and have such terms reviewed periodically with legal counsel;
- utilize an inventory control system that automatically generates purchase orders at set reorder points, considering lead time, safety stock, stock status, and preferably economic order quantities;
- set up procedures to assure prompt follow-up on vendor complaints and inquiries;
- assure receipt of the purchase order by forwarding a copy to the vendor and asking that acceptance be acknowledged by returning the copy to the purchasing department;
- automatically cancel open purchase orders after the specified delivery date;
- periodically visit the vendor's facilities to check on the progress of orders and to verify quality performance (i.e., take preventive measures to assure desired results and to expedite the order).

467

Exhibit 10-5 (continued)

Analyze Performance

- Review "was-is" reports whenever the account status of vendors is substantially altered (e.g., when vendors are approved as suppliers of additional product lines, special order merchandise, or increased amounts of purchases);
- review emergency purchases in an attempt to identify means of avoiding such purchases in the future;
- analyze lead times experienced versus lead times desired;
- investigate and follow up on the reasons for unusual rejection rates at incoming quality control inspection points, as well as at inspection points during the production process;
- periodically review the economics of make versus buy decisions as well as the options to purchase leased assets and the appropriateness of exercising such options.

PROBLEM: Companies frequently do not exercise control over freight costs resulting in waste and inefficiencies.

SOLUTION: Have transportation arrangements evaluated per purchase, taking advantage of the buyer's right to request the particular means by which goods are to be delivered. Specifically, consider:

- use of the appropriate commodity rate for freight,
- use of carload or truckload quantities,
- the possibility of pooling shipments with other shippers as a means of lowering costs,
- the in-transit stopovers or in-transit privileges as well as special services that are available at a small extra cost (drop shipments can yield cost savings),
- the relative costs, delivery dates, and risk of damage or theft across various transportation alternatives,
- acquiring transportation facilities for the company's use.

Also, have the transportation department review freight billings prior to payment. Consider using banking services that certain banks offer for processing and paying freight bills; otherwise the typical high volume of small freight bills can be extremely costly to handle and process.

RECEIVING

PROBLEM: Inadequate delivery instructions can result in higher freight costs and inefficiencies in inventory handling.

SOLUTION: Use preprinted purchase order forms with instructions to vendors to deliver goods only to the receiving location per expected delivery date to avoid backlogs within the receiving department.

PROBLEM: Vendors frequently overcharge for postage.

SOLUTION: Have receiving personnel list the postage or charge on incoming packages on the receiving report for subsequent comparison to the amount charged on the invoice.

PROBLEM: Receiving personnel who inadequately account for goods received can cause inefficiencies and overpayment of creditors.

SOLUTION: Instruct receiving personnel

- to count cartons and compare the count to bills of lading and similar shipping documents and to sample a few cartons on the receiving dock before accepting goods (material in boxes and containers should always be checked by picking a few at random, opening them, and inspecting their contents; furthermore, receiving personnel, not drivers, should break the seals on incoming trucks and should compare seal numbers to the bill of lading for load verification; have the carrier sign and date the bill of lading as support for subsequent invoices),
- to complete a copy of the purchase order (on which quantities were omitted to assure an independent count) and then to have an independent party reconcile the count with the quantities entered on the original purchase order),
- to periodically test scales used for weighing receipts,
- to implement weighing routines by statistical sampling,
- on how to handle customer returns and partial shipments,
- to immediately report shortages, rejections, et cetera, to buyers, accounting, and traffic organizations (in addition, over and under shipments that are within allowable company practice limits should be reported),
- to separate the receiving location from storage and shipping areas.

Have the storing function verify the work of the receiving department by performing an independent count and inspection of goods received and notifying the accounting department of their findings for subsequent comparison to receiving reports.

Exhibit 10-5 (continued)

PROBLEM: The paperwork for proper control over receiving reports can be time-consuming and costly to prepare.

SOLUTION: Use a one-write system whereby a log and the receiving document are created simultaneously; the log can then be used to account for sequentially issued receiving reports.

PROBLEM: Often businesses have difficulties at cut-off in recording purchases in the appropriate accounting period.

SOLUTION: Inform the receiving department of the official cut-off date and have receipts stamped before and after cut-off. Also, the receiving department should maintain a log of receipts for the five days preceding through the five days following the official cut-off date to facilitate a proper cut-off.

ACCOUNTS PAYABLE

PROBLEM: Uncontrolled liabilities can result in poor operating decisions and problems with suppliers.

SOLUTION: Stamp each invoice upon receipt as to date and time and stamp all copies of invoices received, except the original, to clearly indicate that they're duplicates. Prevoucher listings establish immediate control over vendors' invoices before being matched with receiving reports and purchase orders and even before voucher preparation. Record invoices upon receipt in a register or maintain an invoice file entering the amounts of the invoices into the accounts as "unaudited vouchers." Review the unprocessed invoices periodically. Similar control should be maintained for debit memoranda for returned merchandise.

Tax calendars and tickler files (i.e., chronological records of "to do's" or due dates) can be particularly useful in assuring proper recording of accrued liabilities, as can the periodic review of entries, balances, contracts, and similar documents which are likely to be sources of additional accruals.

File clerks should control invoices and similar documents by using a sign-out log whenever documents are removed.

PROBLEM: Frequently invoices which vary in amount from physical evidence of the amount owed are approved for payment.

SOLUTION: Reconcile amounts to all available physical evidence of the debt, such as meter readings and completion reports.

PROBLEM: Too often collections from suppliers of balances that are due a company are not routinely monitored, resulting in lost working capital.

SOLUTION: The accounts payable department should furnish a list of vendors with debit balances to both the purchasing agent and the credit manager on a monthly basis for their follow-up for procurement possibilities or collection of the balance due. Especially follow up on all accounting offsets of accounts receivable with accounts payable.

PROBLEM: Invoices and vendor statements come in such a variety of forms that their conversion to computer input can be extremely costly.

SOLUTION: Use purchase orders supported by comparable receiving reports as source data for Accounts Payable, dispensing with invoices as an input form.

PROBLEM: Recordkeeping requirements can be costly.

SOLUTION: Consider a computer or mechanized bookkeeping machine that can simultaneously prepare checks, vouchers, and a voucher register or payroll register, as well as an earnings card.

PRODUCTION AND CONVERSION

PROBLEM: Control over production and related cost flows is often lacking, resulting in an insufficient data base from which policies can be formulated concerning pricing, production processes, and overall operations.

SOLUTION: Utilize the following control techniques:

Exhibit 10-5 (continued)

Labor

- Train employees on time-reporting procedures and require completion of work tickets, sign-in sheets, crewsheets, idle time reports, overtime reports, and time cards (separate labor tickets should be required for rework);
- require preapproval of overtime, shift changes, and department changes;
- require supervisory review and sign-off on such quantity factors as hours, pieces, or days;
- investigate reasons for idle time, overtime, and excessive delays in work completion;
- require prompt reporting of terminated employees (particularly to payroll) and investigate causes of employee turnover;
- implement an employee scheduling system;
- place time clocks in a conspicuous location and have a management representative observe employees punching in and out each day;
- periodically compare (on a test basis) the number of employees entering work for a given day with the number of time cards in the punched-in slots and the number of employees leaving work for the day with the number of time cards in punched-out slots;
- adequately control time cards of absentees and those individuals leaving the company;
- compare the hours on time records to job tickets, foremen's reports of employees' time, and similar production records;
- implement an incentive and budget structure that encourages control;
- analyze departments' budget variances and labor efficiency and compare average compensation rate trends with industry data;
- conduct research, engineering, and time studies, maintaining security over all such research, and selling the ideas to employees to obtain their cooperation (such studies might involve the sequence of production, equipment use, and the selection of inspection points);
- encourage intercommunication on ways of improving the production process;
- consider social or community issues when contemplating expansion and new production processes since such issues can affect employee morale and liability;
- train employees on precautions in the job and investigate all accidents;
- try to assign meaningful work to employees and consider positive morale effects of having support facilities for food and rest;
- utilize magnetic badges as a means of authorizing particular employees' access to work area;
- set up procedures to assure prompt follow-up on employees' complaints and inquiries (particularly with respect to payroll).

The Production Process

- Periodically evaluate the economic payoff of alternative equipment and production processes, including automation possibilities and related costs in the form of constrained flexibility and adaptability;
- encourage engineering to consider costs whenever making design changes or similar adjustments to production processes;
- control expenditures for construction and installation of new means of production by the same procedures as other operating expenditures;
- implement a production plan that gives priority to known customer orders and maintains operations at levels that preclude layoffs in excess of a set percentage of the authorized labor force;
- utilize linear programming and other operations research techniques for planning input mixes and vary the mix to exploit current market prices;
- require that all products be inspected before transfer to finished goods and reworked or scrapped if they do not meet the company's quality standards;
- utilize statistical methods for quality control tests;
- investigate excessive delays.

Cost Flow Accounting

- Implement a standard cost system and a variance analysis reporting system; prepare periodic reports explaining to management the differences between standard and actual costs (even if standard costs are not tied into the general ledger, unit standard costs should be available for comparison);
- maintain a projects-in-progress subsidiary ledger;
- utilize detailed factory work orders to document estimated costs per job or process, as well as maintenance and repair expenditures; in addition to enhancing control by providing a benchmark by which actual costs can be evaluated, such work orders give notice of equipment retirements, thereby facilitating their control;
- periodically compare performance to industry trends;
- have a system for accurate and prompt reporting of completed production (including completed construction projects) and provide for frequent collection and storage of inventory and self-constructed assets; when transferring finished goods, be certain to relieve work-in-process for the appropriate quantity and related cost.

PROBLEM: Sometimes redundant information collection activities are performed by payroll and production (or cost accounting).

SOLUTION: Consider using mechanized labor collection stations that simultaneously record both production labor and time worked for payroll purposes.

PROBLEM: When disposing of production-related equipment, controls are frequently inadequate and relevant considerations are ignored.

SOLUTION: Require written approval for the removal or disassembly of property and prohibit the sale of such property to direct competitors.

470

Exhibit 10-5 (continued)

INVENTORY

PROBLEM: Frequently accounting records misstate the value of inventory, resulting in faulty management decisions, particularly regarding sales, purchases, and production.

SOLUTION: Require periodic reporting of

- slow-moving items,
- obsolete items (and causes of obsolescence),
- overstocks and understocks,
- damaged items (and causes of damages),

and adjust accounting records whenever appropriate. Since standard costs can greatly influence recorded values, require a periodic review of standards, particularly overhead rates. Maintain separate records of inventory held by outsiders and periodically confirm these inventory balances. Specifically, the accounting department should maintain perpetual records for

- raw materials,
- purchased parts,
- supplies,
- work-in-process,
- finished goods,
- consignments-out,
- inventory in hands of suppliers and processors,
- inventory in warehouses,
- consignments-in,
- returnable containers in hands of customers,
- inventory (such as packing materials) held on behalf of third parties,
- items charged off but physically on hand (like small tools and obsolete stock).

PROBLEM: Storage space for inventory is frequently limited, yet inventory accessibility is critical.

SOLUTION: Consider the following ideas to gain efficiencies in inventory storage:

- place more bulky items in more remote areas;
- utilize shelving, racks, bins, and proper stacking to optimize space, permitting room for storage of similar merchandise yet to arrive;
- clearly identify locations, adequately leaving aisles and using conveyors or similar means for transporting inventory;
- obviously, the payoff to the above procedures will depend on the physical safeguards including fire protection over the stored inventory.

If public warehouses have to be used, remember that they tend to be high-cost storage and their use entails a loss of control over and accessibility to a company's merchandise. For these reasons, the company should consider expanding its own facilities and when public warehouses are used, only homogeneous items to which current access is unlikely to be required should be stored in such locations. Furthermore, goods held at public warehouses should be confirmed monthly and reconciled to the company's records.

Whenever inventory is stored in more than one location, separate ledger accounts should be established per location.

PROBLEM: Inventory investment is often excessive relative to normal operating volume.

SOLUTION: Have a clear statement of criteria for holding inventory, such as:

- only products with sales greater than a stated dollar amount are carried in finished goods, or
- only products with inventory carrying costs that are less than a set percentage of selling price are to be carried in standard products inventory, or
- inventory levels are to be less than a stated number of months' sales.

Also, maintain stock records of raw materials, parts, and supplies that show maximum and minimum reorder points and reorder quantities.

Consider the ABC inventory classification system for monitoring individual items' inventory levels:

471

Exhibit 10–5 (continued)

- First, do a value analysis of inventory item by item, with

  A = high value items that are critical to the production or merchandising process,

  B = lower value items that are also critical to operations,

  C = small-value items.

- Second, carefully monitor classes A and B by cycle counts.

PROBLEM: Frequently companies overlook the cost savings available from adequately controlling and efficiently disposing of scrap.

SOLUTION: Utilize central stockrooms and central gathering locations for scrap and junk. Reconcile scrap inventory records, spoilage reports, and reports on equipment disassembled and scrapped with the scrap held in central locations. Explicitly consider whether scrap is in its most advantageous form in the sense of generating revenue. Require examination of waste and salvage materials before disposal. Solicit bids on scrap. Following the sale, reconcile scrap disposition reports, including equipment disposition forms, to the quantity of scrap reported in central gathering locations.

PROBLEM: Frequently physical inventories are performed in a sloppy manner resulting in both inefficiencies and inaccurate adjustment of books-to-physical.

SOLUTION: Issue formal inventory instructions which stress

- the necessity of controlling inventory tags, count sheets, and worksheets, and the appropriate way of completing each of these forms,
- the necessity of no erasures on tags and the handling of voided tags and voided count sheets,
- the requirement that all inventory items be tagged,
- the use of count teams, including a second count team to verify the first team's counts (particularly for large dollar items),
- the use of counters familiar with stock and able to identify and describe the stock being counted,
- that employees do not work excessive hours at counting (rotate count teams if necessary),
- acceptable methods of determining quantity [e.g. use of ratio scales (or weight counts) for high-quantity, low-cost inventory like nuts and bolts],
- the cut-off of receipts and deliveries,
- the importance of segregating goods that are not part of inventory and having a good physical arrangement of stock,
- the handling of damaged or obsolete inventory items, as well as slow-moving items,
- effective control over any documentation that is forwarded to an inventory comptometer service.

PAYMENT

PROBLEM: While checks are a preferred means of disbursement over cash, from a control perspective, they are subject to the risk of alteration.

SOLUTION: Print checks on special paper to make it difficult to alter the payee's name or the amount. Use a mechanical check signer with a device for physically controlling signed checks (e.g., a locked compartment); protective writing devices such as a check protector should inscribe amounts and be used at the earliest opportunity possible to provide the most effective protection. In addition, restrict check signing to executives without access to accounting records or cash, and have checks mailed directly to the payee by the check signer or by someone under the control of the check signer. A company policy that prohibits the misstating of dates on checks is also a good control measure as is the requirement of a manual signature for checks over a set amount whenever a facsimile signature is in use.

PROBLEM: Risk exposure of loss through defalcations is greatest in the area of cash, particularly disbursements.

SOLUTION: Have an independent party investigate payments to officers, directors, and employees (other than for compensation) as well as checks payable to banks, lending institutions, and attorneys for unusually large amounts. Control transfers between bank accounts by using a clearing account or other record to insure that both sides of the transfer are recorded in the same period.

PROBLEM: Employees entrusted with valuable assets including cash and unissued checks periodically leave the business.

SOLUTION: Maintain control by changing safe combinations periodically and whenever those personnel who are responsible for valuable assets leave the business. Update the listing of authorized signatures for bank accounts to assure that terminated employees are deleted from the listing.

PROBLEM: Improper timing of payments can result in lost discounts and lost earnings from cash investments.

SOLUTION: Establish a company policy of taking profitable cash discounts whenever offered and always defer payment date until the appropriate due date, in light of such discounts. Periodically review unpaid items in the voucher register and reconcile them to the accounts payable control account. Such a review is facilitated by putting the date of payment and check number in the voucher register for paid items. Another useful device is the tickler file.

Exhibit 10–5 (continued)

PROBLEM: Sometimes immediate payment is required and the available time is inadequate to process the payment through the normal disbursements cycle.

SOLUTION: Maintain a petty cash fund on an imprest basis (i.e., the total amount of cash plus petty cash vouchers reconciles to a set fund balance) in an amount that is reasonable in relation to the level of anticipated expenditures. Set the amount of currency funds so that reimbursement is necessary at least once a month to assure reasonably current recording of disbursements from the fund. Set a policy as to which payments are permitted to flow through the funds and require approvals of such payments. Data supporting disbursements should be designed to make alterations difficult and should be receipted by the recipient of the funds. Forcing the accounts payable regular routine to be followed for most disbursements permits the purchasing department to do a better job. Specifically, consider setting reasonable limits on the

- size of individual disbursements,
- extent to which personal checks of employees are cashed,
- loans and advances (e.g., for wages) that are made from such funds as a means of maintaining control over the fund.

Require an inventory of the cash funds periodically on a surprise basis by one who is independent of the fund. One person should have primary responsibility for the fund and responsibility should be fixed by making reimbursement checks payable to the custodian (this precludes denial of accountability). All reimbursements should be by check.

PROBLEM: The accounting (or audit) trail may be approached from several directions, depending on the objective of the information user, making it difficult to locate the desired document.

SOLUTION: Use multicopy checks, filing one copy numerically as the cash disbursements journal, filing one copy alphabetically by payee, and filing one copy with its related voucher. Banks frequently offer the service of sorting canceled checks by check number and preparing bank reconciliations for customers; such procedures enhance the ability to locate canceled checks as well as overall control.

PROBLEM: Numerous small checks can be costly to process.

SOLUTION: Consider using bank drafts as a payment instrument.

PROBLEM: Long outstanding checks result in an unwarranted working capital commitment.

SOLUTION: Write-off old outstanding checks.

PROBLEM: Stamps are easily pilfered items and the related clerical costs of mailing can be significant.

SOLUTION: Use a postage meter; this will decrease the cost of sealing and stamping envelopes, will provide a simple means of accounting (i.e., simply read the amounts on the register dials), and will decrease the exposure of the business to misappropriation.

ACCOUNTING

PROBLEM: "Paper" has a way of multiplying without any information content.

SOLUTION: Make periodic surveys as to the utility of reports to users. Some companies will periodically discontinue distribution of a report to see if anyone misses it. Since distributing copies of useful reports to nonusers represents a waste of resources, a control listing of reports issued, with a check-off system of which reports have been issued and to whom, should be maintained.

PROBLEM: Too often accounting systems stress financial reporting requirements and neglect management information needs.

SOLUTION: Regularly prepare reports on key ratios, trends, and variances, with comparisons to industry performance.

PROBLEM: Control of operating expenses is often lost when detailed accounting records of such expenses are unavailable.

SOLUTION: Maintain the following subsidiary records:

473

Exhibit 10–5 (continued)

- an insurance register,
- a tax register or due date file,
- supplies inventory records,
- experimental and developmental expense cost sheets,
- travel and entertainment expenses, coded by employee (detailing business purpose),

and reconcile these to general ledger control accounts.

PROBLEM: Inadequate monitoring of intangible assets can result in substantial loss of rights to production processes, trade names, and other valuable assets.

SOLUTION: Maintain detailed reports of patents, copyrights, trademarks, brand and trade names, franchises, royalty and license arrangements, lists of customers, and goodwill. Reconcile this information to the general ledger periodically.

PROBLEM: Often reserves, particularly tax reserves, are neglected, resulting in an improper representation of a company's financial position.

SOLUTION: Require a comparison to be made of existing tax reserves with known requirements and estimated requirements for contingencies by internal and external tax specialists. Such factors as the acceptability of depreciation and amortization methods by the IRS should be reviewed.

PROBLEM: Accounting for numerous small dollar assets and related depreciation and amortization expenses can be costly.

SOLUTION: Set a company policy that no costs less than some reasonable dollar limit be deferred.

PROBLEM: The maintenance of detailed property, plant, and equipment records may be beyond the expertise of the regular bookkeeper.

SOLUTION: Have lapsing schedules prepared; these schedules record one-half of the annual depreciation rate in the first and last year of the estimated useful life and typically apply straight-line depreciation to compute the cost and depreciation per year. Once such schedules are prepared by an accountant, the bookkeeper can maintain them and generate adjusting entries. Detailed records should be maintained for assets that are fully depreciated for control purposes.

PROBLEM: The prenumbering of documents by the preparer of the form who has access to unissued documents offers no control, yet frequently businesses have an insufficient number of employees to have someone other than the preparer prenumber documents.

SOLUTION: Have documents prenumbered by the printer and periodically inventory unissued forms, accounting for the numerical sequence of documents to control operations.

PROBLEM: Despite the availability of independent checks on operations by parties external to the company, the checks are frequently not capitalized upon.

SOLUTION: Require prompt follow-up on third parties' (particularly on vendors') complaints.

PROBLEM: Consolidation procedures can be time-consuming if inter-company transactions are not separately recorded.

SOLUTION: Record inter-company transactions in separate accounts.

PROBLEM: Errors are frequently made in posting accounts.

SOLUTION: Utilize machine proofs, whereby the preparation of such records as accounts payable and the purchase journal with the distribution of purchases by department can be combined while the machine proofs, based on the two recordings of each figure. The assumption of such a proofing machine is that if an error is made, it is unlikely to be repeated a second time. Another alternative is the use of electronic accounting machines that record information on carbon strips on the back of ledger sheets as magnetized spots and compare this information (e.g., account number and balance) to the operator's input to assure, for example, that the correct account is being posted.

Exhibit 10–5 (continued)

GENERAL SAFEGUARDING TECHNIQUES

PROBLEM: No matter how well assets and related accounting records appear to be controlled, unlimited access can thwart otherwise effective controls.

SOLUTION: Limit access and enhance safeguarding techniques by using

- external storage facilities such as banks, safe deposit boxes, and bonded warehouses with dual control required;
- outside services such as armored car services, night deposit facilities, guard services, bank reconciliation services for checking accounts; computer service bureaus, electronic funds transfer systems, independent paying agency staff for distributing payroll, and inventory comptometer services (obviously, it is essential that such services be checked out prior to their use to ensure sufficient control);
- physical barriers, including locked doors and cabinets, safes, and fences with dual control required;
- access restrictions such as magnetic key devices, secret passwords, "do not enter" signs, security guards, closed circuit television, employee badges, and sign-in logs;
- detection and prevention devices including fire alarms, electric sensing and similar monitoring devices, and security guards;
- work area layouts that provide maximum visibility by supervisors, guards, detectives, and customers.

In general, visitors, customers, outside truckers, contractors' employees doing work, and employees should be restricted to areas in which they have business. Guards should be given written instructions as to

- the handling of visitors, inspectors, salesmen, et cetera—including whom to admit and when;
- the pass system in operation for the removal of all materials from the premises; and
- the required logs to account for those people who are admitted or who leave the premises before and after normal operating hours.

Whenever keys are distributed to the entrance, gate, storerooms, warehouses, and similar areas of safekeeping, detailed records should be maintained. In addition, locks should be changed whenever key employees who have been entrusted with such keys either terminate or are transferred.

As an overall means of limiting exposure to defalcation, fidelity bonding of all employees handling valuables is essential. Consider using a tickler file to assure that such insurance, as well as property and loss-of-records insurance, is renewed on a timely basis. (A tickler file is simply a chronological filing of things to do.)

475

flicts between control and operating efficiency and potential conflicts between control procedures and incentive schemes, the systems evaluator can enhance the operating efficiency of the cost of sales or production cycle in any organization.

JUST-IN-TIME (JIT) INVENTORY

Just-in-Time (JIT) refers to a production philosophy that is intended to increase velocity and reduce waste through minimization of inventory held. This idea is also referred to as a World Class Manufacturing Environment (WCM).[3] Rather than viewing inventory as a buffer that is necessary and desirable in the operating cycle of a business, the JIT philosophy views inventory as that which should be eliminated, since it largely covers up various problems in the organization. In a sense, the idea is that a buffer is not needed in a well planned operation. Of course, some have noted that the growth of JIT among Japanese businesses, in part, is attributable to the greater geographical proximity of suppliers and customers, as well as a prevalence of cross-holdings and extremely long-term business relationships. It is frequent that when a business decides to relocate or expand, the supplier does likewise.

In contrast, a geographically dispersed setting, as is common in the United States, with independent suppliers that may not be used over the long term and may not be willing to accept the responsibilities attendant with JIT supply commitments all act to hinder a total adoption of JIT. A company cannot afford to have no raw materials and a production line laying idle due to faulty supply linkages.

The terms pipeline inventory, safety stock, anticipation stock, and hedge inventory are carry-overs from a functional approach to inventory. The JIT philosophy pushes for production of all products at all times, with a stable level through varying mix—reflecting rates rather than lots. The production system operates as a pull system, focusing on a make-to-order rather than a make-to-stock system. A critical facet of such a system is that purchases be made from JIT vendors. In a pure sense, inventory would be acquired at a variable rate that equaled the rate of customer orders and instantaneous work-in-process would occur, rather than raw materials as such in a "holding" bin. An added dimension of JIT is an expectation that system improvements will be constant. This would translate to shorter order cycles with reduced ordering and holding costs.

Remember that in self-evaluation, a JIT company considers anything that is produced over that which is necessary is waste. Likewise any ordering for future needs is an incompatible perspective to a JIT approach. In other words, inventory is not viewed as an investment but rather as an asset that is likely to shrink if ordered in advance of need. Yet, large quantity discounts could encourage such

---

[3] R. J. Schonberger, *World Class Manufacturing: The Lessons of Simplicity Applied* (New York: The Free Press, 1986).

purchases, but these discounts would be virtually precluded by the very fact that a JIT vendor would be most unlikely to offer such a purchasing arrangement. Note that policies often discussed in tandem with JIT include: total quality control (TQC), total productivity maintenance (TPM), and employee involvement (EI).

The advent of JIT suggests the need for adjustments to the traditional approach to controlling inventory. Specifically, the dollar risk exposure due to inventory levels is dissipated and the auditor's attention to this "asset base" is definitionally less. The risk is more one of constant supply, reliability of suppliers, and effective monitoring of the rates that drive the inventory process. From a control perspective, this suggests added attention to the selection of supplier and supplier contracting processes. It suggests that the purchasing arrangements are not geared to lot levels but rather have to be carefully coordinated with the entire manufacturing and distribution operations of the organization. By definition, the JIT philosophy integrates an ongoing monitoring of inventory levels. Similarly, by definition, the manufacturing system is defined to include the distribution system, since finished goods should arise only at the end of such a system. The handling of inventory is expected to result in value added. When movement merely relocates but adds no utility, that would be one example of an item to be minimized through improved planning and operating of the production and distribution processes.

A particularly interesting thought to keep in mind is that adoption of JIT may in and of itself be one of the most effective controls to design into the cost of sales or production cycle.

THE SERVICES INDUSTRY REVISITED

Chapter 9 included considerable attention to the increase of services relative to goods and attendant control issues. The advent of JIT and related manufacturing and inventory handling practices, including robotics in various plants, speaks to the continuing education needs of those who provide professional services to such aspects of business.

A key control issue in the service industry relates to the manner of compensating employees. Compensation must be at an adequate level but not so excessive as to deter complaints and suggestions from being forwarded from employee to supervisor. In other words, deterring turnover is good up to a point, but if an individual could not find a suitable substitute for a present position, he or she may be hesitant to complain or bring problems to others' attention. The real problem is that the employees feel imperiled by the prospect of losing an excessively rewarding position.

Oftentimes commissions are a facet of compensation and whenever they exist, control questions of importance include: what is the basis of the commission, is it intuitively justifiable, and reasonably determined without undue influence of the employee; are the commissions so high that the loyalty of the employee becomes excessive in a manner conducive to management override; and have incentives been created that may well be at odds with such organizational objectives as enhancing quality control or customer satisfaction?

Costing services can be particularly difficult when certain aspects of the service are not traditionally tracked or captured in the reporting system. For example, does travel time of employees get tracked? If not, a client in another state may well be costing the firm unduly from an employee morale point of view, from a return on investment perspective, and from the mere fact that job effectiveness is harmed by fatigue induced through travel demands. A key control of use in the cost of sales cycle for professional firms is to capture all time associated with the firm's operations, including travel and associated delay times.

This would be an appropriate juncture to review the discussion of professional services and attendant control ideas put forth in Chapter 9, in light of your increased understanding of the cost of sales cycle. Competency issues, supervision practices, and availability of "tools of production" are clearly relevant controls in such a cycle, though introduced in an earlier chapter.

ADDITIONAL EXAMPLES

The Appendix to this chapter provides additional examples of the interrelationship of errors, control risk, control procedures, tests of control, and substantive tests (Exhibit 10–6 and 10–7) for the cost of sales or production cycle. Documentation suggestions are also provided.

APPENDIX

Exhibit 10–6

Example of Linkage Among Control Risk Assessment, Tests of Controls, and Substantive Tests

1. Evaluation of Controls over Production and Cost Accounting

Strong Controls	Weak Controls
Production orders are authorized by initials, as are materials and labor forms	Foreman prepares material requisitions and time summaries without any independent check
Production orders are prenumbered, sequence checks are performed, and blank forms are well controlled, the same is true for material and labor forms	Material requisitions and time cards are not prenumbered or accounted for and blank forms are not well controlled
Reports on materials used and labor are reviewed, as indicated by initials	
Both issue slips and time cards are reconciled to materials used and labor reports	Standard costs are not in use
Inventory received is reconciled to production	
All inventory entries are independently reviewed and approved	

2. Tests of Controls Deemed to Be Effectively Designed and Judged Likely to Be Cost Beneficial to Perform

   Obviously, the test work does not apply to the weak controls.

Control Objectives for Which Procedures Are Being Tested	
Authorization	• Examine a sample of production orders, material forms, and labor forms, noting initials.
Completeness	• Observe where and how blank forms are secured and then scan files of production orders, material forms, and labor forms for missing numbers.

Exhibit 10–6 (continued)

Accuracy and Approval	• Examine a sample of reports on materials used and labor for initials, as evidence of an independent review.
Accuracy	• Examine reconciliations and how differences identified were resolved.
Accuracy and Approval	• Examine entries for evidence of their independent review and approval.

3. Prepare a bridging work paper for the effects of observed strengths and weaknesses of control design and the results of the control risk assessment and related tests of control on substantive testing. The strengths of control support less extensive test counts of finished inventory and limited testing of the linkage between use reports and journals.

The weaknesses of control suggest a need for

—more extensive test counts of work-in-process inventory.
—tracing, to jobs, from cost accounting records to test the completeness of materials and labor charges.
—vouching of materials costs to invoices and labor costs to employee contracts.
—vouching of prices used in year-end extension of inventory quantities to supporting documentation.

Exhibit 10–7

Payroll: Risks and Controls—A Case Example

Case Setting:

In connection with an examination of the financial statements of the Olympia Manufacturing Company, a CPA is reviewing procedures for accumulating direct labor hours. He learns that all production is by job order and that all employees are paid hourly wages, with time and a half for overtime hours.

Olympia's direct labor-hour input process for payroll and job-cost determination is summarized in the following flowchart:

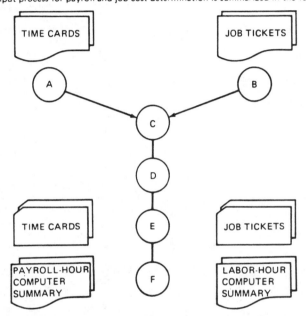

Steps A and C are performed in timekeeping, Step B in the factory operating departments, Step D in payroll auditing and control, Step E in data preparation (keypunch), and Step F in computer operations.

Required:

For each input-processing Step A through F:

1. List the possible errors or discrepancies.

2. Cite the corresponding control procedure that should be in effect for each error discrepancy.

Note: Your discussion of Olympia's procedures should be limited to the input process for direct labor hours, as shown in Steps A through F in the flowchart. Do not discuss personnel procedures for hiring, promotion, termination, and pay rate authorization. In Step F do not discuss equipment, computer program, and general computer operational controls.

Step	Possible Errors or Discrepancies	Control Procedures
A	1. Time may be improperly reported by employees.	1. a. Timekeeping for payroll hours should be an independent function. b. Time clocks should be used under the observation of timekeeping. c. Strict rules should be enforced requiring each employee to punch his or her own time card. d. Timekeeping should make periodic floor checks of employees on duty.

Step	Possible Errors or Discrepancies	Control Procedures
	2. Payroll may be padded by timekeeper.	2. a. Employees should be paid directly by paymaster. b. Personnel department should advise payroll audit and control and the computer department of new hires and terminations.
	3. Employees may work unauthorized overtime hours.	3. A procedure for authorization of overtime should be devised, and timekeeping should determine that required authorizations are made.
B	4. Employees may not work effectively during the hours reported to timekeeping, or they may disguise inefficiencies by spreading excess hours to other jobs.	4. a. Employees should report hours by job, preferably by using a time clock. b. Supervisor should review and approve job tickets, and timekeeping should check to see that these approvals are made. (The effectiveness of this system depends on the supervisor's ability to evaluate the time spent on particular jobs and his or her conscientious review of the job tickets.) c. Employees should be instructed to assign actual hours to jobs. Either the supervisor or timekeeping should enforce this policy.
	5. Overtime work on a job may not be authorized, and the job may not be charged at the premium overtime rate.	5. Timekeeping should check required authorizations and appropriately note hours that should be charged at the premium rate.
C	6. Job tickets and time cards may not be in balance.	6. Absolute balancing may be impractical or unnecessary for cost accumulation, allocation, or control; reasonable difference limits should be established by appropriate authority. Differences can be made to fall within established limits by a. Having the timekeeper balance hours per time card with hours per job tickets and resolve differences, or b. Programming computer to zero balance total hours on job tickets with total hours on time card by employee. Differences exceeding established limits would be printed out as exceptions for follow-up by payroll audit and control and/or timekeeper.
D	7. Time cards and job tickets may be lost in transit from timekeeping to payroll audit and control.	7. a. Timekeeping should promptly forward time cards and job tickets accompanied by a transmittal slip denoting the number of employees for which time is being reported. Payroll audit and control should reconcile the number of employees reported with the master-payroll record, considering employees on vacation, out sick, and so forth. b. To ensure that all cards have been accounted for, timekeeping can prepare a hash total of employee numbers for both time cards and job tickets. These totals can be included in the transmittal slip described under (a) above.
	8. Payroll audit and control may total hours incorrectly in preparing the control total for the batch transmittal form.	8. If this is a common error, payroll audit and control should recompute all control totals. If it is an uncommon occurrence, it can be handled as an exception printout from the computer.
E	9. Time cards and job tickets may be lost in transit from payroll audit and control to data preparation.	9. Payroll audit and control should batch time cards and related job tickets. A consecutively numbered transmittal sheet should accompany each batch and contain a control total, such as total hours. This control total should be compared with total shown by keypunch machine.
	10. Keypunch operator may transcribe data incorrectly.	10. Keypunching should be verified by another operator. Errors also will be detected by using batch controls.
	11. The employee identification number may have been recorded or carried forward improperly.	11. Employee identification numbers should contain a self-checking digit, and the computer should be programmed to test the validity of each employee's number.
F	12. Time cards and job tickets may be lost in transit from data preparation to the computer.	12. Supplementing the programmed computer checks, payroll audit and control should check the computer output hours against its input log.
	13. Errors detected by programmed computer controls may not be reentered in the system.	13. Payroll audit and control should maintain an error log.

CPA exam adapted, November 2, 1972, question 3.

Exhibit 10–7 (continued)

A Field Example in Which Analytical Procedures Were Used in Lieu of Detailed Tests

Payroll is, perhaps, one of the more intuitive settings for an "overall test." In general terms, we speak of multiplying the pay rate by the number of hours worked or the salary level by the number of employees, thereby arriving at aggregate payroll expense. However, we all know that several other factors can influence payroll expenses and that the audit objective is likely to require more precision than such a general formula can provide. While this is, most likely, the case, it may be relatively easy to identify those "other factors" that have substantial effects on the recorded expense numbers and to incorporate them in the analytical procedures. This is exactly what was done in the following field example that resulted in an "expected or explained payroll balance" that was within 3% of the recorded payroll.

- The procedure relies upon last year's audited payroll expense as the basis to which the current period should relate.
- The auditor recognizes a change in the number of employees as well as the level of fringe benefits as being important elements of recorded expense.
- The auditor breaks out those attributes that are not expected to increase or decrease as a function of the number of employees. This is critical to analytical procedures; such effects are "NOISE" when a key relationship such as "employees to payroll" is being analyzed.
- Since quantity and price tend to be the basic components of most economic relationships, the auditor needed to quantify the overall effect of wage changes when analyzing payroll expense. Note that the auditor was careful to incorporate the cost-of-living adjustment and to appropriately reflect that portion of the year in which each change in wage rates was effective.
- By such a detailed approach, the auditor was able to derive an "expected payroll expense" within 1% of the recorded number, supporting the judgment that no further audit work was deemed to be necessary.
- The increase in health insurance, if an employee deduction, should not make a difference.
- Some would prefer to focus on the change in the various benefit costs, tying this change to the number of employees to infer the reasonableness of the amounts.
- The footnoted "*1/1/82 wage increase" might be more effectively evaluated through a tie-in to the expected number of employees and hours worked.
- A need exists to examine client records and to obtain data from production operations as distinct from the accounting area.

This payroll application ought to be compared and contrasted with the typical detailed testing approach of drawing a sample of 54 employees.

Setting:

Prior to 1981, payroll was detail tested with satisfactory results. Based on a planned rotation of audit emphasis, no detail payroll testing is to be performed in 1982. A walk-through of the payroll system will be conducted to ensure our understanding of key controls and procedures and to ensure that the payroll system has not changed significantly. We will employ certain analytical procedures to determine that payroll and related benefits are reasonable.

The walk-through was performed at interim and confirmed that no changes had been made to the payroll system. Two employees were selected from each of the five payroll subsystems for whom source documents were traced through the system.

- Pay was determined to be appropriate.
- Source documents were appropriately approved.
- The amounts were traced into the timebook and the total for the timebook was tied into the payroll distribution.
- The payroll distribution was properly posted to the general ledger.

Worksheet Summarizing Analytical Procedures Performed for Payroll

Payroll Subsystem	Avg. Number of Employees	Payroll Expense	Adjusted Payroll Expense	Fringe Benefits	Fringe Benefits As a % of Adjusted Payroll
Subsystem 1		99,832		25,532	
Subsystem 2		31,740		8,208	
Subsystem 3		22,770		5,838	
Subsystem 4		8,822		2,260	
Subsystem 5		17,222		4,740	
Rounding Difference		<2>		<2>	
Subsequent Reclassification		132			
Per 1982 Consolidated Statement	6,392@	180,516	178,045	46,576	26.2%√
Per 1981 Consolidated Statement	6,768@	185,546	174,280	40,784	23.4%√
Increase <Decrease>	<376>	<5,030>	3,765	5,792	
% Increase <Decrease>	<5.6%>	<2.7%>	2.2%	14.2%	

@ Accumulated from monthly report on employees, services, and compensation; an average for the year was calculated.

Exhibit 10–7 (continued)

√ Reviewed benefit cost file and noted the following increases over 1981:

    (1) Increase in Health Insurance of 23.7% (paid by employee)
    (2) Increase in base amount (subject to tax) for Retirement Tax
    (3) Increase of 23.7% in % of salary the employer contributes to retirement; 1/1/81, 9.5% of maximum monthly salary of
        $1,850 increased on 1/1/82 to 11.75% of maximum monthly salary of $2,025
    (4) Increase of 17% in early retirement tax
    (5) Increase in cost of dental insurance, life insurance, etc.

The above increases were partially offset by a 5.6% decrease in the average number of employees. Fluctuation appears reasonable.

	12/31/81	12/31/82
Total Payroll Expense	185,546,000	180,516,000
Effect of Incentive Compensation		
(Deducted since relates to earnings, not number of employees)	<6,466,000>	909,308
Effect of Pension/Profit-Sharing		
(Deducted since relates to earnings, not number of employees)	<4,800,000>	<3,380,000>
	174,280,000	178,045,308
1/1/82 Increase in Wages of $.35 per hour	4,927,104*	
7/1/82 Increase Due to 3% Cost of Living Adjustment	2,614,200**	
7/1/82 Increase in Wages of $.22 per hour	1,548,518***	
Subtotal	183,369,822	
Effect of decrease in number of employees	<10,473,104>****	
	172,896,718	
NET OTHER DIFFERENCE	5,148,590*****	
(5,148,590 ÷ 178,045,308 = 2.9%)	178,045,308	

*1/1/82 Wage Increase		**7/1/82 Cost of Living Increase	
1981 employees	6,768	1981 Gross Pay	174,280,000
Hours per year	×2,080	3% Adjustment for	
$.35 per hour increase	×.35	for one-half year per cost	
		of living adjustment records	×1.5%
	4,927,104		2,614,200

***7/1/82 Wage Increase		****Effect of Decrease in Employees	
1981 employees	6,768	Decrease in Number of Employees	376
Hours per year	×2,080	1982 Average Salary	
$.22 per hour increase for		($178,045,308 ÷ 6,392)	×27,854
one-half year	×.11		10,473,104
	1,548,518		

***** Due to nature of reasonableness tests, this 2.9% difference does not appear to be unreasonable. No further work deemed necessary.

11

How to Design and Evaluate Internal Accounting Controls for Financing and Nonroutine Transactions

"A smattering of everything, and a knowledge of nothing."[1]

This quote comes to mind when reading of the diverse financial instruments permeating the market place, some of which are cited in Exhibit 11–1. How they have evolved can sometimes be linked to particular events, as reflected in Exhibit 11–2, but more often, a smattering of information is available as to the purpose underlying an instrument and the real knowledge of attendant risks is woefully lacking. Witness the junk bond market, leveraged buy-outs, management buy-outs, and the potpourri of defensive maneuvers aptly named green mail and poison pills. In 1988, RJR Nabisco's $5 billion outstanding bonds lost 20% of their value

---

[1] William D. Hall, *Accounting and Auditing: Thoughts on Forty Years in Practice and Education* (Chicago: Arthur Andersen & Co., 1987), p. 27.

Exhibit 11–1

Innovative Financing

Negotiable CDs	Options On Futures
Eurodollar Accounts	Options On Indexes
Eurobonds	Money Market Funds
Sushi Bonds	Cash Management Accounts
Floating-rate Bonds	Income Warrants
Puttable Bonds	Collateralized Mortgages
Zero Coupon Bonds	Home Equity Loans
Stripped Bonds	Currency Swaps
Options	Floor-Ceiling Swaps
Financial Futures	Exchangeable Bonds

Source: Merton H. Miller, "Financial Innovation: The Last Twenty Years and the Next," *Journal of Financial and Quantitative Analysis* (December 1986), pp. 459–471.

---

on the announcement of a leveraged buyout.[2] Household International Inc. attracted the SEC's attention when its "poison pill" was seen as entrenching management. Specifically, if someone were to buy or control voting rights for 30% or more, a rights offering would be triggered permitting Household shareholders to buy shares in the acquirer at half price.[3]

The third major control cycle deals with financing and nonroutine transactions, and encompasses

—management functions—involving cash balances, financial reporting, and general controls, and

—financing activities—including debt and equity transactions and related dividend, interest, and miscellaneous expense accounts.

The implementation of the internal control design and evaluation process, outlined and demonstrated in prior chapters, will now be described for financing and nonroutine transactions. The explanations provided will include examples of control problems that have been observed for a wide cross-section of industries. Details as to how such problems can be identified and corrected through the application of the recommended approach to analyzing controls will be discussed.

---

[2] "Where is the Limit?" *Time* (December 5, 1988), pp. 40–47.

[3] Gelvin Stevenson, "A Poison Pill That's Causing A Rash of Lawsuits," *Business Week* (April 1, 1985, No. 2888), pp. 54–58.

Exhibit 11–2

**Major Impulses for Financial Innovation:
Regulations & Taxes**

EURODOLLAR MARKET

Regulation Q in the United States placed a ceiling on the rate of interest that commercial banks could offer on their time deposits but did not apply to dollar-denominated time deposits in overseas branches ⇒ competitive bidding in late 1960s and early 1970s which persists today, despite elimination of Regulation Q.

EUROBOND MARKET

Late 1960s required a 30% withholding tax on interest payments on bonds sold in the United States to overseas investors, so the market for dollar-denominated bonds for non-U.S. citizens moved from New York to London and other money centers; despite repeal of the withholding provision, the Eurobond Market thrives most likely due to its bypass of new-issue SEC prospectus requirements.

SWAPS

Initiated in Britain to avoid British government restrictions on dollar financing by British firms and sterling financing by non-British firms.

ZERO-COUPON BONDS

In 1981 a tax change occurred but more important was a technical flaw in the Treasury Department regulations interpreting U.S. tax laws. The permitting of a linear approximation for computing implicit interest inflated the present value of interest deductions so that a taxable corporation could come out ahead by issuing a long-term deep discount bond and *giving* it away. The Treasury corrected the blunder in 1983, but Japanese treat appreciation as capital gains exempt from tax and moreover restrict the value of foreign bond holdings by Japanese pension funds—both effects creating demand for zero-coupon bonds. Since corporate zeroes were scarce, some innovators strip coupons from U.S. Treasury bonds and sell them as zeroes.

Source: Merton H. Miller, "Financial Innovation: The Last Twenty Years and the Next," *Journal of Financial and Quantitative Analysis* (December 1986), pp. 459–471.

SEGREGATING INCOMPATIBLE FUNCTIONS

As in Chapters 9 and 10, the objective of segregating duties is to ensure that no single individual is placed in such a position that (s)he can perpetrate and conceal errors and irregularities while performing regularly assigned duties. This objective can be obtained by segregating three principal activities: authorization of transactions, custody of assets, and accounting for transactions. Nonroutine transactions, including financing activities, pose a particular problem in designing controls because their relative infrequency may cause management to give them inadequate attention. A thorough understanding of a client's operations will help you identify the various nonroutine transactions that may occur and will suggest how to segregate the responsibility for such transactions. Exhibit 11–3 details the critical segregation of duties which is likely to prove useful in maintaining control over financing and nonroutine transactions.

Interpreting Exhibit 11–3

Following the approach illustrated in Chapters 9 and 10, Exhibit 11–3 is organized with the owner-manager's ability to effectively intervene wherever duties are not properly segregated in order to review the work being performed by the employees who are assigned incompatible duties. Exhibit 11–3 uses the three-column structure of the earlier chapters to emphasize the substantial control benefits three-man operations derive from carefully assigning operating and control duties among the small number of available employees. However, the three-column structure is expanded upon by identifying the separate duties within each department which, if performed by different individuals, would enhance control even more than the basic three-way assignment of duties.

Exhibit 11–3 is subdivided into six components of financing and nonroutine transactions:

(1) management of cash balances,
(2) financing activities—debt,
(3) financing activities—equity,
(4) financial reporting,
(5) internal auditing, and
(6) other general controls.

All revenue and expense charges are presumed to have been appropriately recorded in the revenue and cost-of-sales cycle, with the sole exception of dividends and interest charges related to financing activities. However, attention is directed to the control of adjusting and nonstandard journal entries, some of which are likely to relate to nonroutine revenue and expense items. Since financing and equity transactions are less routine, the form and availability of standardized authorization and control documents differ from the revenue and cost-of-sales cycle. However, the same general rules apply to the formal segregation of duties

Exhibit 11–3

Critical Segregation of Duties for Financing and Nonroutine Transactions

OWNER-MANAGER

☐ = Space for initials of individual responsible for this duty.

AUTHORIZATION

Management of Cash Balances

FINANCIAL MANAGEMENT
☐ Prepare Budget of Working Capital Needs.
☐ Secure Board of Directors' Approval.

Financing Activities—debt

TREASURY
☐ Negotiate and Renegotiate Debt Obligations—Have Schedule of Required Financing Prepared and Debt Service Requirements.
☐ Authorize Restrictive Covenants and Terms (Amount, Timing, and Conditions) of Debt Agreement, Including Acceptable Sources of Funds, Desired Debt-to-Equity Ratio and Trustee Appointment; Document Approval.

Financing Activities—equity

TREASURY
☐ Authorize Stock Transactions (Including Treasury Stock Transactions) in Compliance with Board's Criteria and State of Incorporation Regulations—Including Changes in Par and Stated Value of Stock.

☐ Sign Stock Certificates (Designated Signer per Board); Examine Stock Being Replaced for Appropriate Cancellation.
☐ Countersign Stock Certificates (Designated Signer per Board)—Both Signatures Required to Validate Stock; Examine Stock Being Replaced for Appropriate Cancellation.

Financial Reporting

BOARD OF DIRECTORS
☐ Authorize a Chart of Accounts, Complete with Descriptions of Each Account.

Internal Auditing

BOARD OF DIRECTORS/AUDIT COMMITTEE
☐ Reports to a Sufficiently High Level of Authority That Findings Receive Consideration and Appropriate Action—i.e., Organizational Position Includes Direct Access to Board.
☐ Authorized Charter, Standards, and Audit Plan.

Other General Controls

BOARD OF DIRECTORS/TOP MANAGEMENT
☐ Management's General and or Specific Authorization of
—postings,
—transfers between accounts, and
—adjustments to account balances.
Assign Authorization Levels for Standard and Nonstandard Journal Entries and Adjustments of Accounts; Maintain File of Authorized Signatures.
Issue Clear
—Organization Charts
—Job Descriptions
—Policy and Procedures Manual
—Internal Audit Department Activity Description
—Long-Range Plans.
Promptly Prepare Board of Directors' Minutes.

TREASURER
☐ Approve Board Minutes.

CUSTODY

Management of Cash Balances

CASHIER
☐ Arrange for Lockboxes, Immediate Deposits at Geographically Dispersed Locations, Centralized Cash Resources, and Other Techniques for Minimizing Idle Cash.

Financing Activities—debt

TREASURER'S DEPARTMENT—ASSET CONTROL
☐ Control Prenumbered
—Debentures
—Notes
—Commercial Paper
—Similar Debt Instruments.
☐ Independent Trustee over Sinking funds.

Financing Activities—equity

TREASURER'S DEPARTMENT—ASSET CONTROL
☐ Maintain Control over Blank Stock Certificates; Cancel and Attach Stock Certificates to Be Replaced To the New Certificates to Be Issued; Control Stock Option Forms.
☐ Physical Control over Treasury Stock, Segregated from Other Certificates; Register Treasury Stock in Company's Name.
☐ Per Class of Stock, Employ an Independent:
Transfer Agent   Registrar   Dividend Paying Agent
☐ Account for Sequence of Stock Certificates, Including Blank Forms via Physical Inspection.

Financial Reporting

SECRETARY
☐ Maintain Control Listing of Reports Issued; Check Off Reports as Issued.
☐ Collect Supplementary Data—Minutes of Directors' and Shareholders' Meetings; Descriptions of New Regulations; Input from Legal Counsel and Both Internal and External Auditors; Collect Tax Information.

Internal Auditing

BOARD OF DIRECTORS/AUDIT COMMITTEE: REGARDING INTERNAL AUDIT
☐ Full, Unrestricted Access to Assets, Records, and Operations of Entity to Perform Financial and Operational Audits.

Other General Controls

ACCOUNTING—FORMS CONTROL
☐ Maintain Control over Blank Prenumbered
—Standard Journal Entry Forms
—Standard Elimination and Reclassification Entries
—Standard Translation and Consolidation Formats
—Standard Reporting Formats.

Exhibit 11–3 (continued)

OWNER-MANAGER

ACCOUNTING

Management of Cash Balances

REPORTING FUNCTION
☐
Prepare a Timely Cash Flow Report; Quantify Opportunity Cost of Idle Cash.

GENERAL LEDGER ACCOUNTING
☐
Review and Approve Journal Entries Made to Cash; Reconcile Cash Flow Report to General Ledgers.

Prepare Bank Reconciliation, Tying to Cash per Books.

Financing Activities—debt

LIABILITIES
☐
Monitor Compliance with Bond Covenants and Effects of Proposed Debt Adjustments on Such Covenants; Report on Cost of Debt. Tie Records to Treasury Department Documentation.

Prepare Schedule of Payments; Amortize Discounts and Premiums; Maintain Detailed Books; Accrue Interest.

GENERAL LEDGER ACCOUNTING
☐
Maintain the Control Accounts.

Review and Approve Journal Entries; Reconcile Detailed Books with General Ledger; Check Interest Calculations.

Reconcile Activities' Agreement to Board of Directors' Minutes; Periodically Substantiate Recorded Balances; Tie in Records to Actual Securities.

Financing Activities—equity

EQUITIES
☐
Maintain the Stock Certificate Book; Account for the Sequence of Stock Certificate Numbers per Records.

Maintain Stockholder Ledger; Accrue Dividends.

GENERAL LEDGER ACCOUNTING
☐
Reconcile Stockholder Ledger to Stock Certificate Book and to General Ledger; Reconcile Reported Dividend Checks to Stockholder Ledger and General Ledger's Recorded Liability.

Reconcile Transfer Agent's and Registrar's Report on Shares Outstanding to General Ledger Control Accounts; Reconcile Activities' Agreement to Board of Directors' Minutes.

Financial Reporting

REPORTING FUNCTION
☐
Prepare
—Financial Statements
—Governmental Reports
—Regulatory Statements
—Tax Returns
for Management and Financial Reporting Purposes.

CONTROLLER
☐
Review External Audit Reports; Check Financial Reports for Reasonableness via Comparison of Ratios, Trends, and Variances from Budgeted Data; Reconcile Prior Year's Statements to Current Year's; Check Financial Statement's
—Math
—Tie-in to Trial Balance
—Elimination and Reclassification Entries
—Agreement to Source Information Like Exchange Rates
—Agreement to Consolidation Entries
—Compliance with GAAP and Adequacy of Disclosures.

Internal Auditing

INTERNAL AUDIT DEPARTMENT
☐
Prepare Formal Written Reports after Verbally Discussing Results with Auditee; Follow up on Auditee's Responses.

INTERNAL AUDIT DIRECTOR
☐
Approve Written Reports. Prepare Activity Report for Board. Periodically Meet with Board.

Other General Controls

GENERAL ACCOUNTING
☐
Record Nonstandard Journal Entries and Standard Journal Entries, as Appropriate; Tie to Underlying Support; Maintain Sufficiently Detailed Records for Valuation Adjustments, e.g., Records for Investments, Depreciation Computations, Estimation of Warranties, et cetera.

GENERAL LEDGER ACCOUNTING
☐
Make Postings to General Ledger; Regularly Prepare Trial Balance and Promptly Investigate Any Amounts Out-of-Balance.

Review and Approve Nonstandard Journal Entries and Test Standard Entries for Propriety; Compare Actual Entries to Closing Schedule to Ensure All Required Entries Have Been Booked.

Compare Agreement of Board of Directors' Minutes with Recorded Transactions; Ensure That Records Are Retained as Required by Law and as Needed by Management; Independently Review Journal Entries and Supporting Documentation; Regularly Test Reconciliation of Control Accounts to Related Subsidiary Records; Regularly Test Preparation of Trial Balance, Promptly Investigating Any Errors or Amounts Out-of-Balance.

and formal evidence that such segregation in fact is present. The individuals authorizing transactions should do so in writing and should not have access to the assets to which their authorizations relate, or to the records that account for such transactions. A dual authorization procedure is generally preferred. Both parties authorizing transactions should check their propriety and compliance with general and specific authorizations, objectives, and criteria set by the Board of Directors and management. Custody over both issued and unissued documents is a critical control procedure, particularly when those documents have intrinsic value—such as stock certificates and debentures, or are capable of influencing the accountability of assets—such as standardized journal entry forms. In financing activities, additional custody responsibilities are typically assigned to independent third parties: trustees, transfer agents, registrars, and dividend-paying agents. Such external custody can greatly decrease the risk exposure of an entity when compared to the internal control of such functions. Accounting activities are those relating to initial entries in the accounting records and those that summarize and exercise control over the journal records through review and reconciliation procedures. The concept that review controls are effective only when a party other than the preparer of a document reviews it for accuracy and propriety is repeatedly reflected in Exhibit 11–3, as it was in Chapters 9 and 10. The intention is to increase the likelihood of detecting errors.

Exhibit 11–3 lists 44 different tasks for segregation but, as explained earlier, this does not imply that a minimum of 44 staff employees must be available for such activities. In fact, four of the responsibilities are specifically designed to be assumed by third parties—the trustee, transfer agent, registrar, and dividend-paying agent. In addition, the party in general ledger accounting who reviews and approves journal entries in five of the six subdivisions of Exhibit 11–3 could be one individual. Similarly, the same party may be responsible for authorizing many of the transactions that are listed; as noted in the exhibit, the Board of Directors is likely to be involved in many of the authorization procedures. In smaller organizations, the owner-manager will assume numerous responsibilities listed in the exhibit and is thereby capable of creating a reasonable level of control.

How to Use Exhibit 11–3

Become familiar with operations and put the initials of the party performing 44 tasks on the exhibit in the spaces indicated. Initials appearing more than once within one of the three columns on the exhibit cause little concern, although they do indicate an absence of cross-checks and an increase in risk exposure from careless errors. If one individual accounts for a transaction from the beginning to the end of the accounting trail, no real protection exists against errors in the recording process.

> EXAMPLE: The internal auditor noted that certain general journal entries were prepared and approved by the same individual. To ensure that journal entries have been properly prepared and adequately documented, they should

be reviewed and approved by a responsible official other than the preparer. No real control within recordkeeping now exists.

The more important control concerns arise whenever duties are not appropriately segregated across the three columns. Exhibit 11–3 should permit you to both identify the control flaw and interpret the added risk exposure that arises from combining incompatible functions.

> EXAMPLE: An internal audit department is most useful when it is primarily concerned with objectively appraising controls and company operations, independent of normal day-to-day accounting operations, yet internal auditors have been assigned normal or recurring accounting and recordkeeping responsibilities. The result is that internal auditors may not be sufficiently independent to evaluate operations objectively. How can they be expected to judge, in an unbiased manner, operations that they themselves performed?

While Exhibit 11–3 is easier to use as a basis for designing controls, it is equally simple to apply in an internal control evaluation of existing controls. The terms in which it is expressed are so general that any critical segregation of duties missing in an organization can be identified by matching specific people to the individual duties and interpreting the consequence with respect to risk exposure. The probability of such risk will be clarified in the next stage of system analysis, but first consider the potential ill effects of other factors on what might otherwise appear to be an effective separation of duties.

Watch for These Factors That Can Adversely Affect Control and Segregation of Duties

At times, the use of initials on Exhibit 11–3 will not identify weaknesses in controls because other factors are relevant in evaluating the effectiveness of the apparent segregation of duties. The types of factors that may have adverse effects include *family ties* between employees who occupy authorization, custody, and/ or accounting responsibilities, and *temporary "sharing" of duties* during breaks, lunch time, and vacations among employees who have incompatible duties.

Apparent dual controls may not actually exist. Often, the initials on Exhibit 11–3 will be distinct, yet these types of factors will exist and warrant the attention of the systems evaluator.

> EXAMPLE: An entity has an established policy that two officers authorize program changes; one of the signatures on the form has consistently been that of the director of internal auditing. The intent has been to document his awareness of the changes, rather than to signify his approval authority.
> SOLUTION: In fact, his name should be removed from the form to preclude an assumption that he is involved in the initiation of program changes.

At first glance, the above example would have appeared reasonable—two different employees are approving program changes. However, since only one of the individuals has line authority and the second has been "rubber stamping" the change as a mere acknowledgment that a change has been made, no dual control has in fact existed. In addition to creating a facade of control, this situation also has a potential adverse effect on the perceived independence of the internal auditor. The real cost to the entity could include the increased external audit fee that stems from the external auditors' decision that they cannot rely on an internal audit department that performs operational duties, as well as the poor relationship between auditee and internal auditor that could stem from the perception that the internal auditor lacks independence.

Code Exhibit 11–3 for These Adverse Factors

The systems evaluator must remain aware of the numerous adverse factors that potentially could influence controls. One way to explicitly consider such factors is to code initials onto Exhibit 11–3 that reflect

(a) family relationships,
(b) those individuals who are assuming permanent and temporary duties in other operating areas,
(c) the apparent access by others to assets under particular individuals' control, and
(d) the handling of specific transactions known to involve a conflict-of-interest.

The use of such a coding scheme enables the systems evaluator to better assess the effectiveness of segregated duties as an internal accounting and operating control.

CONSIDER USERS OF ACCOUNTING INFORMATION SYSTEMS WHEN ASSESSING CONTROLS

Exhibit 11–4 highlights some of the key users of accounting information. In considering the design of the record-keeping facet of an economic enterprise, it is important to keep all of these parties in mind, since their information demands often have to be met due to contractual agreements and/or regulation. Highlighted within Exhibit 11–4 is the internal user, which is characterized as a managerial accounting concern which can easily differ from the concerns focused on by financial accounting. Nonetheless, the core records of an entity in the typical accounting department would include those depicted in Exhibit 11–5. Importantly, the journals and subsidiary ledger and ledger system provide cross-checks via the double entry system of accounting. Yet, to make this information available to a wide variety of users and compatible with a number of operating and nonfinancial pieces of information, companies are beginning to take advantage of developing software and not only mechanizing the accounting system but also making data base management systems (DBMS) operative. Assuming such an information framework is in place, attention can be directed to the controls over the process.

Exhibit 11–4

Users of Accounting Information

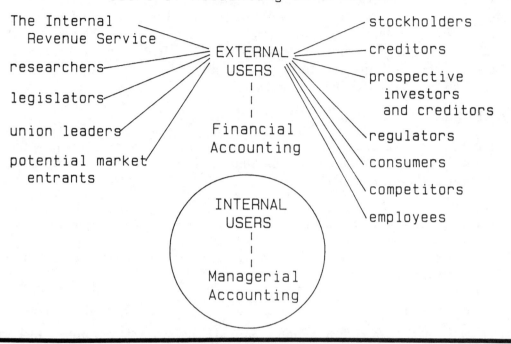

Exhibit 11–5

The Interrelationship of Journals and Ledgers

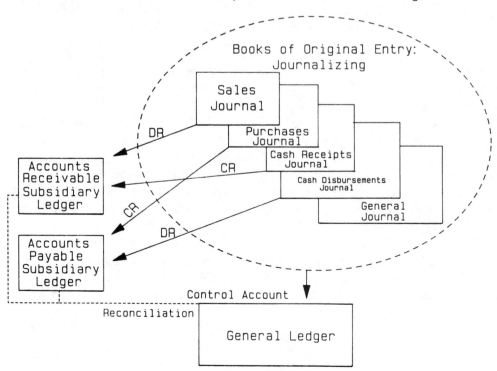

MAINTAINING COMPLETE ACCOUNTING RECORDS

Once the systems designer has established the critical segregation of duties or the systems evaluator has identified the apparent segregation of duties and related strengths and weaknesses, what information is available to document the fact that each of the tasks outlined in Exhibit 11–3 has actually been performed? As discussed earlier in this guide, tests of control frequently involve observation and inquiry techniques. However, a strong system of control will create an accounting trail that requires employees to document the performance of both operating and control duties, thereby stressing the employees' accountability. This trail provides physical evidence that designed controls are in operation.

Forms for Assuring Complete Accounting Records

Exhibit 11–6 provides the systems designer and evaluator with a standard by which to assess the completeness of the accounting trail. The documents presented underlie financing and nonroutine transactions and, if properly completed and controlled, can be expected to assist an entity in recording all valid and authorized transactions in the appropriate period and in the proper account, at the correct amount. Obviously, the format of the various documents, as well as the terms that are applied to each of the forms, should be tailored to the client's operations. However, as noted in Exhibit 11–6, each document has a purpose which should be common across entities and is intended to assist the system designer in understanding the "why" of each form. The catchall nature of the transactions, relative to the revenue and cost of sales cycles, will result in greater variation in the form and content of documentation across entities. Exhibit 11–6 should be augmented by a formal set of journals, subsidiary ledgers, and a general ledger, routinely reconciled, as well as a management reporting system tailored to users' needs. The source documents, however, are the means by which control over summary accounting records and management reports is obtained, and they form the critical foundation of any entity's information system. The information system may be manual or computerized, but in either case, the basic information content reported in this exhibit should be available.

How to Use the forms

Match the system's forms to these source documents. Compare the source documents that have been proposed, or those that are currently being used by the entity for its financing and nonroutine transactions, to those outlined in Exhibit 11–6. A one-to-one comparison should be possible although certain forms may be combined or subdivided by an entity. Any missing forms will flag a break in the accounting trail and a possible weakness in the control system. For example, the absence of standard prenumbered journal entry forms increases the possibility

Exhibit 11–6

Assuring Complete Accounting Records—Use and Control of the Following Forms Will Assist in Recording All Valid and Authorized Financing and Nonroutine Transactions in the Appropriate Amount, Account, and Time Period

FINANCING

LOAN COMPLIANCE CHECKLIST

\# _____   Date _____

Preparer: _____

Purpose: To Document Compliance with Debt Covenants; If Noncompliance Exists, Lender Is to Be Contacted for the Purpose of Obtaining a Waiver.

Tie-in to Debt Agreement: _____

Check If Covenant Is Currently Met	Financial Statistic Restricted by Debt Agreement	Required Level	Current Level
_____	_____	_____	_____
_____	_____	_____	_____
_____	_____	_____	_____
_____	_____	_____	_____
.	.	.	.
.	.	.	.
.	.	.	.

Other Provisions: _____
_____
_____
_____

Is Entity in Compliance with the Above Provision? _____
_____
_____

Action Needed: _____

Action Approved: _____

Waiver Request Date: _____

Waiver Received: _____

Subsequent Action or Follow-up Required: _____
_____

Check & Compliance Complete: _____

Final Approval: _____

Purpose: To document compliance with debt covenants or receipt of waiver for any covenants not met.

Exhibit 11–6 (continued)

GENERAL ACCOUNTING

Date _____

CHART OF ACCOUNTS

Account Number	Account Name	Description
0010	Petty Cash	Cash in Petty Cash Funds
0020	Cash	Cash on Hand
0030	Cash in Bank	Cash on Deposit
•	•	•
•	•	•
•	•	•

Prepared by: _____

Approved by: _____

Final Approval: _____

Purpose: To document all authorized accounts for use in the financial reporting system, thereby encouraging consistency in accounting for transactions.

Exhibit 11–6 (continued)

STANDARD JOURNAL ENTRY FORM

\# _____   Date _____

Preparer: _____

Nature of Transaction: _____

_____

Supporting Documentation (attach, if possible; provide document numbers

whenever possible): _____

_____

_____

Accounts to Be Debited	Accounts to Be Credited	Amounts to Be Debited	Amounts to Be Credited
_____		_____	
_____		_____	
_____		_____	
_____		_____	
_____		_____	
	_____		_____
	_____		_____
	_____		_____
	_____		_____
	_____		_____

Approval: _____

Supervisor's Approval: _____

Purpose: To establish control over all journal entries, documenting their support and
approval.

Exhibit 11-6 (continued)

STANDARD ELIMINATION
AND RECLASSIFICATION ENTRIES

\# _____   Date _____

Preparer _____

Nature of Eliminating Entry(ies): _____

_____

Supporting Documentation (attach, if possible; provide document numbers
whenever possible): _____

_____

Eliminating entry(ies):

_____

_____

_____

_____

_____

_____

Nature of Reclassification _____

_____

Supporting Documentation (attach, if possible; provide document numbers
whenever possible): _____

_____

Reclassification entry(ies):

_____

_____

_____

_____

_____

_____

_____

Approval: _____

Supervisor's Approval: _____

Purpose: To establish control over all elimination and reclassification entries, documenting
their support and approval.

Exhibit 11–6 (continued)

**CONTROL SHEET—
CLOSING ENTRIES**

\# _____   Date _____

Preparer: _____

Closing Entries Planned	Check-off Entries as They Are Booked	Second Review
Adjusting Entries:		
Interest		
Depreciation		
Amortization		
Depletion		
Allowance for Un-collectibles		
Warranties		
Deferred Taxes		
Pension Liability		
Contingent Liability		
•		
•		
•		
Close-Out Entries:		
Revenue Accounts		
Expense Accounts		
Other Nominal Accounts		
Retained Earnings		

Reviewed By: _____

Review Date: _____

Purpose: To ensure booking of all authorized closing entries and to document the prescribed review process.

Exhibit 11-6 (continued)

REPORTING

CONTROL LISTING OF
REPORTS ISSUED

\# _____

Preparer _____

Authorization for Report Issuance	Date Issued	Report(s) Issued	Quantity	Recipient of Report	Other Details

Listing Reviewed by: _____

Date Reviewed: _____

Purpose: To establish control over all reports and to document authorizations as to who receives which reports.

- -

Other Forms That Will Be Tailored to Client Operations:

— Standard Reporting Forms
— Checklist of Additional Disclosures Required
— Standard Transaction & Consolidation Forms
— Stock Certificates
— Debentures; Notes; Commercial Paper; Similar Debt Instruments

of recording unauthorized journal entries or of omitting authorized journal entries from the books.

Compare the contents of each document. After a one-to-one match, the contents of each document should be scrutinized and compared to the format described in Exhibit 11–6.

Look for missing information. Any missing information may flag a break in the accounting trail and a related weakness in controls. For example, the existence of standard journal entry forms that are not prenumbered poses the risk of having documents lost, yet not detecting such losses through routine control procedures. Exhibit 11–6 helps to assure that controls are not overlooked and in that sense can direct you through the control procedures for financing and non-routine transactions.

Caution: A physical trail of forms may be deceptive. However, such a physical trail of forms can also be deceptive. It is always possible that despite prenumbered standard journal entry forms, the prenumbering is ineffective as a control because no one is assigned to account for the sequence of such forms. The probability that an entity will maintain a complete set of accounting records will rest largely on the presence of general control consciousness.

WHAT TO LOOK FOR WHEN EVALUATING
THE CONTROL ENVIRONMENT

The proper performance of control procedures requires that the employees understand their responsibilities. It is also essential that managers recognize control requirements and be actively involved in the development and mainte-nance of controls. As discussed in Chapters 9 and 10, the overall control envi-ronment is essentially the same for all cycles.

Checklist for Determining Whether There Is an Effective
Environment for Control

Exhibit 11–7 provides a checklist tailored to financing and nonroutine trans-actions as a reminder of the primary factors to consider in evaluating whether an entity has an environment conducive to effective control over this cycle. The quality of general control consciousness serves as a basis for predicting the plau-sibility of specific controls operating effectively and should be reviewed by the systems evaluator as one of the first steps in reviewing controls. As the systems review progresses, the results of the Exhibit 11–7 analysis should be considered and updated to reflect new information.

Exhibit 11–7

Checklist To Determine Whether There Is an Environment for Effective Control (Emphasis Is Placed Upon Financing and Nonroutine Transactions)

_____ 1. Is the organizational structure conducive to control, providing a clear definition of responsibilities and segregating the duties of authorization, custodianship, and recordkeeping?

_____ 2. Are accounting policies and procedures and job descriptions communicated via manuals?
If so, do the following manuals provide instructions as to each of the procedures delineated below?

CASH PLANNING
_____Cash Flow Budgets
_____Interface with Capital Projects, Financing, and Other Operating Departments
_____Corporate Objectives
_____Acceptable Investment Forms for Current Working Capital Balances
_____Means of Lowering Required Cash Balances for Operations

FINANCING MANUAL
_____Lender Selection Criteria
_____Requirements to Compare Available Sources of Capital
_____Desired Debt-to-Equity Mix
_____Coordination of Borrowing and Financing Activities with Operating Departments
_____Negotiation Procedures
_____Long-term Planning to Facilitate Future Borrowing and Stock Issuance
_____Debt Convenants—Acceptable Restrictions
_____Deviations from Established Procedures

GENERAL ACCOUNTING PROCEDURES MANUAL
_____Documentation Requirements
_____Authorized Levels of Approval
_____Follow-up Responsibilities
_____Required Report Forms
_____Supplementary Disclosure Requirements
_____Consolidation Procedures
_____Currency Translation Techniques
_____Dissemination of Reports

INTERNAL AUDITING STANDARDS & PROCEDURES
_____Organizational Status
_____Reporting Responsibilities
_____Access to Records and Assets
_____Objectives
_____Communications with Auditees
Audit Procedures, Including:
_____• Programs
_____• Working Papers
_____• Statistical Sampling
_____• Computer Auditing Techniques
_____• Control Evaluation Approach
_____• Compliance Test Work
_____• Substantive Test Work
_____• Dual-Purpose Testing
_____• Operational Audit Procedures
_____Interface with External Auditors
_____Interface with Other Third Parties
_____Code of Ethics
_____Actions When Fraud Is Suspected or Detected

Exhibit 11-7 (continued)

_____ 3. Are personnel selection methods, company training programs, supervisory practices, and performance evaluation techniques conducive to control, providing assurance that an adequate number of employees are available to perform both operating and control duties related to financing and nonroutine transactions?

_____ 4. Are vacations mandatory, and are provisions made for competent replacements to perform all of the assigned duties of the vacationing employees?

_____ 5. For positions of trust, are employees' duties rotated, including bookkeepers' rotation among the various ledgers? (Note that cash on hand should be counted and reconciled before rotating custodians, and similar accountability checks should be invoked prior to rotation of other jobs.)

_____ 6. Is Board designation of authorized approvers of financing activities and general journal entries required and are signature files of authorized personnel maintained?

_____ 7. Is fidelity bonding insurance coverage adequate? (Employees handling cash, investments, and similar valuables should be bonded.)

_____ 8. Are there provisions for reasonable protection against fire, explosion, other natural disasters, and/or malicious destruction of records, of processing facilities, and of other assets of the entity? Such provisions should include adequate loss-of-records insurance coverage as well as adequate insurance coverage of assets. Backup files for EDP records are essential and should be stored at an off-site location.

_____ 9. Is access to cash, financing and accounting records, and critical forms—both issued and unissued—permitted only in accordance with management criteria which reflect control objectives (i.e., is access limited to those persons whose duties require such access)?

_____ 10. Is record retention adequate?

_____ 11. Are accounting data periodically reviewed, tested, and compared to budgets, variance and exception reports, and nonfinancial reports generated outside of the accounting department by internal auditors or by individuals who are independent of generating the accounting data? Do operating personnel rely on such data for decision-making?

_____ 12. Are recorded balances of cash and similar related transaction activity periodically substantiated and evaluated through physical inventory confirmation and through a review of legal documents? Are the adjusting journal entries that result consistent with an adequate control environment?

UNDERSTANDING OF UNDERLYING TRANSACTIONS IS AN IMPORTANT ASPECT OF MOVING TOWARD WELL-CONTROLLED OPERATIONS

The financing and management of equity areas of operations are increasingly complex, creating real challenges to managers and those striving to create a well-controlled environment for decision making. Given the rapidly changing environment, a critical aspect of such control is education of decision makers as to what is and is not known about proposed actions. A few examples of recent developments in our understanding of economic transactions will be provided to illustrate the use of such knowledge in proposed decisions. Control in such judgmental decision areas must come largely in the form of a support system that ensures decision makers are knowledgeable and take advantage of the information available to enhance their evaluation of options.

Contracting

In the process of administering legal aspects of transactions, personnel involved in this nonroutine cycle may face queries such as whether to become involved in a joint venture opportunity or whether to enter a particular type of contracting arrangement. As depicted in Exhibit 11–8, any class of transactions poses a number of unique questions that need to be answered to evaluate the attractiveness of a particular contracting opportunity. A new line of business may be fraught with pitfalls of which decision makers are unaware. An effective control structure will include a set of guidelines on approaching such new lines of business or novel transactions which ensures an adequate understanding and information set to reach a well-reasoned decision.

Exhibit 11–8

Things to Look for in a Franchise Contract

1. Does it cover all aspects of the franchise agreement such as training and management advice?
2. Can it be renewed? Are there additional fees at the time of renewal?
3. Can the franchise be transferred? Do you need permission from the franchisor?
4. When can a franchisor buy back a franchise? How is the price determined?
5. Under what circumstances can a franchise be terminated? How much notice must the franchisor give before terminating?
6. Is a certain size of operation specified?
7. Is there an additional fixed payment each year?
8. Is there a percentage of sales payment? Is it fair?
9. Must a specific amount of material be purchased? From a specific source?
10. Can the franchisee engage in other business?
11. Is arbitration used to settle disputes?
12. What is the term of the contract?
13. Does the franchisee have exclusive rights to a territory? For how long?

Leo G. Lauzen, "Franchising: Another Strategy to Start Your Own Business," *Management Accounting* (July 1984), p. 53.

Letters of Credit and Bankers' Acceptances

Frequently trade is desired between two firms which are widely separated, meaning that the shipment of goods from one firm to the other would require several weeks. In negotiating such a trade, a stalemate can arise due to the seller being unwilling to ship goods until he knows he is going to be paid and the buyer being just as unwilling to pay until he knows the goods have been shipped. The method of financing which has arisen to eliminate this stalemate is the Letter of Credit. The buyer can apply for a Letter of Credit as he would request any unsecured loan. Upon approval, the bank would issue a Letter of Credit addressed to the seller which agrees to pay the seller, on the buyer's behalf, the stated sum of money when the seller delivers the documents evidencing shipment to his bank, according to the documentation requirements and payment terms of the Letter of Credit. Thus the buyer is given the prestige and financial backing of his bank. As is typical, clients utilize irrevocable Letters of Credit, meaning modification or cancellation can take place prior to the expiration date only with the consent of all parties to the Credit. While payment "at sight" of the documents can be specified, companies typically specify time drafts—payment a certain number of days (not exceeding 180) after the presentation of the documentation of shipment. These time drafts result in the creation of Bankers' Acceptances. When the seller presents shipping documents which fulfill the requirements of the Letter of Credit, the seller's bank writes on the face of the time draft the word "accepted" to indicate the bank has accepted the obligation to pay the seller and the authorized persons at the bank sign the draft. The date and place payable are also indicated. Such a Banker's Acceptance represents a short-term investment for which a secondary market exists; therefore, a seller desiring immediate payment can sell the Acceptance at a discounted price.

The journal entry on the books of the client to record purchases from foreign manufacturers is

    Dr.   Freight-in
    Dr.   Letters of Credit and Acceptances Expense
         Cr.   Acceptances Payable
         Cr.   Accounts Payable—Shipper

A commission is charged by the bank for both Letters of Credit and Bankers' Acceptances; these charges should be appropriately recorded as an expense item. Further, if the client indirectly pays for the discount on Acceptances incurred by the seller in order to obtain immediate payment by means of paying a higher price for the goods purchased, this interest expense should be properly segregated and reported appropriately.

These activities create control needs from an accounting and information perspective. Irrevocable letters should have deadlines, required documentation for use should be detailed, and related costs should be analyzed, to ensure optimal financing approaches.

Dividends

Turn to Exhibit 11–9 for a set of potential explanations and problems with such explanations regarding dividend policy. Before determining the dividend declaration, participants in the decision process should be aware of the factors thought to be relevant or irrelevant, based on research and conventional wisdom to date.

Exhibit 11–9
Competing Explanations of Why Dividends Exist and Related Problems With Each Explanation

Explanation: Investments are risky and dividends hedge against the possibility firms will go bankrupt before distributing those assets that have been saved up to the stockholders.

Problem: No bird-in-the hand results since investors often reinvest dividends in stock.

Explanation: Dividends signal companies' well-being, promoting confidence, higher stock prices, and more investment capital.

Problem: Why not use other cheaper methods of signalling? Why would people believe the signal when it's just as easy and rational for poor firms to declare dividends as it is for effective firms?

Explanation: Different investors have different preferences for dividends, creating a clientele effect.

Problem: Investors should prefer capital gains to dividends (or be indifferent) and given the costs of paying dividends and having to raise new capital, the clientele effects are not intuitively persuasive.

Exhibit 11–9 (continued)

Explanation:	Dividend payments force companies to raise capital, which subjects managers to monitoring by the capital markets.
Problem:	Why wouldn't other monitoring devices be used instead of dividends?

Explanation:	Dividends push debt-equity ratios up, preventing the transfer of too much wealth from stockholders to bondholders. Dividends are ex post adjustments for imperfect expectations.
Problem:	Why not renegotiate terms in some other manner?

Source: Frank H. Easterbrook, "Two Agency-Cost Explanations of Dividends," *American Economic Review* (Vol. 74: 650-9, September 1984).

ESOPs

Another example of a vehicle being used in a variety of settings is the leveraged ESOP that is usually accomplished by adopting an Employee Stock Ownership Plan, establishing a related trust, and then having the ESOP borrow needed cash from a lender, with the company guaranteeing such loan and committing to repay. Shares are commonly used as collateral for the loan, with the ESOP trust paying cash to the company for stock of equal value. Annual tax-deductible cash contributions to the ESOP trust are made by the company to facilitate amortization of the loan, with the trust paying the lender upon receipt of contributions. The overall effect is that the loan proceeds are available to the company and stock is transferred first to the ESOP trust and then allocated to employees, usually in a manner tied to the loan repayment. This is one of the three-party transactions mentioned in the opening paragraphs of this chapter that will be revisited later.

Leveraged ESOPs have been discussed as a joint employee benefit plan and financing tool. Motivation of employees, deterrent to potential takeovers, and effective financing whereby pre-tax dollars can be used to pay off ESOP loans are among the advantages frequently cited. However, the verdict is still out as to the return on ESOPs, as suggested by the evidence summarized in Exhibit 11–10. The only statistically significant finding was that ESOP firms in which the non-managerial employees participate in corporate decision making through work groups and committees were observed to improve in productivity, relative to the pre-ESOP period. Of course, no clear causal link could be established. Beyond

Exhibit 11–10

Table I.1: Prior Studies on ESOPs and Corporate Performance

Study	ESOP sample	Comparison	Measure	Finding Improve	Finding Significant
Profitability:					
Conte and Tannenbaum (1978)	Some non-ESOPs	Industry Averages	Pretax Profits to Sales	Yes	No
Tannenbaum, Cook and Lohman (1984)	Some non-ESOPs	Matched Firms	Pretax Profits to Sales	No	No
Livingston & Henry (1980) Brooks, Henry, & Livingston (1982)	Stock Purch. Plans	Matched Firms	Nine Profitability Ratios	Neg Ests[a]	Mixed
Hamilton (1983)	In One Industry	Matched Firms	Net Profits to Net Sales	Some Yrs	No
			Net Profits to Net Worth	Some Yrs	No
			Net Profits to Net Capital	Some Yrs	No
			Net Sales to Net Worth	Yes	Some Yrs
Bloom (1985)	Publicly Traded	Matched Firms	Gross Return on Capital	Mixed Est	Mixed
		Matched Firms and Before and After	Gross Return on Capital	Yes	No
Productivity:					
Marsh and McAllister (1981)	Only ESOPs	Industry Averages	Compensation to Sales	Yes	NR[b]
Hamilton (1983)	In One Industry	Matched Firms	Net Sales per Employee	Yes	No
Bloom (1985)	Publicly Traded	Matched Firms	Sales per Employee	Mixed Est	Mixed
		Marched Firms and Before and After	Sales per Employee	Mixed Est	Mixed
Growth Rates:					
Rosen and Klein (1983)	Some non-ESOPs	Industrial Sector	Employment	Yes	NR
Bloom (1985)	Publicly Traded	Matched Firms	Employment	Neg Ests	Yes
		Matched Firms and Before and After	Employment	No	No
Trachman (1985)	Some in High Technology Firms	High Techn. Firms	Employment Sales	Yes No	NR NR
Quarrey (1986)	Only ESOPs	Matched Firms and Before and After	Employment Sales	No Yes	NR Yes

[a]Negative estimates are only noted if statistically significant.

[b]Not Reported

Source: GAO/PEMD-88-1 ESOPS and Corporate Performance, "Employee Stock Ownership Plans: Little Evidence of Effects on Corporate Performance," (October 1987), Appendix I, p. 47.

some question regarding benefits, disadvantages to ESOPS exist, including: the limit on deductions to generally 25% of payroll, administrative costs, equity dilution with related decline in earnings per share, and repurchase obligations to participants. If the control structure were lacking in ensuring decision makers' appreciation of such pros and cons, then the design of that structure would be flawed.

Treasury Stock

As just mentioned, repurchase obligations can arise, creating the whole question of treasury stock, its potential uses, and related effects on one's own market position.

The major effects of treasury stock buybacks include tax effects of cash distributions, an influence on investment and financing decisions, and the dissemination of information to investors. Buybacks can also reflect conflicts of interest between the holders of different classes of securities.

Related accounting questions are what effects do buybacks have on earnings per share, percentage of equity outstanding, or the recording of accounting for mergers, options, or other compensatory vehicles?

Prior research has documented these conclusions:

—significant positive returns are realized by common stockholders of repurchasing firms within one day of the repurchase announcement.

—the positive value changes in common stock are generally permanent increases.

—although an increase in stock prices subsequent to repurchase announcements is observed, after the execution of the repurchase, stock prices move lower, though not as low as before the announcement.

—owners of convertible securities also realize positive effects from stock buybacks. (All classes of securities receive some benefit).

—most firms repurchasing their own shares through a tender offer are small, closely held firms and this has been interpreted as a signal by such firms in lieu of raising dividends.

—results for open market purchases are less conclusive.

—stock repurchase announcements elicit significantly higher price responses than do dividend announcements.

Four hypotheses have been in the literature regarding theories underlying the repurchase of one's own stock:

—DIVIDEND HYPOTHESIS whereby firms pay a premium to the redeeming stockholders which is a sort of dividend.

—LEVERAGE HYPOTHESIS which holds that repurchases of stock on borrowed funds rather than with internal financing results in a tax subsidy which increases share value by the present value of the accrued tax savings.

—BONDHOLDER EXPROPRIATION HYPOTHESIS which predicts that the rise in stock prices is at the expense of bond prices (although research to date indicates that the negative effect on bond prices is mitigated by the positive information effects).

—SIGNALLING HYPOTHESIS which holds that buybacks are means of transmitting information about the firm to both shareholders and potential investors. Note that since repurchases are expensive, it is believed that only firms with relatively larger undervaluations would use this signalling device. It is also noted that most repurchased common stock is reissued through stock options and deferred pension plans. Such a transfer of stock from outsiders to insiders is seen as positive.[4]

Again, this type of research evidence and conventional wisdom is what is needed as a part of the supporting information system for decision makers. This information can be accessed in a variety of ways, including establishing liaison with various consulting specialists with whom decision makers are encouraged to converse as part of the quality control system.

International Settings

Beyond understanding the nuances in a technical sense of sophisticated transactions, the scope of the decisions now prevalent include numerous international dimensions. Due to the interplay of culture, political, and economic factors, a facet of control has to be the training of personnel to appreciate the context of international decision making and the types of processes likely to be effective. While offered in a humorous tone, the examples of why business was lost in various international settings, as described in Exhibit 11–11, bear out the need for education. The various decision makers' understanding is a critical component of control structure.

Do Employees Understand Control Policies?

An understanding of control is essential to the effective performance of control procedures. In performing internal audit activities, professional staff should con-

---

[4] Theo Vermaelen, "Common Stock Repurchases and Market Signalling," *Journal of Financial Economics* (9; 1981), pp. 183–193, and adapted from Jacqueline Power, "Stock Buybacks: The Effect on Stock Prices," Texas A&M University Ph.D. Paper (1987).

Exhibit 11–11
The Intricacies of International Business:
Causes of Lost Business

- In Tokyo, decisions are made by large teams, scrutinizing details. If a negotiator can't answer their questions, he will lose face.
- In Riyadh, a businessman
  —sat back in his chair and exposed the sole of his shoe and this constituted an insult,
  —then passed documents with his left hand, which Muslims consider unclean, and finally
  —refused coffee, implying criticism of the host's hospitality.
- A businessman in the Far East used a rubber stamp on the back of the business card to translate to the native tongue; the firm's slogan was similarly printed. Yet, the absence of the same quality print on both sides of the card was viewed as an insult, and the slogan was viewed as over aggressive.
- An American businesswoman in Europe overlooked the exchange of business cards and was considered impolite.
- An American accountant doing business in Western Europe dressed in synthetic fabrics, wore a stupid tie, and had several pens and pencils in his front pocket. Only natural fibers are accepted; synthetics cause one to be viewed as a yokel. Ties that are copies of regimentals cause ill feelings and clutter in one's front pocket is considered unsightly.
- A businessman in Latin America shook hands as usual, not realizing that handshakes last about twice as long there and pulling one's hand away too fast creates an impression of rejection.
- An American made a strong-selling presentation, with several jokes integrated, to Europeans. He made a couple of adverse remarks regarding competitors, referred to some local industry gossip, and related information gained in a personal conversation the prior day. The results were devastating: the jokes weren't understood, knocking the competition was viewed as gauche, and the repeating of private conversation was interpreted to mean that the American could not be trusted. Madison-Avenue-style hype does not do well with Germanic, Nordic, and British peoples; dispassionate objectivity emphasizing facts is far more effective.
- Not attentive to the fact that Arabic is read from right to left, a pictoral sequence of a U.S. marketer of laundry detergents showed soiled clothes on the left, the product in the middle, and clean clothes on the right. Arabs interpreted this to mean that the detergent took clean clothes and left them soiled!
- The assumption that Spanish words with identical spellings have identical meaning throughout Latin America is erroneous. The Parker Pen Company designed ads for its ballpoint pen called Bolla, meaning "ball" ac-

Exhibit 11–11 (continued)

cording to the dictionary, only to discover (IN TIME) that this term, depending on the region, also meant a revolution, a lie, or an obscene gesture. Other companies have not been so fortunate in timely detection of similar problems.

Adapted from Neil Chesanow, *The World-Class Executive*, "How To Do Business Like a Pro Around the World," *Macmillan Executive Summary Program* (Vol. 2, No. 3, March 1986), pp. 1–8.

---

sider the risk profile of various areas of operation and proceed to perform the most effective and efficient review possible.

EXAMPLE: While one entity's internal audit department reviews existing internal controls before performing substantive audit tests, in most instances audit personnel rely on prior knowledge of the particular operation and do not alter the established audit scope.

SOLUTION: The review of internal controls utilizing appropriate questionnaires, flowcharts, and related documentation can provide a sound basis for determining the scope of audit test work. The audit emphasis would then be on those areas with weaker internal controls, with correspondingly less time expended on areas with stronger internal controls. Current procedures suggest a certain lack of understanding by internal auditors of the auditing process.

EXAMPLE: Similarly, another entity's internal audit staff relied upon the treasury department's explanations for bank account reconciliations in preference to examining evidence themselves. The role of the auditor and the importance of objective strong forms of evidence are apparently not understood by the professional staff.

The most common problem with comprehension as it applies to financing and nonroutine transactions is with respect to generally accepted accounting principles. The following situation is far too common.

EXAMPLE: A company did not allocate a portion of its cost of shares to the stock that was received in a stock dividend or stock split. Unless the entire issue is sold in the same accounting period, the gain or loss on the sale of such issues will be misstated. The company should allocate an appropriate portion of the costs of an issue of stock to shares of that issue which are received in a stock dividend or a stock split.

SOLUTION: To improve the control environment, employees should be encouraged to check with the company's controller whenever they are uncertain as to the appropriate accounting treatment for a transaction. In addition, continuing education of accounting employees should be encouraged, and internal auditing should be requested to review those account areas that may pose difficulties to personnel in determining the appropriate recordkeeping process. The standard journal entry forms should require approval, with particular emphasis on account distribution and the manner in which charges have been calculated.

The improper application of a particular control-related procedure or employees' apparent ignorance of controls as they perform operating and accounting duties implies an ineffective control environment in the sense of checklist items #2, 3, 4, and 11 of Exhibit 11–7.

Be Alert for Sloppy Application of Controls

Of course, employees may understand controls yet be sloppy in applying such controls. The result can be the destruction of a potentially adequate control system.

EXAMPLE: A wholesaler of durable goods has redeemed shares that have not been effectively canceled nor are they completely endorsed; frequently they are endorsed in blank and on the back of the certificate by the original owner.

SOLUTION: Redeemed certificates should have complete endorsements and be clearly and effectively canceled on their face to prevent reuse of the certificate. Canceled certificates should be attached to the related issue stubs in the stock certificate book and the remaining open stubs balanced periodically to the general ledger. The fact that some certificates were canceled suggests that the employees were aware of a control procedure; they were simply careless in applying the procedure.

Accounting Practices

A similar problem can arise with accounting practices.

EXAMPLE: A company accounted for its treasury stock in a variety of ways, including charging the entire balance against retained earnings.

SOLUTION: Generally accepted accounting principles reflecting the intent of management, upon acquisition, should be applied to treasury stock transactions. The result will be a retained earnings balance that is more reflective of actual operating results over the years. In addition, treasury stock and capital stock accounts will more properly reflect stock repurchases.

The inconsistent application of accounting methods reflects sloppy performance. As a minimum, the employees could research the manner in which treasury stock transactions were most recently applied and be consistent with past practice. Of course, more importantly, the established practice should comply with generally accepted accounting principles.

Sloppy Use of Budget or Activity Schedules

At times, the sloppy application of controls comes in the form of the sloppy use of a budget or activity schedule.

EXAMPLE: The internal auditor's schedule should be realistic and attainable, designed to encompass all significant areas of operation. However, the internal audit department did not conduct all the scheduled audits, hence all the critical operations have not been reviewed.

Had the activity schedule been well designed and applied with care, the entity would have assurance that its most critical operations were effectively reviewed.

The sloppy application of controls would be reflected by mixed responses to items #1, 2, 3, 6, 8, and 9 on Exhibit 11–7. In addition to control problems created by employees' misunderstanding of procedures or their sloppy application of controls, significant problems in maintaining effective control are created by the inadvertent or purposeful circumvention of control.

Check for Circumvention of Existing Controls by Employees

The overall effectiveness of control will depend on the employees' intentions to comply with the substance of the control techniques being applied, regardless of the ease with which the controls could be circumvented.

Ineffective controls over nonroutine transactions. For example, a certificate of incorporation can be viewed as one means of maintaining existing capital structure and ensuring compliance with protective convenants in loan agreements.

> EXAMPLE: A company has a debt agreement that requires capital structure not be changed and cash dividends not be paid without prior consent by the lender. Last year the company altered its certificate of incorporation to change its authorized capital structure and to issue its special "class B" stock to certain officers of the company. Cash dividends were paid to the holders of the special stocks.

> SOLUTION: The lender could declare the loan to be immediately payable or could accelerate the due-date of the loan. The lender should be notified as to the facts and a waiver on these provisions should be obtained.

The ability to change the certificate of incorporation, that control that was perceived to ensure compliance with existing debt agreements, resulted in no control over such debt covenants. Apparently, the entity has assumed that officers' stock and related dividends are sufficiently different from the other stock outstanding that they need not be considered when evaluating compliance with debt covenants.

It is all too common to justify not applying a procedure or not complying with set controls due to the "unusual or nonroutine" nature of the transaction, yet it is imperative that control over such transactions be just as effective as control over routine operations. Employees should be encouraged to process all nonroutine transactions just as similar routine transactions are processed. Hence, cash receipts from sales of property are processed through the same system as cash receipts from sales. Cash disbursements for investments are processed in a manner similar to cash disbursements for purchases. Transactions involving officers' stock are subjected to the same controls and check procedures as other investors' stock. The circumvention of routine controls for unusual transactions can substantially increase a company's risk exposure.

Controls That Are Not Applied

Sometimes a designed control is effectively circumvented simply by never applying that control.

EXAMPLE: Although internal audit has an audit program for each engagement, the completion of the steps on the audit program is not supported by either initials or the signature of the auditor performing the procedure. Since the audit program is an integral part of any audit, a signed or initialed copy of the audit program should be filed with the audit working papers for each audit performed. The advantages to signing or initialing the audit program steps include

—creating a permanent record as to who has performed the audit work,
—eliminating the possibility of missing an audit step, and
—when more than one auditor is included, minimizing the possibility of duplicating procedures.

The internal auditors have effectively circumvented the control of "sign-offs" on audit programs.

Available Controls Are Not Instituted

A similar "circumvention" occurs when an available control, common at most entities, is not designed or instituted.

EXAMPLE: An internal audit director did not have professional staff maintain time records; as no billings were made within the entity, no such detail was required.

Yet informal time records that summarize man-hours per major audit area reflect the department's involvement in audit activities, facilitate the evaluation of audit emphasis, and signal the need for realignment of efforts and resources. Time records are also useful for job planning and control.

A control environment can effectively deter the omission and effective circumvention of key controls by requiring that personnel be adequately trained and that their job responsibilities be clearly delineated. Affirmative replies to items #1, 2, and 3 of Exhibit 11–7 are required for an effective control setting.

To demonstrate the types of questions one might pose to detect omitted controls in the treasury function, consider Exhibit 11–12.

Telltale Signs of Control Problems

If signs of control problems were not flagged in the course of initially completing Exhibit 11–7, subsequent audit procedures that are applied in order to gain an understanding of controls and the effectiveness with which they are being applied may flag a problem. For example:

—How committed does management appear to be to maintaining effective control?

Exhibit 11–12
Key Internal Control Questions Related to the Treasury Function

—Is there a clear definition of the treasury function?

—Where are the securities owned by the corporation stored, and how are they protected?

—Where can a complete listing of all of the bank accounts of the corporation, both foreign and domestic, be obtained?

—Have levels of authority regarding the expenditure of funds by various corporate officers and other executives been clearly established?

—Has provision been made for fidelity bond insurance to cover company personnel?

—Has provision been made to ensure that employees in sensitive control areas are rotated periodically and that they are taking annual vacations? Is the separation of duties in these areas adequate?

—What provision has been made for periodic inventory or confirmation of securities?

—Have specific policies been set forth in writing regarding the uses which may be made of surplus funds?

—Has provision been made for continuing or periodic review of general routines and safeguards over cash, including surprise counts?

—Has provision been made for periodically reviewing the services furnished by the banks and the charges, if any, for those services?

—What are the established criteria for selecting banks?

—Are reconciliations of all bank accounts performed regularly?

—Is there a provision for investigating the background of new employees?

—Have rules in regard to conflicts of interest been established and published?

—Are there written procedures which cover the treasury function?

Source: Adapted from CIA Examination (The Institute of Internal Auditors), May 1978, Part II, Question 31, Solution p. 17.

—How is this commitment reflected in the allocation of resources?

—Have objectives of the company with operating and control implications been set in a consistent manner?

—Have legal requirements been considered and met by management?

—Have tax laws been considered in decision making?

Each of these questions, if answered in the negative, implies some inadequacies in the information system of management and its commitment to control. These inadequacies could well be telltale signs of control problems.

EXAMPLE: An entity requested that its external auditors assist it in the preparation of a detailed internal audit program. However, the responsibilities of the internal auditor were not considered a full-time duty. Accordingly, the time of the individual given the title of "Internal Auditor" has been consumed by numerous special projects. Therefore, no phase of the internal audit program has been implemented.

SOLUTION: If the entity is to accomplish its objectives, a full-time position should be established for the internal audit function.

EXAMPLE: A well-defined investment program recognizes three risks:

—unsafe investments,
—lack of liquidity, and
—inadequacy of interest return, relative to the cost of funds.

Sometimes a company will add other considerations to the development of an investment program. For example, some companies resolve to maintain a portion of funds as an investment in minority-owned credit unions. Yet when this policy was followed, the target interest requirements were not met. For example, certain credit unions have paid no dividends for over two years.

SOLUTION: Try to avoid conflicting resolutions, and monitor consequences of set policies.

EXAMPLE: A company's affiliate did not meet legal requirements that its net assets be equal to at least one quarter of the issued capital stock.

SOLUTION: Either the company should be dissolved, or management should take action within the three-year period permitted by law to meet the requirements.

EXAMPLE: A bank had apparently not considered paying a stock dividend, in spite of an excessive balance in undivided profits. The present money and capital tax laws are uncertain; however, unless the bank anticipates paying dividends with the balance in undivided profits, there is no clear reason to maintain the balance at its present size, thereby risking tax exposure and related difficulties.

Telltale signs of control problems may be flagged by mixed responses (as Exhibit 11–7 is updated by information gained in the course of the review and testing of controls) to items #1, 2, 3, 8, 9, 10, 11, and 12.

Weigh Telltale Signs of Control Problems Against Risk Exposure

However, such telltale signs of control problems may not translate into errors and the loss of control. Compensating controls may exist for observed flaws in the control system. The key questions are what types of errors and irregularities can occur and what procedures exist to prevent or detect these errors and irregularities. The completion of Exhibit 11–7 raises questions as to potential problems but does not assess the entity's risk exposure.

GUIDELINES FOR ASSESSING RISK EXPOSURE

As described in Chapters 9 and 10, three major risks exist for an entity's control system:

(1) it loses valid documents, failing to record the underlying transactions, or it permits bogus documents to enter the data base;

(2) it inaccurately records transactions; or

(3) it permits the removal of assets.

What Can Go Wrong—and How to Prevent or Detect Errors and Defalcations

These three risks are presented in Exhibit 11–13 along with those controls that are typically present in a control system to reduce such risks. This general list serves as a reference in selecting controls, and is as applicable to financing and nonroutine transactions as it is to the cycles described in Chapters 9 and 10. Caution: Remember, as emphasized in the prior chapters, that some redundancy of control procedures can enhance control; however, few entities would require all the controls cited in Exhibit 11–13. In fact, were all of the procedures instituted, operating efficiency would probably suffer. However, a basic set of controls over financing and nonroutine transactions is critical to all entities.

Critical Sources of Risk

Financing and nonroutine transactions pose three primary areas of risk as delineated in Exhibit 11–13.

(1) the employee in charge of cash management conceivably could misappropriate assets,

(2) those involved in general journal entries could cover up a misappropriation of assets if safeguarding controls were inadequate, and

(3) financial statement representations could be in error due either to mistakes or to intentional fraud.

In general, the cash receipt and disbursement controls, as well as the checks and balances in record keeping, should be sufficient to prevent or detect the extraction of resources and the accounting cover-up of such an extraction of assets or financial misrepresentations to third parties. The systems evaluator must recognize that these critical sources of risk exist and that the key controls—or some compensating controls that meet the same control objective—as outlined in Exhibit 11–13 are needed to prevent or detect an error or irregularity.

Risk evaluation for the purpose of assigning internal audit resources has been considered in a number of company settings along a variety of dimensions. It seems that the top priority is to consider the results of prior audits as a risk indicator. A fraud or formal exception in the form of a major audit finding in a prior audit would indicate the potential for serious problems. A second consideration that merits attention are changes in management. Often change weakens control and increases the need for increased scrutiny. In particular, changes in management may be accompanied by changes in other personnel, lines of business, and systems.

Hand-in-hand with the above two risk indicators is the control environment

Exhibit 11–13

What Could Go Wrong and What Controls Can Preclude or Detect Such Errors and Defalcations?

The Risk Profile of Financing and Nonroutine Transactions

GENERAL TYPES OF RISKS AND RELATED CONTROLS TO REDUCE THESE RISKS

Loss of Documents or Input of Bogus Documents

- —Authorization Procedures
- —Competent Employees
- —Segregation of Duties
- —Batch Controls
- —Systematic Stamping of Time and Date on Documents Upon Receipt
- —Systematic Filing of Documents
- —Filing of Support Documents with Related Vouchers and Journal Entry Forms
- —Sign-out Log When Documents Are Removed from an Area
- —Set Policy of Only Permitting Copies of Documents to Leave the Filing Area
- —Stamping of Duplicate Invoices or Creditors' Statements for Financing Transactions
- —Clear Voiding and Retention of Documents
- —Cancellation of Used Documents
- —Accounting for Numerical Sequence
- —Periodic Inventory of Unissued Forms
- —Matching of Key Documents
- —Follow-up on Unmatched, Unpaid, Unreceived, and Open Items
- —Periodic Independent Tests, Both Vouching and Retracing

Inaccurate Recording of Transactions

- —Authorization Procedures
- —Competent Employees
- —Segregation of Duties
- —Utilization of Performance Measures Conducive to Accurate Reporting
- —Batch Controls
- —Clerical Checks of Original Documents and Intermediate Summaries
- —Validity Checks
- —Limit Checks
- —Review of "Was-Is" Reports (to Summarize, for Example, Changes to a Master File)
- —Exception Reports
- —Tickler Files for Accruals (Chronological Reminders of When to Record What Entries)
- —Independent Review of Journal Entries and Postings
- —Independent Reconciliation of Subsidiaries to Controlling Accounts
- —Comparison of Independently Generated Reports Such as Those Generated By Transfer Agents, Trustees, and Creditors
- —Reconciliation of Stock Agent's Statements to the General Ledger
- —Quick Follow-up on Lenders', Stockholders', and Others' Complaints
- —Confirmation of Asset Balances Held Elsewhere, Including Collateral Held by Lenders and Trustees
- —Utilization of Imprest Basis Funds

Removal of Assets

- —Authorization Procedures
- —Formal, Well-Controlled Hiring Practices
- —Segregation of Duties
- —Access Restrictions and Physical Safeguards— Particularly over Documents That Can Easily Be Converted to Cash, Such as Paid-Up Life Insurance Policies
- —Tighter Controls over Highly Liquid Assets
- —Tighter Controls over Items That Are Easily Pilferable, Due to Their Size and Mobility
- —Use of a Security Department, Well Trained as to Means by Which Defalcations Have Occurred in the Past
- —Automatic Accounting Checks and Balances
- —Periodic Reconciliation of Books-to-Physical-Cycle-Counts

Exhibit 11-13 (continued)

CRITICAL SOURCES OF RISK FOR FINANCING AND NONROUTINE TRANSACTIONS AND CONTROLS INTENDED TO REDUCE SUCH RISK

What Could Go Wrong?	Key Controls to Prevent or Detect Extraction of Resources	Key Controls to Detect Accounting Cover-Up
CASH ON HAND OR ON DEPOSIT COULD BE MISAPPROPRIATED	—Require a Surprise Count by an Independent Party of Those Funds That Are Controlled by the Employee Who Is Entrusted with Cash Management. —Require an Independent Test of Supporting Documents for Account Transfers, Deposits, or Withdrawals Initiated by the Employee Who Is Entrusted with Cash Management.	• Require an Independent Party to Compare Recorded Activity in the Cash Account with Detailed Records. • Require an Independent Party to Test the Detailed Cash Transactions.
TANGIBLE ASSETS COULD BE MISAPPROPRIATED	—Institute Safeguarding Procedures for Storage and Movement of Assets.	• Require an Independent Party to Periodically Compare Tangible Assets to Detailed Property Ledgers. • Require an Independent Party to Periodically Review General and Adjusting Journal Entries That Affect Property-Related Accounts.
FINANCIAL POSITION COULD BE MISREPRESENTED	—Comply with Recordkeeping Control Procedures to Prevent Misrepresentation to Creditors, Stockholders and Other Third Parties; Misrepresentations Can Result in Liability Claims and the Disruption of Operations Due to Demands by Creditors for Immediate Payment.	• Establish an Internal Audit Department and Require That the Professional Staff Review Financial Representations. • Undergo an Examination by External Auditors.

of various operations. A control culture is conducive to reduced risks. Of course, a related consideration is how complex the operations are which are being controlled and what implications that complexity has for the monitoring process. Different products, services, processes, eclectic information systems and technologies in place, and the extent of standardization and documentation of controls are among related considerations.

The size of the business, related to materiality of operations, is always a risk consideration, in tandem with the time since the last audit of a particular function or project, since both relate to potential exposure. Alongside these two pragmatic risk indicators are qualitative evaluations of the auditors' confidence in operating management and the belief of both managers and the auditors that a particular auditee's operations are politically sensitive. For example, one might ask: what would be the implications if a particular type of finding were to arise and then be publicly disclosed? Environmental issues, employee and pension related matters, officers' salaries, and related areas may lie in such a domain.

Auditing the Financing and Administrative Cycle's Related Accounting Estimates

The auditor is required by GAAS to evaluate the reasonableness of clients' accounting estimates in the context of the financial statements taken as a whole. Both subjective and objective factors should be considered by the auditor with an attitude of professional skepticism, especially in relation to subjective factors. SAS 57 identifies the following examples of accounting estimates related to the financing and administrative cycle:

Financial Instruments:	Accruals:
—Valuation of Securities —Trading Versus Investment Security Classification —Probability of High Correlation of a Hedge —Sales of Securities with Puts and Calls	—Compensation in Stock Option Plans and Deferred Plans Litigation: —Probability of Loss —Importance of Loss[5]

The manner in which control structure can be helpful in containing risk exposure related to accounting estimates is discussed in Chapter 9.

---

[5] AICPA, SAS 57, "Auditing Accounting Estimates" (New York, AICPA: April 1988), p. 8.

Controls for Prevention and Detection

The timeliness of detection and the preferability of prevention controls over detection controls are important considerations of an evaluator in performing a systems review. For example, the record-keeping checks and balances provide preventive and prompt detection controls over financial representations, whereas internal and external audits are directed at the detection of errors and irregularities. Although the threat of an audit and the increased risk of discovery may deter a fraud, the audits themselves do not have any other *a priori* preventive power. Many would take issue with the idea of classifying audits as controls, since they tend to serve as a check function. However, they are likely to be the sole check (albeit limited) on intentional misrepresentations by top management. The important use of Exhibit 11–13 is in identifying those special controls that are critical to overseeing financing and nonroutine activities and the implied risk exposure from either not having these controls or finding, through control related test work, that they are ineffective.

CONSIDERING OPERATING EFFICIENCY: COMMON PROBLEMS AND PROVEN SOLUTIONS

The evaluation of controls involves gathering in-depth knowledge of operations, assessing the entity's risk exposure, and suggesting ways in which the entity might be more effective and efficient in exercising both accounting and operating control over transactions. As financing and nonroutine transactions are considered, numerous operating problems are found to be common, and various solutions have been implemented and found to be effective in both profit-making and not-for-profit entities. Several of these problems and solutions are presented in Exhibit 11–14.

Anticipating Control Needs So They Can Be Met

Many times the problem is one of knowing how to anticipate control needs so that they can be efficiently met.

EXAMPLE: An important task for internal auditors of banks is the review of employees' savings accounts, since these pose greater risk exposure than the typical customer's account. The numeric listing of savings accounts, however, does not lend itself to a feasible method of identifying which savings accounts in the file represent employee accounts. The identification process will take a period of time to complete.

SOLUTION: Had the control problem of related parties been considered when the savings account numbers were assigned, significant time savings may well have resulted.

Exhibit 11–14

Operating Efficiency Considerations—Means of Enhancing Operating and Internal Controls and Responding to Common Problems Encountered in Financing and Nonroutine Transactions

MANAGING CASH BALANCES

PROBLEM: The optimal strategy for planning working capital and investment policies has been difficult to determine.

SOLUTION: Keep in mind that liquidity, security, and profitability are relevant in selecting the appropriate investment mix. Many entities have found it useful to hire consultants with industry experience to compare their working capital investment mix to their competitors' mix. Beyond the type of investments that are advisable, ways of minimizing working capital commitments by

—offering cash discounts,
—tightening credit standards, and
—using lock boxes at dispersed locations with one-day deposit to a central location

warrant consideration. CPAs can assist clients in such analyses.

RECORDKEEPING/SYSTEMS

PROBLEM: Errors have been made in reporting taxable income as tax exempt and vice versa.

SOLUTION: Maintain detailed records of the exempt and nonexempt earnings.

PROBLEM: The calculation of the monthly amortization of unearned discounts on mortgages for both book and tax purposes is a time-consuming process.

SOLUTION: Rather than making such calculations manually, use a computer with a subsequent manual review for reasonableness. Clerical errors will decline and efficiency will improve.

PROBLEM: Many systems are being automated without effective control.

SOLUTION: Accounting and EDP personnel should coordinate to assure that the transition occurs smoothly. It is important that internal controls be carefully monitored throughout the process to determine that no weaknesses go undetected or unaddressed. Internal audit personnel should be assigned to review all procedural changes for this new systems package and a formal procedure should be adopted to have internal audit review all new financial systems that are implemented to insure that there are no deficiencies in internal controls. Such reviews should occur prior to the utilization of a new system in order to prevent inefficient changes after installation. In addition, an environmental audit should be performed of the new computer facility.

Exhibit 11–14 (continued)

INTERNAL AUDITING

PROBLEM: Operations are geographically dispersed and difficult to control.

SOLUTION: Create a full-time internal audit department to objectively appraise the company's operations and to evaluate and report on accounting procedures, financial data, and the extent of compliance with management policies at each location.

PROBLEM: The expense of an internal audit department is such a substantial cost that management is hesitant to establish such a position.

SOLUTION: To justify the expense, utilize a profit center approach, whereby the internal audit department is required to justify its budget by demonstrating profitable results that it has helped to produce throughout the company when the audit department's suggestions are adopted.

PROBLEM: The internal audit staff's abilities and experience are not commensurate with the duties assigned.

SOLUTION: Initiate an educational program both in-house and via continuing educational courses. To avoid similar difficulties in future hiring, specify the desired level of education, training, and work experience for job applicants to qualify for the position. The past policy of hiring new college graduates should be altered to ensure that the department's expertise is complemented with experienced personnel.

PROBLEM: The internal audit department has been rather disorganized in its activities.

SOLUTION: Prepare and utilize a long-range plan as to the department's manpower requirements, scope and timing of financial and operational audits, attendance at training schools, and assistance to the independent auditors in performing the entity's year-end audit and reviewing the entity's internal controls. Clear criteria should be established as to how internal auditors can be used. Short-term plans should be prepared annually to support long-range plans. The budget process that identifies immediate requirements can be the vehicle for the annual short-term plans by expanding them to include training, hiring, and other requirements. These annual plans can then be used to monitor the degree of accomplishment made each year.

PROBLEM: Reports by internal auditors do not appear to carry much weight with the auditees.

SOLUTION: Send copies of the report to the Audit Committee of the Board of Directors to insure managers' follow-up.

PROBLEM: Internal audit reports seem to be ineffective.

SOLUTION: Require that auditees evaluate and investigate the reported findings and recommendations and submit a detailed response to management. Internal auditing should appropriately follow up previously submitted reports to determine that recommendations are being implemented and errors or deficient procedures are being promptly corrected.

Exhibit 11–14 (continued)

PROBLEM: A company has experienced problems with its sales quotation practices and its service departments.

SOLUTION: Operational audits of sales quotations could be designed to determine if sales quotations are being used on a timely basis, are thorough, and are responsive to the prospective customer's needs. Operational audits of service departments could be designed to determine if written reports are being prepared for all service calls and whether such reports are sufficiently complete to provide adequate information to ascertain the warranty position of the equipment being serviced.

PROBLEM: The time and expense of both internal and external audits are continually growing.

SOLUTION: Appoint an audit coordinator. This individual should have a substantial understanding of accounting and the ability to produce results on a timely basis by exercising authority at an interdepartmental level. Original data like new loan agreements and corporate minutes should be gathered, audit schedules prepared, and explanations obtained for auditors' inquiries.

PROBLEM: A company has to reach a decision as to whether to acquire other companies.

SOLUTION: Have the internal audit department perform acquisition reviews and assist in the financial evaluation of acquisition prospects.

PROBLEM: Currently, the internal audit department is engaged in numerous activities which ordinarily would be considered outside its scope of operations. These activities include maintaining the books and records of the company, determining minimum lease rental payments for inclusion in the annual report, and other activities which preferably would be handled and coordinated by the internal audit department.

SOLUTION: The internal audit department should have a separate "charter," spelling out its responsibilities, objectives, functions, et cetera, so that internal audit does not become engaged in these nonaudit areas. The charter should be approved by upper management so that the internal audit department is seen as an integral part of the company.

EXAMPLE: During the year a new loan agreement was consummated that contains numerous and complex covenants. The controller or his designee should monitor these covenants on a monthly basis to prevent defaults and to obtain timely waivers in the event of default. To facilitate timely and complete monitoring, a checklist of the various debt covenants should be made available so that the employee can efficiently perform assigned duties.

SOLUTION: The monitoring problem can be anticipated at the time the complicated debt agreement is negotiated. Concurrent preparation of a control checklist by the negotiator will insure its completeness and potential effectiveness as an efficient monitoring device. Similar time saving is possible from planning for employees' efficient use of information concerning trust agreements.

EXAMPLE: Trust agreements were on file, but the abstracts of such agreements were not available. Substantial time efficiencies can be realized from not having to refer to formal trust agreements when questions arise. The abstracts should be reviewed by legal counsel and by the treasurer before they are placed in the files.

SOLUTION: Not only can day-to-day operations be aided by considering time savings when preparing information sources, but one-time or periodic activities like internal auditors' confirmation procedures similarly can accrue savings through careful planning of various means by which operating and control needs can be merged.

EXAMPLE: Bank auditors primarily use positive confirmations for asset accounts and negative confirmations for liability accounts.

SOLUTION: To save money, a negative-type rubber stamp or a separate card insert could be used, to confirm sections of the annual mailings of the savings accounts' information returns and the mortgage statements.

Often, entities overlook simple ways of integrating operating and control procedures and fail to draw upon available resources to accomplish these procedures' objectives. For example, entities can use their Controller's Department to actively participate in the review and evaluation of the company's system of internal controls, but they often fail to do so. By considering the specific suggestions in Exhibit 11–14 and being aware of ways of efficiently combining operating and control duties in a manner that minimizes conflicts between such procedures, the systems evaluator can enhance those operations that relate to financing and nonroutine transactions.

CREATIVE FINANCING

Creative financing has emerged in a number of corners of the economy in the 1980s and 1990s, often including the offering of new financial instruments. These instruments blur the distinction of debt and equity and are often directed toward intentionally combining attributes of both types of securities. Due to the inexperience with some of these instruments, related risks are often uncertain.

Leveraged buy-outs (LBOs) in the 1980s, in particular, often involved the use of higher proportions of debt financing that virtually ensured the need for liquidations of certain aspects of the business merely to meet debt service requirements. The term "management buy-out" (MBO) is used when managers are the purchasers of the business, frequently taking a company private and then later returning the company to a public status. A number of reasons may exist for MBOs including a threat of takeover, a desire to avoid regulatory barriers to certain planned restructuring activities, or an entrepreneurial goal set by managers. MBOs frequently entail cutbacks and minimization of administrative costs, since the contention is that when managers become owners, many of the traditional agency or stewardship problems are eliminated.

A threat that emerges as novel financing approaches are adopted is that risk exposures will not be effectively identified and necessary controls will fail to be implemented. A control structure is needed that guides a decision maker to evaluate, document, and periodically check performance. Moreover, cost-cutting must concurrently give attention to controls. While a change in the incentives of the participants in an organization clearly justifies some restructuring, controls are intended to address unintentional errors as well. In other words, detective controls in order to know when an error is made and its implications remain important even in owner-manager operations.

Due to the nature of unique financial packages and leveraged buy-outs, a number of diverse risks will emerge: debt covenants restricting certain types of activities may very well be more foreboding than usual; risks attendant to "fire selling" of assets or business branches to create liquidity can be substantial; and reporting problems can lead to regulatory attention due to the informal guarantees, in-substance defeasance actions, and equity-debt hybrid instruments that must be classified on the balance sheet but appear not to "fit"—hence, the "mezzanine section" as defined by the Securities and Exchange Commission for redeemable preferred stock. A risk analysis framework should be in place to ensure careful attention to each major risk and a proposed means of continually monitoring such risks.

THREE-PARTY TRANSACTIONS

One trait of creating financing is an increasing incidence of transactions that have more than the traditional two parties involved. For example, the in-substance defeasance arrangement alluded to earlier involves a business that borrows from one party and then, in lieu of paying that party back directly, chooses to place the present value of future payments to the lender, in the form of low-risk securities, in the hands of a third party. The advantages to the borrower include convenience, control of timing of the financial statement effect, and removal of the debt from the face of the balance sheet. Yet, in stark contrast to the tradition of an arm's-length transaction underlying most numbers in the financial statements and involving negotiation of two parties on either side of a transaction, this setting does not require the consensus of the borrower and lender. Moreover, if the third party is selected by the borrower, which is likely to be the case, added risk can emerge regarding the appropriate asset transfer and investment requirements. While contingency obligations can still provide some protection to the lender, the nature of the implicit controls of the transaction process have no doubt been altered. This is suggested by the observation that the SEC declared a moratorium on in-substance defeasance from August 1982 until December 1983. This was lifted only after the Financial Accounting Standards Board had issued FASB Statement No. 76.

As three or more parties participate in a number of economic transactions, attention needs to be directed to supplanting lost implicit controls with a set of control processes that ensure the reasonableness of the decision and a monitoring of its consequences. To provide an example of how the absence of such a system can result in excessive risk for an entity, consider a bank setting. A particular company has been told that credit is not available from the bank due to the risk exposure of that industry. When the company confers with a major customer, that entity agrees to borrow money for financing, contingent on certain conditions that virtually make the original company the borrower, in substance. Yet, the bank analyzes the credit prospect of the customer, not realizing how dependent that customer is on the supplier who the bank earlier judged to be too risky to extend credit. Such a triangular arrangement can result in far underestimated risk exposures by the bank, hidden debt financing for the supplier, and a bit of a sham transaction in terms of the apparent borrowing posture of the customer. Off-balance sheet financing, such as the possibilities cited in Exhibit 11–15 should be familiar to decision makers who are assessing their own and others' risk exposure. A similar example is provided by the article reprinted in Exhibit 11–16, which describes swaps and the related problems in effectively evaluating banks' risk position. A later chapter will describe asset securitization, which

Exhibit 11–15

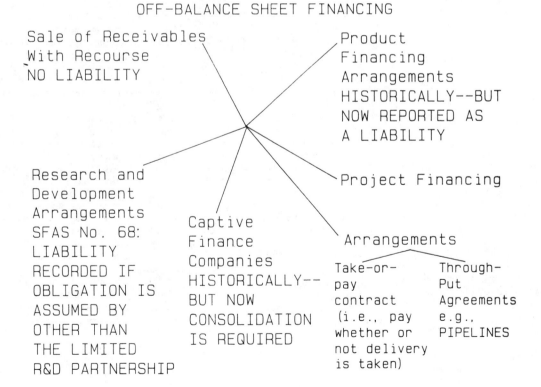

OFF–BALANCE SHEET FINANCING

Sale of Receivables With Recourse NO LIABILITY

Product Financing Arrangements HISTORICALLY––BUT NOW REPORTED AS A LIABILITY

Research and Development Arrangements SFAS No. 68: LIABILITY RECORDED IF OBLIGATION IS ASSUMED BY OTHER THAN THE LIMITED R&D PARTNERSHIP

Captive Finance Companies HISTORICALLY–– BUT NOW CONSOLIDATION IS REQUIRED

Project Financing

Arrangements

Take-or-pay contract (i.e., pay whether or not delivery is taken)

Through-Put Agreements e.g., PIPELINES

Exhibit 11–16

Liability management by means of swaps

Swaps provide a market in liabilities which enhances the ability of borrowers to reduce exposure to the risks arising from interest-rate movements. This market in liabilities allows company treasurers to manage liabilities as well as assets. Steward Hughes and Keith Redhead discuss the swaps explosion and suggest that this new market may have left some banks heavily exposed to risks of default.

One of the most dramatic developments in the financial world during the 1980s has been the growth of swaps. Withing five years the swap market has developed from nothing to a business worth hundreds of billions per year.

Swaps are exchanges of liabilities. A borrower with a floating-interest-rate liability may seek to exchange it for a fixed-interest-rate liability, or a borrower with a debt denominated in one currency may want to exchange it for one denominated in another currency. Swaps may be motivated by attempts to gain from views as to the future courses of interest rates or exchange rates, or by the desire to hedge the risk of adverse movements of interest or exchange rates.

We shall concentrate on the hedging potential, although the speculative uses will be readily apparent.

Hedging interest risk

Floating-rate loans expose the debtor to the risk of increases in the interest rate. A debtor may wish to avoid this risk by taking out a fixed-rate loan but find that, owing to insufficient credit standing, he is unable to borrow at fixed rates or can only do so at a particularly high rate of interest. The borrower could obtain funds on a floating-rate basis and attempt to swap the floating-rate liability for a fixed-rate liability, thereby obtaining fixed-rate funds.

The swap may be carried out directly between the two liability holders or may involve a bank as intermediary. In the latter case the bank might take the role of counter-party to both participants, thereby bearing the risk of default by either party and eliminating the need for the participants to investigate the creditworthiness of the other. This has the additional advantage of allowing anonymity of the parties. It also facilitates swapping by debtors of relatively low credit-worthiness.

Figure 1 illustrates a case in which a bank operates as intermediary.

Borrower A has taken a loan from lender A at a floating rate of interest but would prefer the certainty provided by a fixed-rate loan. The bank agrees that it will provide borrower A with the funds required to pay the interest on the floating-rate loan and accept interest payments at a fixed rate. Lender A is unaffected, his debtor continues to be borrower A and interest payments continue to be received from that source. Lender A need never know that the swap has taken place. Meanwhile borrower A has simulated a fixed-rate liability.

The bank seeks to match its commitment by finding a fixed-rate borrower (B) wanting to swap a fixed-rate liability for a floating one, perhaps because borrower B expects interest rates to fall. Borrower B agrees to pay interest to the bank on a floating-rate basis whilst receiving interest on a fixed-rate basis, the latter being used to meet the fixed-rate commitments to lender B. By swapping borrower B simulates a floating-rate loan whilst lender B retains both its fixed-rate receipts and its original debtor. In effect the two borrowers service each other's debt via the bank.

If the bank is unable to find a borrower B which can be matched with borrower A, it may take over the role of borrower B itself. The bank would thus borrow at a fixed rate and swap its liability with borrower A. The bank effectively converts its fixed-rate debt into a floating-rate one whilst borrower A converts a floating-rate debt into a fixed-rate one.

When acting as counterparty to both borrowers, whether or not it has taken the role of borrower B, the bank faces the risk that a borrower could default. A default would leave the bank exposed to an interest rate risk. The remaining customer may be receiving a high rate of interest and paying a low one. The original matching allowed losses from transactions with one customer to be offset by the corresponding gains from the deal with the matched customer. Once one of the two counter-parties defaults the bank is exposed to the possibility of losses, and indeed it seems that a customer from whom the bank is making gains is the most likely to renege on its agreement.

The danger is also present where the bank has taken the role of borrower, since the bank could find itself paying a high fixed rate to lender B whilst receiving a low rate of return from the funds raised.

Accounting aspects

Swaps are somewhat different from other instruments of financial risk management in that they involve a company in swapping one group of costs for another group of costs. These arrangements therefore need to be reflected in the financial statements in the usual manner. Since in this case the company is attempting to hedge interest rate risk, it is entirely appropriate that the resulting revenues and expenses should appear in the accounts on an accruals rather than a cash-flow basis. Thus interest payments and receipts arising from the swap transaction should be included in the income statement as they are earned and incurred rather than when they are paid and received.

These simple types of interest-rate swap arrangements commit each party to the agreement to the payment of the interest cost on the other party's borrowing. Thus, in so far as the income statement is concerned, the interest cost on the other party's borrowing over the relevant accounting period will be charged to the profit and loss account on an accruals basis. These swap arrangements will clearly affect the income statements of both parties to the swap and also that of any intermediary to the swap such as a bank. This is illustrated in the following example.

Let us assume that a commercial company whose fixed interest charges on its loan amount to £100,000 over a particular accounting period has made a swap arrangement with a manufacturing company whose variable interest charges on its loan over the same accounting period turn out to be £90,000. The swap takes place through an intermediary such as a bank, which charges a swap arrangement fee of £1,000 to each company.

In such circumstances, the commercial company's profit and loss account would be charged with the £90,000 interest payment on the manufacturing company's loan in

Exhibit 11–16 (continued)

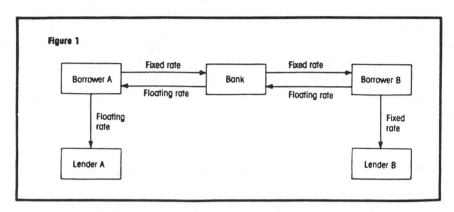

Figure 1

Profit and loss extract for commercial company		
Interest on its own loan		£100,000
Less: Payment received from bank under swap arrangement	(£100,00)	
Plus: Payment made to bank under swap arrangement	£90,000	
Plus: Swap arrangement fee	£1,000	
		(£9,000)
Amount charged to profit and loss account		£91,000
Profit and loss extract for manufacturing company		
Interest on its own loan		£90,000
Less: Payment received from bank under swap arrangement	(£90,000)	
Plus: Payment made to bank under swap arrangement	£100,000	
Plus: Swap arrangement fee	£1,000	
		£11,000
Amount charged to profit and loss account.		£101,000
Profit and loss extract for bank		
Net interest payments made to commercial company under swap		
(£100,000 − £90,000)		(£10,000)
Net interest payments received from manufacturing company under swap		
(£100,000 − £90,000)		£10,000
Swap arrangement fees		£2,000
Gross profit from swap		£2,000

addition to its own swap arrangement fee of £1,000. The manufacturing company would similarly be charged with the £100,000 interest payments of the commercial company along with its own swap arrangement fee of £1,000. The income statement of the bank would, of course, reflect both these transactions. Thus, the profit and loss account extracts of the commercial company, manufacturing company and bank would appear as shown here.

Swaps provide a market in liabilities which enhances the ability of borrowers to reduce exposure to the risks arising from interest rate movements. Swaps have been agreed for periods of as much as 30 years into the future and hence provide scope for hedging over much longer periods than futures, options and FRAs allow for. This market in liabilities allows company treasurers to manage liabilities as well as assets. However, the explosive growth of this very new market may have left some banks heavily exposed to risks of default. ☐

Source: Steward Hughes, "Liability Management By Means of Swaps," *Management Accounting* (January 1987), pp. 42, 43.

involves more than two parties and poses risks of the nature described herein. Substance over form is an important concept throughout business and accounting.

Control systems need to be in place that maintain the credibility of the information system on which decision makers rely. These must include attention to "other parties," sometimes unnamed in the contractual arrangement, that create attendant risks to a particular transaction. A control process that requires explanations and representations as to how funds are to be used and includes corroboration of business relationships with other parties is the type of approach conducive to a successful achievement of control objectives.

ADDITIONAL INSIGHTS

An Appendix to this chapter lends additional insights. Due to the substantial risk exposure associated with check fraud, Exhibit 11–17 provides details on means of deterring such fraud. Exhibit 11–18 provides a control checklist for investments, securities, and real estate holdings, while Exhibit 11–19 clarifies those types of corporate actions that typically require stockholders' approval. Exhibit 11–20 provides additional examples of tests of controls and related objectives for the financing and nonroutine transactions cycle.

APPENDIX

Exhibit 11–17

Deterring Check Fraud

Check fraud is estimated to cost business more than $4 billion every year. Not only does it exceed fire loss, but it is more than four times armed robbery. Handwritten checks are easily altered as to

- payee's name
- amount
- signature

Many type-written and computer-generated checks are likewise vulnerable.

Check protection systems can be vulnerable if impressions are weak or signature imprints are too simple. Such systems are enhanced through use of custom name die, macerated amounts, exclusive ink cartridge use, locked in security, and check positioning guards with automatic repeat/clear. Engraved signature plates with intricate design patterns stifle forgery.[6]

To protect the payee's name, some systems, after the check is written, macerate through the name with pin-hole perforations the word "warranted." This ensures there is no smooth area on which to write, virtually precluding alterations. To protect check amounts, dollar amounts are perforated through the check and printed with indelible ink that is absorbed by paper fibers to make alterations difficult. Similarly, signatures can be protected by using a hand engraved plate that macerates the signature into the check with pin-hole perforations and by using "live" indelible ink. For computer checks, the check signer can automatically macerate an embossed pattern over the amount area.[7]

Other pointers for crime stopping include: spelling out company and incorporated since these are too easy to adjust in their abbreviated form and filling the space for payee with a line if not filled by the payee's name. Court cases have found

"The maker of check is obliged to use all due diligence in protecting it . . ."

Leather manufacturers' Bank vs. Morgan, Et. Al., 117 U.S. 1196.[8]

---

[6] Described in brochure of F&E Check Protector Company, College Station, Texas, 1986.

[7] F. E. Hedman brochure, "4 Billion Dollar Check Fraud Folio," Chicago, Illinois (1985).

[8] Further information of possible interest is E. E. Hoffman, *Billion Dollar Check Racket* (3rd Edition, 1976), Renway Publishing Co. [Library of Congress No.: HG1696.H6 332.9 62-16034].

Exhibit 11-18

Control Checklist for Investments, Securities, and Real Estate Holdings, with Related Objectives

	Yes	No
1. Validity: Does the entity maintain documentation to support account entries, e.g., broker's advice and journal entries?	___	___
2. Completeness: Is an investment security ledger maintained, detailing all securities held and all security transactions?	___	___
3. Accuracy: Is the investment security ledger regularly balanced to the general ledger with respect to both principal and accrued interest totals?	___	___
4. Safeguarding and Proper Period: Have procedures been established to ensure prompt collection of all coupon interest income or other income due on the investment security portfolio? (*Note:* This relates to the revenue cycle.)	___	___
5. Accuracy, Validity, and Disclosure: Are there established procedures to identify related parties, including any association between brokers and officers, directors or employees?	___	___
6. Authorization and Safeguarding: Have procedures been established to control the officers' authority to purchase and sell securities?	___	___
7. Validity: Are routine legal procedures followed that will produce valid titles, and evidence thereof to all property?	___	___
8. Accuracy: Is real estate promptly appraised?	___	___
9. Safeguarding: Is a current appraisal obtained for real estate to be sold, as a basis for establishing a sales price?	___	___
10. Existence and Valuation: Are properties periodically inspected?	___	___

	Yes	No
11. Existence and Valuation: Do inspections indicate both the condition of the property and its occupancy status?	___	___
12. Safeguarding and Valuation: Are maintenance procedures in effect, ensuring that properties will retain their market value?	___	___
13. Classification: Are separate subsidiary records maintained to each parcel, documenting items capitalized expenses, rentals, and the like?	___	___
14. Accuracy and Completeness: Are subsidiary ledgers for real estate balanced monthly to the general ledger?	___	___
15. Completeness and Validity: Are complete files maintained for each parcel of real estate?	___	___
16. Safeguarding: Is effective control maintained over rental income? (*Note:* This relates to the revenue cycle.)	___	___
17. Propriety: Does the entity's advertising for the sale or rental of real estate holdings comply with regulations including governmental agencies' advertising guidelines?	___	___
18. Safeguarding: Are agents bonded who manage properties and collect rent?	___	___
19. Safeguarding: Are security deposits properly controlled?	___	___
20. Safeguarding: Are negotiable securities held under dual control?	___	___
21. Safeguarding: Is the accounting function separate from the security transactions?	___	___
22. Existence and Completeness: Are negotiable securities periodically counted and verified with the general ledger?	___	___

Exhibit 11–19

Corporate Actions That Typically Require Stockholders' Approval and Should Be Recorded in Minutes of Stockholders' Meetings

- Election of directors.

- Stock issuances and retirements.

- Stock voting arrangements.

- Authorization of new classes of securities.

- Waiving of preemptive rights.

- Sale of all or significant parts of business.

- Merger of business.

- Significant acquisitions of other companies.

- Meeting arrangements.

- Stock option, bonus, or profit-sharing plans for key personnel.

- Selection of independent auditors (unless delegated to board of directors.)

- Amendments to articles of incorporation and bylaws.

- Liquidation of corporation.

Exhibit 11–20

Examples of Tests of Control and
Related Audit Objectives and Questions

Audit Question to Which Test May Relate	Tests of Control
Completeness: Are stock certificates controlled so as to ensure accountability over all such certificates?	Ascertain whether stock certificates are prenumbered and account for their numerical sequence.
Safeguarding: Are unissued and redeemed securities controlled to prevent unauthorized use?	Examine evidence of effective control over redeemed notes and bonds, canceled equity securities, and unissued securities.
Completeness: Are all issues and dividends recorded?	Trace documentation of stock issues and dividends to record.
Completeness and Accuracy: Are all proceeds and disbursements recorded?	Trace proceeds and disbursements to records, and check their accuracy.
Proper Period: Does the client have controls to ensure timely payment of debt obligations?	Review client's calendar of principal payments and interest payments.
Safeguarding: Are controls over dividend payments effective, or is there a substantial risk of excess payment?	Examine policies regarding use of imprest bank account for dividend payments, and test compliance with such policies.
Authorization: Are charges to equity accounts authorized and accurate?	Review summary of changes in equity balances, recompute, test for board of directors' approval, and reconcile to the entity's records.
Propriety and Safeguarding: Is there regulatory or legal exposure for improper financing activities?	Review lawyer's opinion that the entity's equity and debt issuances have complied with the state's and the SEC's requirements.

12

How to Handle Control Concerns Unique to Computer Systems

"A computer does not substitute for judgment any more than a pencil substitutes for literacy. But writing without a pencil is no particular advantage."

Robert McNamara[1]

As implied by the quote, computers are likely to be an indispensable part of economic enterprise which continually require thought and attention from a control perspective if they are to achieve the objectives of a well-run entity.

The advent of the computer has posed some unique control concerns for you as an auditor. In many cases, electronic data-processing (EDP) systems combine incompatible functions, making it necessary to have compensating controls to restrict the ability of employees or other parties to commit and effectively conceal errors or irregularities. Determining who is performing a particular accounting or control function is not always simple in an EDP setting. Typically the programmer who prepared the related program is considered to be the party performing the function. However, that programmer may change positions within

---

[1] Edited by James Charlton, *The Executive's Quotation Book: A Corporate Companion* (New York: St. Martin's Press, 1983), p. 63.

the entity and may have key responsibilities in an area for which (s)he also prepared computer programs. The time period over which the programmer is considered to be performing control checks can be extremely long and can complicate the evaluation of whether or not duties are incompatible.

The segregation of duties implies that personnel in a position to perpetrate errors do not also perform functions that make it possible for them to conceal their errors. Due to the concentration of control procedures and accounting data for numerous operating cycles within the EDP department, weaknesses can have far greater audit significance than would be the case for a manual system.

Since EDP systems have data recorded in machine-sensible form, rather than in visible manual records, it is possible for someone to alter the data files without leaving any evidence. An EDP system's information, which is relatively invisible without the use of a computer, is analogous to a set of books in a foreign language which must be interpreted before the "represented facts" are visible, or a diamond inventory which has to be examined by a qualified appraiser before its value can be known. Just as the interpreter's and appraiser's objectivity and qualifications would have to be established prior to using the interpreted or appraised "output," the computer's interpretation of the data files and the processing of interest must be determined to be reasonably reliable. Hence, data's invisibility demands that alternative auditing techniques to those appropriate in a manual setting be applied.

The use of printed reports as a basis for performing audit procedures is likely to be precluded by the sheer volume of data being processed by an entity. Hence, computer-assisted audit techniques are typically essential for the efficient performance of tests of control. Besides, the invisibility of the audit trail will probably constrain the usefulness of any printed report that might be generated for your review.

HOW EDP AFFECTS THE AUDITOR'S EXAMINATION

An important consideration in assessing how EDP affects your examination is the availability of data (1) used to enter information into the computer, (2) retained in data files, and (3) generated for output. Your data needs may not be met in other than machine-readable form. Or the period in which the data exist may be too short for you to utilize effectively. If information is entered directly onto the computer, input documents may not even exist. You must determine how the client's documentation practices and data retention procedures affect the timing of audit procedures; special requests for data retention may have to be made. During the planning phase, the availability of data for *substantive testing*, *sampling*, and *analysis via computer-assisted audit techniques* warrants special consideration. Often data that relate to management decision-making, although not basic accounting records, can be of particular use in performing analytical procedures. Of course, you must be reasonably satisfied that the information is reliable before you use it as a basis for audit reliance.

The invisibility of information also creates the chance that errors that would be obvious to people reviewing the data and related transactions will be missed by the EDP system, due to shortcomings in the program and built-in edit checks. When an error is made in an EDP environment, particularly in programming, the effects of such an error are potentially much greater than any single error in a manual system. "Invisible" rounding errors can result in millions of dollars being lost. Not only are the raw data and related information invisible without the assistance of a computer, but also most control procedures for computer systems are invisible in the sense that no documentary evidence of the procedures' performance is typically available, as it would be for a manual system. For example, programs related to accounts payable will frequently match purchase order, receiving report, and vendor invoice information as a basis for "approving" vouchers for payment, yet leave no visible evidence that such documents were properly matched.

Reviewing the Controls over the Maintenance and Processing of Programs

You must obtain reasonable assurance that the computer program performing programmed control procedures has not had unauthorized changes made to it during the period under review *before* reliance can be placed upon programmed controls. Therefore, you will review the controls over the access to and changing of computer programs before proceeding to review the programmed control procedures. Interdependent controls should be evaluated in the most efficient manner to ensure that detailed review and control test procedures are not wasted. Once you have gained assurance that there are adequate controls over the maintenance and processing of computer programs to which the test data are being submitted, the test work on detailed control procedures can proceed.

Testing controls. If in the EDP environment there is visible evidence that procedures were performed—such as the documentation of program changes for each EDP application and approval of those changes, as well as computer-generated error listings or other correction reports—then tests of control are performed in the same manner as for a manual accounting system. However, if visible evidence is lacking, the tests of control will require such techniques as the use of test data. The test deck should try to trigger the key checks in the application program to determine that the control procedures are in operation for the computer process. At times, generalized audit software can be applied to existing data files to detect error conditions that should have been detected by programmed controls.

Tracing errors. Tracing an error, particularly assigning responsibility for an error, can be much more difficult in an EDP system than in a manual system. This problem can be made more troublesome by the "multiple record" conditions in some EDP systems. Since a voucher register can be produced by ledger account, vendor, or in aging sequence, the question can be posed: which is the voucher register and do all multiple records have identical contents? Finally, the very nature of EDP systems makes changes to such systems expensive, if not implausible, making it necessary to anticipate information and control needs at the point in time that the EDP systems are designed and initially implemented.

This multiple record problem is likely to become more acute with the advent of the microcomputer. An executive may pull a portion of a data base from the mainframe onto a micro for adjustment and evaluation purposes and forget to update the adjustments on the main computer system. Two sets of books can evolve: the one in use for decision making on the micro and the one that is accessible to all other parties and used for other operational and reporting purposes. As the rate of growth of microcomputers is considered, the multiplicity of records can be predicted to be a growing problem in establishing control over EDP.

Key Characteristics That Distinguish Computer Processing from Manual Processing

Characteristics that distinguish computer processing from manual processing and their effect on control risk assessment include the following:

1. The nature of transaction trails—the chain of evidence that connects account balances or other summary results to original transactions and calculations. Such trails may only exist in computer-readable form or may exist for only a short period of time within an EDP environment.
2. The uniformity with which transactions are processed. The random errors expected in a manual system are virtually eliminated while programming errors will systematically generate incorrect results for all like transactions that are processed.
3. The manner in which duties are segregated. The EDP activity will commonly combine duties that would typically be segregated in a manual system, and to achieve control, other procedures are necessary in an EDP setting. These procedures include the establishment of a data control group intended to prevent or detect processing errors or irregularities and the segregation of duties within the EDP group. In particular, the segregation of EDP from user department personnel and the establishment of controls over the access to data and the computer programs are important mitigating controls.
4. The potential for errors and irregularities from unauthorized access, the absence of visible evidence that the system, program, or data file has been accessed, and the decreased involvement of people who might be capable of spotting problems. The period over which problems remain undetected can be extremely long.
5. The potential provided by EDP for management to exercise greater supervision over operations through the use of analytical tools.
6. The computer's ability to initiate and/or execute transactions automatically. Authorizations and control procedures may not be documented in

a manner that is analogous to that of a manual system. Often the application program has limit and reasonableness checks to assure the execution's consistency with management's specific and/or general authorizations.

Some Knowledge of EDP Is Essential

In auditing a computer environment, you are not permitted to "audit around the computer." In other words, the computer cannot be treated as a "black box" under any circumstances. You must gain some knowledge of EDP activities in order to form a decision regarding auditing procedures to be performed and the degree of your reliance on controls involving EDP applications. The extent of knowledge gained need not be in-depth. The degree of depth will be strongly correlated with the significance of EDP applications. Significance relates to how material the effect of errors or irregularities in EDP activities would be on the financial statements under examination.

Note: An important consideration in evaluating the significance of applications is to remember that the EDP procedures performed both "in-house" and by outside service centers are relevant.

All these attributes of EDP systems and related audit procedures suggest control concerns that imply

—increasing training needs for CPAs and others who conduct audits,

—differing control evaluations and related testing procedures from a manual system,

—complementary evaluation and testing procedures for service centers,

—greater involvement by auditors in EDP systems designed to ensure
  • the establishment of an audit trail that facilitates the tracing from summary to transaction documents and vice versa,
  • adequate control checks,
  • reasonable compensating controls where the combination of incompatible controls is deemed to be unavoidable, and
  • sufficient competence in clients' EDP staff to ensure adequate system maintenance and control.

The latter point can be a major stumbling block, particularly when clients believe that their acquisition of a minicomputer does not demand the services of knowledgeable EDP personnel.

THE MINICOMPUTER—NOT A MINI-CONTROL PROBLEM

A minicomputer is difficult to define with the rapidly changing hardware and software technology in EDP systems. Some contend the term should be replaced by microcomputer, while others contend that the growing capabilities of micros justify their classification as minicomputers. This latter term is emphasized in this handbook, although it is intended to encompass micros. In contrast to defining hardware, a minicomputer environment is comparatively easy to define:

—the minicomputer is typically located in a user department rather than in an EDP department,

—the minicomputer has little if any physical security,

—the staff operating the minicomputer is small and frequently has rather limited EDP expertise,

—the programs used on the minicomputer are typically application systems supplied by the manufacturers or software houses, rather than being developed in-house,

—most of the input is entered from an online terminal device and may be edited, verified, and balanced as it is entered,

—the user's staff input most of the data, typically through terminal devices, and

—most data files are available for inquiries and direct updating.

Due to the lack of personnel trained in computers, care should be taken to

• document data processing procedures to be followed and
• appropriately train personnel.

File errors arise from four main sources:

1) loading incorrect files;
2) machine failure;
3) incorrect re-run procedure; and
4) incorrect data.

These, in part, can be addressed through training.

Physical security can be enhanced by log-on procedures and by disabling the microcomputer for data processing by removing critical software each night and restoring it each morning.

A useful control is to design data processing applications with printouts at frequent intervals which have control totals that can be (and are) traced to the general ledger accounts. All files should carry control totals of the following information:

• number of records on file;
• age of records;
• average access—hit rates;

- obsolete—slow moving records; and
- number of additions/deletions since earlier date, possibly since generation.

Auditors can ask for printouts of files on the system, use retrieval packages, and take advantage of the computer to write programs.

The result of such a minicomputer environment is a relative absence of any segregation of duties. Often, by simply sitting at a terminal a user has access to the entire data base of a company and can

—initiate transactions,

—record transactions,

—have effective custody of the company's assets, and

—alter files with no record of having used the system.

A rigid (hard) disk is used for system software and programs in use, with auxiliary storage on flexible floppy disks.

---

* Since backing up files is a separate task, it may not be done unless the organizational procedures and controls are properly supervised; steps include:

- properly label backup diskettes
- store backup diskettes in a separate secure location
- control use of backup diskettes to restore files via supervisory personnel
- assign a library function to a person with other compatible duties

---

Microcomputers or personal computers are used in:

- Planning
- Accounting Functions
- Decision Analysis
- Maintaining Local Files
- Word Processing
- Statistical Analysis

Typically, microcomputers are used for specialized data processing in large organizations, and a wide range of data processing in smaller organizations—including inventory, accounts receivable, payroll purchasing, and general ledger, as well as word processing for correspondence and reports. Computers replace bookkeeping machines or manual recording. Electronic worksheet applications support a wide variety of accounting functions. Micro uses entail

- —Analytical Procedures
- —Audit Sampling
- —Internal Control Review and Evaluation (Risk Assessment)
- —Flowcharting
- —Workpapers
- —Graphics

Standards for the control of computer applications should be written and published in the organization. The standards should cover

- software design
- control levels and audit trails
- access levels
- categorization of confidentiality
- operational procedures
- file handling procedures and security
- output control standards
- contingency arrangements[2]

Establishing Effective Controls over Minicomputers

The problem is a combination of the lack of physical security, uncontrolled access, and the high probability that computerized controls are absent from the operating systems and application programs, which conceptually would have been capable of monitoring the use of the minicomputer. Hence a minicomputer is not a mini-control problem. In fact, the control objectives of an entity with an EDP system are analogous to those of an entity with a minicomputer, yet the controls that typically exist in the two environments run the entire spectrum of possibilities. You will find that the minicomputer environment poses some particular control problems, many of which stem from the relative absence of segregated duties.

Segregation of duties. When one person is responsible for a minicomputer installation, the environment is similar to a one-person accounting department in a manual accounting system. Consider how controls are established in a one-person accounting operation. As discussed in earlier chapters, the critical seg-

---

[2] Financial and Management Accounting Committee of the International Federation of Accountants, *Control of Computer Applications*, Study 1 (October 1985), p. 19.

regation of duties in any entity is the separation of the authorization of transactions, accounting for transactions, and custody of assets.

This segregation can be accomplished by requiring that someone external to the accounting department authorize transactions and that some other third party exercise physical control over assets. Often the party authorizing transactions is an owner/manager.

In a minicomputer environment, the requirement of initial authorization or of post-approval of transactions that have been initiated by the computer can similarly result in effective control. In considering the custody of assets, you should be alert to the frequency with which EDP personnel or those using minicomputers have direct or indirect access to assets. Most often, direct access involves cash or checks that come into the computer area, while indirect access exists when EDP operators "prepare" those documents that control the movement of assets, e.g., shipping orders for inventory. For control to be effective, access to such documents and assets should be restricted to a small group of authorized persons who do not have incompatible duties or over whom compensating controls can be designed. The same type of logic process that dictates that a person recording disbursements should not also be responsible for the performance of a bank reconciliation applies to an EDP environment. If a computer is being utilized to print checks and record disbursements, the information generated by the computer to reconcile the account balance should be received by some person who did not enter the information into the computer to execute the payment process. This would be an example of a potential compensating control over EDP operations.

Restricting access to the accounting records. Of course, even with the establishment of supervisory controls it is essential that access to the accounting records be restricted, to help ensure data integrity. Some idea of the scope of the control problem is provided by these available statistics: in 1970 the number of data communications terminals installed was less than 250,000, yet by 1975, a million were installed, and by 1980, three million.[3] The restriction of access to input devices for an on-line system can be accomplished in a variety of ways.

Checklist of Controls over Minicomputers

Exhibit 12–1 summarizes controls that are of particular use to an entity that uses a minicomputer. These controls include concerns for system access, data integrity, auditability, and systems recovery.

You should consider whether the controls delineated in Exhibit 12–1 are present at minicomputer installations of clients and should recommend those controls that are missing, yet are believed to be potentially cost/beneficial to client operations.

---

[3] Perry, William E. and Jerry Fitzgerald, "Designing for Auditability," *Datamation* (August, 1977), pp. 46–49.

Exhibit 12–1

Controls over Minicomputers

Access to Input Devices

- Physically lock terminals and, of course, exercise adequate control over the keys.
- Require a password to log onto the terminal and to
  - —enter data,
  - —read data, or
  - —alter data.
- Consider password restriction to particular types of data, e.g.,
  - —password grants access to inventory data,
  - —password does not grant access to receivables data, and to particular types of activities, e.g.,
  - —password only grants access to read data,
  - —password grants access to both read and enter data.
- Periodically change passwords and keys.
- To avoid discovery of passwords, suppress their printing when entered on the terminal or camouflage the form in which the password is printed.
- Educate employees as to the importance of maintaining the secrecy of their passwords, particularly from their fellow employees.
- When a party attempts repeatedly to log onto a terminal with an incorrect password, the system can temporarily "lock out" that terminal from gaining access to the minicomputer.
- Establish automated logging and reporting procedures for
  - —attempts to gain access to restructured information,
  - —error reversals, and
  - —overrides.

User Controls

- If practical, users should maintain cumulative totals of master file balances that can be compared to the minicomputer's master file balances as a balancing control.
- If no separate total of input transactions is maintained prior to data entry, some check on a per-document basis should be performed, such as extension checks and overall reasonableness checks.

User Controls (Continued)

- Have exception reports generated for review by users—for example, report all purchases and sales over $1,000 and all credit customers with balances that are older than 90 days.
- Users should review computer-generated reports for overall reasonableness by
  - —applying ratio analyses,
  - —making comparisons to the budget,
  - —evaluating trends and fluctuations from trends.
- The initiation of data entry, as well as the correction, re-entering, and re-submitting of all rejected and unposted items should be the responsibility of the users.

Adequacy of the Audit Trail

- Whenever the minicomputer generates accounting transactions automatically, it is imperative that the actions taken during processing can be identified, and this can be done if a transaction log file and master file record are maintained.
- The log and record files can be the basis for printing out the detail of transactions processed and master file changes made; such detail can be reviewed by users to ensure the reasonableness of the processing and to check that totals tie to users' totals.

Maintenance of Computer Services

- Adequately train employees operating the minicomputer to ensure against accidental destruction of records.
- When available, use internal labels on all applications, subprograms, and files to help ensure that the appropriate files are being processed; if internal labels are unavailable, use external labels (color codings and disk covers) and have the operator check such labels prior to processing.
- Require supervisory approval of overrides of internal labels and log all such overrides.
- Consider the method of recovery from major or minor interruptions; maintain
  - —adequate control over transaction log files,
  - —copies of master files and programs as backup and for off-site storage.

546

Maintenance of Computer Services (Continued)

—backup power, when possible, i.e., backup batteries for short-term use,

—procedures for recovery from an interruption or system failure, including access to information on the status of each file, where to resume processing, and which backup files need reloaded.

- Regularly perform prevention maintenance on computer equipment.
- Record equipment failures in a log showing the time, date, and apparent reason for the failure.

Segregated Duties

- Ensure that physical custody of assets is segregated from minicomputer operations.
- Use a librarian function to restrict operators' access to programs and to data files.
- If an automated data file librarian system is used, available output should be reviewed by installation management.
- Have users who are segregated from the minicomputer operations exercise controls over input and output.
- Have a party not involved in minicomputer operations ascertain that documentation is adequate; that party may be a CPA.
- Rotate operating responsibility for each application, if possible.
- Require all employees to take annual vacations of at least five consecutive calendar days.

Completeness and Accuracy of Data Entry

- Program the computer to use a standard format for data entry and to prompt users for any missing data.
- Have computer request the user to sight-verify the data entered before processing.
- Incorporate on-line computer editing, whereby
    —data codings,
    —numeric versus alphabetic characters, and
    —magnitudes
are checked against valid codes and limit checks for reasonableness and propriety.

Control over Facilities

- Assign responsibility for physical control of programs and data files to an employee other than the operator.
- Operators should maintain a console log as to what jobs were processed.
- In lieu of a console log, the entry and termination of each job processed can be recorded into a magnetic file as an audit trail.
- The console log or magnetic file (system activity logs) should be reviewed by the operator's supervisor; the console log should be maintained over systems testing and other less routine processing activities.
- Special controls should exist over those utility programs that are capable of changing programs and data without leaving an audit trail, such as passwords, known only to supervisors, or "off-line" storage of programs, with access to storage controlled by supervisors.
- Unusual differences in sequence or processing time should be investigated.

Maintenance of Data Integrity

- Generate batch totals, i.e., counts of transactions, debit and credit totals, and summaries of daily transactions.
- The transaction log should summarize the batch totals per shift and this summary record should be made part of the master file.
- To assist in identifying errors, a master file control record of opening and closing balances of records processed per shift should be created and balanced periodically to the total numbers generated when the entire master file is processed.

Physical Security

- Establish controls over checks, negotiable instruments, and other sensitive documents produced by the computer.
- Locate minicomputers away from public entrances and exits, hallways, or other areas of heavy traffic.
- Locate terminals in areas that are supervised.
- Do not leave terminals unattended when "logged on."
- Write programs that "log off" terminals after so many minutes of inactivity.
- Consider the use of guards, alarms, or surveillance devices to detect intrusion and fire.
- Accompany service personnel and other visitors while around the computers.

Exhibit 12–1 (continued)

Systems Development

- Require that standards be set for design, programming, programming changes, and testing, and that user approvals be required for design and changes to processing activities.
- Test files, not live files, should be used in debugging programs.
- When testing a new program intended to produce similar output to an old program, the new program should be run in parallel with the existing one for at least one processing cycle, with a comparison made of the results.
- In purchasing application systems software, confirm
  —the adequacy of processing controls
  —testing and documentation, and
  —users' approval of selected software.
- To prevent unauthorized modifications to programs
  —control access to production programs, data files, and computers, and
  —require user approval to changes in production programs.

Systems Development (Continued)

- Program library activity logs should be protected from operator overrides or alterations.
- Access to source code can be controlled via passwords, "read only" locks on programs, and use of a compiled version of programs for day-to-day processing.
- Use of source code can be controlled by restricting access to source language compilers.
- If minicomputers have an interpretive programming feature, the maintenance of the program in source code poses a greater risk of change to such code; this feature can be effectively used in development and testing but must be carefully controlled and, if possible, avoided when the program is placed in normal operations.

Report Distribution Controls

- Set limits on the number of copies of each report and its distribution.
- Set limits on the frequency with which a report is prepared.
- Maintain an output log to record the distribution of all output reports and documents.

548

GETTING THE AUDITOR, USER, AND TOP MANAGEMENT INVOLVED IN THE SYSTEMS DESIGN

Auditors should make a practice of advising clients to involve the auditor in the systems design and development phase of converting from a manual to a minicomputer processing system. An explanation to clients that minicomputers can affect auditors' work and their related audit fees, as well as the risk exposure of each client's operations to defalcations, accidental errors, and losses, can motivate clients to consult with their auditors before actually purchasing and installing a minicomputer. In this manner, common control problems may be avoidable at a reasonably nominal cost, in contrast to the cost of changing a system that is already installed. By alerting clients to the fact that minicomputers are not a minicontrol problem, you can assist clients to make improved decisions as to what minicomputer should be acquired and how the organization of the entity and day-to-day operations should be altered to retain adequate control. Changes in normal management and control of data processing primarily concern: (1) RIGIDITY—Lack of flexibility, typically tied to size and flexibility of hardware in a micro setting; (2) VISIBILITY—Identification such as handwriting disappears, and alterations are not visible; and (3) CONTROL—Key application controls for correctness, completeness, security (including authorization), and auditability; controls can be examined by looking at input, processing, storage and output, and access. Personnel policies for EDP are particularly critical. Security checks are needed before hiring and bonding of computer personnel is recommended. To ensure the auditability of a system, auditors' participation in system design is essential.

The System Development Life Cycle Technique: an Effective Approach to Application System Development

One effective approach to application system development is known as the System Development Life Cycle technique. This approach identifies the distinct stages of system development and establishes control points, each of which must be completed before proceeding with each subsequent step of the systems design, development, testing, and implementation process. The involvement of an auditor, the user, and top management is made explicit and communication lines are formalized, as is the entity's concern for costs. The auditors involved may be internal and/or external auditors. However, despite the availability of internal audit staff, a client can benefit from input by the external auditors concerning the systems development process. The client should be made aware of your expertise on such matters, past experience with similar systems development, and the differing control perspective that may be provided by the external and internal auditor. As the systems development plan is prepared, those control points at which external auditors' input is felt to be desirable can be made explicit. To document such involvement, the client may wish to establish a formal sign-off

Exhibit 12–2
System Development Life Cycle

Cycle Stages	Control Points
• Project Definition —User requirements —Uses for the system	(1) Auditor, user, and project leader meet to review the design and work plan and to arrange for communication during the project. (2) Auditor, user, and project leader analyze status quo, its cost, and new information needs. (3) Auditor, user, and project leader design and estimate cost/benefit profile for users and for EDP, and auditor presents findings to top management.
• System Analysis and Design —Overall description of system	(4) Review of (1) through (3) by auditor, users, and team members. (5) Auditor, user, and project leader review detailed design of output reports and auditor reviews adequacy of documentation on system design. (6) Auditor, user, project leader, and design analysts review file requirements and input requirements, particularly their agreement to specifications. (7) Auditor, user, project leader, and EDP personnel review equipment requirements. (8) Auditor, user, and project leader review cost, standards, and management's directions as they relate to system design.
• Detailed Design and Programming —Development of programs —Decisions as to internal components of the system	(9) Auditor, user, project leader and EDP personnel review plans, equipment costs, organization, and communications to provide management with assurance that systems analysis and design are sufficient and timed before the detailed design phase. (10) Auditor, user, project leader review documentation, particularly file systems, interface data handler programs, and program run documents; consider need for daily report to management. (11) Auditor, user, team members, and testers review the detailed system design, test plan, and conversion plan for effectiveness, efficiency, and agreement with design requirements; changes to requirements are documented with explanations.

550

- **System Test**

  —Use the system and check
  - √ Accuracy
  - √ Completeness
  - √ Fulfillment of users' needs

  (12) Auditor, user, testers, and project leader review organization of test team and completeness of plan to ensure all of the system and designed controls are to be tested.

  (13) Auditor, user, and testers develop test data, build master files, review test results, and monitor testing.

- **Conversion**

  —Placing the system in operation

  (14) Auditor, user, EDP operating personnel, and project leader review conversion plan's completeness and staffing and plan communications with top management.

  (15) Auditor, user, and project leader review problems, documentation, and incomplete activities; auditor writes final reports.

- **Operation**

  —Maintenance of operations
  —Control over program changes

  (16) Auditor and user periodically review system and related output, stressing whether system meets specified requirements and the adequacy of documentation.

- **Post-Implementation**

  —Comparison of system to objectives
  —Development and improvement of system

  (17) A few months after installation, users identify problems and auditor, project team, and users attempt to improve application systems.

  (18) Changes pursuant to control point (17) are reviewed.

Adapted from Perry and Fitzgerald (1977).

551

procedure for both internal and external auditors throughout the system development process.

Exhibit 12–2 describes the typical stages of a system development life cycle, as well as the common chronological control points within each stage.

Risks Faced by an Entity During the Design Phase and Post-Installation

In the design phase for an EDP system, an entity faces several risks:

—the commitment of resources to an inadequate plan,

—the development of a system that does not meet users' needs,

—the design of a system that has inadequate controls,

—the installation of an inefficient system from the perspective of operations,

—cost overruns,

—inadequately tested programs,

—the installation of a system with errors, and

—inadequate security controls.

Once the system is installed, security concerns persist and the other risks faced by an entity include

—processing problems that threaten the integrity of the data base,

—the inefficient use of EDP, and

—inadequate communications with users post-installation.

Audit Procedures During the Design Phase and Post-Installation

When an auditor is requested to perform a design-phase audit, the procedures would include

—reviewing controls,

—formulating recommendations regarding controls,

—testing controls,

—reviewing documentation for completeness with respect to both system design and user manuals,

—assessing the adequacy of security,

—reviewing the cost/benefit analysis prepared in the planning stage for overall reasonableness, particularly with respect to dollar and man-hour estimates of costs and benefits and comprehensive consideration of risks,

—appraising the appropriateness of planned applications, and

—testing compliance of design activities with prescribed procedures.

Post-installation, you will be in a position to examine information about applications and procedures as designed, as well as test results of actual performance. The types of errors observed, weaknesses in processing, control inadequacies detected, and security issues all warrant evaluation. A comparison of actual costs and benefits to the design-phase estimates can be made, as can a comparison of operations to stated objectives regarding the timeliness and comprehensiveness of output, the performance of edit and logic checks, the demands for EDP, the efficiency of operations, and the fulfillment of users' needs. An integral part of a post-installation review will be the evaluation of personnel.

Be Prepared for These Four Typical Stages of Growth

Once an EDP system has been developed, the typical stages of its growth should be anticipated in order to ensure smooth operations through effective planning. The typical EDP system evolves through four principal stages of growth:

1st. The newly installed EDP system has to prove itself in terms of basic cost/benefit. The initial computerization of all accounting processing of billings, payables, and payroll is likely to demonstrate the system's usefulness and encourage its acceptance. However, behavioral problems arise from employees who fear computer technology and fear that their jobs will be lost due to the efficiency of the computer. Another problem in this stage is that the computer is frequently placed in the accounting user group's locale, causing the typical problems of a "mini-computer environment" and complicating the eventual transfer of responsibilities for EDP to a separate EDP department.

2nd. Once the mundane, though beneficial, computer processing is on line, employees become creative as to other operating applications of EDP. The joint enthusiasm of employees and EDP personnel disregards costs, priorities, and company goals, stressing only the challenge and enjoyment of achieving another application. The computer is typically applied to budgeting, capital budgeting, forecasting, and similar functions.

3rd. The exorbitant growth of the budget signals a problem to top management which commonly overreacts by setting a policy of no additional EDP applications and by implementing stringent controls over the use of EDP. The result is unhappy EDP personnel, possible suboptimal use of computer facilities, and substantial disruption of operations by management's changes that have been initiated for control purposes.

4th. The so-called maturity stage involves maintaining stable service to users, yet investigating improved applications and keeping an eye toward future technology to ensure that the entity's computer facility does not become obsolete. Inertia can set in, leading to suboptimal use of EDP capabilities.

Ways to Avoid Problems in EDP Development

The alert client will be cognizant of these common stages and will avoid extensive problems in EDP development and growth by

—communicating management plans to employees on a timely and factual basis;

—locating the computer outside of the initial user groups' department in anticipation of long-term use or, as a minimum, appointing an EDP person to be in charge of the facility within the user department to facilitate a subsequent shift of operations toward an EDP department;

—initiating the controls commonly applied in stage 3 early in stage 2 to avoid costly proliferation of applications that are not cost/benefit justified and to ensure budgetary control and operating prioritization of projects in line with company goals; and

—establishing good communication between EDP, top management, and user groups.

Since many companies are unaware of the problems that accompany EDP growth, you should help them plan for the growth of computer activities by advising them to take these critical actions on a timely basis.

An aspect of EDP growth that has special control implications is the advent of data base systems (commonly referred to as data base management systems in the accounting literature, despite the more narrow use of the term DBMS in the EDP literature).

DATA BASES—A SPECIAL CONTROL CONCERN

Historically, operating departments have had their data essentially "locked up" into their own applications. The result is that management analyses that require data from several departments are frequently precluded, at least on a timely basis. To effectively remove such obstacles to performing useful data analyses, management has begun to recognize that data are valuable as a resource for decision-making and has organized data as a single pool or bank from which any combination of available data can be accessed. The data banks are termed data base systems. When in use, they permit more efficiency in programming and unlimited flexibility in data analyses. The single structure of a data bank, in contrast to the structure of numerous data files, each locked to specific applications, not only makes programming comparatively easy, but also simplifies the ease of maintaining the data base. The proliferation of redundant data files for each application can be halted and replaced by the single data set. Database systems may be designed as relational (with a file address) or hierarchical (with different levels used for coding).

The data base management system (DBMS) pool is structured as a group of computer programs that are designed to manage the data base and to provide a linkage between the data base and application programs. Typically a data dictionary is used to describe the content of the data base, key relationships in the data, and access authorities. One party should be assigned responsibility for organizing and protecting the data base; the person assigned such responsibility assumes the title of data base administrator. This person should review all program changes, as (s)he is the only individual with a global picture. Such a perspective is important, as a change in a program could change the logical operations performed on data, the data being accessed, or both. All program changes must be evaluated for their effect upon data and other programs.

DBMS Concerns for Auditors

The DBMS poses additional concerns for auditors as to data integrity, restricted access to data, and effective segregation of duties.

Traditionally, an attempt has been made to restrict access to programs and data files to avoid accidental or intentional unauthorized alteration of the data. In particular, the segregation of accounting records from those having access to assets has been stressed, as has the segregation of operators, from programmers, from systems analysts. The practicality of such a separation of duties in a DBMS setting is questionable, suggesting the need for alternative controls to compensate for past control procedures that are no longer deemed to be applicable. Many companies are restricting direct access to the DBMS to programmers and systems analysts. Managers and their analysts communicate information requests to programmers who effectively use the DBMS to generate a prompt response. As interface software has been improved, direct access to the DBMS has been granted to a greater number of individuals. The client and auditors must give particular attention in such settings to

—limiting access to particularly sensitive data through passwords,

—using "read only" controls to protect data integrity, and

—exercising effective applications control to retain the integrity of the information base for financial reporting purposes and management decision making.

You can assist in the evaluation of the cost/benefit dimensions of changing EDP operations to a data base environment. The benefits are obvious and the costs can be minimized with effective planning and integration of controls at an early stage in the conversion process. The benefits to performing effective ad hoc management studies can be even greater if the entity gains access to available data banks of external information relating to operations and merges such data into the DBMS for access in decision analysis.

Protective controls on DBMS integrity should include:

—preventing deletion of shared data by a single dealer without other users' consent,

—preventing simultaneous updates to a record,

—generating an audit trail of all changes to the data base, and

—providing recreation capabilities after system failures.

To monitor the DBMS integrity, periodically, a sequential review and footing of the data base is desirable. This should include balancing the data base for a given type of segment to the higher level.

GENERAL AND SPECIFIC CONTROL CONCERNS

The term "general control" is applied to controls that relate to all EDP activities, while specific controls, frequently referred to as "application controls," apply to specific accounting tasks. The auditor is responsible for reviewing these controls, understanding the control system, and determining whether assessment of control risk at less than a maximum level on the designed system would be appropriate. If so, compliance with the designed system must be tested. If not, the auditor's understanding of the information and control system is sufficient, without the performance of any control test procedures. As noted in earlier chapters, a walk-through of the EDP system can be useful in helping auditors to understand the flow of information.

AN ILLUSTRATION OF WORKPAPER DOCUMENTATION (UNDERSTANDING OF EDP SYSTEM)

Whether evidence is collected using generalized or specialized audit software or other more traditional tools, the results of gaining an understanding of a system and testing such a system are to be documented in the working papers. Such illustrative documentation appears in Exhibit 12–3.

An important facet of your evaluation of EDP is the assessment of how significant EDP is with respect to the accounting system. Significance is typically defined in terms of the

—quantity of transactions processed,

—dollars of transactions processed,

—nature of transactions processed, and

—nature of the processing itself and how it interfaces with manual procedures.

The more extensive the EDP system, the more critical the concern for control and the greater the likelihood that reliance on internal accounting controls will be cost-beneficial, should the design of the system be adequate for such reliance. The insignificance of EDP supports an auditor's decision not to review EDP. The extent of any review performed should be a function of EDP's significance to the accounting function under examination. The first step in evaluating the adequacy of control design for an EDP system is to review general controls.

Exhibit 12–3

Vinco, Inc.
Tests of Computer Access Controls

Completed by:	Teddy Techo	Date:	9-11-90
Reviewed by:	Lefty Lambert	Date:	9-20-90

AUDIT OBJECTIVES OVER COMPUTER ACCESS:

1. *Physical Access*: Computer hardware, software, and documentation should be protected from unauthorized personnel.

2. *Program Access*: Application programs that process accounting data should be protected from unauthorized changes.

3. *Execution of Programs*: Operating application programs should be available only to personnel with no conflicting duties.

4. *Data Access*: Accounting data should be processed and changed only by appropriate application programs.

SUMMARY OF WORKPAPERS RELATING TO COMPUTER ACCESS OBJECTIVES:

Objective 1—Physical Access:—See G-40 p2—Physical access controls found generally to be good.

Objective 2—Program Access:—See G-40 p3–4

Vinco utilizes a computer librarian package (GULP) licensed by a reputable vendor to maintain control over production and development programs. My tests found that the librarian package was properly installed, integrated with the global access security package (GASP), and maintained by Vinco personnel. Execution of production programs is also subject to GASP as discussed under objective 3.

Objective 3—Execution of Programs:—See G-40 p5

Vinco utilizes a global access security package (GASP) licensed by a reputable vendor. My tests found that this package was properly installed and maintained by Vinco personnel.

Objective 4—Data Access:—See G-40 p5

Vinco uses procedures to ensure that production runs are authorized to process against accounting data and that utilities that access data are secure and utilized only when authorized.

Policies Pervasive to Access Objectives:

Vinco does not have a formalized security policy, but the communication of security policies and procedures provides an acceptable environment given the centralized nature of security administration. I verified

Exhibit 12–3 (continued)

via the INSTALLATION command of GASP that Mr. Footlocker is the only individual with "Security" privilege, which indicates that all new user IDs and changes to access rules must go through Footlocker. Although Mr. Footlocker has several responsibilities outside of the security area, based upon his knowledge of various users, he appears to have adequate time to devote to his security responsibilities.

Objective 1—Physical Access:

On July 10, I toured the data processing department to test physical access control, noting the following:

1. Physical access to the computer room is restricted by a combination lock on the door. Visitors sign a log and are accompanied by authorized personnel.

2. Programmers are segregated from the computer room and do not have access to production programs or data files.

3. There are no dial-in lines.

4. A policy statement issued by the security manager precludes terminal users from distributing their passwords to others, taping the password on their terminal, or leaving their terminal without logging off. The GASP system provides further protection of unattended terminals by logging the terminal off after 10 minutes of inactivity (verified by reviewing the most recent GASP "Installation" report). The security manager, Mr. Footlocker, takes disciplinary action as needed.

Objective 2—Program Access:

Administration: I interviewed Vinco's programming manager (Billy Bob Johnson) and established that the general utility librarian package (GULP) that had been in use when we completed last year's audit was still in use with no modifications. The access rules via GASP preclude any production library "write" access to anyone other than the programming manager, except for certain privileged users as discussed on workpaper G-40. He made available the GULP librarian administration reports generated since the beginning of the year. Selected reports were scanned to determine completeness and appropriate actions.

See also W/P G-30 for tests of controls over changes made to programs in the revenue and payables/disbursements systems and GULP reports examined as part of these changes.

Objective 3—Execution of Programs:

Administration: I interviewed Vinco's security manager (Ralph Footlocker) and established that the global access security package

Exhibit 12–3 (continued)

(GASP) that had been in use when we completed last year's audit was still in use with no modifications. The revenue, payroll, and disbursements/accounts payable systems are all subject to the "Full Implementation" mode of GASP. He reviews all security violation as was evident from the violation logs tor the last several days on his desk which all indicated the follow up action which he had taken on each violation.

User's Privileges: Ralph is the only person with GASP authority to change user's profiles. He has no other incompatible duties. Changes in user's privileges are approved in writing by operational department heads. I inspected the User Attribute Reports (UAR) and the Set Attribute Reports (SAR) generated by GASP for the year to date. The written authorizations for 50 changes were traced to the SAR and the UAR, no exceptions were noted, see W/P G-40-1 [not included as part of this illustration].

In addition, I examined a special run of the GASP administration functions to provide the AUDIT report for the month of July and LISTUSER report for the current date. The AUDIT report, periodically used by Ralph, provides a list of changes to user's profiles. The LISTUSER report provides a list of all users and their privileges. Ralph compared his list to last year's LISTUSER report and all changes of users with the highest privileges were checked. All users with high access privileges seem appropriate to their job functions, see W/P G-40-3 [not included as part of this illustration].

As usual with our audit of Vinco, we requested user profiles be established for our audit use in the preaudit meeting on 7/1/90. We have been using our audit IDs and passwords since that time without problems. On 7/15/90, with the knowledge of Mr. Footlocker, I tried to access programs that were not part of our profile and obtain access with an improper password without success. My unauthorized attempts were properly recorded on the LOGAC report (see below).

Objective 3—Execution of Programs:

Detective Controls: Mr. Footlocker made available the LOGAC (logged accesses) reports generated by GASP for the most recently weekly period (these machine-readable reports are purged weekly). The LOGAC report is produced once a week and immediately whenever an unauthorized access is attempted. Mr. Footlocker reviews the weekly reports to determine if accesses are appropriate with known user profiles. Unauthorized access reports are investigated immediately. I noted his initials on the weekly reports indicating his review

Exhibit 12–3 (continued)

and several notes on some reports noting follow up of unusual accesses. My attempt at unauthorized access on 7/15/90 was immediately reported to Mr. Footlocker on a special GASP LOGAC report.

Objective 4—Data Access:

I identified 10 datasets which are part of the systems of financial audit interest. We obtained the GASP rulesets for these subsets and determined in each case that only the related production programs could access those datasets with "write" access with some exceptions. I followed up on the nature of the exceptions and determined that in each case special access privileges were allowed to resolve production restart problems that could occur during midnight shift processing. In all such cases, special privilege access is logged and reported on the violation reports which are reviewed by Ralph Footlocker and subsequently approved by Sally Smith.

Source: Proposed Guide for the Consideration of Internal Control Structure in a Financial Statement Audit (AICPA: Exposure draft from: January 7, 1989) (Exhibit 6–5), pp. 211–215.

General Controls

General controls for an EDP system are analogous to the overall control environment for a manual system. Weaknesses in such controls will typically imply that the related application of specific controls is also weak. For example, if there is no effective segregation of duties within the EDP function, those application controls that depend on the segregation of functions most likely will be ineffective. A specific example of how a general control can effectively eliminate the usefulness of a specific control involves the importance of controlling program changes. If a client has no established procedures for implementing program changes or evidencing such changes, no assurance exists that what the auditor reviews on a particular date was in fact a part of the EDP application for the entire period of interest. Despite the existence of excellent edit checks in the current programs in use, reliance on such checks is precluded by the absence of any reason to believe these checks were in use prior to and following the auditor's review. In other words, adequate general controls are a prerequisite to adequate specific controls. For this reason, general controls are typically evaluated by the auditor prior to the detailed evaluation of application controls. However, efficiency will sometimes dictate a concurrent review of general and specific controls. The components of general controls are illustrated in Exhibit 12–4.

Exhibit 12–4

General Controls

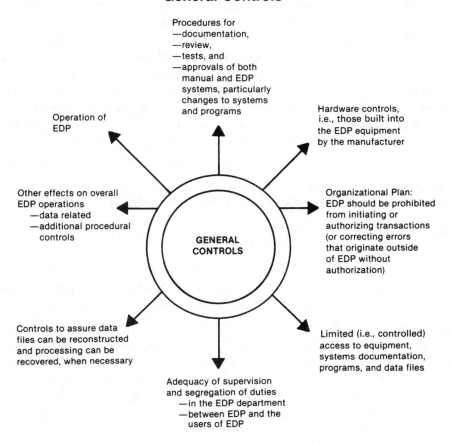

Procedures for
—documentation,
—review,
—tests, and
—approvals of both
   manual and EDP
   systems, particularly
   changes to systems
   and programs

Hardware controls,
i.e., those built into
the EDP equipment
by the manufacturer

Operation of
EDP

Other effects on overall
EDP operations
   —data related
   —additional procedural
      controls

Organizational Plan:
EDP should be prohibited
from initiating or
authorizing transactions
(or correcting errors
that originate outside
of EDP without
authorization)

**GENERAL
CONTROLS**

Controls to assure data
files can be reconstructed
and processing can be
recovered, when necessary

Limited (i.e., controlled)
access to equipment,
systems documentation,
programs, and data files

Adequacy of supervision
and segregation of duties
   —in the EDP department
   —between EDP and the
      users of EDP

Procedures for reviewing general controls. The auditor's procedures for their review typically include

—the examination of systems documentation,

—the review of procedures for granting access to both programs and data files (the librarian's logs, usage records, console logs, time records, and job logs can provide evidence that access has been effectively controlled),

—interviews with EDP personnel on the use of such services,

—observation of the actual operation of the controls,

—discussions with internal audit personnel, when available, to evaluate the effect of internal audit activities on EDP design and operations,

—the tracing of transactions through the system, and

—the completion of such useful audit tools as questionnaires and checklists.

Management reports, studies, and evaluations of EDP systems are frequently available for the auditor's review. In particular, you should obtain assurance that all master file changes are summarized in a listing and returned to the parties initiating such changes or to some third party for a review of the propriety and accuracy of the change. Statistics such as a control total or an item count (e.g., number of changes made to the master file), can be useful for this review process. Clients' reconciliations of control totals generated by EDP with those totals maintained by non-EDP personnel can be reviewed for their reasonableness and timeliness. Beyond some assurance that master file changes are controlled, you will also want to gain assurance that processing is being performed as authorized. A review of controls applied before processing and after processing, in addition to programmed controls that operate during processing, can provide such assurance.

Ensuring effective segregation of duties. The classic segregation of duties for the traditional batch processing EDP system includes the separation of

—operations from programming,

—operations from systems analysts,

—librarian from systems, programming, and operations, and

—an independent data control group from the EDP department if possible or, at a minimum, from systems, programming, and operations.

The underlying intuition of this segregation of functions is that programmers and systems analysts could circumvent many of the designed software controls if they were permitted to operate the computer; assurance that operators do not have access to program documentation and that programmers and systems analysts do not have access to data files is provided by establishing a librarian control function. The so-called independent control group has responsibility for maintaining control totals for data entry, processing, and output to users. To enhance the effective segregation of duties, clients should

—periodically rotate operators,

—require vacations, and

—set a policy that no one other than the operator is to be in the computer room while a program is being run (this is referred to as the requirement of closed-shop operations).

Reviewing documentation. The role of documentation in an EDP setting is critical, since controls are unlikely to be effective without adequate documentation of systems development, systems testing and implementation, systems maintenance, and systems alterations. Documentation should also be available to demonstrate that users' input was considered in the acquisition of software and that internal and/or external auditors reviewed EDP applications at the design stage as a means of ensuring the adequacy of controls and the establishment of an audit trail. Likewise, written specifications, approved by management, should be available as a standard against which existing systems can be evaluated.

Hardware and software controls. Part of the specifications will relate to hardware controls. Hardware should be equipped with automatic error-detection features and should be regularly maintained. Written procedures delineate how the operator is to respond to hardware errors or breakdowns. Operating controls such as the use of header and trailer records that identify the data or program file's name, the number of records, the number of blocks, the date, and the retention period for the file are also important specifications. Run failures due to loss of power, machine failure, lack of resources, operation error, faulty programs, or missing data will lead to abandonment of the run, establishment of the problem, and taking of corrective action. This action should involve:

- establishing the reason for failure;
- a record of what happened;
- a record of what action is taken to correct the failure; and
- rerun the job and record results.

Run instructions should contain details of: what the run does; the files involved; the file versions; action in the event of problems; run sequence; and relationship of the run to other jobs. Users should maintain an operator log stating what happened during the last run and have space for a record of what happens during this run. An operations log should contain: date; jobs run; reason for re-run; problems; and machine failure. Systems software is analogous to application programs in terms of which controls are desirable; approvals, testing and documentation—particularly of software changes—are all important controls.

One facet of software control relates to spreadsheet design.[4] Electronic spreadsheet software can be used to

—develop trial balances and financial statements,

—calculate depreciation,

—test lower of cost or market for inventory,

—perform various analytical procedures,

—monitor audit engagement time and costs, and numerous other procedures.

Spreadsheet programs should be evaluated based on criteria such as:

- Ease of learning
- Ease of use
- Error handling
- Performance
- Versatility, and
- Overall evaluation.

---

[4] *Inforworld* (Feb. 11, 1985), p. 27.

A key consideration in evaluating software is whether systems software was obtained from a reputable manufacturer and has been generally proven reliable. Documentation should be complete and current, and preferably, extensive modifications have not been made to such software.

In dealing with software development, controls should be in place to clarify who owns the rights to software developed by employees. A written instrument is advisable.[5]

Limited access. The concept of limited access to hardware and software implies a concern for physical security. The use of locks, guards, alarms, identification badges, and passwords can contribute to physical security, as can the use of common sense in designing an EDP facility. Its location should not demand that non-EDP personnel pass through the facility, nor should there be any unsupervised entrances and exits from the facility. The usage logs and console logs of an operating system can also control access to EDP, or at least help in the detection of attempted unauthorized access to EDP. Physical security and the use of logs not only assist in deterring intentional destruction, but can also help to avoid such disasters as fires or floods or damage from heat, humidity, or dust particles. These side benefits of security are important in terms of their effect on the likelihood of having to restore or replace lost or damaged files. Exhibit 12–5 simplifies the notion of access by comparing the keys used for a cash box to the analogous access control common in computer systems. Such analogies have appeared in past literature. Access to data should be controlled by knowing

—What is available

—Where

—How it is accessed

—By whom

—For what reasons

Files in computers and in filing cabinets should be clearly labeled as to their nature

OPEN ACCESS   —operational

RESTRICTED ACCESS—operational

CONFIDENTIAL   —authorized access

VERY CONFIDENTIAL —special authority level

CLOSED   —attended access only
                      (two or more people with individual keys
                      which open file when used together)

---

[5] Herbert Swartz, "Examining the Software Ownership Issue," *Journal of Accounting and EDP* (Winter 1989), pp. 42–46.

Exhibit 12–5

Compare Control of Access Over Cash to That of Computers: 7 Keys

Cash Box Control	*Computer Control*
(1) A key to the building	Personal number to start the system, issued only to authorized users
(2) Knowledge of the office in which it is kept	Knowledge of which files to access
(3) A key to the office	Password appropriate to access those files issued only to specific authorized users
(4) A knowledge of the drawer in which the safe key is kept	Knowledge of the access keys appropriate to the file
(5) A key to the drawer	The pre-defined password or code to add as a prefix to the key at a second level of authority
(6) The safe key	The sequence of the key on the file
(7) Knowledge of the combination on the cash-box lock	Knowledge of the actual key code to access the information required at a third level of authority

Note: Change password periodically and change all levels when authorized people resign. [Adopted from past literature.]

Disaster plans. All clients should have formal plans for backup in case of physical disasters or other failures of computer hardware. One facet of an effective backup plan is to routinely store important files, programs, and documentation away from the EDP facility. However, in order to read the files, both programs and computers, as well as related supplies, must be available. Clients should formally arrange for access to compatible computer facilities in case of emergency. Otherwise, the loss from business interruption due to problems with EDP can be substantial, if not crippling to overall operations.[6]

Checklist for formulating and evaluating an EDP disaster plan. Exhibit 12–6 summarizes an approach to formulating and evaluating the adequacy of an EDP disaster plan.

---

[6] Friedman, Stanley D., "Contingency and Disaster Planning in the EDP Area," *Today's Executive* (Price Waterhouse, Autumn, 1982), pp. 5–10.

Exhibit 12–6

Systems Backup—Disaster Plans

I. Assess the Plausible Disaster Types and Levels.

Types*	Levels
fire	equipment failure
water/storm	total facility failure
earthquake	loss of EDP personnel
bomb	time-frame for recovery*
employee disruption	
power shortage	
massive equipment failure	
excessive heat	

When less than a disaster occurs and a short time frame is involved for recovery, a back-up processing plan is initiated, whereas a disaster recovery plan is essential when the EDP site is lost and/or user procedures need to be established.

II. Develop a Set of Alternative Plans, that Adapt to Each Potential Type and Level of Disaster.

III. Test the Feasibility of the Plans and Ensure that Documentation of the Plans is Readily Available Offsite.

IV. Adequacy of Developed Plans can be Evaluated by Determining Whether the Following Questions Have Been Addressed:

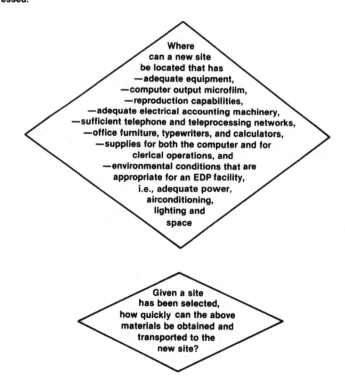

Where can a new site be located that has —adequate equipment, —computer output microfilm, —reproduction capabilities, —adequate electrical accounting machinery, —sufficient telephone and teleprocessing networks, —office furniture, typewriters, and calculators, —supplies for both the computer and for clerical operations, and —environmental conditions that are appropriate for an EDP facility, i.e., adequate power, airconditioning, lighting and space

Given a site has been selected, how quickly can the above materials be obtained and transported to the new site?

Exhibit 12–6 (continued)

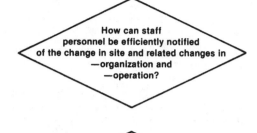

How can staff
personnel be efficiently notified
of the change in site and related changes in
—organization and
—operation?

What skills are
possessed by EDP personnel
and non-EDP personnel that could
offer flexibility to the company in adapting
to various types and levels of disaster, e.g., what if half of
the EDP operators are unavailable, do other
personnel possess the skills necessary
to assume operators'
responsibilities?

Is the
organization
plan for the new site
(and possible concurrent
operation of the old site) delineated
in sufficient detail that each individual
knows his or her responsibilities
and has sufficient guidance
to perform such
duties?

Has offsite
storage provided
assurance as to
the availability of
—operational procedures
(i.e., priority run lists operating manual, computer
run schedules, utilization logs, and restart procedures),
—application software (i.e., program libraries and documentation
and file processing programs),
—system software (i.e., operating system,
computer-based files, and utility systems
and documentation), and
—production files
(i.e., production
data sets)?

Exhibit 12–6 (continued)

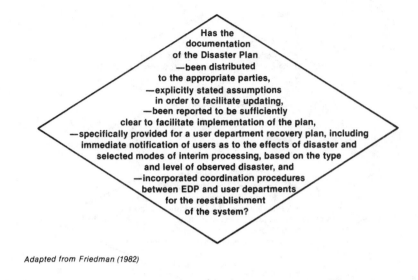

Has the
documentation
of the Disaster Plan
—been distributed
to the appropriate parties,
—explicitly stated assumptions
in order to facilitate updating,
—been reported to be sufficiently
clear to facilitate implementation of the plan,
—specifically provided for a user department recovery plan, including
immediate notification of users as to the effects of disaster and
selected modes of interim processing, based on the type
and level of observed disaster, and
—incorporated coordination procedures
between EDP and user departments
for the reestablishment
of the system?

Adapted from Friedman (1982)

Note: Companies and clients should consider insurance. Regardless of the availability of a disaster plan, losses are expected from system failures. For this reason, clients should consider acquiring business interruption or special EDP risk insurance to help cover the costs of reconstructing data files, recovering processing capabilities, and otherwise restoring the operations of the EDP department. Some indication of the potential risk is provided by IBM in a study that reported that during the period from 1967 to 1978, 352 major data processing disasters occurred: almost half due to fire (49%), 13% from water and storms, 17% from theft, 6% from loss and 15% from other accidents. These statistics support the need for a formal disaster plan.

Be alert to compensating controls. You should expressly consider the effect of general controls upon specific or application controls over EDP. Some apparent weaknesses can be offset by extensive user controls and the owner-manager's involvement in both EDP and non-EDP activities. Very strong application controls may compensate for certain problems in the segregation of duties.

Consider the following setting:

EXAMPLE: As in many small computer shops, a company had two weaknesses:

1. easy access to object code and master files and
2. operation of the computer by programming personnel.

A vital compensating control for these weaknesses is management's daily review of the console log, program update activity, and testing.

It is imperative that you be alert to compensating controls. An effective approach to analyzing general controls, familiar to an auditor, is to ask these questions:

—What types of errors and irregularities could occur, given the general controls of the EDP system?

—Which accounting control procedures should prevent or detect errors and irregularities?

—Are such procedures prescribed and being followed?

Certain application controls may sufficiently diminish the risks that are implied by designed general controls to warrant a testing of controls approach to the audit. Before exploring such tradeoffs, some discussion is warranted as to what constitutes specific or application controls and how these controls can be reviewed.

Specific Controls

The auditor is responsible for having a general understanding of the basic structure of accounting controls. Once this structure is understood, encompassing the structure of general and specific or application controls, the significance of the EDP applications and the anticipated reliance on EDP controls will determine the extent to which the application controls are reviewed. Typically, in-depth reviews are performed only for those application controls on which reliance is planned,i.e., risk is assessed at less than the maximum level .

Specific (application) controls and control procedures. Exhibit 12–7 presents a profile of specific controls. Their objective, the means used to accomplish their objective, the characteristics of the EDP system that are addressed, and the particular control procedures that are commonly applied are delineated. You need not demand that all of the application controls be present, as many are overlapping application controls. Input controls over correctness can include descriptions which are checked when input such as,

—Is field content correct?
  * alpha or
  * numeric
—Does the description exist?
  * match to a file of descriptions such as a customer name.

Data coding can be checked as follows:

—Is the number of digits correct?

—Do the codes exist in the coding system?

—Is the relationship correct—e.g., does the code match with the type of batch?

—Are transposition errors detected by check digits?

Data values can be checked:

—By extension

—By addition

Exhibit 12–7

A Profile of Specific (Application) Controls

OBJECTIVE: To assure that recording, processing, and reporting of data are performed properly.

MEANS: Specific or Application controls.

Categories:

| INPUT CONTROLS | PROCESSING CONTROLS | OUTPUT CONTROLS |

INPUT CONTROLS

- Authorization
- Conversion of data
- Completeness
- Accuracy

PARTICULAR CONTROL PROCEDURES

- Structuring input forms
- Rejection of data:
  —maintenance of an error log.
- Correction of data:
  —by third parties unless error was made by EDP.
- Resubmission of corrected data:
  —follow-through with error log.
- Authorization by:
  —signature or stamp,
  —internal check in program that individual is authorized to both operate the terminal and enter the type of transaction that is requested,
  —fingerprint checking devices,
  —internal check that all supporting documentation is on files prior to processing, e.g., purchase orders and receiving reports are on file to support a disbursement to a supplier,
  —independent review of output,

PROCESSING CONTROLS

PARTICULAR CHARACTERISTICS OF INTEREST:

- Processing performed as prescribed.
- Processing performed only on authorized transactions.
- All authorized transactions are processed.

PARTICULAR CONTROL PROCEDURES

- Balancing of input controls with processing control totals, e.g., run-to-run totals (have automatic listing of out-of-balance batches).
- Use a transmittal document, i.e., a batch total slip attached to documents that are physically transported to help ensure against loss of documents or the input of bogus documents.
- Verification by program of internal label:
  —file identification, and
  —dates.
- Manual verification of external labels and disk covers.
- Program boundary protection, restricting which disks on a disk file can be read from or written on by that application.
- Internal check on file by informing operator as to input received for opera-

OUTPUT CONTROLS

PARTICULAR CHARACTERISTICS OF INTEREST:

- Authorized access to computer reports.
- Checks on the accuracy of processing.

PARTICULAR CONTROL PROCEDURES

- Review of:
  —account listings,
  —reports (particularly exception and discrepancy reports),
  —printed checks, and
  —other output.
- Balancing:
  —reconcile to general ledger,
  —generate error reports.
- Visual scanning or verification:
  —comparison of master file changes to source documents,
  —consider necessity of third-party confirmations.
- Maintenance of control over:
  —machine-sensible files,
  —listings,
  —reports, and
  —other media.
- Distribution:
  —timeliness,
  —restriction to authorized users,

—independent review of input, after processing,

—dollar authorization applied to transactions above a certain amount.

• Edit check for:

—valid characters (zero, blank, alphabetic, numerics),

—valid field size, e.g., 8 digits are expected for a social security number,

—valid field sign, e.g., negative equipment balances would be unexpected,

—missing data by confirming that all data fields are complete,

—valid transaction code, e.g., only sales, cash receipts, sales allowance, and write-off entries are permitted to affect the receivables master file,

—if/then consistency, for example, a disbursement for payroll requires payroll deduction information,

—redundancy.

• Use a read-back approach whereby person entering data verifies input.

• Verification of codings:

—combination of a numerical coding with the first 4 letters of a name can be required, with a check for agreement with the master file,

—self-checking digits—whereby a mathematical formula applied to the digits in the numerical coding always generates an odd or even final digit, unless an error is present—are useful.

• Control over data conversion:

—record counts,

—batch controls—either control totals or nonsense totals such as the sum of social security numbers,

tor's verification prior to processing.

• Periodic management review of operator console log for:

—error messages caused by the operator, or

—indications that label processing and checking are being bypassed.

• Follow-through as to how errors are resolved.

• Program default options—redundant data are programmed in lieu of having to input the data per transaction; for example, a basic 35-hour week could be programmed, with exceptions flagged for overtime or absences.

• Logic checks (these overlap with input edit checks):

—limits,

—feasible range of values (e.g., all positive numbers),

—proper mathematical sign (e.g., subtracting discounts and adding freight costs).

—zero values (i.e., their propriety),

—non-numeric data,

—matching codings to master file,

—between fields,

—self-checking digits,

—cross-footings or extension checks.

• Overflow checks (a limit check based on memory capacity)

• Use of run-to-run totals throughout processing to detect:

—operator errors,

—program errors,

—operating system errors, and

—hardware

• Use parity controls—incorporated by the manufacturers of computers and intended to detect electronic failures in the transmittal of recording of binary-coded data.

—maintenance of confidentiality.

• Establish data retention policies.

• Use tickler files as reminders of review and distribution procedures.

• Maintain error source statistics.

• Periodically undergo an audit.

Exhibit 12–7 (continued)

INPUT CONTROLS (continued)	PROCESSING CONTROLS (continued)	OUTPUT CONTROLS (continued)

—computer editing with limit checks, matching files, and tests for the propriety of numeric versus alphabetic characters in each data field,

—verification by converting data on a dual basis and comparing the results, e.g., keypunch verification,

—exception reporting, e.g., the supplier is not on the approved vendor listing.

- Control over data movement:

—run-to-run totals throughout processing compared to input totals,

—signed receipts acknowledging batch total of physical data received,

—user controls.

- Consider assignment of batch numbering sequence for each processing period, then check for missing numbers; sequence checks are easily applied to preprinted serial numbers on documents.

- For non-batch processing, consider requiring a confirmation or acknowledgment message to be sent to a control point for each input transaction, then tie total confirmations back to original documents.

- List errors and design the programs to halt processing, once a certain number of errors are located in a single batch of input.

- Control rejected records by creating a suspense file.

- Establish recovery/restart procedures for programs exceeding 30 minutes; maintain recovery journals.

- Generating of control report listing:

—program name or number and date,

—labels of input and output tapes,

—control totals,

—error messages,

—results of balancing done by computer.

- Automate error correction, e.g., if invoices do not match with purchase orders, generate debit memoranda.

Adapted from AICPA (1977) and Folsom (1973).

In micros, input will be checked as it is being keyed and rejected there and then. Hence, it is difficult to input incorrect data, but such input can be time-consuming. Control over processing includes: controls over sorting; merging and updating; calculating; and storing. These would entail run-to-run controls. Moreover, a log should be maintained for data movement within the computer for every move that takes place including: a record of who enters, who checks, and a printout of who has done what; the data and their value; the source they were moved from; and their destination. Test programs, runs, and systems will likely include

(1) contrived systems tests—deliberate faults and errors to test validation and control procedures—and
(2) real systems test—using representative real data, e.g., the prior month.

Control amendments of software by consultants and the issue of updated packages should include tests for accidental corruption by malfunction or default by regularly testing files with test data. To ensure only authorized customer, vendor, and employee transactions are processed, a first step should be to verify inclusions of transactional parties on master files. To monitor the integrity of master files, "was—is" reports showing before and after changes can be very useful. One overriding control consideration that affects your evaluation of both general and specific controls, their interaction, and the potential for assessing control risk at less than a maximum level, is the extent to which an EDP system is well-documented.

Recommended Documentation for an EDP Environment

As already suggested, documentation is an integral part of both general and specific controls and is essential to a well-controlled EDP system. You should recommend that clients make documentation standards an integral part of

—systems design,
—systems implementation,
—program testing,
—program changes,
—operations, and
—the interface with EDP users.

The documentation process can be thought of as a means of providing answers to the basic questions—why, how, what, when, and who? This classification scheme for recommended documentation for an EDP system is utilized in Exhibit 12–8. You should evaluate the completeness of clients' documentation procedures relative to the benchmark presented in this figure, and then consider the implications of any missing documentation. For example, if members of the EDP staff quit, could the new employees gain an understanding of the system and their particular duties, based on existing documentation?

Exhibit 12–8

Recommended Documentation for an EDP Environment

WHY?

Defining the problem, explicitly considering human factors affecting system reliability
—Reasons for implementing EDP
—Purposes of operations
—Proposed projects
—Approval
—Assignment of responsibilities—clear distinction of users', EDP staff's, and internal auditors' responsibilities

WHAT IS CURRENT STATUS?

—Narrative descriptions of programs
—Flowcharts or other detail of logic (e.g., logic block diagrams and decision tables)
—Source statements or listings of parameters (source language listings)
—Control features/testing requirements
—Individual program specifications
—File formats and record layouts
—Table of code values used in processing
—Program changes, dates, and authorizations
—Test data specifications
—File maintenance transactions
—Input/output formats
—Operating instructions
—Special features—error detection routines, program switches and similar concerns
—Design review programs to cover planned controls

WHO?

Users require documentation of:
—The system
—Input/output
—Controls, particularly a description of the EDP control group procedures
—Positions responsible for particular controls
—Procedures for correcting errors
—Cut-off procedures for submitting data to EDP
—How they should check reports for accuracy
—Error messages
—Retention policies
—How to review exception and discrepancy reports

HOW?

The Audit Trail
—Systems description
—Systems flowchart
 • data flows
 • paperwork
 • processing steps
 • the relationships of processing steps and computer runs
—Data conversion instructions
—Batch control and transmittal procedures
—Input/output descriptions (examples)
—Clerical instructions on the handling, evaluating, processing, or controlling of documents or operations in the manual portions of EDP systems
—File descriptions
—Control descriptions with specific standards
—Authorizations

WHEN?

—Estimated run times
—Set-up instructions and requirements of the operating system
—Required inputs/outputs—forms and formats (including card layouts)
—Sequence of cards, tapes, disks, and other files and sequence of operations to start, run, and terminate
—Operating description (including required computer switch settings, i.e., external switches to make programs compatible with the computer)
—Operating notes re: program messages, halts, and action required to signal the end of jobs
—Controls
—Instructions to operator, should an emergency arise
—Recovery and restart procedures

Adapted from AICPA (1977) and Mair et al. (1978).

In addition to the documentation described in Exhibit 12–8, the entity that uses a service center for some or all of its EDP activities is faced with additional review, evaluation, and documentation responsibilities.

HOW TO REVIEW CONTROLS AT SERVICE CENTERS

Whenever financial data that could have a material effect on the client's financial statements are processed by a service center, and the user controls external to that service center are inadequate to ensure that errors and irregularities are promptly discovered, the auditor is required to conduct a review of controls at the service center. Often the internal auditors perform such a review on behalf of their employer and the external auditors. Both general and application (specific) controls are to be examined in the review. The nature of such controls is identical to in-house controls, except that if you choose to perform tests of control, it is unlikely that the service center will permit test data to be entered into the processing system. Therefore, you should check source data, control reports, error listings, transaction listings, and management reports in performing control test work. The other available procedure is to trace real transactions through the system; when performed on a broader scope than a walk-through such testing is termed "cycle vouching."

How to Use a Third-Party Review of Service Centers

Due to the commonality of auditors' need for information concerning service center records, third-party reviews of standard packages and systems, performed by an auditor engaged by the service center, have become typical as an efficient means of providing a description of EDP systems and the controls that exist at service centers. However, rarely does a third-party review of a service center involve enough testing to facilitate an auditor's reliance on the service center's controls. Typically, the third-party reviewer only performs limited tests to verify understanding of the system and controls. Since the review typically spans only a short period of time, there is little likelihood that it will be sufficient for control reliance.

The auditor's responsibilities when using third-party reviews are reflected in Exhibit 12–9. When a client is using a tailored processing system that has been designed with the client's involvement in the design, programming, and testing phases of system development, the third-party auditor will often be engaged by the client's auditor rather than by the service center's auditor. Regardless of what party engages the third-party auditor, the nature of the report received and the restricted responsibilities of the third-party auditor are the same. The primary difference is whether any user controls of a client are reviewed by the third-party auditor.

Under all circumstances, the user controls of the client must be carefully evaluated. They may, in fact, provide a basis for the auditor's determination that

Exhibit 12–9

Responsibilities of User's Auditor When Utilizing a Third-Party Review of Service Centers

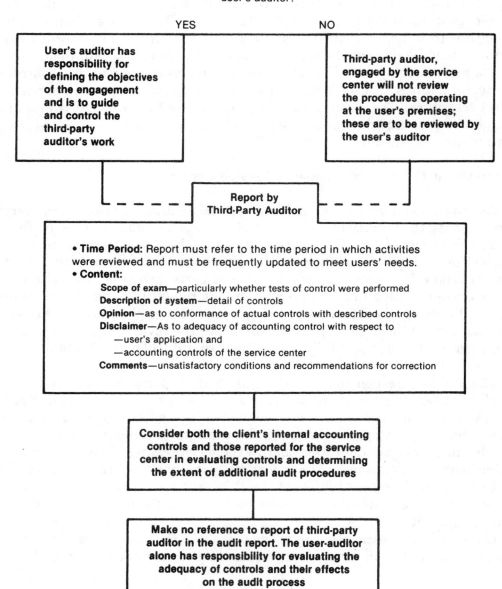

Obtain satisfaction that third-party auditor
- is independent
- has a professional reputation

Is third-party
auditor engaged by
user's auditor?

YES   NO

User's auditor has
responsibility for
defining the objectives
of the engagement
and is to guide
and control the
third-party
auditor's work

Third-party auditor,
engaged by the service
center will not review
the procedures operating
at the user's premises;
these are to be reviewed by
the user's auditor

**Report by
Third-Party Auditor**

- **Time Period:** Report must refer to the time period in which activities were reviewed and must be frequently updated to meet users' needs.
- **Content:**
    Scope of exam—particularly whether tests of control were performed
    Description of system—detail of controls
    Opinion—as to conformance of actual controls with described controls
    Disclaimer—As to adequacy of accounting control with respect to
        —user's application and
        —accounting controls of the service center
    Comments—unsatisfactory conditions and recommendations for correction

Consider both the client's internal accounting
controls and those reported for the service
center in evaluating controls and determining
the extent of additional audit procedures

Make no reference to report of third-party
auditor in the audit report. The user-auditor
alone has responsibility for evaluating the
adequacy of controls and their effects
on the audit process

a review of the service center is not required. Even if a review of the center is required, the user controls are an essential aspect of control over the EDP application and must be considered in evaluating the effect of controls on the audit process.

How to Handle the Special Concerns Posed by Service Centers

A service center can pose some concerns that are not faced by companies who do in-house processing. These include questions as to

—data ownership,

—data confidentiality,

—program access, should the service center terminate operations or relocate, and

—program ownership.

The contractual agreement. The client should resolve these questions when initially negotiating a service center arrangement and should formalize the agreement in a contract. The contract should also, at a minimum, address the following:

—Liability of each party for errors or delays in processing, loss of records, or discontinuance of service center operations.

—Movement of data and reports between the company and service center.

—Insurance coverage of the service center.

—Provisions for termination of services.

—Backup provisions of the service center.

—Fidelity bond coverage of service center employees.

—The privilege of independent or internal auditors to have access to files and programs of the service center.

The auditor will review this contract to ensure that these questions and issues were resolved and will advise the client or company to expand or attempt to adjust the contract, as deemed necessary.

YOUR ROLE IN COMPLYING WITH PRIVACY REGULATIONS

You must give attention to entities' compliance with regulation. An area of regulation affecting EDP systems and related controls is privacy regulation. Government officials concerned over threats to individuals' privacy that are posed by personal data systems have actively promoted privacy regulations such as the Federal Privacy Act of 1974 [Title 5, U.S. Code Section 552a (Public Law 93–579) December 31, 1974] and the Fair Credit Reporting Act of the U.S. effective since

1971. In 1978, 387 pieces of privacy-related legislation were proposed in state legislatures across the country.[7]

Most privacy proposals involve

—restrictions on the use of data, i.e., people must initially give permission for the data to be used in a particular way, as well as for any new use of data sets;

—controls on operating procedures including precautions against disasters, publication of the data base's general content, establishment of procedures to respond to individuals' inquiries and complaints, and the maintenance of a log as to how each person's record is used; and

—the availability of information to individuals, i.e., access to one's own record, ability for individual to request correction of his or her file, and availability of an option to append a statement to a record that has not been corrected to the individual's satisfaction.

While privacy regulations vary by state, their general content implies a need for confidentiality and record-keeping controls and an important role for audit trails regarding how individual data records are used. You should be alert to such requirements, encourage compliance with regulations, and assess the risk exposure for shortcomings in established controls that relate to compliance with privacy regulations.

The privacy regulations also affect your audit process. Should you copy data files for use with generalized or tailored audit software, you are responsible for retaining the confidentiality of such data. Extra precautions are likely to be required for highly sensitive data. Of course, confidentiality is a common aspect of your auditing job; however, retaining the confidentiality of data that are in machine-sensible form creates a need for additional controls that are unique to any EDP environment. Internal labels and password protection within the auditor's EDP system are imperative controls to restrict access to sensitive data.

ENCOURAGEMENT OF INTERNAL AUDIT INVOLVEMENT

Due to the unique characteristics of EDP systems and the "snapshot" limitations of many control test procedures, the external auditor should consider the benefits of internal audit's involvement in EDP activities. Surveys of practicing CPAs have indicated a strong desire for internal auditors to actively evaluate the adequacy of controls during the design phase of new EDP applications. These surveys indicate a consensus by CPAs as to those internal audit activities in EDP that are likely to have a moderate to significant effect on the external auditor's scope and audit approach. They include

---

[7] "Information Technology: The Future Is Bright If . . . ," *Government Executive* (February, 1979), pp. 18–24.

—the monitoring of processing controls via embedded audit routines,

—the use of test data to evaluate processing controls,

—internal auditors' participation during the design phase in specifying both audit trail and control requirements,

—the review of major changes to programs, with an emphasis upon the audit implications of such changes,

—the evaluation of data processing security,

—the surprise inspection of EDP facilities to check compliance with company policies, and

—assistance in design by identifying both problem areas and control needs.

(Complete survey results are reported by Rittenberg and Davis, 1977.)

PERFORMANCE AUDITS IN THE GOVERNMENTAL SECTOR

Increasing attention is directed to computer-based systems by the revised *Yellow Book*, directed toward government audits. Exhibit 12–10 outlines the generally accepted government auditing standards (GAGAS) that detail field standards for performance audits with regard to computer-based systems.

Exhibit 12–10

The Reliability of Evidence from Computer-Based Systems: Field Work Standards for Performance Audits in the Governmental Sector

Reliability of Evidence From Computer-Based Systems

62. When computer-processed data are an important or integral part of the audit and the data's reliability is crucial to accomplishing the audit objectives, auditors need to satisfy themselves that the data are relevant and reliable. This is important regardless of whether the data are provided to the auditor or the auditor independently extracts them. To determine the reliability of the data, the auditors may either (a) conduct a review of the general and application controls in the computer-based systems including tests as are warranted,* or (b) if the general and application controls are not reviewed or are determined to be unreliable, conduct other tests and procedures.

63. When computer-processed data are used by the auditor, or included in the report, for background or informational purposes and are not significant to the audit results, citing the source of the data in the report will usually satisfy the reporting standards for accuracy and completeness set forth in this statement.

Exhibit 12–10 (*Cont.*)

Review of General
and Application
Controls

64. In reviewing the general and application controls, the auditor is to consider the effectiveness of those general controls relevant to the application system being reviewed. General controls are normally applicable to all data processing being carried out within an installation and provide a control environment affecting the applications being processed. Application controls, however, apply on an individual basis, and may vary among applications.

Review of General
Controls

65. General controls include the plan of organization and methods and procedures that apply to the overall computer operations in an agency. In reviewing the general controls, the auditor should determine whether the controls (a) have been designed according to management direction and known legal requirements and (b) are operating effectively to provide reliability of, and security over, the data being processed. The objectives and procedures followed in conducting this work are discussed in the three areas below.

66. Organization and management controls: The auditor should determine whether (a) there is a clear assignment of responsibilities and accountability for planning, managing, and controlling the functions of the data processing organization, (b) personnel are qualified and adequately trained and supervised, and (c) there is proper separation of duties. Such controls will help ensure that the organization's objectives are achieved, and that errors or irregular acts are prevented or detected.

67. Security controls: The auditor should determine whether adequate security is provided over the computer programs, data files, telecommunications network, and input and output materials. These controls, such as physical restrictions and the use of passwords to limit system access, help ensure that only authorized persons are granted access to the computer system for authorized purposes.

68. Systems software and hardware controls: Computer systems are controlled by systems software such as operating, data base management, and program library systems. Systems software and hardware nor-

Exhibit 12–10 (Cont.)

mally include built-in error-checking features to detect any errors during processing. The auditor should be aware (a) of the procedures used to ensure that the systems software and hardware are functioning properly, and (b) that when errors are detected, appropriate and authorized corrective actions are taken. The auditor should also be aware of the controls the systems software can exercise over the system, how these controls can be bypassed or overridden, and how modifications to the software are controlled.

Review of Application Controls

69. Application controls are designed to ensure the authority of data origination, accuracy of data input, integrity of processing, and verification and distribution of output. The auditor should review the application controls upon which the auditor is relying to assess their reliability to process only authorized data and to process them promptly, accurately, and completely. This includes a review of the controls used to ensure that application software and later modifications are authorized and tested before implementation. These controls are intended to protect the integrity of the application software.

Testing for Data Reliability

70. The degree of testing needed to determine data reliability generally increases to the extent that the general or application controls were determined to be unreliable or were not reviewed. Testing procedures could include:
   a. Confirming computer-processed data with independent sources, such as third parties, and knowledgeable internal sources, such as regular users of the data, and suppliers of data.
   b. Comparing the data with source documents, or physical counts and inspections.
   c. Reviewing agency test procedures and results, and processing test transactions through the application.

* When the reliability of a computer-based system is the primary objective of the audit, the auditors should conduct a review of the system's general and application controls.
Source: United States General Accounting Office, by the Comptroller General of the United States, *Government Auditing Standards* (1988 Revision), Chapter 6, pp. 6–18, 6–21.

GUIDELINES FOR PERFORMING THE EDP REVIEW

The scope of an auditor's responsibilities for EDP activities is the same as that scope required for manual activities. To perform an audit, you must understand the flow of transactions through the entire accounting system. The preliminary phase should clarify these same issues:

—What are the types of transactions processed?

—How do the transactions originate?

—What are the significant processing steps?

—What accounting information is maintained across processing cycles?

—What are the significant records and output listings that are likely to be of use?

—How does information interface from one application to another?

To understand such issues, you must be aware of the mode of processing, i.e., manual or EDP, and the extent to which EDP is used. As discussed earlier, clues regarding the extensiveness of EDP use are provided by

—the variety of transactions processed by EDP in a given application,

—the number and types of output reports generated by EDP,

—the quantity, in number and in dollars, of transactions processed by EDP, and

—the relative significance of EDP processing activities to manual processing activities.

This phase of the review process is intended to be deep enough to enable you to design substantive tests. The extent of documentation of your understanding will depend upon the complexity of the accounting system and should support the design of substantive tests.

Preparing a Profile of the Client or Company's Use of EDP

In reviewing an EDP environment, it is frequently useful to prepare a profile of the client's or company's use of EDP. This profile should reflect the nature of the EDP facilities in terms of their organization, hardware, software, personnel, and processing networks. A diagram of the facilities is often useful in evaluating the control environment, as is a summary of the computer application systems, with accompanying statistics on the volume of transactions processed by these systems. The physical control over computer terminals is of particular interest to an auditor. Once your survey is completed in a preliminary review, the depth of understanding is shallow. Little specific knowledge of controls is gained, and only a general perception of the overall control environment has been obtained. In contrast, a detailed review encompasses an understanding of all specific internal accounting controls upon which reliance is planned.

This review is the basis for assessing control risk. If not, whether a manual or an EDP system is involved, you need only document the rationale for your judgment and then proceed with substantive test work. One reason why accounting controls in certain areas of an EDP environment may not be relied upon is that computer-assisted auditing may facilitate a 100% verification of the information of interest. However, any areas for which control risk is assessed to be less than at a maximum level, must be subjected to a detailed review.

PERFORMING THE DETAILED REVIEW

By applying a detailed review, you can identify

—where controls are located—in EDP and/or non-EDP operations,

—how these controls function,

—who performs the procedures,

—whether duties are effectively segregated,

—whether detection of material errors or irregularities would be on a timely basis,

—what EDP general control procedures are essential to the effective operation of application or specific controls on which the auditor plans to rely,

—how effective the important general control procedures are, and

—upon which controls the entity significantly relies.

Tests of Control

As in all tests of control, the issues of interest in determining whether a control structure is subject to less than the maximum level of control risk include:

—whether the prescribed and/or necessary procedures were performed,

—in what manner they were performed, and

—by whom they were performed.

As in a manual system, an EDP system may provide visible evidence that control procedures have been performed; this evidence may take the form of written authorizations, initials, printed control totals, edit listings, exception reports, or error listings. However, such visible evidence will frequently be lacking, implying a need to test the actual operations of the EDP system. The options available include those discussed in earlier chapters concerning computer-assisted audit techniques, such as parallel simulation, controlled reprocessing, the use of test decks, and the review of program codings. A 1977 survey reported that about one fourth of 221 companies used generalized audit software, manual tracing and mapping routines, and test decks in auditing production systems, while about a fifth used parallel operation and tagged transactions for audit purposes.[8] Such procedures by internal auditors provide a starting point for external auditors' review and testing. However, such testing techniques, whether applied by internal or external auditors, make the assumption that effective controls are operative with respect to access to programs used for processing and changes to programs used in EDP. Assurance that this assumption is appropriate might be gained from a mixed control/substantive testing approach to auditing accounting functions that involve significant applications of EDP.

A Recommended Auditing Approach for an On-Line EDP Environment

An auditing approach that warrants consideration in an on-line EDP environment is on-line computer auditing through continuous and intermittent simulation. The technique was specifically designed as a compliance auditing technique for time-sharing systems that can be used to audit internal controls. It essentially simulates the execution of instructions for the application at the same time as the application is processing a transaction. All relevant input to the application is accessible by and shared with the simulation, meaning that the simulation is notified about each transaction entered and each access to the data base by the DBMS. Before the data base is updated and output is generated, the simulation can execute the appropriate instructions that evaluate the internal controls of the application and can verify the results. Should inconsistencies be detected, an exception log can be prepared. A corrective action can be signalled at the time of the failure. The number of transactions audited would be an audit judgment and would be programmed into the simulation process. Selection criteria could be a random sample, a time of day trigger, or an emphasis upon particular types of transactions. For more information on this approach to on-line auditing, see the article by Harvey S. Koch, cited in the references at the end of this chapter.

On-line systems should be controlled by a monitor, protecting against unauthorized access, including maintenance of a log of such significant events as illegal requests or misuse of a file. Terminal polling and call-back procedures are desirable. Either the user identification should be disabled or the terminal shut down after a predetermined number of unsuccessful attempts to access the computer. Similarly, if a terminal sits idle for a certain time, automatic log-off may be desirable. Particular care should be taken to restrict the number of individuals permitted to use critical commands such as overrides. Such restrictions might include only permitting such commands on one or a limited number of terminals. When dial-up access is available, operators should disconnect and call-back preauthorized locations requesting service, as an access control. On-line access logs maintained should be reviewed routinely for unauthorized access attempts.

---

[8] Rittenberg, Larry E. and Gordon B. Davis, "The Roles of Internal and External Auditors in Auditing EDP Systems," *The Journal of Accountancy* (December, 1977), pp. 51–58.

ELECTRONIC DATA INTERCHANGE (EDI)

Electronic data interchange (EDI) is the exchange of documents between the computers of a number of companies, linking suppliers, carriers, manufacturing plants, creditors, and similar contractual parties. As with any transaction, controls to ensure data completeness, accuracy, propriety, timeliness, and auditability are important, but the added dimension of such settings is that internal control is affected by the controls of each of the linked parties. In other words, the controls of a single entity are not the focus; rather, the manner in which that system links to others and the relevant control over such linkages must receive particular attention.

The advantage of EDI is the elimination of paper flow by and large, since electronic links are integrated with the accounting system, inventory management system, and financial reporting. The EDI may be a single hub or one-to-many system or a third-party network, whereby a system acts as a clearing house for a number of network participants. Exhibit 12–11 outlines some key questions related to understanding the environment of EDI and assessing related controls.

Exhibit 12–11

Gaining an Understanding of EDI Related Controls

1) Identify the control boundaries for EDI's

   —sender
   —processor
   —receiver

2) Identify the data transmission controls over the completeness and accuracy of transmissions. EDI systems should include such internal controls as vertical and horizontal redundancy checking and parity checks that ensure transmission protocols. Since EDI permits different modem line speeds and various protocols for communication, chances exist for hardware and software-induced errors; controls need to be established to detect and report such errors and to provide a corrective process.

3) Examine how authorized users gain access to documents in the network and related controls to ensure against unauthorized access. For example, user codes and the rotation and maintenance of passwords with matching user profiles are recommended. Before permitting access for exchanging documents, predesigned user profiles must be provided, verifying trading relationships as a prerequisite to processing; if a match is not achieved, access should be terminated and errors logged to facilitate follow through regarding security violation attempts. A feedback process of periodic reports, particularly by third-party networks, is advisable as to (a) accesses made to the files, (b) dates and times of

Exhibit 12–11 (*Cont.*)

access, and (c) identities of individuals accessing the files. These reports should then be reviewed, and to the degree deemed appropriate, tested, by the auditors.

4) Ensure an adequate audit trail exists at least in machine readable form regarding the interactive on-line system and adjust procedures as needed, in light of what is available or retrievable. Controls should include: validity tests, such as (a) matching the transactions to be retrieved against data maintained on a master or suspense file, and (b) requiring a certain number of data elements for matching to assure the uniqueness of the transaction set; or a review of electronic documents not matched and retrieved by authorized users, with suspense files formed for rejects, ensuring follow-up. The audit trail often will require console logs kept during processing whereby the history of transactions and exception reports for randomly selected transactions are captured onto tapes, journals, or logs to facilitate the audit process.

5) Assess the risk exposure from use of third-party networks that handle a large volume of transactions, including gaining an understanding of that processor's control environment.

6) Ensure you understand who the participants are in EDI and their respective responsibilities: the service bureau often translates documents, checks compliance, performs special editing, translates format for distribution, considers report requests, and performs mailboxing into various electronic mailboxes.

7) Review contingency plans of all the parties to EDI. Backup and restructuring capabilities are particularly critical.

Source: Adapted from Arjan T. Sadhwani, Ill-Woon Kim, and John Helmerci, "EDI's Effect on Internal Controls," *EDPACS* (July 1989), vol. XVII, no. 1, pp. 1–11.

COMPUTER VIRUSES

Beginning in late 1987, computer virus threats led to a number of ideas on how to reduce the threat of infection. A virus is a small piece of computer code that can automatically hide and duplicate itself inside legitimate programs in the system. When triggered, the virus may destroy valuable data and software. The virus can travel from computer to computer attached to the programs on swapped or shared disks and even on new commercial software from virus-infected companies. The use of EDI and various linkages among systems increases the exposure to such problems. Computer viruses have been dubbed with a variety of names:

—Time Bomb is a virus triggered by the computer's clock reaching a certain date and time, ironically triggered frequently to Friday the 13th.

—Logic Bomb is a virus triggered by a certain value that appears in some part of the computer's memory.

—Trojan Horse is an innocent-appearing program that is deliberately infected and circulated publicly.

An important facet of control is to maintain a VACCINE, or program that watches for typical things that viruses do, halts them, and warns the computer operator. In 1988, over 6,000 computers were halted or slowed down for a day and a half due to a "game-playing" experiment of the son of one of the government's top experts on computer security.[9] Software is available for checking for viruses and their application is particularly critical for EDI and various integrated computer networks.

INTEGRATING THE REVIEW OF EDP AND MANUAL CONTROLS— ADVANTAGES AND DISADVANTAGES

In evaluating EDP operations, you should view EDP as an integral part of the entire operations of the client or company. To formulate a review and evaluation of controls for an entity, both manual and EDP controls must be considered. The problem that sometimes arises is a lack of sufficient computer expertise to effectively evaluate the EDP dimension of control. Consequently, whenever operations have some EDP aspects, a computer consultant's services may be essential. However, just as the auditor may lack EDP knowledge, the computer consultant may lack general audit knowledge and a sufficient understanding of the client's operations to form an integrated review of EDP and manual controls.

Using Specialists to Evaluate EDP Controls

A CPA firm, individual practitioner, or internal audit department must evaluate the relative costs and benefits of training the auditor in EDP skills or acquiring consultants' expertise. Of course, one alternative is to attempt to train the consultant in auditing or to train only a subset of auditors in EDP skills. There are several advantages and disadvantages in deciding to utilize various types of specialists to evaluate EDP controls. These are delineated in Exhibit 12–12.

---

[9] N.Y. Times News Service, "Computer Virus Outbreak Not Intended to Cause Harm," *Bryan-College Station Eagle* (November 6, 1988), p. 10A.

Exhibit 12–12

**Advantages and Disadvantages of Utilizing Specialists to
Evaluate EDP Controls**

Advantages	Disadvantages

ASSUMING AN EDP SPECIALIST IS USED:

Advantages	Disadvantages
• (S)he is likely to know the state-of-the-art of computer technology. • The training cost of giving field auditors a sufficient understanding of EDP to evaluate controls is avoided. Besides, it is unlikely that the training would ever be adequate to capture the constantly evolving technology of EDP.	• (S)he is unlikely to have a thorough knowledge of the audit process, or the importance of —audit trails and —controls. In particular, the implications of EDP operations and controls for the entire entity are unlikely to be understood. • Without field auditors who understand EDP, no effective integration of EDP and manual controls is likely to occur in the review and evaluation phase of internal control. It is likely that the CPA would get a good, fair, or poor signal from the specialist and otherwise ignore EDP implications.

ASSUMING AN EDP SPECIALIST, WITH SOME TRAINING AS AN AUDITOR, IS USED:

Advantages	Disadvantages
• The specialist should be able to communicate the control implications of EDP for manual processing systems and help to formulate a more integrated review and evaluation of controls. • The primary concentration in EDP still provides assurance that the specialist knows the state-of-the-art computer technology. • The cost of training the EDP specialist should be less than the cost to train the field auditors. Besides, the problem persists of being unable to train auditors when technological changes are as rapid as observed for EDP activities.	• The EDP specialist is likely to perform only the review of EDP on a particular job, due to the cost/benefit aspects of retaining the individual for other audit duties when EDP applications are present on a number of audit engagements. As a result, the EDP specialist will not have an in-depth knowledge of any particular client's business operations and as a consequence may miss important audit implications or management letter points that an experienced auditor on that engagement would identify.

ASSUMING AN AUDITOR TRAINED AS AN EDP SPECIALIST IS USED:

Advantages	Disadvantages
• The auditor's knowledge of the audit process will minimize the likelihood of key audit implications and management letter points being overlooked. • The auditor is likely to be better able to communicate findings concerning EDP than would an EDP specialist, due merely to the prevalence of professional jargon that can be an obstacle to effective communication across disciplines. • The cost of training a subset of auditors is less than having every field auditor trained in EDP.	• The EDP training of the auditor is unlikely to reach the same level as that obtained by an EDP specialist. As a result, mistakes could be made in reviewing and evaluating the EDP applications and their related controls. • The EDP specialist will have less in-depth knowledge of client operations than members of the typical audit team, since the specialist is likely to be rotated from job to job with sole responsibility for the review of EDP controls.

Exhibit 12–12 (continued)

GENERAL CONCERNS

- The specialist clearly facilitates compliance with existing professional standards.
- The rapidly changing technology of EDP precludes state-of-the-art training of all field auditors, on a cost/benefit basis.
- Basic training of auditors concerning EDP is in no way precluded. In addition, on-the-job-training is likely to be obtained by both the EDP specialist and the auditor in a manner that proves mutually beneficial in formulating an integrated evaluation of internal controls.

- The timing of EDP reviews should be early in the audit process, yet the scheduling of specialists' time may not always mesh with the audit plan. The result can be inefficiencies from either
  - not relying on effective controls, or
  - relying on ineffective controls and having to later extend substantive test work.
- The review and evaluation of controls permeate the entire audit process; however, the extent to which the EDP evaluation is integrated is largely dependent on the timing of the review, the communication capabilities of the reviewer, and the basic understanding of the audit team.

Training Auditors Is Often the Preferred Approach

Initially, many CPA firms used the first approach of relying on an EDP specialist; however, experience demonstrated that the disadvantages were real and costly. As a result, most firms have shifted toward the last alternative in Exhibit 12–12, the training of a subset of auditors as specialists. In addition, a concerted effort has been made to ensure that all auditors have a basic understanding of EDP. Given the growth of EDP and its ever-increasing significance, such a strategy has been essential to ensure an adequate and efficient audit process. While it is clear that all staff auditors are not knowledgeable on state-of-the-art developments, it is also clear that few entities are applying state-of-the-art EDP techniques. As a result, for many computer configurations the audit team will possess the necessary knowledge base to perform an audit without consulting a computer expert. A critical aspect in training field auditors is to ensure that they can accurately evaluate their skills, the degree of complexity of the client's EDP activities, and their ability or inability to assess control risk without the assistance of a computer consultant.

Sophisticated Applications May Require Computer Experts

Sophisticated computer applications utilize higher levels of programmed management decisions and larger equipment. Internally initiated transactions are common, and few detailed reference documents are routinely printed. On-line terminals are available for inquiries and transmission of input data from remote locations for editing and for subsequent batch processing. Most files are in direct access storage for the main computer's use in providing on-line service. User controls are typically impractical, as is a visible transaction trail, due to the sheer volume of transactions. Hence, programmed controls are heavily relied upon, along with the review of numerous exception reports. The transaction trail is typically available via on-line terminals or from microfilm files. The primary updating is done through batch processing, but some real time access complicates the EDP application. As the use of real time becomes extensive, data base systems become prevalent, and programmed controls become even more extensive, the complexity of the EDP application also increases. Typically, memory over 124,000 characters is available for sophisticated computer applications and more than one primary user is involved. Several CPUs are commonly available, and some use of data bases as distinct from more traditional data files is typical. An auditor should be trained to recognize such a sophistication level and typically should involve a computer expert in the review and evaluation of internal control.

Checklist of Control Concerns for Each Type of EDP Environment

Exhibit 12–13 summarizes the wide variety of EDP environments with which an auditor is likely to come in contact and highlights the control concerns for each environment.

A RECOMMENDED APPROACH TO EVALUATING AN EDP ENVIRONMENT

The EDP environment should be analyzed as an integral part of operations in conjunction with the manual system and controls of an entity. In Chapters 9 through 11, five key exhibits are presented per operating cycle that summarize

—the critical segregation of duties,
—key accounting documents,
—control environment considerations,
—error types and controls to prevent or detect such errors, and
—operating efficiency considerations.

For consistency, Exhibits 12–14 through 12–18 are presented to describe these similar concerns in an EDP environment. However, the materials presented earlier in this chapter are important complements to these exhibits' interpretation and to having an understanding of control concerns that are unique to EDP aspects of an entity's system.

Segregating Incompatible Functions

Exhibit 12–14 reflects the importance of identifying the type of system being evaluated before proceeding with an evaluation of control. A minicomputer system, similar to a one-person accounting department, relies on the classic three-way

Exhibit 12–13

Classification Scheme for EDP Environments and Related Control Concerns

Service Center	Minicomputer Environment	Batch Systems	Distributed Systems	On-Line and Real-Time Systems	Data Base Systems
		or Combinations Thereof			
Existence of a contractual agreement.	Have adequate expertise.	Control over batches.	Establish central control over remote processing sites, particularly with respect to systems development and program changes.	Prevention of updating of on-line master files.	Assignment of responsibility to a data base administrator.
Availability of a third-party auditor's report or the performance of a review by the client's auditor.	Segregate duties to extent possible.	Balancing of input data.	Have adequate expertise available at remote processing sites.	Prevention of processing of incomplete or inaccurate data.	Prevention or identification of processing errors.
Ample user controls over processing off premises.	Control access to equipment, programs, and data files to extent possible.	Control over rejected data.		Capability of restoring master files in case of a system breakdown.	Control over access to the data base.
	Document EDP, establishing audit trails and program controls.	Programmed controls over input.		Correct transmittal of data via dual transmission checks and/or message counts.	Capability of restart/recovery in case of a system breakdown.
	Establish editing, verification, and balancing controls over data entry.	Reconciliation of control totals.			

Exhibit 12–14

Critical Segregation of Duties in an EDP Environment

(☐ = *Space for initials of individual responsible for this duty.*)

Authorization

Custody

Accounting

☐ Non-EDP personnel authorize transactions.

MINICOMPUTER ENVIRONMENT

EPD personnel are not to have direct or indirect access to assets. When checks (or similar assets) are processed, a post-review technique via check signers and third-party control of blank checks (or analogous controls) are to be established.

Supervision of accounting activities of EDP is to be established by
—user controls' reconciliation to computer-generated statistics,
—reasonableness checks, and
—users' review of exception reports and other output.

EDP FACILITY

In addition to the basic segregation of duties in a minicomputer environment, the EDP department should, to the extent possible, segregate the following duties:

☐ Systems Analyst

☐ Application Programmers

☐ Computer Operations

☐ File Librarian

☐ Data (input/output) Control Group

592

DATA BASE SYSTEM

In addition to the basic segregation of duties in the minicomputer and EDP facility environments, a Data Base Administrator is needed who

SHOULD HAVE THE FOLLOWING DUTIES

—Defining, organizing, protecting, and controlling data.
—Controlling maintenance-related utility programs.
—Authorizing changes to the data base and library.
—Establishing controls over data base when DBMS is down for maintenance.
—Controlling vendor-supplied utility programs' access to DBMS.
—Reviewing log of library describing additions, changes, programs accessing DBMS, and specifications of information used by program.

SHOULD NOT HAVE THE FOLLOWING DUTIES

—Initiator of transactions.
—Ability to have unsupervised access to the computer.
—Ability to operate the computer.

> NOTE: The DBMS library contains security information as to
> —what programs can access what data and
> —who are the authorized users of various programs;
> the library cannot be altered without the Data Base Administrator's approval. Such changes are made by personnel who are not involved in the development of application programs.

GENERAL PRINCIPLES RELEVANT TO THE SEGREGATION OF EDP-RELATED DUTIES

—Data processing should be prohibited from initiating general ledger or subsidiary ledger entries.
—Knowledge of applications, programming, and documentation should be restricted; each individual should know only what is required to fulfill his or her particular responsibilities.
—Restrict access by technical people to data files and the computer.
—Live data should not be used in testing.
—Rotate personnel involved in sensitive applications.
—Require vacations.
—Retain the distinction between custody of data and accountability for the handling and processing of data.

593

division of duties. As the organization grows to support a separable EDP department, the desirability of segregating duties within that department suggests a second level of control beyond the familiar authorization/custody/accounting division. Finally, as an EDP system increases in complexity and develops a data base system, a data base administrator becomes the key control over the EDP system. Exhibit 12–14 has spaces provided for noting the initials of the key positions that require consideration in evaluating the segregation of duties within an EDP environment. With the advent of the microcomputer, it is likely that distributed systems will proliferate, with their related minicomputer effects on control. As units of operations have processing capabilities, more analyses will be done locally, with only key data being transmitted regionally and nationally—as required for control over operations and for decision-making. The result will be dispersed data bases that may very well call into question the traditional sampling and selection procedures that auditors have been using to test data and related transactions. The relevant universe for testing may not be obvious or practical, and the auditor will have to place greater emphasis on systems design. A firm understanding by the CPA of controls that can be designed into a system to gain assurance of data integrity will become increasingly important due to this

Exhibit 12–15

Assuring Complete Accounting Records
in an EDP Environment

Job Description—EDP Position _____ Department _____ Qualifications		Date _____	
Functions Performed	**% of Time Allocated to Each Function**	**Volume of Activity**	**Other Comments**

PURPOSE: To document EDP personnel's qualifications, tasks, and workload to facilitate management of department, transfer pricing, and personnel replacement.

Exhibit 12–15 (continued)

Input Data Summary Sheet

Date _____

Nature of Input _____(Attach Copy of Form)

Preparer of Summary Sheet _____

Form Number	Form Name	Form Punched Card	Type			Converted to		
			Magnetic Tape	Reprinted Form	Other	Card	Tape	Other

Description of Manual Process: _____

Description of Edit Checks: _____

Description of Controls: _____

Distribution: _____

PURPOSE: To establish control over the data conversion process and to document edit checks, controls, and distribution.

Exhibit 12–15 (continued)

Transmittal Document

Date Prepared _____
Preparer _____

Document	Batch Control Data			
	Items	$	Hash Totals	Other

PURPOSE: To protect against undetected loss or entry of data by maintaining record counts or control totals for documents to be transmitted.

Codes Stored Within Computer Records

Date Documentation Was Prepared _____
Preparer of Documentation _____
Approval of Documentation _____

Code	Interpretation	Use of Function

PURPOSE: To document the meaning of data codings.

Exhibit 12–15 (continued)

**Error Messages—
Programmed Edit and Reasonableness Checks**

Date Documentation Was Prepared _____

Preparer of Documentation _____

Approval of Documentation _____

ERROR MESSAGE	INSTRUCTIONS: HOW TO RESPOND

PURPOSE: To instruct personnel as to how to respond to error messages generated during data entry or processing.

Data Elements

Date Documentation Was Prepared _____

Preparer of Documentation _____

Approval of Documentation _____

Data Element Term (Synonyms)	Meaning	Unit of Measure	Source Picture	Edit Criteria	Applicable Codings	Controls	Security Concerns	Other Comments

PURPOSE: To document the meaning of data elements, including related controls and security concerns.

Exhibit 12–15 (continued)

Record Contents & Layout

Date Documentation Was Prepared _____

Preparer of Documentation _____

Record I.D. _____

Record Title _____

Systems to Which Record Relates _____

File Description _____ File Label _____

Element Number	Data Element Term	ID	Length	Picture	Other Relevant Data

Device Type	JCL	Organi-zation	Hierar-chical File?	Track	Density of File	Bytes Record	Records per Block	Bytes per Block	Fixed or Variable?

Illustrative Example of Record (with Format): _____

PURPOSE: To document the content and layout of EDP records (thereby facilitating the reading, processing, updating, and storage of files).

Exhibit 12–15 (continued)

Program Documentation

Program Title _____

    Identification Number or Code _____

    Preparer of Program _____

Preparer of Documentation _____

Approval of Documentation _____

Description of Program _____

_____

_____

Files Used by Program

File Name	File Number	File Description (Organization and Related Data)

PURPOSE: To describe programs, files accessed by those programs, and the organization of the files accessed, with documentation as to who prepared the programs.

FORMAT DESCRIPTION FOR OUTPUT

Date Specifications Were Prepared _____

    Preparer _____

    Approval of Report Form _____

Report Title: _____

Major Subheadings: _____

Content: _____

Illustrative Example: (see attached copy)

Distribution: _____

PURPOSE: To establish control over form, content, and distribution of output.

Exhibit 12–16

Checklist to Determine Whether There Is an Environment
for Effective Control over EDP

	Yes	No
1. Are duties properly segregated?		
2. Are employees sufficiently qualified to perform their duties?		
3. Are operators subject to periodic rotation?		
4. Are operators required to take vacations?		
5. Are user departments furnished with summary reports on changes to master files and related data?		
6. Are blank checks and negotiable paper, used for printing checks or used in similar processing, under control by someone other than the machine operators?		
7. Are manuals available documenting:		
—programming techniques and procedures?		
—procedures to change programs, including the authorization required for such change?		
—operator instructions?		
—run descriptions?		
—procedure for testing new applications?		
8. Are test data prepared and maintained for new versions of programs and new applications?		
9. Are adequate machine operation logs being maintained?		
10. Is control being effectively exercised over the operator's compliance with prescribed duties?		
11. Do documentation standards exist?		
12. Does a supervisor review documentation for adequacy and completeness and to determine if it is up-to-date?		
13. Is documentation maintained		
—as to reports and other output to be produced by EDP, including a scheduling of the output?		
—as to recipients of the reports?		
14. Are reports and other output checked for reasonableness prior to their distribution?		
15. Has the entity		
—documented a disaster plan?		
—tested planned backup facilities?		
—stored off-premises copies of master files and important programs?		
—adequately maintained equipment?		
—obtained insurance coverage for the effects of an EDP disaster?		
16. Does the entity restrict unauthorized access to EDP?		

Exhibit 12–17

What Could Go Wrong in an EDP Environment and What Controls Can Preclude or Detect Such Errors and Defalcations?

Task	Problem	Control
Creation or initiation of a transaction.	Unauthorized transactions may be entered or inappropriately excluded.	—Written authorization and/or documented approval by non-EDP. —Restrict personnel's access to EDP. —Reconciliation of user controls over input with EDP-generated totals for transactions processed.
Entering of data.	Input can be lost, duplicated, inaccurate, or incomplete.	—Use of preprinted, prenumbered forms. —Sequence checks. —Edit and review checks. —Hash or related totals. —Default options can decrease the need to separately input redundant data—e.g., if all employees pay $5 for parking, program the computer to make the deduction. —On-line instruction for untrained users.
Use of codes as means of —triggering an automatic check and approval, such as a credit check —identifying which records and files are affected by the input —signalling changes to records and instructing how the change is to be made.	Use of erroneous codes, resulting in a loss of data integrity.	—Logic checks. —Master file matching. —Trailer labels. —Transaction totals.
Translation of data from one medium to another.	Errors, loss of data, or addition of bogus data during the translation process.	—Keystroke verification. —Simultaneous preparation through use of multiple copies. —One-time recording techniques.

Exhibit 12–17 (continued)

Physical and electronic transmission of data.	Error, loss of data, or addition of bogus data during the transmission process.	—Use transmittal documents. —Cancel processed documents. —Parity control. —Echo control. —Dual read devices. —Redundancy checks. —Control register. —Run-to-run totals. —Matching items from parallel systems.
Processing of transactions.	Use of wrong file or wrong record. Incomplete or incorrect processing. Untimely processing causing cutoff errors. Loss of files or programs.	—Use of header and file labels. —Logic checks. —Sequence checks. —Run-to-run totals. —Balancing checks. —Overflow checks. —Limit check. —Validity checks. —Use dates in processing and on files. —Redundant processing.
Correction of errors.	Errors may occur in the correction process.	—Generate a transaction trail for follow-up and correction of errors. —Utilize well-qualified personnel. —Consider automated error correction. —Exercise same controls as over original data, i.e., upstream resubmission. —Investigate and try to correct cause of error. —Use suspense files for rejected items.
Storage of data.	Unauthorized access to data. Inaccurate backup to facilitate recovery from system breakdown.	—Establish backup and recovery system. —Use recovery journals. —Use off-premise storage (grandfather, father, son, file backup) with controlled access. —Establish a disaster plan.

Exhibit 12–17 (continued)

Preparation of output (exception reports are of particular importance).	Untimely or lost reports. Excessive volume, precluding effective review and use of output. Errors in output. Improper distribution of output.	—Document authorized distribution. —Encourage users' review of agings, tickler files, and discrepancy reports. —Users should reconcile output to input and review for reasonableness. —Program exception criteria to ensure reports will be useful.
Access to data base merely for inquiry purposes.	Loss of file security.	—Only permit qualified inquiries by authorized parties via the use of passwords and limited access to terminals. —Use "read only" protection on files.

Exhibit 12–18

Operating Efficiency Considerations in an EDP Environment

I. User/EDP Interface

A. Have users been involved in systems development?
B. What is the value of the information being produced?

Via interview techniques, ascertain:
1. timeliness of reports
2. accuracy of reports
3. actual use of reports
4. steps taken based on computer-generated information
5. tangible benefits of EDP.

Via inspection techniques, ascertain:
1. whether the reports being generated are practical for use—the volume of exception reports may suggest that inappropriate parameters are in use to generate such reports,
2. whether the reports appear to be sufficient for optimally accessing available information for use by decision-makers.

Via industry experience, consider whether EDP use compares to competitors.

C. Consider the efficiency savings that could result from
1. greater involvement of users in systems design,
2. creation of a formal users' feedback communication link,
3. conversion of current detailed reports to exception reports to encourage their increased use,
4. production of reports on a request-only basis, rather than on a regular basis,
5. informing users as to data that are available and requesting that they identify opportunities for effectively utilizing such information.

Exhibit 12–18 (continued)

II. Operations
- A. Is the physical setting conducive to efficient operations? Through observation procedures, assess the adequacy of
    1. space
    2. air conditioning,
    3. power lines and backup power,
    4. anti-static floor covering,
    5. cleanliness of environment (housekeeping),
    6. location, i.e., out of traffic flow and preferably physically secure,
    7. fire detectors,
    8. maintenance of equipment.
- B. Are the hardware devices in use operating efficiently and are they optimal? Often an EDP expert is required to evaluate hardware. However, the auditor should be alert to signs of trouble:
    1. Does a hardware monitor indicate a level and nature of use that is consistent with the equipment design?
    2. Does the hardware preclude the use of particular software programming or data base structures that could create efficiencies in operations?
    3. Are bottlenecks observed in processing?
    4. How reliable is the hardware, based on past experience and other available data?
    5. Is the medium used for storage compatible with efficient processing?
        a. Are files requiring frequent updating of a minor percentage of records stored on disk to facilitate direct access?
        b. Are files requiring close to 100% updating, with little need for direct access to individual records stored on magnetic tapes, a cheaper storage medium than disk space?
- C. Are the software systems in use operating efficiently and are they optimal? Again, an EDP expert may be required for an in-depth evaluation. However, the auditor can check
    1. the compatibility of programming languages with their planned use:
        a. is Cobol in use for basic business applications?
        b. is Fortran exclusively applied to higher-level mathematical applications?
        c. are the languages in use obsolete, requiring large expenditures to achieve system and software compatibility?
    2. whether the trade-off between processing efficiency and ease of programming changes has been explicitly considered:
        a. are programs that are used repetitively and changed rarely using assembly language?
        b. are programs requiring frequent adjustments using compiler language?
    3. whether a software monitor indicates a level and nature of use that is consistent with the cost of acquisition and maintenance of existing software;
    4. whether software simulation has been applied to evaluate various factors' effect on the EDP work and potential opportunities for savings;
    5. if available software has been used to ease programming and documentation responsibilities of EDP, such as
        a. source-language generators that create COBOL programs from brief specifications,
        b. decision-table generators that create source code from decision tables,

Exhibit 12–18 (continued)

      c. data management systems that do item *a* in this list and create logic modules for file design and maintenance,

      d. flowchart generators that produce logic flowcharts from source language;

   6. if available software to assist in testing and in improving processing efficiencies has been used, such as

      a. test-data generators that create large test decks from parameter cards,

      b. language optimizers that eliminate unnecessary program steps.

D. Do operator procedures appear to be efficient?

E. Are supervision and management reports adequate for efficient and controlled operations?

   1. Is there a computer operating schedule?

   2. Are statistics available on

      a. equipment use,

      b. EDP personnel's time,

      c. the cost of programming and related testing procedures,

      d. system failures,

      e. software reliability,

      f. program productivity?

F. Consider the efficiency gains that may be possible from

   1. improving the physical settings,

   2. changing the hardware devices,

   3. altering the software systems,

   4. using monitoring devices,

   5. formalizing operating procedures,

   6. maintaining additional logs for the purpose of generating more useful management reports.

III. Overall Considerations

A. In the information-gathering processes, are controls over applications redundant or unnecessary?

B. Is a manual system duplicating the computerized system?

C. Could savings accrue from

   1. automating manual operations or

   2. switching from computerized to manual operations?

D. Are both long-range and short-range planning applied to EDP activities? While recognizing the cost of change, such planning should consider

   1. applications,

   2. hardware,

   3. software,

   4. communication channels.

E. Consider the efficiency gains from

   1. eliminating redundant processing controls,

   2. eliminating redundant processing,

   3. converting from manual to automated systems or vice versa,

   4. initiating formal planning procedures.

trend and the growing use of micros by both small and large entities. Exhibit 12–19 presents a collage that compares and contrasts the EDP environment of the 1960s with that of the 1980s.

Forms for Assuring Complete Accounting Records

Exhibit 12–15 provides illustrative documents' format for an EDP system. The purpose of each document is noted to assist the system designer in understanding the "why" of each form. Of course, flowcharts and the many documents listed in Exhibit 12–8 would augment these forms to provide an auditor with a basic understanding of operations.

Checklist for Evaluating the Control Environment

Exhibit 12–16 focuses on the control environment. Obviously the checklist must be used in the context of the system under review. In the case of a micro-computer, for example, the appropriate segregation of duties will be evaluated differently than in a data base setting.

What Can Go Wrong—and How to Prevent or Detect Errors and Defalcations

Exhibit 12–17 is an effective means for the auditor to apply the recommended approach to designing and evaluating controls. It summarizes those stages of EDP operation in which errors can occur and suggests which controls would be effective at preventing or detecting possible problems. Many of the controls overlap, since a logic check in processing provides a detective check on data entry.

Guidelines for Evaluating Operating Efficiency

Exhibit 12–18 provides ideas for management letter comments concerning EDP.

A future application of the computer may be to assist the CPA in evaluating internal controls. Computer technology's capacity to deal swiftly and accurately with higher complex systems of relationships can facilitate the application of artificial intelligence models to components or possibly to complete audit activities. Descriptions of one automated approach to the evaluation of controls, TI-COM-II, are provided by Bailey et al.

Common Control Problems and Solutions in an EDP Environment

Rather than integrating numerous examples of common problems in an EDP environment throughout Chapter 12, an appendix has been prepared. The appendix to Chapter 12 summarizes typical problems and their implications. Means

Exhibit 12–19

A Contrast of the Past and the Present

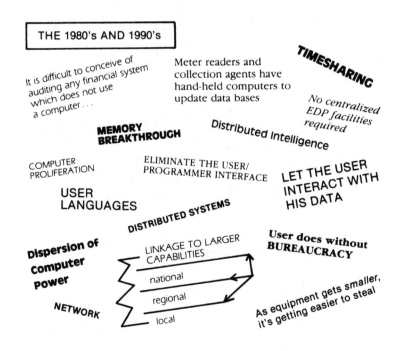

THE 1960's AND 1970's

RESPONSIBILITY SEGREGATED FROM CONTROL

ALIENATION OF USER FROM CENTRALIZED EDP

USER-EDP ANTIPATHY

USER/PROGRAMMER INTERFACE—LAYERS OF SEPARATION FROM PROCESSING

User→Programmer→Job Control→Programs→Higher Level Language Like Cobol→Compilers→Machine Language Programs→Operating System→Instructions in Microcode to Hardware→Hardware

THE 1980's AND 1990's

It is difficult to conceive of auditing any financial system which does not use a computer...

Meter readers and collection agents have hand-held computers to update data bases

TIMESHARING

No centralized EDP facilities required

MEMORY BREAKTHROUGH

Distributed Intelligence

COMPUTER PROLIFERATION

ELIMINATE THE USER/PROGRAMMER INTERFACE

LET THE USER INTERACT WITH HIS DATA

USER LANGUAGES

DISTRIBUTED SYSTEMS

User does without BUREAUCRACY

Dispersion of Computer Power

LINKAGE TO LARGER CAPABILITIES

national

regional

local

NETWORK

As equipment gets smaller, it's getting easier to steal

by which the problems might be corrected are also described. Subject indices are provided to facilitate the usefulness of the appendix as a quick reference for evaluating and communicating EDP-related control problems.

Continuous auditing is increasingly important with the high tech environment of current business operations. Exhibit 12–20 describes how audit facilities can be adapted into clients' network.

Exhibit 12–20

Integration of Audit Facilities Into Clients' Network: Effect on Practice of Auditing and Staff Qualifications

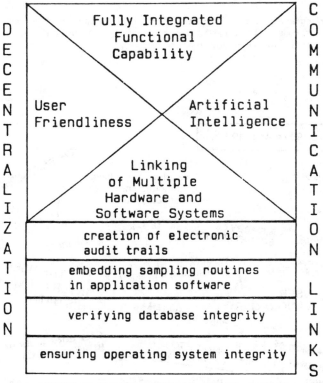

SYSTEM DEVELOPMENT LIFE CYCLE:
Shortened cycle leads to a more critical role for change

COMPUTER ASSISTED DESIGN, ENGINEERING,
AND MAINTENANCE-FREE SOFTWARE

Source: Adapted from Andrew D. Bailey, Jr., Lynford E. Graham, James V. Hansen, "Technological Development & EDP," *Research Opportunities in Auditing: The Second Decade* (American Accounting Association: Auditing Section, 1988).

REFERENCES

American Institute of Certified Public Accountants, *The Auditor's Study and Evaluation of Internal Control in EDP Systems* prepared by the Computer Services Executive Committee (New York: AICPA, 1977).

Bailey, A. D., Jr., J. Gerlach, R. P. McAfee, and A. B. Whinston, "Office Automation," *Handbook of Industrial Engineering*, Salvendy ed. (New York: John Wiley & Sons, Inc., Forthcoming).

Birtle, William, Barry Hawkins, and Walter Pugh, "Accounting Controls in a Minicomputer Installation," *Journal of Systems Management* (December, 1979), pp. 12–17.

Darrow, Joel W. and James R. Belilove, "The Growth of Databank Sharing," *Harvard Business Review* (November–December, 1978), pp. 180–190.

Folsom, Donald J., "A Control Guide for Computer Systems," *Management Accounting* (August, 1973), pp. 49–55.

Friedman, Stanley D., "Contingency and Disaster Planning in the EDP Area," *Today's Executive* (Price Waterhouse, Autumn, 1982), pp. 5–10.

Gibson, Cyrus F. and Richard L. Nolan, "Managing the Four Stages of EDP Growth," *Harvard Business Review* (January–February, 1974), pp. 76–88.

Goldstein, Robert C. and Richard L. Nolan, "Personal Privacy Versus the Corporate Computer," *Harvard Business Review* (March–April 1975), pp. 62–70.

Holmes, Fenwicke, W. Holmes, "Distributed Data Processing," *Journal of Systems Management* (July 1977), pp. 10–12.

"Information Technology: The Future Is Bright If . . . ," *Government Executive* (February, 1979), pp. 18–24.

Johnson, Everett C., Jr., "Applying SAS-3 in Your Audit Practice," *California CPA Quarterly* (December, 1976), pp. 23–29.

Koch, Harvey S., "On-Line Computer Auditing Through Continuous and Intermittent Simulation," *MIS Quarterly* (March, 1981), pp. 29–41.

Mair, William C., Donald R. Wood, and Keagle W. Davis, *Computer Control & Audit* (Florida: The Institute of Internal Auditors, 1978).

Mason, John O., Jr., "Minicomputer Controls and Their Audit Impact," *EDP Audit Symposium 1979/80 Proceedings*, edited by Joseph L. Sardinas, Jr. (University of Massachusetts at Amherst, 1979), pp. 133–174.

Nolan, Richard L., "Computer Data Bases: The Future Is Now," *Harvard Business Review* (September–October, 1973).

Porter, W. Thomas and William E. Perry, *EDP Controls and Auditing,* Third Edition (Boston, MA: Kent Publishing Company, 1981).

Reneau, J. Hal, "Auditing in a Data Base Environment," *The Journal of Accountancy* (December, 1977), pp. 59–65.

Rittenberg, Larry E., *Auditor Independence and Systems Design* (Florida: The Institute of Internal Auditors, 1977).

Rittenberg, Larry E. and Gordon B. Davis, "The Roles of Internal and External Auditors in Auditing EDP Systems," *The Journal of Accountancy* (December, 1972), pp. 51–58.

Sardinas, Joseph, John G. Burch, and Richard Asebrook, *EDP Auditing—a Primer* (New York: John Wiley & Sons, 1981).

Warner, Paul D., "Audits of Service-Center-Produced Records," *The CPA Journal* (January, 1975), pp. 25–28.

Also see 9 footnotes and source citations for each exhibit.

Note: Another useful reference is available from the Office of Policy of the United States General Accounting Office, Assessing the Reliability of Computer-Processed Data (September 1990).

Appendix

**Recommended Solutions to Common Control Problems
in an EDP Environment**

Segregation of Duties

PROBLEM: The size of the EDP operation makes it impractical to have an adequate segregation of duties.

SOLUTION: In light of this limitation, computer system usage logs should be implemented and regularly reviewed by both the EDP manager and a responsible official external to the EDP department. Consideration should also be given to obtaining additional bonding coverage of the EDP manager and the operator.

PROBLEM: Due to the limited number of personnel, there is an unavoidable overlap of functional duties; high-level EDP management is too involved in day-to-day operations. The separation of duties is weak and warrants consideration by management.

SOLUTION: Remove routine operating responsibilities from the purview of high-level EDP management, and consider expanding personnel. Increase users' oversight responsibilities.

PROBLEM: The duties within the EDP department are not well segregated.

SOLUTION: A Data Control Group position should be established to perform the following functions currently performed by the operations staff:

—scheduling,
—balancing of input control totals,
—reconciliation of output, and
—distribution.

This would provide an important segregation of duties and functions within the EDP department.

PROBLEM: Operations personnel are not rotated between shifts or applications. This practice enables an individual to continually have access to the same processing activity and, accordingly, exposes the system to manipulation and fraud.

SOLUTION: Internal control would be strengthened if operations personnel were rotated between applications and required to take vacations so that they are absent for at least five consecutive days.

PROBLEM: The computer control section reconciles certain key user reports and, as part of that reconciliation, creates input data—primarily changes and adjustments. While the reconciliation activities by themselves are proper, the creation of correcting entries should be made outside of the data center.

SOLUTION: All correcting entries are to be initiated by non-EDP personnel.

PROBLEM: EDP prepares payrolls, has control over the facsimile signature plate, and also maintains physical control over the blank payroll checks that are not prenumbered.

SOLUTION: These should be removed from the EDP department. Checks should be prenumbered.

PROBLEM: Granted, the Systems and Programming Department needs to have terminals for testing. However, since the programs that are intended to prevent these terminals from accessing live files are written by Systems and Programming, no control really exists. Obviously, the programs could be changed.

SOLUTION: Hence, special monitoring is required of all activity from these machines. The machines should have locks and their keys should be controlled by internal audit. A special report of all activity from these machines should be produced and regularly reviewed.

PROBLEM: Maintenance procedures for application systems permit programmers to move program changes from test to production libraries. Therefore, application programs can be changed and placed into production libraries without the awareness of programming management.

SOLUTION: An individual within the computer operations staff should be made responsible for moving applications into production status.

PROBLEM: Present policy permits a programmer to schedule hands-on time on the computer. Generally, this time will be scheduled on a weekend when only a part-time operator is on duty. During this period, the programmer has access to all master data files, production codes, and, of course, to computer hardware. It is therefore possible for a programmer to make unauthorized changes to master files.

SOLUTION: The present policy should be modified so that some record of the data files and production programs used during attended time is kept. If this is impractical, the present practice should be discontinued.

PROBLEM: The segregation of duties between programmers and operators is poor.

SOLUTION: Have computer operators to program tests. Other advantages to this approach include the use of more experienced operators for testing, greater ability to schedule testing with the normal workload, greater efficiency in the use of personnel.

Access to Physical Facilities

PROBLEM: Files are not locked during nonworking hours. This problem is compounded by the distribution policy for computer room keys, which allows nonsupervisory and noncompany personnel (i.e., building maintenance people) to hold keys to the computer room.

SOLUTION: Access should be restricted to computer operators, their supervisor, and those individuals who absolutely require access to the computer room.

PROBLEM: The security of the computer room is insufficient.

SOLUTION: The computer room door should be locked after the last shift and on weekends. A policy of restricting computer room access to only authorized persons should be developed. A physically secure and fireproof check vault, secluded from the main stream of traffic, should be constructed. Keys should be issued to only those individuals who need access to the computer room or check vault, and should never be left in a place that is accessible to anyone who might wish to obtain them. The signature plate should be kept in a secure place other than the computer room vault and out of the custody of the EDP department.

PROBLEM: The computer room doors are secured by locks that require the use of a magnetic card in order to be opened. At present, the first shift supervisor is responsible for the control of these magnetic cards, but this system provides no means of determining if a card is missing, since there is no master list of cards, but only a list of card numbers issued.

SOLUTION: A master list of cards should be completed and controlled. Unissued cards should be maintained in the security closet.

PROBLEM: Access to the computer room is controlled by an electronic access control system which can be circumvented through a secondary entranceway that requires only a magnetically encoded card for entrance.

SOLUTION: Access to the computer room should be limited to the main entrance, which requires both the magnetically encoded cards and a cypher unit.

PROBLEM: Security of the minicomputer and sensitive files is inadequate.

SOLUTION: Access to the room housing the minicomputer should be controlled through a combination door lock, because system tapes, passwords, and other sensitive data are contained therein.

PROBLEM: Access to the data center computer room is controlled by a cipher-locked door. The combination has not been changed in several months. There is no procedure for periodically changing the combination. The risk of unauthorized access and damage to hardware increases as the effectiveness of an unchanged combination decreases over time.

SOLUTION: The cipher-lock combination should be changed on a periodic basis, e.g., at least monthly and any time the combination has been compromised.

PROBLEM: Backup documentation is inadequate.

SOLUTION: To reduce the possible loss that could occur in case of fire, natural disasters such as tornadoes, or the acts of malicious employees, an off-site rotation of master files and program documentation on a timely basis is important. To decrease the exposure to potentially malicious employees, those individuals who have been terminated as employees should not be granted access to EDP facilities at any point in time after they have been informed of their termination.

Physical Facilities

PROBLEM: Inadequate arrangements have been made for procedure in case of a fire.

SOLUTION: Two fire extinguishers should be in the computer room and one in data entry areas. Water sprinkler heads, carbon dioxide nozzles, and halon nozzles should be considered for installation.

PROBLEM: If a fire should occur, the water damage could be substantial.

SOLUTION: To diminish the chance for water damage, EDP facilities should switch from the current sprinkler system which has its overhead pipes constantly full. Systems are available that keep overhead pipes empty until an emergency arises. There is a second safety mechanism that sets off an alarm and waits for 30 seconds to permit users to turn off the system, should the sprinklers not be necessary, or to turn off the machinery and cover it up, if possible, before spraying water.

PROBLEM: The wall that currently separates the computer room from a frequently used hallway is not of solid construction and is deemed to be highly vulnerable to fire; hence, it is not adequate to provide equipment and files with reasonable protection from unauthorized access or accidental damage.

SOLUTION: Both heat and smoke sensors should be installed in the ceiling and under the floor. To guard against the hazard of fire, the data center should be constructed of material that is more fire resistant than the material currently used. Consideration should be given to the creation of a tape library room that is separate from the computer room and that has a lockable door and high fire resistant rating.

PROBLEM: A computer printer creates a great number of dust particles from computer paper which can cause equipment breakdowns.

SOLUTION: The printer should be physically isolated from the remainder of the EDP facility whenever possible, i.e., in another room.

Systems Development

PROBLEM: The manual accounting system results in the unnecessary hiring of clerical help and a duplication of duties.

SOLUTION: Conversion to computers would save many hours of manual posting and would also provide management with a data base from which variance and trend analyses could be extracted.

PROBLEM: Recordkeeping was automated, but the full benefits of the automated system have not been realized since the old manual accounting system is still being maintained.

SOLUTION: Eliminate the manual accounting system since it has been automated and is no longer needed.

PROBLEM: The burden on EDP is excessive. Even minor increases in stored data could result in overloading the storage capabilities of the system, requiring costly and inefficient re-programming.

SOLUTION: Due to this situation, a policy ought to be adopted which requires formal requests for all new EDP applications. Such requests should include, along with other pertinent data, the following information:

—frequency of reports,
—distribution requirements,
—usefulness of the reports.

The EDP manager should determine the effect of requests on the EDP schedule, storage capabilities, et cetera, and make a recommendation to the Vice-President of Finance who should then identify the cost/benefit relationship of the requested application and approve or decline the request.

PROBLEM: Duplicate systems and unnecessary hardware expenses have resulted from expansion activities.

SOLUTION: A separate responsibility or profit center should be established to function as an EDP service subsidiary. Its services should be made available to other subsidiaries on a fee-paying basis. Other subsidiaries could choose to utilize the EDP service, their own system, or outside services. If properly designed, the profit center would deliver quality service at competitive prices and reduce EDP costs for the consolidated group.

PROBLEM: The internal audit group is not involved in systems development. Presently, project teams include representatives from management, data processing, and user departments. The control concerns that are unique to an EDP environment include the organization and operation of the computer center, hardware and software management, input and output, and computer controls—including controls over user activity, data, EDP management, computer operations, the computer library, and systems development and programming.

SOLUTION: To ensure that attention is given to these concerns, an internal auditor should be involved as an advisor to project teams for system development.

PROBLEM: Management has not evaluated the effectiveness with which EDP resources are being used or alternatives available to create additional EDP resources.

SOLUTION: Periodically, the present utilization of computer resources should be evaluated, as should future requirements for new systems. Such alternatives as implementation of a multiprogramming environment, expansion of the hours of operation, or acquisition of additional hardware should be considered.

PROBLEM: Short-term objectives are being stressed at the expense of long-term objectives.

SOLUTION: Long-range plans should be developed to handle future EDP requirements over the next three to five years. Planning considerations should include

(1) present EDP configurations, systems, capabilities, etc., and their adaptability to future needs;
(2) present company size and future expansion or reduction plans that would impact the EDP operations; and
(3) increases in the present systems requirements arising from the potential applications for present subsidiaries.

Management should be closely involved in the development of computer systems; a System Review Committee should be appointed.

PROBLEM: No scheduling of operations is routinely performed.

SOLUTION: To realistically plan for new EDP applications that require test time and to increase the effectiveness of equipment and personnel resources for normal production processing, written schedules of EDP work, by day and by period, should be maintained.

PROBLEM: No criteria have been set as to service centers' required user controls for consideration in selecting which center the company will be using.

SOLUTION: Prior to the final selection of a service center, management should establish requirements for effective user controls for inclusion in the criteria to be met by the center selected. At a minimum, such user controls should include batch controls on dollar amounts entered and hash totals on account numbers or other document control numbers. All such control numbers should be taken prior to transmitting the data for processing and compared to the resulting computer output. All procedures should be documented by filing the applicable control tapes or tickets with the output.

PROBLEM: The planning of whether to acquire and/or develop software is insufficient.

SOLUTION: The alternatives of in-house development, contracting for programming services, and the purchasing of available packages from manufacturers, software houses, and other utilities ought to be given consideration, with comparisons made of cost, support, flexibility, and satisfaction potential.

PROBLEM: Revisions to programs are not always tested prior to their use in production. One risk of not thoroughly testing program changes is that further program errors may develop which will have to be corrected, causing delays in system output.

SOLUTION: If the testing is performed in advance of the need for the live results, such risks can be reduced.

PROBLEM: Improper calculations resulted from an error in the computer program.

SOLUTION: To help prevent such occurrences, a responsible individual should review and manually test the output of all programs for propriety.

PROBLEM: Coordination and communication between EDP and cost accounting are essential. Past program changes have resulted in incorrect calculations.

SOLUTION: Before implementing a change, sufficient review, approval and parallel testing should be performed by both the EDP and accounting departments.

PROBLEM: While adequate controls exist over the implementation of a new system, the modification of systems is not well controlled. Currently, user departments contact the programmer who is responsible for the system, and (s)he modifies it and places the new program into production, subject only to the testing and review of that programmer. The documentation of such modifications is inadequate, eliminating an audit trail for system changes. In addition, a supervisory review of changes is effectively hindered.

SOLUTION: A signed programming request form should be submitted to the applications programming department for all program modifications. The request should be reviewed with the programmer who modifies and tests the results. The manager of the applications department should verify its correctness. A source listing of the modified program and a card deck should be submitted to the EDP Operations Department. However, approval of updates must be obtained from the Technical Support Group before any such programs are run.

PROBLEM: No procedure is curently available to track program modifications.

SOLUTION: Systems and programming personnel should be assigned user numbers for the library. Then the directories can be printed by user number, providing each person a listing of those programs in their library. When test programs become production programs and are implemented, user numbers can be changed. The individual directories by user number can serve as a reminder to the systems and programming personnel in updating status codes and in showing management who is modifying each program. The production status of programs helps to prevent them from being altered, i.e., there is a requirement that production programs must be copied and modifications made to the copy.

Input/Output

PROBLEM: Batch control sheets are maintained by accounting and compared to EDP output. However, the control sheets are discarded after the comparison is made.

SOLUTION: The sheets should be initialed to document the comparison and filed for subsequent review purposes.

PROBLEM: Documents entering data processing are logged before being keypunched. However, the number of documents returned by data processing after keypunching is not checked against the logged input figures.

SOLUTION: An employee should perform the check and sign the log to fix responsibility.

PROBLEM: Attention is being directed primarily to the correction of errors in the output of the entity's two service bureaus.

SOLUTION: Input controls should be established. These should include review, approval, item counts, and similar checks on input data.

PROBLEM: The input and output controls over service bureau functions are not operating effectively. The service bureau is not providing sufficient control totals and details of changes in data to enable personnel to compare control totals submitted with totals received.

SOLUTION: Request that the service bureau provide you with desired control totals.

PROBLEM: Procedures to account for checks prepared by a service bureau are inadequate.

SOLUTION: A control log should be utilized to record, as a minimum, the dates the checks were delivered, the dates they were returned, their numerical sequence, and the disposition of unused checks.

PROBLEM: Data entry screens are poorly designed. Data enters the system on "free form" screens that do not schematically match input. In addition, all data entry screens depend on the user to input the proper series of key words. This system of data entry places too much responsibility on the user/operator and fails to take advantage of modern data entry terminal capabilities.

SOLUTION: Utilize such capabilities as

—displaying descriptive information,
—specifying numeric-only or alphabetic-only fields,
—automatically tabbing the cursor, and
—submitting standard information on predesigned fields; for example, the keyboard will "lock up" if alphabetic entries are made in a field defined as numeric.

The rationale provided for not altering the screen design was that it would result in increasing line and data entry time because additional characters would have to be transmitted. Despite increased data entry time, the total time may very well decrease for the following reasons:

(1) Excess line time is already incurred, since the current screen design requires the user to depress the "enter" key several times per

original document. The revised screen design would not require the excessive use of this key.

(2) Excess time is presently incurred in reading and writing information on disks for storage, since only intermediate stages of storage can be accomplished until that point in time when the entire transaction has entered the system. The revised screen design would allow sections of the original document to be permanently stored. Thus, reading and writing on disks would be performed only once per section.

(3) Excess time is incurred in transmitting keywords to the central computer. The revised screen design would eliminate the need to transmit keywords, thus decreasing the number of characters input and minimizing the data entry time.

PROBLEM: Computer operators are required to manually record input and output record counts for control purposes.

SOLUTION: Instead, internal processing controls should be used to ensure that the output from one program is received properly as input to a subsequent program.

PROBLEM: Internal file labels are not in use for all programs with tape file input to verify the identity of these files.

SOLUTION: Such labels help to ensure the accuracy in file set-up prior to processing, and should be used.

PROBLEM: In reviewing the operations exception report, cases of mis-distributed reports were identified.

SOLUTION: To protect confidential information, the report distribution procedure should be re-evaluated to ensure that reports are sent to the proper users.

PROBLEM: No exception reports are currently being prepared.

SOLUTION: Exception reports should be generated, reviewed, and approved, reflecting the results of limit, validity, field, and similar edit tests. Otherwise, unauthorized or inaccurate data may enter the information base.

PROBLEM: Supervisors are not periodically reviewing the unauthorized entry reports that are available through system requests.

SOLUTION: These reports summarize unsuccessful attempts to access on-line records and may highlight unauthorized attempts to process transactions. They should be reviewed periodically.

PROBLEM: There is inadequate reconciliation and balancing of output reports to ensure that all data received were processed.

SOLUTION: Output control totals and balancing procedures should be used.

PROBLEM: When service bureaus are in use, their reports frequently constitute the permanent accounting records of an entity. Yet one organization was observed filing the majority of computer reports in card folders by month, in a rather loose manner, and upon examination, several monthly reports could not be located.

SOLUTION: A permanent binder should be used for report maintenance.

PROBLEM: The EDP input/output control group has no formalized operational procedures.

SOLUTION: The responsibilities of the group should include

—scheduling of input and output,
—follow-up of data not received on a timely basis from user departments,
—recording of input data in control logs with control totals to be used for subsequent balancing purposes,
—ensuring that only authorized data are processed,
—controlling items rejected, maintaining a log of these items to provide a means to verify that the rejected items are re-entered into the system,
—balancing all output reports to control totals, and
—distribution of output to user departments.

In addition, a log should record all program maintenance activities.

Operations

PROBLEM: The use of terminals is not well controlled.

SOLUTION: For terminal security, user identification numbers, transaction codes, and full sign-on/sign-off controls are needed. A transaction log should be maintained.

PROBLEM: Updates to files may be done with the use of a sign-on password. The present system employs the use of a last name to sign on. A control weakness exists in that last names do not provide the degree of secrecy desired.

SOLUTION: Individual identification numbers should be used.

PROBLEM: Idle terminals do not automatically deactivate or become suspended to preclude unauthorized use.

SOLUTION: The system should automatically log off terminals that are idle for more than ten minutes, saving the current file to avoid loss of data.

PROBLEM: The EDP system does not balance the prior day's master file totals plus the current day's activity to the new master file totals.

SOLUTION: Master file balancing provides protection against on-line posting errors and erroneous program changes and should be a routine procedure.

PROBLEM: The present job accounting system does not provide the information necessary for optimizing the job schedule or for identifying the need for additional hardware.

SOLUTION: The system should be adjusted so that it provides a record of the computer system resources used by each job run on the system, permitting the measure of performance, utilization, excess capacity, and the like.

PROBLEM: All on-line systems drop records during system failures and fail to update pointers.

SOLUTION: Consequently, programs should be developed for restart/recovery capability to detect the problems promptly and to reapply dropped transactions.

PROBLEM: There are no formalized procedures for producing backup tapes of master and transaction files and computer programs.

SOLUTION: Backup tapes should be prepared. Program and operations documentation, as well as files, should be stored off-site.

PROBLEM: The off-site backup location for files is the home of one of the members of the data processing department.

SOLUTION: It would be preferable to store the master files at another operating unit or at the service bureau.

PROBLEM: The storage of backup files is very cumbersome.

SOLUTION: The use of microfilm or microfiche should be considered as a means for storing complete systems documentation off-site.

Disaster Plan

PROBLEM: There is no disaster or contingency plan.

SOLUTION: There should be a formal plan that

—identifies essential systems,
—determines input and output requirements,

—identifies a backup mode of operation, which may be manual, mechanical, or a combination of the two,

—identifies a suitable alternative site(s) that will support the needed processing requirements,

—includes, if possible, a formal agreement with the backup site(s) for providing such services, and

—provides the administration framework for plan activation and implementation

PROBLEM: In the event of an extended computer downtime, the EDP department has an informal agreement to have the entity's data processing done at an outside service bureau.

SOLUTION: A specific contractual agreement with an outside service bureau should be obtained.

PROBLEM: Despite the likely feasibility of running current applications on any compatible service bureau equipment, this has not been investigated either formally or informally. In the event that machine backup is required, conversion must be swift and that requires prior planning.

SOLUTION: A contingency plan should be prepared and kept up to date as to those service bureaus or centers that can accommodate the company's applications. The disaster plan should be tested on a regular basis, perhaps semiannually.

PROBLEM: Insurance coverage for the cost of reconstructing information either lost or destroyed while in the hands of an outside service center is inadequate.

SOLUTION: Blanket bond coverage in this area should be periodically reviewed. Insurance coverage should be provided for the cost of recreating lost files, rewriting destroyed programs, and making payments for the use of alternative equipment.

Processing

PROBLEM: While a computer system's log is being generated daily, indicating all activity taking place during the day by operator, its only current purpose is to aid personnel in the event of a breakdown.

SOLUTION: The log should be reviewed daily by a responsible person in order to determine that only proper, authorized applications are being run on the computer.

PROBLEM: There is no regular review or comparison of the EDP listing of computer applications actually processed to the listing of computer applications that are scheduled to be processed. The principal reason for such a review is to determine that only authorized applications scheduled to be processed were actually processed. In other words, such a review reduces the risk of processing unauthorized computer applications.

SOLUTION: The review should be performed at the end of each day and all exceptions should be investigated and cleared with EDP management.

PROBLEM: A file was destroyed during system testing.

SOLUTION: Header labels with specific codings and program edits would help to prevent files from being destroyed or improperly used. In addition, a formal retention plan with external labels on the file could help to assure that a file is kept until no longer needed.

PROBLEM: Computer terminals can be used as both input and output devices for file maintenance transactions and information retrieval. Teleprocessing protection is currently inadequate.

SOLUTION: To control access and prevent unauthorized file changes, unique terminal identifier codes and personal passwords should be established. Computer programs can validate the terminal identifier and password for various transactions. Reports of valid terminal transaction and of invalid attempts to access files should be produced and carefully reviewed. Specific transactions can be subjected to increased control by requiring a special supervisor's key to be inserted in the terminal. A special report should then be produced showing these supervisory override transactions. Identifier codes should be changed on a periodic basis.

PROBLEM: The EDP department has security code protection of critical programs available for use, yet has not utilized this feature. This security protection could prevent confidential or critical programs from being listed or copied without special release codes.

SOLUTION: The security numbers should be used and should be controlled by internal audit.

Library Function

PROBLEM: Program listings are not adequately controlled.

SOLUTION: Program listings should be stored in locked cabinets when not in use. A library procedure should be established for controlling access and updates to the listings.

PROBLEM: Tapes are being kept outside of the tape library, and the exact count of tapes that should be kept in the library is unknown. There is the risk of unauthorized removal of data files or programs; unauthorized data can be brought into the data center and processed against production files.

SOLUTION: When not in use in the computer room, all tape files should be properly stored in the tape library. With the exception of those tapes required for outside storage or outside processing, tapes should not be removed from the tape library.

PROBLEM: The librarian software that is currently in use does not provide the ability to determine if changes have been made to production system programs. Nor is there a way to determine which version of the program was active during a given time period.

SOLUTION: A new package should be obtained that provides a management trail of production system changes and also indicates what version of a program was active during a production run.

Documentation

PROBLEM: No written documentation exists for certain application programs. Besides creating problems if turnover occurs, the absence of documentation could create operational inefficiency and/or errors and would require excessive time to make any necessary program changes.

SOLUTION: Written documentation should be developed.

PROBLEM: The entity has no formal data processing policy and procedure manual.

SOLUTION: A manual should be developed to provide control over the EDP function and should cover

—comprehensive written job descriptions,
—formal procedures for forms control and record retention,
—minimum program documentation requirements,
—program coding conventions,
—procedures for changing application programs or operating systems, and
—off-site rotation of master files and program documentation.

PROBLEM: The documentation of the EDP system is insufficient.

SOLUTION: Standard manuals should include

—applications design,
—programming,
—data center operations,
—operating systems,
—communications, and
—user interface.

PROBLEM: The EDP standards manual is incomplete with respect to application software maintenance and development.

SOLUTION: The following procedures should be incorporated into the EDP standards manual:

—initiation procedures,
—conceptual design,
—detailed design,
—development

- program efficiencies
- programming conventions
- testing conventions,

—implementation, and
—production system support.

PROBLEM: Sufficient information is available in the standards manual for a vendor's software source code to be identified and accessed; files stored within any direct access library can be identified.

SOLUTION: Documentation identifying system software libraries should be removed from the standards manual. In addition, specialized systems utilities may be used to identify sensitive software programs resident in direct access devices. Consequently, the availability of systems documentation to these utilities should be more closely controlled.

PROBLEM: Certain transactions may be suppressed from printing on the daily transaction journals. The primary internal control objective of such journals is to ensure that only valid data is used to update the systems. Yet this objective is clearly not being met because transactions may not appear on the journals. Therefore, the system is exposed to possible manipulation.

SOLUTION: The capability of suppressing printing should be eliminated.

PROBLEM: When packaged software is modified or enhanced internally, documentation is not kept up to date.

SOLUTION: Procedures should be established to update documentation on a timely basis whenever software is modified or enhanced.

13

Putting It All Together: How to Produce a Global Picture of an Entity's Controls

"Our plans miscarry because they have no aim. When a man does not know what harbour he is making for, no wind is the right wind."

Seneca
(4 B.C.–A.D. 65)[1]

Plans are an important part of realizing objectives. Among such plans must be a systematic way of integrating and evaluating the results. This chapter explores such a process, in order to ensure, as cited in the introductory quote that an "aim" exists and that the "right wind" is recognized and used to its greatest advantage in forming a knowledgeable professional judgment.

Once you have evaluated each of the major operating cycles of an entity, as well as the effects of EDP on those cycles, the evaluations per cycle must be combined to form a global picture of the entity's controls. This picture can then

---

[1] Quoted by Donald A. Leslie, FCA, *Materiality: The Concept and Its Application to Auditing—A Research Study* (Canada: The Canadian Institute of Chartered Accountants, 1985), p. 114.

be used either to evaluate the remaining audit plan or to support an opinion on the system for a comprehensive review engagement. While the cycles are an extremely useful organizational approach to evaluating controls, an audit is directed at the total entity's financial statements. Similarly a comprehensive review engagement is intended to produce an opinion on the entire system of controls.

For this reason, each of the parts of a control system should be pieced together to provide assurance that the sum of the parts appropriately reflects each cycle's evaluation. If a control flaw that was immaterial per cycle but when combined with minor flaws in other cycles becomes material, you must recognize this fact. This recognition depends upon an evaluation of control from a global perspective.

COMBINE THE ANALYSIS PER CYCLE INTO AN AUDIT PLAN

From the entity's perspective, each cycle is only one piece of its intricate operations, and only when each of the pieces is combined can you evaluate the overall control picture of the entity. The control picture is essential to finalizing an audit plan. Of course, the auditor typically relies on only a subset of the controls in a subset of the entity's control cycles. Nevertheless, the overall picture is an essential perspective, as the global perspective will facilitate an in-depth knowledge of the entity's operations.

If the control evaluation and review procedures applied in the audit setting to each of the cycles involved an assessment of control risk at the maximum level, the design of the control system is either too weak to warrant reliance or too expensive to test relative to available substantive testing alternatives. In such a setting the audit plan, assuming the entity is auditable, will reflect a substantive testing approach.

On the other hand, the quality of control will often vary across the cycles. You must evaluate how this differential affects the ability to rely on the controls selected for testing. A severe weakness in one aspect of a cycle may not have any bearing on the quality of another control within that cycle or in controls in other cycles. On the other hand, a single flaw in an area like bank reconciliations could very well complicate the reliance decision for the revenue, production, and financing cycles. Although you have systematically considered interactions with other cycles of operations in the course of evaluating each cycle during the design and evaluation phase, the interactions are clearest when the cycles can be simultaneously analyzed for the cumulative effects of control weaknesses. Assuming that the interactions were appropriately evaluated while performing the field work concerning internal controls, the next step is to plan the rest of the audit engagement.

Simplistically, for any cycle where the controls are deemed to be effective in both design and operation at either preventing or detecting errors and irregularities, an assessment of control risk at less than the maximum level is feasible and, based on test results, supportable. The audit plan can explicitly adjust the nature, timing, and extent of substantive audit work. However, even when less than a maximum level of control risk is assessed, and supported, you may have detected some weaknesses in control in the course of performing audit work. The ramifications of the control weaknesses that have been observed can be analyzed by using the risk exposure worksheets described earlier. In addition, the professional literature provides a distinction between material and immaterial control weaknesses.

RECONSIDER THE RISK EXPOSURE WORKSHEETS AND IDENTIFY REPORTING RESPONSIBILITIES

The risk exposure worksheets compared the magnitude of potential errors adjusted for their frequency, to the perceived high, medium, and low levels of risk for operations. This comparison has been encouraged as a useful means by which managers can perform cost/benefit evaluations of alternative control designs. A review of such worksheets will provide you with a perspective as to which controls are of greatest importance to management. The reasonableness of management's frequency and magnitude estimates can be reviewed by studying the supporting documentation accumulated by management in forming their opinions. For example, has the total volume of transactions potentially affected by the weakness been considered? In reviewing these analyses by management, regardless of how persuasive and definitive the analyses might be in establishing that the correction of an observed control weakness would not be cost/beneficial, you are still faced with a responsibility to view risk from a slightly different angle. Specifically, you must address the issue of whether the observed control weaknesses are, in fact, material weaknesses. The material/immaterial dichotomy will assist you in adjusting audit procedures to compensate for severe control weaknesses and in meeting reporting obligations, as they pertain to material weaknesses.

Risk exposure worksheets help you to know management's beliefs as to the cost/benefit picture for correcting various observed weaknesses, but they cannot be used to influence reporting obligations.

How to Identify Material Weaknesses

The definition of a material weakness follows:

> . . . a condition in which the auditor believes the prescribed procedures or the degree of compliance with them does not provide reasonable assurance that errors or irregularities in amounts that would be material in the financial statements being audited would be prevented or detected within a timely period by employees in the normal course of performing their assigned functions (AU § 320.69).[2]

---

[2] Statement on Auditing Standards No. 20, "Required Communication of Material Weaknesses in Internal Accounting Control." While reportable conditions has replaced this primary attention of SAS No. 20, CPAs may still choose to disclose material weaknesses as distinct from other types of significant weaknesses.

Exhibit 13–1

Flowchart of Pre-Engagement and Planning Activities

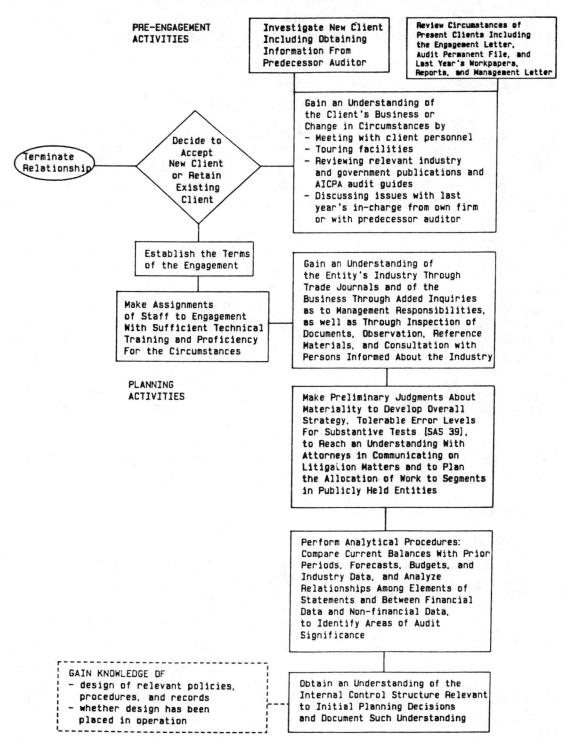

PRE-ENGAGEMENT
ACTIVITIES

Investigate New Client
Including Obtaining
Information From
Predecessor Auditor

Review Circumstances of
Present Clients Including
the Engagement Letter,
Audit Permanent File, and
Last Year's Workpapers,
Reports, and Management Letter

Terminate
Relationship

Decide to
Accept
New Client
or Retain
Existing
Client

Gain an Understanding of
the Client's Business or
Change in Circumstances by
- Meeting with client personnel
- Touring facilities
- Reviewing relevant industry
  and government publications and
  AICPA audit guides
- Discussing issues with last
  year's in-charge from own firm
  or with predecessor auditor

Establish the Terms
of the Engagement

Make Assignments
of Staff to Engagement
With Sufficient Technical
Training and Proficiency
For the Circumstances

Gain an Understanding of
the Entity's Industry Through
Trade Journals and of the
Business Through Added Inquiries
as to Management Responsibilities,
as well as Through Inspection of
Documents, Observation, Reference
Materials, and Consultation with
Persons Informed About the Industry

PLANNING
ACTIVITIES

Make Preliminary Judgments About
Materiality to Develop Overall
Strategy, Tolerable Error Levels
For Substantive Tests [SAS 39],
to Reach an Understanding With
Attorneys in Communicating on
Litigation Matters and to Plan
the Allocation of Work to Segments
in Publicly Held Entities

Perform Analytical Procedures:
Compare Current Balances With Prior
Periods, Forecasts, Budgets, and
Industry Data, and Analyze
Relationships Among Elements of
Statements and Between Financial
Data and Non-financial Data,
to Identify Areas of Audit
Significance

GAIN KNOWLEDGE OF
- design of relevant policies,
  procedures, and records
- whether design has been
  placed in operation

Obtain an Understanding of the
Internal Control Structure Relevant
to Initial Planning Decisions
and Document Such Understanding

Exhibit 13–1 (continued)

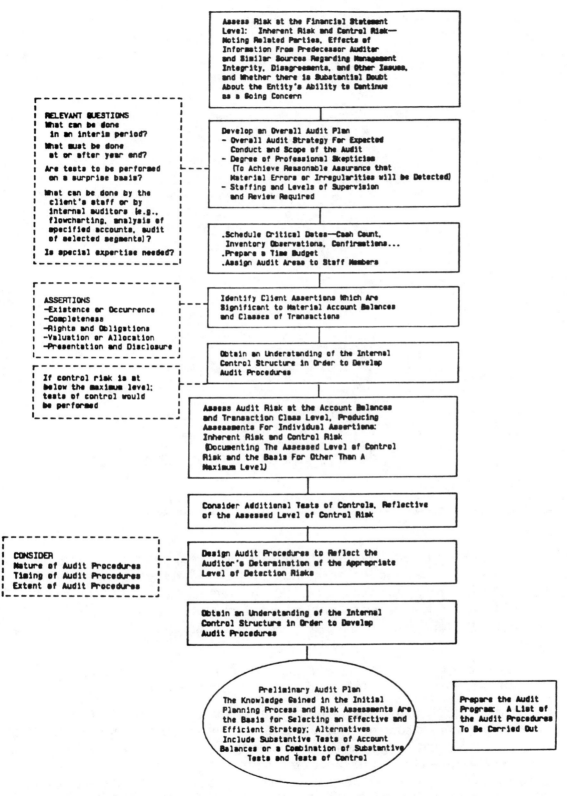

Assess Risk at the Financial Statement Level: Inherent Risk and Control Risk— Noting Related Parties, Effects of Information From Predecessor Auditor and Similar Sources Regarding Management Integrity, Disagreements, and Other Issues, and Whether there is Substantial Doubt About the Entity's Ability to Continue as a Going Concern

RELEVANT QUESTIONS
What can be done in an interim period?
What must be done at or after year end?
Are tests to be performed on a surprise basis?
What can be done by the client's staff or by internal auditors (e.g., flowcharting, analysis of specified accounts, audit of selected segments)?
Is special expertise needed?

Develop an Overall Audit Plan
- Overall Audit Strategy For Expected Conduct and Scope of the Audit
- Degree of Professional Skepticism (To Achieve Reasonable Assurance that Material Errors or Irregularities will be Detected)
- Staffing and Levels of Supervision and Review Required

.Schedule Critical Dates—Cash Count, Inventory Observations, Confirmations...
.Prepare a Time Budget
.Assign Audit Areas to Staff Members

ASSERTIONS
-Existence or Occurrence
-Completeness
-Rights and Obligations
-Valuation or Allocation
-Presentation and Disclosure

Identify Client Assertions Which Are Significant to Material Account Balances and Classes of Transactions

Obtain an Understanding of the Internal Control Structure in Order to Develop Audit Procedures

If control risk is at below the maximum level, tests of control would be performed

Assess Audit Risk at the Account Balances and Transaction Class Level, Producing Assessments For Individual Assertions: Inherent Risk and Control Risk (Documenting The Assessed Level of Control Risk and the Basis For Other Than A Maximum Level)

Consider Additional Tests of Controls, Reflective of the Assessed Level of Control Risk

CONSIDER
Nature of Audit Procedures
Timing of Audit Procedures
Extent of Audit Procedures

Design Audit Procedures to Reflect the Auditor's Determination of the Appropriate Level of Detection Risks

Obtain an Understanding of the Internal Control Structure in Order to Develop Audit Procedures

Preliminary Audit Plan
The Knowledge Gained in the Initial Planning Process and Risk Assessments Are the Basis for Selecting an Effective and Efficient Strategy; Alternatives Include Substantive Tests of Account Balances or a Combination of Substantive Tests and Tests of Control

Prepare the Audit Program: A List of the Audit Procedures To Be Carried Out

Source: This flowchart represents a composite of suggestions from Rita J. Hopewell, a professor at California State University at Dominguez Hills, from a preliminary draft of a proposed Guide for the Consideration of Internal Control Structure in a Financial Statement Audit (AICPA, File Ref. 3046), and from SAS 53 (Section 316), 55 (Section 319), 56 (Section 329), and 59 (Section 341). Professor Hopewell's suggestions to include such an overall framework are appreciated.

Exhibit 13–2

Development of Overall Audit Plan

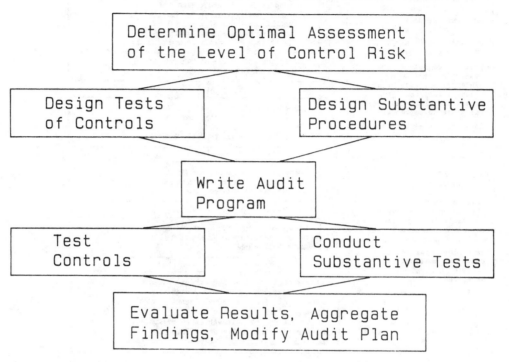

The decision process for identifying such weaknesses is described in Exhibit 13–3. As the flowchart indicates, auditor judgment defines the necessity of particular control procedures and their relative materiality during the review of controls. In other words, you as auditor could formulate a risk exposure worksheet that would be similar to management's cost/benefit analyses. There are two critical questions:

(1) Can a material error occur as a result of this control weakness?
(2) If it occurred, would it be detected within a reasonable time period?

A risk exposure analysis will focus on preventive controls that might compensate for observed control weaknesses, and detective controls that could operate to locate errors and irregularities permitted by the control weaknesses.

The objective of the analysis would be to pose a question as to the largest error that's possible due to the control weaknesses observed, and the probability of such an error occurring, undetected. The frequency of such a lack of detection would also have to be considered. If the resulting total error could be material, control design alone has served as a basis for identifying weaknesses.

Exhibit 13–3

The Decision Process for Identifying Material Weaknesses in Internal Accounting Control*

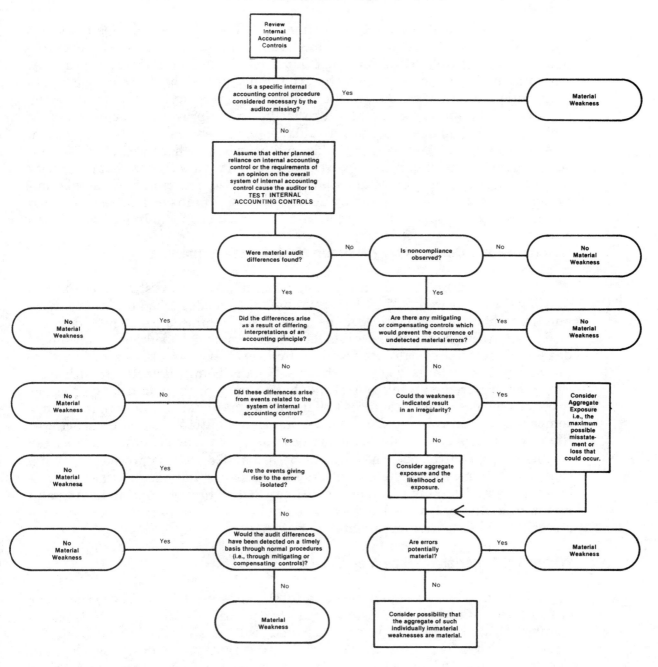

*Peat, Marwick, Mitchell and Company granted permission to utilize this exhibit originally prepared by the author for the firm's Senior Seminar in-house training program related to internal control.

A Key Element: Your Evaluation of Compliance with Controls

A key element in applying the definition of material weaknesses relates to your evaluation of the client's or company's compliance with prescribed preventive and detective controls. To perform an evaluation, you must understand both what the duties of the employees are and how the employees can be expected to perform such duties. In other words, are the competence, integrity, and general understanding of the employees sufficient to facilitate the prevention or detection of material errors and irregularities, should they occur? Are employees who perform internal control procedures responsible to some person whose work they are not reviewing? For example, if an employee is entrusted with verifying that purchases are made from authorized vendors and is supervised by the individual who initiated the order, the employee may not feel that it is in his or her best interests to point out to the superior mistakes that were made in the purchasing process.

Compensating Controls May Render Weaknesses Immaterial

The detailed review of control design for the revenue, cost of sales, and financing cycles, as well as for EDP environments, has described desired controls and the implications of not having particular control procedures. These detailed design analyses are the initial basis for defining material weaknesses in control design. No tests of control are required to discern such weaknesses. The mere knowledge that a large volume of transactions is being subjected to either no control or an extremely weak control and that no compensating controls are present to offset such design flaws suffices to flag a material weakness. Bear in mind that compensating controls could encompass internal auditors' tests of transactions, the owner-manager's involvement in operations, or other general controls; the compensating control need not always be a detailed control procedure. While control design may be ineffective in preventing errors and irregularities, it may be effective in detecting problems on a timely basis through routine testing and review procedures. Timely detection capability is sufficient to make an otherwise material weakness into an immaterial weakness.

When Will Material Weaknesses Exist?

If the control design signals no material weaknesses, the next issue is whether controls are sufficiently strong to warrant testing and whether such testing, assuming control compliance is demonstrated, will be a cost/beneficial basis for reducing substantive test work. For now, assume that control design is adequate to good, and tests of control are performed. Under what circumstances will you conclude that material weaknesses exist in the control system?

Returning to Exhibit 13–3, if no material audit differences are noted and compliance with designed controls is observed, no material weakness has been detected. Similarly, if there are mitigating or compensating controls that would prevent the occurrence of material errors despite noncompliance with designed controls, no material weakness has been detected. However, if material audit differences are discovered in the course of testing controls and were not due to differing interpretations of accounting principles, events unrelated to the internal accounting control system, or isolated events, the probability is that a material weakness does exist. The only condition under which the weakness would not be judged material under such circumstances is if the observed material audit differences would have been detected on a timely basis through normal procedures. In other words, if compensating or mitigating controls were in existence, even material audit differences, discovered during testing, could signal no more than an immaterial weakness in controls. All of these potential settings and additional possibilities involving situations in which material audit differences are not found, yet noncompliance is observed, are portrayed in Exhibit 13–3.

Note: An important facet of the decision process involves the consideration of whether the events that have given rise to the test errors are related to the system; the source of errors must be determined. Recall that errors may arise from the misunderstanding of instructions, mistakes of judgments, and fatigue or distraction of the personnel responsible for performing control procedures, as opposed to arising from a weakness in the control system.

Reporting Responsibilities

Statement on Auditing Standards No. 60 requires reporting "matters coming to the auditor's attention that, in his or her judgment, should be communicated to the audit committee because they represent significant deficiencies in the design or operation of the internal control structure, which could adversely affect the organization's ability to record, process, summarize, and report financial data consistent with management's assertions in the financial statements."[3] There is no requirement that this communication be in writing; however, to demonstrate compliance with the intent of the standards, formality is strongly encouraged. If communication is oral, the auditor should carefully document the time and content of the discussion in the working papers. Public reporting of reportable conditions or material weaknesses is not required. The auditor must, of course, adjust audit procedures to reflect observed control weaknesses, but (s)he can do so and can issue a clean audit report in spite of the presence of a material weakness.

Note the Distinction Between a Material Weakness in Control and a Material Misstatement in Financial Statements

An important distinction exists between a material weakness in control and a material misstatement in financial statements. The former can occur and have

---

[3] SAS No. 60, "Communication of Internal Control Structure Related Matters Noted in an Audit" (New York: AICPA, April 1988), pp. 1–2.

no effect on the reported financial statements. The possibility of material error is not synonymous with actual material error in the financials. You as auditor can do enough substantive test work to provide assurance to report users that no material error exists in the financial reports.

A simplistic analogy can be applied to crime-prevention practices by a shopkeeper. If you were aware of the shopkeeper's practice of not locking his shop when it is unattended, you would probably say that there was a possibility of material losses by that shopkeeper due to the absence of basic safeguarding controls. You might even deem the possibility of loss probable. Yet at any given point in time you could enter the shop as an auditor, take an inventory, and perform an examination of the financial statements, reaching the conclusion that the financial statements fairly portray the financial position of the entity. Apparently, the shopkeeper has not yet experienced material losses due to the material weakness in control. A clean audit report is appropriate for past operations, but the problem persists that unlocked doors are ineffective safeguards against the significant loss of assets.

Key Factors to Consider in Reporting Material Weaknesses

In reporting material weaknesses, two considerations may warrant inclusion in your communication of material weaknesses. The first concerns the past communication of the same weaknesses and the second relates to management's judgment as to the cost/benefit picture with regard to a particular control procedure. Obviously the latter can account for a need for the former. If management has judged the correction of a material weakness to be more costly than justified by the potential benefits of such correction, that material weakness will persist and your reporting will become repetitive. When management has explained that its cost/benefit analysis has indicated that the costs of correcting the material weakness exceed the benefits derived from such a correction, how should you adjust reporting practices? In all cases the material weakness must still be reported, but you can augment such a disclosure with the statement that management believes costs exceed benefits for the particular controls involved. You should not judge the propriety of management's cost/benefit analysis, as management has the responsibility for establishing an entity's control system and for making the cost/benefit tradeoff decisions required in designing a control system. However, if desired, you can issue an explicit disclaimer on the stated belief of management.

Common disclosure practice is to distinguish prior years' repetitive comments on control from new suggestions communicated for the first time this year. In reviewing prior years' comments, frequently a concise reminder will appear in the current year's report, with a reference to the prior year's report for further details. This decreases the redundancy in reporting, yet meets the reporting responsibilities delineated by the professional standards. When such a comment is also accompanied by a synopsis of management's beliefs as to cost/benefit, a balanced picture of the control issue is presented, which effectively communicates management's role in system design. In addition, rapport with management is likely to be enhanced when its beliefs are communicated concurrently with disclosures of control weaknesses.

A final factor warrants explicit attention when reporting on material (as well as immaterial) weaknesses; that factor is management's reaction to the suggestion, beyond information relating to its cost/benefit analysis. For example, has management taken or does it plan to take corrective action? If the client or company, made aware of a material weakness, has taken corrective actions prior to the issuance of your report, you can mention such actions *if* the design of the corrective actions is reviewed and the application of the new or revised controls is tested. Otherwise, no mention of past corrective action by the CPA is permitted. However, the CPA is permitted to cite the intentions and plans of management to correct the observed weaknesses if the CPA has received evidence of such positive reactions by management.

The focus to this point has been on the auditor's reporting responsibilities. For a comprehensive review engagement, which will be discussed in considerable depth in a later chapter, an auditor has clear public reporting responsibilities with respect to material weaknesses. The content of such a report should parallel that which would be presented to top management except that the knowledge base of the users of these types of reports does require consideration when drafting comments. Although reporting issues are primarily the subject matter of a later chapter, it may be useful at this juncture to review one example of how a material weakness might be reported.

An Example of a Material Weakness

One of the more common material weaknesses involves a lack of properly segregated duties. As an example, consider one client's purchasing activities within the cost of sales cycle.

Citing the weaknesses. A person who is responsible for initiating the acquisition and/or disposition of assets should not also be responsible for the physical custodianship of company assets. Yet the parts manager of each of the client's branches now has the authority to initiate purchases and to remove inventory from stock; the parts manager also has responsibility for the physical control of inventory on hand.

Current practice does not involve a consistent use of purchase orders, and when the purchase orders are used, they are typically not completed properly. No control has been established over unused and outstanding purchase orders. Generally, no independent approval of purchase orders is obtained.

When goods are delivered from the suppliers, they are often received and checked by the same person who placed the original order. Sometimes this same person then uses the delivery tickets to update the entity's perpetual inventory records.

As invoices are received from suppliers, they are immediately forwarded to the parts department where they are matched with the corresponding delivery tickets and purchase orders—if they have been used. After such matching, the invoices are sent to the accounting department for initial recording.

Effects of these weaknesses. These weaknesses, in the opinion of the client's auditor, seriously undermine management's efforts to effectively control the entity's inventories and purchases. Several problems could arise as a result, including

- —the unauthorized purchasing of assets and unidentified inventory "shrinkage" as a result of the lack of appropriately segregated duties,
- —a loss of both time and money from the duplication of purchasing duties at each branch; in particular, quantity discounts and optimal pricing opportunities may be foregone by such a decentralized approach,
- —an inability to effectively follow up and expedite outstanding purchase orders, since documentation of such orders is typically unavailable,
- —the loss of delivery tickets and/or invoices resulting in
  - unnecessary reordering
  - lost time in processing invoices
  - lost time in reconciling vendors' statements, and
- —the absence of reliable purchasing data for use in planning cash flows and generating forecasts.

Ways to Improve Weaknesses—and Their Advantages in Terms of Operating Efficiency and Control

Internal controls could be greatly improved by centralizing the purchasing function, permitting exceptions to this centralized approach when absolutely necessary. Requisition requests should be prenumbered, approved by the supervisors of the parts departments, and forwarded to the centralized purchasing function. Multiple copy prenumbered purchase orders should be used and controlled, with one copy going to the accounts payable department for subsequent matching to the invoices. Similarly, multiple copy prenumbered receiving reports should be used for all goods received. Again, a copy of the form should be distributed to accounts payable for matching to the purchase order and invoice. In addition, the purchasing department should receive a copy of the receiving report to verify that the purchase has been filled as ordered.

When invoices from suppliers are received, they should be forwarded directly to the accounts payable department on a timely basis where they can be matched to the appropriate purchase orders and receiving reports. A voucher system could be extremely useful to the accounts payable department as a means of controlling invoices. If such a system is not established, the practice should be adopted of having the mail opener prepare a list of invoices received, a copy of which could be used by the accounts payable department as a control listing of invoices being processed.

Invoices should be approved by designated officials, and dual approval required for purchases over a certain dollar amount. Each invoice should be stamped to facilitate the documentation of various control procedures. The stamp should provide a checklist, requiring initials by the individuals that check (1) the mathematical accuracy of the invoice, (2) the agreement of the quantities ordered and received to the quantities billed, and (3) the invoice for proper approval. Frequently, the stamp also includes information as to account distribution or secondary reviews by a supervisor.

The adjustment of perpetual inventory records for acquired inventory should be made by employees outside of the parts or purchasing departments. The adjustments should be made in batches, with reconciliations performed to the updated records. Since inventory records are maintained on the computer, the computer edit printouts can assist in the reconciliation process. To maintain control over the accounting records, the parts department should have inquiry access only to the perpetual records.

Accounting personnel should periodically account for the numbered sequence of purchase orders and receiving reports.

The disclosure approach. In this example, the CPA has

—cited the weaknesses,

—identified their predictable effects as material,

—suggested specific means of improving the weaknesses, and

—highlighted both operating efficiency and control advantages of instituting the recommended control changes.

This type of a disclosure approach is common in communications to management. For public reporting purposes disclosures are typically restricted to stating the weakness and its possible effects.

Note: In communicating weaknesses to management, the CPA should emphasize that these are the material weaknesses (or reportable conditions) detected in the course of determining how controls are to affect the scope of the audit examination. Since all areas of control have not been selected for study, since testing of controls was not performed in areas where substantive tests were more economical, and since there is an inherent risk that items selected for testing may not include existing errors and irregularities, material weaknesses could exist, yet be undetected.

HOW TO INTERPRET THE RESULTS OF TESTS OF CONTROLS

Areas in which material weaknesses were not detected in the design phase were potential candidates for tests of control. Those areas that had average-to-good controls and for which tests of control were deemed to be cost/beneficial were subjected to test procedures. Interpreting the test results is a critical phase of the auditor's judgment process.

Consider Its Effect upon the Auditor's Assessment of Control Risk

In planning tests of control, the auditor set an acceptable error rate for the population and then proceeded to draw a sample to support whether the observed errors in compliance for that sample indicated that the population would fall within the acceptable error range. As discussed in earlier chapters, any compliance deviations observed were analyzed qualitatively to see if systematic patterns appeared that might indicate critical breakdowns in the system or inherent flaws in complying with prescribed controls. If compliance errors appear to be random, they are probably caused by random human errors which are inherent in any control system. In contrast, a systematic error may flag a programming problem in an EDP application or a turnover in staff that was not followed by sufficient training to ensure the effective compliance with designed controls.

When compliance deviations fall within the acceptable error range and no systematic pattern appears in the observed deviations, the auditor has support for assessing control risk at less than the maximum level. In fact, if the sample evidence supports more effective compliance than anticipated, control risk can be assessed at an even lower level, and substantive tests' nature, timing, and extent can be adjusted even more than initially planned, due to the entity's strong controls.

What to do if the error rate is outside the acceptable range. In contrast, if the observed error rate is outside of the acceptable range of error, you must perform more audit work than originally planned.

Expanding the sample size. If the deviations observed are thought to be due to the drawing of an unrepresentative sample, you may choose to expand the sample size as a means of supporting expectations. *Caution*: This is both a risky and a potentially expensive procedure. As the number of observed deviations increases, the sample size commensurate with a low error rate quickly balloons. Furthermore, if your reason for the unexpected findings is wrong, you may perform the additional testing and still fall short of the desired results.

Identifying and correcting the cause of deviations. Another alternative involves identifying the cause of the deviations, having management take corrective action, and then testing the corrected system as well as estimating the effects of the observed weakness in controls. Several means are available for identifying the cause of compliance deviations.

Statistical check using a runs test. If an auditor wishes to test whether a temporary breakdown in the control system has resulted in the compliance deviations, it is possible to statistically test the probability by using a runs test. Essentially, a *zero/one* coding is used where a *zero* corresponds to transactions with no compliance problem and a *one* corresponds to observed compliance deviations, and the probability of the ones clustering around a breakdown, as opposed to being randomly distributed through the population, is evaluated. As described by Whittington and Adams (1982),

—two deviations out of 7 transactions,

—three deviations out of 18 transactions, and

—four deviations out of 31 transactions

would all suggest that at a 95% level of confidence, for a control system with a normal deviation rate of 5%, a temporary compliance breakdown has occurred. Of course, a greater number of deviations or a fewer number of transactions than these three cut-offs would simply increase the likelihood of a temporary breakdown. Once this statistical test has been applied, the timing and nature of the breakdown can be investigated. Perhaps the reason for the breakdown was that a regular employee was on vacation. In this setting, the magnitude of the transactions processed during the vacation period can be estimated and the materiality of the weakness can be evaluated. The entity can review the set of transactions processed during this period, if deemed necessary, and can improve controls to encompass some formal on-the-job training of substitutes who are to cover for employees on vacation. The result of such an investigation may be a sufficient evidential base to warrant reduction of control risk at less than the maximum level in spite of the observed deviations.

Qualitative runs in deviations. Beyond the statistical check for chronological "runs" of deviations, you should consider qualitative "runs" in deviations. For example, have all deviations involved a particular employee, a particular supplier, or a particular customer?

Testing compensating controls. An important question also concerns what preventive or detective controls failed and whether compensating controls are available that would have detected the problems uncovered in the sample. If compensating controls are available, you may choose to test such controls as a basis for reducing the level of control risk, rather than focusing additional attention on the controls initially selected for review.

If compliance deviations exceed the tolerable error rate for a given area of control, if no pattern is detectable that might resolve or permit the estimation of the deviations' effects on overall control and the related accounting records, and if no alternative compensating controls are available for testing, your assessment of control risk at less than a maximum level for that control area is unsupportable. You must revise the original audit plan to reflect risk at the maximum level in that area of operations, and the nature, timing, and extent of substantive test work must be appropriately adjusted to provide the necessary evidential base for formulating an audit opinion.

Consider Its Effect on the Audit Plan

The effect of control risk assessment on an audit plan has already been discussed in an earlier chapter. For example, a test of control of the revenue cycle may support smaller sample sizes for substantive test work, use of negative confirmation requests rather than positive confirmation requests, and/or the performance of a substantial amount of test work prior to year-end. Exhibit 13–4

Exhibit 13–4

Summary of Audit Approach Existence, Occurrence, Rights

CLIENT: _____VINCO, INC._____ BALANCE SHEET DATE: ___12–31–x4___
Prepared by: _____Roger Smith_____ Date: __9–15–x4_____
Reviewed by: _____Paul Harmon_____ Date: __10–2–x4_____
    Account(s): _____Receivables/Revenues_____
    Assertion(s): _____Existence, Occurrence, Rights_____

Summary of Inherent Risks:

- All sales are to well-known food stores and retail liquor distributors, which reduces risk of non-existence (i.e., little risk that receivables are from non-existent customers)
- No receivables are pledged or factored

Summary of Relevant Internal Control Structure Policies and Procedures:

- Strong control environment reduces risk of misstatements throughout financial statements (see C-10)
- Strong accounting system and control procedures over customer master file and authorization and recording of sales (see R-20, R-30, R-40)

Summary of Tests of Controls:

- Testing of control environment by inquiry and observation and various other tests (see details at C-10, C-30, and C-40)
- Testing of accounting system and control procedures by inquiry and observation of appropriate company personnel and examination of evidence (see details at R-20, R-30, R-40, R-50, R-70, R-80, R-90, R-100, R-110, G-10, G-30 and G-40)

Risk Assessment:

- Low, based on very strong internal control structure factors relating to these assertions

Summary of Substantive Tests:

- Analytical procedures (with comparisons between years and to budget) including volume sales by product line, average sales price by product line, days sales in receivables
- Confirmation of a small sample (high tolerance for sampling error) of customers selected randomly from the 10/31 A/R trial balance
- Analytical procedures applied to activity in the "roll forward" periods from 10/31 to 12/31

Note: Cross-referenced working papers are not presented.

Source: *Guide for the Consideration of Internal Control Structure in a Financial Statement Audit* (AICPA: draft form January 7, 1989), p. 216, Exh. 6–6.

Exhibit 13–4 (continued)
Other Examples of Audit Planning Implications

Account	What Information Would You Collect?	How Would You Use This Information in Analytical Procedures?	What Would Be the Expected Effect of Such Analytical Procedures Work on the Audit Plan, Relative to Last Year's Audit?
Accounts Receivable	• Number of Customers • Credit Ratings of Customers • Payment Terms; Discount Policies • Stability of Balances, Relative to History • Competitors' Experiences • Changes in Customer Base, Credit Extension Practices, or Sales Policies • Aging Schedule • Budgeted Data • Shipment Data • Recurring Analyses of Sales and Collections by Management	• Comparison to Prior Year • Comparison to 3- to 5-Year Trend • Comparison of Budget to Actual • Comparison of Client's Ratios and Balances to Competitors' Data • Tie-in of financial data to information in the management system, such as total shipments and number of customers, perhaps linking current period's receivables to last month's shipment—depending on the payment terms • Review of analyses by management with follow-up on unusual fluctuations and corroboration of significant items noted	• Focus Detailed Test Work on Unusual Items and In Operating Aspects Undergoing Change, e.g., stratify confirmation work to address areas of flux of areas presenting problems in the past—perhaps drop shipments, certain classes of customers, and particular product lines result in the greater risk of under or overstatements, disputed items, or collection difficulties • Reduce sample size for confirmation work, thereby reducing extent of necessary alternate procedures • If receivables can be assessed as reasonable, work in cash receipts could either be reduced to nonsales receipts, or potentially eliminated if such "other" receipts are insignificant
Allowance for Doubtful Accounts	• Industry Experience • Nature of Disputes, i.e., simi-	• Comparison of Client's Experience to that of the Industry	• Rather than having to look over the current year's disputed items, an historical profile as

Exhibit 13–4 (continued)

Account	What Information Would You Collect?	How Would You Use This Information in Analytical Procedures?	What Would Be the Expected Effect of Such Analytical Procedures Work on the Audit Plan, Relative to Last Year's Audit?
	larities or patterns in the past • Economic Conditions • Industry Characteristics of the Customer • Base Credit Ratings of Customers • Stability of Receivable Balances • Past Recovery Experience on "Over 90-Day Accounts" • Aging Schedule • Data as to Management's Recurring Analysis of Uncollectibles (NOTE OVERLAP OF INFORMATION COLLECTED ACROSS ACCOUNT AREAS)	• Historical Trends • Mathematical Extension of Aging Schedule, Based on Past Recoveries and Percentage of Receivables Related to Highly Disputed Items or Troubled Customers • Percentage Relationship to Sales and Receivables • Focus on Large Fluctuations or Upon Changes in Credit Terms	to those types of sales or selling terms (such as shipping instructions) which have been disputed could serve as a benchmark for assessing overall reasonableness • Inquiry Procedures could be reduced by first analyzing that data used by management on a recurring basis and then only discussing "unusual items"
Inventory	• Receiving Report Statistics and Production Date • Shipment Statistics • Average Pricing Data for Last Year and This Year	• Mathematical Analysis of: Beginning Inventory (units) + Receiving Statistics on Production Information − Shipments Expected Inventory in Units × Last Year's Average Price × CPI Conversion Factor Expected Inventory Balance	• Only observe inventory at warehouses with unusual variances • If overhead component is stable, rely on total inventory tests, in lieu of detail testing overhead allocations

Exhibit 13–4 (continued)

Account	What Information Would You Collect?	How Would You Use This Information in Analytical Procedures?	What Would Be the Expected Effect of Such Analytical Procedures Work on the Audit Plan, Relative to Last Year's Audit?
	• CPI Related to Product Line(s) • Historical Relationship of Overhead to Total Price • Plant Capacity and Storage Capabilities • Stability of Balances Across Time • Changes in Purchasing, Production, Shipment, or Pricing Practices that are Expected to Affect Inventory Balance • Market Conditions and Prices	• Historical Comparison of relative balances across time and across warehouses • Stability of Overhead Component in the Inventory Valuation • Compare balances to capacity of production and storage facilities for overall reasonableness • Assess whether net realizable value is questionable based on price data from the market	• Consistent relationships over time with respect to the effects of purchases, sales, and overhead on inventory suggest that cutoff problems are unlikely—in the absence of some change in operations or potential effects of incentive compensation schemes on the risk of smoothing practices • If pricing changes primarily reflect inflation, analytical procedures may provide sufficient assurance that inventory pricing is reasonable without detailed testing
Warranty Provision	• Industry Experiences • Historical Claim Experiences • Nature of Product Line and Its Independence or Dependence on Economic Conditions (for example, during bad times economically, postponement of new pur-	• Check Consistency of Client and Industry Statistics • Extrapolate Past Experience, Adjusting For Changing Economic Conditions	• Regardless of how management computes the provision, if it's reasonable based on industry and historical experiences, it would appear to be acceptable; therefore, the analytical procedures work may very well preclude the need for a detailed review of the client's approach or extended

Exhibit 13–4 (continued)

Account	What Information Would You Collect?	How Would You Use This Information in Analytical Procedures?	What Would Be the Expected Effect of Such Analytical Procedures Work on the Audit Plan, Relative to Last Year's Audit?
	chases leads to higher use of warranty agreements by customers)		discussions as to whose judgment is more accurate
Payroll	• Number of Employees in Prior Year and This Year • Union Contract Terms or Pay Scales • Subclassifications of Hourly Versus Salary Employees and Breakdowns by Plant • Number of New Employees • Number of Employees Terminated • Historical Data on Deductions from Pay • Current Computational Guidelines For Payroll Taxes, etc.	• Mathematical Extension—Compare last year's number of employees to this year, corroborating newly hired and terminated figures by tying inquiry results to the records, and adjust for pay rates • Do Analyses by Subclassifications, applying guidelines and by Plant	• Eliminate detailed testing • Only observe payroll at plants appearing unusual (thereby directing the audit work where the greatest risk seems to exist)
Repair and Maintenance	• Historical Profile of Dollars "Automatically Expensed" and the Percentage of Repairs and Maintenance	• Compare historical Percentages to Current Book Values • Adjust for Factor Capturing Expected Increase Due to	• Eliminate detailed tests if repair and maintenance figures appear reasonable (This is particularly true given planned tests of payables)

Exhibit 13–4 (continued)

Account	What Information Would You Collect?	How Would You Use This Information in Analytical Procedures?	What Would Be the Expected Effect of Such Analytical Procedures Work on the Audit Plan, Relative to Last Year's Audit?
	Represented • Age of Equipment • Historical Repair and Maintenance Experience • Competitors' Experiences	Older Average Age of Equipment or Decrease Due to Recent Replacements • Compare Client's Percentage Relationships to Those of Competitors	
Accounts Payable	• Age of Payables • Cash Disbursement statistics • Economic Condition • Liquidity Pressures • Receiving Report Statistics • Pricing Data • Payment Terms Extended • Discount Policy	• Mathematically Extend Receiving Statistics By Price, Adjust For Payment Terms and Disbursements, then Compare to Book Values • Compare Age of Payables, Economic Condition, Liquidity Pressures, and Payment Terms to Historical Experience	• Reduce Sample Size of testing payables, e.g., accept lower level of confidence or less precision in testing
Fixed Assets	• Competitors' Fixed Asset balances • Changes in Plant Capacity, Production Statistics, or Production Processes • Last Year's Balance • Market Prices for Assets	• Review Client's Balances in Relation to Industry; Assess Reasonableness of Changes, in Light of Known Business Changes of the Client • Compare Self-constructed Asset Values to Market Prices for Similar Assets	• Eliminate Vouching of Fixed Asset Additions, particularly due to Statistical Testing of Payables—Why test these "payables" twice?

presents a summary of the audit approach to testing the assertions of existence, occurrence, and rights as they relate to receivables and the revenue cycle for an illustrative company. Note the linkage of control risk to both inherent and detection risk, as reflected in plans for substantive tests. Audit plan implications of various analytical procedures for a variety of accounts are also detailed. While these examples merely reinforce ideas illustrated in earlier chapters, what has not yet been discussed is how observed weaknesses in control, particularly material weaknesses, affect the audit plan.

In performing a review of control, you may have concluded that certain areas of control design were insufficient to warrant assessment of control risk at less than a maximum level. The observed weaknesses that were judged to preclude assessment of control risk at less than a maximum level must be evaluated as to their potential effect on the financial statements under examination. The results of such an evaluation will be an integral part of setting the scope of the audit examination. You may be able to compensate for the material weaknesses by increasing the audit scope, or you may be forced to issue a qualified report or a disclaimer.

The effect of a material weakness on the audit scope and the audit report should be carefully documented in the working papers. As already emphasized, the existence of a material weakness does not mean that a material error exists, it simply implies the potential for material errors even if such errors have not as yet occurred. In a sense, a material weakness has a futuristic dimension; the material error could well result in the future, due to the present material weakness in control.

An emphasis has been placed on restricting control evaluation to an understanding of controls, when they are judged to be either inadequate for lowering control risk assessment or not cost/beneficial to test. However, whenever material weaknesses are suspected, they should be sufficiently investigated to determine that they are or are not present and to evaluate their effect on the audit plan.

Two considerations involve the effect of material weaknesses on companies' compliance with the Foreign Corrupt Practices Act (FCPA), and interim financial reporting practices of the entity. While a CPA cannot express an opinion as to whether a client is in compliance with the FCPA, since such compliance is essentially a legal question, (s)he must be concerned about the probability of noncompliance, monetary ramifications of noncompliance, and disclosure requirements as to illegal acts.

Illegal Acts. When the evaluation and/or testing of controls has caused you to believe that illegal acts may have occurred, inquiries should be made of management, legal counsel, and other specialists, as deemed necessary, to obtain an understanding of both the nature of the acts and their possible effects on the financial statements. Additional audit procedures may be necessary to investigate such matters. The presence of

—unusual or questionable explanations as to the purpose of certain transactions,

—unauthorized transactions,

—improperly recorded transactions, or

—untimely or incomplete records of transactions

may lead you to suspect the possibility of illegal acts. Inquiry procedures as to loss contingencies and regulatory matters may uncover illegal acts.

Evaluating materiality. Once the illegal act has been identified, you must evaluate its materiality. What effects do the acts have on the financial statements? What is the related contingent monetary exposure from violating the laws involved? This exposure would include fines, penalties, and anticipated damages. The disclosure question is similar to that for any loss contingency—is it probable and reasonably estimable or is it possible and reasonably estimable? As explained in Statement on Auditing Standards No. 53:

> If the auditor has concluded that the financial statements are materially affected by an irregularity, the auditor should insist that the financial statements be revised and if they are not, express a qualified or an adverse opinion on the financial statements, disclosing all substantive reasons for his opinion.

(pp. 11, 12)[4]

An illegal act that has been detected should be reported to the audit committee—an organization that is high enough to ensure that appropriate action can be taken as to remedial actions, adjustments and disclosures in the financial statements, or disclosures in other reports used by the client. The level of authority required is the Board of Directors or the Audit Committee in accordance with SAS No. 53. You must, in particular, evaluate the implications of the illegal action for assessment of control risk and reliance on management's representations.

How illegal acts affect the auditor's report. Suspected or discovered illegal acts may affect your report in one of several ways:

(1) if the suspected act cannot be verified, a qualification of the opinion or a disclaimer may be required due to a scope limitation;

(2) if the act can be determined to have occurred, its effects have been judged to be material, and the client has failed to properly account for or disclose the act, a qualified or adverse opinion would reflect the departure from generally accepted accounting principles;

(3) if the effects of the act cannot be estimated, modification of your report to reflect the existing uncertainty would be appropriate.

Of course, a client may refuse to accept any modification of the audit report, in which case the professional literature suggests that you withdraw from the engagement, document in writing to the client's Board of Directors the reason for withdrawal, and consult legal counsel. SAS No. 53 notes duties to disclose related

---

[4] SAS No. 53, "The Auditor's Responsibility to Detect and Report Errors and Irregularities" (New York: AICPA, April 1988).

to: Form 8-K, SAS No. 7 when communicating with successor auditors, subpoenas, and to certain funding agencies. Due to ethical obligations of confidentiality, discussion with legal counsel is recommended. Exhibit 13–5 summarizes the nature of disclosures required in the event of an auditor change.

What to do if the illegal act is immaterial. If an illegal act is deemed to be immaterial, you should evaluate how the client responds to your information regarding the act. If appropriate consideration is not given to the illegal act, the auditor should further evaluate the effects on the ability to rely on management's representation, and on the CPA firm's continued association with the client. The professional standards suggest that the auditor consider withdrawing from the engagement or disassociating the CPA firm from any future relationship with the client.

An illegal act may cause the auditor to question all management represen-

---

Exhibit 13–5

**DISCLOSURES REQUIRED
WHEN CHANGING AN AUDITOR**

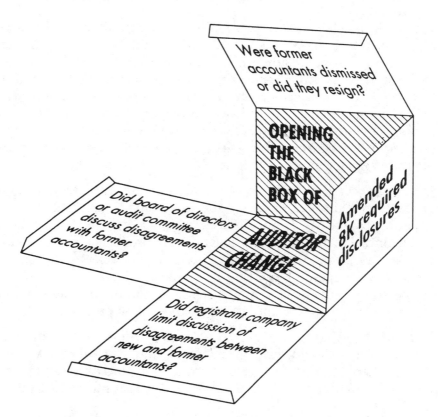

Source: Concurrently prepared for *Auditing*, second edition (Boston, MA: PWS-Kent, 1991), Exhibit 16–17.

tations, making inquiry procedures useless, management override more probable, and the assessment of control risk at less than a maximum level unsupportable. Hence, illegal acts are a special consideration in interpreting the results of tests of control. The initial evaluation of the control environment of the entity may have to be completely revised in light of such discoveries. Exhibits 13–6 and 13–7 detail audit procedures in response to irregularities and illegal acts under existing GAAS.

Interim reporting practices. The effect of observed material weaknesses and reportable conditions on interim financial reports needs to be evaluated to ensure that disclosure practices are adequate. If the CPA is associated with interim statements in the capacity of performing a limited review, particular procedures are required. Any weaknesses identified in an annual examination are to be considered in designing inquiries of management and other employees as to changes in the internal accounting control system since the audit examination, and the accounting controls applicable to the interim financial statements, as contrasted with those used for annual financial statements.

The CPA who has consistently observed large year-end adjustments to the financial statements due to poor internal accounting controls should either discourage interim reporting or discuss a means of disclosing the uncertainty that exists regarding the interim financial information.

Examples of Effects of Control Weaknesses on the Audit Plan

The most severe effect of a control weakness might be viewed as the CPA's inability to perform an audit of the entity's financial statements. In such a case, the CPA may either withdraw from the engagement or issue a disclaimer. However, in many cases even material weaknesses in accounting controls can be considered in setting an audit scope in a manner that suffices to provide the evidence necessary to issue a clean audit report.

One of the most likely effects of control weaknesses will be to shift the timing of the audit work from an interim date to year-end work. A second predictable effect is that the strongest audit procedures available for substantive test work will be applied. Examples might include:

—physical observation of securities in addition to confirmation procedures;

—positive, as opposed to negative, confirmation of customers;

—confirmation of payables in addition to detailed testing;

—complete physical inventories of fixed assets; and

—extensive cut-off tests.

Sample sizes will be larger than anticipated if assessment of control risk at less than the maximum level had been possible. In addition, tests of substantive balances may be stratified to reflect particular weaknesses in controls. For example, if inventory is being tested and material weaknesses in purchasing have

Exhibit 13–6

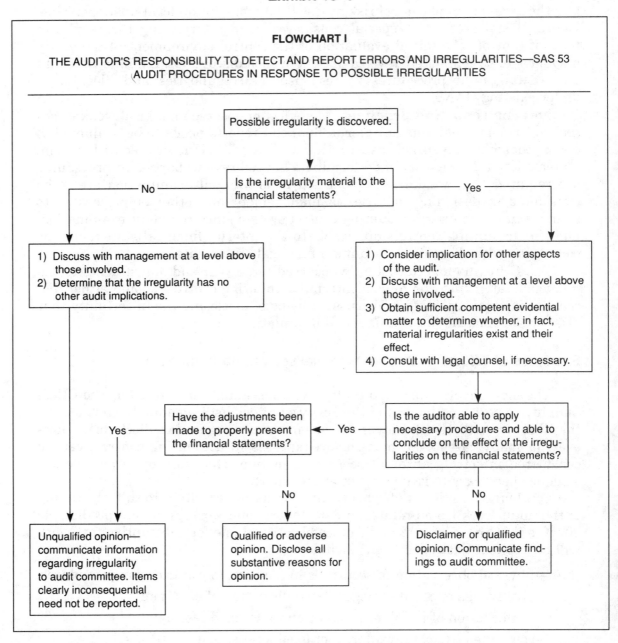

FLOWCHART I

THE AUDITOR'S RESPONSIBILITY TO DETECT AND REPORT ERRORS AND IRREGULARITIES—SAS 53
(AUDIT PROCEDURES IN RESPONSE TO POSSIBLE IRREGULARITIES)

Source: Wayne E. Carnall, "Flowchart Summary of the New SASs," *The CPA Journal* (April 1989), p. 48. Reprinted with permission from *The CPA Journal,* April 1989, copyright 1989.

Exhibit 13–7

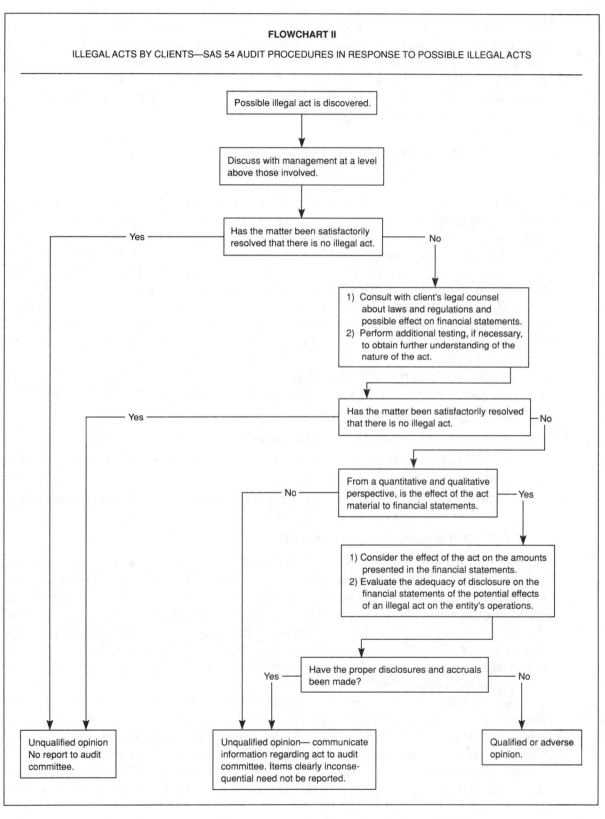

FLOWCHART II

ILLEGAL ACTS BY CLIENTS—SAS 54 AUDIT PROCEDURES IN RESPONSE TO POSSIBLE ILLEGAL ACTS

Possible illegal act is discovered.

Discuss with management at a level above those involved.

Has the matter been satisfactorily resolved that there is no illegal act.

Yes   No

1) Consult with client's legal counsel about laws and regulations and possible effect on financial statements.
2) Perform additional testing, if necessary, to obtain further understanding of the nature of the act.

Has the matter been satisfactorily resolved that there is no illegal act.

Yes   No

From a quantitative and qualitative perspective, is the effect of the act material to financial statements.

No   Yes

1) Consider the effect of the act on the amounts presented in the financial statements.
2) Evaluate the adequacy of disclosure on the financial statements of the potential effects of an illegal act on the entity's operations.

Have the proper disclosures and accruals been made?

Yes   No

Unqualified opinion No report to audit committee.

Unqualified opinion— communicate information regarding act to audit committee. Items clearly inconsequential need not be reported.

Qualified or adverse opinion.

Source: Wayne E. Carnall, "Flowchart Summary of the New SASs," *The CPA Journal* (April 1989), p. 49. Reprinted with permission from *The CPA Journal,* April 1989, copyright 1989.

been identified for a particular branch, more extensive test counts and related samples may be planned for the inventory balances of that operating branch. The objective of the auditor is to gain assurance that financial statements are fairly presented, and an efficient means of collecting a sufficient base is to perform expanded tests of those areas and balances in which problems are expected to occur with a higher probability.

HOW TO ADAPT THE APPROACH TO A SYSTEMS DESIGN MAS ENGAGEMENT

The discussion through this point has focused on the auditor's evaluation and testing of internal accounting controls. However, a CPA will often be called upon to provide management advisory services (MAS), sometimes called management consulting services (MCS), to clients that involve the design of information systems and related internal accounting controls. It should be evident that the considerations affecting the design of a system of controls parallel those that affect the evaluation of a system of controls. Those controls that the auditor would deem to be strong and effective controls in an entity's control system would be desirable controls to install in a new system or to add as improvements to an existing system.

In each of the primary cycle chapters (9, 10, and 11), as well as in Chapter 12 on computers, five exhibits were presented, summarizing the cycles' and EDP's

—critical segregation of duties,

—accounting records that would provide a complete audit trail,

—checklist for determining whether an environment exists for effective control,

—risks, i.e., what could go wrong and what controls could preclude or detect such errors and defalcations, and

—operating efficiency considerations.

These exhibits and related discussions were presented to guide control system designers, as well as evaluators of existing controls. Since the most efficient point in time to establish controls in an information system is when it is designed, an effort should be made to incorporate as many control concepts as possible in the design phase, without overdoing the controls to the point where redundant controls are excessive. Of course, some overlapping of controls is good, but the efficiency of controls is paramount if the designer wishes to motivate an entity's employees to comply with prescribed controls.

As the systems designer reviews the exhibits of Chapter 9 through 11, the context of the specific entity's operations, the risk profile of the entity, and management's control objectives should be the principal considerations in selecting the particular control design to be installed. Chapter 12 focused on EDP and specifically discussed the life cycles of an EDP environment. The points discussed as to the design and implementation approach for an EDP system can easily be translated to a manual system. In each situation, employees should be involved in the design phase, documentation of the developing system should be maintained, testing of newly installed procedures should be performed, and a post audit and periodic monetary review should be completed. The evaluator of controls should distinguish necessary controls from desired controls. The costs of excluding necessary or critical controls from a systems design should be carefully explained to the entity in order to optimize overall control. The use of risk exposure worksheets in explaining the adequacy of proposed or existing controls can aid the evaluator in explaining the design alternatives.

Be Cognizant of the Long-Term Considerations Involved in Designing a System

The major difference in designing a system as opposed to evaluating a system in operation is that the former requires long-term considerations. For example, even if current budget constraints preclude the acquisition of more than two of the selected computer terminals, the location of these terminals must nevertheless reflect the expected growth of EDP. Similarly, even if three terminals bearing a different trade name from that on which inquiry procedures were applied could be purchased for a price similar to the two trade name terminals, the long-term effects of changing the brand of the computer acquired and its capabilities would most likely cause the designer to purchase the two terminals that are manufactured by the selected company. One inevitable long-term effect on design is employee turnover, bearing out the critical importance of procedures manuals, training programs, and other explicit plans for creating reasonably smooth operations in spite of the turnover of personnel.

Employee Involvement Should Be Encouraged

In the MAS setting, the CPA should utilize a basic understanding of control, with an industry and company-specific understanding of operations, to design efficient controls that appear to be feasible as effective controls. Then the exhibits in Chapters 9 through 11 can be used to evaluate and improve upon the designed system. The employees who will be responsible for carrying out the designed control procedures should be informed of the procedures' *objective* and *planned operation*. The employees should be encouraged to critique the control design and to offer their suggestions. The concept of cost/benefit should underlie all control design decisions, and this concept should be explained to employees to facilitate their consideration of economics when making suggestions, as well as their understanding as to why certain suggestions may not be adopted by management.

Maintaining Independence and Objectivity

In choosing to do systems design work, the independence issue should be considered by the CPA as well as the internal auditor. To ensure objectivity, internal auditors should avoid designing and implementing systems which they will be expected to audit at a later date. However, internal auditors should review proposed designs and offer suggestions as to control enhancements. To date, despite numerous expressions of concern by regulators as to the negative effect that MAS work might have on the CPA's independence and objectivity as an auditor, investigators by the Public Oversight Board have reported no evidence that MAS is in actual conflict with auditing. However, the CPA would do well to distinguish between the "bread and butter" product of auditing and the typical one-time audit engagement, evaluating the effect of the latter on the appearance of independence as an auditor.

A CPA firm's use of different professional staff members for audits and for MAS engagements is one means of diminishing any potential objectivity problems in evaluating controls. Another important point to remember is that while the CPA proposes a design for an information or a control system, the client actually decides whether to accept the design, how it ought to be adjusted, and what facets are or are not cost/beneficial. In other words, the CPA is an advisor, not the decision-maker in an MAS engagement. This fact has been the classic focal point in explaining why the MAS engagement does not serve to impair objectivity. The other point commonly cited by CPAs is liability exposure. If a CPA were to find a flaw in a system of internal accounting control which (s)he had designed, the liability exposure that could result from not recognizing and identifying the weakness to management would be far too great for the CPA not to disclose the problem.

Given these arguments, the cost efficiencies of having one CPA firm perform multiple services typically encourage entities to use a single CPA firm for both audits and MAS engagements, including those engagements intended to design and/or improve the control system. Many companies' boards have expressed in the proxy statements their opinion that the selected non-auditing and MAS services performed by the auditing firm in no way impair that firm's independence in rendering services. "Outsourcing," or using outside consultants in lieu of internal resources, for projects such as information systems, is increasingly popular.

SYNOPSIS

Audit plans will reflect the results of internal control evaluation and testing procedures. In particular, any detected weaknesses must be identified as either material or immaterial. If material, the CPA has a responsibility to inform top management. CPAs also have internal reporting responsibilities for any illegal acts that are detected. Tests that support assessment of control risk at less than a maximum level will result in the alteration of the nature, timing, and extent of substantive test work in a manner that reduces the total amount of substantive test work. Tests of control that flag material weaknesses in control will be the basis for modifying the audit plan to compensate for such weaknesses. The analysis of each control cycle, when "put together," provides an outline not only for the evaluation of controls but also for the design of new systems or for MAS engagements to improve existing controls.

REFERENCES

American Institute of Certified Public Accountants, Statement on Auditing Standards No. 53, "The Auditor's Responsibility to Detect and Report Errors and Irregularities" (New York: AICPA, April 1988).

American Institute of Certified Public Accountants, Statement on Auditing Standards No. 54, "Illegal Acts by Clients" (New York: AICPA, April 1988).

American Institute of Certified Public Accountants, Statement on Auditing Standards No. 20, "Required Communication of Material Weaknesses in Internal Accounting Control" (New York: AICPA, August 1977). [Also see SAS No. 60, 1988.]

Whittington, O. Ray and Steven J. Adams, "Temporary Breakdowns of Internal Control: Implications for External and Internal Auditors," *Journal of Accounting and Finance* (Summer, 1982), pp. 310–319.

14

How to Prepare Effective Management Letters

On legislating truth

First Umpire: Some 'r balls and some 'r strikes, and
I calls 'em as I sees 'em.

Second Umpire: Some 'r balls and some 'r strikes, and
I calls 'em as they'r.

Third Umpire: Some 'r balls and some 'r strikes, but
none of em ain't nothin' 'til I calls 'em.

Anonymous

As the introductory quote suggests, opinions are likely to differ as to what various observations on control mean. The profession has recently moved away from the material weakness demarcation of SAS No. 20 toward the reportable conditions guidance of SAS 60, in part to embrace a broader spectrum of professionals' judgment on "significant deficiencies in the design or operation of the internal control structure."

While the auditor is not obligated to search for reportable conditions, those identified are required to be communicated to audit committees. A recommended report form appears in SAS No. 60, as reflected in Exhibit 14–1. Note that the language does not have as many admonitions as to the limitations of control as was common in predecessor communications. An explanation of the reasons for such a posture and some questioning of this posture is reflected in the article reprinted in Exhibit 14–2.

Of interest in the final reaction of the Auditing Standards Board is the following prescription from SAS No. 60:

> Because of the potential for misinterpretation of the limited degree of assurance associated with the auditor issuing a written report representing that no reportable conditions were noted during an audit, the auditor should not issue such representations.

(Paragraph 17)

This shows some attention to concerns for effective communication.

Exhibit 14–1

Suggested Form for Communicating Reportable Conditions

In planning and performing our audit of the financial statements of the ABC Corporation for the year ended December 31, 19XX, we considered its internal control structure in order to determine our auditing procedures for the purpose of expressing our opinion on the financial statements and not to provide assurance on the internal control structure. However, we noted certain matters involving the internal control structure and its operation that we consider to be reportable conditions under standards established by the American Institute of Certified Public Accountants. Reportable conditions involve matters coming to our attention relating to significant deficiencies in the design or operation of the internal control structure that, in our judgment, could adversely affect the organization's ability to record, process, summarize, and report financial data consistent with the assertions of management in the financial statements.

[Include paragraphs to describe the reportable conditions noted.]

This report is intended solely for the information and use of the audit committee (board of directors, board of trustees, or owners in owner-managed enterprises), management, and others within the organization (or specified regulatory agency or other specified third party).

Source: Statement on Auditing Standards No. 60, "Communication of Internal Control Structure Related Matters Noted in an Audit" (AICPA, New York: April 1988), paragraph 12.

Exhibit 14–2

The Irony of Responding to Regulators' Pressures: The Case of Management Letter Precautionary Representations

Wanda A. Wallace

Wanda A. Wallace, Ph.D., CPA, CMA, CIA, is The Deborah D. Shelton Systems Professor of Accounting at Texas A&M University.

Pressures are being placed on the accounting profession from every direction, including the Dingell Committee, the Treadway Commission, and the Securities and Exchange Commission (SEC). The House Energy & Commerce Oversight and Investigations Committee (the Dingell Committee) has been and continues to hold hearings on the accounting profession, challenging the effectiveness of the current audit service. The National Committee on Fraudulent Financial Reporting (Treadway Commission) has analyzed auditors' responsibilities for detecting and reporting on fraud, recommending extended services. Both domestic and Canadian arms of the accounting profession are addressing the "expectations gap." This term addresses an apparent difference which exists between what the public expects of the auditor and what is received.

Concern for communicating effectively is characterized by such actions as the Securities and Exchange Commission's recent approval of condensed reporting practices in annual reports. Observers have asserted that communications are overly complex, deterring users' understanding. Of interest are some observers' assertion that the public perceives an audit report as ensuring strong internal accounting controls, an absence of fraud, and a low business risk of investment, yet the accounting profession responds that the current audit process is not specifically designed to provide such assurances. The response of the Auditing Standards Board has been the issuance of ten proposed standards intended, in part, to close the "expectations" and communication gap.

In evaluating the accuracy of regulators' claims and the adequacy of the profession's response, at least two warnings are heard. One voice contends that unless we respond to regulators' pressures, the age of self-regulation will end. The other voice warns that if we merely sway with the regulators' pressures, we may well bend so far, that we will cause our own demise by promising more than can be delivered. While this paper in no way distinguishes the relative merits of these two positions, it does document the irony which can result from the profession's attempts to respond to regulators' pressures over time concerning one aspect of auditors' services. The case at hand relates to the communication of control-structure related matters noted in an audit—commonly referred to as management letters.

Prior to the Foreign Corrupt Practices Act (FCPA), auditors commonly prepared management letters in diverse formats, delineating internal control points of potential use to clients. These letters became the focus of attention following the FCPA, with suggestions put forth to more formally report on internal accounting controls. The SEC proposed mandatory reports on internal control and the Auditing Standards Board drafted Statement on Auditing Standards No. 20 and No. 30 to require communication of material weaknesses and

This article is based on a research project funded by a grant from the Peat, Marwick, Mitchell Foundation through its Research Opportunities in Auditing Program. The views expressed herein are those of the author and not necessarily those of the Peat, Marwick, Mitchell Foundation.

Exhibit 14–2 (continued)

provide direction for CPAs' reports on control. As a result of Congressional, SEC, and self-regulatory discussions, management letter content shifted.

This paper will document past practice with respect to the use of precautionary representations in control-related communication. An evolution toward increased use of such representations coincides with the timing of regulatory action. The purpose of such language was to communicate more effectively. Examples of the types of representations made are provided for the reader's consideration. Ironically, the Auditing Standards Board's recent proposal for change would eliminate virtually all precautionary language for the express purpose of more effective communication. Thus the paradox arises: how can it be both ways? If reactionary behavior to regulators results in inconsistent behavior, is there not reason to pause and explore substantive implications of change? While the evidence described relates to only one recent exposure draft, some thought-provoking analogies are cited. Implications for the practice community are described, although those are largely provided for contemplation rather than as policy prescriptions.

DATA BASE

The nature of management letters' control-related disclosures, as well as changes over time, can be documented by examining management letters' content. This research analyzes 101 companies' management letters from 1975 to 1979. The companies represent random samples, stratified for similar representation of SEC and non-SEC client companies, from more than one Big Eight firm. Due to the sensitivity of the data requested, the CPA firms providing the letters required that (1) neither their names nor the number of participating CPA firms be disclosed, (2) only the researcher would be given access to the management letters provided, and (3) the letters would be submitted "blind," i.e., with all client names deleted and limited information provided.

Specifically, 45 of the companies were SEC registrants and 56 were not. The assets of the companies ranged from under $500,000 to $10 billion, with a mean of $393 million and a median of $35 million. Virtually every industry code was represented, with 51 companies in manufacturing, mining, oil, or contracting, 11 in transportation, communications, and utilities,

14 in wholesale and retail trade, 17 in banking, credit, insurance, real estate, and business services, and eight in health, education, government, or other lines of business.

The researcher developed a coding framework to reflect the letters' contents. Of particular interest in this analysis is the incidence of precautionary representations appearing in management letters' introductory comments. Specifically, what language has been used by auditors to warn readers not to expect too much of their management letters?

RESEARCH QUESTIONS

The questions of interest are (1) what is the typical content of management letter precautionary representations, (2) have management letters changed in content, with respect to precautionary representations, after the FCPA and related pressures came to bear on the profession, and (3) do communications to SEC companies differ from those to non-SEC companies? The first research issue concerns the nature of precautionary representations. The second query is directed at an aggregate level, across all companies. The third issue explores differential reporting practices. One could contend that if change were primarily due to regulations being imposed, SEC companies would reflect change, but little change would be observable among companies which are less likely to be in the public eye. On the other hand, a carry-over effect to non-SEC companies could reflect a perception of real value for such communications. If that were the case, the advisability of change away from such communications would merit careful scrutiny.

Prescriptive writings have continually demanded increased clarity in disclosures to management and third parties. Operational measures of the content of management letters, recommended in response to regulatory pressures, include the following specific disclosures:

- the audit engagement is unable to disclose all weaknesses,
- a weakness in control does not necessarily lead to a modification of the audit opinion,
- the principal safeguard against irregularities is internal control, as distinct from the audit process alone,
- there are inherent limitations in internal control, and
- most weaknesses in control which are cited are unlikely to be material in nature.

Exhibit 14–2 (continued)

RESEARCH FINDINGS

Exhibit 1 presents descriptive statistics (average values) of the percentage of management letters reviewed which contained each of these types of disclosures in 1975 and 1979. Since the FCPA became law in December 1977, the 1975 to 1979 comparison is expected to offer a pre-post perspective on how precautionary disclosures changed in response to the various pressures in the late 1970s. Details are provided for the total sample, as well as for SEC and non-SEC subsamples.

The commentaries reflect wording endorsed by the AICPA which was expected to clarify the limited scope of auditors' work on controls, as well as inherent shortcomings in any control system. To provide insight on whether the average values differ between 1975 and 1979 for the sample companies, the difference in average value is computed and then tested to see if it has statistical significance. If not, then the difference is likely to be a random fluctuation that is virtually equivalent to no change (a zero difference) over time. However, if significant at the .05 level, the difference is likely to be a real change in reporting practice 95 out of 100 times (often referred to as having "95 percent confidence" that a change has occurred). The technical term for the comparison of values over time for a fixed number of companies is "paired sample t-test." The important focal point in Exhibit 1 is the significance of each t-value. Any value less than .05 is likely to be a real change from 1975 to 1979.

Non-SEC firms are observed to cite the lack of modified audit opinion with significantly greater frequency in 1979 than 1975 (at a .021 level of significance, we have 98 percent confidence that the 23 percent of letters examined in 1979 which contained such wording, represented a real change from 1975, in which no such phrasing appeared). Similarly, non-SEC entities' letters referenced an absence of material weaknesses in 18 percent more letters in 1979 than 1975 (significant at a .042 level, providing 96 percent confidence that a real change occurred, rather than a random fluctuation). In contrast, SEC companies experienced a significantly lower frequency of references to no modification of an audit opinion in 1979, relative to 1975. Yet, the emphasis on no material weaknesses being identified was significantly greater in 1979 than 1975.

No other significant differences are observed for SEC companies (at a .05 level, which is a generally accepted benchmark representing a 95 percent confidence threshold). This suggests that certain precautionary representations had already evolved by 1975 for those client settings in which those communications were deemed to be relevant. The added attention to material weaknesses is likely to be in direct response to the FCPA for public companies. Yet, similar attention by non-SEC companies suggests that this additional disclosure was judged to have value beyond mere regulatory compliance.

An analysis of the significance of differences in SEC versus non-SEC companies within a single year indicated that in 1979, non-SEC companies were more likely to be told that engagements would not necessarily disclose all weaknesses[1] and letters to them were more likely to include a statement related to inherent limitations in controls.[2] Given the auditor's choice of relying on controls or performing substantive tests, and the expectation that such reliance is more common for large public companies than non-SEC companies, it seems reasonable that the precautions would be deemed more important in the latter case. This finding reaffirms the substantive value attributed to such representations, apart from regulation.

Additional evidence of perceived value is provided by the fact that another type of communication has encouraged this sort of qualifying language on inherent weaknesses to be incorporated: management reports. Not only has such wording been observed,[3] but it has become relatively commonplace.

---

[1] The technical term for this comparison is a group t-test, since instead of pairing observations for a single company across time, the comparison is being made at one point in time between two groups—in this case SEC and non-SEC entities with averages of .25 and .68 respectively, as reported in Exhibit 1. The resulting t-value is 2.79 which is significant at a .006 level providing 99.4 percent confidence that a real difference is observable.

[2] The t-value is 2.60 which is significant at a .011 level, providing 98.9 percent confidence that a real difference exists.

[3] Wanda A. Wallace, "How Not to Communicate Material and Immaterial Weaknesses In Accounting Controls," *Auditing Symposium VI, Proceedings of the 1982 Touche Ross University of Kansas Symposium on Auditing Problems*, edited by Donald R. Nichols and Howard F. Stettler (Lawrence: School of Business, University of Kansas, 1982).

Exhibit 14–2 (continued)

EXHIBIT 1

A COMPARISON OF THE MANAGEMENT LETTER CONTENT IN 1975 TO 1979

(Paired Sample t-tests)

	Total Sample			SEC Entities			Non-SEC Entities		
	Average Value 1975	Average Value 1979	Difference (t-value) Significance	Average Value 1975	Average Value 1979	Difference (t-value) Significance	Average Value 1975	Average Value 1979	Difference (t-value) Significance
The engagement would not necessarily disclose all weaknesses	.42	.40	.02 (.24) .81	.25	.25	0 (—) —	.73	.68	.046 (.37) .715
Frequency with which the letter mentions: 1 = yes; 0 = no; No modification of the audit opinion	.15	.13	.02 (.28) .784	.23	.08	.15 (2.22) .032	0	.23	−.227 (−2.49) .021
Principal safeguard against irregularities is internal control	.29	.15	.145 (1.18) .244	.28	.10	.175 (.96) .343	.32	.23	.091 (.81) .427
Inherent limitations exist in controls; cost/benefit considerations are relevant	.21	.16	.05 (1.14) .260	.13	.08	.05 (1.43) .160	.36	.32	.046 (.44) .665
No material weaknesses were identified:	.05	.24	−.19 (−3.83) .000	.03	.23	−.20 (−3.12) .003	.09	.27	−.182 (−2.16) .042

Exhibit 14–2 (continued)

THE PARADOX

As language of a qualifying nature has evolved, probably in response to past regulatory pressure, apparently miscommunications have resulted. Consider the explanation in the recent exposure draft of the AICPA of why SAS No. 20 and sections of SAS No. 30 should be superseded:

> Management, audit committees, and others responsible for internal control in an entity have indicated that they have difficulty understanding the auditor's report on material weaknesses in internal control identified in a financial statement audit.[4]

The Auditing Standards Board's exposure draft also deletes references to the limited purpose of the study and evaluation of internal control and the disclaimer of an opinion on the system of internal control taken as a whole. In discussing this proposal, Jerry D. Sullivan, Chairman of the Auditing Standards Board, explained that all of this qualifying language had virtually undermined the intended information content of management letters.[5]

Hence, the irony arises. The key historical change toward disclosures concerning material weaknesses, prompted by regulation but voluntarily extended to the less regulated sector of CPA firms' client base, is about to be rescinded. In this day of regulatory pressures to effectively communicate and close the expectations gap, changes are being encouraged which pose a paradox. By removing qualifying language as recently proposed, the profession may increase expectations regarding the completeness of control-related disclosures. Depending on how the notion of "reportable internal control conditions" is enacted, users may have problems discerning severe control problems from those reported merely because improvement is possible. The result may not be the more effective communication claimed by the exposure draft. Whenever regulation, over time, creates reactionary moves by the profession in opposite directions, the rationale for such inconsistent behavior merits examination.

Is it possible that the present wave of response by the profession to outside pressures— a response contrary to that encouraged in the late 1970s—may return us to the practices of 1975 or earlier? Is this progress or peril? Auditors have recognized a special kind of communication problem in developing precautionary representations in the management letter:

Users may expect too much unless warned to the contrary. Hence, the observed precautions in 1975 increased by 1979 and became particularly prevalent in the non-SEC sector. However, under current pressures to reclarify what the profession has been trying to clarify, it is now suggested that the auditor remove the precautionary representations.

Why the paradoxical result from the regulatory pressure? What has changed to justify an opposite policy prescription to a similar concern for communication? Action merely to be demonstrably responsive to regulators can lead to inconsistent behavior. As such inconsistencies arise, it would seem wise to defer a decision until a substantive reason for diametrically opposed strategies in responding to a single concern over time can be identified. If none exists, then attention should be directed toward a consistent enhancement of disclosure. Proposed actions to remove precautionary language may well expose auditors to liability rather than praise: the very liability the representations were intended to protect against in the first place.

PERHAPS AN ANALOGY...

This management letter example has far more troublesome analogies. Recent exposure drafts on errors and irregularities, as well as illegal acts, would seem to promise detection of material fraud. Is is possible that pressures by regulators are again encouraging less effective communication? Is the profession promising more than it can deliver?

A NEED FOR EVALUATION

The lessons of the past decade, including the circular approach to first communicating material weaknesses and limitations of control systems, then proposing to rescind such disclosures, would seem to suggest a need for careful evaluation of regulators' suggestions before their adoption. Rather than focusing on form, the profession must give attention to substance. Just as an accountant discerns proper

---

[4] AICPA Auditing Standards Board, "Exposure Draft: Proposed Statement on Auditing Standards: The Communication of Control-Structure Related Matters Noted In An Audit," February 14, 1987, p. 1.

[5] Claremont McKenna-Touche Ross Conference on Emerging Issues in Auditing, Presentation on March 19, 1987.

Exhibit 14–2 (continued)

revenue recognition from the substance of transactions, rather than from their form, the profession needs to focus on the substance of audit activities and internal control issues and align the form of disclosure with such substance. If users understand such substance, communication will be effective. If, instead, the form of disclosure follows the whims of regulatory (often disjointed) pressures, the ironic pattern of circular motion may dominate real progress.

CONCLUSION

Communications regarding controls have been an issue which arises periodically in the regulatory setting. Much as we have witnessed the SEC's turnabout from restricting CPAs' association with forecasts to a position of endorsing CPAs' association and even chastising the profession for non-association, we are likely to witness other changes in regulatory attitudes and suggested action. Despite the consistent focus on effective communication, the policy prescription has shifted *from* a need to communicate the presence of material weaknesses and limitations tied to the scope of audit work *to* a contention that no such language would represent clearer communication. Given the pre-1975 evolution of precautionary representations, their extension in 1979 subsequent to considerable regulatory pressure, including the FCPA, and their carryover to the non-SEC sector, reason exists to believe such disclosures have value. Before such communications are rescinded, their purpose should be considered, the consequences of their removal should be assessed, and the inconsistency with past behavior to the same problem reconciled. This implies a policy prescription of no reactionary response to pressure without evaluation of historical precedents and likely ramifications.

Source: Wanda A. Wallace, "The Irony of Responding to Regulators' Pressures: The Case of Management Letter Precautionary Representations," *Accounting Horizons* (Volume Two—Number One, March 1988), pp. 88–93.

As implied by the reporting in Exhibit 14–2, I would suggest more conservative wording. Note that SAS No. 60 states

> The provisions in this Statement should not be viewed as precluding an auditor from communicating to a client a variety of observations and suggestions regarding its activities that go beyond internal control structure related matters. Such matters may deal with operational or administrative efficiencies, business strategies, and other items of perceived benefit to the client.

(Paragraph 19)

Given this position, the recommendations set forth herein for management letters should be considered distinct from SAS No. 60.

During the course of an audit engagement, the auditor becomes extremely knowledgeable as to the entity's operations and, in particular, the system of internal accounting control. Inefficiencies in operations and weaknesses in controls are likely to come to the auditor's attention as auditing procedures are applied and the audit opinion is formulated. Often the auditor will bring a substantial amount of industry-specific and general-business knowledge of the audit engagement, automatically utilizing such experience as a benchmark in becoming familiar with an entity's operations and in evaluating controls.

Typical business practices of all companies, such as fidelity bonding of employees, efficient cash management through lockbox systems and similar procedures, and record maintenance, will be routinely reviewed and, if the entity does not follow similar practices, the value of the differing approaches will be assessed as the auditor takes the business approach to auditing and gains an in-depth understanding of operations. Practices that are peculiar to the industry, such as self-insurance strategies, financing mechanisms, promotional strategies, employee compensation packages, terms of sale, and service programs, are similarly reviewed, relative to competitors' practices, to evaluate their reasonableness and plausible means by which the entity might improve them.

As comparisons are made in the normal course of an audit engagement, the auditor may routinely share the results of such analyses with the auditee. This sharing may be done either on an informal basis or through a formal report, typically referred to as a management letter.

Although an informal oral communication of suggestions is acceptable, a written report is preferable. A formal management letter is likely to be more carefully prepared than an oral communication, with a thorough analysis of the particular entity's circumstances and specific recommendations. It provides a record of past services and can be used as a reference in evaluating management's reactions to recommendations. Perhaps most importantly, a written document does not run the risk of misinterpretation, distortion, and faulty recall that exists in verbal communications. The possibility of misunderstanding is reduced by issuing a written report.

A VOLUNTARY SERVICE BY THE AUDITOR

As already explained, CPAs are required to report to the audit committee any reportable conditions that come to the auditor's attention during the course of the audit (SAS No. 60). The CPA is not required to provide recommendations regarding operations and/or internal accounting controls to the audit client. However, the voluntary service of providing clients with a so-called management letter or, as a minimum, of verbally discussing CPAs' observations and suggestions, is common practice. Clients have come to expect that a complementary service, or by-product, of the audit is the management letter, and although the report is typically formulated for internal use, some creditors will request access to such a letter to gain additional insight into the client's operations and control systems.

Within the client's organization, line managers, top management, and the Board of Directors typically review the management letter from the CPA. This three-level review helps to

—ensure that the person responsible for the operations and control-related practices being critiqued is aware of the suggestion;

—provide oversight to line managers so as to encourage them to carefully consider the CPA's suggestions; and

—make the Board of Directors aware of management's operating and control-related decisions that are at variance from those commonly observed or specifically recommended by the auditor.

The client at times will request that the management letter give special attention to a particular area of operations or facet of the control system. For example, if cash management has been troublesome, bad debts excessive, changes in processing from a manual system to electronic data processing systems widespread, or management policies recently altered, the CPA is frequently asked to share industry expertise as to how effective these operations appear to be and how they might be enhanced. The extent to which such issues can be addressed by the CPA based on the typical scope of the audit may be limited and, in fact, the CPA may suggest an extended scope or a special engagement for the purposes of meeting the client's requests.

However, the audit process itself is likely to provide the CPA with some insights that can effectively be communicated to management in a manner that could improve its efforts to optimize the return to stockholders. While a voluntary service of CPAs, the management letter has become such an accepted practice that competitive forces are likely to bear down upon that CPA who does not try to constructively communicate means by which controls can be improved and operations made more efficient. Internal auditors commonly include management letter-type suggestions in their reports on audit findings. Similarly, system evaluators are expected to be alert to control and efficiency enhancements.

Planning for Efficient Drafting of Management Letters

Of course, the management letter's value will depend on its content as well as on the entity's understanding of the letter's basis, limitations, and potential uses. While perceived as a voluntary service by-product, the management letter does create incremental direct costs as the auditor or evaluator assimilates suggestions and polishes the communication device for such recommendations. To minimize these costs and to preserve the primary thrust of the engagement, the auditor must efficiently integrate the process of formulating a management letter within the audit process. The means of doing so is to encourage all members of the audit staff to be cognizant of opportunities for control and efficiency improvements throughout the audit and to document such opportunities in the working papers as the audit is conducted. This encouragement should be formalized as a step in the audit program. The working papers in which suggestions and problems are documented in anticipation of developing a management letter, should be separately filed to facilitate easy access when the letter is to be drafted. Since the control suggestions could lead to more efficient audits, auditors will frequently draft a management letter at an interim date, encouraging expedient adoption of particular recommendations, in time for year-end audit work. Hence, the voluntary service is at times a semi-annual reporting process that effectively provides the entity with lead time to consider changes. The semi-annual report is then followed up, at year-end, with the auditor providing feedback to the entity as to how such changes were accomplished and what additional recommendations were formulated during the remainder of the audit process. A similar approach can be taken by the systems evaluator. The effective management letter, particularly one that is drafted in the most efficient manner, depends upon the auditor's or evaluator's understanding and advanced planning of its form and content.

SUGGESTED FORM AND CONTENT OF MANAGEMENT LETTERS

The management letter is often drafted in a letter format, and it is addressed to management, rather than to stockholders, as is frequently the case with the audit report. Since March of 1977 when the Securities and Exchange Commission approved a rule proposed by the New York Stock Exchange (NYSE) that all domestic companies listing common stock of the NYSE be required to establish an independent audit committee,[1] many management letters are addressed to the audit committee. The composition of such committees is a set of Board of Director members who are not members of management; the perceived independence of such a committee is expected to ensure an objective consideration of the external auditor's recommendations. The management letter, in its introductory paragraphs, should clarify the basis for the report and what it is and is not intended to represent. In drafting the management letter, the auditor or evaluator should keep in mind who will be reading it. If the intended readers include nonaccountants, extended explanations will be appropriate throughout the text of the report.

Basis for the Recommendations

The CPA may point out that the primary purpose of the audit examination is to form an opinion as to the financial statements. In conducting the examination, internal accounting controls are evaluated, and reliance is frequently placed upon tests of the internal accounting controls, in addition to the substantive test evidence gathered concerning the reasonableness of account balances. In the course of conducting such procedures, some opportunities for improving control and/or operations are commonly identified. The client should be reminded that the audit

—does not constitute a comprehensive study or evaluation of the control system,

—would not necessarily disclose all weaknesses,

—cannot be relied upon to disclose irregularities, and adequate methods of internal control serve as the principal safeguard against irregularities,

---

[1] Harold M. Williams, "Audit Committees—The Public Sector's View," *The Journal of Accountancy*, September 1977, p. 72.

—does not provide a basis to evaluate the operating economics and practical application of the enclosed recommendations, and

—appropriately compensated for any observed weaknesses in internal accounting control, hence the management letter does not modify the audit opinion.

In other words, the basis for the recommendations is a set of audit procedures primarily directed at the reasonableness of financial statements, rather than at the evaluation of controls and overall operations. What's more, any control system, as well as any audit engagement, faces inherent limitations with respect to fraud. No systematic cost/benefit evaluation of existing controls or recommendations for changes in control is performed in the course of an audit engagement. The basis for recommendations is limited and must be augmented by management's evaluation of the risk involved where weaknesses exist, the need for positive action, the cost of such action, and, in particular, the effects of proposed changes in control and operations on efficiency and good customer service. Of course, the CPA should strive not to communicate ridiculous suggestions, and if the feasibility of the suggestion is uncertain, the CPA might choose to acknowledge this in the management letter.

One means by which the CPA can effectively acknowledge that he or she is not oblivious of cost/benefit concerns, yet has not devoted substantial time to their consideration, is to include the following sentence:

> While we have tried to recommend only solutions that are practical to implement, management should evaluate the cost and benefit of each matter described herein and act upon those items that are economical and beneficial.

The clarification of the basis for recommendation;

(1) reminds the CPA and the client that the management letter is intended to be a by-product, rather than a separate engagement, hence its content is generally restricted by the objectives and scope of the audit, and

(2) highlights the inherent shortcomings of the report, particularly the relative absence of any cost/benefit framework to guide the formulation of suggestions.

Note: If the CPA is providing a management letter at an interim date, the letter should reference the preliminary audit work as providing the basis for the recommendations outlined in the report.

How to Handle Extended Studies Requested by the Client

As suggested earlier, the client may request an extended study of a particular area, to be incorporated in the management letter. If this is the case, the CPA should describe the extended basis for the recommendations. For example, state that as requested by management, the operations of the internal audit department were reviewed in greater depth than necessary in order to provide suggestions for improving the organization and operation of the internal audit group.

Since the CPA may not review all functional areas of a client's operations in a single audit engagement, (s)he will often adopt a rotational plan, emphasizing different aspects of the accounting and administrative systems each year. In this manner, all control areas are reviewed (as a client service) within a set period. The CPA should communicate such a rotational approach, and will of course refer to the rotational plan in the audit program. For certain clients, such as broker/dealers, a fairly precise basis for the review of the client's control system can be referenced:

> Internal accounting control has been evaluated as required by SEC Rule 17a–5 to provide reasonable assurance that material weaknesses are disclosed.

In other words, in drafting the management letter the CPA should consider the initial part of the letter to be analogous to the scope paragraph of the auditor's report.

Take the Opportunity to Offer Future Services to the Client

After outlining the basis for the recommendations, the CPA should take the opportunity to offer future services to the client. Specifically, CPAs should state that

—discussion of the management letter points is welcomed,

—they would be happy to assist the company personnel in evaluating the cost/benefit ratio of alternative solutions to problems identified in the management letter, and

—they would be pleased to assist in the implementation of any desired actions, particularly in those areas where lack of time or skill by the client might otherwise prevent such action.

Later in the letter, the CPA may want to reemphasize this willingness to service the client's needs with respect to a particular suggestion. For example, if the CPA recommends a conversion to a computerized system, the client's selection of appropriate software might be optimized by having the CPA provide a comparative analysis of alternative software packages. Similarly, the implementation of a new perpetual inventory system might be easier if management advisory services were provided by the CPA in both the design and the implementation phase.

One example of phraseology for communicating a willingness to assist in data processing conversion follows:

> Our management advisory group can offer expertise in further determination of the need for data processing guidance as to the most appropriate types of equipment (or outside servicing) for your company, and assistance in the obviously critical stage of implementation of the new system.

At this point in the letter, the CPA can acknowledge the assistance that has already been provided with respect to the management letter points. For example, the CPA might state that the opportunities for enhancing existing internal checks and balances were discussed with management as the audit progressed and have subsequently been reviewed in detail to formulate practical recommendations. The CPA may wish to emphasize that the recommendations are being formalized to provide a record against which to measure implementation. The suggestion to management that the control points are worth pursuing as they represent improvements that can enhance management's ability to deal with substantive problems outside of the day-to-day operating requirements of the business, may also be appropriate in communicating the CPA's interest in and enthusiasm about the benefits from implementing the control and efficiency suggestions.

When Corrective Action Has Been Taken

The past discussions with management may have already resulted in improvements to operations and/or the control system. The CPAs may wish to acknowledge that

> . . . where corrective action has been taken subsequent to our review it has been noted herein. However, we have not substantiated the effectiveness of such measures through actual testing or observation.

The last sentence is particularly important since it provides a clear picture of the basis of subsequent reports on management's reactions to suggestions. The basis is strictly an inquiry procedure, whereby management has described its corrective actions.

Alternatively, if the CPA is reasonably assured that effective actions have been taken, the management letter may report as follows:

> In addition, certain other matters were brought to management's attention, corrected immediately, and accordingly excluded from the following observations.

Emphasize the Combined Efforts of CPAs and Management

A related point may be emphasized concerning the dual effort of management and the CPAs in developing the suggestions delineated in the management letter. For example, the CPA may state that involvement with management at all levels provided an excellent opportunity for the exchange of ideas toward this report, which reflects the results of mutual efforts toward enhancing internal controls and operating efficiencies. Such an acknowledgement not only gives appropriate credit to cooperative managers but also reminds the CPA of the importance of discussing problems and suggestions with line managers. Employees are a rich resource for the CPA in gaining an understanding of why operations are being conducted in a particular manner, what the cause of problems are likely to be, and how feasible particular suggestions might be, given both operating and control concerns.

Suggested Steps to Take When the Client Requests That No Management Letter Be Provided

An occasion may arise in which the client has specifically advised the CPA that no management letter is desired. As a voluntary service, the management letter does not have to be provided by the CPA. However, the CPA may wish to remind the client explicitly of this request, both orally and in writing, to make sure that the client is aware of the CPA's willingness to provide a management letter should the client decide that the service might be of use. Verbal communication of suggestions may still be appropriate, as well as some discussion with the client as to the potential value of the management letter.

At times the request for no management letter may be due to some misunderstanding. For example, the client may feel that significant incremental costs are incurred in developing such a report, or that an explicit written report could endanger its credit standing or suggest that the company is not in compliance with the control provisions of the Foreign Corrupt Practices Act (FCPA).[2] By clarifying such issues, the auditor's service may be enhanced. With respect to the creditor, the client may be advised that the report is intended for internal use and that distribution to the creditor would in no way be required. In addition, the CPA's willingness to speak with the creditor to ensure that the relative importance of the various suggestions is understood, should the creditor be given the management letter, can be expressed. With respect to the FCPA, a cost/benefit framework in which management evaluates the adequacy of controls is generally recognized; this framework is separate from the CPA's suggestions and can serve as a justification for not adopting particular suggestions or for accepting a given level of risk in the existing control system. The concept that "ignorance is bliss" or that "no documentation is preferred" is inconsistent with the substance of the FCPA. In fact, the documentation of a review process, in which weaknesses are identified and calculated and a cost/benefit framework is developed by management, is likely to serve as support that management has complied with the provisions of the Act.

The explicit request by the client that a management letter not be provided may also serve as a performance report to the CPA. The client's feedback suggests that past management letters have been of little or no use. The CPA should critically review past reports and try to identify their strengths and weaknesses as a client service. A discussion with the client may well be warranted. The CPA could then try to improve the next set of verbal suggestions to management,

---

[2] Congress, Title 1 of Public Law No. 95–213 (December 19, 1977). [The internal accounting control provisions are codified in Section 13(b)(2)(B) of the Securities Exchange Act of 1934, 15 U.S.C.78m(b)(2)(B).]

subsequently inquiring whether management might, in light of these comments, want the CPA to again formalize recommendations in a management letter.

The final possibility that suggests itself, when the client explicitly requests that no management letter be provided, is that management does not wish to know of operating and control problems, nor does management intend to react to any such problems. This attitude of management has implications for the CPA in evaluating the control environment of the client. The audit risk faced with such a client is clearly greater than that faced with a client who is interested in enhancing controls and being made continually aware of operating inefficiencies and control problems. The ability of the management to carry out its stewardship responsibilities should be assessed as well as the advisability of retaining such a management team as a client. Whatever the decision, the CPA should discuss any concerns with the client to ensure that the lack of attention to controls and efficiency is intentional, rather than due to a lack of understanding by management. A valuable educational service can be provided by the CPA if management obtains an understanding of the role of internal accounting control as well as the potential benefits that can accrue from the CPA's management letter service. On the other hand,the CPA as a businessman must ascertain that the risk of servicing particular clients is commensurate with the return from that client, and a management profile that suggests a disregard for the control environment may be an important determinant in choosing not to provide future services to a particular company.

Although the emphasis in this chapter is upon the CPA's preparation of a management letter, both internal auditors and system evaluators will face similar considerations when transmitting control and operating suggestions or reacting to entities' requests not to transmit such suggestions.

The Significance of Control Points

The preliminary discussion in the management letter should clearly state the relative significance of the control points that follow. For example, you might state that no material weaknesses[3] were identified. Or, a more appropriate statement may be

> . . . the items discussed below are not considered material weaknesses; however, if allowed to persist, they may evolve into material weaknesses.

A detailed investigation of management letters identified a number of rather severe comments in management letters that can be characterized as indicated by the categories described in Exhibit 14–3. The relative frequency of such comments among 101 management letters is reflected with examples of specific comments provided. Frequencies exceed 101 since multiple comments (at times ex-

---

[3] AICPA, Statement on Auditing Standards No. 60 "Communication of Internal Control Structure Related Matters Noted in an Audit" (New York: AICPA, April 1988) does not require or preclude such designation.

Exhibit 14–3

The Incidence of Severe Comments in Management Letters

Nature of Problem
[Frequency]

Examples

*Arm's Length Concern
[7]

(1) Bank employees' savings accounts are not periodically reviewed.
(2) Employees have access to their own files in the bank.
(3) Disbursements to officers are often signed by the recipient.
(4) Advances to employees until the sale of their residences should have Board approval.
(5) Warehouse sales to stores have inter-company profit recorded, resulting in overstated inventories.

*Misstatement of Financial
Statements Is Nature of
Concern
[420]

(1) Improper cut-off misstates reported income.
(2) Intercompany profits have not been eliminated, causing a misstatement of the company's financial position.

*Basic Control Is Missing
[623]

(1) No password control over the computer terminals or the accounting files is in use.
(2) Operating responsibilities are unclear.
(3) Variance analysis data is not generated to facilitate basic follow-up.
(4) No control is maintained over inventory movement between locations.
(5) Employees are not bonded.
(6) Double shipments are occurring.
(7) No editing checks are built into the program.

*Control Environment
Problems (Issues That
Permeate the Entire
Operation of the Client)
[218]

(1) No document control exists.
(2) The tellers' override key is not controlled.
(3) Inadequate physical safeguards exist over the computer facilities.
(4) The accounting department and general operations are inadequately staffed.

Exhibit 14–3 (continued)

Nature of Problem *[Frequency]*	*Examples*
Control Environment **Problems (CONTINUED)**	(5) Tellers open new accounts without review.
	(6) Internal auditors can authorize program changes and are involved in systems planning and design.
	(7) No clear definition of responsibilities exists; no formal operating or accounting manuals have been prepared.
	(8) Checks are cashed from receipts.
	(9) Controls are regularly circumvented.
	(10) There is wide access to customer files, including one's own file.
	(11) No budgets are used.
	(12) Petty cash disbursements are not documented.
	(13) A computer systems log is available in the event of breakdown but is not regularly reviewed to confirm the propriety of use.
	(14) When the EDP system was first used, it was not tested against a manual reconciliation.
	(15) The system of receiving was circumvented for goods purchased for resale.
	(16) Currently affected departments are not required to formally respond to management with respect to internal audit findings and recommendations.
	(17) Invoices are forwarded for payment without copies of purchase orders or receiving reports attached.
	(18) Invoices were approved without receiving reports, causing old unmatched reports to be on file, thereby defeating the receiving report system.

*Control Environment
Problems (CONTINUED)

ceeding 100 pages in a single management letter) are common. When discussing significance, attention should be directed to the nature of the problem, in tandem with consideration of how that nature may influence assessment of materiality.

Focus on "Constructive Suggestions" Rather Than "Weaknesses"

Rather than as a "weakness" orientation, often the recommendations are better described as "constructive suggestions." For example:

> We believe that the following comments are deserving of your attention and recommend the adoption of our suggestions for improvement after giving consideration to the operating economics and practical application of the suggestions within the operating framework of your company.

The emphasis is upon the opportunities to improve rather than upon weaknesses that exist in the control system.

Take Care to Communicate the Significance of Suggestions

Care should be taken to clearly communicate the significance of the suggestions delineated in the management letter. Vague descriptive terms like "important" and "significant" do not effectively communicate. The CPA's primary measure of significance is *material* or *immaterial*. Within the group of weaknesses or set of recommendations that are identified as immaterial, the CPA at times may be able to quantify or describe the magnitude of the benefits that might accrue from adopting a particular suggestion. This is an effective means of communicating the relative importance of the suggestion. Frequently, the CPA can provide little more than a descriptive explanation of how the suggestions might better segregate duties, reduce risks, enhance customer relations, or otherwise benefit the client. In such cases, the client has the responsibility for evaluating the relative significance of the suggestion but is provided with the CPA's perception as to the breadth of the suggestions' effects on controls and operations.

Separate Material Recommendations from Immaterial Comments

If the management letter has both material and immaterial weaknesses, you should acknowledge this fact in the initial paragraphs of the management letter, assuring the reader that those weaknesses deemed material will be appropriately highlighted. One effective communication device is to use two major subheadings in organizing suggestions by which to segregate the material recommendations from the immaterial comments.

Since material weakness has a very specific definition in the external auditing literature, as discussed in an earlier chapter, it is advisable to repeat that definition in the text of the management letter. The assessment by management of whether or not particular suggestions are "material" in their effects will probably differ from the external CPA's perception of materiality. In addition to the cost/benefit dimension of management's evaluation of materiality, there is an operating dimension to the evaluation process above and beyond accounting effects of the various recommendations. To further clarify the distinction between material weaknesses in accounting controls and the fairness with which financial statements are presented, a sentence to the effect that no modification of the audit opinion was necessary should be included in the introduction to the management letter.

Suggestions for Preparing a Balanced Communication Device

The management letter has traditionally been a communication device that has stressed the negatives. The weaknesses and problems in operations and controls are outlined, with recommendations as to how they might be improved. In part, the negative bias is aggravated by the CPA's unnecessarily harsh and critical descriptions of existing problems. Rather than stressing what is wrong, thereby emphasizing one party's responsibility, the auditor should stress the potential for improvement, with more general phraseology that is unlikely to insult a particular employee. The negative bias of the management letter can be corrected by giving attention to positive findings with respect to efficiency and control, or should be explicitly acknowledged in the introductory paragraphs of the management letter.

The more common practice is to retain the negative bias of the report but to acknowledge that such a bias is intentional and perhaps unfair to the entity. The following paragraphs suggest alternative approaches to communicating the intentional bias:

> This letter by nature is critical, i.e., only deficiencies are noted, and it does not include our observations on the many strong features of the company's organization and internal control.
>
> This letter addresses those weaknesses that we believe should be brought to the attention of management, and accordingly does not recite the many sound controls that presently exist.

While this approach is an efficient use of space, problems can be created, particularly at the interpersonal level, with the auditee.

Identify Strengths in the Client's Control System

Discussions with internal audit directors have disclosed their general annoyance at the negative bias of management letters and the general unwillingness of CPAs to include some positive information in such reports. These directors state that suggestions from the CPAs as to their internal audit department's organization, size, and activities are common, but in conjunction with these comments, no acknowledgment is given to the quality of the department's work, the internal auditor's cooperation with the external auditors, the ability of the external CPAs to rely upon the internal auditors' working papers in reducing their tests, or the incorporation of suggestions in the management letter that overlap those previously identified by the internal auditors. While more space in the management letter should be allocated to weaknesses in controls, since these require support as well as explanations of suggested means of correcting the problems, some space should be allocated to identifying particular strengths in the entity's control system.

Obviously, as strengths are acknowledged, internal managers and auditors are given their due credit and can improve their standing in the organization. This will enhance the interpersonal relationships between the auditee and external auditor and is likely to increase the level of cooperation provided by the client's employees. The external CPA is often perceived as a policeman who detects and reports problems and has little capacity for rewarding performance or improving performance in a manner that will accrue real benefits to the individual employee. This misperception has been perpetuated by CPAs who overlook the opportunity to give some "balanced" report on controls and operations in the text of the management letter. Some CPAs have tried to communicate their intentions by using phraseology such as "our comments are not intended to be a criticism or reflection on any individual employee" or "our suggestions should not be construed as a reflection upon the integrity of any officer or employee of the company." However, more specific positive statements would provide a more balanced report.

Warning: One word of warning is appropriate. The audit engagement does not provide a basis for expressing an opinion on the overall adequacy of controls, nor will it necessarily provide a perspective to the CPA as to the quality of compliance with controls in the various operating cycles. Therefore, the positive remarks should be just as carefully qualified as to their basis as are the negative remarks concerning operations and controls. A later chapter will consider in depth the reporting issues related to internal control; at this juncture, the CPA is merely reminded that such issues exist and require attention when drafting a management letter. In addition to acknowledging positive aspects of controls and operations, you should take the opportunity to express appreciation to management for their courtesies and cooperation. The dependence of the auditor or evaluator upon management's cooperation in order to perform an efficient examination suggests the importance of expressing gratitude for such cooperation, thereby encouraging similar support for future periods.

A Prototype for an Introduction to Management Letter Recommendations

This chapter's comprehensive discussion of those considerations that are expected to affect the form and content of the introductory paragraphs to a management letter provides a basis from which a prototype introductory form for such communication devices can be drafted. Exhibit 14–4 presents one possible report form for the introductory paragraphs that precede the specific suggestions.

Exhibit 14–4

An Introduction to Specific Management Letter Recommendations

February 20, 1991

Dear <u>(President's Name and Possibly the Board of Directors)</u>:

In accordance with generally accepted auditing standards, we have obtained a sufficient understanding of the internal control structure to plan the audit and determine the nature, timing and extent of the audit tests that were necessary to express an opinion on the 1990 financial statements.

Our study and evaluation of the entity's system of internal accounting control were not designed for the purpose of making detailed recommendations and would not necessarily disclose all weaknesses in the existing system. Our audit procedures have been appropriately adjusted to compensate for any observed weaknesses. Although we have recommendations concerning various procedural, control, and general matters, our review did not disclose any weaknesses in internal accounting control that we consider to be material weaknesses. A material weakness is defined for our purposes as

> a condition in which we believe that the prescribed procedures or the degree of compliance with them does not provide reasonable assurance that error or irregularities in amounts that would be material in the financial statements being audited would be prevented or detected within a timely period by employees in the normal course of performing their assigned functions. (AU§320.69)

We have not reviewed the internal control and accounting procedures subsequent to February 20, 1991, the date of our accountants' report.

As the primary purpose of our exam is to form an opinion on the financial statements, you will appreciate that reliance must be placed on adequate methods of internal control as your principal safeguard against irregularities which a test exam may not disclose. The objective of internal accounting control is to provide reasonable, but not absolute, assurance that assets are safeguarded against loss from unauthorized use and that financial records are reliable for preparing financial statements in accordance with generally accepted accounting principles and for maintaining the accountability for assets. The concept of reasonable assurance recognizes that the cost of a system of internal accounting control should not exceed the related benefits; to operationalize this concept, management is required to formulate estimates and judgments of the cost/benefit ratios of alternative controls.

There are inherent limitations that should be recognized in considering the potential effectiveness of any system of internal accounting control. Errors

Exhibit 14–4 (continued)

can result from misunderstanding of instructions, mistakes of judgment, carelessness, fatigue, and other personnel factors. Control procedures whose effectiveness depends upon the segregation of duties can be circumvented by collusion or by management. What's more, any projection of internal control evaluations to future periods is subject to the risk that the procedures may become inadequate because of changes in conditions or due to the deterioration of the degree of compliance with control procedures.

As an adjunct of our audit we remained alert throughout for opportunities to enhance internal controls and operating efficiency. These matters were discussed with management as the audit progressed and have subsequently been reviewed in detail to formulate practical recommendations. Our suggestions should not be construed as a criticism of or a reflection on the integrity of any officer or employee of the company. In fact, the involvement with management at all levels provided an excellent opportunity to exchange ideas and formulate these recommendations. The courtesies and cooperation of employees facilitated the efficient performance of audit procedures, particularly the assistance by your internal audit department. In reviewing this report, it is important to remember that your company's existing many sound controls are not recited; this letter by nature is critical for the purpose of suggesting means of improving control and operations. Not only can the adoption of our suggestions enhance the audit trail and reduce audit fees, but more importantly, incorrect business decisions that could result from the use of inaccurate and incomplete data can be avoided.

This letter has been prepared solely for your information and may be distributed at your discretion to your employees, regulatory authorities, and your bonding company; we request that you confer with us prior to distributing the report to other third parties. In this manner, we can communicate with creditors and other parties you may desire to have review the report, to ensure that its contents are understood.

We welcome discussion of the ideas expressed herein and would be pleased to assist in the implementation of any desired actions. Let us now turn to our specific suggestions. . . .

Drafting Specific Suggestions

Following the introductory paragraphs, various formats are possible for delineating specific suggestions. A subheading to distinguish between material and immaterial weaknesses has already been recommended. In addition, a table of contents, grouping weaknesses and efficiency suggestions by operating and control cycle, greatly facilitates the entity's review of the specific management letter points. If the entity has divisions or subsidiaries, comments should be organized by operating unit to help the entity in distributing suggestions to the appropriate managers. In this table of contents a distinction can be drawn between those suggestions that also appeared in prior years' management letters and those that are appearing in a management letter for the first time. This type of distinction

(1) communicates the CPA's or evaluator's continuing concern for those control points, and
(2) facilitates the entity's review of prior years' reactions to these suggestions and future management plans that relate to such recommendations.

A Table Approach

While many auditors and evaluators prepare management letter points in paragraph form, a table approach can add clarity to the individual suggestions. A parsimonious set of headings that can be used follows:

	Implication or	Suggested
Comments	Risk to the Company	Corrective Actions

A somewhat more developed set of headings might include:

					Inclusion
	Current	Consequences	Suggested	Type of	in Prior
Cycle	Situation	of Situation	Changes	Weakness	Years' Letter
				Material	Yes
				or	or
				immaterial	no

How to Develop Each Point

Whether in paragraph form or in table form, each management letter point should be developed in the following manner:

(1) Identify the cycle and particular accounts to be affected by the suggestion.
(2) Describe the status quo, including specific audit evidence whenever possible; differentiate between the "form" of the supporting evidence and the "substance" of the problem. (For example, accounting errors may be due to understaffing or to incompetence, rather than the need for other than a manual accounting system.)
(3) Clearly delineate the potential and/or actual consequences of not implementing some change in the controls or operations under discussion; whenever possible, quantify the losses and describe the breadth of ef-

fects—i.e., are employees, customers, suppliers, and/or stockholders affected by this problem?

(4) Suggest a means of correcting the situation, being as specific and as practical as possible in formulating constructive recommendations.

(5) Make the nature of the problem evident, to help management in discerning the importance of various suggestions, by specifying whether weaknesses are material or immaterial.

(6) If the control point is repetitive from prior years, remind management of this fact as a means of communicating the CPA's or evaluator's perception of the continuing importance of that particular control suggestion.

In communicating the substance of the control suggestions, the auditor or evaluator should try to discriminate between the various controls' effects on

—the accuracy of account balances,

—the completeness of accounting records,

—the safeguarding of assets, and

—the efficiency of operations.

In addition, if the CPA or evaluator has identified that a weakness is due to the misunderstanding of policies or noncompliance with designed controls, rather than to the complete absence of the policy or control, this finding should be communicated, as the entity's response will differ depending on the particular circumstance. If a request by the entity led to a particular suggestion, you should reference that request. For example, you may state: "You also requested that we share with you our thoughts on investment practices in the industry."

Similarly, if the control suggestions discussed had already been identified by management and/or the internal audit department prior to the auditor's examination, this past recognition should be acknowledged. In addition, if management actions have already been taken to improve or to correct the situation, you should appropriately give credit for such past and ongoing activities.

Should you have reservations as to the practicality of a particular suggestion, explicitly remind the client's managers that they alone are in a position to evaluate the relative merits of the suggestions. You may wish to state any reservations you have as to the feasibility of implementing suggestions, including the expected time frame over which the change could be made operative. If the reservations stem from a lack of information as to management's intentions or as to cost data, flexible wording can effectively communicate the issue that management should address in evaluating alternatives. Both advantages and disadvantages to implementing a particular suggestion should be reported.

Providing a Management Letter Implementation Plan

One approach to assisting the entity in reacting to recommendations is to provide a management letter implementation plan. The content of such a plan is best described by presenting the headings that might appear on a summary table that provides an implementation plan:

Recommendation	Individual Responsible	Participation Required	Completion Date

When available, cost data should be provided, if not in dollar terms, in man-hour terms. For example, "a change in the procedures manual will require two weeks of a supervisor's time." If the CPA or evaluator has particular strengths in assisting in the implementation of a management letter suggestion, this expertise and willingness to assist the entity, as well as related costs, can be communicated with the implementation plan. In addition to an implementation plan, you should consider providing sample forms for the entity's use in adopting particular suggestions. For example, a sample petty cash voucher might speed up the entity's implementation of recommended procedures that are intended to establish control over the petty cash fund.

Including Management's Comments: Advantages and Drawbacks

A final consideration in drafting individual suggestions should be the potential advantages of including management's comments on each suggestion, within the body of the management letter. The advantages of such an approach are that

—the CPA's or evaluator's interaction with managers is documented,

—management is given the opportunity to express reservations as to the feasibility and advisability of implementing various suggestions,

—a formal statement by management of planned and past activities to correct problems can work as a record against which implementation actions can be evaluated, and

—the CPA or evaluator is provided with information that can be of use in determining whether the repetition of particular management letter points in subsequent years' letters is warranted, if no action is taken by the entity in the current period.

However, accompanying such advantages are disadvantages that stem from providing management with an opportunity to justify its inaction. Political overtones may implicitly or explicitly enter the management letters, as managers assume at times a defensive posture in describing why policies and controls exist in their present state and why change may well be unwarranted. If the management letter is to be reviewed by the Board of Directors and/or the Audit Committee, operating managers can apply substantial pressure upon the CPA as to what material should or should not be included in the management letter. This pressure can be exaggerated by requiring formal commentaries from managers regarding each control point. What's more, the formalized reaction by management, within the auditor's management letter, may give the appearance that the auditor condones management's remarks and plans.

Hence, the CPA should assess the political and control environment of the client; the ability of users of the report to appreciate that these are managers' remarks that are incorporated, without editing, and without endorsement by the CPA; and the reasonableness with which management is likely to assimilate formal remarks—i.e., will managers take the time necessary to evaluate the recommendations prior to that point in time that the management letter is to be formally submitted to the president and/or the board? These considerations are also relevant to the internal auditor and system evaluator.

Sample Suggestions from Management Letters

Exhibit 14–5 provides some sample suggestions from management letters that exemplify the points raised herein as to how to draft specific recommendations. The first suggestion relates to the cash disbursement cycle and clearly states current practice and the perceived problem. The entity apparently believes that attaching check copies to the invoices is sufficient documentation of payment. However, the auditor points out in the second paragraph of the suggestion that the current system would permit reuse of invoices and supporting documentation to support further payments. A specific suggestion capable of eliminating this risk exposure of the entity is proposed: the cancellation of each invoice and related document. The success of such a procedure will, of course, depend on the appropriate segregation of duties. The entity is reminded of this fact by the explicit suggestion as to what duties should not be performed by the employee who is given responsibility for stamping the invoices and documents as "paid."

The second suggestion also concerns cash, but focuses on the authorization of expenditures via the check-signing function. In this setting, authorization exists, but the auditor points out that dual authorization provides improved control over an asset that, being easily transferable and negotiable, is greatly exposed to misuse. The auditor in this situation has two alternative suggestions, either of which would accomplish the dual control objective. When the auditor can identify alternative and equally favorable means of correcting problems, (s)he should make a practice of communicating such alternatives to the client.

The third suggestion focuses upon an efficiency suggestion, rather than a control weakness. It describes current practices in specific terms, and how these appear to diverge from an opportunity to generate higher interest revenue and to deter slow payment practices. The opportunity given to management to reply to the suggestion uncovers a consideration that was apparently overlooked by the auditor—a legal consideration pertaining to contract and usury laws for various states. What's more, management appears to consider that certain business reasons warrant interest rates that diverge from the prime rate in certain cases. However, when such rates are "deemed appropriate," the entity has expressed an intention to charge interest rates that are closer to the prime rate. This com-

Exhibit 14–5

Examples of Specific Management Letter Suggestions

CASH DISBURSEMENTS

Vendors' invoices and supporting documents are not effectively canceled when paid. Instead, check copies are attached to vendors' invoices and supporting documents to indicate payment.

These invoices and supporting documents should be marked or canceled upon payment in a manner that will render them ineffective as support for further payments. This can be accomplished by applying a "paid" stamp to each invoice and supporting document immediately after the signing of the checks. That person who cancels the invoices and documents should not be connected with either the preparation of invoices for payment or the writing of checks.

CASH

Presently, company checks require only one signature. Furthermore, the authority for both the signing and preparing of company checks rests with the same individual.

Implications

This weakness potentially limits the effectiveness of management's efforts to safeguard the company's cash balances against errors and irregularities. Due to the nature of the asset, internal controls affecting cash should be assessed on a continual basis and upgraded whenever possible. Even relatively "minor" weaknesses in control over cash balances can result in serious problems.

Suggestions

Require dual signatures on all company checks over a specified dollar amount, or utilize a signature machine with dual key control.

ACCOUNTS AND NOTES RECEIVABLE

Currently, whenever accounts receivable are over 180 days old, the company negotiates interest terms on notes receivable for 6% to 8%. Given that the prime interest rate has ranged from 12% to 18%, these notes represent low interest financing to customers and may well encourage their slow payment practices.

We suggest you change your credit terms by informing customers that interest rates approximating the current prime rate will be charged on delinquent accounts receivable which are transformed to notes receivable,

Exhibit 14–5 (continued)

unless other terms are explicitly negotiated in advance. In this manner, customers should be prompted to pay off their notes.

Management Commentary

We believe this suggestion has merits, but we have concern that contract requirements and usury laws may vary across the states with which we do business, requiring alternative maximum allowable rates. We plan on striving to identify accounts receivable that should be renegotiated to notes receivable on an earlier basis than the 180-day practice that you have cited. When we do so, we will try to obtain the best interest possible and, when deemed appropriate and permitted by law, we will charge a rate approximating the prime rate.

INVENTORY

During our review of the company's final priced-out inventory listing, three keying errors that resulted in a significant overstatement of quantities were identified. The overstatement of inventory of $500,000 was detected by the client's and our review of a descending dollar listing for unusual items. The errors were obvious and should have been detected at an earlier date by the client, had such a review been performed during the normal inventory compilation procedures. As an example, two errors physically counted as 25 were keyed at 25,000. We strongly recommend that such a review procedure be instituted as a formal step in the inventory compilation process.

Management Commentary

The descending dollar listing was reviewed for reasonableness by company personnel, but these errors that you cite were overlooked. We will institute a more formal review, including a computer program that will report the percentage and unit increases and decreases per inventory category, from year to year.

---

mitment by management can serve as a benchmark in future periods to evaluate whether notes receivable are being negotiated at which might be deemed to be a more reasonable rate of interest.

The final suggestion reported in Exhibit 14–5 exemplifies how the auditor can effectively report specific audit evidence to bear out the significance of a particular control weakness. The management response provides the opportunity for management to provide the defense that, in fact, the recommended procedure had been performed, yet the reported errors had persisted in spite of the procedure. While committing the company to take a more formal approach to the procedure, management simultaneously describes an additional action that is intended to capture the type of error that escaped the attention of personnel when the rank-ordered dollar amounts were reviewed. This computer program should highlight unusual changes for particular inventory classifications, thereby avoiding misstatements in the inventory balances in future periods. This plan of management demonstrates an additional advantage to the inclusion of management's commentary in the body of the management letter. Alternative and additional reactions by management, which may not have been suggested by the auditor but which, nevertheless, accomplish the same objectives as would the implementation of specific recommendations of the auditor, are formalized for subsequent follow-up.

Including Graphs to Depict Problems and Related Costs

The suggestions in Exhibit 14–5 can be used as prototypes in drafting the individual recommendations for control and efficiency improvements that are intended to follow the introductory paragraphs presented in Exhibit 14–4. These suggestions can be effectively expanded upon by including graphs depicting the nature of the problem and its related costs. For example, the third suggestion in Exhibit 14–5 could be accompanied by the illustration provided in Exhibit 14–6 to bear out the foregone interest revenue in past years and that anticipated in the future if present policies persist. Whenever possible, the auditor should acknowledge control strengths in particular areas that relate to weaknesses and improvements that are being discussed and should enhance the positive/negative balance of the management letter by reporting on management's past actions and current plans to react to existing problems.

In preparing graphs, attention should be directed to a proposal that is just beginning to be analyzed: standards regarding financial graphics, i.e., a summary regarding accountants' responsibility in the presentation and use of graphs in financial reporting. While only tangentially related to management letter correspondence, of interest are the findings in past studies highlighting a number of common practices in graphing which can be misleading:

(1) a change in a base line so that the horizontal line reference is lacking, leading to physical measurements that are not proportional to the data represented.
(2) use of a rate-of-change graph,
(3) inclusion of multiple amount scales,
(4) placement of the most irregular stratum at the top of the graph,
(5) careful choice of the years to be presented,
(6) reversal of time series, and
(7) variation of the scale range.[4]

---

[4] Barbara G. Taylor and Lane K. Anderson, "Misleading Graphs: Guidelines for the Accountant," *Journal of Accountancy* (October 1986), pp. 126–134.

Exhibit 14–6

Effectively Integrating Graphs and Similar Illustrations in Presenting Management Letter Points: An Example

Effectively Integrating Graphs and Similar Illustrations in Presenting Management Letter Points: An Example.

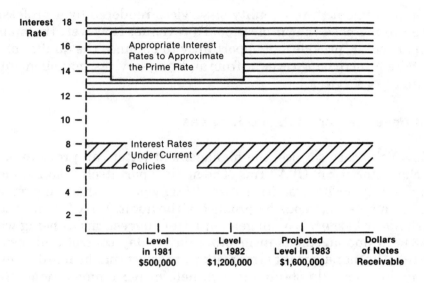

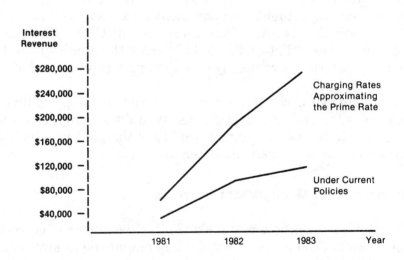

Such pitfalls should be avoided as graphics are used in communicating via management letters.

HOW IMPROVING THE QUALITY OF MANAGEMENT LETTERS CAN INCREASE REVENUE

Any improvement in the quality of services rendered by a professional can be expected to increase that professional's revenue. However, the management letter, in particular, provides an opportunity to enhance the quality of customer services, thereby increasing revenue from auditing services, management advisory services, and tax services.

Increased Revenue from Auditing Services

While a voluntary service, the management letter can prove to be a distinguishing characteristic of CPA firms. The audit report itself is sometimes viewed as a fairly homogeneous product across CPAs, whereas the management letter is likely to be a heterogeneous by-product of the audit. If a CPA can successfully distinguish his or her firm's management letter suggestions as being worthwhile contributions to management in meeting day-to-day control and operating responsibilities, the management is more likely to select that firm to deliver auditing services, as the means to obtaining such helpful recommendations. Should the CPA firm not utilize this reporting by-product to distinguish itself, competing CPAs, known to provide valuable management letter suggestions, might successfully attract audit clients away from their present CPA. Of course, the implication of such an action is that a CPA could increase the number of audit clients, thereby increasing auditing revenue, by establishing a reputation for sound and useful management letters.

Beyond attracting new clients, a CPA firm known for providing valuable management suggestions can more easily justify audit fees higher than those of its competitors, due to the overall higher quality of the product—including both the audit report and the management letter.

Increased Revenue from Management Services

The ability to identify problem areas and effective means of correcting such problems is indicative of competence in providing management advisory services. The CPA firm, via the management letter, has the first opportunity to describe its ability to provide assistance in studying and/or implementing alternative recommendations. Given the CPA's demonstrated knowledge of operations, a built-in advantage to hiring the CPA over other available consultants, not knowledgeable as to the company's particular control and operating systems, is evident. The expected result is increased revenue from management advisory services, as a direct result of formulating constructive practical recommendations in the management letter and supporting the relative merits of such suggestions.

The presumption in this discussion has been that the management letter content has proven valuable to the CPA's clientele. This is perhaps an appropriate time to repeat some implicit suggestions made earlier in this chapter. As comments are considered for inclusion in the management letter, the CPA must carefully consider the facts as to the present situation or procedures upon which recommendations are based. The suggestions should be well thought out within the context of client operations, and should be practicable. Vague commentaries as to areas that management ought to investigate or the communication of casual observations and ideas that have not been structured to communicate clearly the problem, its implications, its significance, and means of improvement are inadequate. If problems are of an industry-specialist nature or deal with administrative and/or tax matters, the CPA on the job should contact professionals with experience in these areas, either within the CPA firm or outside it, to ensure that the suggestions are appropriate. The CPA should recognize that the quickest way to lose the confidence of a client, with regard to any client services offered, is to report impractical recommendations or to make recommendations based on incomplete or erroneous information.

One means of avoiding inappropriate suggestions is to discuss a draft of the management letter with company officials, for the express purpose of confirming that the factual basis of the suggestions, as well as the inferences drawn from this basis, are reasonable. The company's views can be considered and explicitly included in the management letter, if desired.

For recommendations from prior years, the CPA should take particular care to evaluate whether the repetition of these points is warranted and, if so, how the CPA can effectively integrate management's past reactions and an explanation of why actions to date have been inadequate in addressing the particular problem.

As an overall approach, the CPA should emphasize business recommendations as well as internal accounting control suggestions. This approach is more likely to distinguish the CPA's management letter as being of value beyond the client's normal expectations. In addition, the client's reception of internal control and accounting-related recommendations is likely to be more enthusiastic when combined with operating efficiency recommendations. This enthusiasm can evolve into client revenue dollars for the CPA firm.

Increased Revenue from Tax Services

In discussing the means of ensuring high quality management letters, the importance of conferring with specialists in technical areas was acknowledged. One group of specialists of particular importance is the tax-planning group within a CPA firm. Frequently the auditor has tax expertise and can provide both audit and tax services in the course of an engagement. However, tax-planning opportunities, identified in the course of the audit engagement and communicated via the management letter, can lead to extended tax services. Again, the CPA who performs the audit is in the unique position of understanding client operations and organizational structure in a manner conducive to identifying opportunities for tax savings. In addition, tax problems stemming from client practices, such as the means of documenting travel and entertainment expenses, can be identified. Such insights and expertise as to client activities can be shared within a CPA firm across audit and tax personnel in order to supply tax services at a lower cost to the client than might be incurred if another CPA or lawyer were hired purely for tax services. As anticipated for management advisory services, this lower cost opportunity is likely to attract the client toward the use of the same CPA firm for both tax and audit services. By explicitly incorporating tax suggestions in the management letter, the CPA firm can effectively increase its revenue from tax services, as the client is encouraged to follow up on tax-saving opportunities and is made aware of how the CPA can assist in tax-planning activities.

SYNOPSIS

Management letters, though a voluntary service, provide you with an opportunity to communicate control and efficiency suggestions that reflect your expertise, particularly your understanding of an entity's operations. Since recommendations will relate to operating and tax matters, as well as accounting and control procedures, they may lead to increased demand for both management advisory and tax services. The management letter's ability to enhance a CPA's revenue from auditing, management advisory, and tax services depends upon the value of the recommendations made and the effectiveness with which suggestions are communicated. Of course, the timeliness of suggestions is crucial, as is the follow-up on these suggestions in subsequent periods, if top quality service is to be provided. A prototype for the introductory paragraphs of a management letter, as well as an exemplary form for specific recommendations in the management letter, are provided in Exhibits 14–4 and 14–5.

An appendix to this chapter provides various classification schemes for management letter points, which may be useful in organizing communication of control suggestions.

APPENDIX

Organization of Detailed Management Letter Comments

In research on management letter content, the following classification schemes have been useful in describing the nature of findings: account orientation—balance sheet and income statement; operating and control cycles; other control issues; events and systems creating control points; and reporting issues. These are provided both as a "memory jogger" of classes of potential control points and to facilitate organization of management letters.

Balance Sheet

ASSETS

Cash—Petty
Cash—Undeposited
Cash—Bank
Dividend Imprest Bank Account
Marketable Securities
Accounts Receivable—Trade
Accounts Receivable—Other (including Due from Bank Accounts and Employees' Receivables)
Allowance for Uncollectibles (chargebacks, delinquent loans)
Notes Receivable—Customers (revolving credit, related reserves, & deferred payment plans)
Notes Receivable—Other (officers and employees)
Interest Receivable
Other Receivables

Inventory—Raw Materials
Inventory—Work-in-Process
Inventory—Finished Goods (special order items, insurance policies, tickets)
Inventory @ Interim: LIFO Provisions (an interim reporting emphasis)
Rental Inventory

Inventory—Other Than Goods for Sale (small tools, service inventory, defective parts)
Inventory—Testing for Quality; Recording of Costs for Engineering

Prepaid Insurance
Prepaid Rent
Prepaid Advertising
Prepaid Advertising—Barter Agreement
Prepaid Salaries (Advances)
Other Prepaids
Investment Tax Credit—Deferred
Repurchase Agreements—Investments
Long-Term Investments (art objects and collateral)
Cash Surrender Value of Life Insurance
Property
Plant
Equipment
Trucks
Furniture & Fixtures
Construction Work-in-Process
Other Fixed Assets (safe deposit boxes)
Accumulated Depreciation
Goodwill

Balance Sheet (continued)

ASSETS (continued)

Patents
Leases
Copyrights
Franchises
Operating Rights
Natural Resources
Investment in Oil and Gas Operations
Other Intangibles

LIABILITIES

Accounts Payable—Suppliers
Accounts Payable—Other
Unearned Revenue
Savings Accounts for Banks and Savings & Loans
Trust Accounts
Notes Payable—Short-term
Letters of Credit
Health Claims Reserves & Accident and Liability Claims
Interest Payable
Wages Payable
Taxes Payable—Employee Related (Payroll)
Property Taxes Payable

Taxes Payable—Income Tax Related
Accrued Liabilities
Perfect Attendance & Paid Vacation Accrual
Notes Payable—Long-Term (Debentures)
Bonds Payable
Officers' Employment Contracts—Related Liability
Warranty Accruals (reserves, rebates & trade-ins)
Pension Liability
Lease Liability
Contingent Liability

OWNERS' OR STOCKHOLDERS' EQUITY

Common Stock
Preferred Stock
Stock Dividends
Stock Options
Profit-Sharing
Retained Earnings Appropriation
Reserve for Self-Insurance
Treasury Stock
Fund Equity

Income Statement

Revenue—Sales (including patient fees and related contract information)
Sales Returns and Allowances (charge backs; credit memos)
Revenue—Interest
Revenue—Other than Lease, Franchises, Gain & Loss on Asset Disposals, Dividend, Rental, Royalty (fees for book rentals; part sales back to supplier)

Commissions
Dividend Income
Rental Income
Lease Revenue
Royalty Revenue
Franchise Revenue
Gain, Loss on Asset Disposals
Scrap-related, or Sale of Obsolete Items
Cost of Goods Sold—Purchase Related (freight; vendor approval)

Income Statement (continued)

Cost of Goods Sold—Production Related (labor costs; subcontractor advances; cost overruns)

Cost of Goods Sold—Service Related (mortgage loans; hospitals)

Purchase Returns (debit memos)

Loss and Damage Claims (overcharge claims)

Cancellation and Charges Resulting from Unfulfilled Minimum Purchase Commitments

Discounts (cost of goods sold related to customers' discounts)

Payroll Expense

Bonuses

Bad Debt Expense (write-offs; mortgage loan defaults)

Home Office Administrative Expenses (selling, general, and administrative)

Travel and Entertainment Expenses

Depreciation Expense

Amortization Expense

Depletion Expense

Property Tax/Use Tax Expense

Rental Expense

Royalty Expense

Lease Expense

Interest Expense (dividends for banks and for savings and loan associations)

Research and Development Costs

Insurance Expense

Sales Tax Expense

Tax Expense—Employee Related (Payroll)

Income Tax Expense

Earnings Per Share

Other

OPERATING/CONTROL CYCLES

Revenue Recognition

Receiving

Order Entry & Invoicing (including control over invoices)

Credit Approval

Disbursements (including their control, stamping documents paid, accounting for number of checks signed with a facsimile signature)

Shipping & Processing of Orders (satisfying of shipping terms)

Production Labor & Standards (variances and standard costs)

Inventory—Physical Inventory Related

Inventory—Obsolescence Related

Inventory—Cost System or Valuation Related

Inventory—Consignment Related (@ subcontractors)

Inventory—Warehouse Related

Capitalize versus Expense Decisions (start-up costs)

Insurance Coverage (Bonding; Key-Man Life)

Debt Agreements (Covenant Compliance)

Other (continued)

OPERATING/CONTROL
 CYCLES (continued)

Tax Exemption
Closing Entries
Budgets and Overall Control of
 Forecasting
Data Processing Controls (insur-
 ance for disaster plan)
Document & Asset Control

OTHER CONTROL ISSUES

Owner/Management Oversight
 (vigilance is particularly important when there are a small
 number of employees)
Internal Control Systems: A
 Worldwide Plan Exists to Adopt
 and Evaluate Its Controls (audit
 committees, operational audits,
 establishment and expansion of
 the internal audit department)
Change in External Auditors'
 Scope and Coverage
Vaguely Defined Responsibilities;
 Inadequate or No Operating
 Manuals; No Organizational
 Chart; Unclear Accounting Policies
Accounting Personnel: Quantity
 and Quality Issues (turnover;
 too small for ideal internal control)

EVENTS AND SYSTEMS
 CREATING CONTROL
 POINTS

Lock Box System
Wire Transfers
Joint Ventures
Investee Companies—Equity Ac-
 counting (capital contributions
 in training schools)
Subsidiary Companies (redundan-
 cies in systems development;
 more control is desirable)
Discontinued Operations
Employees' Savings Plan
Medical Reimbursement Plan

Stock Purchase Plan
Use of Service Bureau—EDP

REPORTING ISSUES

Translation of Foreign Currency
Format of Statement of Condition
SEC Registration (10-Q's)
Interim Reports (stress AJEs
 other than LIFO; timeliness;
 use to management)

15

Performing Comprehensive Reviews of Internal Accounting Control Systems

"Every corporation's business is conducted by some standard. If it is not formulated systematically at the top, it will be formulated haphazardly and impulsively in the field. And top management will be called on to defend practices that were unnecessary and unintended."

John C. Biegler[1]

One means to both understand the practices in place and form a basis for demonstrating that the standard in practice is what is intended is to proceed beyond the audit process to the performance of a comprehensive assessment of control structure.

Generally accepted auditing standards require a sufficient understanding of the internal control structure to plan the audit and determine the nature, timing, and extent of tests to be performed. Since the auditor's decision to assess control risk at less than a maximum level depends on both control design and the efficiency of control tests relative to substantive tests, there is no assurance that the audit

---

[1] "Rebuilding Public Trust in Business," *Financial Executive*, 45 (June 1977): 29.

will provide evidence concerning the quality of controls, even if the system of controls is well designed. However, a service expressly tailored to provide such evidence is available. The engagement is termed a comprehensive review of an internal accounting control system. Such a review encompasses a detailed review of controls, as well as the testing of designed controls. The objective of a comprehensive review engagement is to provide reasonable assurance that

—assets are safeguarded,

—transactions are executed as authorized, and

—data are recorded properly, providing a basis for the preparation of financial statements in accordance with generally accepted accounting principles (GAAP) and for the accountability of assets.

HOW THE ENGAGEMENT DIFFERS FROM THE AUDITOR'S STUDY AND EVALUATION OF INTERNAL ACCOUNTING CONTROL

The auditor's primary attention to internal accounting control stems from the necessity of

—determining the auditability of an entity,

—understanding the flow of information through the entity's operations, and

—performing an efficient audit that recognizes the entity's investment in controls.

The auditor has no responsibility for forming an opinion on the adequacy of designed controls, except for their adequacy in making an entity auditable. The auditor's objective is to formulate an opinion as to the fairness of financial statements. It is widely recognized that an entity with material weaknesses in its internal accounting controls can nevertheless prepare financial statements that are fairly presented, accompanied by a "clean" or unqualified audit report. The auditor can simply adjust the nature, timing, and extent of tests to compensate for such known weaknesses. For example, if controls over fixed assets are poor, the auditor may deem it necessary to take a physical inventory of fixed assets at year-end. In this manner, (s)he can obtain assurance that recorded assets actually exist and are in the physical control of the entity. The condition of the asset can also be observed. Of course, determining the actual ownership of the assets requires an evidential base beyond simply observing that assets are in the physical possession of the entity. Titles and bills of sale will have to be examined, and tests of cash disbursements and cash receipts will help to confirm that unrecorded asset purchases and sales have not occurred.

The auditor's attention to controls is directed by the risk profile of the entity in various segments of operations. In part, this risk profile relates to materiality. For example, immaterial accounts may get no control test attention, even though the entity may have concern over controls related to these accounts. The consequence of the low volume and/or low dollar amount of transactions processed is that the exposure of the entity, as well as the auditor, to losses related to that area of operations is minimal. The clearest picture of the role of materiality in an audit engagement emerges from a comparison of audits of subsidiaries to audits of the consolidated entity. A subsidiary that represents only 5 percent of a conglomerate's business is unlikely to receive attention from an auditor whose objective is to form an audit opinion on the consolidated entity. Obviously, such an opinion gives little insight as to the extent to which the subsidiary's operations are controlled. A separate audit of the subsidiary might well involve a detailed review of controls and testing, but the consolidated audit is unlikely to incorporate any such procedures. The audit objective will influence the amount of information on controls that is obtained in the course of an engagement, just as control design and the relative efficiency of audit procedures influence the amount of knowledge of controls gained by the auditor.

The auditor, at best, is in a position to provide negative assurance concerning internal accounting controls. In other words, in the course of the audit engagement nothing may come to the auditor's attention that represents a material weakness in control or problems with the entity's overall control environment. However, the auditor is unlikely to have performed a detailed review of all major aspects of internal accounting control. (S)he is even less likely to have tested all the controls that may be essential elements of an adequate control system. Only those controls for which less than the maximum level of control risk is planned are evaluated in detail and tested in the course of an audit engagement, and they may represent only a small percentage of the overall control system. Without a thorough detailed review and control testing process, the auditor cannot express an opinion on the system as a whole, or present a data base that supports the operation of a system that is in compliance with overall control design. It is not surprising to find these limitations of the evidential base of an auditor when (s)he directs data gathered for an audit toward the resolution of how adequately all entity's controls are designed and how well they operate.

Rarely does evidence collected for one engagement's objectives also meet the objectives of a separate engagement, without modification. For example, an audit will not in and of itself supply all the information necessary for effective tax-planning services to be provided. Certain procedures will have to augment the audit process in order to deliver the two products demanded by the entity. In a similar manner, the internal accounting control facet of the typical audit must be expanded if an opinion on that system is to be provided by the CPA.

CLARIFYING THE NATURE OF AN ENGAGEMENT

Engagement letters are strongly encouraged to ensure that a clear understanding of services to be performed exists, particularly their inability to be relied on for the disclosure of errors, irregularities, or illegal acts. Exhibit 15–1 presents excerpts from an illustrative engagement letter for review engagements, including attention to clarifying responsibility for the internal control structure. Similar engagement letters are recommended in all types of engagements. Nonetheless, as Exhibit 15–2 displays, many CPA firms do not use engagement letters, for a variety of reasons, as depicted in Exhibit 15–3.

Exhibit 15–1

Review of Financial Statements—Illustrative Engagement Letter Clarifying Responsibility for the Internal Control Structure

(Appropriate Salutation)

This letter is to confirm our understanding of the terms and objectives of our engagement and the nature and limitations of the services we will provide.

We will perform the following services:

1. We will review the balance sheet of XYZ Company as of December 31, 19XX, and the related statements of income, retained earnings, and cash flows for the year then ended, in accordance with standards established by the American Institute of Certified Public Accountants. We will not perform an audit of such financial statements, the objective of which is the expression of an opinion regarding the financial statements taken as a whole, and, accordingly, we will not express such an opinion on them. *A review does not contemplate obtaining an understanding of the internal control structure or assessing control risk, tests of accounting records and responses to inquiries by obtaining corroborating evidential matter, and certain other procedures ordinarily performed during an audit.* Our report on the financial statements is presently expected to read as follows: . . .

Our engagement cannot be relied upon to disclose errors, irregularities, or illegal acts, including fraud or defalcations, that may exist. However, we will inform you of any such matter that comes to our attention.

Our fees for these services . . .

We shall be pleased to discuss this letter with you at any time.

If the foregoing is in accordance with our understanding, please sign the copy of this letter in the space provided and return it to us.

Sincerely yours,

_____

(Signature of accountant)

Acknowledged:
XYZ Company

_____

President

_____

Date

Source: AICPA File Ref. No. 2000 (March 23, 1989), pp. 9–10. This guidance is a part of the public record, is being revised at the time of this writing, and is not yet published. It is provided purely for illustrative purposes.

Exhibit 15-2

Engagement Letter Usage

Frequency of Engagement Letter Usage By Type of Engagement and Firm Size

Firm Size

Level of Frequency	Individual Practitioner		One Office		Local/ Regional		National		Composite Total	
	N	%	N	%	N	%	N	%	N	%
Always										
Compilation	135	(17)	151	(20)	65	(40)	21	(78)	372	(22)
Review	268	(45)	352	(50)	108	(68)	25	(96)	753	(51)
Audit	444	(74)	553	(78)	146	(90)	24	(92)	1167	(78)
Usually										
Compilation	215	(28)	250	(34)	54	(33)	3	(11)	522	(31)
Review	142	(24)	212	(30)	37	(23)	1	(4)	392	(27)
Audit	76	(13)	99	(14)	10	(6)	1	(4)	186	(12)
Rarely										
Compilation	288	(37)	255	(35)	38	(23)	3	(11)	584	(34)
Review	111	(19)	99	(14)	12	(8)	0	(0)	222	(15)
Audit	38	(6)	45	(6)	7	(4)	1	(4)	91	(6)
Never										
Compilation	138	(18)	78	(11)	7	(4)	0	(0)	223	(13)
Review	71	(12)	38	(5)	1	(1)	0	(0)	110	(7)
Audit	42	(7)	9	(1)	0	(0)	0	(0)	51	(3)
TOTALS										
Compilation	776	(100)	734	(100)	164	(100)	27	(100)	1701	(100)
Review	592	(100)	701	(100)	158	(100)	26	(100)	1477	(100)
Audit	600	(100)	706	(100)	163	(100)	26	(100)	1495	(100)

Source: Glenn E. Sumners, Richard A. White, and Raymond J. Clay, Jr., "The Use of Engagement Letters in Audit, Review, and Compilation Engagements: An Empirical Study," *Auditing: A Journal of Practice & Theory* (Spring 1987), p. 118.

Exhibit 15–3

Reasons for Nonuse of Engagement Letters

Frequency of Reasons for Nonuse of Engagement Letters By Firm Size

	Sole Practice		One Office		Local/ Regional		National		Total
	N	%	N	%	N	%	N	%	N
a. Client Resistance—									
●Compilation	72	(12%)	61	(12%)	15	(16%)	0	(0%)	148
●Review	30	(10%)	37	(11%)	5	(12%)	0	(0%)	72
●Audit	9	(6%)	16	(10%)	6	(29%)	1	(33%)	32
b. Unnecessary for Level of Service—									
●Compilation	355	(57%)	273	(48%)	50	(55%)	3	(43%)	678
●Review	103	(35%)	75	(23%)	14	(33%)	0	(0%)	192
●Audit	40	(28%)	15	(10%)	4	(19%)	0	(0%)	59
c. Only Required for New Clients									
●Compilation	135	(22%)	124	(22%)	19	(21%)	1	(14%)	278
●Review	95	(32%)	89	(27%)	13	(30%)	0	(0%)	197
●Audit	45	(31%)	50	(33%)	8	(38%)	0	(0%)	103
d. Continuing Clients Updated only as circumstances change—									
●Compilation	190	(30%)	233	(41%)	39	(43%)	3	(43%)	462
●Review	103	(35%)	171	(52%)	19	(44%)	1	(100%)	293
●Audit	62	(43%)	92	(60%)	8	(38%)	2	(67%)	162
Total Reasons Checked									
●Compilation	752		691		123		7		1,573
●Review	331		372		51		1		755
●Audit	156		173		26		3		358

Note: The percentages represent the percent of respondents that checked that specific reason for nonuse of engagement letters. Since a respondent could check more than one reason, the percentages do not total to 100 percent.

Source: Glenn E. Sumners, Richard A. White, and Raymond J. Clay, Jr., "The Use of Engagement Letters in Audit, Review, and Compilation Engagements: An Empirical Study," *Auditing: A Journal of Practice & Theory* (Spring 1987), p. 119.

Admittedly, the CPA has responsibility for reporting material weaknesses, upon discovery, to top management and voluntarily reports suggestions for improving internal control via management letters. However, the material weaknesses disclosure is a negative assurance form of disclosure, and the content of the management letter is similarly restricted by the type of audit procedures and extent of control review performed by the CPA. In other words, the audit contributes to the evidential base concerning controls, but is frequently little more than a first step.

PERFORMING A COMPREHENSIVE REVIEW

If an audit was largely a substantive test audit, the first responsibility of a CPA who has been engaged to perform a comprehensive review is to extend the CPA's understanding of control structure beyond that required to fulfill the second standard of fieldwork, to a detailed study, essential to a comprehensive review engagement.

Typically, this detailed review is performed and documented by the completion of internal accounting control questionnaires and checklists, the preparation of flowcharts, and the description of controls via memoranda. The design of controls is evaluated as a basis for identifying the critical control points that must be tested in order to form an opinion as to the adequacy of the control system. The objective of a comprehensive review is to identify all material weaknesses, hence all aspects of operations that might have a weakness that could be material must be scrutinized. The concept of materiality directs the comprehensive engagement in a manner that is similar to an audit, hence certain aspects of control will receive only minimal attention because they apply to an insignificant dollar amount of transactions. The physical locations of a multi-unit entity that are visited for the purpose of performing an audit engagement are likely to correspond to those locations that would need to be visited for a comprehensive review. However, the type of procedures performed at each location may very well differ. While the audit requires detailed review and tests of only those controls upon which the auditor intends to rely, all major control areas must be tested when performing a comprehensive review of internal accounting controls. Beyond the typical materiality considerations, a comprehensive review that relates to the provision of an information base adequate to permit the preparation of financial statements in accordance with GAAP can add a dimension to the materiality evaluation.

How a Client's Reporting Practices Can Influence the Comprehensive Review Engagement

An entity's reporting practices can influence the scope of a comprehensive review engagement. If an entity regularly reports on a quarterly or monthly basis and issues such reports to the public, the materiality of control areas should be reviewed in the context of such interim reports. In contrast, the auditor typically has concern for materiality measured on an annual basis. The CPA performing a comprehensive review poses the question: would this control area be capable of having weaknesses that are material to interim reports? If so, that area is a major control area that must be reviewed on a detailed basis and tested.

Understanding a Client's Operations

In approaching a comprehensive review of internal accounting controls, the CPA has to apply basic procedures similar to those required in an audit. The CPA must understand the client's line of business and the flow of information through the operating system. Such an understanding is of particular use in identifying significant control areas. The client's control environment must be evaluated and a preliminary review performed. One aspect of client operations assumes particular importance in a comprehensive review engagement: management's control objectives. The CPA needs to understand the objectives of a control system, the general and specific controls designed to meet these objectives, and the mitigating circumstances that might be expected to decrease the significance of weaknesses in designed controls. Typically this understanding is gained by examining control system documentation and by interviewing the client.

Evaluating and Testing General Controls

The CPA should first evaluate the design of general controls. Often these general controls will be compliance tested before the CPA proceeds to the detailed review of specific controls. Since general controls can provide assurance that specific controls are being performed, the testing of the former provides a foundation for evaluating the adequacy of controls. The probability of compliance with designed controls can be better estimated, tests of control can be more efficiently designed, and the need to investigate mitigating controls that reduce the negative effects of apparent control weaknesses can be more easily assessed by first evaluating and testing general controls.

In evaluating general controls, the CPA must determine whether any material weaknesses are present. This thought process is identical to that described for an audit engagement.

Examples of General Controls

The general controls of particular interest are those that aid in motivating compliance with internal accounting controls or in detecting noncompliance. The motivators can be in the form of operating reports, internal financial reports, budgets, and variance analyses that are

    —routinely prepared,

    —reviewed by management,

    —periodically reviewed and/or tested by internal auditing, and

—designed to reflect control compliance or to facilitate the detection of non-compliance.

Another effective motivator relates to the extent of supervision within the entity's operations. Adequate supervision enhances employees' understanding of controls and can help to reinforce employees' perceptions that control duties are important. Supervision, like variance analyses, internal auditors' involvement in a control system, and management's monitoring of controls via various reporting mechanisms, serves as a means of detecting noncompliance with controls. This detection capability of such general controls also has some "threat value" in motivating employees, i.e., some employees will be motivated to perform control procedures simply because they fear discovery of their noncompliance.

The existence of general control capabilities does not ensure that general controls are in use. For example, weekly reports on the activities of the receiving department of a company may be routinely produced. Yet if no person monitors such reports, compliance is not achieved. Similarly, if an internal audit department is saddled with operating responsibilities that impair the independence of its staff and preclude the effective performance of internal audits, designed controls are not in operation.

Compliance with general controls is typically tested through inquiry, observation, and inspection procedures. If the entity has an internal audit function, it will be reviewed in considerable depth as to its independence, competency, and effectiveness as a control over the entire system of controls. This is likely to entail a review of the internal audit department's charter, reports, and working papers, in addition to observation and inquiry procedures. The quality of general controls, with respect to both design and compliance, can influence the CPA's procedures in evaluating and testing specific controls. Often the extent of tests of specific control procedures can be reduced based on the results of the tests of general controls.

The general controls discussed here assume a major role in establishing a control environment. In addition, the segregation of duties, the competence of employees, organizational structure, and similar variables cited in earlier discussions of the control environment and how it relates to each control cycle are relevant to the question of whether or not general and specific controls of an entity are adequate.

A useful framework in considering general controls is provided by what have been proposed by quality assurance groups for evaluating data processing. The ideas presented in Exhibit 15–4 can be similarly applied to a number of other aspects of operations.

Evaluating Compensating Controls

Assume the control environment of an entity is deemed to be rather poor. What compensating or mitigating controls might diminish the effect of poor general

Exhibit 15–4

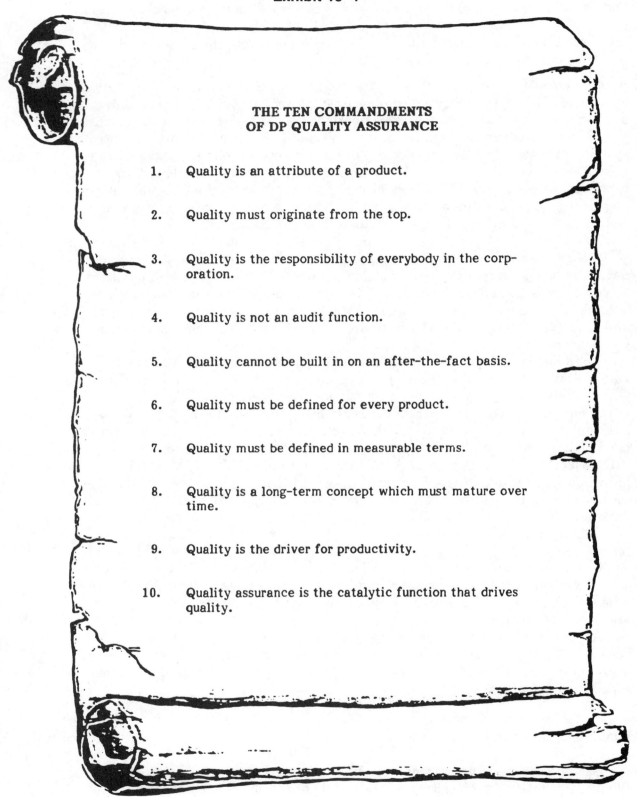

**THE TEN COMMANDMENTS
OF DP QUALITY ASSURANCE**

1. Quality is an attribute of a product.

2. Quality must originate from the top.

3. Quality is the responsibility of everybody in the corporation.

4. Quality is not an audit function.

5. Quality cannot be built in on an after-the-fact basis.

6. Quality must be defined for every product.

7. Quality must be defined in measurable terms.

8. Quality is a long-term concept which must mature over time.

9. Quality is the driver for productivity.

10. Quality assurance is the catalytic function that drives quality.

Source: *Hatching the Data Processing Quality Assurance Function* by William E. Perry, p. 109.

controls? In an owner/manager small business environment, the supervision of operations by the owner may well lessen many of the control problems associated with the lack of strong, well-designed general controls. Similarly, an entity may have a control that although not designed to operate as a particular control procedure, nevertheless can prevent or detect the error or irregularity for which the designed control is either lacking or inoperative.

Example: Assume that an important general control relates to the safeguarding of assets and is expected to include physical security measures with respect to inventory on hand. The auditor discovers that security is only on duty in the evening. However, the inventory is heavy equipment, which cannot be easily moved or hidden. In addition, signed requisitions are required to remove equipment from the storage facility.

In this setting, the requisitioning procedure combined with the physical nature of the inventory constitutes an effective compensating control for the lack of physical security measures during the normal work hours. In contrast, if the inventory were easily pilferable, if numerous entrances and exits were present, and/or if easy means of avoiding the clerk in charge of filling requisitions were available, the auditor could not accept the requisitioning procedure as an adequate compensating control.

Specific Control Evaluation

Once the general controls, in light of the effect of compensating or mitigating controls, have been evaluated, you will direct attention to the specific controls of the entity. In gaining an understanding of the control environment, the entity was requested to describe the entity's control objectives and the means by which the system was to fulfill each objective. The control objectives, beyond the maintenance of a general consciousness, should include

—the proper authorization of transactions,

—the proper accounting for transactions, and

—the adequate safeguarding of assets.

Exhibit 15–5 summarizes the relevant dimensions of each of these specific control objectives. You should check the entity's control objectives for completeness: is each of the necessary dimensions in Exhibit 15–5 encompassed by the designed control system? What control procedures are expected to meet each objective?

A common practice in system design is to incorporate redundant controls to accomplish key control objectives. The logic underlying this practice is a sort of fail-safe approach to ensuring a back-up for noncompliance with designed controls that can result from random human error or from the intentional circumvention of controls. Obviously, such redundancy can be expensive, and you should be alert to cost/benefit dimensions of planned redundancy and provide suggestions to the

Exhibit 15–5

Specific Control Objectives—Their Relevant Dimensions

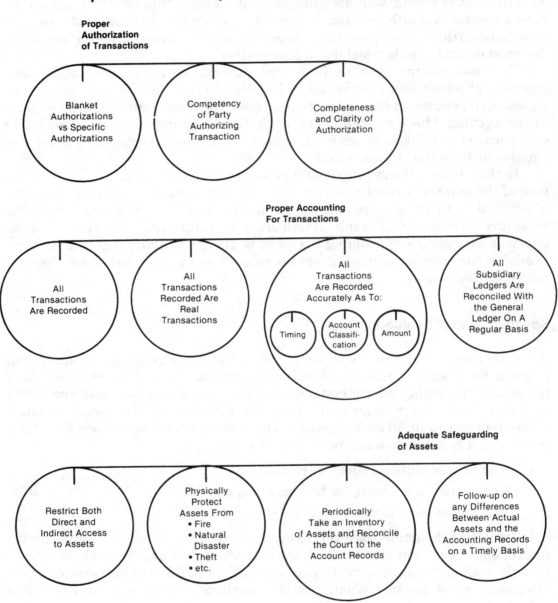

entity regarding the desirability of either increased or decreased redundancy, as deemed appropriate. You are interested in collecting an evidential base for evaluating the general adequacy of the control system and can frequently collect sufficient information from examining only one control procedure out of a set of redundant controls. That control procedure deemed to be essential in reaching the specific control objective is the procedure that should receive your attention.

Performing a Walk-Through

The first step in evaluating the designed specific control procedure of interest is to ensure that your documentation of this procedure is accurate. The walk-through procedure, already discussed, is a valuable means of gaining a clear understanding of how a control procedure operates. In performing a walk-through, you should continually collect additional information on the general control environment:

—Does the entity's personnel appear to be competent?

—Do the duties appear to be adequately segregated?

—Is supervision adequate?

—Have independent checks on employees' performances been established?

The effectiveness of specific procedures will be influenced by such environmental characteristics.

The transactions utilized for the walk-through procedure, if appropriately selected (e.g., from the perspective of a designed statistical sampling plan), can become part of the sample used in testing. Testing of controls in a comprehensive review engagement is no different from such testing in an audit engagement.

The Relevant Time Dimension

The unique consideration in a comprehensive review engagement in planning how to perform test of control procedures is that the relevant time dimension will frequently differ from the annual audit setting. The comprehensive review engagement may be expected to result in an opinion on the adequacy of internal accounting controls at a particular point in time. If this is the case, tests of control should be applied as close to that date as possible, or you should gain assurance that any changes to the system of internal accounting controls have been so well controlled that tests of control performed at an earlier date, or directed at an annual period, provide an adequate basis to comment on the adequacy of the controls as of the particular date of interest.

The extent to which the testing of controls can be clustered around the report date will depend, in large part, on the nature of the controls themselves and, in particular, on the frequency with which the control procedures are applied. For example, a control that is applied on an annual basis will require review at the time that control is operative. By the same token, controls performed on a quarterly basis will require review of at least the last quarter's application of control procedures.

Rather than reporting on controls at a particular point in time, comprehensive review engagements can be designed to yield a report on internal accounting controls for a particular period of time, such as the past quarter or the past year. The period selected will guide the planning of tests of control, although the nature and frequency of controls will similarly affect the period of time over which control procedures will need to be tested. If the period of time selected relates to a critical system change, such as a conversion from a manual to a computerized system, both of the systems in operation over the period will have to be tested.

The result of the various reporting bases for comprehensive review engagements is that the population of transactions of interest can drastically shift across engagements. Whenever the population changes, the sampling units subjected to testing also change. The extent of tests necessary before an opinion can be formed on the adequacy of controls will also be affected by the scope of the engagement. However, as noted in an earlier chapter, population size has only a minor effect upon sample sizes that are required to draw reasonably precise inferences.

Drawing Conclusions

As is the case with any professional engagement, judgment is the primary professional skill that is applied in forming an opinion. In the comprehensive review engagement the opinion is not directed at dollar balances; the attest function is directed at the adequacy of internal accounting controls. Many controls, particularly general controls, can be tested only through such procedures as observation and inquiry; statistical results from such procedures are unavailable.

Key Considerations Involved in Using Statistical Measures of Performance

However, for a large number of controls, especially specific controls, you will be able to apply a statistical sampling plan and generate statistical measures of system performance. To do so, judgment still plays as large a role as in nonstatistical tests, since you must determine the desired level of confidence for tests, what constitute compliance deviations for the procedures examined, and how many deviations are acceptable in order for controls to be reported as adequate.

Recall the smoke/fire argument of how compliance deviations might be expected to relate to accounting misstatements and also recall the crude rule of thumb of 3 to 1. The claim has been made that no more than one of three observed deviations actually leads to misstatement. If this rule of thumb is extended to relate to the common materiality guideline of 3% to 5% used in the audit setting, the implication would be that a 9% to 15% compliance deviation rate might be expected to have material misstatement implications. Using the floor as a conservative approach, the CPA would strive to reach assurance that compliance deviations are at a rate of less than 9 percent if a particular control procedure is to be deemed to be operating effectively. Remember, however, that this rule of thumb is extremely crude. As elaborated upon in Chapter 4, testing of controls is not designed to provide evidence as to the amount of monetary error.

Assume that you chose to use the 9 percent rule of thumb, and estimated a 12% possible upper error limit for a particular procedure. How should you proceed? First, consider whether there is any reason for believing the sample drawn might be unrepresentative. If so, by extending the sample you may well obtain evidence that the 9 percent desired limit does apply to the entity, as originally expected. Second, consider whether there are compensating or mitigating controls that can be tested to provide evidence of adequate controls, despite the poor performance of the control procedure that was initially selected for testing. Third, consider whether the findings indicate that the observed weakness in controls is a material weakness. Fourth, discuss with management how such weaknesses might be corrected and encourage prompt attention to them. Be certain that the client understands that if the condition is corrected prior to the report date, such correction will be verified and noted in the CPA's report. In fact, if the report is issued for a particular date, rather than for a period of time, and if the correction is made prior to that date, no reference to the material weakness will be made in the CPA's report.

Determining Whether Material Weaknesses Exist

The determination of whether control weaknesses are material is the same whether the evaluation is in an audit context or is being performed for a comprehensive review engagement. In a comprehensive review engagement all weaknesses that are not deemed to be material should be considered in total, to ensure that their combined effect is not a material weakness. This procedure is analogous to the auditor's accumulation of immaterial monetary errors for the purpose of evaluating their combined effect on the fairness of financial statements. The evaluation of controls for a comprehensive review engagement does not entail the collection of evidence as to the dollar effects of any material or immaterial weaknesses in controls upon reported financial statements.

Note: In order to avoid any misconception by report users that such evidence has been collected, the CPA should include a statement in the opinion on controls that the entity's financial statements were not examined, nor were the effects of material weaknesses upon any past or current financial statements determined by the CPA.

Is an Adverse Opinion Appropriate?

Most often, material weaknesses will be cited as exceptions in the CPA's report, resulting in a qualified opinion on controls. However, some material weak-

Exhibit 15–6

The Comprehensive Review Process

Gain an understanding of client operations.

Request that the client describe
- control objectives, and
- the system design to meet such objectives.

Whenever possible, utilize the client's documentation of the control system.

Document the system of controls, identifying the major control areas.

Evaluate and test general controls.

Consider controls that may compensate for observed weaknesses.

Advise the client of observed weaknesses and encourage prompt corrective action. Inform the client that such action
- could eliminate the need for disclosure of observed material weaknesses if the comprehensive review report is as of a particular date, or
- will be noted in the auditor's report to demonstrate management's responsiveness to observed problems.

Determine whether material weaknesses exist in general controls.

Identify specific control objectives and the key control procedures to be examined.

Consider the effects of general control on specific controls and perform tests of control.

Consider controls that may compensate for observed weaknesses.

Confirm the effectiveness of corrective actions taken.

Determine whether material weaknesses exist in specific controls.

Evaluate the combined effect of immaterial weaknesses to determine whether, jointly, they constitute a material weakness.

Evaluate whether observed material weaknesses are sufficiently pervasive to require an adverse opinion.

nesses may be so extensive in their effects that the CPA will deem that an adverse opinion is appropriate. An observed problem with control compliance may stem from the effective circumvention of well-designed controls. If this circumvention of controls is infrequent and narrow in scope, it is likely to be a material weakness requiring disclosure. If, however, it is frequent and widespread within the entity, it is likely to result in the issuing of an adverse opinion on the control system. In other words, the general control environment has permitted extensive override of controls, making the specific control procedures in the system ineffective.

Overview of the Comprehensive Review Process

Exhibit 15–6 provides an overview of the comprehensive review process. Once the CPA has concluded as to (1) the presence of material weaknesses, (2) the actions by management that affect disclosure practices with respect to observed weaknesses, and (3) the necessity of issuing an adverse opinion, (s)he can proceed to prepare a report on controls. Specific reporting issues are addressed in Chapter 17. However, before proceeding to discuss reporting options, it is useful to explicitly consider how a comprehensive review engagement can be effectively combined with an audit engagement to generate cost savings for a client.

SAVINGS AVAILABLE THROUGH THE COMBINATION OF COMPREHENSIVE REVIEW ENGAGEMENTS AND AUDITS

If the same CPA is engaged to perform an audit and a comprehensive review engagement, economies can accrue to the client. Since both engagements require an understanding of client operations and a review and evaluation of controls, the tasks underlying these two requirements need only be performed once. If the audit engagement is expected to involve any reliance on internal accounting controls, such controls have to be documented and tested. This documentation can be used in the comprehensive review engagement, as can the control test results. These overlapping learning, documentation, and testing procedures are obvious sources of cost savings. However, if a CPA knows in advance of planning an audit engagement that a comprehensive review engagement will also be performed, additional cost savings can accrue from considering the evidential requirements of the joint engagement.

As already discussed, a comprehensive review engagement requires that all major control areas be evaluated and control tested. Given this requirement, the cost/benefit relationship of control and substantive tests for audit purposes changes drastically. The marginal cost of tests of control for the audit engagement, given the review engagement, is zero, implying that the auditor should plan for the maximum possible reliance on internal accounting controls. Substantive test procedures that would otherwise be considered more economical than tests of control can be reduced or eliminated, because the tests of control must be performed in any case in order to fulfill the requirements of the comprehensive review engagement. If the audit and comprehensive review engagements were performed by different CPAs or if the timing of the two engagements was not synchronized, such planning would be impossible, meaning that both substantive tests and tests of control would be performed, even if redundant from a joint product perspective.

Not only is the audit plan influenced by the anticipated test of control procedures for a review engagement, but the plan for the comprehensive review engagement is likewise influenced by the anticipated needs of an audit engagement. A comprehensive review engagement may apply to a particular date or a period of time that is less than a year. When this is the situation, tests of control are typically performed for the time period closest to the date or period on which the CPA plans to report. Yet, as mentioned earlier in this chapter, a CPA has the option of testing controls over changes in a system of internal accounting controls and using the favorable results of such tests as a basis for performing tests over a longer or an earlier period than that time frame close to the date of the report on the comprehensive review engagement. Since a CPA who is performing a joint audit and review engagement knows that the relevant population for testing of controls for audit purposes is the entire year's transactions, the tests of control for review purposes should similarly be structured over the entire year. The CPA in this setting will perform observation, inquiry, and other available test procedures to gain assurance that control procedures tested for audit purposes are representative of the control system in operation for the date or period of time to which the comprehensive review engagement relates. Since the audit engagement provides information on the effect of control weaknesses on the financial statements, substantive test results provide additional assurance that the controls subjected to tests over the annual period were also in operation during the most recent period surrounding the year-end date (assuming that is the date of the report concerning the comprehensive review). The performance of tests of control that can meet the joint requirements of the audit and comprehensive review engagement generates cost savings for the client.

SAVINGS AVAILABLE THROUGH COORDINATING THE DOCUMENTATION OF CONTROLS BY MANAGEMENT WITH THAT OF THE CPA PERFORMING THE COMPREHENSIVE REVIEW AND THE CPA PERFORMING THE AUDIT

Even if a client decides to use different CPAs to perform the audit and comprehensive review engagements, cost savings can accrue from management's thorough documentation of controls. The client's preparation of a description of the control system is likely to be much less costly than the CPA's preparation of such documentation. Of course, the CPA can greatly assist the client in the documentation process through the

—provision of clear specifications as to what should be included in the system description,

—training of client personnel as to how such documentation can be prepared, and

—distribution of standardized system documentation forms, such as checklists and flowchart instructions.

The client should be encouraged to document the specific objectives of the internal control system and the control procedures that have been designed to achieve the objectives. The documentation would be expected to include procedures manuals, flowcharts, and descriptive memoranda as to controls. Often, control checklists may have been used by management, the entity's board, or the internal auditors in their evaluation of controls, and may be made available to the CPAs as a basis for the comprehensive review of controls and the preliminary phase of the study and evaluation of controls for the audit engagement.

By instructing the client as to the necessity of providing documentation for all major control areas, the CPA can ensure that the system description maintained by clients will fulfill the requirements for both review and audit engagements. At the same time, the system description will assist management in meeting its control objectives. The overall control environment is improved as

—management gains a thorough understanding of controls,

—system design is evaluated on an ongoing basis, and

—formal job descriptions and procedures manuals are available to employees to clarify their duties and responsibilities.

A system description would yield such improvements.

Client Representation Letter

The CPA who performs a comprehensive review engagement will request that the client make a representation as to the appropriateness of designed controls and the adequacy of compliance with designed controls. The system description will provide a basis from which the client can evaluate control design and a benchmark with which the actual performance of control procedures can be compared. The form of the client's representation letter would be expected to be something like Exhibit 15–7.

Depending on the timing of the engagements, the working papers of the CPA performing the audit can be reviewed by the CPA performing the comprehensive review engagement or vice versa. The CPA's review of the client's system description and evaluation of weaknesses may yield additional cost savings to the client if the CPAs cooperate in the documentation phase of the evaluation and review of controls.

Exhibit 15–7

A Client Representation Letter for a Comprehensive Review Engagement

Dear _____ (CPA Firm):

As you requested, we are writing to acknowledge our understanding that based on your comprehensive review of our internal accounting control system, you will attest to whether our system, as a whole, provides reasonable, but not absolute, assurance that

- assets are safeguarded,
- transactions are executed as authorized, and
- data are recorded properly, providing a basis for the preparation of financial statements in accordance with generally accepted accounting principles and for the accountability of assets.

We recognize our responsibility for maintaining a system of internal accounting controls that provide such assurance. Of course, system design reflects our cost/benefit judgments, and due to the inherent limitations of any control system, cannot be expected to prevent or detect all errors and irregularities.

We have provided you with a system description, including procedures, manuals, flowcharts, checklists, and descriptive memoranda. This system is currently in operation, and our system description represents all information that we believe to be of interest to you in performing the comprehensive review engagement. In particular, we are not aware of any irregularities or significant adjustments to the accounting records.

This letter is intended to formally confirm our previous oral representations to you.

Sincerely,

_____

(Client's Authorized Representative(s),
Typically the President or Chief
Executive Officer and the Chief
Financial Officer)

SYNOPSIS

The comprehensive review engagement is an extension of the study and evaluation of controls performed for audit purposes. It entails the detailed review and testing of each major control area of an entity for the purpose of issuing a report on the adequacy of the control system as a whole. A review engagement, when combined with an audit engagement, can generate cost savings relative to the performance of such services by two separate CPA firms. In addition, an entity can generate savings by preparing a thorough description of its control system and by encouraging its CPAs to cooperate with each other whenever different firms are utilized for audit and review engagements.

The CPA should explain to clients the scope of the comprehensive review engagement relative to the audit, the objectives of such an engagement, the responsibility of the client for representations pertaining to system design and current operations, and the type of report to expect. In addition, the various cost savings that can be realized from advanced preparation and planning and from using a single CPA firm for the audit and comprehensive review engagements should be explained to clients. These discussions with clients will improve professional relationships and are likely to lead to future engagements.

A summary of many key points in this chapter is provided by considering the Accounting Series Publication of the United States General Accounting Office entitled *Standards for Internal Controls in the Federal Government* (1983). General standards include: (1) providing reasonable assurance that objectives are accomplished; (2) maintaining supportive attitudes toward controls; (3) having competent personnel; (4) identifying control objectives; and (5) establishing effective and efficient control techniques. Specific standards encompass clear and available documentation, appropriate recording of transactions and events, execution of transactions and events by authorized personnel, separation of duties, adequate supervision, and limited access to resources and effective accountability for resources. An audit resolution standard calls for prompt resolution of audit findings. These ideas guide comprehensive reviews of controls in the Federal Government, a topic that is explored further in later chapters of this *Handbook*.

At the time of this writing, a proposed attestation standard is on public record that discusses many of the issues explored herein for engagements directed at "Reporting on Management's Report on the Effectiveness of an Entity's Internal Control Structure." Excerpts from such guidance may serve as useful reference materials and are included as an Appendix to this chapter.

APPENDIX

Excerpts from the Proposed Statement on Standards for Attestation Engagements: Reporting on Management's Report on the Effectiveness of an Entity's Internal Control Structure over Financial Reporting

EXAMINATION ENGAGEMENT

11. The practitioner's objective in an engagement to examine and report on management's report on the effectiveness of the entity's internal control structure is to express an opinion about whether management has a reasonable basis for its opinion that the entity maintained an effective internal control structure as of a point in time based upon the control criteria. To express such an opinion, the practitioner accumulates sufficient evidence about the design and operating effectiveness of the entity's internal control structure to attest to management's assertions, thereby limiting attestation risk to an appropriately low level.

12. Performing an examination of management's report on the effectiveness of an entity's internal control structure involves (a) planning the engagement, (b) obtaining an understanding of the internal control structure, (c) testing and evaluating the design effectiveness of the internal control structure policies and procedures, (d) testing and evaluating the operating effectiveness of the internal control structure policies and procedures, and (e) forming an opinion about management's report.

Planning the Engagement

13. *General Considerations*. Planning an engagement to examine and report on management's assertions about the effectiveness of the entity's internal control structure involves developing an overall strategy for the expected conduct and scope of the engagement. The practitioner should consider factors such as the following when developing an overall strategy for the engagement—

- matters affecting the industry in which the entity operates, such as economic conditions, government regulations, and technological changes
- matters relating to the entity's business including its organization, operating characteristics, capital structure, distribution methods, etc.
- knowledge of the entity's internal control structure obtained during other professional engagements
- the extent of recent changes, if any, in the entity, its operations, or its internal control structure

- management's process for evaluating the effectiveness of the entity's internal control structure using the control criteria and type and extent of related documentation
- preliminary judgments about materiality levels, inherent risk, and other factors relating to the determination of material weaknesses
- the type and extent of support underlying the design and operation of the internal control structure
- the nature of specific internal control structure policies and procedures designed to achieve the objectives of the control criteria and their significance to the internal control structure taken as a whole
- preliminary judgments about the effectiveness of the internal control structure

14. *Multiple Locations.* A practitioner planning an engagement to examine management's report on the effectiveness of the internal control structure of an entity with operations in several locations should consider factors similar to those he or she would consider if performing an audit of the financial statements of a multi-location entity. It may not be necessary to understand and test controls at each location. In addition to the factors listed in paragraph 13, the selection of locations should be based on factors such as the (a) similarity of business operations and internal control structures at different locations, (b) the degree of centralization of records, (c) the effectiveness of control environment policies and procedures, particularly those that affect management's direct control over the exercise of authority delegated to others and its ability to effectively supervise activities at various locations, and (d) the nature and amount of transactions executed ¬and related assets at the various locations.

Testing and Evaluating the Operating Effectiveness of Internal Control Structure Policies and Procedures

22. To evaluate the operating effectiveness of the internal control structure, the practitioner performs tests of relevant control structure policies and procedures to obtain sufficient evidence about the operating effectiveness of the policies and procedures to support the opinion in the report. Those tests might include inquiries of appropriate personnel, inspection of relevant documentation, observation of the entity's operations, and reapplication or reperformance of the internal control structure procedure.

23. The sufficiency of evidence obtained is a matter of professional judgment. A practitioner may wish to consider matters such as the following when making these decisions—
    - significance of the control to achieving the objectives of the control criteria

- the nature and extent of tests of the operating effectiveness of internal control structure policies and procedures performed by the entity, if any
- risk that compliance with the control policy or procedure will break down, which might be assessed by considering the following matters—
  a) whether there are changes in the volume or nature of transactions that might adversely affect control design or operating effectiveness
  b) whether there are changes in controls
  c) the degree to which the control relies on the effectiveness of other controls (for example, control environment policies and procedures or computer general controls)
  d) whether there are changes in key personnel that perform the control or monitor its performance
  e) whether the control relies on performance by an individual or on electronic equipment
  f) the complexity of the control policy or procedure
  g) whether there is more than one control that achieves an objective

- the nature of the control policy or procedure

24. Management or other entity personnel may perform tests of the operating effectiveness of certain internal control structure policies and procedures and provide the practitioner with the results of such tests. The results of such tests may have been sufficient to enable management to report on the effectiveness of the internal control structure; however, such tests are not sufficient to enable the practitioner to opine on management's report. Although the practitioner may consider the results of such tests when evaluating the operating effectiveness of control structure policies and procedures, it is the practitioner's responsibility to obtain sufficient evidence to support his or her opinion. When evaluating whether sufficient evidence has been obtained, a practitioner should consider that evidence obtained through his or her direct personal knowledge, observation, reperformance, and inspection is more persuasive than information obtained indirectly, such as from management or other entity personnel. Further, judgments about the sufficiency of evidence obtained and other factors affecting the practitioner's opinion, such as the materiality of identified control deficiencies, should be those of the practitioner.

25. The nature of the particular policies and procedures influences the nature of the test of controls the practitioner can perform. For example, the practitioner may examine documents for control structure policies or procedures for which documentary evidence exists. However, doc-

umentary evidence does not exist for all control structure policies and procedures (for example, segregation of duties or some controls performed by a computer). For these policies and procedures, the practitioner may, for example, observe the control in operation or use computer-assisted audit techniques to test their effectiveness.

26. The period of time over which the practitioner should perform tests of controls is a matter of judgment; however, it varies with the nature of the control policies and procedures being tested and with the frequency with which specific control procedures operate and policies are applied. Some control structure policies and procedures operate continuously (for example, controls over sales) while others operate only at certain times (for example, control policies and procedures over the preparation of interim financial statements and control policies and procedures over physical inventory). The practitioner should perform tests of controls over a period of time that is adequate for him or her to determine whether the control structure policies and procedures necessary for achieving the objectives of the control criteria are designed and operating effectively as of the date selected by management in its report.[1]

27. Management may include in its report a statement about the effectiveness of control policies and procedures related to interim financial reporting. For example, management may include in its report a statement about the effectiveness of control policies and procedures related to the preparation of the interim financial statements during the year. Depending on management's statement, the practitioner should consider whether to perform tests of controls over control policies and procedures in effect during a single quarter or whether he or she should also perform tests of controls over additional quarters to form an opinion about the effectiveness of such policies and procedures in achieving the related interim reporting objectives.

28. Prior to the date as of which it reports, management may change the entity's internal control structure policies and procedures to address control deficiencies or simply to make it more effective or efficient. When management has changed certain policies and procedures before the date as of which it reports, the practitioner may not need to consider superseded control structure policies or procedures. For example, if the practitioner determines that the new control policies or procedures achieve the related objectives of the control criteria and

[1] Ordinarily, management will report on the effectiveness of the entity's internal control structure as of the end of the entity's fiscal year. If management selects a subsequent date for its report, the practitioner should perform additional procedures during the subsequent period to evaluate the effectiveness of internal control structure policies and procedures and form an opinion on management's report.

that they have been in effect for a sufficient time to permit the practitioner to assess their design and operating effectiveness by performing tests of controls, the practitioner would not need to consider the design and operating effectiveness of the superseded control structure policies or procedures.

Source: AICPA File Ref. No. 4287 (March 15, 1991), pp. 6–9, 14–19. This guidance is a part of the public record, is being revised at the time of this writing, and is not yet published. It is provided purely for illustrative purposes.

16

Control Problems by Industry Type

"Replicating human judgment with skepticism and independence."

Anonymous

The above definition of auditing depicts an attitude that when applied effectively can lead to particularly astute control risk assessments. One can view the systems evaluator as stepping into the shoes of managers and replicating their judgments on control design and implementation and then changing shoes and viewing that system from the defrauder's perspective, as well as from the employee's vantage point with respect to error possibilities. What could go wrong; how might it be detected?

In considering the skepticism element of this judgment process, it is relevant to note that an understanding of past research can better prepare the evaluator. For example, the Treadway Commission shared the somewhat surprising finding that defalcations are more likely to arise when economic times are good. Apparently growth takes off, liquidity is inadequate, and short-run strategies, at times including misrepresentation, are used. When economic times begin to sour, these "best laid plans" are not as easily reversed as first envisioned and the scope and

Exhibit 16–1

Relative Importance of Control Environment Dimensions
in Explaining Error Patterns

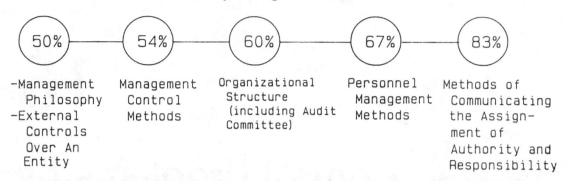

consequences of the fraud become evident.[1] Similarly, research has shown that approximately 80% of internal thefts are committed by one employee acting alone.[2] This bears out the importance of segregated duties.

Research suggests that a second opinion outperforms individual judgments. The implication is that group decision making and a careful review process[3] can be expected to improve performance.

Of similar interest is research that explains advantages of redundant and compensating controls and the key conditions under which advantages can be anticipated:

"If the control components are functioning in such a way that they are *not capable* of correcting errors that are present in the input information but can *further contaminate* the correct input, then the reliability of the output information decreases as an additional control component is introduced into the series.

However, when the controls are in operation (either part of the time or all the time . . .) and they are capable of correcting errors that are present in the input . . . , the reliability of the output information increases as more components are introduced into the system, provided the probability . . . that the controls do not contaminate a correct input is high enough."[4]

In considering the relationship of various control environment elements and the deterrence of errors, research indicates, as displayed in Exhibit 16–1 that the most crucial element is an effective means of communicating the assignment of

[1] National Commission on Fraudulent Financial Reporting, *Report of the National Commission on Fraudulent Financial Reporting* (1987).

[2] The Institute for Financial Crime Prevention, "Red Flags: What Every Manager Should Know About Internal Crime," Training Information (1986 brochure).

[3] K. T. Trotman and P. W. Yetton, "The Effect of the Review Process on Auditor Judgments," *Journal of Accounting Research* (Spring 1985), pp. 256–267.

[4] Rajendra P. Srivastava, "A Note on Internal Control Systems with Control Components in Series," *Accounting Review* (July 1985), pp. 504–507.

Exhibit 16–2

Everyday Impressions

Extremely Positive	*Moderately Positive*	*Neutral*	*Moderately Negative*	*Extremely Negative*
COMPETENCY				
• Keeps Up to Date with Professional Development • Takes the Time to Teach Subordinates • Finishes Reports on Time • Is Innovative	• Delegates Responsibility to Subordinates • Is an Officer in a Professional Organization • Has Worked for a "Big 6" Public Accounting Firm	• Works on Weekend • Reads the Newspaper in the Office Every Morning	• Is Evasive When Responding to Auditor's Questions about Department's Activities • Puts Off Unpleasant Personnel Decisions	• Cannot Explain Budget Variances • Blames Subordinates for Manager's Mistakes
INTEGRITY				
• Tells the Payroll Department About a Case of Overpayment in Paycheck • Returned a Lost Wallet in Tact • Called Supplier to Tell . Them That Company Was Underbilled	• Returns Phone Calls Promptly • Switched Suppliers When Heard a Rumor About the Supplier's Honesty	• Takes Customers to Lunch • Only Takes Two to Three Day Vacations	• Drinks Coffee from the Office Pot, But Does Not Contribute to the Coffee Fund • Copies Office Software for Personal Use	• Takes Credit for Report Written by Subordinate • Brags About Under-Reporting Income to the IRS

Source: Adapted from Urton Anderson and Garry Marchant, "The Auditor's Assessment of the Competence and Integrity of Client Personnel," Working Paper (July 23, 1988), Presented at the Eighth Symposium on Auditing Research at The University of Illinois (October 13–15, 1988) and later published in *Auditing*: *A Journal of Practice & Theory*.

Exhibit 16–3

Procedures for Assessing Control Risk

Procedures to Obtain an Understanding of the Internal Control Structure		Additional Tests of Controls
Provides Evaluation of Design and Placed in Operations	**Tests of Controls Provide Evaluation of Operating Effectiveness**	
1. Previous Experience with the Entity 2. Inquiries of Appropriate Entity Personnel 3. Inspection of Documents and Records 4. Observation of Activities and Operations		1. Previous Experience with the Entity 2. Inquiries of Appropriate Entity Personnel 3. Inspection of Documents and Records 4. Observation of Activities and Operations 5. Reperformance of application of the policies and procedures
Scenarios A and B	**Scenario C**	**Scenario D**

Scenario A: Assess control risk at the maximum because the client has not designed or placed in operation relevant control structure policies or procedures

Scenario B: Assess control risk at the maximum because it is considered inefficient to evaluate the effectiveness of the design and operation of control structure policies and procedures

Scenario C: Assess control risk below the maximum based upon evidential matter obtained about the effectiveness of the design and operation of control structure policies and procedures obtained while understanding the internal control structure

Scenario D: Obtain a further reduction in the assessed level of control risk based upon additional tests of controls

Source: *Guide for the Consideration of Internal Control Structure in a Financial Statement Audit* (AICPA: draft form January 7, 1989), p. 62, Exhibit 4–2.

authority and responsibility.[5] This is very consistent with the "tone at the top" focus of the Treadway Commission. Personnel management methods are the next most critical element. One aspect of such a process is assigning job descriptions in a manner that addresses the needs of the entity. The Appendix to this chapter reports on research related to job descriptions for internal audit posts and may be helpful in both designing and evaluating such descriptions.

Research has also been performed to address how competency and integrity traits are evaluated. Exhibit 16–2 provides examples of how decision makers describe determinants of everyday impressions of others' competency and integrity. This research may be useful in trying to apply control structure guidance.

While a general framework is available to guide control risk assessment, as depicted in Exhibit 16–3, it is useful to consider the likely results of such procedures on an industry basis.

THE BANKING INDUSTRY

The media has directed considerable attention not only to the savings and loan failures and related costs but also to perceived risks in the banking industry. Highly leveraged transactions have become more common. Off-balance sheet financing exposure continually grows. International challenges multiply, and regulatory environments shift. As a result, both operating and auditing banks has increased in complexity.

Since 1986, 354 banks have reported annual losses every consecutive year. Write-offs as a percentage of loans has risen from 0.84% in 1986 to 1.16% as of October 1990. Since 1987, U.S. banks have been failing at the rate of 200 per year, whereas in 1980, 10 a year was the norm.[6] Profits have eroded from 1981 to the third quarter of 1986, with return on assets for all banks dropping from 0.76% to 0.68%. Since 1980, the banks' share of financial assets fell from 35% to 32% by the end of 1985. The big banks have dropped their return on equity from 1980 to 1985: 14.4% versus 9.6%. Since businesses use the commercial paper market, wholesale lending has paralleled the buggy whip and commercial and industrial lending slipped from 43% to 27% from 1974 to 1985.[7] From 1984 through 1987, bankcard chargeoffs jumped 348%; installment loan chargeoffs nearly doubled.[8] If a recession sets in, its effects on equity capital have been projected to yield a decline of 40% to 75%. Among reform proposals is an early warning signal for regulators to flag problems, such as undiversified portfolios, and improvement

---

[5] Richard Kreutzfeldt and Wanda A. Wallace, "Control Risk Assessments: Do They Relate to Errors?" *Auditing: A Journal of Practice & Theory* (Waterloo Conference Supplement, Volume 9, 1990), pp. 1–26.

[6] Brett Duval Fromson, "Will the FDIC Run Out of Money?" *Fortune* (October 8, 1990), pp. 119–127.

[7] Leah Nathans, "Why the Banks Are in a Bind," *Business Month* (April 1987), pp. 34–37.

[8] Michael Violano, "Recovery Systems: Oases in the Bad Loan Desert," *Bankers Monthly* (February 1989), pp. 51–56.

of bank accounting to carry loans and investments at market. Where no liquid market exists for an asset, as is the case for nonperforming assets, the use of a proxy for what that loan realistically should be earning has been suggested in order to discount its value, such as the prime rate plus a few points.[9]

Proposed Accounting Changes

In concert with such a position, the AICPA's Accounting Standards Executive Committee (AcSEC) has decided to issue a statement of position mandating extensive disclosures about the market values of debt securities held for investment or possible sale and about unrealized gains and losses inherent in those securities. This statement is expected to be effective for December 31, 1990. Deliberations are continuing as to possible changes in accounting. SEC Chairman Richard C. Breeden expressed the view that "reflecting market prices in the valuation of debt securities held by banks and savings institutions is absolutely essential to fair financial reporting;" an AcSEC statement is expected shortly and would likely be applicable to December 31, 1991.[10]

The off-balance sheet risk sources that are addressed by the proposed statement of FASB that dates to 1987 includes: credit commitments written; standby and commercial letters of credit issued; financial guarantees written; commitments to purchase or sell financial instruments at predetermined prices; futures contracts and forward commitments; interest rate and foreign currency swaps; and options written (including interest rate caps and floors). Specifically omitted from the proposed statements are the following: insurance contracts, other than financial guarantees and investment contracts; lease contracts; unconditional purchase obligations; employers' (plans') obligations for various employee benefits; financial instruments of a pension plan; extinguished debt and any assets held in trust in connection with an insubstance defeasance of that debt. This is due to their treatment under other GAAP provisions.

In addition to describing "per class of instrument" with off-balance sheet risk, associated face, contract, or notional amount and a description of such instruments and any related amounts recognized on the balance sheet are to be disclosed. A discussion of the nature and terms, including the accounting policy being followed, and credit, liquidity, and market risks would be required if the proposal progresses. The credit risk disclosures would include the amount best portraying the accounting loss that would be incurred if the counterparty to the instrument failed completely to perform under the terms of the contract and collateral for the amount due proved to be of no value. The company's policy is also to be described with respect to its requiring of collateral to support financial instruments subject to

---

[9] Brett Duval Fromson, "Will the FDIC Run Out of Money?" *Fortune* (October 8, 1990), pp. 119–127.

[10] "AcSEC Continues Debate on Accounting for Debt Securities," *The CPA Letter*, Vol. 70, No. 13 (October 1990), p. 1.

credit risk, and information regarding access to the collateral. The nature and a description of the collateral would also be a required disclosure. The FASB has proposed disclosures of concentrations of credit risks in individual counterparties and in groups of counterparties having similar characteristics.[11]

Insurance Related Debates and Institutions' Condition

Insured deposits are being hotly debated not only in relationship to thrifts and banks but also in relationship to Fannie Mae and Freddie Mac instruments.[12] The condition of insured banks as of September 30, 1988 as reported to the FDIC and the Federal Home Loan Bank Board follows:[13]

Description FDIC INSURED BANKS	Number	% of Total	Assets in Billions	% of Total	GAAP Capital in Billions
Insolvent Banks (negative capital per GAAP)	81	0.6	$ 20.6	0.6	$ (0.6)
Barely Solvent (GAAP capital between 0 and 2% of assets)	140	1.0	19.4	.6	.2
All Other Banks	13,466	98.4	3,332.7	98.8	214.9
Total	13,687	100.0	$3,372.7	100.0	$214.5

A number of proposals have been made to address sources of "abuse" that stem from the relative cheapness of the federally insured deposits, including adjusting premiums paid by various financial institutions.[14] Some have called for deregulation and others have suggested various remedial efforts by regulators.

Bank Frauds

National statistics compiled by the FBI on bank fraud and embezzlement cases that have been closed rose from $282 million in losses in 1983 to $860.6 million in 1987, a 205% increase, related to 7,811 versus 11,807 cases—an increase

---

[11] Ernst & Young, "Current Issues in the Financial Services Industries" (October 1989); and Ernst & Young, "Risk-Based Capital: Developing a Strategy and Implementation Plan" (October 1989).

[12] Martin Mayer, "First S&Ls, Now Fannie Mae and Freddie Mac," *The Wall Street Journal* (September 4, 1990), p. A14.

[13] Mary B. Molloy, and Walter M. Primoff, "The S&L Crisis—Putting Things in Perspective," *The CPA Journal* (December 1989), pp. 12–26.

[14] "The Board's Variables Premium Proposal Targets Credit Risk," *Savings Institutions* (July 1984), pp. 164–165.

of 51%. The percentage of involved individuals that are not affiliated with the victim institution has increased from 15.5% in 1983 to 38% in 1988. Losses from fraud by outside individuals in 1987 reached almost $900 million higher than the total of inside and outside fraud in 1983. Combinations of internal employees and outside individuals have been involved in cases numbering 35 in 1983 and 72 in 1987. In middle market lending, it is recommended that due diligence be exercised including client interviews, database reviews, public records search, and source interviews (e.g., with suppliers, clients, present and former managers and employees, adversaries in a lawsuit, and trade union officials), in order to control exposure to fraud.[15]

An FDIC survey of insured banks that failed from 1980 to 1982 found fraud and embezzlement by insiders were a major factor in 15% of the failures, and credit losses on loans to insiders were a major factor in 27% of the cases.[16] Faulty or fraudulent appraisals were a contributing factor at 322 savings institutions that have failed or had serious problems during 1983 through 1986. Reappraisals in 11 of the 12 districts of the Federal Home Loan Bank Board in 1984 valued properties at 58% of the original values, on average, with 17% to 65% ratios observed.[17]

Increasing Auditors' Skepticism

In his testimony before the House Banking Committee, AICPA President Philip Chenok noted that the number of cases alleging audit failure involved only four-tenths of 1% of all audits of public companies performed over the last six years. Yet, increased auditor skepticism has been called for, particularly as it relates to the treatment of Acquisition and Development (ADC) loans that provide for balloon payments several years after granting such debt. Apparently, some institutions have avoided default on such loans by eagerly restructuring or renewing such loans. Other areas requiring greater scrutiny involve the legitimacy of real estate appraisals, transactions with affiliates, conflicts of interest, the role of passive investors, and excessive compensation.

Enhanced communications between auditors and regulators is the focus of an AICPA Statement of Position: "Inquiries of Representatives of Financial Institution Regulatory Agencies," as well as the Financial Institutions Reform, Recovery and Enforcement Act of 1989.[18]

This context for auditor skepticism includes attention to operating and control

---

[15] Bryan J. Krezanoski, "Due Diligence in Middle Market Lending," *The Journal of Commercial Bank Lending* (July 1989), pp. 19–25.

[16] L. William Seidman, "The Role of Outside Auditors in Today's Banking Industry," *Issues in Bank Regulation* (Autumn 1986), pp. 20–24.

[17] Beth M. Linnen, "Development Loan Debacles Teach Tough Lessons," *Savings Institutions* (February 1986), pp. 70–75.

[18] Mary B. Molloy, and Walter M. Primoff, "The S&L Crisis—Putting Things in Perspective," *The CPA Journal* (December 1989), pp. 12–26.

practices. Consider, as an example of a key exposure area, activities tied to appraisal practices.

Realty Loan Losses and Appraisal Issues

In 1985 and 1986, attention was directed to realty loan losses:[19] according to the Federal Deposit Insurance Corp., real estate loan losses of commercial banks jumped to $731 million in the second half of 1985, or 92.4% higher than the first half of that year, while nonperforming real estate loans rose 11% to $6.63 billion. Nonperforming figures include: loans that are 90 days or more past due (for banks with less than $300 million in assets) and nonaccrual loans (for banks with more than $300 million in assets).[20]

Though primarily cited as a problem of thrifts, inflated appraisals of commercial real estate led to demand for increased reserves. Of particular concern were acquisition, development, and construction (ADC) loans on commercial real estate since these sometimes involved equity participation loans, whereby rather than a loan, a direct investment in property is being made, with attendant risks—particularly given the downturn in the real estate market and disinflation.[21] Regulators directed attention to banks, with guidelines requiring bankers to reexamine appraisals on property pledged as collateral to make sure the appraisals reflect current market values and targeted examinations by the comptroller of the currency, particularly of Texas and California banks.[22] Both real estate and energy-related problem loans led to large increases in loan loss provisions and future loan growth slowed from a 20% to 30% asset growth to around 10% in 1985.[23]

Safeguards Against ADC Loan Problems

Safeguards pursued by some banks who faced problems from acquisition, development, and construction loans include: avoidance of high front-end fees; deferral of income generated through profit participations on construction loans until the loan is paid off; requirement of firm, personal guarantees or significant equity on the part of the borrower on all construction loans; imposition of performance standards, including timeliness of construction, quality of construction,

---

[19] Richard B. Schmitt, "Realty Loan Losses at Banks, S&Ls Grew In '85 Second Half, May Worsen in '86," *The Wall Street Journal* (May 29, 1986), Column 1, p. 5(W).

[20] Richard B. Schmitt, "Realty Loan Losses at Banks, S&Ls Grew In '85 Second Half, May Worsen in '86," *The Wall Street Journal* (May 29, 1986), Column 1, p. 5(W).

[21] Monica Langley, "Many Thrifts Ordered to Raise Reserves For Any Commercial-Realty Loan Losses," *The Wall Street Journal* (October 1, 1985), col. 3, p. 2.

[22] Edwin A. Finn, Jr., "U.S. Probing Major Banks on Adequacy of Reserves for Real Estate Loan Losses," *The Wall Street Journal* (November 13, 1985), col. 2, p. 2(W).

[23] John P. Forde, "Problem Loans Put Dent in Texas Bank Profits," *American Banker*, Vol. 150 (July 15, 1985), p. 3(2).

budget compliance, and timeliness of leasing or sales, whereby if not met, draws for interest will not be paid and, instead, must come out of the developer's pocket; and recasting of past loan documentation to implement more stringent loan terms and to obtain additional collateral and liability as necessary.[24]

Bank Examiners Get Tougher

By 1990, the financial press reported that bank examiners were getting tougher on loan-loss allowances.[25] Specifically, examiners were reported to be increasingly concerned that economic stress be reflected, beyond historical experiences. The process of evaluation by examiners includes: (1) their review of the bank's loan portfolio classifications, delinquency and nonaccrual lists, the commercial loan trial balance, and management's latest internal allowance assessment; (2) their comparison of the general allocation with historical loss exposure based on volume and types of loans, i.e., the average net chargeoff ratios for sub-portfolios of construction, real estate, consumer, and commercial loans, adjusted for level, severity, and trends of loan classifications, delinquencies, and nonaccruals per subportfolio; (3) the degree of basis-point adjustments to the ratio from (2) for internal factors such as underwriting standards, charge-off policies, and management considerations; (4) the degree of basis-point adjustments to the ratio from (3) for external factors such as deterioration of specific industries and national and local economic conditions; and (5) comparison of the examiners' range of reasonable allowance, determined in part by an intensive asset-quality examination on a loan-by-loan basis, to test the accuracy of problem loan identification and rating systems, compliance to chargeoff and nonperforming policies, and management's estimate of loss in the portfolio.[26]

In 1990, declining real estate values in the Northeast provoked banking regulators to express concerns, and stock prices of several Northeastern banks were observed to fall. Real estate values have declined by 5% or more in Boston, New York, and Hartford, Connecticut over the past year.[27]

The importance of loan losses to financial viability is evidenced both intuitively and in various banks' attempts to conceal their experiences. Albert[28] reports on an Oklahoma bank that tried to conceal $3 million in loan losses from regulators and investors. Upon discovery, the losses led to the key investor's rejection of an

---

[24] Beth M. Linnen, "Development Loan Debacles Teach Tough Lessons," *Savings Institutions* (February 1986), pp. 70–75.

[25] John P. Danforth, and Jeffrey L. Puchalski, "Comment: Examiners Get Tougher On Loan-Loss Allowances," *American Banker*, Vol. 155 (February 28, 1990), pp. 4, 19, and 22.

[26] John P. Danforth, and Jeffery L. Puchalski, "Comment: Examiners Get Tougher On Loan-Loss Allowances," *American Banker*, Vol. 155 (February 28, 1990), pp. 4, 19, and 22.

[27] Katherine Morrall, "Weakening Northeast Real Estate Market Raises Concerns: Loss Reserves Mount, While Stock Prices Decline," *Savings Institutions* (April 1990), pp. 11–14.

[28] Andrew Albert, "Concealed Loan Loss at Failed Oklahoma Bank," *American Banker*, Vol. 149 (October 10, 1984), pp. 2(2), 23.

option to purchase the bank's stock. The loan problems were attributed somewhat to the energy industry but principally to mismanagement and imprudent lending.

Legislative Effects: Deductibility for Loan-Loss Reserves

Bank practices with respect to loan loss reserves can be substantially influenced by legislation. One significant event involves the deduction for loan-loss reserves for tax purposes. In 1986, a forecast was made that eliminating the deduction and paying out the reserves as income would cost the industry $3 billion[29] to $8 billion in taxes.[30] Note that in 1986, the banks were permitted to deduct from income a reserve up to 0.6% of their total loans. As explained by Rogers and Logan,[31] the Tax Reform Act of 1986 eliminated the percentage method of calculating the bad debt deduction for all banks and the reserve method for large banks (those over $500 million average adjusted assets). Special guidelines apply to "financially troubled" banks which have nonperforming loan-to-equity ratios in excess of 75%. This ratio is calculated using quarterly average values for nonperforming loans and bank equity. Other tax reforms also affected financial institutions[32] both in 1986 and in later years.[33]

Regulators Call on Auditors

Regulators have called for auditors to use their business expertise both to help bankers via management letters in monitoring their operations and establishing controls and in evaluating loan portfolios, with their added skills of business acumen applied, regarding borrowers' risks. Dialogue with audit committees concerning asset quality is encouraged, as is particular concern over managers whose primary goal is growth (*Journal of Accountancy*, February 1985).

The SEC is thought to direct special attention to large adjustments to loan loss provisions, as they raise questions as to the provision's adequacy in prior periods. Spreading is not a permissible option, as loan losses should be charged off as they occur. The bank audit guide provides a number of pointers to auditors including attention to:

"—the current trend of delinquencies
—loans classified by supervisory agency examiners

---

[29] Bartlett Naylor, "Lobbyists Predict Congress Will Retain Loan-Loss Reserve Deduction for Banks," *American Banker* (June 18, 1986), pp. 1, 23.

[30] Bartlett Naylor, "Sen. Packwood Reopens Door on Bank Taxes: But Promises 2d Look at Loan-Loss Deduction," *American Banker*, Vol. 151 (August 8, 1986), pp. 1(2), 12.

[31] William A. Rogers, and David Logan, "Banks' Bad Debt Deduction," *Bankers Monthly* (November 1987), p. 24.

[32] Mina J. Knoll, and Stuart Zwerling, "Bad Debt Deduction and Other Tax Reform Changes Affect Thrifts," *Bankers Monthly* (December 1987), p. 24.

[33] John C. DeCelles, Tommy Snow, Anthony J. DeCellis, and Kathleen Shelton, "Bank and Thrift Bad Debt Deduction Planning," *The Tax Adviser* (January 1989), p. 38.

—excessive loan renewals and extensions

—the absence of current financial data related to borrowers and guarantors

—borrowers experiencing such problems as operating losses, marginal
working capital, inadequate cash flow or business interruptions, such
as voluntary conversions due to fire loss or condemnations

—loans secured by collateral that is not readily marketable or is susceptible to deterioration in realizable value

—loans in industries experiencing economic instability

—inadequate documented loans" (*Journal of Accountancy*, February
1985, pp. 22, 24)

Other risk areas highlighted include accounting for float, particularly deposit float
on a net basis, and related controls over associated deposit liabilities, such as
restrictions on withdrawals until receipt.

By identifying such risk exposures, peculiar to the industry, attention can
be directed toward controls in place to address such risks. The following discussion
offers suggestions on how financial institutions can enhance control via diversification and credit insurance practices and through better evaluation of credit
and risk. Risks and proposed controls peculiar to leveraged buyouts and capital
restructuring are discussed. A number of accounting developments to which control systems will need to adapt are likewise described.

Diversification Strategies

Rose[34] suggests that many bankers under-manage the risk in their com-
mercial-loan portfolios. Specifically, relationships among default probabilities are
often not considered: specific loans' default is emphasized, with scant attention
to collective risks. A loan that lowers risk of simultaneous default through co-
variance considerations should be preferred. Empirical research suggests that
roughly 10% of all industries were negatively correlated from 1973 through 1980.
The correlation of losses between the chemical and the textile industries amounted
to a −0.34. In other words, every 1% increase in loss rates among chemical
producers was associated with approximately a 0.34% decrease in loss rates among
textile makers. The intuition of this inverse correlation is plausible, since chem-
icals are widely used in fabric manufacture, so decreased chemical prices would
benefit textiles (and rising prices would hurt textiles).

The evidence also suggests a −0.65 correlation from 1973 through 1980
between general contractors and the textile industry, and a great deal of positive
correlations among food manufacturing and retail furniture, as well as other retail
and some services industries. Oliver, Wyman & Co., a New York-based consultant
to the financial services industry demonstrated that through use of such historical

---

[34] Sanford Rose, "How to Materially Lower Volatility of Loan Losses," *American Banker*, Vol.
155 (February 20, 1990), p. 4(2).

patterns in forming a loan portfolio, the standard deviation could be lowered by 32% in a subsequent period. Hence, banks can materially improve prospective credit quality through retrospective analysis. The benefits of decreased volatility of loan losses are numerous. One piece of related evidence is a study of the top 50 banks from 1982 to 1986 which demonstrated a strong inverse relationship between risk and stock performance: a drop of 10 basis points in the standard deviation of loan losses would have boosted the stock returns of these banks by around 3.5 percentage points per year during that period, based on the researchers' findings.[35]

Credit Insurance

Credit insurance programs have been described, whereby commercial banks and lending institutions are provided a synthetic put option on portfolios correlated to borrower assets for large single loans or books of similar loans and a hedge strategy for a portfolio of dissimilar loans.[36] The point is made in such proposals that potential solvency of commercial banks ties to three risks: interest rate risk, independent credit risk, and systematic credit risk. While tools are readily available for "gap management," "duration," and "immunization" of the first risk and the second is intended to be covered by the interest rate spread in light of large loan portfolios, the last risk is very troublesome. Credit risk associated with the economic environment at large is referred to as systematic credit risk, i.e., that which cannot be diversified away, such as loans to farmers or real estate developers. Since interest rate spreads are directed to randomly occurring defaults, they are ill-equipped to cover massive defaults. Clustered defaults are epitomized by regional loans (e.g., those to Brazil) and industry loans (e.g., energy related). The strategies to address systematic credit risk depend on there being claims on the borrower's assets that are traded actively and continuously in the marketplace, or more practically, those of others whose financial and/or real assets are highly correlated with the systematic element inherent in the borrower's ability to repay the loan (stock may serve such a role).

The types of factors to consider include cost of input, price of output, quality of output, and quantity of output. A put option can be constructed on a basket of traded financial instruments which is correlated most closely with the value of borrower assets, updated to reflect the composition of such assets. If stock is proposed as a natural hedge, problems can arise due to regulatory proscriptions, inverse associations of market value of stock and bonds, and movement of the two values apart due to wealth redistribution risks—although it has been sug-

---

[35] Sanford Rose, "How to Materially Lower Volatility of Loan Losses," *American Banker*, Vol. 155 (February 20, 1990), p. 4(2).

[36] David F. Babbel, "Insuring Banks Against Systematic Credit Risk," *The Journal of Futures Markets* (John Wiley & Sons, Inc.), Vol. 9, No. 6 (1989), pp. 487–505.

gested that well designed debt covenants can limit such risks. In approaching a hedge portfolio, the market value of the loan portfolio can be estimated indirectly for a bank with actively traded stock and liabilities, netting tangible property and nonloan investments or by focusing on current loan characteristics—stated interest rate, maturity, quality, and industry sector. One possibility cited is to have short futures and forward positions in the S & P 500 stock index as a hedge to a broadly diversified loan portfolio.

Those proposing such plans acknowledge that due to incomplete markets, alternatives to diversifications arise and quantity risk can be hedged often through borrowers by having crop insurance, hail insurance, or strike insurance obtained. Moreover, rather than hedging a loan to a nonpublic company manufacturing farm equipment directly, the linkage of farmers' wealth to land prices, agricultural commodity prices, interest rates, and exchange rates open up vehicles for using a variety of financial instruments. Regulatory attitudes are presently a barrier in pursuing some of these recommendations, as are the incomplete nature of markets, the nature of required expertise to facilitate implementation, and the cost of the program itself.[37]

An Example of Understanding Exposure for Undiversified Portfolios

Concern for undiversified portfolios of loans is not really novel. For example, in 1985, Morgan Guaranty Trust Co. of New York and Chase Manhattan Bank were reported to have analyzed their holdings and found they had a large share of the steel industry's credits relative to other money-center banks. The result was that the banks determined they would be increasingly selective in steel lending. Banks' exposure was cited as understated due to the steel industries' use of creative financing arrangements that result in contingent liabilities and off-balance sheet financing; examples are financing of iron ore and metallurgical coal suppliers on a production-payment arrangement basis which appear as loans to mining companies but clearly are dependent for payment on steelmakers' ability to accept the ore.[38]

Of interest is the observation that while savings associations were subject to federal regulations that restricted the amount of commercial loans to one borrower to 15% of the institution's capital and surplus, 23 of 26 institutions reviewed by the General Accounting Office were in violation of the loans to one borrower regulation.[39] Hence, the lack of diversification has been cited as problematic in other sectors of the financial markets than in banking.

---

[37] David F. Babbel, "Insuring Banks Against Systematic Credit Risk," *The Journal of Futures Markets* (John Wiley & Sons, Inc.), Vol. 9, No. 6 (1989), pp. 487–505.

[38] J. Ernest Beazley, "Banks Fret Over Exposure in Steel Industry," *The Wall Street Journal* (May 2, 1985), p. 6.

[39] United States General Accounting Office, Testimony, "Resolving The Savings And Loan Crisis: Billions More and Additional Reforms Needed," Statement of Charles A. Bowsher, Comptroller General of the United States, Before the Committee on Banking, Housing, and Urban Affairs, United States Senate (April 6, 1990), GAO/T-AFMD-90–15.

The Five Cs of Credit

The elementary components of lending, known as the five "Cs" of credit include: capital, capacity, character, collateral, and the conditions of business.[40] An area of management recommended by Stern[41] is monitoring of "run-of-the-mill bad debts and problem loans that are generated each year in a retail banking network." Necessary information for such monitoring includes: risk measures for the industry to which a loan is being extended; the examination of managerial ability—assessed by computing the proportion of management decisions that went wrong, i.e., total losses divided by quantities of management decisions—and controls over advances; trend of bad debt experience in the bank on a detailed basis; region concerned; debt amount; age of the account from its opening until declared bad; and various benchmarks, analyzed by industry as well as by region to reflect the median value of debt, the relationship of age of bad debt accounts to the size of the losses incurred.

Qualitative considerations in tandem with attention to such patterns include: management discretionary limits for both new and old business, the efficiency and effectiveness of the bank inspectorate, and the typical period a manager stays at a branch. Unstated items include the temper, morale, and team spirit of the organization, and the real organization structure, as well as unusual conditions like civil disorder or strife. Evidence exists that decision makers in lending decisions will often use compensatory decision models, meaning that strengths along one dimension of a prospective borrowing setting can at times be offset by weaknesses elsewhere.[42] The type of information used in monitoring also influences decisions: for example, non-GAAP financial statements are seen as less useful for lending and less complete, and survey research further suggests that interest premiums are charged for reviews, relative to audited information.[43]

Why Loans Go Bad

In exploring why loans go bad, technical causes include: fraud, character, industry problems, weak analysis, and market risk. Managerial problems include: seniorities (whereby internal miscommunication occurs because junior officers perceive that the senior officer wants the loan to be made); the halo effect (participants are held in high regard and the credit is inadequately reviewed); joint venture problem—again due to perceived participation of quality partners but no

---

[40] Jeremy F. Taylor, "Credit Risk and the Logic of Lending," *Bankers Monthly Magazine* (May 15, 1986), pp. 22, 23, and 35.

[41] Michael Stern, "Bad Debt Analysis of a Loan Portfolio," *Bankers Magazine*, Vol. 167, No. 3 (May/June 1984), pp. 73–76.

[42] Stanley F. Biggs, Jean C. Bedard, Brian G. Gaber and Thomas J. Linsmeier, "The Effects of Task Size and Similarity on the Decision Behavior of Bank Loan Officers," *Decision Sciences*, Vol. 31, No. 8 (August 1985), pp. 970–987.

[43] William M. Baker, "How Non-GAAP Financial Statements Affect Loan Officers and Borrowers," *The Journal of Commercial Bank Lending* (May 1990), pp. 23–29.

clear arrangement has been made to stand behind such a venture; credit being managed in the wrong place (i.e., sufficient expertise is not available to address specialized industry of collateral control considerations); down market; strategy problems such as inadequate and inappropriate staffing, inadequate knowledge of law or custom, insufficient language proficiency, or market proximity; and loans booked not as approved, i.e., the deal ultimately concluded varies materially from what was approved and the people involved in the credits are usually no longer in the bank's employ.[44] Concerns must be directed to borrowers' financial difficulties, as the following words could well hold:

> "How did you go bankrupt?" Bill asked.
> "Two ways," Mike said. "Gradually and then suddenly."
>
> > Ernest Hemingway,
> > *The Sun Also Rises*

Early detection of problem loans is possible by paying attention to signs of trouble including declining sales and profits, deteriorating receivables, inadequate cash flows, slow inventory turnover, extended trade payables, poor management of cash and the bank relationship, industry problems, changes in key stockholders, change in accountants, and rapid growth. Early warning systems include stressing monthly reviews of financial statements, close contact with borrowers, regular analysis of industry trends, attentiveness to bank auditors' reports, and reorientation of loan officers toward credit management and away from selling. Discipline should be imposed on borrowers, encouraging asset divestment, overhead reductions, the finding of new management, changes in marketing strategy, arranging of mergers or acquisitions, capital infusion by stockholders, and modification of loans when appropriate.[45]

"The Judge Hates a Bossy Lender"

Ironically, care must be exercised in such remedial and disciplinary activities, as reflected by the following:

The Judge Hates a Bossy Lender *by Richard Greene*

"When you talk to lawyers, they immediately bring up the Farah Manufacturing case. Problems there started in 1976 when William Farah, the apparel company's chief executive officer, found his company in deep trouble. Several banks that had lent the company millions of dollars successfully pushed Farah out of his job and put in their own management. Unfortunately for

---

[44] David L. Eyles, "Why Do Loans Go Bad?" *The Bankers Magazine* (January–February 1988), pp. 9–12.
[45] David A. Bradlow, "Early Detection of Problem Loans," *The Journal of Commercial Bank Lending* (April 1986), pp. 48–55.

the bankers, the company's troubles got worse. By threatening a proxy fight, Farah regained control in 1978, and he seems to have orchestrated a turnaround. In the meantime, however, the company sued the banks, claiming their involvement damaged it. Finally, a Texas court awarded Farah Manufacturing $18.9 million.

Obviously, Farah is an extreme situation. Bankers rarely install new managements. But it points up the problem. It is clear that at some point bankers can exert so much influence on a company that they become liable for its failure, but no one knows the limits. (*Forbes*, October 10, 1983, p. 102)"

In 1985, a Federal appellate court ruled that reasonable notice was required when calling a demand obligation and affirmed a $7.5 million judgment against Irving Trust Company. The largest judgment to date ($26 million) was rendered against Bank of America for lender misconduct. The Hunt brothers have sued 23 financial institutions for $3.6 billion, alleging a multitude of collusive and wrongdoings by individual banks. Suggestions to address these fairly recent developments include: exercising care in file maintenance; clarifying and simplifying loan agreements; properly structuring the workout team; and carefully planning enforcement action.[46] Other important perils include prolonged decline in commodities' prices, successive years of severe bad weather, depressed housing industry, and protectionist policies' effect on sales,[47] as well as problems of uninsured collateral and environmental exposure due to the control or ownership of collateral which has hazardous substances.[48]

Keys to Success

Studies of successful banks suggest a road to success by setting the tone, e.g., not being too adventuresome and establishing a credit culture that focuses on sound credit as being the top priority. Personal connection is emphasized, as is retention of well trained and quality employees. Selectivity is a byword in lending, and loan limits are set conservatively to ensure group decision making. Ongoing monitoring is encouraged, and philosophies are reflected in such views as that expressed by Alexander Kyman of City National:

"At our bank, having a problem credit does not get you into trouble.
Hiding a problem credit gets you fired." (p. 60)

---

[46] David G. Heiman, and Gregory M. Gordon, "Lender Liability: Dodging Bullets With Procedures for Managing Problem Loans," *The Journal of Commercial Bank Lending* (December 1986), pp. 15–21.

[47] Bob A. Hedges, "Risk Management: Part 2—Identifying Loss Exposures," *The Journal of Commercial Bank Lending* (November 1985), pp. 19–28.

[48] John C. Thomas, and Eric B. Nilsson, "Issues in Lending . . . Avoiding Pitfalls in Real Estate Loan Workouts," *The Journal of Commercial Bank Lending* (September 1989), pp. 28–36.

Watch lists are encouraged and asking for help is encouraged. Moreover, internal examiners are used to formally review problems loans.[49]

Bank Examiners' Viewpoint

Major reasons for banks to experience loan problems, according to bank examiners include: self dealing, whereby credit is overextended on an unsound basis to a bank's directors (or their interests), is not avoided; earnings are over emphasized relative to considerations of loan soundness; credit principles are compromised without adding vigilance to the credit monitoring process; incomplete credit information is obtained; failure to obtain and enforce repayment agreements; complacency through dependence on oral statements or lack of adequate supervision of old and familiar borrowers; poor selection of risks; overlending; and reacting to competition in a manner that compromises credit principles.[50] Lending experience is emphasized as an important factor in effectively assessing risk;[51] members of workout groups require technical, personal, and group skills, as well as "street smarts" and accounting, legal, managerial, and analytical skills.[52]

An example of "street smarts" is an appreciation of the fact that background work is needed in order to ensure the creditor will be able to realize on a guarantee, should that become necessary.[53] Another trait of effective lending officers is that they master the art of observation, effectively "kicking the tires" of the borrowers[54] and take time to perform contingency planning.[55] Problems related with insiders have been particularly visible in analyses of the thrift industry[56] and could well be shared by various banking institutions. Incentives to motivate management to act in the best interests of various stakeholders have also been lacking in the

---

[49] Steve Cocheo, "Giving Credit Where Credit Is Due," *ABA Banking Journal* (July 1990), pp. 59–63.

[50] Thomas Hoar, "An Examiner's Perspective On Loan Problems," *The Journal of Commercial Bank Lending* (May 1988), pp. 36–42.

[51] Mark N. Moore, Edgar L. Smith II, Joseph J. Herr, Robert D. Lowrie, Roy C. Postel, William R. Breisch, Fred Wittowske, Norman J. Greenfeld, "Opinion Survey . . . Exploring the Function of Loan Review," *The Journal of Commercial Bank Lending* (October 1988), pp. 48–53.

[52] Till A. Bruett III, "Managing a Loan Workout Department," *The Journal of Commercial Bank Lending* (February 1988), pp. 44–50.

[53] David Snowdon, "Spilled Milk: A Troubled Loan, A Useless Guarantee," *The Journal of Commercial Bank Lending* (October 1988), pp. 67–70.

[54] Thomas J. Gryp, "Management Evaluation: The Lost Art of Lending," *The Journal of Commercial Bank Lending* (February 1988), pp. 4–8.

[55] George F. Weinwurm, "Survival Principles for Middle Market Lenders," *The Journal of Commercial Bank Lending* (January 1988), pp. 11–24.

[56] United States General Accounting Office Testimony, "Failed Thrifts: Resolution Trust Corporation and 1988 Bank Board Resolution Actions," Statement by Richard L. Fogel, Assistant Comptroller General, General Government Programs, Before the Committee on Banking, Finance and Urban Affairs House of Representatives (April 2, 1990), GAO/T-GGD-90–29.

thrift sector[57] and questions have recently been posed about the banking sector's incentives, such as an emphasis on volume or short-term profit in lieu of focusing on credit quality.

Risks Associated With Networks

A source of risk to banks is the use of various networks. For example, the Clearing House Interbank Payments System (CHIPS) in 1984, shuttled close to 100,000 transactions, totaling close to $300 billion, among the 130 large financial institutions. Although the system began in the early 1970s, not until 1984 was attention directed to the credit risks attached to use of the system. Limits on the electronic network were tested as bilateral credit limits, whereby each participant established a limit of the net amount of payments it is willing to accept from each of the other participants (in case one should fail). Intraday risk, arising in any given business day since credit is extended, with the actual exchange of dollars or net settlement occurring at the end of the day, can be a critical exposure.[58]

Wire transfers pose a number of risks. Consider what can go wrong. The transfer can be made in the wrong amount, go to the wrong place, sent twice, or not at all. Moreover, wrong entries associated with that transfer can be recorded. These errors can pose substantial exposure. Using predesigned forms, batch totals, comparison of forms for data entry to subsequent reports, balancing and reconciling activities, automation of entries, and, of course, daily balancing can all serve as useful controls. When a transfer form is submitted in writing, the signatures are to be verified. If the transfer from elsewhere is over the phone, then the form is initiated internally. A critical control would seem to be to send confirmations to customers on all wire transfers.

Ironically, this control is at times undermined by the procedure that confirmations are sent out by wire transfer personnel. It is important that such personnel not only be separated from such a responsibility but also that they be unable to intercept such confirmations. In other words, the parties responsible for such confirmations should be physically separated from those responsible for wire transfer handling. Always keep in mind the concern that a wire transfer employee might initiate transfers and then tamper with customer confirmations. The idea is that the confirmation operate as a control over unauthorized transfers from the inside; this can only happen if other than the insiders handling such transfers have confirmation responsibilities.

---

[57] United States General Accounting Office, Report to the Chairman, Committee on Banking, Housing, and Urban Affairs, U.S. Senate, and the Chairman, Committee on Banking, Finance and Urban Affairs, House of Representatives, "Failed Thrifts: FDIC Oversight of 1988 Deals Needs Improvement" (July 1990), GAO/GGD-90-93.

[58] Robert Trigaux, "CHIPS Opts for Slower Growth to Reduce Credit Risks to Banks: Payment System's Operator Tests New Limits on Network," *American Banker*, Vol. 149 (August 3, 1984), pp. 2(2)-6.

In assessing risk, consider the value of the transactions handled (often large for wire transfers), the volume of transactions (similarly large), and the liquidity or negotiability of the assets involved (the most liquid of possibilities). All of these factors suggest that wire transfers are a substantial risk exposure of financial institutions.

Stock Market Reactions

An interesting observation concerns the stock market's reaction to loan loss reserve adjustments. When Citicorp added $3 billion to its loan loss reserves due to troubled foreign loans, its stock was observed to jump more than 7 points after the announcement on May 18, 1987.[59] The financial press observed

> The surest way for a bank to get its stock up is for it to announce a huge charge-off for a bum loan. It's too bad Penn Square never was public—shareholders would have been rolling in it.[60]

Such tongue-in-cheek commentary speaks to possible expectation gaps in the marketplace.

Disclosure Issues

Disclosure issues have been discussed by the Financial Accounting Standards Board and the media: the proposal to disclose the credit risk of all financial instruments, including future cash receipts and payments, interest rates, and market values of all financial instruments in their portfolios was greeted with support of the spirit of the disclosures but resistance as to feasibility. Specifically, many instruments, it is claimed, cannot be marked to market because the banks do not know the risk-adjusted cost of their own products or because secondary markets have not yet developed for many of their assets. Not only is rigorous pricing information lacking on their own products, but banks usually lack a data base of usable historical information on the performance of these instruments. The 1987 exposure draft on financial instruments would apply to any company using such instruments as interest rate swaps, standby letters of credit, and options; it is a facet of a larger project on financial instruments and off-balance sheet financing. Some contend that market value information on a loan lacks usefulness unless that loan is being sold and that the stated rate on the loan tells little. Others have cited information on pricing and maturities to be proprietary, suggesting that competitive harm would result from the proposed disclosures.[61]

---

[59] Anise C. Wallace, "Money-Center Banks—A Bad Bet?" *New York Times*, Vol. 136, Col. 4 (May 31, 1987), p. F10 (N).

[60] Alan Abelson, "Up & Down Wall Street—banks prepare for bad debt," *Barron's* (June 22, 1987), pp. 1, 51.

[61] Lisabeth Weiner, and John P. Forde, "Plan to Force Banks to Disclose Risk is Criticized," *American Banker*, Vol. 152 (December 2, 1987), pp. 2(2)–22.

Strategic Approaches to Evaluating Risk

Strategic approaches by banks should address interest rate, liquidity, event, and operations risks. Assets held vary in risk, with holding of state and municipal bonds, as an example, being of higher risk than U.S. government securities; within U.S. government agencies' claims, non-U.S.-backed mortgage-backed securities (MBS) private issues are of higher risk than Government National Mortgage Association (GNMA) or Federal National Mortgage Association (FNMA) issues; mortgage backed strips are of even higher risk. Off-balance sheet items pose differential risks, with sales and repurchase agreements, asset sales with recourse, forward agreement to purchase assets, and securities lent when at risk being of greatest risk, relative to commercial letters of credit or unconditionally cancellable commitments with original maturity of a year or less.[62]

Interest rate exposure can be evaluated by comparing market values of an instrument at various interest rate levels, by discounting cash flow projections, by considering principal and interest payments, and through option-based simulations incorporating assumptions on loan prepayments and deposit withdrawals for each interest rate scenario.[63]

Spillover effects among banking institutions are extremely common, not just with respect to market reactions to loan loss announcements and industry practice accounting and tax issues. For example, when the billionaire Hunt family made headlines losing millions on silver speculation, three Hunt-controlled companies owed $210 million to several banks. Many of these loans were nonperforming, affecting banks, parent banks, and numerous involved parties.

Leveraged Transactions

In 1988, more than 300 leveraged buy-out (LBO) deals were reportedly completed, aggregating around $100 billion. Estimates suggest that LBO loans outstanding approximate $200 billion. As of January 26, 1989, a handful of the largest U.S.-based banking companies publicly acknowledged LBO exposures: Citicorp reported $5 billion, Bankers Trust reported $2.7 billion, Wells Fargo reported $3 billion, BankAmerica reported $1.3 billion, Bank of Boston reports $2.2 billion, and Continental Bank Corporation reports $1 billion. Similar disclosures are anticipated in other annual reports. Such business is seen as lucrative due to attractive margins, large up-front fees, and the ability to largely mitigate interest rate concerns through hedges, swaps, caps, and similar rate protection practices for floating-rate debt. In mid-1989, statistics suggested that most banks had less

---

[62] Ernst & Young, "Current Issues in the Financial Services Industries" (October 1989); and Ernst & Young, "Risk-Based Capital: Developing a Strategy and Implementation Plan" (October 1989).

[63] Ernst & Young, "Current Issues in the Financial Services Industries" (October 1989); and Ernst & Young, "Risk-Based Capital: Developing a Strategy and Implementation Plan" (October 1989).

than 10% of total loans in LBOs and that as a percentage of equity, LBO exposures seldom exceed 100% and commonly are less than 50%. Of course, total commitments increase these percentages. Nonetheless, exposures seem to be well diversified along industry and geographic lines, although some regional banks have concentrated in local markets.[64]

Definition Clarified by OCC

Yet these statistics could be ineffective in capturing risk exposures since definitions of highly leveraged transactions differ and voluntary disclosures are the basis of inferences drawn. Indeed this is part of the reason the Federal Reserve, the Office of the Comptroller of the Currency (OCC), and the FDIC issued an October 1989 common definition of highly leveraged transactions (HLTs) which all banks must report:

> a loan is classified as highly leveraged if it finances a leveraged buy-out, acquisition, or recapitalization of a business. It also comes under the HLT heading if 75% of the borrower's capital is debt, or if the transaction doubles the borrower's liabilities and results in more than 50% of capital being debt, or if the bank itself designates the loan as highly leveraged. (*Standard & Poor's*, 1990, p. B11)

However in February 1990, regulators revised such guidelines by relaxing some parameters, specifically permitting exclusion of loans of less than $20 million from the HLT classification and likewise permitting reclassification from HLT once a loan has performed for two years. This revision is thought to be particularly important to regional banks who reportedly sold HLT loans when the original regulation was set, since they feared their average loan exposure of $10 million would be viewed as resulting in too risky a portfolio. The new standard applies to 1989 10-K reports and was announced to have effects of increasing prior disclosed HLTs, e.g., Bank of America announced its HLT portfolio would increase up to 50% in January 1990 and Banker's Trust reported that its definition of $3.3 billion in September 1989, when subject to the regulators' definition would become $3.9 billion (similarly Security Pacific's September 30, 1989 $2.6 billion becomes $4.5 billion, though with much of this tied to factoring, the revised definition may lower this announced exposure.) (*Standard & Poor's*, February 15, 1990, p. B11).

Regulatory Review

The OCC in November 1989 announced a quarterly review initiative, targeting banks with 2% or more of their assets devoted to HLTs. The concerns stemmed in part from the observation that at the end of 1988, 9% average participation by 11 large multinational banks rose to 17% in mid 1989. The following

---

[64] Gregory Root, "What If . . . Banks Do Not Control LBO Credit Risks," *The Journal of Commercial Bank Lending* (June 1989), pp. 16–20.

statistics are provided in company reports as of September 30, 1989 (*Standard & Poor's*, February 15, 1990, p. B11):

Billions of Dollars of Highly Leveraged Transactions as of 9/30/89 in Relation to 12/30/89 Financial Statistics

Banks	HLT Loans Outstanding	Net Loans	Assets	Common Equity	% Assets	% Equity
Citicorp	5.6	155.4	230.6	8.2	2.43	68
Chemical Bank	3.8	41.9	71.5	2.8	5.3	137
Wells Fargo	3.4	41	48.7	2,456	6.98	138
Chase Manhattan	3.2	73.4	107.4	3.2	2.98	100
Bankers Trust	3.1	18.4	55.7	2.1	5.57	148
Bank of New York	3.1	34.6	48.9	2.36	6.34	131
Manufacturers Hanover	3.1	36.5	60.5	2.9	5.12	107
Security Pacific	2.6	60.6	83.9	4.11	3.09	63
Bank of Boston	2.5	24.2	39.2	1.88	6.38	133
First Chicago	1.4	28.4	47.9	2.3	2.92	61
Bank of America	1.2	72.5	98.8	4.9	1.21	24

The new reporting requirements are intended to enable investors to better compare the riskiness of a bank's portfolio, restraining bank's leeway in reporting. To meet such requirements, financial institutions need an effective information system that is well controlled. In the presence of an improved information context, banks may be able to avoid such media observations as that offered almost two years to the day from the 1987 Black Monday: the Dow Jones Industrial average fell 190 points on October 13, 1989 and many attributed the decline to Citicorp's and Chase's inability to round up other potential lenders to finance the proposed management buy-out of UAL (*Standard & Poor's*, February 15, 1990, p. B11).

Others have also expressed discomfort with LBOs; for example, managers of City National state their avoidance of foreign loans, agricultural loans, energy loans, and LBOs. In the words of Alexander Kyman,

> Acts of God and fraud will take care of giving you some level of bad debt . . . You shouldn't go out of your way to find bad risks.[65]

Internal Controls Called For by OCC

Leveraged buyouts, management buyouts, and capital restructurings have accelerated the volume and size of creative, highly leveraged transactions (HLTs)

---

[65] Steve Cocheo, "Giving Credit Where Credit Is Due," *ABA Banking Journal* (July 1990), pp. 59–63.

of banks and these have taken the place of many traditional (and somewhat scarce) commercial lending opportunities. Complex transactions are commonly involved, including: secured debt, mezzanine financing (including junk bonds), and equity ownership, in which financial institutions may invest, arrange, underwrite, or participate. These have attracted regulators' attention. The Office of the Comptroller of the Currency Issues Examining Circular (EC) 245 discusses internal control issues tied to such transactions. It calls for banks to: (1) set in-house limits on exposure for individual credits, specific industries, and the aggregate HLT portfolio, (2) have a separate loan approval process by qualified personnel, (3) monitor the HLT portfolio, including tracking statistics on industry concentration, type of financing, risk rating of the portfolio, aging of the portfolio, and performance relative to expectations, (4) establish controls over distributions and participations, and (5) watch for conflicts of interest. Care is to be taken in separating fees for advisory services from origination fees.

Syndications and Participations

Loan syndications and participations involve a lead bank that organizes and facilitates a transaction—syndication involves a number of funding sources, while participation means the lead bank funds the entire amount and then sells participating interests in the loan to other investors. Certain participations are in-substance syndications, as the Emerging Issues Task Force (EITF) has defined their equivalence as whenever within 60 days of the date the loan is initially funded, the enterprise sells at least 50% of the loan to other independent institutions and the risks and rewards are shared proportionately by all enterprises from the date of the sale. FASB No. 91 "Accounting for Nonrefundable Fees and Costs Associated With Originating or Acquiring Loans and Initial Direct Costs of Leases" calls for deferral of income of other than insubstance syndication activities when syndicated loans are not retained.

Other Accounting Matters

Key accounting and tax-related management concerns relate to how to report payments on interest rate swaps, i.e., as miscellaneous income and expense, rather than as interest income or expense for tax purposes. Similarly, when investing in collateralized mortgage obligations (CMO), care needs to be taken to allocate cash receipts between income on their investment and a return of their investment. Other issues being addressed by the SEC and standard setters involve accounting for third world debt treatment, good bank/bad bank transactions that have considerable tax advantages, and in-substance foreclosures.[66]

---

[66] Ernst & Young, "Current Issues in the Financial Services Industries" (October 1989); and Ernst & Young, "Risk-Based Capital: Developing a Strategy and Implementation Plan" (October 1989).

APPLICATION OF ANALYTICAL PROCEDURES TO BANKS

The framework introduced earlier for using analytical procedures in risk assessment can be adapted to banks as reflected in Exhibit 16–4. Key indicators used in bank failure prediction can be integrated in such risk assessments.

A major area in which modeling has been applied is to assess going concern risk. In such studies, predictor variables related to banks tend to follow certain general financial features:

> bank size; loan exposure; capital adequacy; asset quality; operating perform-
> ance; and liquidity. Size is measured using the natural logarithm of total assets.
> Loan exposure variables include the proportion of total assets represented by
> (1) construction loans, (2) real estate loans, and (3) agricultural loans . . . ,
> [as well as] (4) the aggregate credit to officers (loans to insiders) as a proportion
> of net loans.
>   Measures designed to capture the adequacy of bank capital include (1)
> primary capital to adjusted assets, (2) total capital to total loans, and (3) the
> raw measure of total equity capital when measuring primary and total capital
> [i.e., rather than adding the allowance for loan losses back to equity capital,

Exhibit 16–4

Analytical Procedures: Banks and Insurance Companies

Examples of Adaptation to Banking ...

Key Analytics: An Overview

Exhibit 16–4 (continued)

**Analytical Procedures Using Key Financial Data and Ratios
for A Fire & Casualty Insurance Company**

Consider the following example of a report on key analytics and their interpretation.

In addition to our examination, we have also performed a financial analysis using the National Association of Insurance Commissioners (NAIC) Insurance Regulatory Information System to assist management of the Association in assessing the financial condition and results of operations of the Association.

The following schedules represent a series of statistical tests to assist management in the evaluation of the Association with regard to solvency, stability and general financial condition. It should be emphasized that these tests are not intended to replace or eliminate the need for other financial and management reviews, but rather serve as indicators of areas which may need further attention. The tests may indicate the possibility of financial difficulties or poor trends, but are not in themselves indicative of adverse financial condition because these financial conditions can only be judged by knowledgeable people taking all pertinent facts into consideration.

A "usual range" of ratio results has been established from studies of the ratios for companies that have become insolvent or have experienced financial difficulties in recent years. Falling outside the usual range is not considered a failing result. For example, an increase larger than "usual" in surplus or in premium is not necessarily unsound. Furthermore, in some years it may not be unusual for financially sound companies to have several ratios with results outside the usual range. Indeed, when a fundamental variable (such as surplus) is significantly affected by outside forces (e.g., a drop in the stock market), many of the calculated values will not fall within their normal or usual range.

*ANALYTICAL PROCEDURES ON
KEY FINANCIAL DATA AND RATIOS*

Financial analysis is important for appraising the solvency and stability of insurance companies.

Financial analysis of insurance companies follows the same basic principles applied to the study of any corporation's financial structure and therefore includes an analysis of liquidity, leverage, profitability and growth.

Over the years a set of basic measurement statistics has been developed and is composed of five categories of financial ratios for property and casualty insurance companies which encompass:

• basic operating statistics

Exhibit 16–4 (continued)

- capacity statistics
- liquidity statistics
- profitability statistics
- reserve statistics

Exhibit I includes the ratios and analysis that will be applied to operating results in order to assess its financial strengths and weaknesses and identify unusual fluctuations and variations.

Exhibit I

Financial Analysis for Property and Casualty Insurance Companies

A. *Basic Operating Statistics*

　1. Loss Ratio

- measures fundamental cost of underwriting operations
- gives general indication of quality of business written and adequacy of premium rates
- calculation

$$\text{Loss Ratio} = \frac{\text{Losses Incurred \& Loss Expenses Incurred}}{\text{Premium Earned}}$$

　2. Expense Ratio

- expresses the relationship between underwriting expenses and premiums
- measures operating efficiency and effectiveness
- calculation

$$\frac{\text{Expense Ratio}}{\text{(Financial Basis)}} = \frac{\text{Other Underwriting Expenses Incurred}}{\text{Premium Earned}}$$

$$\frac{\text{Expense Ratio}}{\text{(Trade Basis)}} = \frac{\text{Other Underwriting Expenses Incurred}}{\text{Premiums Written}}$$

　3. Combined Ratio
- summarizes in one statistic overall underwriting performance
- calculation

$$\frac{\text{Combined Ratio}}{\text{(Financial Basis)}} = \text{Loss Ratio} + \frac{\text{Expense Ratio}}{\text{(Financial Basis)}}$$

$$\frac{\text{Combined Ratio}}{\text{(Trade Basis)}} = \text{Loss Ratio} + \frac{\text{Expense Ratio}}{\text{(Trade Basis)}}$$

Exhibit 16–4 (continued)

B. *Capacity Statistics*

1. Kenney's "Fire" Ratio

   - similar to a current ratio
   - calculation

   $$\text{Kenney's "Fire" Ratio} = \frac{\text{Policyholders' Surplus}}{\text{Unearned Premium Reserve}}$$

2. Kenney's "Casualty" Ratio

   - similar to a debt-to-equity ratio
   - calculation

   $$\text{Kenney's "Casualty" Ratio} = \frac{\text{Premiums Written}}{\text{Policyholders' Surplus}}$$

3. Cover Ratios

   - popular benchmarks for judging whether company is overextending its capital through rapid premium growth
   - calculation

   $$\text{Cover Ratio "1"} = \frac{\text{Loss Reserves \& Policyholders' Surplus}}{\text{Premiums Written}}$$

   $$\text{Cover Ratio "2"} = \frac{\text{Loss Reserves for Workers' Compensation}}{\text{Premiums Written in Workers' Compensation}}$$

   $$\text{Cover Ratio "3"} = \frac{\text{Admitted Assets}}{\text{Premiums Written}}$$

C. *Liquidity Statistics*

1. Liquidity Ratio

   - similar to an "acid test" or quick ratio
   - measures ability to meet obligations as they come due
   - calculation

   $$\text{Liquidity Ratio} = \frac{\text{Cash \& Invested Assets (Market Value)}}{\substack{\text{Unearned Premium Reserve \& Loss and} \\ \text{Loss Adjustment Expense Reserves}}}$$

D. *Profitability Statistics*

1. Investment Earnings Ratio

   - expresses the relationship between net investment income and average admitted assets

Exhibit 16–4 (continued)

- narrowly defined measure of investment return

$$\text{Investment Earnings Ratio} = \frac{\text{Net Investment Income Earned}}{\text{Average Admitted Assets}}$$

2. Investment Profit Ratio

- includes realized gains (losses) in investment return to produce an overall index of investment performance

$$\text{Investment Profit Ratio} = \frac{\text{Net Investment Gain or Loss}}{\text{Average Admitted Assets}}$$

3. Return on Net Worth

- relates profits to policyholders' surplus
- can be calculated on statutory basis or GAAP basis
- summarizes overall operating success relative to net resources

$$\text{Return on Net Worth} = \frac{\text{Net Income}}{\text{Policyholders' Surplus}}$$

$$\text{GAAP Return on Net Worth} = \frac{\text{GAAP Net Income}}{\text{GAAP Policyholders' Surplus}}$$

4. Adjusted Return on Net Worth

- includes unrealized gains (losses) in total return for the period
- calculation

$$\text{Adjusted Return on Net Worth} = \frac{\text{GAAP Net Income \& Change in Unrealized Appreciation (Depreciation)}}{\text{GAAP Policyholders' Surplus}}$$

E. *Reserve Statistics*

- estimations of loss reserves has significant impact on financial statements
- judging the accuracy with which these reserves are established and maintained is fundamental
- development tests measure the accuracy of prior years' reserve levels

OUTLINE OF TESTS
DECEMBER 31, 1982

OVERALL TESTS

- *Premiums to surplus*—Used to gauge companies' insurance exposure, i.e., the higher the premiums written the higher exposure of surplus to loss variations.

Exhibit 16–4 (continued)

- *Change in writings*—Large change, although not necessarily unfavorable, may indicate instability in premium writings.
- *Surplus aid to surplus*—Used to determine contribution to surplus of commissions on insurance ceded to non-affiliated companies. Large amounts of surplus aid to surplus may indicate company is undercapitalized for volume of business.

PROFITABILITY TESTS

- *Two year adjusted underwriting ratio*—A measure of the underwriting profit margin for two year period.
- *Two year overall operating ratio*—A measure of the overall profitability of the company. Total of underwriting ratio and investment returns for two-year period.
- *Investment yield*—A loosely defined measure of investment return. Ratio expresses net investment income as percentage of the average amount of investment during the year.
- *Change in surplus*—A measure of the improvement or deterioration in the company's financial condition for the year.

LIQUIDITY TESTS

- *Liabilities to liquid assets*—A rough approximation of the company's ability to meet its obligations in a timely fashion.
- *Agents' balances to surplus*—Used as an indication of the degree to which solvency depends upon an asset often difficult to collect in the event of liquidation.

OUTLINE OF TESTS
DECEMBER 31, 1982

RESERVE TESTS

- *One year reserve development to surplus*—Used to test accuracy with which the outstanding claims for last year were recorded and to examine reserving practices.
- *Two year reserve development to surplus*—As with the one year development ratio, this is another indicator of the accuracy with which the company has established reserves for losses and may lead to an examination of reserving practices.

Exhibit 16–4 (continued)

- *Estimated current reserve deficiency to surplus*—An estimate of the adequacy of current reserves recorded by the company.

SUMMARY OF TEST RESULTS
DECEMBER 31, 1982

	Association Results	Usual Industry Range
Overall Tests		
Premiums to surplus	122.3%	<300%
Change in writings	+10.9%	<+33%;>−33%
Surplus aid to surplus	0.7%	<25%
Profitability Tests		
Two year adjusted underwriting ratio	100.3%	<110%
Two year overall operating ratio	87.2%	<100%
Investment yield	9.8%	<9.9%;>4%
Change in surplus	+13.2%	<+50%;>−10%
Liquidity Tests		
Liabilities to liquid assets	51.7%	<105%
Agents' balances to surplus	4.1%	<40%
Reserve Tests		
One year reserve development to surplus	4.2%	<25%
Two year reserve development to surplus	7.7%	<25%
Estimated current reserve deficiency to surplus	17.1%	<25%

Note—For the Association there are no test results falling outside usual industry range.

Exhibit 16–4 (continued)

*FURTHER CONSIDERATIONS WHERE RESULTS
OUTSIDE USUAL RANGE*

Premiums to Surplus

If result is indicated as unfavorable then the following should be considered.

1. Is the company a member of a group of affiliated companies? If so, it is necessary to consider the ratio for the group.
2. Is the company profitable? Are profits stable or increasing?
3. Where is the company's business concentrated? Property business does not need as low a ratio as liability because liability losses are more unpredictable.
4. Does the company have adequate protection against large losses or catastrophes?
   Each of the above may contribute to lessen the adverse implication of an otherwise unfavorable ratio.

Change in Writings

If significant increase, include the following consideration in the report.

1. Expansion with new product lines or new market areas.
2. Addition to agency force.
3. Increase due to economic up turns.

If significant decrease include the following considerations in report.

1. Withdrawal from certain product lines or market areas.
2. Reduction of agency force.
3. Decrease due to economic down turns.
4. Other.

Surplus Aid to Surplus

If value is unfavorable we should consider recomputing several of the tests that include surplus in the calculation to remove surplus aid.

Two Year Adjusted Underwriting Ratio

If ratio is outside usual range we will need to consider the results of loss reserving tests with respect to over or under-reserving, because loss reserves increase or decrease loss expenses and numerator in the ratio.

Investment Yield

If results outside usual range, include following additional comments. A result below the lower value in the range may indicate:

Exhibit 16–4 (continued)

1. The company is investing for capital gain and not income. If this is the case we need to determine the real value of the underlying investments.
2. Large investment in associated or affiliated companies.
3. Large investment in home office facilities.
4. Large investments in tax exempt bonds meaning lower yields but not subject to tax.

A result above the usual range may indicate investments in questionable assets. We will need to determine whether liquidity and safety of principal are being sacrificed for short-term gain.
If the results lie outside the normal range we would therefore need to perform in-depth analysis of investment portfolio.

Changes in Surplus

If decrease greater than 10% include following:

1. Dramatic decline in ratio may be accompanied by poor underwriting and/or investment results therefore these need to be considered, especially investments yield and underwriting ratio.
2. Large capital gains and losses, capital transactions dividends to stockholders, changes in non-admitted assets, change in surplus aid from reinsurance, etc. may cause the decrease.

Liabilities to Liquid Assets

If value above 105% include:
A value above 105% may indicate that the company may be heading for insolvency. Before making such a judgment we need to consider the following:

1. The adequacy of reserves and proper valuation.
2. Mix and liquidity of assets.
3. Amount by which amortized value of bonds exceeds market.

Agents Balances to Surplus

If the ratio is greater than 40% then we should consider the following:

1. A close analysis of agents' balances to determine whether balance over 90 days due is included as admitted assets.

One and Two Year Reserve Development to Surplus Tests

If the results are consistently outside the range then we need to take a closer look at reserving policies.

Exhibit 16–4 (continued)

Estimated Current Reserve Deficiency to Surplus

> If reserve development tests on current estimated reserve deficiency indicate that surplus is significantly overstated, some of the other tests should be reperformed using adjusted surplus.

it is subtracted in a sort of double jeopardy manner, consistent with understatement] . . .

Asset quality predictor variables include various measures of substandard loans as a proportion of either gross loans, primary capital, or total assets. The call report includes the following separate categories of substandard loans: (1) loans past due over 90 days; (2) loans for which interest accrual has been suspended; (3) total nonperforming loans, which is the sum of past due and nonaccrual loans; and (4) loans that have been restructured. Two additional asset quality predictor variables are the ratio of net chargeoffs to total loans, and the ratio of provision for loan losses to total assets.

Measures designed to capture operating performance include: (1) total interest income to total assets (yield), (2) total interest expense to total assets, (3) net interest income to total assets, (4) return on total assets, (5) return on total equity capital, (6) undivided profit and capital reserves to total assets, and (7) income before extraordinary items. Non-operating performance measures include (1) total noninterest income to total assets, (2) total overhead expense to total assets, and (3) security gains (losses) and gross extraordinary items to total assets.

Liquidity measures include: (1) short-term assets less large liabilities to total assets [measures the gap between short-term liquid assets and large deposits, providing an indication of the Bank's ability to produce cash should depositors make large withdrawals], (2) large time deposits to total assets, and net loans to total assets [i.e., measuring the proportion of total assets that is nonliquid].[67]

For analysis purposes, this research has examined commercial banks that have and have not failed, forming peer groups into 9 size demarcations, based on asset size: $0 to $10 million, $10 to $25; $25 to $50, $50 to $100, $100 to $300, $300 to $500, $500 million to $1 billion, $1 billion to $5 billion, and over $5 billion. The variables that did not display significant differences between failed and non-failed institutions were construction and real estate loan proportions of total assets, total capital to total loans, net interest income to total assets (spread), total noninterest income to total assets, security gains (losses) and gross extraordinary items to total assets, return on total equity capital, income before extraordinary items, and the raw measure of total equity capital.[68] Considerable

---

[67] Timothy B. Bell, Gary S. Ribar, and Jennifer R. Verchio, "Neural Nets vs. Logistic Regression: A Comparison of Each Model's Ability to Predict Commercial Bank Failures," Submitted to Cash Flow Accounting Conference in Nice, France Working Paper (May 1990).

[68] Timothy B. Bell, Gary S. Ribar, and Jennifer R. Verchio, "Neural Nets vs. Logistic Regression: A Comparison of Each Model's Ability to Predict Commercial Bank Failures," Submitted to Cash Flow Accounting Conference in Nice, France Working Paper (May 1990).

explanatory power, in excess of 90% has been observed in predicting failed banks using logit and neural nets.[69]

To demonstrate a similar application of analytical procedures based on company entities of interest to those that have failed, Exhibit 16–4 continues with an example from the insurance industry. Key ratios are explained and comparisons made between a hypothetical company and ranges within which those ratios are expected to lie.

Failures of entities in any industry can provide useful lessons to others. According to a study by a panel of the House Government Operations Committee, fraud and misconduct play a part in nearly one-third of all commercial bank closings and more than three-fourths of all savings association failures. While federal regulators estimate the savings industry's restoration will cost $45 billion to $50 billion, private analysts put the price tag as high as $100 billion.[70]

THRIFTS

Before shifting from financial institutions, it is useful to consider the thrift industry and conclusions drawn by the General Accounting Office as to sources of risk. "The types of direct investment activities these thrifts started, continued, or expanded included[71]

- providing funds to developers to acquire land and construct buildings with little or no developer equity;
- investing in real estate, including ownership in anything from raw land to a residential development to an established income-producing property;
- investing in equity securities, such as corporate shares of stock and investment in joint ventures; and
- investing in service corporations and operating subsidiaries which engaged in lines of business not related to the thrift industry."[72]

The observed weaknesses in failed thrifts examined by the General Accounting Office are reported in Exhibit 16–5. A key exposure identified was that thrifts would acquire subsidiary businesses without adequate appraisals. This led to

---

[69] Research assistance in preparing this discussion of financial institutions was provided by Karen Cravens, a CPA and Ph.D. student at Texas A&M University; her assistance is most appreciated.

[70] "Fraud Tied to One-Third of Bank Closings," *Battalion* (October 20, 1988), p. 8 [Washington (AP)].

[71] United States General Accounting Office (GAO), "Thrift Failures—Costly Failures Resulted From Regulatory Violations and Unsafe Practices," (GAO/AFMD-89-62, June 1989), p. 27.

[72] Through its proposed risk-based capital guidelines, the Bank Board has designated certain activities as having more risk. Under the proposed rule, those activities found at the failed thrifts and enumerated above would be in the highest-risk category. Thus, the proposed rule would require a thrift engaging in such activities to maintain three to six times the capital required for traditional mortgage lending activities. However, according to the Bank Board, with proper diversification and sound management, the nontraditional activities can be appropriate and desirable assets for a thrift, notwithstanding the greater risk they entail.

Exhibit 16–5

Characteristics of 26 Failed
Thrifts in Our Sample

	Number of thrifts	Percent
Weaknesses cited		
Inaccurate recordkeeping or inadequate controls	26	100
Change from traditional to higher-risk activity	26	100
Inadequate credit analysis	24	92
Inadequate appraisals	23	88
Excessive loans to one borrower	23	88
Growth with jumbo deposits	21	81
Transactions with affiliates	21	81
Conflicts of interest	20	77
Acquisition, development, and construction lending	19	73
Passive board of directors or dominant individual	19	73
Excessive compensation	17	65
Inadequate project analysis	17	65
Faulty loan disbursements	17	65
Change in control	16	62
Actions taken		
Supervisory agreement signed with district bank	22	85
Enforcement action taken by Bank Board	9	35
Criminal referrals	19	73
Civil suits filed by Bank Board	16	62

Source: United States General Accounting Office (GAO), "Thrift Failures—Costly Failures Resulted From Regulatory Violations and Unsafe Practices" (GAO/AFMD-89-62, June 1989), p. 15.

Bank Board guidance on factors a thrift should consider when acquiring a business, specifying that:

- "thrifts should obtain an adequate independent appraisal to substantiate the value of the business entity,
- the purchase price should be based on operating results for the current year and the three years prior to acquisition, and
- the Board of Directors should review all documentation relative to the acquisition before approving the price and value of the purchase."[73]

The problem of appraisals, already cited for the banking industry, likewise permeates thrifts. "To illustrate, when one thrift made a loan of over $54 million to a borrower who bought an office complex, it relied on a borrower-ordered appraisal. Examiners found that the appraisal did not accurately assess the property's value because, among other reasons, it did not consider

- that more than half of the rentable space in the complex was already obligated by leases and options to lease at rates that were 50% below the current market prices, and
- that occupancy levels were low in nearby comparable properties as a result of newly built office buildings.

[73] United States General Accounting Office (GAO), "Thrift failures—Costly Failures Resulted From Regulatory Violations and Unsafe Practices" (GAO/AFMD-89-62, June 1989), pp. 28–29.

Examiners also noted instances in which thrifts did not obtain feasibility studies for development projects. For example, a thrift in California lent $40 million to one borrower, principally to build condominiums and a shopping center, but no feasibility studies were done. Examiners stated that adequate feasibility studies would have shown that the area was already overbuilt with condominiums and shopping facilities before the loans were made. This thrift expects to lose over $10 million on this project.

Numerous other underwriting practices in which thrifts engaged, although not always a violation of regulations, were considered unsafe by examiners. These include the following conditions:

- Borrowers had little or no equity in property or projects.
- Thrifts lent an amount that equaled or exceeded the purchase price or the appraised value of collateral.
- Loan approval terms were not followed.
- Borrowers were released from any personal liability to repay a loan."[74]

The role of control has been much debated, the view has been put forth by the General Accounting Office, as reflected in Exhibit 16–6. "A weak economy

Exhibit 16–6

Matrix of Combined Effects of Economy, Management, and Internal Controls

Source: United States General Accounting Office (GAO), "Thrift Failures—Costly Failures Resulted From Regulatory Violations and Unsafe Practices" (GAO/AFMD-89-62, June 1989), p. 65.

---

[74] United States General Accounting Office (GAO), "Thrift Failures—Costly Failures Resulted From Regulatory Violations and Unsafe Practices" (GAO/AFMD-89-62, June 1989), p. 34.

tends to expose internal problems which may not be evident when a bank is operating in a strong economy.[75] Therefore, banks with internal control weaknesses were also more vulnerable to adverse economic conditions. Conversely, good internal controls tended to serve as a buffer to protect banks from those conditions."[76]

SECURITIZATIONS

Somewhat related to the financial institutions since they first used such transactions is an increasingly applied financing vehicle referred to as securitization. Such a transaction involves transfer of ownership of a group of assets from an originator to a trust or special purpose corporation in exchange for cash. That entity then uses the assets to support asset-backed debt financing and the proceeds are paid to the originator. Often that originator uses the cash for capital expenditures or debt retirement. These arrangements have been a basis for removing loans to lesser developed countries from the financial statements of banks as well as a means of down-sizing financial institutions.

However, companies have likewise used these transactions. For example, Eastern Airlines used this financing option before its demise. Indeed, the approach is expected to create new lines of credit in a manner that achieves off-balance sheet treatment, and may be successful at avoiding debt covenants and "me-first" type rules.

An ongoing use of such securitizations has been observed by financial subsidiaries such as GMAC which transfers car loans periodically and achieves results similar to traditional factoring arrangements. An interesting unanswered question is the degree to which such transactions are tied to efficiency advantages or financial statement consequences whereby consolidation requirements of the FASB Statement No. 94 are circumvented.[77]

From a control perspective, this type of transaction demonstrates:

- the ongoing change in means of altering capital structure that are available to borrowers, lenders, and investors;

- the possibility that control mechanisms such as direct lender oversight, debt covenants, and "me-first" rules can be circumvented;

- the necessity of monitoring new forms of past problems—i.e., some have drawn an analogy to international pyramiding, now disallowed, and the advent of securitization; and

- the importance of footnote scrutiny, since the face of financial statements may omit entire classes of transactions.

---

[75] *Bank Failure: An Evaluation of the Factors Contributing to the Failure of National Banks*, Office of the Comptroller of the Currency, Washington, D.C., June 1988.

[76] United States General Accounting Office (GAO), "Thrift Failures—Costly Failures Resulted From Regulatory Violations and Unsafe Practices" (GAO/AFMD-89-62, June 1989), p. 65.

[77] Financial Accounting Standards Board, Statement No. 94, "Consolidation of All Majority-Owned Subsidiaries (FASB, 1987).

Control structure must be adaptive to change, alert to both form and substance, and wary as to attendant risks associated with new transactions.[78]

GOVERNMENT CONTRACTORS

Companies across a number of industries are government contractors. They are subject to additional risks tied to the highly regulated environment in which government contractors operate, as detailed in Exhibit 16–7. The regulatory at-

---

Exhibit 16–7

Risks Associated with Government Contracting

- Companies are subject to extensive and complex cost accounting and other regulations.
- Business and accounting practices are subject to frequent government scrutiny.
- The government has unilateral rights not found in commercial relationships.
- Cost accounting considerations play a vital role in negotiating pricing and administering government contracts and, consequently, determining the contractor's reported financial position and results of operations.
- Disallowance of incurred costs resulting in reduced earnings
- Contract changes or claims affecting earnings
- Contract losses, if the contractor is unable to meet its contractual obligations requiring the design or manufacture of complex or state-of-the-art products
- Potential for unrealizable investments in equipment and facilities and a general reduction in business activity if government programs and funding policies change
- Possible allegations of defective pricing if the contractor fails to submit current, accurate and complete cost or pricing data
- Possible allegations of fraud for cost mischarging which can lead to loss of contracts, debarment, loss of reputation or criminal penalties assessed against both the contractor and responsible management
- Cash flow problems if progress payments are withheld by the government or retentions are increased because of disputes with the government, noncompliance with regulations, or other problems
- Government audit and other oversight of the contractor's operations

Source: "Industry Audit Guide—Audits of Government Contractors," Prepared by American Institute of Certified Public Accountants Government Contractors Guide Special Committee (Draft: Revised Edition, February 25, 1987), pp. 110–112.

---

[78] The author has benefited from a seminar conducted by Professor Scott Lummer and Marilyn Wiley, at Texas A&M University, Department of Finance, on this topic (held January 25, 1991).

tention and imposition of penalties irrespective of the materiality of a violation creates a particular need to focus on policies and practices related to controls. The key factors considered in evaluating control structure for such industries are cited in Exhibit 16–8. Contractor controls associated with government regulations should include: encouraging communication as to compliance issues; reacting to and communicating results of government audits and reviews; and documenting support for reasonableness of significant cost elements. Inaccurate estimates may increase the risk of defective pricing, creating a particular need for control over the estimating systems and proposal preparation. Exhibit 16–9 prescribes controls in this area of operations. For further insights on the nature of other facets of the control structure, an AICPA industry audit guide is available, as are a number of related government guidance documents.

In 1986, the President's Blue Ribbon Commission on Defense Management put forth a call for various defense industry initiatives on businesses ethics and conduct. The questionnaire suggested as a guideline by which public accountability might be achievable, including a related review report by CPAs, is provided in Exhibit 16–10.

Exhibit 16–8

Factors Relevant to Gaining an Understanding of Contractors' Control System

- Overall control environment
- Compliance with government regulations
- Estimating systems and proposal preparation
- Project administration
- Quality assurance
- Contract costs
- Contract revenues
- Billing
- Change orders
- Claims
- Inventories
- Government-furnished property
- Related-party and interorganizational transactions
- Operational economy and efficiency

Source: "Industry Audit Guide—Audits of Government Contractors," Prepared by American Institute of Certified Public Accountants Government Contractors Guide Special Committee (Draft: Revised Edition, February 25, 1987), pp. 113–114.

Exhibit 16–9

Controls Over Estimating Systems and Proposal Preparation

- Written estimating policies and procedures are maintained.
- Estimates are consistently prepared.
- Prices and quantities are obtained from approved sources.
- Only allowable costs are included in cost estimates.
- Forward pricing and provisional overhead rates are based on current budgets and consistent with the latest management plan.
- Estimates are adequately documented and include support for any management pricing decisions reflected in the final proposal.
- Changes in cost or pricing data are communicated so that proposals and updates to proposals reflect accurate, current, and complete data.
- Subcontractor and vendor proposals are reviewed by the contractor, and that vendors and subcontractors certify that these proposals are accurate, current, and complete.
- Estimates are clerically accurate and independently reviewed by an appropriate level of management knowledgeable of government contracting regulations.

Source: "Industry Audit Guide—Audits of Government Contractors," Prepared by American Institute of Certified Public Accountants Government Contractors Guide Special Committee (Draft: Revised Edition, February 25, 1987), pp. 117–118.

Exhibit 16–10

Illustrative Procedures for Review of Answers to Questionnaire Defense Industry Questionnaire on Business Ethics and Conduct

Before performing procedures, the practitioner should read the *Defense Industry Initiatives on Business Ethics and Conduct*.

1. DOES THE COMPANY HAVE A WRITTEN CODE OF BUSINESS ETHICS AND CONDUCT?

   Determine whether the Company has a written Code of Business Ethics and Conduct.

2. IS THE CODE DISTRIBUTED TO ALL EMPLOYEES PRINCIPALLY INVOLVED IN DEFENSE WORK?

   Determine by inquiry of Company officials and/or by reading relevant documentation how the Company distributes the Code to all employees principally involved in defense work.

Exhibit 16–10 (continued)

3. ARE NEW EMPLOYEES PROVIDED ANY ORIENTATION TO THE CODE?

   Determine by inquiry of Company officials and/or reading relevant documentation how the Company provides an orientation to the Code to new employees.

4. DOES THE CODE ASSIGN RESPONSIBILITY TO OPERATING MANAGEMENT AND OTHERS FOR COMPLIANCE WITH THE CODE?

   Read the code to determine whether it includes (a) the assignment of responsibility for compliance with the Code to operating management and others, and (b) a statement of the standards that govern the conduct of all employees in their relationships to the Company.

5. DOES THE COMPANY CONDUCT EMPLOYEE TRAINING PROGRAMS REGARDING THE CODE?

   Determine by inquiry of Company officials and/or by reading relevant documentation how the Company conducts training programs regarding the Code.

6. DOES THE CODE ADDRESS STANDARDS THAT GOVERN THE CONDUCT OF EMPLOYEES IN THEIR DEALING WITH SUPPLIERS, CONSULTANTS, AND CUSTOMERS?

   Read the Code to determine whether it addresses standards that govern the conduct of employees in their dealings with suppliers, consultants, and customers.

7. IS THERE A CORPORATE REVIEW BOARD, OMBUDSMAN, CORPORATE COMPLIANCE OR ETHICS OFFICE OR SIMILAR MECHANISM FOR EMPLOYEES TO REPORT SUSPECTED VIOLATIONS TO SOMEONE OTHER THAN THEIR DIRECT SUPERVISOR, IF NECESSARY?

   Determine by inquiry of Company officials and/or by reading relevant documentation whether a corporate review board, ombudsman, corporate compliance or ethics office, or similar mechanism exists for employees to report suspected violations.

8. DOES THE MECHANISM EMPLOYED PROTECT THE CONFIDENTIALITY OF EMPLOYEE REPORTS?

   a. Determine by inquiry of members of the corporate review board, ombudsman, corporate compliance or ethics office, or similar mechanism established by the Company whether they understand the need to protect the confidentiality of employee reports.

   b. Determine by inquiry of Company officials and/or by reading relevant

Exhibit 16–10 (continued)

documentation how the procedures employed protect this confidentiality.

9. IS THERE AN APPROPRIATE MECHANISM TO FOLLOW-UP ON REPORTS OF SUSPECTED VIOLATIONS TO DETERMINE WHAT OCCURRED, WHO WAS RESPONSIBLE, AND RECOMMENDED CORRECTIVE AND OTHER ACTIONS?

Determine by inquiry of Company officials and/or by reading relevant documentation how the follow-up procedures established by the Company operate and whether an appropriate mechanism exists to follow-up on reports of suspected violations reported to a corporate review board, ombudsman, corporate compliance or ethics office, or similar mechanism to determine what occurred, who was responsible, and recommended corrective and other action.

10. IS THERE AN APPROPRIATE MECHANISM FOR LETTING EMPLOYEES KNOW THE RESULT OF ANY FOLLOW-UP INTO THEIR REPORTED CHARGES?

   a. Determine by inquiry of Company officials and/or by reading relevant documentation whether an appropriate mechanism exists for letting employees know the result of any follow-up into their reported charges.
   b. Determine by inquiry of members of the corporate review board, ombudsman, corporate compliance or ethics office, or similar mechanism whether the results of the Company's follow-up of reported charges have been communicated to employees.

11. IS THERE AN ONGOING PROGRAM OF COMMUNICATION TO EMPLOYEES, SPELLING OUT AND RE-EMPHASIZING THEIR OBLIGATIONS UNDER THE CODE OF CONDUCT?

   and

12. WHAT ARE THE SPECIFICS OF SUCH A PROGRAM?
   A. WRITTEN COMMUNICATION?
   B. ONE-ON-ONE COMMUNICATION?
   C. GROUP MEETINGS?
   D. VISUAL AIDS?
   E. OTHERS?

Determine by inquiry of Company officials and/or by reading relevant documentation the extent of the Company's ongoing program of communication to employees, spelling out and re-emphasizing their obligations under the Code. Note the specific means of communication and compare to the Company's response to Question 12 of the Questionnaire.

Exhibit 16–10 (continued)

13. DOES THE COMPANY HAVE A PROCEDURE FOR VOLUNTARILY REPORTING VIOLATIONS OF FEDERAL PROCUREMENT LAWS TO APPROPRIATE GOVERNMENTAL AGENCIES?

    Determine by inquiry of Company officials and/or by reading relevant documentation how the Company's procedures operate for determining whether violations of federal procurement laws are to be reported to appropriate governmental agencies.

14. IS IMPLEMENTATION OF THE CODE'S PROVISIONS ONE OF THE STANDARDS BY WHICH ALL LEVELS OF SUPERVISION ARE EXPECTED TO BE MEASURED IN THEIR PERFORMANCE?

    Determine by inquiry of Company officials and/or by reading relevant documentation, such as position descriptions and personnel policies, whether performance evaluations are to consider supervisors' efforts in the implementation of the Code's provisions as a standard of measurement of their performance.

15. IS THERE A PROGRAM TO MONITOR ON A CONTINUING BASIS ADHERENCE TO THE CODE OF CONDUCT AND COMPLIANCE WITH FEDERAL PROCUREMENT LAWS?

    Determine by inquiry of Company officials and/or by reading relevant documentation how the Company monitors, on a continuing basis, adherence to the Code and compliance with federal procurement laws.

16. DOES THE COMPANY PARTICIPATE IN THE INDUSTRY'S "BEST PRACTICES FORUM?"

    Determine by inquiry of Company's officials and/or by reading relevant documentation whether the Company participated in the "Best Practices Forum."

17. ARE PERIODIC REPORTS ON ADHERENCE TO THE PRINCIPLES MADE TO THE COMPANY'S BOARD OF DIRECTORS OR TO ITS AUDIT OR OTHER APPROPRIATE COMMITTEE?

    Determine by inquiry of Company officials and/or by reading minutes of the Board of Directors or audit or other appropriate committee meetings or other relevant documentation whether Company officials have reported on adherence to the principles of business ethics and conduct.

18. ARE THE COMPANY'S INDEPENDENT PUBLIC ACCOUNTANTS OR A SIMILAR INDEPENDENT ORGANIZATION REQUIRED TO COMMENT TO THE BOARD OF DIRECTORS OR A COMMITTEE THEREOF ON THE EFFICACY OF THE COMPANY'S INTERNAL PROCEDURES FOR IMPLEMENTING THE COMPANY'S CODE OF CONDUCT?

Exhibit 16–10 (continued)

Determine by inquiry of Company officials and/or by reading relevant documentation whether the Company's independent accountants are required to comment to the Board of Directors or a committee thereof on the efficacy of the Company's internal procedures for implementing the Company's Code.

Source: Appendix E of "Proposed Interpretation of Statement on Standards for Attestation Engagements, Attestation Standards: Defense Industry Questionnaire on Business Ethics and Conduct," Draft 4/22/87, pp. 31–34.

EVIDENCE OF VARIATIONS IN MANAGEMENT LETTER POINTS ACROSS ORGANIZATIONS OF DIFFERENT SIZE AND INDUSTRY CLASSIFICATION

Management letter points examined for 100 entities over a five-year period vary significantly across entities of different sizes. Large entities receive a greater number of comments, on a percentage basis, although they are frequently of an immaterial nature and often have already been recognized by the auditee's management. The dominant concerns involve documentation safeguards and accuracy errors. Medium-sized operations find approval problems to be of similar gravity, followed by segregation, compliance, and competency (including EDP) issues. Control environment considerations are prevalent. The likelihood that an auditor will mention that an internal control point is being repeated from a prior management letter is invariant to auditee size. The only types of control points which were found to vary across industries relate to approval, documentation, inventory adjustment, segregation, and tax-related issues. Some differences in auditors' comments and management's reactions are observed.

Detailed support for these general inferences follows.

Management letters issued to 100 companies over a five-year period (1975 to 1979) are the basis for the analysis reported herein. Descriptive information is provided in Exhibit 16–11.

ANALYSIS

Although almost 100 categories were used to code the management letter points, by focusing on key management assertions and control objectives, as well as whether the point involved (1) nature of the problem, (2) severity of the problem, (3) management's reactions, and/or (4) auditors' commentaries, it was possible to collapse the analysis to the 15 categories in Exhibit 16–12; 7 categories in Exhibit 16–13; 6 categories in Exhibit 16–14; and 10 categories in Exhibit 16–15, for a total of 38 key classifications. These classifications and the results of chi-square analysis will now be detailed.

Exhibit 16–11

Descriptive Information on Sample Companies

	Manufacturing, Mining, Oil & Contractors (51 entities)	Transportation, Communications & Utilities (8 entities)*	Wholesale & Retail (14 entities)	Banking, Credit, Insurance & Real Estate (17 entities)	Health, Educational, Membership Group, Government, & Non-classifiable (8 entities)
% of Entities Regulated by the SEC	55%	38%	36%	29%	0%
Total Assets:					
Mean Value	482,000,000	315,000,000	71,000,000	195,000,000	11,400,000
(Standard Deviation)	(1,080,000,000)	(630,000,000)	(146,000,000)	(312,000,000)	(20,700,000)
Median	100,000,000	13,500,000	9,500,000	70,000,000	3,666,667
Frequency Breakdown					
≤ $500,000	5	—	—	—	1
$500,000 to $1,000,000	2	—	1	1	5
$1,000,000 to $10,000,000	10	4	6	5	1
$10,000,000 to $100,000,000	7	3	5	4	—
$100,000,000 to $1 billion	15	1	2	7	—
$1 billion to $10 billion	12	—	—	—	—
	51	8	14	17	7*
Total Sales:					
Mean Value	567,000,000	394,000,000	90,800,000	23,800,000	3,550,000
(Standard Deviation)	(1,090,000,000)	(840,000,000)	(157,000,000)	(28,000,000)	(2,508,984)
Median	100,000,000	16,000,000	23,400,000	10,000,000	4,000,000
Frequency Breakdown					
≤ $500,000	2	—	—	—	1
$500,000 to $1,000,000	3	—	—	3	1
$1,000,000 to $10,000,000	9	4	4	7	4
$10,000,000 to $100,000,000	10	2	7	7	—
$100,000,000 to $1 billion	12	2	3	—	—
$1 billion to $10 billion	15	—	—	—	—
	51	8	14	17	6*

* Descriptive information is missing for some companies within the sample.

768

Exhibit 16–12

The Nature of the Problem: The Association
of Management Letter Points with Client Size

ACCOUNT CLASSIFICATION

FREQUENCY PERCENT	< $1 M	> $1 M < $100 M	> $100 M < $10 B	TOTAL
NO COMMENTS	8 8.00	28 28.00	3 3.00	39 39.00
COMMENTS	2 2.00	27 27.00	32 32.00	61 61.00
TOTAL				100 100.00

STATISTIC	DF	VALUE	PROB
LIKELIHOOD RATIO CHI-SQUARE	2	27.038	0.000
CONTINGENCY COEFFICIENT		0.440	
CRAMER'S V		0.490	

ACCURACY ERRORS AND MISSTATEMENTS

FREQUENCY PERCENT	< $1 M	> $1 M < $100 M	> $100 M < $10 B	TOTAL
NO COMMENTS	4 4.00	10 10.00	0 0.00	14 14.00
COMMENTS	6 6.00	45 45.00	35 35.00	86 86.00
TOTAL				100 100.00

STATISTIC	DF	VALUE	PROB
LIKELIHOOD RATIO CHI-SQUARE	2	15.377	0.000
CONTINGENCY COEFFICIENT		0.329	
CRAMER'S V		0.348	

ACCOUNTING TREATMENT

FREQUENCY PERCENT	< $1 M	> $1 M < $100 M	> $100 M < $10 B	TOTAL
NO COMMENTS	7 7.00	28 28.00	5 5.00	40 40.00
COMMENTS	3 3.00	27 27.00	30 30.00	60 60.00
TOTAL				100 100.00

STATISTIC	DF	VALUE	PROB
LIKELIHOOD RATIO CHI-SQUARE	2	17.449	0.000
CONTINGENCY COEFFICIENT		0.373	
CRAMER'S V		0.401	

ALLOCATION AND CUTOFF PROBLEMS

FREQUENCY PERCENT	< $1 M	> $1 M < $100 M	> $100 M < $10 B	TOTAL
NO COMMENTS	7 7.00	16 16.00	0 0.00	23 23.00
COMMENTS	3 3.00	39 39.00	35 35.00	77 77.00
TOTAL				100 100.00

STATISTIC	DF	VALUE	PROB
LIKELIHOOD RATIO CHI-SQUARE	2	29.312	0.000
CONTINGENCY COEFFICIENT		0.441	
CRAMER'S V		0.491	

Exhibit 16–12 (continued)

APPROVAL PROBLEMS AND AUTHORIZATION

FREQUENCY PERCENT	< $1 M	> $1 M < $100 M	> $100 M < $10 B	TOTAL
NO COMMENTS	5 / 5.00	9 / 9.00	0 / 0.00	14 / 14.00
COMMENTS	5 / 5.00	46 / 46.00	35 / 35.00	86 / 86.00
TOTAL				100 / 100.00

STATISTIC	DF	VALUE	PROB
LIKELIHOOD RATIO CHI-SQUARE	2	18.108	0.000
CONTINGENCY COEFFICIENT		0.378	
CRAMER'S V		0.409	

COMPETENCY CONCERNS AND COMPUTERS & SYSTEMS RELATED ISSUES

FREQUENCY PERCENT	< $1 M	> $1 M < $100 M	> $100 M < $10 B	TOTAL
NO COMMENTS	8 / 8.00	15 / 15.00	1 / 1.00	24 / 24.00
COMMENTS	2 / 2.00	40 / 40.00	34 / 34.00	76 / 76.00
TOTAL				100 / 100.00

STATISTIC	DF	VALUE	PROB
LIKELIHOOD RATIO CHI-SQUARE	2	26.671	0.000
CONTINGENCY COEFFICIENT		0.455	
CRAMER'S V		0.511	

ARM'S LENGTH CONCERN

FREQUENCY PERCENT	< $1 M	> $1 M < $100 M	> $100 M < $10 B	TOTAL
NO COMMENTS	7 / 7.00	45 / 45.00	22 / 22.00	74 / 74.00
COMMENTS	3 / 3.00	10 / 10.00	13 / 13.00	26 / 26.00
TOTAL				100 / 100.00

STATISTIC	DF	VALUE	PROB
LIKELIHOOD RATIO CHI-SQUARE	2	4.059	0.131
CONTINGENCY COEFFICIENT		0.198	
CRAMER'S V		0.202	

COMPLIANCE DIRECTED

FREQUENCY PERCENT	< $1 M	> $1 M < $100 M	> $100 M < $10 B	TOTAL
NO COMMENTS	5 / 5.00	12 / 12.00	0 / 0.00	17 / 17.00
COMMENTS	5 / 5.00	43 / 43.00	35 / 35.00	83 / 83.00
TOTAL				100 / 100.00

STATISTIC	DF	VALUE	PROB
LIKELIHOOD RATIO CHI-SQUARE	2	19.609	0.000
CONTINGENCY COEFFICIENT		0.369	
CRAMER'S V		0.397	

INVENTORY ADJUSTMENTS

FREQUENCY PERCENT	< $1 M	> $1 M < $100 M	> $100 M < $10 B	TOTAL
NO COMMENTS	9 / 9.00	35 / 35.00	6 / 6.00	50 / 50.00
COMMENTS	1 / 1.00	20 / 20.00	29 / 29.00	50 / 50.00
TOTAL				100 / 100.00

STATISTIC	DF	VALUE	PROB
LIKELIHOOD RATIO CHI-SQUARE	2	27.955	0.000
CONTINGENCY COEFFICIENT		0.452	
CRAMER'S V		0.506	

NEGATIVE CONFIRMATION AND EXCEPTION POLICY PRACTICES

FREQUENCY PERCENT	< $1 M	> $1 M < $100 M	> $100 M < $10 B	TOTAL
NO COMMENTS	10 / 10.00	55 / 55.00	27 / 27.00	92 / 92.00
COMMENTS	0 / 0.00	0 / 0.00	8 / 8.00	8 / 8.00
TOTAL				100 / 100.00

STATISTIC	DF	VALUE	PROB
LIKELIHOOD RATIO CHI-SQUARE	2	18.126	0.000
CONTINGENCY COEFFICIENT		0.373	
CRAMER'S V		0.402	

DOCUMENTATION SAFEGUARDS, CLARIFICATION, AND COMPLETENESS

FREQUENCY PERCENT	< $1 M	> $1 M < $100 M	> $100 M < $10 B	TOTAL
NO COMMENTS	4 / 4.00	8 / 8.00	0 / 0.00	12 / 12.00
COMMENTS	6 / 6.00	47 / 47.00	35 / 35.00	88 / 88.00
TOTAL				100 / 100.00

STATISTIC	DF	VALUE	PROB
LIKELIHOOD RATIO CHI-SQUARE	2	14.303	0.001
CONTINGENCY COEFFICIENT		0.334	
CRAMER'S V		0.354	

IRREGULARITIES OR LEGALITY CONCERNS

FREQUENCY PERCENT	< $1 M	> $1 M < $100 M	> $100 M < $10 B	TOTAL
NO COMMENTS	7 / 7.00	23 / 23.00	6 / 6.00	36 / 36.00
COMMENTS	3 / 3.00	32 / 32.00	29 / 29.00	64 / 64.00
TOTAL				100 / 100.00

STATISTIC	DF	VALUE	PROB
LIKELIHOOD RATIO CHI-SQUARE	2	11.629	0.003
CONTINGENCY COEFFICIENT		0.318	
CRAMER'S V		0.335	

Exhibit 16–12 (continued)

SYSTEMS REVIEW REQUESTED

FREQUENCY PERCENT	< $1 M	> $1 M < $100 M	> $100 M < $10 B	TOTAL
NO COMMENTS	10 10.00	55 55.00	33 33.00	98 98.00
COMMENTS	0 0.00	0 0.00	2 2.00	2 2.00
TOTAL				100 100.00

STATISTIC	DF	VALUE	PROB
LIKELIHOOD RATIO CHI-SQUARE	2	4.276	0.118
CONTINGENCY COEFFICIENT		0.191	
CRAMER'S V		0.195	

SEGREGATION ISSUES

FREQUENCY PERCENT	< $1 M	> $1 M < $100 M	> $100 M < $10 B	TOTAL
NO COMMENTS	6 6.00	12 12.00	1 1.00	19 19.00
COMMENTS	4 4.00	43 43.00	34 34.00	81 81.00
TOTAL				100 100.00

STATISTIC	DF	VALUE	PROB
LIKELIHOOD RATIO CHI-SQUARE	2	16.997	0.000
CONTINGENCY COEFFICIENT		0.382	
CRAMER'S V		0.414	

TAX RELATED CONSIDERATIONS

FREQUENCY PERCENT	< $1 M	> $1 M < $100 M	> $100 M < $10 B	TOTAL
NO COMMENTS	8 8.00	31 31.00	5 5.00	44 44.00
COMMENTS	2 2.00	24 24.00	30 30.00	56 56.00
TOTAL				100 100.00

STATISTIC	DF	VALUE	PROB
LIKELIHOOD RATIO CHI-SQUARE	2	23.117	0.000
CONTINGENCY COEFFICIENT		0.418	
CRAMER'S V		0.461	

Exhibit 18-13

The Severity of the Problem: The Association of Management Letter Points with Client Size

AUDITOR QUESTIONED MATERIALITY OR MANAGEMENT EXPLICITLY MENTIONED MATERIALITY IN ITS RESPONSE

FREQUENCY PERCENT	<$1 M	>$1 M <$100 M	>$100 M <$10 B	TOTAL
NO COMMENTS	8 / 8.00	31 / 31.00	5 / 5.00	44 / 44.00
COMMENTS	2 / 2.00	24 / 24.00	30 / 30.00	56 / 56.00
TOTAL				100 / 100.00

STATISTIC	DF	VALUE	PROB
LIKELIHOOD RATIO CHI-SQUARE	2	23.117	0.000
CONTINGENCY COEFFICIENT		0.418	
CRAMER'S V		0.461	

MANAGEMENT ACCEPTS COMMENTS

FREQUENCY PERCENT	<$1 M	>$1 M <$100 M	>$100 M <$10 B	TOTAL
NO COMMENTS	7 / 7.00	28 / 28.00	7 / 7.00	42 / 42.00
COMMENTS	3 / 3.00	27 / 27.00	28 / 28.00	58 / 58.00
TOTAL				100 / 100.00

STATISTIC	DF	VALUE	PROB
LIKELIHOOD RATIO CHI-SQUARE	2	12.585	0.002
CONTINGENCY COEFFICIENT		0.327	
CRAMER'S V		0.346	

BASIC CONTROL IS MISSING: THIS IS A CONTROL ENVIRONMENT PROBLEM

FREQUENCY PERCENT	<$1 M	>$1 M <$100 M	>$100 M <$10 B	TOTAL
NO COMMENTS	4 / 4.00	9 / 9.00	0 / 0.00	13 / 13.00
COMMENTS	6 / 6.00	46 / 46.00	35 / 35.00	87 / 87.00
TOTAL				100 / 100.00

STATISTIC	DF	VALUE	PROB
LIKELIHOOD RATIO CHI-SQUARE	2	14.796	0.001
CONTINGENCY COEFFICIENT		0.330	
CRAMER'S V		0.350	

MANAGEMENT EXPRESSES ITS BELIEF THAT THE FINDING OF THE AUDITORS REPRESENTS AN ISOLATED INCIDENT

FREQUENCY PERCENT	<$1 M	>$1 M <$100 M	>$100 M <$10 B	TOTAL
NO COMMENTS	10 / 10.00	55 / 55.00	26 / 26.00	91 / 91.00
COMMENTS	0 / 0.00	0 / 0.00	9 / 9.00	9 / 9.00
TOTAL				100 / 100.00

STATISTIC	DF	VALUE	PROB
LIKELIHOOD RATIO CHI-SQUARE	2	20.604	0.000
CONTINGENCY COEFFICIENT		0.394	
CRAMER'S V		0.429	

Exhibit 16–13 (continued)

MANAGEMENT EXPRESSES SEMI-ACCEPTANCE OF COMMENTS

FREQUENCY PERCENT	< $1 M	> $1 M < $100 M	> $100 M < $10 B	TOTAL
NO COMMENTS	10 / 10.00	51 / 51.00	24 / 24.00	85 / 85.00
COMMENTS	0 / 0.00	4 / 4.00	11 / 11.00	15 / 15.00
TOTAL				100 / 100.00

STATISTIC	DF	VALUE	PROB
LIKELIHOOD RATIO CHI-SQUARE	2	12.298	0.002
CONTINGENCY COEFFICIENT		0.324	
CRAMER'S V		0.343	

MANAGEMENT STATES:
(1) CONTROL EXISTS,
(2) COST-BENEFIT ISSUES ARE INVOLVED,
(3) REASONS EXIST FOR WHY THE MANAGEMENT LETTER POINT HAS NOT YET BEEN IMPLEMENTED,
(4) THAT A QUESTION EXISTS AS TO MATERIALITY OR BENEFITS,
(5) ADDITIONAL INFORMATION IS NEEDED,
(6) FEASIBILITY OF IMPLEMENTATION IS QUESTIONABLE,
(7) WHAT APPEARS TO BE AN EXPLICIT REJECTION OF THE MANAGEMENT LETTER POINT.

FREQUENCY PERCENT	< $1 M	> $1 M < $100 M	> $100 M < $10 B	TOTAL
NO COMMENTS	8 / 8.00	26 / 26.00	3 / 3.00	37 / 37.00
COMMENTS	2 / 2.00	29 / 29.00	32 / 32.00	63 / 63.00
TOTAL				100 / 100.00

STATISTIC	DF	VALUE	PROB
LIKELIHOOD RATIO CHI-SQUARE	2	25.225	0.000
CONTINGENCY COEFFICIENT		0.429	
CRAMER'S V		0.475	

MANAGEMENT STATES THAT ADEQUATE INTERNAL CONTROL EXISTS WITHOUT THIS CONTROL

FREQUENCY PERCENT	< $1 M	> $1 M < $100 M	> $100 M < $10 B	TOTAL
NO COMMENTS	10 / 10.00	53 / 53.00	21 / 21.00	84 / 84.00
COMMENTS	0 / 0.00	2 / 2.00	14 / 14.00	16 / 16.00
TOTAL				100 / 100.00

STATISTIC	DF	VALUE	PROB
LIKELIHOOD RATIO CHI-SQUARE	2	23.640	0.000
CONTINGENCY COEFFICIENT		0.434	
CRAMER'S V		0.481	

Exhibit 16–14

Other Management Reactions: The Association of Management Points with Client Size

AUDITOR OR MANAGEMENT CITED MANAGEMENT ACTIONS TO DATE, OR AUDITOR STATED THAT MANAGEMENT ALREADY RECOGNIZED PROBLEM

FREQUENCY PERCENT	<$1 M	>$1 M <$100 M	>$100 M <$10 B	TOTAL
NO COMMENTS	8 8.00	17 17.00	1 1.00	26 26.00
COMMENTS	2 2.00	38 38.00	34 34.00	74 74.00
TOTAL				100 100.00

STATISTIC	DF	VALUE	PROB
LIKELIHOOD RATIO CHI-SQUARE	2	27.501	0.000
CONTINGENCY COEFFICIENT		0.451	
CRAMER'S V		0.506	

MANAGEMENT CITES MANY KNOWN WEAKNESSES

FREQUENCY PERCENT	<$1 M	>$1 M <$100 M	>$100 M <$10 B	TOTAL
NO COMMENTS	10 10.00	55 55.00	34 34.00	99 99.00
COMMENTS	0 0.00	0 0.00	1 1.00	1 1.00
TOTAL				100 100.00

STATISTIC	DF	VALUE	PROB
LIKELIHOOD RATIO CHI-SQUARE	2	2.118	0.347
CONTINGENCY COEFFICIENT		0.136	
CRAMER'S V		0.137	

MANAGEMENT SAID IT WOULD INVESTIGATE OR WOULD TRY HARDER

FREQUENCY PERCENT	<$1 M	>$1 M <$100 M	>$100 M <$10 B	TOTAL
NO COMMENTS	9 9.00	52 52.00	19 19.00	80 80.00
COMMENTS	1 1.00	3 3.00	16 16.00	20 20.00
TOTAL				100 100.00

STATISTIC	DF	VALUE	PROB
LIKELIHOOD RATIO CHI-SQUARE	2	22.030	0.000
CONTINGENCY COEFFICIENT		0.427	
CRAMER'S V		0.473	

MANAGEMENT GIVES NO FORMAL RESPONSE REGARDING THE SUGGESTION OF THE AUDITOR

FREQUENCY PERCENT	<$1 M	>$1 M <$100 M	>$100 M <$10 B	TOTAL
NO COMMENTS	4 4.00	9 9.00	16 16.00	29 29.00
COMMENTS	6 6.00	46 46.00	19 19.00	71 71.00
TOTAL				100 100.00

STATISTIC	DF	VALUE	PROB
LIKELIHOOD RATIO CHI-SQUARE	2	9.686	0.008
CONTINGENCY COEFFICIENT		0.296	
CRAMER'S V		0.310	

Exhibit 16–14 (continued)

MANAGEMENT SAID IT WOULD KEEP THE SUGGESTIONS IN MIND

FREQUENCY PERCENT	< $1 M	> $1 M < $100 M	> $100 M < $10 B	TOTAL
NO COMMENTS	10 10.00	52 52.00	27 27.00	89 89.00
COMMENTS	0 0.00	3 3.00	8 8.00	11 11.00
TOTAL				100 100.00

STATISTIC	DF	VALUE	PROB
LIKELIHOOD RATIO CHI-SQUARE	2	8.389	0.015
CONTINGENCY COEFFICIENT		0.272	
CRAMER'S V		0.283	

TWO TO THREE YEAR TIME FRAME IS REQUIRED FOR COMPLIANCE

FREQUENCY PERCENT	< $1 M	> $1 M < $100 M	> $100 M < $10 B	TOTAL
NO COMMENTS	8 8.00	46 46.00	16 16.00	70 70.00
COMMENTS	2 2.00	9 9.00	19 19.00	30 30.00
TOTAL				100 100.00

STATISTIC	DF	VALUE	PROB
LIKELIHOOD RATIO CHI-SQUARE	2	14.880	0.001
CONTINGENCY COEFFICIENT		0.363	
CRAMER'S V		0.390	

Exhibit 16–15

Auditor's Comments: The Association of Management Letter Points with Client Size

AN ECONOMIC ORDER QUANTITY APPROACH IS SUGGESTED

FREQUENCY PERCENT	< $1 M	> $1 M < $100 M	> $100 M < $10 B	TOTAL
NO COMMENTS	9 9.00	53 53.00	28 28.00	90 90.00
COMMENTS	1 1.00	2 2.00	7 7.00	10 10.00
TOTAL				100 100.00

STATISTIC	DF	VALUE	PROB
LIKELIHOOD RATIO CHI-SQUARE	2	6.304	0.043
CONTINGENCY COEFFICIENT		0.245	
CRAMER'S V		0.252	

AN EFFICIENCY POINT IS RAISED

FREQUENCY PERCENT	< $1 M	> $1 M < $100 M	> $100 M < $10 B	TOTAL
NO COMMENTS	6 6.00	11 11.00	0 0.00	17 17.00
COMMENTS	4 4.00	44 44.00	35 35.00	83 83.00
TOTAL				100 100.00

STATISTIC	DF	VALUE	PROB
LIKELIHOOD RATIO CHI-SQUARE	2	22.673	0.000
CONTINGENCY COEFFICIENT		0.413	
CRAMER'S V		0.454	

AUDIT EVIDENCE IS CITED IN THE SUGGESTION AND, POSSIBLY STATISTICAL EVIDENCE

FREQUENCY PERCENT	< $1 M	> $1 M < $100 M	> $100 M < $10 B	TOTAL
NO COMMENTS	4 4.00	8 8.00	0 0.00	12 12.00
COMMENTS	6 6.00	47 47.00	35 35.00	88 88.00
TOTAL				100 100.00

STATISTIC	DF	VALUE	PROB
LIKELIHOOD RATIO CHI-SQUARE	2	14.303	0.001
CONTINGENCY COEFFICIENT		0.334	
CRAMER'S V		0.354	

BENEFITS ARE DESCRIBED, DETAILS AS TO ADVANTAGES AND DISADVANTAGES ARE PROVIDED, SPECIFIC SUGGESTIONS ARE MADE, OR USEFULNESS TO FUTURE AUDITS IS CITED

FREQUENCY PERCENT	< $1 M	> $1 M < $100 M	> $100 M < $10 B	TOTAL
NO COMMENTS	4 4.00	8 8.00	0 0.00	12 12.00
COMMENTS	6 6.00	47 47.00	35 35.00	88 88.00
TOTAL				100 100.00

STATISTIC	DF	VALUE	PROB
LIKELIHOOD RATIO CHI-SQUARE	2	14.303	0.001
CONTINGENCY COEFFICIENT		0.334	
CRAMER'S V		0.354	

Exhibit 16–15 (continued)

COMMENTS ARE FUTURE DIRECTED

FREQUENCY PERCENT	< $1 M	> $1 M < $100 M	> $100 M < $10 B	TOTAL
NO COMMENTS	10 10.00	27 27.00	3 3.00	40 40.00
COMMENTS	0 0.00	28 28.00	32 32.00	60 60.00
TOTAL				100 100.00

STATISTIC	DF	VALUE	PROB
LIKELIHOOD RATIO CHI-SQUARE	2	37.899	0.000
CONTINGENCY COEFFICIENT		0.488	
CRAMER'S V		0.559	

THE FOREIGN CORRUPT PRACTICES ACT IS MENTIONED IN REMARKS BY THE CPA

FREQUENCY PERCENT	< $1 M	> $1 M < $100 M	> $100 M < $10 B	TOTAL
NO COMMENTS	10 10.00	52 52.00	27 27.00	89 89.00
COMMENTS	0 0.00	3 3.00	8 8.00	11 11.00
TOTAL				100 100.00

STATISTIC	DF	VALUE	PROB
LIKELIHOOD RATIO CHI-SQUARE	2	8.389	0.015
CONTINGENCY COEFFICIENT		0.272	
CRAMER'S V		0.283	

INTERNAL AUDIT IS MENTIONED

FREQUENCY PERCENT	< $1 M	> $1 M < $100 M	> $100 M < $10 B	TOTAL
NO COMMENTS	10 10.00	38 38.00	0 0.00	48 48.00
COMMENTS	0 0.00	17 17.00	35 35.00	52 52.00
TOTAL				100 100.00

STATISTIC	DF	VALUE	PROB
LIKELIHOOD RATIO CHI-SQUARE	2	70.449	0.000
CONTINGENCY COEFFICIENT		0.588	
CRAMER'S V		0.728	

THE INTERNAL CONTROL POINT IS REPEATED

FREQUENCY PERCENT	< $1 M	> $1 M < $100 M	> $100 M < $10 B	TOTAL
NO COMMENTS	6 6.00	16 16.00	10 10.00	32 32.00
COMMENTS	4 4.00	39 39.00	25 25.00	68 68.00
TOTAL				100 100.00

STATISTIC	DF	VALUE	PROB
LIKELIHOOD RATIO CHI-SQUARE	2	3.709	0.157
CONTINGENCY COEFFICIENT		0.196	
CRAMER'S V		0.200	

POSSIBLE PROVISION OF MANAGEMENT ADVISORY SERVICES IS DISCUSSED

FREQUENCY PERCENT	< $1 M	> $1 M < $100 M	> $100 M < $10 B	TOTAL
NO COMMENTS	10 10.00	50 50.00	32 32.00	92 92.00
COMMENTS	0 0.00	5 5.00	3 3.00	8 8.00
TOTAL				100 100.00

STATISTIC	DF	VALUE	PROB
LIKELIHOOD RATIO CHI-SQUARE	2	1.768	0.413
CONTINGENCY COEFFICIENT		0.098	
CRAMER'S V		0.099	

PREVENTIVE SUGGESTIONS ARE PROVIDED

FREQUENCY PERCENT	< $1 M	> $1 M < $100 M	> $100 M < $10 B	TOTAL
NO COMMENTS	4 4.00	9 9.00	0 0.00	13 13.00
COMMENTS	6 6.00	46 46.00	35 35.00	87 87.00
TOTAL				100 100.00

STATISTIC	DF	VALUE	PROB
LIKELIHOOD RATIO CHI-SQUARE	2	14.796	0.001
CONTINGENCY COEFFICIENT		0.330	
CRAMER'S V		0.350	

Size Differences: The Nature of Problems Cited

The nature of the problems described in management letters can be categorized into the fifteen groups described in Exhibit 16–12. The nature of each problem should be self-explanatory, with the possible exception of the twelfth group: "negative confirmation and exception policy practices." Eight companies had policies that were applied on an exception basis or tested receivable balances periodically using negative confirmations; it was recommended that such policies be applied more uniformly and that positive confirmations be used for periodic testing. Exhibit 16–12 reports the association of management letter points with client size as defined by total revenues, utilizing simple three-way chi-square analysis (comparing entities with revenue less than one million, to those with revenue between one and 100 million and those from 100 million to 10 billion). The significance of the chi-square relationship is reported, alongside both the contingency coefficient and the Cramer's V statistic. These latter two statistics indicate the strength of predicting whether or not a particular type of comment was made, based on knowledge of the size of an entity. The data set relates to 100 entities' comments over a five-year period.

Some key patterns are apparent from a careful examination of Exhibit 16–12. The most common problem encountered by the greatest number of entities was the category of "documentation safeguards, clarification, and completeness" (88 companies). Other common problems are accuracy errors and misstatements and approval problems (cited for 86 companies). Larger entities dominate most of the categories reflected in Exhibit 16–12, even on a percentage basis. For example, only a quarter of smaller firms have account classification comments (two out of eight), while 91% of very large entities had such comments (32 out of 35). The exceptions to this general pattern are arm's length concerns and the request of a systems review, which have no tie-in to size (based on a chi-square analysis at a 0.05 level of significance). In part, this atypical result is tied to the rarity of these types of problems.

No empirical evidence is provided to support the common assertion in the literature that segregation issues are more prevalent in smaller firms. Of course, the nature of the data set raises the question of whether cost-benefit concerns of auditors lead to selective reporting in management letters. Nonetheless, the existence of segregation issues at all but one entity in the $100 million to $10 billion category clearly suggests that the concern permeates control systems at the largest of entities.

Of interest is the small incidence of inventory adjustment concerns at small entities. This may be due to the commonality of CPAs' assistance with inventory adjustments, as a client service to smaller companies.

Severity of problems

While the nature of problems is of obvious interest, of even greater concern is whether the problems cited are severe. As Exhibit 16–13 describes, many of the larger entities' comments were cited as being of questionable materiality or of questionable importance due to existing controls or cost-benefit issues. In nine of the largest entities, managers stated that they believed the auditor's comment related to an isolated incident. Despite such comments, of particular interest is the explicit acceptance of at least one management letter point by the management of 80% of the largest companies (28 out of 35). The implication is that a management letter seems to be made up of primarily immaterial suggestions, some of which are accepted. Yet, of interest, is the common comment that the control point represents the absence of a basic control and, in fact, relates to the control environment. The prevalence of this latter point helps explain why the auditing Standards Board of the American Institute of CPAs has recently directed its attention toward clarifying the role of the control environment in the audit process. The larger entities' comments on the severity of error are far more frequent than small entities' comments, in percentage terms.

Other Management Reactions

More insight as to management's explicit responses to management letter points is provided in Exhibit 16–14. In particular, substantial evidence exists that many companies had already recognized the problems highlighted in the management letter. This may, in part, explain why a number of companies provide no formal response to the auditor. It needs to be emphasized, of course, that not all auditors provide an opportunity for management response. When responses are provided, they tend to be encouraging as to management's plans to investigate the problem, keep suggestions in mind, or implement change over a two- to three-year time frame. In a sense, the latter comment could be viewed as a slightly defensive move to counteract reemphasis of control problems in subsequent management letters. Of interest is the one large company who issued a statement that "many known weaknesses existed." As with comments on the severity of problems, comments on management's reactions are predominantly made by larger companies, on a percentage basis.

Auditor's Comments

Management's reactions may very well depend on the approach that an auditor takes to explaining or justifying a management letter point. For example, as depicted in Exhibit 16–15, the provision of audit evidence and a description of benefits are emphasized, particularly in larger entities' management letters. The preventive nature of the suggestion is also typically explained, and the efficiency aspects of implementing the control point are emphasized. When the comments primarily relate to future concerns, that point is often highlighted.

Obviously, another incentive for adopting a management letter point is the existence of the Foreign Corrupt Practices Act (FCPA). Of interest is the fact that only 11 entities were reminded of this fact by the auditor.

A clear means of emphasizing the importance of a comment is to bring attention to the fact that the problem was cited in a prior management letter. This technique is used by CPAs at all entities; there is no size effect observable. Some of these comments may relate to problems which require a two- to three-year time frame for compliance, as cited in Exhibit 16–14.

An interesting question which is addressed in Exhibit 16–15 relates to CPAs' propensity to cite the availability of management advisory services (MAS) to address various control problems. Only five entities received such comments. Since the CPA firms issuing these management letter points all have large MAS departments, this may well reflect the firms' concerns over "mixing" the marketing of MAS with the provision of a by-product of audit services. Indeed, with the independence issues repeatedly raised by the SEC, this is likely to be a prudent practice of the profession. Of course, the Public Oversight Board's findings may well suggest that such hesitancy to market MAS could lead to efficiency losses by clients.

Two of the items in Exhibit 16–15 tie into auxiliary research questions of interest when reviewing a unique data set such as management letters. Specifically, past literature has cited some resentment of external auditors by internal auditors for not giving due credit to internal auditing for identifying key management letter points. The empirical question raised is whether internal audit is given credit for identifying problems and helping to formulate potential solutions. Indeed, internal auditing is explicitly recognized by all large entities, as reflected in Exhibit 16–15.

The other question of interest relates to whether the economic order quantity (EOQ) is relevant in approaching control problems or obsolete, as some have contended. Given that 10% of the companies represented in the data base received suggestions related to the usefulness of an EOQ analysis, some evidence is provided that this basic model still had relevance as of 1979. This point implies the propriety of directing some attention to EOQ analysis in the basic training of business entities' personnel.

Industry Effects

Management letter points vary both by size and by industry. However, industry differences are far fewer than are size differences. Those internal control points related to "nature of the problem" which differ across industries at a 0.05 level are reported in Exhibit 16–16. The industry groupings used are indicated by standard industry classification (SIC) ranges. The first group includes manufacturing, mining, oil, and contractors. The second group represents transportation, communications and utilities. The third group includes retail, wholesale, and hotels. The fourth group represents banking, credit, insurance, and real estate, while the fifth grouping includes health, educational, membership groups, government, and nonclassifiable codes. All of the transportation, retail, and health groups are reported to face approval and documentation problems. Over three-fourths of the remaining industries have such problems. As expected, the manufacturing group receives the greatest percentage of comments on inventory adjustments, with the retailing group in a close second position. Obviously, the banking group faces virtually no inventory-related problems. All of the retail entities have segregation problems, followed in percentage terms by transpor-

Exhibit 16–16

Problems That Significantly Differ Across Industry Classifications

		SIC ≥ 1000 and ≤ 3999	SIC ≥ 4000 and ≤ 4999	SIC ≥ 5000 and ≤ 5999, or ≥ 7000 and ≤ 7099	SIC ≥ 6000 and ≤ 6799	SIC ≥ 8000 and ≤ 9999	Total Sample	Likelihood Ratio Chi Square (Probability) Contingency Coefficient [Cramer's V]
Approval Problems; Authorization	Comments							
	Frequency	42	11	13	10	9	85	12.511
	(Percentage)	(79.25)	(100)	(100)	(76.92)	(100)	(85.86)	(.014)
	No Comments							
	Frequency	11	—	—	3	—	14	.277
	(Percentage)	(20.75)	—	—	(23.08)	—	(14.14)	[.288]
Documentation Safeguards, Clarification, and Completeness	Comments							
	Frequency	44.00	11	13	10	9	87	10.790
	(Percentage)	(83.02)	(100)	(100)	(76.92)	(100)	(87.88)	(.029)
	No Comments							
	Frequency	9	—	—	3	—	12	.26
	(Percentage)	(16.98)	—	—	(23.08)	—	(12.12)	[.27]
Inventory Adjustments	Comments							
	Frequency	37	3	7	1	3	51	22.888
	(Percentage)	(69.81)	(27.27)	(53.85)	(7.69)	(33.33)	(51.52)	(.000)
	No Comments							
	Frequency	16	8	6	12	6	48	.418
	(Percentage)	(30.19)	(72.73)	(46.15)	(92.31)	(66.67)	(48.48)	[.460]
Segregation Issues	Comments							
	Frequency	42	10	13	10	5	80	9.575
	(Percentage)	(79.25)	(90.91)	(100)	(76.92)	(55.56)	(80.81)	(.048)
	No Comments							
	Frequency	11	1	—	3	4	19	.269
	(Percentage)	(20.75)	(9.09)	—	(15.79)	(44.44)	(19.19)	[.279]
Tax-Related Considerations	Comments							
	Frequency	36	6	6	5	2	55	9.549
	(Percentage)	(67.92)	(54.55)	(46.15)	(38.46)	(22.22)	(55.56)	(.049)
	No Comments							
	Frequency	17	5	7	8	7	44	.294
	(Percentage)	(32.08)	(45.45)	(53.85)	(61.54)	(15.91)	(44.44)	[.307]

783

tation, manufacturing, and banking, respectively. Tax considerations are most prevalent for manufacturing concerns and least likely for entities in the health category. Since some nonprofit and governmental entities are in the latter group, this result is apparent.

Exhibit 16–17 reports those internal control points for which management reactions were provided or on which auditors made comments that significantly differ across industries at a 0.05 level. All entities in the transportation, retailing, and health groups have management letter points supported by audit evidence and described with an emphasis on advantages and the preventive nature of suggestions offered. Management gives no formal response regarding auditors' suggestions for the retail and health groups. Audit evidence is less likely to be cited in support of management letter points for manufacturing or banking. Similarly, benefits are less likely to be cited and the notion of preventive suggestions is less likely to be highlighted. A full half of the manufacturing group had managers providing no formal response to auditors' comments. While the FCPA was not cited for many entities, when it was mentioned, the industry was manufacturing or retailing.

None of the other management letter points reflected in Exhibit 16–12 through 16–15 experienced differences across industries.

Tendencies of auditors to describe support for control points and benefits, as well as to provide preventive suggestions or reminders as to the role of the FCPA vary across industries. In addition, management's propensity to give no formal response regarding auditors' suggestions fluctuates across industry groupings. The most surprising results are the greater number of control points for larger entities relative to smaller or medium-sized auditees, and the applicability of segregation-related issues to the largest of organizations.

It may well be that the nature of the management letter service and perceptions by auditors who draft such letters leads to an emphasis on control suggestions for the larger auditees. Not only may the service be viewed as particularly important in larger engagements, but it may be that cost-benefit considerations lead to far fewer comments being drafted for smaller clients. Nonetheless, it is interesting to track the discernible pattern in disclosures by auditors via the management letter.[79] These research findings provide a context whereby those evaluating control issues in various organizations will have some ideas to concerns of others who have examined entities of similar size or comparable industry mix.

An interesting aspect of past management letters is the incidence of repetitive comments from year to year. It would seem important in such communications, regardless of the industry, size of client, or public status to share the history of reportable conditions in terms of when they were first mentioned, management's reactions, and possible effects of subsequent events.

A profile of research evidence of repeated findings, patterns over time, and the incidence of receiving comments is provided in Exhibit 16–18.

---

[79] This discussion is based on a research project funded by a grant from the Peat, Marwick Foundation through its Research Opportunities in Auditing Program. The views expressed herein are those of the author and not necessarily those of the Peat, Marwick Foundation.

Exhibit 16–17

Auditor's Comments and Management Reactions That Significantly Differ Across Industry Classifications

	SIC ≥ 1000 and ≤ 3999	SIC ≥ 4000 and ≤ 4999	SIC ≥ 5000 and ≤ 5999, or 7000 and ≤ 7099	SIC ≥ 6000 and ≤ 6799	SIC ≥ 8000 and ≤ 9999	Total Sample	Likelihood Ratio Chi Square (Probability) Contingency Coefficient [Cramer's V]
Audit Evidence Is Cited In The Suggestion And, Possibly, Statistical Evidence							
Comments Frequency	44	11	13	10	9	87	10.790
(Percentage)	(83.02)	(100)	(100)	(76.92)	(100)	(87.88)	(.029)
No Comments Frequency	9	—	—	3	—	12	.260
(Percentage)	(16.98)	—	—	(23.08)	—	(12.12)	[.270]
Benefits Are Described, Details As To Advantages And Disadvantages Are Provided, Specific Suggestions Are Made, Or Usefulness In Future Audits Is Cited							
Comments Frequency	44	11	13	10	9	87	10.790
(Percentage)	(83.02)	(100)	(100)	(76.92)	(100)	(87.88)	(.029)
No Comments Frequency	9	—	—	3	—	12	.260
(Percentage)	(16.98)	—	—	(23.08)	—	(12.12)	[.270]
The Foreign Corrupt Practices Act Is Mentioned In The CPA's Remarks							
Comments Frequency	9	—	2	—	—	11	9.614
(Percentage)	(16.98)	—	(15.38)	—	—	(11.11)	(.047)
No Comments Frequency	44	11	11	13	9	88	.243
(Percentage)	(83.02)	(100)	(84.62)	(100)	(100)	(88.89)	[.251]
Preventive Suggestions Are Provided							
Comments Frequency	43	11	13	10	9	86	11.616
(Percentage)	(81.13)	(100)	(100)	(76.92)	(100)	(86.87)	(.020)
No Comments Frequency	10	—	—	3	—	13	.268
(Percentage)	(18.87)	—	—	(23.08)	—	(13.13)	[.278]
Management Gives No Formal Response Regarding Auditors' Suggestions							
Comments Frequency	30	8	13	10	9	70	20.259
(Percentage)	(56.60)	(72.73)	(100)	(76.92)	(100)	(70.71)	(0)
No Comments Frequency	23	3	—	3	—	29	.357
(Percentage)	(43.49)	(27.27)	—	(23.08)	—	(29.29)	[.382]

Exhibit 16–18

Patterns in Recurring Comments

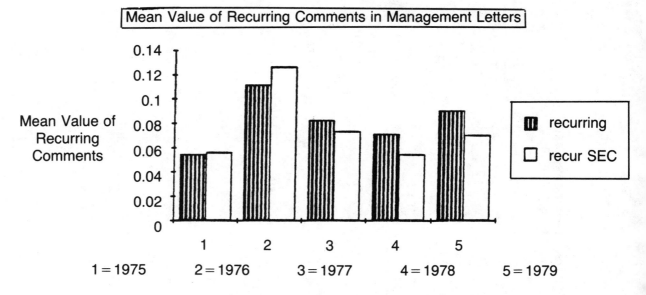

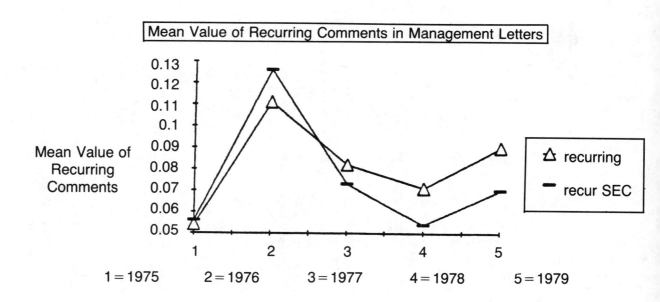

Exhibit 16–18 (continued)

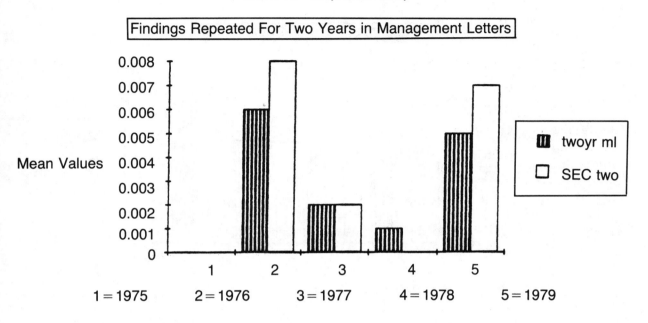

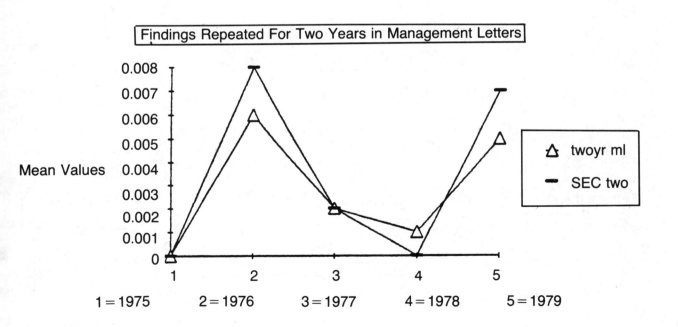

Exhibit 16–18 (continued)

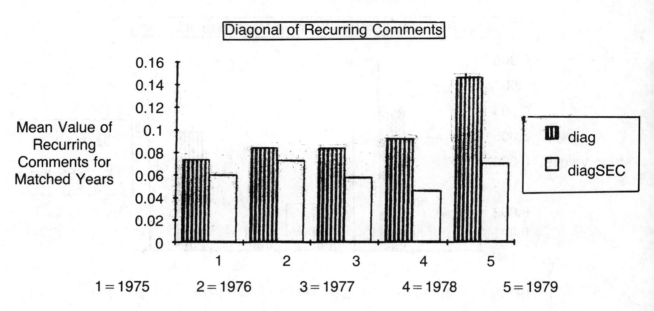

Diagonal of Recurring Comments

Mean Value of Recurring Comments for Matched Years

1 = 1975   2 = 1976   3 = 1977   4 = 1978   5 = 1979

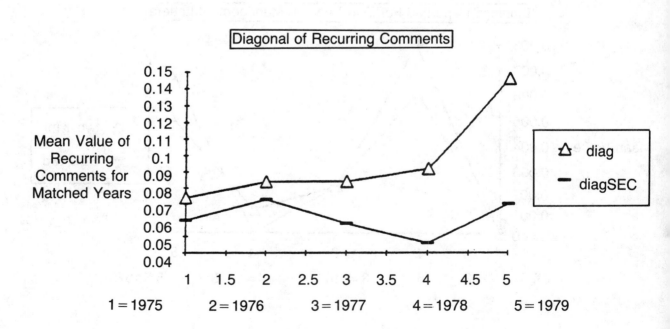

Diagonal of Recurring Comments

Mean Value of Recurring Comments for Matched Years

1 = 1975   2 = 1976   3 = 1977   4 = 1978   5 = 1979

PROFESSIONAL SERVICES

While we could discuss controls in a variety of professional service settings, public accounting firms would seem a particularly appropriate example on which to focus. Peer review activities within the profession have provided an excellent database to consider controls, possible problems, and potential opportunities for improvement. Exhibit 16–19 reprints an article directed to this exact purpose. The inferences drawn have analogies for a broad cross-section of professional service firms. Note also the Appendix, Part I that details internal audit job descriptions.

Exhibit 16–19
Learning from Peer Review Comments

By Wanda A. Wallace and James J. Wallace

Firms enrolled in the AICPA's Quality Review program are concerned about what that first review will turn up. What kind of things is a reviewer likely to find and comment on?

Because the program is new and the results of reviews are confidential, a firm may believe that there is no place to turn to learn of the experience of others. Fortunately, there is a place to look. The practice monitoring system of the AICPA Division for Firms, i.e., Peer Review, has been functioning for about 10 years. The results of these reviews are available to the public.

A major source of information is the letter of comment (LOC) that often accompanies the report on a reviewed firm's quality control system. A LOC is required to be issued when there are matters that resulted in a modification of the standard form of report on the control system or if there are matters that the review team believes indicate there is more than a remote possibility that the firm would not conform with professional standards on accounting and auditing engagements.

In simple terms, the LOC is the means for reporting significant deficiencies in the system of quality control.

A DETAILED LOOK

Substantial literature is available describing, in general, the nature of peer review findings, case examples of the benefits of peer review and its historical development, and the interaction between the profession and regulators. Differences exist in the way commentators have categorized and interpreted these findings. Some, for example, make no distinction between a lack of documentation of supervision and a lack of documentation of whether an audit step has been completed. Given the legal role of working papers, there seem to be benefits obtained by distinguishing such matters, beyond merely expressing a concern for documentation *per se*.

This article avoids generalizations by presenting sufficient detail in describing the nature and implications of letters of comment (LOC) so as to facilitate action. Specificity has led to presenting clear directives for improving quality control. The directives have been formulated from a study of the AICPA public peer review files from 1980 through the first quarter of 1986. All the LOCs on file accompanying peer review reports of SECPS members have been read

and coded as to the subject matter of findings.

ACCEPTANCE AND CONTINUANCE OF CLIENTS

More than a quarter of the LOCs contained a finding related to relationship with clients. The most prevalent problem, reflected in 20% of the filings, was associated with client acceptance and retention policies. Often, no formal documentation was available concerning acceptance and retention decisions and when available, it often was not applicable to smaller engagements requiring fewer than 300 hours. The directives from such findings include:

- The firm's quality control document should specify acceptance and continuation criteria (e.g., consideration of the clients' financial history and inquiries of bankers and attorneys), decision processes, and modes of documentation, including required approval of client acceptance;
- The documentation should be completed for all clients, regardless of size; and
- Self-monitoring of compliance with the quality control document should be exercised, particularly, as to modes of documentation.

Exhibit 16–19 (continued)

Once the decision is made to accept or retain a client, the next step is expected to be an engagement letter. However, its absence was a finding in over 5% of the LOCs. Frequently given reasons were that an engagement letter was not required after the initial engagement or was not required on all clients. Yet, misunderstandings as to the extent of services to be performed can arise in subsequent periods, and clarification of the nature of the service provided may well be of greatest importance for smaller engagements.

. . . source of information is the Letter of Comment . . . that often accompanies the report on a reviewed firm's quality control system.

One firm had a set policy of not having an engagement letter for compilation and review engagements of fewer than 40 hours. Such a policy is hard to understand given the rather nominal time required to tailor an engagement letter to a particular client. Moreover, such limited scope engagements can be the source of confusion, as detailed in past litigation and the horror stories of numerous practitioners and clients. Research suggests that many small clients refer to their CPAs as providing audits, when in fact only review services or compilations are provided. It seems to be in everyone's interest to clarify the nature of each professional arrangement.

Unfortunately, some firms obtain engagement letters, but they are incomplete. The purpose of quality control is not only to establish documentation of the process, but also to avoid errors and omissions. The second set of directives inferred from the LOCs are:
- Establish a firm practice of obtaining engagement letters for all client services, no matter how limited the scope; and

- Be certain such engagement letters are tailored to the specific engagement and do not omit critical details as to the nature of the service commitments, as well as responsibilities undertaken and not undertaken.

LETTERS OF REPRESENTATION

Just as clarity is essential in engagement letters, it is imperative under GAAS to obtain a letter of representation from clients. Yet, findings tied to the absence or limitations of representation letters appeared in almost 8% of the LOCs. Limitations include key omissions in the representation letters, such as no representation as to subsequent events and no signature by the client! Other limitations related to the dating of the letters of representation. Some letters omitted dates, were dated after the engagement, or were dated too early relative to the completion of the CPA's work. The use of a boilerplate form for representation letters at times led to insufficient tailoring of the representations to the engagement. The directives include:
- Require that a complete representation letter be obtained, with both date and signature commensurate with the engagement requirements;
- Establish a review procedure to ensure inclusion in files of a complete and timely representation letter; and
- Take care in training to attune professional staff to the need to tailor boilerplate representation letters to peculiarities of each engagement.

INTERNAL CONTROL COMMUNICATIONS

A common practice of CPAs is to communicate verbally and/or in writing the nature of internal control problems and opportunities for improvements available to clients. However, in 4% of the LOCs, concern was expressed as to the lack of such

communication to clients on internal control matters or problems associated with such potential or actual communications. This was seen by peer reviews as particularly troublesome when material weaknesses had been identified in the working papers. The decisions to verbally communicate were neither documented nor followed through to ensure the client was appropriately informed. These concerns lead to questions concerning compliance with GAAS. Even when decisions were made to communicate in writing, a review of such letters uncovered short-comings in the nature of the communications.

Although recent SASs have altered the form of presentation of communications with clients and others, the lessons of past LOCs direct that firms:
- Clearly document their intentions as to verbal or written communications with clients on internal control matters.
- Assign responsibility to follow through on either decision and carefully document the process upon completion of the communication to avoid any omissions.
- When management letters are issued, establish a review process to evaluate them for completeness, propriety, and clearness before sending the communication to clients; and
- Now that reportable conditions have evolved in tandem with the more traditional concept of material weakness, the nature of communication with clients will require more careful scrutiny to ensure adequate compliance with professional standards.

INDEPENDENCE ISSUES

Presumably, before an engagement of an attest nature begins, the independent status of the firm and engagement team should be effectively evaluated. However, in over 15% of the LOCs, problems arose in this regard. Most often, there was an

Exhibit 16–19 (continued)

absence of a routine confirmation of independence by staff, or an absence of assurance that another firm helping on an engagement was independent. However, there were occasions in which it was found that a partner lacked independence or that the appearance of independence was present due to firm members and family members being on boards of not-for-profit clients. The LOCs suggest a need to:

- Assure periodic use and completion of confirmation procedures concerning independence to ensure their adequacy; and
- Integrate independence guidelines into the training and inspection process to avoid impairment.

SUPERVISION OF AUDIT PERFORMANCE

Planning the Audit

Many of the files contained findings on this topic. Specifically, an absence of a detailed plan of who would be on a job, whether that staff assignment was approved, and whether consideration had been given to issues of "agreed-upon procedures," surprise visits, and staffing requirements characterized the findings. Although budgeting is not generally a quality issue, there were budgeting questions that entailed whether the budget was reasonable, why comparisons of budget to actual had not been made, and why explanations of discrepancies were not in the working papers.

The directive of such findings is:
- Ensure that the planning process includes staff assignment, resource, timing, and budget considerations, as well as commitments for added "agreed-upon procedures."

Work Programs

Approximately 13% of the LOCs expressed problems with either not having a program for an audit or a review engagement, or not approxi-

mately tailoring that program to the engagement. As a result, there could be omissions of key steps. These findings also pointed out that some steps of the audit or review process were not appropriately signed off, which in the absence of adequate working paper documentation to the contrary imply a lack of assurance that such steps were ever performed. Furthermore, instances in which review points had not been cleared left questions as to whether such work had been completed but merely left undocumented.

Supervision of Field Work

Five percent of the LOCs contained findings related to the actual supervision of work, both of the audit process and of work by internal audit. By and large, the concern was that the quality control document either did not deal with supervision or gave too much discretion to engagement auditors or team leaders, some of whom were not partners. Due to inadequate documentation in the workpapers, it was at times difficult to infer the extent of the engagement partners' involvement in the supervision of the planning process, as well as field work. The directives from such findings include:
- In addition to documenting work performed on an engagement, be certain to document how that work was supervised, at each stage of the process and by whom; and
- Such attention is needed both for the audit process and for work done under the supervision of the audit team by internal auditors.

Internal Control

A most pervasive finding in content (about 12% of the LOCs on file) related to internal control assessments. Specifically, some engagements did not document why the professional staff judged that internal control could not be relied upon to some extent or, where internal control could be relied upon but was not,

decided to use an all substantive approach for efficiency reasons. Many failed to tie the tests of control to the subsequent substantive test work. Instances of testing controls without any apparent reliance were noted. Additional problems seemed to arise when EDP processing of transactions was present, particularly outside EDP service bureaus or organizations. About 8% of filings referred to an EDP-related concern.

A most prevalent problem . . . was associated with client acceptance and retention policies.

Sampling

Almost as troublesome as the internal control area was the application of sampling tools, also cited in about 12% of the LOCs. Problems included an absence of any firm practice on the use of statistical tools and noncompliance with GAAS, particularly the provisions of SAS 39. Errors in designing sampling plans and making inferences were cited.

Analytical Procedures

Another conspicuous area in which substantial problems were noted involved the use of analytical procedures; over seven percent of the LOCs referred to this area. Specifically, such procedures tended to be inadequately documented or not applied to key aspects of the audit.

Review of Work

About 20% of the files contain a finding involving issues related to the absence of review by partners or by an independent party. Another common problem is that sign-offs are not appropriately documented. One finding noted that there was no indication of partner review of prior year workpapers, while another noted that one firm does not review the final draft of a 10-K prior to issue. Public files imply that:

Exhibit 16–19 (continued)

• Care is needed to document the review process in a comprehensive manner, particularly pre-issuance (second or concurring partner) reviews; and

• The initialing and dating of review steps are critical facets of evidencing appropriate review and should not only be emphasized in the quality control documentation and training, but also should be monitored periodically through inspection.

Areas of Risk in Which Audit Steps Were Cited as Inadequate

Beyond key types of procedures, such as those related to controls, sampling, and analytical procedures, numerous findings, ranging from 1% to 4% of the LOCs on file, concerned related parties, subsequent events, and confirmations. Absence of attention to these areas, incomplete procedures, or inadequate documentation of work performed characterized the findings. The specific concerns with respect to related parties were the possibility of inadequate identification of related parties and inadequate documentation relative to related-party transactions.

In addition to these concerns, findings were cited involving: communications with predecessor auditors; documentation of the use of internal auditors; the allocation of income tax in a manner not in accordance with professional standards; the absence of a schedule of unrecorded as well as recorded adjustments for each engagement; inadequate confirmation of investments; timeliness of attorney's letters used in the search for contingencies; an absence of accruals for compensated absences; and a lack of documentation of compliance with quality control procedures associated with long-term debt and pension plan disclosures. Global comments included: "documentation of decisions relating to accounting principles and auditing procedures could be im-

proved;" and the need to "inform firm attorney of significant matters" existed. Among the findings was a constant theme that attention to specific accounting principles was lacking, particularly as they may have related to an industry standard, such as for a not-for-profit entity. In addition, there was concern that communication to the managing partner was not sufficiently comprehensive. The disclosure issues were principally the total lack of use of disclosure checklists. Moreover, financial statement checklists had been signed subsequent to the issuance of the report, suggesting a quality control in form only, rather than in substance.

The directives from the findings relate to two key dimensions:

• Training is needed with respect to the aggregation of evidence from tests of controls and substantive tests, as well as the application of tools of analysis relating to EDP, sampling, and analytical procedures; and

• Care must be taken to establish and monitor controls over complex aspects of the audit and reporting process.

Other Findings on Documentation

As noted earlier many findings relate purely to documentation without giving question as to whether the actual underlying audit step had in fact been performed. These findings appeared in over a third of the files. They ranged from a lack of signatures on the working papers to the use of an outdated disclosure checklist.

As to compilations and reviews, concerns were expressed that the firm failed to document the client industry, accounting system, and other general information as required under SSARS 1. At times, verbal communication of policies and procedures was viewed to be excessive, with inadequate written documentation.

Of particular interest were dis-

crepancies such as the dating of field work, according to work papers on an engagement, after the report date, and the presence of divergent expressions of conclusions in the working papers without any apparent reconciliation being sought.

The directives most apparent are:

• Use up-to-date disclosure checklists;

• Maintain disclosure checklists and specialized decision aids for specific industries; and

• Give attention to detail in the working paper process, particularly telltale signs of inconsistencies in both dating and concluding on workpapers. Proper supervision would determine that attention had been directed to such matters.

Reporting

Over a quarter of the files referred to a reporting finding; indeed, a fifth of the files cited an error in a report's content, five percent cited omissions, and just over one percent noted an apparent error in the dating of the report. The detailed findings imply particular trouble spots to which directives should be aimed.

• The auditor's report should be consistent with GAAS, should clarify the responsibility for supplemental information including summarized financial information, and should be dated to correspond to the end of field work.

• Footnote disclosures need to be comprehensive, in accordance with GAAP, with special attention to:
 —pensions
 —interest costs,
 —construction contractors,
 —inventory costing methods,
 —valuation reserve policies,
 —contingencies,
 —stock repurchases,
 —income taxes,
 —five-year maturities of long-term debt,
 and
 —related-party transactions. The

Exhibit 16–19 (continued)

use of a disclosure checklist is strongly encouraged; and

- Classification of accounts should be reviewed carefully, e.g., long-term and short-term debt status and interest expense as an income item.

The files also suggest instances when the working papers' evidence was inadequate to support the type of report issued or the lack of disclosure of some event, such as noncompliance with a debt covenant.

. . . concern was expressed as to the lack of . . . communication to clients on internal control matters . . .

CONSULTATION, TRAINING AND ADVANCEMENT

About one-fifth of the LOCs contained findings in these categories. Most concerns related to consultation. In particular, training of personnel as to when to consult, who to consult with, how to document the consultation, and the advantage of circulating copies of related memoranda to those consulted was not apparent. The documentation of matters requiring consultations was often inadequate, and consultations that should have resulted may not have been made.

Numerous instances arose in which CPA firms made no background check of new hires and maintained incomplete personnel files. Documentation of employee interviews was similarly incomplete. Inattention to training of firm professionals on quality control matters and inadequate library resources for the maintenance of quality work were among the findings.

The lessons to be learned include:

- Carefully screen and document the hiring process of new employees;

- When training professional staff, introduce quality control procedures and give particular attention to the use of consultants;
- Maintain library resources and consultation lists that are up-to-date and able to meet the needs of the professional staff; and
- Consider staff evaluation as documentation on important tasks.

INSPECTIONS AND OTHER QUALITY CONTROL FINDINGS

A fifth of the LOCs were concerned about the inspection process, a tenth about the quality control document, and another tenth about issues including insurance, management advisory services, partner rotation, and reporting practices. Often no inspection was performed, and, if done, it was deemed inadequate and other than on an annual basis. Documentation related to inspections was challenged, as was the scope of the inspection, particularly when it related purely to engagement reviews. A problem was noted of not formalizing findings from the inspection process to ensure follow-up of problems and effective communication with individuals affected by such potential enhancements in quality control procedures.

The quality control document was cited as inadequate in numerous ways implying a directive as follows:

- A quality control document if required by the size of the practice, should be realistic. It should include annual inspection requirements, with related reporting practices, and be up-to-date; furthermore,
- The document should avoid omitting: procedures for communicating the firm's policies to new staff; independence issues; continuance of client concerns; a requirement for a listing of in-house specialists when consultations are required; and personnel matters.

[Editor's Note: Quality control documents are not a mandatory re-

quirement. However, the larger a firm's practice the more likely a quality control document would be needed to effectively articulate the quality control system.]

An added message is that when a peer review or an inspection is performed, monitoring mechanisms must be in place to ensure responsiveness to the findings and corrective action. On numerous occasions, it was noted that no improvements were apparent, despite findings from an earlier peer review or inspection process. Advancement policies were not well developed in many firms, and an absence of personnel review documents and staff evaluation was frequently problematic.

. . . absence of a detailed plan of who would be on a job, whether that staff assignment was approved, and whether consideration had been given to issues of "agreed-upon procedures," . . .

CPE REQUIREMENTS

About a tenth of the LOCs cited a finding related to CPE requirements, typically including a lack of documentation, the failure to meet reporting requirements, or inadequacies in training. The absence of review of CPE training, use of in-house training, evaluation of in-house training, and tracking CPE on an annual basis were highlighted in specific findings. The directives would include:

- Initiate in-house training programs and carefully document their development, evaluation, and scope; and
- Maintain records as required by all of the groups to whom reporting is required.

Exhibit 16–19 (continued)

Table 1 An Analysis of Letters of Comment	
Most Frequent Findings	*Number of Filings Containing Such a Finding*
• Planning guidelines do not exist or, if they do, documentation is inconsistent with such guidelines	52
• Inappropriate disclosures were provided in the financial statements	41
• The firm's quality control document is not updated or is otherwise inadequate; for example, it does not address compilation and review engagements	27
• Extensive use of checklists and standard forms have made the audit mechanical rather than substantive	25
• Evaluations of professional personnel are not performed per engagement and/or are inadequately documented	24
• Annual inspections are not performed or are not adequately followed up	23
• Independence is not documented for compilation engagements	21
• Time budgets are not in writing or fail to be compared to actual hours, particularly on engagements of fewer than 40 hours	19

OVERVIEW

While this article reinforces messages that have appeared elsewhere, such as the need to direct attention to the "tone at the top" of a public accounting firm and to direct attention to each of the key elements of a quality control system, more specificity of direction is detailed herein. The hope is that through systematic consideration of what has "gone wrong" in controls and performance at other CPA firms, current and future practices will be enhanced. *Table 1* re-emphasizes the most frequent findings in past LOCs. These matters merit special attention by firms striving to establish and maintain effective quality control.

If a CPA firm is enrolled in the quality review progam, with oversight being exercised by the AICPA, the areas of practice and quality control likely to catch the attention of the reviewers can be anticipated by learning from history. The role of this article is to share that history and to enhance understanding of lessons learned from LOCs in peer reviews. Ω

Source: Wanda A. Wallace and James J. Wallace, "Learning from Peer Review Comments," *The CPA Journal* (May 1990), pp. 48–53. Reprinted with permission from *The CPA Journal,* May 1990, copyright 1990.

OVERVIEW

This chapter focuses on

- banks and thrifts,
- insurance companies,
- securitization transactions,
- defense contractors,
- research on industry-related and size-related patterns of comments in management letters, and
- professional services, focusing on public accounting firms.

While by no means comprehensive for all industries, this chapter permits more in-depth consideration of how controls need to be tailored to context. Part II of the Appendix to this chapter includes illustrations of internal control breakdowns for several of these industries, according to the Comptroller General's correspondence with the United States House of Representatives member, The Honorable Ron Wyden.

APPENDIX

JOB DESCRIPTIONS AND CONTROL BREAKDOWNS

Part I: How Are Internal Auditing Jobs Commonly Described[80]

A key element to control in all industries is effective personnel management. Since internal audit groups have been recommended by the Treadway Commission for all companies, it may be useful to know what practice suggests are common job descriptions for such posts.

Job descriptions for internal auditors vary widely. To identify commonalities, 206 different job descriptions for close to 100 companies were examined.[81] Frequency analyses were performed on the various dimensions identified from reading the entire data set. At times, in spite of the dominance of one coding, other aspects of a dimension overlap with the primary thrust of the job description. As one example, an emphasis was often placed on the possession of an accounting major, yet other majors were sometimes cited as permissible. This was particularly true at higher level positions. Therefore, a dual frequency analysis was performed: primary thrust and overlapping dimensions. In reviewing the analyses, the counts will average far below 206, since many job descriptions lack embellishment beyond posting the position to be filled.

Educational Background

As depicted in Exhibit 16–20 an emphasis is placed on accounting and business majors at all levels of staffing. Of particular interest is the virtual dominance of "associated fields," i.e., finance, economics, management, business, and computer science, over the accounting major. In many cases, as reflected by a comparison of the 65 total primary frequencies to the 206 job descriptions reviewed, often there is no treatment of the question of which college major is desired of applicants.

---

[80] This research, conducted by Wanda A. Wallace and James J. Wallace, while at Southern Methodist University, is based on data collected for a research project which was funded by a grant from The Institute of Internal Auditors Research Foundation. The views expressed herein are those of the authors and do not necessarily reflect views of the Foundation.

[81] Those wishing further details as to the nature of these companies are referred to demographic statistics presented in *A Time Series Analysis of the Effect of Internal Audit Activities on External Audit Fees*, a research monograph authored by Wanda A. Wallace and published by The IIA.

Exhibit 16–20

College Majors Cited In Job Descriptions

	Staff	Senior	Manager
Accounting Major	3 (—)	13 (—)	— (7)
Other Majors*	23 (—)	2 (23)	— (25)
Substitutions for degrees and additions	10 (—)	2 (3)	5 (3)
No Specifications	3 (—)	—	—
TOTALS	36	17 (26)	5 (35)

	Director	EDP Auditor	Supervisor
Accounting Major	2 (5)	4 (5)	— (5)
Other Majors*	— (25)	1 (25)	— (25)
Substitutions for degrees and additions	— (4)	— (3)	— (4)
No Specifications	—	—	—
TOTALS	2 (34)	5 (33)	— (34)

* Associated Fields = Finance, Economics, Business Management, Business, MBA, Computer Science

Note: The numbers in the parentheses are observations that overlap, e.g., involving both accounting and other majors in job descriptions of senior positions.

Certification or Graduate Work

As Exhibit 16–21 indicates, some job descriptions will cite a preference for a professional certification or for completion of an MBA. The CIA designation would seem to dominate such requirement listings, although bank auditing and computer science certifications are clearly emphasized as well. Once again, with 697 references to certification, it is obvious that many job descriptions virtually ignore such matters.

Exhibit 16–21

College Majors Cited In Job Descriptions

	CPA	CIA	CMA
Staff	4 (—)	18 (—)	3 (—)
Senior	2 (1)	(15)	(3)
Manager	2 (3)	1 (15)	— (3)
Director	— (4)	— (16)	— (3)
EDP Auditor	(3)	1 (15)	— (3)
Supervisor	— (3)	— (15)	— (3)
TOTALS	8 (11)	20 (76)	3 (15)

	MBA	Other*	No Specifications
Staff	1 (—)	8 (—)	6 (—)
Senior	(1)	15 (1)	
Manager	1 (1)	7 (10)	
Director	— (1)	— (16)	
EDP Auditor	— (1)	— (13)	
Supervisor	— (1)	— (16)	
TOTALS	2 (5)	30 (56)	6 (—)

* Other certifications specified = CISA, CBA, and so on.

Desired Qualifications

In addition to formal education and professional certification, many job descriptions specify desirable attributes of future professional staff, as well as past work experience. As Exhibit 16–22 reflects, communication skills are heavily emphasized. The key emphasis is placed on auditing experience, although many organizations permit no such experience.

Exhibit 16–22

I. Desired Attributes Cited In Internal Audit Job Descriptions

EDP Knowledge	Governmental Knowledge	Accounting/Auditing Talent; Business Sense	Technical/Analytical Supervisory Responsibility
3	1	6	19

Creativity	Sound Judgment/ Substantial Concentration Power	Desirable Ethical Attributes	Interpersonal/ Communication Skills
10	11	9	43

Willingness to Travel	No Specifications
1	5

II. Work Experience Specified In Job Descriptions

"Big 6"	Primarily Accounting	Accounting/ Auditing	Primarily Auditing	Industry Related	Government Related
2	1	11	37 (13)	7	3

Supervisory Experience	No Experience or MBA	Company Related	EDP
11	11	4	3

The Nature of the Job

As the four-part Exhibit 16–23 depicts, the nature of the job is most commonly represented as "Accounting/Auditing," though an emphasis is placed upon the constructive task of formulating recommendations. Travel demands are rarely mentioned, perhaps in order to downplay that off-cited problem with an internal auditing career path. The need for continuing education in accounting and auditing is sometimes cited, yet it is an exception to recognize such needs in narrower fields like EDP or interpersonal skills. The final part of Exhibit 16–24 highlights the prevalence of informal job descriptions.

Exhibit 16–23

I. Nature Of Job As Depicted In Job Descriptions

Compliance Work	Approvals [Determinations]	Developments of Recommendations	Checks and Reviews
41	102 (6)	158	109 (12)

Special Reviews	Supervisory	Accounting/Auditing and all others
41	102	206

II. Travel Demands Cited In Job Descriptions

Less than 10%	10–20%	21–50%	Over 50%	No Specifications
5	1	7	2	10

III. Specific Mention Of Continuing Education In Job Descriptions

Accounting/Auditing	Interpersonal	Individualized	EDP	No Specifications
14	2	3	3	10

IV. Formality Of Job Description

	Frequency
No formal job description	7
Clear delineation of purpose and authority	12
Well specified, including qualifications and responsibilities	4
TOTAL	23

Exhibit 16–24

I. Internal Audit—Structure As Referenced By Job Descriptions

	Frequency
Responsible for recommendations being implemented	7 (—)
Reports directly to President	3 (—)
Reports to Audit Committee/Board of Directors	7 (—)
Reports to Vice President of Finance	5 (—)
Reports to Treasurer	4 (—)
Written responses to reports required	3 (—)
Responses are requested	1 (—)
Reports to Commissioner for Program/Management Support	1 (—)
Reports to Director—Financial Services	2 (—)
Serves on Audit Committee of Board of Directors	1 (—)
Reports to Chairman of the Board	1 (—)
Reports to City Council	1 (—)
Reports to Senior Vice President—Regulatory and Customer Relations	— (2)
Reports to Executive Vice President/Comptroller	— (4)
Reports to Executive Officer (Navy)	— (1)
Reports to Assistant Comptroller—Corporate Accounting	— (1)
TOTAL	36 (8)

II. Internal Audit—Responsibilities As Referenced By Job Descriptions

	Frequency
No such statement (missing)	8
Standards of The Institute of Internal Auditors	8
Scope—operational	9
Scope—financial	1
Review audit plans, policies, and procedures	1
Implementation of Federal Audit Requirements	1
Develop audit programs	1
Evaluate adequacy of internal control system and improvements	1
Evaluate adequacy of internal accounting and other data	1
Independence/objectivity of departments maintained	5
Unrestricted access to company records/personnel	2
Implement audit program	1
TOTAL	39

Structure and Responsibilities

The internal auditor's reporting linkage has been emphasized in the Professional Standards of The IIA and is similarly the subject of some job descriptions. Exhibit

Exhibit 16–24 (continued)

16–24 summarizes reporting linkages, as well as the type of responsibilities held by internal auditors, based on a review of available job descriptions.

Observations

The data base emphasizes the wide diversity in job descriptions' format and content, yet serves to suggest possible information that might be incorporated in future descriptions of internal audit positions. Turnover is widely recognized as a problem in the auditing profession. Perhaps that turnover which is undesired could be deterred by providing more informative job descriptions to prospective employees. In particular, if accounting or engineering knowledge were essential, interpersonal skills indispensable, and industry-related work experience critical, then such dimensions should be delineated. If fraud is over 20%, the employer might be well advised to make applicants cognizant of the organization's expectations. Many job descriptions fail to explain where internal auditing fits into the organization's structure or what key responsibilities rest with the department, let alone the particular position to be filled.

Synopsis

By reviewing the content of other entities' job descriptions, more effective means of attracting professional staff which properly "match" the position to be filled can be identified. It would appear that arguments could be advanced for far more detailed job descriptions, as many key qualifications of prospective employees appear to be virtually ignored.

Part II: Control Breakdowns Cited by the Comptroller General

Illustrations of Internal Control Breakdowns

The following cases help to illustrate how internal control breakdowns have contributed to company failures and investor and government losses.

Lockheed

Lockheed received millions of dollars in loan guarantees from the U.S. Government in the early 1970s to stave off bankruptcy. Subsequently, the SEC filed a civil action suit against Lockheed in 1976, alleging numerous internal control and other breakdowns, such as the payment of millions of dollars in bribes to foreign governments through the use of "slush funds" and falsification of financial records. A special committee of the Board of Directors, appointed at the suggestion of the SEC, recommended a number of internal control improvements, including broadening the role of Lockheed's audit committee to oversee Lockheed's financial reporting.

Continental Illinois

During 1984, Continental Illinois National Bank received several billion dollars in federal assistance to avoid closing. A 1985 congressional staff report to a House Banking subcommittee noted that, "The bank's management was more concerned with its aggressive growth strategy and appeared to dismiss the need for compliance with adequate safeguards even though management was made aware of the deteriorating conditions on a number of occasions." An investigation by internal auditors at Continental Illinois found numerous internal control weaknesses, including incomplete and inaccurate recordkeeping, and questionable loans.

Vernon Savings and Loan

Vernon Savings and Loan failed in 1987 following serious weaknesses in Vernon's internal controls. Federal regulators cited Vernon's management for numerous instances of internal control problems and noncompliance with laws and regulations, such as misuse and manipulation of assets; concealment of liabilities; failure to maintain accurate financial records; overstatement of income and net worth; excessive compensations, bonuses, and dividends paid to management and directors; excessive and extravagant perquisites; and dishonest acts and practices.

ZZZZ Best

Investors and creditors lost tens of millions of dollars when internal control weaknesses contributed to the 1987 bankruptcy of ZZZZ Best Company, Inc., a publicly traded carpet cleaning and restoration company. According to federal prosecutors, ZZZZ Best faked contracts and forged accounting records which circulated money through bank accounts of sham companies for the appearance of business activity. Auditors were aware of material internal control weaknesses, but reported them only to the company's management and to the company's audit committee. The public did not learn of these weaknesses until after ZZZZ Best was bankrupt.

Lincoln Savings and Loan

According to the Resolution Trust corporation, the failure of Lincoln Savings and Loan in 1989 will cost taxpayers $2.6 billion. Federal examiners noted a number of internal control weaknesses leading up to Lincoln's failure, such as improper loans, speculative investments, accounting abuses, and numerous related party transactions which enabled the parent company's management to siphon cash for their personal benefit.

Mission Insurance Company and Others

According to a February 1990 congressional report,* internal control breakdowns played a significant role in four insurance company failures (Mission Insurance Company, Integrity Insurance Company, Transit Casualty Company, and Anglo-American Insurance Company). Weak controls, including poor underwriting practices and reckless insurance and re-insurance activities, ultimately led to numerous fraudulent acts. Controls were so bad at one of the failed companies that management had no reasonable idea of how many policies it had issued or how much premium income was due or had been collected. According to the subcommittee, the company's management and auditors were aware of these problems as early as 1979, but the auditors waited until 1984 before threatening to publicly disclose them.

---

* *Failed Promises: Insurance Company Insolvencies,* Subcommittee on Oversight and Investigations, House Committee on Energy and Commerce.

Source: Enclosure I with letter from Charles A. Bowsher, Comptroller General of the United States, to the Honorable Ron Wyden, House of Representatives (May 1, 1991).

17

Reporting Issues

"Purposive influence towards a pre-determined objective."

The Control Revolution by James R. Beniger[1]

The introductory quote offers one definition of control, which clarifies the reason so many types of reports are foreseeable and currently envisioned by SAS No. 30.

Many alternative report forms relate to internal control. An attest function exists for comprehensive review engagements, with CPAs issuing reports as to the adequacy of entire systems of control. Limited negative assurance types of reports on control can also be issued by CPAs. These sometimes relate to regulatory reporting guidelines and frequently are a by-product of the financial statement audit. In addition to these reports on control systems that are issued by CPAs, reports by management have become common, and they typically include disclosures concerning internal control. The CPA has responsibility for reviewing such management disclosures to make sure that they are reasonable and consistent with other representations made in the annual report. Since management disclosures often describe the CPA's role in reviewing internal controls, it is partic-

---

[1] Cited in presentation by a spokesperson for Coopers and Lybrand entitled "A New Study on Internal Controls," at Management's Responsibilities—The New Requirements By The SEC And Congress," sponsored by the Executives Enterprises and held on December 4–5, 1990 at the New York Hilton.

ularly important that the CPAs review the accuracy with which their duties, responsibilities, and alternative services are reported. The overstatement in some management reports of CPAs' involvement in evaluating internal accounting controls is so misleading that it could well have liability implications for the profession. The careful monitoring of management reports to prevent such overstatements is a critical responsibility of the CPA.

INTERNAL CONTROL REPORTING OPTIONS, ACCORDING TO STATEMENT ON AUDITING STANDARDS NO. 30

Comprehensive review engagements were discussed in the prior chapter; the report that is issued on such engagements is the subject matter of Statement on Auditing Standards (SAS) No. 30, "Reporting on Internal Accounting Control." Also discussed in Statement No. 30 are reports on internal accounting control that are based solely on work done in an audit engagement and special purpose reports that may involve an opinion on all or part of an entity's system of control. Exhibit 17–1 summarizes these possible report forms that are related to internal accounting control, distinguishing between the purpose, scope, use of the report, and opinion content for each type of engagement. Exhibit 17–1 is based entirely on SAS No. 30.

Opinion on Entity's System of Internal Accounting Control

The first report form described in Exhibit 17–1 relates to comprehensive review engagements. The exhibit highlights the distinction between a review of controls with the intention of expressing an opinion on a system and a review of controls for auditing purposes.

Purpose. While a review of internal control for auditing purposes facilitates the setting of an audit strategy and is only an intermediate step of the audit, it is the end product in an engagement to express an opinion on the entity's system. While the auditor can choose to document information flows and not to identify or test specific controls beyond gaining an understanding of control, the CPA performing an engagement to express an opinion on controls must check the specific controls over all significant transactions. The procedures followed to study and evaluate internal accounting controls are identical except that *the decision on whether to rely upon controls has no limiting role in an engagement to express an opinion on the control system.*

Scope. The scope of an engagement to evaluate controls requires the CPA to determine whether prescribed procedures are being applied in a manner that provides reasonable assurance that assets are safeguarded, that financial records are reliable, and that financial statements can be prepared. In contrast, the auditor's concern is with the effect of controls on the nature, timing, and extent of audit procedures.

Exhibit 17-1

The Distinction Between an Evaluation of Internal Accounting Controls for Purposes of Expressing an Opinion on Financial Statements, a Comprehensive Review of Internal Accounting Controls for Purposes of Issuing a Report Expressing an Opinion on the System, and Other Internal Control-Related Engagements*

Possible Report Forms Related to Internal Accounting Control:	Opinion on Entity's System of Internal Accounting Control as of a Specified Date/During a Specified Period of Time	Report on Entity's System Based Solely on a Study and Evaluation of Internal Accounting Control Made as Part of an Audit	Report on All or Part of an Entity's System Based on Regulatory Agencies' Pre-established Criteria	Special-Purpose Reports on All or Part of an Entity's System
Purpose	To determine whether management has reasonable assurance that assets are safeguarded, financial records are reliable, and financial statements can be prepared.	Intermediate step in forming an opinion on the financial statements which provides the basis for determining the nature, timing, and extent of audit procedures.	To meet regulators' reporting requirements.	To meet special information requests which do not require an opinion on the system taken as a whole.
Scope	Assess susceptibility of the entity's assets to misuse, the overall control environment of the entity, the effect of recent operating and control changes, the significance of classes of transactions and related assets, and then utilize available knowledge of the entity to —conclude whether the entity's control procedures are suitably designed to achieve the objectives of internal accounting control; —determine whether such prescribed procedures are being applied; and —evaluate the total system.	While entire system is reviewed, testing of the system is limited to those prescribed control procedures on which the auditor relies; no testing is performed on —procedures not satisfactory for the auditor's purposes; or —procedures for which the audit effort required to test compliance exceeds the reduction in audit effort possible through control reliance.	Per specifications of regulatory agency.	Per specifications of party engaging the accountant.
Use	No restrictions on the use of this report. - - - - - - - - - - - - - - - - - - May serve as basis for reliance on internal accounting controls for the auditor since the nature of the procedures is the same.	Restricted use: management, specified regulatory agencies, or other specified third parties.	Restricted use: management or specified regulatory agencies.	Restricted use: management, specified regulatory agencies, or other specified third parties.

805

Possible Report Forms Related to Internal Accounting Control:

Opinion

Opinion on Entity's System of Internal Accounting Control as of a Specified Date/During a Specified Period of Time	Report on Entity's System Based Solely on a Study and Evaluation of Internal Accounting Control Made as Part of an Audit	Report on All or Part of an Entity's System Based on Regulatory Agencies' Pre-established Criteria	Special-Purpose Reports on All or Part of an Entity's System
Scope	Restricted Use.	Restricted Use.	Restricted Use.
Date	Limited Purpose (GAAS).	Matters Covered by Study.	Scope and Nature of Accountant's Procedures.
Responsibilities of Management	Disclaim Opinion on Whole.	Whether Tests of Control Were Performed.	Disclaimer on System as a Whole.
Objectives—Report Does Not Affect Audit Report	Would Not Necessarily Disclose All Material Weaknesses in the System.	Objectives and Limitations of Both Internal Accounting Control and the Accountant's Evaluation of It.	State Accountant's Findings.
Inherent Limitations	Negative Assurance Regarding Material Weaknesses.	Conclusions Based on Criteria, i.e., Adequate for Agency's Purpose (Study/Audit).	
Opinion That System as a Whole Prevents or Detects Material Errors or Irregularities	Material Weaknesses Were Considered in Determining Audit Tests—Report Does Not Affect Audit Report.	Material Weaknesses Disclosed Even If Not Material by Agency's Criteria (but not responsible for comprehensiveness of agency's criteria).	
In Accordance with Standards Established by AICPA	If Immaterial Weaknesses Are Included in Some Reports and Excluded from Others, Be Able to Justify Any Exclusion.	Can Disclose Immaterial Weaknesses, Recommendations for Corrective Actions, and Description of Actions Taken If Reviewed and Tested.	
Disclose Material Weaknesses (and Immaterial Weaknesses, if desired)			
Qualify Report for Scope Restrictions, or Disclaim, if Substantial Restrictions			
State if Management Believes Costs Exceed Benefits—Do Not Express a Related Opinion, But Issue Disclaimer if Desired			
Do Not Mention Corrective Actions Unless Design Is Reviewed and Application Is Tested			

* Peat, Marwick, Mitchell & Co. granted permission to utilize this exhibit, originally prepared by the author for the firm's Senior Seminar in-house training program related to internal control.

Note: At the time of this writing, SAS No. 30 has not been updated to reflect the SAS on reportable conditions or the control structure. The effect of such changes (likely to evolve) should be considered as this exhibit is interpreted.

Use. The report form is for unrestricted use and provides an opinion on the internal accounting control system as a whole, if an engagement to evaluate controls is requested, whereas an audit can only provide a disclaimer with some negative assurance provided regarding material weaknesses.

Exhibit 17–1 acknowledges that a report on a comprehensive review engagement is unrestricted in its use; it is intended as a publicly available report form. It further notes that a comprehensive review engagement is separate from an audit in the sense that its purpose and scope are entirely different, yet it does not have to be entirely separate in the sense that evidence collected during an audit to document and evaluate controls can be relied upon as part of the evidential base for forming an opinion on the system of controls. Similarly, if the engagement to review controls precedes the audit, evidence collected in forming an opinion on the entity's control system could be relied upon in the study and evaluation of internal accounting control for audit purposes (provided, of course, that the timing of the audit procedures that provided the evidence is acceptable in either engagement). These points were also discussed in Chapter 15.

Opinion. In delineating the content of an opinion on a comprehensive review engagement, Exhibit 17–1 suggests that the related responsibilities of management be stated. Those responsibilities include the design of a control system that reflects management's estimates and judgments as to the cost/benefit relationship of available control procedures and compliance with the prescribed system to ensure the adequacy of overall control.

Effect of the control report on the audit report. Exhibit 17–1 suggests that the objectives of the engagement be made explicit, particularly the fact that the internal control report is intended to have no effect upon the audit report. This is of particular importance when material weaknesses are disclosed in the report on internal accounting controls. The phrasing could be as follows, if the CPA for the comprehensive review engagement were also the auditor:

> These control conditions were considered in the determination of the nature, timing, and extent of audit procedures so that no modification of the audit report on the financial statements was required.

If another CPA were to perform the audit, the comprehensive review report might state:

> We have not examined the financial statements of the client and are not in a position to express an opinion on the effect, if any, of control conditions on the financial statements of the client for any period.

Inherent limitations in the control system. Since no control system is perfect, an important communication to report to users, as cited in this exhibit, is that inherent limitations exist for all designed systems. Typical of the wording found in the professional literature is a statement to the following effect:

> Inherent limitations in any control system may permit errors or irregularities to occur and not be detected by the system. Since any designed control system

can become inadequate if conditions change or if prescribed procedures are not followed, projection of any control evaluation into the future may be inappropriate.

Cost/benefit considerations. The remaining items in the exhibit that relate to comprehensive review engagements are self-explanatory, with the possible exception of the point regarding management's beliefs as to a particular control's desirability from a cost/benefit perspective. The CPA will, at times, be told that a control condition will not be corrected because the costs of improving or instituting a control are expected to exceed any related benefit from correcting an observed weakness. The CPA is advised to acknowledge management's beliefs but should not give an opinion as to whether or not management's judgment is "correct." Management has the unique capability of evaluating proposed system changes from both an operating and a control perspective. The CPA is in no position to second-guess management, nor is that the role of the CPA for reporting purposes. The comprehensive review engagement is intended to report on the adequacy of the system that is in operation, regardless of its relative efficiency from a cost/benefit perspective.

Disclosing material weaknesses. Of course, the CPA will frequently advise management, via a management letter, of conditions that appear to be inefficient. When material weaknesses are observed in a control system, the CPA should provide constructive suggestions as to how such weaknesses could be corrected. Timely advice on control weaknesses can facilitate management's prompt action which, in some circumstances, will obviate the need to disclose the weakness in a report on the control system issued for a particular date. If the report is issued for a period of time, the observed material weakness would have to be reported, but the CPA can also cite management's past corrective actions, provided (s)he has some assurance that these actions have been effective. Whenever management's corrective actions obviate disclosure or are a part of the accountant's report, the CPA has responsibility to review and test the new control procedures to gain assurance that the material weaknesses have been eliminated.

If management has not had the opportunity to implement changes, but has developed plans as to how the material weaknesses will be corrected, the CPA may wish to describe such plans in the report on internal accounting controls.

Report on Entity's System Based Solely on a Study and Evaluation of Internal Accounting Control Made as Part of an Audit

If an audit client wishes to receive some negative assurance as to the quality of controls but does not wish to incur the cost of a comprehensive review engagement, a reporting alternative is available.

Purpose, scope, and use. As noted in Exhibit 17–1, a report on an entity's controls can be issued based solely upon a study and evaluation of internal accounting control made as part of an audit. This by-product of an audit will be restricted in its use as well as its scope. As the exhibit outlines, the review of controls in the audit is an intermediate step in the audit process which requires an understanding of controls, but a detailed review of testing of only those control procedures on which the auditor plans to rely.

Opinion. Due to the absence of testing in many control areas, any control report issued solely based on audit procedures is restricted in its use. This restricted use is stated in the opinion issued by the auditor, as is its limited purpose—as indicated in Exhibit 17–1. A disclaimer further emphasizes that the whole system of controls has not been evaluated. A warning is issued to users of the report that all material weaknesses are not necessarily disclosed by such a "limited purpose" review of controls, although negative assurance regarding material weaknesses can be provided. The auditor further assures report users that if material weaknesses are reported, these were appropriately considered for auditing purposes and in no way influence the audit report. If an auditor chooses to outline immaterial weaknesses in such a report, their classification as immaterial should be made very clear. Furthermore, if a report to management includes immaterial weaknesses, while reports to regulatory agencies do not, their exclusion from the reports to regulators must be defensible.

Disclosures common to both report forms. The arrows connecting column one of Exhibit 17–1 to column two are intended to point out similarities in the disclosures provided in an opinion on an entity's control system and those provided in the report based solely on the study and evaluation of controls made as part of an audit. For example, management's responsibility for establishing and maintaining controls, the inherent limitations of any steps of internal accounting control, the disclosure of material (and, if desired, immaterial weaknesses), and the identification of cost/benefit explanations provided by management as to why certain controls are missing, are disclosures common to both report forms.

Report on All or Part of an Entity's System Based on Regulatory Agencies' Pre-established Criteria

Purpose, scope, and uses. The third column of the exhibit emphasizes the limited and tailored scope and purpose of the control reports issued based on regulatory agencies' criteria. The use of such reports is typically restricted to management and specified regulatory agencies, although some regulations may include public filings.

Opinion. As an example, the Securities and Exchange Commission (SEC) has control-related reporting requirements for broker-dealers. The SEC requires that an audit be conducted in a manner that provides the CPA with reasonable assurance of the discovery of any material inadequacies in the accounting system, the internal accounting control procedures for safeguarding securities, or the procedures followed in complying with Rule 17a–13 [17 CFR 240.17a–13]. Any material inadequacies identified must be reported as part of the annual audit report and the chief financial officer of the broker or dealer must be notified of such weaknesses. That officer, in turn, is to notify the SEC; if the broker or dealer fails to give such notice, the CPA must do so. As reported in the *Federal Register* (December 30, 1975, page 15):

> A determination of a material inadequacy may, in many instances, require completed audit procedures in a particular area, appropriate review at the decision-making level by management and the independent accountant, and possible consultation with counsel . . . and [should] be completed in the shortest time possible.

The regulations prescribe the nature and form of the reports. They also define a material inadequacy as

> any condition which has contributed substantially to or, if appropriate corrective action is not taken, could reasonably be expected to (i) inhibit a broker or dealer from promptly completing securities transactions or promptly discharging his responsibilities to customers, other broker-dealers or creditors; (ii) result in material financial loss; (iii) result in material misstatements of the broker's or dealer's financial statements; or (iv) result in violations of the Commission's recordkeeping of financial responsibility rules to an extent that could reasonably be expected to result in the conditions described in parts (i), (ii), or (iii) [*Federal Register*, December 30, 1975, p. 24].

While this definition includes in part (iii), the primary basis for CPAs' concern in either an audit or a comprehensive review engagement, even if it did not include such a proviso the CPA would always be required to apply such a criterion in identifying material weaknesses. In a regulatory setting, this criterion is augmented in whatever manner is required by the regulatory agencies for whom the control reports are being prepared.

The American Institute of Certified Public Accountants in a 1960 publication on Special Reports recommended that a phrase be added to the scope paragraph of short-form audit reports on brokers and dealers to the effect that the auditor had performed a review of the internal control system and the procedures for safeguarding securities. The Institute recommended that this phrase be included in reports to jurisdictional agencies but be optional for reports to customers. In addition to the scope adjustment as to what was done by the CPA, a context for the procedures is helpful to financial statements. This can be communicated by following the statement in the short-form report that the CPA performed "such other auditing procedures as we considered necessary in the circumstances," with a statement to the effect that these procedures included "the audit procedures prescribed by the Securities and Exchange Commission or other jurisdictional agency."

The CPA has no responsibility for evaluating the comprehensiveness of the agency's criteria, but rather is placed in a position of testing compliance with the regulators' pre-established criteria. The broker-dealer report form is only one of numerous plausible control-related reports that might be issued to regulatory agencies by a CPA.

Special-Purpose Reports on All or Part of an Entity's System

Special-purpose reports are the subject matter of the last column of Exhibit 17–1. This column related to reports other than those issued primarily for regulatory agencies. Exhibit 17–2 illustrates an internal control report in accordance with generally accepted governmental auditing standards (GAGAS).

Exhibit 17–2

Report on Internal Control Structure in Accordance with GAGAS when Reportable Conditions Have Been Noted

In planning and performing our audit of the financial statements of [name and entity] for the year ended June 30, 19X1, we considered its internal control structure in order to determine our auditing procedures for the purpose of expressing our opinion on the financial statements and not to provide assurance on the internal control structure.

The management of [name of entity] is responsible for establishing and maintaining an internal control structure. In fulfilling this responsibility, estimates and judgments by management are required to assess the expected benefits and related costs of internal control structure policies and procedures. The objectives of an internal control structure are to provide management with reasonable, but not absolute, assurance that assets are safeguarded against loss from unauthorized use or disposition, and that transactions are executed in accordance with management's authorization and recorded properly to permit the preparation of financial statements in accordance with generally accepted accounting principles. Because of inherent limitations in any internal control structure, errors or irregularities may nevertheless occur and not be detected. Also, projection of any evaluation of the structure to future periods is subject to the risk that procedures may become inadequate because of changes in conditions or that the effectiveness of the design and operation of policies and procedures may deteriorate.

For the purpose of this report, we have classified the significant internal control structure policies and procedures in the following categories [identify internal control structure categories].

For all of the internal control structure categories listed above, we obtained an understanding of the design of relevant policies and procedures and whether they have been placed in operation and we assessed control risk.

Exhibit 17–2 (continued)

We noted certain matters involving the internal control structure and its operation that we consider to be reportable conditions under standards established by the American Institute of Certified Public Accountants. Reportable conditions involve matters coming to our attention relating to significant deficiencies in the design or operation of the internal control structure that, in our judgment, could adversely affect the entity's ability to record, process, summarize, and report financial data consistent with the assertions of management in the financial statements.

[Include paragraphs to describe the reportable conditions noted].

A material weakness is a reportable condition in which the design or operation of the specific internal control structure elements does not reduce to a relatively low level the risk that errors or irregularities in amounts that would be material in relation to the financial statements being audited may occur and not be detected within a timely period by employees in the normal course of performing their assigned functions.

Our consideration of the internal control structure would not necessarily disclose all matters in the internal control structure that might be reportable conditions and, accordingly, would not necessarily disclose all reportable conditions that are also considered to be material weaknesses as defined above. However, we believe none of the reportable conditions described above is a material weakness.

We also noted other matters involving the internal control structure and its operation that we have reported to the management of [name and entity] in a separate letter dated August 15, 19X1.

This report is intended for the information of the audit committee, management, and [specify legislative or regulatory body]. This restriction is not intended to limit the distribution of this report, which is a matter of public record.

Source: AICPA, SAS 63 (Section 801), "Applicable to Governmental Entities and Other Recipients of Governmental Financial Assistance" (April 1989), pp. 21–22.

Purpose. CPAs may be requested to issue reports on the design of controls, with no attention to compliance, or they may be requested to review controls over only a part of the entity's system of controls. An example of the latter would be a special report that addresses the safeguarding of customers' securities in a trust department of a bank. Another example of a special-purpose report, discussed in Chapter 12, concerns internal accounting control at service centers.

Scope. A service center auditor may issue a report on control design and/or control compliance and may define the scope of an examination as a segment of the organization, rather than the entire entity. Provided the segment distinguishes between its assets and its activities, no particular problem is posed by concentrating on a segment of operations rather than the total operations of an entity.

Opinion. A report on system design essentially reflects inquiry and observation procedures that are directed at a review of system documentation. Other than applying a walk-through to confirm a basic understanding of the information flows and designed controls, the CPA performs no tests of control. A report on system design will be as of a particular date and will describe those aspects of the internal accounting control system that are relevant to the intended report users. Typically, control objectives, designed procedures, and the CPA's opinion as to whether the system is adequately designed will be discussed in the special report. As is the case with any report on controls, a statement describing the inherent limitations of internal accounting controls and the risk of projecting control conditions should be included. The description of controls may be accomplished by attaching the client's documentation of the control system to the auditor's report, since design specifications are nothing more than client representations, in any case. When reporting on design, the CPA should explicitly state that no tests of control have been performed. In expressing an opinion on design, the CPA should stress the fact that control objectives would be achieved if designed control procedures were complied with satisfactorily. It is likewise advisable for the CPA to state the intended distribution of the report.

If a CPA expands the client service to a report on control design and tests of control of the design, the service center auditor will state the judgment reached as to whether the system description conformed to actual operating and control procedures during the period covered by the service auditor's report. At times, only that segment of a service center that executes transactions for others will be of interest to the users of the control report. However, even if reporting on only a segment of the service center's operations, the CPA will utilize the entire center's financial statements as a benchmark for evaluating the materiality of observed weaknesses. This is necessary because the financial position of a segment of the center's operations lacks meaning. In reporting on a control engagement related to a segment of operations, it is imperative that the scope paragraph clearly state which of the segments have been examined and that the opinion paragraph clearly states to what segment of operations the opinion relates. The objectives of control should be stated as pertaining to the prevention or detection of errors or irregularities in amounts that would be material to the entire entity's financial statements.

The service centers on which special-purpose reports might be issued include centers providing computer services, insurers maintaining accounting for ceded reinsurance (the assumption by one insurer of risk originally undertaken by another insurer), trust departments of banks and similar entities, mortgage bankers or savings and loan associations that service loans for others, and shareowner accounting organizations for investment companies. As Exibit 17–1 indicates the scope and nature of procedures, the restrictions on use, the accountants' findings, and the disclaimer on the system as a whole, when appropriate, are important components of special-purpose reports. The items in the first column with arrows extended would commonly be included in both regulatory agencies' reports and special-purpose reports on control. At the time of this writing, the amendment or superseding of SAS No. 30 (Section 642) is under consideration. In addition, proposals have been made for eventual revision of the auditor's standard report. The wording discussed to date would add one of the following sentences to the scope paragraph, after the second sentence of the report form described in SAS No. 58 (Section 642):

- They also require the consideration of the internal control structure to the extent necessary to plan the audit.[2]
- They also require the consideration of the internal control structure to the extent necessary to plan the audit, and not to provide assurance on that structure.[3]

Concern exists that the document containing the auditor's report on financial statements, on occasion, inappropriately associates the name of the auditor with the internal control structure. Therefore, a proposal is under consideration to modify the standard report in such a setting to include the following paragraph after the scope paragraph:

> In planning and performing our audit, we considered X company's control structure in order to determine our auditing procedures for the purpose of expressing our opinion on the financial statements and not to provide assurance in the internal control structure. Accordingly, we do not express an opinion or any other form of assurance on the internal control structure of X Company taken as a whole.[4]

A final topic under current discussion is whether an attestation standard should be developed regarding the CPA's review of management's assertions about the effectiveness of an entity's internal control structure. Such guidance is likely to be developed.[5]

Materiality Concepts

Financial Accounting Standards Board Statement of Financial Accounting Concepts No. 2, "Qualitative Characteristics of Accounting Information" defines *materiality* as

---

[2] "Reporting on Internal Control," File Ref. 4287 (AICPA, March 17, 1989), p. 104. This is part of the public record but is subject to revision and is not yet published guidance.

[3] ibid, p. 105.

[4] ibid, p. 106

[5] ibid, pp. 197–210.

the magnitude of an omission or misstatement of accounting information that, in the light of surrounding circumstances, makes it probable that the judgment of a reasonable person relying on the information would have been changed or influenced by the omission or misstatement.

The discussion explicitly recognizes the importance of making materiality judgments in light of the situation, considering both quantitative and qualitative factors. For example, the possibility of noncompliance with a debt covenant, illegal payments, or inadequate disclosure of related party transactions could influence the qualitative materiality of otherwise quantitatively immaterial errors.

Materiality has been given such operational definitions as the rule-of-thumb for profit-oriented enterprises of the least of

- 5% of normal pre-tax income where such income exceeds $2 million;
- 5%–10% of normal pre-tax income where normal pre-tax income is less than $2 million or where there is not widespread public ownership;
- 1% of gross revenues,

and for nonprofit organizations

- ½% of normal gross revenues.[6]

However, such conventions do not have consensus among auditors,[7] due to the large number of factors necessary to satisfy unique audit settings. Indeed, one study identifies 52 factors relevant to the evaluation of materiality.[8]

The diversity of materiality assessments by various professionals is reflected in Exhibit 17–3, as are reprints of two articles: (1) the first inventories materiality guidelines in the accounting literature and (2) the second performs a small sample analysis of how different rules of thumb compare when applied in practice. An appreciation for such variation in judgment is a useful context from which material weaknesses in controls can be evaluated in professional literature and practice.

The Decision Process

The identification of material weaknesses has two stages. The first stage focuses on control design, while the second stage focuses on tests of control. The second stage is only performed in those areas of control on which reliance by the external auditor is planned. Of course, if a CPA is asked to express an opinion

---

[6] M. Jennings, P. Reckers, and D. Kneer, "A Source of Insecurity: A Discussion and An Empirical Examination of Standards of Disclosure and Levels of Materiality in Financial Statements," *Journal of Corporation Law* (Spring 1985).

[7] M. Jennings, D. Kneer, and P. Reckers, "A Reexamination of the Concept of Materiality: Views of Auditors, Users and Officers of the Court," Unpublished Working paper, Arizona State University (1986).

[8] J. W. Pattillo, "The Concept of Materiality in Financial Reporting," *Research Study Published by the Financial Executives Research Foundation* (1976).

Exhibit 17–3

Materiality: Judgment, Professional Literature, and Practice Comparisons

Mean Thresholds of Materiality

	Inventory Loss	Eminent Domain	Lawsuit	Bribe
CPAs	$1,850,000	$2,350,000	$1,700,000	$430,000
	(11%)	(14%)	(10%)	(3%)
	[1,400,000]	[1,400,000]	[1,600,000]	[325,000]
Attorneys	$2,100,000	$1,500,000	$ 650,000	$450,000
	(13%)	(9%)	(4%)	(3%)
	[1,800,000]	[1,600,000]	[560,000]	[550,000]
Judges	$1,980,000	$1,900,000	$1,200,000	$250,000
	(12%)	(11%)	(7%)	(2%)
	[2,100,000]	[2,100,000]	[2,000,000]	[250,000]

( ) Percentage of income
[ ] Standard Deviation

Mean Thresholds of Materiality

Subjects:	Obsolete Inventory	Eminent Domain	Lawsuit	Bribe	Product Line Loss
CPAs	$1,980,000	$2,350,000	$1,850,000	$1,040,000	$2,490,000
	(12%)	(14%)	(11%)	(6%)	(15%)
	[1,900,000]	[2,000,000]	[1,860,000]	[1,540,000]	[2,060,000]
Credit Managers	$2,000,000	$1,590,000	$1,220,000	$ 695,000	$1,960,000
	(12%)	(10%)	(7%)	(4%)	(12%)
	[2,030,000]	[1,890,000]	[1,570,000]	[1,160,000]	[2,160,000]
CFAs	$2,010,000	$1,990,000	$1,420,000	$ 920,000	$1,930,000
	(12%)	(12%)	(9%)	(6%)	(12%)
	[2,090,000]	[2,090,000]	[1,780,000]	[1,520,000]	[2,150,000]
Bankers	$3,000,000	$2,830,000	$1,880,000	$1,450,000	$3,380,000
	(18%)	(17%)	(11%)	(9%)	(20%)
	[2,020,000]	[1,950,000]	[1,800,000]	[1,830,000]	[2,150,000]

Aggregate Means:

CPAs	$1,940,000	Obsolete Inventory	$2,270,000
CMs	$1,490,000	Eminent Domain	$2,220,000
CFAs	$1,650,000	Lawsuit	$1,610,000
BKs	$2,510,000	Bribe	$1,040,000
		Product Line	$2,470,000

( ) Percentage of income
[ ] Standard Deviation

Source: Marianne Jennings, Dan C. Kneer, and Philip M. J. Reckers, "A Reexamination of the Concept of Materiality; Views of Auditors, Users, and Officers of the Court," *Auditing: A Journal of Practice & Theory* (Spring 1987), pp. 108–112.

Exhibit 17–3 (continued)

AN INVENTORY OF MATERIALITY GUIDELINES IN ACCOUNTING LITERATURE

By **James H. Thompson, Ph.D., CPA,** *Associate Professor of Accountancy, University of Mississippi, University, MS;* **Thomas G. Hodge, CPA,** *Assistant Professor at Northeast Louisiana University, Monroe, LA; and* **James S. Worthington, Ph.D., CPA,** *Associate Professor of Accounting, Auburn University, Auburn, AL*

Editor:
Douglas R. Carmichael, Ph.D., CPA
Baruch College

Accounting is often described as an art. Accordingly, decisions are usually based on professional judgment after considering the facts and circumstances of each situation. Although pronouncements by standard-setting bodies provide guidance, it is often general rather than specific. Because specific quantitative guidelines are rare, materiality decisions in practice can be difficult. Indeed, the standard-setting bodies have often been criticized for not providing more specific quantitative guidelines.

The concept of materiality provides an excellent example. Authoritative accounting pronouncements provide few specific quantitative guidelines concerning materiality, therefore, determining materiality is largely a matter of judgment. Accountants continually face situations involving materiality judgments, not only in day-to-day accounting decisions but also in their role as independent auditors. This article summarizes the sources in which specific guidance is provided on the subject of materiality.

A search of authoritative pronouncements was made using the National Automated Accounting Research System (NAARS), an automated electronic database. The following pronouncements were considered: Accounting Research Bulletins (ARBs), Accounting Principles Board Opinions (APBs), AICPA Accounting Intepretations (AINs), Statements of Financial Accounting Standards (FASs), and FASB Interpretations (FINs). Specific quantitative guidelines and judgment items associated with those guidelines were identified and compared to the findings across the different pronouncements. The following terms and variations of such terms were used in the search of the pronouncements: material, substantial, significant, and percent. Once a pertinent source was located, a printed copy of the original pronouncement was examined and evaluated to determine whether a reference was applicable to this study. This analysis of the authoritative accounting pronouncements reveal that selected percentages are often provided as materiality guidelines. The alternative percentages provided in the accounting pronouncements are identified and summarized by judgment area in *Table 1*.

In addition to percentages, authoritative pronouncements also provide selected guidance about "judgment items" which may be used as a basis for mate-

Exhibit 17–3 (continued)

Table 1
Quantitative Materiality Guidelines

Judgment Area	Pronouncement			Criteria
	Number	Paragraph	Percent	
Stock dividends				
Cut-off	ARB 43	.7 & .13	20–25%	Point at which relative size of shares issued influences unit market price
Stock split	ARB 43	7. & .15	20–25%	Point at which intent of shares is to reduce unit market price to obtain wider distribution
Earnings per share				
Report dilution	APB 15	.14	3%	Compare simple EPS to diluted EPS
Treasury stock method	APB 15	.38	20%	Compare shares obtainable to shares outstanding at year end
Common stock equivalent	FAS 85	.3	66⅔%	Compare effective yield to current average Aa corporate bond yield
Business combinations				
Combinations—pooling unless companies are independent	APB 16	.46	10%	Combined intercorporate investments compared to outstanding voting shares
Combinations—pooling method	APB 16	.47	90%	Outstanding voting shares of investee
Investments in common stock				
Equity method—significant influence	APB 18	.17	20–50%	Outstanding voting shares of investee
Cost method—no significant influence	APB 18	.17	20%	Outstanding voting shares of investee
Consolidation method	ARB 51	.2	50%	Outstanding voting shares of investee
Leases				
Capital lease	FAS 13	.7	75%	Compare lease term to economic life of leased property
Capital lease	FAS 13	.7	90%	Compare present value of minimum lease payments to fair value of leased property
Capital lease—exception	FAS 13	.7	25%	Compare lease term to economic life of leased property's life
Sale-leaseback-test				
for transfer of rights	FAS 28	.3	10%	Compare present value of rental for leaseback to fair value of assets sold

Exhibit 17–3 (continued)

Table 1—continued
Quantitative Materiality Guidelines

Judgment Area	Pronouncement Number	Paragraph	Percent	Criteria
Sales of real estate				
Accrual method	FAS 66	.45	10%	Percent of cumulative payments compared to sales price
Percentage of completion method	FAS 66	.46	10%	Percent of cumulative payments compared to sales price
Installment method	FAS 66	.47	20%	Percent of cumulative payments compared to sales price
Accrual method	FAS 66	.45	90%	Percent of projects collected in full within certain time periods
Percentage of completion method	FAS 66	.46	90%	Percent of projects collected in full within certain time periods
Accrual method	FAS 66	.45	20%	Specified down payment size compared to sales price
Significant receivable	FAS 66	.27	15%	A receivable in excess of 15% of certain types of financing
Oil and gas activities				
Significant activities—revenues	FAS 69	.8	10%	Compare revenues of oil and gas activities to combined revenues
Significant activities—assets	FAS 69	.8	10%	Compare identifiable assets of all oil and gas activities to combined identifiable assets
Significant activities—profit or/loss	FAS 69	.8	10%	Compare results of operations of oil and gas activities to greater of combined operating profits of all segments with profits or combined operating losses of all segments with losses
Segment reporting				
Industry—revenue	FAS 14	.15	10%	Compare segment revenue to combined revenues
Industry—operating profit or loss	FAS 14	.15	10%	Compare absolute amount of segment operating profit or loss to greater of combined operating profit of all segments that did not incur an operating loss or combined operating loss of all segments that incurred an operating loss
Industry-identifiable assets	FAS 14	.15	10%	Compare segment identifiable assets to combined identifiable assets

Exhibit 17–3 (continued)

Table 1—*continued*

Quantitative Materiality Guidelines

Judgment Area	Pronouncement Number	Paragraph	Percent	Criteria
Substantial portion of operations explained	FAS 14	.17	75%	Compare combined revenues from sales of all reportable segments to combined revenues
Disclosed dominant segment	FAS 14	.20	90%	Compare revenue, operating profit or loss and identifiable assets to combined totals
Foreign operations	FAS 14	.32	10%	Compare revenue or assets to combined totals
Geographic area	FAS 14	.33	10%	Compare revenue to combined revenues
Major customers	FAS 30	.6	10%	Compare revenue to combined totals
Segment information for investee	FAS 24	.5	50%	If 50% of investee is owned, report if criteria in FASB 14.15, 14.32, or 14.39 are met
Defined benefit pension plans				
Disclosure of investments	FAS 35	.28	5%	Compare investments to net assets available for benefits
Amortization of unrecognized gains and losses	FAS 87	.32	10%	Compare gains and losses to projected benefits obligation or gains & losses market-related value of plan assets
Foreign currency translation—highly inflationary economy	FAS 52	.11	100%	Defined as having specified cumulative inflation over a 3-year period
Related party transactions				
Principal owners	FAS 57	.24	10%	Percent ownership or beneficial ownership of voting interest for disclosure
Investees	FAS 57	.2	50%	Percent ownership of investee for disclosure

---

riality judgments. These items are not themselves percentages for determining materiality, they both suggest certain comparisons.

In many materiality judgments, a comparison of an individual item to 1) income before extraordinary items, 2) net income, or 3) the trend of earnings, is suggested. Sometimes, judgment is required based simply on the nature of the event, such as an extraordinary item. In other situations

Exhibit 17–3 (continued)

the pronouncements leave the determination open-ended by suggesting that "other appropriate criteria should be considered." The alternative judgment items provided in the accounting pronouncements are identified and summarized by judgment area in *Table 2.*

Based on an analysis of Tables 1 and 2, several observations can

---

Table 2

Factor Base Materiality Guidelines

Judgment Area	Pronouncement Number	Paragraph	Criteria
Accounting changes	APB 20	.38	Effects of change on income before extraordinary items, net income, or trend of earnings
Accounting errors	APB 20	.38	Effects of errors on income before extraordinary items, net income, or trend of earnings
Disclosure of accounting policies and acounting principles	APB 22	.12	Materiality affects financial position, changes in financial position, or results of operations
Interim financial reporting			
Extraordinary items	APB 28	.21	Compare interim extraordinary items to estimated income for year
Other unusual or infrequent items	APB 28	.21	Compare to operating results for interim periods
Cumulative effect of change in accounting principles and correction of errors	APB 28	.29	Relate to estimated income for year or trend of earnings and to interim periods
Seasonal variation	APB 28	.18	Disclose material variations
Changes in accounting estimates	APB 28	.26	Compare to interim earnings
Prior period adjustments	FAS 16	.13	Consider material when compared to income from continuing operations for year, trend of income from continuous operations, or other appropriate criteria
Extraordinary events			
Unusual and frequent	APB 30	.24	Relate to income before extraordinary items, trend of earnings before extraordinary items, or other appropriate criteria
Unusual or infrequent	APB 30	.26	Based on nature of event and financial effects

Exhibit 17–3 (continued)

Table 2—continued
Factor Base Materiality Guidelines

| | Pronouncement | | |
Judgment Area	Number	Paragraph	Criteria
Leases			
Capital	FAS 13	.60	Record asset and liability when sub-stantially all of benefits and risks incident to ownership are transferred
Net investment balances in	FAS 13	.47	Present components of net investment balances leveraged when a significant part of revenues, net income, or assets
Income tax items			
Investment tax credit	AIN-APB 4, #1	.2	Relate to income tax provision, net income, and trend of earnings
Income tax expense	FAS 96	.27	Disclose significant components of income tax expense attributable to continuing operations
Reconciling items	FAS 96	.28	Disclose significant components of income tax expense attributable to continuing operations
Nonpublic company—reconciling items	FAS 96	.28	Disclose nature of reconciling items
Net operating loss and tax	FAS 96	.29	Disclose separately significant NOL or tax credit carryforwards for which credit carryforwards any tax benefits will be applied to reduce goodwill and other noncurrent intangible assets
Troubled debt restructuring-gains	FAS 4	.8	Classify as extraordinary if material in aggregate based on income before extraordinary items, trend of earnings before extraordinary items, or other appropriate criteria
	FAS 15	.21	
	APB 80	.24	

be made. *Table 3* shows that only 10% of authoritative accounting pronouncements contain specific materiality percentages, and only 6% give judgment items. The percentage of pronouncements giving these guidelines has changed little since the FASB assumed the responsibility for setting accounting standards—12% of the FASB's Statements give materiality percentages compared to 10% of the APB's Opinions, and 5%

Exhibit 17–3 (continued)

Table 3

Number of Accounting Pronouncements Providing Materiality Guidelines

| | | Number Providing Materiality Guidelines | | | |
| | | Quantitative | | Factor Base | |
Type of Pronouncement	Number Issued (as of 6/30/88)	Number	Percent	Number	Percent
Accounting Research Bulletin (ARBs)	9*	2	22%	0	0%
Accounting Principles Board Opinions (APBs)	31	3	10%	5	16%
Statements of Financial Accounting Standards (FASs)	98	12	12%	5	5%
Financial Accounting Standards Board Interpretations (FINs)	38	0	0%	0	0%
Total Number of Pronouncements	176	17	10%	10	6%

* ARBs 43–51

of the FASB's Statements give judgment items compared to 16% of the APB's Opinions. Interestingly, a pronouncement that specifies a percentage generally does not give a judgment item. In fact, only one pronouncement (SFAS 13) gives both a percentage and a judgment item.

A majority (nine out of 17) of materiality percentages (see Table 1) are investment-related. These pronouncements provide standards of accounting for stock dividends, earnings per share, business combinations, investments, and segment reporting. The remaining pronouncements that give percentages relate to specialized accounting practices. For example, four pronouncements give materiality percentages for decisions involving related party transactions, foreign currency transactions, oil and gas accounting, or real estate transactions. Two pronouncements give materiality percentages related to leases and pensions, respectively.

The influence of the SEC and other government agencies is evident in several pronouncements that contain materiality percentages. When APB 15, APB 16, and APB 18 were issued (late 1960s and early 1970s), the accounting profession and the APB were coming under increasing political pressure. The SEC issued Accounting Series Releases (ASRs) pertaining to leases, pensions, related party disclosures,

Exhibit 17–3 (continued)

and disclosure of significant oil and gas related activities before the APB and the FASB also issued pronouncements in those areas. Indeed, when SFAS 25 was adopted, the FASB refused to adopt the SEC's 10% rule found in ASR No. 257. This rule is used to determine if a company has significant oil and gas related activities. When SFAS 69 was adopted, the SEC's 10% rule for determining significant oil and gas producing activities was included.

Tables 1 and *2* are presented to assist practitioners in making the materiality decisions that are demanded in today's accounting and auditing environment.

Source: James H. Thompson, Thomas G. Hodge, and James S. Worthington, "An Inventory of Materiality Guidelines In Accounting Literature," *The CPA Journal* (Vol. LX/No. 7, July 1990), pp. 50, 52–54. Reprinted with permission from *The CPA Journal*, July 1990, copyright 1990.

Exhibit 17–3 (continued)

A Comparison of Various Materiality Rules of Thumb

The implementation of Statement on Auditing Standards (SAS) No. 47 "Audit Risk and Materiality in Conducting the Audit" has been a difficult and controversial process. The Statement requires that auditors make a "preliminary judgment about materiality levels" in planning the audit, yet provides limited guidance on how this measure should be determined. Furthermore, although the Statement suggests that this judgment "may or may not be quantified," it asserts that the auditor "generally plans the audit primarily to detect errors that he believes could be large enough, individually or in the aggregate, to be *quantitatively* material to the financial statements." Significant implementation difficulties have arisen as to how auditors are to operationalize planning materiality in the absence of a quantitative definition. In response, several "rules of thumb" have emerged from both practice and academic

research. For instance, all of the following have been suggested as ways of arriving at a preliminary judgment about materiality:
• Percentage of pretax income or net income;
• Percentage of gross profit;
• Percentage of total assets;
• Percentage of total revenue;
• Percentage of equity;
• Blended methods involving some or all of these definitions (e.g., compute some combination of the above and find the average);
• "Sliding scale" methods which vary with the size of the entity (e.g., KPMG Peat Marwick's "audit gauge").

While all these definitions represent plausible methods for quantifying materiality, it seems possible that the resulting materiality measures could significantly differ. Since "planning materiality" should affect the scope of both tests of controls and substantive tests, such differences might be of importance. Thus, it is hypothetically

possible that two auditors auditing otherwise similar entities might generate differing scopes of audit procedures, solely based on the "planning materiality" definition used. Likewise, audit procedures for the same client could differ substantially from year to year depending on how materiality is operationalized by the audit team each year.

The objective of this article is to compare the magnitude and stability of alternative "rule of thumb" planning materiality definitions using actual financial data for 1977 to 1986 from the Standard and Poor's annual Compustat database for the following companies:
1. Concord Fabrics Inc.—Textile Manufacturing.
2. Mott's Supermarkets—Retail Groceries.
3. Golden West Financial Corp.—Savings & Loans.

We selected three companies to represent fairly typical manufacturing, retail and financial companies to keep them within the range of clients of most CPAs and we selected companies somewhat smaller than the av-

Exhibit 17–3 (continued)

erage within the industries.

Five separate materiality measures were computed for comparison within and between companies:

1. 5% of average pre-tax income (using a 3-year average).

2. Sliding scale of gross profit depending on firm size (i.e., 5% of gross profit if between $0 and $20,000; 2% if between $20,000 and $1,000,000; 1% if between $1,000,000 and $100,000,000; ½% if over $100,000,000).

3. ½% of total assets.

4. 1% of total equity.

5. ½% of total revenues.

These and other measures of materiality are discussed in D. A. Leslie, *Materiality and its Application to Auditing*, (Canadian Institute of Chartered Accountants, 1985). These measures are used for convenience and not because they have any authoritative support. In practice, an even wider array of measures are being used today.

Tables 1 and 2 present the absolute and relative size obtained for

planning materiality for each company, on average, over the period from 1977 to 1986. To address the relative magnitude of the measures, the last three rows of *Table 1* provide comparisons of largest to smallest, largest to second largest, and second smallest to smallest. This was done to identify cases where one measure might have differed extremely from the others. For example, the ratio of the largest to the smallest measures ranged from 3.1 for Concord to 13.3 for Golden West.

In order to address whether our results were specific only to the three companies selected, we computed the same ` measures for all companies in the same industries as these firms. Our analysis showed that the ratios of largest to smallest measures for these three firms were somewhat conservative when compared to industry averages (i.e., 5.3 for all textile manufacturers, 8.9 for all retail grocers, and 18.8 for all savings and loans). These findings illustrate that substantial differences in quantitative

materiality measures are obtained, depending on the definition chosen. Extending the analysis, these differences could translate into sizable differences in audit scopes (and audit costs) as a function of the measure utilized. To the extent that a CPA firm uses rules of thumb such as these, one might speculate that the selection of a given materiality measure could also affect a CPA firm's competitive position for obtaining and retaining audit clients.

By examining the value in the last two rows, it is evident that the largest measure for all three companies tends to swamp even the second largest measure. Conversely, the smallest measures tend to be fairly close in magnitudes.

Table 2 summarizes rankings of the five materiality measures. The numbers of years where the given measure was largest and smallest are shown parenthetically. As seen in the table, the revenue-based measure was largest for the manufacturer and the retailer for all ten years. Likewise,

Exhibit 17–3 (continued)

Table 1

Absolute Size of Materiality Measures and Ratios (000s Omitted)

	Concord Fabrics Inc.	Mott's Supermarkets	Golden West Financial
Materiality Measures			
1. 5% of Average of Income	$150	$240	$ 3,560
2. Sliding Scale	180	510	N/A
3. ½% of Total Assets	200	220	35,760
4. 1% of Equity	210	240	2,680
5. ½% of Revenues	470	1310	3,730
Ratios:			
Largest to Smallest	3.1	6.0	13.3
Largest to Second Largest	2.2	2.6	9.6
Second Smallest to Smallest	1.2	1.1	1.4

Table 2

Rankings of Materiality Measures 1977–86

	Concord Fabrics Inc.	Mott's Supermarkets	Golden West Financial
Materiality Measures			
1. 5% of Average of Income	5[8]*	4[4]	3[4]
2. Sliding Scale	4[2]	2	N/A
3. ½% of Total Assets	3	5[6]	1[10]
4. 1% of Equity	2	3	4[4]
5. ½% of Revenues	1[10]**	1[10]	2[2]

* Number of years the measure ranked the smallest.
** Number of years the measure ranked the largest.

Exhibit 17–3 (continued)

the asset-based measure was largest for the financial institution. The smallest measure results varied between measures much more, with the income-based measure tending to be among the smallest for all three companies.

The results of this "small sample" study provide empirical evidence that, among five commonly employed "rules of thumb" definitions for materiality, sizable differences can occur depending upon the industry of the client and the definition chosen. For example, for the financial company examined, the largest of the materiality measures was, on average, over 13 times bigger than the smallest measures over the period 1977 to 1986. Such large differences in materiality definitions would presumably lead to correspondingly large differences in audit scope decisions, depending on which definition is chosen to quantify "planning materiality." The differences may also carry over into the pricing of audit services by different auditors for the same client, and thus affect the competitive market for audits. While more evidence is needed, it appears that additional authoritative guidance would be helpful. As evidence, given the lack of quantitative guidelines from the FASB, at least one Big 8 firm has developed its own materiality guidelines to ensure intra-firm decision consistency. Perhaps it is time for the profession as a whole to follow suit.

Source: Kurt Pany and Stephen Wheeler, "A Comparison of Various Materiality Rules of Thumb," *The CPA Journal* (June 1989), pp. 62–63. Reprinted with permission from *The CPA Journal*, June 1989, copyright 1989.

---

on the overall system of internal accounting control, stage two would be performed on all significant control areas.

Recall that Exhibit 13–3 shows the process of identifying material weaknesses in control, emphasizing the various interpretations of the results of tests of control.

Material weaknesses may be resolved by increasing the audit scope or by issuing either a qualified report or disclaimer. The auditor should document the effect of reportable conditions and may wish to direct special attention to the effect of material weaknesses on the audit scope and the audit report in the working papers. Of particular concern to the CPA making interim statements is the likely effect of observed material weaknesses on interim financial reports. The existence of a material weakness, however, does not mean that there is a material error; it merely implies the possibility of material errors. In that sense, material weaknesses have a futuristic dimension.

Reporting Responsibilities

Professional pronouncements include a requirement that reportable conditions be communicated to the audit committee:

Although [SAS 60, Section 325] . . . does not require that the auditor separately identify and communicate material weaknesses, the auditor may choose or the client may request the auditor to separately identify and communicate as material weaknesses those reportable conditions that, in the auditor's judgment, are considered to be material weaknesses." (SAS 60, Section 325, p. 5, paragraph 15)

As noted earlier, communication need not be in writing but, if oral, should be carefully documented in the working papers as to both the time and content of the discussion. No report to the public is required. As already suggested, it is possible for the auditor to adjust audit procedures in order to reflect observed weaknesses in control, including material weaknesses, in order to form an evidential base that can support the issuance of an unqualified or clean audit report. However, from a litigation point of view, communication of material weaknesses in a formal written manner may be advisable. Consider the 1989 report in the *Wall Street Journal* that Arthur Young & Co. was appealing a 1987 case in which a California state court ruled that the accounting firm was liable for $4.2 million in damages to investors who relied on unaudited quarterly financial statements of a computer company, which collapsed.

A jury rules that, had our firm issued a letter on the material weaknesses of the company's internal controls, management wouldn't have issued the interim financial statements," says Carl Liggio, general counsel of Arthur Young. [Lee Berton, "Law: Suits Against CPAs Are More Creative—And More Common" (February 8, 1989), p. B8]

Reporting Material Weakness

The various report forms in Exhibit 17–1 require that material weaknesses be disclosed. While SAS No. 30 outlines the possible report forms related to internal accounting control that can be prepared by the CPA, it provides no directions or illustrations as to how disclosures regarding material weaknesses can be communicated in a meaningful form—particularly to the general public. When various professionals who prepare or use reports on internal control were asked by the author to evaluate the ramifications of a set of internal control points related to control weaknesses, widely diverse reactions were observed. For example, mutual fund and financial analysts saw the absence of audit committees and internal auditors as having a far more negative effect on control than did CPAs. The interpretation of control weaknesses for small entities relative to large entities ranged from the feeling that small entities could frequently be managed effectively without many of the formal procedures and practices of a larger entity, to the opinion that weaknesses could be even worse for the small entity that is not as financially sound and that may be merely a marginal participant in an industry. CPAs widely recognize the difficulty in interpreting disclosures of weaknesses in accounting controls, without some specific context and some reasonably in-depth knowledge of the entity's operations. Since disclosure practices are supposed to have explicit, complete, and unequivocal content with facts that are apparent to prudent investors, the diverse interpretation of control disclosures that has been reported in past research (see Wallace, 1982) is troublesome. In addition to the interpretation problem, there is some risk of losing competitive advantages.

Take care that trade secrets on control procedures are not disseminated. Survey evidence indicates concern that control reports may disclose proprietary information. There are two primary risks that could create a competitive disadvantage to the reporting companies:

(1) specific information on existing controls that were developed through the expenditure of a significant amount of resources can be "given away" to the competition through control disclosures; and

(2) the public disclosure of a control system's weak points makes the entity vulnerable to exploitation. Of particular interest is the fact that when internal accounting control reports are obtained by the Federal Home Loan Board, they are unavailable to the public—based on conversations with one representative of the Board—because the information on material weaknesses could be utilized to "beat the control system" of a financial institution (see Wallace, Spring 1982, p. 22).

The implication of these risks is that entities and CPAs should take care in preparing control disclosures to assure that trade secrets on optimal control procedures are not disseminated and that the inevitable risk exposure that might stem from disclosing control weaknesses is appropriately limited.

How to describe material weaknesses. While explicitly considering these potential interpretation problems and the risks related to particular disclosures, the CPA should carefully describe material weaknesses by indicating

—the control objective not being met,

—the errors and irregularities that could occur, due to this weakness, and

—whether the weakness relates to control design or compliance with control design.

The idea is to effectively communicate risk exposure. While the primary dichotomy of material versus immaterial weaknesses quantifies risk, the description of the type of error or irregularity that might result is of particular interest to the user of the report in interpreting the specific assets or financial statement line items that are exposed to risk of loss and misstatement. The literature has suggested that disclosures be made as to the volume of transactions processed by an entity in particular areas of control weakness, to assist in the users' interpretation of control reports. However, such suggestions have not become a part of typical disclosure practices.

Examples of disclosures concerning material weaknesses for each operating cycle. Exhibit 17–4 presents numerous examples of disclosures con-

Exhibit 17–4

Examples of Disclosures Concerning Material Weaknesses
for Each Operating Cycle

Revenue or Income-Producing Cycle

Cash Sales tickets are prenumbered but not accounted for, resulting in the possibility of unrecorded sales.

Cash receipts are not vouchered upon receipt and the cash receipt book is not controlled by means of prenumbering the book's pages. The lack of such a control limits the effectiveness with which management can safeguard the company's cash balances against errors and irregularities. Due to the nature of the asset, even relatively minor weaknesses in control can result in serious problems.

The accounts receivable subsidiary ledger is not being reconciled to the general ledger. No assurance exists of proper accounting records and appropriate billing practices.

The entity has a substantial amount invested in certificates of deposits. Consideration should be given to establishing securities records in sufficient detail that a ready check can be made of all essential information, particularly the promptness with which income is received.

Heavy reliance is placed on finance companies in determining customers' credit worthiness and in following up on delinquent accounts. Recently the company has experienced significant losses resulting from customer default on recourse financing arrangements. We urge management to consider hiring an in-house credit manager.

Regulations require that mortgage loan officers review the need for flood hazard insurance. Yet, no written documentation exists that indicates where flood insurance is and is not required. Hence, no written evidence exists that this important procedure was performed.

When loans are made to builders with whom the entity has experience, no current financial statements are obtained from those builders. This lack of current information could well result in the inadequate safeguarding of assets.

Loan interest calculated on a monthly basis results in an effective interest rate that exceeds the stated annual percentage rate. This situation could cause problems with respect to truth-in-lending requirements.

Customers' signed authorizations supporting requests for changes to the master file of names and addresses are not in use, nor is someone other than the teller responsible for processing such requests. As a result, customers' accounts are not being adequately safeguarded from irregularities.

The Association does not follow the general practice of obtaining written authorization from customers who request that no mail be sent to them. Since "no mail accounts" effectively eliminate communication with these customers by management, examiners, and auditors, such written authorization is essential.

Cost of Sales or Production Cycle

Petty cash is maintained in an unlocked box in the vault compartment, accessible to virtually all employees.

Petty cash funds have been expanding in amount. They are not being maintained on an imprest basis. At the time of replenishment, the petty cash vouchers are not being properly canceled.

Exhibit 17–4 (continued)

The fund has been used for payroll advances. Vouchers are prepared, signed by the employee, and the amounts noted are deducted from the subsequent pay check. Such a practice is not in line with the purpose of maintaining the petty cash fund, and it effectively eliminates control over cash disbursements via requiring payments by check.

The head bookkeeper prepares checks, prepares the cash disbursements journal, signs checks, and has access to all records. Such a lack of segregated duties permits control to be exercised over the accounting records by a person who also handles or controls cash transactions without any intervention by another person to provide some cross-check. As a result, errors and irregularities could occur that would be very difficult and perhaps impossible to detect.

Blocks of blank checks are periodically sent to branch locations to facilitate small disbursements. However, no initial control is established over those check numbers that are transferred. Checks are separately keypunched into the general ledger without any control features to ensure that all checks have been entered correctly. Checks involving transfers between bank accounts are not recorded on a timely basis, but are recorded at the end of the month, based on check copies. No batch totals or other input controls are used. Due to recent cash flow difficulties, a large number of written checks have been held for extended periods, without any security measures. As a result, the entity cannot have assurance that all disbursements were appropriate, recorded accurately, or recorded in the correct time period for financial statement reporting purposes.

Company checks require only one signature. Furthermore, authority for both signing and preparing checks rests with the same individual. This absence of properly segregated duties could result in inappropriate cash disbursements.

Loan disbursement checks are being made payable to other than the borrower. This is not in compliance with prescribed procedures and may facilitate irregular disbursement practices.

Branch bank accounts are being reconciled by a person who has cash-receiving, cash-disbursing, or recording-of-cash functions. This lack of segregated duties removes the effectiveness of reconciliations as a control check.

Bank reconciliations contain reconciling items that have been carried forward from month to month. If bank reconciliations are to provide an effective safeguard against the misuse of cash, all reconciling items should be cleared promptly. We noted bank accounts that have checks outstanding for as many as nine years.

Current payroll procedures call for departmental supervisors' approval of hours worked, distribution of pay, and maintenance of custody over unclaimed wages. Time clocks are not in use as a basis for the preparation of payroll. Changes, additions, and deletions to the master file for payroll can be generated by the department requesting the adjustment, and confirmation that such changes have been made is received directly by the party making the request, rather than by the party that is responsible for approving personnel changes for the entity. As a result, unauthorized erroneous or irregular payroll disbursements are possible without detection.

Subsidiary ledgers for withholdings from independent truckers' receivables are incorrect due to program logic errors. This programming error has existed for three years without correction.

The company purchases a large quantity of material on a cash on delivery (C.O.D.) basis. Often, no supporting documents are available when the payment is made, other than a check request. The possibility exists of paying for more than is received and of issuing a duplicate payment when an invoice is received on a subsequent date.

When goods are purchased for resale, such orders originate in the sales department, rather than being subjected to the controls of the purchasing department. Proper handling and ac-

Exhibit 17-4 (continued)

counting for such goods is not ensured by such an effective circumvention of purchasing controls.

The entity's parts department personnel have custodianship responsibilities as well as authority to make sales to customers. Invoices that are generated manually, rather than by the computer, are processed by the parts department to reflect the reduction in inventory that results from the sale. No control exists to ensure that the reductions noted in the record are accurate or posted on a timely basis. When credit memos are issued to customers, often information noted is incomplete and no separate approval of the transaction is required. The parts sold according to completed invoices are not reconciled to deletions from inventory, nor are general ledger inventory accounts tied back to perpetual records on a daily basis, due to timing differences in processing. As a result, unauthorized removal of inventories, erroneous and untimely recording of inventory depletion on both perpetual and ledger records, and unauthorized or erroneous issuance of credit memos are all possible problems.

Financing and Nonroutine Transactions—Including Safeguarding, General Accounting, and EDP Considerations

Extra keys to the tellers' cash boxes and to vault compartments are typically stored in a key vault that requires two keys for access. However, this designed control feature is circumvented when either the manager or the assistant manager is not on duty, as both keys are then placed in the custody of the one individual on duty.

No procedures exist to check that officers and employees are not processing transactions in their own bank accounts. Nor is an independent officer performing at least an annual review of officers' and employees' accounts. No assurance exists that the records are accurate or that assets are being effectively safeguarded.

The cash balance of the entity is excessive in terms of normal operating requirements. Cash disbursements are not centralized, demand deposits are high, and earnings from the investment of such funds are being foregone.

Journal entries lacked proper authorization and explanation. Frequently, documentation supporting entries could not be located. Erroneous or irregular entries could be recorded in the accounting records under the current conditions of control compliance.

The chart of accounts has not been altered for numerous years, despite the need for specialized accounts to ensure accurate financial records that meet both tax and financial statement reporting needs. Intercompany accounts should be created to facilitate the elimination of intercompany amounts at year-end. The lack of a full set of detailed accounts has resulted in diverse account classification practices across branches for similar income and expense items.

The client does not effectively monitor the data processing service bureau-produced records. The center's daily audit report, summarizing supervisory overrides, changes, or removals of hold conditions, activity in inactive accounts, and similar events, is not reviewed, nor are the records generated by the center subjected to any tests of mathematical accuracy. As a result, control is not effective over information processed by the service center.

Management has investigated the feasibility of obtaining insurance coverage to protect it against expenses and losses from the suspension of computer center operations and has found that such coverage is not available on an individual basis. However, we recommend that this matter be brought to the attention of the "user group" of the computer center to determine if such coverage might be obtainable under the auspices of the center itself.

cerning material weaknesses for each operating cycle. Most of the disclosures relate to control design, although noncompliance with controls or circumvention of designed controls is explicitly cited in a few of the disclosures. Several items are brief, as the effects of the observed weakness are evident from the description of the weakness. Some disclosures could clearly have adverse effects on the competitive position of the entity, such as the truth-in-lending issue regarding interest charges on loans. Other disclosures, such as the lack of safeguards over petty cash, inadequate controls over employees' and officers' accounts, and the ease of master file changes to payroll records and customer names and addresses, could all be abused to increase the risk exposure of the entity to the reported control weaknesses. A common practice that may help deter such negative ramifications is the inclusion, in the report, of management's corrective actions. A simple statement that the client "has taken appropriate control procedures to correct this observed weakness" or "plans to take" such action will suffice. Of course, the CPA, as already noted, is responsible for testing the effectiveness of such corrective action, if it is to be cited in the control report.

Additional perspective on internal control weaknesses and descriptives on material weaknesses within the government setting are offered in Exhibit 17–5.

Exhibit 17–5

Material Weaknesses Disclosure in the Government Sector

Principal Findings

| Internal Control Weaknesses Affect Program Management and Accountability | Strengthening internal controls in the federal government will require a continuous emphasis by agency managers and a sustained commitment from the administration and the Congress. While GAO has seen progress since passage of the Financial Integrity Act, serious internal control problems remain. Solutions are often complex and may require an investment in funds which can be difficult in times of federal budget deficits. |

Internal control weaknesses reported by agencies under the act cover a broad range of government programs and operations such as accounting and financial management, procurement, debt collection, and property management. More than a third of the remaining weaknesses were first reported by agencies in 1983 or 1984, and a number of them were well known years before the act's passage. Reported internal control problems have serious consequences. Some examples follow.

- The Department of Defense cannot account for over $600 million in advances made by foreign customers for weapons systems purchases.
- Medicaid recipients and providers of Medicaid services abusing the system may have cost the federal government at least $54 million, and possibly as much as $400 million in 1985, although internal control weaknesses were identified in 1978.
- Weaknesses in agencies' collection systems remain and delinquencies in nontax debt owed the federal government have grown by 55 percent in 3 years to $24 billion.

Exhibit 17–5 (continued)

- Agencies paid almost 25 percent of their bills late, thereby incurring millions of dollars annually in interest penalties. They also paid close to a quarter of their bills too soon, thus costing the government at least $350 million annually in lost interest.
- The Social Security Administration, which has long-standing accounting system problems, credits workers with $58.5 billion less in earnings than does the Internal Revenue Service, a difference which may result in underpayments to an estimated 9 million beneficiaries.
- The basic lack of internal controls over its $160 billion inventory, which Defense cites as the most serious departmentwide problem, has, among other things, reportedly allowed explosives to fall into the hands of extremist organizations.

Agency self-evaluations of internal control systems have resulted in identifying 229 new weaknesses in 1986. Identifying weaknesses is an important aspect of the act and is an important step toward achieving the act's objectives. It shows that agencies and the administration are committed to implementing the act by recognizing that federal managers must continuously focus on identifying and correcting internal control problems.

Actions To Strengthen Internal Controls Continue	Agencies continue to correct their internal control problems and reported in 1986 that they had corrected more than two-thirds of their material weaknesses reported since 1983. Following are some examples.

- The Navy reported that it had strengthened internal controls to ensure the security of classified material and physical security at several commands and activities.
- The Army said it had corrected internal control weaknesses which had caused flying hour funding requirements to be overstated by $130 million.
- The Department of the Treasury reported that it installed a system which improved the reliability and efficiency of accounting operations for billions of dollars in U.S. savings bonds.

Verifying that control weaknesses are promptly and effectively corrected is an essential task in this process. GAO found instances where (1) corrective measures taken had not completely corrected the identified weaknesses and (2) actions to resolve audit findings, which could potentially save millions of dollars, had been delayed, in some cases for years.

The Defense Department, for instance, reported it had corrected over two-thirds of the material weaknesses it identified since 1983. Although we did not confirm that the reported actions have been taken, following are some examples of significant improvements reported for 1986.

- The Air Force reported that, through strengthening internal controls, it reduced by 32 percent the value of Air Force "undefinitized contractual actions," which had surged to a level of $12.9 billion at the end of fiscal year 1985. Undefinitized contractual actions authorize the start of work prior to finalizing pricing agreements between the government and the contractor. The Air Force also stated that through verifying and correcting data, which are key controls, it has been able to ensure that the number of expendable spare parts for F100 aircraft engines is sufficient to meet Air Force mission requirements.

Exhibit 17–5 (continued)

- As part of an effort to address serious internal control weaknesses in its health care activities, the Army reported that it had completed verification of active duty Army physicians' credentials and that it had taken actions to increase the exchange of such information among the Army, state medical boards, and the American Medical Association. The Army also stated that weak internal controls which led to errors in an Army model for determining flying hour requirements for its pilots had been corrected. Mistakes related to the flaws in the model had contributed to a $130-million overstatement of funding requirements.
- The Navy reported it had strengthened internal controls to ensure the security of classified material and physical security and had implemented automated controls and guidance to prevent duplicate payments made by Navy finance centers.
- The Department of Labor reported that it had corrected several internal control weaknesses in its Mine Safety and Health Administration's regulations which had impaired the investigation of mine accidents and injuries and the reporting of these data.
- Treasury reported having installed a system to improve the reliability and efficiency of accounting operations for billions of dollars in U.S. savings bonds.
- The Department of Energy reported correcting a number of internal control weaknesses which were key to effective administration of its Petroleum Pricing Violation Program. The objective of the program is to investigate petroleum pricing violations, recover overcharges, and make restitution to injured parties.
- HHS reported that SSA had completed acquisition of a hardware back-up and implementation of a contingency plan for its principal ADP center.

As highlighted below, our work has confirmed that there has been some progress in correcting identified internal control weaknesses.

- In 1983 and 1984, the Department of Transportation reported material weaknesses in the Urban Mass Transportation Administration's (UMTA) bus grants program, which cost $336.5 million in fiscal year 1986. The weaknesses resulted in UMTA's approving funds for additional buses for some transit systems which already had more buses than they needed. Transportation reported the weaknesses as corrected in 1985. To correct the problem, UMTA had (1) issued guidelines governing federal assistance for the purchase, rehabilitation, and stockpiling of buses to ensure that grantees properly manage their bus fleets, (2) increased monitoring of grantee bus management practices through triennial reviews, and (3) withheld or denied funds for the acquisition of buses by grantees with excess buses. In an April 1987 report, we noted that corrective actions were being adhered to by UMTA's regional offices, which administer the program. (See GAO/RCED-87-97, April 28, 1987.)
- In August 1987, we reported that the Department of the Interior's Bureau of Land Management had essentially corrected a major internal control weakness in its management of royalties due the government for drilling and mining activities on federally-owned land. Between 1976 and 1984, the Bureau's failure to promptly readjust federal coal leases had resulted in an estimated loss of $187 million in royalty and rental payments. Our review of readjustments scheduled for 1985 and 1986 found that all but one of the scheduled readjustments had been made on time. (See GAO/RCED-87-164, August 25, 1987.)

Exhibit 17–5 (continued)

Agencies Do Not Consistently Ensure Effective and Prompt Actions	An important step in strengthening internal controls is verifying that planned actions have been implemented as envisioned and that the completed corrective actions have been effective. During our review of agencies' 1986 Financial Integrity Act reports, we noted some differences in how agencies defined completed corrective actions.

For example, Defense generally included corrective action plans in its reports which showed specific tasks and estimated completion dates. Some of the tasks called for an evaluation as to whether the corrective actions have been effective before considering a weakness corrected. On the other hand, Defense, as well as other agencies, sometimes considered a weakness as having been corrected through the issuance of policy guidelines or plans for corrective actions.

Audits are another tool to help managers detect and correct internal control problems, and the Financial Integrity Act calls for prompt resolution of audit findings. However, as we recently reported, managers are not always effectively or expeditiously availing themselves of this tool.

Corrective Actions Taken Were Not Always Effective

Although, as discussed in the previous section, a number of corrective actions have been effective, we also found some instances where, contrary to agencies' reports, this was not the case. Following are some examples.

- In August 1987, we reported that the Bureau of Indian Affairs' Housing Improvement Program, which provides housing assistance grants to families in 271 tribes, continued to contain internal control weaknesses and that the agency did not have adequate assurance that the most needy Indian families were being served and that funds were being properly spent. Based on issuance of a model contract to be used by all tribes that have contracted to manage the program, the Department of the Interior reported the weakness as corrected in its 1984 Financial Integrity Act report. However, based on recently completed work, we concluded that, although the model contract is a positive step toward improving program effectiveness, the material weakness reported by Interior in 1983 still existed. (See GAO/RCED-87-148, August 5, 1987.)
- The Department of Housing and Urban Development (HUD) reported deficiencies in the appraisal review process for its Single-Family Housing Insurance Program as a material weakness in its 1983 and 1984 Financial Integrity Act reports. Based on actions to improve appraisers' performance and its supervision over them, the Department reported this problem as corrected in 1985. We reported in September 1987 that, although some corrective actions were implemented, we found that HUD still was not adequately monitoring appraisers' performance or properly controlling the field review process. The program has experienced billions of dollars of losses since its inception. Internal control weaknesses and adverse economic conditions in certain areas of the country contributed to the program's $629 million loss in fiscal year 1986. (See GAO/RCED-87-165, September 30, 1987.)
- In its 1983 Financial Integrity Act report, the Department of Labor cited material weaknesses in its Federal Employees Compensation Act Program, including deficiencies in assuring the accuracy and reasonableness of payments made to medical providers. Labor reported in 1986 that the final action to correct the weaknesses, the establishment of a medical

Exhibit 17–5 (continued)

fee schedule to limit payments to the program's medical providers, was completed. However, in a subsequent review, we found that this medical fee schedule covered less than half of the program's medical payments and that additional controls were needed to limit payments to medical providers not covered by the schedule, such as hospitals and pharmacies. (See GAO/IMTEC-88-9, December 1987.)

Audit Follow-Up Systems Not Always Effective

Audits are tools for agency managers to help detect problem areas and find solutions to improve internal control weaknesses. However, agencies' 1986 Financial Integrity Act reports and our recent review of recommendations made by Defense internal auditors, suggest that not all agencies are fully availing themselves of these tools.

Managers are required to have a follow-up system to ensure that internal control weaknesses reported in their Financial Integrity Act reports are promptly and effectively implemented. In addition, as prescribed by the act, the Comptroller General's internal control standards include an audit resolution standard which requires managers to take prompt, responsive action on all findings and recommendations made by auditors.

Agencies' Actions To Strengthen Internal Controls

Status of Material Weaknesses Reported by Agencies During Fiscal Years 1983 Through 1986

Agency	Number of material weaknesses		
	Reported	Corrected	Pending
Agriculture	401	314	87
Commerce	27	22	5
Defense	316	217	99
Education	42	28	14
Energy	8	4	4
EPA	12	10	2
GSA	25	24	1
HHS	258	229	29
HUD	47	13	34
Interior	114	69	45
Justice	14	8	6
Labor	26	14	12
NASA	19	6	13
SBA	44	30	14
State	16	5	11
Transportation	84	60	24
Treasury	37	6	31
VA	25	13	12
Total	**1,515**	**1,072**	**443**

Exhibit 17–5 (continued)

Serious Internal Control Weaknesses Remain

Comparison of the Number of Agencies Reporting Material Weaknesses by Category

Category	Number of agencies[a]			
	1983	1984	1985	1986
Procurement	14	14	13	13
Grant, loan, and debt collection management	13	13	14	11
Eligibility and entitlement determinations	9	10	9	8
Cash management	12	12	12	13
Automated data processing	10	14	17	17
Property management	14	15	16	16
Financial management and accounting systems	17	17	17	17
Personnel and organizational management	10	12	11	16

[a]The 23 agencies reviewed included 6 Defense agencies (Office of the Secretary of Defense, Army, Navy, Air Force, the Defense Logistics Agency, and the Defense Security Assistance Agency). Because the 6 agencies were included in one report to the Congress and the President, the figures in this table are based on a total of 18 agencies. Information in the remaining tables in this report is also based on these 18 agencies.

Source: United States General Accounting Office, Report to Congress, "Financial Integrity Act," (GAO/AFMD-88-10), pp. 3, 4, 13, 28–31, 46–50.

In addition to accountants' reports on control, another source of information on controls is available to financial statement users—the management report.

REPORTS BY MANAGEMENT: DISCLOSURE PRACTICES IN THE PAST AND THEIR LIABILITY IMPLICATIONS FOR THE PROFESSION

Reports by management have been recommended by the Committee on Auditor's Responsibilities and the American Institute of Certified Public Accountants' Special Advisory Committee in its report entitled "Tentative Conclusion and Recommendations of the Reports by Management." In addition, the Financial Executives Institute has endorsed the practice of issuing management reports in annual reports to shareholders. Management reports were noted to have appeared in 38% of annual reports reviewed by *Business Week* (April 16, 1978) compared to only four of those companies' disclosures in the prior year. Similarly, a 1979 study of 305 companies of the Fortune top 1,000 indicated that 40% had issued management reports relative to 23% in 1978 (see Beresford et al, 1980). This widespread reporting practice has ramifications for CPAs because these reports commonly discuss the role of the CPA and the internal control system of the entity. When these issues are discussed together, misleading statements may be made that imply greater involvement in control evaluations by the auditor than is actually the case for the typical audit engagement.

In particular, disclosures in past management reports regarding the requirements of generally accepted auditing standards and the nature of internal control have lacked precision. As discussed at length in prior chapters, a CPA makes an economic choice as to the level of control risk and may perform steps to gain an understanding of the control structure and no more. When attention is directed at detailed controls, it focuses only on those controls on which the CPA intends to set control risk at less than a maximum level, and these controls are properly termed "internal accounting controls" as distinct from "internal controls." Operating or administrative controls encompass far more than internal accounting controls, yet are not subjected to review or testing by the CPA, beyond their direct effect on accounting controls. The audit engagement alone does not provide a basis for reporting on the adequacy of internal controls or internal accounting controls. The sole control-related requirement is that material weaknesses that come to the auditor's attention during the audit engagement be communicated to top management. Under generally accepted auditing standards there is no requirement that each control be evaluated or that every material weakness be identified. When a weakness is cited, its materiality is evaluated relative to financial statements, which may be a different criterion that those applied by management or various users of an entity's information when they are evaluating the adequacy of controls.

In spite of these facts about CPAs' prescribed activities, past survey results reported by the Commission on Auditors' Responsibilities have documented the belief of bankers or financial analysts, and shareholders that an audit exam means that the CPA has evaluated the adequacy of the accounting system. This belief is being encouraged by imprecise disclosures in management reports. The nature of internal control, particularly regarding its limitations, is not adequately discussed in management reports, creating a wrong impression that well-designed controls somehow guarantee that fraud has not and will not occur. Few disclosures by management acknowledge the role of cost/benefit considerations, and many reports use the term "internal control" as though it were synonymous with internal accounting control. The key problem in reporting practices is the loose coupling of discussions of the adequacy of internal accounting controls and descriptions of independent auditors' activities. For example, in reviewing the audit committees' activities, reports will frequently state that the committee discussed the internal auditors' and independent CPAs' evaluation of internal accounting controls or their opinions on the adequacy of internal accounting controls.

As reported in Exhibit 17–6, a number of different CPA firms provide services to the companies, and many of the disclosures make no distinction between internal controls and internal accounting controls. The evidence suggests a widespread practice by the profession of implicitly condoning imprecise control-related disclosures by clients via their management reports. Exhibit 17–6 includes a couple of examples of wording in 1985 reports, suggesting that the 1980 practices have

Exhibit 17–6

Disclosures in Management Reports Related to Auditors' Formation and Expression of Opinions on Internal Control

Client's Name (Year for Which Annual Report Was Examined)	CPA Firm	Management Report's Phrasing
Aluminum Company of America (1980)	Coopers & Lybrand	[Internal auditors and independent CPAs] "discuss their evaluation of internal accounting controls."
The Continental Group, Inc. (1980)	Deloitte Haskins & Sells	"The results of their (internal and external auditors') audits, their opinions on the adequacy of internal accounting controls" [are discussed].
General Electric Company (1980)	Peat, Marwick, Mitchell & Co.	"The public accountants . . . discuss . . . their opinions on the adequacy of internal financial controls."
General Motors Corp. (1979)	Deloitte Haskins & Sells	"Deloitte Haskins & Sells . . . discuss . . . their opinions on the adequacy of internal accounting controls."
Getty Oil Company (1980)	Arthur Andersen & Co.	"The independent auditors . . . discuss . . . opinions on the adequacy of internal controls."
Goodyear Tire & Rubber Company (1980)	Price Waterhouse & Co.	"Price Waterhouse & Co. . . . discuss . . . their opinions on the adequacy of internal controls and the quality of financial reporting."

Exhibit 17–6 (continued)

Client's Name (Year for Which Annual Report Was Examined)	CPA Firm	Management Report's Phrasing
Honeywell, Inc. (1979)	Deloitte Haskins & Sells	"The independent auditors . . . discuss . . . the adequacy of internal accounting controls."
IC Industries (1980)	Peat, Marwick, Mitchell & Co.	"Independent Certified Public Accountants . . . discuss . . . the adequacy of internal controls."
International Harvester Company (1979)	Deloitte Haskins & Sells	"Independent public accountants . . . discuss . . . their opinions on the adequacy of internal accounting controls."
Lockheed Corporation (1980)	Arthur Young & Co.	"Independent accountants . . . discuss . . . their opinions on the adequacy of financial records . . . and the system of internal controls."
Monsanto Company (1979)	Deloitte Haskins & Sells	"Independent auditors . . . discuss . . . the adequacy of internal accounting controls."
National Steel Corp. (1980)	Ernst & Whinney	"Independent public accountants . . . discuss the adequacy of financial controls."
RCA Corp. (1980)	Arthur Young & Co.	"Independent public accountants . . . discuss . . . the adequacy of internal accounting controls."
Union Carbide Corp. (1980)	Main Hurdman & Cranstoun	"Independent and internal auditors . . . discuss . . . the adequacy of internal accounting controls."

Exhibit 17–6 (continued)

Client's Name (Year for Which Annual Report Was Examined)	CPA Firm	Management Report's Phrasing
Westinghouse (1981)	Price Waterhouse & Co.	"Independent accountants . . . discuss . . . their comments on the adequacy of internal accounting controls."

Similar disclosures in 1985	CPA Firm	Management Report's Phrasing
GTE Corporation (1985)	Arthur Andersen & Co.	"Meets periodically with . . . the public accountants to review internal accounting controls"
Dayton Hudson Corporation (1985)	Ernst & Whinney	"The results of the auditors' examinations and their opinions of the adequacy of our internal controls and the quality of our financial reporting are regularly reviewed by the committee"

persisted. Some improvement was apparent in a subset of reports. For example, some management reports focused far more on audit committees' responsibilities:

> The Audit Committee of the Board of Directors, consisting entirely of Directors who are not employees of NCR, monitors the accounting, reporting and internal control systems of NCR. (1984 annual report, p. 35)

The problem with such imprecision is its potential legal ramifications, as well as its effect on individuals' decision-making.

With respect to the former, courts have already contested, though unsuccessfully, the limited evaluation and reporting responsibilities of auditors regarding internal controls [see Ernst & Ernst v. Hochfelder (425 U.S. 185 (1976)), and Adams v. Standard Knitting Mills, Inc. (1976, ¶ 95, 683)]. The commonality of management report disclosures that claim an extended audit function is likely to provide added impetus to litigation disputes. With respect to investors' decisions, both creditors and investors may incorrectly assess the risk profile of operating entities if they believe the auditor's attest function encompasses an opinion on the adequacy of internal controls. Errors in evaluating risk, in turn, imply the misallocation of financial resources.

THE AUDITOR'S RESPONSIBILITY FOR REVIEWING MANAGEMENT'S STATEMENTS

Statement on Auditing Standards No. 8, "Other Information in Documents Containing Audited Financial Statements," requires that the auditor read other information such as the management report, and consider whether such information, or the manner of its presentation, is materially inconsistent with information, or the manner of its presentation, appearing in the financial statements. If the auditor becomes aware of a material misstatement of fact, though not a material inconsistency, the matter should be discussed with the client. This statement suggests that CPAs have been reviewing management reports as part of generally accepted auditing standards and have either deemed the imprecision of control-related disclosures to be immaterial or have failed to persuade clients to revise their disclosures. Most likely the former situation has prevailed. Obviously, the individual CPA must judge the importance of implicit miscommunication of auditors' responsibilities, but little doubt exists that constructive suggestions by the CPA concerning disclosures in management reports could greatly enhance the clarity with which both managements' and auditors' control-related responsibilities are communicated.

SUGGESTIONS THE CPA CAN MAKE CONCERNING DISCLOSURES ON INTERNAL CONTROL

Management reports should encompass

—a statement to the effect that management is responsible for designing controls that provide reasonable but not absolute assurance (i.e., a listing of control objectives would follow),

—acknowledgment that such design is intended to reflect cost/benefit judgments by management since controls should be cost-justified if they are to be established,

—recognition that the maintenance of control is an ongoing process and is management's responsibility, i.e., managers regularly appraise controls,

—a qualification that effective systems depend upon competent employees, (i.e., similar key qualifiers would be listed),

—a reminder that inherent limitations exist in any system of internal control, and

—explicit recognition of external auditors' limited responsibilities with respect to controls, including the fact that
- internal accounting controls, not internal controls, are reviewed,
- generally accepted auditing standards require tests of controls only to the extent deemed to be necessary for auditors' assessment of control risk at less than a maximum level, and
- an issuance of a management letter is distinct from a report on the adequacy of internal accounting control.

Specific reference to material weaknesses by management should, of course, be consistent with auditors' findings. However, no statement should imply that the auditor has provided assurance that no material weaknesses exist. In other words, the CPAs should encourage their clients to inform report users of the role of controls, their limitations, and auditors' restricted involvement with control evaluation. The primary role of management in establishing and monitoring controls should be emphasized.

Obviously, management reports typically concern a variety of subjects beyond internal accounting control, and each of these topics also warrants review by the CPA. However, it is the control-related discussion, with particular emphasis upon external auditors' responsibilities, that is of concern as a reporting issue involving internal accounting control.

HISTORICAL PRESSURES RELATED TO CONTROL REPORTING

The diversity of services described herein is, in part, due to the disagreement over the users' desire for extensive information on internal controls. The SEC proposed, in April 1979, that internal control reports be audited and required for publicly held companies. But, as described in the article reprinted in Exhibit 17–7, after 950 letters protesting the proposal were received, the SEC withdrew its proposal and encouraged voluntary disclosures of the adequacy of entities' control systems. SAS No. 30 was issued in large part to show the various types of voluntary reporting.

Exhibit 17–7

Internal Control Reporting—950 Negative Responses*

Although SAS 30 offers guidance for auditors in reporting on internal accounting control, mandatory reporting is not at issue today. Yet the withdrawal of the SEC proposal leaves open many questions on this subject—inconsistencies within the proposal and auditing literature. In this article there is a discussion of flaws in the SEC's claim that reports on material weaknesses will be useful to investors, as well as problems with the SEC's expectations and proposal of monitoring and estimating the cost of private sector initiatives for public reporting on controls.

Exhibit 17–7 (continued)

Indeed, the Commission continues to believe that management disclosure concerning, and auditor involvement with, issuers' systems of internal accounting control have important values that can be achieved without undue cost or other burdens. (SEC, 1980, p. H-11, IV)

These are the concluding remarks of the SEC in the Withdrawal on June 6, 1980 of their April, 1979 proposal to require a Statement of Management on Internal Accounting Control. Despite the staff's acknowledgment that the original proposal provoked more negative responses than any other proposed rule on accounting, the SEC appears to have wavered only slightly from its initial stance. The Withdrawal Statement reports that

Approximately 550 commentators viewed the Commission's rule proposals as an attempt to require management to report on its compliance with the FCPA (Foreign Corrupt Practices Act) as distinguished from a medium for meaningful disclosures to investors. (Emphasis added.)

Yet, the SEC persists in stating

The withdrawal of these proposals at this time should not be interpreted as a change in the commission's views concerning the importance of effective systems of internal accounting control and of management reporting on and auditor examination of such controls. (Emphasis added.)

What the Withdrawal Statement does is pose an ultimatum. After the SEC monitors

issuer practice in voluntarily providing management statements on internal accounting control and in engaging independent accountants to report on such statements . . . through the spring of 1982 . . . should the Commission's monitoring effort or the comments which it receives identify a specific need for further Commission action, the Commission stands ready to take whatever appropriate regulatory action may be indicated. (Emphasis added.)

In light of this SEC promise to mandate disclosures in the absence of private sector action, it is important that the profession understand what constitutes action in the eyes of the Commission. If reasons exist for questioning the propriety of the SEC's expectations, these reasons should be presented to elicit the Commission's reactions, to direct the profession's development, and to ensure against the misinterpretation of private sector disclosure practices.

The purpose of this article is to provide evidence of primary flaws in

Exhibit 17–7 (continued)

the SEC's analysis of the value of internal accounting control disclosures and consequent problems with the SEC's expectations and proposed means of monitoring "private-sector initiatives for public reporting on internal accounting control." Literature citations, market evidence, and survey findings provide support for the critique.

Reliable Financial Statements in Spite of Inadequate Control

In the SEC's 1979 proposal, the Commission states: "An effective system of internal accounting control has always been necessary to produce reliable financial statements," and the Withdrawal reiterates this assertion.

While difficult to evaluate with such ambiguous language as "effective," "necessary," and "reliable," these statements seem to contradict the accounting and auditing literature. It is widely recognized that a clean audit report can be issued to a company with a poor internal control system.

> It should be understood that when an auditor gives a certificate on the financial statements of a company, he is not necessarily endorsing, or completely satisfied with, the system of internal check and control he finds in effect. He has to take it as he finds it for the current examination, and determine how far it should influence the scope and extent thereof.[1]

While influencing the risk of the auditor, a poor control system will be compensated for through substantive tests to assure that the auditor has the evidential base required to attest to financial statement reliability.

The ability of auditors to compensate for poor controls is supported by the infrequency of audit opinions which are qualified due to problems involving internal accounting control systems. A review of the *Disclosure Journal* indicates that out of all the filings with the SEC, including disclaimers and qualified opinions by auditors, less than 10 companies annually have inadequacies in the internal control system which influence the audit opinion. The SEC Proposal and Withdrawal overstate the "need" for control reports when they claim such controls are essential for reliable financial statements. Further, due to the judgment involved in selecting reporting practices which can significantly affect financial statement reliability, the mere existence of an adequate control system does not preclude the preparation of unreliable financial reporting.

Evidence Is Available on Costs and Benefits

The SEC in its Withdrawal refers to the costs and benefits "asserted" by commentators and points to its intention to evaluate voluntary efforts of registrants to engage independent auditors to examine and publicly report on their system of internal accounting control as a basis for evaluating the

Exhibit 17–7 (continued)

actual costs of such examinations. The inference that only assertions as to the cost/benefit tradeoffs exist ignores the ability to measure such cost and benefits by observing the current market equilibrium and the current demand for and related costs of providing internal control reports to commercial lending officers and private placement debt officers.

It is an empirical fact that market forces have led to accountants' reports on internal control in only two companies' annual reports: J. P. Morgan & Co., Incorporated, and Bankers Trust New York Corporation. This indicates that auditors can furnish these reports but there is little market demand for them. The existence of only two such public disclosures reflects consumers' cost-based valuation of internal control reports.

Even stronger support for the low valuation of auditors' reports on internal control is provided by the fact that commercial lending officers and private placement analysts, in a position to demand internal control reports without the inclusion of such information in annual reports, rarely require them (based on interview and survey evidence collected by the author). Even management letters, normally available to managers and potentially available to such third parties at nominal or no cost to the borrowers, are rarely requested. Based on discussions with loan officers, they are only requested from small to medium-sized companies considered high-risk investment prospects, and the reports are then only useful in raising the right questions. Most officers state that the report would be meaningless without direct access to management to discuss the issues addressed in the management letters.

A direct measure of demand for internal control related information is available from the examination of bonding indentures and covenants. Since companies are rewarded for contracting to supply information for monitoring bonding covenants at the times of entering into covenants, i.e., by being able to sell the securities at higher prices with the covenants than without them, the companies have incentives to fill information requests by third parties and to provide the most useful means of monitoring their performance to third parties. Yet, the required types of reports specified in bond covenants do not include management letters or other internal accounting control reports.

SEC's Proposed Basis for Calculating Costs of Auditor Examination of Controls

In light of the current market equilibrium and disclosure practices in the private placement markets, if an increased number of voluntary reports on internal accounting control with auditor examinations are observed, the underlying demand for such disclosures is properly attributed to the SEC and its regulatees' desire to deter future rule-making by the Commission.

Exhibit 17–7 (continued)

Investors' "need" for such reports will remain unsupported. It can be predicted that those companies which voluntarily opt for such reports will be highly regulated ones like banking institutions that believe that without such voluntary action, the reports are likely to be mandated; or companies that have low marginal costs related to such reports. Hence, the data reviewed by the SEC as a basis for assessing the actual cost of its withdrawal proposal will be systematically understating the costs of imposing the disclosure on all SEC registrants.

The voluntary issuers' cost data will provide only a least cost or minimum floor from which to evaluate the incremental costs of auditors' examination of control reports. Those companies for which control reports are deemed not to be cost beneficial (even in light of the possible benefit of deterring regulation) will not be included in the data base. Yet, subsequent regulation from the SEC would be likely to encompass all registrants.

A mandatory CPA examination of controls would fall with the greatest severity on smaller registrants. Not only does the traditional "little GAAP" argument apply, but the quality of controls is typically less for smaller companies because of the scale of operations. The business itself does not require sophisticated controls to conduct normal business, and frequently owner-managers are considered reasonable replacements for numerous controls typically found in larger companies. Subjective attributes like loyal employees are also likely to play a role in assessing control adequacy. Bankers who lend to small businesses state that personal acquaintance with the owner/manager is the primary information used in the lending decision. In light of current control practices and credit relations of small businesses, there are two central problems with applying a regulation similar to the SEC 1979 proposal. First, auditors are likely to be unwilling to rely on subjective support for system adequacy, e.g., employee loyalty, or to accept the owner/manager's presence as an "adequate" control. Hence, smaller companies will be forced to implement more objective, though unnecessary, control measures; based on the status quo, these controls will not be cost justified. Second, if creditors have direct access to small business, it is unlikely that a report by a CPA on general control adequacy will be of any use whatsoever. Further, since other small business investors are frequently knowledgeable of the operations and personally acquainted with management, the same argument applies.

These problems with regulation also exist with voluntary issuance of auditors' reports on control. It is unreasonable for the SEC to expect the majority of businesses, particularly small businesses, to undergo auditors' examination of internal control in the absence of creditors' or investors' demand for such information, given the substantial costs related to such an audit extension.

Exhibit 17–7 (continued)

One possible alternative for the SEC would be to exempt smaller registrants from both the SEC's expectations of voluntary reporting and subsequent regulation, as offered in the 1979 Proposal. Yet, "most of the problems related to internal control systems are concerned with medium-sized and smaller companies just entering the public market." (*Financial Analysts Journal*, May–June 1980, p. 79). If an internal control report is to be required (or expected through voluntary actions), there is no clear rationale for exempting smaller companies.

SEC's Focus in Estimating Actual Costs Too Narrow

Not only is there a predictable bias in the data base proposed by the SEC as useful in evaluating the cost of regulation similar to the 1979 Proposal, but there is a predictable exclusion of relevant cost factors.

The concept of describing uncorrected material weaknesses in the annual report assumes:

- Management should be placed in a defensive position when not correcting material weaknesses, i.e., it is desirable to pressure management to implement controls to correct cited "material weaknesses";
- Some benefit is derived from the implied "bad information" that material weaknesses exist in the internal control system;
- A description of a material weakness can be understood without thorough knowledge of the internal accounting control system of the entity;
- Users will comprehend that a material weakness does not translate to a probable loss;
- Such reported weaknesses cannot be utilized to "rip-off" resources;
- Significant competitive disadvantages will not result;
- Users comprehend auditors' current responsibility, particularly the absence of a cost/benefit analysis of controls; and
- There is a significant problem with weaknesses in the control systems of corporations and this information is of value.

If any one of these assumptions is in error, extensive "misinformation" will be communicated through public reporting of material weaknesses. The third and fourth points may well be the most critical.

The risk exposure due to a given control weakness is a judgment which may differ across business managers and across auditors. There are even cases where a material weakness is also a material strength to a control system. The classic example is in the owner-managed company where owner participation replaces numerous controls involving segregation of duties in larger entities. Yet from a creditor's perspective, the dependence

Exhibit 17–7 (continued)

primarily on the owner can be an extremely risky proposition. In the auditing literature, decisions that are matters of judgment are rarely described because of the professional expertise and information required to evaluate the circumstances. Ordinarily, an opinion is "better left unexplained." For instance, when an auditor lacks independence, he simply states that fact, not explaining, for example, that the lack of independence is based on his wife's ownership of 5% of the client's stock. Such an explanation could confuse the user, implying that he should reassess whether the auditor is indeed lacking independence. A measure of overall system adequacy or risk exposure appears to be a superior means of discussing internal controls when compared with the proposed alternative of listing material weaknesses, which implies users have some basis for evaluating the importance of the individual weaknesses.

A survey by the author in 1979 indicates there is substantial diversity in the interpretation of the effect of internal control points on report users' assessment of management. This observed diversity suggests that the report form of a management letter or a listing of material weaknesses alone is inadequate to provide a basis for evaluation of a company's management. The respondents noted that it was impossible to evaluate the internal control points without knowing more about the company and the context of the control suggestion.

Similarly, description of the means of evaluating internal accounting controls implies that the user of the report can meaningfully incorporate such information in an investment decision. Yet, without in-depth knowledge of an entity, evaluating the appropriateness of a review technique is extremely difficult. The disclosure of the basis for the management opinion, suggested in the original SEC proposal and in the Withdrawal statement, will likely be uninformative and its effect will be much like an advertising marketing reaction: what "sounds" best. For example, if one company has a periodic inventory system with six spot-checks a year, while another firm has a perpetual inventory system but poor control over the accessibility of inventory, which firm's description of the approach to controlling inventory is preferred? If one firm follows "common industry practices" while another "unlike, other companies in this industry . . ." adopts a unique control of approach to controls, how can this be evaluated? To give an adequate description of internal control, the length of disclosures would be excessive. To give less, particularly with some description, is misleading in the inference that "information" is being made available; data, perhaps, but certainly not information.

The questionable information content of proposed disclosures is supported empirically by a survey (reported in the *Financial Analysts Journal*, May–June, 1980) of 112 Chartered Financial Analysts, 60% to 70% of whom believed that a report on internal accounting controls could not lead

Exhibit 17–7 (continued)

to valid inferences about the quality of management, the likelihood of embezzlement or other impropriety, the reliability of audited financial statements (in addition to the auditor's opinion), the reliability of unaudited financial information or compliance with the FCPA (p. 79—Survey by Holzmann).

In light of such questionable benefits the costs related to internal control regulation of registrants would be expected to affect the capital formation process by encouraging more private debt placements.

An investigation of financial disclosure in a competitive economy, indicates that disclosures interfering with management's legitimate right to make decisions (in this case, the selection of internal control policies), should be viewed as "disfunctional" and as having a harmful effect on capital formation. In addition, the disclosure of material weaknesses in control systems can have a competitive impact. Despite the problems with such reports in terms of information content, some users will evaluate such disclosures as "bad news" and reallocate resources. Further, there is some possibility that the information will be sued to "beat the control system" of the entity, and thereby "rip-off" assets of a company which otherwise were adequately safeguarded. Some "trade secrets" may be disseminated in control related disclosures.

The application of the ruling to all companies will clearly alter the relative wealth positions of small and large ones as well as those in industries with differing control practices. Business conditions can be expected to lead to adequate controls for large companies, with those businesses with very liquid assets necessarily having more extensive control systems. Hence, the relative costs of conforming with regulations are not uniform across companies. Competitive disadvantages from financial disclosure are possible when the costs of disclosure fall unevenly on competing companies. Consideration should be given to the cumulative costs to the company (of disclosure) as well as to the effects of disclosure on hardship cases which may be so severe as to imperil some companies' survival.

Lifting Limitation on Materiality Would Be Cost Prohibitive

In its Withdrawal of the 1979 Proposal, the Commission reemphasizes

the fact that the internal accounting control provisions of the FCPA (Foreign Corrupt Practices Act) are not limited by a standard of materiality. Those provisions require the design and maintenance of a system of internal accounting control which provides reasonable assurance of achievement of the objectives of internal accounting control. However, the Commission does recognize that certain weaknesses in internal accounting control are more sig-

Exhibit 17-7 (continued)

nificant than others. Therefore, the Commission believes that, for disclosure purposes, the focus of such a management statement should encompass, at a minimum, the adequacy of the issuer's controls over matters about which shareholders reasonably should be informed.

Despite this invitation to invoke a materiality guideline, a footnote in the Withdrawal suggests that, in light of the federal securities laws, some otherwise immaterial control difficulties may have to be disclosed, for example, if related to a significant inventory adjustment. Further, the message is clear that the concept of reasonable assurance, with the application of cost/benefit criteria, is being promoted in preference to any materiality limit.

Not only will an audit directed by concern for financial statement materiality fail to uncover all immaterial inadequacies, but it is also likely that auditors will deem certain system flaws to be material despite cost/benefit justification for exclusion of the control as sanctioned in the SEC proposal. Further, in light of the absence of cost/benefit analyses in the current performance of audits, it is not entirely clear that CPAs can make such an analysis in meaningful terms, despite the SEC's proposal to charge CPAs with such responsibility. There is some doubt that any advantage accrues from having the auditor redundantly assess cost/benefit tradeoffs. In fact, the trend of other government agencies is to avoid redundancy when possible, for example, "The comptroller now cautiously admits that . . . bankers may be just as capable of recognizing good and bad credits as the examiners are! The examiner is not allowed possible reliance upon internal loan review if [certain] . . . criteria are met.[2] Since auditors may very well not be "just as capable" as management in evaluating costs and benefits, a separate evaluation requirement seems senseless.

If the SEC persists in its preference for a report and related auditor's examination on internal control without materiality limitations, the reporting process would be cost prohibitive with respect to the auditor's role. It would alter the entire auditing process and, by definition, is impossible to justify in cost/benefit terms. If a control is of no consequence in determining the overall fairness of financial statements, of what use is information concerning that control? Even the SEC's Regulation SX, Rule 1.02 states

> The term "material," when used to qualify a requirement for furnishing information . . . limits the information required to those matters to which an average prudent investor ought reasonably to be informed . . .

At the very least the statement infers the unreasonableness of requiring immaterial disclosures.

Exhibit 17–7 (continued)

Continued Lack of Clarity Poses Reporting and Cost Concerns

The SEC 1979 proposal and Withdrawal, just as the Foreign Corrupt Practices Act, utilize the accounting and auditing literature extensively. In describing the objectives of internal accounting control, it is cited that reasonable assurances should be provided that "The recorded accountability for assets was compared with the existing assets at reasonable intervals and appropriate action was taken with respect to any difference." While the above requirements are generally understood by CPAs in private practice, it appears that the regulators enforcing the FCPA have a different perception of "reasonable intervals." Most review techniques are performed annually and traditionally have been considered sufficient. Yet, the SEC's questioning of all large fourth quarter adjustments as possible violations of the FCPA implies that periodic inventory systems may be inadequate. If such interpretations are anticipated by regulators, more clarification of the internal accounting control objectives is essential for effective implementation of the proposal or some similar reporting practice. There is evidence that the SEC is making

> unrestrained use of Section 15(c) (4) in contested proceedings, particularly coupled with far-reaching provisions of the Foreign Corrupt Practices Act . . . whether Congress intended that the Commission be so armed, and whether such an administrative weapon is in the public interest . . . become issues for judicial or legislative resolution.[3]

While ambiguity may be desirable from the regulators' perspective, the regulated companies require clarification as to the expectations and planned enforcement activities of the SEC regarding the FCPA and future reports by management and auditors on internal accounting control.

In its proposal, the SEC recognizes management's unique position in assessing the adequacy of the internal controls in cost/benefit terms and the importance of evaluating such controls in the specific context of the single entity. Yet, as suggested earlier in this article under "misinformation" communication, the SEC still expects the public to appropriately evaluate the material weaknesses of a company as well as management's explanations regarding its lack of action. If the SEC admits the peculiarity of each decision to a given entity, and assigns responsibility for that decision to management, why encourage financial statement users to "second-guess" management with insufficient information on the entity's circumstances?

Overstatement of Existing Auditor Involvement

The Withdrawal focuses on SAS No. 20 and SAS No. 8—as well as the proposed SAS on Reporting on Internal Accounting Control, now SAS

Exhibit 17–7 (continued)

No. 30, 1980—as evidence of substantial auditor involvement in the examination of internal accounting controls. The Withdrawal does acknowledge that the auditor is required to inform the registrant of any information of which he is aware including weaknesses in internal accounting. However, the SEC does not acknowledge that the auditing process now permits a review of controls with no testing of those controls that are not relied upon by the auditor. Hence, an inference that the auditor already essentially has control examination responsibilities constitutes an overstatement.

Further, a footnote in the Withdrawal acknowledges

> Certain commentators suggested that it is not clear that Statement on Auditing Standards No. 8 would apply to an omission (as opposed to a misstatement) of disclosure of an internal accounting control weakness in a statement of management on internal accounting control. The Commission encourages the Auditing Standards Board to take whatever action is necessary to make clear that the provisions of the Statement are applicable to such omissions.

This "back-door" attempt to require public reporting of material weaknesses by auditors is extremely questionable. How does the auditor discern "Where a management statement includes an assessment of the effectiveness of internal accounting control?" Does a simple description of the logic of the control system suffice? And, what if management qualifies its statement with the reasonable assurance, cost/benefit based language of the SEC?

In an article in the May 1980 *Journal of Accountancy*, Douglas Carmichael explains

> the reasonable assurance standard would allow management to avoid disclosing weaknesses if it could justify the costs of correction as exceeding the benefits of reducing the risk of an error or irregularity. In other words, a material amount of assets could theoretically be at risk, but the risk would not be disclosed if cost of correction exceeded the potential monetary effect.

Finally, the SEC seems to interpret the proposed SAS on internal control reports as suggesting that future voluntary auditing engagements to evaluate and publicly report on systems of internal accounting control can be expected to become common. First, the SEC fails to acknowledge that the proposed SAS (now SAS No. 30) provides guidelines not only for reports on Internal Accounting Control based on a separate engagement, but also for reports based solely on a study and evaluation made as part of an audit. In the Withdrawal Statement, the SEC provides no information as to whether such limited reports would fulfill the SEC's expectations of voluntary initia-

Exhibit 17-7 (continued)

tives. Further, the SEC refers to the proposed SAS as capable of providing a framework for assessing the costs of such examinations. It is, of course, imperative that the SEC distinguishes between the report types outlined in the SAS in order that the SEC avoid the further understatement of the costs of past proposals (already predicted in this article). Second, the mere presence of a pronouncement says nothing of companies' demand for control review. In fact, as demonstrated by J. P. Morgan and Bankers Trust, there have been no barriers to public reports and official guidelines for reports have long been a part of generally accepted auditing standards. It is an overstatement by the SEC to infer future demand for control reports merely due to the availability of another SAS.

* This paper is based on a research project which was funded by a grant from the Peat, Marwick, Mitchell Foundation through its Research Opportunities in Auditing Program. The views expressed herein are those of the author and do not necessarily reflect the views of the Peat, Marwick, Mitchell Foundation.

[1] Walter A. Staub, "Auditing Developments During the Present Century," Harvard University Press, 1942.

[2] Bruce Adamson, "Current Examination Procedures," *The Journal of Commercial Bank Lending*, January 1979.

[3] Dennis J. Block and Nancy E. Barton, "Administrative Proceedings to Enforce the Foreign Corrupt Practices Act," *Securities Regulation Law Journal*, 1979.

Source: *CPA Journal* (January, 1981), pp. 33–38. Reprinted with permission from *The CPA Journal,* January 1981, copyright 1981.

PROPOSED REPORT ON MANAGEMENT'S RESPONSIBILITIES

The Securities and Exchange Commission in its Release No. 33–6789, issued in July 1988, proposed rules to require that registrants present a report of management's responsibilities that is in line with the recommendations of the Treadway Commission. Specifically, the proposed management report would:

a. Be required in Forms 10-K and N-SAR (registered management investment companies) and in annual reports to security holders

b. Contain a description or statement of management's responsibilities for the preparation of the registrant's financial statements and other financial information, and for establishing and maintaining a system of internal control directly related to financial reporting

c. Include management's assessment of the effectiveness of the registrant's system of internal control and a statement as to how management has responded to any significant recommendations concerning such controls, made by its internal auditors and independent accountants.[9]

---

[9] Margaret Ruffin Horwath, presentation entitled "A Report on Management's Responsibilities" on December 4, 1990. The following discussion is largely adapted from her presentation at an Executives Enterprises program intended to update business participants as to the status of this proposal.

The report would include management's acknowledgment of responsibilities beyond the establishment and maintenance of internal control systems. Beyond speaking to reasonable assurance as to the integrity and reliability of financial reporting, the proposal calls for a statement as to how management has responded to any significant recommendations concerning the system of internal control made by its internal auditors or those performing an equivalent function and the independent accountants. The idea is to address reportable conditions as set forth by SAS No. 60. The proposal envisions a report at a point in time, i.e., as of the most recent fiscal year end, rather than for the entire period. Subsequent events are expected to be considered. Signature by principal executives would be required. The registrant's independent accountant, in accordance with GAAS would be required to read the disclosures and consider whether a material misstatement of fact appears. This considers specifically SAS No. 8, 55, and 60, among other aspects of GAAS.

DIFFERENCES FROM THE 1979 PROPOSAL

The 1979 proposal was criticized, in part for its apparent replication of language from the Foreign Corrupt Practices Act (FCPA). In contrast, the 1988 proposal includes a materiality threshold and avoids direct correlation to the FCPA. The 1979 proposal used a "devise and maintain" requirement related to the period concept, whereas the 1988 proposal is a point-in-time focus.

REACTIONS TO THE 1988 PROPOSAL

A total of 189 letters had been received by the SEC by the October, 1988 comment period's expiration. These are still being analyzed by the SEC, but a related discussion indicated that many respondents were concerned with the scope applied by the proposal and favored attention to financial statement representations rather than operations (53 favored this lesser scope). Concerns were expressed regarding how foreign operations might be addressed. The proposed requirement of a response to significant recommendations received substantial opposition, with commentators expressing concerns including: (1) the potential for confusion that might result from disagreements between management and auditors; (2) difficulty in explaining such points in a concise manner; and (3) the excessive attention to mere recommendations as opposed to weaknesses. About half of the respondents wanted some sort of minimum standard provided regarding materiality and qualitative factors. The point-in-time focus raises questions as to when problems are identified and corrected and what types of related disclosures are called for. About 40 respondents requested flexibility on such matters. Regarding signatures, a good many of the respondents felt the signature proposal was redundant, given the 10-K was signed.

In discussing the proposal, it was pointed out that while costs would be associated incrementally with the preparation of the report and related assessments, no additional work would be required for the auditor beyond reading the report. The associated benefits perceived included increased financial statement users' understanding of management's responsibilities, as well as the role of auditors, in tandem with responsiveness to Congressional initiatives. Of interest is the observation that in July, 1990, Big 6 support was expressed for CPAs' reporting on managements' reports, as then proposed by the Wyden bill.[10]

Recent Congressional Activity

Congressmen Dingell and Wyden in 1990 proposed an amendment to the S&L Crime Bill that would have:

> —required management of each issuer subject to the FCPA to include a report in each Form 10-K and annual report to shareholders containing, among other things, an assessment of the adequacy of the registrant's internal control system;
> —require an auditor's report on management's assessment;
> —generally codify certain auditing standards concerning related party transactions, the detection of "illegal acts," and the issuer's ability to continue as a going concern; and
> —require auditors to report illegal acts directly to the Commission if (after assuring itself that the issuer's audit committee is aware of the illegal act) the auditor concludes: the illegal act has a material effect on the issuer's financial statements, the failure of management and the board to take timely and appropriate remedial action is reasonably expected to warrant qualification of the auditor's resignation, and the board has not given the Commission a copy of the auditor's conclusion within one business day of receipt.[11]

PROPOSED STATEMENT ON STANDARDS FOR ATTESTATION ENGAGEMENTS

The AICPA has drafted a proposed statement entitled "Reporting on Management's Report on the Effectiveness of an Entity's Internal Control Structure Over Financial Reporting" (File Reference No. 4287, September 12, 1990). This proposal would prescribe that practitioners focus on internal control structure policies and procedures in terms of their significance to achieving the objectives of the control criteria rather than consider specific policies and procedures in isolation. The examination engagement requires that the practitioner accumulate "sufficient evidence about the design and operating effectiveness of the entity's

---

[10] Financial Executives Institute, "Congressional Hearings on Proposals to Expand Auditor Responsibility to Detect and Report Illegal Activities" (Wyden Bill) (August 10, 1990), Volume 17, No. 1.

[11] Margaret Ruffin Horwath, presentation entitled "A Report on Management's Responsibilities" on December 4, 1990. The following discussion is largely adapted from her presentation at an Executives Enterprises program intended to update business participants as to the status of this proposal. This discussion appeared within the outline prepared and distributed by Ms. Horwath.

internal control structure to attest to management's assertions, thereby limiting attestation risk to an appropriately low level." The proposal requires SAS No. 60 on reportable conditions to be applied in such engagements. In addition, the practitioner is required to communicate, preferably in writing, any material weaknesses noticed.

Attention is directed in the proposal to evaluating material weaknesses and the need when evaluating individual weaknesses to identify the amounts of errors or irregularities that might occur and remain undetected and the risk of errors or irregularities that is likely to be different for the various amounts within that range. The combined effect of individually immaterial weaknesses also merits consideration as to the range of distribution of errors or irregularities that might occur in the same accounting period from two or more such weaknesses, their joint risk of such occurrence being material, and the relationship of the exposure to a single or different control objective.

Exhibit 17–8 presents the report form suggested in the proposed pronouncement. Exhibit 17–9 describes the wording for communicating material weaknesses, including discussion of how to phrase disagreements with management.

Exhibit 17–8

Proposed Report Form: "Reporting on Management's Report on the Effectiveness of an Entity's Internal Control Structure Over Financial Reporting"

The following is the form of report a practitioner should use when he or she has examined management's report on the effectiveness of an entity's internal control structure as of a specified date.

Independent Accountants' Report

(Introductory Paragraph)

We have examined the accompanying [*title of management report**] on the effectiveness of W Company's internal control structure over financial reporting as of December 31, 19XX.

(Scope Paragraph)

Our examination was made in accordance with standards established by the American Institute of Certified Public Accountants and, accordingly, included obtaining an understanding of the internal control structure, testing and evaluating the design and operating effectiveness of the internal control structure policies and procedures, and such procedures as we considered necessary in the circumstances.

Exhibit 17–8 (continued)

(*Inherent Limitations Paragraph*)

Because of inherent limitations in any internal control structure, errors or irregularities may occur and not be detected. Also, projections of any evaluation of the internal control structure to future periods is subject to the risk that procedures may become inadequate because of changes in conditions, or that the degree of compliance with the procedures may deteriorate.

(*Opinion Paragraph*)

In our opinion, W Company maintained an effective internal control structure over financial reporting as of December 31, 19XX, based upon (identify established or stated criteria).

REPORT MODIFICATION

The practitioner should modify the standard report if any of the following conditions exist:

- There is a material weakness in the entity's internal control structure.
- There is a restriction on the scope of the engagement.
- The practitioner's opinion is based, in part, on the report of another practitioner.
- Management has not disclosed in its report a significant subsequent event that has occurred since the date as of which management reports.

Material Weaknesses

If the examination discloses conditions that, individually or in combination, result in one or more material weaknesses, the practitioner should modify the report. The nature of the modification depends on whether management reports the weakness and on the significance of the weakness and its effect on achieving the objectives of the control criteria.

* The practitioner should identify the management report examined by reference to the report title used by management in its report. Further, he or she should use the same description of the entity's internal control structure as management uses in its report.

Source: AICPA, Proposed Statement on Standards for Attestation Engagements Entitled "Reporting on Management's Report on the Effectiveness of an Entity's Internal Control Structure Over Financial Reporting," (File Reference No. 4287, March 15, 1991, paragraphs 39–41.

Exhibit 17–9

Modifying Reports for Material Weaknesses and Disagreements

The following is the form of report, modified with explanatory language, that a practitioner should use when he or she has identified a material weakness in the entity's internal control structure and management has reported the weakness in its report.

Independent Accountants' Report

(*Standard introductory, scope, and inherent limitations paragraphs*)

(*Opinion Paragraph*)

In our opinion, management has a reasonable basis for its opinion that, except for the effect of the material weakness described in its report,* W Company maintained an effective internal control structure over financial reporting as of December 31, 19XX, based upon the (*identify established or stated criteria*).

(*Explanatory Paragraph*)

As stated in management's report, the following material weakness exists in the design or operation of internal control structure policies and procedures of W Company in effect at (*date*). (*Describe material weakness.*) A material weakness is a condition that precludes the entity's internal control structure from providing reasonable assurance that material misstatements in the financial statements are prevented or detected on a timely basis.**

Disagreements With Management. In some circumstances, management may disagree with the practitioner over the existence of a material weakness and, therefore, not include in its report a description of such weakness and its effect on achieving the objectives of the control criteria. In such cases, the practitioner should express either a qualified or adverse opinion on management's report, depending on the significance of the weakness and its effect on achieving the objectives of the control criteria.

Independent Accountants' Report

(*Standard introductory, scope, and inherent limitations paragraphs*)

(*Explanatory Paragraph*)

Our examination disclosed the following material weakness in the design or operation of internal control structure policies and procedures of W Company in effect at (*date*). (*Describe material weakness.*) A material weakness is a condition that precludes the

Exhibit 17–9 (continued)

entity's internal control structure from providing reasonable assurance that material misstatements in the financial statements are prevented or detected on a timely basis.

(Opinion Paragraph)

In our opinion, except for the effect of the material weakness described above, management has a reasonable basis for its opinion that W Company maintained an effective internal control structure over financial reporting as of December 31, 19XX, based upon the control criteria.

If management has implemented control procedures to correct a material weakness reported by the practitioner, the practitioner should not refer to this corrective action unless he or she is satisfied that the procedures are designed and operating effectively for a sufficient period of time.***

If management's report contains a statement that management believes the cost of correcting the weakness would exceed the benefits to be derived from implementing the new policies and procedures, the practitioner should disclaim an opinion on management's cost/benefit statement. Sample language the practitioner may use to disclaim an opinion on management's cost/benefit statement follows:

We have not examined management's cost/benefit statement and, accordingly, we do not express an opinion or any other form of assurance on it.

Management Report That Includes a Material Weakness Issued in Conjunction with Audit. If the practitioner issues an examination report on management's report on the effectiveness of the entity's internal control structure with his or her audit report on the entity's financial statements, the following sentence should be included in the paragraph of the examination report that describes the material weakness:

These conditions were considered in determining the nature, timing, and extent of audit tests to be applied in our audit of the 19XX financial statements, and this report does not affect our report dated *(date of report)* on these financial statements.

Scope Limitations

An unqualified opinion on an entity's internal control structure can be expressed only if the practitioner has been able to apply all the procedures he or she considers necessary in the circumstances. Restrictions on the scope of the engagement, whether imposed by the client or by the circum-

Exhibit 17–9 (continued)

stances, may require the practitioner to qualify or disclaim an opinion. The practitioner's decision to qualify or disclaim an opinion because of a scope limitation depends on his or her assessment of the importance of the omitted procedure(s) to his or her ability to form an opinion on the internal control structure.

The following is the form of report a practitioner should use when restrictions on the scope of the examination cause the practitioner to issue a qualified opinion.

Independent Accountants' Report

(Standard introductory paragraph)

(Scope Paragraph)

Except as described below, our examination was made in accordance with standards established by the American Institute of Certified Public Accountants and, accordingly, included such procedures as we considered necessary in the circumstances.

(Standard inherent limitations paragraph)

(Explanatory Paragraph)

Our examination disclosed the following material weaknesses in the design or operation of internal control structure policies or procedures of W Company in effect at (*date*). A material weakness is a condition that precludes the entity's internal control structure from providing reasonable assurance that material misstatements in the financial statements are prevented or detected on a timely basis. Prior to December 20, 19XX, the Company had an inadequate system for recording cash receipts, which prevented the Company from recording cash receipts on accounts receivable completely and properly. Therefore, cash received could be diverted for unauthorized use, lost, or otherwise not reported properly to accounts receivable. Although the Company implemented a new cash receipts system on December 20, 19XX, the system has not been in operation for a sufficient period of time to enable us to obtain sufficient evidence about its operating effectiveness.

(Opinion Paragraph)

In our opinion, except for the effect of matters we may have discovered had we been able to examine evidence about the effectiveness of the cash receipts system, management has a reasonably objective basis for its opinion that W Company maintained an effective internal control structure over financial reporting as of

Exhibit 17–9 (continued)

December 31, 19XX, based upon the (*identify established or stated criteria*).

When restrictions that significantly limit the scope of the examination are imposed by the client, the practitioner generally should disclaim an opinion on management's report on the effectiveness of the entity's internal control structure.

* The practitioner should use the same language as management to describe the effect of a material weakness on the entity's internal control structure.
** This description of a *material weakness* differs from the definition of a *material weakness* discussed in paragraph 37. Although a practitioner should consider the definition in paragraph 37 when determining whether a material weakness exists, the description above should be used to describe a material weakness in the practitioner's report since it is clearer to the report user.
*** See guidance in paragraph 26.

Source: AICPA, Proposed Statement on Standards for Attestation Engagements Entitled "Reporting on Management's Report on the Effectiveness of an Entity's Internal Control Structure Over Financial Reporting" (File Reference No. 4287, March 15, 1991), paragraphs 43–53.

Management's Report Form

Management's report can take a variety of forms. An illustration of a possible report form is provided by the AICPA in its proposed attestation engagement standard and appears in Exhibit 17–10.

Exhibit 17–10

Example of a Management Report

The following is an example of a management report containing a paragraph that describes, among other matters, management's assessment of the effectiveness of the entity's internal control structure over financial reporting.

MANAGEMENT'S REPORT ON FINANCIAL REPORTING

The management of ABC Company and its subsidiaries has the responsibility for preparing the accompanying financial statements and for their integrity and objectivity. The statements have been prepared in conformity with generally accepted accounting prin-

Exhibit 17–10 (continued)

ciples and are not misstated because of material fraud or error. The financial statements include amounts that are based on management's best estimates and judgments. Management also prepared the other information in the annual report and is responsible for its accuracy and consistency with the financial statements.

The corporation's financial statements for the years ended December 31, 19X0 and 19X1, have been audited by XYZ Co., independent certified public accountants, elected by the shareholders. Management has made available to XYZ Co. all the corporation's financial records and related data, as well as the minutes of stockholders' and directors' meetings. Further, management believes that all representations made to XYZ Co. during its audit were valid and appropriate.

Management of the corporation has established and maintains an internal control structure in conformity with the control criteria developed by the Financial Executives Research Foundation for effective internal control structures. The internal control structure is designed to provide reasonable assurance about the reliability of the financial reporting process over the preparation of both annual and interim financial statements. Further, the internal control structure over financial reporting is designed to provide for an appropriate division of responsibilities and is documented by written policies and procedures that are communicated to employees with significant roles in the financial reporting process and updated as necessary. Management continually monitors the internal control structure over financial reporting to ensure its effectiveness. Management also has considered XYZ Co.'s recommendations concerning the corporation's internal control structure over financial reporting and has taken appropriate actions to respond to such recommendations. Based on the results of its evaluations, management believes that, as of December 31, 19X1, the entity has an effective internal control structure over financial reporting in conformity with the control criteria developed by the Financial Executives Research Foundation for effective internal control structures.

[Other matters may be discussed in other sections of the management report. However, the auditor's report should refer to the specific section of the report on which he or she is attesting.]

Source: AICPA, Proposed Statement on Standards for Attestation Engagements Entitled "Reporting on Management's Report on the Effectiveness of an Entity's Internal Control Structure Over Financial Reporting" (File Reference No. 4287, September 12, 1990), Appendix.

ERRORS OR IRREGULARITIES AND ILLEGAL PAYMENTS: RESPONSIBILITIES AND RELATED REPORTING PRACTICES[12]

In addition to directing attention to contingencies, the auditor has the responsibility, within the inherent limitations of the auditing process (such as flaws in audit procedures; necessary cost-benefit considerations; and risks created by management override of controls, collusion, forgeries, or unrecorded transactions), to plan the engagement so as to provide reasonable assurance of detecting material errors or irregularities.

Statement on Auditing Standards No. 53 [Section 316] "The Auditor's Responsibility to Detect and Report Errors and Irregularities" provides guidance to the CPA as to what to do when there is an indication that errors or irregularities may exist. Errors are defined as unintentional mistakes, while irregularities are intentional distortions including misrepresentations by management and fraud. Professional skepticism should be the auditor's attitude in setting the audit scope and in gathering evidence. Circumstances outlined in SAS No. 53 [Section 316] that should make the auditor question whether material errors or irregularities exist include affirmative answers to the following: (1) Are there differences in control accounts and subsidiary records, or similar discrepancies within the double-entry accounting system? (2) Are there confirmations that disclose discrepancies in reported accounts and customers' representations? (3) Are there abnormally low response rates to confirmations, relative to the rates expected? (4) Have the transactions been improperly documented? (5) Are some transactions not recorded in accordance with management's general or specific authorization? and (6) Are there unusual transactions at or near the year-end?

If no evidence is obtained to suggest the existence of irregularities, the auditor is to remain skeptical throughout the course of an audit. Professional standards emphasize that the subsequent discovery of errors and irregularities does not, in itself, indicate the auditor's inadequate performance, owing to the audit's own inherent limitations. But if the CPA discovers irregularities during the audit, he or she is required to adequately inform the audit committee of both irregularities and material errors (unless clearly inconsequential). The CPA should find evidence of their existence and quantify their effect and perhaps should consult legal counsel. Finally, the auditor may need to qualify his or her report, issue an adverse opinion or a disclaimer, and/or withdraw from the engagement, with a letter to the Board of Directors of the findings and reasons for the withdrawal. The auditor should evaluate the irregularities' effect on the audit engagement.

ILLEGAL ACTS

The auditor must similarly watch for illegal acts (including illegal political contributions, bribes, and other violations of laws and regulations). If an auditor has reason to believe that illegal acts may have been committed, he or she first

---

[12] Adapted from Wanda A. Wallace, *Auditing*, 2nd Edition (Boston, MA: PWS-Kent, 1991).

should gain an understanding of both the nature of the acts and their possible effects on the financial statements [SAS 54, Section 317]. The auditor should do this by talking to management, legal counsel, and other specialists, as is deemed to be necessary. The reading of the minutes and performance of tests of details of transactions or balances may be useful procedures. Inquiries of management concerning the client's compliance with laws and regulations are required [SAS 54, Section 317]. Inquiries may similarly be directed toward a client's policies to prevent illegal acts and its use of directives and periodic representations of the client concerning compliance with laws and regulations.

Information That May Raise a Question

Examples of what might make the CPA suspicious are the client's offering unusual or questionable explanations for certain transactions and the auditor's discovering unauthorized or improperly recorded transactions or untimely or incomplete records of transactions. Other information which would raise a question includes: investigations by governmental agencies; enforcement proceedings; payment of unusual fines or penalties; violations cited by regulatory agencies in reports made available to the auditor; large payments for unspecified services to consultants, affiliates, or employees or excessive commissions or agents' fees; unusually large payments in cash or cashiers' checks payable to bearer, unexplained payments to government officials or employees; and failure to file tax returns or to pay similar fees such as duties. The CPA then must gauge the illegal acts' materiality, including their effect on the financial statements and any related contingent monetary exposure from fines, penalties, and anticipated damages. Implications for other aspects of the audit must also be considered.

Disclosure

Any material effect will ordinarily require disclosure in the financial statements. All illegal acts should be reported to the client at a level high enough to ensure that there will be remedial actions, adjustments, and disclosure. The auditor should be assured that the audit committee or others of equivalent authority (i.e., the board if no audit committee exists) is adequately informed with respect to illegal acts coming to the auditor's attention. The auditor should describe the act, circumstances, and its effects. Communication can be oral or written. Furthermore, the CPA must consider the implications of the illegal acts for reliance on management's representations and on controls. Exhibit 17–11 tells the reporting consequences of illegal acts. If the client refuses to accept a modified audit report, then the auditor should withdraw from the engagement, document in writing to the client's Board of Directors the reason for withdrawing, and consult legal counsel.[13]

---

[13] Statement on Auditing Standards No. 17, "Illegal Acts by Clients" (New York: AICPA, January 1977), Superseded by SAS No. 54 (Section 317).

Exhibit 17–11

Reporting Effects of Illegal Acts

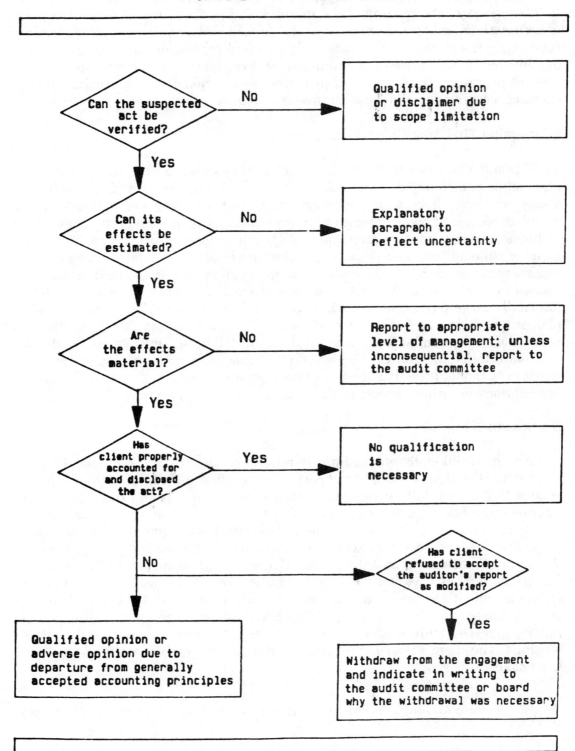

Can the suspected act be verified? — No → Qualified opinion or disclaimer due to scope limitation

Yes ↓

Can its effects be estimated? — No → Explanatory paragraph to reflect uncertainty

Yes ↓

Are the effects material? — No → Report to appropriate level of management; unless inconsequential, report to the audit committee

Yes ↓

Has client properly accounted for and disclosed the act? — Yes → No qualification is necessary

No ↓ →

Has client refused to accept the auditor's report as modified?

Yes ↓

Qualified opinion or adverse opinion due to departure from generally accepted accounting principles

Withdraw from the engagement and indicate in writing to the audit committee or board why the withdrawal was necessary

Other Circumstances: Governmental Audits

At times auditors accept greater responsibility for the detection of illegal acts. In particular, an audit in accordance with the Single Audit Act of 1984 will involve testing and reporting on governmental units' compliance with certain laws and regulations applicable to Federal financial assistance programs. The Appendix provides citations to relevant control literature concerning governmental audits.

REFERENCES

American Institute of Accountants, Committee on Auditing Procedure, *Audits of Brokers or Dealers in Securities* (New York: American Institute of Accountants, 1956).

American Institute of Certified Public Accountants, *Special Reports*, Application of Statement on Auditing Procedure No. 28 (New York: AICPA, 1960).

American Institute of Certified Public Accountants, Statement on Auditing Standards No. 8, "Other Information in Documents Containing Audited Financial Statements" (New York: AICPA, December 1975).

American Institute of Certified Public Accountants, Statement on Auditing Standards No. 30, "Reporting on Internal Accounting Control" (New York: AICPA, 1980).

Beresford, Dennis R., James J. Doyle, and Gary A. Zell, "On Trial—Voluntary Internal Control Reports," *Financial Executive* (September, 1980), pp. 14–19.

The Commission on Auditors' Responsibilities, *Report on Tentative Conclusions* (New York: AICPA, 1977).

The Commission on Auditors' Responsibilities, *Report, Conclusions, and Recommendations* (New York: American Institute of Certified Public Accountants, 1978).

Federal Register, Vol. 40, No. 250, "Chapter 11—Securities and Exchange Commission [Release No. 34–11935] Focus Broker-Dealer Reports" (December 20, 1975), pp. 14–26 [59706–59718].

Financial Executives Institute, letters to members, June 6, 1978.

Special Advisory Committee, "Tentative Conclusions and Recommendations: Reports by Management," File Ref. No. 4267 (AICPA, December 8, 1978).

Wallace, Wanda A., "Should CPAs' Reports On Internal Control Be Required? Survey Evidence on the Effects of Such a Requirement," *Akron Business and Economic Review* (Spring, 1982), pp. 20–23.

Wallace, Wanda A., "How Not to Communicate Material and Immaterial Weaknesses in Accounting Controls," *Auditing Symposium VI*, editors Donald R. Nichols and Howard F. Stettler (Kansas: University of Kansas, 1982), pp. 27–64.

[Also see sources included in footnotes throughout the chapter.]

APPENDIX

Control-related Guidance for Governmental Audits

"Internal Controls in Federal Entities

However, similar proposals to strengthen attention to internal controls have been enacted for federal entities. For example, the concept of management reporting is well established by the Federal Managers' Financial Integrity Act of 1982 (FMFIA) and the Chief Financial Officers Act of 1990 (CFO Act). The FMFIA requires ongoing evaluations and annual public reports by heads of executive branch departments on the adequacy of internal accounting and administrative controls, as well as corrective measures to fix identified material weaknesses. Moreover, the FMFIA requires that internal controls provide reasonable assurance that obligations and costs are in compliance with applicable laws. The CFO Act extends the management reporting concept to government corporations and requires CFOs of executive branch departments to issue an annual report on the financial condition of their departments which includes a summary of internal control weaknesses discussed in the latest FMFIA report.

Also, auditor reporting on both internal controls and compliance with laws and regulations is mandated by government auditing standards. These standards require that auditors' findings related to their examination of internal controls and of compliance with laws and regulations be made public. These reports are made in addition to auditors' opinions on financial statements.

Another important point is the broad view of internal controls used to frame the requirements relating to federal entities. The scope of this definition covers virtually all administrative and managerial aspects of the entities' operations. This is in sharp contrast to a more traditional, narrower view of internal controls that specifically relates only to financial statements."

Source: Enclosure II in correspondence from the Comptroller General of the United States to the Honorable Ron Wyden, House of Representatives dated May 1, 1991 [B-240516].

Other Guidance:

Office of Management and Budget Proposed Revision of Circular A-102 printed in the *Federal Register,* June 9, 1987, pp. 21816–18, "Uniform Administrative Requirements for Grants and Cooperative Agreements to State and Local Governments" and related notice in same source, pp. 20178–79.

Chief Financial Officers Act of 1990, to amend title 31, United States Code, H.R. 5687, One Hundred First Congress of the United States of America at the Second Session (January 23, 1990).

U.S. General Accounting Office, Office of Policy, *Assessing Internal Controls in Performance Audits* (September 1990), GAO/OP-4.1.4.

U.S. General Accounting Office, Office of Policy, *Assessing Compliance with Applicable Laws and Regulations* (December 1989), GAO/OP-4.1.2.

U.S. General Accounting Office, Office of Policy, *Assessing the Reliability of Computer-Processed Data* (September 1990), GAO/OP-8.1.3.

Office of Inspector General, *Interim Standards for Inspections* (President's Council on Integrity and Efficiency, August 1990).

AICPA Auditing Standards Division, "Exposure Draft: Proposed Statement on Auditing Standards—Compliance Auditing Applicable to Governmental Entities and Other Recipients of Governmental Financial Assistance" (April 9, 1991), File 2353.

18

Adapting the Design and Evaluation of Controls to Not-for-Profit Entities

"Before a senate subcommittee, one CPA reported an agency had made a profit of $5,226,000 when another reported a loss of $6,448,000. The dispute concerned the recognition of interest revenue."[1]

Such accounts of what appear to be disparate results from information systems of government and nonprofit entities raise questions as to the credibility of the underlying information system and associated control systems. Consider the multiple announcements regarding the level of the federal deficit! Indeed, to make any of the numbers more comprehensible, Former Congressman Joseph J. DioGuardi, through an organization he chairs named Truth in Government, prepared the following summary of each taxpayer's personal obligation for the national debt.

This sort of report is consistent with the representation that all tax revenue

---

[1] "Two Accountants Disagree on RFC 'Profits,'" *The Journal of Accountancy* (June 1950), p. 467.

U.S. TAXPAYER
PERSONAL CREDIT CARD STATEMENT

FISCAL YEAR 1989
(OCTOBER 1, 1988 – SEPTEMBER 30, 1989)

Description	Charges	Payments
Previous Balance Due (Your Share – beginning of year)	$18,511.50	
Purchases During Year (Your Share)		
Social Security and Medicare	$2,886.41	
National Defense	2,759.55	
Income Security and Welfare	1,243.33	
Health	439.92	
Education, Training, Employment	324.52	
Agriculture, Natural Resources	300.29	
Transportation	251.12	
Administration of Justice	85.42	
Other	559.94	
Payments Received During Year (Your Share)		
Individual Income Taxes		$4,051.73
(Thank you for your prompt payment)		
Social security taxes and contributions		$3,267.42
Other		$1,688.03
Totals	$27,362.00	$9007.18
Finance Charge (Your share of Interest on the National Debt)	$1,539.22	
NEW BALANCE DUE (Your Share – end of year)	$19,894.04*	

Previous Balance	Purchases	Finance Charges	Payments	Balance Due
$18,511.50	$8,850.50	$1,539.22	- $9,007.18	$19,894.04

* Note: This statement is based on the cash accounting system still used by the Federal government, not the Generally Accepted Accounting Principles used by most state governments and private industry. Thus this statement makes no allowance for accrued expenses not yet payable or unfunded future liabilities, such as the future costs of the S&L bailout, the long-term social security shortfall, expected future loan defaults, etc. Inclusion of these items could as much as triple the balance due.

Source: Final Monthly Statement of Receipts and Outlays of the United States Government for FY 1989 (Financial Management Service, Department of the Treasury); CRS 1989 estimate of 110 million joint and individual income tax-payers.

This information supplied by **TRUTH IN GOVERNMENT**, 34 Locust Avenue, Rye, NY 10580 • **(914) 967-7438.**
Hon. Joseph J. DioGuardi, CPA, Chairman.

collected west of the Mississippi is required merely to pay the interest on the national debt.

There are 82,000 units of government (state, counties, cities, towns, special districts, and so on) in the United States. The spectrum of local government activities is depicted in Exhibit 18–1. It is estimated that 25,000 local governments will exceed the $100,000 Federal funds "threshold," thus triggering a "single

Exhibit 18–1

Local Government Activities

Revenue—

- taxes, special assessments, licenses, fees, fines, and grants from higher levels of government
- control over revenue is often limited via grant provisions and the sharing of revenues
- indirect cost reimbursements

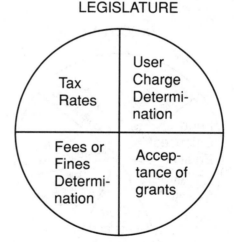

Services—

- delivery of services to citizens
- maintenance of inventories and supplies via purchasing activities

Exhibit 18–1 (continued)

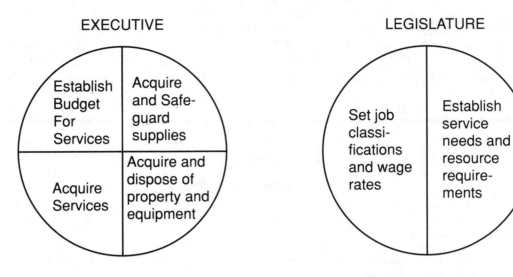

EXECUTIVE

- Establish Budget For Services
- Acquire and Safe-guard supplies
- Acquire Services
- Acquire and dispose of property and equipment

LEGISLATURE

- Set job classi-fications and wage rates
- Establish service needs and resource require-ments

Finance—

- collects cash at a number of locations
- manages financial resources

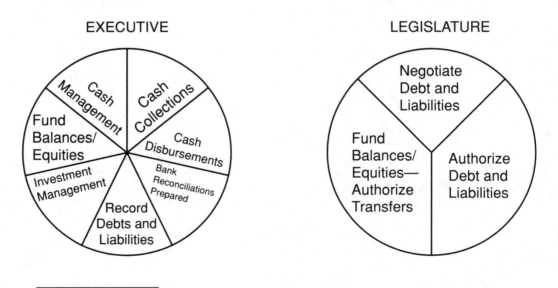

EXECUTIVE

- Cash Management
- Cash Collections
- Fund Balances/ Equities
- Cash Disbursements
- Investment Management
- Bank Reconciliations Prepared
- Record Debts and Liabilities

LEGISLATURE

- Negotiate Debt and Liabilities
- Fund Balances/ Equities— Authorize Transfers
- Authorize Debt and Liabilities

Administrative—

- considerations of specific control objectives
- expenditures for the executive branch

Exhibit 18–1 (continued)

EXECUTIVE   LEGISLATURE

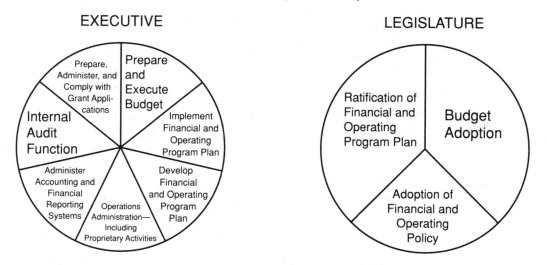

Source: Adapted from Ernst & Whinney, *Guide to the Ernst & Whinney Audit Approach—Government Supplement* (June 1982).

Exhibit 18–2

Alternative Modes of Classifying Expenditures

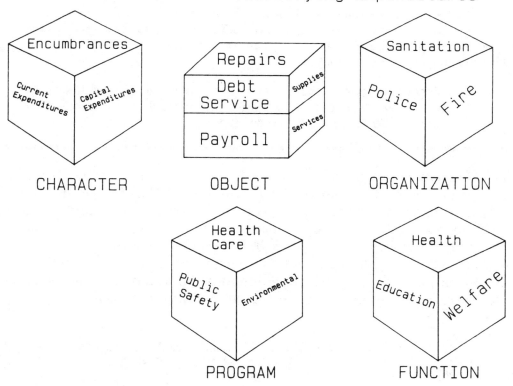

Exhibit 18–3

UNIVERSE OF NONBUSINESS* ORGANIZATIONS

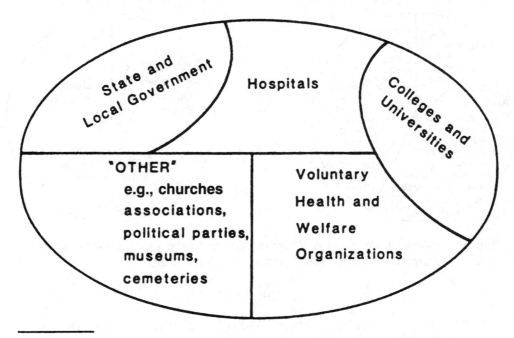

* The terms nonbusiness, nonprofit, and not-for-profit are often used interchangeably to refer to the same organizations. There appears to be a trend toward
identifying the nonbusiness universe as above and reserving the term nonprofit
for the nongovernmental nonbusiness entities.

Source: Mary Alice Seville, "The Evolution of Voluntary Health and Welfare Organization Accounting: 1910–1985," *The Accounting Historians Journal*
(Vol. 14, No. 1, Spring 1987), pp. 58.

audit."[2] The nature of expenditures made by such units is suggested by Exhibit
18–2. When one considers that SEC registrants total 11,000, there is no doubt
that the governmental sector is an important facet of the economy and the market
for audit services. Of similar importance is the universe of nonbusiness organizations, as diagrammed in Exhibit 18–3. In this chapter control considerations
related to government and nonprofit entities are the focal point.

Audits of not-for-profit entities represent a significant share of the market
for audit services. Although the cycle approach of this guide to the evaluation of

---

[2] AICPA Auditing Standards Board Planning Subcommittee, March 20, 1986—Revised, Proposals of AICPA Task Force on Quality of Government Audits—Section I (File Ref. No. 1110),
February 4, 1987.

internal accounting controls has emphasized profit-making organizations, it can be adapted to not-for-profit entities.

RECONCILING FUND ACCOUNTING WITH THE CYCLE APPROACH

Fund accounting refers to an accounting system whereby several sets of self-balancing accounts, designated as funds, are established in the books of an entity. These funds are used to segregate the records of various aspects of operations in order to reflect the various stewardship responsibilities of the entity's management. For example, a local government unit will typically have a general fund for day-to-day government operations, a special revenue fund for dollars earmarked for such purposes as schools, museums, and parks, a capital property fund for the acquisition of capital facilities, a special assessment fund for public improvements levied against particular property owners, and a debt service fund to accumulate and invest bond proceeds. If the governmental unit is involved in proprietary activities, such as operating a public utility, a separate enterprise fund is created. Internal service funds will be established for maintenance services, municipal garage, and similar functions that would be business activities if customers other than the government were permitted access to such services. Finally, the government may need to create trust and agency funds for resources held on behalf of a third party or administered as trust funds. Beyond these basic funds, self-balancing groups of accounts termed the general fixed asset account group and the general long-term debt account group are essential to accounting for the unit's assets and debt obligations.

Exhibit 18–4 defines key terms in fund accounting and illustrates the likely organization of funds.

While some of the funds fit neatly into the three-way cycle approach discussed in earlier chapters, others contain all three elements of the cycle classification scheme. Some funds reflect revenue, expenses, and financing activities of an aspect of the entity's operations. Such is the case for a municipally owned public utility's enterprise fund. Similarly, the general fund will reflect revenues and expenditures, as well as some of the results of financing activities, at least indirectly. In contrast, the special revenue and assessment funds are clearly part of the revenue cycle of operations. In any case, in spite of the lack of profit motivation, operations parallel those of a profit-oriented company. Every operation generates some sort of revenue, incurs related expenses, and obtains capital for investment.

The Simplest Way to Reconcile Fund Accounting with the Cycle Approach

The easiest way for a CPA to reconcile fund accounting with the cycle approach is to

—envision the type of activities to be performed by the entity,

—classify such activities as to their relationship to cash receipts (revenues), cash disbursements (most often, cost of sales), or finance and nonroutine activities.

—identify the specific funds affected by the activities, and

—then proceed to identify the control objectives and related procedures, as would be done for any entity on which a review of internal controls was being performed.

This reconciliation can be done across the various not-for-profit entities, including churches, hospitals, health and welfare agencies, colleges, and govern-

---

Exhibit 18–4

Fund Accounting

Key Definitions:
- FUND—A fiscal and accounting entity with a self-balancing set of accounts recording certain assets, related liabilities, and residual equities or balances, and the changes in them, which are segregated for specific activities or to meet certain legal or administrative objectives or restrictions.
- FUND BALANCE—The difference between fund assets and liabilities; the fund equity.
- ACCRUAL BASIS—A basis of accounting that recognizes the effects of transactions or events on the net resources of an entity when they take place, regardless of when cash is received or paid.
- PROPRIETARY FUNDS—Those funds used to account for a government's ongoing organizations and activities that are similar to those often found in the private sector. Proprietary funds are classified into one of two fund types, enterprise and internal service, depending on the primary users of the fund's services.
- AGENCY FUND—A fund used to account for and report on assets held by a government as an agent for individuals, private organizations, other governments, or other funds.
- EXPENDABLE TRUST FUND—A trust fund used to account for and report on financial resources that may be spent for designated purposes
- GOVERNMENTAL FUNDS—Those funds generally used to account for and report on governmental-type activities. Depending on the sources of financial resources and the nature of the activities reported, governmental funds are classified into one of four fund types: general, special revenue, debt service, and capital projects.
- EXPENDITURES—In governmental funds, decreases in net financial resources from other than interfund transfers and refunding of general long-term capital debt.

Exhibit 18–4 (continued)

- REVENUES—In governmental funds, increases in net financial resources from other than interfund transfers and the issuance of general long-term capital debt. Governmental fund revenues usually result from taxation and other nonexchange transactions or events.

- FIDUCIARY RESOURCES—Those funds used to account for and report on assets held by a government in a trustee or agency capacity for individuals, private organizations, other governments, or other funds. These funds, known as the trust and agency fund types, include expendable trust, nonexpendable trust, pension trust, and agency funds.

- FLOW OF FINANCIAL RESOURCES MEASUREMENT FOCUS—A measure of the extent to which financial resources obtained during a period are sufficient to cover claims incurred during that period against financial resources, and the net financial resources available for future periods. This is accomplished by measuring the increases and decreases in net financial resources and the balances of and claims against financial resources using an accrual basis of accounting.

- ACCOUNT GROUPS—Self-balancing sets of accounts used to account for and report on certain general fixed assets and certain long-term capital debt associated with and arising from the flow of financial resources measurement focus of the governmental funds.

- GENERAL FIXED ASSETS—Capital assets that are not assets of any fund, but of the governmental entity as a whole. General fixed assets are associated with and arise from governmental-type activities and most often result from the expenditure of the financial resources of governmental funds.

- CAPITAL ASSETS—Long-lived, tangible assets (for example, equipment, buildings, land, and infrastructure) obtained or controlled as a result of past transactions or events.

- GENERAL FIXED ASSETS ACCOUNT GROUP—A self-balancing group of accounts that reports certain general fixed assets.

- GENERAL LONG-TERM DEBT ACCOUNT GROUP—A self-balancing group of accounts that reports the unmatured principal of general long-term capital debt.

- INTERPERIOD EQUITY MEASUREMENT—The measure of whether current-year revenues were sufficient to pay for current-year services. A measure of interperiod equity would show whether current-year citizens received services but shifted part of the payment burden to future-year citizens or used up previously accumulated resources. Conversely, such a measure would show whether current-year revenues were not only sufficient to pay for current-year services, but also increased accumulated net resources.

Exhibit 18–4 (continued)

Expendable Funds

Nonexpendable Funds
(Self-sustaining Going Concerns
with a Capital Maintenance
Objective)

Combined Statement of Financial Position

Governmental Funds:	Fiduciary Funds	Fiduciary Funds		Proprietary Funds:
• Current orientation				Activities analo-gous to private
• Liquidity focus used to finance governmental functions	Operating Statement	Funds held for others	Operating Statement	sector commercial accounting princi-ples
Budget versus actual comparisons				

General Fund-	Capital Project Fund-	Trust Funds	Statement of	Enterprise Fund-
• Period orientation	• Project orientation		Change in Financial	Business-like
• Current operations	• Creates fixed assets	and	Position (cash flows)	activities; ac-counts for income
• Only unrestricted fund	with future service po-			and capital main-
Special Revenue Fund-	tential: acquisition and	Agency Funds	Trust Funds	tenance
• Period orientation	construction of major			
• Accounts for restricted	capital facilities	Governmental		Internal Service
revenue services	Special Assessment Fund-	Unit Acts As		Funds-
Debt Service Fund-	• Project orientation	A Trustee or		Account for cost-
• Period orientation	• Deleted by GASB	Agent		reimbursed goods
• Accumulates financial	Statement 6 as a "ge-			and services
resources for payment	neric fund": funds			among govern-
of principal and inter-	from levies to finance			mental units
est on general long-	special projects are			
term debt	now combined with			

one of the other ge-
neric fund types
based on whether
they are service or
capital improvement in
nature; note that the
former would include
street lighting, snow
removal, and street
cleaning and would be
in the General, Spe-
cial Revenue, or En-
terprise Fund Assess-
ment = user charges

These funds account for fixed assets and long-term
liabilities, requiring no use of account groups.

The capital project basis is an agency fund activity
if the unit has no obligation to pay should property
owners default. If commitment exists, it is recorded
in capital projects and debt service funds.

To maintain accountability
of long-term assets and
liabilities, accounting
entities that are not
fiscal entities are
established, i.e., the
account groups do not
contain financial resources

General Fixed Assets
Account Group-
Relate to entire governmental
unit rather than specific
funds. Infrastructure
assets like sewer systems
can be included; such
reporting is optional.

General Long-term
Debt Account Group-
Relate to entire governmental
unit rather than specific funds.

ment. The primary difference in the fund approach per entity is in jargon. For example, colleges and universities use the following fund groups: current, loan, endowment, annuity and life income, plant, and agency funds. Hospitals use operating, specific purpose, plant replacement and expansion, and endowment funds. However, in spite of terminology differences, similarities exist across not-for-profit entities with regard to control problems that result largely from the fund accounting process and the nature of not-for-profit operations.

Control Problems Unique to Not-for-Profit Entities—and How to Solve Them

Interfund transfers. Perhaps the most critical control problem with respect to fund accounting involves interfund transfers. Since the entire structure of fund accounting is intended to ensure an appropriate stewardship function over separate operations and related funds of an entity, only authorized interfund transfers should be made. Generally speaking, interfund transfers should be discouraged. The reason is simple: the operations of any single fund can be camouflaged through transfers. Operating deficits of a city government might be offset by the transfer of profits from a municipally owned utility or from improper classification of capital projects funding. A concern exists for debt covenant compliance as well, since the creditors of a municipally owned utility are likely to specify those conditions under which set amounts can be transferred to the governmental unit.

Incomplete recording of transactions. Beyond exposure to manipulation through interfund transfers or the effects of noncompliance with debt covenants, fund accounts can be misstated as a result of the incomplete recording of transactions. Since each fund is self-balancing and several funds may be affected by a single transaction, the bookkeeper is not assured of a signal that only half of an entry has been recorded. The double entry system provides checks within each fund, but not across funds. Another complication is the set of accounts, as distinct from funds that are normally separate and unconsolidated items. It is easy to overlook an update to the fixed asset account when acquiring an asset, as the only entry required to achieve an apparent balance is the cash disbursement for the equipment. The use of a tickler file, formal stamps documenting account classifications, and similar devices, will assist a bookkeeper in completely reflecting the transactions throughout the fund and account system of the entity.

Separating restricted balances from unrestricted balances. A third problem peculiar to not-for-profit entities and reflected in fund-accounting practices is the difficulty of finding an effective means by which restricted balances can be properly separated from unrestricted balances. Restricted gifts, bequests, and donations must be treated as instructed by the donor. Designated assets should not be recorded as restricted funds but should be handled as specified by those making the designations. Analyses of fund balance transactions are essential as a means of supporting the unrestricted and restricted control accounts in the general ledger. Funds that are held in trust by outside parties need to be controlled via the accounting records. In order to ensure that donors' and the Board's instructions are followed, an organized chart of accounts to distinguish restricted and unrestricted fund balances is needed; this will facilitate the segregation of restricted investments and other assets both physically and in their accounting treatment from unrestricted investments and other assets.

Restricted monies frequently come to organizations like governmental units and universities in the form of grants. A key issue is how to recover overhead in such grants and how to appropriately control the revenue and related expenditures per grant. A useful approach is to set up separate accounts per grant and then formalize a cost allocation plan that will ensure that indirect costs are recouped to the fullest extent possible. The control issues faced are similar to those affecting businesses that have job-costing systems and work on government contracts.

Accounting for restricted funds can be facilitated, in part, by establishing separate funds or accounts within each fund. Authorization procedures, inferfund transfers, and controls over monitoring procedures will enhance the adequacy with which donor restrictions and grant monies are managed.

Fund accounting can also pose control problems due to its deceptive nature. The existence of separate funds gives the impression that each fund's assets have been similarly segregated, yet no necessary relationship exists between the books and actual physical control over assets. The implication, of course, is that not-for-profit entities need to establish physical control and segregation of various funds' assets—particularly of restricted assets. Such procedures are largely independent of the accounting records. It is common for entities with six separate funds to maintain one bank account. While six bank accounts may be excessive, the separation of restricted funds from unrestricted funds probably has merit.

Three Practices Unique to Fund-Accounting Environments That Should Be Considered When Establishing and Monitoring Controls

Three practices in fund-accounting environments add controls for which no clear parallels exist in the business setting. These practices include the

—formality of appropriations,

—use of encumbrances, and

—actual entry of budgeted amounts into the entity's fund-accounting system.

Appropriations. Although businesses set budgets that are approved by top management, many not-for-profit organizations have legal appropriations made. Appropriations are sometimes item-by-item restrictions on asset flow and expenditures. Any changes to appropriations typically require approval by the same body that initially made the appropriations. This dollar-accountability enhances control by the governing body but decreases control and flexibility by operating management. The effects of the latter can be loss of talented managers, manipulative games growing as a means of gaining flexibility through intra-account transfers, and budget padding to ensure some margin of control. Each of these effects should be considered in establishing controls and in monitoring the control environment.

Encumbrances. Encumbrances recognize purchase orders as claims against available resources. A business entity typically records purchases when they become legal obligations, i.e., upon delivery. However, the intention of a commitment of resources clearly arises when the purchase order is originated, and that intention can be formalized in fund accounting as encumbrances. This technique, typically applied by governmental units, controls against over-committing funds and may help to avoid double orders and similar errors in the purchasing cycle.

Entry of budgeted amounts into the fund-accounting system. While both profit and not-for-profit entities generate budgets, governmental units go a step further by actually recording appropriations and estimated revenues in the accounts. The result is a continuous monitoring device for judging compliance of operations with budgets. Again, this control, like the control over appropriations, can have an adverse effect. While compliance with a well-defined budget is to be encouraged, flexible budgeting and adaptation to changing conditions is also desirable. Controls can be established that help to ensure that procedures exist for such adaptive actions, whenever necessary.

Of course, budgeting approaches in and of themselves can be important aspects of overall control. Exhibit 18–5 describes common methods, alongside their respective advantages and disadvantages. Note that in exploring the control environment, a systems evaluator should focus on the segregation of duties related to

—budget preparation,
—budget adoption,
—budget execution, and
—budget reporting.

Moreover, law should require an awareness of budgets and budgetary procedures which ought to entail budgeting of all significant activities and citizen input through budget hearings. Prescribed procedural controls should include timely explanations of differences in actual expenditures and budgeted amounts.

Encourage Consolidated Financial Statements

A final aspect of fund accounting that warrants mention is the difficulty such an accounting approach creates in gaining a clear picture of the total entity's operations. Often a general fund can reflect a surplus due to an interfund transfer

Exhibit 18–5

Budgeting Alternatives

Line Item Budgeting	Advantages	Disadvantages
Budgets per unit of the organization the production function via line-item cost control	• Facilitates control • Restricts discretion as to input mix such as payroll versus supplies • Can couple with other budgeting techniques to compensate for disadvantages • Easy tie-in to actual expenditure information, facilitating comparisons of budget to actual	• Voluminous • No information as to objectives • Over emphasis on costs • Encourages "spending" of entire line item versus effective strategies altering input mix • Tends to permit slack budgeting (i.e., excess requests)

Program and Performance Budgeting	Advantages	Disadvantages
Specifies objectives, activities, and resources per activity with a program orientation. Since objectives are often in terms of output, performance is easily evaluated. In the 1960s, the approach was often referred to as PPBS, an acronym for planning, programming, and budgeting system. Multi-year planning with cost-benefit analysis of alternatives was the focal point	• Focuses on objectives • Requires understanding of operations to perform an activity analysis • Uncovers waste and inefficiencies fairly effectively • Fosters coordination among activities • Can be coupled with line-item budgeting by designing crosswalk which clarifies where line items "fit" into the programs being budgeted • Can apply to a subset of core programs to reduce cost	• Difficult to quantify output—particularly dimensions of such output • Tends to emphasize efficiency and economy, with little attention to equity • Requires information beyond the financial accounting system • Requires tracing and allocation of indirect costs • Does not, alone, facilitate control over finances

Incremental Budgeting	Advantages	Disadvantages
This year's budget is increased by a set amount or percentage to determine next year's budget	• Budgets are stable and predictable, facilitating easy management • Saves unnecessary scrutinizing of line items • Today's experiences may be the best predictor • Some of the problems can be addressed by using a decremental approach when resources are tight • Uses the accounting system	• Expands expenditures automatically leading to waste and inefficiency • Has to consider prior year's budgeted data due to the considerable delay in the reporting and audit process

Exhibit 18–5 (continued)

Zero-Base Budgeting	Advantages	Disadvantages
Nothing is automatically budgeted for the next year. Every dollar of expenditure must be justified. Related guidelines were issued during the Carter Administration by the Office of Management and Budget (OMB)*. The approach emphasizes all managers' involvement, evaluation of discrete activities with set objectives, an analysis at different budget amounts or performance levels (i.e., alternative "decision packages,") and development of a rationale for reallocations. All programs have "sunset reviews" whereby programs have to justify their existence. Moreover, all decision packages must be rank ordered.	• Avoids protecting "budgetary sacred cows" • Not biased upwards as is an incremental approach; it is particularly useful as resources become scarce • Increases the rationality of the budgeting process	• Artificial concept, given fixed costs and mandated multi-year commitments • Prioritization was difficult and sometimes impossible • Managers were encouraged to play games like the "Washington Monument trick" whereby low priorities are assigned to important items as a means to ensure funding of less important items • Monumental paper work • Very time consuming • Disrupts the status quo, being excessive in fostering a defensive attitude

* U.S. Office of Management and Budget, "Zero Base Budgeting," Bulletin No. 77-9 (April 19, 1977).

Source: Adapted from James L. Chan, *Governmental and Nonprofit Accounting Concepts, Standards, and Uses of Information* (May 1987), Chapter 2 (Manuscript from University of Illinois-Chicago Circle).

from a municipally owned public utility and the separate fund for capital projects can be woefully inadequate, yet undetectable from an examination of each fund balance in a relative vacuum. Recently, the practice of presenting consolidated financial statements for cities and states has been encouraged. Even if a consolidation is not done for public reporting purposes, a comprehensive picture of operations can be an extremely useful control tool for management and the board overseeing the operations of a not-for-profit entity. This practice should be encouraged by the auditor or system evaluator.

Note that comprehensive annual financial reports (CAFRs) are comprised of a number of disclosures as illustrated in Exhibit 18–6. The CAFR is, in turn, a component of the reporting pyramid, as illustrated in Exhibit 18–7, that commonly includes combined statements.

Exhibit 18–6

COMPREHENSIVE ANNUAL FINANCIAL REPORT (CAFR)

Management Introduction (CEO Letter)

Combined Statements

Combining Statements

Individual Fund Statements

Notes To The Financial Statements

Schedules

Narrative Explanations

Statistical Tables

May Be Issued Separately

General Purpose Financial Statements

Exhibit 18–7

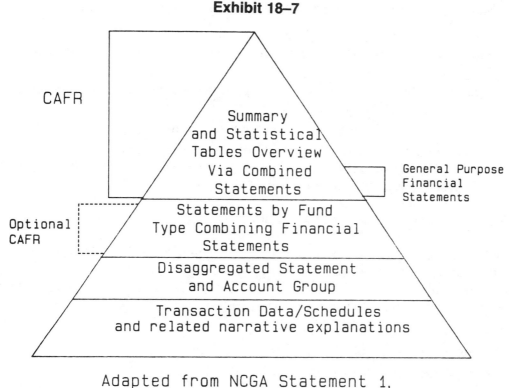

Adapted from NCGA Statement 1,
Illustration by "The Financial Reporting Pyramid"

OPERATING DISTINCTIONS BETWEEN PROFIT AND NOT-FOR-PROFIT ENTITIES THAT INFLUENCE CONTROLS

Beyond fund-accounting concerns, certain dimensions of not-for-profit operations create unique control issues that are not faced by business organizations.

Establishing Control over Voluntary Contributions

One of these dimensions relates to the means by which revenue is generated. While profit organizations sell inventory and services, not-for-profit organizations frequently give goods and services to nonpaying customers relying on donations as the primary revenue source for operations. Contributions do not lend themselves to control in the manner that inventory and even services do. Audit trails will flag missing inventory and expenses, and for those providing services, hours expended will suggest what level of revenue is reasonable. In contrast, no benchmark is easily available from the accounting records to use in judging the reasonableness of recorded contributions. To exercise control over contributions, an entity must

> —control the issuance of solicitation materials during fund-raising campaigns,
>
> —make it common knowledge that pledges will be acknowledged by correspondence with donors,
>
> —issue prenumbered receipts for donations, and
>
> —segregate the duties of handling pledge cards from the handling of cash receipts, as well as have fund-raising activities performed by a party who is independent from the organization.

Establishing Control over a Tax Program

Of course, not all not-for-profit entities depend on voluntary support. Government entities, for example, have nonvoluntary support via taxation. This revenue source also poses unique control issues, not faced by profit-generating entities. Effective administration of a tax program relies upon

> —accurate property assessments,
>
> —timely updating of property improvements,
>
> —the approval of tax rates in the political forum, and
>
> —enforcement of tax payment through the courts and/or the seizure of property.

Adequate means of reporting and paying taxes must be available, including means of reflecting legislated rate reductions—such as those frequently granted to veterans and the elderly. The controls established should deter kickbacks, errors in recordkeeping, and improper handling of cash receipts. They should ensure timely follow-up for enforcement so that taxpayers can be effectively motivated to fulfill their tax responsibilities. Detailed procedures for enforcing payments should be prescribed to avoid costly mistakes and to promote efficiency.

Establishing Control over Service Fees

Many not-for-profit entities set service charges that are analogous to product prices. However, these charges frequently are not intended to cover the total costs of the services and are commonly subject to government approval. For example, college tuition at a state university will not tend to be commensurate with the total costs of education, nor can tuition increases be initiated without the legislators' agreement. The control implications of service fees are identical to those of any business revenue cycle, except that

> —the planning and budgeting phases, as well as the administrative control over such operating decisions as pricing, must explicitly balance the ex-

pected coverage of costs by the service charges versus contributions and must incorporate the political process, and

—the measures used to evaluate and monitor operations must involve other than simple comparisons of revenues from service charges to costs.

Controls Should Direct Attention to the Political Process

As the political process is considered, the legislators' role can be viewed as parallel to that of a board of governors or trustees at a hospital or university. The board's decisions are likely to mold operations, yet the board members may be politically elected or appointed and have no vested interest in the entity, whereas a substantial number of the directors for a profit-making entity would tend to have such a vested interest. This difference in incentives warrants considerations by management in setting strategies and in inferfacing with such boards or political bodies. If elections are controlling the boards, then elections are likely to be based on equal votes by some defined "membership," with no proportional weighting to reflect investment in the entity, as would be typical for profit organizations. The principal role of the political process in shaping the operations of not-for-profit entities suggests controls must direct attention to this process. For example, careful guidelines as to eligible members for the board should be prescribed to avoid conflicts of interest and to encourage the election or appointment of qualified individuals. An information link to the political process must be established to facilitate adequate planning and controls by operating management. Finally, to ensure well-planned and controlled operations, means must be established of effectively communicating to the board

—key operating goals, objectives, and problems,

—the diverse views of the various constituencies being represented by the board,

—the ramifications of proposals under consideration, and

—appropriate means of evaluating the entity's performance.

Evaluating Employees and Overall Operations

The last point may pose the most difficult control issue—how to effectively evaluate employees and overall operations. Some means of reflecting the services of the entity, beyond mere financial statistics, is imperative. Social accounting strides have been made in the corporate sector and the General Accounting Office's involvement in operational auditing has led to the development of numerous output, efficiency, and performance measures. The CPA can assist not-for-profit entities in identifying useful measures of their services, accumulating supporting information, and putting a reporting and evaluation system into operation. Such a system is an integral part of establishing an adequate control environment and encouraging competent employees not to leave the organization.

CONTROLLING INFORMATION AND OPERATIONS BEYOND THE INTERNAL ACCOUNTING CONTROL SYSTEM

Comparison of the operations of profit and not-for-profit entities suggest that accounting information assumes a much smaller role in controlling the not-for-profit entity. Information on political factors, service operations, and effective means of generating contributions is essential in meeting the not-for-profit entity's objectives. As a result, you should go beyond the internal accounting control system in order to effectively evaluate the entity's operations, the viability of continued existence, the critical control environment, and the detailed control system. In going beyond the internal accounting control system, the scope of the system to be examined can best be defined by assessing the desired "output." Specifically, what information is desired to adequately safeguard assets, control day-to-day and long-term operations, and publicly report on operations.

Reviewing Statistics to Assist in Developing an Information Base

Some ideas as to useful statistics for control purposes can be gained by reading the statistical disclosures made by not-for-profit entities in their annual reports.

Municipalities frequently provide demographic statistics as to their population, average age of their residents, median education, median income of residents, types of businesses in the locale, the region's unemployment rate, and the land area encompassed by the municipality. In addition, the number of municipal employees and types of services provided and the tax rates, assessment values, and collection experience of the municipal unit are disclosed. Exhibit 18–8 diagrams common statistical information.

For educational institutions, information as to the types of educational and residential services provided by the institution and the number of students enrolled is stressed. Ratios of faculty to students, class sizes, and success ratios on standardized exams such as the CPA exam, bar exam, and similar certification programs are similarly emphasized.

For hospitals, the number of patient beds, the days such beds were occupied, the average length of patient stay, and the nature of services rendered are frequently reported.

A review of statistics generally reported suggests that a not-for-profit entity should develop an information base that details

—the nature of services provided,

—the nature of the groups being serviced,

—the quantity of services performed,

—the subsequent experience of parties who have received services, and

—the total capacity of the entity to provide services.

Exhibit 18–8

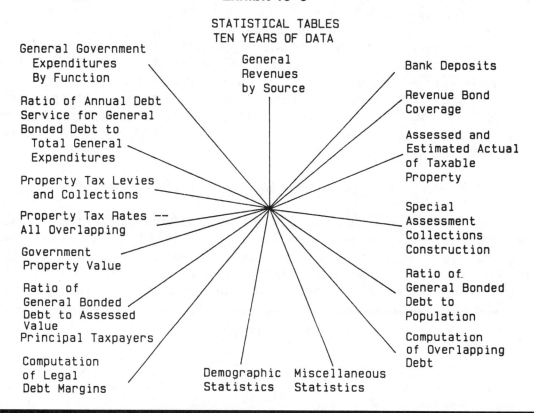

STATISTICAL TABLES
TEN YEARS OF DATA

General Government
  Expenditures
  By Function

Ratio of Annual Debt
Service for General
Bonded Debt to
  Total General
  Expenditures

Property Tax Levies
  and Collections

Property Tax Rates --
All Overlapping

Government
Property Value

Ratio of
General Bonded
Debt to Assessed
Value
Principal Taxpayers

Computation
of Legal
Debt Margins

General
Revenues
by Source

Demographic   Miscellaneous
Statistics   Statistics

Bank Deposits

Revenue Bond
Coverage

Assessed and
Estimated Actual
of Taxable
Property

Special
Assessment
Collections
Construction

Ratio of
General Bonded
Debt to
Population

Computation
of Overlapping
Debt

The GASB has issued a series of Service Efforts and Accomplishments Research Studies that provide a number of recommendations on such statistics.[3] Of course, the use of service efforts and accomplishments data creates incentives. Care must be taken to consider possible incentive effects and what adverse situations could arise. By identifying potential problems, such as those in Exhibit 18–9, offsetting control practices can be put in place.

Augmenting the Information System by Controls That Limit Liability Exposure

This information base will require the same types of input, processing, and reporting controls that are typically applied to accounting data. Since not-for-

---

[3] As examples, see Wanda A. Wallace, *Service Efforts and Accomplishments Reporting: Its Time Has Come—An Overview* Chapter Seven "Mass Transit" (The Governmental Accounting Standards Board), 1990, pp. 157–185; and Wanda A. Wallace, Robert W. Parry, Jr., Florence C. Sharp, and Jannet Vreeland, *Service Efforts and Accomplishments Reporting: Its Time Has Come—An Overview* Chapter Five "Fire Department Programs" (The Governmental Accounting Standards Board), 1990, pp. 119–139.

profit entities are typically service oriented, the information system can be augmented by controls that help to limit subsequent liability exposure. For example, documentation of services provided should include the authorization of specific services by the physician, board, or other appropriate party, depending on the nature of operations. The quantity of services performed should be reviewed for reasonableness and for agreement with authorized services. The reports as to subsequent experience, such as fatalities for a hospital or employment experiences of the student body of a government jobs program or of a university, should be monitored as a means of evaluating operating performance and improving operations when weaknesses are noted.

Facilitate Feedback from Customers and Contributors

Beyond establishing a data base for internal operations and to report on the subsequent experiences of parties serviced, a feedback loop should be formalized that facilitates input from current, past, and even prospective users of and contributors to the entity's services. Due to the voluntary nature of much of the support of not-for-profit operations, as well as the service orientation of operations,

---

Exhibit 18–9

INCENTIVE EFFECTS

Potential Problems

Mass Transit
% of Trains on Time, i.e., Within 3 Minutes of Scheduled Departure and Arrival

When a Train is late, no incentive exists to service it and minimize the time frame that it is late, i.e., only the 3-minute benchmark matters

Hospitals
% of Patients Who Die

Deters treatment of fatally ill patients and encourages their early release

Education
% of Students Earning a Passing Score on a Standardized Examination

Attempts may be made to deter poorer students from taking the exam, thereby minimizing their influence on the metric, or the spoon-feeding of exams may occur

. . .

Exhibit 18–9 (continued)

Potential Problems

Police
Number of Burglaries,
With an Excess of
$500 Stolen

*May repeatedly measure
losses at $499 to avoid
tarnishing of metric*

Fire
Number of Calls to
Suppress Fires

*Fails to encourage preventive
measures and may deter
responses for nonfire
purposes, e.g., bomb scares
or the like*

Driving Bureau
Number of Driving
Tests Administered

*Those taking the test can
be repeatedly failed, forcing
retakes, and enhancing the
overall metric in an
unintended manner*

. . .

it is important that qualitative performance measures be available to the entity. Profit-oriented companies can get full feedback as to operations via the market; if service is inadequate, product quality poor, price too high, or if some similar flaw exists, the message of the consumer will be delivered in the form of lower sales. The not-for-profit entity does not have an analogous market measure of operations. While extremely inefficient and ineffective operations will eventually show up as decreased contributions and, possibly, fewer people seeking the entity's services (assuming some similar not-for-profit organization is available), a much more timely reaction can be received and reacted to by facilitating customers' and contributors' informal input. Controls must be established to ensure that all such input is read, evaluated, and, when appropriate, acknowledged and/or made operational by the entity. Input with no visible effect can frustrate customers and donors so that the established feedback loop has adverse effects. However, formal procedures to express appreciation for input and to enact those suggestions that are cost/beneficial will be recognized as sincere efforts by the entity to meet its operating objectives.

Information Chain Between the Entity and Parties Affecting Its Operations

The final chain of information required for the not-for-profit entity is that chain between the entity and the principal parties affecting its operations, i.e.,

—external managers, like city councils and boards of governors or trustees,

—the constituency, members and/or donors,

—the users of services,

—creditors, and

—regulatory agencies.

The focus here is not on feedback as much as it is on being aware of these parties' activities and making them aware of the entity's needs and activities. Such an information chain is likely to require personnel and lobbying commitments on the part of the not-for-profit entity, as well as resource commitments for research and public relations. To control this type of information chain, a careful network of authorization must be constructed and operating procedures involving these third parties should be defined in formal manuals.

Your role in not-for-profit entities should be to assist managers in recognizing the need to control operations and information flows beyond the generation of financial statement information and then to assist the entities in designing and evaluating such controls on a continuing basis.

OPPORTUNITIES FOR PROVIDING INTERNAL CONTROL-RELATED SERVICES TO GOVERNMENT

While no internal control system provides a guarantee against fraud, it does diminish the opportunities for fraud and increases the probability of fraud detection. Such controls are sorely needed at the state and federal government level. A poll by the Federal Bureau of Investigation, reported in the *Wall Street Journal* (September 11, 1980), ranked corruption by state and local officials as the most widespread white-collar crime problem. Such corruption includes kickbacks to purchasing agents, inspectors, legislators and judges, and fraud in the handling of federal funds. An earlier article in the *Wall Street Journal* (December 18, 1978) reports on the widespread cheating of government due to lax auditing and lax controls at federal agencies. The article discusses frauds that involve such cheating as

—substituting sub-grade material on government contracts,

—overcharging expenses on government contracts,

—nonpayment of student loans,

—filing for Veterans Administration reimbursements for fictitious students,

—filing of false Medicare claims by medical doctors,

—serving spoiled food to disadvantaged children, and

—food-stamp fraud.

The General Accounting Office (GAO) is on record as stating that every time the Justice Department investigators have gone looking for fraud in federal programs, "They have found it," and an experienced congressional investigator reportedly estimates that "there's probably $10 wasted for every one stolen." On November 5, 1982, the Director of the Office of Management and Budget issued a directive to government agencies, OMB Circular A-123, that requires a tighter system of internal management controls for the agencies. Past control weaknesses are cited to have resulted in intolerable losses, including

— unauthorized payroll checks issued to Defense Department clerks and then friends, due to the lack of segregated duties,

— benefit checks printed by computers in amounts far in excess of the amount due because no control totals were in use,

— social security payments made to deceased persons, and

— expensive electronic equipment lost due, in part, to failure to perform periodic inventories to identify security problems.

The GAO has reported (see document AFDM-81-73) that 29% of detected fraud cases involve government employees, 18% involve Federal assistance recipients, and 12% involve business entities. The involvement of employees, "customers," and "suppliers" has definite implications for the auditor, as well as for the design of control systems.

GAO Hotline

As one means of uncovering fraud and mismanagement, a GAO toll-free Fraud Hotline has been established [(800) 424-5454]. In its 9-year existence, 94,000 calls have been received, of which 13,992 cases have warranted further review. Of the calls warranting further review, 70% were received from anonymous sources. Part of these anonymous calls were from federal employees. Altogether, calls from federal employees totaled 26.2% of those warranting further review.

Calls not written up were for reasons such as the caller lacked specific information or the allegation did not involve a federal program. Those callers who had information on nonfederal matters were directed to the appropriate state or local agency.

With 13 of the 19 statutory IG offices now providing toll-free hotlines and with the establishment of the President's Council on Integrity and Efficiency to coordinate the efforts of the IG offices, the role of the GAO Fraud Hotline has taken on different dimensions. The composition of the 13,992 cases receiving further review is described in Exhibit 18–10. Examples of specific problems uncovered by the GAO are provided in Exhibit 18–11.[4]

---

[4] United States General Accounting Office (GAO), "Fraud Hotline—9-Year GAO Fraud Hotline Summary" (GAO/OGC/OSI-88-1FS, April 1988), pp. 2–3.

Exhibit 18–10

Experiences with Fraud Hotlines

The following chart shows the percentage for each participant category of the 13,992 cases we referred for further review.

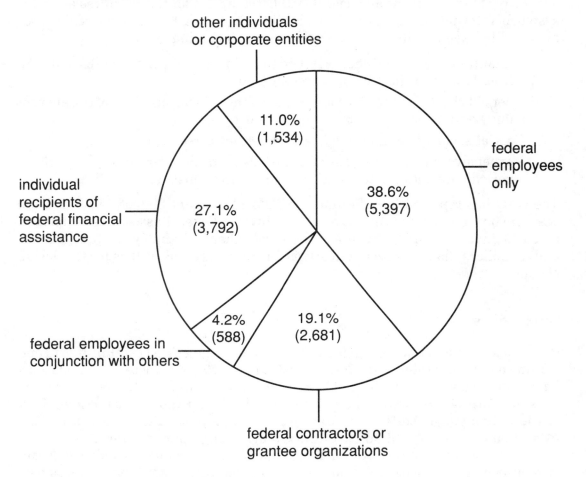

In the largest category, "federal employees only," we found 891 reports of employee work-hour abuse, 654 allegations of private use of government property, 605 allegations of noncompliance with established agency procedures or policies, 597 reports of improper financial transactions, 338 allegations of theft, 192 reports of purchasing unnecessary equipment, 158 allegations of awarding unneeded contracts, and 1,962 other allegations of fraud and mismanagement.

In the second largest category, "individual recipients of federal financial assistance," we found 1,161 allegations of improper receipt of welfare benefits and 823 of improper receipt of disability benefits. There were also 676

Exhibit 18–10 (continued)

cases of improper receipt of social security benefits, 249 instances of improper receipt of food stamps, 195 reports of housing subsidy abuse, 178 instances of improper receipt of veterans' benefits, and 510 miscellaneous allegations.

Source: United States General Accounting Office (GAO), "Fraud Hotline—9-Year GAO Fraud Hotline Summary" (GAO/OGC/OSI-88-1FS, April 1988), p. 6.

Exhibit 18–11

Examples of Fraud Hotline Cases

—A caller contacted the Hotline to allege that an Army commander of a special forces group ordered some of his noncommissioned officers and enlisted men to wrongfully use government tents and vehicles to support a local civilian horse show in which his daughter was a participant. After the show, the Commander ordered his personnel to remove these tents. The allegation was referred to the Department of Defense Inspector General for investigation, who substantiated the allegations. The Commander received a letter of reprimand from the Commanding General for his actions. Also, the Commanding General has sent formal notification to all other Commanders reminding them of applicable Army regulations.

—An anonymous caller alleged that Department of Commerce employees were manipulating the evaluation of technical proposals to keep one contractor in the running for a contract. The contractor's technical proposal did not comply with the requirements of the evaluation. We referred this allegation to the Department of Commerce Inspector General, who conducted an audit in this area and noted that a full-scale $500 million production contract may result from this technical proposal. Although the IG could not fully sustain the allegation, serious management deficiencies were identified involving inadequate accountability for evaluations, inadequate criteria for judging proposals, and problems in the source-selection process. The agency took corrective action to resolve these deficiencies.

—A caller alleged that a government inspector was covering up nonperformance of a janitorial contractor at a Naval installation because the contractor had hired the inspector's girlfriend. The caller also alleged that the same inspector was taking gratuities from the contractor and socializing with contractor personnel. This allegation was referred to the Department of Defense Inspector General, and the Naval Investigative Service (NIS) conducted the investigation. Although NIS did not find that

Exhibit 18–11 (continued)

the contractor was inadequately performing on the contract, they did find a gambling ring that was operating at the installation with government and contracting personnel involved. As a result, the government inspector was suspended for three days, and another government employee was convicted in a local court and given six months probation. Four other government employees were given either letters of caution or reprimand. In addition, three contract personnel were convicted in a local court, placed on six months probation, and debarred from working at the installation. Another resigned his position with the contractor.

—A caller from Minnesota told the Hotline that a local housing authority had illegally spent Housing and Urban Development funds for planning fees, salaries, benefits, and equipment for the city. The writer provided evidence documenting the allegation. The Hotline referred the matter to HUD's Office of Inspector General. Auditors substantiated the allegation. The housing authority returned $13,336 to the federal treasury.

—An anonymous informant alleged that a farmer was actually operating a commercial trucking business for hire and ignoring various state and federal regulations. The GAO Hotline referred this case to the Department of Transportation Inspector General, who directed the Federal Highway Administration (FHWA) to investigate the case. The FHWA substantiated the allegation. The farmer was found to be violating a number of regulations, which included using uncertified motor vehicle operators and poor recordkeeping. The farmer agreed to comply with the federal regulations he was violating. FHWA plans to monitor this carrier's business.

—A caller alleged that a Navy contractor was falsifying and altering air freight bills to increase shipping costs on Navy purchases. This allegation was referred to the Department of Defense Inspector General, and an investigation was conducted by the Naval Investigative Service. Although the government did not prosecute the contractor, the government took administrative action and recovered over $1,100 from the contractor.

Source: United States General Accounting Office (GAO), "Fraud Hotline—9-Year GAO Fraud Hotline Summary" (GAO/OGC/OSI-88-1FS, April 1988), pp. 10–13.

Department of Defense

A key aspect of audits of defense contractors by the Department of Defense (DOD) is whether defective pricing has occurred. This relates to the nature of information supplied by contractors in the contract negotiation process. Auditors evaluate contractors' cost estimating systems, as well as performing post-award audits. The Defense Contract Audit Agency (DCAA), an independent agency within DOD is credited with $9 billion being eliminated in contractor cost claims (DCAA, 1988 Report on Activities). Within the DOD, investigations of the Inspector General suggest the nature of fraud against the government, as reflected in Exhibit 18–12—including a profile of case activity and related dollar losses. Exhibit 18–13 summarizes open cases.

A key aspect of deterring fraud relates to controls in place to punish defrauders upon discovery. Exhibit 18–14 depicts the nature of administrative and punitive actions taken by the Department of Defense (DOD). The DOD has particularly focused on timely identification and reporting of internal control weaknesses as a key deterrent to fraud.

Exhibit 18–12

Closed DOD Fraud Cases Referred for Prosecution, by Activity, Fiscal Years 1984 and 1985[a]

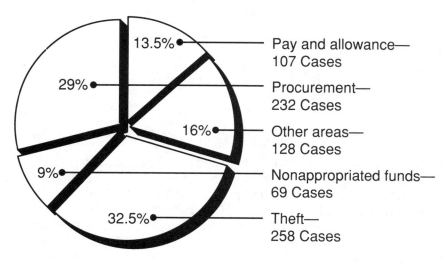

Cases: 794

[a] Data on closed DOD fraud cases referred for prosecution for fiscal years 1986 and 1987, provided by the DOD OIG in its comments on this report, showed that of 789 closed cases during that period, 43.5% were procurement; 22.9%, theft; 14.7%, pay and allowance; 4.2%, nonappropriated funds; and 14.7%, other areas. Thus, the theft category has decreased the most as a percentage, while procurement has increased the most.

Exhibit 18–12 (continued)

**Dollar Losses by Type of Closed DOD Fraud Cases Referred
for Prosecution, Fiscal Years 1984 and 1985[a]**

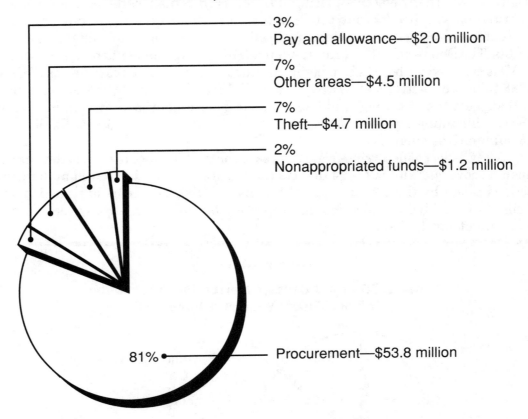

3%
Pay and allowance—$2.0 million

7%
Other areas—$4.5 million

7%
Theft—$4.7 million

2%
Nonappropriated funds—$1.2 million

81% Procurement—$53.8 million

Cases: 794
Losses: $66.2 million

[a] Data for fiscal years 1986 and 1987 provided by the DOD OIG showed that losses of $134.5 million were 73.7% from procurement; 13.1%, pay and allowances; 5.6%, theft; 0.1%, nonappropriated funds; and 7.5%, other areas. Thus, since the data we analyzed for fiscal years 1984 and 1985, procurement losses have decreased as a percentage of losses and those for pay and allowances have increased. The total losses of $134.5 million for the 789 cases in fiscal years 1986 and 1987 are substantially larger than the $66.2 million reported for about the same number of cases in fiscal years 1984 and 1985.

Exhibit 18–12 (continued)

**Dollar Losses by Type of Closed DOD Procurement Fraud
Cases Referred for Prosecution,
Fiscal Years 1984 and 1985[a]**

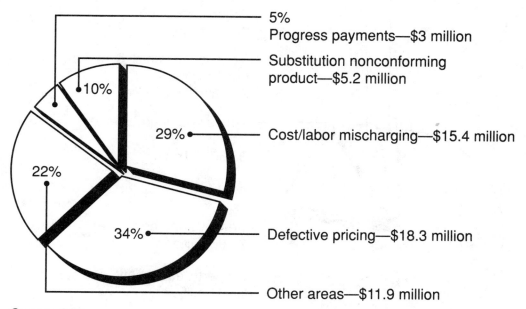

5%
Progress payments—$3 million

Substitution nonconforming
product—$5.2 million

Cost/labor mischarging—$15.4 million

Defective pricing—$18.3 million

Other areas—$11.9 million

Cases: 232
Losses: $53.8 million

[a] For fiscal years 1986 and 1987, DOD informed us that there were 343 procurement cases involving total losses of $99.1 million. The percentage of dollar losses was 30.4% for substitution/nonconforming product; 26.3%, cost/labor mischarging; 18.5%, defective pricing; 4.3%, progress payments; and 20.5%, all other areas. Thus, the percentage for the substitution/nonconforming product category has increased substantially, while that of the defective pricing category has gone down.

Exhibit 18–12 (continued)

**Dollar Losses by Type of Theft Cases Referred for Prosecution,
Fiscal Years 1984 and 1985**

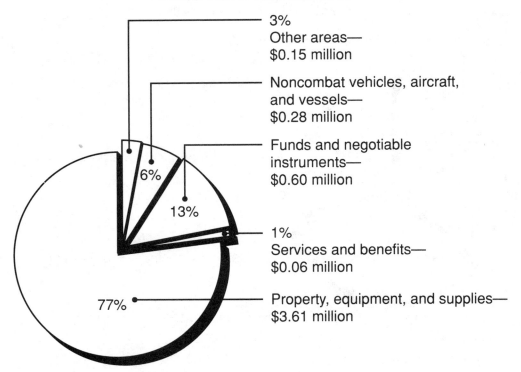

3%
Other areas—
$0.15 million

Noncombat vehicles, aircraft,
and vessels—
$0.28 million

Funds and negotiable
instruments—
$0.60 million

1%
Services and benefits—
$0.06 million

Property, equipment, and supplies—
$3.61 million

Cases: 258
Losses: $4.7 million

An example of a theft of government supplies involved employees of a company that delivered copier paper to 53 DOD facilities. The individuals stole almost 900 cases of paper valued at about $30,000 by removing the paper from various facilities without authorization in some instances and shorting deliveries in others. Four individuals pleaded guilty to the theft. Their sentences included fines and restitutions of $4,764 and various probation and community service terms.

Another example involved four individuals who stole about $43,000 worth of aluminum landing mats from firing ranges and sold the items to a steel company for almost $6,000. This case was declined for prosecution due to weak or insufficient evidence. The case file did not include evidence of any action taken.

A theft in the noncombat vehicle category occurred when a youth entered an unsecured office, stole athletic uniforms and the keys to a van, and drove off in the van.

Source: United States General Accounting Office (GAO) "DOD Fraud Investigations—Characteristics, Sanctions, and Prevention" (GAO/AFMD-88-5BR, January 1988), pp. 19–21, 24.

Exhibit 18–13

Type of Open Procurement Cases Reported
to the Secretary of Defense
(April 1, 1985, Through March 31, 1986)

Type	Number of Cases	Percentage	Estimated Dollar Loss	Percentage
Cost and/or Labor mischarging	50	33.8	$278,632,831	71.9
Defective pricing	21	14.2	56,554,202	14.6
Product substitution nonconforming product	32	21.6	32,068,222	8.3
Progress payment claims	15	10.1	11,549,000	3.0
Contractor kickbacks	6	4.1	3,650,000	.9
Bribery/solicitation of bribe	11	7.4	1,000,000	.3
Undelivered product	3	2.0	486,240	.1
Conflict of interest	5	3.4	400,000	.1
Other procurement cases	5	3.4	3,056,504	.8
Total	148	100.0	$387,396,999	100.0

In one of the cost and/or labor mischarging open cases, a DCAA audit uncovered suspected cost escalations on over 300 spare parts in 3,200 contracts, resulting in an estimated loss of over $100 million. The contractor had allegedly been manipulating cost transfers from one contract to another over a 6-year period. As of August 12, 1987, the case was pending and will be presented before a grand jury.

In one of the defective pricing open cases, a subcontractor was allegedly overpricing spare parts for a missile warning system contract. Based on the subcontractor's overpricing, the contractor was charging from 70% to 2,472% more than the Federal Supply Schedule prices, resulting in an estimated loss to the government of $2 million.

Source: United States General Accounting Office (GAO), "DOD Fraud Investigations—Characteristics, Sanctions, and Prevention" (GAO/AFMD-88-5BR, January 1988), p. 28.

Exhibit 18–14

**Administrative Actions Taken Against DOD Employees
(232 Actions)**

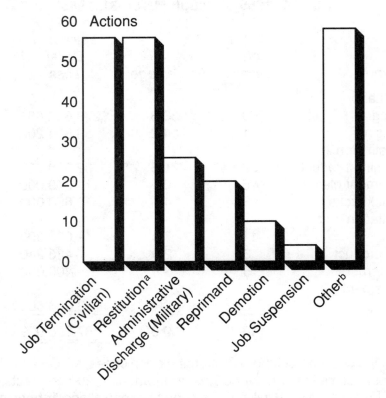

^a Includes garnishment of wages

^b "Other" includes such things as increased supervision and being temporarily transferred to another job

Exhibit 18–14 (continued)

**Administrative Actions Taken Against
Contractors/Vendors (202 Actions)**

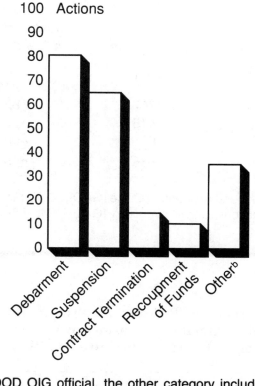

[a] According to a DOD OIG official, the other category includes such actions as additional contract supervision, increased audit activity, withholding additional orders, and in the future holding the contractor/vendor as a nonresponsible bidder.

Exhibit 18–14 (continued)

**Selected Punitive Actions Taken Against Those Who
Defrauded DOD Programs, Fiscal Years 1983–87**

Fiscal Year	Suspensions	Debarments	Total Suspensions and Debarments	Justice Criminal Convictions
1983	195	85	280	207
1984	134	260	394	192
1985	225	357	582	333
1986	470	415	885	344
1987	393	505	898	307
Total	1,417	1,622	3,039	1,383

Source: United States General Accounting Office (GAO), "DOD Fraud Investigations—Characteristics, Sanctions, and Prevention" (GAO/AFMD-88-5BR, January 1988), pp. 36–38.

Evaluating Materiality

An interesting overview of "Risk and Materiality in Governmental Audits" and research on their determination is provided by William A. Hillison and Rhoda Caudill Icerman, both of the Florida State University (Working Paper, July 1989):

> The 1972 "Yellow Book" of the General Accounting Office (GAO) provided general guidance for reporting materiality. The GAO noted that reports and statements should contain the information necessary for users—management, the electorate, creditors, grantors, and others—to form an opinion on the effectiveness of the stewardship exercised by public officials. Consideration should be given to materiality, defined as the relative importance or relevance of an item included in or omitted from a financial or operation report. Six specific indicators of materiality were identified that could be used individually or in combination:
>
> 1. Absolute dollar amount
> 2. Ratio of amount of an item to an appropriate base figure
> 3. Length of life of an asset
> 4. Importance of the item to the accomplishment of the mission
> 5. Importance to the maintenance of adequate controls, such as a matter of small discrepancies
> 6. The characteristic of the items involved, such as indications of malfeasance or misfeasance (p. 52)

The 1988 revision of the GAO "Yellow Book" provides equally general guidance. In addition to consideration of the dollar amount of the item, determinants of materiality (and risk) can be based on qualitative factors such as:

a. Amount of revenues and expenditures.
b. Newness of the activity or changes in its conditions
c. Adequacy of internal controls
d. Results of prior operations
e. Level and extent of review or other form of independent oversight
f. Adequacy of the internal controls for ensuring compliance with laws and regulations
g. Management's adherence to applicable laws and regulations
h. Audit report users' expectations
i. Public perceptions and political sensitivity of the areas under audit
j. Audit requirements (pp. 3–13 and 3–14)

In implementing the Single Audit Act, OMB Circular A-128 provides specific guidance to auditors concerning the materiality of items discovered in the audit. Section 13.a requires

All fraud abuse, or illegal acts or indications of such acts, including all questioned costs found as the result of these acts that auditors become aware of, should normally be covered in a separate written report . . .

Thus, once discovered, the materiality threshold for reporting questioned costs, illegalities, and acts of abuse is zero. Users of Single Audit reports have the right to conclude that if no items were reported, then no items were discovered. However, this same assumption does not hold for financial statement errors.

To explore the degree of auditor consensus regarding materiality in the governmental sector, over 200 governmental auditors were asked to evaluate a set of cases and identify what would be considered planning materiality. Their focus in formulating a number varied greatly, as did the numbers attached to each basis.

Focus of Materiality Decision

Selected as Focus	Number	Percent
Individual Funds Balances	43	21
Total of Fund Balances	42	20
Total Assets	40	19
Revenues	26	12
Expenditures	20	10
Net of Revenues—Expenditures	7	3
No Response	31	15
Total	209	100%

Mean Percentage Planning Materiality
149 of 209 Subjects

Basis	Mean Percent	Variance	NOB*	Percent Selecting	
				5%	10%
Individual Funds Balances	6.3	3.7	27	70%	13%
Total of Fund Balances	5.3	3.0	42	52%	24%
Total Assets	8.6	11.9	35	59%	27%
Revenues	5.1	3.3	21	50%	24%
Expenditures	5.2	3.3	19	39%	24%
Net of Rev-Expend	4.4	1.3	5	80%	0

* Number of observations differ since a number of subjects indicated the focus of the materiality judgment but failed to provide a percentage.

The Trend Toward Using Independent External CPAs Among Federal, State and Local Governments

Although the general accounting office has primary audit responsibilities for federal government operations, many agencies also utilize independent external CPAs for management service and audit engagements. One reason for this use of external CPAs is inadequate staffing of the GAO and similar positions. In many government programs no audits have been performed, and a GAO survey of 418 federal agencies found that a third had not been audited from fiscal year 1974 through 1976 despite their receipt of more than 20 billion governmental dollars. In many cases, government programs have been subjected to an audit only once in 10 to 15 years. To meet management and control needs, the use of external auditors is likely to increase.

As the state and local government markets are viewed, the participation of external auditors is likely to be even greater than at the federal level due to the general trend of state governments not to expand and even to reduce the size of state audit departments. It has become increasingly popular, based on remarks by Charles A. Bowsher, Comptroller General of the United States, for government units, including state audit departments, to contract with CPA firms to provide audit services. Even municipalities with qualified auditing departments have increasingly hired private CPA firms for annual audits, reportedly due to bond underwriters' requests for complete audits by external CPAs, as well as the government units' belief that private accounting firms can do a better job.

Jack Gary, manager of the audit division of the Treasury's revenue-sharing program in 1977, had predicted:

> In the next 10 years this public—municipal and state—accounting could be the biggest area in the whole accounting business. (See Lynch, 1977, p. 21, cited in the references.)

A major reason for his prediction is the federal revenue-sharing program's provision that in three years all municipalities that receive at least $25,000 in funds must have an independent audit done on their financial statements. The provision applied to about 11,000 municipalities in 1977. In addition to demands for financial statement audits, a potential exists for increased demand for pension plan audits. More than 30% of the bigger municipal pension plans are not audited annually, yet increasing attention to unfunded pension liabilities and the problems with social security are likely to increase governmental units' accountability for pension funds.

Generally Accepted Government Auditing Standards (GAGAS)

The revised "Yellow Book" describes Generally Accepted Government Auditing Standards (GAGAS), a summary of which appears as an Appendix to this chapter. Exhibit 18–15 diagrams aspects of GAGAS and bears out the central

---

Exhibit 18–15

Overview of Standards

GENERALLY ACCEPTED GOVERNMENT AUDITING STANDARDS (GAGAS)

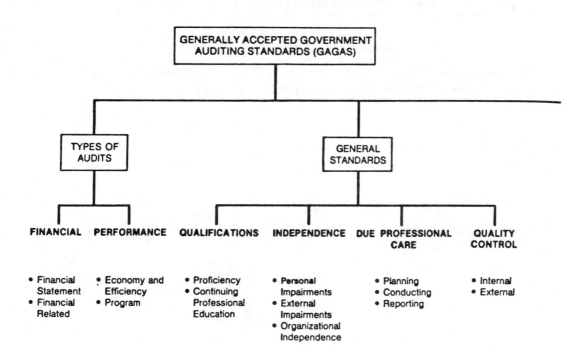

Exhibit 18–15 (continued)

GENERALLY ACCEPTED GOVERNMENT AUDITING STANDARDS (GAGAS)   **(Continued)**

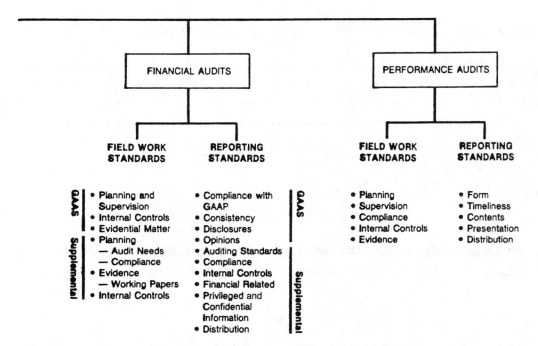

Source: United States General Accounting Office, *Government Auditing Standards* (1988 Revision), Appendix B.

Exhibit 18–15 (continued)

Internal Control Related Requirements

The fourth field work standard for government performance audits is:

An assessment should be made of applicable internal controls when necessary to satisfy the audit objectives.

Management is responsible for establishing an effective system of internal controls. The lack of administrative continuity in government units because of continuing changes in elected legislative bodies and in administrative organizations increases the need for an effective internal control system.

Internal controls include the plan of organization and methods and procedures adopted by management to ensure that its goals and objectives are met; that resources are used consistent with laws, regulations, and policies; that resources are safeguarded against waste, loss, and misuse; and that reliable data are obtained, maintained, and fairly disclosed in reports.

The need to assess internal controls and the focus of that assessment varies with the objectives of the audit.

a. An assessment is required in audits having as objectives the assessment of the adequacy of particular internal controls. Here, the auditor should design steps and procedures to assess the effectiveness of the prescribed control procedures or actual control practices.

b. An assessment of internal controls is a natural adjunct in audits having as their objectives an assessment of the adequacy of the process (e.g., procedures and practices) for carrying out a particular program, service, activity, or function. Here, the auditor should design steps and procedures to determine if controls needed in the process exist and if the existing controls are adequate to achieve the desired objectives.

c. An assessment may be necessary in audits having as objectives determining the underlying cause of unsatisfactory performance (e.g., lack of improvement achieved by recently installed automation intended to increase productivity). Here, if the unsatisfactory performance could occur from weaknesses in internal controls, the auditor should design steps and procedures to assess the adequacy of those specific controls that if weak could cause the unsatisfactory performance.

The focus of the assessment of internal controls varies with the objective of the audit being conducted.

a. Economy and efficiency audits: The auditors may assess those policies, procedures, practices, and controls applicable to the programs, functions, and activities, under audit to the extent necessary, as determined by the audit objectives.

Exhibit 18–15 (continued)

b. Program audits: The auditors may assess those policies, procedures, practices, and controls which specifically bear on the attainment of the goals and objectives specified by the law or regulations for the organization, program, activity, or function under audit to the extent necessary, as determined by the audit objectives.

Auditors may be required or contracted to audit or assess particular internal controls. Such assessments should be made in accordance with the standards in this statement.*

Internal auditing is an important part of internal control, and the auditors should consider this in conducting the audit. Where an assessment of internal controls is called out, external auditors should consider the extent to which the work of the internal auditors can be relied upon to help provide reasonable assurance that internal control is functioning properly and to prevent duplication of effort.**

In view of the wide range in the size and nature of government organizations, programs, activities, and functions and in view of their organizational structures and operating methods, no single pattern for internal audit and review activities can be specified. Many governmental entities have these activities identified by other names, such as inspection, appraisal investigation, organization and methods, or management analysis. These activities assist management by reviewing selected functions.

* Examples include the Federal Managers' Financial Integrity Act of 1982 (Public Law 97–255) and the laws of several states.
** See chapter 3, paragraph 37 for guidance the auditor should follow when relying on the work of others.

Source: United States General Accounting Office, By the Comptroller General of the United States, *Government Auditing Standards* (1988 Revision), pp. A-1, 13–16.

---

role of internal controls in the various types of audits. Note that these audits relate to a broad spectrum of activities at the federal government, as depicted in Exhibit 18–16, in addition to the local level. Of interest is the General Accounting Office's issuance of an exposure draft on December 29, 1982 entitled "Standards for Internal Controls in the Federal Government," which contained the following definition:

Internal controls are a plan of organization and all the methods and procedures (techniques) the management of an entity adopts to help it achieve four basic management objectives:

- Ensure adherence to laws, regulations, and policies

Exhibit 18–16

Federal Government Activities

ALLOCATION:	who receives which public good services as prescribed by budgeting procedures
DISTRIBUTION:	adjustment of wealth and income levels toward a "fairness" concept
STABILIZATION:	application of fiscal policies to achieve high employment, price stability, and economic growth
PRODUCTION:	of goods not totally private in nature

PRODUCTION (continued):

- public good characteristics
- free-ridership possibilities as well as those private in nature but produced to achieve governmental goals:
  * equity-oriented goods like housing projects for low-income families
  * education-related products intended to enhance society
  * monopolies granted on the premise of efficiency, such as utilities

REVENUE GENERATION:
- taxation
- sells goods and services
  * toll roads
  * user fees (e.g., community pool)

- Ensure that reliable data are obtained, maintained, and properly disclosed in reports
- Promote economy, efficiency, and effectiveness of operations
- Safeguard resources against loss due to errors and irregularities

COMPLIANCE AUDITING

The AICPA has issued guidance on testing and reporting on compliance with laws and regulations in engagements under generally accepted auditing standards, *Government Auditing Standards*, the Single Audit Act of 1984,[5] and in

---

[5] This Act of Congress is applicable to governmental units receiving $100,000 or more per year through federal financial assistance programs. The Act substantially increases compliance and control testing that is directed at the entity's federal financial assistance program receipts and expenditures.
"The Evolution of the Single Audit: A 20-Year Process" by Clifford D. Brown and Priscilla Burnaby [*Accounting Horizons* (June 1988), pp. 47–52] describes how this Act has and continues to evolve.

other engagements. It has also provided guidance on the reporting on the internal control structure under Government Auditing Standards.[6]

Governmental Accounting Standards Board has pointed out that governments apply GAAP in an environment of numerous legal and contractual considerations, reflected in fund structures and unique principles and methods.[7] This requires auditors to assess risk associated with possible violations of laws and regulations. Procedures to do so entail: gaining an understanding of such laws and regulations; inquiring of management, legal counsel, and state and federal auditors; and review of agreements (including grants and loans) and minutes.

An example of an auditor's report on compliance when the auditor's procedures disclosed no material violations is presented in Exhibit 18–17.

Single Audit Act

The Single Audit Act requires reports by the auditor on financial statements, a supplementary schedule of federal financial assistance and an internal control structure of policies and procedures relevant to federal financial assistance programs. Audit procedures may involve: review of plans and procedures; detailed review of files to test expenditures, recipients, and related records; contact with cognizant agencies as to prior or pending disallowances; confirmation work; and attainment of a representation letter.

Exhibit 18–18 illustrates a report on compliance with requirements applicable to major Federal Financial Assistance Programs. In meeting the general audit requirements under the "Single Audit" initiative, the *Compliance Supplement* for Single Audits prescribes tests in the areas of

- political activity, i.e., prohibiting the use of federal funds for partisan political activity (Hatch Act and Intergovernmental Personnel Act of 1970)
- Davis-Bacon Act, i.e., requiring that laborers working on federally-financed construction projects be paid a wage not less than the prevailing regional wage established by the Secretary of Labor
- civil rights
- cash management, requiring recipients of federal financial assistance to minimize the time elapsed between receipt and disbursements of that assistance
- relocation assistance and real property acquisition
- federal financial reports

In such audits, the role of the government's external control system is emphasized.[8]

---

[6] AICPA File Ref. No. 2353, *Compliance Auditing* (December 9, 1988).

[7] GASB, *Codification of Governmental Accounting and Financial Reporting Standards*, Section 1200.103.

[8] AICPA Auditing Standards Board Planning Subcommittee, March 20, 1986—Revised, proposals of AICPA Task Force on Quality of Governmental Audits—Section I (File Ref. No. 1110), February 4, 1987.

Exhibit 18–17

Compliance Audit Report

[Addressee]

We have audited the financial statements of [name of entity] as of and for the year ended June 30, 19X1, and have issued our report thereon dated August 15, 19X1.

We conducted our audit in accordance with generally accepted auditing standards and *Government Auditing Standards*, issued by the Comptroller General of the United States. Those standards require that we plan and perform the audit to obtain reasonable assurance about whether the financial statements are free of material misstatement.

Compliance with laws, regulations, contracts, and grants applicable to [name and entity] is the responsibility of [name of entity]'s management. As part of obtaining reasonable assurance about whether the financial statements are free of material misstatement, we performed tests of [name of entity]'s compliance with certain provisions of laws, regulations, contracts, and grants. However, our objective was not to provide an opinion on overall compliance with such provisions.

The results of our tests indicate that, with respect to the items tested, [name of entity] complied, in all material respects, with the provisions referred to in the preceding paragraph. With respect to items not tested, nothing came to our attention that caused us to believe that [name of entity] had not complied, in all material respects, with those provisions.

This report is intended for the information of the audit committee, management, and [specify legislative or regulatory body]. This report is a matter of public record.

Firm's Signature
City, State
August 15, 19X1

Source: AICPA, SAS 63 (Section 801), "Applicable to Governmental Entities and Other Recipients of Governmental Financial Assistance" (April 1989), p. 13.

Exhibit 18–18

Independent Auditor's Report on Compliance with Requirements That Govern Each Major Federal Financial Assistance Program

To the City Council
City of Example, Any State

We have audited the City of Example, Any State's, compliance with the requirements governing types of services allowed or unallowed; eligibility; matching, level of effort, or earmarking; reporting; [describe any special tests and provisions]; claims for advances and reimbursements; and amounts claimed or used for matching that are applicable to each of its major federal financial assistance programs, which are identified in the accompanying schedule of federal financial assistance, for the year ended June 30, 19X1. The management of the City of Example is responsible for the City's compliance with those requirements. Our responsibility is to express an opinion on compliance with those requirements based on our audit.

We conducted our audit in accordance with generally accepted auditing standards, *Government Auditing Standards*, issued by the Comptroller General of the United States, and OMB Circular A-128, "Audits of State and Local Governments." Those standards and OMB Circular A-128 require that we plan and perform the audit to obtain reasonable assurance about whether material noncompliance with the requirements referred to above occurred. An audit includes examining, on a test basis, evidence about the City's compliance with those requirements. We believe that our audit provides a reasonable basis for our opinion.

The results of our audit procedures disclosed immaterial instances of noncompliance with the requirements referred to above, which are described in the accompanying schedule of findings and questioned costs. We considered these instances of noncompliance in forming our opinion on compliance, which is expressed in the following paragraph.

In our opinion, the City of Example, Any State, complied, in all material respects, with the requirements governing types of services allowed or unallowed; eligibility; matching, level of effort, or earmarking; reporting; [describe any special tests and provisions]; claims for advances and reimbursements; and amounts claimed or used for matching that are applicable to its major federal financial assistance programs for the year ended June 30, 19X1.

Firm's Signature

City, State
August 15, 19X1

Source: AICPA, SAS 63 (Section 801), Applicable to Governmental Entities and Other Recipients of Governmental Financial Assistance" (April 1989), pp. 36–37.

OMB Circular A-128 requires the auditor to select and test a representative number of expenditures from each major program as a means to restrict detection risk. The Compliance Supplement contains other suggested procedures that the auditor should consider in determining tests of compliance with specific requirements. [These relate to types of services, eligibility, matching and level of effort, reporting, cost allocation, special requirements, and monitoring of subrecipients.]

Evaluation of Audit Procedures. An auditor must evaluate whether the recipient governmental unit complied with all laws and regulations that could have a material effect on each major program. To accomplish this objective, the auditor should consider for each major program the effect of instances of noncompliance that were identified in the audit. Specifically, the auditor should consider:

- The frequency of noncompliance identified in the audit;
- The adequacy of a primary recipient's policies and procedures for monitoring subrecipients and the possible effect of any noncompliance identified by the primary recipient or the subrecipients' auditors; and
- The existence of any questioned costs, and whether they are material to the program.

Reporting Responsibilities

An auditor has extensive reporting responsibilities under the Act. In addition to the reports required under GAGAS, the auditor must issue the following reports on the governmental unit's federal financial assistance programs:

- A report on the internal controls used in administering each program;
- A report on a supplementary schedule showing total expenditures for each of the governmental unit's federal financial assistance programs; and
- A report on compliance with laws and regulations identifying all findings of noncompliance and questioned costs.

OMB Circular A-128 requires the governmental unit to make these reports available for public inspections within 30 days after the audit is completed. Copies of the audit reports must be submitted to the governmental unit being audited, and to the cognizant agency requiring or arranging for the audit. The cognizant agency must then provide copies of the auditor's reports to each federal department or agency that provided federal assistance funds to the recipient.

The classification of a cost as a questioned cost varies among agencies since the criteria for such classification may have been established by law when the program was authorized and funded, or may have been established through regulations issued by the agency. Generally, the criteria relate to:

- Unallowable costs—specifically not allowed under the general and special requirements or conditions of the program;
- Undocumented costs—charged to a program for which detailed documentation does not exist;
- Unapproved costs—the auditor cannot find evidence of required approval, or the cost was not provided for in an approved budget; and
- Unreasonable costs—incurred that may not reflect the actions of a prudent person, or assigned to in-kind contributions an unreasonably high valuation.

In evaluating the effect of questioned costs on the opinion on compliance, the auditor considers the best estimate of total costs questioned for each major program (likely questioned costs), not just the questioned costs specifically identified (known questioned costs). The auditor should relate the number of instances of noncompliance that resulted in known questioned costs to the number of transactions examined. For example, if audit sampling was used, the auditor would project the amount of known questioned costs identified in the sample to the population items in the major program.

The auditor must then report any instances of noncompliance found in accordance with GAGAS and any resulting known questioned costs. The auditor is not required to report likely questioned costs. [All material weaknesses that have come to the auditor's attention during the audit should be described, citing condition, criteria, effect, and cause.]

Source: Adrian Fitzsimons and Marc Levine, "SAS No. 63: An Analysis of Compliance Auditing Standards," *The Practical Accountant* (February 1990), pp. 34–53.

Issues of Audit Quality and Related Recommendations for Control Over Procurement

A GAO investigation of 150 governmental audits selected using statistical sampling techniques found 32 with severe standards violations, 25 evidencing unsatisfactory performance, and 63 with no problems or minor problems. Three-fourths of the audits with something more than minor problems involved CPA firms who were not members of the Division.[9]

One recommendation made by the GAO has been for Federal Officials and others to review the audits they receive to ensure that they are of high quality. To promote such quality, reports to the accounting profession, via state boards, are encouraged. Consistent with earlier discussion, follow-up action when problems are detected are critical to retaining quality control. Exhibit 18–19 suggests the responsiveness of the accounting profession to referrals, and as Exhibit 18–20 suggests, a process is in place to provide comfort of future enforcement action.

In light of the 1985 and 1986 reports by the GAO citing adverse affects on audit quality, questions have been raised about the manner in which audits are procured in the governmental sector. Indeed, when considering this procurement process, the following attributes were identified as critical:

- competition
- solicitation
- technical evaluation
- written agreement

The GAO found that 58% of the entities studied failed to meet these four criteria and 46% of these entities' CPA audits were deemed to be of unacceptable quality. In contrast, 17% of companies meeting the four criteria for procurement suffered from unacceptable quality audits.

The GAO proceeded to recommend means of enhancing procurement of audit services. These are presented in Exhibit 18–21. While uniquely tailored to considering CPA service procurement, these recommendations may well apply to other services as well. Exhibit 18–22 provides the GAO's recommendations when soliciting audit services.

Timeliness

Once auditing services are obtained, follow-up to ensure timeliness of reporting is an important control practice. As reflected in Exhibit 18–23, federal loan programs for HUD and FmHA multi-family housing programs have suffered from untimely filings. Because many audit reports are received late, the GAO recommended that each agency should have a system with written procedures

---

[9] Letter to The Honorable Jack Brooks from the AICPA dated February 27, 1987 (File No. A-8-702).

Exhibit 18–19

Disciplinary Actions Taken by State Boards on Completed Referrals

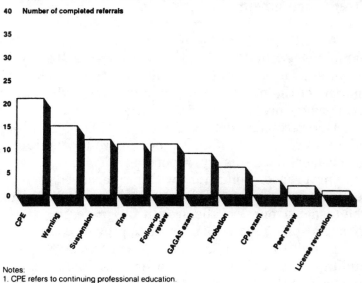

40 Number of completed referrals

35

30

25

20

15

10

5

0

CPE · Warning · Suspension · Fine · Follow-up review · GAGAS exam · Probation · CPA exam · Peer review · License revocation

Notes:
1. CPE refers to continuing professional education.

2. GAGAS refer to generally accepted government auditing standards.

3. The number of completed referrals does not total 36 because most state boards imposed more than one disciplinary action on each referral.

Disciplinary Actions Taken by the AICPA on Completed GAO Referrals

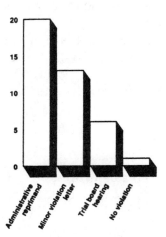

25 Number of completed referrals

20

15

10

5

0

Administrative reprimand · Minor violation letter · Trial board hearing · No violation

Note: Sixteen of the 20 administrative reprimands required that the CPA take continuing professional education and have a follow-up work product reviewed by the AICPA. The remaining four required only continuing professional education.

Source: United States General Accounting Office (GAO),"CPA Audit Quality—A Status Report on the Accounting Profession's Enforcement Efforts" (GAO/AFMD-88-28, April 1988), pp. 16, 24.

Exhibit 18–20

Typical Enforcement Process Used by State Boards of Accountancy

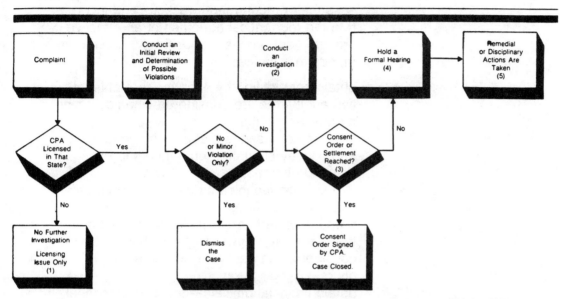

(1) The state board receives a complaint (audit referral) and determines whether it has jurisdiction over the CPA involved. If the CPA does not hold a license to practice public accountancy from the state, the state board does not investigate the complaint because the board has no jurisdiction over the CPA and cannot impose disciplinary action. However, the state board may seek an injunction if the CPA is required to have a license to practice in the state.

(2) An investigator for the state board reviews the audit in question and the specific charges made in a complaint. In some states, the investigator may examine previous audits by the CPA to determine if the problem is a recurring one and whether any mitigating circumstances exist. At the conclusion of the investigation, a report is made to the state board outlining specific findings and, in some cases, recommending disciplinary actions.

(3) A state board often uses a consent order or a stipulated settlement to resolve a complaint. These legal documents describe actions, usually remedial, which the CPA agrees to take rather than proceed to a formal hearing. With either document, the state board allows the CPA, within limitations, to be involved in negotiating the final disciplinary actions.

(4) During a formal hearing, the state board, as a quasi-judicial body, has authority to reach final decisions on the severity of the auditing standards violations. If warranted, the state board can impose disciplinary actions.

(5) All decisions reached through a state board's formal hearing process are subject to appeal.

Source: United States General Accounting Office (GAO), "CPA Audit Quality—A Status Report on the Accounting Profession's Enforcement Efforts" (GAO/AFMD-88-28, April 1988), p. 61.

Exhibit 18–21

Recommended Practices When Procuring Audit Services

Recommendations

GAO recommends, among other things, that entities that procure CPA services carefully assess their procurement practices and incorporate the four critical attributes of an effective procurement process. Specifically, GAO recommends that entities

- obtain competition by ensuring that at least two audit firms are considered when selecting a qualified auditor,
- prepare solicitations that are comprehensive and convey all audit requirements to interested audit firms,
- use specific technical factors in selecting a qualified audit firm,
- prepare written agreements which hold both the entity and the audit firm accountable,
- consider using multiyear agreements, preferably of a 5-year duration,
- obtain financial officials—qualified personnel with specialized knowledge of governmental accounting and auditing—to assist in planning and implementing their procurement processes, and
- consider the benefits of using audit committees both to help plan and to oversee entities' procurement processes.

In addition, GAO endorses the formulation of detailed procurement guidance as an important vehicle to improving audit quality. The results of GAO's work should be useful in this effort. GAO believes the guidance can be best accomplished by all interested organizations working together under the auspices of an intergovernmental organization facilitating the project or by GAO leading the project with the assistance of an advisory committee.

Source: United States General Accounting Office (GAO), "CPA Audit Quality— A Framework for Procuring Audit Services" (GAO/AFMD-87-34, August 1987), pp. 6–7.

Exhibit 18–22

Suggested Provisions for Solicitation Documents

Regardless of the type of solicitation document used, entities can increase the likelihood of obtaining a quality audit when the solicitation document is comprehensive and accurately conveys all the details and requirements of the audit. The following represents a list of suggested provisions that we believe entities should include in any solicitation document. Although these provisions should be present, the extent to which the entity elaborates on them should coincide with the size of the audit engagement and procurement method used.

(1) Administrative Information:

- background information on the entity;
- schedule of government funds by project or grant to be audited;
- description and magnitude of the entity's accounting records;
- description of the entity's computer system(s), if applicable;
- name and number of a contact person at the cognizant federal agency;
- period to be audited;
- term of contract engagement; and
- availability of prior audit reports and working papers.

(2) Work and Reporting Requirements:

- auditing standards to be followed;
- extent to which entity would assist firm;
- specific scope of audit work to be performed;
- number and types of reports required;
- list of restrictions, such as copy services or work space;
- exit conference requirements;
- specific audit guide or program to be followed; and
- minimum audit requirements under applicable laws such as the Single Audit Act.

(3) Time Requirements:

- date records would be ready for audit;
- dates for completing interim phases, such as fieldwork completion and draft report preparation;
- date of contract award;
- date final report is due;
- working paper retention requirements; and
- workpaper availability requirements for cognizant agency when applicable.

(4) Proposal Information:

- evaluation criteria against which the proposal will be judged and
- entity's right to reject proposal.

Exhibit 18-22 (continued)

(5) Contractual Information:

- provision stipulating recourse in the event of poor quality work,
- provision for Equal Employment Opportunity,
- provision for termination of contract, and
- provision for administrative and/or legal remedies for contract violations.

Source: United States General Accounting Office (GAO), "CPA Audit Quality—A Framework for Procuring Audit Services" (GAO/AFMD-87-34, August 1987), pp. 59–60.

---

requiring program officials to provide written follow-up on late reports and time frames for when follow-up action should be taken. Moreover, each agency should designate an official to ensure that its procedures are followed.

Guidelines for Preparing Control Suggestions for Municipalities

The municipal sector has been a leader in the area of communicating to the public internal control commentaries by external CPAs and by state auditors. Past research regarding the content of such disclosures suggests that more care needs to be taken by CPAs in preparing control suggestions for municipal units. The disclosures frequently leave unanswered questions regarding risk exposure, cost/benefit issues, and the meaning of diversity of report form. The difficulty, in part, is a lack of guidelines for reporting on material weaknesses or immaterial weaknesses in controls. Some CPA's reports on control are several pages long while others are a brief statement of two or three control recommendations. Some

---

Exhibit 18–23

Timeliness of Audit Report Filings for HUD and FmHA

Receipt of Annual Audit Reports

Receipts of reports	Number	Percent
Received on time	146	30
Received late:		
1-30 days	149	30
31-60 days	59	12
61-365 days	93	19
Not received within 1 year	47	9
Total	**494**	**100**

Source: United States General Accounting Office (GAO), "CPA Audit Quality—Improved Controls Are Needed to Ensure Quality Audits of Federal Loan Programs" (GAO/AFMD-88-3, May 1988), p. 16.

reports include the auditee's response, while others do not. Report users are left guessing:

—Is a long report a sign of extensive problems?

—Are city management's responses that indicate recommendations are not going to be followed a signal of poor management?

—If a recommendation is made for improved documentation of travel expenses, does that mean losses have occurred from inappropriate travel expenditures?

—How can the reader interpret the difference between possibilities for error and probabilities for error?

—What dollar effect on financial statements might result from control weaknesses?

Since the CPA knows that management letters are frequently made public by municipal units, a concerted effort should be made to improve the quality and clarity of disclosures. The approach should be similar to that used for material weaknesses, and a clear demarcation should be made between those commentaries that are intended to be material and those intended to be immaterial. An explanatory statement that the CPA's comments are intended as constructive suggestions requiring a cost/benefit evaluation by management to assess their desirability as new or revised control procedures would be advisable. A more detailed critique of past control reports and samples of internal control reporting practices in the municipal sector are provided by the author in an article that appears in the *Accounting Review* (July, 1981), should additional information be desired. However, the basic message is that the profession's services with respect to control disclosures are demanded by the municipal sector and efforts should be taken by each CPA to ensure consistent and informative disclosure practices.

Educating Government Entities About Controls

In recommending controls, you should strive to educate governmental entities as to how the control procedures can be effectively implemented and monitored. Two internal controls that are particularly popular in county government include required approval by the County Board of expenditures over a set dollar amount and required competitive bidding for expenditures over a set dollar amount. In many cases, these are made a part of state law. Of course, to maintain the effectiveness of these two controls, the County Boards must use precision in authorizing expenditures, as well as strive to prevent the effective circumvention of either control by the breaking down of large purchases into numerous small dollar amounts.

Example: A classic illustration of the failure of designed controls was provided by the Cook County Board, in its dealings with snow-lease pacts, as reported by William Juneau in the *Chicago Tribune*. Apparently a sweetheart deal was arranged to lease 14 pieces of snow equipment for three years for $937,170, when the pieces could have been purchased for only $650,000. The Board approval requirement may or may not have been met, depending on one's definition of what was approved. The Board acknowledged its granting of "permission to negotiate a leasing agreement," and county officials interpreted this as "giving permission to sign a lease contract." Beyond this miscommunication, both the board approval and competitive bidding requirements for most leases in excess of $5,000 could be claimed to have been effectively circumvented by the county officials' signing of seven different lease contracts which resulted in monthly payments per lease of less than $5,000. When the situation was publicly announced, an additional internal control was suggested; the county's computer could be programmed to reject any checks that exceeded $5,000 unless information was fed into the computer showing that the board has approved the payment. It was claimed that the breaking down of invoices to below $5,000 would be ineffective in circumventing controls because when invoices are due to a single payee, they are accumulated for payment. Hence, the seven lease payments would aggregate to a check that exceeded $5,000. The Cook County experience demonstrates the usefulness of detective controls, in addition to preventive controls, and the importance of enforcing compliance with designed controls. Mere control design, even when in the form of legislation, is no assurance of compliance.

Examples of fraud and control problems at the federal, state, county, and local levels of government abound. They all represent opportunities to provide control-related services that can enhance both the effectiveness and the efficiency of government operations.

UNIQUE CONTROL CONSIDERATIONS FOR A HOSPITAL

The Medicare-Medicaid Anti-Fraud and Abuse Act of 1977 (Public Law 95–142) has a motivating effect for hospitals similar to the Foreign Corrupt Practices Act's effect on corporations in encouraging the improvement of designed systems of internal accounting control and the timely monitoring of such systems' operations. In addition, the numerous reporting requirements of the National Health Planning and Resources Development Act of 1974 (Public Law 93–461) require effectively controlled information systems. Of course, proprietary hospitals and not-for-profit hospitals have similar operations that can be viewed through the same cycle approach as applied to any service-oriented business entity.

Specifically, the revenue cycle will encompass patient charges and their collections, as well as investment income. The cost-of-sales cycle will encompass physicians' and other employees' salaries and fringe benefits, supplies, and the acquisition, use, repair, and retirement of property, plant, and equipment. The financing and nonroutine transaction cycle will include the management of financial resources, fund balances, and administration. Administration encompasses internal audit, tax, and budgetary matters. The control objectives are essentially the same as for any entity, except that additional emphasis is placed on

—regulatory requirements

—provisions for third-party settlements, particularly with insurance companies and the government,

—fund balance restrictions, and

—the maintenance of accurate data to facilitate patient care.

Since hospitals are one of those industries that are highly regulated, a continuous review of legislation and regulations is essential to ensuring compliance. This is particularly true of cost-reimbursement regulations, as these comprise a large portion of a hospital's revenue. Rate regulations require that rate setting be approved and be consistent for services provided to various patient classifications. Due to the nature of the service at hospitals, stock-outs of inventory or obsolescence of items like blood supplies have critical effects on patients, employees, and the hospital as an organization. Liability consequences abound. Also, the condition of patients upon arrival at a hospital may be one of helplessness. The result is an added trustee type of function for the hospital whereby responsibility exists for preventing the misappropriation of the patient's valuables. These special circumstances imply additional concerns for the control system of hospitals beyond those typically found in a business organization.

Patient data bases are critical. These must include

—patient identification,

—complete biographical data,

—sufficient financial data to facilitate the payment for services

—patient allergies and similar so-called "alert" data,

—test results,

—drug profile and medication administration records,

—physicians' orders,

—medical activities to date, and

—future plans for care.

Furthermore, for patient safety it is imperative that such data bases be available at all times, i.e., immediate back-up must exist should the normal system fail.

Of equal importance is the updating of care facilities and the competency and adequacy of the medical staff. Closed hospitals attribute their closures primarily to the following factors:

—financial bankruptcy,

—replacement by new facilities,

—low occupancy,

—outdated facilities, and

—lack of medical staffing.

Each of these operating problems should be solvable if adequate information and control systems are established.

Since a hospital is a service operation, the ability to control access to the services provided, particularly by management and employees, is difficult. Controls must be established to avoid irregular use of patient services, and these controls must be tailored to the service nature of the product by focusing on the providers of the service (in addition to the typical physical safeguard procedures that are applied to inventory in business entities) in order to prevent misuse of products.

MATERIAL WEAKNESSES IN THE NOT-FOR-PROFIT SECTOR—AN EXAMPLE

The nature of material weaknesses in a not-for-profit entity is no different from that in a profit organization. However, it may be useful to review a report on material weaknesses at a hospital. The weaknesses reported all relate to the revenue cycle of the operation. Together, the weaknesses materially affect the entity's ability to control patient revenue and accounts receivable. The weaknesses relate to the recording of revenue, the generation of billings, and the processing of cash receipts.

The bases for recording patient revenue and preparing billings to third-party payors are forms that are not prenumbered. Furthermore, these forms are not submitted to the billing department from all ancillary departments and physicians on a daily basis. They should be submitted daily, and a numerical sequence should be established via prenumbering. Such prenumbered forms should be verified as being complete, and missing items should be investigated. Reconciliations of such forms to daily activity should be performed. As daily bills are prepared, the originating form number should be noted on the bills. Now, no cross-reference is noted, hence no assurance is provided that all revenue is being recorded or that billings are being provided on a timely basis. A further disadvantage of no cross-reference is that the investigation of questions relating to billings is rather difficult. A cross-reference, combined with the orderly filing of originating forms, would greatly enhance the ease of such investigations. The filing could be on a daily basis, with forms ordered per day by type of service rendered and type of payment expected.

No detailed subsidiary records of accounts receivable are maintained, making it impossible to perform any monthly reconciliations. If the entity established billing logs to account for all billings and payments from each third party payor, and by self-payors, the logs could be reconciled to the "Third Party Receivable Balances" and the "Self-Pay Receivable Balances" in the general ledger. Such logs would be of particular use in following up on past due accounts.

Tied to the absence of subsidiary records is the lack of any reconciliation process to detect and correct errors that have been made in updating self-pay receivable ledger cards. Confirmations with customers have disclosed errors, such as those arising from recording services prior to the date the services were rendered, clerical mistakes, and incomplete computations.

The poor follow-up procedures have led to high uncollectibles and a substantial number of write-offs. Yet no formal approval procedures have been established for write-offs, nor is there adequate documentation to easily distinguish them from collections or to identify which account is being written off. An employee with no receivables or cash receipts responsibility should approve write-offs.

The hospital has failed to integrate revenue, billings, accounts receivable, and cash receipts in processing activities to facilitate monthly reconciliations to the general ledger. In light of the large number of small dollar balances processed, the proportion of billings subject to disallowance by third-party payors, and the substantial number of uncollectible accounts, a monthly reconciliation of

> Beginning Accounts Receivable
> + Billings
> − Cash Receipts
> _____
> Ending Accounts Receivable

would greatly enhance the control system for the revenue cycle.

A related problem that requires correction in order for timely reconciliations to be performed concerns cash receipts. An arbitrary rule of thumb states that if receipts are small, they need not be recorded on a daily basis, nor is it deemed necessary to make a bank deposit under such circumstances. This practice exposes cash receipts to loss and eliminates the potential control provided by timely accounting records. In addition, if cash receipts are particularly heavy, the normal courier is not entrusted with the large deposit. Until alternative arrangements can be made or numerous trips taken by the courier, substantial sums of money are exposed to increased risk by their retention on the premises of the hospital. When the courier returns with the validated duplicate deposit slip, no efforts are made to compare the deposit with either the initial control listing over mail receipts or the cash receipts journal. The hospital should

—record all cash receipts on a daily basis,

—make daily bank deposits,

—arrange for more than one person to take cash receipts to the bank throughout the day, whenever receipts are particularly heavy, and

—arrange for an independent party to receive the validated duplicate deposit slip and compare it to both the recorded mail receipts and the cash receipts journal balance.

As the material weakness is described, it should be evident that the control principles are no different from these applied to the revenue cycle of a profit-oriented entity. While the terminology of "third-party logs" is distinctive, the concept of ensuring that all revenue is recorded, follow-up of uncollectibles facilitated, cash receipts safeguarded, and accounting records prepared on a timely basis applies to all entities that operate to provide goods and services.

A MEDICARE EXAMPLE FROM THE GAO

A discussion of the need to strengthen controls over payments by Medicare Intermediaries is provided by the General Accounting Office (November 1988 Report to Congress GAO/HRD-89-8). Samples tested uncovered the following types of error

- No record of beneficiary entitlement to types of services claimed
- Services are shown after benefits stopped
- Services are shown after the patient died
- Master record shows health maintenance organization pays for services
- Part A cash deductible was underapplied
- Part B deductible has not been met
- Full inpatient reimbursement days have been overutilized[10]
- Error in full coverage days
- Error in coinsurance days
- Error in lifetime reserve days
- Error in lifetime psychiatric days
- Claim overlaps a previously accounted claim

These suggest that master record computer edits have not been followed through to ensure resolution of intermediaries' potential claims. Indeed as of July 1987, a backlog of 2 million unresolved errors were identified, with an age averaging over a year. To improve controls, the General Accounting Office suggests that the administrator:

- include all errors detected by master record computer edits in its unresolved claims file (RTI file) until intermediaries confirm that they have been fully resolved;
- add requirements to CPEP that will assure that intermediaries (1) resolve those types of errors that raise significant payment questions and (2) correct systems weaknesses that allow the errors to occur; and
- revise CPEP to assure follow-up on actions by intermediaries to resolve errors purged from the RTI file in early 1988, especially those that raise significant questions.

---

[10] Medicare provides full reimbursement (less a deductible of up to $520) for up to 60 days of hospitalization, after which time part of the reimbursement becomes the responsibility of the patient.

AN EXAMPLE OF CONTROL DESIGN CONSIDERATIONS FOR A NOT-FOR-PROFIT ENTITY: THE CHURCH

The nature of operations of a church can frequently lead to control problems. Since the church is the center of both religious and social activity, the temptation exists, following religious services, for those who collected the offerings to simply stash the offering plates into some seemingly "safe place" for later counting and recording by the sole financial employee of the organization—typically called the financial secretary. The aura or "halo effect" of church members' perceptions of one another or of visitors to the church creates an assumption that no party is capable of wrongdoing with respect to church contributions. The loyal bookkeeper who is expected to perform the tasks of depositing cash collections, reconciling bank accounts, approving and signing checks, and preparing financial statements is never viewed in the same light as the bookkeeper for a business. Surely, the church members believe, a dedicated servant for the church is beyond the need for control. In some sense, the religious environment is expected to deter both errors and malfeasance.

Apparent Controls May Be Inoperative

Certain controls that appear to exist in a church are inoperative as a matter of practicality. For example, pledge envelopes may be prenumbered with an implied objective of improving control over cash receipts. Yet the consistency with which church members use prenumbered contribution envelopes in proper order, without missing any weeks, is at considerable odds with the consistency, for example, of customers' monthly mortgage payments, accompanied by prenumbered payment cards. The latter carries a financial penalty if the payments are late or documentation is inadequate, whereas the former has no such related jeopardy. The result is that the numerical sequence of documents such as contribution envelopes cannot typically be considered an effective control over receipts.

When some segregation of duties is established at a church, practical considerations frequently result in a loss of the desired separation of duties. As an example, it is desirable to have the financial secretary serve as recordkeeper and to have no custody of assets. Yet if the financial secretary is the only salaried employee except for the clergy, it is likely that a petty cash fund will have to be placed in the secretary's custody to facilitate day-to-day financial operations. The effective segregation of duties is further complicated by the use of volunteers to perform many of the church duties. Their motivation to comply with prescribed duties and their ability to make the required time commitment to complete their duties as prescribed can vary substantially from that of paid employees.

Generally speaking, the informality of church operations can serve as the key obstacle to achieving effective control. The practice of requiring written authorizations for purchasing church items such as flowers, decorations, or wine appears to impugn the honesty of the individuals involved, and is surely, in the minds of church members, "much too formal" a management approach! The mere idea of formal controls is perceived to be inconsistent with the community zeal of the organization. The formality of operations can probably be promoted by a CPA most effectively on efficiency grounds. To successfully market a formal approach, the availability of a "most effective" means by which the church can meet its objectives, with no necessary loss of community spirit, should be emphasized. Considering the fact that in the United States annual church contributions are recorded in billions of dollars, the magnitude of savings from improved controls can be substantial. An emphasis on avoiding "honest mistakes" may prove effective in persuading a church organization to exchange some degree of informality for more effective control. A related problem in obtaining a strong control environment is the common lack of trained personnel, particularly with respect to accounting.

Encourage Churches to Use Cash-Accounting Systems

Churches should be encouraged to utilize cash-accounting systems that are double-entry systems, using fund-accounting techniques. Each fund will be a separate set of self-balancing accounts that will facilitate the management of restricted assets; these funds typically include a general fund, benevolence fund, building fund, missions, and debt retirements. Transfers between funds should require authorization to the Finance Committee. The rationale for encouraging a cash basis of accounting is the uncertainty of the collection of pledges and the common lack of accounting training by either the treasurer or the financial secretary of a church.

Cash basis accounting is intuitive and is consistent with the recordkeeping by individuals. The double-entry system is recommended due to its built-in checking capability—if the books are out of balance, an error is flagged for prompt follow-up. A journal should be maintained as the detailed record of transactions and posted to a ledger that is designed to summarize disbursements to date for the fiscal year, budgeted amounts, and unencumbered balances. You can assist in designing such a system and in providing basic education as to how the books can be maintained. A congregation can improve its control by electing the best qualified individuals into positions on the finance and audit committee, as well as into the treasurer's role. Once a congregation has recognized the desirability of a strong accounting and control system, formal procedures can be established.

Suggested Organizational Structure for Churches

Exhibit 18–24 illustrates a desirable organizational structure for a church, including an effective approach to segregating duties. The procedures assigned to each major participant in the financial affairs of a church are delineated. Whenever feasible, the members of the money-counting team should be periodically rotated.

Exhibit 18–24

A Suggested Organizational Structure for Churches

AUDIT COMMITTEE

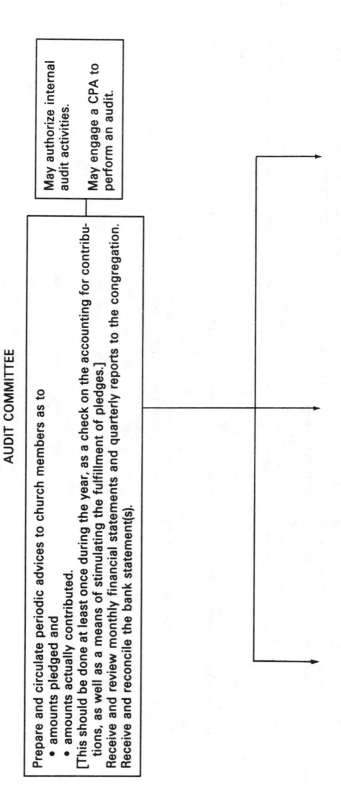

Prepare and circulate periodic advices to church members as to

- amounts pledged and
- amounts actually contributed.

[This should be done at least once during the year, as a check on the accounting for contributions, as well as a means of stimulating the fulfillment of pledges.]

Receive and review monthly financial statements and quarterly reports to the congregation.

Receive and reconcile the bank statement(s).

May authorize internal audit activities.

May engage a CPA to perform an audit.

933

Exhibit 18–24 (continued)

AUTHORIZATION FUNCTION:

Finance Committee

—Dual check signers.

—Authorize particular individuals to make purchases as permitted by the budget, with written committee approval of purchases over a set dollar amount; utilize requisitions with complete purchase information including estimated cost.

—Approval of invoices by person ordering and receiving materials or service.

—Examination of supporting documentation and cancellation of documents.

—Mailing of checks.

—Review of monthly financial statements.

CUSTODY FUNCTION:

Cash Treasurer and Money-Counters

—Handling of cash contributions from offerings.

• Utilize two or more money-counters.

• Have money-counters prepare a triplicate report on receipts, including a contribution record of any designated use of the contributed funds and of pledge envelopes—copy #1 retain, #2 to bookkeeping, #3 to audit committee with empty pledge envelopes, bearing notations of any discrepancy in stated and actual content of the envelopes.

• Require prompt deposit at bank, e.g., use the bank's night depository and distribute a copy of the deposit slip to the audit committee, retaining a copy with the count sheet.

—Handling of cash receipts from Sunday School or similar educational sessions.

• Have each class secretary turn over receipts to two money-counters who come to each classroom, or

• have each class secretary, in front of class members, seal receipts in an envelope, to be opened only by the authorized money-counters.

—Mail receipts should be controlled by authorizing two people to open incoming mail, maintain a record of receipts and distribute copies to the bookkeeper and to the audit committee; all checks should be restrictively endorsed upon receipt.

—Establish an imprest basis petty cash fund, requiring support for fund replenishment.

ACCOUNTING FUNCTION:

Financial Secretary (Bookkeeper)

—Record keeping responsibilities.

—Preparation of checks and corresponding support for disbursements—check sufficiency of budget and cash balances.

—Prepare for the finance and audit committees' review, monthly statements of

• receipts and disbursements,
• financial position,
• funds flow per fund, and
• quarterly statements for the congregation.

Other Useful Control Practices

Additional control practices that can prove to be useful to a church include

—the performance of some internal audit work by the finance or audit committee of the church,

—the requirement that most disbursements be made by check,

—the encouragement of donors to make payments by check,

—the requirement that prenumbered receipts be given for any cash donations collected other than at offerings or educational settings,

—the physical safeguarding of assets via safes and similar devices,

—the formal record of operating and control duties in a procedures manual, and

—the fidelity bonding of both members and employees who have access to church assets in an amount equivalent to the maximum dollar amount that is exposed to loss

While budgets are commonly established, not-for-profit entities will often use them as authorizations for expenditures rather than as planning devices to more effectively control operations. This latter use can be encouraged by CPAs through the education of church members and employees. A program budget should be encouraged for such activities as Sunday School and other educational programs and for mission work. These program goals should be combined with line item budgets for the clergy's salaries, utility expenses, and other normal overhead items. Suggestions as to both line item and program budgets should be obtained from the general church membership, particularly from those who are actively involved in educational programs, mission work, and similar special projects.

Churches are increasingly recognizing the benefits of having an external audit or, as a minimum, of obtaining the management services of a CPA. Either engagement will require the CPA's review of controls and will offer an opportunity for client service in the form of recommended improvements to the accounting and control system of the entity.

Establishing Controls over Church Property

Beyond the central concern for cash, controls should also be established over property of the church. A receiving function at the church can help to ensure that goods are in good condition upon receipt and were delivered as ordered. Annual inventory should be taken of capital assets, and signed records should document the borrowing of any assets from the church. Investments can be controlled via dual access to a safety deposit box. In addition to physical safeguards such as locks to secure facilities when they are not in use, safeguards against fire should be installed and adequate insurance coverage maintained.

SYNOPSIS

Fund accounting provides both advantages and disadvantages from a control perspective. As an astute professional, you can assist not-for-profit entities in turning the fund-accounting practices into real advantages and in avoiding the potential detrimental effects of strait-jacket appropriations or of an unclear picture of the global operations of an entity. To do so requires an understanding of both fund accounting and the operating distinctions between the not-for-profit entity that typically uses fund accounting and the profit-oriented entity. The basic cycle approach to control evaluation applies to the not-for-profit entity, with a mere adjustment for the jargon that is applied to such entities' accounting records— i.e., revenues are, at times, cash receipts while recorded expenses may well be equivalent to expenditures. However, the cycle approach must be expanded from the accounting system orientation that suffices in profit organizations to an information system orientation for the not-for-profit entity that measures services, performance, and output in other than dollar terms. This broader system interfaces with the external environment to ensure that an information base is available to both internal and external management for decision making. The definition of a material weakness for a not-for-profit entity is identical to that for a profit entity, as are the definitions of basic control concepts like the critical segregation of duties and the adequate safeguarding of assets. However, the nature of governmental units, hospitals, churches, and other organizations poses special control concerns that warrant attention. This chapter is intended to demonstrate the unique nature and scope of some controls in a not-for-profit environment, as well as the overwhelming similarity of the nature and scope of most controls to a business setting, with the primary exception that a higher priority is necessarily set on social accounting measures for the not-for-profit entity.

REFERENCES

Ellis, Loudell O., "Internal Control for Churches·and Community Organizations," *The CPA Journal* (May, 1974), pp. 45–48.

Henke, Emerson O., *Accounting for Nonprofit Organizations*, Second Edition (California: Wadsworth Publishing Company, Inc., 1977).

Hospital Information Systems, issue editor Thomas K. Shaffert (Maryland: Aspen Systems Corporation, Summer, 1978).

Ignatius, David, "Duping Uncle Sam: Widespread Cheating of Government Is Laid to Laxness of Agencies," *The Wall Street Journal* (December 18, 1978), pp. 1, 32.

Juneau, William, "Safeguards Urged in Wake of County Snow-Lease Pacts," *Chicago Tribune* (September 12, 1980), Section 3, p. 14.

Keister, Orville R., "Internal Control for Churches," *Management Accounting* (January, 1974), pp. 40–42.

Leathers, Park E. and Dr. Howard P. Sanders, "Internal Control in Churches," *The Internal Auditor* (May/June, 1972), pp. 21–25.

Lynch, Mitchell C., "Accounting Firms Drawn More Heavily Into Hazy World of Municipal Finance," *The Wall Street Journal* (November 29, 1977), p. 21.

———, "Paying the Piper: Soaring Pension Costs for Public Employees Plague States, Cities," *The Wall Street Journal* (May 5, 1978), p. 1.

McNeil, Dorothy and Robert Williams, "Wide Range of Causes Found for Hospital Closures," *Hospitals, J.A.H.A.* (December 1, 1978), pp. 76–81.

Prentice, Karol Beth, "Church Accounting: Good Intentions and Good Accounting," *The Woman CPA* (April, 1981), pp. 8–14.

The Wall Street Journal, "Corruption by State and Local Officials Tops FBI Field Poll" (September 11, 1980), p. 14.

Wallace, Wanda A., "Internal Control Reporting Practices in the Municipal Sectors," *The Accounting Review* (July, 1981), pp. 666–689.

[Also see footnotes throughout the chapter.]

APPENDIX

Summary of Statement on Government Auditing Standards

I. Introduction

A. Purpose

1. This statement contains standards for audits of government organizations, programs, activities, and functions, and of government funds received by contractors, nonprofit organizations, and other nongovernment organizations.

2. The standards are to be followed by auditors and audit organizations when required by law, regulation, agreement or contract, or policy.

II. Types of Government Audits

A. Purpose

1. This chapter describes the types of audits that government and nongovernment audit organizations conduct, and that government organizations arrange to have conducted. This description is not intended to limit or require the types of audits that may be conducted or arranged.

2. In conducting these types of audits, auditors should follow the applicable standards included and incorporated in this statement.

B. Financial Audits

1. Financial statement audits determine (a) whether the financial statements of an audited entity present fairly the financial position, results of operations, and cash flows or changes in financial position in accordance with generally accepted accounting principles, and (b) whether the entity has complied with laws and regulations for those transactions and events that may have a material effect on the financial statements.

2. Financial related audits include determining (a) whether financial reports and related items, such as elements, accounts, or funds are fairly presented, (b) whether financial information is presented in accordance with established or stated criteria, and (c) whether the entity has adhered to specific financial compliance requirements.

C. Performance Audits

1. Economy and efficiency audits include determining (a) whether the entity is acquiring, protecting, and using its resources (such as personnel, property, and space) economically and efficiently, (b) the causes of inefficiencies or uneconomical practices, and (c) whether the entity has complied with laws and regulations concerning matters of economy and efficiency.

2. Program audits include determining (a) the extent to which the desired results or benefits established by the legislature or other authorizing body are being achieved, (b) the effectiveness of organizations, programs, activities, or functions, and (c) whether the entity has complied with laws and regulations applicable to the program.

(continued)

D. Understanding the Audit Objectives and Scope

1. Audits may have a combination of financial and performance audit objectives, or may have objectives limited to only some aspects of one audit type.

2. Auditors should follow the appropriate standards in this statement that are applicable to the individual objectives of the audit.

E. Other Activities of An Audit Organization

1. Services other than audits: The head of the audit organization should establish policy on which audit standards from this statement should be followed by the auditors in performing such services. However, as a minimum, auditors should collectively possess adequate professional proficiency and exercise due professional care for the service being performed.

2. Investigative work: The head of the audit organization should establish policy on whether the audit standards in this statement, or some other appropriate standards, are to be followed by the employees performing this work.

3. Nonaudit activities: The head of the audit organization should establish policy on what standards in this statement are to be followed, or whether some other appropriate standards are to be followed, by the employees in performing this type of work.

III. General Standards

A. Qualifications: The staff assigned to conduct the audit should collectively possess adequate professional proficiency for the tasks required.

B. Independence: In all matters relating to the audit work, the audit organization and the individual auditors, whether government or public, should be free from personal and external impairments to independence, should be organizationally independent, and should maintain an independent attitude and appearance.

C. Due Professional Care: Due professional care should be used in conducting the audit and in preparing related reports.

D. Quality Control: Audit organizations conducting government audits should have an appropriate internal quality control system in place and participate in an external quality control review program.

IV. Field Work Standards for Financial Audits

A. Relationship to AICPA Standards

1. The standards of field work for government financial audits incorporate the AICPA standards of field work for financial audits, and prescribes supplemental standards of field work needed to satisfy the unique needs of government financial audits.

2. The field work standards of the AICPA and the supplemental standards in chapter 4 of this statement apply to both financial statement audits and financial related audits.

(continued)

B. Planning:

1. Supplemental planning field work standards for government financial audits are:

a. Audit Requirements for all Government Levels: Planning should include consideration of the audit requirements of all levels of government.

b. Legal and Regulatory Requirements: A test should be made of compliance with applicable laws and regulations.

(1) In determining compliance with laws and regulations:

(a) The auditor should design audit steps and procedures to provide reasonable assurance of detecting errors, irregularities, and illegal acts that could have a direct and material effect on the financial statement amounts or the results of financial related audits.

(b) The auditor should also be aware of the possibility of illegal acts which could have an indirect and material effect on the financial statements or results of financial related audits.

C. Evidence (Working papers)

1. The AICPA field work standards and this statement require that: A record of the auditors' work be retained in the form of working papers.

2. Supplemental working paper requirements for financial audits are that working papers should:

a. Contain a written audit program cross-referenced to the working papers.

b. Contain the objective, scope, methodology and results of the audit.

c. Contain sufficient information so that supplementary oral explanations are not required.

d. Be legible with adequate indexing and cross-referencing, and include summaries and lead schedules, as appropriate.

e. Restrict information included to matters that are materially important and relevant to the objectives of the audit.

f. Contain evidence of supervisory reviews of the work conducted.

D. Internal Control

1. The AICPA field work standards and this statement require that: A sufficient understanding of the internal control structure is to be obtained to plan the audit and to determine the nature, timing, and extent of tests to be performed.

(continued)

V. Reporting Standards for Financial Audits

A. Relationship to AICPA Standards

1. The standards of reporting for government financial audits incorporate the AICPA standards of reporting for financial audits, and prescribes supplemental standards of reporting needed to satisfy the unique needs of government financial audits.

2. The reporting standards of the AICPA and the supplemental standards in chapter 5 of this statement apply to both financial statement audits and financial-related audits.

B. Supplemental reporting standards for government financial audits are:

1. Statement on Auditing Standards: A statement should be included in the auditors' report that the audit was made in accordance with generally accepted government auditing standards. (AICPA standards require that public accountants state that the audit was made in accordance with generally accepted auditing standards. In conducting government audits, public accountants should also state that their audit was conducted in accordance with the standards set forth in chapters 3, 4, and 5.)

2. Report on Compliance: The auditors should prepare a written report on their tests of compliance with applicable laws and regulations. This report, which may be included in either the report on the financial audit or a separate report, should contain a statement of positive assurance on those items which were tested for compliance and negative assurance on those items not tested. It should include all material instances of noncompliance, and all instances or indications of illegal acts which could result in criminal prosecution.

3. Report on Internal Controls: The auditors should prepare a written report on their understanding of the entity's internal control structure and the assessment of control risk made as part of a financial statement audit, or a financial related audit. This report may be included in either the auditor's report on the financial audit or a separate report. The auditor's report should include as a minimum: (a) the scope of the auditor's work in obtaining an understanding of the internal control structure and in assessing the control risk, (b) the entity's significant internal controls or control structure including the controls established to ensure compliance with laws and regulations that have a material impact on the financial statements and the results of the financial related audit, and (c) the reportable conditions, including the identification of material weaknesses, identified as a result of the auditors' work in understanding and assessing the control risk.

4. Reporting on Financial Related Audits: Written audit reports are to be prepared giving the results of each financial related audit.

5. Privileged and Confidential Information: If certain information is prohibited from general disclosure, the report should state the nature of the information omitted and the requirement that makes the omission necessary.

(continued)

6. Report Distribution: Written audit reports are to be submitted by the audit organization to the appropriate officials of the organization audited and to the appropriate officials of the organizations requiring or arranging for the audits, including external funding organizations, unless legal restrictions, ethical considerations, or other arrangements prevent it. Copies of the reports should also be sent to other officials who have legal oversight authority or who may be responsible for taking action and to others authorized to receive such reports. Unless restricted by law or regulation, copies should be made available for public inspection.

VI. Field Work Standards for Performance Audits

A. Planning: Work is to be adequately planned.

B. Supervision: Staff are to be properly supervised.

C. Legal and Regulatory Requirements: An assessment is to be made of compliance with applicable requirements of laws and regulations when necessary to satisfy the audit objectives.

1. Where an assessment of compliance with laws and regulations is required: Auditors should design the audit to provide reasonable assurance of detecting abuse or illegal acts that could significantly affect the audit objectives.

2. In all performance audits: Auditors should be alert to situations or transactions that could be indicative of abuse or illegal acts.

D. Internal Control: An assessment should be made of applicable internal controls when necessary to satisfy the audit objectives.

E. Evidence: Sufficient, competent, and relevant evidence is to be obtained to afford a reasonable basis for the auditors' judgments and conclusions regarding the organization, program, activity, or function under audit. A record of the auditors' work is to be retained in the form of working papers. Working papers may include tapes, films, and discs.

VII. Reporting Standards for Performance Audits

A. Form: Written audit reports are to be prepared communicating the results of each government audit.

B. Timeliness: Reports are to be issued promptly so as to make the information available for timely use by management and legislative officials, and by other interested parties.

C. Report Contents

1. Objectives, Scope, and Methodology: The report should include a statement of the audit objectives and a description of the audit scope and methodology.

2. Audit Findings and Conclusions: The report should include a full discussion of the audit findings, and where applicable, the auditor's conclusions.

(continued)

3. Cause and Recommendations: The report should include the cause of problem areas noted in the audit, and recommendations for actions to correct the problem areas and to improve operations, when called for by the audit objectives.

4. Statement on Auditing Standards: The report should include a statement that the audit was made in accordance with generally accepted government auditing standards and disclose when applicable standards were not followed.

5. Internal Controls: The report should identify the significant internal controls that were assessed, the scope of the auditor's assessment work, and any significant weaknesses found during the audit.

6. Compliance With Laws and Regulations: The report should include all significant instances of noncompliance and abuse and all indications or instances of illegal acts that could result in criminal prosecution that were found during or in connection with the audit.

7. Views of Responsible Officials: The report should include the pertinent views of responsible officials of the organization, program, activity, or function audited concerning the auditors' findings, conclusions, and recommendations, and what corrective action is planned.

8. Noteworthy Accomplishments: The report should include a description of any significant noteworthy accomplishments, particularly when management improvements in one area may be applicable elsewhere.

9. Issues Needing Further Study: The report should include a listing of any significant issues needing further study and consideration.

10. Privileged and Confidential Information: The report should include a statement about any pertinent information that was omitted because it is deemed privileged or confidential. The nature of such information should be described, and the basis under which it is withheld should be stated.

D. Report Presentation: The report should be complete, accurate, objective, and convincing, and be as clear and concise as the subject matter permits.

E. Report Distribution: Written audit reports are to be submitted by the audit organization to the appropriate officials of the organization audited, and to the appropriate officials of the organizations requiring or arranging for the audits, including external funding organizations, unless legal restrictions, ethical considerations, or other arrangements prevent it. Copies of the reports should also be sent to other officials who may be responsible for taking action on audit findings and recommendations and to others authorized to receive such reports. Unless restricted by law or regulation, copies should be made available for public inspection.

VIII. AICPA Generally Accepted Auditing Standards

A. General Standards

1. The examination is to be performed by a person or persons having adequate technical training and proficiency as an auditor.

(continued)

2. In all matters relating to the assignment, an independence in mental attitude is to be maintained by the auditor or auditors.

3. Due professional care is to be exercised in the performance of the examination and the preparation of the report.

B. Standards of Field Work

1. The work is to be adequately planned and assistants, if any, are to be properly supervised.

2. A sufficient understanding of the internal control structure is to be obtained to plan the audit and to determine the nature, timing, and extent of tests to be performed.

3. Sufficient competent evidential matter is to be obtained through inspection, observation, inquiries, and confirmations to afford a reasonable basis for an opinion regarding the financial statements under examination.

C. Standards of Reporting

1. The report shall state whether the financial statements are presented in accordance with generally accepted accounting principles.

2. The report shall identify those circumstances in which such principles have not been consistently observed in the current period in relation to the preceding period.

3. Informative disclosures in the financial statements are to be regarded as reasonably adequate unless otherwise stated in the report.

4. The report shall either contain an expression of opinion regarding the financial statements, taken as a whole, or an assertion to the effect that an opinion cannot be expressed. When an overall opinion cannot be expressed, the reasons therefor should be stated. In all cases where an auditor's name is associated with financial statements, the report should contain a clear-cut indication of the character of the auditor's examination, if any, and the degree of responsibility he is taking.

Source: United States General Accounting Office, *Government Auditing Standards* (1988 Revision), Appendix A.

SINGLE AUDIT REPORTING ON COMPLIANCE

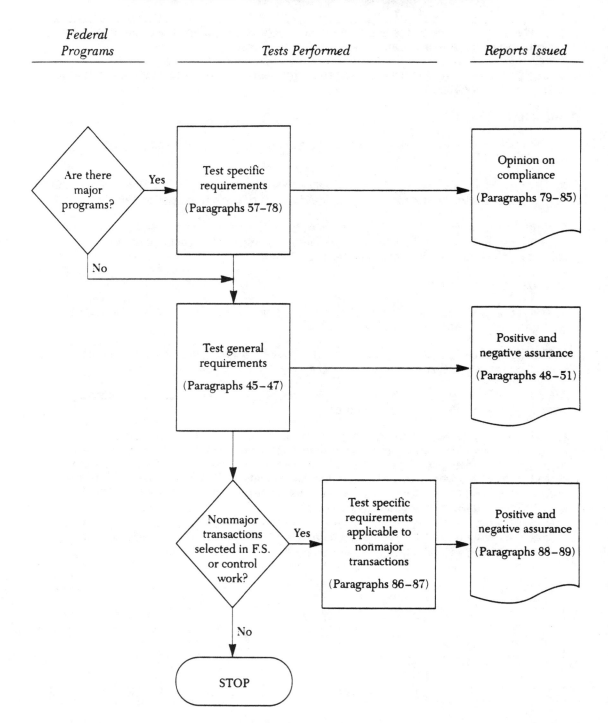

Federal Programs   *Tests Performed*   *Reports Issued*

Are there major programs?

Yes → Test specific requirements (Paragraphs 57–78) → Opinion on compliance (Paragraphs 79–85)

No → Test general requirements (Paragraphs 45–47) → Positive and negative assurance (Paragraphs 48–51)

Nonmajor transactions selected in F.S. or control work?

Yes → Test specific requirements applicable to nonmajor transactions (Paragraphs 86–87) → Positive and negative assurance (Paragraphs 88–89)

No → STOP

Note: Paragraph references relate the AICPA Auditing Standards Board's Exposure Draft of Proposed Statement on Auditing Standards entitled "Compliance Auditing Applicable to Governmental Entities and Other Recipients of Governmental Financial Assistance" (April 9, 1991), File 2353, the source of this chart, Appendix C, p. 36.

19

Litigation Support Considerations

"Public agencies are very keen on amassing statistics—they collect them, add them, raise them to the nth power, take the cube roots and prepare wonderful diagrams. But what you must never forget is that every one of those figures comes in the first instance from the village watchman, who just puts down what he damn pleases."

Sir Josiah Stamp[1]

As the quote suggests, what is done with data should first consider its source and credibility. These are words to especially keep in mind when working in a litigation support environment. The question must be raised: what types of controls existed in the environment in which the information was first collected? Are such controls reliable? Can the information deemed credible be collected and/or transmitted in a manner subject to little risk exposure? What controls are necessary to maintain credibility of the information collected? How might the data be effectively analyzed to not only control the quality of the information itself, but also the nature of inferences drawn?

---

[1] Cited in George W. Downs and Patrick D. Larkey, *The Search for Government Efficiency* (Philadelphia: Temple University Press, 1986).

THE ADVERSARIAL CONTEXT

Two aspects of the litigation environment are particularly important to keep in mind from a control perspective: first,there are clear vested interests and sources of bias on each side of the conflict and second, the "other side" of that adversarial relationship should be expected to take a fine-toothed comb through the various documents and analyses put forth in describing economic events and their consequences. The adversarial nature of the proceeding is a two-edged sword. Its very nature creates bias, limits on the degree of cooperation extended, and game-playing incentives. Yet, it likewise encourages due care in preparation of information and demands integrity in the presentation of facts.

ASSIMILATING EVIDENCE

The discovery process is steeped in legalities but offers an opportunity to those involved to assimilate evidence relevant to the issues in dispute and the surrounding context for such issues. The quality of discovery will depend to some degree on the understanding of questions in dispute, the nature of the information system in place, and the control context in which the information was developed. Hence, an understanding of information systems and related control procedures, as they typically operate, provide an important framework for structuring information requests and ensuring sufficient insight into data quality to begin to draw inferences.

The various control system design issues described throughout this *Handbook* should provide a vantage point to consider

—the types of information likely to be available

—the best controlled source for the information

—the plausibility of being able to corroborate the reasonableness of such information

—and isolation of those aspects of the information system likely to have the greatest relevance.

Depositions can be a forum to acquire the same types of insights and understanding as to the control structure, responsibilities of individuals, and likely implementation problems as one would commonly obtain in the interview process during a systems analysis.

Often a time crunch is at hand as information is being assimilated and a very real limit exists in that one cannot continually "go back to the well." Importantly, if some request is overlooked that has relevance, the "other side" can retrieve that information and effectively use it to counter the analysis you put forward. This speaks to the need for "completeness" as issues are identified, risk exposures assessed, and cost/benefits evaluated.

EVALUATING THE EFFECTIVENESS OF CONTROL PRACTICES IN OTHERS' ASSIMILATION

In reviewing others' data bases and analyses, a sense of whether they have exercised due care can be obtained in a manner similar to that used to evaluate the role of internal audit. In other words, some sense of competency, objectivity, and performance is desired, with respect to those preparing the information and performing various analyses. Some of this information will be self-evident from vitas and exhibits prepared and put forward. However, the deposition testimony and detailed analysis of performance as represented in supporting documents are likely to be particularly critical sources of information to evaluate the credibility of the claims and evidence being put forward.

Simple tests of agreement between data bases assembled or accessed by you and those evaluated by the party on the other side of the dispute are a good first step. Exhibits should be decipherable, supportable, and not deceptive in the message being presented. Tell-tale signs of a lack of objectivity in presenting information in a credible manner would include:

- excessive white space in graphing, such that scales are not appropriately adjusted and as a result make certain aspects look different from what they would if an optimal, scale-adjusted portrait were generated
- quantitative models that fail to relate to that which they are represented to simulate and fail normal types of reasonableness tests
- omission of disclosures as to necessary assumptions
- subtle maneuvers that apply "tricks" that inflate or deflate consequences without straight-forward justification of such adjustments

These are only a few of the means of inferring the quality of the arguments to be brought forward in terms of their credibility and reasonable objectivity. Often the competence of the individual can concurrently be inferred from such steps of evaluating work made available.

You can uncover problems with the quality of data sets and evidence being assimilated through alertness to (1) missing information, (2) the picking and choosing of benchmarks, (3) the unexplained substitution of certain data or proxies for what would seem to be available from another source, and (4) unjustified inflation, deflation, or indexing and transformations of raw data.

The control practices exercised by parties providing data through discovery, including the party on the opposing side of a dispute are important facets to understand in trying to evaluate the appropriate data on which to rely in one's own analysis. The point is to appreciate the control structure, evaluate control risk, and to obtain sufficient documentation and information to permit some testing of the presumptions you have thereby formed as to the controls in place over the evidence being assimilated.

COMMUNICATION

Understanding the controls established and operative in the evidence collection and presentation process is important. However, as important is the ability to communicate such controls, both in evaluating others' evidence and in supporting one's own analyses. This communication can be facilitated by keeping a sort of log of information as it is obtained and of steps taken as they become relevant to the evaluation process. For example, the nature of representations in the depositions, in affidavits, in verbal dialogue, and in documentary evidence should be understood in a manner that paints a clear picture as to overall control and credibility of evidential sources. Steps taken to corroborate impressions as to competency, objectivity, and performance should be documented similar to a working paper approach, whether formalized or simply informally analyzed only in one's mind. Finally, as one moves forward in setting forth one's own analysis, whether directed at others' ideas or developing one's own ideas, caveats should be clearly set forth. Sources of information and known limitations should be documented. Importantly, the consequences of such limitations should be evaluated. If something cannot be resolved, it is far better if that item works in an opposite direction in its effects to that which one is trying to demonstrate.

In other words, conservatism is warranted, lest someone attribute your results to that one assumption, missing piece of evidence, or omitted step in the analysis. While it may seem ironic to work against one's self, the idea is to anticipate that someone is about to scrutinize your work with the most critical of vantage points in mind.

Often, issues tied to control and data availability are questions of fact. Corroboration should be sought through testimony or documents to support such facts. If certain benchmarks are selected because they are deemed to be relevant by operating managers, then representations to such an effect become an important part of the control process. Just as assumptions are tested when they are important facets of a management's planning process or attempts to avoid going concern problems, the participant in litigation support should test assumptions invoked to the fullest extent merited by the case at hand.

POTENTIAL PITFALLS

In a litigation setting a number of potential pitfalls can arise, particularly as controls are tested and analyses proceed. Exhibit 19–1 lists some specific concerns. Foremost in an adversarial setting is a need to understand what others have done and how it might relate to the points you wish to address. The easiest step in ensuring such understanding is via REPLICATION. I would liken this suggestion to the notion of a "walk-through." Recall that one of the primary purposes of a walk-through was to prove to one's self that they had a reasonable understanding of how things worked by actually generating and/or following a

Exhibit 19–1

POTENTIAL PITFALLS

≡ ≡ ≡ ≡ ≡ ≡ ≡ ≡ ≡ ≡ ≡ ≡ ≡ ≡ ≡ ≡ ≡ ≡ ≡

What was done? REPLICATION

Practical vs. Statistical SIGNIFICANCE

COMMUNICATION

Use POPULATION descriptives

Guard DATA integrity

SOFTWARE selection

Research Design

---

transaction through the system from start to finish, incorporating both operational steps and, most importantly, control procedures.

If you can replicate another's analysis, you by definition begin to understand that evidence. If you are unable to replicate the analysis, it may suggest:

- the analysis is not being performed as initially described
- while performed as described, other information is necessary for replication, such as assumptions invoked or intermediary steps in generating information or computing quantitative information
- .errors have been made by the party preparing the analysis

Which of these three is the explanation will hopefully be resolvable through discovery and/or deposition evidence.

SIGNIFICANCE IN WHAT SENSE?

An important consideration in evaluating evidence and designing one's own analysis is to distinguish between practical and statistical significance. It may be practically insignificant that $100,000 changed hands, even though that amount within a sample could easily have a significant influence on comparisons being drawn via statistical tools. A key consideration relates to the influence of sample sizes on statistical significance. Exhibit 19–2 describes the possibility that bigger may not be better, since very large sample sizes can virtually create statistical

Exhibit 19–2

Is Bigger Necessarily Better?

Just as the saying "bigger is better" implies, many presume that a larger sample size is always preferable. While it is the case that larger samples reduce sampling error and enhance the reliability and precision of estimates formulated, a possibility exists of producing statistical significance in the absence of practical significance. In other words, if you take a large enough sample, almost anything is statistically significant, due to the extremely tight precision available for drawing inferences. Yet the magnitude of the amount may be of no interest from a practical perspective.

Indeed, some have even argued that smaller samples should be far more persuasive than large samples because if something is found to be of statistical significance, it has to be a very substantial effect in order to have the discernible effect noted statistically. In contrast, something of no consequence can be made to appear to be statistically significant, merely by enlarging the sample size. Of course, since small sample artifacts can arise, some balance as to sample size determination is desirable.

---

significance. The point is raised in the latter part of that exhibit that a small sample size that is totally consistent with some proposition should actually be of greater practical significance, perhaps, even if statistical significance is precluded due to sample size constraints.

The context will help one determine whether both practical and statistical significance have been reached, presumably the preferable conclusion. It is troublesome to claim differences that can be shown to have either no practical importance or no statistically discernible distinction. To provide one example, a

Exhibit 19–3

Practical Significance Implies Value

"A man who knows the price

of everything and the

value of nothing"

Source: Oscar Wilde's play, Lady Windermere's Fan (Act III),

published in 1893

---

party may observe that price increased by 3% as a result of some event, yet if the precision around the point estimate is 5% at the expected degree of reliability, the statistical implication would be that the 3% difference lacked significance. Indeed, such a difference was an expected fluctuation due to mere chance, given the manner in which the evidence had been collected and evaluated. Exhibit 19–3 comes to mind. We must not only know the price or quantity of interest, but we must understand its underlying meaning, value, or in our terms herein, its practical significance.

COMMUNICATION

As already alluded, the nature of the communication process is critical to a litigation environment. If judge, arbitrator, or jury cannot understand the facts, your analysis, and your concerns regarding others' analyses, then the best thought-out evaluation is for naught. Graphics can be powerful tools to demonstrate relationships and key points. Analogies are also helpful tools in making points come alive and have relevance to the listeners.

POPULATION DESCRIPTIVES

Although samples will be one of the major means by which analyses have proceeded, since such samples are intended to be inferred back to the population of interest, it is extremely useful to provide descriptive statistics on that population. A number of common descriptive statistics are available for use in such presentations. Exhibit 19–4 illustrates commonly used measures for an assumed population of six inventory values. Bar graphs and frequency distributions such as that depicted in Exhibit 19–5 are similarly useful. As depicted, such a picture can bear out divergence from a normal, symmetrical, bell-shaped curve. In this

---

Exhibit 19–4

Descriptive Statistics—Population Parameters

Data Set: Six Inventory Items, Valued at
$200 $500 $600 $600 $700 $1,000

Term	Value	Description
Minimum:	$ 200	Lowest Value
Maximum:	1,000	Highest Value
Median:	600	Middle Value
Range:	800	Maximum–Minimum
Mode:	600	Most Frequently Occurring

Mean: $\dfrac{\$200 + \$500 + \$600 + \$600 + \$700 + \$1,000}{6}$ = $600 Average*

Standard Deviation: $\sqrt{\dfrac{\begin{array}{l}(200 - 600)^2 + (500 - 600)^2 + \\ (600 - 600)^2 + (600 - 600)^2 + \\ (700 - 600)^2 + (1,000 - 600)^2\end{array}}{6}}$ = $238 Dispersion Around the Mean**

Skewness:
(Considered Normally
Distributed if
Close to Zero
i.e., within ±.5)

$\dfrac{3\,(\$600 - \$600)}{238} = 0$

Deviation from
Symmetry
around the
median***

$* \ \mu_x = \dfrac{\sum\limits_{i=1}^{N} x_i}{N}$

$** \ \sigma_x = \sqrt{\dfrac{\sum\limits_{i=1}^{N} (x_i - \mu_x)^2}{N}}$

$*** \ s_k = \dfrac{3\,(\mu_x - M_e)}{\sigma_x}$

Where
x_i = element in population
N = number of elements in population
$\sum\limits_{i=1}^{N}$ = sum of the N elements
μ_x = mean
σ_x = standard deviation
s_k = skewness
M_e

Exhibit 19–5
Frequency Distribution

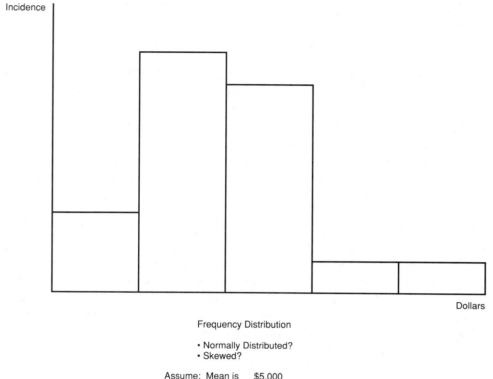

Incidence

Dollars

Frequency Distribution

• Normally Distributed?
• Skewed?

Assume: Mean is $5,000
        Median is $4,000

What does this suggest?

Skewness with a few large dollar items

setting, the higher mean than median suggests a skewed distribution. This, in turn, can provide an important justification for stratifying a population for analysis purposes. One common technique is an 80/20 rule that suggests 80% of the dollars or transactions may involve, for example, only twenty percent of the customer base. In such a case, a stratification of the largest 20% from the remaining population may yield a more symmetrical distribution of the remaining items of interest, such as smaller dollar invoice values. Better coverage of large dollars can result from focusing on the 20%.

DATA INTEGRITY

Referring back to the potential pitfalls listed in Exhibit 19–1, another key concern as population descriptives begin to be provided and other analyses follow, is to guard data integrity. One central source of information, with controls in place to monitor changes to the data set, should be established. Alterations to the data base should be well documented and care should be taken not to generate conflicting analyses due to changing underlying data sets. Access to the raw data should be limited and back-up of information is imperative.

SOFTWARE SELECTION

Just as the raw data needs to be protected, software needs to be selected with care, as the integrity of the analysis will link to the appropriateness and credibility of the software accessed. Mainstream software packages should be used when available and critical computations should be double-checked either through use of a spreadsheet and detailed computations or through a parallel test relative to other available software programs. Since many software approaches involve numerous data sets, iterative analyses, and various adjustments to data sets for discovered additional data or corrections to existing data, it is especially important to maintain a good audit trail as a control on the software's application.

The saying "garbage in—garbage out" can too easily apply unless care is taken to both select and track the use of software. Keep in mind that even widely used software can have "bugs," some of which are generally known. Steps should be taken to gain comfort regarding the reasonableness of the software selected for the task at hand. Quality controls built into the software should be explored, such as what happens if memory is exceeded or if insufficient information is provided? Damage control is important in any process, but particularly in being warned if some automatic "fix it" is invoked by a self-helping software routine. To exemplify the concerns I have in mind, consider how missing observations are treated by your software; whether models defined automatically include a constant term or require model specification by the user; and what happens when a non-unique solution is obtained by the program.

RESEARCH DESIGN

Just as the raw data and mode of analysis must be controlled, the overall evaluation needs to be controlled through an effective research design.[2] Specifically, the objectives should be understood, the resources available should be identified, the limitations and assumptions should be itemized and as reasonably addressed as is possible, and the methodology should be appropriate for the analyses at hand. Research design includes understanding the strengths and weaknesses of alternatives, selecting at times a multimethod approach, and taking care in drawing inferences that the conclusions are reasonably supported by the evidence at hand. Once again, clear analogies track to the more common systems evaluator's domain.

---

[2] See Wanda A. Wallace, *Accounting Research Methods*: *Do The Facts Speak For Themselves?* (Homewood, Illinois: Irwin Publishers, 1991).

To assess a control system and test its ability to operate in conformance with design and in a manner that provides reasonable assurances requires a research design that happens to take the form of an audit or systems engagement plan, with accompanying working paper documentation in a variety of forms. Increasingly, workshop forums and creative means of gaining feedback on risk exposures and controls' effectiveness have joined the more traditional formal documentation procedures.

OPPORTUNITIES FOR ANALYSES

Assuming the pitfalls cited in Exhibit 19–1 provide a useful context for proceeding, a number of questions present themselves as to how to proceed with analyses. As Exhibit 19–6 suggests, a number of places exist to use statistics, with certain considerations kept in mind. Options are outlined and elaboration is provided on Bayesian statistics and applications to controls in audit settings. Exhibit 19–6 expands upon the descriptive statistics already described, to entail plots, correlations, chi-square analyses, various modeling and sampling procedures, and the attendant pitfalls of such techniques. These are the topics to which we now turn.

Statistics can be used throughout litigation settings and for a number of other

---

Exhibit 19–6

Types of Analyses and Where to Apply Them

- ## USE OF STATISTICS...WHERE?

- ## CONSIDERATIONS

- ## DESCRIPTIVES & PLOTS

- ## CORRELATIONS & CHI-SQUARE

- ## REGRESSION ANALYSIS & ARIMA

- ## SAMPLING

- ## PITFALLS

Exhibit 19–6 (continued)

THE USE OF THE BAYESIAN APPROACH IN AUDITING: THE STATE-OF-THE-ART

by
Mohammad J. Abdolmohammadi
Boston University

More than two decades ago, Birnberg (1964) suggested the use of Bayesian statistics in auditing. Although much research has followed, there is no formal incorporation of this approach in any U.S. accounting firm, most likely due to technical and computational complexities to be discussed in this essay. With the increasing use of computers in auditing, however, interest in the use of complex statistical techniques such as the Bayesian approach is increasing. This interest may be because computers would allow the automation of many of the details of a statistical method, relieving the auditor of dealing with such complexity. For example, expert systems are now being developed for use in auditing (see Chandler, 1985). Most of these expert systems (e.g., the EDP-Xpert developed by Messier and Hansen, 1984) explicitly use a Bayesian methodology to update prior information. The Bayesian approach is a systematic method of integrating non-sampling and sampling evidence and provides the potential for greater efficiency (at the same level of planned effectiveness) over the classical approach currently used.[1]

The objectives of this essay are (1) to briefly explain what the Bayesian approach is and how it relates to auditing, and (2) to identify some major problems related to operationalization of the Bayesian approach which suggest fruitful research directions. The next two sections discuss each of these objectives, respectively, followed by a final conclusion section.

The Bayesian Approach in Auditing

The Bayesian statistical approach is based on a theorem advanced in the eighteenth century by an English clergyman, Thomas Bayes, to measure conditional probabilities. This theorem states that a decision-maker's state of knowledge about some uncertain parameter of interest (such as compliance errors or account balances) can be represented by a set of probabilities called prior probabilities. These prior probabilities can then be revised as additional information is collected. The updated prior probabilities (called posterior probabilities) serve as the basis for making decisions. Bayes's theorem can be presented in the following basic form:

$$P(A_i|B) = \frac{P(A_i) \cdot P(B|A_i)}{\Sigma P(A_i) \cdot P(B|A_i)} \quad (1)$$

where $P(A_i)$ = prior probability of event A_i

$P(B|A_i)$ = likelihood of information B given that event A_i occurs

$P(A_i|B)$ = posterior probability of event A_i given information B

$\Sigma P(A_i) \cdot P(B|A_i)$ is a standardizing factor such that the sum of all possible posterior probabilities will be equal to one.

Exhibit 19–6 (continued)

For a simple auditing example, suppose that having studied the system of internal controls of a client (and perhaps the previous year's audit results), John Doe, the auditor, is able to express his client's compliance error possibilities as 3%, 5%, or 7%, as reported in column (a) of Table 1.

Furthermore, suppose that John has also quantified (either subjectively, or based on historical data on similar audits) the probabilities of each of the compliance error possibilities as reported in column (b). Column (b) probabilities sum to one, since they represent the probability distribution of the only assumed error possibilities.

Now suppose that John collects futher evidence by taking a sample of 100 sales invoices and observes four compliance errors (4%). The likelihood of this sample result, given actual population error rates of 3%, 5%, or 7%, is found in statistical tables of binomial distribution as reported in column (c).[2] Column (d) represents the numerator of the Bayes model in (1) and column (e) provides the posterior probabilities of the error possibilities. Finally, column (f) represents the cumulative probabilities of the three possible compliance errors in column (a). Thus, the Table shows that there is an 89% chance that the error rate is 5% or less.

If John has a maximum tolerable error rate of 5% and would like to have an 89% confidence level, the Bayesian revision result indicates no need for further sampling or extended audit procedures. Using classical statistical methods, on the other hand, would have resulted either in further sampling or extended substantive procedures for the following reason: Using classical statistical methods, John would have concentrated only on sample results. A 90% confidence level in Arens and Loebbecke (1984, p. 406), for example, would show the computed upper error rate for a sample of 100 with four errors to be 7.8%. Based only on the sample, this indicates that the population error rate might be significantly greater than John's maximum tolerable error rate of 5%. In contrast, using both nonsampling and sampling information indicates that

Table 1

John Doe's Compliance Error Judgments

(a) A_i	(b) $P(A_i)$	(c) $P(B|A_i)$*	(d) = (b) • (c) $P(A_i) P(B|A_i)$	(e) = (d)/Σ(d) $P(A_i|B)$	(f) Cum. Prob.
A_1 = 3%	.30	.1706	.0512	.32	.32
A_2 = 5%	.50	.1781	.0891	.57	.89
A_3 = 7%	.20	.0888	.0178	.11	.00
Total	1.00		m(d) = .1581	1.00	

* From the table of binomial distribution (Winkler, 1972, p. 468) for n = 100 and r = 4.

Exhibit 19–6 (continued)

there is an 89% chance that the population error rate may not exceed 5%. Thus, in this hypothetical example, the use of Bayes's theorem resulted in capturing valuable information on prior knowledge, which is normally lost in classical statistical methods.

The above discussion revolves around the assumption that there are only three exclusive and exhaustive error possibilities. In a more realistic situation, the number of error possibilities is numerous or perhaps even infinite (continuous). Bayes's theorem still applies, although some mathematical complexities arise. Winkler (1972) shows that in the case of many standard probability distributions, this is not a major problem. For example, Corless (1971) and Crosby (1981) present evidence that (PA_i) takes the form of a standard beta distribution in compliance testing. Approximation of the parameters of this distribution follows certain relationships. The same would be true for the normal distribution as well as other standard distributions. To update prior probabilities in the case of a continuous distribution, the procedure presented in Table 1 is replaced by the use of calculus and involves much detailed work, most of which can easily be automated. A discussion of the mathematical details is beyond the scope of this essay. The interested reader is referred to Winkler (1972) and Abdolmohammadi and Berger (1986).

Research Opportunities

As shown in Table 1, the Bayesian approach systematically combines the auditor's prior information, reflected in a prior probability distribution (hereafter called PPD), with sample results. The Bayesian approach thus requires the auditor to quantitatively and formally express, and later use, prior knowledge, reducing the need for large sample sizes or generating greater confidence for the same level of sampling.

The operationalization of the Bayesian approach provides both an opportunity and a challenge for researchers and practitioners. Here are some examples: First, how does one quantify PPDs? To establish PPDs one needs a quantification method. There are many of these methods available in the behavioral literature. Abdolmohammadi (1985a) identifies eight methods that are particularly relevant to auditing tasks and notes that only four of these methods have been studied in auditing.

The four methods examined in auditing research are Cumulative Distribution Function (CDF), Probability Density Function (PDF), Equivalent Prior Sample Information (EPS) and Hypothetical Future Sample Information (HFS). While Corless (1972) studied the feasibility of CDF and PDF in compliance error estimations, Solomon et al. (1982) studied the feasibility of CDF in account balance estimation. These researchers reported high levels of inconsistency between auditors and across techniques. This inconsistency was also reported by Felix (1976) between subjects and across CDF and EPS in compliance error estimations. The inconsistencies in Felix

Exhibit 19–6 (continued)

(1976) were less than those of Corless (1972) perhaps due to the training Felix provided subjects. Crosby (1981) replicated Felix (1976) and reported less inconsistency between CDF and EPS. Solomon et al. (1984) reported high variations in EPS in account balance estimations. Abdolmohammadi (1985b) found EPS and CDF to be more difficult than PDF and HFS for auditors to use. Finally, Abdolmohammadi and Berger (1986) found PDF to generate PPDs closer to audited values than EPS, CDF and HFS.

Four promising methods not yet studied are Odds or Ratio Estimation (ORE), Distribution Parameter Estimation (DPE), Graphical or Diagrammatic Representation (GDR), and the PERT-based method of Most Likely, Minimum and Maximum (LMM) values. As argued in Abdolmohammadi (1985a), while ORE and PDF are particularly congruent to compliance error estimation, LMM and GDR have potential in account balance estimation. Comparative study of these quantification methods is needed to identify the most cost-effective ones. Some methodological suggestions are offered in Abdolmohammadi (1985a) to do this.

Second, once prior probabilities are quantified, how should they be evaluated? One method of evaluation is to compare the assessed prior with the auditor's beliefs. This comparison, of course, is not easy since measures of real beliefs are difficult to arrive at. Instead, researchers have concentrated on the magnitude of heuristics and biases present. For example, Kinney and Uecker (1982) studied the

comparative anchoring and adjustment bias of two alternative modes of probability assessment in auditing. Other biases to be included in future research include availability, motivational and representativeness biases.

Another method of evaluation of PPDs relates to the comparison of such distributions with actual outcomes. The problem is that actual outcomes are seldom known in auditing. Here researchers have offered many surrogates such as historical frequencies of errors or account balances. This analysis, which is termed calibration, attempts to develop a correspondence between prior probabilities and historical frequencies (or frequency of events at a given point in time). But, as Chesley (1984) argues, if the frequency of events is known and has relevance to the future, why should one assess PPDs rather than using empirical frequencies? Other researchers have suggested consensus of auditors as a surrogate for accuracy of prior distributions. In a recent survey of 27 very experienced, policy-making partners and nine managers of several accounting firms, Wright and Abdolmohammadi (1986) found that auditors consider reliability (i.e., consistency of a method over time or over different cases at a given time) to be as important as accuracy followed by such factors as cost and ease-of-use of a method. Consensus was considered the least important factor. Thus, research on the comparative reliability of various PPDs and other important attributes seems necessary.

Third, how should auditors be

Exhibit 19–6 (continued)

trained for PPD assessment? There is a need for "optimal" training materials. Although different training approaches exist, no research has evaluated their comparative merits in auditing. The author favors a computer-based, on-line, user-friendly training-assessment-feedback mechanism, where the auditor is provided hands-on experience with PPD assessments. The PPD assessed, for example, could immediately be drawn in graphical form and presented to the auditor for any desired changes, along with summary information such as mean and median. The purpose is to provide the auditor the opportunity to change the PPD as necessary to best reflect beliefs. Feedback has been suggested by researchers (e.g., Spetzler and Stael von Holstein, 1975) to improve the ability of auditors to properly reflect PPDs, but while the pencil-and-paper medium does not allow rapid feedback, the computer would easily do so in a matter of seconds.

Fourth, once PPDs are assessed, how would the integration of priors and sample results take place? As Table 1 shows, once the data in column (b) are available, statistical tables or mathematical computations would provide the data in column (c), leaving columns (d) through (f) as routine computations. All of these can be programmed. In fact, the sample size decision can also be automated, based on the PPD presented in column (b) and the auditor's desired confidence level. The author has developed a prototype of such a Bayesian-assisted

sampling system. The initial testing indicates that development of such a decision support system is quite feasible, although much detailed work remains to make the system operational in actual audit settings.

Conclusions

Much conceptual work has been done in support of the applicability of the Bayesian approach in auditing. Some empirical evidence has also been accumulated on the efficiency of the Bayesian vis-a-vis the classical approach and on appropriate PPD quantification techniques. However, additional research is needed in resolving issues, some of which were identified in this essay. The Bayesian statistical approach appears to be a natural extension of the classical approach and, in my opinion, is going to be a widely used method in the future. The auditing profession is showing significant interest in decision support and expert systems, and a Bayesian assisted decision support system seems to be a logical outcome. In fact, Hansen and Messier (1985) report that 13 out of their 17 auditor participants considered sampling as a good area of application of decision aids. As one policy-making partner from a Big Eight firm recently related: "The Bayesian method has so much promise that it is going to be used in the firm in the next few years in one way or another." This essay has identified key areas needing attention by researchers and practitioners that will help to make this promise a practical reality.

Exhibit 19–6 (continued)

References

Abdolmohammadi, M. J., "Bayesian Inference Research in Auditing: Some Methodological Suggestions," *Contemporary Accounting Research 2* (Fall 1985a), pp. 76–94.

Messier, W. F. and J. V. Hansen, "Expert Systems in Accounting and Auditing: A Framework and Review," in *Decision-Making and Accounting*: *Current Research*, S. Moriarity and E. Joyce (eds.) (University of Oklahoma, 1984), pp. 182–202.

Solomon, I., J. L. Krogstad, M. S. Romney and L. A. Tomassini, "Auditors' Prior Probability Distributions for Account Balances," *Accounting, Organizations and Society 7* (1982), pp. 27–41.

———, "Bayesian Inference in Substantive Testing: An Ease-of-Use Criterion," *Advances in Accounting 2* (1985b), pp. 275–289.

———, "Efficiency of the Bayesian Approach in Compliance Testing: Some Empirical Evidence," *Auditing*: *A Journal of Practice and Theory* (forthcoming 1986).

———and P. Berger, "A Test of the Accuracy of Probability Assessment Techniques in Auditing," *Contemporary Accounting Research* (forthcoming 1986).

Birnberg J. G., "Bayesian Statistics: A Review," *Journal of Accounting Research* (Spring 1964), pp. 108–116.

Chandler, J., "Expert Systems in Auditing: The State-of-the-Art," *The Auditor's Report 8* (Summer 1985), pp. 1–4.

Chesley, G. R., "Discussant's Comments On: Calibration of Subjective Probability Assessments: A Methodological Perspective," in *Decision Making and Accounting*: *Current Research*, S. Moriarity and E. Joyce (eds.) (University of Oklahoma, 1984), pp. 101–105.

Corless, J. C., "Assessing Prior Distributions for Applying Bayesian Statistics in Auditing," *The Accounting Review* (July 1972), pp. 556–566.

Crosby, M. A., "Bayesian Statistics in Auditing: A Comparison of Probability Elicitation Techniques," *The Accounting Review* (April 1981), pp. 355–365.

Felix, W. L., Jr., "Evidence on Alternative Means of Assessing Prior Probability Distributions for Audit Decision Making," *The Accounting Review* (October 1976), pp. 800–807.

Hansen, J. V. and W. F. Messier, Jr., "A Preliminary Test of EDP-Xpert," (working paper, University of Florida, 1985).

Kinney, W. R., Jr. and W. C. Uecker, "Mitigating the Consequences of Anchoring in Auditor Judgments," *The Accounting Review* (January 1982), pp. 55–69.

———, Tomassini, L. A.; M. B. Romney; and J. L. Krogstad, "Probability Elicitation in Auditing: Additional Evidence on the Equivalent Prior Sample Method," *Advances in Accounting I* (1984), pp. 267–290.

Spetzler, C. S. and C. A. S. von Holstein, "Probability Encoding in Decision Analysis," *Management Science* (November 1975), pp. 340–358.

Exhibit 19–6 (continued)

Winkler, R. L., *Introduction to Baye-sian Inference and Decision* (New York: Holt, Rinehart and Winston, 1972).

Wright, A. and M. J. Abdolmoham-madi, "Modeling Auditor Weights of Key Criteria in Evaluating Alternative Sampling Approaches: A Guide for

Researchers," *Advances in Account-ing* (forthcoming, 1986).

[1] For empirical evidence of this, see Abdol-mohammadi, 1986.

[2] For rationale and the binominal table, see Winkler (1972).

Source: *Auditor's Report* (Volume 9, Num-ber 2, Winter 1986), pp. 1–4.

---

valuation, consulting, and auditing purposes. Potential applications are depicted in Exhibit 19–7. MCS is an acronym for Management Consulting Services; otherwise, the exhibit is relatively self-explanatory.

Considerations in choosing such applications include the ability to communicate techniques and conclusions and the strength of persuasiveness often pro-

---

Exhibit 19–7

Some Potential Applications

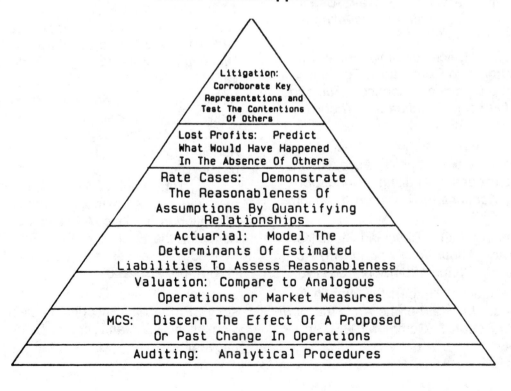

Litigation: Corroborate Key Representations and Test The Contentions Of Others

Lost Profits: Predict What Would Have Happened In The Absence Of Others

Rate Cases: Demonstrate The Reasonableness Of Assumptions By Quantifying Relationships

Actuarial: Model The Determinants Of Estimated Liabilities To Assess Reasonableness

Valuation: Compare to Analogous Operations or Market Measures

MCS: Discern The Effect Of A Proposed Or Past Change In Operations

Auditing: Analytical Procedures

'vided by statistics. Which statistic to apply in what setting will largely be a function of the nature of the data set and the underlying assumptions of a particular statistical tool.

DESCRIPTIVES AND PLOTS

As Exhibit 19–4 displayed, a great deal of information can be communicated through the use of simple descriptive statistics. Beyond those measures depicted, often interquartile distributions are useful at showing either the heterogeneity of the population or its homogeneity. This would amount to sorting a data set and then identifying those amounts that constitute the largest 25% of the population and so on.

Beyond descriptives, a picture can tell a thousand words! Plots of raw data and interrelationships, or lack thereof, between two variables can be very useful and communicate with ease. Exhibit 19–8 provides some examples of scatter diagrams. To put some words to the pictures, graph a could be viewed as demonstrative that the price had little effect on the volume of sales. Graph b might clearly show that commissions are a variable expense that track closely with sales dollars. Graph c on the other hand may track how the revenue fell as the number of customers lost to another company infringing on a patent increased. Graph d explains why some relationships do not take a one to one or unidirectional pattern. Indeed, as one example, growth may require expansion of facilities up to a point and then the relevant range of operations may be such that the incremental facilities cost not merely flattens, but on a per unit basis turns down drastically as the number of units handled increases. Graph e refers to the realistic probability that relationships are not as clean cut as those depicted in b through d. Rather, associations pictured between only two variables at a time often require other considerations to be made to really understand how they interact with one another.

CORRELATIONS AND CHI-SQUARE

Correlation statistics can quantify the pictures depicted in scatter diagrams. For example, the graphs b and c in Exhibit 19–8 are likely to have accompanying correlations in the approximate amount of $+.95$ and $-.95$, respectively. Correlations lie between -1 and $+1$, depending on the slant of the line. The positive correlation means the two variables move in the same direction, whereas the negative correlation means that the two variables move in an opposite direction. The closer to an absolute value of one, the stronger the association, whereas a zero correlation means no discernible systematic linear pattern between the two variables. Hence, graph d in Exhibit 19–8 would be expected to have close to a zero correlation, since half of the time it goes up and half of the time it goes down.

A layman's interpretation of a .95 correlation would be that approximately 95% of the time that one variable lies above its mean or average value, the other variable likewise lays above its respective mean or average value.

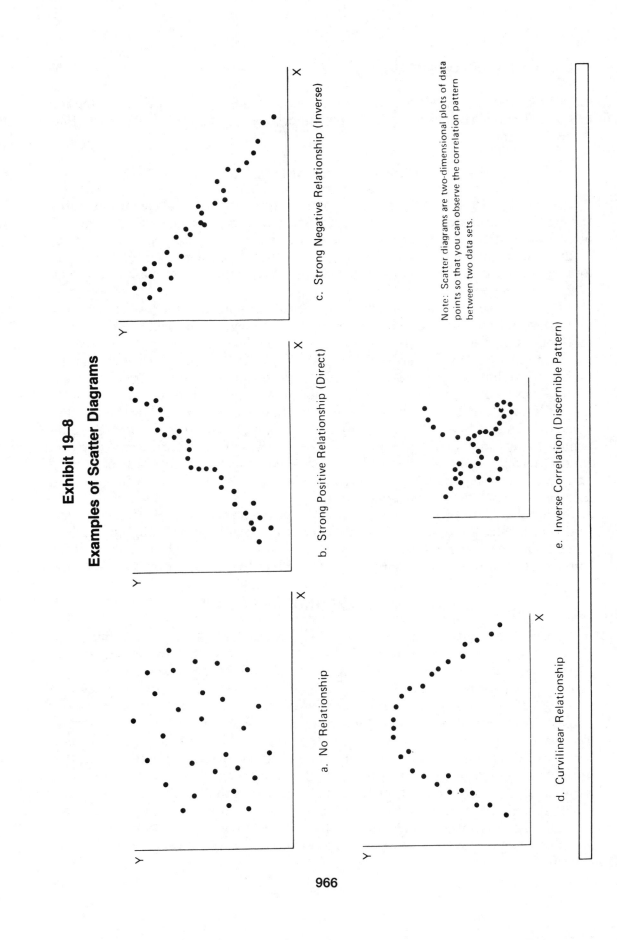

Exhibit 19—8

Examples of Scatter Diagrams

a. No Relationship

b. Strong Positive Relationship (Direct)

c. Strong Negative Relationship (Inverse)

d. Curvilinear Relationship

e. Inverse Correlation (Discernible Pattern)

Note: Scatter diagrams are two-dimensional plots of data points so that you can observe the correlation pattern between two data sets.

Since correlations require a linear relationship and use information that has normal distributions as underlying assumptions for computational purpose, another tool that does not require such assumptions is often used. That tool is Chi-Square, a so-called nonparametric analysis tool. The notion of parametric is that underlying distributional assumptions apply, whereas nonparametric means that such assumptions can be set aside. Importantly, Chi-Square can be used for qualitative information, while correlations depend more on a continuous type variable such as dollars of invoices.

Exhibit 19–9 depicts the approach to Chi-Square: the formation of a contingency table. The idea is to demonstrate whether a relationship exists between the size of a company, characterized as small, medium, or large, and the industry in which that company operates. If a pattern emerges whereby certain industries tended to be systematically smaller than others, the types of colored areas in Exhibit 19–9 would be expected to emerge. The test for Chi-Square compares the incidence of frequencies in the various cells of the contingency table, relative to an equal distribution (i.e., a random pattern) among the six cells in this setting.

Exhibit 19–9

Chi-Square Analyses

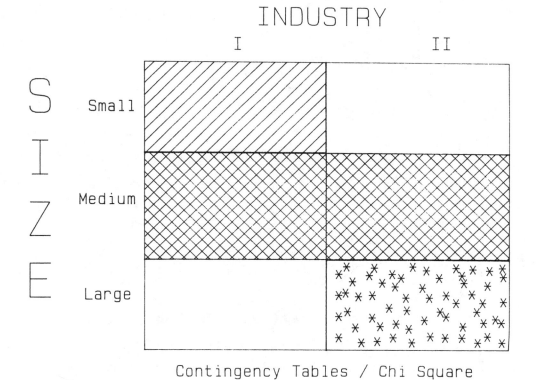

Contingency Tables / Chi Square

Chi-Squares can be computed for contingency tables of a variety of sizes. A number of software packages are available to compute these and related statistics.

The null hypothesis may be tested by

$$\chi^2 = \sum_{i=1}^{r} \sum_{j=1}^{k} \frac{(O_{ij} - E_{ij})^2}{E_{ij}}$$

where O_{ij} = observed number of cases categorized in ith row of jth column

E_{ij} = number of cases expected under H_0 to be categorized in ith row of jth column

$\sum_{i=1}^{r} \sum_{j=1}^{k}$ directs one to sum over all (r) rows and all (k) columns, i.e., to sum over all cells

The values of χ^2 yielded are distributed approximately as chi square with $df = (r - 1)(k - 1)$, where r = the number of rows and k = the number of columns in the contingency table.

To find the expected frequency for each cell (E_{ij}), multiply the two marginal totals common to a particular cell, and then divide this product by the total number of cases, N [i.e, the corresponding row total multiplied by the corresponding column total, divided by the total number of observations].

This reduces to the following formula for 2 × 2 contingency tables:

$$\chi^2 = \frac{N\left(|AD - BC| - \frac{N}{2}\right)^2}{(A + B)(C + D)(A + C)(B + D)} \qquad df = 1$$

where the cells are defined as:

A	B
C	D

[**Source:** Sidney Siegel, *Nonparametric Statistics for the Behavioral Sciences* (New York: McGraw-Hill Book Company, Inc., 1956), pp. 104–110.]

REGRESSION ANALYSIS AND ARIMA

Regression analysis is a term applied to linear modeling, whereby a set of data points are described as to the tendency of various attributes to be systematically related. Regression analysis can be used to analyze time-series data, cross-sectional data, or a combination of such data. This possibility is reflected in Exhibit 19–10. An example of time-series would be to gather monthly information from the beginning of 1987 through to the end of 1990 to describe the association between various expenses and the volume of operations, as a means of evaluating cost behavior. Other environmental factors expected to influence such expenses might likewise be included in the model.

A cross-sectional data set might be to examine 30 branch banks, one relative to the other, to evaluate which branch banks are unusual. This might point out a particular branch that had an unusual interest return from its accounts, relative to all other banks in the model. A pooled approach would potentially use all of the monthly data for the 1987 to 1990 time frame for each of the 30 branch banks, creating 48 monthly observations multiplied by 30 units, or 1,440 data points. In pooling, homogeneity of the years being collapsed together is quite important, and the interpretation of parameters of the model is often difficult. Hence, the pooled approach requires more assumptions and tends to be more difficult to explain and interpret.

Exhibit 19–10

Regression Modeling

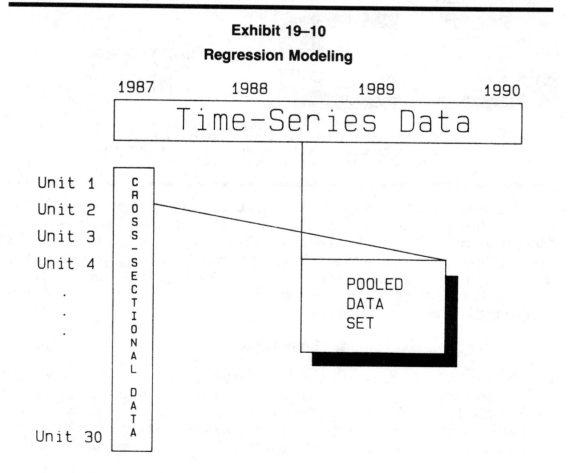

Exhibit 19–11

Time-Series Processes

Combine persistency characteristics of a constant-mean model with the unpredictable behavior of a random-walk model

AUTOREGRESSIVE PROCESSES
    a tendency to revert to some mean level over long periods

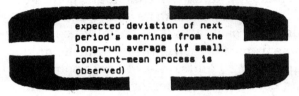
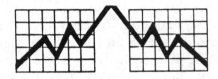

SMOOTHING MODELS (MOVING AVERAGE MODELS are one subset)
    partially eliminate or smooth out chance factors in
reported numbers to provide a best guess of earnings next period

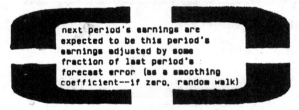
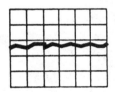

Adapted from Paul A. Griffin, _Research Report: Usefulness
to Investors and Creditors of Information Provided by
Financial Reporting_, Second Edition (Stamford, Connecticut:
Financial Accounting Standards Board, 1987), pp. 60–61

The term ARIMA is used in Exhibit 19–6 and refers to Autoregressive Integrated Moving Average Techniques, one of which is regression analysis. Time-series processes of the ARIMA variety are often thought of as tracking patterns in a single data series, rather than stressing interrelationships between variables, as is the common regression technique. Exhibit 19–11 provides an example of how an autoregressive or moving average pattern might be communicated, should that be used for modeling purposes.

SAMPLING

Chapter 7 of this _Handbook_ described sampling in some detail. The considerations set forth regarding sampling plans, sample size determination, sample selection, evaluation of results, and qualitative factors are all important to keep in mind when sampling is applied in a litigation setting. The burden of proof as to representativeness will likely be placed on the individual applying sampling.

PITFALLS

All of the statistical tools discussed herein have their pitfalls. The assumptions invoked may not fit the data set. The complexity of the application may be cumbersome to communicate. The analysis may fail to address the focal issues in dispute. Ironically, one of the better tools for evaluating the analysis process in litigation support is provided from the computer domain. In Exhibit 19–12, an

---

Exhibit 19–12

Quality Assurance Factors

In data processing, we need to look at the attributes of quality in order to understand the components of quality and as a basis for measuring quality. The following are the commonly accepted quality attributes for data processing:

FACTORS	DEFINITION
CORRECTNESS	Extent to which a program satisfies its specifications and fulfills the user's mission objectives.
RELIABILITY	Extent to which a program can be expected to perform its intended function with required precision.
EFFICIENCY	The amount of computing resources and code required by a program to perform a function.
INTEGRITY	Extent to which access to software or data by unauthorized persons can be controlled.
USABILITY	Effort required to learn, operate, prepare input, and interpret output of a program.
MAINTAINABILITY	Effort required to locate and fix an error in an operational program.
TESTABILITY	Effort required to test a program to ensure it performs its intended function.
FLEXIBILITY	Effort required to modify an operational program.
PORTABILITY	Effort required to transfer a program from one hardware configuration and/or software system environment to another.
REUSABILITY	Extent to which a program can be used in other applications—related to the packaging and scope of the functions that the programs perform.
INTEROPERABILITY	Effort required to couple one system with another.

Source: William E. Perry, *Hatching the Data Processing Quality Assurance Function* (Orlando, Florida: Quality Assurance Institute), pp. 13–14.

Exhibit is provided that is from a quality assurance initiative on data processing. Yet, the quality attributes of an EDP environment clearly apply to a litigation support setting.

The correctness of the research design and the reliability of various tests applied are particularly critical. However, one must not lose sight of the need for cost-efficient approaches. The data integrity, as well as the integrity of various software and modes of communication applied, have been showcased as key considerations throughout litigation support. The communication considerations in litigation support would seem to link to usability. Since the litigation process is iterative, with changing data sets, exhibits, and sequential discovery, the ability to adapt one's analysis and maintain the integrity of the data base is critical. Periodic means of testing the approach and flexibility in modifying the approach in light of new information can be crucial. Portability can be important due to the need to merge data from a variety of places and to potentially adjust analyses on the spot, in the presence of hypotheticals or new facts that are revealed. If a single procedure can be applied to more than a single aspect of the analysis, then the communication obstacles are less troublesome.

Finally, the term interoperability recognizes that numerous systems may have to be linked in the course of data collection, translation, and analysis. Remember that litigation disputes often span a large number of years, meaning that system changes arose in the course of tracking the original data and may well have to be considered in retrieving information for subsequent analyses.

Exhibit 19–12 is a particularly useful benchmark to keep in mind, not only while evaluating computer systems, but when setting a strategy for litigation support activities as well.

CLOSING COMMENTARY

Litigation support activities are increasingly information intensive, and statistics are increasingly in use. The appendix to this chapter addresses the acceptability of modeling techniques as support in the courtroom. Keep in mind as you review its content, the quote from one judge in a courtroom setting:

> "too many use statistics as a drunk man uses a lamp-post—for support, and not for illumination."

The materials herein and those in the accompanying Appendix are intended to encourage an appreciation for the role of control concepts in providing effective litigation support services and, in particular, for avoiding pitfalls in applying the powerful tools of statistics that are readily available and are useful in evaluating information.

Appendix

The Acceptability of Regression Analysis as Evidence in a Courtroom — Implications for the Auditor

Wanda A. Wallace

ABSTRACT

Despite numerous academic articles concerning the application of regression analysis as an audit tool, the acceptability of the tool in the legal setting has not been explored. This article reviews court cases involving the application of regression analysis, analyzing factors which influenced the evidentiary force given to testimony that was reliant on regression analysis. Some general issues involved in the use of such statistical evidence, as well as the effect of the "hearsay" rule on individual testimony in jury settings, are discussed. Since no cases have involved regression applications to the audit, no direct proof exists of whether or not the use of regression analysis in analytical review would be considered acceptable in a court of law. However, actual cases where regression analysis has been used in court suggest that if the technique is clearly explained in submitting testimony, if the rationale for the selection of variables is included in the working papers, and if violations of the regression assumptions are investigated, legal support exists for accepting the *application of regression* as evidence. Further, the ability of the evidence to withstand a technical rebuttal (typical of academicians' critique of empirical studies) is demonstrated. Recommendations are provided as to how to approach model building based on the analysis of relevant court cases.

GIVEN the litigation environment of public accounting, a concern which naturally arises when new auditing techniques are introduced is whether such techniques will be acceptable in court. Will a judge deem that the auditor was a prudent person exercising due audit care when a

Wanda A. Wallace holds the Marilyn R. and Leo F. Corrigan, Jr. Trustee Professorship, Southern Methodist University.

new auditing technique has been applied? In many cases the response to this question becomes clear only after implementation of the technique. However, if the technique is not unique to auditing, it is possible to find legal support for applying the new tool by investigating its use by other professionals. This opportunity for investigation exists with respect to regression analysis. Such an investigation can suggest means of improving the evidentiary force of the new audit tool, as well as means of preparing the person who is applying the technique for the courtroom setting, should such an occasion arise.

Regression analysis is a well-known statistical tool which is taught at universities across the country. This technique utilizes the relationship between two or more quantitative or qualitative variables so that one variable can be predicted from the other, or others. It has audit potential as a planning tool, a substantive testing technique, and a tool for special studies (see Tummins and Watson, 1975; Deakin and Granof, 1976; and Albrecht and McKeown, 1977). Regression analysis has recently been implemented by two international accounting firms and is under consideration by other firms for future use in analytical review procedures (Stringer, 1975; Akresh and Wallace, 1982; and Wallace, forthcoming). While the academic literature has discussed the application of regression analysis (Kinney, 1978) and problems with its application (Kinney and Salamon, 1979, and Wallace, 1979), the overall reception of the tool in the legal setting has not been explored in the literature. Regression analysis, in fact, has already been tested in court. In Wade v. Mississippi Cooperative Extension Service [372 F. Supp. 126 (N.D. Miss. 1974), aff'd, 528 F.2d 508 (5th Cir. 1976)], the discrediting of the foundation of regression analysis was attempted, with a claim that its application to the field of social science violated sound statistical procedures. The

court rejected the contentions, and a door was opened for the future use of regression analysis. Its future use has been repeatedly accepted as legitimate evidence, as reflected in the following words of the judge:

Regression analysis is a professionally accepted method of analyzing data.[1] [Brown v. Moore, 428 F. Supp. 1123, 1128 (S.D. Ala. 1976), aff'd, 575 F.2d 298 (5th Cir. 1978)]

The purpose of this article is to review the court cases involving the application of regression analysis, in order to provide insight regarding the acceptability of the statistical tool as evidence in a court of law. Dicta, or the various judges' opinions, are the focal point of analysis in gaining an understanding of how the regression evidence submitted in past cases has been evaluated. For example, in what circumstances have judges been hesitant to assess the regression evidence or to rely thereon? What aspects of the regression evidence were persuasive to the judge in reaching a decision? Dicta are frequently cited in arguing court cases; such language in cases is often cited by later courts as having persuasive power. However, technically speaking, only the holdings of each case, which state the narrow findings of the court predicated on the specific facts of the case,

[1] This same statement is found in the judge's opinion for Civil Action No. 75-297-P, Bolden v. City of Mobile, Alabama [423 F. Supp. 384, 388 (S.D. Ala. 1976)].

The data base for this research was provided by Price Waterhouse. The author gratefully acknowledges the useful comments of Nancy B. Hogan, JD, Adjunct Professor at Southern Methodist University, and George Sullivan, JD, Assistant Professor at Rochester Institute of Technology. The views expressed in this article, however, are solely those of the author.

become part of common law, carrying the absolute weight of the law as the critical legal precedents. The case quotations presented are not cited as authorities for a single proposition but rather as a means of understanding the courts' analysis of and stated reliance upon regression evidence. Further, the case transcripts frequently suggest statistical and nonstatistical issues which are relevant to the auditor's application of regression analysis in preparing working paper documentation and in anticipating courtroom cross-examinations, should the use of regression analysis as an audit tool be given attention in legal or regulatory proceedings.

METHOD

A search of the Supreme Court decisions beginning in 1938, the Federal Court of Appeals decisions beginning in 1945, Federal District Court decisions beginning in 1960, and the Court of Claims decisions[2] beginning in 1977 located seventeen court references to regression analysis.[3] Abstracts of these cases were reviewed and five cases were selected for in-depth review, based on their application to a business context and/or the apparent emphasis placed on the use of regression analysis. The author's review of the other twelve cases raised similar issues to those described herein, and several supporting case citations are integrated throughout the content analysis of the five selected cases and related literature. In addition, law reviews and legal treatises were reviewed for discussions of statistical evidence and the use of regression analysis. References are integrated throughout this article.

The five cases to be discussed in detail are:

(1) *Trans World Airlines, Inc. v. Hughes* [308 F. Supp. 679 (S.D.N.Y. 1969), aff'd, 449 F.2d 51 (2d Cir. 1971) rev'd sub nom.

Hughes Tool Co. v. Trans World Airlines Inc., 409 U.S. 363 (1973)].

(2) *Texas Instruments v. United States* [407 F. Supp. 1326 (N.D. Texas 1976), modified, 551 F.2d 599 (5th Cir. 1977)].

(3) *Kirksey v. City of Jackson, Mississippi* [461 F. Supp. 1282 (S. D. Miss. 1978), vacated on other grounds, 625 F.2d 21 (5th Cir. 1980), readopted, 506 F. Supp. 491 (S.D. Miss. 1981), aff'd, 663 F.2d 659 (5th Cir. 1981)].

(4) *Kyriazi v. Western Electric Co.* [461 F. Supp. 894 (D.C.N.J. 1978), aff'd, 647 F.2d 388 (3d Cir. 1981)].

(5) *Pennsylvania v. Local 542, Operating Engineers* [469 F. Supp. 329 (E.D. Pa. 1978), aff'd, 648 F.2d 922 (3d Cir. 1981)].

As is true of statistical evidence in general, regression analysis has been used primarily in civil rights litigation, particularly in voting rights and employment discrimination cases (Dawson, 1973). However, regression applications are also quite common in regulatory proceedings before the Commodity Exchange Authority, the Federal Power Commission, the Securities and Exchange Commission, the Federal Communications Commission, and similar regulatory agencies (Finkelstein, 1973).

TWA v. HUGHES

Preference for Precision

While it can be expected that the methodology of regression analysis, which

---

[2] These cases are provided in the General Federal Library, United States Code data base of LEXIS.

[3] The key words used were "Regression Analysis or Analytic: Review or Bayesian Statistic:" where the colons allow different endings to the words to be selected. Twenty-two total citations were located, eighteen of which related to regression analysis.

is accepted by mathematicians and statisticians, would also be acceptable in a courtroom,[4] its relative evidentiary weight cannot be as easily anticipated. In the TWA v. Hughes case, the judge discusses the rules for computing the amount of damages in an antitrust case:

> ... the trier of the facts must use the most precise proof available, that even where a defendant by his own wrong has prevented a more precise computation, the award may not be based on speculation or guesswork, and that the award must be predicated on a just and reasonable estimate of the damage, based on relevant data [p. 685, citing Bigelow v. RKO Radio Pictures, Inc., 327 U.S. 251 (1946)].

These rules are applied to the case:

> The special master rejected the comparative profit studies because there was a more precise method of ascertaining damages, which was the method he used [p. 694].

Hence, a warning is issued regarding the degree of acceptance of various quantitative and statistically-based testimony. Implicit in the judge's comments is the message that more precise evidence is preferred and will tend to overrule other testimony. This preference is also discussed by the judge when he addresses the factors which count against noticing the defendants' "proposition of indisputability" (i.e., the acceptance of facts as true without hearing testimony, such as accepting the fact that "October 5, 1982, was a Tuesday"):

> First, the subject of the proposition is not scientific, historical, geographic or statistical matter of the kind courts are most willing to notice. Instead it is a garden variety proposition about who did what, when and where [p. 684].

Thus, in the opinion of the judge, *statistical* evidence is clearly desirable and compares favorably to other evidence — particularly relative to nonstatistical evidence. Its desirability is directly related to its ability to capture the essence of the problem as reflected by precision measures. For example, having a reasonably low standard error for a regression model would provide evidence that the essence of the relationship being modeled had been captured.

The dicta suggest that a comparative advantage exists for regression analysis relative to nonstatistical predictions, since the precision of statistically based procedures can be quantified. As observed in Brown v. Gaston County Dyeing Mach. Co. [457 F.2d 1377, 1382 (4th Cir. 1972)], "Elusive, purely subjective standards must give way to objectivity if statistical indicia ... are to be refuted." It would appear that the usual advantages of statistical sampling relative to nonstatistical sampling in terms of its defensibility can be expected to hold for regression analysis relative to more subjective and informal analytical review procedures.

The potential weight of statistical evidence is exemplified in numerous quotations, such as the judge's words in Ford v. White [430 F.2d 951, 954 (5th Cir. 1970)]: "These figures require little comment.

---

[4] However, some may be surprised to learn that other skills taught across the country, such as hypnotism or — more related to the analysis at hand — pooling of cross-sectional and time-series data, have not been accepted as scientifically valid [see People v. Ebanks, 117 Cal 652, 49 P 1049], or have been deemed "meaningless" [see Southern Louisiana Area Rate Cases, 428 F. 2d 407, 436 n. 91 (5th Cir.) cert. denied, 400 U.S. 950 (1970)], respectively. Similarly, the literature predicts that Bayesian statistics do not "provide judicially acceptable methods for meeting critical presuppositions of the method," i.e., an acceptable way of quantifying the prior distribution (see Baldus and Cole, 1980, p. 304).

They speak for themselves." The figures involved were simple percentage comparisons of jury selections to master jury lists for the purpose of highlighting discriminatory selection procedures. If such weight is provided to simple analyses, one can infer that more sophisticated, powerful analyses should be dominant in persuasive power, if effectively presented.

The Role of Assumptions

However, as analyses become more sophisticated, they tend to become more heavily reliant on assumptions made by the model builder. This is largely due to the preference for constructing parsimonious models, the usual presumption that historical trends will persist, and the inclusion of forecasted independent variables (i.e., those variables intended to explain and predict the variable of interest) when drawing inferences. The question arises as to whether the courts are aware of the role of assumptions in such statistical approaches and whether the judges have been receptive to regression evidence, even when hindsight has demonstrated that the model builder's assumptions were wrong.

The idea that experts' testimonies are based on assumptions is clearly acknowledged in the TWA v. Hughes case, as is the basis for such assumptions:

> The assumption made by TWA's expert was justified on the facts as to the time of year and passenger demand [p. 690].

The necessity of using data available at the time of the analysis as a basis for assumptions and statistical inference is further discussed when the judge reviews conflicting testimony as to what "would have occurred" in the absence of the illegal acts of the defendants.

> I have determined that TWA has not established that a prudent and competent management of TWA acting independently and free of any control or interference on the part of Toolco would and should have calculated in the Spring of 1955 the amount of the financial requirements of TWA for the jet aircraft age. It is also my determination that an independent and prudent TWA management would not have accepted the recommendation of Drexel Harriman Ripley that TWA sell in May 1955 $55.5 million (net proceeds) in common stock of TWA.

> For me to find to the contrary would in my opinion endow Drexel Harriman Ripley and an independent prudent Board of TWA in 1955 with a prescience, wisdom and perfection of timing that exceeds the natural capacity of the most experienced men acting without the benefit of hindsight [p. 695].

Thus the role of hindsight as an unfair advantage is acknowledged; yet if predictions are representative of what eventually occurs, such information is regularly considered by the judge in evaluating the quality of the testimony. As an example, the judge in reviewing the subject matter being predicted concludes:

> The suggested finding that it was not unusual for an airline to cut back initial jet orders covers only part of the relevant fact. The remainder is that such an airline would, *and did*, at the same time increase orders for other models [p. 688]. (Emphasis added.)

Similarly, in explaining why profit on the sale of stock is not attributable to the illegal acts of the defendants, the judge states:

> At that time [1963], the end of the ill effects of defendants' control, the stock was selling at about $32 a share compared with $86 a share at the date of sale. Therefore, the high value that the TWA stock reached in 1966 had nothing to do with the acts of the defendants [p. 693].

Again, the actual stock prices post facto affect the evaluation of submitted evidence. Courts are similarly motivated to embrace statistical results that accord with common sense [Jones v. New York City Human Resources Administration, 391 F. Supp. 1064 (S.D.N.Y. 1975)].

The essential role of assumptions in applying statistical tests and the distinction between available data and hindsight are thereby acknowledged by the judge, with the additional acknowledgement that hindsight and common sense expectations can be effectively used in support of predictions, when they are consistent with assumptions. The court's stated preference[5] for more precise evidence whenever available, coupled with the court's awareness of the role of assumptions, suggests clear advantages to a statistically-based analytical review, as opposed to primarily informal review procedures.

TEXAS INSTRUMENTS v. UNITED STATES

This case parallels TWA v. Hughes: (1) objections were not directed at the acceptability of regression analysis — the only dispute concerned an assumption regarding an input to the model, i.e., the rate of return; (2) the court clearly acknowledged the necessary role of assumptions in making statistical predictions;[6] and (3) the judge recognized the unfairness of using hindsight to assess whether the statistical methods applied were reasonable.

The Texas Instruments v. United States case involves several disputes with the Internal Revenue Service, one of which involves an area in which regression analysis was applied. The point of contention concerns whether the plaintiff is entitled to deductions made to its employee pension trust during the years 1968 and 1969 in light of past overfunding. The court finding in 1976, upheld in 1977, was that the corpora-

tion's contributions to a qualified employee pension trust were ordinary and necessary, even though the trust was overfunded. The statistical conclusions of a national, well reputed actuarial firm were the basis for such contributions. The nature of the statistical evidence is discussed by the judge:

> Texas Instruments introduced evidence at trial to show that the assumptions underlying its contributions were derived from data organized and reduced according to the highest standards and methods of actuarial science. Indeed, the only attack made on TI's assumptions by the Service is that in retrospect the rate of return expected on the monies invested under the pension plan was underestimated and the employee turnover rate was overestimated in 1968 and again in 1969. Yet such variance is to be expected at times during the forty- to sixty-year lifetime over which the basic assumptions underlying TI's pension plan are to be functional. Certainly blind adherence to assumptions which are improperly derived or which become invalid predictors over the lifetime of a trust would be persuasive evidence that contributions made upon these assumptions were extraordinary and unnecessary, but the evidence in this case demonstrated that TI was carefully attempting to hew a path through the uncertain future using computers, surveys, regression analysis and past experience as its cutting edge. While blunt, the tools used by TI are the only ones available to mortal man to predict the inscrutable future. In the instant case, it is clear that

---

[5] The Supreme Court reversed prior rulings by finding that, legally speaking, Hughes had no liability exposure, since the regulatory agency had approved the various investment and operating actions of Hughes. Hence, the legal force of the regression evidence was removed, but the court's approach to analyzing the regression evidence remains relevant.

[6] Also note Treas. Reg. S1.404(a) - 3(b) for a discussion of the need to consider the assumptions used in deriving a discount rate.

TI contributed monies to its pension fund, not in blind adherence to an arithmetic scheme, but out of a well reasoned faith that the average figures chosen as a basis for its contributions would prove accurate in the long run. [See Philadelphia Suburban Transp. Co. v. Smite (52-2 USTC ¶9381), 105 F. Supp. 650, 655 (E.D. Pa. 1952)].

. . . the Service would ask this court to penalize the employer if that employer's good faith predictions proved inaccurate and it mistakenly overfunded its pension plan in the short run. Id. at 651. Congress should not have required that the employer should walk such a narrow and treacherous path . . .

I conclude therefore that the contributions in this case were ordinary and necessary within the meaning of Section 404 (a) because they were based upon assumptions which were honestly, conscientiously, and scientifically derived, and because they were in good faith applied in 1968 and 1969 [pp. 1334, 1335].

The Texas Instruments case clearly upheld the use of regression analysis by actuaries.

KIRKSEY v. CITY OF JACKSON, MISSISSIPPI

In this case the judge explicitly accepts the conclusions drawn from regression analysis and states that such findings *establish* the relationship claimed by the expert witness.

The Kirksey v. City of Jackson, Mississippi action centers on the contention that the present at-large system of electing the mayor and two city commissioners abridges the rights of the city's black citizens. The suit was dismissed due to the plaintiffs' failure to prove any lack of access in the electoral process, either in slating, registering, or voting; and the failure to prove discriminatory intent in retaining the form of government. However, the

testimony involving regression analysis was accepted as valid. The judge acknowledged that a pattern of racially polarized voting was "established" [p. 1283] to have existed. The evidence on polarization was based on regression analysis; this regression application is described in the judge's opinion.

Five black candidates sought seats on the Jackson City Council in 1969 and 1973 municipal elections, and all were defeated. In addition, the referendum submitted to the electorate of Jackson for a change in the form of city government to a mayor-council form was defeated. The results of all these elections and the unsuccessful referendum were analyzed . . . . Based upon 1970 Census data, Dr. Henderson computed the racial composition of all the Jackson voting precincts, and then compensating for socio-economic status, used the election results and a computer program to perform . . . regression analysis of the election returns by precinct . . . . Regression analysis is a process which singles out from a group of variables the independent variable which best predicts values of the dependent variable, and thus can best explain the variance between the two . . . . The dependent variable was the vote received by the candidates studied, and race was the independent variable whose influence on the vote received was measured by the regression . . . . The regression analysis showed that the best predictor of the votes received by the black and white candidates for municipal offices was the racial composition of the population of the precincts, and other factors such as socio-economic status were never significant predictors of the voting patterns [p. 1289, 1290].

The judge further states the court's agreement with the conclusions drawn from the regression analysis application:

This court agrees with Dr. Henderson's conclusions that there is a clear pattern of racially polarized voting in Jackson with whites voting overwhelmingly for white candidates for municipal office and blacks voting almost overwhelmingly for black candidates [p. 1290].

KYRIAZI v.
WESTERN ELECTRIC CO.

One of the more telling cases involved a dual presentation of regression applications. In Kyriazi v. Western Electric Co. the plaintiff first presented a graphical illustration of how salary was related to age — in other words, a scatter plot of a simple regression relationship — and the middle 50 percent of employees were marked on the graph. This evidence was deemed to be "persuasive" [p. 943] in demonstrating that an employee, even under the improperly low ratings being awarded by Western Electric, did not receive the salary to which the employee was entitled. Yet a multiple regression model intended to demonstrate the employer's discrimination against a class of employees was labeled unhelpful to the court, primarily because the expert's testimony was not comprehensible to the court. Obviously, the additional rigor provided by the multiple regression analysis relative to the graphical presentation should have been more persuasive, but its explanation was woefully inadequate for the court's needs.

The court, at least at this stage, is simply not prepared to accept or adopt the regression analysis of plaintiff's expert, Dr. John Ullman. The court found Dr. Ullman's testimony unhelpful in determining this issue, in large part because his criteria and their valuations were quite arbitrary and subjective, and frankly, in larger part because *his testimony was simply not comprehensible to the court.* There will have to be a second stage in this case, at which time we will determine the amount of damages the class, or any member of it has sustained [p. 914]. (Emphasis added.)

Hence, consideration of the testimony is postponed to a later hearing which will determine the amount of damages to be awarded. (It should be noted that the use of statistics in estimating damages is common [see Joseph, 1975 and Greenberg, 1976], although regression is more sophisticated than the typical technique applied.)

It appears that the primary problem with the regression application was one of communication. Due to the typical unfamiliarity of judges, lawyers, and jurors with such a technique, ample time must be devoted to properly explaining the statistical approach. It is essential to clearly describe the technique, its purpose, its limitations, and its advantages as a statistical tool in order to ensure that the court considers the regression-related testimony, assigning the appropriate evidentiary weight.

The judge's objection regarding the subjective, arbitrary criteria included in the regression model is not a criticism of the tool itself, but only of components of the model. Clearly, selection of variables must be based on some theory of reasonably objective criteria, and an explanation of how variables were selected should be incorporated in testimony involving the application of regression analysis. The apparent misuse of a statistical tool does not constitute grounds for rejecting the tool; it merely makes one cognizant of the conditions under which the tool should not be applied.

The overall acceptance of statistical methods by the courts is reflected by the following facts:

A prima facie case of discrimination under Title VII may be made on statistics alone; albeit the reliability of those statistics depends upon all the surrounding facts and circumstances [Civil Rights Act of 1964, §701 et. seq. as amended 42 U.S.C.A. §2000 et. seq. (p. 895)].

[Once established] the defendant has the burden of coming forward with 'countervailing evidence of his own' regarding fallacies or deficiencies in the data offered by the plaintiff [Dothard v. Rawlinson, 433 U.S. 321 (1977)].

[Further] the defendant can effectively rebut a prima facie case by introducing statistics of its own which explain why minority groups are under-represented [Wolf, 1978].

PENNSYLVANIA v. LOCAL 542, OPERATING ENGINEERS

In this case, point estimates with reported significance levels as derived from regression analysis provide the primary evidence for the court's decision. Despite statistical experts' rebuttals of the regression evidence — typical of academic criticism of regression applications — the court is persuaded by the regression findings.

Persuasive Testimony

Perhaps the most persuasive legal support for the evidentiary weight placed upon regression analysis applications is provided in Pennsylvania, et al, v. Local 542, Operating Engineers. The judge states:

The foundation of this case rests on the statistical documentary and testimonial evidence of discriminatory departures from and applications of the union hiring hall . . . . Upon balance I find Dr. Siskin's testimony to be credible, persuasive and accurate on these subjects . . . . The testimony of the other experts who differ does not cause me to repudiate or modify my finding as to Dr. Siskin's credibility [pp. 342, 351].

Siskin estimated the labor force size of racial minority males between 18 and 65 years of age who were qualified to perform the work of operating engineers by applying regression analysis to adjust for labor-force participation, education, occupation, and census undercount. Disparities be-

tween the racial composition of the labor force and the membership of a labor union representing operating engineers were significant enough to indicate racially discriminatory membership practices.[7] In concluding that the disparities in the hours worked and wages obtained between white and minority union members indicated racial discrimination, the regression analysis used by Siskin to define the two groups appropriately sought to equalize the factors of age, lists of employees and applicants at different trade levels, seniority, branch of union, and jurisdictional district. Siskin estimated that whites on the average worked 97.5 hours more than minorities in 1972 and earned $749 more. Hence, point estimates with reported significance levels as derived from regression analysis provided the primary evidence for the court's decision. However, the reason for claiming this case to be an important precedent in the application of the regression tool to auditing is that statistical experts presented rebuttals of the regression evidence typical of academic criticism of regression applications, and the court was still persuaded by the regression findings.

Rebuttal Evidence Pertaining to the Regression Application

The extensive rebuttal of the regression application attempted by several expert witnesses failed to uncover any substantial flaws. The flaws claimed were similar to any critique of empirical applications of regression analysis:

(1) Was the population appropriate?
(2) Were proper variables used?

---

[7] The labor force was 11.5 percent minority, whereas the union minority composition as of 1971 was 4.4 percent; this represents a statistically significant disparity.

(3) Why weren't particular variables included in the model?

However, in this case the judge declared that "speculation is not effective rebuttal" [p. 368]. The case provides the following guidelines:

(1) those questioning a regression application should rerun the analysis with recommended model adjustments;
(2) hindsight is considered to be an unfair advantage and is to be explicitly distinguished from model adjustments made based on information that was available at the date of the original analysis;
(3) data availability is cited as an acceptable explanation, as well as measurement error, for omitting selected variables;
(4) perhaps most importantly, the intuition of a model should be consistent with its objectives.

As an example of the importance of recognizing the "intuition" underlying a model, the court in this case pointed out that the objective of the case was to demonstrate that the existing labor pool was unrepresentative of the area's population and therefore that any attempt to draw inferences from those areas of the city from which current employees were hired was considered by the judge to be absurd. Similarly, when a proposal was made that education was a key omitted descriptor variable in the model, demonstrating why minorities were not hired, the court dismissed the claim as unreasonable in light of the fact that many of the members of the employee group did not even have their high-school diplomas. This intuition point was also critical in James v. Stockham Valves and Fittings [559 F.2d, 310, 332 (5th Cir. 1977)]; the judge observed that two ex-

planatory variables, intended to describe wages by productivity measures ("skill level" and "merit rating"), would actually incorporate existing discrimination. In addition, education — not a job requirement, yet correlated to race — was included in the biased model. The biased regression model was not accepted as evidence that discrimination had not occurred in the Stockham Valves and Fittings case; intuition had not guided the model builder in selecting relevant yet objective explanatory variables.

Hindsight, while not sufficient to penalize a regression analysis, as already discussed, can be used as additional support for any inferences drawn from regression. Specifically, witnesses in the Pennsylvania v. Local 542 case claimed that minorities did not desire to secure the union jobs or, in other words, a general lack of motivation was present. This lack of motivation, they argued, should have been included as a relevant determinant of minority employment. However, the plaintiff's ability to quantify the large number of minority applications over the recent past was acknowledged as supportive of the fact that such an attribute was not a necessary distinguishing descriptor variable that might explain observed differences between actual and expected levels of minority employment.

Other assertions by the rebutting witnesses included

(1) the inappropriateness of a linear model and
(2) the lack of availability of detailed documentation of each step of the model-building process.

These criticisms were not granted any importance because the primary expert witness had acknowledged the potential problem with the quantification of significant findings by using the simplifying linear model; moreover, other parties had the ability to replicate the model-building process and to demonstrate, if actually possible, some fatal flaw in the estimation process which might have yielded an inappropriate regression relationship. The rebutting witnesses' decision not to replicate this process was deemed evidence of the appropriateness of the regression model selected.

The rebutting experts' tendency to criticize without adequate evidence of their claims is reflected in the judge's statements below:

Dr. Perl (another expert witness) raises the question of the propriety of looking to any static figure representing the minority labor pool at any given time because the composition of the union has developed over a period of years. Consistent with the usual approach of Dr. Wachter, Dr. Perl declines to develop any substitute statistical measure or to indicate whether such a measure would disproportionately affect minority labor pool composition. I believe the measure chosen from the most recent Census data is an effective one for purposes of generating a (rebuttable) statistical conclusion [p. 374].

It is clear that the defendants believed it sufficient principally to raise theoretical questions about the value of Dr. Siskin's analysis and in most instances chose to do no more with the burden on defendants to "defeat" plaintiffs' prima facie case by demonstrating inaccuracies or insignificance, this is patently insufficient. But apart from the burden of proof question (for this is not a case in which the evidence is at equilibrium) defendants have simply not raised any tangible or credible reason why Siskin's labor pool estimate should be viewed as anything less than persuasive [p. 375].

This dismissal of the rebuttal pervades the judge's opinion. For example, the judge addresses Dr. Wachter's claim that Siskin's analysis of hours and wages is misleading:

He [Dr. Wachter] did not, however, perform any duplicative study which might suggest a different result. *He does not dispute the appropriateness of regression analysis in general as a way of isolating a disparate race effect in hours and wages* [p. 377]. (Emphasis added.)

While this article focuses on regression, other cases reviewed, involving a variety of forms of statistical evidence, indicate that disputes frequently arise over what the relevant population and time frame are from which data should be sampled for analysis. There is usually no controversy over the statistical technique itself. (For example, see Hazelwood School District v. United States [444 U.S., 299, 307 (1977)].) The implication for auditors is that working paper documentation should include rationales for the selection of specific variables and particular information sources, including explanations as to why certain obvious data sources were not utilized.

COURT ACCEPTANCE OF REGRESSION AS A STATISTICAL TOOL

The Wade v. Mississippi Cooperative Extension Service, cited earlier, involved the trial court's partial reliance upon plaintiffs' evidence, utilizing regression analysis to hold that the plaintiffs had established a prima facie case of discrimination in hiring and promotion.

In its brief to the Fifth Circuit, defendants attempted to discredit the foundation of the regression analysis. [Brief for Appellants at 13-24, Wade v. Mississippi Coop. Extension Serv., 528 F.2d 508 (5th Cir. 1976)].

The Fifth Circuit rejected defendants' contentions . . . (and) held that the regression analysis was valid . . . [Hallock, 1977, p. 27].

In discussing the court's stand, Hallock (1977) cites the court's preference for evidence with which it was more familiar (in this case, specific instances of discrimination were cited as "corroborative evidence" of disparities — p. 514). Hallock concludes that while regression is an acceptable tool of analysis, care must be taken in its application and in the presentation of findings, if it is to be persuasive. Of course, corroborative evidence based on simpler analyses can effectively assist in gaining acceptance of regression analysis results, as can documented case examples that are consistent with a regression model. (For example, 40 specific cases of discrimination were recounted in International Brotherhood of Teamsters v. United States [431 U.S. 340, 338 (1977)] to bring "the cold numbers convincingly to life" [p. 339].)

Vain attempts have even been made to convince courts that "the potential which inheres in statistics in general for misleading the court or misstating the truth" is grounds for deeming statistical evidence to be unreliable [Sledge v. J.P. Stevens & Co., Inc., 585 F.2nd 625, 635 (4th Cir. 1978)]. In spite of the dismissal of such claims, key limitations on the use of statistics have been cited in the legal literature, and these limitations will likely apply to statistical analyses, including regression analysis, and constrain its application in certain settings. These limitations include:

(1) Size of the sample — the "small universe" is deemed a constraint in the sense that, by mathematical reasoning, the smaller the group, the greater the possibility that a chance variation will occur.
(2) Relevance — statistics must compare relevant groups (this concept was suggested earlier in discussing the rebuttal to Siskin's evidence in the Local 542 case).

(3) Statistics are unlikely to help in establishing an individual's claim, though useful in establishing patterns.
(4) Judicial discretion in evaluating evidence — considerable judicial mistrust of statistics remains. Such skepticism arises from the great potential for misuse and distortion of statistical evidence. In Keely v. Westinghouse Electric Corp. the court stated that "too many use statistics as a drunk man uses a lamppost — for support, and not for illumination." (See Whitten, 1978, pp. 1041-1044, for an in-depth discussion of these limitations).

These limitations emphasize the importance of having adequate sample sizes when performing regression analysis, and reinforce issues raised earlier in the case analyses.

The third issue raised above has, very likely, been one of the "Achilles' heels" of statistical evidence in a court of law.

Criticism of statistical proof has also been directed to the use of probabilistic inference as to a particular, historic fact . . . . The danger arises when statistical techniques are applied to questions which are too specific to be addressed without distortion. For example, one could not assert that racial prejudice motivated Jones' reprimand of Smith on a certain date simply because a regression shows that race has an impact on advancement at Jones' plant. The uses [of regression analysis] . . . are to make inferences about gross processes, not particular incidents. [See *Harvard Law Review* (Vol. 89:387, 1975), p. 417 for citations.]

Courts should not be encouraged to allow entire cases to be determined by statistics from which the inferences drawn are unreasonable; they should be encouraged to view the evidence just as an auditor views the regression evidence collected for an audit: as one part of a set of both statistical and non-statistical evidence which, when combined, provides a basis for inferences to be drawn regarding a particular event and its corresponding financial statement representation. In this manner statistical methods can be utilized where they have relative strengths; for example, in determining remedies for individuals [Sweeney v. Board of Trustees of Keene St. College, 569 F.2d, 169, 179 (1st Cir. 1978) vacated and remanded, 99 S. Ct. 295 (1978)]. This type of point estimate in discrimination suits is analogous to the CPA's estimate of book values. Yet the usefulness of any such statistical measures "depends on all of the surrounding facts and circumstances" [International Brotherhood of Teamsters v. United States, 431 U.S. 324, 340 (1977), citing Hester v. Southern Ry., 497 F.2d 1374, 1379-81 (5th Cir. 1974)].

ANOTHER SOURCE OF SUPPORT

In addition to court cases clearly accepting the technique of regression analysis into testimony, numerous rate hearings in the public utility sector have involved the application of regression analysis (see Brigham and Crum, 1978). In fact, in hearings conducted by the Oregon Public Utility Commission, the Commission has ruled that the capital asset pricing model (CAPM) should be the primary means to determine required rates of return on equity (see Robichek, 1978 for a related discussion). The use of the CAPM, a regression model with substantial support in the modern finance literature, has been disputed regarding the particular model's application; however, these disputes do not focus on the regression tool itself. Finkelstein (1973) presents an excellent review of the use of regression analysis in administra-

tive proceedings, and provides numerous citations.

STATISTICS AS LEGAL EVIDENCE

"According to the Supreme Court, statistical proof of a significant disparity in treatment can constitute a prima facie case in class actions, and shift the burden of going forward with evidence to the opposing party" [Hallock, 1977, p. 9; see Franks v. Bowman Transp. Co., 424 U.S. 747, 772 (1977)]. However, admonitions in existing literature concerning the use of statistics as legal evidence clearly apply to the regression technique (Zeisel, 1968) and should be considered to ensure that the appropriate evidential weight is accorded to the statistical information.

Figure 1 presents a synopsis of points raised in the legal literature that relate to the probable evidentiary value of regression results. First, the desirable qualities of legal proof are delineated, then the well-known threats to validity, reliability, and the statistics' stability are described. The literature guides the attorney on how to cross-examine statistical evidence to uncover such threats (see *American Jurisprudence Proof of Facts*, 1965 and 1977). By anticipating the relevant issues, a regression model builder can document the decision process that addressed each of the various questions.

The CPA may utilize regression analysis as a tool for management advisory services in supporting rate requests, documenting annexation payments between cities and counties, and formulating similar estimates for various client settings. In this case, the CPA is likely to serve as an expert witness and the relevant Federal Rules of Evidence, described in Figure 1, are of interest. However, the critical concern occurs in the audit engagement when the regression procedure is applied as an auditing tool to collect analytical review evidence.

FIGURE 1
A Synopsis of Relevant Legal Literature Relating to the Probable Evidentiary Value of Regression Results

QUALITIES OF IDEAL PROOF

- Relevance
  - Facial, i.e., Do numbers claim to describe an issue that would be considered relevant to the substantive law?
  - Validity, i.e., Do numbers describe what they claim to describe; is the research methodology appropriate?

IF BOTH, CONSISTENT RESULTS WILL BE OBSERVED THAT PERMIT COMPARISONS AND QUANTITATIVE STANDARD-SETTING BY COURTS. PRESUMABLY, PREDICTABILITY WOULD IMPROVE AND GREATER RELIANCE COULD BE PLACED ON THAT PREDICTABILITY.

- Conceptual Simplicity
  - Is the underlying logic intuitively comprehensible?
  - Can legal significance be evaluated without a secondary analysis?
  - Do numbers describe observable occurrences in real populations?

IF ALL OF THESE CONDITIONS ARE MET, OVERALL RELIABILITY IS ACHIEVED.

THREATS TO VALIDITY

- Measurement error in variables
- Flaws in research design
- Errors in transferring and submitting raw data to the computer
  - Are any precautions taken to ensure that no input errors are made?
  - What happens if an error is detected?
- Program Errors
  - On average, one man-made mistake is made for every 100 program instructions; what is the debugging process?
- Completeness of models, i.e., have all relevant variables been included?
- Meeting the underlying assumptions of the estimation process
- Sampling error
  - Is sample size sufficient?
  - How much variability is left unexplained?

THREATS TO RELIABILITY

- Use of irrelevant, unstable, or incomprehensible data
- Use of data for an inappropriate time period
- Comparison of noncomparables
- Use of data or models that do not meet the underlying statistical assumptions
- Disregard of the effects of chance

THE RELIABILITY OF REGRESSION ANALYSIS CAN BE NO GREATER THAN THE MODEL'S VALIDITY. TIED TO ERRORS IN MEASURES, ERRORS IN DATA, SAMPLE SIZE PROBLEMS, AND THE ABILITY OF THE DATA TO MEET UNDERLYING ASSUMPTIONS.

SOURCES OF INSTABILITY AND VARIABILITY

- Research sampling
- Measurement error
- Sampling error
- Random shocks from unknown or unknowable factors
- Nonrandom samples
  - How representative is the sample?
  - How relevant is the sample?

RELEVANT FEDERAL RULES OF EVIDENCE

- Rule 702 expanded scope of expert testimony: can testify if the expert's knowledge "will assist the trier of fact to understand the evidence or to determine a fact in issue."
- Can exclude an expert's testimony if it "may tend to confuse or mislead the jury" [Schwabe, Inc. v. United Shoe Mach. Corp., 297 F.2d 906 (2d Cir.), cert. denied, 369 U.S. 865 (1962)].
- Can exclude an expert's testimony if (s)he acts as a summary witness and does not "add a component of expertise" [U.S. v. Brown, 548 F.2d 1194 (5th Cir. 1977)].
- Rule 703 provides that an expert may base an opinion on inadmissible facts or data, "if of a type reasonably relied upon by experts in a particular field in framing opinions or inferences upon the subject."

EXPERT WITNESSES

- Acceptability of testimony tends to be greater if "the expert acknowledges the questionable reliability of the underlying information, thus indicating that he has taken this factor into consideration in forming his opinion" [Judge Becker in Zenith Radio Corp. v. Matsushita Electric Industrial Co.; 505 F. Supp. 1313 (E.D. Pa 1980)].
- Make certain that the expert does not exceed his or her expertise as acquired through practical experience, scientific study, training, or research.
- The expert should be informative and able to make jargon comprehensible and meaningful to a layman if (s)he is to be persuasive.
- When not based upon facts in his own knowledge or upon his own personal observation, the expert witness should base the opinion upon facts testified to at the trial which, for the purposes of the expert's testimony, are assumed to be true [Carlton v. Bielling (Fla. App.) 146 So. 2d 915].

RECOMMENDED PROTOCOL BASED ON A REVIEW OF ADMINISTRATIVE PROCEEDINGS

- Designate relevant data and utilize it for modeling before refining the estimation with other data
  - This ensures that the model is not dismissed due to the data
  - Subsequent proceedings would be simplified
- Objections should be accompanied by calculations
  - To enable decision makers to appraise their importance
  - To demonstrate a superior analysis that effectively quantifies speculation
- Decision makers should select the model that most usefully describes data rather than judgmentally combining models
- A finding based on raw data cannot be more precise than a finding based on a model of that data

Adapted from: *American Jurisprudence* (1967)
American Jurisprudence Proof of Facts (1965 and 1977)
Baldus and Cole (1980)
Finkelstein (1973)
Zoeller (1982)

In such a setting, the CPA could be called upon as a skilled witness to make observations and testify as to what he or she has observed and how conclusions were drawn in applying the technique. In addition, the CPA firm is likely to have an expert witness whose job it is to view the facts stated by the CPA and to state an opinion based on such facts. For example, the expert may be called upon to support the statistical application in more technical terms and to confirm that the method employed by the CPA was appropriate. Figure 1 describes some useful qualities of an expert witness and some effective approaches to presenting testimony.

As noted earlier, regression testimony has been accepted in administrative proceedings, and these applications have been reviewed by Finkelstein (1973). Based on his review, four "protocols" as to how regression model building should proceed, how cross-examinations should be documented, and what types of decisions would be reasonable by fact finders in such hearings were developed. These are listed in Figure 1 and correlate well with the inferences drawn from the five in-depth analyses of court cases presented earlier.

Legal Proof

One of two key legal problems which appear most relevant to considering the CPA's use of regression analysis concerns the requirements of legal proof.

In accepting testimony, certain requirements of legal proof can be expected to influence the evidentiary force of an auditor's application of regression as an evidence-gathering technique. The auditor will be the party applying the technique, in a role similar to the actuary's role as the user of regression analysis; there will not merely be an expert witness presenting post-facto support for one side of an issue. The hearsay rule suggests that whenever the auditor has applied regression analysis as an audit tool, he or she will be expected to testify concerning that regression application. This is due to the hearsay rule's emphasis that a witness be "required to speak as to his own knowledge" (Chamberlayne, 1919, p. 672). This puts the witness under oath, subject to the penalty for perjury, and facilitates cross-examination by the adversary (Morgan, 1948). When this rule is combined with the observed actions by courts to dismiss evidence that is not clearly presented, an audit implication arises: if auditors are to apply regression in the field, they must be trained not only in its use and analysis, but also in its "proper interpretation" and in those statistical criteria that are built into the regression time-sharing package utilized in an audit. While detailed knowledge of the statistics is not required, an intuitive understanding of and ability to explain the nature of regression analysis, potential applications, and the technique's weaknesses are essential.

A second relevant aspect of legal proof is known as the "falsus in uno, falsus in omnibus doctrine"; or, in other words, a witness's entire testimony can be dismissed if it is found to be untrue in a single instance. The auditor, aware of this tendency of the courts, can prepare acceptable audit evidence by meticulously documenting his chain of statistical inferences so that a third party could complete an identical analysis if desired. In addition, the auditor can be warned to distinguish between correlation, or that form of evidence provided by the regression tool, and causality, that attribute that can only be inferred from additional audit investigation.

> Any statistical method of examining data can provide information about certain characteristics of a defendant's business, but it may not disclose the causes of those characteristics [Finkelstein, 1966 — cited by Joseph, 1975].

Regression offers a directing tool to the auditor, as well as a tool to check the reasonableness of client explanations for business fluctuations. However, investigation of outliers will be an important part of the audit process to augment the statistical evidence presented. The courts have recognized the correlation/causality distinction:

> [I]t is statistically true that there have been no forest fires on Manhattan Island since the "Smokey the Bear" advertisements have been displayed in New York subways. However, it is not commonly accepted that this statistic proves the value of advertising [Louis v. Pennsylvania Indus. Dev. Auth., 371 F. Supp. 877, 885 n. 14 (E.D. Pa 1974) cert. denied, 420 U.S. 993 (1974)].

The auditor must similarly recognize this distinction — both in applying the tool and in presenting audit evidence in a court of law, if he or she wishes the testimony to be given legal weight.

A basic understanding of issues relevant to a user of the regression tool, and knowledge of when a concern raised in court should be directed to the statistical expert witness for the firm, can prevent the dismissal of regression-based evidence which might occur if the credibility of the auditor were to be lost in cross-examination. Legal proof is subject to double scrutiny (see Zeisel, 1968, p. 248). The initial acceptance of regression analysis as a relevant, acceptable, and scientific data-analysis technique can be supported by past legal cases, but the ability of regression to stand up against that second level of scrutiny — cross-examination — depends entirely on the auditor's working paper documentation and ability to assume some witness responsibilities, and on the availability of an expert witness who is capable of responding to highly technical statistical questions that arise.

Any imaginable statistical presentation, being fundamentally empirical, is going to depend upon data which are subject to criticisms which a skillful opponent can blow up extravagantly [Dawson, 1976, p. 899].

It is imperative that a witness be sufficiently knowledgeable to preclude such exaggerations from being successful. Otherwise, regression assumptions can be "statistical mine fields" in a court of law [Jones v. New York City Human Resources Administration, 391 F. Supp. 1064, 1072 (S.D.N.Y. 1975)]. The courts have demonstrated a willingness to rely on experts in the interpretation of statistical analysis [see *Harvard Law Review*, 1975, p. 419 for citations].

The experts' experience in presenting regression evidence in discrimination cases and in agency proceedings can be evaluated to formulate useful regression model-building techniques that address the legal jeopardies that can exist as an attorney cross-examines the CPA and/or statistical expert on the plausible effects of the various "threats" reported in Figure 1. An effective means of gaining some appreciation of why particular regression model-building approaches are useful in the courtroom is to review the relative advantages and disadvantages (or limitations) of regression analysis. Figure 2 summarizes the frequently cited strengths and weaknesses of the regression tool and then proceeds to summarize model-building and model-presentation recommendations.

Legal Uncertainty

The second key legal problem that appears relevant to considering the CPA's use of regression analysis is the legal uncertainty problem. This refers to the fact that some uncertainties relevant to the application of a statistical tool are likely to be de-

FIGURE 2
A Critique of the Regression Tool and Recommendations
for Model Building and Model Presentation

ADVANTAGES OF REGRESSION ANALYSIS

The analysis can be used to support other statistical analyses that are simpler, such as average and range computations or past observations [see Cargill, Inc. v. Hardin, 452 F.2d 1154, 1168-69 (8th Cir. 1971), cert. denied, 406 U.S. 932 (1972)].

Several variables can be handled simultaneously without an unduly large sample, providing an overall measure of an effect after other factors are accounted for.

Regression coefficients can be evaluated to determine the relative weights of various factors.

Regression coefficients can be compared to general knowledge to evaluate their reasonableness and validity.

Explanatory variables can be either dichotomous or interval-scaled.

A prediction is formulated as to what the value of a particular variable of interest would be if values similar to those used in estimating the regression model were observed as explanatory variable values.

The availability of time-series and cross-sectional techniques facilitates the performance of both types of modeling to provide mutual confirmation of the statistical findings. In fact, regulatory agencies have noted that such an approach "goes far . . . to offset the criticisms leveled against each of the studies separately" [Domestic Passenger Fare Investigation Phase 7, No. 21866-7 (C.A.B., Apr. 9, 1971)].

LIMITATIONS & DISADVANTAGES OF REGRESSION ANALYSIS

The technique is not as direct or intuitive as simple descriptive statistics.

As an evidentiary tool, regression models cannot conclusively prove anything; they can only describe statistical relationships which, when combined with other relevant findings, can be available for descriptive and causal inferences (inferences are easiest to make when no relationship is revealed; i.e., disconfirming evidence is intuitively strong).

Models can be deceptive, since the chance always exists that some legitimate variable excluded from the model, but highly correlated with the selected explanatory variable, was, in fact, the causal factor. Causal theory is the key; explanatory power and numbers alone are not enough to resolve this potential proxy effect.

Assumptions are subtle and mathematically based; the holding of assumptions is not obvious merely from looking at the regression results, yet it's imperative to the accuracy of estimates.

The effect of deviations from underlying assumptions on the reliability of models is not always clear.

The relevant range must be explicitly considered, as estimations using explanatory variable values outside of the relevant range are expected to have greater error.

As models get more complex, the economic theory involved is likely to become more debatable, leading to rejection of the statistical model. The result is frequently the acceptance of a simpler regression, while a multiple regression relationship is played down as being less useful [Southern Louisiana Area Rate Cases, 428 F.2d 407, 436 n. 91 (5th Cir.), cert. denied, 400 U.S. 950 (1970)].

FIGURE 2 (Continued)

Model-Building and Model-Presentation Recommendations

Since no model in the social sciences will meet all requirements for the "perfect regression," all models tend to be vulnerable to criticisms.

- Focus on comparative test results of alternative models rather than on theoretical arguments.
  — Evaluate plausibility of alternative causal theories.
  — Evaluate the inherent plausibility of the selected model.
  — The consistency of results across models simplifies the interpretation of the relationship, whereas inconsistent results pose a proxy question.

The objective is to identify the model that "fits" the data best, yet avoids overfitting.

- Stepwise regression analysis should assume no more than a supporting role, due to multicollinearity problems.

Utilize restraint in selecting variables to avoid multicollinearity and the overfitting of data; select variables on substantive and legal grounds. Analyze the theoretical foundation of cause and effect.

A Critique of the Regression Tool and Recommendations for Model Building and Model Presentation

- Start with a simple regression model reflecting an intuitive understanding, and use the model as a benchmark in evaluating subsequent runs that control for other relevant variables.
- Build up one at a time; since it's technically possible to increase the significance of a variable by including another variable, it is best to demonstrate significance in smaller models, too.

Utilize both correlation coefficients and regression coefficients in evaluating relationships, as well as scatter diagrams. While correlation coefficients measure the consistency of the relationship between variables, and the overlap in average values of the quantity being described for high and low values of the descriptor or explanatory variable(s), no quantitative measure of the units of change in one variable, associated with increases in the other variable, is provided. This latter measure is obtained from regression coefficients. The scatter diagram helps to illustrate that the underlying assumptions of regression analysis are met, as well as to highlight the extent to which data overlap and cluster with respect to various measurements. The square of the correlation coefficient measures the percentage of the total variation in the variable being modeled that is explained by changes in the characteristic being used as an explanatory variable.

Most courts have followed the conventions of social science which set .05 as that level of significance below which chance explanations become suspect. An example of reliance on this absolute standard is provided in Pennsylvania v. O'Neill [473 F.2d 1029, 1030-31 (3rd Cir. 1973)]. Other cases have used "p-values" in evaluating significance [e.g., Dendy v. Washington Hosp. Center, 581 F.2d 990, 991 (D.C. Cir. 1978)]. The so-called Castaneda or Hazelwood "two or three standard-deviation" rule basically holds that if a large sample is available, the expected and observed values are significantly different if they are more than two to three standard deviations apart. [See Castaneda v. Partida, 430 U.S. 482, 496 n. 17 (1977), 97 S. Ct. 1272, 1281 n. 17 (1977), and the further development in Hazelwood School District v. United States, 433 U.S. 299, 308, 311 ns. 14 and 17, 97 S. Ct. 2736, 2742-43 ns. 14 and 17 (1977)].

FIGURE 2 (Continued)

However, the level of significance adopted by a court will be influenced by the costs and benefits of the possible errors and their trade-offs. The Supreme Court explicitly considered Type I (chance of saying something is wrong when it's right) and Type II (chance of saying something is right when it's wrong) errors in the context of a criminal conviction in Ballew v. Georgia [435 U.S. 223, 234, 98 S.Ct. 1029, 1036 (1978)]. Both practical and statistical significance are relevant [see Boston Chapter, N.A.A.C.P. v. Beecher, 504 F.2d 1017, 1024 n. 13 (1st Cir. 1974) cert. denied 421 U.S. 910 (1975)]. These benchmarks should be considered in evaluating statistical results.

Court findings will rest on all evidence in the case. Hence, small sample sizes can be supported from collateral and qualitative evidence. Of course, inconsistency with collateral information may convince a fact finder that statistical results are a coincidence.

Confidence intervals have been used in court [see Green v. Missouri Pacific R.R. Co., 523 F.2d 1290, 1294 (8th Cir. 1975), and Ensley Branch, N.A.A.C.P. v. Seibels, 14 F.E.P., 670, 681-682 (N.D. Ala. 1977)]. These can be effective measures in communicating the effect of chance and sampling error on regression estimates.

NOTE: This figure was largely adapted from Baldus and Cole (1980), Finkelstein (1973), and a review of court cases involving regression analysis as a form of statistical evidence.

---

cided only in the very trial for which the evidence is prepared. For example, is the regression model applicable only to a particular division of a company, or does it similarly apply to the total company's account balances? The proper way of solving such a problem is to *sample* from both levels of financial data and tabulate the results for each separately. The other type of uncertainty of interest to an auditor concerns the level of precision at which the statistical "answers" will be relevant. It is popular to contest that:

(1) the sample is not large enough to permit any reliable conclusion,
(2) there are not enough cases to add up to any significance, or
(3) the statistics themselves are biased [Joseph, 1975, p. 888 — see this reference for court citations].

Often a precise answer comes at the price of some contamination and even pos-

sible bias — such as the building of a regression model that uses current unaudited accounting data as explanatory variables. It is essential that the auditor test for such contamination and bias (e.g., through alternative auditing procedures, including the testing of correlations between internally and externally generated data) as a means of lending credibility to the precision levels obtained. Correlation coefficients have been effectively presented in court to test validation [United States v. City of Chicago, 549 F.2d 415, 430 (7th Cir. 1977), cert. denied 434 U.S. 875 (1977)]. One court concluded: "Statistical doubt is cast on the test's validity by its failure to correlate at all with any of the subjective ratings or with the overall objective ratings" [Boston Chapter N.A.A.C.P. v. Beecher, 504 F.2d 1017, 1024 n. 12 (1st Cir. 1974) cert. denied, 421 U.S. 910 (1975)].

Further, a precision definition by the auditor which reflects his materiality judgment, while still subject to the review of the court, is likely to be an acceptable criterion for utilizing evidence from a regression analysis. The auditor must remember the distinction between legal significance and statistical significance; however, the few cases that have addressed the concept of significance have employed statistical theory. [See Albermarle Paper Co. v. Moody, 422 U.S. 405, 430-431, 437 (1975), which focuses on a .05 level of significance.] Of particular interest is the court's acceptance of the statement that "the 95 percent level of confidence was the one ordinarily used by practicing statisticians" as a justification of the confidence level utilized in statistical analyses in the absence of any strong reason for preferring a more or a less stringent level [Katz, 1975].

> Examples of concepts already fully embraced by courts include measuring standard deviation, analyzing sample size, testing hypotheses by 95 percent confidence intervals, and determining how large a statistical disparity is judicially cognizable [see *Harvard Law Review*, 1975, p. 416 for citations].

A distinction also exists between practical significance (a magnitude consideration that depends on substantive legal issues, value judgments, and related costs of Type I versus Type II errors) and statistical significance [Boston Chapter N.A.A.C.P. v. Beecher, 504 F.2d 1017, 1024 n. 13 (1st Cir. 1974), cert. denied 421 U.S. 910 (1975)].

> Whether (statistical) evidence is convincing enough to require the burden of persuasion to shift will thus depend on judicial estimates of probability . . . . Judges are faced with the problem of drawing a line between what is a significant disparity and what is an insignificant disparity. They will frequently (compare to) . . . selections . . . made randomly [Joseph, 1975, p. 890]. It is certainly possible to provide statistical evidence and to

provide such a case that "the mind of justice, not merely its eyes, would have to be blind to attribute such an occurrence to mere fortuity" [Avery v. Georgia, 345 U.S., 559, 564 (1953)].

As suggested by the court cases reviewed herein, regression analysis is not a new source of evidence, nor is it dissimilar from other statistical evidence in its general acceptability by the courts (probabilistic testimony in the U.S. dates back to 1868 and is now generally accepted in civil cases, with slight inroads to criminal cases [see Van Matre and Clark, 1976 and Randall and Frishkoff, 1976]). It is apparent that statistical evidence is playing a growing role in litigation. (Not surprisingly, given that legislation, such as 31 U.S.C. 826-1 [1964], permits the use of statistical sampling in the examination of vouchers for governmental expenditures; statistics has become a matter of law.)

A further concern of the auditor focuses on the differences between jury trials and rulings by a judge or agency. The earliest general acceptance of statistical evidence was observed in proceedings before administrative agencies, in antitrust cases, and in surveys of what the law calls the "state of mind" of the witness — often involving consumer awareness, trademark disputes, and cases centering on misleading or false advertising. The implication is that statistical evidence in a nonjury setting is probably more readily accepted. One explanation that is commonly offered is that attorneys have well-established patterns of thought which can be exploited to the advantage of an expert witness. Another explanation is that the judge can cross-examine the witnesses until a clear understanding of the regression technique is obtained, easing the possible problem with communicating sophisticated statistical analyses.

Jurors may be impressed with the mystique of mathematical demonstrations but may be unable to assess their relevance [Joseph, 1975, p. 893].

Hence, in explaining and responding to statistical evidence, the auditor must be wary of incomplete documentation and explanations in the working papers and in oral testimony. However, statistical evidence has been successfully introduced in an ample number of jury cases [see Katz, 1975 and Van Matre and Clark, 1976 for several examples].

Based on the court cases reviewed herein and those discussed in the literature, in either setting the CPA and/or expert witness on statistics will need to devote a considerable amount of time and effort on the witness stand to explaining, in terms comprehensible to attorneys, judges, *and jury members*, the procedures used and the conclusions drawn. Some similar witness responsibilities are likely to be placed upon the auditor, since any regression testimony will involve the application of the tool by the "typical professional auditor." The perspective is analogous to Texas Instruments v. U.S., in which the firm applied regression analyses in its estimation of pension funds. The importance of the CPA's witness responsibilities is probably heightened in a jury trial, in which confusion regarding methodology is more likely to occur, as a function of the number of people involved.

More variation can be expected in the jurists' tendency to rely on a particular expert witness. As a consequence, the auditor will require training in the appropriate audit settings for applying regression, the weaknesses of the technique being applied, and the "proper" interpretation of results. The individual auditor's testimony is likely to be relied upon to an extent similar to that of the statistical expert on such issues.

The courtroom experience of statistical methodology as means of contributing materially to shortening the trials of complex cases has encouraged acceptance of such evidence. As universities provide training for future lawyers involving enough statistics and probabilities to enable them to be better informed and, therefore, more knowledgeable and appreciative of statistical evaluations, the frequency with which the nonacceptance of regression analysis is observed due to complexity of testimony (e.g., Kyriazi v. Western Electric Co.) will substantially decline. However, it can be expected that:

The weight to be accorded the statistics [will] vary. Much [will] depend on the correctness, completeness and comprehensiveness of the figures presented [Joseph, 1975, p. 889].

Just as the "Best Evidence Rule" combined with the "Eminently Reasonable Rule" permits summaries of documents to carry evidentiary force (see Sawyer, 1967), the potential of regression analysis as courtroom evidence, particularly when raw data are made accessible to third parties who wish to review field applications, should be substantial.

CONCLUSION

Regression analysis has been recommended and used by CPAs in performing an audit but has not yet been tested in court. Its defensibility has been questioned by practitioners interested in but somewhat hesitant to implement the tool introduced in the academic literature as a useful auditing technique. In the litigious environment of audit practice, this "gun-shy" attitude is not surprising. However, evidence exists that courts have not only accepted testimony which relies on regression models, but have attributed substantial evidentiary

force to such models and their implications. The critical question, "Does the incorrect use of regression analysis expand
liability relative to no use of regression
analysis?" in the audit setting remains to
be tested.

As is true of statistical sampling, the incorrect use of regression analysis clearly
makes the auditor vulnerable (Copeland
and Englebrecht, 1975). However, if the
technique is clearly explained in submitting
testimony, if the rationale for the selection
of variables is included in the working
papers, and if violations of assumptions,
such as linearity, are investigated, past
court cases suggest that the application of
regression to the audit will be considered
not only a valid, but a worthwhile and, in
fact, preferred approach to performing an
examination. A synopsis of the implica-

tions for auditors who use regression,
based upon the cases and legal literature
that have been reviewed, is presented in
Figure 3. The potential formalization of
analytical review through the use of regression analysis will provide the auditor with a
quantitative basis of defense. It is expected
that such a quantitative basis will reduce
vulnerability to legal liability claims. In
fact, the review of court cases involving the
application of regression analysis established legal support for both the acceptability of the statistical tool in a court of
law and the courts' preference for statistical evidence relative to nonstatistical evidence. Statistical methods of decision
making and of evaluation of evidence in
circumstances involving uncertainty can be
expected to be both appealing and convincing to legal professionals.

FIGURE 3
Implications for the Auditor

- Meticulously document the chain of statistical inferences in a regression application — the recorded details in the working papers of a regression procedure should facilitate completion of an identical analysis by a third party.

  Specifically document:

  (1) the relevant population and time frame for the data sampled in the regression analysis (when considered necessary, document tests of reasonableness of the data selected, e.g., a comparison of regression results obtained when a division's data are utilized with those results obtained when company-level data are analyzed);
  (2) the adequacy of sample size;
  (3) the rationale for the selection of variables;
  (4) consideration of possible "omitted variables" with the rationale for not including such desired measures — e.g., cost/benefit issues, no available measure of desired variable, or unreliable data;
  (5) why a level of precision other than 95 percent is used; and
  (6) the investigation of potential violations of the underlying assumptions of regression.

- Some witness responsibilities are likely to be placed on the auditor, implying the auditor must be trained in:
  — the appropriate audit settings for applying regression,
  — the weaknesses of the technique being applied,
  — the "proper" interpretation of results,
  — and those statistical criteria built into the regression time-sharing package about which *detailed* knowledge of the individual auditor is not required.

- In explaining and responding to statistical evidence, the auditor must be wary of incomplete documentation and explanations in the working papers and in oral testimony. The auditor should appropriately qualify evidence according to the results of the investigation of underlying assumptions of a given model.

- Have an expert witness available who is capable of responding to highly technical questions and who is able to explain clearly the regression technique.

REFERENCES

Akresh, Abraham D. and Wanda A. Wallace, "The Application of Regression Analysis for Limited Review and Audit Planning," *Fourth Symposium on Auditing Research* (University of Illinois at Urbana-Champaign, 1982), pp. 67-128; 147-161.

Albrecht, William Steve and James C. McKeown, "Toward an Extended Use of Statistical Analytical Reviews in the Audit," *Symposium on Auditing Research II* (University of Illinois, 1977), pp. 53-69.

American Jurisprudence, 2d edition, State & Federal, Volume 31, "Expert and Opinion Evidence" (Rochester, New York: The Lawyers Cooperative Publishing Co., 1967), pp. 487-758.

American Jurisprudence Proof of Facts, Volume 16, 273, §14, 15, 16, and 28 (1965); 2d edition, Volume 14, 173, §8, 9, 18, and 36 (1977).

Baldus, David C. and James W.L. Cole, *Statistical Proof of Discrimination* (New York: McGraw-Hill Book Company, Inc., 1980).

Brigham, Eugene F. and Roy L. Crum, "Reply to Comments on Use of CAPM in Public Utility Rate Cases," *Financial Management* (Autumn, 1978), pp. 72-76.

Chamberlayne, Charles Frederick, *Handbook on the Law of Evidence* (New York: Matthew Bender & Company, Inc., 1919).

Copeland, Ronald M. and Ted D. Englebrecht, "Statistical Sampling — An Uncertain Defense Against Legal Liability," *The CPA Journal* (November, 1975), pp. 23-27.

Dawson, John M., "Probabilities and Prejudice in Establishing Statistical Inferences," *Jurimetrics* (Summer, 1973), pp. 196-199.

_____, "Scientific Investigation of Fact — The Role of the Statistician," *The Forum* (Chicago: Spring, 1976), pp. 896-917.

Deakin, Edward B. and Michael H. Granof, "Directing Audit Effort Using Regression Analysis," *The CPA Journal* (February, 1976), pp. 29-33.

Finkelstein, Michael O., "Regression Models in Administrative Proceedings," *Harvard Law Review* (Vol. 86, 1973), pp. 1442-1475.

Greenberg, Ronald David, "Quantitative Aspects of Legal Analysis," *The Insurance Law Journal* (October, 1976), pp. 589-607.

Hallock, Marcy M., "The Numbers Game — The Use and Misuse of Statistics in Civil Rights Litigation," *Villanova Law Review* (November, 1977), pp. 5-34.

Harvard Law Review (Note), "Beyond the Prima Facie Case in Employment Discrimination Law: Statistical Proof and Rebuttal," Vol. 89:356 (December, 1975), pp. 387-422.

Joseph, Michael E., "Evidence: Statistical Proof in Employment Discrimination Case," *Oklahoma Law Review* (Vol. 28, 1975), pp. 885-894.

Katz, Leo, "Presentation of a Confidence Interval Estimate as Evidence in a Legal Proceeding," *The American Statistician* (November, 1975), pp. 138-142.

Kinney, William R., Jr., "ARIMA and Regression in Analytical Review: An Empirical Test," *The Accounting Review* (January, 1978), pp. 48-60.

_____ and Gerald L. Salamon, "The Effect of Measurement Error on Regression Results in Analytical Review," *Symposium on Auditing Research III* (University of Illinois: The Board of Trustees, 1979), pp. 49-64.

Morgan, Edmund M., "Hearsay Dangers and the Application of the Hearsay Concept," *Harvard Law Review* (December, 1948), pp. 177-219.

Randall, Boyd and Paul Frishkoff, "An Examination of the Status of Probability Sampling in the Courts," *Auditing Symposium III* (University of Kansas, May 13-14, 1976), pp. 83-102.

Robichek, Alexander A., "Regulation and Modern Finance Theory," *The Journal of Finance* (June, 1978), p. 703.

Sawyer, L.B., "The Lawyer, the Statistician, and the Internal Auditor," *The Internal Auditor* (Summer, 1967), pp. 9-18.

Stringer, Ken W., "A Statistical Technique for Analytical Review," *Supplement to the Journal of Accounting Research* (1975), pp. 1-9.

Tummins, Marvin and Hugh J. Watson, "Advantages of Regression Analysis Over Ratio Analysis," *The CPA Journal* (May, 1975), pp. 35-38.

Van Matre, Joseph G. and William N. Clark, "The Statistician as Expert Witness," *The American Statistician* (February, 1976), pp. 2-5.

Wallace, Wanda A., "Discussant's Response to 'The Effect of Measurement Error on Regression Results in Analytical Review,'" *Symposium on Auditing Research III* (University of Illinois: The Board of Trustees, 1979), pp. 70-81.

_____, "Analytical Review: Misconceptions, Applications and Experience — Part I & Part II," *The CPA Journal* (January 1983), pp. 24-37, and forthcoming in February, 1983.

Whitten, David, "Statistics and Title VII Proof: Prima Facie Case and Rebuttal," *Houston Law Review* (May, 1978), pp. 1030-1053.

Wolf, Benjamin S., "The Role of Statistical Evidence in Title VII Cases," *Boston College Law Review* (July, 1978), pp. 881-898.

Zeisel, Hans, "Statistics as Legal Evidence," *International Encyclopedia,* Vol. 15 (New York: Crowell Collies & MacMillan, 1968), pp. 246-250.

Zoeller, Donald J., "The Economics Expert: An Expanding Role in Antitrust Litigation," *The National Law Journal* (July 19, 1982), pp. 15-18.

Source: Wanda A. Wallace, "The Acceptability of Regression Analysis as Evidence in a Courtroom—Implications for the Auditor," *Auditing: A Journal of Practice & Theory* (Vol. 2, No. 2, Spring 1988), pp. 66–89.

20

Overview, Challenges for the Future, and Unanswered Questions

"The most successful businessman is the man who holds onto the old just as long as it is good, and grabs the new just as soon as it is better."

Robert P. Vanderpeol[1]

Knowing when change is appropriate and represents an improvement is a critical skill in conducting any economic enterprise. This *Handbook* intentionally retains key concepts and approaches proven to be useful in its first edition, but expands beyond that framework to integrate developments in a broad cross-section of regulation, practice, and research that suggest a need for change. One of the most visible changes from a public accounting vantage point relates to SAS No. 55, which was met during its development by a number of criticisms, while being championed by others.

---

[1] *The Executive's Quotation Book: A Corporate Companion*, Edited by James Charlton (New York: St. Martin's Press, 1983), p. 22. Copyright © 1983 by James Charlton. Reprinted with special permission from St. Martin's Press, Inc., New York, N.Y.

To provide some insights as to the likelihood that this is one aspect of practice that the creator of those words recounted as the introductory quote might suggest be "grabbed" as "better," Exhibit 20–1 reprints a thoughtful essay by the then Chairman of the Auditing Standards Board. Many ideas discussed are controversial. I would disagree, for example, with the extent to which Mr. Sullivan suggests that sampling is inapplicable to today's technological setting when one considers tests of control. Yet, the point he raises which addresses a paramount

---

Exhibit 20–1

A NEW WAY OF THINKING ABOUT THE AUDITOR'S STUDY AND EVALUATION OF INTERNAL CONTROL

by
Jerry D. Sullivan
Director of Audit Policy
Coopers & Lybrand
Chairman, Auditing Standards Board
Before the Auditing Section of the
American Accounting Association
Annual Luncheon
August 17, 1987 - Cincinnati

If I were speaking to this group in ordinary times as Chairman of the ASB, I would probably think it appropriate to talk about such matters as the role of research in setting auditing standards, my long-range goals for the ASB, areas of practice where authoritative guidance was needed, and board activities over the past year.

And if I were speaking to my fellow practitioners, to corporate managers or directors, or, as has increasingly been the case these days, to legislators and regulators, I would surely be speaking about:

- First, the exposure drafts of 10 new auditing and attestation standards the ASB issued last February, the dramatic effects they will have on auditors' responsibilities, and what has occurred since the end of the exposure period;
- Second, the draft Report of the Treadway Commission on Fraudulent Financial Reporting issued in June, and how it would directly and indirectly affect auditors' responsibilities; and
- Third, the work of the Dingell Committee and my prognosis for its likely impact on auditing standards and auditors' responsibilities.

I have the distinct impression, however, that the single action that has provoked the most controversy and the greatest interest in academic circles has been the ASB's proposal of a wholesale revision of Auditing Standards Section 320 on *The Auditor's Study and Evaluation of Internal Control*. I view this exposure draft, entitled *The Auditor's Responsibility for Assessing Control Risk*, to be the most important of the proposed new standards and the "link document" to many of the other exposure drafts.

I would like to focus on what this exposure draft does and does not require of the auditor, the tenor of

Exhibit 20–1 (continued)

INTERNAL CONTROL (continued)

the comments the Board has received to date — particularly those from the academic community — and my own personal reaction to those comments, which I hope is not significantly at variance with the views of the majority of the Board. I know that this is a highly controversial and emotionally charged issue. While I and other Board members have definite views on each of the major issues, our minds are not closed, and we're willing to listen, respond, and learn from you.

In terms of a broad overview, the proposed Statement was issued with two objectives in mind:

(1) To emphasize the importance of internal control to audit planning by broadening the auditor's responsibility in that area.

(2) To clarify and bring up to date the guidance on the auditor's study and evaluation of internal control by incorporating the concepts concerning audit evidence and audit risk that have evolved in practice and have been established in auditing standards issued subsequent to Section 320, namely, SAS 31 on evidential matter and SAS 47 on audit risk and materiality.

The proposed Statement replaces the concept of internal control in Section 320 with the broader concept of the control structure. The control structure consists of three elements: (1) the control environment, (2) accounting systems, and (3) control procedures.

The concept of the control structure recognizes that components of each of these three elements may be relevant to an entity's ability to record, process, summarize, and report financial data consistent with management's assertions in the financial statements. Consequently, they each provide a form of control that may be relevant in an audit. This concept precludes the need for the artificial and sometimes confusing distinction between administrative and accounting controls used in Section 320 in identifying controls relevant in an audit.

The proposed Statement unifies these three elements into a single concept and provides an expanded discussion of the characteristics of each of them. It also includes the notion that the accounting system is part of the control structure. While Section 320 discusses the control environment and accounting systems, it provides only limited guidance about why the auditor considers them, and focuses almost entirely on control procedures. The discussion of the control environment in Section 320 is so skimpy that it is not referred to in the topical index to the codification. Moreover, Section 320 does not require any understanding of control procedures for audit planning purposes unless the auditor intends to rely on them.

The proposed Statement requires the auditor to obtain an understanding of *each* of the three elements of the control structure sufficient to plan the examination, including such audit planning considerations as the auditability of the financial statements, the causes of potential material misstatements in financial statements and the risk that such misstatements will occur, the design of tests of financial statement balances, and the determination of the appropriate detection risk for financial statement assertions. The Statement provides guidance to the auditor in determining the extent of understanding of each element

that is necessary for audit planning, as well as the procedures to perform to obtain that understanding. The Statement provides similar guidance when the auditor extends the assessment of control risk in the expectation of obtaining support for a conclusion that control risk is low for particular financial statement assertions.

SAS 47, *Audit Risk and Materiality in Conducting an Audit*, defined control risk and established the auditor's basic responsibility for assessing it. The proposed Statement replaces the concept of the study and evaluation of internal control with the SAS 47 concept of assessing control risk. In addition, in what I think should be a help to both textbook writers and students, the proposed Statement discusses the control structure in relation to the auditor's responsibility for assessing control risk for financial statement assertions. This responsibility is similar to the responsibility discussed in Section 320 concerning the study and evaluation of internal control to determine if there is a basis for reliance on controls, but it is couched in terms that reflect the emphasis in SAS 31 on management's assertions.

Section 320 does not require the auditor to study and evaluate specific internal controls to determine whether they can be relied on. Similarly, the proposed Statement does not require the auditor to assess control risk for control structure elements specifically to determine if that risk is less than 100 percent. It does, however, require the auditor to consider the extent of understanding of control structure elements that is necessary for audit planning. That understanding may provide a basis for concluding that control risk is limited for some financial statement assertions.

For the first time, the literature would recognize what I think is often true in practice, namely, that an auditor may use information about an entity's control structure obtained in prior examinations in determining the scope of control structure work necessary for the current examination. And, in what is surely one of the most controversial aspects of the SAS, it acknowledges that an auditor's conclusion about the level of control risk for a financial statement assertion may be low enough to preclude the need for any tests of financial statement balances to restrict detection risk for that assertion.

Largely because of SAS 31 and 47, the Statement clarifies and updates terminology, such as substituting "control structure" for "internal control system," "assessing control risk" for "study and evaluation of internal control," "conclusion about the level of control risk" for "reliance on internal control" (which recognizes that reliance need not be an on-off switch but could take place along a continuum), and "control structure elements relevant to financial statement assertions" for the terms "accounting controls" and "administrative controls." More importantly, the exposure draft does not use the terms "compliance tests" and "substantive tests," substituting "control risk assessment procedures" and "tests of financial statement balances," respectively.

Now let me turn to the reactions of the exposure draft. Many of the comments clearly indicate that — substantive issues aside — as it is written, this is a very complex document and is very difficult to understand. In developing it, the Board members became so comfortable with the concepts that had been discussed over

Exhibit 20–1 (continued)

a two-year period that we lost sight of the fact that those who had not shared in our discussions would find certain areas of the draft did not contain sufficient explanations, which could lead to misinterpretations.

Turning to substantive issues raised by commentators — and so many specific points and so many variations on a particular theme were raised that I can cover only what I believe are the major, threshold issues — I would like to address three broad concerns that we have been hearing.

The first is the misperception that the Board's approach to assessing control risk creates opportunities for the auditor to accept weak evidence as support for audit planning judgments. In particular, some believe that the Statement weakens the evidence needed to support a reduced assessment of control risk in the following ways:
- It will lead to "conversational auditing" in the form of casual "walk-throughs" that follow one or two transactions through the accounting system.
- It allows for a restriction of tests of account balances based on "soft" evidence about the control environment.
- It allows the auditor to reduce his control risk assessment based on the preliminary understanding.
- It allows evidence gathered in prior years to influence the control risk assessment.

Let me consider each of these thoughts. As to the notion of the walk-through being a weak form of evidence, that's simply not true. It's not what the Board intended, and it's not what the SAS says. The concept of a walk-through is relevant only in the context of determining whether particular policies and procedures *have been placed in operation* — as part of obtaining the required minimum understanding of each of the three elements of the control structure necessary to plan the audit. The walk-through concept — and that term is not used in the document nor is it really the appropriate term — is not relevant to determining whether control structure policies and procedures *are operating as prescribed*, that is, in making an extended risk assessment with the intent of being able to support an assessment of control risk as low.

Concerning the client's control environment, about the only thing you can do to understand it is to examine one or a few applications of a particular policy or procedure and observe the related actions and documents. You can't compliance test specific procedures by reperforming them to obtain an understanding of management's and the board's overall attitude, awareness, and actions.

But this does not mean that the auditor obtains the required understanding of the control environment by casual chit-chats with enterprise management. Rather, that understanding involves making judgments based on observing actions and documents — and the SAS says so. The questionnaire that my firm has developed for assessing the control environment, for example, requires the auditor to consider over 60 separate factors on our smallest audit clients — based on evidence, not on "gut feel." The evidence may not be obtained by reperforming management's actions, but it comes from observing the policies and procedures in operation and the actions taken by management, and that's not exactly "soft" evidence.

The criticism that the Statement permits a reduction of control risk based on the preliminary understanding is related to a concern that the exposure draft permits reliance on controls without the performance of compliance tests. In a sense, that's correct. But as stated, it's very misleading. First of all, one doesn't rely or not rely on controls — one assesses risk. And an auditor can assess risk as being something less than 100 percent without performing compliance tests.

Moreover, the original concept of "compliance testing" was never intended to accommodate an evaluation of the control environment or the accounting system. It was originally intended as a means of obtaining evidence about the effective functioning of control procedures, and primarily involved tests of transactions to determine if specific internal accounting control procedures were operating effectively. The concept was later understood to include, where appropriate, inquiry and observation, but it was still directed to control procedures.

Thus, an auditor can in fact understand the control structure sufficiently to plan the audit *and* to assess control risk as less than 100 percent without performing compliance tests of transactions. The auditor can, and does at present, use the evaluation of the control environment and the accounting system to reduce his assessment of control risk. But other types of procedures — such as inquiry and observation, which don't easily lend themselves to audit sampling — are necessary and appropriate to support an understanding of the control environment and the accounting system.

(Incidentally, this is one of the two main reasons that the exposure draft avoided the word "compliance." The other is that many people confused the concepts of compliance testing of controls and compliance audits — that is, audits of compliance with laws, regulations, and controls — which require substantive tests of management's assertions of compliance. As another aside, my guess is that we will restore the term "substantive testing," but not the term "compliance testing.")

Furthermore, I don't believe that the traditional concept of compliance testing of controls over transactions — which generally involves sampling — even has much relevance for evaluating the operation of specific control procedures — not in an age when transactions are processed by computers and not by people.

Just to assure myself on this point, I went back and looked at C&L's internal control questionnaires. We use three different questionnaires, one for each major system, on our larger clients, covering controls over both transactions and files, as well as EDP general controls.

For one significant transaction in one system, the auditor typically considers and documents over 100 pieces of information. All require evidence; all require judgment; and many firms, including mine, have developed or are developing sophisticated audit tools and decision support systems to help us make those judgments. None require reperformance on controls using sampling — the traditional compliance test — although sampling is not precluded, if in the auditor's judgment, based on the design of the control procedures, that's the appropriate way to obtain the necessary evidence that a particular aspect of the control structure is functioning effectively.

Exhibit 20–1 (continued)

For very large enterprises, even if it were possible to apply traditional compliance tests of transactions to the intricate processing of financial information in complex distributed data base systems, which are the types of environments in which extended risk assessments are made today, it just wouldn't be practical. Moreover, it would ignore controls over program security and program changes and maintenance — the very controls that management relies on.

Turning to the issue of using evidence gathered in prior years as part of the risk assessment process, I believe that while this concept is new to the authoritative literature, it is not new to audit practice. I understand that this concept is already imbedded in some firms' auditing manuals, and I believe that all auditors, consciously or not, take prior years' results into account in assessing risk.

In fact, to sum up this entire issue about judgments based on weak evidence, let me express my belief that auditors have always — Section 320 notwithstanding — used their understanding of the control environment and the accounting system and the results of prior years' audits to assess control risk at less than 100 percent. And well they should. What we have, then, is a change in the literature to reflect practice.

The second major concern I want to address is related to the statement in the SAS that "when, in the auditor's judgment, the control risk (together with the inherent risk) for a specific assertion or related audit objective results in an audit risk that is appropriately low, the auditor need not apply any tests of financial statement balances to restrict detection risk for that specific assertion or related audit objective," other than those required by other SASs, such as confirmation of receivables and observation of inventories.

In a word, can there be complete reliance on controls? Some commentators have read the exposure draft that way and have been highly critical, particularly because they see this as a major change from Section 320, and a very undesirable change. It is important to address this issue head-on.

One of the problems is that the existing literature — Section 320 — is unclear on the issue of complete reliance on controls. The auditor is told to not place complete reliance on internal control to the exclusion of other auditing procedures with respect to particular *account balances and classes of transactions*, but the section is silent about complete reliance at the individual assertion and audit objective levels.

I don't think we should read too much into that silence. For example, I don't think we should try to fathom the original intent of the framers of Section 320, simply because the notions of audit assertions and their relation to audit objectives were not explicitly addressed in the literature at that time. I personally read Section 320 as permitting complete reliance on controls for specific assertions related to particular accounts, but that's probably because that's what I think the answer should be.

But no matter. If it's right to permit complete reliance on controls at the individual assertion level, let's get it explicitly into the literature. Section 320 tells us that the fundamental reasons for not permitting complete reliance on controls are the inherent limitations on the effectiveness of accounting control, namely, human er-

ror caused by misunderstanding instructions, mistakes of judgment, carelessness, distraction, or fatigue; collusion; management override of controls; and the ineffectiveness of controls in preventing wrong estimates and judgments that enter into the financial statements.

These are valid points; there are limitations on the effectiveness of controls. But these limitations may be completely irrelevant to achieving a low level of audit risk with respect to certain specific assertions regarding certain specific accounts. Moreover, we should not ignore the facts that substantive tests directed at one assertion frequently provide evidence about other assertions. Is it, then, so hard to imagine complete reliance on *tested* controls for specific assertions? I really don't think so.

The third, and final, issue I want to address is whether we really had to kill Section 320. Why couldn't we have simply amended it where it needed fixing?

Section 320 evolved on a piecemeal basis over the last 35 years. It is a combination of three Statements on Auditing Procedure issued between 1949 and 1972 and was later amended by eight Statements on Auditing Standards. Several other SASs have either introduced or altered major auditing concepts that should have been incorporated into Section 320 but were not. The combination of these factors has created a hodge-podge of professional standards pertaining to the study and evaluation of internal control. Many elements of those standards are inconsistent with current auditing concepts and terms.

No one can deny that there are compelling reasons for merely fixing 320 where it's broken. There's a lot of good stuff in old 320, and perhaps some of that good stuff was lost in the exposure draft. We will be looking closely at this issue. There's no doubt that 320 clearly warned us against the dangers of generalized or overall control evaluations. I believe that the exposure draft's focus on relating specific control structure elements to specific assertions is adequate to prevent the auditor from offsetting or averaging control strengths and-weaknesses, but if the Board feels this needs to be made more explicit, who but a logician would object?

However, I am convinced — as was the Board when the decision was made — that so much of 320 has to go, and so many new concepts and principles have to be added, that is far more appropriate to completely rewrite it than it is to try to patch it up. Just think of what 320 would look like if the 21 paragraphs on definitions were removed. And I must say I just can't imagine trying to integrate the concepts of risk assessment at the assertion level into 320 as it stands today.

How much of Section 320 can be saved is a judgment call. But I promise you that the Board will analyze it and will once again carefully consider whether any portions that were lost in the exposure draft should be restored. But I'm not promising you that you'll be happy with the results, unless you've undertaken a similar analysis.

To sum up: There *have* been many thoughtful responses to the exposure draft. The Board is considering them all carefully and will surely revise the draft to make its intent clearer and to provide more examples. On the basis of discussions at both the Board and task force levels, and because of the interest in the subject

Exhibit 20–1 (continued)

matter by regulators and legislators, however, I believe
that the Board will issue the statement before the end
of this year. Our analysis to date indicates that all the
flaws identified during the exposure process are fixable
— in this document, as well as in the other nine proposed standards.

I want to thank many of you for thoughtful insights
— they will contribute considerably to improving the
final standard.

Source: Jerry D. Sullivan, "A New Way of Thinking About the Auditor's Study and Evaluation of Internal Control," *The Auditor's Report* (Volume 11, Number 1, Fall 1987), pp. 1–5.

role for aspects of the control environment and general controls is extremely consistent with discussions contained throughout this *Handbook*.

This self-regulatory initiative in response to the so-called "Expectations Gap" has developed alongside a number of regulatory initiatives. While many are still in the proposed stage—management reports on controls, potentially with auditor association; interim reporting association; reporting responsibilities directly to regulators—they are directed at ensuring accountability of all of those involved with controls. As an example of the synergy of self-regulation and regulation, consider the topic of interim financial reporting.

An exposure draft under consideration by the Auditing Standards Board would expand the auditor's responsibility for communicating with audit committees to include matters related to interim financial information of regulated entities. This amendment would be applied to all SEC engagements and to financial institutions that report to the Comptroller of the Currency, FDIC, Federal Reserve Bank, and the Office of Thrift Supervision. In specific terms, the proposal would require the auditor to communicate, as soon as he or she becomes aware (through certain specified means) that interim financial information that has been filed or is expected to be filed with the regulatory agency is materially misstated or is likely to be materially misstated. Moreover, the auditor would evaluate whether the audit committee and management had taken appropriate follow-up action upon notification of the likely misstatement.

Reportedly, as a result of findings of the Special Investigations Committee of the SEC Practice Section of the AICPA, the Auditing Standards Board is likewise considering a revision to SAS No. 36 on "Review of Interim Financial Information," including providing guidance on what specific knowledge the accountant should obtain about the client's internal control structure and its accounting and financial reporting practices where no prior audit basis exists.[2]

---

[2] Gary L. Holstrum, "ASB Topics of Importance to Educators and Researchers" (June 10, 1990), printed in *The Auditor's Report* (Summer 1990).

The advent of regulators' attention both within and outside the profession have directed attention to matters of interim reporting which may increase the demand for continuous auditing and increase the central consideration of controls as a vehicle for lending greater credibility to interim reports and disclosures.

As such regulation has increased, some have called for research as a basis for such action; see Exhibit 20–2 for one example. One quote that comes to mind is "All change is not growth, as all movement is not forward." (ANONYMOUS)

Exhibit 20–2

A RESEARCH RESPONSE TO THE DINGELL HEARINGS

by

John J. Willingham, Peat, Marwick, Mitchell & Co.

and

Peter D. Jacobson, Peat, Marwick, Mitchell & Co.

Introduction

All things considered, Representative Dingell's hearings on the accounting profession have thus far attracted relatively little attention among parties outside of the profession and the SEC. Press coverage could have been wider, even discounting the co-incidental and competitive appearance of Margaret Thatcher before Congress on the first day of the hearings. The level of attention may be explained by the pattern of the hearings: two days of witnesses on the profession and the SEC followed by a series of hearings on individual cases (e.g., ESM and Beverly Hills Savings and Loan). Individual cases are less likely to generate charges applicable to the profession as a whole. Whatever the reasons, the hearings do not seem to have riveted the attention of a wide audience. Nevertheless, the hearings should be of interest to audit researchers because they can bring to light worthy research topics and highlight needs for follow-up research in areas already under study.

The hearings in the late 1970's held by Senator Lee Metcalf and Representative John Moss provide a precedent because they led to research. To take just one example, the accusation that accounting and auditing standard setting was controlled by a monolithic set of eight large accounting firms led Marsha Puro (1985) to analyze responses to seven FASB exposure drafts. She found that the allegation was unsupported by the data and uncovered the fact that "the only group that regularly opposes the position taken by a majority of the Big Eight is the AICPA," an interesting finding because the Metcalf staff had charged that the AICPA was the instrument for Big Eight control of accounting standard setting.

We cite Puro's work not because an allegation hostile to the profession was punctured, but because it was, at least in part, undertaken and pursued to help settle a politically sensitive issue. She doubtless would have reported that the Metcalf allegation was supported by the data had that been the case. However, the implied distinction between disinterested research and politically motivated research raises a subject that should be addressed in an article such as this: Is it appropriate to orient research resources toward politically sensitive subjects?

There are two ways of looking at this question. First, should research be avoided because of its political sensitivity? Second, should research be encouraged because of its political sensitivity? The answer to the first question should be obvious from the academic tradition of pursuing truth. Certainly if research is unbiased and is worthwhile without regard for its potential political consequences, it should always be pursued. The cause of audit research would surely suffer if worthy research subjects are avoided merely because they are politically sensitive. Therefore, if useful research subjects can be identified by analyzing the product of a political process such as the hearings, involvement in politics should not stand in the way of pursuing the research.

The answer to the second question is also "yes," again assuming the research is unbiased. Researchers can perform a public service by shedding light on politically controversial issues. Such research can contribute to more orderly and constructive dialogue among practitioners, regulators, and congressmen. The need for such research is underscored by the limitations of the hearing process. Testimony from selected witnesses too often produces a clash of unsupported opinions. Even a consensus of opinions is more likely to be misleading if it is not based on research.

The AAA's commitment to the public-service aspect of audit research is already a part of the hearing records in the form of a letter from President Doyle Z. Williams to Representative Dingell prior to the start of the hearings. President Williams (1985) wrote, "We have an ample supply of able researchers in accounting willing to aid your inquiry in any way possible. Please feel free to call on us." We are not aware of any effort by Dingell's staff to take advantage of the AAA's generous offer, but the same objective can be achieved by research following a post-hearing identification of issues. Moreover, this retrospective approach might be more effective because researchers would be freed from time pressures imposed by the subcommittee's agenda.

POTENTIAL RESEARCH TOPICS

Audit Quality

The broadest issue at the hearings has been the

Exhibit 20–2 (continued)

quality of the performance of independent auditors. This issue underlies the debates on the effectiveness of the SEC and self-regulatory institutions. Thus, one cluster of researchable topics centers around the question of how to measure the quality of the auditor's performance. It is easy to discount the glib equivalency between "audit failure" and "business failure" that has too often been voiced at the hearings as a measure of the auditor's performance. The equivalency is incompatible with the wording of the unqualified audit report, has no basis in the securities laws, and has no precedent in the enforcement actions of the SEC. But after the false equivalency has been demolished, the question remains.

Part of the answer lies in determining an appropriate measure of the rate of audit failure. Comparisons of the number of lawsuits alleging audit failure to the number of audits performed are surely relevant and have been cited, but the measure raises as many questions as it answers. The incidence of such allegations does not correlate directly with performance levels. Accounting firms often settle cases because of prospective legal costs and risks to their reputations, factors that may be independent of the quality of the audit. And the number of verdicts against accountants does not necessarily mean that uniform measurement criteria have been applied in reaching verdicts. Moreover, litigated engagements that are apparently identified as audit failures may exclude unlitigated engagements with the same characteristics. These points suggest that some hard thought on the measurement of audit failure would be helpful.

It would also be helpful to develop more specific measures of the quality of audits not considered failures. Progress on this subject should be of particular interest to the research community because of its efforts to improve audit technology. Work on evaluating audit quality has already appeared (e.g., Mock and Samet, 1982), but more seems in order.

New approaches could be employed. The model of audit risk from Statement on Auditing Standards No. 47 could be used to help focus a portion of the research. The Statement defines audit risk as the "risk that the auditor may unknowingly fail to appropriately modify his opinion on financial statements that are materially misstated," and it defines the components of audit risk as inherent, control, and detection risk (paragraphs 2 and 20). The evaluation of audit quality would thus be based on evaluating what the auditor did to reduce audit risk to an appropriately low level. It would thus be necessary to analyze which audit steps contribute directly to the reduction of audit risk and which do not.

For example, appropriate "training and proficiency as an auditor" is a prerequisite to audit quality, but it does not itself reduce audit risk. Substantive evidence of the correctness of an account balance, on the other hand, does directly reduce audit risk. The role of review in reducing audit risk is less clear. Is it solely a quality control ensuring that appropriate evidence is obtained? Or does it, in specified circumstances, provide evidence that reduces audit risk? For instance, when a complex accounting treatment is reviewed for propriety, has a procedure been reperformed providing the same evidence, or has ad-

ditional evidence been obtained? How can a reviewer's disagreement that leads to a revised accounting treatment be reconciled with the idea that no new evidence can be provided by a review? Researchers would also have to define the circumstances under which the assessment of inherent risk constitutes audit evidence that reduces audit risk. Such issues suggest that a clearer understanding of the nature of audit evidence may be essential in developing measures to evaluate audit quality.

Independence

The hearings have raised questions about the effect on independence of performing management advisory services (MAS) for audit clients. This is hardly a new issue, having been discussed well before the Metcalf hearings aired the subject in 1977. It was studied by the Cohen Commission (1978) and by the Public Oversight Board (1979), and a number of articles have appeared since then.[1] However, recent findings by McKinley, Pany, and Reckers (1985) suggest the need for additional research.

Their approach differed from that of previous survey studies because the subjects (bank loan officers) were placed in a "realistic" situation, reviewing loan application information and making a loan recommendation, whereas previous survey studies elicited subjects' evaluations of whether auditors appear more or less independent given situations in which the auditor had provided some form of MAS. McKinley et al. found that the provision of MAS did not change the loan decisions and did not decrease average perceptions either of the reliability of the financial statements or of the independence of the auditors. Prior research using the survey approach had indicated that perceptions of auditor independence were negatively affected by the performance of MAS.

The Dingell hearings have also considered another aspect of the independence question, "opinion shopping." The prevalence of opinion shopping is unknown, and evidence of its dimensions in today's audit environment would clearly be valuable. So too would additional evidence of the effectiveness of the SEC's Form 8-K in disclosing auditor-client disagreements because the 8-K disclosure requirements are partly designed to discourage opinion shopping. However, there have been a few recent studies pertinent to these issues. Hall and McConnell (1985) examined inconsistencies among auditors in disclosing management disagreements and Chow and Rice (1982) provide data relevant to evaluating opinion shopping.

In July the SEC issued a request for comments on opinion shopping and how to improve disclosures of "opinion shopping" situations.[2] The timing of the SEC suggests the influence of criticisms voiced at the

---

[1] See McKinley, et al. (1985) for a review of the prior research in this area.

[2] SEC Release No. 33-6594, July 1, 1985. See also SEC Release No. 33-6592, July 1, 1985, which contains a proposal to expand requirements to report disagreements with former accountants.

Exhibit 20–2 (continued)

hearings. The comments may provide additional ideas for needed future research.

The independence issue is part of a larger subject—whether there has been a decline in the level of public confidence in auditors. As Representative Dingell said at the opening hearing, "Public faith in the reliability of financial statements depends upon public perception of the outside auditor as an independent professional." Many statements at the hearings thus far have suggested that public confidence in the auditor's performance has waned, and there is a danger that the very occurrence of the hearings will be considered evidence that such a decline has taken place. This would be an unpleasant irony since the hearings should in part be trying to ascertain the true nature of the auditor's standing with users of financial statements. As it happens, Peat Marwick (1984) commissioned an independent, broadly-based, national survey that indicated a high level of public confidence in independent accountants. However, the auditor's relationship to third-party users of financial statements is so essential to the success of the audit process that such work is needed periodically.

Self-Regulation

The profession's self-regulatory institutions were altered in a number of ways during and after the hearings by Moss and Metcalf in the 1970s, but some of the criticisms at the current hearings sound like an echo. The Metcalf staff study asserted in 1976 that the eight largest accounting firms controlled the self-regulatory mechanisms, and members of Dingell's subcommittee, Representative Wyden in particular, has made a similar charge: i.e., that the same people make the rules, interpret them, and enforce them. There is room for considerable additional research on the various issues this charge raises. And the usefulness of the research would go well beyond its contribution to settling the political charges. More should be known about the sociology and constitutional structure of the profession. Among worthy topics are: the degree of influence exercised within the AICPA by firms of various sizes; under what circumstances, if any, coalitions are formed; the role of the permanent staff; and the relationship between the interests of the AICPA as a trade organization and the interests of its various constituents. Enough is known about the behavior of institutions in our society to be skeptical of the assumption that a trade organization representing groups with varying interests can give those interests equal consideration all of the time or can be free of a unique self-interest of its own. But we cannot get a reliable picture of these matters without detailed study. The mere assumption that the largest always maintain control is not an approach for obtaining reliable facts on the matter, especially when it is obvious in the accounting profession that "largest" and "majority" are not synonymous.

There are more specific issues bearing on the efficacy of self-regulation. Two stand out: the role of the Public Oversight Board, whose independence was questioned at the hearings, and the effectiveness of peer review, which is the heart of the self-regulatory system set up in the late 1970s. Research on how to improve the peer review process could make a long-term contribution to the profession and its ability to serve the public.

Conclusion

The research subjects cited above are intended to show the relevance of the Dingell hearings to the agenda of audit research. But it would be premature even to suggest that a thorough list of additions could be prepared. Any such list must await the completion of the hearings and issuance of the printed transcript. It is unlikely that the colloquies in the transcript will recognize that the hearings can contribute to research, but such a contribution may turn out to be one of the hearings' more enduring legacies.

References

AICPA, *Statement on Auditing Standards No. 47*, "Audit Risk and Materiality in Conducting an Audit," 1983, paragraphs 2 and 20.

Chow, Chee and Steven Rice, "Qualified Audit Opinions and Auditor Switching," *The Accounting Review* (April 1982), pp. 326-335.

The Commission on Auditors' Responsibilities, *Report, Conclusions, and Recommendations* (New York), 1978, pp. 94-104.

Dingell, John D., "Opening Statement of the Honorable John D. Dingell, Chairman, Committee on Energy and Commerce," February 20, 1985, p. 2.

Hall, Thomas and Donald McConnell, "Audit Firm Consistency in Disclosing Auditor-Client Disagreements," *Collected Abstracts of the American Accounting Association's Annual Meeting*, August 19-21, 1985, Reno, Nevada, p. 81.

McKinley, Sue, Kurt Pany and Philip M.J. Reckers, "An Examination of the Influence of CPA Firm Type, Size, and MAS Provision on Loan Officer Decisions and Perceptions," *Journal of Accounting Research* (forthcoming, Fall 1985).

Mock, Theodore J. and Michael G. Samet, "A Multi-Attribute Model for Audit Evaluation," *Auditing Symposium VI, Proceedings of the 1982 Touche Ross/University of Kansas Symposium on Auditing Problems,* eds., Donald R. Nicholas and Howard F. Stettler.

Peat, Marwick, Mitchell & Co., *Independent Auditors: How the Profession is Viewed by Those it Serves, A National Survey Conducted by Opinion Research Corporation and Research Strategies Corporation* (New York: Peat, Marwick, Mitchell & Co.), 1984.

Public Oversight Board, *Scope of Services by CPA Firms* (New York), 1979.

Puro, Marsha, "Do Large Accounting Firms Collude in the Standards-Setting Process?" *Journal of Accounting, Auditing & Finance* (Spring 1985), pp. 165-177.

Williams, Doyle, *Accounting Education News* (January 1985), p. 17.

Source: John J. Willingham and Peter D. Jacobson, "A Research Response To The Dingell Hearings," *The Auditor's Report* (Volume 9, Number 1, Fall 1985), pp. 1–4.

The need to integrate research considerations in policy setting is being increasingly recognized. Such inquiry can provide one control to avoid unproductive change. These calls for research have been heard by the research community, and a number of interesting findings have evolved, many of which are recounted throughout this *Handbook*.

A POTPOURRI OF RESEARCH FINDINGS: FOOD FOR THOUGHT

To expand on such discussions, consider a number of suggestions in the literature that help to assess means of implementing regulation and conforming with generally accepted standards of practice.

- One approach cited for detecting and deterring management fraud is to track data on prospective and current clients' illegal activities and civil litigation (i.e., corporate recidivism). The idea is that the more successful actions are against a company by government authorities and private parties, the more likely the learning of criminal behavior by perpetrators associated with such a corporate environment, and the higher the probability of current or future offenses.[3]
- Checklists have been criticized due to their being
  (1) incapable of translating the experience or sound reasoning intended to be captured by each red flag or combinations thereof;
  (2) inappropriate implications that equal weights are to be applied per flag or indicator
  (3) prone to overload users to an extent that the checklist is treated in a perfunctory manner, rather than as determinants of an overall assessment as intended and
  (4) the provider of false security in their apparent comprehensiveness which suggests that all relevant factors have been considered.[4] Research suggests that while the use of checklists may increase the comprehensiveness and uniformity of data acquisition, no difference in assessment accuracy was discernible in the absence of fraud and a dysfunctional effect was observed in terms of identifying the existence of fraud.[5]
- Empirical evidence is at hand from a sample of 186 audit engagements in six broad industries that as detailed information on 731 detected errors was tracked, those results indicated that as assessed internal controls weakened, the frequency of errors increased and were more likely to have

---

[3] Robert K. Elliott and John J. Willingham, *Management Fraud: Detection and Deterrence* (Petrocelli Books, Inc., 1980).

[4] James K. Loebbecke, "Assessing the Risk of Material Irregularities," Working Paper, University of Utah (February 10, 1988), later published in *Auditing: A Journal of Practice & Theory* (1989).

[5] Karen V. Pincus, "The Efficiency of a Red-Flags Questionnaire for Assessing the Possibility of Fraud," Working Paper at University of Southern California (January 1987).

an effect on income. In weaker internal control settings, it was found that the predominant direction of errors was towards understatement, suggesting the need for different audit strategies. As controls deteriorate, a greater frequency of "routine" errors was observed; all control settings have been observed to have cut-off and mechanical errors.[6]

- Research on disclosures surrounding auditor litigation activities—649 cases from 1960 to 1988 for the then Big Eight and the largest non-Big Eight found that a small number of cases (39) accounted for nearly half of the total disclosures in the *Wall Street Journal*. These were characterized as "high impact" cases, with a 6.6-year time frame in which the cases were discussed from a number of vantage points. These cases typically involved management fraud and severe financial distress. Disclosures have increased steadily from the 1960s into the 1970s and the 1980s. Over half of the cases were mentioned only once, around the filing date; of those in which final resolution information was announced, 90% involved confirming audit failure allegations.[7]

- The size of internal audit department investments appears to be strongly associated with organization size, as measured by both assets and employees, regulated industry and public environment, and to a lesser extent complexity and external auditors' use or reliance on internal audit. Findings are consistent with the rule-of-thumb cited in past literature of an average standard of one auditor per 1,000 employees, with a median of 1.33.[8]

- Expert judgment in an audit team setting has been demonstrated to be a function, in part, of the perceived reliability of the source, even to the extent that evidence gathered from a reliable source but transmitted by a senior who is viewed by a manager as less reliable, will likely be discounted and underutilized.[9]

- A sample of 260 companies was used to identify characteristics associated with the creation of an internal audit department. Those creating such departments were observed to be significantly larger, more highly regulated, more competitive, more profitable, more liquid, more conservative

---

[6] Arnold Wright, "The Relationship Between Assessments of Internal Control Strength and Error Incidence, Detection & Cause," Working Paper, Northeastern University (February 1989).

[7] Zoe-Vonna Palmrose, "An Analysis of Public Disclosures of Litigation Against Independent Auditors," Working Paper from the University of Southern California (September 1989).

[8] Wanda A. Wallace, Paulette R. Tandy, and Nancy L. Wilburn, "Determinants of the Investment in the Internal Audit Department," Working Paper at Texas A & M University (1990 draft).

[9] E. Michael Bamber, "Expert Judgment in the Audit Team: A Source Reliability Approach," *Journal of Accounting Research*, Vol. 21, No. 2 (Autumn 1983), pp. 396–412. Of similar interest is the finding when evaluating the relative quality of evidential sources integrated into an audit program that considerations include: competence—reflecting less biased, more reliable, and relevant information—sufficiency, and cost (in order from greatest to least important). This result is reported by Arnold Wright and Theodore J. Mock, "Evidential Planning Decisions—A Multi-Attribute Investigation," Working Paper, USC (July 1986).

in accounting policies, more competent in their management and accounting personnel, and subject to better management controls. Key operational variables that discriminated companies without internal audit departments from those with such departments included: the degree of regulation, decentralization, size, the duration of association with present auditors, the existence of an audit committee, EDP control, and pressures by external parties on management to achieve budgetary goals. The qualitative attribute of internal audit most related to both the overall quality of the control environment and the decreased incidence of errors was the independence of internal audit in terms of the propriety of reporting level. From a benefit perspective, external auditors reported a 10% reduction in the number of hours incurred and greater flexibility in performing work in off-peak periods when internal auditing was present.[10]

- Control over information systems has been reported as troublesome in some mass transit operations. For example, the Office of the Inspector General for the New York City Metropolitan Transportation Authority (MTA) (October and December 1986) reports: "That on-time performance and key station throughput performance statistics were grossly inaccurate, providing as evidence a reported 80.1% on-time statistic in the MTA's information system, whereas auditors' direct observation of the same 442 trips at 16 terminals resulted in a 61.8% measure."[11] This and similar evidence on the verifiability of service efforts and accomplishments data, and the possibility that control structure is not yet conducive to truthful reporting calls for action.

- Research suggests that auditing procedures do not have the same reliability in all circumstances. Indeed, another study reports that an audit program which is flexible, facilitating a reaction to specific contexts is advantageous relative to standard procedures applied to all audits.[12]

- Firms disclosing large discretionary write-offs—sometimes interpreted by the popular press as a sign of earlier misstatements in the information system—are larger than other firms in their industries in terms of revenues and assets and are more debt intensive. They tend to underperform their industries in return on assets and return on equity, with significantly lower

---

[10] Wanda A. Wallace and Richard W. Kreutzfeldt, "Distinctive Characteristics of Entities With An Internal Audit Department and the Association of the Quality of Such Departments With Errors," *Contemporary Accounting Research* (Spring 1991), pp. 485–512.

[11] Wanda A. Wallace, *Research Report: Service Efforts and Accomplishments Reporting: Its Time Has Come—Mass Transit* (Norwalk, Connecticut: Governmental Accounting Standards Board of the Financial Accounting Foundation, 1991), p. 22.

[12] Eric E. Spires and James A. Yardley, "Empirical Studies on the Reliability of Auditing Procedures," *Journal of Accounting Literature*, Vol. 8 (1989), pp. 49–75 and A. Wright and T. J. Mock, "Towards a Contingency View of Audit Evidence," *Auditing: A Journal of Practice & Theory* (Fall 1985), pp. 91–100, respectively.

security returns in periods before, coincident with, and following announcement of the write-off.[13]

- Evidence exists that accounting firm policies concerning tests of control affect auditors' evaluation of the strength of such tests of control. The implication is that firms' specific policies must be understood prior to evaluating some aspect of the audit approach. As one example, auditors from firms providing caution that inquiry and observation are relatively weak derived less assurance from inquiry and observation than auditors from other firms. This could cause overreaction to weaknesses in inquiry and observation, trading off audit efficiency or, in the absence of the warning, perhaps other firms' auditors are deriving too much assurance from those same procedures and are imperiling audit effectiveness.[14] Other inferences drawn from this research include the idea that (1) scanning increases reliance when used with document inspection and (2) reperformance and scanning do not appear to be differentiated by the average auditor.

- Reliability theory has been useful as a framework for modeling controls and considering expert system approaches.[15]

- Some have recommended that auditors assign weights to internal control questionnaire responses based on a subjective ranking of each question's importance. The sum of the weights of the positive answers is then used to quantify the quality of controls.[16] One problem evidenced in a number of research papers is that "large differences among auditors exist in evaluating the importance of different types and levels of internal control."[17] This is one explanation given for some researchers' difficulty in documenting the sensitivity of audit programs to controls and changes therein.[18]

- Auditors consider the underlying nature of test-of-control evidence in their judgments, such as different objectives of testing controls like "by whom" and "how well" controls were being applied. There are findings that some

---

[13] John A. Elliott and Wayne H. Shaw, "Big Baths as Accounting Procedures to Manage Perceptions," Working Paper from Cornell University (July 1988, preliminary version 2, September 1988); later published in *Journal of Accounting Research*.

[14] Eric E. Spires, "Auditors' Evaluations of Test-of-Control Strength," Working Paper at The Ohio State University (June 1988).

[15] R. D. Meservy, A. D. Bailey, and P. E. Johnson, "Internal Control Evaluation: A Computational Model of the Review Process," *Auditing: A Journal of Practice and Theory* (Fall 1986), pp. 44–74; R. P. Srivastava, "Auditing Functions for Internal Control Systems with Independent Documents and Channels," *Journal of Accounting Research* (Autumn 1986), pp. 422–426; and B. Srinidhi and M. Vasarhelyi, "Reliability Theory and Internal Control Evaluation," *Auditing: A Journal of Practice and Theory* (Spring 1986), pp. 64–76.

[16] G. R. Brown, "Objective Internal Control Evaluations," *Journal of Accountancy* (November 1962), pp. 50–56.

[17] William L. Felix, Jr. and Marcia S. Niles, "Research in Internal Control Evaluation," *Auditing: A Journal of Practice and Theory* (Spring 1988), p. 50.

[18] J. J. Willingham and W. F. Wright, "Financial Statement Errors and Internal Control Judgments," *Auditing: A Journal of Practice and Theory* (Fall 1988), pp. 57–70.

evidence, when added with other results ends up providing more assurance than would be implied by the sum of the parts. The propriety of such a synergy type effect has yet to be explored.[19] One important element to control in any research related to tests of controls is the importance of the control under consideration, since it has been found to interact with the strength of tests of control as evaluated by auditors.[20]

- In understanding how business operates and decisions are made, the role of taxes must be appreciated and viewed from a strategy perspective.[21]

- A study of 245 internal EDP auditors suggests that significant factors affecting the use of concurrent EDP audit techniques are the involvement of internal auditors in the development of new systems, the maturity level of the EDP audit function, and the degree of complexity of the computerized systems as well as type of complexity.[22]

- Some have hypothesized that the selection of computer audit technique is in large part a function of the stability of the computerized application. An unstable application leads to less sophisticated techniques and a greater focus on substantive test work, whereas a stable application leads to greater use of tests of control.[23]

- An improvement in internal controls from inadequate to adequate is observed to coexist with a decrease in average audit hours by 52%.[24]

- Research of client traits and related errors for 110 audits of 55 manufacturing companies in the United Kingdom suggests that budget pressure and return on total assets appeared frequently as situations which were associated with errors in financial statements presented for audit. Personnel problems were also noted to be associated with the size of errors. Measures of control risk traits were rarely associated with errors detected, but limitations of the research design are acknowledged which may be responsible for such results.[25]

---

[19] Eric E. Spires, "Combinations of Audit Evidence: Model and Tests of Model," Ohio State University (October 1989 Working Paper).

[20] Eric E. Spires, "The Interaction Between Control Importance and Tests of Controls in Auditors' Control Reliance Decisions," Working Paper at The Ohio State University (March 1990).

[21] Myron Scholes and Mark Wolfson, *Taxes and Business Strategy: A Global Planning Perspective* (Englewood Cliffs, New Jersey: Prentice Hall, In Progress).

[22] Lawrence C. Mohrweis, "An Empirical Investigation of Factors Affecting the Use of Concurrent EDP Audit Techniques," Working Paper at Indiana University (September 1987).

[23] Uday S. Murthy, "The Relationship Between the Stability of Computerized Accounting Applications, Computer Audit Strategy and Audit Risk: An Empirical Investigation," Working Paper/Dissertation Proposal, Indiana University (November 1988).

[24] Kathryn M. Means and Paul M. Kazenski, "Improved Internal Controls Can Cut Audit Costs," *Management Accounting* (January 1987), pp. 48–51.

[25] Raymond N. Johnson, "Auditor Detected Errors and Related Client Traits—A Study of Inherent and Control Risks in a Sample of U.K. Audits," *Journal of Business Finance & Accounting*, Vol. 14, No. 1 (Spring 1987), pp. 39–64.

General Inferences

A review of this listing of research projects suggests that

—we could enhance our evaluation of control through use of new tools and better use of existing tools . . . particularly interaction effects among varied sources of evidence;

—poorer controls as they relate to errors create larger understatement risks, which suggest completeness assertions may be substantial risk exposures, suggesting the advisability of greater use of analytical procedures and similar reasonableness tests,

—media blitzes could be creating an atmosphere of crisis through mere redundancy and a clear selection bias toward sensational reporting

—incentives would appear to exist to enhance controls and means of doing so are available

—behavioral influences, and firm policy, have perceptible effects on decision making

—context influences tests of controls and related inferences.

These examples of research contributions and implications are provided to reinforce a major point revisited throughout this *Handbook*:

> Controls are extremely dependent on competent people who stay abreast of change and adapt as appropriate.

Competency is essential to stay aware of these types of developments, insights, and potential opportunities for application. Indeed, participation in such research and development on control dimensions could be an important facet of ensuring quality assurance throughout an organization.

A number of resources are available to assist individuals at being up-to-date and accessing relevant information on such developments as well as practice prototypes. Database examples include NAARS, NAARS Literature, NEXIS, INFOBANK, EXCHANGE, DISCLOSUREII, SPECTRUM, ABI/INFORM, PREDICASTS (PTS), STANDARD & POOR's, and various items likely to be in libraries.[26] These tools can help to determine preferred practice, perform statistical comparisons, evaluate potential clients, and find relevant literature. Use of such systems raises questions as to how to choose the optimal selection, set-up, support structure, and applications.[27] Exhibit 20–3 reprints an article concerning auditors' use of on-line data bases that addresses some of these issues. Attention to building

---

[26] Andrew P. Gale, "Data Bases: An Accountant's Choice," *Journal of Accountancy* (December 1985), pp. 111–122 and Hortense Goodman, "NAARS: The CPA's Electronic Shoe Box," *Journal of Accountancy* (December 1985), pp. 125–132.

[27] Felix Pomeranz, "Auditors' Use of On-Line Data Bases," Florida International University (March 17, 1987 Working Paper).

Exhibit 20–3

Auditors' Use of On-Line Data Bases*

By Felix Pomeranz

On-line data bases represent an emerging audit tool, which promises to contribute importantly to audit efficiency and effectiveness.

This article reports the results of a research study directed to the extent of accountants' usage of on-line data bases, the reasons for non-usage, and the potential for increased usage in audit applications. To determine actual levels of utilization within *practice offices*, the study focused on organizations in South Florida; the subjects included public accounting firms of various sizes, internal audit departments of major corporations sited in the area, and a sprinkling of government entities of the State of Florida.

Widely disparate approaches to use of the on-line data bases were found. There was divergence with respect to the nature of the applications, and the position levels of the users. However, discussions with users identified a considerable number of potential audit applications.

Background

In the "Omni On-Line Data Base Directory" Owen Davis and Mike Edelhart explained that data bases are resources which contain "facts that people will want to use and that (such a) collection is not static." They also noted that "a base is something you build upon, and (that) data bases by and large, are information resources designed to get started."[1]

Use of the data bases involves many considerations, including selection of data bases, cost and billing aspects, quality control, and training. But the primary focus of this article is on expanding the usefulness of the data bases to an independent public accountant or to an internal auditor.

Practice Today

The first part of this article discusses the state of the art as it relates to audit use of on-line data bases.

Data Base Utilization

The data bases mentioned most frequently by the respondents, are shown in Appendix 1, grouped by distributor;

HEADNOTE: *Considerable improvement and economics in many audit steps may be achieved through experienced use of software to obtain information concerning numerous classifications of financial facts from data bases. The author, experienced in research and practice in this area, reports on a study made of such use in a variety of circumstances, and urges further use and study. The appendices portray a typical use of data bases in an engagement.*

---

* The National Center for Automated Information Retrieval Inc., underwrote the author's research.

[1] Davies, Owen, and Edelhart, Mike "*Omni Online Data Base Directory,*" Collier Books/McMillan Publishing Company, New York, 1985. p. 2.

Exhibit 20–3 (continued)

APPENDIX 1
DATA BASES MENTIONED MOST FREQUENTLY

The data bases mentioned most frequently by the respondents are listed below, grouped by distributor. A brief description has been provided of the contents of each data base.

<u>Mead Data Central</u>

LEXIS

Law cases, administrative decisions, attorney general opinions, regulatory material, and other legal documents. Some libraries, such as GENFED and STATES, contain materials not classified by subject area. Other libraries such as FEDSEC contain material specific to a particular area of law.

NAARS

Financial statements, footnotes, and auditors' reports for more than 4,000 companies for each year covered by the library; a separate literature file contains all current and superseded authoritative and semiauthoritative promulgations of the AICPA, the FASB, and the SEC, including the Emerging Issues Task Force.

NEXIS

Full text articles from 11 major newspapers, 38 magazines, 50 newsletters, and a variety of newswires. Information about pending litigation, potential clients, business actions, government activities, technology, and general news.

EXCHANGE

Analyses from leading banking, brokerage and research firms on finance, economy, demographics of countries, business prospects of companies and industries, and selected SEC registrants.

DIALOG

ABI/INFORM

Abstracts of principal articles appearing in more than 660 business and management periodicals worldwide. Emphasis is placed on company case histories, competitive intelligence, new product development, and facts relevant to business decision making.

DISCLOSURE FINANCIALS

Detailed financial information on over 10,000 public companies. The information is derived from reports filed with the SEC. The financial information includes quarterly statements, annual sources and uses of funds, 30 common financial ratios, price and earnings information, and up to five years of historical annual income statements and balance sheets.

DISCLOSURE/SPECTRUM OWNERSHIP

Detailed and summary ownership information for approximately 5,000 public companies.

---

the Appendix also contains a brief description of the contents of each data base.

Reasons for Data Base Selection

In general, the accountants surveyed did *not* select data bases by matching documented needs to available products. "Low cost" was mentioned as a selection criterion by one accounting firm—a circumstance which appears to conflict with the accounting stereotype.

> *. . . the primary focus . . . is on expanding the usefulness of the data bases to an independent public accountant or to an internal auditor.*

Essentially, data bases *were* chosen, because 1) someone had heard that they were available; and 2) because it was thought that a data base could fill a particular need.

Cost Recovery by Public Accountants

The firms asserted that they followed the practice of charging part of the cost of the data base and of the time of the researcher to the client involved. However, the charge varied from a low of 20 percent to 100 percent of aggregate billable amounts. Moreover, a charge to the client's account was not synonymous with invoicing: Actual bills varied between 50 percent and 100 percent of amounts entered on the records. Taken at face value, these numbers indicate that the data bases often are loss leaders; discussion with several partners did not elicit any explanation, other than that the partners did not feel comfortable with the results, and were reluctant to pass the charges on to clients.

The Nature of the Applications

The applications encountered during the survey were ranked in descending order of popularity. Most of these applications have been discussed elsewhere; they will not be commented on in depth.

• Analytics, to compare a client to others in its industry. In the author's view, this application usually requires thorough knowledge of the client's business. The value of the

Exhibit 20–3 (continued)

application varies directly with the effort expended by the auditor and with the knowledge applied to formulate expected relationships.

- Obtaining a better understanding of current developments in the client's industry to evaluate business risk.
- Inquiring into the backgrounds of executives of potential clients.
- Searching the professional literature to document support for technical positions.
- Searching for examples of accounting treatments or disclosures.
- Obtaining timely notice of pending changes to the tax laws, or of changes to IRS regulations, forms, and publications.

. . . data bases were chosen, because . . . they . . . could fill a particular need.

The greatest number of applications occurred on the first five usages listed, and averaged 1 to 20 applications per respondent per month.

Who Are the Users

The primary users were audit staff members, technical specialists, and librarians. In general, considerable importance was attached to giving an auditor an influential user role. However, a reading of Appendix 2 will convince readers of the need for *senior* audit personnel, that is, partners and managers, to take an active part in on-line data base applications.

User training

Reliance was placed on user manuals, followed by vendor courses, free practice time, toll-free telephone numbers, and on-the-job training. Almost all discussants stressed the need for constant practice, and repeated exposure to searches.

Quality Control Aspects

Differences existed as to the position level of the person responsible for developing search approaches; the job titles ran from "audit staff" to partner. In two cases the development of the search approach was a joint venture between a technical specialist (a trained librarian) and an auditor. The approval of search approaches ran a similar gamut of rank and titles. The review of results—in light of search objectives—was usually performed by a partner or manager.

Constraints

In order of frequency constraints included:
- Too costly.
- Didn't know about it.

- Not user friendly.
- Not cost effective, given lack of practice, plus "customary" turnover in accountants' offices.

What Must be Done to Expand Usage

There was general agreement that *demonstrable* increases in audit efficiency and effectiveness, greater user friendliness and apparent cost effectiveness would foster increased data base utilization.

Observations

Many auditors have found it difficult to use the data bases, or to acquire the requisite efficiency and effectiveness. A partial answer may lie in the development of software focused toward helping an *auditor* to identify the most promising data base and to structure his search; also, an additional computerized decision aid could help the auditor to distinguish between "simple" and "complex" applications; if this were done, a technical information specialist could become involved in complex applications only, via an audit firm's internal communication network.

. . . the auditor would become sensitized to potential problems as a basis to further investigation.

Some respondents reported that data base vendors had given little or no attention to that segment of the accounting and auditing market that performs on the "firing line." Mead Data Central has carved out an important niche bearing on accounting rules and tax work via NAARS and LEXIS; however, Mead has done little to help auditors in evaluating inherent risk, and in managing audit risk. And, to the best of the author's knowledge, DIALOG has not marketed aggressively to professional auditors.

Increasing competition among data base vendors, accompanied by breakthrough in storage technology, may motivate vendors to devote greater attention to practitioners. In the final analysis, innovation will have to come from the auditors themselves. The remainder of this article focuses on potential applications from a practitioner's perspective.

"Master the Possibilities"

Auditing applications can be slotted into one of two nondiscrete categories: 1) Tasks involving the financial statements as a whole; 2) procedures affecting one or more individual accounts. The first category relates to the obtaining of an understanding of the client's industry, business, and systems to identify inherent risk. In the case of a new client, these procedures should help the auditor decide whether to accept the client. In the case of a recurring client, the auditor would become sensitized to potential problems as a basis to further investigation.

Exhibit 20–3 (continued)

APPENDIX 2
MINICASE: RESULTS OF ON-LINE DATA BASE INQUIRIES DISCOVER CORP.

The auditor conducts his initial search in a data base which represents a collection of file indexes of other data bases: DIALOG'S DIALINDEX. The search identifies data bases which contain documents referring to Discover; data bases thought to be particularly pertinent are:

Data Base Number and Name	Document Count
100: Disclosure Financials	2
133: Standard & Poors, Descriptions	1
148: Trade and Industry Index	10
548: M&A Filings	1

Next, the auditor examines file 133 which contains a description of Discover. The company is in the business of acquiring interests in oil and gas properties for subsequent sale to others for development, while retaining an interest in such properties. The record also lists the Company's primary and secondary SIC codes, which will be helpful in subsequent comparisons of Discover to others in the same industry. And, the names of officers and directors are given, facilitating possible searches in biographical data bases, or in legal data bases.

The auditor learns that Congress Corporation owns 29.9 percent of the common stock, and that J. M. Gross, a corporate director, owns 10.6 percent. Congress Corporation appears to have a connection with Discover's Board Chairman, although the nature of the relationship has not been made clear. The auditor dockets the relationship between Congress and the Chairman for further inquiry.

The file includes a summarized statement of earnings and finances for each of the three years ended August 31, 1986 (thousands omitted):

	1986	1985	1984
Revenues	$ 4,992	$ 4,468	$ 6,668
Net Income	d8,003	d2,735	d1,000
Income per share	d3.28	d1.13	d.50

The auditor, aware of Discover's recent financial performance, refers to File 100: Disclosure Financials. The File includes information for three quarters ended since the last fiscal year. The most recent quarter, May 31, 1987, shows a small profit, due primarily to decreases in expenditures; the fluctuations are included in the auditors "To Do" list of matters for inquiry:

Receivables decreased from $ 1,915,000 to $ 803,000; consequently there is less available in the way of working capital that could be turned into cash, if additional expenditures had to be made for development of oil and gas wells. However, it is uncertain whether such expenditures are contemplated, whether the nature of Discover's stated business requires such expenditures, or whether such expenditures are mandated by contracts with shareholders or otherwise. If Discover is engaged merely in holding land—in spite of its misleading name—the somewhat limited nature of that activity could negatively influence its property valuations.

There could be a further question: In the light of Discover's apparent business, the origin of the receivables would seem to raise questions; the receivables may not have been acquired in the ordinary course of business; there may be disclosure or valuation issues.

Investments were shown as $ 469,000 in 1986; no comparable item existed in 1985. Again, there are disclosure and valuation questions.

Research and development expenditures were substantial in 1986, $ 743,000, but dropped to virtually nothing in 1987. This may reflect a change in Discover's business, or discretionary management of expenditures. Unwillingness, or inability, to make these expenditures, as well as capital expenditures, could have serious effects.

Selling, general, and administrative expenses declined precipitously in 1987, raising issues of unrecorded liabilities or of expense deferrals.

In 1986 zero funds were generated by operations; dividends were paid out of working capital, as were capital expenditures, in the amounts of $ 732,000 and $ 604,000, respectively. Again, if either capital expenditures or research and development expenditures had to be made, Discover could be in difficulty, given its inability to generate significant cash flow.

File 148: Trade and Industry Index, discusses quarterly earnings and dividends for the past two years. Results for the last reported quarter, May 31, 1987, were unfavorably affected, because a major customer exercised a contractual right to decline takedown of gas for a quarter. The auditor must identify the incidence of such contractual rights, the market conditions under which such rights are likely to be exercised, and the possible effect on the company's ability to continue in business.

File 548: M & A Filings revealed that J. M. Gross, previously mentioned as a director, and as holder of an important interest in Discover, had acquired a 7.37 percent interest in another public company, Topeka, Inc. He had offered to manage a restructuring of that company. Instead, Topeka, Inc. entered into a contract to sell substantially all assets of a subsidiary. The Discover officer commenced an action to declare the sale of Topeka's assets void, because prior approval of two thirds of shareholders had not been obtained. If and when a stockholders' meeting is convened, J. M. Gross may solicit proxies against the sale; Gross may also consider ways in which either he or Discover may become more active in Topeka's management. The reported investment by J. M. Gross resembles the investment shown on the books of Discover in 1986. Also, since 1986 Topeka's market price, as shown on the American Stock Exchange, has fallen by half its value.

Exhibit 20–3 (continued)

Tasks in the first category include:

• Identify significant legal actions—civil, criminal or regulatory—to which the client, or its executives, may have been subject.

• Inquire into information that may point to insolvency. Examples include negative trends, default on loan agreements, arrearages in dividends, denial of credit from suppliers, non-compliance with statutory capital requirements, etc.

... auditors may use information available 'on-line' to evaluate managerial judgments as applied to individual accounts.

• Review filings with regulatory agencies for the names of related parties, and for other entities in which officers and directors have ownership or other interests.

• Refer to financial publications for unfamiliar customers or for the identities of other parties to transactions of questionable merit.

Secondly, auditors may use information available, "on-line" to evaluate managerial judgments as applied to individual accounts. When the auditor develops his program for the audit of individual accounts, he does so to substantiate management's assertions. Assuming that the auditor has decided to rely on the system, and that compliance tests have established the auditor's entitlement to such reliance, some assertions will be corroborated by the functioning of the system or by physical examination. But, other assertions involve managerial judgments: Valuation, rights and obligations, reporting and disclosure.

The pervasive importance of management judgments is reflected in a recent study by the SEC concerning "surprise" writeoffs. The writeoffs were classified as follows: Asset impairments, plant closings and restructurings, writedowns and writeoffs of investments, and writedowns and writeoffs of goodwill.[2] Additional comments are appropriate pertaining to the testing of management judgments.

Historically, auditors have tested management judgments by scrutinizing client-furnished documentary evidence. Also, attempts have often been made to confirm information with third parties. However, the on-line data bases have equipped the auditor with a new tool.

The following opportunities come to mind; the list is by no means complete:

• *Accounts receivable.* Review adequacy of allowance for doubtful accounts vis-a-vis others in the same industry, or

bearing the same SIC codes; review open sales commitments in a search for possible losses, in light of industry conditions; evaluate customer credit worthiness by examining the files of credit granting agencies.

• *Inventories.* Review the nature of items and quantities on hand in light of market forecasts and economic conditions. Assess carrying values for obsolete or slowmoving articles, considering market conditions, customer preferences, changes in selling prices, capacity in the industry, and changing technology.

• *Property, plant, and equipment.* Compare client's policies to others with pertinent SIC codes with respect to depreciation and amortization policies, carrying values, and maintenance expenditures. See whether the industry has experienced idle capacity, abandoned property, or property held for sale.

• *Investments.* Develop information for appropriate valuation of restricted securities, non-marketable securities, or other investments which may have suffered impaired values. With respect to joint ventures, check the treatment to the books of the partner.

• *Goodwill.* Identify dispositions of major parts of the business to search out possible declines in value.

• *Contingencies.* Develop estimates in light of economic conditions, settled litigation, and government regulations. Check for "open" regulatory actions, fines, or assessments.

Case Study

A brief case study was conducted to illustrate audit applications of on-line data bases; the study was limited to tasks involving the financial statements as a whole: inquiring into information that may point to insolvency, and reviewing filings with regulatory agencies. Only DIALOG data bases were consulted, because the audit literature has been sparse with respect to this data base wholesaler. The assumption was also made that the user auditor had been assigned to perform a first year audit. The company itself was selected at random; the name of this entity was changed to Discover Corp. (Discover).

The use of data bases to accomplish a variety of audit tasks is consistent with current developments in data storage technology ...

The specific and significant results of the searches are discussed in Appendix 2. Among other serious open questions, the auditor was alerted to potential going concern issues and to valuation questions, involving accounts receivable, investments, and property, plant and equipment. All searches combined took less than two hours, at a data base cost of $175. In resolving open questions, the auditor will make additional use of the data bases, as discussed in foregoing

---

[2] Fried, Dov et al, "Surprise Writeoffs—Financial Reporting, Disclosure, and Analysis." cited in *Draft Report of the National Commission on Fraudulent Financial Reporting*, April 1987, p. 107.

Exhibit 20–3 (continued)

paragraphs in connection with the audit of individual accounts.

Conclusions

This article suggests that on-line data bases can help auditors perform more efficient and effective audits. The use of data bases to accomplish a variety of audit tasks is consistent with current developments in data storage technology; there are staggering increases in storage capacity. Among other benefits, the on-line data bases will provide auditors with new tools for testing management judgments independently. Ω

Source: Felix Pomeranz, "Auditors' Use of On-Line Data Bases," *The CPA Journal* (February 1988), pp. 14–22. Reprinted with permission from *The CPA Journal*, February 1988, copyright 1988.

---

user-friendly access to such tools can be expected to enhance control design, implementation, and evaluation.

THE PRACTICE ENVIRONMENT

Having commented on regulation and research, the question arises as to what is the nature of the practice environment being faced? One obvious element is technology, which creates numerous challenges in the education domain, similar to the challenge of tracking and choosing among research findings as to those results that really seem to lead to "better" practice. As Exhibit 20–4 poses the question, which technology is appropriate for which setting? The key to any such choice and subsequent control structures that can maintain and enhance the results of the choice rely on a clear understanding of the tools at hand. Exhibit 20–5 bears out this recommended axiom—applicable to various aspects of technology and conceptual materials developed throughout this *Handbook*.

FIELD EXAMPLES

Evidence exists that companies are investing in such know-how and applying technology in field applications. These examples span the last decade.

- One major company details how it has used Critical Path Analysis for large construction projects' scheduling and assessing the reasonableness of related capital budgets from a control perspective.

- One report tells how Monte Carlo simulation was used to assess cash flow related to check clearance, allowing projection of an optimum bank versus book balance.

- An internal audit department uses MARK IV and similar systems to extensively analyze computer files and make data selections, including aging of accounts payable payment dates, performing file comparisons to highlight audit exceptions, and applying statistical sampling and other quantitative methods, Mark IV was likewise used to write an audit program to forecast

Exhibit 20–4

NEW TECHNOLOGY AND
ACCOUNTING PRACTICE

by
Lynford E. Graham, Jr.
Jean C. Wyer
Coopers & Lybrand

The Promise of Technology

It's easy to be enchanted by the technologist's siren
song of "bits and bites, MIPS and mice," and be drawn
away from the more prudent focus of managing the introduction of technology to your office. Technology is a
major competitive issue in many businesses today, and
is no less so in the public accounting profession. From
the technology employed in delivering audit services,
to the specialized systems and management consulting
services offered by the large CPA firms, new
technologies are shaping who delivers services, what
services are delivered, and how they will be delivered
to clients. For example, recent public disclosures about
the merger of two Big-8 CPA firms have cited the need
to establish consulting specialties as a moving force in
the decisions.

The growth of technology as a basic business
strategy leads to management challenges. We are still
faced with solving old problems, but the new
technologies offer us many more choices than ever
before as to how we solve those problems. For example,
laser disks and special hardware placed at the engagement site can be used to research firm policy and professional pronouncements when needed. Alternatively,
improved telecommunications software makes possible
the sharing of central data bases for a similar search
using basic portable microcomputers with modems.
The delivered service may be similar, but the
economics of delivery may be quite different, depending on hardware and software costs; distribution and
maintenance costs; frequency of use; and so forth.

The positioning of new technology in the audit environment is no special feat. Money will solve that problem. But overcoming the natural "kid in the candy
store" and "first kid on the block" approaches to investments in technology takes restraint and careful
management. Finding the right application for the
right technology is critical to the implementation
process.

Exhibit 20–4 (continued)

NEW TECHNOLOGY (continued)

Properly managed, the introduction of technology will address important business problems and deliver either efficiencies or quality improvements or both, while probably increasing job satisfaction for those affected. For example, the focus of ExperTAX, an expert system developed by C&L for corporate tax accrual and planning, grew out of a business opportunity as identified in research with the audit and tax staffs. The solution exploited the then available technology to deliver a system to enhance quality and ensure greater consistency; improve staff job satisfaction; and provide training value to the audit staff. Also, the technology employed in building ExperTAX made it economical to maintain, and since its introduction, the product "shell" has been recast and used for solving additional problems through other applications within the firm.

Technologies for the Nineties

An important focus for the decade ahead will be the more widespread application of an important lesson we have been learning for many years: The process of tool development and implementation is inextricably linked to problem solving. Technology rarely solves problems directly. The creative application of technology to a well-defined and understood problem is more likely to lead to a solution. The central focus was and will be the well-defined and understood problem, a point overlooked in many discussions of technology.

Some DSS (Decision Support Systems) and ESS (Executive Support Systems) developers are today on the leading edge of understanding and managing the difficult and complex relationships between technology and people. While DPS (Data Processing Systems) have a well-defined and oft-cited system development life cycle and structural development process, those technologies and approaches may be less than satisfactory for economically building systems to support professionals and executives. Current DSS methodology focuses on early user feedback from rapid prototyping and incremental system development, as made possible by new computer tools. These approaches recognize that at the start of a project, system specifications in complex environments are often impossible to identify. Such alternative system development processes would most likely be successful in environments that include "custom" rather than "routine" work; the presence of interactive processes; a critical need for the system to adapt to the user; and an inability to completely specify functionality at the front end of the project. Thus, the alternative system development strategies and tools that support them will play a critical role in developing systems for auditing.

Communications are central in the service-oriented public accounting practice. The frustrations of playing "telephone tag" rank high on the list of problems facing auditors responsible for managing engagements. Word processing alternatives will redefine the traditional relationship between the field auditor and the administrative support staff. Electronic transmission of documents and mail will speed the work flow. Voice mail has the advantage of communicating a technical

message exactly as the sender intended, without the risk of something "getting lost in the translation."

Microcomputer-based tools are clearly the auditor's work environment of the future. The ability to communicate between or network different systems is critical to the evolution of computer usage in the practice of accounting. How these powerful machines are linked to office mini and mainframe systems and to client systems will determine their practical effectiveness. As rumors of the "486" chip and beyond circulate, it appears that what is needed is always just "around the proverbial corner." The trick is to deliver effective support tools in today's (or yesterday's) environments because that is where your hardware investment lies. The size of the required hardware investment makes constant adjustment impossible. So auditors will have to adapt to incremental changes and those managing technological implementation will be faced with difficult decisions about timing the shift to new generations of technology.

With increased system memory and horsepower, more "intelligent" support systems can be made practical to help deliver information and advice on an "as needed" basis to aid staff and leverage firm resources and valuable expertise. Systems will also help structure, organize, and guide the auditor through the maze of complexity that is part of the modern practice environment. Desktop publishing will add a new efficiency and quality to the proposal and presentation process, conserving valuable staff and administrative resources. Easy word processing and simple spreadsheet functions already meet the basic needs of engagement teams. Innovative ways to process these electronically generated documents will be the key to exploiting the productivity gains these programs have already made possible.

Not only is an understanding of technology important to applying it in the practice of auditing, but also it is fundamental in delivering appropriate services to fulfill the auditor's attest function and advise clients on critical business matters. Auditing "around the technology" will be as archaic and risky a philosophy as auditing "around the computer" has become. Clients are moving swiftly to implement new technologies as competitive tools, sometimes exposing themselves to considerable business risks that the auditor must understand. Less visual examples can be drawn from data processing systems, but one can easily imagine a single, minimally controlled automated share trading system that may operate well in a stable market but behave disastrously during a stock market crash. The lesson is that one must understand the system and technology in order to know its limits and assess its control structure. No direct link to risk assessment can be made by just knowing that "expert systems" or "telecommunications" were involved. With the increasing emphasis in professional standards on the control environment in assessing audit risk, controls over technology and its effective organizational implementation become more visible in the audit process.

Education and the New Technologies

Two issues are at the confluence of new technologies

Exhibit 20–4 (continued)

and education:

- How to teach people to use the new tools, and
- How new technologies will change the way we educate across all subjects

The first phase of teaching technology involved educating students on how to create and maintain it. Many of us learned to program in our first computer courses, because applications software was not sufficiently developed. If one wanted to use technology, one had to be able to create instructions from fairly basic building blocks.

The current approach to teaching technology is to dedicate significant amounts of time to teaching specifics of applications packages. Knowledge of direct programming, while still useful for those who develop systems, is not necessary for the average user. Teaching the various applications requires significant time and effort. In fact, a whole sub-industry of providers of software training has grown up to support continuing education and, in some cases, pre-entry (i.e. before employment) education in application packages.

In the future it is likely that direct, dedicated training in the uses of technology will become much less prevalent. As our definition of "user-friendly" evolves to include much more sophisticated assistance, the gap between the computer novice and the computer expert will narrow. A higher level of general computer understanding and experience will reduce the gap from the bottom, and better design of the human-software interface will reduce it from the top.

Some software applications can be made intuitively obvious to the user, greatly reducing the need for any training. Since ExperTAX was released to our general practice, its user manual has consisted of a single page of instructions, policy, and guidance. No formal training for the use of the system is needed; only a short orientation to the tool and its capabilities and firm policies is presented. Savings from reduced training efforts can pay for additional development costs to further refine the software and its user interface.

Future generations of software also can reduce the training requirements by capitalizing on what their users already know. Providing an on-line help facility capable of cross-referencing commands from familiar packages will allow users to begin using new software quickly. There is already at least one example of a new generation product including a help function that references the command sequences of a competing product. Users can utilize many of the functions of the new product with no training.

Those applications that require significant transfer of knowledge to new users will likely do so through enhanced help functions. Intelligent, context-specific assistance embedded in the actual software will make training virtually transparent to the user. This type of instruction is automatically tailored to the user's needs and minimizes the time spent learning new programs. The movement of training for new technologies to intuitive designs and embedded training will allow a reduction of time spent in education for initial uses. This is good news for those of us who want to stop debugging software problems and get back to education.

The impact of new technologies on education is the subject of much speculation. While dreams of swift and radical change in pedagogy are sometimes voiced, most visions of the future are more temperate. Perhaps the experience with instructional television has taught us to be more careful in our initial estimates.

Computer based training (CBT) and video technology, including interactive applications and teleconferencing, have many benefits. It is argued that they increase consistency of what is taught; stimulate student interest; and increase the speed of learning. When used with repeated audiences, they often have lower implementation costs than traditional teaching methods. Current computer technology is good at teaching structured material; future developments will provide better support for teaching less structured tasks. Video presentations allow the communication of human interaction in a life-like manner that can be quite effective. The combination of the two in an interactive teaching tool holds great promise. However, realization of the promise will require careful development.

There are a number of problems with switching from current lecture/textbook based methods to more technology based methods. Most new technological applications require large amounts of resources, including both money and commitment, for development. They also alter the socialization process that is impounded in our current methods and will reduce the benefits from the peer teaching model that is often used in accounting firm's continuing education.

The efficiencies available from the use of CBT to teach structured material will probably guarantee its use for the transmission of some of the technical parts of pre-entry and continuing education in accounting. The real challenge for educators will be to use the classroom time that is liberated by this transfer in creative ways to teach subjects for which the computer does not have a relative advantage.

Throwing technology at a problem, primarily for the sake of using it, will rarely result in significant improvements in the educational process. We must be continuously open to the potential of new technologies while demanding that they meet a real need. The long-term success of the implementation of the new technologies in education will require a thorough understanding of the educational process; a careful selection of technology appropriate to the problem; and a sufficient investment of resources and commitment.

Suggested Research

The application of technology in delivering services as well as the changes in auditing necessitated by our clients' applications of technology may provide a number of fertile research topics. The emergence of computer security as a central issue and the behavioral impact that continued system developments will have on practice are but a few issues that are worthy of consideration. Readers interested in likely research topics emerging from current trends will enjoy *Research Opportunities in Auditing: The Second Decade*, edited by A. Rashad Abdel-Khalik and Ira Solomon and published in 1988 by the Auditing Section of the American Accounting Association. The third chapter is devoted to the research implications of "Technological Development and EDP."

Source: Lynford E. Graham, Jr. and Jean C. Wyer, "New Technology and Accounting Practice," *The Auditor's Report* (Volume 12, Number 3, Summer 1989), pp. 1–4.

Exhibit 20–5

The Critical Role of Understanding

Sampling

Generalized Audit Software

Modeling

Spread Sheets

Other Mechanized Procedures

AXIOM:

```
Any professional judgment should
be understood before it is
implemented in mechanized form.
```

---

audit plans for the next five years, thereby assisting in planning manpower and projects—the forecast considers prior audits and audit frequencies.

- Use of data bases such as laboratory standards published by groups like the Consumer Product Safety Commission facilitate evaluations of quality assurance and such activities as compliance with laboratory protocol.

- Statistical Analysis System (SAS) has been applied to perform multiple file extracts and comparisons on a computerized purchase order system, permitting cross-validation of information on user authorization tables versus actual users and facilitating statistical profiles of the related data base files.

- Video tapes are increasingly used in training.

- Computers have been used to create procedures allowing seventeen identical fields in payroll and personnel files to be compared and exceptions highlighted for follow-up.

- Analytics are commonly used in planning audits and evaluating profitability, particular income streams and expenses of interest, financial position, growth, asset quality, and monthly trends within key functional areas.

- Exposure analysis models are in use to aid in allocation of staff time according to the highest level of calculated exposure.

- Audit relevance is maintained through constant adjustment of tools, to match rapidly changing industry and economic settings, as well as developing product lines.

- Auditors' time is recorded and a time project printout automated, accessible by audit project, by audit activity, or by vacation, time off, and similar considerations.

- A focus on training of auditors in new concepts related to technology is apparent within audit plans.

- Preinstallation reviews are common, as are simulations of disaster recovery.

- Statistical Package for the Social Sciences (SPSS) is used to perform data analysis, including histograms, tabulations, cross-tabulations, and regression analysis.

- Regression analysis has been used to model external auditors' fees to assess their reasonableness—some have used as a comparative benchmark the model authored by Wanda A. Wallace entitled "Internal Auditors Can Cut Outside CPA Cost," in the *Harvard Business Review* (April 1984, pp. 16, 20).

- CULPRIT, a generalized report writing language produced by the Cullinane Corporation is used to summarize data, draw random samples, and to show managers computerized reports they could be receiving from their own data.

- Libraries of in-house prepared programs are available, tailored to sampling application, random number generation, and simulations of various tax systems such as state income tax withholdings (as a check on the production program).

- Emphasis is placed on eclectic backgrounds of internal audit staff members, including statistics, economics, industrial engineering, and computers, among others.

- Exhibit 20–6 displays a cost-effectiveness matrix which has been found to be particularly helpful in nonprofit entities when qualitative attributes were being compared one to the other. In a sense, the matrix can be used as a filtering tool. Once it is applied, it may well be necessary to add other factors, but such factors are unlikely to have relevance until "indecisiveness" is at hand (unless initial measurements are woefully inadequate.

Exhibit 20–6

Cost-Effectiveness Matrix of Decision Criteria

		Cost of A Relative to B		
		A < B	A = B	A > B
Effectiveness of A Relative to B	A < B	?	Choose B	Choose B
	A = B	Choose A	No Difference	Choose B
	A > B	Choose A	Choose A	?

Adapted from Daniel B. Fishman, "Development of a Generic Cost-Effectiveness Methodology for Evaluating Patient Services of a Community Mental Health Center," National Conference on Evaluation in Alcohol Drug Abuse, and Mental Health Programs (3 April 1974), as reported by James E. Sorensen and Hugh D. Grove, "Cost-Outcome and Cost Effectiveness Analysis: Emerging Nonprofit Performance Evaluation Techniques," Accounting Review (July 1977), pp. 658-675.

Innovation is apparent among companies' internal auditors, although some inertia to change exists, in part, due to a trait we nurture among auditors: skepticism, as highlighted in Exhibit 20–7. Balance must be maintained between a state of Missouri's "SHOW ME" attitude and the avoidance of obsolescence as the environment and numerous other factors change.

Exhibit 20–7

Try to Nurture Skepticism

PROFESSIONAL
SKEPTICISM

COMPLEXITY

A key challenge has to do with the complexity of the decision environment in which we operate. At the risk of sounding trite, things are not as simple as they once seemed to be. Consider the recently reported observation that in the Art Buchwald case, the judge seems to have rewritten contracts; whether or not his is an accurate depiction, the very presence of debate on such a possibility will likely create legal uncertainty about contracts' reliability and thereby raise the cost of doing business. The unintended result could be to stifle economic activity, and importantly from the perspective of the systems designer and evaluator, the weight of documentary evidence may at times be imperiled.[28]

Beyond complexity from legality of contracts between limited parties is the added complexity that arises from social contracts. In part, this is one aspect of the so-called contingency fee in the legal system. Regardless of whether it achieves its intended purpose, descriptive evidence is at hand that liability, insurance premiums, and a variety of products' prices have increased with the advent of contingency fees. This so-called tort tax has been estimated at $300 billion a year.[29] Hence, a challenge to the control structure entails avoiding exposure, identifying problems, responding to claims, and effectively conducting evidence collection and evaluation.

The challenge in such a goal is apparent when one considers the nuances of the issues involved. For example, a mixture of golf and stock tips reportedly landed middle-class Memphis professionals in the middle of an insider trading case setting.[30] One rule of thumb placed in the media regarding "hot tips" is that "If you overhear it, it's legal. If someone who is an insider intentionally tells you, it's illegal."[31] The problems when substance and form fail to be aligned are obvious.

Beyond legal quandaries, the international setting is growing in importance relative to domestic enterprises. The International Accounting Standards Committee (IASC), on January 1, 1989, released its exposure draft 32 (ED32) that called for "Comparability of Financial Statements."[32] Yet, others contend that countries exhibit such substantial economic and cultural differences that preclude accounting figures from having the same interpretation even if generated by the same accounting principles; the implementation of ED32 could even decrease

---

[28] L. Gordon Crovitz, "Coming to America: The End of Contracts," *The Wall Street Journal* (January 9, 1991), p. A10.

[29] Gordon Crovitz, "Contingency Fees and the Common Good," *The Wall Street Journal* (Friday, July 21, 1989), p. A14.

[30] Thomas E. Ricks, "Dangerous Game: How 4 Pals Who Mixed Golf and Stock Tips Landed in the Rough," *The Wall Street Journal* (July 21, 1989), pp. A1 and A6.

[31] James B. Stewart, "Hot Tips Can Mean Trouble With SEC If You Aren't Careful," *The Wall Street Journal* (July 21, 1989), p. A6.

[32] Ralph Reinertsen, "An International Perspective," Edited by Jonathan Grant, *The Auditor's Report*, Volume 13, Number 2 (Spring 1990), pp. 1–2.

information to user groups.[33] The manner in which some countries sort such issues out is to avoid global markets, yet that is unlikely to be an effective long-term strategy. Markets are changing and both approaches to business and controls will need to adapt. Information systems are just one facet of adaptation. Language and cultural barriers may be gradually overcome with training, technology, and experience; however, it is likely to be a gradual adaptation.

Tied with contractual, legal, and international complexities, is the result of media coverage of a spectrum of issues with differing degrees of credibility and accuracy. Consider the intriguing headlines: "Peat denies Brent Walker audit resignation" and "What's in a name?"—Asks D&T.[34] The latter describes a dispute related to mergers as to who can use what name, and local Public Accountants Board decisions (in this case, a decision in Singapore).

Perhaps the most prominent example of disputes in the press among the media and the subjects of the article is apparent in the case of Ernst & Young. As recounted in a Letter to the Editor of the *Wall Street Journal* on December 11, 1990, a December 3, 1990 story had created unfortunate publicity for the firm and an untrue rumor. Despite direct conversations with the reporter and no apparent source for corroboration, the rumor was printed.[35] The message would seem to be that as we access increasing amounts of information, we should again be "professionally skeptical," as depicted in Exhibit 20–6, as to its actual information content.

What comes to mind is a quote attributed to Abraham Lincoln:

> If you call the tail of a dog a leg, how many legs does the dog have?" When others would inevitably answer "5," he would smile and respond "No. You can call the tail a leg all day, but it doesn't make the tail a leg . . ."[36]

UNANTICIPATED CONSEQUENCES

Uncertainties in various information markets lead us to evaluate the likelihood of unanticipated consequences. In the presence of increasingly complex and decentralized operations, coupled with information that might be manipulated in some fashion, the possibility of differentiation instead of desired integration can easily be an unanticipated consequence of organizational politics. This very

---

[33] Frederick D. S. Choi and Richard M. Levich, *The Capital Market Effects of International Accounting Diversity* (Homewood, Illinois: Dow Jones-Irwin, 1990).

[34] "Peat Denies Brent Walker Audit Resignation," *The Accountant*, Issue No. 5841 (September 1990), p. 3.

[35] William L. Gladstone and Ray J. Groves, Co-Chief Executives Ernst & Young, "Ernst & Young Scotches a Rumor," *The Wall Street Journal* (December 11, 1990), p. A13.

[36] Adapted from Irving Stone's novel about the wife of Abraham Lincoln, as cited by Wanda A. Wallace in *Auditing*, Second Edition, from PWS-Kent.

Exhibit 20–8

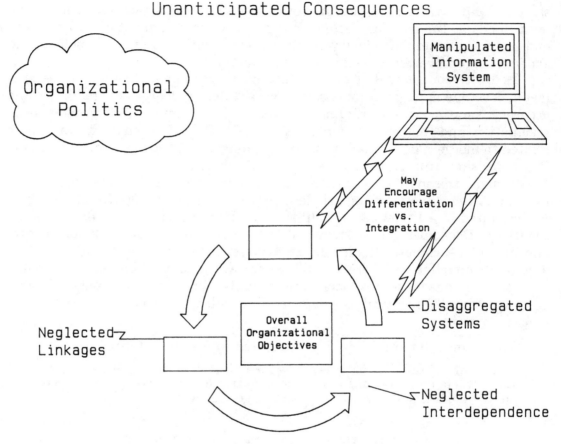

Unanticipated Consequences

undesired result is depicted in Exhibit 20–8. As implied in that diagram, inter-dependencies must not be neglected and overall organizational objectives need to be reinforced.

Local optimization, in part, may result from ineffective communication within the organization and insufficient adaptation to changes in the environment. For example, to what extent have so-called MEGATRENDS (a term used by the author John Naisbitt) been recognized and responded to in the development, implementation, and monitoring of control? Exhibit 20–9 characterizes the megatrends of the 1980s and 1990s and hypothesizes some of the related control implications.

Exhibit 20–9

Megatrends in Controls

—Look at John Naisbitt's 10 Megatrends & Implications—

1. INDUSTRIAL SOCIETY EVOLVING TO AN INFORMATION SOCIETY

   —value of information has increased as has the need to maintain its reliability
   —change in audit trail for service-oriented business is evident
   —role of data bases and analytical procedures is one of increased importance

2. FORCED TECHNOLOGY HAS RESULTED IN HIGH TECH/HIGH TOUCH

   —computer skills are indispensable
   —impersonalization heightens the need for interpersonal skills in the control evaluation process
   —fraud implications have resulted: behavior is affected by perception that defrauding a computer is not the same as defrauding a person, as well as a tendency to "excuse" the computer
   —is technology artificial intelligence or automatic ignorance—related myths
   —optical disk storage, optical scanning, and other devices will make on-line availability and access to reference libraries easier, enhancing controls via improved information
   —standardized internal control questionnaires and form entry devices can be automated via software that can assist in generating flowcharts and ratings

3. NATIONAL ECONOMY EVOLVING TO A WORLD ECONOMY

   —international auditing and accounting standards must be considered in control design
   —new risks: data flow across international boundaries, property rights, reporting standards, currency exchange fluctuations, and attendant risks of a political, cultural, and economic nature
   —travel implications, such as controls that limit the number of key managers on a single flight
   —personnel needs: language and cultural appreciation

4. SHORT TERM FOCUS HAS BECOME A LONGER TERM FOCUS

   —criteria for evaluating results of control evaluations and operational audits are likely to include longer-term considerations

Exhibit 20–9 (continued)

—a cycle approach is likely to be the focus rather than a one-year management program for control evaluation

—independence of the systems evaluator: lesser likelihood of imperiling the longer-term attribute of independence for shorter-term operational needs

5. CENTRALIZATION HAS BEEN REPLACED BY DECENTRALIZATION

—multilocation audit problems arise, as well as more expensive audits

—control issues: threats of override of controls and problems common in microcomputer settings

—organizational issues pose challenges for control design

6. INSTITUTIONAL HELP IS LESS EMPHASIZED THAN SELF-HELP

—responsibility and professionalism enhancement should improve controls

—grass-roots suggestions are increasingly common: auditees' input on ways to address control and operating problems facilitate improved control structure

—training evolution: self-study and tailored continuing education will be increasingly prominent

—reference materials are increasingly on-line, facilitating effective referencing

7. REPRESENTATIVE DEMOCRACY HAS SHIFTED TOWARD A PARTICIPATING DEMOCRACY

—this reinforces trends of increased auditees' input, including suggestions as to prioritization of risks, control design, and implementation of control

—more discussion of level of involvement and nature of assistance among control designers and those responsible for implementing and monitoring controls

8. HIERARCHIES HAVE SHIFTED TO NETWORKING

—more emphasis has to be placed on informal communication lines with inquiry procedures and, possibly, positional analysis techniques

—increased team orientation in decision-making

—computers have evolved from mainframe configurations to microcomputers, for which networking capabilities are critical and can pose substantial control problems

—advances in teleprocessing capabilities and networking structures will facilitate audits from central locations

Exhibit 20–9 (continued)

9. DECLINES IN THE NORTH AND BOOMS IN THE SOUTH

—plant closings, expansion, and related problems pose special control problems, including a number of valuation issues

—shortages of services in the south create resource problems and encourage "flexible shifts" and similar practices, with attendant control implications

—attraction of personnel is a more critical objective with related control needs

10. EITHER/OR FOCUS HAS BECOME MULTIPLE OPTION ORIENTATION

—"multiple career paths" are increasingly common, creating training and hiring control challenges

—multidimensional aspects of controls and the mix of investment in controls, internal auditing, and external auditing are increasingly evident

—various time allocations of auditors' time are observed, e.g., operational auditing vs. financial auditing

—innovative auditing using database monitoring with extraction and analysis abilities, applying quantitative, qualitative, and database analytics

---

COMMUNICATION

One of the key aspects of the megatrends development is the critical merger of technology and communication. Interpersonal skills are increasingly valued as one has more of his or her time dominated by hardware, software, fax, and numerous types of technology. In some ways, technology helps us to communicate more carefully. Indeed, that was the experience reported by public accounting firms as they developed expert systems: only by placing a curtain between the experts and the novice who was being directed to follow guidance were the details of the thought process sufficiently communicated to begin the development process.[37]

Of course, technology can also garble communications. Consider the software with a glitch. In such a circumstance, one deterrent to mass distribution of such software is the possibility that software firms will be held liable for costly errors.[38]

---

[37] Dennis Kneale, "How Coopers & Lybrand Put Expertise Into Its Computers," *The Wall Street Journal* (November 14, 1986), p. 25. Also see Steven P. Galante, "Your Loan Office Next Time May Be an 'Expert' on a Disk," *The Wall Street Journal* (December 8, 1986), p. 25.

[38] Hank Gilman and William M. Bulkeley, "Can Software Firms Be Held Responsible When a Computer Makes a Costly Error?" *The Wall Street Journal* (August 4, 1986), p. 15.

While "as-is" warranties are extended, it is uncertain whether limited liability will be maintained. Given the increasing involvement of public accounting firms in computer related consulting and software development, special attention to quality control over software prior to distribution either internally or externally would seem desirable.[39] Of course, just as there is no such thing as a perfect internal control system, given the number of ways in which a software package might be applied, other than its original intended use, some exposure will persist, even in the presence of strong controls.

Another obstacle to effective communication appears to be a hesitancy on companies' part to admit when they have been duped. As a result, cases are on record of individuals who have been chronic and successful embezzlers from numerous employers over many years. One case in point involved a 20-year period, six employers, repeated discovery, but a decision by employers not to press charges. In a sense, such employees are like a virus that gets passed along to someone else. Clearly, the communication process between the current employer and the prospective employer is anything but ungarbled.[40]

What is needed is better communication that will set up a control culture which is antithetical to such behavior. One means of obtaining greater objectivity in the process and, perhaps, to remove the ego element from having been duped, is to increase the role of public directors. Some have proposed public directors that would be full-time, well-staffed "limited public directors" to help clean up "demonstrated delinquency" and assume social responsibilities. Court appointees or those proposed by regulatory agencies could be designated as in-house probation officers to receive the bad news of any such internal corporate investigation.[41]

In part, such a role is carried out by an audit committee in the sense that they do meet with managers and auditors and try to objectively evaluate the state of control. SAS 61 requires communication by auditors to audit committees of

—their responsibility under generally accepted auditing standards

—significant accounting policy

—management judgments and accounting estimates

—significant audit adjustments

—other information in audited financial statements

—disagreements with management

—consultation with other accountants

---

[39] Paul B. Carroll and Lee Berton, "Arthur Andersen Unveils Software to Aid Companies in Designing Own Programs," *The Wall Street Journal* (April 1, 1988), p. 12—This article reports that Arthur Andersen will have revenues from computer consulting exceeding $1 billion in 1988, or 40% of its worldwide revenue. It describes the availability of Foundation, a software to aid clients in designing their own computer programs.

[40] Bryan Burrough, "The Embezzler: David L. Miller Stole From His Employers And Isn't in Prison," *The Wall Street Journal* (September 19, 1986), pp. 1, 8.

[41] "Public Directors: A Possible Answer to Corporate Misconduct?" *The Wall Street Journal* (March 23, 1976), vol. LVII, no. 57, p. 1.

—major issues discussed with management prior to retention

—difficulties encountered in performing the audit.

Creating such dialogue, along with communicating reportable conditions, is an important liaison for increasing the likelihood of an auditor having open lines of communication to those leading corporate governance.

THE THIRD WAVE

In line with the megatrend projections and similar writings, a number of likely patterns will emerge for the future of our profession. Exhibit 20–10 provides the author's expectations as to the future use of technology.

The timeline recognizes what is likely to happen in field applications of technology. Today, the use of micro-based aids, including sampling software and analytics, is largely at the discretion of the individual auditor. Those with an analytic bent, good computer skills, and/or an environment in which partners promote the use of technology, frequently apply available resources. However, no feedback loop exists to reinforce such behavior and inconvenience often gives way to manual approaches to day-to-day audit activities. Since available software is distributed by librarians, no system is established to monitor use, assess results, or pool

Exhibit 20–10

Timeline of Field Applications of Audit Technology

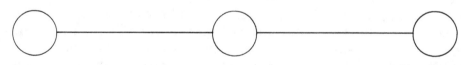

| Today | 5 Years Later | 10 Years Later |

```
LOTUS                      CONTINUOUS SAMPLING          INTEGRATED SAMPLING
COMPUTER TEMPLATES            SYSTEMS (RETRIEVAL            AND TESTING OF
PRACTICE AIDS                 MECHANISM)                    DATA BASES
 . WORD PROCESSING         DECISION SUPPORT SYSTEMS      EXPERT SYSTEMS
 . WORKING PAPER SET-UP     . TO SELECT AMONG             . ROUTINE APPLICATION
SAMPLING--SOFTWARE            STATISTICAL SAMPLING        . EXTENSIVE USE
ANALYTICS                     APPROACHES                    IN TRAINING
 . RATIOS                   . TO PERFORM BASIC           DATA BASE DEVELOPMENT:
 . PREDICTIVE MODELS          ANALYTICS                     ONGOING MONITORING AND
                            . TO ASSIST IN PLANNING         COMPARISON AMONG CLIENTS
                              THE AUDIT--SCHEDULING       BAYESIAN FRAMEWORK
                              FOCUS AND ATTENTION           FOR AUDIT PROCESS
                              TO USE OF PLANNING
                              MATERIALITY AND INTERNAL
                              AUDIT RESOURCES
                           SOPHISTICATED MODELING TOOLS
                            . MULTIPLE REGRESSION ANALYSIS
                            . MARKET-BASED SCREENING
```

experiences. Reliance on technology can produce efficiency gains, but the skeptical auditor needs evidence that technology-based audit tools are effective. Hence, reports on the relative use of different sampling approaches, analytic tools, and predictive models should be developed. Results of such applications should be shared among the professional staff, including information on the costs of such applications. Comparisons ought to be made between non-technology-based audits versus settings in which more innovative approaches are used.

Effectively, a "sales effort" is needed beyond "these tools are available." Inertia is a fact of life. A tendency to carry on prior years' audit steps exists, and it takes too long for every auditor in the firm to build up individual experience with each technological advance in order to consider its use. A mind set needs to be created that change is expected, a "zero base" audit approach has merit, and assessment of pooled experiences can be a basis for individual auditors' selection of audit approaches and reliance thereon.

FIVE YEARS LATER

The "Five Years Later" time frame recognizes elements in place, proposed standards, and the inevitable consequences of data base management systems and extended robotic applications by clients. Continuous monitoring of systems to ensure against program changes, systematic error, or other contamination of on-line data bases will be essential. This is due to both audit risk considerations and firms' decision needs. Yet, integrated test facilities (ITFs) are unlikely to be pervasive in their current form. Instead, mechanisms will be in place which retrieve a random sample of current transactions, copy them, and transmit the resulting data base to the auditor.

Present use of practice aids and software will expand to a set of decision support systems (DSS) which are routinely applied to audit clients. Envision a simulation-based DSS which makes inquiries and then describes the relative size of samples to be drawn, depending on the sampling approach selected. Advantages and disadvantages of each approach will be summarized, and each step of sample selection and evaluation will be addressed by the DSS. Such a system will establish firm standards for nonstatistical approaches to sampling to develop a "floor" or minimum permissible level of coverage. This will deter any present tendency to avoid formal sampling because the sample sizes implied are too large. Moreover, the simulation capabilities of the DSS eliminate most of the confusion as to which sampling technique ought to be applied.

A simple decision support system is likely to be applied to clients' trial balances and data bases for the purpose of performing basic analytics. This would entail reasonableness checks, such as how does productive capacity compare to sales and warehouse facilities? Do the dollar sales per customer seem reasonable? Are ratios comparable to the industry? Are there patterns in sets of ratios which suggest potential problems or strengths?

A number of computational techniques for scheduling staff and allocating materiality are likely to be built into present practice aids. An interactive guide to reflecting the effect of internal auditors on engagement planning could be an integral part of such decision support tools. Again, simulation analysis of the effects of altering available staff, planning materiality, or the extent of use of internal auditing would likely be a desirable decision aid in such systems.

Within five years, the general training provided in statistics and audit coursework should include an appreciation for the potential of sophisticated modeling tools. With sufficient investment in training and the pooling of field results, application of multiple regression analysis for substantive test purposes could well become commonplace. Moreover, public companies under audit could be screened using a variety of market-based filters. The concept of such a tool is to build on the well-recognized concept that stock price reflects all publicly available information, not merely accounting information. Hence, if long-term risk adjusted returns fall below the general market's level, both business risk and audit risk are likely to increase. The result of applying screening tools routinely to public companies is that an early warning signal of potential problems is obtained.

Note that both the basic analytics decision support and the market-based screening tool would rely on data bases such as Dun and Bradstreet, Citibank, COMPUSTAT, CRSP, or other sources of industry information or security price data.

10 YEARS LATER

By "10 Years Later," the sophistication of continuous sampling systems, in my opinion, will extend far beyond mere retrieval. Mini-expert system algorithms will sample and test data base interrelationships and transmit to the auditor summary reports. Only exceptions will be transmitted in detail.

The decision support systems five years from now will be replaced by expert systems which will be routinely applied to most engagements. Such systems will be applicable to key judgments which pervade most audits. For example, expert systems are likely to be developed for

- fee proposals,
- engagement planning,
- materiality allocation and extrapolation from disaggregated account level to the overall client level,
- sampling scope and execution of the sampling plan including its evaluation,
- basic analytical procedures,
- quality control over more sophisticated modeling tools,
- internal control evaluation, with a focus on computer considerations,
- substantive work in judgmental areas such as various allowances and deferrals, and
- going concern assessments.

The expert systems will be introduced in training, thereby reinforcing the idea that they can be as commonplace in the field as are word processing tools today. The pedagogical advantages of expert systems are considerable, since they document the reason for various decisions when users make inquiries.

Presently DBASE packages are widely used and RBASE approaches are increasingly applied. Relational data bases and their integration with audit technology will develop rapidly. Within the decade, beyond accessing clients' in-house data bases, audit firms will have their own data bases developed on client portfolios. These data bases may summarize PAJEs, the nature of risks and operating problems, and key analytics to which other similar companies' performance can be compared. Expert system packages will monitor such statistics within the client portfolio and facilitate a reporting and evaluation process whereby the auditor of a private company can compare that entity with similar entities audited by the firm.

Within 10 years, an overall audit framework will be mechanized which will link various stages of the audit process using an approach that is Bayesian in nature. The framework will be flexible in permitting judgmental adjustments to the algorithm, but will attempt to minimize judgmental inconsistencies and biases and document the rationale for critical professional judgments. While the Bayesian framework may actually apply Bayes' Theorem, it is possible that elements of Prospect Theory belief systems, or other research developments could be integrated. Throughout the development of technology's application to the audit, an emphasis is likely to be placed on sensitivity analysis of results and explanation of rule-based decisions. Such capabilities avoid a black-box or definitive rule application by permitting the decision maker to understand the decision support tool and to evaluate implications of varying from certain assumptions. This reinforces the strong view that technology should assist rather than replace the decision maker.

RESEARCH AND DEVELOPMENT

The timeline implies the research and development activities depicted in Exhibit 20–11. The foundation of the program recognizes the importance of information flow as to the "performance" of technology. Subsequent stages of development focus on ease of access of technologically based tools. Ongoing attention has to be paid to the training of professional staff.

FACTUAL vs. JUDGMENTAL DATA

As one considers expert systems, sampling, analytical techniques, and a Bayesian framework for decision making, one question often posed is how such advanced techniques relate to the type of data of interest to the auditor. Exhibit 20–12 attempts to illustrate this interrelationship. First and foremost, factual data by necessity will blend into judgmental data. In terms of audit risk, the

Exhibit 20–11

Research and Development Activities

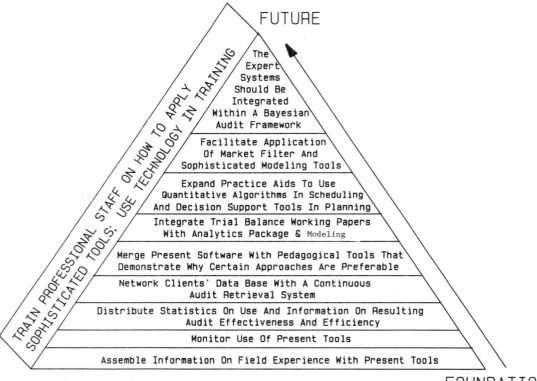

factual data tends to be less problematic. Sampling approaches can be applied to factual data. Linear programming can be applied to factual characteristics of the audit process, such as scheduling considerations. An expert system is depicted as a lined portion of the setting which blends factual and judgmental data. Uncertainty must be present to merit an expert system but some consensus of a factual nature must also exist to support the rule-base development of such systems. The small size of the lined area of the illustration emphasizes the rather small scope expected for individual systems. Too large a scope expands the development and testing phase to such an extent that obsolescence is problematic. Moreover, computer capabilities often restrict the number of decision trees to be considered, creating a capacity problem for large systems.

Modeling permeates a combination of factual and judgmental data. Multiple regression analysis can concurrently consider the relationship of a number of variables of relevance to a judgment, without forcing the specification of a particular definition by the decision maker. Hence, if a reserve for loan loss is expected

Exhibit 20–12

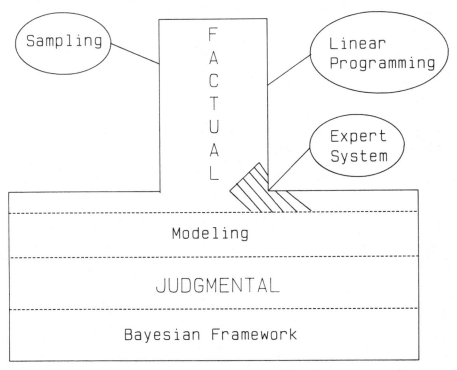

The Relationship Of Data Type and Audit Techniques

to reflect economic, industrial, demographic, and customer-specific attributes, all of this can be made a part of the model.

As the number of judgments begins to explode through the progression of a particular audit engagement, a Bayesian framework is likely to be of assistance. This objective approach to combining judgmental priors with both statistical and nonstatistical evidence accumulated in the course of an audit permits control over the consistency of aggregate judgments across audit engagements. The advantage of such a framework is the avoidance of known cognitive limitations of individual decision makers.

Overall, a key misconception seems to exist that analytical modeling techniques are more applicable to factual than judgmental data. On the contrary, factual data can be explored using a variety of techniques including sampling, EDP auditing, recomputation, and modeling. Whereas, judgmental data's primary tool is modeling. Think of regression analysis as a reflection of the key items considered by the decision maker. The advantage of specifying such quantitative and qualitative components is that the data can objectively quantify the actual interrelationship of the variables. These statistical measures can be compared to the auditor's expectations and provide a reasoned basis for evaluating the fairness of presentation of judgmental accounts.

THE SYSTEMS-ORIENTED AUDIT AND SAMPLING

Controversy exists as to the implications of a systems-oriented audit with respect to the application of particular audit techniques. In particular, is sampling applicable to such an audit?

The systems-oriented audit primarily recognizes the need for continuous auditing and management's increased reliance on data bases in day-to-day decision making. If controls lapse for a week, the economic consequences of bad decisions due to bad information can be considerable. The implication appears to be an orientation toward on-line evaluation and considerable expertise among EDP auditors. The long-range inference is that all auditors will have to be EDP auditors. With this perspective in mind, the nature of sampling plans does change.

The first obvious change is depicted in Exhibit 20–13. Rather than wait until the transaction is trapped in a data base and apply post-facto sampling at interim and year end, the auditor will sample transactions on-line. This will require a different perspective in sample size specification. Rather than having a single population from which to sample, the concept adjusts to recognition that the source of the population, i.e., the system, could be altered over time. Hence, a time-based stratification to ensure continuous auditing will be needed. Given the large number of implied strata, sample sizes are likely to get larger as a result of on-line monitoring. The key toward maintaining efficiency with such samples will be the development of mini-expert systems that test the samples and generate documentation of such tests, with trapping of only those sample points which are exceptions. Since this may require considerable time for development, in the short-term the focus will be to trap the larger samples, retrieve them on a regular basis, and apply some tests, perhaps through concurrent processing, as a means of achieving comfort.

The importance of the timeliness element in monitoring is brought home by the EDP fraud literature. The ease with which computers can be programmed to lie or conceal the truth is problematic. As the retrieval system is designed for on-line sampling, consideration must be given not only to strata effects of time, but also to alternative bases for designing strata.

Exhibit 20–14 notes that editing algorithms of the client are likely to vary with respect to the scope of transactions tested, the Post-Facto Sampling threshold which triggers certain checks, the nature of the edit check used (e.g., field length, alphabetic character check, or limit check), and the frequency with which controls are applied. These control peculiarities should be reflected in stratifying the population of transactions for sampling purposes. The more stringent such controls, the more likely the auditor can direct a larger percentage of testing to the exception reports generated by the client's control system. This implies redefining populations as exception items rather than the full population of transactions. Ob-

Exhibit 20–13

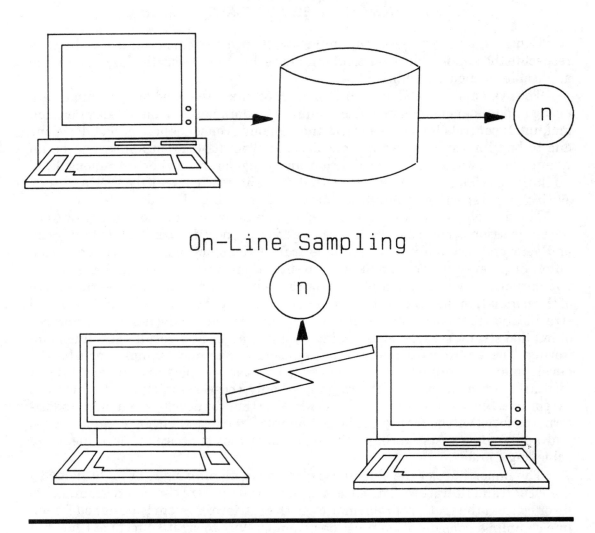

Post-Facto Sampling

On-Line Sampling

viously, care would be needed in extrapolating the results to the exception population.

Although some have contended that systems orientations may decrease the relevancy of sampling since a computer error tends to contaminate the entire population, it would appear that the relevancy of sampling has actually increased. The key difference is we are not drawing conclusions to the population of all transactions, but rather to the population of transactions generated in the same time frame as the one sampled. The focus is on dynamic change in the systems.

Exhibit 20–14

Edit Algorithms: Input/Process/Output Controls

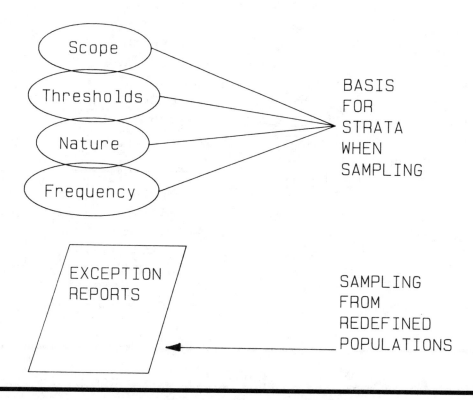

DATA BASE DEVELOPMENT

A key obstacle in artificial intelligence is development of an associative memory flexible enough to retrieve stored experiences that approximately match an arbitrary new situation. While relational data base systems are powerful, presently it is necessary to access data with such software and then apply other software for analysis. As yet, it has not been possible to couple expert systems with relational data base systems. The necessity of having to construct knowledge bases per expert system is a key problem in progressing toward the ideal dual use of artificial intelligence and large relational data bases. More development in technology is required.

Another key motivation for developing such a data base relates to the validation of expert systems. By their very nature, expert systems are built from one or a small sample of decision makers. When an assertion is made that a affects b, a certainty factor has to be applied as to the nature of the effect. An empirical data base could be tremendously helpful in quantifying such factors, checking

Exhibit 20–15

Uses of a Data Base

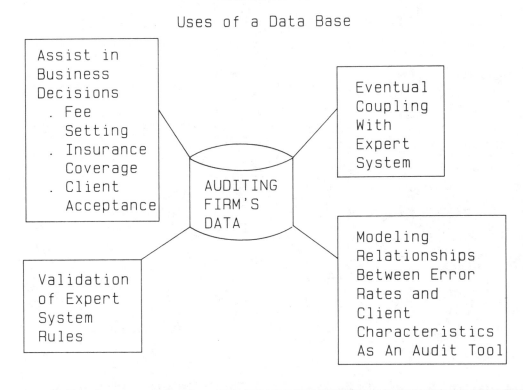

the reasonableness of rules, and avoiding decision rules that cannot be substantiated.

The multiple applications of an audit firm's data base, as described herein, are summarized in Exhibit 20–15.

In considering the overall audit process with such a data base and analytical approach to applying technology, quantitative algorithms will go into planning and risk analysis. Sampling will likely be applied to testing of controls. However, numerous other means of gathering evidence are likely. Sophisticated modeling can provide substantial substantive test evidence, and decision support systems could prove extremely useful in the financial reporting process.

THE INFORMATION REVOLUTION

The third wave philosophy recognizes the information revolution as having started around 1955 and expects that technologies of such an age will include the transistor, the computer, and some form of accountability. This *Handbook* focuses on control concepts intended to address the decentralization, quality focus, and need for adaptation to change. A major call for research as to accountability technologies has been registered.[42] This *Handbook* includes attention to service efforts and accomplishments data and to transactions involving more than two parties.

The latter poses a substantial accountability question. For example, assume that car manufacturer A advertises a warranty on new cars of a set amount that it offers to the dealerships for that manufacturer. Also assume that the dealer has other prospective warranties offered, such as insurance policies by third parties. Further assume that unbeknownst to the customer, the dealer purchases warranty coverage from the third party insuror rather than the manufacturer. Finally, assume the insuror begins to have financial woes and is unable to meet its commitments. Who loses? Clearly, we have a customer demanding services, presumably blaming the car manufacturer and the car dealer for any problem of warranty coverage. The dealer saved money, presumably at the time of sale and, if unconcerned with reputation effects, may not be damaged on the short run. The insuror apparently made a short-term profit and plans to liquidate or is merely a poor business risk that was not effectually monitored by the dealer, since he or she viewed the customer as the risk bearer.

The challenge is to establish sufficient controls that the accountability structure encourages behavior that is in everybody's best interest, if that is feasible. The "everybody" focus historically was on the two primary parties to the exchange, but greater than two-party exchanges clearly result in a set of interests that are countervailing and conflicting. One might envision a restrictive clause in the manufacturer's agreement with dealers that if alternative warranty providers are used and the service lapses in any manner, then a second warranty must be purchased from the manufacturer, at the dealer's expense. Such an approach would increase the incentives for the dealer to carefully evaluate the providers of warranty coverage, since even a short-term stake exists, beyond the longer-term reputation effects. While "unfair competition" may be claimed by the third party insuror, there is little doubt that the reputation of the manufacturer is at risk and some coverage of that investment seems viable.

If such a contractual arrangement would begin to avoid the present described dilemma, then how can the accounting records effectively capture the respective risks? The answer must be far greater attention to contingencies, guarantees, residual interests, and what are so often off-balance sheet items under today's accounting framework. While footnote disclosure is sufficient for notification or signalling purposes, based on efficient markets research, the question nonetheless arises of efficiency in measurement. Would it not be more efficient to bring such details onto the face of financial statements in a manner that was reasonably consistent and comparable, at least within industries if not across industries? Beyond accountability concerns, increased focus is being directed toward quality.

---

[42] Many of these analogies stem from a presentation by Bob Elliott of Peat Marwick Main entitled "The Third Wave Breaks on the Shores of Accounting Education" (1990 KPMG Faculty Symposium in Montvale, New Jersey, September 27, 1990).

Of course, one would expect improved accountability might well encourage improved quality.

Quality

Service quality is characterized as tangibles, reliability, responsiveness, assurance, and empathy. This suggests that a product related service may well differ from a pure service. The nature of who the customer is (individual or business) and the experience level of the customer would seem to be particularly relevant in evaluating quality and in anticipating a reasonably efficient market along the quality dimension for a particular good. Expectations may be that service will be adequate, will be desired at some level, or will be perceived to have been delivered at some other level. Research studies suggest that reliability is the key dimension for customers and that nothing else can compensate for such a factor. Customer service throughout the process that surprises or exceeds expectations of the customers will build a rapport with such customers. To attain this result, quality must be integrated as part of the design of a service system. Particularly critical are the contact people, i.e., those (service providers) who come into contact with the customer.

An expectation exists on the part of customers that the suppliers of services will "play fairly." Rapport can be enhanced by explaining practices to customers, educating those customers about the nature of the service that is being purchased, and listening to the customers' concerns. The root cause of quality malaise is related to leadership: a need exists for high standards, a service vision, an interest in details, field experience, and high integrity.

One approach to evaluating quality is to consider success factors. These are detailed in the popular press as well as academic journals and tend to include:

1) complementary skills, discipline, and mutual respect of partners
2) sensitivity to needs of the industry
3) willingness to take a risk
4) research program orientation versus a project orientation, i.e., a long-term rather than a short-term focus
5) attention to theoretical foundation as empirical research is pursued
6) not understanding executives' interest in theory
7) hard work
8) luck . . .[43]

Note the deja vu experience as we close the loop, beginning with the Deming philosophy and now returning to his "14 Points for Management":

[1] Create constancy of purpose for the improvement of product or service.
[2] Adopt that new philosophy.

---

[43] A. Parasuraman and Leonard L. Berry, "A Research Program on Service Quality," presented at Texas A & M University on April 20, 1990.

[3] Cease dependence on mass inspection.

[4] End the practice of awarding business on the basis of the price tag alone; instead minimize total cost by working with a single supplier.

[5] Improve constantly and forever every process for planning, production, and service.

[6] Institute training on the job.

[7] Adopt and institute leadership.

[8] Drive out fear.

[9] Break down barriers between staff areas.

[10] Eliminate slogans, exhortations, and targets for the workforce.

[11] Eliminate numerical quotas for the workforce and numerical goals for management.

[12] Remove barriers that rob people of pride of workmanship, including the annual rating or merit system.

[13] Institute a vigorous program of education and self-improvement for everyone.

[14] Put everybody in the company to work on accomplishing the desired transformation.[44]

In considering this thrust for quality, consider the encouraging signs that are provided in recent testimony before Congress:

- "The Commission shall share reports and other information concerning any potential mismanagement, fraud, and abuse on the part of an issuer with any independent public accountant performing an audit of the issuer under this title, except when such sharing would impair an investigation or litigation." p. 16

- "We suggest that the following language be added to your bill: "All audits required by this title should be performed only by an independent public accountant who has received a peer review within a time interval set by the Commission. Reports on peer reviews shall be available for public inspection." p. 14

- "Any additional auditor responsibility that Congress may wish to impose would be accompanied by protection for "good faith" fulfillment of such responsibilities." p. 9[45]

---

[44] "Deming's Way Out Of The Crisis," *Industry Week* (June 20, 1988), p. 91.

[45] The House of Representatives Subcommittee on Telecommunications and Finance Committee on Energy and Commerce, Washington, D.C. 20515, "Hearing on Proposed Legislation Concerning Measures to Expand Auditor Responsibility to Detect and Report Illegal Acts," Witness: Charles A. Bowsher, Comptroller General of the U.S., General Accounting Office (and Mr. James R. Doty, General Counsel for the SEC, Mr. Don Neebes, Chairman of the Auditing Standards Board of the AICPA, and Mr. John Spiegel, Executive Vice President and CFO of Sun Trust Banks, Inc. on behalf of the American Bankers Association (August 2, 1990).

Exhibit 20–16

INTENT IS TO FACILITATE

o Management's Evaluation of Control

o Management's Improvement of Control

o Auditors' Assessments of Control

o Regulators' Understanding of Managers' Ability
  to Self-Assess Controls in a Coherent and
  Reasonably Consistent Manner Even in the
  Presence of Divergent

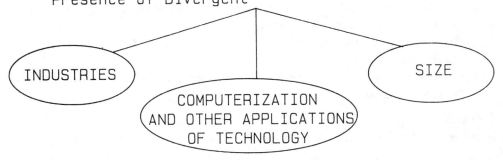

o Regulators' and Other Stakeholders'
  Consideration of Related Disclosure Issues

These points of view speak to cooperative efforts, endorsement of positive effects of self-regulation, and acknowledgment that to establish a workable framework, some safe harbor protection is appropriate. While the bill being discussed was not passed during 1990, most anticipate that the topic will be revisited and that legislation will eventually be forthcoming. No doubt, new responsibilities on all of the various parties involved in the control process for economic entities will pose challenges. The intent of this *Handbook* is reflected in Exhibit 20–16. It is my hope that the pages of this *Handbook* are of assistance in working through today's and tomorrow's challenges effectually to achieve an improved control structure.

Index